# Annotated Teacher's Edition

# ¡Qué chévere! 4

## Contributing Writers

Sarah W. Link

Jenn Carter

Charisse Litteken

EMC Publishing

ST. PAUL, MINNESOTA

**Associate Publisher:** Alejandro Vargas

**Development Editor:** Kristin Hoffman

**Director of Production:** Deanna Quinn

**Production Editor:** Bob Dreas

**Production Specialist and Designer:** Leslie Anderson

AP® is a registered trademark of the College Board, which was not involved in the production of, and does not endorse, this product.

Care has been taken to verify the accuracy of information presented in this book. However, the authors, editors, and publisher cannot accept responsibility for Web, e-mail, newsgroup, or chat room subject matter or content, or for consequences from application of the information in this book, and make no warranty, expressed or implied, with respect to its content.

**Trademarks:** Some of the product names and company names included in this book have been used for identification purposes only and may be trademarks or registered trade names of their respective manufacturers and sellers. The authors, editors, and publisher disclaim any affiliation, association, or connection with, or sponsorship or endorsement by, such owners.

We have made every effort to trace the ownership of all copyrighted material and to secure permission from copyright holders. In the event of any question arising as to the use of any material, we will be pleased to make the necessary corrections in future printings. Thanks are due to the aforementioned authors, publishers, and agents for permission to use the materials indicated.

ISBN 978-0-82197-687-6 (print)

© 2017 by EMC Publishing, LLC
875 Montreal Way
St. Paul, MN 55102
Email: educate@emcp.com
Website: www.emcp.com

Printed in the United States of America
24 23 22 21 20 19 18 17 16      2 3 4 5 6 7 8 9 10

# Table of Contents

From the Publisher                                                    T5

Scope and Sequence                                                   T6
    Level 1                                                        **T6**
    Level 2                                                        **T8**
    Level 3                                                        **T10**
    Level 4                                                        **T12**
    Level 5                                                        **T14**

Introduction                                                         T16
    ACTFL World-Readiness Standards for Learning Languages         **T16**

Walk-through: Student Edition                                        T18

Walk-through: Annotated Teacher's Edition                           T28

Program Resources                                                    T32
    Teacher Materials                                              **T32**
    Student Materials                                              **T32**
    Passport®                                                      **T33**

Philosophy and Approach                                              T34
    World Language Learning in the 21st Century                    **T34**
    Oral Proficiency in the 21st Century                           **T35**
    Differentiated Instruction                                     **T36**
    Blended Learning Environment                                   **T37**
    Pre-AP Spanish Language and Culture                            **T38**
    Common Core State Standards                                    **T38**

Correlation of Common Core State Standards                          T39

Classroom Apps and Games                                            T45
    Apps                                                           **T45**
    Games                                                          **T46**

# From the Publisher

Greetings, Spanish teachers! As you know, speaking another language is more important than ever in a globalized world that requires skilled workers who can communicate across borders and understand cultural similarities and differences. This poses a great challenge for you because many of your students don't understand this reality. They lack the motivation to learn another language or simply don't see the purpose. *¡Qué chévere!* speaks to this challenge. It seeks to motivate your students to discover the value and importance of learning a language and become enthusiastic and passionate participants in the learning process.

*¡Qué chévere!* is an engaging program that develops students' communication skills by providing ample speaking and writing practice in contextualized situations, working with partners and in groups.

*¡Qué chévere!* integrates language practice with culture—its practices, products, and perspectives—to create a rich learning environment. Students compare Spanish-speaking cultures to their own, and in doing so, they deepen their knowledge of both.

The *¡Qué chévere!* series is centered on the five C's of the revised ACTFL Standards:

- **Communication:** Students work in the Interpersonal, Presentational, and Interpretive modes.
- **Cultures:** Students investigate the Practices, Products, and Perspectives of Spanish-speaking cultures.
- **Connections:** Students connect to other disciplines such as geography, math, and ecology.
- **Comparisons:** Students compare their culture(s) to the Spanish-speaking cultures they encounter in the program.
- **Communities:** Students build communities at school and outside the classroom by reaching out to Spanish speakers in their region and around the world.

Technology, social media, music, and travel are some of the themes in the *¡Que chévere!* series that will engage your students and motivate them to learn Spanish. Throughout the program, your students have opportunities to develop their critical thinking and problem-solving skills as well to begin preparing for the AP exam as early as Level 1.

Content in the series is regularly re-entered, and concepts are reinforced in the supplemental materials. These components enrich *¡Qué chévere!* textbook instruction. You can meet the diverse needs of your students by choosing from a variety of interactive program components and audio resources. These supplemental materials are described in this Annotated Teacher's Edition and will be delivered through our new language learning environment, Passport®.

*¡Qué chévere!* students easily become global citizens who are: communicative as they interact orally in dialogues, interviews, and surveys, and practice writing everything from lists to reports; knowledgeable about Spanish language and its cultures; inquisitive about diverse subject areas; reflective about human values, perspectives, and their own learning process; and open-minded about cultural practices, products, and perspectives that differ from their own.

## Level 1, Unidades 1–10

| | Unidad 1 | Unidad 2 | Unidad 3 | Unidad 4 | Unidad 5 |
|---|---|---|---|---|---|
| **Essential Question** | How do people reach out to communicate with others? | How does education promote understanding of different cultures? | How do major cities tell their stories? | How do cultural values shape relationships in Hispanic countries? | How do key activities in a society reflect its values? |
| **Objetivos** | **Lecciones A & B**<br>• ask for and give names<br>• ask and tell where someone is from<br>• ask for and state age<br>• ask and tell how someone is feeling<br>• express courtesy<br>• ask for and state the time | **Lecciones A & B**<br>• identify people and classroom objects<br>• ask for and give names<br>• ask or tell where someone is from<br>• discuss school schedules<br>• describe classroom objects and clothing<br>• say some things people do<br>• state location<br>• talk about how someone feels | **Lecciones A & B**<br>• talk about places in the city<br>• make introductions and express courtesy<br>• ask and answer questions<br>• discuss how to go somewhere<br>• say some things people do<br>• say where someone is going<br>• talk about the future<br>• order food and beverages | **Lecciones A & B**<br>• talk about family and relationships<br>• express possession<br>• say some things people do<br>• state likes and dislikes<br>• describe people and things | **Lecciones A & B**<br>• talk about electronics<br>• describe everyday activities<br>• express strong feelings<br>• talk about days, dates, and holidays |
| **Vocabulario** | **Lección A**<br>Greetings<br>Farewells<br>Alphabet<br>Names<br>Numbers 0–20<br>Spanish-speaking countries<br><br>**Lección B**<br>Greetings<br>Farewells<br>How people are doing<br>Courtesy expressions<br>Time<br>Numbers 21–100 | **Lección A**<br>Identifying people<br>Saying where a person is from<br>Classroom objects<br><br>**Lección B**<br>Class schedule<br>Days of the week<br>Colors<br>Clothing<br>Technology items | **Lección A**<br>Places in a city<br>Introductions and responses<br>Suggestions and invitations<br>Transportation<br><br>**Lección B**<br>Places in a city<br>Foods<br>Restaurant dining | **Lección A**<br>Family relationships<br>Possession<br><br>**Lección B**<br>Leisure-time activities<br>Relationships with friends<br>Likes and dislikes<br>Descriptions | **Lección A**<br>Electronic equipment<br>Weekly schedule<br>Leisure-time activities<br><br>**Lección B**<br>Dates<br>Special days<br>Numbers (101–999,999)<br>Months |
| **Gramática** | **Lección A**<br>Punctuation<br>Definite articles and countries<br>Cognates<br><br>**Lección B**<br>Formal/Informal<br>Telling time | **Lección A**<br>Subject pronouns and the verb *ser*<br>Using definite articles with nouns (singular and plural)<br>Using indefinite articles with nouns (singular and plural)<br><br>**Lección B**<br>*Repaso rápido:* Nouns<br>Using adjectives to describe<br>Present tense of *-ar* verbs<br>*¿A qué hora?*<br>*Repaso rápido:* Present tense of *-ar* verbs<br>The verb *estar* | **Lección A**<br>Making introductions: *te, le, les*<br>Using contractions: *al/del*<br>*Repaso rápido:* Question words<br>Asking questions<br>The verb *ir*<br><br>**Lección B**<br>*Ir a* + infinitive<br>*Repaso rápido:* Conjugating regular *-ar* verbs<br>Present tense of *-er* verbs | **Lección A**<br>*Repaso rápido:* Adjectives<br>Possessive adjectives<br>*Repaso rápido:* Conjugating regular *-er* verbs<br>Present tense of *-ir* verbs<br>*Repaso rápido:* Using *estar* to express location<br>Describing people and things with *estar*<br><br>**Lección B**<br>Using *gustar* to state likes and dislikes<br>Using *a* to clarify or emphasize<br>Uses of *ser* and *estar* | **Lección A**<br>The verb *tener*<br>*¡Qué* (+ adjective/noun)*!*<br>Direct objects and the personal *a*<br>Direct object pronouns<br><br>**Lección B**<br>The verb *venir*<br>Using the present tense to indicate the future<br>Using the numbers 101–999,999<br>Asking for and giving the date |
| **Cultura** | **Lección A**<br>Una gran celebración<br>Abrazos, besos y más<br><br>**Lección B**<br>La cortesía en el mundo hispanohablante<br>Más sobre saludos | **Lección A**<br>El español en tu vida<br>La influencia hispana en los Estados Unidos<br><br>**Lección B**<br>El intercambio estudiantil<br>El colegio | **Lección A**<br>De visita en la Ciudad de México<br>El Parque de Chapultepec<br><br>**Lección B**<br>La Plaza de las Tres Culturas<br>La comida de las tres culturas | **Lección A**<br>Descubre los dos idiomas de Puerto Rico<br>La isla del encanto y su gente encantadora<br><br>**Lección B**<br>La evolución de la familia dominicana<br>Dos dominicanos famosos: El merengue y la bachata | **Lección A**<br>Costa Rica: País pequeño pero de gran riqueza<br>Costa Rica: Un país pacífico y patriótico<br><br>**Lección B**<br>Días de fiesta en Nicaragua<br>La procesión de los perros |
| **Lectura informativa** | Visita las maravillas del mundo hispanohablante | Las notas en el colegio | El metro de la Ciudad de México | Los nombres de familia | Unas vacaciones de aventura |
| **Lectura** | El mundo hispanohablante | Puentes y fronteras de *Gina Valdés* | Frida Kahlo, una artista universal, famosa e importante | El béisbol: Un deporte nacional | Las fiestas Darianas |

| Unidad 6 | Unidad 7 | Unidad 8 | Unidad 9 | Unidad 10 |
|---|---|---|---|---|
| What does a house and its contents tell us about the people who live there? | How does geography affect the sports and leisure of a nation? | How do routines inside and outside the home reflect cultural values? | What can you learn about a country from the products and services it provides? | How do ancient civilizations live on in the present? |
| **Lecciones A & B**<br>• identify items in the kitchen and at the dinner table<br>• express obligations, wishes, and preferences<br>• discuss food and table items<br>• point out people and things<br>• describe a household<br>• tell what someone says<br>• say how someone is doing | **Lecciones A & B**<br>• talk about leisure-time activities<br>• discuss sports<br>• say what someone can do<br>• discuss length of time<br>• describe what is happening<br>• talk about the seasons and weather<br>• indicate order | **Lecciones A & B**<br>• talk about household chores<br>• say what just happened<br>• ask for and offer help<br>• talk about the past<br>• identify and describe foods<br>• discuss food preparation<br>• make comparisons | **Lecciones A & B**<br>• describe clothing<br>• identify parts of the body<br>• express disagreement<br>• talk about the past<br>• discuss size and fit<br>• describe accessories<br>• discuss price and payment | **Lecciones A & B**<br>• discuss past actions and events<br>• talk about everyday activities<br>• talk about future plans<br>• discuss interesting places to visit in the Spanish-speaking world |
| **Lección A**<br>Objects in a kitchen<br>Table setting and cleanup<br>Foods<br>At the dinner table<br><br>**Lección B**<br>Rooms and floors of a house<br>Describing a home<br>How someone is doing (*tener* idioms) | **Lección A**<br>Leisure-time activities<br>Entertainment<br>Sports<br>Time expressions<br><br>**Lección B**<br>Seasons<br>Weather<br>Sports<br>Leisure-time activities<br>Ordinal numbers | **Lección A**<br>Household chores<br><br>**Lección B**<br>Foods<br>Shopping in a market | **Lección A**<br>Clothing<br>Shopping in a department store<br>Parts of the body<br><br>**Lección B**<br>Shopping in a department store<br>Gift ideas<br>Jewelry<br>Size and fit<br>At the cash register | |
| **Lección A**<br>Expressing obligation with *tener que* and *deber*<br>Stem-changing verbs: *e → ie*<br>Demonstrative adjectives<br><br>**Lección B**<br>The verb *decir*<br>Expressing wishes with *querer* or *gustaría*<br>*Repaso rápido:* Regular present tense verbs<br>Stem-changing verbs: *e → i* | **Lección A**<br>Stem-changing verbs: *o → ue* and *u → ue*<br>Expressions with *hace*<br>Present progressive<br>*Repaso rápido:* Direct object pronouns<br>Present progressive with direct object pronouns<br><br>**Lección B**<br>Verbs that require special accentuation<br>Present tense of *dar* and *poner*<br>Describing people using *-dor* or *-ista*<br>Using ordinal numbers | **Lección A**<br>*Repaso rápido:* Direct object pronouns<br>Indirect object pronouns<br>*Acabar de*<br>Present tense of *oír* and *traer*<br>Preterite tense of *-ar* verbs<br><br>**Lección B**<br>Making comparisons<br>*Repaso rápido:* Preterite tense of regular *-ar* verbs<br>Preterite tense of *dar* and *estar* | **Lección A**<br>Adjectives as nouns<br>*Repaso rápido:* Preterite of *-ar* verbs<br>Preterite tense of *-er* and *-ir* verbs<br>Preterite tense of *ir* and *ser*<br>Affirmative and negative words<br><br>**Lección B**<br>Diminutives<br>Preterite tense of *leer, oír, ver, decir, hacer,* and *tener*<br>*Repaso rápido:* Prepositions<br>Using prepositions | **Lección A**<br>*Repaso rápido:* The preterite tense of *gustar*<br><br>**Lección B**<br>*Repaso rápido:* Verb phrases |
| **Lección A**<br>Los venezolanos y sus casas<br>Los venezolanos y su comida<br><br>**Lección B**<br>Las diferentes casas colombianas<br>El patio | **Lección A**<br>Argentina: Un país de mucha variedad<br>El río de Buenos Aires<br><br>**Lección B**<br>La geografía y la identidad chilena<br>Naturaleza, tradiciones y deportes chilenos | **Lección A**<br>La vida diaria en España<br>¿Cómo viven los chicos españoles?<br><br>**Lección B**<br>Los domingos en casa en España<br>¿Dónde compran los alimentos los españoles? | **Lección A**<br>Panamá, país comercial<br>El Canal de Panamá<br><br>**Lección B**<br>Los productos de Ecuador<br>Unas islas únicas en el mundo | **Lección A**<br>Perú: Una civilización antigua<br>Perú hoy<br><br>**Lección B**<br>Una antigua civilización en el presente<br>Descubriendo Tikal |
| La gente y las viviendas en otras regiones de Venezuela | Los deportes en Argentina | ¿Quién hace qué? | Un día en el centro comercial | Viajar a Machu Picchu: Siete consejos para el viajero |
| La pobre viejecita<br>de *Rafael Pombo* | Rapa Nui | Una moneda de ¡Ay!<br>de *Juan de Timoneda* | El mercado de Otavalo | El libro sagrado de los mayas |

# Scope and Sequence

## Level 2, Unidades 1–10

| | Unidad 1 | Unidad 2 | Unidad 3 | Unidad 4 | Unidad 5 |
|---|---|---|---|---|---|
| **Pregunta clave** | What role does technology play in people's lives? | What do people do to feel well? | How do people interact with cities? | What brings people together? | How do local products reflect the cultural heritage of a region? |
| **Objetivos** | **Lecciones A & B**<br>• talk about ecology<br>• discuss technology<br>• talk about everyday activities<br>• seek and provide personal information<br>• state what is happening right now<br>• talk about the future<br>• talk about the past<br>• express negation or disagreement | **Lecciones A & B**<br>• identify objects in a bathroom<br>• discuss daily routine<br>• discuss personal grooming<br>• seek and provide personal information<br>• point out someone or something<br>• talk about the past<br>• discuss health<br>• identify parts of the body<br>• give and take instructions | **Lecciones A & B**<br>• talk about places in a city<br>• ask for and give directions<br>• tell others what to do or not to do<br>• give advice and make suggestions<br>• discuss what is sold in specific stores<br>• talk about everyday activities<br>• discuss whom and what people know<br>• identify parts of a car | **Lecciones A & B**<br>• discuss activities at a special event<br>• describe in the past<br>• identify animals<br>• discuss details about the past<br>• express past intentions<br>• talk about nationality<br>• add emphasis to a description<br>• discuss size<br>• indicate possession | **Lecciones A & B**<br>• name some foods<br>• talk about the past<br>• talk about what someone remembers<br>• express an opinion<br>• describe clothing<br>• ask for advice<br>• state what was happening at a specific time<br>• describe how something was done<br>• express length of time |
| **Vocabulario** | **Lección A**<br>Technology and communication<br>Environmental issues<br>**Lección B**<br>Vacations<br>Everyday activities | **Lección A**<br>Daily routines<br>**Lección B**<br>Parts of the body<br>Activities and health | **Lección A**<br>Places in the city<br>Stores<br>Directions<br>**Lección B**<br>Directions<br>Neighborhood and neighbors<br>Everyday activities<br>Driving<br>Parts of a car<br>Traffic signs | **Lección A**<br>Amusement parks<br>Zoo animals<br>Nationalities<br>**Lección B**<br>The circus<br>Wild and farm animals | **Lección A**<br>Supermarket, fish, meats, and seafood<br>Metric system<br>Menu<br>**Lección B**<br>Clothing<br>Everyday activities<br>Food and dining |
| **Gramática** | **Lección A**<br>*Repaso rápido:* Present tense of -ar, -er, and -ir verbs<br>*Repaso rápido:* Present tense of verbs with irregularities<br>*Repaso rápido:* The present progressive<br>*Repaso rápido: ir a*<br>*Repaso rápido:* Preterite tense of -ar verbs<br>Preterite tense of -er and -ir verbs<br>**Lección B**<br>*Repaso rápido:* The preterite tense<br>Irregular preterite-tense verbs<br>Negative and affirmative expressions<br>*Repaso rápido:* Direct and indirect object pronouns<br>Using direct and indirect object pronouns together | **Lección A**<br>Reflexive verbs<br>The word *se*<br>Preterite tense of reflexive verbs<br>*Repaso rápido:* Demonstrative adjectives<br>Demonstrative pronouns<br>**Lección B**<br>Verbs that are similar to *gustar*<br>More on reflexive verbs<br>Prepositions | **Lección A**<br>Informal affirmative commands<br>Formal and plural commands<br>*Nosotros* commands<br>**Lección B**<br>*Conocer* vs. *saber*<br>Negative commands | **Lección A**<br>Imperfect tense<br>Verbs irregular in the imperfect: *Ser, ir,* and *ver*<br>*Repaso rápido: Ser* vs. *estar*<br>Adjectives of nationality<br>**Lección B**<br>Special endings: *-ísimo/a* and *-ito/-ita*<br>Adjective placement<br>Possessive adjectives: Long forms<br>*Lo* with adjectives/adverbs | **Lección A**<br>*Repaso rápido:* The preterite tense<br>Preterite vs. imperfect tense<br>Present tense of *reír* and *freír*<br>Irregular preterite-tense verbs<br>**Lección B**<br>The imperfect progressive tense<br>Adverbs ending in *-mente*<br>*Repaso rápido: Hace* (+ time) *que*<br>*Hacía* (+ time) *que* |
| **Cultura** | **Lección A**<br>El lenguaje cibernético<br>Las redes sociales<br>**Lección B**<br>Internet gratis en todo el mundo<br>Conexión antes, durante y después de un viaje | **Lección A**<br>La moda de la mano de un hispano<br>De Colombia al *glamour* de Hollywood<br>**Lección B**<br>Sentirse bien de manera natural<br>La importancia de los intérpretes médicos | **Lección A**<br>Pequeña iglesia sobre pirámide grande<br>Una gran ciudad sobre un lago seco<br>**Lección B**<br>Barrios mágicos<br>Puntos mágicos en Coyoacán | **Lección A**<br>Diversión y educación para los más jóvenes<br>Diversión popular salvadoreña en San Miguel<br>**Lección B**<br>El circo social<br>Teatro callejero | **Lección A**<br>El origen de las frutas tropicales<br>Sabor sobre ruedas<br>**Lección B**<br>Ciudad pionera textil<br>Ropa y arte de Puerto Rico |
| **Lectura informativa** | La voz de los indígenas en la internet | Un *boom* dominicano en Nueva York | Parkour en México | La conservación de las tortugas marinas en El Salvador | Una cadena de sabor en la costa caribeña |
| **Lectura literaria** | Las abejas de bronce<br>de *Marco Denevi* | Apolvenusina<br>de *Yoss* | Polidor: leyenda mexicana de Guadalajara<br>*Anónimo* | Platero y yo<br>de *Juan Ramón Jiménez* | Cuando era puertorriqueña<br>de *Esmeralda Santiago* |

| Unidad 6 | Unidad 7 | Unidad 8 | Unidad 9 | Unidad 10 |
|---|---|---|---|---|
| What makes a place a home? | How do people stay informed? | What makes a tourist attraction? | How do people create a better future for themselves? | How do people benefit from living in a global society? |
| **Lecciones A & B**<br>• describe a household<br>• talk about family<br>• tell someone what to do<br>• state wishes and preferences<br>• talk about everyday activities<br>• invite someone to do something<br>• make a request<br>• express doubt, emotion, and uncertainty<br>• state hopes and opinions | **Lecciones A & B**<br>• say what has happened<br>• discuss the news<br>• talk about a television broadcast<br>• describe people and objects<br>• identify sections of newspapers and magazines<br>• relate two events in the past<br>• talk about a radio broadcast<br>• talk about soccer | **Lecciones A & B**<br>• express emotion<br>• talk about everyday activities<br>• talk about the future<br>• plan a vacation<br>• state what is probable<br>• make travel and lodging arrangements<br>• use the twenty-four-hour clock<br>• talk about schedules<br>• express logical conclusions<br>• talk about hopes and dreams | **Lecciones A & B**<br>• discuss careers<br>• express events in the past<br>• relate two past events<br>• talk about hopes and dreams<br>• state wishes and preferences<br>• discuss the future<br>• express uncertainty<br>• express doubt<br>• advise and suggest<br>• express emotion<br>• identify and locate countries | **Lecciones A & B**<br>• talk about past actions and events<br>• apply technology to find information on the Spanish-speaking world<br>• talk about art in some Spanish-speaking countries<br>• discuss contemporary Hispanic culture<br>• talk about the future<br>• discuss travel and employment opportunities<br>• state wishes and preferences |
| **Lección A**<br>Home and family<br>Household items and everyday activities<br>Household chores<br><br>**Lección B**<br>Household rules and expectations<br>Household appliances | **Lección A**<br>News and television programs<br>Everyday activities<br><br>**Lección B**<br>Newspapers<br>Radio<br>Soccer | **Lección A**<br>Vacations, travel agencies, and food<br>Emotions and dreams<br><br>**Lección B**<br>Airports and hotels<br>The twenty-four-hour clock | **Lección A**<br>Careers and jobs<br>Problems of the world<br>Hopes and dreams<br>Personal relationships<br><br>**Lección B**<br>Body language<br>Nationalities<br>Future plans | |
| **Lección A**<br>*Repaso rápido:* Stem-changing verbs<br>The subjunctive<br>Irregular subjunctive verbs<br>Using an infinitive instead of the subjunctive<br><br>**Lección B**<br>The subjunctive with verbs of emotion and doubt<br>The subjunctive with impersonal expressions | **Lección A**<br>The present perfect tense and past participles<br>The present perfect tense of reflexive verbs<br>Participles as adjectives<br><br>**Lección B**<br>The past perfect tense<br>*Repaso rápido:* The passive voice<br>More on the passive voice | **Lección A**<br>*Repaso rápido:* The future tense with *ir a*<br>The future tense<br>The future tense: Irregular forms<br><br>**Lección B**<br>The twenty-four-hour clock<br>The conditional tense<br>The conditional tense of irregular verbs | **Lección A**<br>*Repaso rápido:* Uses of *haber*<br>Present perfect subjunctive<br>More on the subjunctive<br><br>**Lección B**<br>*Repaso rápido:* The subjunctive<br>*Repaso rápido:* The future tense<br>*Repaso rápido:* The conditional tense | |
| **Lección A**<br>Hogares coloniales<br>Hogares sobre un lago<br><br>**Lección B**<br>Un hogar latinoamericano<br>La casa del Sol | **Lección A**<br>Noticias de ayer, hoy y mañana<br>Información interactiva<br><br>**Lección B**<br>Domingo, día de deportes<br>Información en lengua indígena | **Lección A**<br>Una gran salsa de tomate<br>Fiesta con toros<br><br>**Lección B**<br>El horario de los españoles<br>Atracción para turistas jóvenes | **Lección A**<br>Premios y honores para hispanos<br>Talentos mexicanos<br><br>**Lección B**<br>Ayudando a las comunidades<br>Inmersión cultural para mejorar el futuro | **Lección A**<br>Ciudades hermanas<br>Hermanas del centro y del norte<br><br>**Lección B**<br>Una mirada al cielo<br>Investigación en el frío |
| Los bohíos | Actor talentoso | Atracción para deportistas | El viaje de egresados | Misterios de Norte a Sur |
| Vivir para contarla<br>de *Gabriel García Márquez* | El viejo goleador<br>de *José Cantero Verni* | Lazarillo de Tormes<br>*Anónimo* | Lazarillo de Tormes<br>*Anónimo* | El negro<br>de *Rosa Montero* |

## Level 3, Unidades 1–10

| | Unidad 1 | Unidad 2 | Unidad 3 | Unidad 4 | Unidad 5 |
|---|---|---|---|---|---|
| **Pregunta clave** | ¿Cómo se relfeja la cultura de un país en las actividades de su gente? | ¿Cómo se ve la presencia hispana en Estados Unidos? | ¿Cómo se manifiesta la historia de un país en su cultura actual? | ¿Cómo se difunde la cultura dentro y fuera de un país? | ¿Cómo se transportan las personas en otros países y adónde van? |
| **Objetivos** | **Lecciones A & B**<br>• greet friends<br>• talk about school activities<br>• describe others in terms of personality<br>• talk about sports and after-school activities<br>• talk about after-school jobs<br>• describe occupations<br>• describe movies and programs<br>• talk about likes and dislikes<br>• express an opinion | **Lecciones A & B**<br>• describe family members<br>• express negation or disagreement<br>• name different areas of a house and household items<br>• talk about activities in progress<br>• make generalized statements<br>• talk about daily routine<br>• describe emotions and relationships<br>• talk about household chores<br>• tell others what to do | **Lecciones A & B**<br>• classify news in corresponding sections<br>• talk about activities of the media<br>• talk about how long something has been going on<br>• comment on news and events in the media<br>• recall and talk about events in the past<br>• react to news events<br>• link parts of sentences | **Lecciones A & B**<br>• describe your personality and that of your friends<br>• talk about personal relationships<br>• make apologies<br>• express events in the past<br>• describe people and things<br>• talk about family relationships<br>• give recommendations and advice<br>• receive and place phone calls<br>• talk about actions that lasted for an extended time | **Lecciones A & B**<br>• give advice about driving in the city<br>• identify road signs<br>• tell others what to do<br>• ask for and give directions<br>• make generalizations about what's important, useful, and necessary<br>• talk about train travel<br>• talk about camping activities<br>• make requests, suggestions, and demands |
| **Vocabulario** | **Lección A**<br>Greetings<br>School-related activities<br>Descriptions<br><br>**Lección B**<br>After-school activities, jobs<br>Types of movies<br>Likes and dislikes | **Lección A**<br>Family members<br>Descriptions<br>Household items and activities<br><br>**Lección B**<br>Daily routine<br>Emotions<br>Household items and placement | **Lección A**<br>Sections of a newspaper<br>Activities of the media<br>Events in the past<br><br>**Lección B**<br>News<br>Events in the past | **Lección A**<br>Descriptions<br>Feelings<br>Relationships<br>Apologies<br><br>**Lección B**<br>Family relationships<br>Giving orders and advice<br>Using the phone | **Lección A**<br>Driving<br>Road signs<br>Giving directions<br><br>**Lección B**<br>Train travel<br>The country<br>Camping activities |
| **Gramática** | **Lección A**<br>*Repaso rápido:* El presente de indicativo<br>Los verbos que terminan en *-cer, -cir*<br>Usos del presente<br>*Repaso rápido:* Número y género de los adjetivos<br>Usos de *ser* y *estar* con adjetivos<br><br>**Lección B**<br>Usos de *qué* y *cuál/cuáles*<br>El verbo *ser* para describir ocupaciones o profesiones<br>*Repaso rápido:* El verbo *gustar*<br>Para expresar opiniones: Otros verbos como *gustar* | **Lección A**<br>*Repaso rápido:* Expresiones afirmativas y negativas<br>Más sobre expresiones afirmativas y negativas<br>*Repaso rápido:* Los pronombres de complemento directo e indirecto<br>El presente progresivo<br>El uso de *se* en expresiones impersonales<br><br>**Lección B**<br>Los verbos reflexivos<br>Otros usos de los verbos reflexivos<br>Acciones recíprocas<br>Los mandatos informales afirmativos<br>*Repaso rápido:* Expresiones de lugar | **Lección A**<br>*Repaso rápido:* El pretérito<br>Verbos irregulares en el pretérito<br>Otros verbos irregulares en el pretérito<br>*Repaso rápido:* Expresiones de tiempo con *hace*<br>El imperfecto<br><br>**Lección B**<br>Usos del pretérito y del imperfecto<br>Cambios de significado en el pretérito y el imperfecto<br>El participio pasado y el pluscuamperfecto<br>Los pronombres relativos *que, quien(es)* | **Lección A**<br>*Repaso rápido:* Más sobre verbos y pronombres<br>Los complementos directos e indirectos en una misma oración<br>*Repaso rápido:* Los participios pasados y el pretérito perfecto<br>La posición del adjetivo y su significado<br><br>**Lección B**<br>Los mandatos negativos informales<br>Los usos de la preposición *a*<br>El imperfecto progresivo | **Lección A**<br>Los mandatos formales singulares y plurales<br>Los mandatos con *nosotros*<br>*Repaso rápido:* Preguntar y pedir<br>El subjuntivo: Verbos regulares y con cambios ortográficos<br><br>**Lección B**<br>El subjuntivo: Verbos irregulares y más expresiones impersonales<br>El subjuntivo: Verbos con cambio de raíz<br>*Para* y *por*<br>Más sobre el subjuntivo |
| **Cultura** | **Lección A**<br>El sabor de Colombia<br>Bogotá: Centro cultural de talla mundial<br><br>**Lección B**<br>Un país donde el béisbol es rey<br>Venezuela y la televisión | **Lección A**<br>Un sueño en común<br>La Florida: Para muchos, un segundo hogar<br><br>**Lección B**<br>¡Mi casa es su casa!<br>La familia hispana llega a Hollywood | **Lección A**<br>España, un país donde el presente y el pasado se encuentran día a día<br>Fiestas en España<br><br>**Lección B**<br>Costumbres arraigadas en el pasado<br>La familia real española | **Lección A**<br>Puerto Rico: La isla de varias culturas<br>La clave musical de Puerto Rico<br><br>**Lección B**<br>Embajadores dominicanos de renombre<br>Donde los jóvenes les susurran a las ballenas | **Lección A**<br>¿Cómo se movilizan los porteños?<br>¿Adónde vamos a bailar tango?<br><br>**Lección B**<br>De punta a punta: El transporte en Chile<br>Un viaje al sur chileno |
| **Lectura informativa** | El mundo de Botero | Un homenaje para los artistas latinos en Estados Unidos | El mundo del entretenimiento y el espectáculo en España | ¿Cómo se comunican hoy los adolescentes? | Una sonrisa en la vida diaria |
| **Lectura literaria** | La idea que da vueltas<br>de *Gabriel García Márquez* | Once<br>de *Sandra Cisneros* | De la segunda salida de Don Quijote<br>de *Miguel de Cervantes Saavedra* | A Julia de Burgos<br>de *Julia de Burgos* | Dos palabras<br>de *Isabel Allende* |

| Unidad 6 | Unidad 7 | Unidad 8 | Unidad 9 | Unidad 10 |
|---|---|---|---|---|
| ¿Por qué viaja la gente a otros países? | ¿Cómo se relaciona la comida que se consume en un país con su cultura? | ¿Qué se hacía en el pasado para mantenerse saludable y qué se hace en la actualidad? | ¿Cómo se refleja la cultura de un lugar a través de lo que está de moda? | ¿Qué puede hacer la juventud actual para mejorar su futuro y el del planeta? |

**Lecciones A & B**

| Unidad 6 | Unidad 7 | Unidad 8 | Unidad 9 | Unidad 10 |
|---|---|---|---|---|
| • make travel plans<br>• make weather predictions<br>• talk about events that will take place in the future<br>• express doubt or certainty about certain facts<br>• make lodging arrangements<br>• state wishes and preferences<br>• make requests in a polite manner<br>• describe a visit to a national park<br>• express emotions, likes, and dislikes | • talk about grocery shopping<br>• describe foods in terms of flavor and freshness<br>• make comparisons<br>• single out something<br>• discuss food preparations<br>• express accidental occurrences<br>• talk about good manners<br>• order food in a restaurant<br>• make complaints<br>• avoid using a word already mentioned | • talk about minor accidents<br>• express future events<br>• talk about situations that would have happened<br>• talk about symptoms and remedies<br>• ask for and provide medical information<br>• express length of time<br>• discuss ways to stay fit<br>• express what someone would do in a specific situation<br>• talk about a healthy diet | • describe hairstyles<br>• express hypothetical situations<br>• describe clothes and accessories<br>• describe colors<br>• talk about the cleaning and tailoring of clothing items<br>• specify conditions under which things will be done<br>• say to whom things belong<br>• talk about handicrafts | • talk about projects for the future<br>• talk about careers<br>• prepare for a job interview<br>• evaluate work conditions<br>• refer to indefinite or unknown subjects<br>• talk about future technologies<br>• express wishes and hopes for the future<br>• discuss environmental problems, their causes, and solutions |

| Unidad 6 | Unidad 7 | Unidad 8 | Unidad 9 | Unidad 10 |
|---|---|---|---|---|
| **Lección A**<br>Travel plans<br>Weather<br>Airport<br><br>**Lección B**<br>Lodging arrangements<br>National parks<br>Outdoor activities<br>Wildlife | **Lección A**<br>Food<br>Shopping in an outdoor market<br>Comparisons<br>Cooking<br><br>**Lección B**<br>Good manners at a party<br>Ordering food | **Lección A**<br>Emergencies at a clinic<br>Parts of the body<br>At the hospital<br>Symptoms<br>Remedies<br><br>**Lección B**<br>Fitness<br>Nutrition | **Lección A**<br>Hairstyles<br>Clothes<br>Colors<br><br>**Lección B**<br>At the dry cleaner<br>Sewing notions<br>Handicrafts | **Lección A**<br>Professions<br>Plans for the future<br>Job interview<br><br>**Lección B**<br>Future technologies<br>Space and science<br>The environment |

| Unidad 6 | Unidad 7 | Unidad 8 | Unidad 9 | Unidad 10 |
|---|---|---|---|---|
| **Lección A**<br>El subjuntivo con cláusulas adverbiales<br>El futuro<br>El subjuntivo para expresar duda y negación<br><br>**Lección B**<br>El condicional<br>Otros usos del condicional<br>El subjuntivo con verbos que expresan emociones | **Lección A**<br>*Repaso rápido:* El comparativo<br>El comparativo de igualdad<br>El superlativo<br>La voz pasiva<br>*Estar* y el participio pasado<br>Más usos de *se*<br><br>**Lección B**<br>El imperfecto del subjuntivo<br>El subjuntivo después de pronombres relativos<br>La nominalización y el pronombre relativo *que* | **Lección A**<br>*Repaso rápido:* El verbo *doler*<br>Los tiempos compuestos: El futuro perfecto y el condicional perfecto<br>Expresiones con *hace / hacía… que*<br><br>**Lección B**<br>El imperfecto del subjuntivo con *si*<br>*Repaso rápido:* Preposiciones y pronombres<br>Preposiciones seguidas de infinitivo | **Lección A**<br>El presente perfecto del subjuntivo<br>El pluscuamperfecto del subjuntivo<br>*Cualquiera*<br>Adjetivos para describir colores<br>*Repaso rápido:* Los diminutivos y los aumentativos<br><br>**Lección B**<br>El subjuntivo en cláusulas adverbiales<br>*Repaso rápido:* Los adjetivos y pronombres posesivos<br>Otros usos del infinitivo<br>Usos del gerundio y del participio pasado | **Lección A**<br>Verbos que terminan en *-iar, -uar*<br>Usos del subjuntivo y del indicativo<br>*Repaso rápido:* El subjuntivo con sujeto indefinido<br><br>**Lección B**<br>*Repaso rápido:* El futuro perfecto<br>Más sobre el imperfecto del subjuntivo<br>*Repaso rápido:* Las formas del subjuntivo<br>*Repaso rápido:* Los usos del subjuntivo<br>*Repáso rápido:* Más sobre los usos del subjuntivo |

| Unidad 6 | Unidad 7 | Unidad 8 | Unidad 9 | Unidad 10 |
|---|---|---|---|---|
| **Lección A**<br>Lo mejor de Panamá<br>Otras atracciones turísticas<br><br>**Lección B**<br>Costa Rica, ¡un país esencial!<br>Visitantes siempre bienvenidos | **Lección A**<br>Manjares con altura<br>El mercado tradicional<br><br>**Lección B**<br>Platos peruanos con tradición<br>Lo mejor de la cocina peruana | **Lección A**<br>La salud en Guatemala: Antes y ahora<br>Medicina tradicional maya<br><br>**Lección B**<br>Juegos del pasado<br>¡En forma! en San Pedro Sula | **Lección A**<br>Una tradición que no pasa de moda<br>Los mariachis, siempre de moda<br><br>**Lección B**<br>La artesanía mexicana y la industria de la moda<br>¿Qué está de moda en el mercado? | **Lección A**<br>Los jóvenes en medio de la crisis<br>Alternativas para un futuro mejor<br><br>**Lección B**<br>¡Explora tu río!<br>España mira hacia el futuro |

| Unidad 6 | Unidad 7 | Unidad 8 | Unidad 9 | Unidad 10 |
|---|---|---|---|---|
| Centro de Observación de la Ampliación en Colón | La quinua, el "grano de oro" codiciado por el mundo | La naturaleza también sana | La leyenda de Pascualita, el maniquí viviente de Chihuahua | Los jóvenes de la ESO ven su futuro muy negro (aunque se esfuercen) |

| Unidad 6 | Unidad 7 | Unidad 8 | Unidad 9 | Unidad 10 |
|---|---|---|---|---|
| Emboscada del tiempo<br>de *Marco Aguilar* | Cocinero en su tinta<br>de *Gustavo Rodríguez* | La rana que quería ser una rana auténtica<br>de *Augusto Monterroso* | El eterno femenino<br>de *Rosario Castellanos* | Vuelva usted mañana<br>de *Mariano José de Larra* |

## Level 4, Unidades 1–10

| | Unidad 1 | Unidad 2 | Unidad 3 | Unidad 4 | Unidad 5 |
|---|---|---|---|---|---|
| **Pregunta clave** | ¿Cómo se refleja la idiosincrasia de una nación en el trato de su gente? | ¿Qué se aprende cuando se viaja al extranjero? | ¿Qué aspectos socioculturales de un país afectan el futuro de su gente? | ¿Cómo se refleja la herencia cultural de un país en las prácticas familiares? | ¿Qué factores afectan la situación económica de un país y de su gente? |
| **Objetivos** | • greet friends<br>• ask questions and express emotion<br>• describe people and things<br>• point out someone or something<br>• write an informal e-mail<br>• write a persuasive essay<br>• understand cultural perspectives of Cuba | • use words and terms related to traveling<br>• make travel plans<br>• identify people<br>• talk about present activities<br>• talk about the future<br>• compare and contrast<br>• write a social network post<br>• write a tourist pamphlet<br>• understand cultural perspectives of Spain | • identify professions<br>• use vocabulary related to school and future success<br>• discuss the school enrollment process<br>• describe daily activities<br>• talk about present activities<br>• express obligations and probability<br>• write a formal letter<br>• write a recommendation<br>• understand cultural perspectives of Peru | • use words and terms associated with the home<br>• describe household chores<br>• talk about events in the past<br>• narrate events in the past<br>• explain how long something has been occurring<br>• write an informal letter<br>• write an account of what happened<br>• understand cultural perspectives of Bolivia | • use words and terms associated with banking and the business world<br>• talk about personal finances<br>• talk about situations that have and had happened<br>• refer to people and objects<br>• talk about likes and dislikes<br>• make generalized statements<br>• write a résumé<br>• write a summary<br>• understand cultural perspectives of Mexico |
| **Vocabulario** | Greetings<br>Farewells<br>Introductions<br>To ask for information<br>To ask for help<br>Courtesy expressions<br>Expressions of excitement and disappointment<br>*Comparación y contraste:*<br>   to ask, question, why, because, for | Airport expressions<br>Travel<br>Customs<br>Train station<br>At a hotel<br>Traveling in Spain<br>Horoscopes<br>*Comparación y contraste:*<br>   expressions for the word "time" | Preparing for college<br>Being a student<br>Homework<br>People in a school<br>Professions and careers<br>School buildings<br>*Comparación y contraste:*<br>   to fail, to take, expressions with *acabar*, other idiomatic expressions | Rooms and objects in the house<br>Chores<br>Meals<br>Family and relatives<br>*Comparación y contraste:*<br>   to know, to meet | Jobs and professions<br>Job search<br>Transactions with money<br>At the bank<br>Loans<br>Business expressions<br>*Comparación y contraste:*<br>   to think, to come |
| **Gramática** | Los interrogativos y las exclamaciones<br>Los sustantivos y artículos<br>Los adjetivos<br>Los demostrativos | Los pronombres personales<br>El presente del indicativo<br>El tiempo futuro<br>Las comparaciones | Los verbos reflexivos<br>Los usos de *ser* y *estar*<br>Los verbos *haber, hacer, tener, nevar* y *llover*<br>Expresiones de obligación y probabilidad<br>Las preposiciones *en* y *de* | Las formas del pretérito<br>Las formas del imperfecto<br>El pretérito vs. El imperfecto<br>El verbo *hacer* en expresiones temporales | Las formas del presente perfecto y del pluscuamperfecto<br>Los pronombres en función de complemento directo, indirecto o de preposición<br>El verbo *gustar* y verbos similares<br>Usos especiales del pronombre *se*<br>Las preposiciones *a* y *con* |
| **Cultura** | Cuba<br>Así somos y así nos saludamos<br>¿Cuestión de léxico o filosofía?<br>El vínculo de la amistad | España<br>Madrid: Arte por todas partes<br>Verde encanto<br>¡A visitar lo que es nuestro! | Perú<br>Con la mira puesta en el futuro<br>Del elitismo a la meritocracia<br>Diversidad y educación en Perú | Bolivia<br>Mujeres: El eje central de la familia boliviana<br>El matrimonio en la cultura aymara<br>El aguayo | México<br>La importancia de la economía<br>La economía real<br>Beneficios del teletrabajo |
| **Lectura informativa** | Fragmentos del discurso de Barack Obama sobre la reanudación de relaciones entre EE. UU. y Cuba | 2015, Año del Quijote<br>Cospedal celebra que "nuestro personaje más universal" acercará Castilla-La Mancha al mundo para crear riqueza | Verano en Cusco<br>Vida en Cusco | Las trabajadoras del hogar se asocian y ofrecen servicios domésticos por hora | El 59 % de los universitarios mexicanos no cuenta actualmente con un empleo |
| **Escritura** | Un correo electrónico informal<br>Un ensayo persuasivo | Una publicación en una red social<br>Un folleto turístico | Una carta formal<br>Una recomendación | Una carta informal<br>Un relato | Una hoja de vida<br>Un resumen |
| **Lectura literaria** | Dos patrias<br>   de *José Martí* | He andado muchos caminos<br>   de *Antonio Machado* | El alacrán de fray Gómez<br>   de *Ricardo Palma* | Las medias rojas<br>   de *Emilia Pardo Bazán* | Autorretrato<br>   de *Rosario Castellanos* |

| Unidad 6 | Unidad 7 | Unidad 8 | Unidad 9 | Unidad 10 |
|---|---|---|---|---|
| ¿Cómo cambia el cuidado de la salud según la época? | ¿Qué problemas conlleva la vida urbana y cómo se resuelven? | ¿Cómo afectan las decisiones políticas la identidad cultural de un país? | ¿Qué aspectos de la cultura de un país se reflejan en sus fiestas y tradiciones? | ¿Cómo afecta la situación política y social de un país a los medios de comunicación? |
| · talk about health and well-being<br>· talk about symptoms, illnesses, diagnoses, and treatments<br>· identify body parts<br>· make requests, suggestions and demands<br>· indicate ownership<br>· fill out a medical form<br>· write an argumentative essay<br>· understand cultural perspectives of Chile | · discuss issues related to living and shopping in a big city<br>· identify foods and clothing items<br>· discuss hypothetical situations<br>· talk about situations that would have happened<br>· describe actions<br>· write a comparative essay<br>· write an informal e-mail<br>· write a letter to the editor<br>· understand cultural perspectives of Argentina | · use terms and words associated with geography, the environment and current events<br>· express hypothetical situations<br>· make positive and negative statements<br>· avoid using a word already mentioned<br>· analyze social and environmental issues<br>· write a biography<br>· understand cultural perspectives of Puerto Rico | · use terms and words associated with celebrations<br>· incorporate infinitive verb forms<br>· decide which preposition to use in specific situations<br>· add emphasis to a description<br>· discuss holidays in Colombia and the Spanish-speaking world<br>· write a persuasive letter<br>· understand cultural perspectives of Colombia | · use terms and words associated with print and electronic communication<br>· talk about what is currently happening<br>· say what will have and would have happened<br>· express hypothetical and contrary past actions<br>· avoid using a word already mentioned<br>· write a persuasive essay<br>· understand cultural perspectives of Honduras |
| Health maintenance<br>Emergency room<br>Emergency situations<br>Health symptoms<br>Treatments<br>Parts of the body<br>Doctor's office<br>Recommendations and advice<br>*Comparación y contraste:*<br>  false cognates | In the city<br>In the street<br>Clothing and accessories<br>Food<br>Shopping in the market<br>*Comparación y contraste:*<br>  to leave, to put | Geography<br>Natural phenomena<br>The economy<br>Ethnic groups<br>Politics<br>*Comparación y contraste:*<br>  quedar | Celebrations<br>Holidays<br>Traditions<br>Legends<br>Artisans<br>*Comparación y contraste:*<br>  looks and appearance, to miss, date | Types of communication<br>Expressions on the telephone<br>At the post office<br>The press<br>Film and theater<br>Computer<br>Radio and television<br>Video<br>*Comparación y contraste:*<br>  but |
| El subjuntivo<br>El imperativo formal de *Ud.* y *Uds.*<br>El imperativo familiar de *tú* y *vosotros*<br>El imperativo de *nosotros* | El subjuntivo en cláusulas adjetivales<br>El subjuntivo en cláusulas adverbiales<br>El imperfecto del subjuntivo<br>El subjuntivo en oraciones independientes<br>Los adverbios | El tiempo condicional<br>Las cláusulas condicionales con *si*<br>El presente perfecto del subjuntivo<br>Expresiones afirmativas y negativas<br>La voz activa y pasiva | Los usos del infinitivo<br>Las preposiciones *por* y *para*<br>Los usos de algunas preposiciones<br>Los diminutivos y los aumentativos | El gerundio<br>El futuro perfecto y el condicional perfecto<br>El pluscuamperfecto del subjuntivo<br>Los usos de los pronombres relativos *que* y *quien(es)* |
| **Chile**<br>Medicina mapuche en el siglo XXI<br>Un médico rural, un médico integral<br>La salud en el mundo virtual | **Argentina**<br>Buenos Aires y el tránsito<br>Cuando lo abandonado vuelve a cobrar vida<br>De ciudad ideal a ciudad sumergida | **Puerto Rico**<br>La construcción de la puertorriqueñidad<br>El idioma y la cultura<br>Nueva ola migratoria de la isla al continente | **Colombia**<br>El carnaval y la cumbia<br>La Leyenda Vallenata<br>Noviembre es pura fiesta en Cartagena | **Honduras**<br>Los medios de comunicación hondureños<br>Una ley para el periodismo<br>Asociación de Medios Comunitarios en Honduras |
| Los momentos que marcaron la evolución de la medicina y la salud en Chile | Una tragedia que no admite más disputas ni dilaciones | La crisis lleva a universitarios puertorriqueños a emigrar en masa a EE. UU. | ¿Triqui triqui enfrentado a los angelitos? | Virgilio Andrade: en 50 años de radio sufrí amenazas, marginación y exilio |
| Una historia clínica<br>Un texto argumentativo | Un ensayo comparativo<br>Un correo electrónico informal<br>Una carta de lectores | Una biografía | Una carta persuasiva | Un ensayo persuasivo |
| Walking Around<br>  de *Pablo Neruda* | Los dos reyes y los dos laberintos<br>  de *Jorge Luis Borges* | Cuando era puertorriqueña<br>  de *Esmeralda Santiago* | Un señor muy viejo con unas alas enormes<br>  de *Gabriel García Márquez* | Hombres necios<br>  de *Sor Juana Inés de la Cruz*<br>Peso ancestral<br>  de *Alfonsina Storni* |

## Level 5, Unidades 1–10

| | Unidad 1 | Unidad 2 | Unidad 3 | Unidad 4 | Unidad 5 |
|---|---|---|---|---|---|
| **Título** | ¡De viaje! | Viajes con desafíos | Jóvenes, sus valores y retos | Comida y salud | ¿Cómo eres? ¿Quién eres? |
| **Temas** | • Los desafíos mundiales<br>• La belleza y la estética<br>• La vida contemporánea<br>• Las familias y las comunidades | • Los desafíos mundiales<br>• Las familias y las comunidades<br>• La vida contemporánea<br>• Las identidades personales y públicas | • Las familias y las comunidades<br>• Los desafíos mundiales<br>• Las identidades personales y públicas | • Las familias y las comunidades<br>• La ciencia y la tecnología<br>• Los desafíos mundiales | • Las identidades personales y públicas<br>• Las familias y las comunidades<br>• La vida contemporánea<br>• Los desafíos mundiales |
| **Comunicación** | • Hablar sobre viajes, experiencias y destinos turísticos<br>• Describir hoteles<br>• Analizar hábitos y preferencias en los viajes<br>• Investigar y predecir sobre destinos turísticos populares en países hispanos | • Hablar de viajes que no son por ocio<br>• Hablar del impacto del turismo en el medio ambiente<br>• Discutir y comparar la inmigración<br>• Hablar sobre las travesías y retos de deportistas de alto riesgo | • Hablar de los jóvenes y sus cambios<br>• Hablar de las aficiones de los jóvenes<br>• Identificar a los jóvenes solidarios<br>• Discutir las metas y aspiraciones de los jóvenes<br>• Hablar de la gente joven y sus desafíos | • Hablar de la comida y la salud<br>• Discutir el tema del hambre mundial<br>• Hablar del impacto de la tecnología en nuestra comida | • Hablar sobre la fama y los famosos<br>• Charlar de la personalidad y la identidad<br>• Opinar sobre el impacto de los hispanos en Estados Unidos<br>• Hablar de puentes de unión entre culturas en Estados Unidos<br>• Hablar del maltrato y opresión a comunidades |
| **Gramática** | • Presente, pretérito e imperfecto del indicativo | • Género<br>• Conectores o nexos<br>• Verbos como gustar<br>• Pretérito e imperfecto del indicativo | • Presente del subjuntivo (nominal)<br>• Imperfecto del subjuntivo | • Mandatos<br>• Se impersonal<br>• Tiempos perfectos<br>• Participio pasado<br>• Subjuntivo nominal y cláusulas con si | • Subjuntivo adjetival y adverbial<br>• Subjuntivo con expresiones impersonales<br>• Preposiciones |
| **Tapitas gramaticales** | • lo que<br>• al + infinitivo<br>• es importante que + subjuntivo, cuando + indicativo/subjuntivo<br>• gran/grande + sustantivo<br>• tiempos perfectos<br>• para que + subjuntivo<br>• género y número de policía y taxista<br>• dos adverbios terminados en -mente seguidos | • e<br>• aunque + indicativo/subjuntivo<br>• construcciones recíprocas con nos<br>• diario, mensual, anual<br>• ya no, ni… ni<br>• sino, pero, sino que<br>• por mucho que + subjuntivo<br>• al + infinitivo | • ser, estar, haber, hacer, tener<br>• por/para | • sustantivos, artículos y adjetivos<br>• pronombres dobles<br>• expresiones con que<br>• prefijo des- | • lo + adjetivos<br>• nexos |
| **Cultura** | • Película Diarios de motocicleta<br>• El archipiélago de San Blas, Panamá<br>• Los indios kuna<br>• Destinos turísticos en España<br>• Hoteles originales y con encanto<br>• Transporte preferido por los hispanos en EE. UU. | • El Camino de Santiago<br>• La integración de comunidades hispanas en E.E. U.U.<br>• Inmigrantes y emigrantes en diferentes países de habla hispana<br>• Turismo y medio ambiente | • Los niños soldados y las Farc<br>• La generación de los ni-nis<br>• Las tribus urbanas<br>• El realismo mágico | • Los freegans<br>• La alimentación<br>• La escasez de alimentos<br>• La comida como Patrimonio de la Humanidad<br>• Los alimentos alterados genéticamente | • La identidad latina y estereotipos<br>• La diversidad entre los latinos y los latinos en EE. UU.<br>• Latinos famosos, imagen e influencia |
| **Lecturas** | • Un destino para Robinsones del siglo XXI<br>• Conozca España<br>• Machu Picchu (Perú)<br>• Dulces (y originales) sueños<br>• (Los latinos) viajan y gastan más<br>• Una noche en el Museo del Prado (España) | • Pedro en el Camino de Santiago<br>• El impacto del turismo en el medio ambiente<br>• Spanglish, Carta de Cristina a la universidad<br>• La vuelta al mundo a pie<br>• Naranjas | • ¿Por qué los millennials influyen tanto en el marketing?<br>• ¿Por qué los jóvenes no se van de casa?<br>• Pequeños soldados<br>• Los niños y niñas de la calle<br>• Alba | • El mate… su historia<br>• Y el chocolate espeso<br>• Toda la verdad sobre los superalimentos<br>• El mundo en desequilibrio<br>• Menús del futuro<br>• Fragmento de Como agua para chocolate (Laura Esquivel) | • Enamoradictos<br>• La identidad latina traspasa etiquetas<br>• Crítica a Sofía Vergara y Modern Family<br>• La isla bajo el mar<br>• La sombra del viento |

| Unidad 6 | Unidad 7 | Unidad 8 | Unidad 9 | Unidad 10 |
|---|---|---|---|---|
| Naturaleza y medio ambiente | La tecnología y el futuro | ¡Qué arte! | Comunidades y costumbres | Historia y actualidad |
| • Los desafíos mundiales<br>• La ciencia y la tecnología<br>• La vida contemporánea<br>• Las familias y las comunidades<br>• Las identidades personales y públicas | • La ciencia y la tecnología<br>• La vida contemporánea<br>• Las familias y las comunidades<br>• Los desafíos mundiales | • La belleza y la estética<br>• La vida contemporánea<br>• Las identidades personales y públicas<br>• Las familias y las comunidades<br>• Los desafíos mundiales | • Las familias y las comunidades<br>• Las identidades personales y públicas<br>• La vida contemporánea<br>• Los desafíos mundiales | • La vida contemporánea<br>• Los desafíos mundiales<br>• Las identidades personales y públicas<br>• Las familias y las comunidades |
| • Hablar sobre desafíos ecológicos y soluciones<br>• Hablar sobre las energías renovables<br>• Leer e investigar sobre animales en peligro de extinción y medidas de protección | • Hablar del impacto de la tecnología<br>• Opinar de los avances tecnológicos<br>• Charlar de las adicciones a las redes sociales<br>• Hablar del futuro<br>• Charlar sobre los inventos | • Hablar de las bellas artes<br>• Estudiar y comparar el arte de varios artistas hispanos<br>• Discutir la música y su impacto en la comunidad<br>• Charlar sobre la influencia de las telenovelas y el cine<br>• Hablar de la moda<br>• Debatir sobre la controversia en el arte | • Hablar sobre las tradiciones hispanas<br>• Comparar tradiciones hispanas con las de EE. UU.<br>• Escribir correos formales e informales<br>• Dialogar sobre la importancia de la lengua en una comunidad<br>• Hablar sobre comunidades y su impacto en la sociedad | • Conocer algunos de los principales procesos históricos del siglo xx<br>• Hablar de sus dimensiones sociales, económicas, culturales y políticas<br>• Desarrollar habilidades interpretativas, analíticas, culturales, reflexivas y de investigación<br>• Analizar eventos históricos de diversas épocas incorporando y contrastando varias experiencias nacionales |
| • Tiempos perfectos<br>• Participios<br>• Gerundios<br>• Futuro<br>• Repaso de tiempos verbales<br>• Mandatos de *nosotros* | • Verbos con preposición<br>• Cognados y falsos cognados<br>• Expresiones impersonales<br>• Subjuntivo o indicativo<br>• Formación de verbos a partir de sustantivos<br>• Formación de sustantivos a partir de verbos | • Repaso de tiempos<br>• Mandatos<br>• Adjetivos descriptivos | • ¡Qué…!<br>• Repaso de los tiempos verbales<br>• Expresiones de tiempo: *llevo, hace, hacía, tardar, aún, todavía*<br>• Cláusulas con *si*<br>• Uso de *como* y *de* en el condicional<br>• Algunos usos de *ser* y *estar*<br>• Nexos<br>• Género de sustantivos | • Participio pasado<br>• Nexos<br>• Indicativo o subjuntivo<br>• *Ser, estar, haber, tener*<br>• Repaso de tiempos verbales |
| • usos del condicional | • *sino, si no, pero*<br>• *mientras que* + indicativo/subjuntivo | • participios pasados<br>• expresiones con *hacer(se)*<br>• *cuando* + subjuntivo<br>• verbos con objeto indirecto | • *Ponerse, volverse, hacerse, llegar a ser* | • artículo + pronombre posesivo (el mío, el tuyo…)<br>• *lo* + adjetivo/adverbio<br>• *quedar* y verbos similares<br>• *a pesar de que, como, pues, ya que, puesto que, en vista de que*<br>• *por* y *para* |
| • Los retos medioambientales de los países de habla hispana<br>• Los indígenas y su respeto por el medio ambiente<br>• El impacto del monocultivo en la Amazonia<br>• El cambio climático y medidas para combatirlo | • El fenómeno *hacker*<br>• La privacidad en la era de la internet<br>• La tecnología y el futuro<br>• Las profesiones del futuro<br>• La búsqueda de vida en otros planetas | • El patrimonio arqueológico y artístico<br>• La música hispana y la de las comunidades latinas en EE. UU.<br>• El flamenco<br>• La arquitectura de Antonio Gaudí<br>• Las telenovelas y su impacto social<br>• El *Guernica* y la Guerra Civil española | • La sobremesa<br>• Tradiciones de fin de año<br>• La celebración del 5 de mayo<br>• La Fiesta del Sol<br>• El Día de los Muertos y el Día de Todos los Santos<br>• Otras fiestas y tradiciones en países hispanos<br>• Lenguas y dialectos<br>• Mitos hispanos | • Las Abuelas de la Plaza de Mayo<br>• El Canal de Panamá<br>• El camino hacia la paz en Colombia<br>• Ernesto «Che» Guevara<br>• La colaboración entre EE. UU. y Latinoamérica<br>• Raíces democráticas en los países hispanos<br>• La Guerra Civil española<br>• Las tres culturas de Córdoba en el siglo xii<br>• Evita Perón<br>• Las hermanas Mirabal |
| • Crisis ambiental en América Latina<br>• Árboles para la Tierra<br>• Las cucarachas tienen personalidad<br>• Arrasando la Amazonia en nombre del progreso (de las multinacionales)<br>• Fragmento de *La casa de los espíritus* (Isabel Allende)<br>• "¿No oyes ladrar los perros?" (Juan Rulfo) | • Los jóvenes y las nuevas tecnologías<br>• Profesiones del futuro<br>• ¿Eres adicto a Facebook?<br>• Misión: vivir para siempre en Marte<br>• El robot de tus sueños (y pesadillas)<br>• Fragmento de *Cien años de soledad* (Gabriel García Márquez) | • La música tiene un papel en la comunidad<br>• Crítica de arte reprueba comercialización de Frida Kahlo<br>• Gaudí<br>• Polémica sobre los patrimonios de la humanidad en los museos<br>• El impacto de las telenovelas<br>• El *Guernica* | • Los indígenas: los sacrificados<br>• Lenguas indígenas en agonía<br>• 10 de noviembre: Día de la Tradición Argentina<br>• El deporte rey<br>• Fragmento de *La casa de Bernarda Alba* (Federico García Lorca)<br>• Una comunidad unida | • Romance junto al Guadalquivir (Luis Novas)<br>• Fragmento de *Santa Evita* (Tomás Eloy Martínez)<br>• Fragmento de *Noticia de un secuestro* (Gabriel García Márquez)<br>• Fragmento de *La casa de los espíritus* (Isabel Allende)<br>• El tiempo de las mariposas |

*¡Qué chévere!* was designed to give Spanish teachers a program that focuses on the three modes of communication—interpersonal, presentational, and interpretive—while ensuring their students become proficient in the five skill areas. Based on an extensive survey of Spanish educators as well as focus groups and discussion groups, the textbook program responds to teachers' expressed interests and priorities. In *¡Qué chévere! 4*, the vocabulary presentations are set in a narrative style accompanied by up-to-date and engaging photos. This style allows students to review previously learned expressions while gaining exposure to new expressions in context. Grammar explanations and exercises are designed to review previously learned concepts, build proficiency, and prevent fossilization. Students learn to read informative and literary texts as part of this Pre-AP program. Activities move from mechanical and meaningful to communicative and then progress to creative and open-ended projects. An essential question frames all the learning in any given unit. Each unit has a theme, for example, interpersonal relationships or health and well being.

Because paired, small group, and cooperative group activities are at the heart of today's student-centered classroom, *¡Qué chévere!* offers many opportunities for students to work with their classmates on activities and projects that have clear guidelines and expectations. Students assume a more active role in their learning as they focus on how to learn as well as how to integrate language and culture. Opportunities for critical thinking can be found throughout the program, for example, in comparing Spanish-speaking cultures to a student's own culture, as well as in the *Analice* questions that accompany the culture, informative, and literary reading selections.

Since a modern challenge in world language instruction is reaching all students—those with varying abilities, backgrounds, interests, and learning styles—the *¡Qué chévere!* program has many opportunities beyond the textbook to help meet those needs. The Annotated Teacher's Edition provides suggested activities for different types of learners, from those with special needs to those who would benefit from having their learning style met.

Finally, the *¡Qué chévere!* program was written to incorporate the National Standards. Included here are the revised ACTFL Standards.

## ACTFL World-Readiness Standards for Learning Languages

### Communication

**Communicate Effectively in More Than One Language in Order to Function in a Variety of Situations and for Multiple Purposes**

**Interpersonal Communication (formerly Standard 1.1)**: Learners interact and negotiate meaning in spoken, signed, or written conversations to share information, reactions, feelings, and opinions.

**Interpretive Communication (formerly Standard 1.2)**: Learners understand, interpret, and analyze what is heard, read, or viewed on a variety of topics.

**Presentational Communication (formerly Standard 1.3)**: Learners present information, concepts, and ideas to inform, explain, persuade, and narrate on a variety of topics using appropriate media and adapting to various audiences of listeners, readers, or viewers.

### Cultures

**Interact with Cultural Competence and Understanding**

**Relating Cultural Practices to Perspectives (formerly Standard 2.1)**: Learners use the language to investigate, explain, and reflect on the relationship between the practices and perspectives of the cultures studied.

**Relating Cultural Products to Perspectives (formerly Standard 2.2)**: Learners use the language to investigate, explain, and reflect on the relationship between the products and perspectives of the cultures studied.

## Connections

**Connect with Other Disciplines and Acquire Information and Diverse Perspectives in Order to Use the Language to Function in Academic and Career-Related Situations**

**Making Connections (formerly Standard 3.1)**: Learners build, reinforce, and expand their knowledge of other disciplines while using the language to develop critical thinking and to solve problems creatively.

**Acquiring Information and Diverse Perspectives (formerly Standard 3.2)**: Learners access and evaluate information and diverse perspectives that are available through the language and its cultures.

## Comparisons

**Develop Insight into the Nature of Language and Culture in Order to Interact with Cultural Competence**

**Language Comparisons (formerly Standard 4.1)**: Learners use the language to investigate, explain, and reflect on the nature of language through comparisons of the language studied and their own.

**Cultural Comparisons (formerly Standard 4.2)**: Learners use the language to investigate, explain, and reflect on the concept of culture through comparisons of the cultures studied and their own.

## Communities

**Communicate and Interact with Cultural Competence in Order to Participate in Multilingual Communities at Home and Around the World**

**School and Global Communities (formerly Standard 5.1)**: Learners use the language both within and beyond the classroom to interact and collaborate in their community and the globalized world.

**Lifelong Learning (formerly Standard 5.2)**: Learners set goals and reflect on their progress in using languages for enjoyment, enrichment, and advancement.

Welcome to *¡Qué chévere!*!

**A**

**¿Sabía que...?**
La Terminal 4 del aeropuerto Adolfo Suárez Madrid-Barajas es uno de los íconos arquitectónicos de la ciudad. Inaugurada en 2006, llama la atención del viajero por su diseño ondulado y sus colores, que representan el arco iris.

Unidad

# 2

# El atractivo de viajar

**B**

**D**

Escanee el código QR para mirar el video "De tapas".

Conocer las costumbres típicas de otros países es uno de los atractivos de viajar. ¿En qué consiste la costumbre española de "ir de tapas" o "tapear"? Explique en detalle su respuesta.

pregunta clave

**?**

¿Qué se aprende cuando se viaja al extranjero?

**F**

**Mis metas**

**En esta unidad:**

▶ Usaré expresiones relacionadas con viajes dentro y fuera del país.

▶ Usaré los pronombres personales y los verbos regulares e irregulares en el presente de indicativo.

▶ Me familiarizaré con la riqueza artística, natural e histórica de España.

▶ Distinguiré el significado de palabras y frases según el contexto.

▶ Usaré correctamente el futuro de los verbos regulares e irregulares.

▶ Leeré un artículo sobre la celebración del *Año del Quijote* en España y los motivos de esta celebración.

▶ Publicaré mi opinión sobre "Gigantes", el logotipo del Quijote 2015, en una red social.

▶ Crearé un anuncio publicitario para promocionar el turismo en diferentes regiones de España.

▶ Desarrollaré nuevas destrezas de vocabulario.

▶ Usaré los comparativos y las diferentes formas del superlativo en español.

▶ Leeré el poema "He andado muchos caminos" del español Antonio Machado.

**C**

**E**

¿De quién es esta famosa obra de arte y cómo se llama?

España

cuarenta y cinco **45**

---

**A**

***¿Sabía que...?*** presents an interesting fact connected to the unit theme and country or region of focus.

**C**

The **map** for each unit highlights the featured country or region from the Spanish-speaking world.

**E**

A **culture question** is accompanied by a photo. Students will watch for the photo and the answer to the question in one of the culture readings of the unit.

**B**

Each unit features a video short giving a glimpse into the daily life of a Spanish-speaking teen. Students can scan the **QR code** to watch the video.

**D**

Unit content is centered on a ***Pregunta clave*** that anchors learning.

**F**

**Learning objectives** encourage students to anticipate the unit content.

## Vocabulario 1

**A** **¡Nos vamos de viaje!** 🎧 **B**

### En el aeropuerto

Acuérdese de estas recomendaciones para viajeros, sobre todo si es la primera vez que viaja al extranjero.
- Confirme sus reservaciones antes del viaje y recuerde que debe estar en el aeropuerto con tres horas de anticipación para vuelos internacionales y dos para vuelos nacionales.
- Diríjase al mostrador de la línea aérea para facturar su equipaje. Tome precauciones si no quiere pagar por exceso de equipaje.
- Quítese cualquier artículo personal de metal antes de pasar por el detector de metales en el control de seguridad.
- Presente su visa, pasaporte y pasajes en emigración y, luego, diríjase a la sala de espera y manténgase allí hasta el momento de abordar el avión.

**C**

### En la sala de espera

**D** Última llamada para los pasajeros del vuelo 357 de Iberia, directo a la ciudad de Madrid. El avión está preparándose para el despegue.

### En el avión

Siga las indicaciones de la tripulación a todo momento. En caso de turbulencia o de aterrizaje forzoso, mantenga la calma (no van a estrellarse) y haga lo que indique el (la) piloto o el (la) auxiliar de vuelo.

¿Cambiamos de asiento? Pedí uno de ventanilla o de pasillo, pero ya no había.

Tengan la amabilidad de apagar sus computadoras. Ya estamos próximos a despegar.

Abróchate el cinturón de seguridad que ya vamos a aterrizar.

### Al bajarse del avión

- Después de pasar por inmigración, recoja su equipaje y pase por la inspección de aduana.
- Si está haciendo escala y pierde su vuelo de conexión, vaya al mostrador de la línea aérea donde lo/la ayudarán.
- Si lo necesita, generalmente hay una oficina de cambio (de moneda) en la planta baja del aeropuerto.

 El inspector revisará sus maletas y maletín de mano para ver que no lleve contrabando.

 Consulte el monitor de salidas y llegadas de vuelos para saber a qué hora sale su vuelo de conexión.

### En el hotel

Al llegar al hotel, diríjase a la recepción para inscribirse y pedir la llave de su habitación. Recuerde que el botones puede ayudarle a subir o bajar su equipaje. Si tiene algún problema, no dude en hablar con el gerente del hotel.

¿Podría decirme si la Srta. Amelia Cárdenas aparece en su lista de huéspedes?

¿Te acordaste de darle una propina?

¡Por supuesto!

Claro que sí. Un momento, por favor.

### Para conversar 🎧 **E**

**P**ara hacer planes de turismo:

Queremos conocer España y nos gustaría hacer unas reservaciones. ¿Puede ayudarnos?

¿Les interesa viajar en coche, en barco, o en ferrocarril?

¿Desean viajar en primera clase o clase turística?

¿Cuánto cuesta un pasaje de ida y vuelta a...?

¿Tienen servicio de coche cama y coche comedor en este tren?

¿Qué hacemos si tenemos que cancelar o posponer el viaje?

¿A qué hora sale/llega...?

El tren sale del andén número...

¡Pasajeros al tren!

---

**A** The *Vocabulario 1* title provides the theme of the unit vocabulary.

**B** All textbook audio is recorded by a native speaker so students are exposed to different accents from around the Spanish-speaking world.

**C** Up-to-date photos engage students and provide a context for the vocabulary.

**D** Previously learned and new vocabulary expressions are presented in narrative form in context.

**E** *Para conversar* presents structures in meaningful context.

**F** **emcpassport.com** indicates that more support activities related to this page's content can be found in digital supplements.

**T19**

## Gramática A

### El tiempo futuro

El futuro de los verbos regulares se forma añadiendo al infinitivo las siguientes terminaciones.

| Futuro de verbos regulares | | |
|---|---|---|
| **viajar** | **volver** | **ir** |
| viajaré | volveré | iré |
| viajarás | volverás | irás |
| viajará | volverá | irá |
| viajaremos | volveremos | iremos |
| viajaréis | volveréis | iréis |
| viajarán | volverán | irán |

Los verbos irregulares en futuro tienen cambios en la raíz, pero no en las terminaciones.

A veces se puede seguir un patrón (*pattern*) en la conjugación de estos verbos, como se ve a continuación.

*Viajaremos a Sevilla este verano.*

| Futuro de verbos irregulares | | | |
|---|---|---|---|
| **Cambio en la raíz** | **Infinitivo** | **Raíz** | **Futuro** |
| | caber | cabr- | cabré |
| | haber | habr- | habré |
| Se omite la **e** del infinitivo. | poder | podr- | podré |
| | querer | querr- | querré |
| | saber | sabr- | sabré |
| | poner* | pondr- | pondré |
| | salir | saldr- | saldré |
| La **d** reemplaza la **e** o **i** del infinitivo. | tener* | tendr- | tendré |
| | valer | valdr- | valdré |
| | venir | vendr- | vendré |
| Se omiten las letras **ec** y **ce**, respectivamente | decir | dir- | diré |
| | hacer* | har- | haré |

*Los verbos que se derivan de estos, como **suponer**, **mantener** y **deshacer**, se conjugan con la misma terminación en el futuro: **supondré**, **mantendré**, **desharé**, etc.

### Un poco más B

**Haber**, cuando se usa como verbo impersonal, se conjuga solamente en la tercera personal del singular.

**Hay** mucha gente en el aeropuerto.

**Habrá** mucha gente en el aeropuerto.

Se conjuga en todas las personas cuando se usa como verbo auxiliar en la formación de los tiempos compuestos. Ver futuro perfecto, p. 409.

Ya **habremos reclamado** el equipaje cuando pasemos por la aduana.

---

### 33 El horóscopo del mes C

Complete el horóscopo con el futuro del verbo indicado.

**Capricornio**
Ud. (**1.** *salir*) de todas sus deudas mediante la oferta de trabajo que le (**2.** *ser*) ofrecida muy pronto.

**Cáncer**
Un amigo (**15.** *venir*) a buscarlo con planes para el futuro. (**16.** *valer*) la pena considerar su oferta.

**Acuario**
Busque la compañía de sus amigos. Ellos le (**3.** *ayudar*) con sus problemas, y su vida social (**4.** *comenzar*) un nuevo ciclo.

**Leo**
Ud. (**17.** *sufrir*) una traición. (**18.** *tener*) que cuidar sus actos al hablar con parientes y amigos.

**Piscis**
Ud. (**5.** *sentir*) que el estudio es aburrido y (**6.** *tener*) dificultades, pero muy pronto (**7.** *poder*) resolverlas.

**Virgo**
El día 15 Ud. (**19.** *recibir*) la visita inesperada de un amigo que le (**20.** *contar*) sus penas y (**21.** *haber*) que consolarlo.

**Aries**
Ud. (**8.** *recibir*) dinero. Aproveche para dar fiestas. Muy buenos amigos (**9.** *buscar*) su compañía.

**Libra**
Uno de sus pasatiempos le (**22.** *producir*) dinero y (**23.** *firmar*) grandes contratos con compañías muy importantes.

**Tauro**
Sus planes (**10.** *empezar*) a dar frutos. Ud. (**11.** *ganar*) más dinero y (**12.** *hacer*) el viaje soñado.

**Escorpión**
Sus planes de viaje (**24.** *tomar*) un rumbo positivo. (**25.** *conocer*) Sudamérica y (**26.** *encontrar*) la felicidad y el amor.

**Géminis**
Ud. (**13.** *tener*) momentos de duras luchas interiores. No se desanime; no (**14.** *ser*) nada muy grave.

**Sagitario**
Piense antes de aceptar un trabajo; de lo contrario (**27.** *tener*) muchos problemas que lo (**28.** *poner*) en dificultades.

---

**A** *Gramática* explains grammatical concepts clearly and concisely with charts and examples.

**B** *Un poco más* provides additional information related to the grammar explanation.

**C** The *actividades* that follow the grammar explanation progress from mechanical to meaningful to communicative.

T20

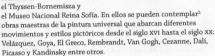

# *Cultura*

¿Qué se aprende cuando se viaja al extranjero?

**A**

**B** ## Madrid: Arte por todas partes

### 21 Comprensión

1. ¿En qué zona del país está ubicada Madrid?

2. ¿Qué deben visitar los viajeros que aman la pintura?

3. ¿Por qué se dice que Madrid es como un "museo al aire libre"?

*La Puerta de Alcalá*

Muchas cosas pueden decirse de Madrid: que es la residencia oficial de los reyes de España, que es la capital del Estado español, que es una mezcla perfecta de modernidad y tradición. Pero para describir esta ciudad, situada en el corazón geográfico del país, la mejor palabra es "arte".

En Madrid, el "Paseo del Arte" es el recorrido obligado[1] de los viajeros que aman la pintura. Este itinerario incluye tres museos ubicados a pocos metros de distancia: el reconocido[2] Museo del Prado, el Thyssen-Bornemisza y el Museo Nacional Reina Sofía. En ellos se pueden contemplar[3] obras maestras de la pintura universal que abarcan diferentes movimientos y estilos pictóricos desde el siglo XVI hasta el siglo XX: Velázquez, Goya, El Greco, Rembrandt, Van Gogh, Cezanne, Dalí, Picasso y Kandinsky entre otros.

*Las meninas de Diego de Velázquez*

Pero en Madrid el arte no se limita a las grandes pinturas. Caminar por esta ciudad es como recorrer un museo al aire libre. Hermosos monumentos e impresionantes obras arquitectónicas aparecen casi en cada esquina: el Palacio Real, la plaza de Cibeles, la Puerta de Alcalá o el parque del Retiro, que perteneció a la monarquía española hasta fines del siglo XIX y donde se encuentra el maravilloso Palacio de Cristal. La zona del centro antiguo, llamado "viejo Madrid", está poblada de plazas con tabernas[4] de tapas, restaurantes y comercios tradicionales, como la Plaza Mayor. Y la mejor parte es que el viajero descubrirá enseguida que los lugares más emblemáticos[5] de Madrid son también los más queridos por sus habitantes: en la concurrida[6] Puerta del Sol, por ejemplo, el turista podrá sentir plenamente el ritmo y la intensidad de esta ciudad.

¹ all-important tour   ² renowned   ³ admire   ⁴ bars   ⁵ representative   ⁶ crowded

### 22 Analice

1. ¿Qué cree Ud. que significa el hecho de que los habitantes de Madrid también visiten sus lugares más emblemáticos?

2. ¿Qué práctica gastronómica de su país se parece al tapeo español?

🔍 **Búsqueda:** paseo del arte madrid, plaza mayor, puerta del sol

**C** ### Prácticas

"Ir de tapas" o "tapear" es una de las costumbres más típicas de España. Es una forma de socializar, relacionarse y pasar un rato divertido al tiempo que se consumen pequeñas porciones de alimento, siempre acompañadas de una bebida. Originalmente, las "tapas" se servían sobre la boca de la jarra o el vaso de bebida, de modo que "tapaba" (*covered*) el recipiente. Así se originó su nombre. "Tapear" es una costumbre española que se ha convertido en un símbolo de identidad del país.

## Verde encanto 🎧

A la hora de elegir un destino, son muchas las razones que pueden atraer al viajero: disfrutar la belleza de un paisaje natural, enriquecerse con la cultura local o alojarse en un hotel de ensueño. Y hay un lugar donde todo eso es posible: la España verde, conformada por Galicia, Asturias, Cantabria y el País Vasco. Allí, en el litoral[1] norte español, con más de 2000 kilómetros de costa sobre el océano Atlántico y el mar Cantábrico, la naturaleza se asoma al mar y le ofrece innumerables paisajes de todos los verdes imaginables.

La España verde es un espacio ecológico que incluye acantilados[2], montañas, dunas, bosques, islas, ríos y playas. Por su belleza y biodiversidad, muchos de ellos han sido declarados Reserva de la Biosfera por la UNESCO, por ejemplo, el Parque Nacional de Los Picos de Europa, que abarca Cantabria y Asturias, y que además es el espacio protegido más extenso de España.

*España, un país rico en paisajes naturales*

Pero ser una valiosa reserva de flora y fauna (donde se puede observar una gran variedad de especies ornitológicas[3] o la mayor población de osos pardos en libertad de toda Europa) no impide que la España verde sea también un lugar lleno de historia. Lo que en otra época fueron antiguas líneas ferroviarias, trazados[4] de vías romanas, rutas y calzadas pecuarias[5] son hoy una red de senderos que el turista puede recorrer a pie, en bicicleta o a caballo.

La riqueza del patrimonio cultural español también se refleja en la oferta hotelera de esta zona. El visitante puede alojarse en mansiones que datan del siglo XV, acogedoras casas de labranza[6] reformadas u hoteles rurales o costeros que pueden incluir una gran torre medieval de piedra. En la España verde, el encanto no tiene fin.

¹ coast   ² cliffs   ³ species of birds   ⁴ lines   ⁵ livestock routes   ⁶ farmhouse

**F** 🔍 **Búsqueda:** españa verde, unesco

**G** ### Productos 🎧

El Transcantábrico es un tren turístico que recorre la España verde, desde San Sebastián hasta Santiago de Compostela. Creado en 1983 con la idea de imitar al clásico *Orient Express*, este hotel de lujo sobre rieles está considerado el mejor del mundo. Tiene vías especiales que le permiten circular por lugares a los que los trenes normales no pueden acceder.

*El Transcantábrico es un tren de lujo.*

**D** ### 23 Comprensión

1. ¿Por qué se llama "España verde" a la región norte del país?

2. ¿Cuál es el espacio protegido más grande de España?

3. ¿Qué sitios de interés histórico puede conocer el viajero en esta región de España?

**E** ### 24 Analice

1. ¿Qué características cree Ud. que debe tener un lugar para ser declarado Reserva de la Biosfera por la UNESCO?

2. ¿Qué diferencia cree que hay entre alojarse en un hotel que es un edificio moderno y uno que tiene muchos años de historia?

emcpassport.com
LA 3

60   sesenta   |   *Unidad 2*                    *Unidad 2*   |   sesenta y uno   61

---

**A** The *Pregunta clave* guides students to uncover the depth and richness of the culture.

**B** *Cultura* readings present topics of high interest that highlight the products, perspectives, and practices of the unit's country of focus.

**C** *Prácticas* reveals patterns of social interactions and behaviors within the highlighted culture.

**D** *Comprensión* questions ensure that students understand the key points of the reading.

**E** *Analice* questions encourage a deeper analysis of the reading and often ask students to make comparisons between their own culture and the culture of focus.

**F** *Búsqueda* provides key word searches to expand the culture topic beyond the classroom.

**G** *Productos* highlights the tangible and intangible creations of the highlighted culture.

# Walk-through: Student Edition

## Vocabulario 2

emcpassport.com
WB 6–8

### A  Comparación y contraste: ¡Ojo con estas palabras!

En español, al igual que en inglés, hay varias formas de expresar el concepto de **tiempo**. Preste atención, pues su uso depende del contexto.

¿Cuántas **veces** has venido a Madrid?

Muchas veces, pero **cada vez** que vengo, me gusta más.

time —
- tiempo
- vez (veces)
- hora
- rato
- época

| | |
|---|---|
| **tiempo** *a period or duration of time* | —¿Cuánto **tiempo** vas a estar en Madrid?<br>—Voy a quedarme una semana. |
| *time in the abstract* | —¿Quieres acompañarme al Museo del Prado? Hace mucho **tiempo** que quiero ir.<br>—Claro que sí. |
| **una vez** *once, one time* | —¿Nunca has ido al museo? |
| **cada vez** *each time* | —Sí. Fui **una vez** hace mucho tiempo y me encantó. Por eso, **cada vez** que |
| **otra vez** *again* | vuelvo a España, quiero ir a visitarlo **otra vez**. |
| **a veces** *sometimes* | —En cambio, yo le ido al museo en muchas oportunidades. **A veces** lo he |
| **veces** *times, occasions* | hecho por gusto propio, pero muchas otras **veces** he tenido que hacerlo para llevar a amigos que quieren visitarlo, como tú. |
| **hora** *time of day* | —¿Sabes a qué **hora** abren el museo hoy? |
| **hora (de)** *the proper time to do something* | —No sé. Creo que abren a las diez. ¿Qué **hora** es?<br>—Ya es **hora de** irnos. Acuérdate que no tenemos mucho tiempo.<br>—Por supuesto. ¡Ya es **hora**! |
| **rato** *a short time, a while* | —¿Cuánto tiempo piensan estar en el museo? |
| **época** *time during a season, historical time* | —Solo vamos a estar un **rato**. En estos días de verano hay demasiados turistas.<br>—Es verdad. Vienen muchos turistas en esta **época** del año. |
| **Para expresar la idea de** *to have a good time* use **divertirse** y **pasarlo bien**. | —¿Cómo les fue en el museo? **¿Se divirtieron?**<br>—Claro que sí. **Lo pasamos muy bien.** |

### B  27  ¿Otra vez?

Primero, complete las oraciones con las palabras del recuadro. Luego, empareje las preguntas de la izquierda con las respuestas de la derecha.

| tiempo | vez | otra vez | cada vez | veces | hora | rato | época |
|---|---|---|---|---|---|---|---|

1. ¿____ de viaje?
2. ¿Por qué te gusta viajar en esta ____ del año?
3. ¿Fuiste alguna ____ al restaurante Lakasa?
4. ¿Sabes qué ____ es?
5. ¿A qué ____ sale tu vuelo?
6. ¿Quieres que te acompañe un ____?
7. ¡Cuánto ____ está atrasado el vuelo!

A. A las seis y veinte. Es ____ de despedirnos.
B. Sí, varias ____. La comida es deliciosa.
C. Sí, dentro de un ____ salgo para Madrid.
D. Porque no hay muchos turistas y es la ____ de conciertos.
E. Cálmate. ____ que vuelas te pones nerviosa.
F. Por favor, acompáñame hasta que sea ____ de abordar.
G. Son las cinco y cuarenta. ¡Cómo pasa el ____!

### ¡Comunicación!

### C  28  ¡El mundo en la palma de la mano!  👥  Interpersonal Communication

Imagine que Ud. trabaja en una agencia de viajes y está ayudando a dos clientes, Jairo y Elisa, a planear su viaje de luna de miel. Represente la situación con dos compañeros, turnándose para pedir y dar información. Incluyan los siguientes temas en su conversación, como se ve en el modelo.

- Lugar de destino
- Itinerarios
- Clases de vuelos, escalas y conexiones
- Precios y formas de pago aceptadas
- Ofertas de paquetes especiales que incluyan pasajes, comida y alojamiento

¿Han viajado al Caribe alguna vez?

MODELO  Agente:  ¿En qué tiempo del año les gustaría viajar?
Jairo:  Bueno, la boda es en junio, pero tenemos cierta flexibilidad.
Elisa:  Sabemos que el verano es época de temporada alta.
Agente:  Muy bien. En ese caso...

---

**A**

***Comparación y contraste*** highlights potentially troublesome expressions whose meanings might fool a native English speaker.

**B**

Students demonstrate their understanding of the ***Comparación y contraste*** expressions in a follow-up activity.

**C**

Students engage in a communicative activity, expanding their comprehension and use of these troublesome expressions.

# A Lectura informativa

### Antes de leer

Un personaje literario se convierte en un clásico universal cuando se sabe de él aunque no se haya leído la obra en la que aparece. ¿Qué sabe Ud. sobre don Quijote de La Mancha?

B

## Estrategia

### Hacer conexiones

Usar sus conocimientos previos y hacer conexiones entre lo que ya sabe y la información que se presenta en el texto lo ayudará a comprender mejor lo que lee.

### 40 Comprensión

1. ¿Por qué el año 2015 es importante para el castellano y la literatura universal?

2. ¿Qué tipo de obra es *Don Quijote*?

3. ¿Qué clase de héroe es don Quijote?

### 41 Analice

¿Qué características cree Ud. que debe tener una obra literaria para convertirse en un clásico universal?

---

### 2015, Año del Quijote

**ALVARO OCTAVIO LARA HUERTA    14 de enero 2015 20:11:52**

Este 2015 será un año importante para el castellano y la literatura universal, ya que se cumple el cuarto centenario[1] de la publicación de *El ingenioso hidalgo don Quijote de la Mancha* (la segunda parte de la novela). [...]

A finales de 1615 salía a luz uno de los textos más importantes para el mundo de las letras y el máximo referente[2] para la lengua española. La primera novela moderna que ha sido traducida prácticamente a todos los idiomas y solo superada en ediciones por la Biblia.

Una obra que conjuga[3] la comedia, la poesía, el drama y la caballería[4] de una forma extraordinaria que ha cristalizado al personaje principal Alonso Quijano, don Quijote, en un símbolo de la cultura hispanoamericana que lo mismo ha tocado el cine, las artes visuales, la música y, por supuesto, la literatura, convirtiéndose en ese eterno espíritu libre, sabio e inquebrantable[5].

Seguramente el idealismo de don Quijote invadirá los eventos culturales del presente año, pues siempre es una delicia volver a los clásicos para redescubrir su actualidad y frescura, aun después de 400 años. La inventiva y "sabiduría popular" impregna cada frase, situación y diálogo a lo largo de los 74 capítulos que integran la obra con un sinfín[6] de recursos literarios.

El *Quijote* se ha vuelto un ícono de libertad y justicia, el héroe humanizado, la utopía alcanzable, la locura más realista, la razón de la sinrazón.

Cervantes con el *Quijote* se convirtió en el mayor y más longevo inspirador de la creación artística. La lucidez y grandeza reflejada en su obra cumbre[7] ha influenciado lo mismo a poetas, críticos, filósofos, literatos, intelectuales y dramaturgos, entre otros. [...]

El *Quijote* lo es todo: una parodia, una novela de aventuras, un tratado de la mente, un cuento picaresco, una historia de amor que no termina de sorprendernos en las rendijas del discurso[8].

---

[1] four hundred year anniversary    [2] example    [3] combines    [4] chivalry    [5] unyielding
[6] endless number    [7] masterpiece    [8] interwoven throughout the story

---

Castilla-La Mancha    CIUDADANOS    |    EMPRENDEDORES    |    GOBIERNO    |    PRESIDENTA

## Cospedal celebra que "nuestro personaje más universal" acercará Castilla-La Mancha al mundo para crear riqueza

**08/01/2015, Presidenta, Castilla-La Mancha**

*Subraya que el año 2015 hará que Castilla-La Mancha sea un referente conocido en cualquier parte del mundo en ámbito de la producción artística*

*Asegura que el logotipo ganador, 'Gigantes', "constituye una representación del Quijote y de nuestra tierra, clara, sencilla y reconocible pero, a su vez, vanguardista e innovadora"*

La presidenta del Gobierno de Castilla-La Mancha, María Dolores de Cospedal, ha destacado que nuestra región va a utilizar este año "a nuestro personaje literario más conocido y a nuestro escritor más universal" para dar a conocer al resto del mundo las bellezas de nuestra cultura, patrimonio e historia, y a partir de ahí "que sean acicates[1], todos ellos, para nuestro crecimiento económico".

Así lo ha manifestado Cospedal durante la presentación del logo del IV Centenario de la publicación de la Segunda Parte del Quijote, donde se ha referido a la magnífica posibilidad que supondrá para el turismo cultural en nuestra tierra, "para que visitantes de otras partes de España y del mundo vengan atraídos por todo lo que representamos y que esa representación lo sea de lo que es esta tierra nuestra, el corazón de España".

Cospedal ha subrayado que este año 2015, "hará que en el ámbito de la producción artística, Castilla-La Mancha sea un referente conocido en cualquier parte del mundo". [...]

### Un reto[2] importante

María Dolores de Cospedal ha hecho hincapié en[3] el "importante reto" que supone la celebración del IV Centenario de la publicación de la Segunda Parte del *Quijote*, "porque esta conmemoración es muy nuestra, porque no hay un personaje de ficción más conocido que don Quijote y tenemos la obligación de mirar al frente y cumplir ese reto con creces[4], como estoy convencida que vamos a hacer".

Por ello, la presidenta regional ha hecho referencia a toda una serie de actividades que se llevarán a cabo[5] a lo largo del año, "que van a plasmar[6], a través de las artes escénicas, de la música y exposiciones, la conmemoración de la obra más universal en lengua castellana y también dar a conocer el talento que hay en nuestra región".

Estos acontecimientos, ha señalado la presidenta, tendrán su continuación en el año 2016 con la conmemoración del IV Centenario del fallecimiento de Miguel de Cervantes. [...]

---

[1] stimuli    [2] challenge    [3] has emphasized    [4] exceeding expectations    [5] will take place    [6] express

 **Búsqueda:** don quijote, miguel de cervantes, cuarto centenario del quijote, castilla-la mancha

---

### 42 Comprensión

1. ¿Qué beneficios le traerá a Castilla-La Mancha la celebración del IV Centenario de la publicación de la Segunda Parte del Quijote?

2. ¿Por qué este aniversario es una oportunidad magnífica para el turismo cultural en la región?

3. ¿Qué tipo de actividades planea el gobierno de Castilla-La Mancha para celebrar el aniversario?

### 43 Analice

¿Qué lugares de su país atraen visitantes por su relación con obras literarias famosas?

---

**A**  *Lectura informativa* integrates the unit theme and country of focus in an informal, authentic, non-fiction reading.

**B**  *Estrategia* includes pointers on how to read successfully the upcoming selection and be more proficient readers in general.

**C**  *Comprensión* questions ensure that students understand the key points of the reading.

**D**  *Analice* questions encourage a deeper analysis of the reading and often ask students to make comparisons between their own culture and the culture of focus. They also connect to Common Core State Standards.

## *Vocabulario 3* **A**

### Mejore su comprensión

Familiarizarse con este vocabulario le ayudará a leer "He andado muchos caminos" más adelante, y a mejorar su comprensión auditiva.

**a lomos de mula vieja** *exp. figurado:* Sin prisa, como si fueran (*as if they were*) montados en una mula vieja que anda despacio por su edad.

**andar** *v.* Ir de un lugar a otro a pie.

**apestar** *v.* Dar muy mal olor.

**atracar** *v.* Llegar una embarcación a tierra.

**borracho** *s.m.* Persona que está bajo los efectos del alcohol.

**cabalgar** *v.* Ir a caballo.

**callar** *v.* No hablar, en silencio.

**camino** *s.m.* Por donde se va de un sitio a otro.

**caravana** *s.f.* Grupo de personas que viajan juntas.

**danzar** *v.* Bailar al ritmo de una música.

**¡Eso sí que es!** Exclamación de afirmación cuyas iniciales deletrean la palabra *socks*.

**fresco/a** *adj.* Temperatura agradablemente fría.

**laborar** *v.* Trabajar la tierra.

**mar** *s.m.* Masa de agua salada que cubre la mayor parte de la superficie de la tierra.

**melancólico/a** *adj.* Triste.

**navegar** *v.* Viajar en una nave.

**palmo** *s.m.* Medida de longitud.

**pedantones al paño** *exp.* Personas sabelotodo.

**ribera** *s.f.* Borde del mar o de un río.

**soberbio/a** *adj.* Orgulloso.

**sombra** *s.f.* Imagen oscura reflejada por la luz en una superficie.

**soñar** *v.* Representar algo en la mente mientras se duerme.

**taberna** *s.f.* Lugar sencillo donde se sirven comidas y bebidas.

**tierra** *s.f.* Mundo; suelo donde crecen las plantas.

**tristeza** *s.f.* Sentimiento que tiende al silencio y al llanto.

**un poco molesto/a** *adj.* Algo disgustado(a).

*Caminos y veredas del norte de España*

**vereda** *s.f.* Camino estrecho formado por el paso de personas y ganado.

**vino** *s.m.* Bebida alcohólica que se obtiene de las uvas.

---

**B** **48 Identifique al intruso**

Diga qué palabra no pertenece al grupo y explique por qué.

MODELO atracar / navegar / cabalgar
**Cabalgar no tiene que ver con embarcaciones.**

1. vino / camino / taberna
2. palmo / melancólico / tierra
3. tristeza / caminos / caravanas
4. pedantón / sombra / soberbio
5. mar / vereda / ribera
6. soñar / danzar / andar
7. atracar / callar / tierra
8. cabalgar / molesto / mula

---

**B** **49 ¿Cuál corresponde?**

Complete las oraciones que siguen con la palabra del recuadro que corresponda según el contexto.

| | | | |
|---|---|---|---|
| vino | laboran | melancólicas | navegan |
| andar | palmos | soberbia | camino |
| | atracan | borracho | |

1. Ese hombre es un ___ que se la pasa bebiendo ___ de taberna en taberna.
2. Esos barcos inmensos ___ por el mar y ___ en sus riberas.
3. Esos campesinos ___ de sol a sol y viven de trabajar su par de ___ de tierra.
4. La tristeza es el gran mal que afecta a las personas ___.
5. Ella es una persona ___ y orgullosa que se cree mejor que todos los demás.
6. Mañana tenemos que llegar a nuestro destino y todavía nos falta ___ gran parte del ___.

---

**C** **50 El problema de una turista**

Escuche el relato "El problema de una turista". Luego, Ud. oirá la primera parte de una pregunta y tres terminaciones posibles. Seleccione la letra de la respuesta con la terminación más lógica. La oración y las terminaciones se leerán dos veces.

1. **A.** ... no puede comprar ropa en un almacén.
   **B.** ... puede comprar ropa sin saber hablar inglés.
   **C.** ... puede comprar ropa porque habla inglés.
2. **A.** ... no comprar nada más.
   **B.** ... salir del almacén.
   **C.** ... comprar unos calcetines.
3. **A.** ... trata de explicarle lo que quiere.
   **B.** ... le explica lo que quiere.
   **C.** ... le habla en inglés.

*Una señora quiere comprarle unos calcetines a su esposo.*

4. **A.** ... la sección para caballeros.
   **B.** ... donde debe pagar.
   **C.** ... varios artículos de vestir.
5. **A.** ¡Eso sí que es!
   **B.** ¿Qué es eso?
   **C.** ¡Eso no es!

---

**A** ***Vocabulario 3*** presents students with additional vocabulary that will aid in comprehension of a short audio story on the following page as well as the ***Lectura literaria*** at the end of the unit.

**B** Two follow-up activities allow students to practice the newly-presented vocabulary.

**C** Students listen to a short ***relato*** (which incorporates expressions from ***Vocabulario 3***) and answer follow-up comprehension questions.

## A Lectura literaria

### He andado muchos caminos
#### de Antonio Machado

### B Sobre el autor

Antonio Machado (Sevilla 1875–Colliure 1939) es uno de los poetas más importantes de la Generación del 98 en España. Esta generación la formaron intelectuales españoles que reflexionaban sobre la situación de España tras la pérdida de sus últimas colonias en América y el Pacífico. Antonio Machado, conocido como "el poeta del pueblo," describió los pueblos de España y sus gentes en su poesía íntima y melancólica. Entre sus obras más importantes destacan *Soledades, Galerías y otros poemas* (1899–1907) y *Campos de Castilla* (1912).

*Antonio Machado*

### C Antes de leer

Machado dice en sus poemas que la mejor forma de conocer un país y su gente es caminando por sus caminos.

1. ¿Ha viajado de esta forma alguna vez?
2. ¿Ha conocido a alguien especial durante un viaje? Comparta su experiencia con sus compañeros/as de clase.

### D Estrategia

**El tema**

El tema de un poema es el punto de enfoque o concepto que el poeta desarrolla a través de sus ideas. En la poesía el tema no siempre es evidente. Por eso, para identificarlo, se requiere analizar el lenguaje y reflexionar sobre las ideas que el poeta trata de comunicar.

### E  59  Practique la estrategia

En "He andado muchos caminos" Machado hace alusión a la gente sencilla y humilde que ha conocido por los caminos y veredas de España (la buena gente), al tiempo que censura a la gente soberbia y arrogante que se siente superior a todos los demás (la mala gente). Es en el fondo una crítica de las clases sociales en España. Busque en el poema dos ejemplos que ilustren a estas personas y dé su interpretación.

| Versos del poema | Buena gente | Mala gente | Interpretación |
|---|---|---|---|
| "...y pedantones al paño que miran, callan y piensan que saben porque no beben el vino de las tabernas." | | ✓ | No beben en las tabernas porque son lugares frecuentados por gente humilde, y si lo hacen, solo miran a la gente y piensan que son mejores que ellos y, por eso, no se toman ni la molestia de hablarles. |
| | | | |
| | | | |

### F  60  Comprensión

1. ¿Qué quiere decir Machado cuando habla de "caravanas de tristeza" en la segunda estrofa, y a quiénes se refiere con esta metáfora?
2. ¿A quiénes se refiere Machado en los versos 16 a 18?
3. ¿Qué actitud de la gente se refleja en los versos 25 y 26?

### 61 Analice

Explique la ironía que se expresa en los versos 29 y 30.

### He andado muchos caminos
#### de Antonio Machado

He andado muchos caminos,
he abierto muchas veredas[1];
he navegado en cien mares,
y atracado[2] en cien riberas[3].

5   En todas partes he visto
caravanas de tristeza,
soberbios[4] y melancólicos
borrachos de sombra negra,

y pedantones al paño[5]
10  que miran, callan y piensan
que saben, porque no beben
el vino de las tabernas.

Mala gente que camina
y va apestando[6] la tierra...

15  Y en todas partes he visto
gentes que danzan o juegan,
cuando pueden, y laboran
sus cuatro palmos de tierra[7].

Nunca, si llegan a un sitio,
20  preguntan adónde llegan.
Cuando caminan, cabalgan
a lomos de mula vieja[8],

y no conocen la prisa
ni aun en los días de fiesta.
25  Donde hay vino, beben vino;
donde no hay vino, agua fresca.

Son buenas gentes que viven,
laboran, pasan y sueñan,
y en un día como tantos,
30  descansan bajo la tierra.

*He andado muchos caminos.*

[1] paths, trails   [2] anchored   [3] shores   [4] haughty   [5] pretentious   [6] polluting   [7] handspans of land   [8] on the backs of old mules

### Después de leer

Cada paso que andamos ayuda a hacer nuestro camino en la vida. ¿Qué paso ha sido especialmente significativo en su vida? Compare su experiencia con la de un(a) compañero/a y, luego, compartan sus experiencias con el resto de la clase.

---

**A** *Lectura literaria* is an authentic reading by an author from the country of focus. It complements the unit theme as well as provides practice in reading authentic literary selections.

**B** *Sobre el autor* gives background about the author, such as information on writing style or preferred topics/themes.

**C** *Antes de leer* activities connect to the theme of the text and prepare students for what they are about to read.

**D** *Estrategia* includes pointers on how to be a successful reader in Spanish.

**E** *Practique la estrategia* allows students immediate practice using the *Estrategia* in an activity directly connected to the upcoming reading.

**F** *Comprensión* questions ask students to demonstrate understanding of the text.

## A Para concluir

? Pregunta clave
¿Qué se aprende cuando se viaja al extranjero?

### Proyectos

#### B A ¡Manos a la obra!

Imagine que su clase de español celebra el IV Centenario de la publicación de *Don Quijote* en una jornada especial para conmemorar la obra.

A su grupo, le han asignado hacer una representación con alguno de estos personajes:

- Don Quijote
- Sancho Panza
- Dulcinea del Toboso

Primero, deben buscar información en la internet sobre el personaje elegido. Tomen nota sobre sus características: su aspecto físico, su personalidad, la relación con otros personajes. Luego, elijan un diálogo breve del libro en el que participe el personaje elegido. Busquen las expresiones que no entiendan en el diccionario o pidan ayuda a su profesor. Por último, representen el diálogo frente al resto de sus compañeros.

*Don Quijote y Sancho Panza*

#### C B En resumen

Imagine que Ud. ha hecho un largo viaje por España y, a su regreso, le piden que escriba un artículo sobre su experiencia para la sección de viajes de una revista.

Primero, imagine el itinerario de su viaje a partir de la información que se presenta en las tres lecturas de Cultura. Luego, complete la tabla para organizar lo que ha aprendido en su viaje por España en cada lugar que ha visitado.

| | |
|---|---|
| Atractivo natural | |
| Atractivo cultural | |
| Atractivo artístico | |
| Atractivo histórico | |

Por último, escriba su artículo haciendo énfasis en todo lo que ha aprendido sobre la cultura española gracias a su viaje.

---

#### D **¡A escribir!** directs students to use lesson vocabulary, grammar, and cultural information to construct formal and informal writings.

#### E Additional **cross-curricular** projects may be connected to art, math, science, history, music, literature, etc.

#### D C ¡A escribir! Conéctese: la geografía

Investigue información en la internet sobre la Ruta de Don Quijote. Imagine que Ud. hizo una parte del recorrido de esa ruta cuando estuvo en España. Ud. acaba de llegar y todo el mundo quiere saber cómo le fue. Escriba un párrafo sobre su experiencia y publíquelo en su red social favorita para así compartir todo lo que aprendió sobre España y su cultura al hacer este recorrido.

**Para escribir más**

Primero...
Después...
Luego...
Al final...
Un día...
Al otro día..

#### E D Paseo del Arte Conéctese: el arte

Elija uno de los museos del "Paseo del Arte" de Madrid. Busque su sitio web y averigüe qué colecciones de artistas españoles posee. Tome notas acerca de las obras más relevantes. Incluya datos como el título de la obra, el nombre del artista, el año en que fue terminada y el movimiento artístico al que pertenece. Busque imágenes de algunas de las obras y comparta la información que reunió con el resto de la clase.

#### E Se hace camino al andar Conéctese: la literatura

Lea y escuche el poema "Caminante, son tus huellas" de Antonio Machado y, luego, compárelo con "He andado muchos caminos", el poema que leyó en esta unidad. ¿En qué se parecen? ¿En qué se diferencian? Escriba sus respuestas en un diagrama de Venn y justifíquelas con citas textuales de los poemas.

**"Caminante, son tus huellas"**
de *Antonio Machado*

Caminante, son tus huellas
el camino, y nada más;
caminante, no hay camino,
se hace camino al andar.
Al andar se hace el camino,
y al volver la vista atrás
se ve la senda que nunca
se ha de volver a pisar.
Caminante, no hay camino,
sino estelas en la mar.

"Caminante, son tus huellas"    "He andando muchos caminos"

Los dos se refieren al camino de la vida.

---

**A** **Para concluir** is end-of-unit project-based learning. Students apply all language skills and prior knowledge to complete the activities.

**B** **¡Manos a la obra!** is a hands-on activity where students do research and collaborate with a group to complete a project.

**C** **En resumen** is an analysis of the unit's cultural information. Students use charts to organize their knowledge in order to draw conclusions that answer the **pregunta clave**.

**abordar** to board
**acordarse/recordar** to remember
el **aeropuerto** airport
**a lomos de mula vieja** on the backs of old mules
el **andén del tren** train platform
**abrocharse el cinturón** to fasten one's seatbelt
**andar** to walk
**apagar** to turn off
**aparecer** to appear, to be listed
**apestar** to pollute, to stink
**¿A qué hora...?** At what time...?
el **asiento de pasillo** aisle seat
el **asiento de ventanilla** window seat
el **aterrizaje forzoso** forced landing
**aterrizar** to land
**atracar** to anchor
el/la **auxiliar de vuelo** flight attendant
el **avión** airplane
**ayudar** to help
**bajar** go down, bring down
el **barco** boat
el **borracho** drunkard
el **botones** bellman
**cabalgar** to ride
**callar** to keep quiet
el **camino** path, road
**cancelar** to cancel
la **caravana** caravan
la **clase turista** economy class
**consultar** to check
el **coche** car
el **coche cama** sleeping car
el **coche comedor** dining car
el **control de seguridad** security
**con tres horas de anticipación** three hours in advance
**confirmar las reservaciones** to confirm reservations
**¿Cuánto cuesta...?** How much does...cost?
**danzar** to dance
**dar** to give
**desear + inf.** to want, to wish
**despegar** to take off
el **despegue** takeoff
el **detector de metales** metal detector
**dirigirse a** to walk to

**¡Eso sí que es!** That's it!
**Estamos próximos a...** We are about to...
**estrellarse** to crash
**facturar el equipaje** to check luggage
el **ferrocarril** train
**fresco/a** fresh
el/la **gerente** manager
la **habitación** room
**hacer** to do, to make
**hacer camino** to forge a path
**hacer escala** to have a layover
**hacer una parada** to make a stop
**hacer reservaciones** to make reservations
el **hotel** hotel
**indicar** to indicate
la **inmigración** immigration
**inscribirse** to register
la **inspección de aduana** customs inspection
el/la **inspector(a)** inspector
**ir a + inf.** to be going + inf.
**laborar** to work
**¿Les interesa...?** Are you interested in...?
la **lista de huéspedes** guest list
la **llave** key
**llevar contrabando** to carry illegal goods
el **maletín de mano** carry-on luggage
**mantener la calma** to keep calm
**mantenerse** to stay, to remain
el **mar** sea
**melancólico/a** melancholy
el **monitor** monitor
el **mostrador de la línea aérea** airline counter
**navegar** to navigate
la **oficina de cambio (de moneda)** currency exchange office
**pagar por exceso de equipaje** to pay for excess baggage
el **palmo de tierra** handspan of land
el **pasaje de ida y vuelta** round trip ticket
el/la **pasajero/a** passenger
**¡Pasajeros al tren!** All aboard!
el **pasaporte** passport
**pasar por...** to go through...

los **pedantones al paño** people who are pedantic to the core
**perder el vuelo** to miss the flight
el/la **piloto** pilot
la **planta baja** ground floor
**posponer** to postpone
**presentar** to show
la **primera clase** first class
la **primera vez** the first time
la **propina** tip
**querer + inf.** to want + inf.
**quitarse** to remove, to take off
la **recepción del hotel** hotel lobby
la **recomendación** recommendation
**recoger** to pick up
**revisar** to inspect
la **ribera** shore
la **sala de espera** waiting room
la **salida y llegada de vuelo** flight departure and arrival
**salir** to leave
**seguir las indicaciones** to follow directions
el **servicio** service
**soberbio/a** pompous
la **sombra** shadow
**soñar** to dream
**subir** to go up, bring up
la **taberna** tavern
la **tierra** land, earth, soil
**tomar precauciones** to take precautions
la **tripulación** crew
la **tristeza** sadness
la **turbulencia** turbulence
la **última llamada** last call
**molesto/a** annoyed
la **vereda** path, trail
**viajar al extranjero** to travel abroad
el **viaje** trip
el/la **viajero/a** traveler
el **vino** wine
la **visa** visa
el **vuelo de conexión** connecting flight
el **vuelo directo** direct flight
el **vuelo internacional** international flight
el **vuelo nacional** domestic flight

The Spanish-English *Vocabulario* contains the key vocabulary for the unit and is a useful reference tool.

# Walk-through: Annotated Teacher's Edition

## Margin Icons

 Flipgrid

 Avenue

Video short

Audio

**WB** Workbook

**LA** Listening Activities

**FC** Flash Cards

**T** Test

## B Reference Desk

1. This unit's country of focus is Chile, which occupies a long and narrow coastal strip of land wedged between the Andes mountains and the Pacific Ocean. The country borders Peru, Bolivia, and Argentina, and also includes Easter Island, Desventuradas, Salas y Gómez, and the Juan Fernández Islands.
2. Chile has the longest seacoast in the world, stretching from Peru all the way to Punta Arenas, one of the southernmost cities in the world. However, its widest point measures just 217 miles.

## C Culture

**Products/Practices: Information**
The Mapuche are the original inhabitants of central and southern Chile, and the most numerous indigenous population in South America (about 1.4 million). **Machis** are central to Mapuche medicine; they possess knowledge of herbal remedies and are also believed to have spiritual powers. **Machis** are usually women.

## Culture

**Products/Practices: Activity**
Ask students to create a list of questions they have about Chile. As students progress through the unit, encourage them to document the answers they find in their Culture Journals. If any questions remain unanswered, provide suggestions for resources where students might find this information.

### E ¿Sabía que...? 1.2, 2.1, 2.2
La medicina ancestral mapuche todavía se practica y convive con la medicina moderna. Para hacer un diagnóstico, el machi o chamán canta acompañado por el *kultrún* (tambor ritual) en una ceremonia llamada *machitún*. Todos los productos curativos de la medicina mapuche provienen de la tierra.

## D Essential Instruction

1. Begin with a discussion of the **Pregunta clave**. Ask students to consider how health care changes over time.
2. Point out Chile on the map. Ask students to share what they know about the country.
3. Draw attention to the culture photo and question. Encourage students to watch for the photo and the answer later in the unit.
4. Point out the QR code, the video question, and the screen shot from "**Visitas inesperadas.**" Encourage students to watch the video as many times as they like.
5. Have students read and ask questions about **Mis metas**.

226

---

**A** **Margin icons** denote the supplemental materials that support the page content.

**B** **Reference Desk** provides additional information on cultural, linguistic, and pronunciation notes, and other relevant information related to page content.

**C** Side panel features include additional resources on **Culture**, **Critical Thinking**, **Connections**, **Communication**, **Games**, and ideas for **TPR** activities.

**D** **Essential Instruction** is preparation help for the day's lesson; these tips suggest a logical order of approach.

**E** **ACTFL Standards** are placed at point of use on the student pages of the ATE.

# Unidad 6

# Salud y bienestar

Escanee el código QR para mirar el video "Visitas inesperadas".

En esta historia de visitas y situaciones inesperadas, la madre de Alex se da cuenta de que él está enfermo y llama al médico para que vaya a hacerle una consulta en casa. ¿Qué síntomas tiene Alex, qué dice el médico y qué le recomienda?

Chile

*Pregunta clave*

¿Cómo cambia el cuidado de la salud según la época?

¿Qué papel desempeña el *machi* o *chamán* en la cultura mapuche?

## Mis metas

### En esta unidad:

- ▶ Usaré expresiones relacionadas con la salud y el bienestar, enfermedades, diagnósticos y tratamientos.
- ▶ Repasaré las formas y usos del presente del subjuntivo.
- ▶ Leeré sobre la medicina mapuche en Chile, la medicina rural y la salud en el mundo virtual.
- ▶ Distinguiré el significado de palabras y frases según el contexto.
- ▶ Usaré correctamente los mandatos de **Ud.** y **Uds.**
- ▶ Leeré un artículo sobre los momentos que marcaron la evolución de la medicina y la salud en Chile.
- ▶ Crearé una historia clínica con base en una entrevista entre un médico y un paciente.
- ▶ Escribiré un ensayo argumentativo con base en un segmento sobre la medicina complementaria y la medicina convencional.
- ▶ Desarrollaré nuevas destrezas de vocabulario.
- ▶ Usaré correctamente los mandatos de **tú**, **vosotros/as** y **nosotros/as**.
- ▶ Leeré el poema *"Walking Around"* del chileno Pablo Neruda.

doscientos veintisiete **227**

---

**RESOURCES** **F**

📹 Visitas inesperadas

🅰 Avenue

Answers

**G** **Video question** *Respuesta posible:* Alex tiene fiebre, le duele la garganta y la espalda y se siente muy cansado. El médico dice que tiene una gripe común, que tome ibuprofeno para la fiebre, que tome mucho líquido y que descanse.

**Culture question**
El machi o chamán es la persona encargada de los tratamientos médicos en la cultura mapuche.

### Reference Desk

1. Ask students to read the **Pregunta clave** and speculate about the theme of the unit and the vocabulary and culture they might encounter.
2. Draw attention to the screen shot from "**Visitas inesperadas**." Ask them to guess where these people are.
3. Remind students with eBook access they can click on the red country on p. 227 to link directly to Wikipedia.

---

## Multiple Intelligences **H**

### Naturalist
Ask these students to research the varied landscapes and habitats of Chile, and prepare a geographical profile of the country. They can submit their profiles via Avenue.

### Verbal-Linguistic
Review and preview the unit vocabulary and grammar by asking questions such as: **¿Qué podemos hacer para mantener la salud? ¿Alguna vez has sufrido una fractura o golpe fuerte? ¿Dónde? ¿Qué le recomiendas a una persona que se siente muy estresada?**

227

---

**F** **Resources** includes icons of supplemental materials that enhance the contents of that page.

**G** Answers to the video question and culture question from the unit opener are provided at point of use.

**H** **Multiple Intelligences** provides tips on how to reach students who are naturalist, bodily-kinesthetic, musical-rhythmic, verbal-linguistic, visual-spatial, or mathematical-logical learners.

## [Textbook spread pages 228–229]

**RESOURCES**

 ¡Más vale prevenir que curar!

WB Activities 1–2

FC Unidad 6

### Reference Desk

1. Mention that **sala de emergencias** is sometimes referred to as **sala de urgencias**.
2. You may want to review other verbs during this presentation (e.g., **herirse**, **lastimarse**).

**A** **Communication**

Presentational: Paired Practice
Have students tell a partner about an accident they or someone they know has had. Did they have to go to the doctor or the hospital? What treatment did they have to undergo? How long did it take them to recuperate?

**Communication**

Interpersonal/Presentational: Cooperative Groups
Ask students to work in groups to dramatize two or three situations that demonstrate someone having an accident and others coming to help. Have each group choose one situation to role-play for the class.

**Expansion**

Write the five senses (**el gusto, el oído, el olfato, el tacto, la vista**) on the board and have students name the parts of the body they associate with each sense.

---

### Vocabulario 1

#### ¡Más vale prevenir que curar! 1.2

**Cuándo ir al consultorio del médico**

Keepira profunda

Es importante que te hagas un examen médico cada año aunque te sientas bien. La enfermera revisará tu peso y tu presión arterial, te tomará la temperatura y te hará un análisis de sangre y de orina. Luego, el médico te examinará.

Ve al médico si tienes fiebre y dificultad para respirar y si te duele la garganta y no dejas de toser. Puede ser solo gripe, pero también es posible que tengas otra enfermedad o una infección que requiera antibióticos o algún otro tratamiento.

**Cuándo ir a la sala de emergencias**

Ve a la sala de emergencias si te enfermas de gravedad o si tienes un dolor agudo constante en cualquier parte del cuerpo. Puede ser algo grave que necesite atención inmediata. Si ese es el caso, es posible que te lleven ahí mismo al quirófano para hacerte una operación.

También debes ir a la sala de emergencias si te caes y te rompes algún hueso. Allá te tomarán rayos equis para hacer un diagnóstico. Si te fracturas la pierna o el pie, es posible que tengas que estar enyesado por un tiempo y que tengas que caminar con muletas o usar una silla de ruedas.

**Cuándo pedir auxilio**

Pide auxilio y llama una ambulancia si presencias un accidente, si alguien se estrella o es atropellado y debe ser llevado al hospital. Y recuerda: conduce siempre con cuidado. ¡No quieras ser el muerto o el herido de gravedad en esa camilla!

228 doscientos veintiocho | Unidad 6

---

**El cuerpo humano: partes externas**

la cabeza
la espalda
la rodilla
el brazo
el codo
la pantorilla
el pie
la mano
la muñeca
los dedos
las uñas
la boca
el pelo
el pecho
el cuello
el hombro
la cintura
la pierna
el tobillo

**La cara**

el ojo
la nariz
los labios
la ceja
las pestañas
la mejilla
la oreja

**El cuerpo humano: órganos internos**

los pulmones
el corazón
el hígado
los riñones
el estómago
las venas
la sangre

**Para conversar**

Para intercambiar información en el consultorio del médico:

—Tengo los ojos superirritados y no dejo de estornudar. Creo que tengo una infección, pero soy alérgico a los antibióticos y no sé qué hacer.

—No se preocupe. Lo que tiene es alergia. Le recetaré otros medicamentos para aliviar los síntomas. Mientras tanto, póngase boca abajo que ya mismo le voy a aplicar una inyección. Verá que pronto se sentirá mucho mejor.

—Generalmente duermo bien, pero ya llevo varios días sin poder hacerlo y, luego, paso el día entero bostezando. Estoy preocupado.

—No se preocupe. Ud. sufre de insomnio. Le voy a recetar unas pastillas para dormir, pero sería buena idea ver a un psicólogo si el problema continúa.

Unidad 6 | doscientos veintinueve 229

---

**RESOURCES**

 El cuerpo humano: partes externas
El cuerpo humano: órganos internos
Para conversar

### Reference Desk

1. You may want to present additional words for the body, such as **la barbilla, la cadera, el cerebro, el dedo del pie, la frente, la lengua, el muslo**, and **la piel**. The terms **los intestinos** and **el ombligo** are presented later in the unit.
2. Explain that **la oreja** refers to the outer ear, and **el oído** indicates the inner ear.

**Communication**

Interpersonal: Paired Practice
In pairs, have students take turns describing a part of the body, for example, **Los uso para nadar y para abrazar a mi madre.** Their partner must guess the word (**los brazos**).

**Expansion**

Give sentences that use expressions related to parts of the body, e.g., **Luis se encogió de hombros; Marta tiene cara de enojada; ¿Tengo monos en la cara o qué?** Have the class try to guess their meaning.

**TPR**

Say aloud the names of different parts of the body. Have students point to where they are located on the body.

---

**Essential Instruction**

1. Before playing the audio, have students scan the vocabulary on pp. 228–229 and pick out cognates. They can work in pairs and practice pronouncing these words.
2. Ask students to brainstorm a list of reasons why someone would visit a doctor.
3. Play the audio for **¡Más vale prevenir que curar!** Pause occasionally to ask comprehension questions.
4. Personalize the vocabulary presentation by asking students how long it has been since their last physical. Depending on your class's comfort level, you could ask about any emergency room trips or hospital stays.

**B** **Differentiated Learning**
Heritage Learners
Health and medical vocabulary may vary by region; for example, most Spanish speakers use **la gripe** for *flu*, but in Colombia and Mexico **la gripa** is more common. Ask heritage learners what terms they know that are synonyms of the ones presented on pp. 228–230.

**C** **Learning Styles**
Visual Learners
Have students make their own flash cards for the new terms from **Vocabulario 1**. Tell them to use note cards, and to write the Spanish term on one side and draw or paste a picture on the other side.

228

229

---

**A** **Communication** provides additional activities for students to interact with classmates in the interpersonal and presentational modes.

**B** **Differentiated Learning** provides tips on how to accelerate, decelerate, adapt, and expand material as well as tips to engage heritage learners.

**C** **Learning Styles** provides tips on how to reach students who are auditory, visual, or kinesthetic learners.

**A**

Answers to activities are placed in the margins.

**B**

**Critical Thinking** provides activities for students to apply higher order thinking skills to newly learned information.

**C**

**Pre-AP** provides ideas on how to prepare students for the AP exam.

**D**

**Expansion** provides ideas on how to go beyond the activities on the page and can be employed depending upon students' interest and ability level.

---

 Flipgrid

 Medicina mapuche en el siglo XXI Prácticas

LA Activity 4

**A** Answers

10
1. Debido a la migración masiva a las ciudades.
2. Los machis y los médicos convencionales se derivan pacientes unos a otros según la dolencia que padezca.
3. Para los mapuches, es una manera de mantener vivas sus tradiciones, aun en la gran ciudad. Para el resto de la población, es una manera de acceder a tratamientos alternativos.

11 Ⓔ *Las respuestas variarán.*

**Reference Desk**

Students can do a Flipgrid post reacting to any of these cultural readings.

**B** **Critical Thinking**

**Analyzing and Comparing**

Ask students to consider what impediments there are to alternative medicine in the United States.

**C** **Pre-AP** Ⓐ

Have students respond to the **Pregunta clave**, in spoken or written form, using information from the readings on pp. 238–240. Students should also include a comparison between their own community/culture and Chile.

---

🇨🇱 *Cultura* Ⓐ  **1.2, 2.1, 2.2**

**?** Pregunta clave

**1.2, 2.1, 2.2**
**10 Comprensión**

1. ¿Por qué se pueden encontrar chamanes mapuches en la gran ciudad?
2. ¿Cómo se combinan la medicina mapuche y la convencional?
3. ¿Qué ventajas tiene la colaboración entre medicina mapuche y medicina convencional?

### Medicina mapuche en el siglo XXI 🔊

Puede parecer de ciencia ficción, pero no lo es: en Chile es posible encontrar un chamán o médico mapuche en una gran ciudad moderna como Santiago. Históricamente, la medicina tradicional de los mapuches (los indígenas del sur chileno) se limitaba al ámbito rural. Sin embargo, con la migración masiva a las grandes ciudades, muchos sanadores[1] mapuches han abierto en ellas consultorios privados donde ofrecen una alternativa terapéutica.

La medicina mapuche se basa en la herbolaria, que es el uso de plantas y hierbas con fines curativos, y es ejercida por el machi o chamán. Pero lo más interesante de esta alternativa es que no excluye las prácticas médicas convencionales. Por el contrario, ambas se combinan y complementan. Los machis ofrecen a los pacientes tratamientos muy distintos a los de la medicina occidental, pero los pacientes aseguran que no hay conflicto: a veces son los mismos médicos quienes los derivan[2] a un machi (por ejemplo, cuando se trata de problemas asociados con el estrés) o viceversa: el machi manda los pacientes al médico (por ejemplo, cuando sus dolencias[3] requieren una cirugía).

*Los chamanes mapuches siguen teniendo vigencia en la actualidad.*

**1.3, 2.1, 2.2, 4.2**
**11 Analice**

1. ¿Qué opina Ud. de los tratamientos alternativos, naturales o tradicionales?
2. ¿Cree Ud. que en su país las personas recurren a la medicina alternativa tanto como en Chile?

Esta colaboración intercultural recibe el apoyo del Ministerio de Salud de Chile, que desde hace años reconoce la medicina mapuche y permite el ejercicio libre[4] de los machis. De hecho, hay más de 150 plantas medicinales estudiadas y reconocidas por ese organismo. Para la comunidad mapuche, es una oportunidad imperdible[5] de mantener su cultura viva dentro de una gran ciudad. Para el resto de los chilenos, es una posibilidad de complementar y mejorar el cuidado de su salud.

[1]healers  [2]refer  [3]ailments  [4]free practice  [5]unique

🔍 **Búsqueda:** medicina mapuche, machi mapuche, chamán mapuche, programa salud y pueblos indígenas chile

**Prácticas** 🔊 **2.1**

En Chile, según una encuesta del Ministerio de Salud, más de la mitad de las personas han recurrido en algún momento a la medicina alternativa para tratar problemas de salud. Esta práctica se ha difundido tanto entre los chilenos porque los mismos profesionales de la medicina convencional tienen una mirada positiva al respecto y muchos de ellos se especializan también en disciplinas de la medicina complementaria, como la homeopatía y la acupuntura.

*Muchos médicos chilenos recurren también a la medicina alternativa.*

238  doscientos treinta y ocho  |  Unidad 6

---

### Un médico rural, un médico integral 🔊 **1.2, 2.1, 2.2**

Es posible que, al pensar en la medicina rural en América Latina, imaginemos un médico que, en solitario y maletín en mano, visita muy esporádicamente[1] a sus pacientes en lugares remotos. Pero las cosas cambian. Si bien es cierto que en el ámbito rural hay factores que dificultan el acceso a la salud, como las largas distancias o la falta de equipamiento especializado en las pequeñas clínicas, también hay muchos programas en los que los médicos trabajan en equipo para mejorar el sistema rural de salud.

En la Universidad de Chile, los estudiantes de medicina del último año de la carrera deben cursar un Internado Rural. Se trata de una experiencia integradora, en la que los internos se incorporan durante cuatro semanas a la vida rural: viven allí, se relacionan estrechamente con la comunidad y aprenden a apreciar sus condiciones de vida.

*Los médicos rurales tienen una relación muy cercana con sus pacientes.*

Durante esta experiencia, ponen en práctica sus conocimientos mediante actividades de promoción, prevención y atención primaria. Uno de los aspectos más enriquecedores es que los internos visitan a pacientes que no pueden asistir a la clínica. Así, entran en su hogar, conocen a su familia y forma de vida, conversan con ellos, les entregan medicamentos y resuelven situaciones clínicas agudas[2]. Este tipo de atención personalizada no es habitual ni posible en un consultorio moderno del sistema urbano de salud. En el internado rural, los futuros médicos adquieren una visión abarcadora[3] y alternativa de los problemas del paciente, sin dejar de lado ningún detalle. Así se preparan para ser médicos integrales.

[1]seldom  [2]acute  [3]wide-ranging

🔍 **Búsqueda:** medicina rural en chile, internado rural universidad de chile

**1.2, 2.1, 2.2**
**12 Comprensión**

1. ¿Qué dificultades presenta el ámbito rural para el acceso a la salud?
2. ¿Qué se hace en Chile para mejorar el sistema de salud rural?
3. ¿Qué tiene de particular el ejercicio de la medicina rural?

**1.3, 2.1, 4.2**
**13 Analice**

1. ¿Qué opina Ud. de la mirada más abarcadora de la medicina rural u otras medicinas alternativas?
2. ¿Hay alguna práctica de la medicina de los pueblos originarios de su país que esté reconocida por la medicina convencional? ¿Cuáles?

**Productos** 🔊 **1.2, 2.2**

El Museo Nacional de Medicina de Chile contiene equipos e instrumental médico, libros, documentos y fotografías de la historia de la salud chilena. Los visitantes pueden acceder allí al patrimonio histórico no solo de la medicina convencional sino también de la medicina mapuche. En el museo hay un rehue (tronco de árbol que simboliza el poder), dos cultrum, o tambores, y una pipa usada por los machis. Hay también una pequeña muestra de las plantas medicinales de varias culturas precolombinas, que luego se incorporaron a la farmacopea española durante la conquista y, junto con los baños termales, sirvieron para aliviar las enfermedades de los conquistadores.

*Los cultrum usados por los machis en la medicina mapuche*

Unidad 6  |  doscientos treinta y nueve  **239**

---

**RESOURCES**

 Un médico rural, un médico integral Productos

Answers

12
1. Las largas distancias o la falta de equipamiento especializado en las clínicas.
2. Un Internado Rural obligatorio para los estudiantes de medicina que los acerca al medio rural y a sus condiciones de vida.
3. Tiene un enfoque personalizado, más abarcador del paciente y su entorno.

13 Ⓔ *Las respuestas variarán.*

**Reference Desk**

The **rehue** and **cultrum** form key parts of a **machitún** ceremony. A **rehue** is a tree trunk that has steps carved into it. It is placed at a vertical angle into the earth and used as a kind of altar during **machitún**. A **cultrum** (or **cultrún**) is a drum made of wood and animal skin.

**D** **Expansion**

Have students go online and take a virtual tour of the **Museo Nacional de Medicina** through the museum's website. Have them say what parts they would be most interested in visiting and why.

---

**Essential Instruction**
1. Point out the **Pregunta clave**, and tell students to keep it in mind as they complete these cultural readings.
2. Have students preview the titles and photos on pp. 238–240. Ask them to predict what they will learn about Chile.
3. Remind students of the photo and question from the unit opener. Ask where they can find the answer (in the second paragraph on p. 238).

**Differentiated Learning**
**Expand**
Have students research online to learn more about **machitún** ceremonies. Have them find out where they usually take place, how the **machi** determine the patient's ailment and treatment, how the **rehue** and **cultrum** are used, and the names and descriptions of some medicinal plants that might be used.

**Multiple Intelligences**
**Verbal-Linguistic**
Point out the words on this page that derive from Mapudungun, the language of the Mapuche in Chile. Ask students to research its history, basics of phonology and grammar, and how many people speak the language today. You might also ask them to find out which names of Chilean places derive from Mapudungun.

## Teacher Materials

**Annotated Teacher's Edition** includes margin notes featuring games and activities, cultural information, and teacher suggestions.

**eATE** includes the full Annotated Teacher's Edition plus all program resources.

- **Textbook Audio Program and Audio Files** includes the transcripts for the textbook audio as well as access to all recordings for vocabulary, narratives, and activities.
- **Workbook Teacher's Edition** includes the answers to the student activities that reinforce vocabulary, grammar, and cultural information.
- **Listening Activities Teacher's Edition and Audio Files** includes additional listening comprehension activities as well as the audio and answer key.
- **Tests with Answer Key and Audio Files** includes one test per unit to assess speaking, listening, reading, and writing based on unit vocabulary, grammar, and culture. Two versions are offered to allow flexibility on the part of the instructor.

**ExamVIEW®** is software preloaded with the assessments from the **Tests** that can be adapted, printed, and administered to students.

## Student Materials

**Textbook** has the core material to engage and motivate life-long Spanish learners.

**eBook** includes all textbook activities that are interactive and give immediate feedback; access to the video shorts; and all audio for vocabulary, narratives, and listening activities.

**Workbook** has activities that reinforce vocabulary, grammar, and cultural information.

**eWorkbook** includes interactive activities with immediate feedback.

**eListening Activities** includes interactive listening activities with immediate feedback.

**Flash Cards** provide extra vocabulary practice.

## Passport®
www.emcpassport.com

### The Learning Environment for the Spanish Classroom of Tomorrow...Today!

Passport® "brings it all home" with its unique anytime, anywhere learning platform. In the classroom, at home, on the go, students connect to curriculum, culture, classmates, and communities as well as showing what they know.

**Teachers can:**
- Assign activities from the eBooks (eBook, eWorkbook, eListening Activities); assign project-based learning modules; engage students in cultural enrichment activities (videos, news, and songs); and check oral proficiency through video-based performance tools
- Track student progress and grades
- Provide individualized video or written feedback
- Communicate with classes
- Access all program resources
- Incorporate blended learning

**Students can:**
- Access materials anytime, anywhere
- Complete assignments and practice activities
- Work on project-based tasks
- Receive immediate feedback
- Submit work
- Track progress

### Passport® at a Glance

 **Discover** – Students connect to core curriculum via their eBooks and other supplemental materials

 **Create** – Students complete ready-made, IPA-aligned projects that engage them in real-life situations while employing the three modes of communication—Interpretive, Interpersonal, and Presentational

 **Expand** – Students explore language and culture through virtual tours, news articles, video documentaries, and music

 **Share** – Students post for peers their opinions, ideas, stories and more, using this video-based tool

 **Perform** – Students demonstrate oral proficiency through video assessment tasks

# World Language Learning in the 21st Century

Our world is becoming an increasingly diverse, globalized, and complex, media-saturated society. Our 21st-century learners need a learning environment that is designed to inspire analysis, synthesis, evaluation, and reflection, as well as provide opportunities for problem-solving and creating meaningful, relevant projects in a collaborative environment. So what are the critical skills and multiple literacies that our students will need in order to successfully participate in the global community of today's world? How do we successfully engage these students and prepare them for the world of work?

ACTFL, collaborating with the Partnership for 21st Century Skills, sought to address these and other critical questions via the 21st Century Skills Map. The map, outlined below, helps teachers plan and guide instruction, while giving concrete examples to administrators and policymakers across the country. (Examples of activities in the Novice, Intermediate, and Advanced ranges can be found at www.actfl.org.)

**Here are the twelve skills statements from the ACTFL World Languages 21st Century Skills Map and their topics:**

1. **Communication**
   Students as effective communicators use languages to engage in meaningful conversation, to understand and interpret spoken language and written text, and to present information, concepts, and ideas.

2. **Collaboration**
   Students as collaborators use their native and acquired languages to learn from and work cooperatively across cultures with global team members, sharing responsibility and making necessary compromises while working toward a common goal.

3. **Critical Thinking and Problem Solving**
   Students as inquirers frame, analyze, and synthesize information as well as negotiate meaning across language and culture in order to explore problems and issues from their own and different perspectives.

4. **Creativity and Innovation**
   Students as creators and innovators respond to new and diverse perspectives. They use language in imaginative and original ways to make useful contributions.

5. **Information Literacy**
   Students as informed global citizens access, manage, and effectively use culturally authentic sources in ethical and legal ways.

6. **Media Literacy**
   Students as active global citizens evaluate authentic sources to understand how media reflect and influence language and culture.

7. **Technology Literacy**
   Students as productive global citizens use appropriate technologies when interpreting messages; interacting with others; and producing written, oral, and visual messages.

8. **Flexibility and Adaptability**
   Students as flexible and adaptable language learners are open-minded, willing to take risks, and accept the ambiguity of language while balancing diverse global perspectives.

9. **Initiative and Self-Direction**
   Students as life-long learners are motivated to set their own goals and reflect on their progress as they grow and improve their linguistic and cultural competence.

10. **Social and Cross-Cultural Skills**
    Students as adept language learners understand diverse cultural perspectives and use appropriate socio-linguistic skills in order to function in diverse cultural and linguistic contexts.

11. **Productivity and Accountability**
    Students as productive and accountable learners take responsibility for their own learning by actively working to increase their language proficiency and cultural knowledge.
12. **Leadership and Responsibility**
    Students as responsible leaders leverage their linguistic and cross-cultural skills to inspire others to be fair, accepting, open, and understanding within and beyond the local community.

# Oral Proficiency in the 21st Century

"I want to learn how to speak the language" is the most common goal of world language learners. But what is oral proficiency, and how do learners demonstrate their progress toward this goal?

At the center of the ACTFL World-Readiness Standards are the three modes of communication. The interpersonal and the presentational modes are focused on both oral and written communication. In the interpersonal mode learners engage in conversation, provide and obtain information, express feeling and emotion, and exchange opinions. This mode occurs in two-way, spontaneous exchanges that involve negotiation of meaning and are based on unrehearsed prompts. Activities and strategies include debates, discussions, phone calls, video chats, asking for and giving directions, and conversations with friends about making plans.

In the presentational mode, learners present information, concepts, and ideas to an audience of listeners or readers on a variety of topics. It is one-way, planned, and can be rehearsed. There is no feedback from another person. Some activities and strategies include creating videos, presenting a story, delivering a speech, creating a public service announcement, recording podcasts, or presenting a skit or play.

Teachers can assess language performance using a rubric that measures proficiency in terms of ability to use the language effectively and appropriately in real-life situations. Students need to demonstrate what they "can do." *Linguafolio®* is an excellent source for "can do" statements at different proficiency levels. The "can do" statements are a perfect resource to use to create learner targets for each thematic unit, help students set personal goals, and provide a clearer explanation to parents about what their children are learning in their Spanish class.

Open-ended performance assessments are the best way to determine growth in oral proficiency. Each assessment needs to be designed to show what a student is able to do with the language in order to elicit meaningful feedback. Rubrics and feedback should be put in student-friendly terms, so students know what they can do to improve. EMC's learning environment, Passport®, provides ready-made rubrics for its project-based learning modules as well as for its oral proficiency tasks and assessments. It also provides opportunities for teachers to provide individualized, meaningful feedback to students.

With *¡Qué chévere!* students gain practice in the three modes of communication in vocabulary and structure activities, in reading authentic informational and literary texts, in listening to authentic audio, and in the *Proyectos* section. The goals section on the Unit Opener page makes it clear to students what material they will be responsible for learning and helps them take ownership of this content from the beginning. The final projects are designed to showcase student learning and make students feel successful, engaged, and purpose-driven in their Spanish language learning experiences with *¡Qué chévere!*

# Differentiated Instruction

Differentiated instruction occurs when teachers design learning to meet individual student needs. It differentiates among **content** (the materials students need to learn); **process** (the practice provided by the material); **products** (activities and projects in which students apply learning); and, according to Carol Ann Tomlinson, fosters a positive **learning environment** (the way the classroom functions and feels). *¡Qué chévere!* is designed to meet differing ability levels and learning styles. Below are a few examples from *¡Qué chévere!* that correspond to these aspects of differentiated instruction.

## Content

1. **Use reading materials for different ability levels.**

   Options to reach all reading levels are included in *¡Qué chévere!* through reading strategies, recorded readings by native Spanish speakers, basic comprehension questions, and post-reading analysis questions. Within the Annotated Teacher's Edition, wraparound notes include Multiple Intelligences, Special Needs Students, Learning Styles, and Differentiated Learning (to accelerate, decelerate, adapt, and expand content to fit student needs) to help teachers reach students of diverse reading levels.

2. **Present materials visually and auditorily.**

   For visual learners, *¡Qué chévere!* includes many activities based on an illustration, a photo, or realia. These students will also benefit from the eVisuals and electronic flash cards to learn vocabulary. Students are encouraged to use graphic organizers throughout *¡Qué chévere!* to help them organize ideas and analyze and evaluate texts. The program also builds listening skills with the supplemental Listening Activities, video offerings, and online offerings.

3. **Use materials that result in analysis and evaluation.**

   While some students may feel most comfortable in the knowledge, comprehension, and application areas of Bloom's taxonomy, *¡Qué chévere!* also challenges students to develop critical thinking skills such as analysis (*Analiza* questions), evaluation (graphic organizers), and synthesis (Essential question).

## Process

1. **Provide opportunities for students to work in pairs and groups.**

   Students learning with *¡Qué chévere!* receive many opportunities to work cooperatively in pairs and groups, both within the classroom and online.

2. **Adapt instruction to meet multiple intelligences and other learning styles.**

   Different learning styles are built into the activities of *¡Qué chévere!*; suggestions for implementation appear in the Annotated Teacher's Edition wraparound notes.

3. **Provide differentiated testing.**

   With *¡Qué chévere!*, social learners can engage in project-based assessment rather than traditional test taking.

## Products

1. **Provide opportunities for communication.**

   With the *¡Qué chévere!* program, students participate in dialogues (interpersonal communication); write memos, emails, postcards, etc. (presentational communication); and make presentations based on online research (interpretive/presentational communication).

2. **Provide challenging and engaging tasks.**

   The activities in *¡Qué chévere!* move from those that are mechanical to those that are meaningful, creative, and open-ended, including opportunities for pair and group work.

3. **Provide a variety of final projects based on learning styles.**

   Students have the opportunity in *¡Qué chévere!* to pursue thematic, project-based assessments.

## Learning Environment

People passing by your classroom will see a lot of activity when you teach with *¡Qué chévere!*, but it is a good idea to provide some quiet days to keep all your students comfortable. A *Pregunta clave* ties unit content together meaningfully and allows for reflection in culture journals and pair and group discussions. *¡Qué chévere!* technology allows your students to engage with video, audio, electronic flash cards, and more, using a variety of mobile devices. This variety allows your students to have fun while they learn at their own pace because you have planned and organized instruction that accommodates their interests and that respects their abilities and learning styles.

# Blended Learning Environment

### What Is Blended Learning?

Blended learning occurs when teachers combine face-to-face learning with online learning. With self-paced e-learning, students experience differentiated learning. In a blended learning environment, many activities that may have previously taken place during classroom time are moved online. In one model, students might meet in the traditional classroom only a couple times per week and do the rest of their learning online. For blended learning with *¡Qué chévere!*, students can access materials anytime, anywhere with EMC's Passport®.

### What Does Passport® Provide?

EMC's Passport® supports student-directed and project-based learning, interpersonal communication, and performance tasks. Within this digital environment, students **discover** the content of *¡Qué chévere!* anytime, anywhere through eBooks, listening activities, and other supplemental materials; **create** meaningful, project-based tasks centered in IPA-aligned modules; **expand** their linguistic and cultural horizons through virtual tours, video documentaries, and current news articles; **share** opinions, ideas, and perspectives through short video posts; and **perform** to demonstrate their cultural knowledge and oral proficiency through video tasks.

### What Kind of Blended Learning Experience Can I Create for My Students with *¡Qué chévere!*?

Today's students are digitally literate, interactive, experiential, and social, and they possess strong visual-spatial skills. They look for fast response times and are adept at moving quickly from one task to another. You might consider using face-to-face learning to introduce new concepts and allow for oral interpersonal communication and presentational sharing; self-paced learning for slower-paced and advanced learners; and online learning for all students to conduct interpretive research, create interpersonal written practice, and prepare presentational projects.

# Pre-AP Spanish Language and Culture

The new AP Spanish Language and Culture exam is centered around themes, incorporates overarching essential questions, and focuses on the three modes of communication (interpersonal, presentational, interpretive). It relies on abundant authentic print, audio, and video materials; it also requires students to comprehend cultural perspectives and compare cultures. These are some ways in which *¡Qué chévere!* prepares students for the AP Spanish exam:

- Units are organized thematically, for example, *La vida urbana* and *Fuentes de información*.
- All units have an essential question, or *Pregunta clave*, around which students frame their learning, for example, *¿Qué problemas conlleva la vida urbana y cómo se resuelven?*
- Culture readings in the program take students to all Spanish-speaking locations around the world. Specific *prácticas, productos*, and *perspectivas* of these cultures are pulled out for examination. Students also make comparisons between their culture and the target culture in this section.
- Authentic audio recordings (interviews, podcasts, etc.) allow for student engagement with authentic listening experiences. Textbook activities in *¡Qué chévere!* practice listening comprehension, and there are also supplemental listening activities for students to complete online.
- In *Lectura informativa* and *Lectura literaria*, students are exposed to authentic texts from throughout the Spanish-speaking world (news articles, short stories, poems, excerpts from plays and novels) that they analyze using critical thinking skills.
- The *Proyectos* allow students to build communities within the classroom and outside of school as well as make connections to other disciplines.
- Students who use *¡Qué chévere!* will master all five C's of the ACTFL Standards, learning to use Spanish in real-life settings (Communities), demonstrating an understanding of Spanish-speaking cultures (Culture), incorporating interdisciplinary learning (Connections), making comparisons between their cultures and Spanish-speaking cultures (Comparisons), all the while communicating in Spanish (Communication).

# Common Core State Standards

The Common Core State Standards (CCSS) initiative seeks to raise academic standards for students and provide articulation of academic standards among states. The CCSS is designed for courses in English Language Arts, History/Social Studies, Science, and Technical Subjects, each containing four strands: Reading, Writing, Speaking and Listening, and Language. Having CCSS drive curricula will result in new assessment benchmarks for students.

*¡Qué chévere!* was designed with the CCSS in mind. It emphasizes the purpose behind the communication by labeling activities that provide interpersonal (speaking-listening or writing-reading), interpretive (reading, listening, viewing), and presentational (writing, speaking, representing visually) communication. The goal of the program is to move students from novice, to intermediate, to advanced proficiency levels by the time they complete the five levels of *¡Qué chévere!*. Connections activities in *¡Qué chévere!* that are specific to history and science allow students to learn about historical and scientific contributions made by key figures in the Spanish-speaking world. Technology skills are developed in sections where students are encouraged to do additional research online using provided search words, and in the *Proyectos* section, where activities allow for individual, pair, and group work using various tools: the Internet, video, smartphones, and online programs. *¡Qué chévere!* uses the CCSS to make sure all students are ready for post-secondary learning, entry into the working world, and becoming global citizens.

# Correlation of Common Core State Standards

| Common Core State Standards—ELA | Standards for Learning Languages | ¡Qué chévere! Level 4 |
|---|---|---|
| **READING** | | |
| **Key Ideas and Details** | | |
| 1. Read closely to determine what the text says explicitly and to make logical inferences from it; cite specific textual evidence when writing or speaking to support conclusions drawn from the text.<br>2. Determine central ideas or themes of a text and analyze their development; summarize key supporting details and ideas.<br>3. Analyze how and why individuals, events, or ideas develop and interact over the course of a text. | **Interpretive Communication (Standard 1.2)**<br>· Demonstrate comprehension of content from authentic audio and visual resources. | 2, 3, 4, 5, 6, 7, 8, 9, 11, 13, 14, 15, 16, 17, 18, 19, 21, 22, 23, 25, 26, 27, 28, 29, 30, 31, 34, 35, 36, 37, 38, 39, 40, 41, 42, 43, 46, 47, 48, 49, 50, 51, 52, 53, 54, 57, 58, 59, 60, 61, 62, 63, 66, 67, 68, 69, 70, 71, 73, 74, 75, 76, 77, 78, 79, 80, 81, 83, 84, 85, 87, 88, 89, 90, 91, 94, 95, 96, 97, 98, 99, 100, 101, 103, 104, 105, 107, 108, 109, 110, 111, 112, 114, 115, 116, 117, 118, 120, 121, 122, 123, 124, 125, 126, 127, 128, 129, 130, 131, 132, 135, 138, 139, 140, 141, 142, 143, 144, 145, 146, 147, 148, 149, 150, 151, 152, 153, 154, 158, 159, 160, 161, 163, 164, 165, 166, 167, 168, 169, 170, 172, 174, 175, 176, 179, 182, 183, 184, 185, 186, 187, 188, 189, 190, 191, 192, 193, 194, 195, 196, 197, 200, 201, 202, 203, 204, 205, 206, 207, 208, 209, 210, 211, 212, 213, 215, 216, 218, 219, 220, 221, 222, 225, 226, 228, 230, 232, 233, 234, 235, 236, 238, 239, 240, 241, 242, 244, 245, 247, 248, 249, 251, 252, 253, 254, 255, 256, 257, 258, 259, 260, 262, 263, 264, 266, 267, 268, 269, 270, 272, 273, 274, 275, 276, 279, 280, 281, 282, 283, 286, 287, 288, 289, 290, 292, 293, 295, 296, 297, 298, 299, 300, 301, 302, 304, 305, 308, 309, 310, 311, 313, 314, 316, 317, 320, 321, 322, 323, 324, 326, 327, 328, 329, 331, 332, 334, 335, 336, 337, 338, 339, 340, 341, 342, 345, 346, 348, 349, 350, 351, 353, 354, 355, 356, 357, 358, 359, 360, 361, 362, 363, 364, 365, 366, 367, 368, 370, 372, 373, 375, 376, 377, 378, 379, 380, 381, 382, 383, 384, 387, 388, 390, 391, 392, 393, 395, 396, 397, 398, 399, 400, 401, 402, 403, 404, 405, 406, 407, 408, 409, 411, 412, 413, 414, 415, 416, 418, 419, 420, 421, 422, 423, 424, 426, 427, 428, 429, 430, 431, 433. |
| | **Cultures: Practices and Products (Standard 2.1 and 2.2)**<br>· Examine, compare and reflect on products, practices, and/or perspectives of the target culture(s). | 4, 6, 7, 11, 13, 14, 15, 16, 21, 22, 23, 26, 27, 30, 35, 36, 37, 39, 40, 41, 42, 52, 60, 61, 62, 63, 68, 73, 74, 75, 78, 79, 80, 81, 86, 87, 89, 94, 98, 99, 103, 104, 105, 110, 111, 114, 117, 118, 119, 120, 133, 134, 135, 141, 143, 144, 147, 148, 150, 151, 152, 158, 164, 165, 166, 167, 174, 175, 177, 178, 188, 190, 193, 194, 195, 200, 201, 202, 206, 207, 212, 215, 217, 220, 221, 223, 224, 225, 226, 232, 233, 234, 235, 238, 239, 240, 244, 248, 249, 251, 254, 258, 259, 261, 262, 263, 264, 272, 279, 280, 281, 287, 292, 293, 298, 301, 303, 304, 305, 309, 320, 321, 325, 331, 332, 338, 340, 341, 343, 344, 345, 346, 348, 349, 351, 352, 356, 360, 361, 362, 363, 366, 370, 372, 373, 374, 375, 380, 381, 385, 386, 388, 390, 391, 401, 402, 403, 415, 416, 417, 418, 427, 428, 430, 431, 432. |
| | **Connections: Acquiring New Information (Standard 3.2)**<br>· Acquire information from other content areas using authentic sources. | 6, 7, 10, 11, 13, 14, 15, 16, 19, 26, 27, 29, 30, 35, 36, 37, 39, 40, 41, 42, 43, 46, 47, 51, 52, 58, 59, 60, 61, 62, 63, 66, 67, 68, 69, 70, 71, 73, 74, 75, 76, 77, 78, 79, 80, 81, 83, 84, 85, 86, 87, 88, 89, 90, 91, 94, 98, 99, 100, 102, 103, 104, 105, 106, 107, 110, 111, 112, 114, 116, 118, 127, 128, 129, 130, 131, 135, 139, 140, 143, 144, 147, 148, 152, 158, 164, 167, 183, 188, 190, 192, 194, 195, 200, 201, 202, 206, 207, 212, 215, 225, 229, 232, 233, 234, 235, 240, 244, 251, 254, 263, 268, 272, 292, 293, 298, 305, 309, 320, 321, 331, 332, 345, 362, 372, 402, 416, 417, 428, 431. |
| **Craft and Structure** | | |
| 4. Interpret words and phrases as they are used in a text, including determining technical, connotative, and figurative meanings, and analyze how specific word choices shape meaning or tone.<br>5. Analyze the structure of texts, including how specific sentences, paragraphs, and larger portions of the text relate to each other and the whole.<br>6. Assess how point of view or purpose shapes the content and style of a text. | **Interpretive Communication (Standard 1.2)**<br>· Derive meaning from expressions found in culturally authentic texts.<br>· Understand the purpose of a message and point of view of its author.<br>· Identify the distinguishing features (e.g. type of resource, intended audience, purpose) of authentic written and aural texts. | 2, 3, 4, 5, 6, 7, 8, 9, 10, 11, 13, 14, 15, 16, 17, 18, 19, 20, 21, 22, 23, 24, 25, 26, 27, 29, 30, 31, 32, 33, 34, 37, 38, 39, 40, 41, 43, 46, 47, 50, 52, 53, 54, 55, 56, 57, 58, 59, 60, 61, 62, 63, 64, 66, 67, 68, 69, 70, 71, 72, 73, 74, 75, 76, 77, 78, 79, 80, 81, 82, 83, 84, 85, 86, 87, 88, 90, 91, 94, 95, 96, 97, 98, 99, 100, 101, 102, 103, 104, 105, 106, 107, 108, 109, 110, 111, 112, 113, 114, 115, 116, 117, 118, 120, 121, 122, 123, 124, 125, 126, 127, 128, 129, 130, 131, 132, 135, 138, 139, 140, 141, 142, 143, 144, 145, 146, 147, 148, 149, 150, 151, 152, 153, 154, 158, 159, 160, 161, 163, 164, 165, 166, 167, 168, 169, 170, 172, 174, 175, 176, 179, 182, 183, 184, 186, 187, 188, 189, 190, 191, 192, 193, 194, 195, 196, 197, 200, 201, 202, 203, 204, 205, 206, 207, 208, 209, 210, 211, 212, 213, 215, 216, 218, 219, 220, 221, 222, 225, 226, 228, 229, 230, 232, 233, 235, 236, 238, 239, 240, 241, 242, 244, 245, 247, 248, 249, 251, 252, 253, 254, 255, 256, 257, 258, 259, 260, 262, 263, 264, 266, 267, 268, 269, 270, 272, 273, 274, 275, 276, 279, 280, 282, 283, 286, 287, 288, 289, 290, 292, 293, 296, 297, 298, 299, 300, 301, 302, 304, 305, 308, 309, 310, 311, 313, 314, 316, 317, 320, 321, 322, 323, 324, 326, 327, 328, 329, 331, 332, 334, 335, 336, 337, 338, 339, 340, 341, 342, 345, 346, 348, 349, 350, 351, 353, 354, 355, 356, 357, 358, 359, 360, 361, 362, 363, 364, 365, 366, 367, 368, 370, 372, 375, 376, 377, 378, 379, 380, 381, 382, 383, 384, 387, 388, 390, 391, 392, 393, 395, 396, 397, 398, 399, 400, 401, 402, 403, 404, 405, 406, 407, 408, 409, 411, 412, 413, 414, 415, 416, 418, 419, 420, 421, 422, 423, 424, 426, 427, 428, 429, 430, 431, 432, 433. |
| | **Cultures: Practices and Products (Standards 2.1 and 2.2)**<br>· Compare and reflect on products, practices, and/or perspectives of the target culture(s). | 2, 4, 5, 8, 14, 15, 26, 27, 36, 39, 40, 41, 42, 58, 60, 61, 62, 63, 73, 79, 86, 87, 88, 90, 116, 117, 118, 119, 120, 133, 134, 141, 147, 150, 151, 152, 164, 165, 166, 167, 175, 177, 178, 193, 194, 195, 206, 207, 220, 221, 223, 224, 226, 238, 239, 240, 249, 251, 258, 259, 261, 262, 264, 279, 280, 281, 292, 293, 301, 303, 304, 320, 321, 322, 325, 331, 332, 338, 340, 341, 343, 344, 346, 348, 349, 351, 352, 356, 360, 361, 362, 363, 366, 370, 372, 373, 374, 375, 380, 381, 385, 386, 388, 390, 391, 401, 402, 403, 415, 416, 417, 418, 427, 428, 430, 431. |
| | **Connections: Reinforce Other Disciplines (Standard 3.1)**<br>· Demonstrate knowledge and understanding of content across disciplines. | 3, 4, 6, 7, 9, 10, 11, 13, 14, 15, 17, 20, 21, 22, 23, 24, 25, 26, 27, 28, 29, 30, 31, 32, 33, 34, 35, 36, 37, 38, 39, 40, 41, 42, 48, 49, 50, 51, 52, 53, 55, 56, 58, 59, 60, 61, 62, 63, 64, 65, 66, 68, 69, 70, 71, 72, 73, 74, 75, 76, 77, 78, 79, 80, 81, 82, 83, 84, 85, 86, 87, 88, 89, 90, 96, 97, 98, 99, 100, 101, 102, 103, 104, 105, 107, 108, 110, 111, 113, 114, 115, 116, 117, 120, 126, 127, 128, 129, 132, 134, 140, 143, 144, 147, 148, 157, 158, 164, 167, 169, 174, 175, 176, 177, 178, 183, 188, 190, 192, 193, 200, 201, 202, 206, 207, 212, 215, 220, 221, 223, 224, 232, 233, 234, 235, 238, 243, 244, 253, 254, 259, 260, 262, 268, 272, 279, 287, 292, 293, 297, 301, 302, 304, 325, 331, 336, 338, 339, 340, 341, 343, 344, 345, 372, 377, 379, 380, 381, 386, 394, 406, 407, 417, 420, 427, 428, 430, 432. |
| | **Comparisons: Language (Standard 4.1)**<br>· Evaluate similarities and differences in language use and idiomatic expressions between the target language and one's native language. | 2, 5, 6, 7, 8, 9, 11, 12, 16, 21, 22, 23, 24, 37, 41, 43, 51, 52, 56, 58, 63, 66, 68, 71, 73, 79, 80, 82, 84, 85, 87, 88, 91, 94, 95, 98, 99, 106, 107, 110, 111, 113, 114, 115, 135, 143, 144, 153, 158, 188, 190, 196, 200, 201, 202, 212, 215, 218, 232, 233, 234, 235, 241, 244, 254, 257, 263, 272, 282, 287, 298, 305, 323, 337, 345, 353, 354, 357, 358, 395, 396, 397, 404, 409, 421, 423. |
| | **Comparisons: Cultures (Standard 4.2)**<br>· Evaluate similarities and differences in the perspectives of the target culture(s) and one's own culture(s) as found in multimedia and digital/print resources. | 2, 6, 7, 11, 26, 27, 28, 36, 37, 43, 52, 63, 68, 80, 84, 85, 91, 94, 98, 99, 110, 111, 114, 116, 133, 134, 143, 144, 150, 158, 165, 188, 190, 193, 194, 195, 200, 201, 223, 202, 206, 212, 215, 217, 232, 233, 234, 235, 238, 239, 240, 244, 248, 254, 272, 279, 281, 287, 293, 298, 320, 321, 332, 345, 352, 361, 362, 372, 375, 401, 430, 432. |

| Common Core State Standards—ELA | Standards for Learning Languages | ¡Qué chévere! Level 4 |
|---|---|---|
| **Integration of Knowledge and Ideas** | | |
| 7. Integrate and evaluate content presented in diverse formats and media, including visually and quantitatively, as well as in words.<br>8. Delineate and evaluate the argument and specific claims in a text, including the validity of the reasoning as well as the relevance and sufficiency of the evidence.<br>9. Analyze how two or more texts address similar themes or topics in order to build knowledge or to compare the approaches the authors take. | **Interpretive Communication (Standard 1.2)**<br>· Interpret content from authentic multimedia and digital/print resources. | 2, 3, 4, 6, 7, 8, 9, 10, 11, 13, 14, 15, 16, 17, 19, 20, 21, 22, 23, 24, 26, 27, 28, 29, 30, 31, 32, 33, 34, 35, 36, 37, 38, 39, 40, 41, 42, 43, 46, 47, 48, 49, 50, 51, 52, 53, 54, 55, 56, 57, 58, 59, 60, 61, 62, 63, 64, 66, 67, 68, 69, 70, 71, 72, 73, 74, 75, 76, 77, 78, 79, 80, 81, 82, 84, 85, 86, 87, 88, 89, 90, 91, 94, 95, 96, 97, 98, 99, 101, 102, 103, 104, 105, 106, 107, 108, 109, 110, 111, 112, 113, 114, 115, 116, 117, 118, 120, 121, 122, 123, 124, 125, 126, 127, 128, 129, 130, 131, 132, 135, 138, 139, 140, 141, 142, 143, 144, 145, 146, 147, 148, 149, 150, 151, 152, 153, 154, 158, 159, 160, 161, 163, 164, 165, 166, 167, 168, 169, 170, 172, 174, 175, 176, 179, 182, 183, 184, 185, 186, 187, 188, 189, 190, 191, 192, 193, 194, 195, 196, 197, 200, 201, 202, 203, 204, 205, 206, 207, 208, 209, 210, 211, 212, 213, 215, 216, 218, 219, 220, 221, 222, 225, 226, 228, 229, 230, 232, 233, 234, 235, 236, 238, 239, 240, 241, 242, 244, 245, 247, 248, 249, 251, 252, 253, 254, 255, 256, 257, 258, 259, 260, 262, 263, 264, 266, 267, 268, 269, 270, 272, 273, 274, 275, 276, 279, 280, 281, 282, 283, 286, 287, 288, 289, 290, 292, 293, 295, 296, 297, 298, 299, 300, 301, 302, 304, 305, 308, 309, 310, 311, 313, 314, 316, 317, 320, 321, 322, 323, 324, 326, 327, 328, 329, 331, 332, 334, 335, 336, 337, 338, 339, 340, 341, 342, 345, 346, 348, 349, 350, 351, 353, 354, 355, 356, 357, 358, 359, 360, 361, 362, 363, 364, 365, 366, 367, 368, 370, 372, 373, 375, 376, 377, 378, 379, 380, 381, 382, 383, 384, 387, 388, 390, 391, 392, 393, 395, 396, 397, 398, 399, 400, 401, 402, 403, 404, 405, 406, 407, 408, 409, 411, 412, 413, 414, 415, 416, 418, 419, 420, 421, 422, 423, 424, 426, 427, 428, 429, 430, 431, 433. |
| | **Cultures: Practices and Products (Standards 2.1 and 2.2)**<br>· Compare and reflect on products, practices, and/or perspectives of the target culture(s). | 4, 8, 14, 15, 16, 26, 27, 35, 36, 39, 40, 41, 42, 60, 61, 62, 63, 73, 74, 75, 76, 79, 86, 103, 104, 105, 116, 118, 119, 120, 150, 133, 134, 135, 141, 147, 148, 152, 164, 165, 166, 167, 175, 177, 178, 193, 194, 195, 206, 217, 220, 223, 224, 225, 226, 238, 239, 240, 251, 258, 259, 261, 262, 263, 264, 279, 280, 281, 292, 293, 301, 303, 304, 305, 320, 321, 322, 325, 331, 332, 338, 341, 343, 344, 346, 348, 349, 351, 352, 356, 360, 361, 362, 363, 366, 370, 372, 373, 374, 375, 380, 381, 385, 386, 388, 390, 391, 401, 402, 403, 415, 416, 417, 418, 427, 428, 430, 431, 432. |
| | **Connections: Reinforce Other Disciplines (Standard 3.1)**<br>· Make cross-curricular connections. | 6, 7, 10, 11, 12, 13, 14, 15, 20, 21, 22, 23, 24, 26, 27, 28, 29, 30, 31, 32, 33, 34, 35, 36, 37, 38, 39, 40, 41, 42, 46, 47, 48, 49, 52, 53, 54, 55, 56, 57, 58, 59, 60, 61, 62, 64, 66, 67, 68, 69, 70, 71, 72, 73, 74, 85, 75, 76, 77, 78, 79, 80, 81, 82, 83, 84, 86, 87, 88, 89, 90, 94, 95, 98, 99, 100, 101, 102, 103, 104, 105, 106, 107, 108, 109, 110, 111, 112, 113, 114, 115, 116, 117, 120, 126, 127, 128, 129, 132, 134, 139, 140, 143, 144, 147, 148, 157, 158, 164, 167, 169, 174, 175, 176, 177, 178, 183, 188, 190, 192, 193, 200, 201, 202, 206, 207, 211, 212, 215, 220, 221, 223, 224, 232, 233, 234, 235, 243, 244, 253, 254, 258, 259, 260, 262, 268, 272, 279, 292, 293, 297, 298, 301, 302, 303, 304, 325, 331, 336, 338, 339, 340, 341, 343, 344, 345, 371, 372, 377, 379, 380, 381, 386, 394, 406, 407, 415, 416, 417, 427, 428, 430, 432. |
| | **Comparisons: Cultures (Standard 4.2)**<br>· Evaluate similarities and differences in the perspectives of the target culture(s) and one's own culture(s) as found in multimedia and digital/print resources. | 6, 7, 11, 26, 27, 37, 41, 52, 63, 68, 70, 77, 79, 80, 86, 98, 99, 110, 111, 114, 133, 134, 143, 144, 150, 158, 165, 188, 190, 193, 194, 195, 200, 201, 202, 206, 212, 215, 217, 223, 232, 233, 234, 235, 239, 240, 244, 248, 254, 272, 279, 281, 287, 293, 298, 320, 321, 345, 352, 361, 362, 366, 372, 401, 430, 432. |
| | **Communities: Beyond the School Setting (Standard 5.1)**<br>· Analyze the features of target culture communities (e.g. geographic, historical, artistic, social and/or political). | 3, 9, 10, 11, 13, 14, 15, 16, 19, 26, 27, 28, 29, 30, 34, 35, 36, 39, 40, 41, 42, 48, 53, 58, 59, 60, 61, 62, 63, 66, 70, 71, 73, 74, 75, 76, 77, 78, 79, 81, 82, 84, 85, 86, 87, 88, 89, 90, 94, 95, 100, 103, 104, 105, 112, 115, 116, 134, 135, 148, 183, 225, 263, 305, 309, 406. |
| **Range of Reading and Level of Text Complexity** | | |
| 10. Read and comprehend complex literary and informational texts independently and proficiently. | **Interpretive Communication (Standard 1.2)**<br>Monitor comprehension and use other sources to enhance understanding.<br>· Apply critical reading skills to authentic written and aural sources. | 2, 3, 4, 5, 8, 9, 10, 11, 12, 13, 14, 16, 17, 18, 19, 20, 21, 22, 23, 24, 25, 26, 27, 28, 29, 30, 31, 32, 33, 34, 35, 36, 38, 39, 40, 41, 48, 49, 51, 53, 54, 55, 56, 57, 58, 59, 60, 61, 64, 65, 66, 69, 70, 71, 72, 73, 74, 75, 76, 77, 78, 79, 81, 82, 83, 84, 85, 86, 87, 88, 90, 96, 97, 100, 101, 102, 106, 107, 108, 109, 112, 113, 115, 116, 117, 118, 120, 121, 122, 123, 124, 125, 126, 127, 128, 129, 130, 131, 132, 135, 139, 140, 141, 142, 145, 146, 147, 148, 149, 150, 151, 152, 153, 154, 158, 159, 160, 161, 163, 164, 165, 166, 167, 168, 169, 170, 172, 174, 175, 176, 179, 182, 183, 184, 185, 186, 187, 189, 191, 192, 193, 194, 195, 196, 197, 203, 204, 205, 206, 207, 208, 209, 210, 211, 213, 216, 218, 219, 220, 221, 222, 225, 226, 228, 229, 230, 236, 238, 239, 240, 241, 242, 245, 247, 248, 249, 251, 252, 253, 252, 625, 256, 257, 258, 259, 260, 263, 264, 266, 267, 268, 269, 270, 273, 274, 275, 276, 279, 280, 281, 282, 283, 286, 288, 289, 290, 292, 293, 295, 296, 297, 299, 300, 301, 302, 304, 305, 308, 309, 310, 311, 313, 314, 316, 317, 320, 321, 322, 323, 324, 326, 327, 328, 329, 331, 332, 334, 335, 336, 337, 338, 339, 340, 341, 342, 346, 348, 349, 350, 351, 353, 354, 355, 356, 357, 358, 359, 360, 361, 362, 363, 364, 365, 366, 367, 368, 370, 372, 373, 375, 376, 377, 378, 379, 380, 381, 382, 383, 384, 387, 388, 390, 391, 392, 393, 395, 396, 397, 398, 399, 400, 401, 402, 403, 404, 405, 406, 407, 408, 409, 411, 412, 413, 414, 415, 416, 418, 419, 420, 421, 422, 423, 424, 426, 427, 428, 429, 430, 431, 433. |
| | **Comparisons: Cultures (Standard 4.2)**<br>· Compare and reflect on products, practices, and/or perspectives of the target culture(s) and one's own culture. | 5, 6, 7, 14, 15, 16, 26, 27, 37, 41, 42, 52, 63, 68, 77, 79, 80, 86, 88, 98, 99, 110, 111, 114, 133, 134, 135, 143, 144, 150, 158, 165, 188, 190, 193, 194, 195, 200, 201, 202, 206, 212, 215, 217, 223, 225, 232, 233, 234, 235, 238, 239, 240, 244, 248, 254, 263, 272, 279, 280, 281, 287, 293, 298, 305, 320, 321, 345, 352, 361, 362, 366, 372, 375, 401, 430, 432. |
| | **Communities: Beyond the School Setting (Standard 5.1)**<br>· Interpret authentic written and aural texts within the communities of the target language. | 2, 3, 4, 5, 8, 9, 10, 13, 14, 15, 16, 17, 19, 20, 21, 22, 23, 24, 25, 26, 27, 28, 29, 30, 31, 32, 33, 34, 35, 36, 38, 39, 40, 41, 42, 43, 46, 47, 48, 49, 50, 51, 53, 54, 55, 56, 57, 58, 59, 60, 61, 62, 64, 66, 67, 69, 70, 71, 72, 73, 74, 75, 76, 77, 78, 79, 81, 82, 83, 84, 85, 86, 87, 88, 89, 90, 91, 94, 95, 96, 97, 100, 101, 102, 103, 104, 105, 106, 107, 108, 112, 113, 115, 116, 135, 139, 140, 148, 183, 192, 225, 229, 263, 268, 305, 309. |

| Common Core State Standards—ELA | Standards for Learning Languages | ¡Qué chévere! Level 4 |
|---|---|---|
| | WRITING | |

| | | |
|---|---|---|
| 1. Write arguments to support claims in an analysis of substantive topics or texts using valid reasoning and relevant and sufficient evidence. 2. Write informative/explanatory texts to examine and convey complex ideas and information clearly and accurately through the effective selection, organization, and analysis of content. 3. Write narratives to develop real or imagined experiences or events using effective technique, well-chosen details, and well-structured event sequences. | **Presentational Communication (Standard 1.3)** Present information, concepts, and ideas to an audience of listeners or readers on a variety of topics. · Produce a variety of creative oral and written presentations (e.g. original story, personal narrative, script). · Retell or summarize information in narrative form, demonstrating a consideration of audience. · Create and give persuasive speeches and write persuasive essays. · Produce expository writing. | 14, 18, 19, 20, 28, 29, 32, 33, 34, 36, 41, 42, 49, 51, 55, 56, 57, 58, 59, 60, 61, 62, 65, 72, 73, 76, 77, 86, 89, 90, 102, 108, 109, 113, 116, 117, 118, 119, 120, 121, 126, 127, 128, 129, 130, 131, 132, 133, 134, 146, 147, 150, 151, 152, 156, 159, 160, 163, 164, 165, 166, 167, 171, 172, 174, 175, 176, 177, 178, 186, 187, 191, 193, 194, 195, 198, 203, 204, 205, 206, 207, 208, 209, 211, 214, 217, 220, 221, 222, 223, 224, 231, 237, 238, 239, 240, 243, 245, 246, 248, 249, 250, 251, 252, 257, 258, 259, 260, 261, 262, 269, 271, 273, 277, 280, 281, 285, 286, 291, 292, 293, 294, 295, 296, 301, 302, 303, 304, 314, 318, 319, 320, 321, 322, 324, 325, 327, 329, 330, 331, 332, 333, 334, 335, 338, 339, 340, 341, 342, 343, 344, 352, 359, 360, 361, 362, 363, 365, 369, 370, 371, 372, 373, 374, 375, 380, 381, 382, 383, 384, 385, 386, 392, 394, 398, 400, 401, 402, 403, 406, 407, 410, 415, 416, 417, 418, 425, 426, 427, 428, 429, 430, 431, 432. |
| | **Comparisons: Language (Standard 4.1)** Demonstrate understanding of the nature of language through comparisons of the language studied and one's own. | 6, 7, 11, 12, 16, 28, 30, 31, 37, 39, 40, 41, 49, 50, 52, 53, 68, 71, 72, 80, 81, 96, 97, 98, 99, 101, 110, 111, 114, 135, 143, 144, 148, 153, 158, 188, 190, 196, 200, 201, 202, 212, 215, 218, 225, 232, 233, 234, 235, 241, 244, 254, 257, 263, 272, 287, 298, 305, 323, 337, 345, 353, 354, 357, 358, 364, 367, 368, 404, 409, 421, 422, 423. |

| | | |
|---|---|---|
| 4. Produce clear and coherent writing in which the development, organization, and style are appropriate to task, purpose, and audience. 5. Develop and strengthen writing as needed by planning, revising, editing, rewriting, or trying a new approach. 6. Use technology, including the Internet, to produce and publish writing and to interact and collaborate with others. | **Presentational Communication (Standard 1.3)** Present information, concepts, and ideas to an audience of listeners or readers on a variety of topics, knowing how, when, and why to say what to whom. · Retell or summarize information in narrative form, demonstrating a consideration of audience. · Self-edit written work for content, organization, and grammar. | 3, 4, 5, 8, 9, 10, 11, 13, 15, 17, 18, 19, 20, 25, 26, 27, 28, 29, 32, 33, 34, 36, 39, 40, 41, 42, 48, 49, 50, 51, 53, 54, 55, 56, 57, 58, 64, 65, 66, 69, 70, 72, 73, 76, 77, 79, 82, 83, 86, 87, 89, 90, 101, 102, 107, 109, 113, 116, 117, 118, 119, 120, 121, 126, 127, 128, 129, 130, 131, 132, 133, 140, 141, 146, 147, 150, 151, 152, 156, 159, 160, 163, 164, 165, 166, 167, 171, 172, 174, 175, 176, 177, 178, 186, 187, 191, 193, 194, 195, 198, 203, 204, 205, 206, 207, 208, 209, 211, 214, 217, 220, 221, 222, 223, 224, 231, 237, 238, 239, 240, 243, 245, 246, 248, 249, 250, 251, 252, 257, 258, 259, 260, 261, 262, 269, 271, 273, 277, 280, 281, 285, 286, 291, 292, 293, 294, 295, 296, 301, 302, 303, 304, 314, 318, 319, 320, 321, 322, 324, 325, 327, 329, 330, 331, 332, 333, 334, 335, 338, 339, 340, 341, 342, 343, 344, 352, 359, 360, 361, 362, 363, 365, 369, 370, 371, 372, 373, 374, 375, 380, 381, 382, 383, 384, 385, 386, 392, 394, 398, 400, 401, 402, 403, 406, 407, 410, 415, 416, 417, 418, 425, 426, 427, 428, 429, 430, 431, 432. |
| | **Cultures: Practices and Perspectives (Standard 2.1):** Demonstrate an understanding of the relationship between the practices and perspectives of the cultures studied. | 2, 4, 5, 8, 12, 13, 14, 15, 26, 27, 28, 29, 35, 39, 40, 41, 42, 48, 58, 60, 61, 62, 63, 66, 81, 87, 88, 118, 133, 134, 141, 147, 150, 151, 152, 164, 165, 166, 167, 177, 178, 194, 195, 223, 224, 226, 238, 239, 240, 249, 251, 261, 262, 280, 320, 321, 322, 332, 338, 343, 346, 348, 351, 352, 356, 361, 362, 363, 366, 370, 372, 373, 374, 375, 385, 401, 402, 403, 415, 416, 417, 431. |
| | **Cultures: Products and Perspectives (Standard 2.2)** Demonstrate an understanding of the relationship between the products and perspectives of the cultures studied. | 4, 5, 6, 7, 11, 14, 15, 26, 27, 28, 35, 36, 37, 39, 40, 41, 42, 52, 60, 61, 62, 63, 80, 87, 88, 89, 90, 98, 99, 110, 117, 118, 119, 120, 133, 134, 143, 144, 148, 151, 152, 158, 164, 165, 167, 174, 175, 177, 178, 188, 190, 193, 194, 195, 200, 201, 206, 207, 212, 215, 217, 220, 221, 223, 224, 226, 232, 233, 234, 238, 239, 240, 244, 249, 251, 254, 258, 259, 261, 262, 264, 272, 279, 280, 281, 292, 293, 298, 301, 303, 304, 320, 321, 322, 325, 332, 338, 340, 341, 343, 344, 345, 348, 349, 351, 352, 356, 360, 361, 362, 363, 366, 370, 372, 373, 374, 375, 380, 381, 385, 388, 390, 391, 401, 402, 403, 415, 416, 417, 418, 427, 428, 430, 431, 432. |
| | **Comparisons: Language (Standard 4.1)** Demonstrate understanding of the nature of language through comparisons of the language studied and one's own. | 16, 63, 84, 85, 96, 108, 153, 196, 218, 241, 257, 323, 337, 353, 354, 357, 358, 364, 367, 368, 395, 396, 397, 404, 409, 423. |
| | **Communities: Beyond the School Setting (Standard 5.1)** Use the language both within and beyond the school setting. | 2, 3, 4, 5, 8, 9, 10, 11, 12, 13, 15, 16, 18, 19, 20, 21, 22, 23, 24, 25, 26, 27, 28, 29, 30, 31, 32, 33, 34, 35, 36, 38, 39, 40, 41, 42, 43, 46, 47, 48, 49, 50, 51, 53, 54, 55, 56, 57, 58, 63, 64, 65, 66, 67, 69, 71, 72, 73, 74, 75, 76, 77, 78, 79, 81, 82, 83, 84, 85, 87, 88, 89, 90, 91, 94, 96, 97, 100, 101, 102, 103, 104, 105, 106, 107, 108, 112, 116, 134, 135, 139, 140, 148, 183, 225, 263, 309. |

# Correlation of Common Core State Standards

| Common Core State Standards—ELA | Standards for Learning Languages | ¡Qué chévere! Level 4 |
|---|---|---|
| | | |
| 7. Conduct short as well as more sustained research projects based on focused questions, demonstrating understanding of the subject under investigation.<br>8. Gather relevant information from multiple print and digital sources, assess the credibility and accuracy of each source, and integrate the information while avoiding plagiarism.<br>9. Draw evidence from literary or informational texts to support analysis, reflection, and research. | **Presentational Communication (Standard 1.3)**<br>Present information, concepts, and ideas to an audience of listeners or readers on a variety of topics.<br>• Expound on familiar topics and those requiring research.<br>• Produce expository writing including researched reports.<br>• Use reference tools, acknowledge sources and cite them appropriately.<br>• Demonstrate an understanding of features of target culture communities (e.g. geographic, historical, artistic, social and/or political).<br>• Demonstrate knowledge and understanding of content across disciplines. | 9, 10, 14, 15, 17, 18, 19, 20, 26, 27, 28, 29, 32, 33, 34, 36, 42, 49, 51, 55, 56, 57, 58, 64, 65, 70, 72, 73, 76, 77, 83, 86, 87, 89, 90, 101, 102, 108, 109, 113, 115, 116, 117, 118, 119, 120, 121, 126, 127, 128, 129, 130, 131, 132, 133, 134, 146, 147, 150, 151, 152, 156, 159, 160, 163, 164, 165, 166, 167, 171, 172, 174, 175, 176, 177, 178, 186, 187, 191, 193, 194, 195, 198, 203, 204, 205, 206, 207, 208, 209, 211, 214, 217, 220, 221, 222, 223, 224, 231, 237, 238, 239, 240, 243, 245, 246, 248, 249, 250, 251, 252, 257, 258, 259, 260, 261, 262, 269, 271, 273, 277, 280, 281, 285, 286, 291, 292, 293, 294, 295, 296, 301, 302, 303, 304, 314, 318, 319, 320, 321, 322, 324, 325, 327, 329, 330, 331, 332, 333, 334, 335, 338, 339, 340, 341, 342, 343, 344, 352, 359, 360, 361, 362, 363, 365, 369, 370, 371, 372, 373, 374, 375, 380, 381, 382, 383, 384, 385, 386, 392, 394, 398, 400, 401, 402, 403, 406, 407, 410, 415, 416, 417, 418, 425, 426, 427, 428, 429, 430, 431, 432. |
| | **Interpretive Communication (Standard 1.2)**<br>Understand and interpret written and spoken language on a variety of topics. | 2, 3, 4, 5, 6, 8, 9, 10, 11, 12, 13, 14, 15, 16, 17, 18, 19, 20, 21, 25, 26, 27, 28, 29, 30, 31, 32, 33, 34, 35, 36, 37, 38, 39, 40, 41, 42, 43, 46, 47, 48, 49, 50, 51, 52, 53, 54, 55, 56, 57, 58, 60, 61, 62, 63, 64, 65, 66, 67, 68, 69, 70, 71, 72, 73, 74, 76, 77, 78, 79, 80, 81, 82, 83, 84, 85, 86, 87, 88, 89, 90, 91, 94, 96, 97, 98, 99, 100, 101, 102, 103, 104, 105, 106, 107, 108, 109, 110, 111, 112, 113, 114, 115, 116, 117, 118, 120, 121, 122, 123, 124, 125, 126, 127, 128, 129, 130, 131, 132, 135, 138, 139, 140, 141, 142, 143, 144, 145, 146, 147, 148, 149, 150, 151, 152, 153, 154, 158, 159, 160, 161, 163, 164, 165, 166, 167, 168, 169, 170, 172, 174, 175, 176, 178, 179, 182, 183, 184, 185, 186, 187, 188, 189, 190, 191, 192, 193, 194, 195, 196, 197, 200, 201, 202, 203, 204, 205, 206, 207, 208, 209, 210, 211, 212, 213, 215, 216, 218, 219, 220, 221, 222, 225, 226, 229, 230, 232, 233, 234, 235, 236, 238, 239, 240, 241, 242, 244, 245, 247, 248, 249, 251, 252, 253, 254, 255, 256, 257, 258, 259, 260, 261, 262, 263, 264, 266, 267, 268, 269, 270, 272, 273, 274, 275, 276, 279, 280, 281, 282, 283, 286, 287, 288, 289, 290, 292, 293, 295, 296, 297, 298, 299, 300, 301, 302, 304, 305, 308, 309, 310, 311, 313, 314, 316, 317, 320, 321, 322, 324, 323, 326, 327, 328, 329, 331, 332, 334, 335, 336, 337, 338, 339, 340, 341, 342, 345, 346, 348, 349, 350, 351, 353, 354, 355, 356, 357, 358, 359, 360, 361, 362, 363, 364, 365, 366, 367, 368, 370, 372, 373, 375, 376, 377, 378, 379, 380, 381, 382, 383, 384, 387, 388, 390, 391, 392, 393, 395, 396, 398, 399, 400, 401, 402, 403, 404, 405, 406, 407, 408, 409, 411, 412, 413, 414, 415, 416, 418, 419, 420, 421, 422, 423, 424, 426, 427, 428, 429, 430, 431, 433. |
| | **Cultures: Practices and Perspectives (Standard 2.1)**<br>Demonstrate an understanding of the relationship between the practices and perspectives of cultures studied. | 2, 4, 8, 11, 13, 14, 15, 16, 26, 27, 28, 36, 39, 40, 41, 42, 48, 60, 61, 62, 63, 66, 86, 118, 133, 134, 135, 141, 147, 148, 150, 151, 152, 164, 165, 166, 167, 177, 178, 194, 195, 223, 224, 225, 226, 238, 239, 240, 248, 249, 251, 261, 262, 263, 280, 305, 320, 321, 322, 331, 332, 338, 343, 346, 348, 349, 351, 352, 356, 361, 362, 363, 366, 370, 372, 373, 374, 375, 385, 386, 401, 402, 403, 415, 416, 417, 431. |
| | **Cultures: Products and Perspectives (Standard 2.2)**<br>Demonstrate an understanding of the relationship between the products and perspectives of cultures studied. | 5, 14, 15, 26, 27, 28, 35, 39, 40, 41, 42, 60, 61, 62, 63, 86, 87, 89, 90, 117, 118, 119, 120, 133, 134, 151, 152, 164, 165, 167, 174, 175, 177, 178, 193, 194, 195, 206, 207, 217, 220, 221, 223, 224, 226, 238, 239, 240, 248, 249, 251, 258, 259, 261, 262, 264, 279, 280, 281, 292, 293, 301, 303, 304, 320, 321, 322, 331, 332, 338, 340, 341, 343, 344, 348, 349, 351, 352, 356, 360, 361, 362, 363, 366, 370, 372, 373, 374, 375, 380, 381, 385, 386, 388, 390, 391, 401, 402, 403, 415, 416, 417, 418, 427, 428, 430, 431, 432. |
| | **Connections: Reinforce Other Disciplines (Standard 3.1)**<br>Reinforce and further knowledge of other disciplines through the target language. | 2, 3, 6, 7, 10, 11, 13, 14, 15, 21, 25, 26, 27, 28, 29, 30, 31, 34, 35, 36, 37, 39, 40, 41, 42, 43, 46, 47, 49, 50, 52, 53, 56, 57, 60, 61, 63, 64, 66, 69, 71, 72, 73, 74, 76, 77, 78, 79, 80, 81, 82, 83, 84, 85, 86, 87, 88, 89, 90, 91, 94, 96, 98, 99, 100, 101, 102, 103, 107, 108, 109, 110, 111, 112, 114, 116, 120, 126, 127, 128, 129, 132, 134, 139, 140, 143, 144, 147, 148, 157, 158, 164, 167, 169, 174, 175, 176, 177, 178, 183, 188, 190, 193, 200, 201, 202, 206, 207, 211, 212, 215, 220, 221, 223, 224, 229, 234, 235, 243, 244, 248, 253, 258, 259, 262, 268, 279, 292, 293, 297, 298, 301, 302, 303, 304, 325, 331, 336, 338, 340, 341, 343, 344, 371, 372, 380, 381, 386, 406, 407, 415, 420, 427, 428, 430, 432. |
| | **Connections: Acquiring New Information (Standard 3.2)**<br>Acquire information and recognize the distinctive viewpoints that are only available through the target language and its cultures. | 4, 6, 7, 10, 11, 13, 14, 15, 16, 19, 20, 21, 26, 27, 29, 30, 32, 33, 35, 36, 37, 39, 40, 41, 42, 46, 47, 50, 52, 55, 57, 58, 60, 61, 62, 63, 66, 67, 68, 69, 76, 77, 78, 79, 80, 82, 83, 84, 85, 87, 88, 89, 90, 94, 98, 99, 100, 103, 104, 105, 107, 110, 111, 114, 116, 118, 120, 127, 128, 129, 130, 131, 135, 143, 144, 148, 152, 158, 164, 167, 178, 188, 190, 192, 194, 195, 200, 201, 202, 206, 207, 212, 215, 222, 225, 232, 233, 234, 235, 240, 244, 254, 263, 272, 292, 293, 298, 305, 309, 320, 321, 332, 345, 362, 372, 373, 402, 408, 415, 416, 417, 428, 431. |
| | **Comparisons: Culture (Standard 4.2)**<br>Demonstrate understanding of the nature of culture through comparisons of the culture studied and one's own. | 16, 26, 27, 28, 63, 79, 116, 133, 134, 150, 193, 194, 195, 206, 223, 225, 238, 239, 240, 248, 279, 280, 281, 293, 320, 321, 332, 352, 361, 362, 366, 372, 375, 401, 432. |

| Common Core State Standards—ELA | Standards for Learning Languages | ¡Qué chévere! Level 4 |
|---|---|---|

| Common Core State Standards—ELA | Standards for Learning Languages | ¡Qué chévere! Level 4 |
|---|---|---|
| 10. Write routinely over extended time frames (time for research, reflection, and revision) and shorter time frames (a single sitting or a day or two) for a range of tasks, purposes, and audiences | **Presentational Communication (Standard 1.3)** Present information, concepts, and ideas to an audience of listeners or readers on a variety of topics. · Self-monitor and adjust language production. · Self-edit written work for content, organization, and grammar. | 3, 4, 6, 7, 9, 10, 11, 11, 17, 18, 19, 20, 25, 28, 29, 32, 34, 35, 36, 37, 39, 40, 41, 42, 48, 49, 50, 51, 52, 53, 54, 55, 56, 57, 58, 64, 65, 68, 69, 70, 72, 73, 76, 77, 79, 80, 82, 83, 86, 87, 89, 90, 96, 97, 98, 99, 100, 101, 102, 107, 108, 109, 110, 111, 113, 114, 116, 117, 118, 119, 120, 121, 126, 127, 128, 129, 130, 131, 132, 133, 134, 143, 144, 146, 147, 150, 151, 152, 156, 158, 159, 160, 162, 163, 164, 165, 166, 167, 171, 172, 174, 175, 176, 177, 178, 186, 187, 188, 190, 191, 192, 193, 194, 195, 198, 200, 201, 202, 203, 204, 205, 206, 207, 208, 209, 211, 212, 214, 215, 217, 220, 221, 222, 223, 224, 231, 232, 233, 234, 235, 237, 238, 239, 240, 243, 244, 245, 246, 248, 249, 250, 251, 252, 254, 257, 258, 259, 260, 261, 262, 269, 271, 272, 273, 277, 280, 281, 285, 286, 287, 291, 292, 293, 294, 295, 296, 298, 301, 302, 303, 304, 312, 314, 318, 319, 320, 321, 322, 324, 325, 327, 329, 330, 331, 332, 333, 334, 335, 338, 339, 340, 341, 342, 343, 344, 345, 352, 359, 360, 361, 362, 363, 365, 369, 370, 371, 372, 373, 374, 375, 380, 381, 382, 383, 384, 385, 386, 392, 394, 398, 400, 401, 402, 403, 406, 407, 410, 415, 416, 417, 418, 425, 426, 427, 428, 429, 430, 431, 432. |
|  | **Cultures: Practices and Perspectives (Standard 2.1)** Demonstrate an understanding of the relationship between practices and perspectives of the cultures studied. | 4, 5, 9, 11, 13, 14, 15, 16, 20, 21, 22, 23, 24, 26, 27, 28, 32, 33, 35, 36, 39, 40, 41, 42, 60, 61, 62, 63, 74, 75, 79, 88, 116, 118, 133, 134, 135, 141, 147, 150, 151, 152, 164, 165, 166, 167, 177, 178, 194, 195, 223, 224, 225, 226, 238, 239, 240, 248, 249, 251, 262, 263, 280, 305, 320, 321, 322, 331, 332, 338, 343, 346, 348, 349, 351, 352, 356, 361, 362, 363, 366, 370, 372, 373, 374, 375, 385, 386, 401, 402, 403, 415, 416, 417, 431. |
|  | **Cultures: Products and Perspectives (Standard 2.2)** Demonstrate an understanding of the relationship between the products and perspectives of the cultures studied. | 4, 14, 15, 20, 26, 27, 28, 32, 33, 35, 39, 40, 41, 42, 55, 60, 61, 62, 63, 74, 75, 87, 88, 89, 90, 117, 118, 119, 120, 133, 134, 151, 152, 164, 165, 167, 174, 175, 177, 178, 193, 194, 195, 206, 207, 217, 220, 221, 223, 224, 226, 238, 239, 240, 248, 249, 251, 258, 259, 262, 264, 279, 280, 281, 293, 301, 303, 304, 320, 321, 322, 325, 331, 332, 338, 340, 341, 343, 344, 348, 349, 351, 352, 356, 360, 361, 362, 363, 366, 370, 372, 373, 374, 375, 380, 381, 385, 386, 388, 390, 391, 401, 402, 403, 415, 416, 417, 418, 427, 428, 430, 431, 432. |

| Common Core State Standards—ELA | Standards for Learning Languages | ¡Qué chévere! Level 4 |
|---|---|---|
| 1. Prepare for and participate effectively in a range of conversations and collaborations with diverse partners, building on others' ideas and expressing their own clearly and persuasively. 2. Integrate and evaluate information presented in diverse media and formats, including visually, quantitatively, and orally. 3. Evaluate a speaker's point of view, reasoning, and use of evidence and rhetoric. | **Interpersonal Communication (Standard 1.1)** Engage in conversations, provide and obtain information, express feelings and emotions, and exchange opinions. · Engage in the oral exchange of ideas in formal and informal situations. · Elicit information and clarify meaning by using a variety of strategies. · State and support opinions in oral interactions. · Self-monitor and adjust language production. · Converse in ways that reflect knowledge of target culture communities (e.g., geographic, historical, artistic, social and/or political). | 2, 3, 4, 5, 9, 10, 12, 17, 18, 19, 20, 29, 32, 33, 34, 35, 36, 41, 42, 47, 49, 51, 53, 55, 56, 57, 58, 59, 64, 65, 66, 70, 71, 72, 73, 74, 75, 76, 77, 81, 82, 83, 86, 89, 90, 97, 102, 108, 109, 112, 113, 115, 116, 123, 124, 125, 133, 134, 139, 140, 142, 145, 146, 149, 154, 155, 156, 157, 161, 162, 169, 170, 171, 172, 173, 177, 183, 187, 192, 197, 198, 199, 205, 213, 214, 216, 217, 223, 224, 231, 236, 237, 242, 243, 246, 247, 250, 256, 260, 261, 262, 268, 269, 270, 271, 273, 274, 278, 284, 286, 291, 299, 300, 303, 304, 311, 312, 314, 315, 317, 318, 319, 324, 325, 330, 333, 338, 339, 343, 344, 352, 356, 361, 365, 366, 371, 385, 386, 393, 394, 399, 400, 405, 406, 407, 408, 410, 411, 412, 414, 425, 431. |
|  | **Cultures: Practices and Perspectives (Standard 2.1)** · Use appropriate verbal and non-verbal behavior in interpersonal communication. | 2, 3, 5, 12, 17, 18, 19, 20, 25, 29, 32, 33, 34, 35, 36, 38, 41, 47, 49, 51, 53, 55, 56, 57, 58, 64, 65, 66, 70, 71, 72, 73, 77, 81, 82, 90, 95, 97, 102, 108, 112, 113, 116, 118, 133, 134, 141, 147, 150, 151, 152, 162, 164, 165, 166, 167, 177, 178, 192, 194, 195, 223, 224, 226, 238, 239, 240, 248, 249, 251, 261, 262, 280, 320, 321, 322, 331, 332, 338, 343, 346, 348, 349, 351, 352, 356, 361, 362, 363, 366, 370, 372, 373, 374, 375, 385, 386, 401, 402, 403, 415, 416, 417, 431. |
|  | **Cultures: Products and Perspectives (Standard 2.2)** · Compare and contrast artifacts, themes, ideas, and perspectives across cultures. | 6, 7, 13, 15, 20, 32, 33, 34, 35, 36, 37, 41, 42, 49, 51, 52, 53, 55, 63, 64, 65, 66, 68, 70, 71, 72, 73, 74, 75, 76, 77, 79, 80, 81, 82, 86, 87, 88, 89, 90, 95, 97, 98, 99, 102, 110, 111, 112, 113, 114, 116, 118, 119, 120, 133, 134, 143, 144, 151, 152, 158, 164, 165, 167, 174, 175, 177, 178, 183, 188, 190, 193, 194, 195, 200, 201, 202, 206, 207, 212, 215, 217, 220, 221, 223, 224, 226, 232, 233, 234, 235, 238, 239, 240, 244, 248, 249, 251, 254, 258, 259, 261, 262, 264, 272, 279, 280, 281, 287, 292, 293, 298, 301, 303, 304, 320, 321, 322, 325, 331, 332, 338, 340, 341, 343, 344, 345, 348, 349, 351, 352, 356, 360, 361, 362, 363, 366, 370, 372, 373, 374, 375, 380, 381, 385, 386, 388, 390, 391, 401, 402, 403, 415, 416, 417, 418, 427, 428, 430, 431, 432. |
|  | **Connections: Acquiring New Information (Standard 3.2)** · Use age-appropriate authentic sources to prepare for discussions. | 19, 20, 29, 32, 33, 35, 36, 41, 51, 53, 55, 58, 64, 66, 70, 71, 72, 73, 77, 82, 86, 87, 89, 90, 116, 118, 120, 127, 128, 129, 130, 131, 139, 152, 164, 167, 192, 194, 195, 206, 207, 222, 240, 251, 292, 293, 321, 331, 332, 362, 372, 373, 402, 408, 415, 416, 417, 428, 431. |
|  | **Comparisons: Language (Standard 4.1)** · Demonstrate an awareness of formal and informal language expressions in other languages and one's own. | 3, 4, 5, 12, 17, 20, 32, 33, 36, 41, 42, 47, 49, 55, 56, 57, 58, 64, 66, 71, 72, 73, 77, 78, 79, 81, 82, 86, 95, 97, 102, 108, 112, 116, 153, 196, 218, 241, 257, 282, 323, 337, 353, 354, 357, 358, 364, 367, 368, 395, 396, 397, 404, 409, 421, 423. |
|  | **Communities: Lifelong Learning (Standard 5.2)** · Establish and/or maintain interpersonal relations with speakers of the target language. | 3, 5, 18, 20, 32, 33, 35, 41, 47, 49, 55, 56, 59, 64, 66, 70, 71, 72, 73, 77, 81, 95, 97, 102, 108, 109, 112, 116, 117, 119, 171, 199, 213, 214, 220, 243, 284, 285, 286, 301, 303, 317, 324, 356, 372, 410. |

| Common Core State Standards—ELA | Standards for Learning Languages | ¡Qué chévere! Level 4 |
|---|---|---|
| **Presentation of Knowledge and Ideas** | | |
| 4. Present information, findings, and supporting evidence such that listeners can follow the line of reasoning and the organization, development, and style are appropriate to task, purpose, and audience.<br>5. Make strategic use of digital media and visual displays of data to express information and enhance understanding of presentations.<br>6. Adapt speech to a variety of contexts and communicative tasks, demonstrating command of formal English when indicated or appropriate. | **Presentational Communication: (Standard 1.3)**<br>Present information, concepts, and ideas to an audience of listeners or readers on a variety of topics.<br>• Produce a variety of creative oral presentations (e.g. original story, personal narrative, speech, performance).<br>• Retell or summarize information in narrative form, demonstrating a consideration of audience.<br>• Create and give persuasive speeches.<br>• Expound on familiar topics and those requiring research.<br>• Self-monitor and adjust language production.<br>• Use information about features of target culture communities (e.g. geographic, historical, artistic, social and/or political) in presentations.<br>• Incorporate content across disciplines in presentations. | 5, 13, 15, 17, 18, 19, 20, 29, 32, 33, 34, 35, 36, 41, 42, 47, 49, 51, 53, 55, 56, 57, 58, 59, 64, 65, 66, 70, 71, 72, 73, 74, 75, 76, 77, 81, 82, 83, 86, 87, 88, 89, 90, 95, 97, 102, 108, 109, 113, 115, 116, 117, 118, 119, 120, 121, 126, 127, 128, 129, 130, 131, 132, 133, 134, 139, 140, 146, 147, 150, 151, 152, 156, 159, 160, 162, 163, 164, 165, 166, 167, 171, 172, 174, 175, 176, 177, 178, 186, 187, 191, 192, 193, 194, 195, 203, 204, 205, 206, 207, 208, 209, 211, 214, 217, 220, 221, 222, 223, 224, 231, 237, 237, 238, 239, 240, 243, 245, 246, 248, 249, 250, 251, 252, 257, 258, 259, 260, 261, 262, 269, 271, 273, 277, 280, 281, 285, 286, 291, 292, 293, 294, 295, 296, 301, 302, 303, 304, 312, 314, 318, 319, 320, 321, 322, 324, 325, 327, 329, 330, 331, 332, 333, 334, 335, 338, 339, 340, 341, 342, 343, 344, 352, 359, 360, 361, 362, 363, 365, 369, 370, 371, 372, 373, 374, 375, 380, 381, 382, 383, 384, 385, 386, 392, 394, 398, 400, 401, 402, 403, 406, 407, 410, 415, 416, 417, 418, 425, 426, 427, 428, 429, 430, 431, 432. |
| | **Connections: Acquiring information (Standard 3.2)**<br>• Use age-appropriate authentic sources to prepare for discussions. | 19, 20, 26, 27, 32, 33, 35, 36, 41, 42, 49, 51, 55, 57, 58, 59, 64, 66, 71, 72, 73, 77, 82, 86, 87, 89, 90, 103, 104, 105, 116, 118, 120, 127, 128, 129, 130, 131, 134, 139, 140, 152, 164, 167, 194, 195, 206, 207, 222, 240, 251, 262, 292, 293, 320, 321, 331, 332, 362, 372, 373, 402, 408, 415, 416, 417, 428, 431. |

## Apps

Use these apps* in or beyond the classroom as an effective tool to foster student engagement while promoting active communication in Spanish.

**Assessment:** Gengo Quiz (by Innovative Language Learning) • quizlet.com (quizzes on words and phrases)

**Communication:** **Interpersonal:** Spanish Conversation Master (by JikuSystem) • Learn Spanish Online (by LingQ) • notesinspanish.com (podcasts) • www.mosalingua.com (dialogues) • Busuu-talk (www.busuu.com) **Presentational:** Toontastic (by Launchpad Toys) • Smeet (telecinco.es) • https://getkahoot.com (create quizzes, surveys, etc.) • powtoon.com (create animated videos, presentations) • quia.com (create web pages, games, etc.) • Directr (wistia.com) • Flipogram (video stories with music, flipagram.com) • animoto.com (video voiceover) • piccollage.com (make collages with labels) • Splice (edit video, add effects, by Path 36) • wordeo.com (videos with music and captioning) • Notability (by Ginger Labs) • tellagami.com (create speaking avatar) • Voice Record Pro (great for longer recordings, by Dayana Networks Ltd.) • homestyler.com (design a room) **Interpretive (Listening):** Spanish Conversation HD (dialogues, by redriverpress.com) • Spanish Conversation Master (by JikuSystem) • tunein.com (radio wherever you are) • highschoolspanishapp.com • mangolanguages.com **Interpretive (Reading):** Spanish Test Pro (sentence completion, by ege arge) • duolingo.com (Spanish-to-English translation)

**Crosswords:** Spanish Crossword Puzzles for Kids (with picture cues, by Lyuboz Zhivova) • Learn American Spanish with Crossword Puzzles (Jourist Verlags GmbH) • Words With Friends (by Zynga)

**Culture:** ¡Ya Tú Sabes! (by OpenLanguage) • mangolanguages.com • www.museodelprado.es (click on "APPS") • México es cultura

**Games:** Juego de Palabras (by Berni Mobile) • El Mejor Ahorcado (by Renato Pessanha) • ¡Adivina la palabra! (picture cues to identify words, by Alexandru Halmagean) • play2learn Spanish HD (Clear Vision) • Scrabble Spanish

**Grammar:** conjuguemos.com • Spanish Touch Trainer (by Appocado) • Gengo Grammar (by Innovative Language Learning) • ñ: Learn Spanish Verbs (by Brainscape) • miraispanish.com

**Interactive Language Learning:** Quickstart Spanish (by BBC Active)

**Writing:** evernote.com • Toontastic (create cartoons, by Launchpad Toys) • Book Creator (by Red Jumper) • highschoolspanishapp.com

**Miscellaneous:** History Maps of the World (by Seungbin Cho) • ShowMe (create lessons and remedial materials) • educlipper.net (clip web content for lessons) • Prezi • Moodle

* These apps are for identification purposes and the authors, editors, and publisher disclaim any affiliation, association, or connection with, or sponsorship or endorsement by such owners.

## Games

### El juego del mundo hispanohablante

Presentational Communication

*This game reviews, compares, and contrasts the Spanish-speaking countries in the world.*

Divide the class into two teams. Have one player from the team that begins draw a slip of paper from a bag that has the names of two Spanish-speaking countries on it, for example, *Argentina, España*. The player's objective is three-fold: to say where he or she is from, how he or she got from the first place to the second, and what he or she is going to do there, for example, *Soy de Buenos Aires, Argentina. Fui a España en avión. En España voy a visitar el Museo del Prado en Madrid*. For a bonus point and to incorporate AP practice, the student must make a cultural comparison between the two countries.

### El juego del pretérito y de la cultura

Interpretive/Presentational Communication

*This game is intended to review the preterite and culture, with whatever culture categories you wish to highlight: art, literature, history, daily life, museums, landmarks, names of dishes, etc.*

Divide the class into several groups. Then ask all the groups a question, for example, *¿Cuándo terminó Frida Kahlo la obra "Las dos Fridas"?* Students race to find the answer on their digital devices. The first student to find the answer raises his or her hand, and the teacher sends the student to the board where three columns have been made with these labels: *La literatura, El arte, La historia*. The student writes the answer in the correct column, for example, in the *El arte* category: *Frida Kahlo terminó "Las dos Fridas" en 1939*, earning a point for the right answer and the correct use of the preterite, hence two points for that team. To incorporate AP practice, have student volunteers take two elements from one category on the board and make a short presentation comparing and contrasting them.

### Cuando se fue la luz

Presentational Communication

*This is a writing game played in small groups that practices the preterite and the imperfect.*

Students are in groups of six people. The teacher announces that the power has gone out in town and the objective is to explain what everyone was doing when it went out, using the two past tenses in the same sentence. One person from each group picks a slip of paper from the "places container" (for example: *el museo de arte, el parque de atracciones, el circo, la fiesta, el aeropuerto, el restaurante, en casa*). Then each group member picks a slip of paper from the "persons container" (for example: *yo, tú, el/la abogado/a, Juan y yo/mi padre y yo, etc.*). One student in the group creates a logical sentence, for example, (*el restaurante/ yo*): *Comía una ensalada de tomate en el restaurante cuando se fue la luz*. The next student must use his or her "person" and continue the story using using the preterite and the imperfect correctly, for example, *"De repente, Juan y yo oímos un ruido en la cocina. Teníamos miedo."* One person in the group records the "story," and the team with the most correct sentences at the end wins the round. This game can also be played with a different situation, for example: *Cuando la actriz llegó a la fiesta, cuando empezó a llover, cuando aterrizaron los extraterrestres.*

### El fin de semana

Presentational Communication

This game can be used to review the past, present, future, and conditional tenses.

Divide the class into two teams. For the team that starts, the team members think of something they did this past weekend and raise their hand. The teacher selects the first student to raise his or her hand; the selected student describes his or her weekend, for example, *Fui de compras al centro comercial*. The second student on that team who raised his or her hand repeats the first player's sentence, adds a description, then adds a new activity: *Había mucha gente porque hacía mal tiempo. Después, salí a comer con amigos*. If all sentences are grammatically correct, the team earns five points for the "story." Then the other team takes a turn. The team with the most points at the end of the allotted time wins. (You may want to adopt this game to other topics, such as *De vacaciones*, *Mi año escolar*.)

### El juego de los adjetivos

Presentational Communication

*This game reviews adjectives and the present and past tense using names of famous people.*
Have each student in class write the name of a famous dead person (preferably from a Spanish-speaking country) on a small piece of paper that you put in a hat or bag. Then repeat the activity, having students write the name of a famous person (preferably from a Spanish-speaking country) who is alive. Divide the class into small groups. Have the first player in each group select a name, for example, Gabriel García Márquez. The first player has to say a sentence that uses two adjectives that he or she thinks will get the group to identify the person, for example, *Él fue un gran escritor colombiano*. If the first player gets someone on the team to guess the identity of the famous person with his or her first sentence, that team earns 3 points. If someone in the group guesses after the second sentence, the team earns 2 points. If someone in the group doesn't guess until the third sentence, the team only earns 1 point. After that, the next player selects a name and the game continues.

### ¿Qué harías?

Interpersonal/Presentational Communication

*This game reviews the subjunctive in "si" clauses as well as cultural information.*
Prepare small slips of paper, each containing a potentially hypothetical situation and a Spanish-speaking country, for example, *vivir en Argentina*, *viajar a México*, etc. Divide the class into two teams, and give each student on each team a number. One student draws a slip and must create a hypothetical question: *"Si vivieras en Argentina, ¿qué harías?*" The student on the other team with the corresponding number must reply: *"Si viviera en Argentina, aprendería a bailar el tango en el Barrio La Boca."* The student who asked the question must reply with a different idea: *"Yo no aprendería a bailar el tango en el Barrio La Boca. Yo viajaría a Patagonia para disfrutar la naturaleza."* Each correct sentence earns a point for the team.

# ¡Qué chévere! 4

## Authors

**Graciela Ascarrunz Gilman**
University of California, Santa Barbara

**Nancy Levy-Konesky**
Yale College
Teacher Preparation Program

**Karen Daggett**
Boston College

### Contributing Writer

Miriam C. Álvarez

EMC Publishing®

ST. PAUL, MINNESOTA

**Associate Publisher:**
Alejandro Vargas

**Development Editor:**
Kristin Hoffman

**Director of Production:**
Deanna Quinn

**Production Editor:**
Bob Dreas

**Production Specialist and Designer:**
Leslie Anderson

**Digital Production Specialist:**
Julie Johnston

AP® is a registered trademark of the College Board, which was not involved in the production of, and does not endorse, this product.

Care has been taken to verify the accuracy of information presented in this book. However, the authors, editors, and publisher cannot accept responsibility for Web, e-mail, newsgroup, or chat room subject matter or content, or for consequences from application of the information in this book, and make no warranty, expressed or implied, with respect to its content.

**Trademarks:** Some of the product names and company names included in this book have been used for identification purposes only and may be trademarks or registered trade names of their respective manufacturers and sellers. The authors, editors, and publisher disclaim any affiliation, association, or connection with, or sponsorship or endorsement by, such owners.

**Credits:** Acknowledgements, Literary Credits, and Photo Credits follow the Index.

We have made every effort to trace the ownership of all copyrighted material and to secure permission from copyright holders. In the event of any question arising as to the use of any material, we will be pleased to make the necessary corrections in future printings. Thanks are due to the aforementioned authors, publishers, and agents for permission to use the materials indicated.

Adapted from *Nuevos horizontes: Lengua, conversación y Literatura, 1E* by Graciela Ascarrunz Gilman, Nancy Levy-Konesky, Karen Daggett © 2006 by John Wiley & Sons, Inc. Published by arrangement with John Wiley & Sons, Inc.

ISBN 978-0-82197-681-4

© 2017 by EMC Publishing, LLC
875 Montreal Way
St. Paul, MN 55102
Email: educate@emcp.com
Website: www.emcp.com

# Mensaje a los estudiantes

You have made great progress in your Spanish studies, and now you are ready to continue your journey on the pathway to proficiency in *¡Qué chévere! 4*. Whether you plan to use Spanish in your post-high school studies, for travel abroad, in a volunteer situation or at a job, you now have the basic communication skills to make yourself understood in many settings and situations. You have developed an understanding of other cultures and a sensitivity toward the people from those cultures so that when you travel to Spanish-speaking countries or meet people from there, you can build solid relationships and demonstrate your willingness and ability to be a responsible citizen in a globalized society.

With *¡Qué chévere! 4*, you will be able to master Spanish by augmenting your vocabulary and learning even more about different Spanish-speaking cultures. In addition, you will read authentic non-fiction and literary selections, which means you will be reading materials written for and by native Spanish speakers. You will also listen to authentic audio in the form of interviews, radio programs, and podcasts. Most importantly of all, you will engage in many interpersonal and presentational communication activities in which you will use your Spanish for real-life situations.

Whatever your goals for your newly acquired Spanish skills, you will find a world of opportunities waiting for you after completing *¡Qué chévere! 4*. Have a great year, and enjoy the next stage on the journey!

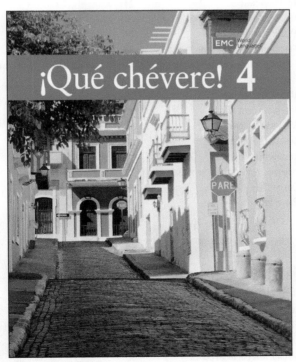

*Cover photo: Viejo San Juan*
*San Juan, Puerto Rico*

# Tabla de contenido

| Unidad 1 | | Cuba |
|---|---|---|

## El trato con los demás — 1

| | | |
|---|---|---|
| Vocabulario 1 | ¡Hombre de buen trato, a todos es grato! | 2 |
| Gramática | Los pronombres interrogativos | 6 |
| | Otras palabras interrogativas | 7 |
| | Pronombres exclamativos | 11 |
| Cultura | Así somos y así nos saludamos | 13 |
| | ¿Cuestión de léxico o filosofía? | 14 |
| | El vínculo de la amistad | 15 |
| Vocabulario 2 | Comparación y contraste: ¡Ojo con estas palabras! | 16 |
| Gramática | Los sustantivos | 21 |
| | El artículo definido | 23 |
| | El artículo indefinido | 24 |
| Lectura informativa | Fragmentos del discurso de Barack Obama sobre la reanudación de relaciones entre EE. UU. y Cuba | 26 |
| Escritura | Un correo electrónico informal | 28 |
| | Un ensayo persuasivo | 29 |
| Vocabulario 3 | Mejore su comprensión | 30 |
| Gramática | Los adjetivos calificativos | 32 |
| | Los adjetivos posesivos | 35 |
| | Adjetivos y pronombres demostrativos | 37 |
| Lectura literaria | Dos patrias | 39 |
| Para concluir | Proyectos | 41 |
| Vocabulario de la Unidad | | 43 |

| Unidad 2 | | España |
|---|---|---|

## El atractivo de viajar — 45

| | | |
|---|---|---|
| Vocabulario 1 | ¡Nos vamos de viaje! | 46 |
| Gramática | Los pronombres personales y su uso | 50 |
| | El presente de indicativo | 51 |
| | Los usos del presente de indicativo | 55 |
| Cultura | Madrid: Arte por todas partes | 60 |
| | Verde encanto | 61 |
| | ¡A visitar lo que es nuestro! | 62 |
| Vocabulario 2 | Comparación y contraste: ¡Ojo con estas palabras! | 63 |
| Gramática | El tiempo futuro | 68 |
| | Los usos del futuro | 71 |
| Lectura informativa | 2015, Año del Quijote | 74 |
| | Cospedal celebra que "nuestro personaje más universal" acercará Castilla-La Mancha al mundo para crear riqueza | 75 |
| Escritura | Publicar en las redes sociales | 76 |
| | Un folleto turístico | 77 |
| Vocabulario 3 | Mejore su comprensión | 78 |
| Gramática | Las comparaciones | 80 |
| | Las comparaciones de igualdad | 83 |
| | El superlativo | 84 |
| Lectura literaria | He andado muchos caminos | 87 |
| Para concluir | Proyectos | 89 |
| Vocabulario de la Unidad | | 91 |

| Unidad 3 | | Perú |
|---|---|---|

## Paso a paso hacia el futuro — 93

| | | |
|---|---|---|
| Vocabulario 1 | Así nos preparamos | 94 |
| Gramática | Los verbos reflexivos | 98 |
| Cultura | Con la mira puesta en el futuro | 103 |
| | Del elitismo a la meritocracia | 104 |
| | Diversidad y educación en Perú | 105 |
| Vocabulario 2 | Comparación y contraste: ¡Ojo con estas palabras! | 106 |

| Gramática | Los usos de **ser** y **estar** | 110 |
| | Los verbos **haber**, **hacer**, **tener**, **nevar** y **llover** | 114 |
| Lectura informativa | Verano en Cusco | 117 |
| | Vida en Cusco | 118 |
| Escritura | Una carta formal | 119 |
| | Una recomendación | 120 |
| Vocabulario 3 | Mejore su comprensión | 121 |
| Gramática | Expresiones de obligación y probabilidad | 123 |
| | Las preposiciones **en** y **de** | 124 |
| Lectura literaria | El alacrán de fray Gómez | 126 |
| Para concluir | Proyectos | 133 |
| Vocabulario de la Unidad | | 135 |

## Unidad 4 — Bolivia

## La vida del hogar — 137

| Vocabulario 1 | En casa nos repartimos los quehaceres | 138 |
| Gramática | El tiempo pretérito | 143 |
| | El tiempo imperfecto | 148 |
| Cultura | Mujeres: El eje central de la familia boliviana | 150 |
| | El matrimonio en la cultura aymara | 151 |
| | El aguayo | 152 |
| Vocabulario 2 | Comparación y contraste: ¡Ojo con estas palabras! | 153 |

| Gramática | El pretérito vs. el imperfecto | 158 |
| Lectura informativa | Las trabajadoras del hogar se asocian y ofrecen servicios domésticos por hora | 164 |
| Escritura | Una carta informal | 166 |
| | Un relato | 167 |
| Vocabulario 3 | Mejore su comprensión | 168 |
| Gramática | Expresiones con **Hace que...** y **Hacía que...** | 170 |
| Lectura literaria | Las medias rojas | 174 |
| Para concluir | Proyectos | 177 |
| Vocabulario de la Unidad | | 179 |

## Unidad 5 — México

## Empleos y finanzas — 181

| Vocabulario 1 | Aduéñate de tus finanzas | 182 |
| Gramática | El pretérito perfecto | 188 |
| | El pluscuamperfecto | 190 |
| Cultura | La importancia de la economía | 193 |
| | La economía real | 194 |
| | Beneficios del teletrabajo | 195 |
| Vocabulario 2 | Comparación y contraste: ¡Ojo con estas palabras! | 196 |
| Gramática | Los pronombres de complemento | 200 |

| Lectura informativa | El 59 % de los universitarios mexicanos no cuenta actualmente con un empleo | 206 |
| Escritura | Una hoja de vida | 208 |
| | Un resumen | 209 |
| Vocabulario 3 | Mejore su comprensión | 210 |
| Gramática | El verbo **gustar** y verbos similares | 212 |
| | Usos del pronombre **se** | 215 |
| | Las preposiciones **a** y **con** | 218 |
| Lectura literaria | Autorretrato | 220 |
| Para concluir | Proyectos | 223 |
| Vocabulario de la Unidad | | 225 |

## Unidad 6 — Chile

## Salud y bienestar — 227

| Vocabulario 1 | ¡Más vale prevenir que curar! | 228 |
| Gramática | El modo subjuntivo | 232 |
| Cultura | Medicina mapuche en el siglo XXI | 238 |
| | Un médico rural, un médico integral | 239 |
| | La salud en el mundo virtual | 240 |
| Vocabulario 2 | Comparación y contraste: ¡Ojo con estas palabras! | 241 |
| Gramática | El modo imperativo | 244 |
| Lectura informativa | Los momentos que marcaron la evolución de la medicina y la salud en Chile | 248 |

| | | |
|---|---|---|
| **Escritura** | Una historia clínica | 250 |
| | Un texto argumentativo | 251 |
| **Vocabulario 3** | Mejore su comprensión | 252 |
| **Gramática** | Mandatos de **tú** y de **vosotros** | 254 |
| | Mandatos de **nosotros** | 257 |
| **Lectura literaria** | *Walking Around* | 258 |
| **Para concluir** | Proyectos | 261 |
| **Vocabulario de la Unidad** | | 263 |

## Unidad 7 — Argentina

### La vida urbana — 265

| | | |
|---|---|---|
| **Vocabulario 1** | Así se vive en la ciudad | 266 |
| **Gramática** | El subjuntivo en cláusulas adjetivales | 272 |
| | El subjuntivo en cláusulas adverbiales | 275 |
| **Cultura** | Buenos Aires y el tránsito | 279 |
| | Cuando lo abandonado vuelve a cobrar vida | 280 |
| | De ciudad ideal a ciudad sumergida | 281 |
| **Vocabulario 2** | Comparación y contraste: ¡Ojo con estas palabras! | 282 |
| **Gramática** | El imperfecto del subjuntivo | 287 |
| | Los usos del imperfecto del subjuntivo | 289 |

| | | |
|---|---|---|
| **Lectura informativa** | Una tragedia que no admite más disputas ni dilaciones | 292 |
| **Escritura** | Un ensayo comparativo | 294 |

| | | |
|---|---|---|
| **Vocabulario 3** | Mejore su comprensión | 296 |
| **Gramática** | El subjuntivo en oraciones independientes | 298 |
| | Los adverbios | 299 |
| **Lectura literaria** | Los dos reyes y los dos laberintos | 301 |
| **Para concluir** | Proyectos | 303 |
| **Vocabulario de la Unidad** | | 305 |

## Unidad 8 — Puerto Rico

### A nuestro alrededor — 307

| | | |
|---|---|---|
| **Vocabulario 1** | Nuestro entorno natural y sociocultural | 308 |
| **Gramática** | El condicional | 313 |
| | Las cláusulas condicionales con **si** | 316 |
| **Cultura** | La construcción de la puertorriqueñidad | 320 |
| | El idioma y la cultura | 321 |
| | Nueva ola migratoria de la isla al continente | 322 |
| **Vocabulario 2** | Comparación y contraste: ¡Ojo con estas palabras! | 323 |

| | | |
|---|---|---|
| **Gramática** | El presente perfecto del subjuntivo | 326 |
| | Expresiones afirmativas y negativas | 328 |
| **Lectura informativa** | La crisis lleva a universitarios puertorriqueños a emigrar en masa a EE. UU. | 331 |
| **Escritura** | Una biografía | 333 |
| **Vocabulario 3** | Mejore su comprensión | 335 |
| **Gramática** | La voz pasiva | 337 |
| **Lectura literaria** | Cuando era puertorriqueña | 340 |
| **Para concluir** | Proyectos | 343 |
| **Vocabulario de la Unidad** | | 345 |

## Unidad 9 — Colombia

### Festejos con tradición — 347

| | | |
|---|---|---|
| **Vocabulario 1** | ¡De celebración en celebración! | 348 |
| **Gramática** | Los usos del infinitivo | 353 |
| | Usos de **por** y **para** | 357 |

| | | |
|---|---|---|
| **Cultura** | El carnaval y la cumbia | **361** |
| | La Leyenda Vallenata | **362** |
| | Noviembre es pura fiesta en Cartagena | **363** |
| **Vocabulario 2** | Comparación y contraste: | **364** |
| |   ¡Ojo con estas palabras! | |
| **Gramática** | Usos de algunas preposiciones comunes | **367** |

| | | |
|---|---|---|
| **Lectura informativa** | ¿Triqui triqui enfrentado a los angelitos? | **372** |
| **Escritura** | Una carta persuasiva | **374** |
| **Vocabulario 3** | Mejore su comprensión | **376** |
| **Gramática** | Los diminutivos y los aumentativos | **378** |
| **Lectura literaria** | Un señor muy viejo con unas | **380** |
| |   alas enormes | |
| **Para concluir** | Proyectos | **385** |
| **Vocabulario de la Unidad** | | **387** |

## Unidad 10             Honduras

## Fuentes de información      389

| | | |
|---|---|---|
| **Vocabulario 1** | ¿Cómo nos comunicamos? | **390** |

| | | |
|---|---|---|
| **Gramática** | El gerundio | **395** |
| **Cultura** | Los medios de comunicación hondureños | **401** |
| | Una ley para el periodismo | **402** |
| | Asociación de Medios Comunitarios | **403** |
| |   en Honduras | |

| | | |
|---|---|---|
| **Vocabulario 2** | Comparación y contraste: | **404** |
| |   ¡Ojo con estas palabras! | |
| **Gramática** | El futuro perfecto y el condicional | **409** |
| |   perfecto | |
| | El pluscuamperfecto del subjuntivo | **411** |
| **Lectura informativa** | Virgilio Andrade: en 50 años de radio | **415** |
| |   sufrí amenazas, marginación y exilio | |
| **Escritura** | Un ensayo persuasivo | **417** |
| **Vocabulario 3** | Mejore su comprensión | **419** |
| **Gramática** | Los pronombres relativos **que** y **quien** (es) | **421** |
| | Otros pronombres relativos | **423** |
| **Lectura literaria** | La voz femenina en Sor Juana Inés y | **427** |
| |   Alfonsina Storni | |
| | Hombres necios | **428** |
| | Peso ancestral | **430** |
| **Para concluir** | Proyectos | **431** |
| **Vocabulario de la Unidad** | | **433** |

| | | |
|---|---|---|
| **Apéndice A** | **Reglas de puntuación y ortografía** | **434** |
| **Apéndice B** | **Los posesivos** | **437** |
| **Apéndice C** | **Los verbos** | **438** |
| **Apéndice D** | **¿Lleva el verbo una preposición?** | **448** |
| **Vocabulario** | **Español / Inglés** | **455** |
| **Índice** | | **469** |
| **Créditos** | | **472** |

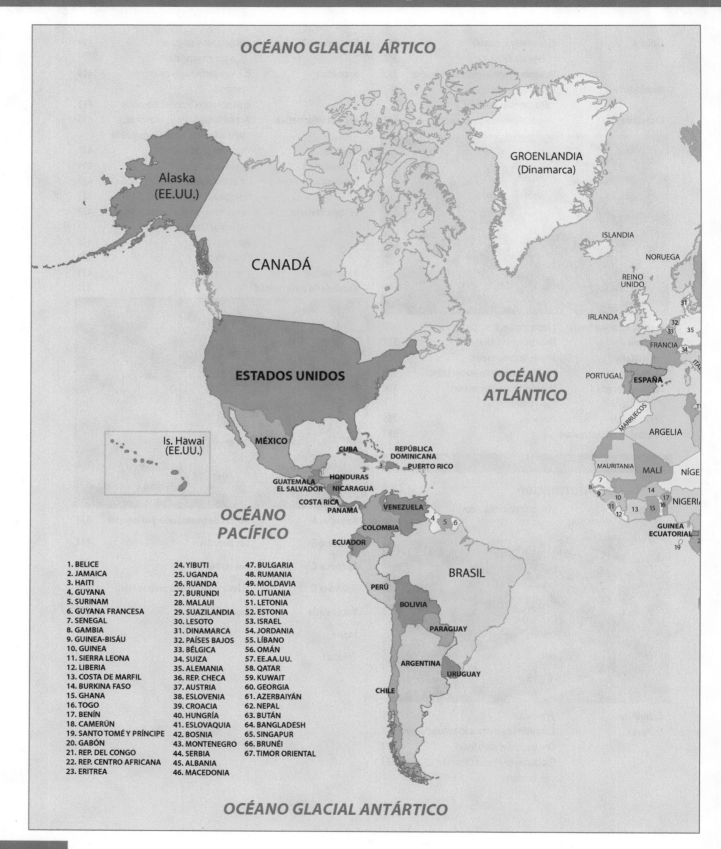

OCÉANO GLACIAL ÁRTICO

GROENLANDIA
(Dinamarca)

Alaska
(EE.UU.)

ISLANDIA

NORUEGA

CANADÁ

REINO
UNIDO

IRLANDA

ESTADOS UNIDOS

OCÉANO
ATLÁNTICO

PORTUGAL    ESPAÑA

FRANCIA

Is. Hawai
(EE.UU.)

MARRUECOS

MÉXICO

ARGELIA

CUBA

REPÚBLICA
DOMINICANA

MAURITANIA    MALÍ    NÍGER

PUERTO RICO

GUATEMALA    HONDURAS
EL SALVADOR    NICARAGUA

COSTA RICA

PANAMÁ    VENEZUELA

NIGERIA

COLOMBIA

GUINEA
ECUATORIAL

ECUADOR

OCÉANO
PACÍFICO

BRASIL

PERÚ

BOLIVIA

PARAGUAY

ARGENTINA

URUGUAY

CHILE

| | | |
|---|---|---|
| 1. BELICE | 24. YIBUTI | 47. BULGARIA |
| 2. JAMAICA | 25. UGANDA | 48. RUMANIA |
| 3. HAITI | 26. RUANDA | 49. MOLDAVIA |
| 4. GUYANA | 27. BURUNDI | 50. LITUANIA |
| 5. SURINAM | 28. MALAUI | 51. LETONIA |
| 6. GUYANA FRANCESA | 29. SUAZILANDIA | 52. ESTONIA |
| 7. SENEGAL | 30. LESOTO | 53. ISRAEL |
| 8. GAMBIA | 31. DINAMARCA | 54. JORDANIA |
| 9. GUINEA-BISÁU | 32. PAÍSES BAJOS | 55. LÍBANO |
| 10. GUINEA | 33. BÉLGICA | 56. OMÁN |
| 11. SIERRA LEONA | 34. SUIZA | 57. EE.AA.UU. |
| 12. LIBERIA | 35. ALEMANIA | 58. QATAR |
| 13. COSTA DE MARFIL | 36. REP. CHECA | 59. KUWAIT |
| 14. BURKINA FASO | 37. AUSTRIA | 60. GEORGIA |
| 15. GHANA | 38. ESLOVENIA | 61. AZERBAIYÁN |
| 16. TOGO | 39. CROACIA | 62. NEPAL |
| 17. BENÍN | 40. HUNGRÍA | 63. BUTÁN |
| 18. CAMERÚN | 41. ESLOVAQUIA | 64. BANGLADESH |
| 19. SANTO TOMÉ Y PRÍNCIPE | 42. BOSNIA | 65. SINGAPUR |
| 20. GABÓN | 43. MONTENEGRO | 66. BRUNÉI |
| 21. REP. DEL CONGO | 44. SERBIA | 67. TIMOR ORIENTAL |
| 22. REP. CENTRO AFRICANA | 45. ALBANIA | |
| 23. ERITREA | 46. MACEDONIA | |

OCÉANO GLACIAL ANTÁRTICO

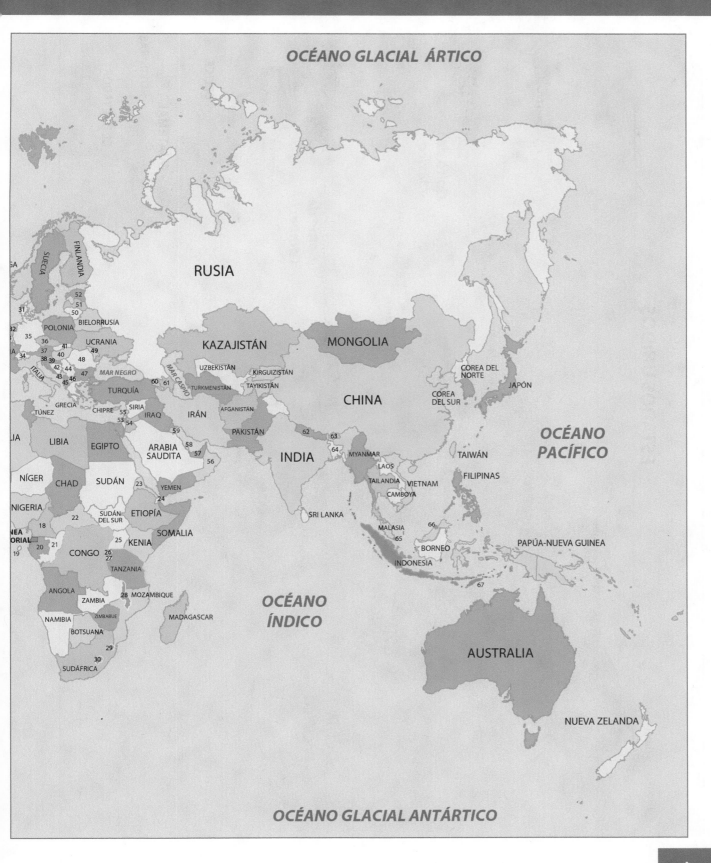

OCÉANO GLACIAL ÁRTICO

RUSIA

SUECIA
FINLANDIA

52
51
50
BIELORRUSIA
31
32
35
POLONIA
36
41
UCRANIA
34
37 40
49
38 39
42 44 48
ITALIA
43 47
45 46

KAZAJISTÁN

MONGOLIA

COREA DEL
NORTE

JAPÓN

MAR NEGRO
60 61
MAR CASPIO
UZBEKISTÁN
KIRGUIZISTÁN
TURQUÍA
TURKMENISTÁN
TAYIKISTÁN

CHINA

COREA
DEL SUR

OCÉANO
PACÍFICO

GRECIA
CHIPRE
SIRIA
55
TÚNEZ
53 54
IRAQ
AFGANISTÁN
IRÁN

LIBIA
EGIPTO
59
PAKISTÁN
62
63
58
ARABIA
SAUDITA
57
56
INDIA
64
MYANMAR

TAIWÁN

LAOS
NÍGER
CHAD
SUDÁN
23
YEMEN
TAILANDIA
VIETNAM
FILIPINAS

NIGERIA
24
CAMBOYA

22
SUDÁN
DEL SUR
ETIOPÍA
SRI LANKA

NEA
ORIAL
18
SOMALIA
66
MALASIA
21
25
KENIA
65
PAPÚA-NUEVA GUINEA
19
20
CONGO
26
27
BORNEO
TANZANIA
INDONESIA

ANGOLA
ZAMBIA
28
MOZAMBIQUE
67

NAMIBIA
ZIMBABUE
MADAGASCAR
OCÉANO
ÍNDICO

BOTSUANA

29
AUSTRALIA
30
SUDÁFRICA

OCÉANO
ÍNDICO

NUEVA ZELANDA

OCÉANO GLACIAL ANTÁRTICO

# MÉXICO

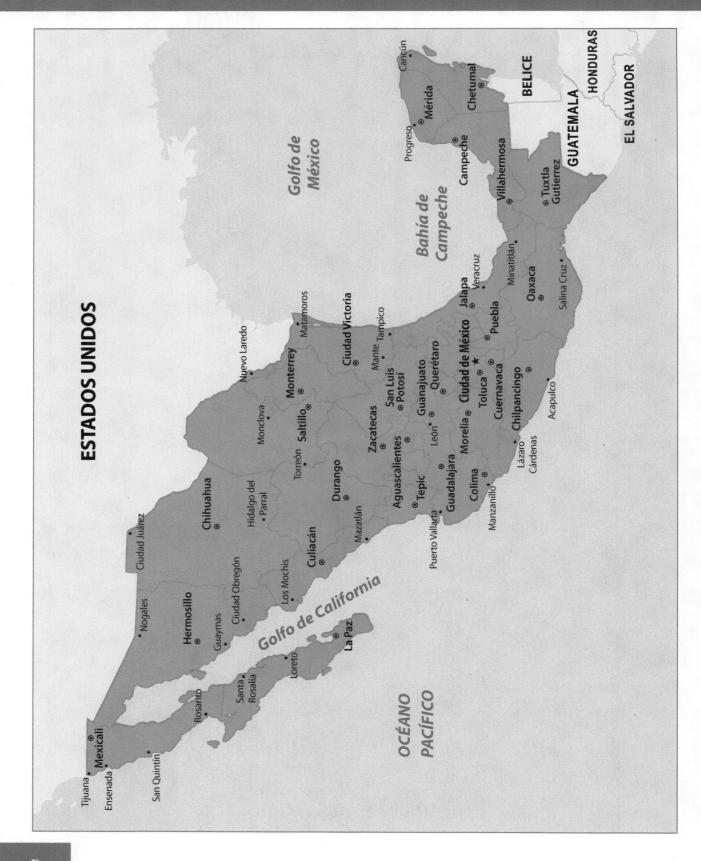

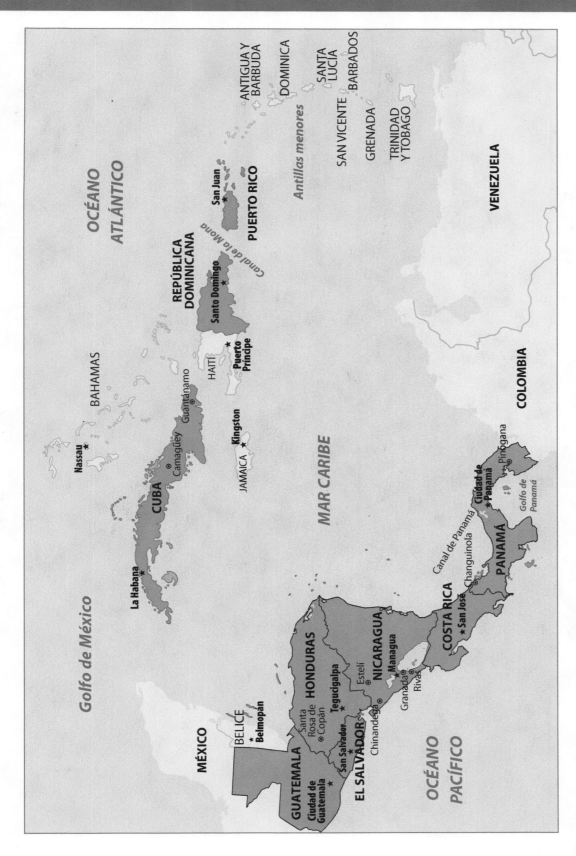

ANTIGUA Y BARBUDA

DOMINICA

SANTA LUCÍA

BARBADOS

SAN VICENTE

GRENADA

TRINIDAD Y TOBAGO

VENEZUELA

*Antillas menores*

OCÉANO ATLÁNTICO

San Juan ★

PUERTO RICO

*Canal de la Mona*

REPÚBLICA DOMINICANA

Santo Domingo ★

BAHAMAS

HAITÍ

Puerto Príncipe ★

COLOMBIA

Guantánamo

Kingston ★

JAMAICA

Camagüey ⊙

CUBA

Nassau ★

MAR CARIBE

Pinogana

*Golfo de Panamá*

Ciudad de Panamá ★

PANAMÁ

La Habana ★

Canal de Panamá

Changuinola ⊙

COSTA RICA

San José ★

Golfo de México

NICARAGUA

Managua ★

Granada ⊙

Rivas ⊙

HONDURAS

Estelí ⊙

Tegucigalpa ⊙

Santa Rosa de Copán ⊙

Chinandega ⊙

BELICE

Belmopán ★

MÉXICO

GUATEMALA

Ciudad de Guatemala ★

San Salvador ★

EL SALVADOR

OCÉANO PACÍFICO

# ESPAÑA

# AMÉRICA DEL SUR

NICARAGUA
COSTA RICA
San José ★
Ciudad de Panamá ★
PANAMÁ
Valencia
Maracaibo
Mérida
Cúcuta
Medellín
Bucaramanga
Cali
Bogotá, D.C. ★
COLOMBIA
Mitú
Puerto España
★ TRINIDAD Y TOBAGO
Caracas
Barcelona
VENEZUELA
Georgetown ★
Paramaribo ★
Linden
Cayenne ★
Puerto Ayacucho
GUYANA
SURINAME
GUYANA
FRANCESA

OCÉANO
ATLÁNTICO

Quito ★
ECUADOR
Cuenca
Piura
Chiclayo
Trujillo
Chimbote
Huaraz
PERÚ
Iquitos
Pucallpa
Huancayo
Ayacucho
Lima
Ica
Cusco
Juliaca
Arequipa
Tacna
Arica
Iquique

Manaus
Belém

BRASIL

BOLIVIA
La Paz ★
Santa Cruz
Cochabamba
Sucre
Tarija
PARAGUAY
Pedro Juan Caballero
Asunción ★
Ciudad del Este

Brasília ★

Río de Janeiro
São Paulo

OCÉANO
PACÍFICO

Antofagasta
Salta
San Miguel de Tucumán
La Rioja
Resistencia
La Serena
Córdoba
San Juan
Santa Fe
Valparaíso
Mendoza
Rosario
Santiago ★
CHILE
Concepción
ARGENTINA
Neuquén
Bahía Blanca
Puerto Montt
Tacuarembó
URUGUAY
Buenos Aires ★
Montevideo ★
Mar del Plata

Pôrto Alegre

OCÉANO
ATLÁNTICO

Rawson
Comodoro Rivadavia
Coyhaique
Río Gallegos
Punta Arenas
Río Grande

Islas Malvinas
(territorio británico
de ultramar)

Georgias del sur (R.U.)

1. Each unit begins with an opener, a spread that provides an overview of the unit goals as well as information and photos related to the country or countries highlighted in the unit. For **Unidad 1**, Cuba is the country of focus. Students will learn more about Cuba throughout the unit, especially in the **Cultura** and **Lectura informativa** sections.
2. **¿Sabía que…?** presents interesting cultural facts about the unit's country of focus.
3. Each unit includes a four to five minute video showing a day in the life of teens across the Spanish-speaking world. The topic relates to the overall theme and may be shown at any point in the unit.
4. Inform students with eBook access they can click on the red country on p. 1 to link directly to Wikipedia and find general information about that region.

## Culture

**Practices: Activity**
Encourage students to keep a Culture Journal. As they progress through each unit of *¡Qué chévere! 4*, students can add country information, facts, personal reflections, and other important cultural details they learn.

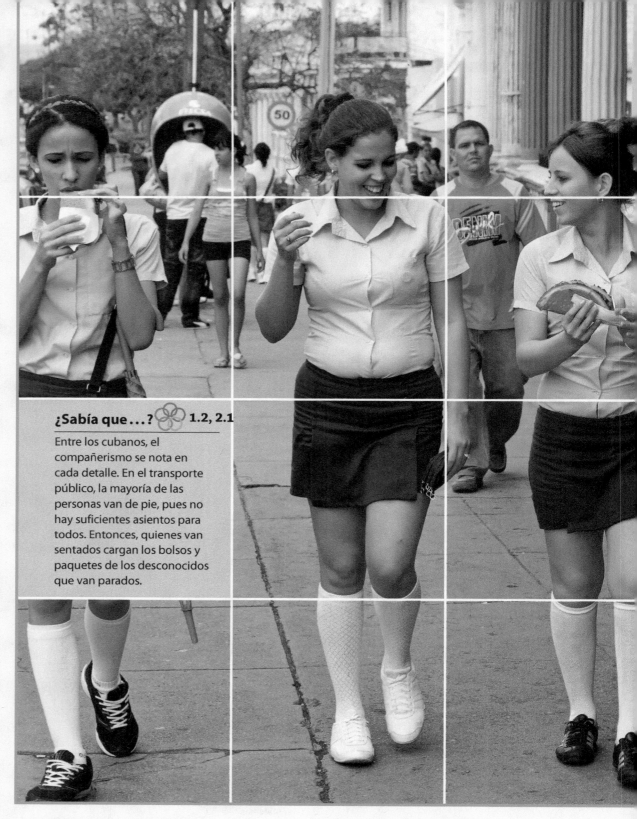

**¿Sabía que…?** 1.2, 2.1

Entre los cubanos, el compañerismo se nota en cada detalle. En el transporte público, la mayoría de las personas van de pie, pues no hay suficientes asientos para todos. Entonces, quienes van sentados cargan los bolsos y paquetes de los desconocidos que van parados.

## Essential Instruction

1. Begin with a discussion of the **Pregunta clave**. Ask students for examples of how the unique characteristics of a nation's people might be reflected in their manners and contact with others.
2. Point out Cuba on the map. Ask students to share what they know about the country.
3. Mention the culture photo and question.

Encourage students to watch for the photo and the answer later in the unit.
4. Point out the QR code, the video question, and the screen shot from "**Encuentros en la red**." Encourage students to watch the vignette as many times as they like.
5. Have students read and ask questions about **Mis metas**.

# 1

# El trato con los demás

Escanee el código QR para mirar el video "Encuentros en la red".

Gracias a las nuevas tecnologías, algunas personas se reencuentran después de muchos años y otras se encuentran por primera vez.

¿A quiénes les sucede esto en esta historia y por qué? Resuma su respuesta en un breve párrafo.

Cuba

### Pregunta clave

**?**

¿Cómo se refleja la idiosincrasia de una nación en el trato de su gente?

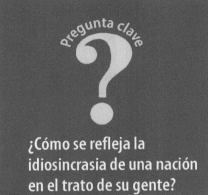

¿Quién es este cantautor y poeta cubano y de qué tratan muchas de sus canciones?

## Mis metas

### En esta unidad:

- ▶ Usaré frases de cortesía para tratar con los demás.
- ▶ Usaré expresiones para pedir información, expresar agradecimiento, acuerdo, sorpresa, y otras emociones.
- ▶ Usaré palabras interrogativas y frases exclamativas para comunicarme.
- ▶ Leeré sobre la forma en que se tratan los cubanos y sobre sus vínculos de amistad.
- ▶ Distinguiré el significado de palabras y frases según el contexto.
- ▶ Distinguiré el género y número de los sustantivos.
- ▶ Usaré correctamente los artículos definidos y los artículos indefinidos.
- ▶ Leeré parte del discurso del presidente Obama sobre la reanudación de relaciones diplomáticas con Cuba.
- ▶ Escribiré un correo electrónico y un ensayo sobre las relaciones diplomáticas con Cuba.
- ▶ Desarrollaré nuevas destrezas de vocabulario.
- ▶ Usaré los adjetivos y los pronombres demostrativos correctamente.
- ▶ Leeré el poema "Dos patrias" del cubano José Martí.

uno **1**

**RESOURCES**

 Encuentros en la red

**Answers**

**Video question** *Los párrafos variarán.*
Aurora y una amiga de su juventud, Candelaria Jaramillo, se encuentran después de mucho tiempo. Valentina, la nieta de Aurora, y Javier, el nieto de Candelaria, se encuentran por primera vez, gracias a la nueva tecnología.

**Culture question**
Se llama Silvio Rodríguez. Muchas de sus canciones tratan de la amistad.

### Reference Desk

1. The **Pregunta clave** is an essential question designed to frame students' learning for the entire unit. This question is repeated in the **Cultura** and **Para concluir** sections. Ask students to read the **Pregunta clave** and speculate about the theme of the unit and the vocabulary and culture they might encounter. Model the pronunciation of **idiosincrasia** (*unique characteristic, trait*) and explain that this word does not carry a negative connotation as it can in English.
2. **Mis metas** is a list of the core content that students will master in the unit. They include vocabulary themes, functions, cultural topics, and grammatical structures.
3. Each unit opener includes a culture photo and corresponding question. The photo is repeated in one of the unit's **Cultura** reading selections, and the accompanying question is answered in that reading. Encourage students to look for the photo and question as they read **Cultura**.

## Special Needs Students

### AD(H)D
The **Mis metas** list can be overwhelming. Work with these students to separate the objectives into categories: vocabulary, grammar, culture, etc. Help students with any unfamiliar wording in the objectives, or translate them into English as needed.

## Multiple Intelligences

### Bodily-Kinesthetic
Use the cultural information in **¿Sabía que...?** to preview the unit vocabulary. Brainstorm polite expressions (e.g., **¿Me puede ayudar con?**). Have groups of students act out riding crowded public transportation in Cuba; they should use the expressions when they bump into each other, need help with their bags, etc.

# *Vocabulario 1*

## ¡Hombre de buen trato, a todos es grato!   1.2

### Para conversar

**P**ara saludar y despedirse:
¿Qué tal?
¿Cómo te ha ido?
Estupendo.
¿Qué me cuentas?
No mucho.
¿Qué hay de nuevo?
Todo igual. / Todo lo mismo.
Adiós.
Nos vemos.
Hasta luego. / Hasta pronto.

**P**ara presentarse y conocerse mejor:
Quiero presentarte a…
Me gustaría presentarte a…
Tanto gusto. / El gusto es mío.
Me llamo… ¿y tú?
¿Cómo te llamas?
¿Cuál es tu apellido?
¿Cuánto hace que…?
¿Qué haces? / ¿A qué te dedicas?
¿Qué opinas de…?
¿Qué te parece si…?

¿Tiene un momento, profesor? Quisiera hacerle una pregunta.

¡Desde luego, Miriam! ¿Qué se te ofrece?

Dígame, Srta. Sánchez, ¿en qué puedo servirle?

Bueno, para empezar, me gustaría saber....

## Para conversar

**P**ara expresar cortesía:
Adelante.
¡Bienvenidos!
Entre y siéntese, por favor.
Pase y tome asiento.
¡Está en su casa!
Disculpe.
Perdone.
Con permiso.
Lo siento (mucho).

**P**ara expresar agradecimiento:
Mil gracias. / Un millón de gracias.
Muchísimas gracias por su amabilidad.
De nada. / ¡No hay de qué!
No sabes cuánto te agradezco.

**P**ara pedir información o ayuda:
¿Cómo se dice...?
¿Qué quiere decir...?
¿Podría hablar con...?
¿Me puede decir/explicar...?
¿Puedes ayudarme?
Quisiera pedirte un favor.

**P**ara expresar acuerdo:
Claro que sí.
¡Cómo no!
De acuerdo.
¡Fantástico!
¡Magnífico!
¡Pero claro!
Por supuesto.
¡Qué bien!
¡Vale!

**P**ara expresar sorpresa:
¿De veras?
¡No lo puedo creer!
¡No me digas!
Qué sorpresa (verte por aquí).

**P**ara expresar otras emociones:
¡Ni hablar!
¡Qué buena (mala) suerte!
¡Qué lástima!
¡Qué pena!
¡Qué va!
¡Ya era hora!

*Unidad 1* | tres | **3**

**Reference Desk**

1. As you go through the expressions, have students identify them as formal, informal, or neutral. For the expressions that use the **tú** form (e.g., **¡No me digas!**), work with students to deduce the **usted** form (**¡No me diga!**), and vice versa.
2. Have students create a Flipgrid post in which they introduce themselves and ask one "ice-breaking" question.

**Communication**

**Interpersonal: Paired Practice**
Ask students to work in pairs to find alternate expressions that can complete the speech bubbles on pp. 2–3 in a logical way. Then have them exchange papers with another pair and role-play the dialogues.

**Expansion**

Have students study the vocabulary on these pages. Then have them close their books. Write the eight category headings on the board and have students list as many expressions as they can for each one.

## Learning Styles
### Auditory Learners
Prepare brief conversations using the expressions from **Vocabulario 1**. Each conversation should take place in a different context, such as asking a classmate for help. Write the contexts on the board for reference. Read the dialogues aloud for the class; they will match each one with the corresponding context.

### Visual Learners
Have visual learners create icons for the various lists of expressions in **Para conversar**, e.g., a waving hand for **Para saludar y despedirse**. They also can use contrasting colors to highlight the formal expressions and the informal ones.

3

**Answers**

**1 Script**

1. Buenos días, profesor. ¿Puedo pasar?
2. ¿Podría hablar con Ud. por un momento?
3. Primero, me gustaría presentarle a mi novio, Marcos.
4. También, quisiera decirle que me siento enferma. No voy a poder tomar el examen hoy.
5. Gracias, profesor, y hasta pronto.

1. ¡Adelante!
2. ¡Claro que sí!
3. Encantado.
4. Lo siento.
5. Cuídese.

**2** *Las explicaciones variarán.*

1. *¡Ni hablar!* No se usa para expresar cortesía.
2. *¡Qué pena!* No se usa para expresar acuerdo.
3. *¡Cuídate!* No se usa para expresar agradecimiento.
4. *¡Qué va!* No se usa para saludar.
5. *De acuerdo.* No se usa para despedirse.
6. *¡No me digas!* No se usa para expresar cortesía.
7. *¡Qué pena!* No se usa para expresar gusto.
8. *¿Qué haces?* No se usa para pedir una opinión.
9. *¿De veras?* No se usa para responder a un saludo.
10. *Con permiso.* No se usa para dar la bienvenida a alguien.

**3**

1. B; 2. A; 3. B; 4. A; 5. A; 6. B

**4**

---

### 1 Tengo que hablar con mi profesor    1.2

Escuche e indique la respuesta correcta.

1. ¡Adelante! / ¡Disculpe!
2. ¡Ni hablar! / ¡Claro que sí!
3. Encantado. / De acuerdo.
4. ¡Qué va! / Lo siento.
5. Cuídese. / ¡Perdone!

### 2 Identifique al intruso  1.2, 1.3

Diga qué expresión no pertenece al grupo y explique por qué.

> MODELO  ¡Por supuesto! / ¡No me digas! / ¡Desde luego!
> **¡No me digas!**
> **No se usa para expresar acuerdo.**

1. ¡Perdone! / ¡Disculpe! / ¡Ni hablar!
2. ¡Fantástico! / ¡Igualmente! / ¡Qué pena!
3. ¡Cuídate! / De nada. / ¡No hay de qué!
4. ¡Qué va! / ¿Qué tal? / ¿Cómo has estado?
5. Adiós. / De acuerdo. / Hasta pronto.
6. Adelante. / Pase, por favor. / ¡No me digas!
7. ¡Qué pena...! / ¡Qué grato...! / ¡Qué placer...!
8. ¿Qué opinas? / ¿Qué te parece? / ¿Qué haces?
9. ¿De veras? / No mucho. / Todo igual.
10. Pase Ud. / Con permiso. / Entre Ud.

### 3 Interacciones 1.2

Complete las siguientes interacciones con la palabra o frase que corresponda según el contexto.

1. Qué sorpresa verte. ¿Qué me cuentas?
   A. Igualmente, ¿y tú?
   B. No mucho, ¿y tú?
2. ¿Podría hablar con Ud. un momento?
   A. Desde luego.
   B. Ya era hora.
3. ¿Qué tal si tomamos un café?
   A. ¡Adelante!
   B. ¡Vale!
4. ¿Puedes hacerme un favor?
   A. Claro, ¿qué se te ofrece?
   B. No sabes cuánto te agradezco.
5. Quisiera presentarle a mi padre Luis Vásquez.
   A. Es un placer, Sr. Vásquez.
   B. Con permiso, Sr. Vásquez.
6. Bienvenido. Siga y siéntese, por favor.
   A. Está en su casa.
   B. Gracias por su amabilidad.

### Essential Instruction

1. Before playing the audio in **Actividad 1**, read through the answer choices as a class. Explain that they will hear a statement or question and they must choose the logical response.
2. For their explanations in **Actividad 2**, point out to students that they can use the phrasing in the category headings on pp. 2–3.
3. Check answers to **Actividad 3** chorally.
4. Have students read **Actividad 4** aloud in pairs.
5. Ask pairs to role-play their conversations from **Actividad 5** for the class.

④
1. ¿Qué tal?
2. ¡Encantada!
3. ¿De dónde eres?
4. Cuánto hace que
5. qué te parece si
6. Estupendo.
7. Te gustaría
8. ¿De acuerdo?
9. Hasta pronto.

⑤ *Las respuestas variarán.*

 **4** **¡Vale!**  **1.2**

A la salida del colegio, Arturo se encuentra con Adriana, una nueva estudiante, y se pone a hablar con ella. Complete su conversación con la expresión del recuadro que mejor corresponda según el contexto.

| | | |
|---|---|---|
| **Hasta pronto.** | **qué te parece si** | **Estupendo.** |
| **¿De dónde eres?** | **¿De acuerdo?** | **¿Qué tal?** |
| **Cuánto hace que** | **¡Encantada!** | **Te gustaría** |

**Arturo:** ¡Hola! __(1)__ Me llamo Arturo.

**Adriana:** __(2)__ Yo soy Adriana.

**Arturo:** No pareces de aquí. __(3)__

**Adriana:** Soy cubana.

**Arturo:** ¿De veras? Yo conozco a muchos cubanos. ¿__(4)__ vives aquí?

**Adriana:** Solo un par de meses.

**Arturo:** ¡Qué bien! Oye, ¿__(5)__ salimos juntos? Así conoces a mis amigos.

**Adriana:** __(6)__ ¿Conocen alguna discoteca chévere para bailar salsa?

**Arturo:** Por supuesto. Nos encanta ir a bailar. ¿__(7)__ ir con nosotros este sábado?

**Adriana:** ¡Como no! Llámame por teléfono y acordamos detalles. __(8)__

**Arturo:** Claro que sí. __(9)__

## ¡Comunicación!

**5** **Necesito un favor** 👥 **Interpersonal Communication**  **1.1**

Represente la siguiente situación con un(a) compañero/a de clase. Imagine que es tarde y tiene que llamar a uno de sus amigos/as para pedirle el favor de que lo lleve al colegio mañana por la mañana pues su carro está en el taller (*repair shop*). Túrnense para hacerse preguntas y responderlas según sea el caso y no se olviden de usar las expresiones que correspondan según la situación.

MODELO
**A:** ¿Elena? Te habla Ana. Perdona que te llame tan tarde, pero necesito un favor. ¿Puedes ayudarme?

**B:** Por supuesto, Ana. Dime qué se te ofrece.

**A:** Bueno, para empezar...

**B:** ....

## Gramática

### Los pronombres interrogativos  1.2

Los pronombres interrogativos **qué**, **cuál(es)**, **quién(es)** y **cuánto(a) / cuántos(as)** hacen el papel del nombre y se usan para hacer preguntas directas sobre las personas y las cosas.

- Use **qué** para pedir una definición o aclaración o para pedir información sobre hechos, fechas, horarios y estado del tiempo.

¿**Qué** es el amor?
Es un sentimiento muy fuerte que liga a las personas.

¿**Qué** pasó?
Hubo un accidente.

¿**Qué** te gusta hacer para divertirte?
Me gusta salir con mis amigos.

¿**Qué** significa: "que liga a las personas"?
Quiere decir que las une.

¿**Qué** fecha es hoy?
Es el 30 de enero.

¿**Qué** tiempo hace en invierno?
Nieva y hace mucho frío.

- Use **qué** en **por qué** y **para qué** para preguntar la causa y el propósito de algo.

¿**Por qué** llegaste tarde?
Porque no tenía transporte.

¿**Para qué** sirve este dispositivo?
Sirve para guardar música.

- Use **cuál** y **cuáles** para hacer preguntas sobre las personas o las cosas en casos en que haya que elegir entre dos o más opciones.

¿**Cuál** es tu nacionalidad?
Soy cubano.

¿**Cuál** es su profesión?
Soy médico.

¿**Cuál** de esos dos chicos te gusta más?
A mí me gusta el alto, ¿y a ti?

¿**Cuáles** son tus películas favoritas?
Las películas de acción.

- Use **quién** y **quiénes** para hacer preguntas sobre la identidad de las personas.

¿**Quién** es él?
Él es mi hermano.

¿**Quiénes** van a ir a la fiesta?
Todos los estudiantes de la clase.

- Use **cuánto(a) / cuántos(as)** para preguntar un número o cantidad.

¿**Cuánto** cuesta este libro?
Cuesta $30.000 pesos.

¿**Cuántos** años tienes?
Tengo dieciséis años.

¿**Cuánta** tarea tienes para mañana?
No tengo tarea para mañana.

¿**Cuántas** personas viajan con Ud.?
Tres. Mi esposa y mis dos hijos.

> **Un poco más**
>
> Cuando **qué** o **cuál(es)** funcionan como adjetivos interrogativos en lugar de pronombres, es decir, cuando acompañan al sustantivo, se prefiere el uso de **qué** en lugar de **cuál(es)**, aun cuando haya que elegir entre dos o más opciones de respuesta.
>
> ¿**Qué país** te gusta más?
> **Which country** do you like most?
>
> ¿**Qué películas** vas a ver esta semana?
> **What (Which) movies** are you going to see this week?

---

# Gramática

## Otras palabras interrogativas  1.2

Las palabras **dónde**, **cómo** y **cuándo** se usan en oraciones interrogativas para hacer preguntas directas sobre el lugar, modo y tiempo en que se realizan las acciones.

- Use **dónde**, **adónde** y **de dónde** para pedir información sobre el origen, procedencia, destino y ubicación de algo o de alguien.

**¿De dónde** son tus padres?
Son de Santiago de Cuba.

**¿Dónde** queda la biblioteca?
Al lado de la cafetería.

**¿Dónde** viven ellos ahora?
Viven en Miami.

**¿De dónde** viene Ud.?
Vengo de Lima, Perú.

**¿Adónde** vas?
Voy a la biblioteca.

**¿Adónde** viaja después?
Voy a la Ciudad de México.

- Use **cómo** para preguntar sobre el estado o características de algo o de alguien y la forma en que se realizan las acciones o los hechos.

**¿Cómo** estás?
Bien, ¿y tú?

**¿Cómo** son los cubanos?
Son muy alegres.

**¿Cómo** te sientes?
Mucho mejor. Gracias.

**¿Cómo** van Uds. al colegio todos los días?
Vamos en autobús.

- Use **cuándo** para preguntar sobre el tiempo en qué ocurren u ocurrieron los hechos u acontecimientos.

**¿Cuándo** es tu cumpleaños?
Es el veintidós de noviembre.

**¿Cuándo** regresaste de tus vacaciones?
Llegué hace una semana.

Hola Lisa, ¿cómo has estado?

### Un poco más

Las palabras interrogativas que aparecen en oraciones declarativas en que se hacen preguntas indirectas, también llevan el acento escrito.

No sé **cómo** lo hiciste.
*I don't know **how** you did it.*

No sé de **qué** me estás hablando.
*I don't know **what** you're talking about.*

## Reference Desk

1. Point out that **¿dónde?** means *where?* and asks for a location. **¿Adónde?** means *to where?* and asks for a destination.
2. After going over **Un poco más**, emphasize that interrogative words always have a written accent, whether in direct (**¿Cuándo llega Luisa?**) or indirect questions (**Quisiera saber cuándo va a llegar ella.**). Contrast this with linking words, which lack the accent: **Yo estaba en casa cuando llegó Luisa.**

## Expansion

As a homework assignment, ask students to find and bring to class an article or interview from Spanish-language online or print media. Tell them to circle the uses of interrogative words, whether in direct or indirect questions. Ask students to explain why each interrogative was used.

## TPR

As a whole-class or large-group activity, have students stand in a circle. Begin by saying an interrogative word and tossing a foam ball to a student. He/she must formulate a question using that word and toss the ball to another student, who will answer the question and then name another interrogative word. Continue until all the interrogatives have been practiced.

## Differentiated Learning

### Expand
Tell students to imagine that an alien creature is visiting your classroom, and it has a lot of questions about everything it sees and hears. Have them write the creature's questions, using the interrogative words on these pages.

### Heritage Learners
Depending on their family's origin, some heritage learners may use question words differently than presented here. For example, in some regions of Latin America, **cuál** is used before nouns when choice is implicit: **¿Cuál libro te gusta más?** In the Caribbean, it is common to use **tú** before the verb in **qué** questions: **¿Qué tú quieres hacer?**

## Communication

**Presentational/Interpersonal:
Paired Practice**

After completing **Actividad 6**, have pairs of students write a dialogue between Adriana and her little sister. They should leave the questions blank so that only Adriana's answers appear. Have students exchange papers with another pair, who will complete the conversation.

---

**6** **¡Qué niño tan curioso!**  **1.2**

Arturo está preparándose para salir y su hermanito, que es un niño muy curioso, quiere saber todo al respecto. Complete sus preguntas con la palabra interrogativa que corresponda según el contexto.

**1.** —¿Con ____ vas a salir?
—Con una amiga.

**2.** —¿____ es, bonita o fea?
—Es muy bonita.

**3.** —¿____ la conociste?
—La semana pasada.

**4.** —¿____ van a ir?
—Al cine.

**5.** —¿____ película van a ver?
—No sé.

**6.** —¿A ____ hora vas a regresar?
—No estoy seguro, y ya no me preguntes más. Tengo prisa.

---

**7** **¿Vamos al cine?**  **1.2**

Arturo quiere volver a salir con Adriana y la llama para saber qué planes tiene. Empareje las respuestas de la columna I con las preguntas de la columna II.

**I**

**Arturo:** __(1)__

**Adriana:** Bien, ¿y tú? ¿Qué hay de nuevo?

**Arturo:** __(2)__

**Adriana:** Sí, pienso ir al cine. Tengo muchos deseos de ver una película española que están anunciando.

**Arturo:** __(3)__

**Adriana:** *Antes que anochezca.*

**Arturo:** __(4)__

**Adriana:** Javier Bardem. Es un actor español muy bueno.

**Arturo:** __(5)__

**Adriana:** Es sobre el autor cubano Reinaldo Arenas.

**Arturo:** __(6)__

**Adriana:** En el cine Rex.

**Arturo:** __(7)__

**Adriana:** En la Plaza de España.

**Arturo:** __(8)__

**Adriana:** A las ocho y media.

**Arturo:** __(9)__

**Adriana:** No te preocupes. Yo te invito.

**II**

**A.** ¿De qué se trata?

**B.** ¿Qué película?

**C.** ¿En qué cine pasan esa película?

**D.** ¿Cuánto cuesta la entrada?

**E.** Hola Adriana, ¿cómo has estado?

**F.** ¿Quién es el actor principal?

**G.** ¿A qué hora la pasan?

**H.** No mucho. Quería saber si ya tienes planes para el sábado.

**I.** ¿Dónde queda el cine Rex?

*¿Tienes planes para el sábado?*

## Essential Instruction

**1.** After checking **Actividad 6** as a class, have pairs of students role-play the conversation.

**2.** Check answers to **Actividad 7** as a class. Then ask pairs to role-play the conversation. Have them sit back-to-back and, if possible, use their cell phones as props.

**3.** Before beginning **Actividad 8**, ask for volunteers to briefly review the uses of **qué** and **cuál**.

**4.** For **Actividad 9**, you may want to generate a list of possible vocabulary on the board for pairs to use in their conversations.

## 8  Mucho en común    **1.2**

Arturo y Adriana quieren conocerse mejor, así que deciden encontrarse el fin de semana. Hablan de películas, libros y música y descubren que tienen mucho en común. Complete sus preguntas con **qué**, **cuál** o **cuáles**, según corresponda.

**Adriana**   Bueno, ahora te toca elegir a ti. ¿ **(1)** es la película que quieres ver?

**Arturo:**   No sé. Quiero ver una película divertida.

**Adriana:**   ¿ **(2)** son tus comedias favoritas?

**Arturo:**   Me encantan las del director español, Pedro Almodóvar.

**Adriana:**   ¿También te gustan los libros cómicos?

**Arturo:**   No, esos no me gustan. Y a ti, ¿ **(3)** libros te gustan?

**Adriana:**   Los libros de comentario social.

**Arturo:**   ¿ **(4)** es tu escritor favorito?

**Adriana:**   Octavio Paz. Es mexicano y fue el ganador del Premio Nobel de Literatura en 1990.

**Arturo:**   ¿ **(5)** libro de Octavio Paz prefieres?

**Adriana:**   *El laberinto de la soledad*, sin duda.

**Arturo:**   ¿ **(6)** sabes de su vida?

**Adriana:**   No solo fue gran escritor sino que también fue diplomático en París y Bombay.

**Arturo:**   Y en música, ¿ **(7)** te gusta escuchar?

**Adriana:**   Música cubana, igual que a ti, me imagino.

**Arturo:**   ¿ **(8)** es tu CD favorito?

**Adriana:**   *Buena Vista Social Club*.

**Arturo:**   ¿ **(9)** canciones te gustan más?

**Adriana:**   "Chan Chan" y "Candela".

**Arturo:**   ¡De acuerdo! También son mis favoritas.

**Adriana:**   Oye, si vamos a ir al cine, debemos irnos ya.

**Adriana:**   ¡Vale!

*Buena Vista Social Club*

## ¡Comunicación!

## 9  ¿Qué te parece si...?   Interpersonal/Presentational Communication     **1.1, 1.3**

Después del cine, Arturo invita a Adriana a un restaurante. Hablan de sus comidas favoritas, deportes y muchos temas más. Con un(a) compañero/a, escriban el diálogo y represéntenlo enfrente de la clase. Sigan el modelo como guía.

> MODELO   A: ¿Qué te parece si vamos a comer? Conozco un lugar donde venden los mejores emparedados de lechón.
>
> B: ¿De veras? Me encantan los emparedados de lechón.

## Special Needs Students
### Dyslexia/Reading Difficulties
These students may struggle with text-heavy dialogues such as those in **Actividades 7** and **8**. You may want to break the dialogues into chunks, and highlight the questions. Read the dialogues aloud while students follow along. Pause after each question for students to determine the answer.

### Social Anxiety
Offer students with social anxiety alternative ways to participate in class. For example, if these students feel comfortable with a particular partner, you may want to partner them for most pair work. You might have them present activities such as **Actividad 9** as an Avenue task, or meet with them individually.

**10**
1. Dónde; 2. Quién; 3. Cuántos;
4. Dónde; 5. Qué; 6. Cómo;
7. Cuántos; 8. Quiénes; 9. Cuántos

1. Tuvo lugar en la Universidad Politécnica José Antonio Echevarría en La Habana.
2. Es estudiante de la universidad.
3. Tiene 22 años.
4. Estudia Pedagogía.
5. Dice que el Estado ha tratado de mejorar la educación.
6. Ha afectado los intercambios académicos, el flujo de información y la adquisición de materiales para la docencia.
7. Más de 80 sitios web dejaron de funcionar de manera sorpresiva, desde el 2007.
8. los estudiantes de las Secundarias Básicas
9. Más de 22.000 estudiantes carecen del equipo que necesitan para adquirir una buena educación.

## Reference Desk

1. The U.S. embargo was first imposed on Cuba in 1960, and was made official in 1962 by President John F. Kennedy. The embargo was in part precipitated by Cuba's trade arrangements with the Soviet Union.
2. You may want to point out that in the second paragraph, **Sin embargo** doesn't refer to the embargo; it means *However*. In this article, the term **bloqueo** is used to refer to the trade embargo.

## Culture

**Perspectives: Activity**
Invite a person of Cuban heritage to the class to talk about his/her culture and experiences. Have students prepare several questions in advance, using different interrogatives. Remind them to use the formal register in their questions.

**10**

---

**10 Juventud cubana**  **1.1, 1.2, 3.2**

Lea el siguiente artículo sobre el testimonio de una estudiante en la audiencia parlamentaria (*parliamentary hearing*) contra el bloqueo en Cuba, la cual tuvo lugar en la sede de la Universidad Politécnica José Antonio Echevarría en La Habana. Luego, complete las preguntas sobre la lectura con las palabras interrogativas que correspondan y, con un(a) compañero/a, túrnense para contestarlas.

○○○  Cuba – Juventud Rebelde

▾ MULTIMEDIA    ▾ ESPECIALES    ▾ BLOGS    ▾ ARCHIVO

JUVENTUD
**rebelde**

**11 DE FEBRERO DEL 2015 11:13:20 CDT**
**DIARIO DE LA JUVENTUD CUBANA**
EDICIÓN DIGITAL

PORTADA   CUBA   INTERNACIONALES   OPINIÓN   CULTURA   CIENCIA Y TÉCNICA   DEPORTES   COLUMNAS

## Una joven ofrece su testimonio sobre los efectos del bloqueo

La joven diputada[1] de 22 años, Jennifer Bello Martínez, estudiante de la carrera de Pedagogía, contó cómo durante su formación académica ha sido testigo de las cuantiosas inversiones del Estado cubano para potenciar[2] la educación.

Sin embargo, «la permanencia del bloqueo económico, financiero, comercial y tecnológico ha afectado el desarrollo de los intercambios académicos, los viajes de estudiantes y profesores, el flujo de información científica, la difusión y retribución[3] adecuada por los resultados dentro de esta esfera, y la adquisición de insumos[4], medios e instrumentos para la docencia[5], la investigación y el trabajo científico en general», comentó.

De entre muchos ejemplos posibles, citó uno en especial: la imposibilidad del acceso pleno a las tecnologías de la información y las comunicaciones. «Solo podemos contar con pocos megas para la búsqueda de bibliografía y para la actividad científica. Por ejemplo, desde el 2007, más de 80 sitios web dejaron de funcionar para nuestro país de manera sorpresiva».

Explicó que en las Secundarias Básicas[6] faltan 420 laboratorios de física y química, en la enseñanza preuniversitaria hay escasez de literatura de autores de habla inglesa y de diccionarios especializados en el idioma, y existen más de 22 mil estudiantes con necesidades educativas especiales que carecen del equipamiento necesario para fortalecer su educación.

[1] representative    [2] strengthen    [3] payment    [4] consumable goods    [5] teaching    [6] high schools

---

1. ¿ ____ tuvo lugar esta audiencia?
2. ¿ ____ es Jennifer Bello Martínez?
3. ¿ ____ años tiene ella?
4. ¿ ____ estudia ella?
5. ¿ ____ cuenta ella con relación a su formación académica?
6. ¿ ____ ha afectado el bloqueo tecnológico el campo de la educación?
7. ¿ ____ sitios web han dejado de funcionar de manera sorpresiva en Cuba en los últimos años?
8. ¿ ____ carecen de laboratorios, libros de literatura inglesa y diccionarios especializados?
9. ¿ ____ estudiantes carecen del equipo necesario para adquirir una buena educación?

## Essential Instruction

1. Begin **Actividad 10** by having students scan the article for cognates. Go over any unfamiliar vocabulary or concepts in the article.
2. Have pairs share their answers to **Actividad 10** with the class.
3. Begin the **Gramática** presentation by reminding students that they already have learned several exclamations in **Vocabulario 1**.
4. Guide the class in completing the first item in **Actividad 11**. Explain that some items will have more than one possible answer.

# *Gramática*

## Pronombres exclamativos  1.2

Los pronombres **qué**, **cómo** y **cuánto** también se usan para formar frases exclamativas.

**¡Qué!** *What a(n)... ! How... !*

| | | |
|---|---|---|
| **¡Qué** aburrido! | **¡Qué** idea más interesante! | **¡Qué** hermoso! |
| **¡Qué** horror! | **¡Qué** bueno! | **¡Qué** sueño tengo! |
| **¡Qué** bonito! | **¡Qué** lástima! | **¡Qué** horrible! |

**¡Cómo!** *How... ! (in what manner)*

| | |
|---|---|
| **¡Cómo** llueve! | **¡Cómo** se divierte Arturo! |

**¡Cuánto/a/os/as!** *How much... ! How many... ! (to what extent) (quantity)*

| | | |
|---|---|---|
| **¡Cuánto** lo siento! | **¡Cuánto** dinero tiene! | **¡Cuánta** gente! |
| **¡Cuánto** ruido! | **¡Cuánto** jaleo *(uproar)*! | **¡Cuántas** preguntas al mismo tiempo! |

---

**11** **¡Qué suerte!**  1.2

Arturo habla con uno de sus amigos sobre Adriana. Dice que tienen muchas cosas en común y se siente afortunado de haberla conocido. Complete algunos de los comentarios que él hace sobre Adriana con la palabra de exclamación que corresponda según el contexto.

1. ¡____ muchacha más interesante!
2. ¡____ me encanta charlar con ella!
3. ¡____ nos divertimos cuando salimos!
4. ¡____ contento estoy de ser su amigo!
5. ¡____ deseos tengo de verla nuevamente!
6. ¡____ lástima que no pueda verla ahora mismo!
7. ¡____ bueno que aceptó volver a salir conmigo!
8. ¡____ sorpresas agradables hay en la vida!

*¡Cómo nos divertimos!*

---

## RESOURCES

| WB | Activities 6–7 |
|---|---|
| LA | Activity 2 |

### Answers

**11**
1. Qué
2. Cómo/Cuánto
3. Cómo/Cuánto
4. Qué
5. Cuántos/Qué
6. Qué
7. Qué
8. Cuántas/Qué

## Reference Desk

1. Point out the written accent on **Qué**, **Cómo**, and **Cuánto/a/os/as** in these exclamations.
2. Model examples of exclamations for students with varying tone and intonation to show how **qué** (+ *noun* or *adjective*) can convey delight (**¡Qué fantástico!**) or dismay (**¡Qué horrible!**). You may also want to teach students that when they are exclaiming about something bad, **¡Ay!** is equivalent to the English *Oh!* For example: **¡Ay, qué lástima!**

---

## Learning Styles
### Auditory Learners

Bring in Spanish-language publications or Internet articles. Read the headlines to the class. For each one, students should provide several logical exclamations.

## Multiple Intelligences
### Verbal-Linguistic

Ask students to write short descriptions of a variety of situations to which people might react favorably, with shock, with delight, etc. Students should read their situations aloud for the class to react, e.g., **Encuentras dinero en la calle. (¡Qué bueno!)**

Answers

**12**

1. B, Qué; 2. H, Qué; 3. A, Qué;
4. F, Qué; 5. G, Cómo; 6. D, Qué;
7. C, Qué; 8. E, Cuánto

**13** *Las respuestas variarán.*

## Reference Desk

1. Around 500,000 Cubans arrived in Miami in the years following the Revolution in Cuba. Today there are approximately 1.2 million Cuban-Americans in the city. Cuban culture has had a pervasive influence in Miami's identity: its cuisine, music, language, politics, and so on.
2. Have students present their situations and reactions to **Actividad 13** in a Flipgrid post.

## Culture

**Products/Practices: Activity**
Divide the class into groups. Assign each group a different aspect of Cuban culture in Miami (e.g., cuisine, festivals, music) and have them research the topic online. Have groups share their findings with the class.

## Expansion

As an extension of **Actividad 12**, ask students to give exclamations that convey the opposite sentiments.

---

**12** ¿Qué diría Ud.?  **1.2**

Imagínese que Ud. está en Miami para visitar a Adriana. Diga cómo reaccionaría en cada situación. Complete las exclamaciones de la columna II y, luego, emparéjelas con las situaciones de la columna I.

**I**

1. Su casa está en Key Biscayne, una linda zona residencial.
2. Su familia le da una gran fiesta de bienvenida al estilo cubano.
3. ¡Su abuela prepara la mejor comida cubana de Miami!
4. Su pobre abuelo está enfermo y no puede asistir a la fiesta.
5. No salen a conocer Miami porque hace muy mal tiempo.
6. Una noche alquilan un DVD.
7. Su hermano, que es médico, atiende a pacientes día y noche.
8. Su hermana es bailarina de ballet clásico.

**II**

A. ¡____ deliciosa!
B. ¡____ casas tan bonitas!
C. ¡____ trabajador!
D. ¡____ buena película!
E. ¡____ talento!
F. ¡____ lástima!
G. ¡____ llueve!
H. ¡____ sorpresa!

---

**13** ¿Cuál sería su reacción?  **1.1**

Con un(a) compañero/a, túrnense para reaccionar a las siguientes situaciones con una frase de exclamación, como se ve en el modelo. Después, piensen en tres situaciones más y túrnense para reaccionar a ellas con frases de exclamación adecuadas.

MODELO   Su mejor amigo le propuso un plan para montar un negocio turístico.
**¡Qué idea más interesante!**

1. Su novio/a se fue de viaje y lleva tres días sin comunicarse con Ud.
2. Se desveló (*stayed up all night*) estudiando para el examen final.
3. Acaba de enterarse de los ingresos anuales de Bill Gates.
4. Hay una manifestación política en la calle donde vive.
5. Contempla una espléndida puesta de sol en una playa del Caribe.
6. Llega al estadio de fútbol y ve que hay más de 100.000 fanáticos allí.

*¡Qué vista tan hermosa!*

## Essential Instruction

1. Complete the exclamations in **Actividad 12** as a class. Then have students match the columns.
2. Point out that the situations in **Actividad 13** can have many different reactions. Provide alternate reactions for the **Modelo**.
3. Mention the **Pregunta clave**, and tell students to keep it in mind as they complete the cultural readings.
4. Pause the recording after each paragraph of the readings and ask **sí/no** questions to check comprehension.
5. For Common Core practice, have students answer the **Analice** questions.

emcpassport.com
 LA 3

## Así somos y así nos saludamos  1.2, 2.1

**Pregunta clave**
¿Cómo se refleja la idiosincrasia de una nación en el trato de su gente?

Si su nación fuera una persona, ¿cómo la describiría? ¿Cuáles son los rasgos[1], el temperamento y el carácter que la distinguen? Si piensa en cómo responder estas preguntas, seguramente se le ocurrirá un conjunto de características que comparten sus connacionales[2] en general. Esas características comunes forman la idiosincrasia de su nación. Un aspecto importante en el que se ve reflejada la idiosincrasia de un pueblo es el trato de su gente.

Los cubanos, por ejemplo, se destacan por su carácter alegre: andan por la vida con una sonrisa dibujada en el rostro. También son imaginativos, extrovertidos y muy conversadores, y se los reconoce por su chispa[3] y su creatividad. Estas características de los cubanos se reflejan en sus saludos y en el trato que tienen con los demás.

Un saludo típicamente cubano es "¿Qué vuelta?", que equivale a "¿Qué tal?". De la letra de una canción de un cantautor argentino que se hizo muy popular en Cuba, proviene el curioso saludo "¿Qué tiras al agua?". Si un hombre se cruza por la calle con un amigo cercano, lo saluda diciendo "Acere, ¿qué volá?", que es una forma muy cubana de decir "¡Hola amigo! ¿Cómo estás?". "Ambia" y "monina" también se usan para referirse a los amigos. Los amigos íntimos cuentan con términos propios, como "ecobio" y "hermano". Cuando un cubano tiene confianza con[4] una persona, puede llamarla "mi sangre" para demostrarle su aprecio. La variedad de saludos y de formas de llamar a los amigos ilustran la idiosincrasia del pueblo cubano.

[1] traits  [2] compatriots  [3] wit  [4] trusts

 **Búsqueda:** idiosincrasia cubana, habla cubana

*"Acere, ¿qué volá?" es un típico saludo cubano.*

### 14 Comprensión  1.2, 2.1

1. ¿Qué cosas conforman la idiosincrasia de una nación?
2. ¿Cómo describiría Ud. la idiosincrasia cubana?
3. ¿Qué términos usan los cubanos para referirse a los amigos?

### 15 Analice 1.3, 2.1, 4.2

1. ¿Por qué cree Ud. que los cubanos cuentan con tantos términos para referirse a los amigos?
2. ¿Qué conclusión puede Ud. sacar sobre el uso de los términos "hermano" y "mi sangre"?
3. ¿En qué se parece o se diferencia el trato entre amigos en Cuba en comparación con el trato en su propia cultura?

## Prácticas  1.2, 2.1

Expresiones informales como "mi vida", "mi corazón" o "cariño" se usan en muchos pueblos de habla hispana para referirse a las personas del círculo íntimo, como la pareja, los amigos cercanos o los familiares. Sin embargo, si uno conversa con un cubano desconocido o alguien que acaba de conocer, no debe sorprenderse si usa esas expresiones. Es muy común que los cubanos las usen cuando conversan con extraños en contextos informales.

*Los cubanos son conocidos por su carácter alegre.*

---

## RESOURCES

| | |
|---|---|
| fg | Flipgrid |
| 🎧 | Así somos y así nos saludamos Prácticas |
| LA | Activity 3 |

**Answers**

**14**
1. Las características que tienen en común las personas de una misma nación.
2. Los cubanos son alegres, creativos y conversadores.
3. Usan *acere*, *ambia*, *monina*, *ecobio* y *hermano*.

**15** 👥 *Respuesta posible:*
1. Los cubanos tienen tantos amigos que crearon muchos términos para llamarlos.
2. *Las respuestas variarán.*
3. *Las respuestas variarán.*

## Reference Desk

1. The expression **¿Qué tiras al agua?** comes from the song "**Dime, ¿qué tiras al agua?**" by the Argentine singer-songwriter Alberto Cortez.
2. Students can do a Flipgrid post reacting to any of these cultural readings.

## Pre-AP

Have students respond to the **Pregunta clave**, in spoken or written form, using information from the readings on pp. 13–15. Students should also include a comparison between their own community/culture and Cuba.

---

**13**

**1.2, 2.1, 3.2**

## 16 Comprensión

1. ¿Para qué usan los cubanos la palabra "compañero"?

2. ¿Cuándo y por qué empezó a desaparecer el término "compañero"?

3. ¿Qué debate se generó con el uso de "señor"?

**3.2**

### Perspectivas

Con respecto a la caída en desuso de la palabra "compañero", dice Diego Rodríguez Molina, comentarista del diario *Granma*, (la publicación oficial del Partido Comunista Cubano): «Los necesarios cambios que impone y exige constantemente la vida no pueden llevarnos a la ingenuidad de modificar de manera tan sutil cuestiones esenciales de nuestro modo de ser». Según la cita, ¿Está Rodríguez Molina a favor o en contra de reemplazar "compañero" por "señor"? Explique su respuesta.

*El periódico cubano* Granma

## 17 Analice   **1.3, 2.1, 3.2**

1. ¿Qué aspectos de la idiosincrasia cubana encierra el uso de "compañero"?

2. ¿Está Ud. de acuerdo o en desacuerdo con la afirmación de Rodríguez Molina? Explique su respuesta.

# ¿Cuestión de léxico o filosofía?  **1.2, 2.1, 3.2**

A veces las palabras no son más que una manera de llamar las cosas. Cualquiera que tenga que presentar a un estudiante de su clase dirá, sin pensárselo dos veces, "Es mi compañero". Pero otras veces las palabras son mucho más que eso. El léxico compartido por un grupo social puede encerrar[1] ecos de una historia común, reflejos de una forma de ser y de sentir. En Cuba, desde la Revolución de 1959, es "compañero" el vecino, el amigo, el dependiente de la tienda y casi cualquier desconocido. Entre los isleños, durante décadas, no hubo un término mejor para saludarse, para llamarse entre sí, para empezar un discurso, para romper el hielo con alguien a quien recién se conoce.

*¿Cómo le va, compañero?*

Pero las cosas están cambiando, y esta expresión que lleva más de 50 años en el trato cotidiano[2] de los cubanos ha comenzado, poco a poco, a desaparecer. Desde mediados de la década de 1990, de la mano de las reformas que apuntaban a una política económica de mayor apertura,[3] el término "compañero" parece haber perdido encanto, tal vez porque no se lleva bien con el ámbito de los negocios. Así, con el tiempo, se empezó a extender en la isla el uso de "señor", que antes quedaba reservado al tratamiento cortés de extranjeros o turistas.

Junto con el nuevo término, surgió el debate. Para algunos cubanos, el cambio no es más que una cuestión de forma. Para muchos otros, el término "compañero" representa mucho más que una simple forma de tratamiento. Es un reflejo de su proceso social, una "fórmula" que tiene el poder de hacerlos sentir más cercanos e iguales. Para algunos cubanos, perder esa palabra significa perder una parte de sí mismos, de su modo de ser y ver la vida.

[1] contain    [2] everyday contact    [3] economic openness

 **Búsqueda:** significado del término "compañero" en cuba, revolución de 1959, reformas políticas en cuba

## Essential Instruction

1. Have students glance at the photos and titles on these pages. Ask them to predict what else they will learn about Cuba.
2. Remind students of the culture photo and question from the unit opener. Ask them to skim the paragraphs to find the answer.
3. If possible, play the song "**Vamos a andar**" so that students can listen as they read the lyrics in **Productos**.

# El vínculo de la amistad

"Más vale un buen amigo que un peso en el bolsillo", dice el refrán popular que mejor define la filosofía de los cubanos sobre el valor de la amistad. En Cuba, decir "amigo" es sinónimo de lealtad, colaboración y apoyo[1] mutuo y desinteresado[2]. En un contexto de crisis económica, las amistades cubanas se construyen día a día a fuerza de escaseces[3] compartidas. En otras naciones, donde la sociedad de consumo es masiva, tal vez no sea tan importante contar con la generosidad de los amigos.

*La amistad tiene un gran valor en Cuba.*

Además de la colaboración, otro elemento que caracteriza a las amistades en Cuba es su gran número. Los cubanos suelen tener muchísimos amigos porque les resulta fácil establecer vínculos con los demás. Son por naturaleza hospitalarios y alegres; cuentan con un gran sentido del humor; y, lo más importante, tienen un carácter extrovertido y abierto.

Cualquier persona de Cuba puede contar que alguna vez conoció a alguien de manera accidental o fortuita[4] y que, un rato después, ya le había contado vida y milagros.[5] ¡Los cubanos pueden hacer amigos en media hora! Esto no ocurre en otras culturas donde las personas son más reservadas, les cuesta ponerse a conversar con desconocidos y jamás se les ocurriría confiarles a ellos sus venturas y desventuras.[6]

En realidad, si un problema tienen los cubanos, no es la soledad; más bien al contrario, ¡a veces la cuestión es el exceso de compañía!

[1] support  [2] lacking in self-interest  [3] scarcities  [4] by chance  [5] life story
[6] ups and downs

**🔍 Búsqueda:** símbolos de amistad en cuba

---

## Productos 🎧 Conéctese: la música   1.2, 2.2, 3.1, 3.2

A lo largo de la historia, muchísimos poetas, músicos y filósofos le han dedicado obras al vínculo de la amistad. Silvio Rodríguez es uno de ellos. Este cantautor y poeta cubano habla de la amistad en muchas de sus canciones. En las estrofas de su tema "Vamos a andar", se celebra la amistad no solo como vínculo interpersonal, sino también como vínculo entre los pueblos de las distintas naciones.

"Vamos a andar,
matando al egoísmo,
para que por lo mismo,
reviva la amistad."

"Vamos a andar,
con todas las banderas
trenzadas (*intertwined*), de manera
que no haya soledad."

*Silvio Rodríguez, cantautor cubano*

---

 1.2, 2.1, 3.2

### 18 Comprensión

1. ¿Por qué son tan importantes las amistades generosas en Cuba?

2. ¿Qué características tienen los cubanos que les ayudan a hacer amistades?

3. ¿Qué experiencia sobre la amistad pueden contar muchos cubanos?

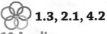 1.3, 2.1, 4.2

### 19 Analice

1. ¿Por qué cree que el contexto socioeconómico influye en el valor que asigna una nación a la amistad?

2. ¿Es fácil hacer amigos en su cultura, como en la cultura cubana, o es difícil? Explique su respuesta.

---

## Differentiated Learning
**Accelerate**
Ask students to re-read the lyrics to **"Vamos a andar"** and identify the main themes. Ask them to relate this to what they read about the term **compañero** on p. 14.

## Multiple Intelligences
**Musical-Rhythmic**
Ask students to research another song by Silvio Rodríguez. Have them compare the song to **"Vamos a andar"** in terms of theme, instrumentation, and lyrics.

## Reference Desk

1. Point out the expression **¡Qué pena contigo!** in the last speech bubble. Encourage students to deduce the meaning from context (*I'm so sorry!; I'm so embarrassed!*).
2. Emphasize that **pedir**, **preguntar**, **preguntar por**, **hacer una pregunta**, and **preguntarse** have separate meanings, and they are not interchangeable. **Pedir** has the additional meaning of "to order" in a restaurant context.
3. The word **por** is also used to express: movement, duration of time, manner or means, reason/cause/motivation, proportion and rate or exchange. There are many popular expressions used with **por**: **por ejemplo**, **por eso**, **por favor**, **por fin**, **por lo general**, **por lo menos**, **por primera vez**, **por supuesto**, and **por última vez**.

## Communication

**Presentational: Paired Practice**
Ask students to write sentences that use the words on this page. They should write sentences about themselves that are true. Then have them get together with a partner and share their sentences. Ask for volunteers to share information about their partners.

# Vocabulario 2

## Comparación y contraste: ¡Ojo con estas palabras! 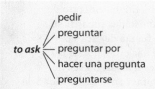 1.2, 4.1

En español, al igual que en inglés, hay varias formas de expresar estas palabras. Preste atención, pues su uso depende del contexto.

to ask
- pedir
- preguntar
- preguntar por
- hacer una pregunta
- preguntarse

**pedir**   *to ask for (something)*
¿Sabes el número del celular de Alex? Se lo **pedí** a Ana, pero no lo tenía.

**preguntar**   *to ask (a question)*
Yo tampoco lo tengo. ¿Por qué no le **preguntas** a Raúl?

**preguntar por**   *to ask for (someone)*
Raúl, llamó una chica **preguntando por** ti, pero no quiso dejar ningún mensaje.

**hacer una pregunta**   *to ask (pose) a question*
¿Y no le **hiciste** ninguna **pregunta** para saber quién era?

**preguntarse**   *to wonder*
A veces **me pregunto** por qué te pago para que seas mi secretaria.

question
- pregunta
- cuestión

**pregunta**   *(an interrogative) question*
Tengo solo **una pregunta**: ¿Cuándo piensas decirle a tu madre lo que estás pensando?

**cuestión**   *an issue, matter, question*
Es solo **cuestión** de tiempo. Tengo que hacerlo en un momento conveniente.

why, because, for
- ¿por qué?
- porque
- a causa de (por)

**¿por qué?**   *why?*
¿**Por qué** hay tantas canciones y poemas sobre el tema de la amistad?

**porque**   *because (used to introduce a clause)*
**Porque** es uno de los principales vínculos de unión entre las personas.

**a causa de… (por)**   *because of (used to introduce a noun or pronoun)*
Había poca visibilidad **a causa de** la lluvia.

## Essential Instruction

1. Model the pronunciation of the vocabulary and have students repeat the words.
2. Personalize the vocabulary presentation by giving additional example sentences about your own life.
3. Check the answers to **Actividad 20** by having two volunteers read the dialogue aloud.
4. Encourage students to use appropriate tone and emotion as they role-play the situations in **Actividad 21**.

## 20 ¡Qué pena contigo!  1.2

Complete la conversación entre Ernesto y Andrea con las palabras del recuadro que correspondan según el contexto.

| pedir | pregunta | pregunté | por qué | pregunté por |
|---|---|---|---|---|
| hacer una pregunta | a causa del | porque | me pregunto | |

**Ernesto:** ¡Hola, Andrea! Casi no te reconozco.

**Andrea:** ¡Claro! Siempre me ves en el gimnasio con ropa deportiva.

**Ernesto:** Esta noche estás hermosa. Ese vestido rojo y el pelo suelto te quedan muy bien.

**Andrea:** ¡Gracias! Tú también te ves muy guapo.

**Ernesto:** El viernes, en el gimnasio, te quería __(1)__ que me invitaras a tu fiesta, pero no tuve el valor de hacerlo.

**Andrea:** ¡Qué pena contigo! Tenía tu invitación en mi mochila pero olvidé dártela. Pero, entonces, ¿cómo sabías dónde quedaba mi casa?

**Ernesto:** Yo le __(2)__ a tu amiga tu dirección y cuando llegué a la fiesta __(3)__ ti.

**Andrea:** Yo __(4)__ por qué me estoy ruborizando (*blushing*) ahora.

**Ernesto:** Supongo que a mí me pasa lo mismo.

**Andrea:** ¿Te puedo __(5)__ ?

**Ernesto:** Sí, claro.

**Andrea:** ¿ __(6)__ te ruborizas?

**Ernesto:** Muy fácil. Vine a tu casa sin invitación __(7)__ me gusta mucho estar contigo. Y ahora, yo también tengo una __(8)__ para ti. ¿Te gustaría salir conmigo?

**Andrea:** ¿Qué dices? No puedo escucharte __(9)__ ruido.

## ¡Comunicación!

## 21 ¿Cómo es su final?  Interpersonal/Presentational Communication 1.1, 1.3

¿Cómo cree Ud. que termina la conversación entre Andrea y Ernesto en la actividad anterior? Compare sus opiniones con las de su compañero/a y, luego, escriban su propio final para el diálogo y represéntenlo enfrente de la clase. Sigan el modelo como guía.

> MODELO
> **Ernesto:** ¿De veras?
>
> **Andrea:** ¡Qué va! Estaba bromeando. Claro que te oí y...

**Answers**

**22** *Las respuestas variarán.*

**23** *Las respuestas variarán.*

**24** *Las conversaciones variarán.*

---

### Reference Desk

Have students choose one statement from **Actividad 23** and create a Flipgrid post in which they state their opinion about it.

---

### Communication

**Presentational/Interpersonal: Paired Practice**

Ask students to write their own letter to Dra. Corazón seeking advice for a problem of their choosing. Then, ask them to exchange letters with a classmate who will draft a response.

---

### Culture

**Productos/Prácticas: Activity**

Ask students to research an advice columnist in a Spanish-speaking country similar to "Dra. Corazón." Have them bring in a portion of the column, and get together in small groups to discuss the nature of the advice given. Ask them to consider whether similar advice would have been given by a U.S. columnist, or if there are cultural influences.

---

## ¡Comunicación!

**22 ¿Qué quieren saber?** 👥 **Interpersonal Communication**  **1.1**

Con un(a) compañero/a, piensen en lo que Uds. quieren saber cuando desean conocer mejor a alguien. ¿Qué clase de preguntas hacen y por qué? Compartan sus ideas y explicaciones, como se ve en el modelo.

MODELO
> **A: Yo le pregunto qué hace en su tiempo libre. Así sé si tenemos gustos en común, ¿y tú?**
>
> **B: Yo le pregunto sobre su familia. Así sé si valora las relaciones familiares.**

**23 En mi opinión...** 👥 **Interpersonal Communication**  **1.1**

Reúnanse en grupos de tres o cuatro estudiantes y, luego, intercambien sus opiniones sobre los siguientes comentarios.

1. Para ser feliz hay que tener muchos amigos.
2. No es normal estar nervioso antes de ir a una fiesta.
3. Cuando una persona es insegura es porque se siente inferior a los demás.
4. Es posible apreciar las cualidades de una persona, tales como la inteligencia, la lealtad, y el sentido del humor en uno o dos encuentros.

**24 No estás solo** 👥 **Interpersonal Communication**  **1.1**

Imagine una conversación entre la consejera de un programa de radio, la doctora Corazón, y David, un joven tímido e introvertido que tiene problemas para hacer amigos y relacionarse con los demás. David llama al programa porque tiene muchas preguntas y no sabe qué hacer. Con un(a) compañero/a, representen la conversación, turnándose para exponer los problemas, hacer las preguntas y ofrecer las posibles soluciones.

MODELO
> **Dra. Corazón:** Mis queridos radio-escuchas, ahora tenemos en la línea a David Delgado de la ciudad de Lima. David, bienvenido a nuestro programa *No estás solo.* Cuéntanos...
>
> **David:** Gracias por su amabilidad, Dra. Corazón. Para empezar, quisiera hacerle una pregunta.
>
> **Dra. Corazón:** ...

---

### Essential Instruction

1. You might want to frame the context of **Actividad 22** as either friendships or romantic relationships.
2. After students complete **Actividad 23**, choose one statement for class discussion.
3. Before beginning **Actividad 24**, brainstorm a few pieces of advice that the doctor might give.
4. You may want to assign the writing portion of **Actividad 26** for homework.

# ¡Comunicación!

## 25 Intercambio de opiniones  Interpersonal Communication  1.1

Intercambie opiniones con un(a) compañero/a acerca de las siguientes preguntas.

1. Si quieres conocer a gente nueva, ¿adónde vas? ¿Qué haces? ¿Cómo empiezas una conversación?

2. Si no conoces muy bien a un(a) muchacho/a y te invita a salir, ¿aceptas su invitación de una vez? Si no, ¿qué haces para conocerlo/a mejor?

3. Si alguien te invita a salir y no quieres, ¿qué haces? ¿Le dices la verdad o buscas excusas para no salir? Explica.

4. ¿Cómo defines la palabra "amistad"?

5. ¿Qué criterio usas para elegir a tus amigos? ¿Qué criterio usan tus amigos? ¿Son diferentes? Explica.

## 26 Amistad por la internet 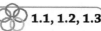 Interpersonal/Presentational Communication 1.1, 1.2, 1.3

Hoy en día, muchas personas hacen amigos y mantienen amistades a través de las redes sociales en la internet. Lea los perfiles personales de estos chicos y chicas de España y, luego, con un(a) compañero/a intercambien opiniones sobre las preguntas que se dan a continuación. Para terminar, escriban su propio perfil, en unas 25 palabras, para buscar amigos en la internet.

• ¿Qué opinan de las descripciones? ¿Son interesantes?

• ¿Dan suficiente información? ¿Cuánta información es necesaria para determinar si quieren comunicarse con la persona en cuestión?

• Si Uds. no creen ser compatibles con estos jóvenes, ¿conocen a alguien que sí pueda serlo? Si sí creen ser compatibles con alguno de ellos/as, qué les preguntarían para conocerlos/as mejor?

• ¿Piensan que se puede iniciar y mantener una amistad de esta manera? Expliquen su respuesta.

○○○  Perfiles personales

### Perfiles personales

**Isabel**

Soy una chica de 18 años y soy de Santiago de Compostela. Me gusta conocer a gente de toda Europa. Me apasiona hacer caminatas, la música rock y aprovechar cada minuto para pasarlo bien. Si eres como yo y piensas lo mismo, escríbeme.

**Lucía**

Tengo 19 años y quisiera conocer a chicos simpáticos y divertidos de Barcelona. Me fascina leer libros de ciencia ficción e ir al Barrio Gótico. Si quieres ir de tapas y caminar por Las Ramblas, ¡vamos juntos!

**Antonio**

Soy de Valencia y me encanta ir a la playa con mis amigos. Tengo 17 años y estudio arte en el colegio. Puedes ver mis pinturas aquí en mi muro. Si te encanta dibujar, pintar o ir a la playa los fines de semana, envíame un mensaje.

**Diego**

¿Te gusta ir a la discoteca? Tengo 20 años y vivo en Madrid. Me encanta salir con mis amigos todos los fines de semana y bailar, y si esto es algo que también te gusta, ¡déjame un mensaje!

### Reference Desk

Create an Avenue task in which students submit their profile from **Actividad 26**.

### Communication

**Presentational/Interpersonal: Cooperative Groups**
Tell students to remove their names from their profiles that they wrote in **Actividad 26**. Collect the profiles and post them around the room. Have students visit the profiles and determine with whom they would have a viable friendship. Afterward, discuss the process as a class. Did any students pick each other? What were the criteria?

### Connections

**Technology**
People in Spanish-speaking countries use worldwide social networks such as Facebook and Twitter, but there are also locally developed social networks, such as **Tuenti** in Spain and **Sonico** in Argentina. Have students go online and visit a social network developed for Spanish speakers. Have them compare and contrast the platform with that of a network in their own country.

### Differentiated Learning

**Decelerate**
Reformulate the questions in **Actividad 25** as a multiple-choice personality quiz.

**Expand**
Have students reformulate their ideas from **Actividad 25** into a list of "dos and don'ts" for forming lasting, healthy relationships. They can submit their lists via an Avenue task.

### Multiple Intelligences

**Mathematical-Logical**
Have students rank the profiles in **Actividad 26** in order of interest to them. Have them explain their rankings.

## ¡Comunicación!

### 27 ¿Demasiada formalidad?  Interpersonal/Presentational Communication  1.1, 1.3

Formen grupos de tres o cuatro compañeros e intercambien ideas sobre los siguientes temas. Al final, hagan un resumen de los diferentes puntos de vista y conclusiones y preséntenlo a la clase.

- ¿Piensan que las presentaciones formales son necesarias entre los jóvenes o que deben eliminarse? (Por ejemplo: "Te presento a...", "Mucho gusto", "El gusto es mío".) Expliquen su respuesta.

- ¿Existen estas formalidades entre sus amigos/as? Si no existen, ¿cómo presentan Uds. a alguien o cómo se presentan Uds. mismos?

- ¿Piensan que el hombre debe ser especialmente cortés con la mujer, que debe abrirle la puerta al entrar a un lugar, cederle el paso o pagar la entrada del cine o la cuenta del restaurante si salen juntos? ¿Cuándo sería apropiado dar estas muestras de cortesía?

- ¿Qué formas de cortesía debe esperar un hombre de una mujer? Expliquen su respuesta.

### 28 ¡No seas aguafiestas! 1.1

**Interpersonal Communication**

Imagine que un(a) joven invita a un compañero/a de clase a una fiesta y esa persona resulta ser todo/a un aguafiestas (*party pooper*). Tiene una actitud súper negativa, se queda en un rincón (*corner*) del salón, ignora a todo el mundo y no quiere hacer nada. No se divierte ni deja que Ud. se divierta. Represente la situación con un(a) compañero/a, turnándose para hacer el papel del aguafiestas y el de su pareja, que trata en vano de convencerlo/a de que cambie de actitud y se divierta.

MODELO    **A:** No te quedes en ese rincón. Ven y te presento a mis amigos.

                 **B:** Perdona, pero no...

                 **A:** Entonces, vamos a bailar o a...

                 **B:** ...

*Me encanta bailar, aunque tenga que hacerlo sola.*

### Essential Instruction

1. Write students' ideas from **Actividad 27** on the board. Can the class reach a consensus on any of the main points?

2. Encourage students to use humor and creativity in their role-plays for **Actividad 28**.

3. As you go over the **Gramática**, ask for volunteers to give additional examples for each bullet point. Write them on the board.

4. Model the pronunciation of the nouns and have students repeat.

# Gramática

## Los sustantivos  1.2

Los sustantivos se clasifican según el género y el número. El género (masculino o femenino) y el número (singular o plural) se determinan por medio de las terminaciones. En español, los sustantivos generalmente van acompañados de los artículos definidos o indefinidos y concuerdan con ellos en número y persona.

| Género y número de los sustantivos | | |
|---|---|---|
| | **Singular** | **Plural** |
| **Masculino** | el amig**o** | los amig**os** |
| **Feminino** | la amig**a** | las amig**as** |

### El género de los sustantivos

- Generalmente los sustantivos que terminan en **-o**, **-al**, **-or**, **-ente** y **-ante** son masculinos.

| **-o** | **-al** | **-or** | **-ente, -ante** |
|---|---|---|---|
| el aprecio | el animal | el color | el accidente |
| el pueblo | el hospital | el amor | el presente |
| el temperamento | el carnaval | el valor | el diamante |

Excepciones:

| | | | |
|---|---|---|---|
| la mano | la catedral | la labor | la gente |
| la señal | la flor | la corriente | la serpiente |

- Algunos sustantivos que terminan en **-ante** y **-ente** y se refieren a personas tienen una sola forma para el masculino y el femenino. Otros tienen formas correspondientes.

| | | | |
|---|---|---|---|
| el agente | la agente | el cliente | la clienta |
| el cantante | la cantante | el dependiente | la dependienta |
| el estudiante | la estudiante | el presidente | la presidenta |

- Los sustantivos que terminan en **-a**, **-ión** (**-ción**, **-sión**) y **-umbre** generalmente son femeninos.

| **-a** | **-ión** | **-umbre** |
|---|---|---|
| la confianza | la ilusión | la costumbre |
| la entrevista | la nación | la incertidumbre |
| la idiosincrasia | la situación | la muchedumbre |

- Los sustantivos que terminan en **-ie**, **-d** (**-dad**, **-tad**, **-ud**) y **-z/-ez** también son, generalmente, femeninos.

| **-ie** | **-d** (**-dad**, **-tad**, **-ud**) | **-z** |
|---|---|---|
| la especie | la amistad | la paz |
| la serie | la generosidad | la escasez |
| la superficie | la actitud | la niñez |

Excepciones:

el día, el tranvía, el mapa, el avión, el lápiz y varias palabras que terminan en **-ma**: el sistema, el problema, el clima, el tema, el programa, el idioma, el drama, el poema

1. You may want to point out that **el arte** is masculine in the singular (**el arte moderno**, **el arte nuevo**), but feminine in the plural (**las bellas artes**, **las artes plásticas**).
2. Remind students that masculine plural nouns that refer to people (e.g., **los jóvenes**, **los turistas**) may indicate a group of only males or a mixed group of males and females. Remind them that even if the group is overwhelmingly female, if males are included the masculine form of the noun is used.
3. Refer students to **Apéndice A** as needed to review accentuation rules.
4. Point out that **abrelatas** and **paraguas** are compound nouns. Additional ones include: **el cubrecamas**, **el lavamanos**, **el parabrisas**, **el quitamanchas**, **el rascacielos**, **el sacapuntas**.

## TPR

Call out a variety of nouns. Students should raise their right hand if the noun is feminine (**lección**), their left hand if the noun is masculine (**carro**), and both hands if it can be either (**estudiante**). Repeat the process to practice singulars and plurals: have students raise their right hand if the noun they hear is singular (**noche**), or their left hand if it is plural (**libros**).

- Los sustantivos que terminan en **-ista** son masculinos o femeninos, según el sexo de las personas.

| Hombre | Mujer |
| --- | --- |
| el periodista | la periodista |
| el turista | la turista |
| el artista | la artista |

## El número de los sustantivos

El número determina si el sustantivo es singular o plural. El plural de los sustantivos se forma añadiendo **-s** o **-es** a la forma singular.

- Si el sustantivo termina en vocal, se añade **-s**.[1]

| Singular | Plural |
| --- | --- |
| la man**o** | las manos**s** |
| el pi**e** | los pie**s** |
| la hor**a** | las hora**s** |

- Si el sustantivo termina en consonante, se añade **-es**.

| Singular | Plural |
| --- | --- |
| la ocasió**n** | las ocasion**es**[2] |
| el pape**l** | los papel**es** |
| la ve**z** | las vec**es**[3] |
| el jove**n** | los jóven**es**[4] |

- Si el sustantivo es de más de una sílaba y termina en **-s**, la forma plural no cambia.

| Singular | Plural |
| --- | --- |
| el lune**s** | los lune**s** |
| el abrelata**s** | los abrelata**s** |
| el paragua**s** | los paragua**s** |

[1] Algunas palabras que terminan en **-í** forman el plural con **-es**: el rubí, los rubíes; el ají, los ajíes.

[2] Con el aumento de una sílaba, el acento escrito no es necesario. (Ver Apéndice A)

[3] La **z** cambia a **c** delante de **e**.

[4] Con el aumento de una sílaba, el acento escrito es necesario. (Ver Apéndice A)

*Las jóvenes van de compras con su mamá.*

### Essential Instruction

1. Personalize the **Gramática** by associating the nouns with people in your class or famous people, places in your community, etc.
2. Drill formation of plurals by calling out singular nouns, and have students give the plural form. Then reverse the drill by calling out plurals, and they give the singular. Finally, do a mix of the two.
3. Tell students they have been using definite and indefinite articles already, and here they will refine their usage.

# Gramática

## El artículo definido  1.2

El uso del artículo definido es más frecuente en español que en inglés. Sirve para indicar a una persona, animal, cosa o idea específica, ya sea concreta o abstracta.

**El** periodista desea hablar con Ud.

**El** motociclismo es un deporte peligroso.

Me encanta **la** música de Shakira.

Queremos **la** paz y **la** libertad.

| Formas del artículo definido | | |
|---|---|---|
| | **Singular** | **Plural** |
| **Masculino** | **el** actor | **los** actores |
| **Femenino** | **la** pregunta | **las** preguntas |

## Usos del artículo definido

- Se usa el artículo masculino singular **el** delante de sustantivos femeninos que comienzan con **a** o **ha**, para facilitar la pronunciación si el énfasis cae en la primera sílaba.

    Mi madre tiene **el a**lma bondadosa.
    **El a**gua del mar es salada.
    **El h**ada es una mujer fantástica que tiene poderes mágicos.

    **Pero: Las a**guas del mar Caribe son claras.

- Cuando el artículo definido **el** sigue a la preposición **de** o **a**, la contracción es necesaria.

    de + el = **del**    La idiosincrasia **del** cubano se refleja en su trato con los demás.

    a + el = **al**    Ellos tratan **al** conocido y **al** desconocido con la misma amabilidad.

- Se usa el artículo definido delante de nombres modificados o con títulos cuando se habla **de** la persona y no **a** la persona (excepto con **don** y **doña**, que nunca llevan artículo).

    **La** señora Ortega llega mañana porque tiene una cita con **el** doctor Vega.

    **Pero:** Buenas tardes, señor Marcos. ¿Cómo está doña María?

- Se usa con los nombres de algunos países. Sin embargo, la tendencia hoy es de no usar el artículo.

    Viví en (**el**) Perú dos años y después pasé un año en (**los**) Estados Unidos.

- Se usa con los nombres de personas y de países cuando están modificados.

    **La** pobre María solo tiene una semana de vacaciones.

    **La** Cuba de hoy atrae a muchos turistas europeos y canadienses.

## Reference Desk

1. Some nouns can take both articles, e.g., **el corte** = *cut* / **la corte** = *court*; **el capital** = *money* / **la capital** = *capital city*; **el cura** = *priest* / **la cura** = *cure*; **el papa** = *the Pope* / **la papa** = *potato*.

2. For the first bullet point, emphasize that this change in article does not make the word masculine. Therefore, the plural takes the definite article **las**. Give additional examples (e.g., **el águila**, **el alba**, **el arma**, **el aula**, **el hambre**) and have students say the singular and plural forms.

3. For the second bullet, point out that if **a** or **de** is followed by the personal pronoun **él** or by an article that is part of a proper name or title, the contraction does not occur: **Estos libros son de él. Ella me habló de El Quijote.**

4. You may want to point out that **don** and **doña** don't have direct translations in English. Normally in English these titles are written as **Don** and **Doña**.

5. For the fourth bullet, mention that with some countries, the article is part of the name and therefore obligatory: **El Salvador**.

6. Some students may feel intimidated by lengthy grammar explanations, or ones that are in Spanish. Point out that these grammar presentations use simple, accessible language and that they can think of grammar as merely a description of how language works.

### Differentiated Learning
**Accelerate/Heritage Learners**
Ask accelerated students or heritage learners to play the role of teacher and conduct this grammar presentation. Allow them time to organize their presentation and prepare additional examples. Encourage the rest of the class to ask follow-up questions.

### Special Needs Students
**Linguistically Challenged**
Provide color-coding to help these students distinguish the different categories of noun endings in **Los sustantivos**. It may also be helpful to compare these nouns to their English counterparts.

## Communication

**Presentational: Cooperative Groups**

Divide the class into three groups, and assign each group a grammar point: **Los sustantivos**, **El artículo definido**, and **El artículo indefinido**. Instruct each group to create a poster summarizing the rules. They should include original examples. Display the posters in the classroom.

## Expansion

Retype a Spanish-language news article, replacing all the definite and indefinite articles with blanks. Using the information learned on pp. 23–24, ask students to fill in the correct articles.

# Gramática

- El artículo definido se usa delante de las partes del cuerpo y la ropa en lugar del adjetivo posesivo.

    Lávese **los** dientes.
    Se pusieron **el** abrigo.
    Los niños levantaron **la** mano.

- Se usa con los días de la semana y las estaciones del año. (Se omite después del verbo **ser** para identificar el día de la semana.)

    Voy de compras **los** sábados.

    **Pero:**   Hoy es lunes.

- Se usa con las fechas y las horas.

    La fiesta es **el** 3 de mayo, a **las** ocho y media.

- Se usa con los nombres de idiomas. (Se omite después de los verbos **hablar**, **aprender**, **estudiar**, **enseñar** y **entender** y las preposiciones **de** y **en**.)

    Me gustan mucho **el** italiano y **el** alemán.

    **Pero:**   Quiero estudiar portugués. Solo hablo español. Háblame en francés.

## El artículo indefinido  1.2

El artículo indefinido sirve para indicar a una persona, animal o cosa en forma general.

| Formas del artículo indefinido | | |
| --- | --- | --- |
| | **Singular** | **Plural** |
| **Masculino** | un coche | **unos** coches |
| **Femenino** | una casa | **unas** casas |

- El artículo indefinido plural **unos/unas** corresponde al inglés *some/a few* y generalmente se omite.

    Tenemos (**unos**) amigos muy buenos.

## Cuándo omitir el artículo indefinido

- Se omite después del verbo **ser** con nombres que indican profesión, religión o nacionalidad, excepto cuando están modificados.

    Mi hermano es mecánico. Es **un** mecánico excelente y su esposa es **una** maestra muy buena.

- Se omite con los verbos **tener**, **llevar** y **haber** cuando no expresan cantidad, especialmente en oraciones negativas.

    ¿Tienes coche? No, pero tengo bicicleta.
    Hace frío y no llevas abrigo.
    Para mañana no hay tarea.

- Se omite cuando el sustantivo va precedido por otras palabras que lo modifican, en lugar del artículo, como: **otro**, **medio**, **cien(to)**, **mil** y **¡Qué… !**

    **¡Qué** chaqueta más bonita! Cuesta solo **ciento** cincuenta dólares.

## Essential Instruction

1. After going over **Gramática**, drill articles by calling out nouns and having students state the noun together with the definite article.
2. Practice indefinite articles by doing a conversion activity. Say a noun with its definite article; students have to give the noun with its indefinite article.
3. Circulate around the room as pairs work on **Actividades 29** and **30** to make sure that they understand these activities.
4. Check answers to **Actividades 29** and **30** by having volunteers role-play the conversations for the class.

## 29 Situaciones y opiniones  1.1, 1.2

Complete el siguiente diálogo con el artículo definido, el artículo indefinido o las contracciones **al** o **del**, según corresponda. Luego, compare sus respuestas con las de su compañero/a para ver si acertaron las respuestas.

**A:** ¿Qué haces si estás cenando en casa de __(1)__ amigas y se te caen los fríjoles __(2)__ plato __(3)__ suelo?

**B:** Recojo __(4)__ frijoles y le pido disculpas a __(5)__ señora de la casa.

**A:** ¿Qué haces si le pides __(6)__ coche a tu amigo para ir __(7)__ cine y te dice que él lo necesita?

**B:** ¡Voy __(8)__ cine caminando!

**A:** ¿Qué haces cuando tienes __(9)__ problema serio?

**B:** Le pido __(10)__ consejo a __(11)__ buen amigo.

**A:** ¿Cuáles son __(12)__ cualidades que más te gustan en __(13)__ persona?

**B:** __(14)__ sinceridad, __(15)__ sensibilidad y __(16)__ ingenio.

**A:** ¿Y cuáles crees que son __(17)__ peores defectos de algunos estudiantes?

**B:** __(18)__ inseguridad y __(19)__ pereza.

**A:** ¿Qué piensas de __(20)__ telenovelas?

**B:** Pienso que __(21)__ son buenas y otras son malas.

## 30 ¡Cuéntame de tu familia!  1.1, 1.2

Complete el siguiente diálogo con el artículo indefinido cuando sea necesario. Luego, compare sus respuestas con las de su compañero/a para ver si acertaron las respuestas.

**A:** ¿Tienes __(1)__ familia grande?

**B:** Sí. Somos ocho. Mi padre, mi madre, __(2)__ hermano mayor, cuatro hermanos menores y yo.

**A:** ¿Qué hacen tus padres?

**B:** Mi padre es __(3)__ veterinario reconocido y mi madre es __(4)__ odontóloga.

**A:** ¿Dónde viven?

**B:** Vivimos a __(5)__ tres cuadras de aquí. Y Uds., ¿acostumbran viajar en las vacaciones?

**A:** Generalmente viajamos a Ecuador, Colombia y Perú porque tenemos __(6)__ amigos en estos países. Hace poco recibimos visita de __(7)__ amiga ecuatoriana. ¡Qué __(8)__ mujer tan especial! Estuvo con nosotros __(9)__ días. Aunque disfrutó su estadía, no estaba acostumbrada a nuestro clima. Cuando salía siempre llevaba puesto __(10)__ abrigo de lana y __(11)__ botas de invierno porque decía que sentía demasiado frío.

**B:** Yo también tengo __(12)__ amigo en Perú. Él nos escribió hace poco diciendo que piensa hacer __(13)__ viaje a Estados Unidos para comprar electrodomésticos para __(14)__ negocio que tiene con __(15)__ chilenos que viven en Lima. ¡Qué sorpresa se va a llevar cuando sepa que yo no tengo __(16)__ microondas en casa! ¡Cómo soy de anticuada!

### Answers

**29**
1. unas; 2. del; 3. al; 4. los; 5. la; 6. el; 7. al; 8. al; 9. un; 10. un; 11. un; 12. las; 13. una; 14. La; 15. la; 16. el; 17. los; 18. La; 19. la; 20. las; 21. unas

**30**
1. una; 2. un; 3. un; 4. —; 5. —/ unas; 6. —; 7. una; 8. —; 9. unos; 10. un; 11. unas; 12. un; 13. un; 14. un; 15. unos; 16. —

### Critical Thinking

**Analyzing**
After students have completed **Actividades 29** and **30**, have them get together with another pair and explain why they used each answer.

### Expansion

Ask students to create their own mini-dialogues. Have them use blanks where the articles should be. Then have them exchange papers with a classmate and fill in the blanks.

### Learning Styles
**Auditory Learners**
Conduct **Actividades 29** and **30** as listening activities. Write the possible answers on the board as a lettered list. As you read aloud the conversation, pause at each blank so that students can call out the corresponding letter.

### Special Needs Students
**Dyslexia/Reading Difficulties**
Create a handout with the information on pp. 23–24 listed in a graphic organizer. This will help students when trying to remember all of the rules and exceptions of articles.

**25**

---

Answers

**Antes de leer**
*Las respuestas variarán.*

**31**

1. A pesar de estar muy cerca, entre los dos países hay una gran barrera ideológica y económica.
2. A pesar de las diferencias entre los dos países, los inmigrantes cubanos contribuyeron a Estados Unidos.
3. Prometió revisar su política hacia Cuba.
4. Reestablecer las relaciones diplomáticas y la embajada estadounidense en Cuba.

**32** *Respuesta posible:*
Los dos países llevan muchísimos años distanciados por posiciones políticas y económicas radicalmente opuestas.

**26**

---

# *Lectura informativa*

 **1.3 Antes de leer**

¿Qué cambios cree Ud. que se producirán en Cuba a partir de la reanudación de relaciones con Estados Unidos?

 **1.2, 2.2, 3.1**

## Estrategia · 1.3, 3.1

**Palabras y frases de transición**

Identificar las palabras y frases de transición sirve para comprender mejor las relaciones de causa y efecto (por lo tanto), las de contraste (pero) y las temporales (mientras tanto).

 **1.2, 2.2**

### 31 Comprensión

1. ¿Por qué es complicada la relación entre Cuba y Estados Unidos?
2. ¿Por qué Cuba y Estados Unidos han sido amigos y enemigos al mismo tiempo?
3. ¿Qué promesa hizo Obama al asumir el cargo de Presidente de Estados Unidos?
4. ¿Cuáles fueron las primeras medidas que tomó el presidente Obama en relación con Cuba?

 **1.3, 5.1**

### 32 Analice

¿Por qué la reanudación de las relaciones entre Cuba y Estados Unidos constituye un hito (*landmark*) en las relaciones internacionales?

## Fragmentos del discurso de Barack Obama sobre la reanudación de relaciones entre EE. UU. y Cuba

Hoy, Estados Unidos de América empieza a cambiar su relación con el pueblo de Cuba.

En el cambio más significativo de nuestra política[1] en más de cincuenta años, terminaremos con un enfoque[2] obsoleto que por décadas fracasó en promover nuestros intereses y, en cambio, comenzaremos a normalizar la relación entre los dos países. A través de estos cambios, es nuestra intención crear más oportunidades para el pueblo estadounidense y para el pueblo cubano y comenzar un nuevo capítulo entre las naciones del continente americano.

La historia entre Estados Unidos y Cuba es complicada. Yo nací en 1961, justo dos años después de que Fidel Castro tomara el poder en Cuba y unos meses después de la invasión en la Bahía de Cochinos, en la que se intentó derrocar[3] a su régimen. En las siguientes décadas, la relación entre nuestros países tuvo lugar frente al trasfondo[4] de la Guerra Fría y la firme oposición de Estados Unidos al comunismo. Solamente nos separan 90 millas. Pero año tras año, se endureció la barrera ideológica y económica entre los dos países.

Mientras tanto, la comunidad de exiliados cubanos en Estados Unidos contribuyó enormemente con nuestro país, en la política, los negocios, la cultura y los deportes. Como otros inmigrantes lo habían hecho previamente, los cubanos ayudaron a reconstruir a Estados Unidos, a pesar de sentir una dolorosa nostalgia[5] por la tierra y las familias que dejaron atrás. Todo esto forjó una relación única entre Estados Unidos y Cuba, al mismo tiempo amigos y enemigos. [...]

Por eso es que, cuando asumí el cargo de Presidente de Estados Unidos, prometí volver a revisar nuestra política con Cuba. Para comenzar, levantamos restricciones para los estadounidenses de origen cubano para que pudieran viajar y enviar giros[6] a sus familias en Cuba. [...]

Primero, he instruido al Secretario de Estado Kerry a que comience inmediatamente las discusiones con Cuba para restablecer las relaciones diplomáticas que han estado interrumpidas desde enero de 1961. En adelante, Estados Unidos restablecerá una embajada estadounidense en La Habana, y funcionarios de alto rango[7] visitarán Cuba.

[1] policy  [2] approach  [3] overthrow  [4] backdrop  [5] yearning  [6] remittances
[7] high-ranking officials

---

En donde podamos promover intereses compartidos, lo haremos, en asuntos como salud, inmigración, antiterrorismo, tráfico de drogas y respuesta a catástrofes. [...]

Segundo, he instruido al Secretario Kerry para que revise la calificación de Cuba como un Estado que patrocina[8] el terrorismo. [...]

En tercer lugar, estamos tomando las medidas para aumentar el transporte, el comercio y el flujo de información de y hacia Cuba. [...] Un aumento del comercio es bueno para los estadounidenses y los cubanos. Por lo tanto, facilitaremos transacciones autorizadas entre Estados Unidos y Cuba. [...]

Desafortunadamente, nuestras sanciones sobre Cuba han negado a los cubanos el acceso a tecnología que ha empoderado[9] a individuos en todo el mundo. Por lo tanto, he autorizado el aumento de las conexiones de telecomunicaciones entre Estados Unidos y Cuba. [...]

Para aquellos que se oponen a los pasos que anuncio hoy permítanme decirles que respeto su pasión y comparto su compromiso con la libertad y la democracia. La cuestión es cómo mantenemos ese compromiso. No pienso que podamos seguir haciendo lo mismo durante más de cinco décadas y esperar un resultado distinto. Además, intentar empujar a Cuba al colapso no beneficia a los intereses de Estados Unidos ni los de los cubanos. [...]

A los cubanos, Estados Unidos les extiende una mano de amistad. Algunos de ustedes nos han buscado como fuente de esperanza, y continuaremos alumbrando una luz[10] de libertad. Otros nos han visto como un pasado intento de colonización para controlar su futuro. José Martí una vez dijo, "la libertad es el derecho que tienen las personas de actuar libremente, pensar y hablar sin hipocresía". Hoy, estoy siendo honesto con ustedes. Nunca podremos borrar la historia entre nosotros, pero creemos que deben estar empoderados para vivir con dignidad y autodeterminación. Los cubanos tienen un dicho sobre la vida diaria: "No es fácil". Hoy, Estados Unidos quiere ser un socio para hacer que la vida de los cubanos ordinarios sea un poco más fácil, más libre y más próspera. [...]

El cambio es duro, en nuestras propias vidas y en las vidas de las naciones. Y el cambio es aún más duro cuando llevamos el peso de la historia en nuestros hombros. Hoy, Estados Unidos elige deshacerse de[11] las cadenas del pasado para poder llegar a un mejor futuro para los cubanos, para los estadounidenses, para todo el hemisferio y para el mundo. [...]

[8] sponsor    [9] empowered    [10] to shine a light    [11] cut loose

🔍 **Búsqueda:** reanudación de relaciones entre estados unidos y cuba, guerra fría, fidel castro

 **1.2, 2.2, 3.2**

### 33 Comprensión

1. ¿Qué opina el presidente Obama sobre el acceso a la tecnología que tienen los cubanos?

2. ¿En qué asuntos se prevé que ambos países trabajen juntos?

3. ¿Qué motivó al gobierno de Estados Unidos a realizar este cambio con respecto a Cuba?

4. Según el presidente Obama, ¿qué dos posiciones tienen los cubanos respecto de Estados Unidos?

 **1.3, 2.1, 3.2**

### 34 Analice

¿Por qué cree Ud. que los cubanos usan la frase "No es fácil" para referirse a la vida diaria?

## RESOURCES

(fg)    Flipgrid

**Answers**

**33**
1. Cuba se ha visto muy perjudicada por las sanciones que le impiden el acceso a la tecnología.
2. Comercio, salud, inmigración, antiterrorismo, tráfico de drogas, etc.
3. Para lograr un mejor futuro para todos.
4. Algunos cubanos consideran a Estados Unidos una luz de esperanza; otros, una amenaza.

**34**  *Respuesta posible:*
Porque no debe ser fácil vivir en un país con las características políticas y económicas de Cuba.

### Reference Desk

1. Students will read a selection by **José Martí** later in this unit.
2. Students can present their ideas from **Actividad 34** in a Flipgrid post.

### Culture

**Products: Activity**
Have students research more about José Martí, including his most famous works and his role in Cuba's fight for independence. Ask them to consider why President Obama chose to quote Martí in this speech.

### Connections

**Economics**
Have students research Cuba's economy. Have them investigate why U.S. sanctions and the fall of the Soviet Union were crippling factors. Invite them to speculate how things might change if relations are restored with the United States.

---

**Differentiated Learning**
**Expand**
Have students write a reaction piece to Obama's speech for the school newspaper. Tell them to include a brief introduction, their opinions, and a short conclusion.

**Special Needs Students**
**Dyslexia/AD(H)D/Visually Impaired**
Allow these students to watch the speech online before attempting to read the selection. This will help them to preview the content and also will aid their comprehension of cognates and main ideas.

**Answers**

**35** *Los correos electrónicos variarán.*

### Reference Desk

1. If possible, bring in a few examples of informal e-mails in Spanish.
2. You might have students submit their e-mails from **Actividad 35** in an Avenue task.
3. The persuasive essay is a key component of the AP® Spanish Language and Culture exam's free-response section.
4. **Actividad 36** contains authentic audio, which is another important part of the AP® Spanish exam.

### Culture

**Perspectives: Activity**
After students read Obama's speech on pp. 26–27 and listen to the authentic audio in **Actividad 36**, ask them to include an entry in their Culture Journals about the speech and Cubans' reactions to it.

### Pre-AP

Have students complete the activities on pp. 28–29 to help them prepare for the writing sections of the AP® exam.

# *Escritura*

## Un correo electrónico informal  1.3

Un correo electrónico es un mensaje similar a una carta, que se redacta en una computadora y se envía utilizando una conexión a la internet. El texto puede variar en extensión y nivel de formalidad según el propósito del mensaje y el destinatario.

### Para escribir un correo electrónico informal

- Escriba la dirección del destinatario y complete el campo "Asunto" con un encabezado breve que capte el interés del lector.
- Empiece el mensaje con un saludo informal, y desarrolle brevemente el tema del que quiere tratar.
- Concluya el mensaje con una frase de despedida informal y fírmelo con su nombre.

## ¡Comunicación!

**35 ¡Ya era hora!** Interpersonal Communication  1.3

Imagine que Ud. se encuentra en la situación de Elena, una joven cubana que llegó a Estados Unidos junto con sus tíos hace un par de años; que sus padres tuvieron que quedarse en Cuba, y que Ud. y sus familiares han tratado por todos los medios de ayudar a sus padres a salir del país, pero no han tenido éxito.

Luego, escríbale un correo electrónico a su tía Alicia contándole las últimas noticias que acaba de escuchar sobre la posible reanudación de relaciones diplomáticas entre Estados Unidos y Cuba. Incluya detalles del discurso del Presidente Obama al respecto, exprese su emoción, y pídale que le ayude con los trámites (*steps*) que sean necesarios para que su sueño de volver a reunirse con sus padres se vuelva realidad.

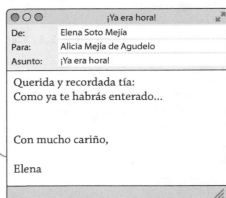

| ¡Ya era hora! |
| --- |
| De: Elena Soto Mejía |
| Para: Alicia Mejía de Agudelo |
| Asunto: ¡Ya era hora! |

Querida y recordada tía:
Como ya te habrás enterado...


Con mucho cariño,

Elena

*Elena le envía un correo electrónico a su tía Alicia.*

## Essential Instruction

1. As a class, read the introductory information about informal e-mails. Give examples of catchy subject lines, and appropriate greetings and closings.
2. You may want to have students peer-edit their e-mails from **Actividad 35**.
3. Read about persuasive essays as a class.
4. For **Actividad 36**, play the audio once and have students just listen. Play the audio a second time and have them take notes.
5. Have students re-read the speech on pp. 26–27. Discuss the key points as a class. Then model how to use the graphic organizer.

# Un ensayo persuasivo  1.3

Un ensayo persuasivo es un texto que tiene como finalidad presentar un punto de vista sobre un asunto para convencer al lector de que adhiera a la postura del autor.

## Elementos de un ensayo persuasivo

Para que un ensayo persuasivo cumpla su propósito, se deben incluir los siguientes elementos:

- **Introducción:**
  Un dato interesante o una declaración convincente que llame la atención del lector, y una o dos oraciones breves que resuman el tema y el punto de vista del autor.

- **Desarrollo del tema o cuerpo del ensayo:**
  Presentación de las razones que respaldan la tesis del autor y evidencia que demuestre que su punto de vista es acertado.

- **Conclusión:**
  Resumen de las razones del autor y reformulación de la tesis para cerrar el ensayo.

> **Para escribir más**
>
> Use las siguientes frases para presentar las razones que respaldan (*support*) su tesis.
>
> En primer/segundo/tercer lugar,
> Por un lado,
> Por otro lado,
> Además,
> No solo…, sino también…

## ¡Comunicación!

### 36 Revolución emocional  Interpretive Communication  1.2, 1.3, 3.2

Escuche este segmento informativo de RTVE.es *A la Carta, radio y televisión española*, sobre la reacción de los cubanos a la decisión del presidente Obama de levantar las restricciones a los viajes y envíos de dinero a Cuba, y tome apuntes de los puntos principales en una hoja aparte.

### 37 En mi opinión... Presentational Communication 1.2, 1.3, 3.2

Vuelva a leer el discurso del presidente Obama en las páginas 26 y 27 y, con base en esa información y la que acaba de escuchar, escriba un ensayo persuasivo sobre la reanudación de relaciones entre Estados Unidos y Cuba. Puede escribir desde su propia perspectiva o bien desde el punto de vista de un cubano que vive en Estados Unidos o un cubano que vive en Cuba. Antes de escribir su ensayo, resuma sus ideas en un organizador gráfico como el que se muestra.

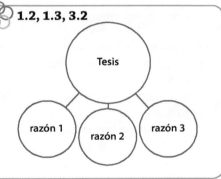

---

**RESOURCES**

🎧 Activity 36

**Answers** _____

**36 Script**

Para los cubanos, Obama es diferente y desde el inicio de su mandato han puesto en él muchas esperanzas. Permitir que los cubano-americanos puedan viajar libremente a la isla es quizás el mayor gesto de la Casa Blanca en décadas.

—Es bueno, es una alegría para nosotros los cubanos.

La revolución emocional será enorme, más de millón y medio de cubanos viven en la otra orilla, pero hasta ahora solo unos ciento cincuenta mil viajaban al año a la isla, tenían que tener sus viajes cada tres años, con esta medida los reencuentros se dispararán.

—Mi mayor deseo sería que viniera Wu a ver a conocer a su hija aquí.

—Todos los cubanos tenemos culpa, entiendes, de las decisiones que... o las disputas que hay ante los dos países.

El alivio para la débil economía cubana también será inmenso. Cuba espera ansiosa una invasión de divisas.

—Para mucho mejor que aquí estamos muy necesitados, aquí la vida es muy cara.

—La economía de nosotros va a mejorar, yo lo veo muy bien todo.

Era un gesto esperado y solicitado por todos los líderes latinoamericanos que han ido desfilando durante este año por la Habana: un acercamiento de Obama a Cuba en vísperas de la Cumbre de las Américas dentro de unos días en Trinidad. Ese será el estreno de una nueva política de Estados Unidos en el continente.

*Los apuntes variarán.*

**37** *Los ensayos variarán.*

---

## Differentiated Learning

### Heritage Learners

Invite heritage learners to share reactions from their cultural communities to President Obama's speech. You may want to have them interview their family members or watch news clips from their family's country of origin.

## Special Needs Students

### Auditory Impairment

Ask these students to listen several times to the recording in **Actividad 36**. You may also want to provide them with a script so that they can follow along and highlight the main points as they listen.

Mejore su comprensión

## Reference Desk

1. The words presented in **Vocabulario 3** are extracted from the audio in **Actividad 41** and the **Lectura literaria** that appears later in the unit. These words are intended for comprehension and expansion only; they will not appear on assessments.

2. Make sure that students are familiar with dictionary abbreviations. If not, guide them in deducing the meaning of **v.**, **s.f.**, and so on.

## Game

**El ahorcado**
Have students practice the new vocabulary by playing Hangman. First demonstrate the game on the board with a short word, such as **velo**.

## TPR

Have students work in pairs. They should take turns acting out the vocabulary for their partner to guess. For example, for **atrasarse**, a student could act out looking at his/her watch and shrugging. Encourage students to exaggerate their gestures. Invite a few pairs to act out some terms for the class to guess.

# Vocabulario 3

## Mejore su comprensión  1.2

Familiarizarse con este vocabulario le ayudará a leer "Dos patrias" más adelante, y a mejorar su comprensión auditiva.

*La vela flameaba dando luz en la oscuridad.*

**aparecer** *v.* Dejarse ver.

**atrasarse** *v.* Llegar tarde.

**bandera** *s.f.* Trozo de tela con colores que representa a una nación o a un grupo de personas.

**batallar** *v.* Luchar para vencer.

**cielo** *s.m.* Espacio en el que están las estrellas y planetas.

**clavel** *s.m.* Flor que tiene el borde superior terminado en picos.

**enturbiar** *v.* Oscurecer.

**estorbar** *v.* Impedir, molestar.

**estrecho/a** *adj.* Apretado.

**flamear** *v.* Despedir llamas.

**lago** *s.m.* Gran cantidad de agua dulce acumulada en depresiones de la tierra.

**llama** *s.f.* Lo que produce algo al quemarse o arder.

**mudo/a** *adj.* Que le falta la capacidad de hablar.

**pasar (una película, un programa)** *v.* Presentar.

**patria** *s.f.* Lugar en el que ha nacido una persona.

**recorrer** *v.* Ir o transitar por un espacio o lugar.

**retirar(se)** *v.* Alejar, ocultar.

**sangriento/a** *adj.* Manchado o cubierto de sangre.

**silencioso/a** *adj.* Que calla, que no hace ruido.

**temblar** *v.* Agitarse con movimientos breves.

**vacío/a** *adj.* Sin nada adentro, desocupado.

**vela** *s.f.* Objeto de cera con una cuerda por dentro que al prenderse produce luz.

**velo** *s.f.* Tela fina y transparente.

**viuda** *s.f.* Mujer casada cuyo esposo ha muerto.

### 38 Sinónimos y antónimos  1.2

Empareje cada palabra con su sinónimo o antónimo, según se indica.

1. antónimo de viuda
2. sinónimo de mudo
3. sinónimo de patria
4. sinónimo de batallar
5. antónimo de estrecho
6. sinónimo de recorrer

A. país
B. casada
C. luchar
D. ancho
E. caminar
F. silencioso

### 39 Así ha sucedido 1.2

Complete las siguientes oraciones con la palabra que corresponda según el contexto.

1. Sabían que solo les quedaban dos opciones: ____ o morir.
   A. temblar    B. batallar    C. flamear

2. La llama de la ____ brillaba en medio de la oscuridad que los rodeaba.
   A. vela    B. luz    C. noche

3. En la noche ____ no se oía ni el sonido de la respiración.
   A. silenciosa    B. triste    C. muda

4. Las estrellas brillaban en el ____ con más luz que nunca.
   A. sol    B. velo    C. cielo

5. Las calles estaban completamente ____, pues nadie se atrevía a salir.
   A. tristes    B. sangrientas    C. vacías

6. Ya no ____ nada en el cine, la radio o la televisión. Todo estaba prohibido.
   A. recorrían    B. pasaban    C. retiraban

## Essential Instruction

1. Model pronunciation of the new vocabulary words and have students repeat. Clarify any unfamiliar words in the definitions.

2. You may want to have students complete **Actividades 38** and **39** in pairs.

3. After checking answers to **Actividad 40**, have students write a few more sentences with terms from p. 30 that were not used.

4. Before playing the audio in **Actividad 41**, remind students that they will hear some of the words from p. 30.

5. For **Actividad 41**, have students listen to the story with their eyes closed. Play it a second time, pausing to ask questions. Then play the rest of the audio and have students select their answers.

## 40 Cuentos de campamento  1.2

Complete las oraciones con la palabra del recuadro que corresponda según el contexto.

| | | |
|---|---|---|
| aparecían | velo | patria |
| muda | temblar | lagos |
| estrechos | viuda | estorbaban |
| llama | enturbiaba | recorrían |

1. La ____ de la hoguera en el campamento se veía desde lejos.

2. Tuvieron que abandonar su ____ y dejar atrás a sus seres queridos.

3. El viento, que anunciaba tormenta, hacía ____ las hojas de los árboles.

4. La tierra que caía de las montañas por la lluvia ____ el agua de los ____.

5. Los caminos se hacían más ____ por toda la nieve acumulada.

6. La ____ iba vestida de negro en memoria de su esposo quien murió en la guerra.

7. Oyeron historias de fantasmas y espíritus que se les ____ en medio de la noche.

8. Iba toda vestida de blanco, y un ____ transparente le cubría la sonrisa en el rostro.

9. Se quedó ____ de sorpresa al verlo y aunque quería, no le salían las palabras.

10. Las ramas caídas de los árboles ____ el paso de los hombres que ____ el bosque.

## 41 La muchacha de la película   1.2

Escuche el relato "La muchacha de la película". Después de oír la pregunta y las tres terminaciones posibles, indique la terminación más lógica. La pregunta y las terminaciones se leerán dos veces.

1. A. ...y ve dos películas.
   B. ...y ve la misma película.
   C. ...y ve muchas películas.

2. A. ...se queda en casa y hace otra cosa.
   B. ...busca en qué cine la pasan y va nuevamente a verla.
   C. ...lee el periódico o va a ver otra película.

3. A. ...por qué le gusta ver la misma película.
   B. ...por qué le gusta ir tanto al cine.
   C. ...por qué va cada día al cine.

4. A. ...un lago muy hermoso.
   B. ...un tren muy pequeño.
   C. ...una muchacha muy hermosa.

5. A. ...un tren muy largo pasa delante de ella.
   B. ...un tren para delante de ella.
   C. ...un muchacho en el tren ve a la muchacha.

6. A. ...la muchacha va a subir al tren.
   B. ...la muchacha va a nadar en el lago.
   C. ...el tren va a llegar un poco más tarde.

**Answers**

**40**
1. llama
2. patria
3. temblar
4. enturbiaba, lagos
5. estrechos
6. viuda
7. aparecían
8. velo
9. muda
10. estorbaban, recorrían

**41 Script**
Un muchacho de 14 años va cada día a ver la misma película. Si el cine ya no pasa la película, el chico busca en el periódico en qué cine la dan y se va nuevamente a verla. Después de varias semanas de ver la misma película y recorrer casi todos los cines de la ciudad, su padre, muy sorprendido, le pregunta al hijo por qué le gusta precisamente esa película:
"Sabes, papá," le responde el chico, "en la película hay una muchacha muy hermosa que desea nadar en un lago. En el momento que ella comienza a desvestirse para entrar en el lago, pasa un tren muy largo delante de ella y yo ya no puedo ver a la muchacha. Pero, papá... como marchan los trenes, yo estoy seguro que uno de estos días el tren se atrasa, pasa por el lago un poco más tarde y yo podré verla."

1. Un muchacho va todos los días al cine...
2. Si el cine deja de pasar la película, el muchacho...
3. Después de varias semanas el padre le pregunta al hijo...
4. El hijo le dice al padre que en la película hay...
5. Cuando la muchacha de la película va a desvestirse...
6. El muchacho está seguro que uno de estos días...

1. B; 2. B; 3. A; 4. C; 5. A; 6. C

## Learning Styles
### Visual Learners
Encourage these students to create a deck of flash cards, with the new vocabulary words on one side and on the other, have them draw or paste a picture to illustrate the term.

### Special Needs Students
**Auditory Impairment**
Provide students with the script of the story and the sentence starters in **Actividad 41**.

## Multiple Intelligences
### Verbal-Linguistic
Encourage these students to create analogies using the vocabulary words on p. 30. For example: **estrecho : ancho : : limpio : sangriento**; **lago : agua : : clavel : flor**.

### Reference Desk

Adjectives ending in **-ú** and **-í** are also common to both masculine and feminine genders. For example: **hindú**, **israelí**, **iraquí**.

### Communication

**Presentational: Cooperative Groups**
Divide the class into two groups. Write adjectives on note cards. As you hold up each card, call out **sinónimo** or **antónimo**. Each group must confer and come up with an appropriate synonym or antonym, and have one member go to the board and spell the word. The first student to write a correct word earns a point for his/her team.

### Expansion

Instruct students to write their name on a piece of paper. Then ask students to list as many adjectives as they can think of to describe themselves.

# Gramática

## Los adjetivos calificativos 🍀 1.2

Los adjetivos calificativos describen al sustantivo con el cual concuerdan en género y número.

| un camin**o** estrech**o** | unos camin**os** estrech**os** |
| una vel**a** encendid**a** | unas vel**as** encendid**as** |

### Género y número de los adjetivos calificativos

* Los adjetivos que terminan en **-o** son masculinos y femeninos los que terminan en **-a**. Los adjetivos que terminan en vocal forman el plural añadiendo **-s** a la forma singular.

| | Singular | Plural | | Singular | Plural |
|---|---|---|---|---|---|
| **Masculino** | mud**o** | mud**os** | **Masculino** | silencios**o** | silencios**os** |
| **Femenino** | mud**a** | mud**as** | **Femenino** | silencios**a** | silencios**as** |

* Los adjetivos que terminan en **-dor** y **-ol** y los adjetivos de nacionalidad que terminan en consonante forman el femenino añadiendo **-a** y el plural, añadiendo **-es**.

| | Singular | Plural | | Singular | Plural |
|---|---|---|---|---|---|
| **Masculino** | conversador | conversador**es** | **Masculino** | español | español**es** |
| **Femenino** | conversador**a** | conversador**as** | **Femenino** | español**a** | español**as** |

| | Singular | Plural | | Singular | Plural |
|---|---|---|---|---|---|
| **Masculino** | portugués | portugues**es** | **Masculino** | alemán | aleman**es** |
| **Femenino** | portugues**a** | portugues**as** | **Femenino** | aleman**a** | aleman**as** |

* Los adjetivos que terminan en **-e** y en consonantes como **-l**, **-n**, **-r** y **-z** tienen una sola forma para el masculino y el femenino y forman el plural añadiendo **-s** y **-es** respectivamente.

| | Singular | Plural |
|---|---|---|
| **Masculino** | importante | importante**s** |
| **Femenino** | importante | importante**s** |

| | Singular | Plural |
|---|---|---|
| **Masculino** | común | comun**es** |
| **Femenino** | común | comun**es** |

| | Singular | Plural |
|---|---|---|
| **Masculino** | difícil | difícil**es** |
| **Femenino** | difícil | difícil**es** |

| | Singular | Plural |
|---|---|---|
| **Masculino** | veloz | veloc**es** |
| **Femenino** | veloz | veloc**es** |

> **Un poco más**
>
> Al formar el plural de los adjetivos que terminan en **-z**, recuerde que la **-z** cambia a **-c** antes de **-e**.
>
> andalu**z**    andalu**ces**
>
> capa**z**    capa**ces**

### Essential Instruction

1. As you review the **Gramática** section **Los adjetivos calificativos**, ask students for additional examples of each type.
2. Test comprehension by providing nouns (e.g., **clase**); students have to say a correct adjective form (**una clase difícil**).
3. Use names of celebrities (e.g., **Javier Bardem**) to practice adjectives of nationality and other descriptive adjectives. Encourage a variety of responses: **Es español. Trabaja en películas estadounidenses. Es buen actor. Es un hombre rico.**

## Posición y uso de los adjetivos calificativos

Como norma general, los adjetivos calificativos se colocan después del sustantivo y sirven para expresar sus propiedades o características, ya sean concretas o abstractas, como se ve a continuación.

- Indican la nacionalidad y creencias políticas, sociales y religiosas de las personas.

  Hay muchos exilados **cubanos** en Estados Unidos que se oponen al gobierno **comunista** de Fidel Castro.

  Su santidad el papa Francisco, el mayor representante de la iglesia **católica**, manifestó su alegría por la reanudación de las relaciones **diplomáticas** entre EE. UU. y Cuba.

- Describen el tamaño, forma y color de algo o de alguien.

  Es una ciudad **pequeña** de estilo **colonial**, con calles **estrechas** de piedra y casas con techos de tejas **rojas** y paredes **blancas**.

  Es una mujer de pelo **negro**, estatura **mediana** y facciones **delicadas**.

- Describen nuevas tecnologías.

  Hoy en día, todo el mundo tiene teléfonos **celulares**, conexión **inalámbrica** y pantallas de **alta definición**.

- Algunos adjetivos como **bueno** o **malo**, que pueden ir antes o después del sustantivo, cambian de forma cuando se colocan antes.

  | | |
  |---|---|
  | Un hombre **bueno** | Un **buen** hombre |
  | Un hombre **malo** | Un **mal** hombre |

- Los adjetivos **peor** y **mejor** siempre se colocan antes del sustantivo.

  Este es el **peor** problema que tenemos y esa es la **mejor** solución.

## Adjetivos que cambian de significado

Los siguientes adjetivos cambian de significado según estén antes o después del sustantivo.

| Adjetivo | Antes del sustantivo | Después del sustantivo |
|---|---|---|
| gran(de) | un **gran** libro (great) | un libro **grande** (big) |
| pobre | el **pobre** hombre (unfortunate) | el hombre **pobre** (poor, penniless) |
| nuevo | una **nueva** casa (new, another) | una casa **nueva** (brand-new) |
| viejo | un **viejo** amigo (of long-standing) | un amigo **viejo** (old, elderly) |
| antiguo | un **antiguo** coche (former) | un coche **antiguo** (old, antique) |

### Un poco más

Los adjetivos calificativos se colocan antes del sustantivo cuando describen una cualidad inherente al sustantivo o cuando se quiere dar énfasis, lo cual ocurre especialmente en el lenguaje literario o poético:

La **blanca** nieve de las montañas resaltaba en la distancia.

"...con **largos** velos y un clavel en la mano, **silenciosa** Cuba, cual viuda me aparece."

---

### Reference Desk

1. Sometimes, more than one adjective will modify the same noun. In this case, one adjective can precede the noun and the other will follow it. For example: **un famoso músico talentoso**.
2. Other common adjectives that change meaning when placed before or after a noun are: **alto**, **cierto**, **diferente**, **puro**, **raro**, **rico**, and **único**.
3. **Ambos**, **mucho**, **otro**, and **poco** generally precede the noun they modify.

### Communication

**Presentational/Interpersonal: Cooperative Groups**
Have students work in groups to write a description of a famous person. They should use a wide variety of descriptive adjectives. Tell them not to include the person's name. Have groups take turns reading their descriptions for the class, who will guess the famous person.

### Game

**Teléfono**
Have students sit in a circle and play Telephone. Model the game by whispering a sentence using descriptive adjectives to a student. The whispered message gets passed around the circle until it reaches the last student, who says it aloud for everyone to hear.

---

### Differentiated Learning
**Accelerate**
Prepare sentences with adjectives that change meaning depending on their placement before or after the noun. Read the sentences for the class, who must supply the correct use of the adjective.

### Learning Styles
**Auditory/Visual Learners**
Show two photos to the class. Read a prepared description of one of the photos. Students must point to the correct photo based on what they hear.

**42**

1. independientes, bella, colonial
2. buena, céntrica, turística
3. básicos
4. climatizadas
5. doble

**43** *Las respuestas variarán.*

## 42 ¿Dónde piensan alojarse?  1.2

Imagine que Ud. va a ir de vacaciones a Cuba con un grupo de estudiantes y están buscando un lugar para hospedarse que no sea muy costoso. Complete las oraciones con las palabras del recuadro haciendo los cambios necesarios según sea necesario.

| | | |
|---|---|---|
| básico | independientes | bello |
| céntrico | colonial | bueno |
| doble | turístico | climatizado |

1. Casa Inés: Se ofrecen dos habitaciones ____ en una ____ casa de estilo ____ .
2. Casa Blanca: Esta es una ____ oportunidad de alojarse en una zona ____ y ____ de la capital.
3. Casa Carmen: Se ofrece habitación con baño y servicios ____ en el barrio de El Vedado.
4. Villa Babi: El calor de La Habana no le afectará en estas habitaciones ____ .
5. Casa Miriam: Aquí hay alojamiento para dos en una habitación ____ con muchas comodidades.

## ¡Comunicación!

## 43 Cualidades en común  Interpersonal Communication  1.1

Piense en cinco cualidades que Ud. busca en un(a) amigo/a y explique por qué son importantes. Ordénelas según su preferencia y, luego, compárelas con las de un(a) compañero/a de clase para ver qué tienen en común.

| | | | |
|---|---|---|---|
| alegre | fuerte | rico/a | cariñoso/a |
| extrovertido/a | religioso/a | cortés | guapo/a |
| romántico/a | honesto/a | sensible | mentiroso/a |
| inteligente | simpático/a | divertido/a | maduro/a |
| sincero/a | educado/a | paciente | tranquilo/a |

**MODELO**  Un amigo/a debe ser honesto/a y sincero/a. Para mí, no hay nada peor que las personas mentirosas.

## Essential Instruction

1. Complete the first sentence in **Actividad 42** as a class. Point out that some adjectives precede the noun, and that students need to make sure the adjectives agree in number and gender with the nouns.

2. Introduce **Actividad 43** by reading through the list of adjectives. Ask students to raise their hand if they hear a word they would use to describe themselves. Then ask if they seek friends who are similar or different.

3. Introduce the **Gramática** section by describing your possessions and those of your students.

# *Gramática*

## ¡Comunicación!

**44** **¿Quién es?**  Interpersonal Communication  **1.1**

Con un(a) compañero/a piensen en cuatro cualidades de las personas famosas y pónganse de acuerdo en las que aplican a cada una de las siguientes personas. Luego, piensen individualmente en otra persona famosa y descríbansela a su compañero/a para que adivine quién es.

*Sofía Vergara*

*Gael García Bernal*

1. Shakira
2. Gael García Bernal

3. Narciso Rodríguez
4. Sofía Vergara

## Los adjetivos posesivos  1.2

Los adjetivos posesivos indican pertenencia, es decir, a quién o quiénes pertenece algo.

| Formas de los adjetivos posesivos | | | |
|---|---|---|---|
| **Singular** | | **Plural** | |
| mi | nuestro/a | mis | nuestros/as |
| tu | vuestro/a | tus | vuestros/as |
| su | su | sus | sus |

- Los adjetivos posesivos concuerdan en número con los sustantivos a los que modifican. Solo la primera y la segunda persona del plural tienen género masculino y femenino.

  Con **nuestra** ambición y **tus** conocimientos, **nuestra** labor tendrá éxito.

*Unidad 1* | treinta y cinco **35**

---

## Special Needs Students
**Dyslexia/Linguistically Challenged/AD(H)D**
Use scaffolding to help students with **Actividad 42**. First, read through the sentences together. Then work with students to underline the nouns in each one. Next have them select a logical adjective for each blank. Finally, have students make sure each adjective agrees in number and gender with the noun it modifies.

## Multiple Intelligences
**Mathematical-Logical**
Survey the class for responses to **Actividad 43**. Ask students to quantify the results and create a graphic representation of the class's preferences.

---

**Answers**

**44** *Las respuestas variarán.*

### Reference Desk

Shakira is a Colombian pop singer with Lebanese roots. She sings in Spanish and English. Gael García Bernal is a Mexican actor who has made many Hollywood movies. Narciso Rodríguez is a Cuban-American fashion designer. Sofía Vergara is a Colombian actress best known in the United States for her role on the TV show *Modern Family*.

### Connections

**Language Arts**
Search online for examples of "diamond" poems, or write your own example on the board. Have students write their own seven-line diamond poems using descriptive adjectives. You may want to assign a topic, such as describing themselves, or have students choose.

### Expansion

Prepare a brief biography for each person listed in **Actividad 44**; use as many descriptive adjectives as possible. Post photos of the four celebrities and assign each picture a number. Read aloud the biographies in random order and have the class match each biography to the correct person.

## Reference Desk

1. Remind students that the number and gender of possessive adjectives must match what is possessed, *not* the possessor. For example: **Nuestras fotos están en la sala. Tus padres trabajan, ¿no?**

2. After presenting **Gramática**, borrow items from students. Walk around the room and ask students if this is their item, e.g., **¿Es tu mochila?** When you find the owner of each item, borrow the items again and ask another student, **¿De quién es esta mochila?**

## TPR

Use possessive adjectives and the **tú** form of commands to ask students to do various tasks. For example: **Dame tu cuaderno. Por favor, tráeme su lápiz.**

---

- Si se necesita aclarar el significado del adjetivo posesivo **su** o **sus**, se usa el artículo definido y una frase preposicional.

| | |
|---|---|
| el/la... de Ud./Uds. | los/las... de Ud./Uds. |
| el/la... de él/ellos | los/las... de él/ellos |
| el/la... de ella/ellas | los/las... de ella/ellas |

### Un poco más

Para contestar la pregunta, "¿Es la casa de Juan o de los García?" indicando que la casa es de los García, se diría: "Es la casa de ellos."

Contestar simplemente: "Es su casa" no es suficiente, porque "su casa" puede significar la casa de él, de ella, de Ud., de ellos, de ellas y de Uds.

## ¡Comunicación!

### 45 ¡Con carácter devolutivo, por favor! 👥 Interpersonal Communication  1.1

Todos tenemos amigos que nunca devuelven las cosas que piden prestadas: ropa, bolígrafos, cosméticos, DVDs y más. De ahí el dicho: "¡Con carácter devolutivo!" Piense en ejemplos de esta situación y túrnese con un(a) compañero/a para comentarlos.

MODELO
A: Imagínate, le presté mi... y mis... a un amigo hace más de un mes y no me los ha devuelto. Nunca le he vuelto a prestar nada.

B: No lo puedo creer. Yo le presté mi... y mis... a una amiga y ella... Por eso decidí...

### 46 Quisiera saber... 👥 Interpersonal/Presentational Communication  1.1, 1.3

Escriba una pregunta sobre cada uno de los temas que siguen y, luego, túrnese con un(a) compañero/a para hacerse las preguntas y responderlas. Después, resuman la información y preséntela a la clase.

MODELO
¿Cuál es tu país de origen?
Mi país de origen es...
Voy a hablarles de mi compañero(a). Su país de origen es... y sus padres... etc.

- País de origen
- Casa de sus padres
- Sus clases

- El colegio (clases / tecnología / deportes / compañeros)
- El tiempo libre / pasatiempos
- ¿...?

### 47 Intercambio Interpersonal/Presentational Communication 1.3

Un estudiante cubano va a pasar un mes con Ud. y su familia en un programa de intercambio estudiantil. Escríbale una carta en la que le describe a su familia, su casa, sus costumbres. Hágale cuatro preguntas sobre su vida en Cuba.

## Essential Instruction

1. To practice **su/sus**, you can follow up **Actividad 45** by placing students in new pairs; they report what their first partner said.

2. For **Actividad 46**, you may want to generate a list of possible vocabulary on the board for pairs to use in their conversations.

3. Before beginning **Actividad 47**, review the basics of writing a letter in Spanish.

4. As you go through **Adjetivos y pronombres demostrativos**, give concrete examples by making statements about objects in your classroom.

# Gramática

## Adjetivos y pronombres demostrativos  1.2

Las palabras **este**, **ese** y **aquel** y sus respectivos femeninos y plurales funcionan como adjetivos demostrativos cuando acompañan al sustantivo que modifican. Funcionan como pronombres cuando hacen el papel del nombre.

**Como adjetivo demostrativo:**
¿Te gusta **este** vestido?
*Do you like **this** dress?*

**Como pronombre demostrativo:**
Sí, pero prefiero **aquel** que está más allá.
*Yes, but I prefer **that one** that is over there.*

| **Formas de los adjetivos y pronombres demostrativos** | | |
|---|---|---|
| | **Singular** | **Plural** |
| **Masculino** | este ese aquel | estos esos aquellos |
| **Femenino** | esta esa aquella | estas esas aquellas |

### Usos de los adjetivos demostrativos

Los adjetivos demostrativos indican la distancia de las personas y las cosas, con relación a la persona que habla. Los adjetivos demostrativos concuerdan en género y número con el sustantivo al que acompañan.

- Use **este** (*this*) para referirse a algo que se encuentra cerca de la persona que habla.

  Compré **este** disco compacto de los Orishas en El Rincón Records en Miami.

- Use **ese** (*that*) para referirse a algo que se encuentra cerca de la persona con quien se habla.

  **Ese** DVD que tienes es el último de Celia Cruz, ¿no?

- Use **aquel** (*that over there*) para referirse a algo que se encuentra lejos de las personas que hablan.

  En **aquella** tienda al otro lado de la calle se puede comprar toda clase de música latina.

### Usos de los pronombres demostrativos

Los pronombres demostrativos hacen el papel del nombre y concuerdan con él en género y número. También se usan para indicar la distancia de las personas o las cosas con relación a la persona que habla, pero sin nombrarlas, para evitar repetición.

—¿Qué flores vas a comprar?

—**Estas** (flores) me gustan mucho, pero voy a comprar **esas** (flores), que son más baratas.

La casa donde viven mis abuelos no es **esta** (casa), es **aquella** (casa).

### Un poco más

Los pronombres demostrativos neutros se refieren a algo no identificado o a una idea abstracta.

¿Qué es **esto**?

**Eso** sí que es un problema serio.

**Aquello** que te dije ya no tiene importancia.

**48**
1. esta; 2. este; 3. Eso; 4. estos;
5. estas; 6. esos; 7. Esa; 8. esto;
9. Ese/Aquel; 10. aquel

**49**
1. esta (noche), adjetivo
2. este (plato), adjetivo
3. Eso, pronombre
4. estos (fríjoles), adjetivo
5. estas (tajadas), adjetivo
6. esos (plátanos), adjetivo
7. Esa (blusa), adjetivo
8. esto, pronombre
9. Ese/Aquel (chico), adjetivo
10. aquel, pronombre

## Reference Desk

Before beginning **Actividad 48**, review the neuter demonstrative pronouns with students. These pronouns do not refer to a specific noun and do not agree in gender and number with anything.

---

**48 ¡No lo puedo creer!**  **1.2**

Complete la conversación entre Marleni y Ernesto con las palabras del recuadro que correspondan según el contexto.

| esta | este | ese | aquel | esto |
|---|---|---|---|---|
| estos | esos | esa | estas | eso |

**Marleni:** —¡Qué suerte! El menú de **(1)** noche está fabuloso. ¿Qué te gustaría comer?

**Ernesto:** —No sé. ¿Qué me recomiendas?

**Marleni:** —Pues, **(2)** plato de arroz con mariscos es fantástico. Es una de las especialidades de la casa.

**Ernesto:** —¿ **(3)** es lo que vas a pedir tú?

**Marleni:** —No, creo que voy a pedir **(4)** fríjoles negros y **(5)** tajadas de plátano maduro. ¿Has comido tajadas de plátano alguna vez?

**Ernesto:** —Sí, y **(6)** plátanos se ven deliciosos. Creo que voy a pedir lo mismo que tú.

**Marleni:** —¡Listo! Llamemos al camarero.

**Ernesto:** —A propósito, Marlen, estás muy bonita esta noche. **(7)** blusa que llevas puesta te queda muy bien.

**Marleni:** —¿Qué es **(8)** ? ¿Un cumplido?

**Ernesto:** —No es un cumplido. ¿No te has dado cuenta? **(9)** chico que está cerca de la puerta no deja de mirarte. Tiene muy buen gusto. ¡Igual que yo!

**Marleni:** —No me sorprende, pero en realidad, no dejan de mirarme a mí sino a ti.

**Ernesto:** —¿Dejan?

**Marleni:** —Sí, ese chico y **(10)** que está allá son mis hermanos. Por eso es que no te quitan los ojos de encima.

**Ernesto:** —¿De veras? ¡No lo puedo creer!

---

**49 ¿Adjetivo o pronombre?**  **1.2, 1.3**

Vuelva a leer la actividad anterior y analice sus respuestas en el contexto de cada oración. Luego, diga qué función (adjetivo o pronombre demostrativo) desempeña cada palabra en ese contexto. Siga el modelo como guía y escriba sus respuestas en una hoja aparte.

MODELO   El menú de **(1)** noche está fabuloso.

El menú de **esta** noche está fabuloso.

**"Esta" funciona como adjetivo, porque aparece junto al sustantivo que está modificando (noche).**

## Essential Instruction

1. Check answers to **Actividad 48** by having a pair of students come to the front of the classroom and role-play the conversation. Use props to give perspective for *here/there/over there.*

2. You may want to have students do **Actividad 49** in pairs.

3. As you go through **Sobre el autor** with the class, pause to ask comprehension questions.

4. Have students complete **Antes de leer** in pairs.

5. Read the **Estrategia** and give examples of metaphors, in English and then in Spanish.

# Lectura literaria

## Dos patrias   **1.2, 2.2, 3.1, 3.2**
### de *José Martí*

### Sobre el autor

José Martí, el poeta cubano por excelencia, nació en la Habana en 1853. Hijo de padres españoles, dedicó su vida entera y su obra a la lucha por la independencia de Cuba de España, primero, y de las políticas imperialistas estadounidenses. Fue el precursor del modernismo en Hispanoamérica. Su dedicación a las letras se hace evidente en sus colecciones de poemas entre las que se destacan *Versos sencillos* (1891) y *Versos libres* (1892). A causa de su actividad política fue encarcelado y deportado a España, donde residió y estudió por un tiempo. Finalmente se estableció en Nueva York, que solo abandonó en 1895 para volver a luchar a Cuba, donde encontró la muerte.

*José Martí*

### Antes de leer  **1.3**

"Dos patrias" es el reflejo del sufrimiento de Martí como cubano en una Cuba que no es libre. El concepto de patria, teniendo en cuenta que vivió exiliado la mayor parte de su vida, es especialmente doloroso en este poema.

¿Cómo cree que se siente alguien que se ha visto obligado a abandonar su país?

### Estrategia  **3.1**

**Recursos estilísticos**

El lenguaje metafórico es un recurso estilístico que usan los escritores para dar a las palabras una dimensión de significado que va más allá del lenguaje literal.

### 50 Practique la estrategia  **1.3, 3.1**

En el primer verso del poema, Martí afirma tener dos patrias. Una es literal, Cuba, y la segunda es metafórica, la noche. ¿Qué cree que simboliza la noche? Busque otros tres ejemplos de lenguaje metafórico en el poema y explique su significado, como se ve a continuación.

| Lenguaje metáforico | Significado |
|---|---|
| Dos patrias tengo yo: Cuba y la noche. | Puede simbolizar la vida del poeta en el destierro. |
| | |
| | |
| | |

**Answers**

**51**
1. Cuba
2. un clavel rojo
3. Quiere decir que la noche es buena para morir o para irse al exilio.
4. La llama roja de la vela que flamea es como la bandera que invita a batallar.

**52** *Respuesta posible:*
Puede referirse al llamado a luchar; se abren las ventanas para que entre la luz, la libertad.

**Después de leer**
*Las respuestas variarán.*

### Reference Desk

1. While footnote glosses are provided, encourage students to determine meaning from context.
2. Point out the numbers in the margin and ask a volunteer to explain how to use them.
3. Have students summarize their ideas from **Después de leer** in a Flipgrid post.

### Connections

**Language Arts**
After completing **Después de leer**, work as a class to review the metaphors in the poem and analyze them. Then have students identify a few feelings and write a few metaphors that capture those feelings. Encourage creativity.

---

# Dos patrias   1.2, 3.1, 3.2
### de *José Martí*

**51 Comprensión** 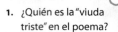 **1.2**

1. ¿Quién es la "viuda triste" en el poema?

2. ¿Con qué imagen representa la idea de la sangre roja de los patriotas que mueren por Cuba?

3. ¿Qué quiere decir: "La noche es buena para decir adiós"?

4. ¿Qué comparación hace Martí entre "la llama de la vela" y "la bandera"?

**52 Analice**  **1.3, 3.2**

¿A qué cree que se refiere el poeta cuando dice: "las ventanas abro, ya estrecho en mí" en los versos 16–17? Explique su respuesta.

Dos patrias tengo yo: Cuba y la noche.
¿O son una las dos? No bien retira
su majestad el sol[1], con largos velos
y un clavel en la mano, silenciosa
5  Cuba cual[2] viuda triste me aparece.
¡Yo sé cuál es ese clavel sangriento
que en la mano le tiembla! Está vacío
mi pecho, destrozado está y vacío
en donde estaba el corazón. Ya es hora
10  de empezar a morir. La noche es buena
para decir adiós. La luz estorba[3]
y la palabra humana. El universo
habla mejor que el hombre.
          Cual bandera
15  que invita a batallar, la llama roja
de la vela flamea. Las ventanas
abro, ya estrecho en mí[4]. Muda, rompiendo
las hojas del clavel, como una nube
que enturbia[5] el cielo, Cuba, viuda, pasa...

[1] as soon as the sun has withdrawn its majesty (has just set)   [2] like   [3] hinders
[4] too narrow (to contain myself)   [5] obscures

*"...Está vacío mi pecho, destrozado ..."*

**Después de leer**  **1.1, 1.3, 3.1, 3.2**

En "Dos patrias" el poeta plantea un dilema: por una parte Cuba reclama la presencia del poeta en la lucha; por otra, la noche se apodera de su espíritu y se deja morir. ¿Cómo le parece que se desarrolla esta idea en el poema? Intercambie sus opiniones con las de un(a) compañero/a y, luego, compárenlas con las del resto de la clase.

**Essential Instruction**

1. Have students read the title and guess what the poem is about.
2. Before they read, have students scan for cognates and words they learned in **Vocabulario 3**. Explain any unfamiliar vocabulary that is not in the glosses.
3. Play the recording, pausing for students to answer the during-reading questions.
4. Read through the **Proyectos** and brainstorm ideas for the tasks. If time is limited, you may want to let students pick a project that appeals most to them.

# Para concluir

## Proyectos

**?** Pregunta clave

¿Cómo se refleja la idiosincrasia de una nación en el trato de su gente?

### A ¡Manos a la obra! 1.1, 1.3, 2.2, 3.1, 5.1

Trabaje con un compañero. Imagine que Ud. es especialista en música cubana y su compañero es periodista y tiene un programa de radio. Lo invita a hablar sobre la historia del dúo Los Compadres, formado por los amigos Francisco Repilado, conocido como "Compay Segundo", y Lorenzo Hierrezuelo.

Busquen información sobre este dúo en la internet, por ejemplo, cuándo se formó, qué tipo de música tocaban, cuántos discos hicieron juntos, alguna anécdota sobre su amistad, etc.

Algunos datos interesantes que pueden mencionar son:

- El nombre del dúo se debe a la forma tradicional de saludarse los vecinos en las zonas rurales de Cuba.
- Repilado recibe el apodo "Compay" porque es la forma de llamar a los hombres en la región oriental de Cuba y "Segundo" porque hacía la segunda voz en el dúo.

Preparen un diálogo de la entrevista con las preguntas que hace el periodista y las respuestas que da el especialista. Pueden grabar su entrevista e incluir algunas canciones de Los Compadres para presentarla al resto de la clase.

### B En resumen Conéctese: el lenguaje 1.3, 2.1, 3.2

La forma de ser y de pensar de los cubanos se refleja en su forma de tratar a los demás ya sean conocidos o desconocidos, familiares, amigos cercanos o amigos íntimos. Piense en las diferentes expresiones que usan los cubanos para dirigirse o referirse a los demás y complete la tabla con la información, como se ve a continuación.

| Expresiones | Usos | Significado o ejemplos |
|---|---|---|
| Acere, ¿qué volá? | Se usa para saludarse entre amigos. | Es lo mismo que decir: "Hola amigo, ¿cómo estás?" |
| | | |
| | | |
| | | |
| | | |

## Reference Desk

1. **Para concluir** provides projects that review the entire unit.
2. Point out the **Pregunta clave**. Explain that completing the **Para concluir** tasks allows them to demonstrate that they can now fully answer this question.
3. In **¡Manos a la obra!** students work in groups or pairs to use what they have learned in a creative way.
4. In **En resumen**, which directly ties in the **Pregunta clave**, students summarize the unit's cultural topics and, if appropriate, information from the **Lectura informativa** and the authentic audio in the **Escritura** section.
5. Ask students to consider the **Pregunta clave** in relation to their own culture.

## Differentiated Learning
### Heritage Learners
Ask heritage learners to interview a family member or friend about any nostalgia or homesickness they might feel for their country of birth. They can compare and contrast this with the feelings expressed in "**Dos patrias**."

## Special Needs Students
### All Categories
Allow for adaptations of the tasks in **Para concluir** depending on student needs. For example, students with speech impairments can submit art or written projects. Students with visual impairments can present audio recordings, etc. Those with social anxiety can complete their tasks through Avenue, etc.

**Answers**

**C** *Los blogs variarán.*

**D** *Los informes variarán.*

**E**

1960: Fidel Castro nacionaliza empresas estadounidenses
1961: Desembarco en Bahía de Cochinos
1962: Kennedy ordena el bloqueo
1980: Crisis migratoria con EE. UU.

*Las conversaciones variarán.*

### Reference Desk

1. In **¡A escribir!** students use the unit vocabulary and grammar to complete a creative writing assignment.
2. The culminating activity or activities in **Para concluir** connect to another content area. Students who are strong in the other content area may prefer these projects.
3. You could create an Avenue task for students to present their findings from **Actividad D**.

### Expansion

Display students' projects in the classroom. Invite other Spanish classes, teachers, and parents to view the projects.

---

**C** **¡A escribir!**  **1.3, 2.1, 3.2, 5.2**

Imagine que Ud. acaba de regresar de La Habana y decide contar en su blog su experiencia en la ciudad. Escriba una entrada sobre la forma de ser de los cubanos, en la que relate las principales características de su idiosincracia. Mencione detalles concretos sobre el trato que recibió y lo que haya observado sobre cómo se relacionan entre ellos. No olvide incluir ejemplos de expresiones de saludo, formas de llamarse entre sí y regionalismos que le hayan parecido interesantes.

**Para escribir más**

apoyo mutuo
carácter alegre
colaboración
comunicativo/a
con chispa
conversador(a)
extrovertido/a
generosidad
hospitalario/a
lealtad

**D** **Una encuesta**  **1.1, 1.3, 3.1**

Repase los puntos principales del discurso de Obama sobre su propuesta de reanudar (*resume*) las relaciones entre Cuba y Estados Unidos. Prepare una encuesta de cuatro preguntas para averiguar la opinión de sus compañeros sobre el tema. Haga preguntas que se puedan responder con "sí" o "no", o bien con "de acuerdo" y "en desacuerdo". Luego, presente un informe de los resultados e incluya gráficas para ilustrarlos.

**REANUDACIÓN DE LAS RELACIONES EE. UU.-CUBA**
¿Cree que será beneficiosa para los cubanos?

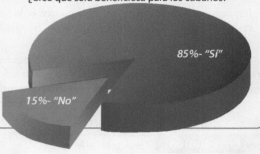

85%- "Sí"
15%- "No"

**E** **Más de cincuenta años**  **Conéctese: la historia** **1.1, 1.3, 2.2, 3.1, 4.2, 5.2**

La importancia histórica de la decisión del presidente Obama de reanudar las relaciones con Cuba queda clara si analizamos la historia del vínculo entre ambos países desde 1959 en adelante. Investigue los sucesos principales de la relación cubano-estadounidense a partir de la Revolución. Complete la línea de tiempo con los datos que faltan y luego compare y comente los sucesos con un compañero.

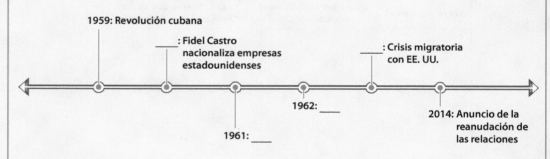

1959: Revolución cubana

____: Fidel Castro nacionaliza empresas estadounidenses

____: Crisis migratoria con EE. UU.

1962: ____

1961: ____

2014: Anuncio de la reanudación de las relaciones

---

### Essential Instruction

1. Begin **Actividad C** by reading through the list. Make sure students are comfortable using these words. Tell students they can also use their charts from **Actividad B** on p. 41 in preparing their writing.
2. For **Actividad D**, tell students they can use a variety of graphic organizers to illustrate their results.
3. For the **Vocabulario de la Unidad 1**, ask students to place the words into categories such as nouns, verbs, greetings, etc.

# Vocabulario de la Unidad 1  1.2

**a causa de (por)** because of
**¿A qué te dedicas?** What do you do for a living?
**Adelante.** Come in.
**Adiós.** Good-bye.
**aparecer** to appear
**atrasarse** to be late
**ayudar** to help
la **bandera** flag
**batallar** to fight
**Bienvenidos.** Welcome.
**Bueno, para empezar...** Well, to begin with…
**casi todos** almost all
el **cielo** sky
el **cine** the movie theater
**Claro que sí./Cómo no./Desde luego.** Of course.
el **clavel** carnation
**¿Cómo has estado?/¿Cómo te ha ido?** How have you been?
**¿Cómo se dice...?** How do you say…?
**¿Cómo te llamas?** What is your name?
**¡Con permiso!** Excuse me! (when passing through a crowd)
**¿Cuál es tu apellido?** What is your last name?
**¿Cuánto hace que...?** How long ago…?
la **cuestión** issue, matter, question
**¡Cuídate!** Take care!
**De acuerdo** OK
**De nada./No hay de qué.** You're welcome.
**¿De veras?** Really?
**Dígame.** Tell me.
**Disculpe./Perdone.** Excuse me.
**El gusto es mío.** The pleasure is mine.
**¿En qué puedo servirle?** How can I help you?
**¡Encantado/a!** Pleased to meet you!
**Entre./Pase.** Come in.
**enturbiar** to obscure
**Es un placer...** It is a pleasure…
**Está en su casa.** Make yourself at home.
**estorbar** to hinder
**estrecho/a** narrow

**estupendo/a** wonderful
**explicar** to explain
**fantástico/a** fantastic
el **favor** favor
**flamear** to blaze
**Fue muy grato...** It was a pleasure…
**hablar** to speak
**hacer una pregunta** to ask (pose) a question
**Hasta la vista.** So long.
**Hasta luego.** See you later.
**Hasta pronto.** See you soon.
**Igualmente.** Same here.
el **lago** lake
la **llama** flame
**Lo siento (mucho).** I am (very) sorry.
**magnífico/a** magnificent
**Me gustaría + inf.** I would like to…
**Me llamo... ¿y tú?** My name is… and yours?
**Mil gracias./Un millón de gracias.** Thank you very much.
**Muchísimas gracias por su amabilidad.** Thanks a lot for your kindness.
**Mucho gusto.** Nice to meet you.
**mudo/a** mute
**Ni hablar.** No way.
**No lo puedo creer.** I can't believe it.
**No me digas.** You don't say.
**No mucho.** Not much.
**No sabes cuánto te agradezco.** You don't know how much I appreciate it.
**Nos vemos.** See you.
**pasar (una película, un programa)** to show (a movie, a program)
la **patria** fatherland
**pedir** to ask for (something)
**Permítame + inf.** Allow me to…
**Pero claro.** Of course.
**¿Podría + inf.?** Could I?
**Por favor.** Please.
**¿Por qué...?** Why…?
**Porque...** Because…
la **pregunta** question
**preguntar por** to ask for (someone)

**preguntar** to ask (a question)
**preguntarse** to wonder
**presentar a** to introduce
**¿Puedes + inf.?** Can you…?
**Qué alegría verte.** How nice to see you.
**¡Qué bien!** Great!
**Qué buena (mala) suerte.** What good (bad) luck.
**¿Qué hay de nuevo?/¿Qué me cuentas?** What's new?
**¡Qué lástima!/¡Qué pena!** What a pity!
**¿Qué opinas de...?** What is your opinion about…?
**¿Qué quiere decir...?** What does…mean?
**¿Qué se te ofrece?** What can I do for you?
**Qué sorpresa...** What a surprise…
**¿Qué tal?** How are you?
**¿Qué te parece si...?** What do you think about…?
**¡Qué va!** No way!
**Quisiera + inf.** May I…?
**recorrer** to go over
**retirar(se)** to withdraw
**saber** to know (information)
**sangriento/a** bloody
**sentarse** to sit down
**silencioso/a** silent
**¡Súper!** Super!
**Tanto gusto en conocerlo/a.** Pleased to meet you.
**temblar** to tremble
**tener un momento** to have a minute
**Todo igual./Todo lo mismo.** Nothing new.
**tomar asiento** to take a seat
**vacío/a** empty
**Vale.** OK.
la **vela** candle
el **velo** veil
la **viuda** widow
**¡Ya era hora!** It is about time!

## RESOURCES

 **T**    Unidad 1

## Reference Desk

1. The **Vocabulario de la Unidad** contains all of the active vocabulary from the unit. Encourage students to use this reference list, since it summarizes the words and expressions that they need to know for the unit test and for future units.

2. Point out that this vocabulary list is in alphabetical order; definite articles appear in the margin of each column.

3. It is a good idea to have Spanish dictionaries available in the classroom, especially if online resources are not always accessible.

## Expansion

Have students work in pairs to determine categories for the words on p. 43. Then have students write lists of the words within these categories.

---

## Differentiated Learning
### Decelerate
Provide students with a matching worksheet with Spanish words in one column and English words in the other.

### Heritage Learners
Ask heritage learners to write down as many synonyms as possible for the words on p. 43.

## Multiple Intelligences
### Verbal-Linguistic
Ask pairs of students to write four conversations using as much of the vocabulary as they can. You may want to set a time limit.

1. This unit's cultural context is Spain, whose area is about the size of Texas. This relatively small country is divided into **17 comunidades autónomas**, which are culturally and linguistically diverse.

2. Tourism forms a major part of Spain's economy. Every year, around 60 million people visit the country, many more than inhabit it (47 million).

3. **Barajas** was built in 1927, and it is Spain's busiest airport, with 40 million people passing through its terminals annually. Terminal 4's award-winning design was conceived by architects Antonio Lamela of Spain and Richard Rogers of the United Kingdom, and built by the Spanish company Ferrovial. It covers an area of 760,000 square meters, making it one of the world's largest terminals.

4. Remind students with eBook access they can click on the red country on p. 45 to link directly to Wikipedia.

## Culture

**Products/Practices: Activity**
Provide each student with a sticky note. Tell students to write one piece of information they know about Spain. Have students bring the note to the board. Group the notes in categories and, as a class, summarize students' background knowledge about the country.

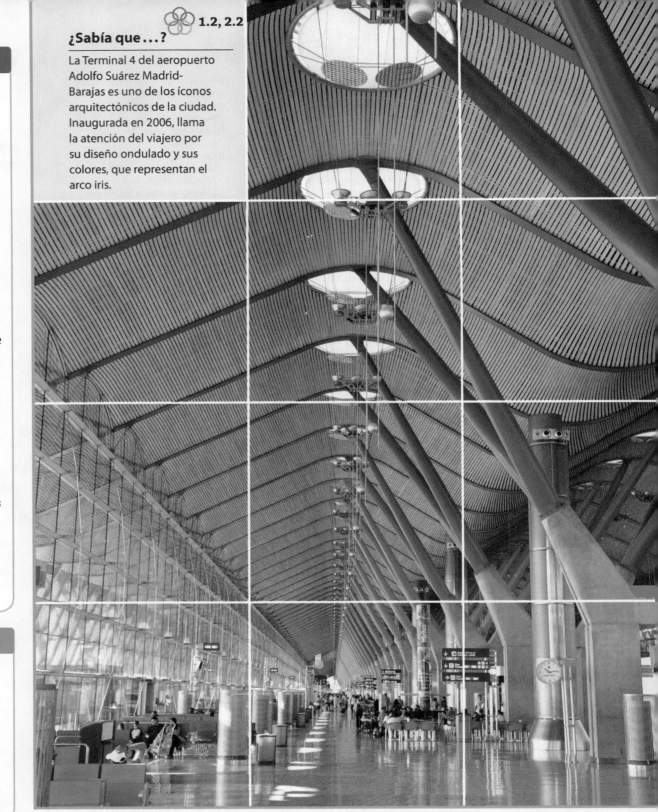

**1.2, 2.2**

**¿Sabía que...?**

La Terminal 4 del aeropuerto Adolfo Suárez Madrid-Barajas es uno de los íconos arquitectónicos de la ciudad. Inaugurada en 2006, llama la atención del viajero por su diseño ondulado y sus colores, que representan el arco iris.

## Essential Instruction

1. Begin with a discussion of the **Pregunta clave**. Ask students for examples of things people learn when traveling abroad. Have them draw on personal experience, if possible.

2. Point out Spain on the map. Ask students to share what they know about the country.

3. Draw attention to the culture photo and question. Encourage students to watch for the photo and the answer later in the unit.

4. Point out the QR code, the video question, and the screen shot from "**De tapas.**" Encourage students to watch the video as many times as they like.

5. Have students read and ask questions about **Mis metas**.

# Unidad

# 2

# El atractivo de viajar

Escanee el código QR para mirar el video "De tapas".

Conocer las costumbres típicas de otros países es uno de los atractivos de viajar. ¿En qué consiste la costumbre española de "ir de tapas" o "tapear"? Explique en detalle su respuesta.

### Pregunta clave

**?**

¿Qué se aprende cuando se viaja al extranjero?

España

¿De quién es esta famosa obra de arte y cómo se llama?

## Mis metas

### En esta unidad:

▶ Usaré expresiones relacionadas con viajes dentro y fuera del país.

▶ Usaré los pronombres personales y los verbos regulares e irregulares en el presente de indicativo.

▶ Me familiarizaré con la riqueza artística, natural e histórica de España.

▶ Distinguiré el significado de palabras y frases según el contexto.

▶ Usaré correctamente el futuro de los verbos regulares e irregulares.

▶ Leeré un artículo sobre la celebración del *Año del Quijote* en España y los motivos de esta celebración.

▶ Publicaré mi opinión sobre "Gigantes", el logotipo del Quijote 2015, en una red social.

▶ Crearé un anuncio publicitario para promocionar el turismo en diferentes regiones de España.

▶ Desarrollaré nuevas destrezas de vocabulario.

▶ Usaré los comparativos y las diferentes formas del superlativo en español.

▶ Leeré el poema "He andado muchos caminos" del español Antonio Machado.

cuarenta y cinco **45**

## Differentiated Learning
### Heritage Learners
Ask heritage learners to share what they know about an airport in their family's country of origin. If possible, have them compare and contrast the airport with one in this country, or with Barajas in Madrid.

## Multiple Intelligences
### Verbal-Linguistic
Review and preview the unit vocabulary and grammar by asking these questions: **¿Te gusta viajar? ¿Adónde fuiste en tu último viaje? En tu opinión, ¿cuál es la mejor forma de viajar? ¿Son más cómodos los aviones que los trenes?**

# Vocabulario 1

## ¡Nos vamos de viaje!  1.2

### En el aeropuerto

Acuérdese de estas recomendaciones para viajeros, sobre todo si es la primera vez que viaja al extranjero.

- Confirme sus reservaciones antes del viaje y recuerde que debe estar en el aeropuerto con tres horas de anticipación para vuelos internacionales y dos para vuelos nacionales.
- Diríjase al mostrador de la línea aérea para facturar su equipaje. Tome precauciones si no quiere pagar por exceso de equipaje.
- Quítese cualquier artículo personal de metal antes de pasar por el detector de metales en el control de seguridad.
- Presente su visa, pasaporte y pasajes en emigración y, luego, diríjase a la sala de espera y manténgase allí hasta el momento de abordar el avión.

### En la sala de espera

Última llamada para los pasajeros del vuelo 357 de Iberia, directo a la ciudad de Madrid. El avión está preparándose para el despegue.

### En el avión

Siga las indicaciones de la tripulación a todo momento. En caso de turbulencia o de aterrizaje forzoso, mantenga la calma (no van a estrellarse) y haga lo que indique el (la) piloto o el (la) auxiliar de vuelo.

¿Cambiamos de asiento? Pedí uno de ventanilla o de pasillo, pero ya no había.

Tengan la amabilidad de apagar sus computadoras. Ya estamos próximos a despegar.

Abróchate el cinturón de seguridad que ya vamos a aterrizar.

### Essential Instruction

1. Before playing the audio, have students look at the vocabulary on pp. 46–47 and pick out cognates. They can work in pairs and practice pronouncing these words.

2. Play the audio for **¡Nos vamos de viaje!** Then have pairs of students take turns reading aloud the text. Encourage them to use proper intonation, and for the "announcements," an official-sounding tone.

3. Personalize the vocabulary presentation by discussing transportation options in your region.

## Al bajarse del avión

- Después de pasar por inmigración, recoja su equipaje y pase por la inspección de aduana.
- Si está haciendo escala y pierde su vuelo de conexión, vaya al mostrador de la línea aérea donde lo/la ayudarán.
- Si lo necesita, generalmente hay una oficina de cambio (de moneda) en la planta baja del aeropuerto.

El inspector revisará sus maletas y maletín de mano para ver que no lleve contrabando.

Consulte el monitor de salidas y llegadas de vuelos para saber a qué hora sale su vuelo de conexión.

## En el hotel

Al llegar al hotel, diríjase a la recepción para inscribirse y pedir la llave de su habitación. Recuerde que el botones puede ayudarle a subir o bajar su equipaje. Si tiene algún problema, no dude en hablar con el gerente del hotel.

¿Podría decirme si la Srta. Amelia Cárdenas aparece en su lista de huéspedes?

Claro que sí. Un momento, por favor.

¿Te acordaste de darle una propina?

¡Por supuesto!

## Para conversar

**P**ara hacer planes de turismo:

Queremos conocer España y nos gustaría hacer unas reservaciones. ¿Puede ayudarnos?

¿Les interesa viajar en coche, en barco, o en ferrocarril?

¿Desean viajar en primera clase o clase turística?

¿Cuánto cuesta un pasaje de ida y vuelta a...?

¿Tienen servicio de coche cama y coche comedor en este tren?

¿Qué hacemos si tenemos que cancelar o posponer el viaje?

¿A qué hora sale/llega...?

El tren sale del andén número...

¡Pasajeros al tren!

*Unidad 2* | cuarenta y siete **47**

## RESOURCES

 Flipgrid

 Para conversar

## Reference Desk

1. Ask questions about travel: **¿Por qué te gusta viajar? ¿Prefieres viajar en coche, en tren o en avión? ¿Tienes pasaporte? ¿Cuáles son las ventajas de viajar en avión? ¿Qué haces para no aburrirte cuando viajas en avión? ¿Es fácil pasar por la aduana al entrar a los EE. UU.?**
2. Point out that **ferrocarril** is a synonym of **tren**.
3. Have students create a Flipgrid post in which they describe their favorite travel memory.

## Communication

**Interpersonal/Presentational: Paired Practice**

Ask pairs of students to create a skit involving two travelers passing through Barajas. Have pairs act out their skits for the class.

## Expansion

Ask students to choose any ten vocabulary words from these pages and write a cloze sentence for each. Model one that has enough context so students are able to fill in the blank with the correct word or expression.

## Learning Styles
### Visual Learners

Create a color visual of each noun or verb phrase found in the vocabulary section. Use the visuals each day instead of flash cards to review vocabulary.

## Special Needs Students
### Reading Difficulties

With presentations that feature paragraphs, have students work in pairs to highlight the key vocabulary. Then have them place the highlighted words into categories, such as **Personas en el aeropuerto**, **Lugares en el aeropuerto**, **Cosas en el avión**, etc.

Activity 1

**1** **Script**

1. ¿Quién debe pasar por la aduana?
2. ¿Quién sube el equipaje en el hotel?
3. ¿Quién deja la llave de la habitación?
4. ¿Quién pierde su vuelo a Madrid?
5. ¿Quién factura su equipaje?

1. el viajero
2. el botones
3. el huésped
4. el turista
5. el pasajero

1. vuelos internacionales
2. vuelos nacionales
3. los dos
4. los dos
5. vuelos internacionales
6. los dos

**3**

1. B; 2. A; 3. D; 4. C; 5. F; 6. E

## Game

### Parejas

Create two sets of cards: one with the Spanish words and the others with simple drawings (or, if necessary, the English translations). Divide the class into pairs and have students shuffle the cards and place them facedown on their desks. They take turns making matches; the person with the most matching cards is the winner.

---

**1** **¿Quién?**  **1.2**

Escuche e indique la respuesta correcta.

1. el inspector / el viajero
2. la tripulación / el botones
3. el huésped / el gerente
4. el botones / el turista
5. el inspector / el pasajero

**2** **Vuelos nacionales e internacionales**  **1.2**

El procedimiento para viajar en avión dentro y fuera del país es similar, pero no es igual. Decida si las siguientes regulaciones aplican solo a los vuelos internacionales o si aplican a los dos: vuelos nacionales e internacionales, como se ve a continuación.

| Regulaciones | Vuelos nacionales | Vuelos internacionales |
|---|---|---|
| **1. Llegar al aeropuerto con tres horas de anticipación** | | ✓ |
| **2.** Estar en el aeropuerto dos horas antes del viaje | | |
| **3.** Mantener la calma en situaciones de emergencia | | |
| **4.** Seguir las indicaciones de la tripulación del vuelo | | |
| **5.** Dirigirse a inmigración después de salir del avión | | |
| **6.** Consultar los monitores de llegada y salida de vuelos si tiene vuelos de conexión | | |

**3** **Dentro y fuera del país**  **1.2**

Empareje cada oración de la derecha con el lugar más apropiado de la izquierda.

1. ¿Va a facturar su equipaje?
2. Favor de abordar el avión por la puerta de salida 8.
3. ¡Pasajeros al tren!
4. Aquí están las llaves de su habitación.
5. Abróchense el cinturón de seguridad.
6. Abra sus maletas, por favor.

**A.** la sala de espera
**B.** el mostrador de la línea aérea
**C.** la recepción del hotel
**D.** el andén de la estación del ferrocarril
**E.** la inspección de aduana
**F.** el avión

### Essential Instruction

1. Before playing the audio in **Actividad 1**, read through the answer choices as a class. Explain that they will hear a question and they must choose the logical answer.
2. You may want to complete **Actividad 2** orally as a class.
3. Expand **Actividad 4** by having students write their own cloze sentences for a partner to complete.
4. Before assigning **Actividad 5**, briefly review how to compose an e-mail in Spanish.
5. Ask a few pairs to act out their skits from **Actividad 6**.

## 4 Al llegar al hotel  1.2

Complete las oraciones con las palabras del recuadro y, luego, colóquelas en orden lógico.

| subir | huéspedes | el botones | la llave | confirmar | una propina |
|-------|-----------|------------|----------|-----------|-------------|

1. Le doy ____ al botones por su ayuda.
2. Voy a la recepción y hablo con la gerente para ____ mi reservación.
3. Afortunadamente, el botones me ayuda a ____ el equipaje hasta el tercer piso.
4. Dice que mi nombre no está en la lista de ____ .
5. A la llegada ____ me saluda cordialmente y me abre la puerta.
6. Al desocupar mi habitación, dejo ____ en la recepción.

## ¡Comunicación!

## 5 ¡Qué mala suerte! **Interpersonal Communication**  1.3

Imagine que hizo un viaje y tuvo todos los problemas que se mencionan a continuación. Escríbale un correo electrónico a su mejor amigo/a y cuéntele en detalle todo lo que pasó.

**A.** Perdió su vuelo de conexión.

**B.** Tuvo que pagar exceso de equipaje.

**C.** Tuvo que posponer el viaje de regreso.

**D.** En el hotel perdieron su reservación.

## 6 Hay que mantener la calma 👥 **Interpersonal Communication**  1.1

Dos amigas, Adriana y Alejandra, están haciendo un viaje a España. Adriana está muy nerviosa porque nunca ha viajado al extranjero y no sabe qué hacer y Alejandra tiene que ayudarla a mantener la calma a cada momento, especialmente en el aeropuerto. Con un(a) compañero/a hagan el papel de las dos jóvenes y representen la situación. ¿Qué diría o haría Adriana? ¿Qué diría o haría Alejandra para ayudarla? Incluyan información relacionada con los temas del recuadro, como se ve en el modelo.

| equipaje | documentos | control de seguridad |
|----------|------------|----------------------|
| inmigración | inspección de aduana | vuelos de conexión |

MODELO — Llegada al aeropuerto

Adriana: ¿Por qué tenemos que estar tan temprano en el aeropuerto?

Alejandra: Como te dije, para vuelos internacionales hay que estar en el aeropuerto con tres horas de anticipación.

---

---

**Answers** _____

 **7**

1. tú
2. yo
3. —
4. —
5. —
6. —
7. —
8. —
9. —
10. —
11. —
12. tú

## Reference Desk

1. You may want to tell students that **vos** is used instead of **tú** in many areas of Latin America, such as the Southern Cone and Central America. **Vos** has its own set of verb endings (**-ás, -és, -ís**).
2. You may want to add **salvo** to this list of words in the last bullet of **Gramática**.

## Expansion

After completing **Actividad 7**, ask students to write another cloze conversation for a partner to complete.

---

# Gramática

## Los pronombres personales y su uso  1.2

Los pronombres personales **yo, tú, Ud.**[1], **él, ella, nosotros/as, vosotros/as, Uds.**, y **ellos/as** hacen el papel del sujeto, el cual concuerda (*agrees*) con el verbo en número y persona. Por esa razón los pronombres personales generalmente se omiten.

> —¿Adónde viaj**as**? (**tú**)      —Viaj**o** a Madrid. (**yo**)

- Los pronombres **Ud.** y **Uds.** se usan con más frecuencia como forma de cortesía.

  > ¿Prefiere **Ud.** un asiento de ventanilla o de pasillo?

- Se usa el pronombre personal para nombrar, aclarar o dar énfasis al sujeto.

  > —¿Quiénes son **ellos**?      —Son mis compañeros de viaje.
  > —¿Tuvieron que pagar por exceso de equipaje?    —**Yo** no, pero **ella** sí tuvo que hacerlo.

- Para dar aún más énfasis al sujeto se puede usar **mismo/a/os/as** después del pronombre personal.

  > ¿**Ud.** canceló las reservaciones?
  > Sí, **yo misma** las cancelé.

- Con el verbo **ser**, en casos enfáticos, el pronombre va después del verbo.

  > —¿Es Ud. el gerente del hotel?    —Sí, soy **yo**. ¿En qué puedo servirle?

- Siempre se deben incluir después de las palabras **según, como, entre, menos, excepto** e **incluso**, pues estas se usan para nombrar al sujeto.
  > **Según ellos**, la recepcionista nunca recibió la reservación.

[1] **Usted** y **ustedes** se abrevian como **Ud.** y **Uds.** en forma escrita.

### Un poco más

**Tú** es la forma familiar que se usa entre amigos y familiares. **Usted** (**Ud.**) se usa cuando una persona habla con personas que no conoce, personas mayores o para mostrar respeto. En los últimos años, sin embargo, ha habido una tendencia a usar más la forma familiar **tú**, sobre todo en España y en el Caribe.

---

**7**   **¿Qué pasa?**    **1.2**

Complete el siguiente diálogo con los pronombres personales que correspondan, cuando sea necesario.

**Daniela:** ¿Eres **(1)** , Javier?

**Javier:** Sí, soy **(2)** . Ábreme la puerta.

**Daniela:** Hola, Javier.

**Javier:** Hola, Daniela. Ya veo que mamá no está. ¿Sabes dónde está **(3)** ?

**Daniela:** No estoy segura, pero creo que **(4)** viene pronto. **(5)** veo que dejó la cena lista, así es que **(6)** voy a poner la mesa.

**Javier:** Daniela, ¿qué pasa? ¿ **(7)** estás nerviosa?

**Daniela:** Un poco. **(8)** acabo de recibir una carta de los abuelos. Quieren que **(9)** los visite en Granada. **(10)** prefiero esperar hasta el otoño, pero **(11)** quieren que viaje de inmediato. Mira, toma la carta y léela **(12)** mismo.

---

### Essential Instruction

1. Give examples for all the words introduced in the last bullet of **Gramática**. After completing the grammar presentation, have students close their books; ask volunteers to summarize the main points.
2. Have students justify each of their answers in **Actividad 7**. Go over the uses as a class.
3. Ask volunteers to act out the dialogues in **Actividad 8**.
4. Point out that **El presente de indicativo** will function as a comprehensive review of the present indicative.

# Gramática

## 8 Fiesta de bienvenida  1.1

Daniela viaja a Granada y cuando llega sus abuelos le tienen una fiesta de bienvenida. Hace diez años que Daniela no está en España y no se acuerda mucho de sus familiares, así es que su abuela tiene que ayudarla a reconocerlos. Con su compañero/a, representen la situación, como se ve en el modelo.

MODELO   Francisco
         **Daniela:** ¿Ese es Francisco?
         **Abuela:** ¡Claro que es él!

1. la tía Sara
2. la hija de Sofía
3. Daniel y Pablo
4. Alejandro
5. los tíos
6. las hermanas García

## El presente de indicativo 1.2

### Conjugación de verbos regulares

| | | | | | | |
|---|---|---|---|---|---|---|
| pregunt**ar** | pregunt**o** | pregunt**as** | pregunt**a** | pregunt**amos** | pregunt**áis** | pregunt**an** |
| comprend**er** | comprend**o** | comprend**es** | comprend**e** | comprend**emos** | comprend**éis** | comprend**en** |
| decid**ir** | decid**o** | decid**es** | decid**e** | decid**imos** | decid**ís** | decid**en** |

### Verbos de cambio radical

Los verbos de cambio radical tienen cambios en la raíz en todas las personas del presente de indicativo, menos **nosotros** y **vosotros**.

**Cambio e → ie**

| | | | | | |
|---|---|---|---|---|---|
| **pensar** | p**ie**nso | p**ie**nsas | p**ie**nsa | pensamos | pensáis | p**ie**nsan |

Verbos como **pensar**: cerrar, comenzar, despertarse, defender, encender, entender, perder, querer, advertir, divertir(se), mentir, preferir, sentir

**Cambio e → i**

| | | | | | |
|---|---|---|---|---|---|
| **pedir** | p**i**do | p**i**des | p**i**de | pedimos | pedís | p**i**den |

Verbos como **pedir**: reír, repetir, seguir, servir, sonreír

**Cambio o/u → ue**

| | | | | | |
|---|---|---|---|---|---|
| **poder** | p**ue**do | p**ue**des | p**ue**de | podemos | podéis | p**ue**den |
| **oler** | h**ue**lo | h**ue**les | h**ue**le | olemos | oléis | h**ue**len |
| **jugar** | j**ue**go | j**ue**gas | j**ue**ga | jugamos | jugáis | j**ue**gan |

Verbos como **poder** y **jugar**: acordar, almorzar, contar, encontrar, mostrar, probar, recordar, rogar, devolver, mover, resolver, soler, volver, dormir, morir

### Un poco más

**Oler** es un verbo único en cuanto al cambio que sufre en la raíz porque ninguna palabra en español comienza con un diptongo. Por eso, es necesario anteponer una **h** al diptongo **ue**, en su conjugación.

---

## RESOURCES

**WB** Activities 3–5

**LA** Activity 2

**Answers**

**8** *Las respuestas variarán.*

## Reference Desk

1. Remind students that Spanish has three moods: the indicative, the subjunctive, and the imperative. Here, they are going to focus on the present indicative tense.

2. Point out that **oler** and **jugar** are unique; **oler** is the only **o → hue** verb, and **jugar** is the only **u → ue** verb.

## Culture

**Products: Activity**
Have students watch a Spanish-language short film that deals with travel, such as ***Volamos hacia Miami***. Have them write any verbs they hear in the present indicative, or ask them to summarize the plot using the present indicative.

## TPR

As a whole-class or large-group activity, have students stand in a circle. Begin by saying a subject pronoun and an infinitive and tossing a foam ball to a student. He/she must formulate a sentence using the two elements, and then name another subject pronoun and an infinitive and toss the ball to another student. You may want to have a list of infinitives on the board for reference.

## Learning Styles
### Auditory Learners
Prepare sentences to read aloud to the class, e.g., **Elena y Marta van a la fiesta.** Pause after you read each one, and students will say the sentence with the correct subject pronoun (**Ellas van a la fiesta.**).

## Multiple Intelligences
### Verbal-Linguistic
Invite students interested in linguistics to investigate the evolution of the pronouns **usted/ustedes** (also, if you prefer, **vos** and **vosotros/as**). Have them find out how this evolution explains why **ustedes** is used in Latin America and **vosotros/as** in Spain.

**Reference Desk**

Work as a class to create a list of additional verbs for each bullet point in **Gramática**.

**Communication**

**Interpersonal: Cooperative Groups**
Put students in small groups. Provide each group a set of cards with infinitives written on each. When a student draws a card, each student in the group must use the verb in a sentence incorporating a different subject.

**Game**

**Charada**
Have students practice the present tense by playing charades. In pairs, students take turns acting out a variety of activities for their partner to guess (e.g., **¿Abres una ventana?**). Once their partner guesses correctly, they should confirm using the **yo** form: **Sí, abro una ventana.**

## Verbos de cambio ortográfico

Los siguientes verbos tienen cambios de ortografía en la primera persona del presente de indicativo.

- Los verbos que terminan en **-ger** y **-gir** cambian la **-g** a **-j** antes de **-o**.

| recoger | reco**j**o | recoges | recoge | recogemos | recogéis | recogen |
|---|---|---|---|---|---|---|
| dirigir | diri**j**o | diriges | dirige | dirigimos | dirigís | dirigen |

Verbos como **recoger** y **dirigir**: coger, escoger, proteger, dirigir, exigir

- Los verbos que terminan en **-guir** pierden la **u** antes de **-o**.

| distinguir | distin**g**o | distingues | distingue | distinguimos | distinguís | distinguen |
|---|---|---|---|---|---|---|

Verbos como **distinguir**: seguir, perseguir, proseguir

- Los verbos que terminan en **-cer** y **-cir** cambian la **-c** a **-zc** antes de **-o**.

| conocer | cono**zc**o | conoces | conoce | conocemos | conocéis | conocen |
|---|---|---|---|---|---|---|
| conducir | condu**zc**o | conduces | conduce | conducimos | conducís | conducen |

Verbos como **conocer** y **conducir**: agradecer, (des)aparecer, (des)obedecer, producir, traducir

- Los verbos que terminan en **-uir** cambian la **-i** a **-y** en todas las formas del presente de indicativo, menos nosotros y vosotros.

| construir | constru**y**o | constru**y**es | constru**y**e | construimos | construís | constru**y**en |
|---|---|---|---|---|---|---|

Verbos como **construir**: destruir, distribuir, huir, incluir

## Verbos irregulares

Los verbos irregulares pueden tener cambios en la raíz, en la terminación o en toda la conjugación.

| caber | quepo | cabes | cabe | cabemos | cabéis | caben |
|---|---|---|---|---|---|---|
| caer(se) | caigo | caes | cae | caemos | caéis | caen |
| dar | doy | das | da | damos | dais | dan |
| decir | digo | dices | dice | decimos | decís | dicen |
| estar | estoy | estás | está | estamos | estáis | están |
| hacer | hago | haces | hace | hacemos | hacéis | hacen |
| ir | voy | vas | va | vamos | vais | van |
| oír | oigo | oyes | oye | oímos | oís | oyen |
| poner | pongo | pones | pone | ponemos | ponéis | ponen |
| saber | sé | sabes | sabe | sabemos | sabéis | saben |
| ser | soy | eres | es | somos | sois | son |
| tener | tengo | tienes | tiene | tenemos | tenéis | tienen |
| venir | vengo | vienes | viene | venimos | venís | vienen |
| ver | veo | ves | ve | vemos | veis | ven |

**Essential Instruction**

1. Review the meaning of any unfamiliar infinitives in **Gramática**.
2. Working as a class, create a graphic organizer of irregular verbs in the present tense. Categories can include: stem-changing verbs, accented verbs, verbs that change in the **yo** form, etc.
3. Check answers to **Actividad 9** orally as a class.
4. Emphasize that there are many different combinations for **Actividad 10**, but that students should look for those that are most logical.

## 9 Ya vamos a aterrizar  1.2

Complete el párrafo con el presente de indicativo del verbo en paréntesis que corresponda según el contexto.

El piloto (**1.** *acabar*) de anunciar que el avión (**2.** *estar*) próximo a aterrizar. Los pasajeros que (**3.** *venir*) dormidos (**4.** *empezar*) a despertarse mientras las auxiliares de vuelo (**5.** *ir*) y (**6.** *venir*), revisando que todo esté en orden para el aterrizaje. Yo (**7.** *tener*) que llenar mi declaración de aduana pero no (**8.** *encontrar*) un bolígrafo en mi maletín de mano. Entonces, le (**9.** *pedir*) uno prestado a la señora que (**10.** *sentarse*) a mi lado y ella (**11.** *reírse*) nerviosa y me (**12.** *decir*) que no (**13.** *entender*) español. Me (**14.** *contar*) que es la primera vez que viaja a España y no (**15.** *saber*) muy bien qué hacer. Yo le (**16.** *decir*) que no debe preocuparse y (**17.** *ofrecerse*) a ayudarla en lo que pueda necesitar. Los dos (**18.** *salir*) del avión conversando animadamente, mientras que otros pasajeros (**19.** *seguir*) hacia su destino final.

## 10 Según sus necesidades   1.1

Con un(a) compañero/a túrnense para hablar de las necesidades especiales que puedan tener los pasajeros de un avión. Use los verbos del recuadro para unir los pasajeros con sus necesidades y expliquen su respuesta, como se ve en el modelo.

| pedir | preferir | insistir en |
|-------|----------|-------------|
| requerir | necesitar | querer |

**MODELO** Un grupo de estudiantes en una excursión

**Un grupo de estudiantes en una excursión necesita un vuelo con tarifas bajas para poder hacer el viaje.**

*Tiene que hacer arreglos especiales si quiere viajar con su mascota en la cabina.*

**Pasajeros**

1. una pareja en viaje de luna de miel
2. un grupo de estudiantes en una excursión
3. una famosa figura pública
4. un hombre o una mujer de negocios
5. una señora de mayor edad
6. una señora con una mascota
7. un señor en silla de ruedas
8. una familia con niños pequeños
9. un personaje importante del gobierno
10. el padre de un niño menor de edad que va a viajar solo

**Necesidades**

vuelo con tarifas bajas

conexión a la internet

más espacio entre asientos

tapones (*plugs*) para los oídos

bebidas gratis

música

reserva anticipada del asiento

películas

cabina más cómoda y amplia

tranquilidad

un DVD de *Río 2*

**Answers**

**9**
1. acaba
2. está
3. vienen
4. empiezan
5. van
6. vienen
7. tengo
8. encuentro
9. pido
10. se sienta
11. se ríe
12. dice
13. entiende
14. cuenta
15. sabe
16. digo
17. me ofrezco
18. salimos
19. siguen

**10** *Las respuestas variarán.*

### Reference Desk

Model the pronunciation of irregular verbs. Remind students that they should only stress the part of the word that carries an accent mark.

### Expansion

For **Actividad 10**, have students write the possible combinations on the board. As a class, vote on the most logical in each case as well as the most creative.

### Special Needs Students
#### Linguistically Challenged
Give these students extra practice with the stem-changing and irregular verbs by having them conjugate verbs using dice (in which each number on the die corresponds to a subject). Tell them to begin with the **e → ie** verbs on p. 51, and practice all infinitives in the list before moving on to the next category. Have them work in pairs so that they can monitor each other's answers.

### Multiple Intelligences
#### Visual-Spatial
Display photos to the class that show people engaged in a variety of activities. Ask students to describe each activity using the present indicative.

**11**
1. puedo
2. Quiero
3. hay
4. hace
5. sale
6. debe
7. Sabe
8. tiene
9. es
10. agradezco

**12** *Las respuestas variarán.*

## 11 Estación de Atocha  1.2

Una viajera llega a la estación de trenes de Atocha en Madrid, pensando que todavía puede tomar el tren expreso para Segovia, pero se equivoca (*is mistaken*). Complete el diálogo con la forma del verbo del recuadro que corresponda según el contexto.

| deber | agradecer | salir | saber | poder |
|-------|-----------|-------|-------|-------|
| hacer | querer | tener | ser | hay |

**Empleado:** ¿En qué __(1)__ servirle?

**Viajera:** __(2)__ comprar un boleto para el expreso a Segovia.

**Empleado:** Lo siento. Ese tren acaba de salir.

**Viajera:** ¿Cómo? ¿Y cuándo sale el próximo tren expreso?

**Empleado:** A esta hora ya no __(3)__ trenes expresos. El próximo tren __(4)__ varias paradas.

**Viajera:** ¿A qué hora __(5)__ el primer expreso mañana?

**Empleado:** A las siete de la mañana, pero Ud. __(6)__ estar en la estación a las seis y media.

**Viajera:** De acuerdo. ¿ __(7)__ Ud. si el tren __(8)__ coche comedor?

**Empleado:** ¡Por supuesto! El servicio de comedor __(9)__ muy bueno.

**Viajera:** Le __(10)__ mucho su ayuda.

*Estación de trenes Atocha, en Madrid, España*

## 12 De vacaciones  1.3, 5.2

Complete las siguientes oraciones con la forma del verbo entre paréntesis que corresponda según el contexto.

> **MODELO** Si estoy de vacaciones, yo... porque... (*preferir*)
> **Yo prefiero ir a una playa tranquila porque me gusta caminar y mirar el atardecer.**

1. Si estoy de vacaciones, yo... porque... (*preferir*)
2. Si tengo que escoger un espectáculo nocturno, yo... porque... (*elegir*)
3. Si quiero hacer deporte, yo... porque... (*ir a*)
4. Si me invitan a cenar en Madrid, yo... porque... (*tener que*)...

## Essential Instruction

1. Begin **Actividad 11** by going over the verbs in the word bank. Have students identify their changes or irregularities, and point out that **hay** is already conjugated.
2. Have pairs act out **Actividad 11**.
3. Model **Actividad 12** by completing item 1 with your own ideas. Encourage creativity.
4. Go over **Gramática**. Emphasize that the present indicative is used much more in Spanish than in English, and the present progressive is used much less. Have volunteers say how they would state the example sentences in English.

# Gramática

## Los usos del presente de indicativo  1.2, 4.1

El presente de indicativo se usa generalmente para hablar de lo que sucede **ahora**, **en este momento**, **en la actualidad**. Sin embargo, el presente también se puede usar para hablar del pasado (presente histórico) o de un futuro cercano. El uso del tiempo presente es mucho más frecuente en español y equivale en inglés al presente simple, al presente enfático y al presente progresivo. (**Hablo** = *I speak, I do speak, I am speaking*.)

- Para expresar acciones generales o habituales:

  **Voy** de vacaciones a Madrid todos los años.

  Siempre **nos reunimos** para ir al cine todos los sábados.

- Para expresar una acción que ocurre al momento de hablar:

  El vuelo no **puede** despegar a causa de la nieve.

  No **encuentro** mi pasaporte. ¿**Sabes** dónde **está**?

- Para hablar de acciones en un futuro cercano:

  **Nos vemos** a las siete en el restaurante.

  **Viajamos** mañana por la noche.

- Como presente histórico, para narrar acciones del pasado:

  En agosto de 1945 **estallan** las primeras bombas atómicas sobre las islas japonesas de Hiroshima y Nagasaki.

  Las explosiones **causan** muchas muertes y **traen** la destrucción de ciudades enteras.

### 13 Llamo para avisarte que...  1.2, 1.3

Sara acaba de llegar al aeropuerto de Madrid y llama a su hermano Gabriel (quien la está esperando) para avisarle que su vuelo ya llegó, pero que se va a demorar en salir porque está esperando para pasar por la aduana. Cambie el inglés al español, usando el tiempo presente para expresar acciones que ocurren al momento de hablar.

¡Hola, Gabriel! *I'm calling you* __(1)__ para decirte que ya estoy en el aeropuerto y que *I'm going through customs* __(2)__ en este momento. ¡Qué proceso más interesante! El aduanero *is inspecting* __(3)__ todo: maletines, bolsos, computadoras, hasta los zapatos de los niños. El pasajero que está delante de mí *is showing* __(4)__ su pasaporte y el oficial *is asking* __(5)__ muchas preguntas. No sé qué, pero algo importante *is happening* __(6)__ aquí, Gabriel. El pasajero está demasiado nervioso, otro inspector se está acercando y tres policías *are observing* __(7)__ todo con mucho interés. Ay, hermano, esto *is* __(8)__ serio, como de película. ¡Ay, no lo vas a creer, pero....!

Ahora, use su imaginación para continuar esta historia en el tiempo presente.

### Answers

13 *Las historias variarán.*
1. Te llamo
2. paso por la aduana
3. inspecciona
4. muestra
5. hace
6. pasa
7. observan
8. es

### Reference Desk

1. Ask students to create a Flipgrid post in which they use the present indicative to talk about their daily routines.
2. Have students present their stories from **Actividad 13** in an Avenue task.

## Differentiated Learning

### Decelerate/Adapt

If students struggle with **Actividad 12**, you may want to provide a word bank of ideas for sentence completion. Guide students in choosing a logical way to complete each sentence that is most true for them and, if needed, provide assistance to conjugate the verbs correctly.

### Heritage Learners

Ask heritage learners to interview their family members about the events surrounding their arrival to this country and their first experiences here. Then have them narrate the stories using the historical present.

**14  Un viaje de urgencia**  **1.1**

Después de pasar solo dos días con su hermano Gabriel, Sara se entera de (*finds out about*) que su esposo necesita una cirugía urgentemente y por eso tiene que regresar inmediatamente a EE. UU. Con un(a) compañero/a representen la conversación entre Sara y Gabriel. Usen el presente para hablar del futuro cercano y túrnense para hacerse las preguntas y responderlas como se ve en el modelo.

> **MODELO**   **Gabriel:** ¿Qué vas a hacer?
> **Sara:** Salgo para Boston de inmediato.

1. ¿Qué vas a hacer?
2. ¿Vas a ir al apartamento primero?
3. ¿Cuándo van a hacerle la cirugía?
4. ¿Crees que vas a llegar a tiempo?
5. ¿Quién te va a recoger en el aeropuerto?
6. ¿Cuándo piensas volver a España?

## ¡Comunicación!

**15  Los mejores incentivos**   Interpersonal Communication  **1.1**

Imagine que Ud. y sus compañeros trabajan en una línea aérea y les han pedido sugerencias para atraer a más pasajeros y mejorar las ventas. Representen la situación y túrnense para hablar de los incentivos que podrían ofrecer para lograr este objetivo.

> **MODELO**   **A:** Yo sugiero restablecer el servicio de comida gratis. ¿Y Uds.?
> **B:** ...
> **C:** ...

**16  ¿Qué recuerdan del pasado?**   Interpersonal/Presentational Communication  **1.1, 3.1**

Con un compañero/a, túrnense para hablar de los siguientes acontecimientos usando el presente histórico. Luego, escriban un breve resumen y preséntelo en frente de la clase.

1. La abdicación del Rey Juan Carlos I de España: En junio de 2014
2. El alunizaje del Apolo 11: En julio de 1969
3. La caída del Muro de Berlín: En noviembre de 1989
4. El asesinato de Martin Luther King, Jr: En abril de 1968

## ¡Comunicación!

**17** **Nada como mi pueblo natal**  Interpersonal/Presentational Communication  1.1, 1.3, 5.2

Muchas personas piensan que no hay nada igual al lugar donde pasaron su niñez. Con un(a) compañero/a, túrnense para hacer y responder preguntas sobre los siguientes temas. Luego, comparen su información con la de otros compañeros y elijan las cuatro ciudades más interesantes para hacer una presentación enfrente de la clase.

1. Nombre del pueblo o ciudad donde nació
2. Sitios históricos importantes del lugar
3. Atracciones y horario de atención al público
4. ...

**18** **¿Cómo es su personalidad?** Presentational Communication  1.1, 1.3

Complete las preguntas de esta encuesta con la forma del verbo entre paréntesis que corresponda según el contexto. Luego, túrnese con un(a) compañero/a para hacerse las preguntas y responderlas. Comparen sus respuestas con las de sus otros compañeros, hagan una tabla con los resultados de la encuesta y preséntenla a la clase.

1. Cuando vas de vacaciones...
   A. ¿____ viajar solo/a? (*preferir*)
   B. ¿Te ____ ir con tu familia o con compañeros? (*gustar*)
   C. ¿____ estar con un grupo turístico organizado? (*querer*)

2. Cuando vas de viaje...
   A. ¿____ en avión? (*viajar*)
   B. ¿____ el tren? (*tomar*)
   C. ¿____ en coche? (*ir*)

3. En un viaje en avión...
   A. ¿____ el equipaje? (*facturar*)
   B. ¿____ un maletín y una maleta? (*llevar*)
   C. ¿____ solo una mochila? (*usar*)

4. Para pasar el tiempo en el avión...
   A. ¿____ revistas o un libro? (*leer*)
   B. ¿____ con las personas que están a tu lado? (*charlar*)
   C. ¿____ la película que pasan y que posiblemente ya has visto? (*ver*)

5. Cuando el avión aterriza...
   A. ¿____ inmediatamente? (*salir*)
   B. ¿____ tu turno para salir? (*esperar*)
   C. ¿____ sentado hasta que todos salgan? (*quedarse*)

**Resultados**

Si tienes 3 o 4 con **A.**, eres una persona solitaria que prefiere no hacer amistades en un viaje.

Si tienes 3 o 4 con **B.**, eres una persona amigable y cortés y te gusta la compañía en los viajes.

Si tienes 3 o 4 con **C.**, eres a veces una persona poco práctica o que está dispuesta a aceptar lo que ofrecen sin protestar.

---

Answers_____

**19**

**A.**

1. Están de vacaciones en Alemania. Están enfermos y no saben cómo buscar ayuda.
2. Los padres tienen calambres en el estómago y mucha fiebre. El niño no se siente mal porque no comió lo mismo que ellos.
3. Sus mayores preocupaciones son el cuidado médico que pueden recibir y qué será del niño.
4. Europ Assistance actúa, paga y resuelve cualquier contratiempo.
5. Pueden ocurrir problemas de enfermedad, accidentes, robos y una multitud de incidentes de viaje.
6. *Las respuestas variarán.*

B. *Los párrafos variarán.*

---

## Reference Desk

1. The French company Europ Assistance was founded in 1963. They provide a wide array of travel assistance, such as medical repatriation, lost luggage insurance, vehicle assistance services, protection against identity theft, and so on.
2. Ask students to identify all irregular verbs in the article.
3. Have students present their narrations from **Actividad 19** in an Avenue task.

## ¡Comunicación!

**19 ¿Qué haría Ud. en este caso?** Interpretive/Presentational Communication 1.1, 1.3, 5.1

Cuando se viaja al extranjero, pueden pasar muchos problemas imprevistos (*unforeseen*).

**A.** Lea este artículo sobre *Europ Assistance*, una compañía de asistencia al viajero y conteste las preguntas que siguen.

1. ¿Dónde están las personas de quienes trata el artículo y en qué situación se encuentran?

2. Describan los síntomas que sienten. ¿Por qué no se siente mal el niño?

3. ¿Cuáles son las dos mayores preocupaciones de estas personas?

4. ¿Cuáles son tres de los servicios que ofrece *Europ Assistance*?

5. ¿Qué problemas pueden ocurrir durante un viaje al extranjero?

6. ¿Qué se puede hacer para prevenirlos?

Esta noche han empezado a darme unos calambres en el estómago. Luego comenzaron los vómitos. Teresa sintió los mismos síntomas un poco más tarde y ahora, a las 6 de la madrugada, estamos encendidos de fiebre. El niño duerme tranquilo. No cenó lo mismo que nosotros. Ni siquiera sabemos cómo pedir un médico. En este hotel solo hablan alemán. Supongo que comprenderán que estamos enfermos pero, ¿adónde nos llevarán?, ¿cuándo?, ¿qué nivel de cuidados médicos vamos a recibir? ... ¿qué será del niño?

Hechos como este pueden ocurrir. Ocurren. Problemas de enfermedad, accidentes, robos y una multitud de incidentes de viaje. En todo el mundo y también en nuestro país. *Europ Assistance* es una compañía de asistencia al viajero. Es la primera, la inventora, la mayor y más experimentada de las compañías de asistencia.

*Europ Assistance* actúa, paga, resuelve sobre el terreno, en el momento en que está ocurriendo el contratiempo[1]. Está con el viajero abonado[2] y no lo deja hasta que este pueda seguir el viaje o haya sido repatriado a su lugar de origen.

[1] mishap  [2] subscribed

**B.** Ahora, imagine que Ud. usó los servicios de *Europ Assistance* durante un viaje al extranjero y quedó muy satisfecho con sus servicios. Narre su experiencia en un breve párrafo y publíquelo en su red social como muestra de agradecimiento. Use las palabras del recuadro al igual que la información del artículo y su propia experiencia como guía.

| proteger | atención médica | enfermedad |
|---|---|---|
| accidente | ayudar | asistencia | hospital |

## Essential Instruction

1. Open **Actividad 19** by asking students if they or their parents have ever purchased travel insurance, or if they have had a mishap while traveling abroad.
2. Have students share their paragraphs from **Actividad 19 Parte B** in small groups.
3. For **Actividad 20**, read through the tour descriptions as a class. Clarify any unfamiliar vocabulary or abbreviations. Then have students discuss the options in pairs and make their choices.

# ¡Comunicación!

## 20 De excursión en Madrid  👥  Interpersonal/Presentational Communication  ❀ 1.1, 1.2, 2.1, 2.2

Imagine que Ud. está en Madrid con un grupo de turistas y que tienen que elegir uno de los tours que se ofrecen en la siguiente guía turística. Represente la conversación que Ud. tendría con uno de sus compañeros de viaje antes de tomar la decisión. Túrnense para hablar de los horarios, precios y actividades que se incluyen en cada recorrido y decidan qué quieren hacer. Luego, informen al grupo sobre su decisión y expliquen el por qué.

---

⚪⚪⚪  Tours Diarios : Madrid

### SANDEMANs new MADRID

Página de inicio | Tours privados | Los guías | **Tours diarios** | Blog

#### El Madrid Dorado

En estas dos horas y media de tour a pie podrás conocer el orgullo, dramatismo, color, arte y estilo característico del mejor Madrid: "El Madrid dorado".

Al este del centro madrileño encontramos el "Barrio de las letras", casa de muchos de los mejores escritores, poetas y comediantes del mundo. Descubre la vida de los escritores más famosos, sus historias oscuras, secretos, enemistades, asesinatos, condenas, y ejecuciones relacionadas con la Guerra Civil y con la Inquisición; paseando por las calles que hoy en día se han convertido en uno de los barrios más importantes de la ciudad, por sus teatros, bares y romanticismo. Visita la Casa de Lope de Vega y la de Cervantes, lugar del nacimiento del Quijote.

#### Madrid de Noche

¡Madrid, la ciudad que nunca duerme! Famosa por su vida nocturna, esta ciudad ha marcado tendencia en lo que a la noche se refiere, tanto en Europa como en el resto del mundo, ¡y queremos que seas parte de ello tú también! Por ello lo que te ofrecemos es una noche para recordar por siempre organizada en dos de los barrios más modernos y vivos de Madrid. Los domingos y lunes ven con nosotros al barrio de Huertas, junto al centro y con una oferta espectacular de bares y discotecas que te harán disfrutar de la noche en el centro de la capital; y de martes a domingo vente a disfrutar de la noche en Malasaña, el barrio alternativo y moderno, hogar de la Movida, que dio origen a la loca noche madrileña!

¡Esta experiencia incluye: retorno ilimitado con nuestra pulsera, entrada a tres bares y una discoteca, con chupitos gratis y ofertas en cada uno de los locales!

¡Ven a disfrutar de la verdadera noche madrileña con nosotros!

#### Tour de Tapas

Este tour te ofrece una forma divertida y asequible de visitar algunos de los mejores lugares de tapas en Madrid con los mejores entendidos en tapas de Madrid. Tu líder de grupo compartirá su pasión por la comida española y los secretos de la gastronomía española. Al final de la noche, habrás hecho nuevos amigos de todo el mundo y disfrutado de una experiencia inolvidable.

**EL MADRID DORADO** ▼

| LUN | | MIÉ | | VIE | SÁB |

| Recogida | Comienzo |
| --- | --- |
| | 14:30h |
| | Plaza Mayor |

€12 Estándar / €10 Estudiante

Reservar ▶ | Leer más ▶

**MADRID DE NOCHE** ▼

| | MAR | MIÉ | JUE | VIE | SÁB |

| Recogida | Comienzo |
| --- | --- |
| | 22:00h |
| | Plaza Mayor |

€12 Estándar / €12 Estudiante

Reservar ▶ | Leer más ▶

**TOUR DE TAPAS** ▼

| LUN | MAR | MIÉ | JUE | VIE | SÁB | DOM |

| Recogida | Comienzo |
| --- | --- |
| | 19:00h |
| | Plaza Mayor |

€14 Estándar / €14 Estudiante

Reservar ▶ | Leer más ▶

**HORARIO Y RESERVAS**

| | MAR | MIÉ | JUE | VIE | SÁB |

Salida de todos los tours

Plaza Mayor
Punto de Inicio 22:00
Frente de la Oficina de Información Turística

---

Unidad 2 | cincuenta y nueve **59**

## Differentiated Learning

### Accelerate
Tell students to imagine that they are on one of the tours in **Actividad 20**. Have them write a detailed e-mail to a friend or blog post relating their experiences. Encourage creativity.

### Expand
Ask students to research in depth a person, place, event, or thing mentioned in **Actividad 20**. Have them create a poster summarizing their findings; encourage them to include at least three visuals.

---

## Answers

**20** *Las respuestas variarán.*

### Reference Desk

1. Point out the use of the 24-hour clock on the web page in **Actividad 20**. Remind students that in many Spanish-speaking countries, the 24-hour clock is used for various types of schedules, such as event listings, train and flight timetables, agendas, etc.
2. Students will learn more about **tapas** in the **Cultura** reading on p. 60.

### Culture

**Practices: Information**
Nightlife in Spain, particularly in Madrid, is renowned. However, this wasn't always the case: the Franco dictatorship meant many years of social restriction. Soon after Franco's death in 1975, an energetic cultural wave known as **la movida madrileña** emerged, bringing with it a widespread feeling of freedom and a reaction against the restrictions of the old regime, and the now-famous **marcha** (*nightlife*).

### Culture

**Products: Activity**
Ask students to research sites of interest and activities in Madrid or another Spanish city. Have them make up their own tour itinerary and write an advertisement blurb for it. They should give their tour a name, and assign it a realistic cost and schedule. Have students present their tours to the class, who can pick which ones they would like to participate in.

**59**

---

# *Cultura*  **AP**

1.2, 2.1, 2.2, 3.1

**¿Pregunta clave**
¿Qué se aprende cuando se viaja al extranjero?

### 1.2, 2.2, 3.1

## 21 Comprensión

1. ¿En qué zona del país está ubicada Madrid?
2. ¿Qué deben visitar los viajeros que aman la pintura?
3. ¿Por qué se dice que Madrid es como un "museo al aire libre"?

*La Puerta de Alcalá*

### 1.3, 2.1, 3.2, 4.2

## 22 Analice

1. ¿Qué cree Ud. que significa el hecho de que los habitantes de Madrid también visiten sus lugares más emblemáticos?
2. ¿Qué práctica gastronómica de su país se parece al tapeo español?

## Madrid: Arte por todas partes

Muchas cosas pueden decirse de Madrid: que es la residencia oficial de los reyes de España, que es la capital del Estado español, que es una mezcla perfecta de modernidad y tradición. Pero para describir esta ciudad, situada en el corazón geográfico del país, la mejor palabra es "arte".

*Las meninas de Diego de Velázquez*

En Madrid, el "Paseo del Arte" es el recorrido obligado[1] de los viajeros que aman la pintura. Este itinerario incluye tres museos ubicados a pocos metros de distancia: el reconocido[2] Museo del Prado, el Thyssen-Bornemisza y el Museo Nacional Reina Sofía. En ellos se pueden contemplar[3] obras maestras de la pintura universal que abarcan diferentes movimientos y estilos pictóricos desde el siglo XVI hasta el siglo XX: Velázquez, Goya, El Greco, Rembrandt, Van Gogh, Cezanne, Dalí, Picasso y Kandinsky entre otros.

Pero en Madrid el arte no se limita a las grandes pinturas. Caminar por esta ciudad es como recorrer un museo al aire libre. Hermosos monumentos e impresionantes obras arquitectónicas aparecen casi en cada esquina: el Palacio Real, la plaza de Cibeles, la Puerta de Alcalá o el parque del Retiro, que perteneció a la monarquía española hasta fines del siglo XIX y donde se encuentra el maravilloso Palacio de Cristal. La zona del centro antiguo, llamado "viejo Madrid", está poblada de plazas con tabernas[4] de tapas, restaurantes y comercios tradicionales, como la Plaza Mayor. Y la mejor parte es que el viajero descubrirá enseguida que los lugares más emblemáticos[5] de Madrid son también los más queridos por sus habitantes: en la concurrida[6] Puerta del Sol, por ejemplo, el turista podrá sentir plenamente el ritmo y la intensidad de esta ciudad.

[1] all-important tour    [2] renowned    [3] admire    [4] bars    [5] representative    [6] crowded

**Búsqueda:** paseo del arte madrid, plaza mayor, puerta del sol

### Prácticas  2.1, 2.2

"Ir de tapas" o "tapear" es una de las costumbres más típicas de España. Es una forma de socializar, relacionarse y pasar un rato divertido al tiempo que se consumen pequeñas porciones de alimento, siempre acompañadas de una bebida. Originalmente, las "tapas" se servían sobre la boca de la jarra o el vaso de bebida, de modo que "tapaba" (*covered*) el recipiente. Así se originó su nombre. "Tapear" es una costumbre española que se ha convertido en un símbolo de identidad del país.

---

## Essential Instruction

1. Point out the **Pregunta clave**, and tell students to keep it in mind as they complete the cultural readings.
2. Have students glance at the photos and titles on pp. 60–62. Ask them to predict what else they will learn about Spain.
3. Remind students of the culture photo and question from the unit opener. Ask where they can find the answer (in the caption).
4. Pause the audio occasionally to check comprehension by asking **sí/no** questions.
5. Have students complete the **Analice** activities for Common Core practice.

# Verde encanto  1.2, 2.2, 3.1

A la hora de elegir un destino, son muchas las razones que pueden atraer al viajero: disfrutar la belleza de un paisaje natural, enriquecerse con la cultura local o alojarse en un hotel de ensueño. Y hay un lugar donde todo eso es posible: la España verde, conformada por Galicia, Asturias, Cantabria y el País Vasco. Allí, en el litoral[1] norte español, con más de 2000 kilómetros de costa sobre el océano Atlántico y el mar Cantábrico, la naturaleza se asoma al mar y le ofrece innumerables paisajes de todos los verdes imaginables.

La España verde es un espacio ecológico que incluye acantilados[2], montañas, dunas, bosques, islas, ríos y playas. Por su belleza y biodiversidad, muchos de ellos han sido declarados Reserva de la Biosfera por la UNESCO, por ejemplo, el Parque Nacional de Los Picos de Europa, que abarca Cantabria y Asturias, y que además es el espacio protegido más extenso de España.

*España, un país rico en paisajes naturales*

Pero ser una valiosa reserva de flora y fauna (donde se puede observar una gran variedad de especies ornitológicas[3] o la mayor población de osos pardos en libertad de toda Europa) no impide que la España verde sea también un lugar lleno de historia. Lo que en otra época fueron antiguas líneas ferroviarias, trazados[4] de vías romanas, rutas y calzadas pecuarias[5] son hoy una red de senderos que el turista puede recorrer a pie, en bicicleta o a caballo.

La riqueza del patrimonio cultural español también se refleja en la oferta hotelera de esta zona. El visitante puede alojarse en mansiones que datan del siglo xv, acogedoras casas de labranza[6] reformadas u hoteles rurales o costeros que pueden incluir una gran torre medieval de piedra. En la España verde, el encanto no tiene fin.

[1] coast  [2] cliffs  [3] species of birds  [4] lines  [5] livestock routes  [6] farmhouse

 **Búsqueda:** españa verde, unesco

### Productos  1.2, 2.2

El Transcantábrico es un tren turístico que recorre la España verde, desde San Sebastián hasta Santiago de Compostela. Creado en 1983 con la idea de imitar al clásico *Orient Express*, este hotel de lujo sobre raíles está considerado el mejor del mundo. Tiene vías especiales que le permiten circular por lugares a los que los trenes normales no pueden acceder.

*El Transcantábrico es un tren de lujo.*

 1.2, 2.2, 3.1

## 23 Comprensión

1. ¿Por qué se llama "España verde" a la región norte del país?

2. ¿Cuál es el espacio protegido más grande de España?

3. ¿Qué sitios de interés histórico puede conocer el viajero en esta región de España?

1.3, 2.2, 3.1

## 24 Analice

1. ¿Qué características cree Ud. que debe tener un lugar para ser declarado Reserva de la Biosfera por la UNESCO?

2. ¿Qué diferencia cree que hay entre alojarse en un hotel que es un edificio moderno y uno que tiene muchos años de historia?

RESOURCES

Verde encanto
Productos

Answers

**23**
1. Es un lugar donde la naturaleza tiene paisajes de distintos tonos de verde.
2. El Parque Nacional de Los Picos de Europa.
3. Puede visitar antiguas líneas ferroviarias o vías romanas y alojarse en antiguas mansiones.

**24** *Respuesta posible:*
1. Un lugar de riqueza natural con una flora y fauna variada o especial.
2. *Las respuestas variarán.*

### Reference Desk

1. Galicia possesses a climate similar to that of Ireland and also traces of Celtic culture; Celtic groups populated the area for centuries.
2. Distribute blank maps of Spain to the class. Have students fill in the places mentioned in these readings.

### Culture

**Products: Activity**
Have students research Spain's **paradores**, which are state-run luxury hotels in historic settings, such as former monasteries, castles, etc. Tell them to choose a **parador** that they would like to visit, and find out all the necessary information in order to stay there.

## Multiple Intelligences

### Verbal-Linguistic
Ask students to research the different languages spoken across Spain. Which ones are official, and in what regions? Ask them also to find out which is a language isolate (**euskera**/Basque). Have them make a language map, look up a few common phrases, and list them in each language.

### Naturalist
Encourage students to learn more about the varied geography and landscapes of Spain, including the Balearic and Canary Islands.

**61**

¡A visitar lo que es nuestro!

## Answers

### Perspectivas
*Las respuestas variarán.*

**25**
1. Lugares que representen un logro artístico, que hayan sido importantes en la historia o sean testimonio de una cultura desaparecida.
2. Integran el paisaje urbano con el entorno natural.
3. Deben garantizar su protección y conservarlos para futuras generaciones.

**26** *Respuestas posibles:*
1. Todos podemos disfrutar de ellos y no serán propiedad exclusiva de ninguna persona individual.
2. Esos lugares deben ser cuidados y preservados para que todos los puedan disfrutar.

**62**

 **1.2, 2.2**

## 25 Comprensión

1. ¿Por qué motivos podría un lugar convertirse en Patrimonio de la Humanidad?
2. ¿Qué relación tienen con la naturaleza algunas Ciudades Patrimonio de la Humanidad de España?
3. ¿Qué compromiso tienen que cumplir las Ciudades Patrimonio?

## 26 Analice **1.3, 2.2, 3.2**

1. ¿En qué sentido se puede decir que los lugares que son Patrimonio de la Humanidad son propiedad de todos?
2. ¿Por qué cree Ud. que es importante que algunos lugares sean Patrimonio de la Humanidad?

### Perspectivas **3.2**

Para Federico Mayor Zaragoza, ex Director General de la UNESCO, el patrimonio cultural es un instrumento de desarrollo: "Al día siguiente de que se declara un patrimonio mundial hay miles de agencias de viajes que ponen: si viaja usted a tal sitio no deje de visitar tal; en esta ciudad hay este patrimonio inmaterial. [...] Usted mire y verá cómo es inmediato el cambio en el número de personas que van a contemplar estas maravillas; por tanto, hay una influencia económica muy directa".

Según Federico Mayor Zaragoza, ¿qué consecuencias tiene para una ciudad que se la declare Patrimonio de la Humanidad?

*Casas colgantes de Cuenca*

## ¡A visitar lo que es nuestro!  **1.2, 2.2**

¿Sabía que Ud. es dueño de un acueducto romano en Segovia? ¿Qué le parece visitar la ciudad donde nació Cervantes, el autor del *Quijote*, que también es suya? En el mundo, hay muchos lugares maravillosos declarados Patrimonio de la Humanidad por la UNESCO y eso significa que nos pertenecen a todos, también a Ud.

Se trata de lugares importantes porque son un logro artístico único o porque fueron influyentes en algún momento de la historia o porque son el testimonio de una cultura desaparecida. Y muchos de ellos se encuentran en España, un país que por tradición, historia, riqueza y variedad tiene una herencia cultural incalculable[1]. Por eso, la UNESCO le ha otorgado[2] el privilegio de ser el tercer país del mundo con más lugares declarados Patrimonio de la Humanidad.

Algunas de las Ciudades Patrimonio de la Humanidad de España, como Córdoba, Toledo o Tarragona, reflejan una mezcla de las transformaciones e influencias de distintas épocas: el Imperio romano, el dominio musulmán, el catolicismo. Un elemento importante en estas ciudades es la integración del paisaje urbano y el entorno natural, por ejemplo, las "casas colgantes" de Cuenca, una ciudad que parece suspendida en el aire.

*La Mezquita de Córdoba*

En las Ciudades Patrimonio se encuentran grandes monumentos como la Mezquita de Córdoba, la Muralla de Ávila, la Universidad de Salamanca o la Catedral de Santiago de Compostela. Los edificios históricos están restaurados y algunos cumplen funciones diversas: centros de exposición y venta de artesanía, galerías de arte, mercados o alojamientos de primera categoría.

El grupo de Ciudades Patrimonio de la Humanidad españolas ofrecen la oportunidad de conocer un legado[3] histórico sobresaliente[4], pero también representan un compromiso universal: el de garantizar su protección y conservación para el disfrute de generaciones futuras.

[1] immeasurable   [2] awarded   [3] legacy   [4] outstanding

**Búsqueda:** unesco, patrimonio de la humanidad españa

## Essential Instruction

1. Display a map of Spain, and point out the locations of the places and cities mentioned in the readings.
2. Encourage students to use a chart or graphic organizer as they progress through the cultural readings. They can write the places mentioned and any key details.
3. Model pronunciation of the new vocabulary on p. 63 and have students repeat the words.
4. Personalize the vocabulary presentation by giving additional example sentences about your own life.

# Vocabulario 2

## Comparación y contraste: ¡Ojo con estas palabras!  1.2, 4.1

En español, al igual que en inglés, hay varias formas de expresar el concepto de **tiempo**. Preste atención, pues su uso depende del contexto.

¿Cuántas **veces** has venido a Madrid?

Muchas veces, pero **cada vez** que vengo, me gusta más.

```
            tiempo
            vez (veces)
time ─────  hora
            rato
            época
```

| | |
|---|---|
| **tiempo** *a period or duration of time* | —¿Cuánto **tiempo** vas a estar en Madrid?<br>—Voy a quedarme una semana. |
| *time in the abstract* | —¿Quieres acompañarme al Museo del Prado? Hace mucho **tiempo** que quiero ir.<br>—Claro que sí. |
| **una vez** *once, one time* | —¿Nunca has ido al museo? |
| **cada vez** *each time*<br>**otra vez** *again* | —Sí. Fui **una vez** hace mucho tiempo y me encantó. Por eso, **cada vez** que vuelvo a España, quiero ir a visitarlo **otra vez**. |
| **a veces** *sometimes*<br>**veces** *times, occasions* | —En cambio, yo he ido al museo en muchas oportunidades. **A veces** lo he hecho por gusto propio, pero muchas otras **veces** he tenido que hacerlo para llevar a amigos que quieren visitarlo, como tú. |
| **hora** *time of day* | —¿Sabes a qué **hora** abren el museo hoy? |
| **hora (de)** *the proper time to do something* | —No sé. Creo que abren a las diez. ¿Qué **hora** es?<br>—Ya es **hora de** irnos. Acuérdate que no tenemos mucho tiempo.<br>—Por supuesto. ¡Ya es **hora**! |
| **rato** *a short time, a while*<br>**época** *time during a season, historical time* | —¿Cuánto tiempo piensan estar en el museo?<br>—Solo vamos a estar un **rato**. En estos días de verano hay demasiados turistas.<br>—Es verdad. Vienen muchos turistas en esta **época** del año. |
| **Para expresar la idea de** *to have a good time* use **divertirse** y **pasarlo bien**. | —¿Cómo les fue en el museo? **¿Se divirtieron?**<br>—Claro que sí. **Lo pasamos muy bien.** |

---

## RESOURCES

**WB**  Activities 6–8

## Reference Desk

1. Emphasize that **tiempo**, **vez**, **hora**, **rato**, and **época** have distinct meanings; they are not interchangeable.
2. For more advanced learners, you may also want to introduce the terms **momento**, **periodo**, and **ocasión** and give a more nuanced explanation of their use to mean *time*.
3. Point out that students can also use **¡Ya era hora!** to say *It is (about) time!*
4. Explain that in Latin America many people use **pasarla bien**; **pasarlo bien** is used in Spain.
5. You may want to teach additional expressions with these words, such as **No veo la hora de…**, **cada vez más/menos**, **una que otra vez**, etc.

## Expansion

Have students work in groups to create a poster with examples, using the words from **Vocabulario 2**. Display the posters in the classroom.

---

## Differentiated Learning

### Expand
Divide Spain into regions and have students work in groups to summarize what they learned about each region in these cultural readings.

### Heritage Learners
Ask heritage learners to teach this vocabulary presentation. Allow them time to prepare, and encourage the use of visuals and their own example sentences.

**27 ¿Otra vez?**  **1.2**

Primero, complete las oraciones con las palabras del recuadro. Luego, empareje las preguntas de la izquierda con las respuestas de la derecha.

| tiempo | vez | otra vez | cada vez | veces | hora | rato | época |
|---|---|---|---|---|---|---|---|

1. ¿____ de viaje?
2. ¿Por qué te gusta viajar en esta ____ del año?
3. ¿Fuiste alguna ____ al restaurante Lakasa?
4. ¿Sabes qué ____ es?
5. ¿A qué ____ sale tu vuelo?
6. ¿Quieres que te acompañe un ____?
7. ¡Cuánto ____ está atrasado el vuelo!

**A.** A las seis y veinte. Es ____ de despedirnos.

**B.** Sí, varias ____. La comida es deliciosa.

**C.** Sí, dentro de un ____ salgo para Madrid.

**D.** Porque no hay muchos turistas y es la ____ de conciertos.

**E.** Cálmate. ____ que vuelas te pones nerviosa.

**F.** Por favor, acompáñame hasta que sea ____ de abordar.

**G.** Son las cinco y cuarenta. ¡Cómo pasa el ____!

## ¡Comunicación!

**28 ¡El mundo en la palma de la mano!** 👥 Interpersonal Communication  **1.1**

Imagine que Ud. trabaja en una agencia de viajes y está ayudando a dos clientes, Jairo y Elisa, a planear su viaje de luna de miel. Represente la situación con dos compañeros, turnándose para pedir y dar información. Incluyan los siguientes temas en su conversación, como se ve en el modelo.

- Lugar de destino
- Itinerarios
- Clases de vuelos, escalas y conexiones
- Precios y formas de pago aceptadas
- Ofertas de paquetes especiales que incluyan pasajes, comida y alojamiento

*¿Han viajado al Caribe alguna vez?*

| MODELO | |
|---|---|
| **Agente:** | **¿En qué tiempo del año les gustaría viajar?** |
| **Jairo:** | **Bueno, la boda es en junio, pero tenemos cierta flexibilidad.** |
| **Elisa:** | **Sabemos que el verano es época de temporada alta.** |
| **Agente:** | **Muy bien. En ese caso...** |

### Essential Instruction

1. Have students fill in the blanks in **Actividad 27** individually; then work as a class to match the columns.
2. For **Actividad 28**, encourage students to arrange their desks and chairs to simulate a travel agency. If possible have them use props as well.
3. Open **Actividad 29** by asking students if their luggage has ever been lost by an airline. Encourage them to draw on personal experience when creating their dialogues.
4. Circulate around the room as students complete **Actividad 30**. Provide additional vocabulary as needed.

**¡Comunicación!**

### 29 Se nos perdió el equipaje 👥 Interpersonal Communication ✿ 1.1

Imagine que después de un largo viaje de vacaciones por España, Ud. y su pareja están esperando en el aeropuerto Logan a que les entreguen las maletas. Después de una larga espera se dan cuenta de que su equipaje no ha llegado. En grupos, representen la conversación que Uds. tienen con el empleado de la línea aérea, el día que presentan su queja y, al otro día, cuando el empleado los llama para darles información del paradero (*whereabouts*) de su equipaje.

MODELO
> A: Disculpe, señor, ya salieron todas las maletas, pero las nuestras no han llegado. ¿Nos puede ayudar?
>
> B: Claro que sí. Para empezar, dígame su número de vuelo y procedencia.
>
> C: Por supuesto. Es el vuelo 756 de Iberia, de Madrid a Boston.
>
> B: …

### 30 Intercambio de ideas 👥 Interpersonal/Presentational Communication ✿ 1.1, 1.3, 5.2

Trabajen en grupos de cuatro estudiantes e intercambien información sobre los viajes. Elijan a una persona del grupo para que tome apuntes y, al final, presenten un resumen de los temas discutidos enfrente de la clase.

MODELO
> A: ¿Cuál creen que es el mejor medio de transporte para viajar?
>
> B: Depende. Si tienes prisa, viajar en avión es mucho más rápido.
>
> C: Estoy de acuerdo. Pero también es mucho más costoso.

*Todo el mundo quiere viajar en los días festivos.*

- ¿Cómo se sienten Uds. cuando viajan por avión? ¿En tren? ¿En autobús? ¿En coche? ¿En barco?

- ¿Qué medio de transporte piensan que es más cómodo y seguro? ¿Por qué?

- En general, ¿cuáles son las ventajas y las desventajas de estos medios de transporte?

- ¿Por qué hay que pasar por la inspección de aduana?

- ¿Qué cosas pueden considerarse artículos de contrabando?

- ¿Por qué revisan los inspectores unas maletas, pero no revisan otras? ¿Qué piensan Uds. al respecto?

---

**Answers**

㉙ *Las conversaciones variarán.*

㉚ *Las respuestas variarán.*

### Reference Desk

For the first bullet of **Actividad 30**, if students do not have travel experience, encourage them to talk about other aspects of these modes of transportation.

### Culture

**Perspectives: Activity**
Ask students to interview Spanish speakers using modified questions from **Actividad 30** or similar ones. If students do not have access to Spanish speakers, have them investigate as much as they can online. Have them compare the information they obtain with their group's opinions about travel.

### Expansion

After completing **Actividad 29**, ask students to write a complaint letter to the airline's customer service department.

---

### Special Needs Students
**Physical Disabilities**
Encourage these students to share their experiences and perspectives about the different modes of transportation mentioned in **Actividad 30**. Which are most accommodating to people with disabilities? If they have traveled abroad, are other countries as accommodating?

### Multiple Intelligences
**Mathematical-Logical**
Have students quantify the class's responses to the first three groups of questions in **Actividad 30** and graph the results. Ask them to report the findings to the class.

## Reference Desk

Barcelona is the capital city of the autonomous region Catalonia (**Cataluña**). The region has two official languages: **castellano** and **catalán**. Barcelona's main railway station, located in the Sants neighborhood, is called **Barcelona-Sants**; the Spanish high-speed **AVE** (**Alta Velocidad Española**) trains began service at this station in 2008.

## Critical Thinking

**Comparing**
Ask students to compare and contrast the transportation systems in Madrid with that of a U.S. city.

## Connections

**Architecture**
Ask students to research several works of Antoni Gaudí that can be visited in Barcelona, such as **Parc Güell**, **Casa Milà**, **Casa Batlló**, or the **basílica de la Sagrada Familia**. Have them analyze the influences and themes in his works.

 **¡Comunicación!**

**31 En la estación del ferrocarril** 👥 Interpersonal Communication ❀ **1.1**

Imagine que Ud. es un agente de la estación de trenes en Barcelona y tiene que ayudar a un señor que quiere cambiar su boleto. El viajero iba a tomar el tren para Madrid a las seis de la tarde, pero se le presentó un contratiempo y necesita tomar el próximo tren. Con un(a) compañero/a, representen la conversación entre el agente y el viajero, y túrnense para pedir y dar la siguiente información, como se ve en el modelo.

> MODELO  **Agente:** ¿En qué puedo servirle?
>
> **Viajero:** Tengo un boleto para Madrid a las seis de la tarde, pero necesito cambiarlo.

- Razón para querer cambiar el boleto
- Hora de salida del próximo tren
- Si sale del mismo andén que el tren de las seis
- Si es un tren de alta velocidad
- Si hace paradas, dónde las hace
- Si...

**32 Servicio de trenes en España** 👥 Interpretive/Interpersonal Communication ❀ **1.1, 2.2, 3.1**

Lea el anuncio de la página que sigue sobre el servicio de trenes en España. Luego, imagine que Ud. piensa pasar un par de meses en Madrid y quiere saber más sobre el sistema de trenes pues quiere viajar dentro y fuera del país. Con un(a) compañero/a, representen la conversación entre Ud. y un empleado de la RENFE —Red Nacional de Ferrocarriles Españoles—, y túrnense para intercambiar información de acuerdo a la lectura y los siguientes temas, como se ve en el modelo.

- Información sobre horarios, paradas y reservaciones
- Transporte dentro de la ciudad y de las afueras a la ciudad
- Transporte desde Madrid a otras ciudades del norte y sur del país
- Transporte desde Madrid a otros países de Europa

> MODELO  **A:** ¿Dónde puedo hallar más información sobre el horario de trenes dentro de la ciudad?
>
> **B:** En el sitio web de RENFE hallará los horarios de todos los trenes suburbanos.

## Essential Instruction

1. Read through the directions for **Actividad 31** and assign **agentes** and **viajeros**. Allow students time to prepare for their roles; help them brainstorm a list of words and expressions if needed.

2. For **Actividades 31** and **32**, have students change roles and repeat the activities.

3. Display a map of Spain so that students can reference it as they read the information on p. 67.

Avenue

**Reference Desk**

**RENFE** is an acronym for **Red Nacional de los Ferrocarriles Españoles**. It was created in 1941 when Spain's railways were nationalized.

**Culture**

**Products: Activity**
Have students work in pairs. Tell them to imagine that they are studying abroad in Madrid. Assign each pair a certain amount of travel money (e.g., 100 euros per person) and tell them to plan a weekend getaway within Spain via train. Have them peruse options on the **RENFE** website, as well as other websites for lodging and meal options. Then have them repeat the activity with an unlimited budget. Would they still choose to go by train, or would they choose another method of transport? Would their destination change? Students can submit their itineraries via an Avenue task.

---

◯◯◯ | Tipos de trenes en España

# Interrail

## Tipos de Trenes en España

Hay diversos tipos de trenes en España en los que podrás viajar tanto de día como de noche. La mayor parte de la red ferroviaria española está operada por RENFE. Utiliza los horarios de trenes de Interrail para comprobar los horarios de los trenes en España.

### Trenes regionales e InterCity en España

La principal red ferroviaria de España está formada por los siguientes trenes regionales e InterCity:

- Los trenes de Media Distancia conectan los destinos regionales con las ciudades más grandes. La red conecta con trenes de alta velocidad de larga distancia y los trenes hacen paradas frecuentes.

- Los Cercanías (trenes suburbanos) son una red de trenes que circulan en las grandes ciudades españolas, incluyendo Barcelona y Valencia.

*Trenes regionales en España*

En los horarios de Interrail los trenes de Media Distancia aparecen como "IR". Es necesario hacer reservas en la mayoría de estos trenes. Los trenes de cercanías no aparecen en este horario. Consulta el sitio web de Renfe para obtener más información sobre las horas de salida.

## Trenes de alta velocidad en España

### Trenes internacionales de alta velocidad en España

Estos trenes de alta velocidad circulan desde y hacia España:

Los trenes Renfe-SNCF en Cooperación conectan Madrid y Barcelona con Francia.

Los trenes Internacional conectan Vigo con Oporto (Portugal).

### Trenes nacionales de alta velocidad en España

La extensa red española de trenes de alta velocidad está operada por trenes modernos que ofrecen un servicio de alta calidad durante tu viaje con Interrail.

*Trenes de alta velocidad en España*

Estos trenes de alta velocidad circulan dentro de España:

- Los trenes Avant circulan en rutas de corta distancia.

- Los trenes AVE alcanzan velocidades de hasta 300 km/h (186 mph) y te llevan de Madrid a Barcelona en menos de 3 horas.

- Los trenes Altaria conectan Madrid con las ciudades del sur de España.

- Los trenes Alvia y Arco operan entre Madrid y algunas ciudades del norte de España como Bilbao y San Sebastián.

- Los trenes Euromed operan en la ruta Barcelona - Valencia - Alicante.

En los horarios de Interrail, los trenes de alta velocidad aparecen como "IC", "ATR-Altaria", "AVE", "A" o "EM". En estos trenes siempre es obligatorio hacer una reserva.

---

**Learning Styles**
**Visual Learners**
Distribute maps of the Iberian Peninsula; make sure that all the cities mentioned in the article on p. 67 are labeled. As they read, have students draw the railway lines that connect the various cities. Have them use color-coding to denote the various lines.

**Multiple Intelligences**
**Bodily-Kinesthetic**
Test comprehension of the article on p. 67 by devising a gesture for each category of train. Then name each train type and students must make the correct gesture.

## Reference Desk

1. Emphasize that with the future tense, the verb endings are always the same, even if the stem is irregular.
2. Remind students that the auxiliary verb *will* does not have an equivalent in Spanish.
3. Point out that the impersonal form of **haber** is the same for singular and plural: **habrá**.
4. Remind students that the future tense can be used in other ways, such as to express probability. Students will review all uses of the future tense on p. 71.

## Expansion

Give each student a paper with a phrase in the infinitive form, such as **vivir en Europa**, **tener tres hijos**, **ser famoso/a**, etc. Have students decide whether or not the information will be true for them, and make an affirmative or negative statement in the future tense, e.g., **(No) Viviré en Europa.** To challenge students, ask them to provide a related follow-up sentence, such as **Compraré una casa en Berlín.** Afterward, ask questions like **¿Quién vivirá en Europa?**

# Gramática

## El tiempo futuro  1.2

El futuro de los verbos regulares se forma añadiendo al infinitivo las siguientes terminaciones.

| Futuro de verbos regulares | | |
|---|---|---|
| **viajar** | **volver** | **ir** |
| viajar**é** | volver**é** | ir**é** |
| viajar**ás** | volver**ás** | ir**ás** |
| viajar**á** | volver**á** | ir**á** |
| viajar**emos** | volver**emos** | ir**emos** |
| viajar**éis** | volver**éis** | ir**éis** |
| viajar**án** | volver**án** | ir**án** |

Los verbos irregulares en futuro tienen cambios en la raíz, pero no en las terminaciones.

A veces se puede seguir un patrón (*pattern*) en la conjugación de estos verbos, como se ve a continuación.

*Viajaremos a Sevilla este verano.*

| Futuro de verbos irregulares | | | |
|---|---|---|---|
| **Cambio en la raíz** | **Infinitivo** | **Raíz** | **Futuro** |
| | caber | cabr- | cabré |
| | haber | habr- | habré |
| Se omite la **e** del infinitivo. | poder | podr- | podré |
| | querer | querr- | querré |
| | saber | sabr- | sabré |
| | poner* | pondr- | pondré |
| | salir | saldr- | saldré |
| La **d** reemplaza la **e** o **i** del infinitivo. | tener* | tendr- | tendré |
| | valer | valdr- | valdré |
| | venir | vendr- | vendré |
| Se omiten las letras **ec** y **ce**, respectivamente | decir | dir- | diré |
| | hacer* | har- | haré |

### Un poco más

**Haber**, cuando se usa como verbo impersonal, se conjuga solamente en la tercera personal del singular.

**Hay** mucha gente en el aeropuerto.

**Habrá** mucha gente en el aeropuerto.

Se conjuga en todas las personas cuando se usa como verbo auxiliar en la formación de los tiempos compuestos. Ver futuro perfecto, p. 409.

Ya **habremos reclamado** el equipaje cuando pasemos por la aduana.

*Los verbos que se derivan de estos, como **suponer**, **mantener** y **deshacer**, se conjugan con la misma terminación en el futuro: **supondré**, **mantendré**, **desharé**, etc.

## Essential Instruction

1. Personalize the **Gramática** by talking about your future plans.
2. Drill conjugation of the future tense by having all students stand. Call on them in random order to say one thing that they (or they and their family/friends) will do next summer.
3. Open **Actividad 33** by asking students what their zodiac signs are. Model pronunciation of the signs in Spanish. Ask them if they believe in astrology, and if they read horoscopes regularly.
4. Have students check their answers to **Actividad 33** in pairs.

**Answers**

## 33 El horóscopo del mes  1.2

Complete el horóscopo con el futuro del verbo indicado.

**Capricornio**

Ud. (**1.** *salir*) de todas sus deudas mediante la oferta de trabajo que le (**2.** *ser*) ofrecida muy pronto.

**Cáncer**

Un amigo (**15.** *venir*) a buscarlo con planes para el futuro. (**16.** *valer*) la pena considerar su oferta.

**Acuario**

Busque la compañía de sus amigos. Ellos le (**3.** *ayudar*) con sus problemas, y su vida social (**4.** *comenzar*) un nuevo ciclo.

**Leo**

Ud. (**17.** *sufrir*) una traición. (**18.** *tener*) que cuidar sus actos al hablar con parientes y amigos.

**Piscis**

Ud. (**5.** *sentir*) que el estudio es aburrido y (**6.** *tener*) dificultades, pero muy pronto (**7.** *poder*) resolverlas.

**Virgo**

El día 15 Ud. (**19.** *recibir*) la visita inesperada de un amigo que le (**20.** *contar*) sus penas y (**21.** *haber*) que consolarlo.

**Aries**

Ud. (**8.** *recibir*) dinero. Aproveche para dar fiestas. Muy buenos amigos (**9.** *buscar*) su compañía.

**Libra**

Uno de sus pasatiempos le (**22.** *producir*) dinero y (**23.** *firmar*) grandes contratos con compañías muy importantes.

**Tauro**

Sus planes (**10.** *empezar*) a dar frutos. Ud. (**11.** *ganar*) más dinero y (**12.** *hacer*) el viaje soñado.

**Escorpión**

Sus planes de viaje (**24.** *tomar*) un rumbo positivo. (**25.** *conocer*) Sudamérica y (**26.** *encontrar*) la felicidad y el amor.

**Géminis**

Ud. (**13.** *tener*) momentos de duras luchas interiores. No se desanime; no (**14.** *ser*) nada muy grave.

**Sagitario**

Piense antes de aceptar un trabajo; de lo contrario (**27.** *tener*) muchos problemas que lo (**28.** *poner*) en dificultades.

**33**
1. saldrá
2. será
3. ayudarán
4. comenzará
5. sentirá
6. tendrá
7. podrá
8. recibirá
9. buscarán
10. empezarán
11. ganará
12. hará
13. tendrá
14. será
15. vendrá
16. Valdrá
17. sufrirá
18. Tendrá
19. recibirá
20. contará
21. habrá
22. producirá
23. firmará
24. tomarán
25. Conocerá
26. encontrará
27. tendrá
28. pondrá

## Communication

**Presentational: Paired Practice**
Have students work in pairs to write a horoscope for their partner, predicting what will happen in the coming week. They should pattern their paragraph after the entries in **Actividad 33** and put the verbs in the infinitive for their partner to conjugate in the future tense.

## Differentiated Learning
**Expand**
Post visuals of astrological signs, and their corresponding dates and characteristics. Have students form groups according to their signs and ask them to discuss and compare their personality traits. Are there commonalities? Do they share any interests or professional plans for the future?

## Special Needs Students
**Dyslexia/AD(H)D**
Work with these students to complete **Actividad 33**. Ask them to focus on the verbs in parentheses, and to consult p. 68 to see if they are regular or irregular. They should then find and underline the subject for each verb. Finally, have them conjugate the forms.

**Answers**

**34**

1. encontrará
2. tendrá
3. habrá
4. podrán
5. tendrá
6. estaremos
7. verá
8. llevará
9. estarán
10. haremos
11. podrán
12. tendrán
13. podrán
14. gustará
15. leeré
16. llamaré
17. haré

**35** *Las conversaciones variarán.*

## Reference Desk

Andalusia's **Costa del Sol** is a world-famous tourist destination on the Mediterranean Sea. Its name was created specifically as part of a marketing effort to attract international tourists.

## Expansion

As a follow-up to **Actividad 35**, ask students to create a video blog review about Hotel Marbella Playa. They can submit it via Avenue.

---

**34 Marbella Playa en la Costa del Sol**  **1.2**

El agente de ventas del Hotel Marbella Playa en la Costa del Sol está en el teléfono explicándole al Sr. Alvarado las ventajas que tendrá si elige este hotel. Complete la conversación, con la forma del futuro de los verbos en paréntesis, según corresponda.

**Sr. Alvarado:** —¿Cómo es su hotel?

**Agente:** —El Hotel Marbella Playa es un hotel de cuatro estrellas. En él Ud. (*1. encontrar*) todas las comodidades de los grandes hoteles.

**Sr. Alvarado:** —Las habitaciones, ¿tienen vista al mar?

**Agente:** —¡Por supuesto! Desde su habitación Ud. (*2. tener*) una maravillosa vista de la playa.

**Sr. Alvarado:** —Y..., dígame, ¿hay muchos turistas?

**Agente:** —Para esa época del año ya no (*3. haber*) muchos turistas y Ud. y su familia (*4. poder*) disfrutar de mucha tranquilidad.

**Sr. Alvarado:** —¿Es fácil llegar al hotel?

**Agente:** —Ud. no (*5. tener*) ningún problema para llegar al hotel y nosotros (*6. estar*) atentos a su llegada.

**Sr. Alvarado:** —¿Qué otros servicios ofrece el hotel?

**Agente:** —Nuestro servicio de comedor es excelente; ya lo (*7. ver*) Ud. Y si desea, el camarero le (*8. llevar*) el desayuno a su habitación. Ud. y su familia (*9. estar*) como en su casa. Recuerde que si viene con su familia nosotros le (*10. hacer*) un descuento especial.

**Sr. Alvarado:** —¿(*11. poder*) mis hijos usar el gimnasio? Son menores de dieciocho años.

**Agente:** —Sí, (*12. tener*) acceso a nuestro gimnasio entre las ocho y las diez de la mañana. Ellos también (*13. poder*) participar en el mini-club, que ofrece muchas actividades para los pequeños. Les (*14. gustar*) mucho el club.

**Sr. Alvarado:** —Bueno, cuando reciba los folletos, yo los (*15. leer*). Si a mi familia le gusta la idea, yo le (*16. llamar*) y (*17. hacer*) reservaciones para la primera semana de junio.

---

¡Comunicación!

**35 ¡Qué pesadilla!** 👥 Interpersonal Communication **1.1**

Imagine que el Sr. Alvarado y su familia llegan al Hotel Marbella Playa y se sorprenden de ver que no hay ninguna de las comodidades que, según el agente, se ofrecían en el hotel. No hay habitaciones con vista al mar, ni gimnasio, ni mini-club. Tampoco hay servicio a la habitación, y el servicio de comedor no tiene nada de excelente. Con un(a) compañero/a, hagan el papel del Sr. Alvarado que viene a quejarse y el empleado del hotel que no tiene idea de los servicios y comodidades que supuestamente se debían ofrecer. Usen su imaginación y sentido del humor, como se ve en el modelo.

> **MODELO**
> A: **Nos dijeron que tendríamos una maravillosa vista al mar.**
> B: **¿Al mar? Ah... Temo que solo tendrán una buena vista del estacionamiento.**

---

## Essential Instruction

1. Check answers to **Actividad 34** by having two volunteers role-play the conversation for the class.
2. Encourage students to use props and to act with expression and gestures during their role-plays in **Actividad 35**.
3. For listening comprehension, have students write the verbs that their classmates use during their presentations in **Actividad 36**.
4. Augment the grammar explanation by giving example sentences that all fit within one context, such as **el presidente de los EE. UU**.

# Gramática

emcpassport.com
WB 11–12
LA 5

## ¡Comunicación!

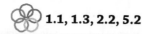 1.1, 1.3, 2.2, 5.2

**36 Dejen volar su imaginación**  Interpersonal/Presentational Communication

Imagine que Ud. y su mejor amigo/a tienen la oportunidad de hacer el viaje que siempre han soñado y, para completar, cuentan con un presupuesto (*budget*) ilimitado. Con un(a) compañero/a, intercambien opiniones y decidan adónde irán y por qué. Luego, describan todos sus planes en un breve párrafo en tiempo futuro y, para finalizar, preséntenlo enfrente de la clase.

MODELO **Nosotros haremos un viaje por Asturias al norte de España. Visitaremos Gijón, Avilés y Oviedo. Iremos en el verano porque...**

## Los usos del futuro 1.2, 4.1

El futuro se usa en los siguientes casos.

- Para expresar una acción que se predice o anticipa desde el momento presente.

  El auxiliar de vuelo **explicará** las medidas de seguridad antes del despegue.
  El piloto anunció que el vuelo **llegará** a tiempo a Málaga.

- Para indicar una orden o mandato.

  No **te quedarás** aquí ni un solo minuto más. **Te irás** ahora mismo.

- Para expresar una conjetura o probabilidad en el presente. Este uso se distingue del uso regular solo por el contexto. No indica una acción que va a ocurrir, sino la probabilidad de una acción que en inglés se expresa con *probably, must* o *I suppose*.

  —¿Qué hora es?
  —**Serán** las nueve. (*It is probably nine.*)

  —¿Por qué no **habrán** llegado?
  —**Se habrá** retrasado el vuelo. (*I suppose the flight was delayed.*)

- La idea del futuro también se expresa por medio del presente, cuando la acción va a tener lugar en un futuro inmediato. A menudo se usa con adverbios de tiempo.

  **Salgo** esta tarde para Bilbao.

- Para expresar algo que va a ocurrir en un futuro cercano se usa **ir a + infinitivo**. Es equivalente del inglés *to be going* (*to do something*).

  **Voy a** hacer mis maletas ahora mismo.

- También es común usar el presente del verbo **querer + infinitivo** con sentido de futuro para pedir o solicitar algo. Es equivalente del inglés *will*.

  ¿**Quieres** ayudarme? (*Will you help me?*)

---

### Answers

36 *Las presentaciones variarán.*

### Reference Desk

1. Ask students to use visuals, a packing list, and a detailed budget of their trip for **Actividad 36**. Also encourage students to use the Internet or travel guides to complete this task. Provide students with a rubric to show how the project will be graded and any other expectations.
2. Ask students to react to their classmates' trip plans from **Actividad 36** via a Flipgrid post.
3. Remind students that the future tense is used less frequently in Spanish than in English.

### Expansion

Ask students to write a short paragraph predicting their lives as adults. Tell them not to include their names. Collect the papers, shuffle them, and read the paragraphs aloud. The class will try to guess who wrote each one.

---

## Special Needs Students
### At-Risk Students/Behavior Problems
Engage these students by asking them to write a list of their favorite singers, athletes, or other role models. Tell them to think of what will happen 10 years from now, and to write two predictions for each person.

## Multiple Intelligences
### Naturalist
Have students research online about the ecological challenges that Spain faces today. Then, using what they learned, ask them to write at least ten sentences explaining what will happen or what things will be like in Spain 20 or 30 years from now.

**Answers**

**37** *Respuestas posibles:*

1. El mes antes del viaje conseguiré el pasaporte, leeré las guías turísticas, llamaré a la línea aérea y haré reservaciones.
2. Una semana antes del viaje compraré ropa nueva.
3. Un día antes del viaje iré al banco y cancelaré el periódico.
4. El día del viaje verificaré el vuelo.

**38** *Las conversaciones variarán.*

1. llamaré
2. viajaré
3. enviaré
4. podré

---

## Reference Desk

**Las Islas Baleares** are an archipelago in the Mediterranean Sea. The four largest islands are **Mallorca**, **Menorca**, **Formentera**, and **Ibiza**. The islands form an autonomous community; the capital is **Palma de Mallorca**. The region has two official languages: Catalan and Spanish.

---

### 37 Tantos preparativos  1.3

Imagine que Ud. está haciendo planes para un viaje al extranjero y quiere hacer una lista de todos los preparativos. Piense en todo lo que tiene que hacer y cuándo tiene que hacerlo. Use las expresiones del recuadro y las fechas que se dan como guía, como se ve en el modelo.

> **MODELO** el mes antes del viaje...
>
> **El mes antes del viaje llamaré a la agencia de viajes para preguntarles si tienen paquetes especiales con todo incluido.**

| pedir información sobre... | llamar a la agencia | hacer reservaciones |
|---|---|---|
| comprar ropa nueva | conseguir el pasaporte | verificar el vuelo |
| cancelar el periódico | leer las guías turísticas | llamar a la línea aérea |
| | ir al banco | |

1. El mes antes del viaje...
2. Una semana antes del viaje...
3. Un día antes del viaje...
4. El día del viaje...

---

### 38 ¡Qué día!  1.1, 1.2

Imagine que Ud. trabaja en una agencia de viajes y se pregunta por qué hoy precisamente todos los clientes desean confirmar, posponer, cambiar o cancelar sus reservaciones. Primero, complete las oraciones con la forma del futuro de los verbos en paréntesis, según corresponda. Luego, túrnese con su compañero/a para representar cada una de las situaciones, dando la información que falta.

1. **Primera llamada**
   —¡Aló! ¿Es la agencia de viajes?
   —...
   —Tengo un pequeño inconveniente y por el momento necesito aplazar mi viaje a las Islas Baleares. Yo (**1.** *llamar*) mañana para darles mi próximo itinerario.
   —No se preocupe...
   —...

2. **Segunda llamada**
   —Soy... Llamo para modificar mi reservación. En vez de viajar el 20 de agosto, yo (**2.** *viajar*) el 30.
   —...

3. **Tercera llamada**
   —Buenos días, estoy llamando para confirmar mi viaje a... Hoy, yo le (**3.** *enviar*) un cheque por la suma total del viaje.
   —¡Vale! Recuerde que...
   —...

4. **Cuarta llamada**
   —Señor(ita), necesito cambiar la fecha de regreso de mi vuelo.
   —...
   —Necesito regresar cuatro días antes. ¿Cree Ud. que yo (**4.** *poder*) regresar el 10 de diciembre?
   —Lo siento, pero...
   —...

---

## Essential Instruction

1. Have students compare their answers from **Actividad 37** in small groups.
2. Complete items 1–4 in **Actividad 38** as a class. Then pair students and have them role-play the conversations. Have them sit back-to-back and use props.
3. Open **Actividad 39** by showing **el País Vasco** on a map of Spain. Have students scan the brochure for unfamiliar vocabulary. Read through the brochure as a class, pausing to ask comprehension questions.

# ¡Comunicación!

**39** ¿Qué te parece? 👥 **Interpersonal Communication** 🌸 **1.1, 1.2, 2.1, 2.2, 3.1**

Imagine que Ud. vive en España y Sofía, una amiga peruana, va a venir a visitarlo. Ella quiere conocer la región de Euskadi (el País Vasco) en el norte de España, y Ud. la llama por teléfono para contarle los planes que ha hecho. Lea el siguiente folleto y, luego, represente la conversación con un(a) compañero/a, turnándose para intercambiar opiniones y finalizar los planes y el itinerario. Usen el futuro en su conversación, como se ve en el modelo.

MODELO
**Ud.:** **Te cuento que ya tengo todo planeado. Primero iremos a Bilbao para no perdernos la celebración de la Semana Grande. ¿Qué te parece?**

**Sofía:** **Me encanta la idea. Y ya estando allá, podremos ir al Guggenheim. Siempre he querido conocerlo.**

# Euskadi

Viajar a **Euskadi** es explorar una rica cultura con raíces prehistóricas. Euskadi viene de *Euskal Herria*, que significa la tierra del euskera, su lengua. Ser *euskaldún* —el que tiene euskera— implica todo un sentido de identidad. Cuando llegues a esa hermosa tierra inmediatamente serás bienvenido Ve a Euskadi y *¡Ondo pasa!*, ¡Pásalo bien! Tres regiones, tres capitales, tres maravillas que te cautivarán por múltiples razones.

❶ Pasea por **Bilbao**, capital de Vizcaya, y experimenta su heterogeneidad: del vanguardista Museo Guggenheim, al neoclasicista teatro Arriaga, de las modernas torres Isozaki Atea a las antiguas Siete Calles del Casco Viejo[1]. En agosto, baila y celebra como todo un bilbaíno en la *Bilboko Aste Nagustia*, la Semana Grande de Bilbao, una fiesta recuperada del acervo[2] popular, con sus *konpartsak* (comparsas[3]) y la *Marijaia*, la Señora de las Fiestas.

❷ Disfruta la variada agenda cultural de **Donostia-San Sebastián**, capital de Guipúzcoa. ¡Por algo es la Capital Europea de la Cultura 2016! Hay de todo: Festival Internacional de Cine, Semana de Cine Fantástico y de Terror, Festival de Jazz y Quincena Musical. No te vayas sin degustar[4] su deliciosa comida; ¡es la ciudad del mundo con más estrellas Michelín por habitante! Prueba también sus típicos *pintxos*, o pinchos.

❸ Camina por **Vitoria-Gasteiz**, capital de Álava, y respira su entorno. Capital Verde Europea en 2012, es un referente mundial en planificación. Recorre sus múltiples parques y, especialmente, su Anillo Verde, una red ecológica que rodea la ciudad. Luego, sumérgete en los contrastes de su historia, desde el casco medieval y edificios románicos, hasta palacetes renacentistas y callejuelas de oficios antiguos: Cuchillería, Herrería, Zapatería...

Definitivamente, visitar Euskadi es para pedir *beste bat*, una repetición, y de seguro que haces muchos amigos. *¡Bai, noski!* ¡Claro que sí!

[1] old historic quarter  [2] heritage  [3] troupes  [4] taste, sample

RESOURCES

 Avenue

Answers _____

**39** *Las conversaciones variarán.*

## Reference Desk

1. Photo 1 shows the Guggenheim Museum in Bilbao, which was designed by Frank Gehry. Photo 2 shows a **pinchos** (**pintxos** in **euskera**) bar. Explain that **pinchos** are similar to **tapas**. Photo 3 shows part of the **Anillo Verde** around Vitoria-Gasteiz.

2. Point out the **euskera** words in the brochure and model their pronunciation. Explain that **euskera** is a language isolate, meaning that its origins are unknown and it does not belong to other language families. During the Franco regime, the speaking of Basque in public was forbidden; however, in the 1980s measures were taken to strengthen the language. Today about half of Basques speak **euskera**; the highest percentages are found in the younger age groups.

3. Explain that the Basque Country actually covers an area that spans a part of France and Spain.

4. Have students submit their finalized itineraries from **Actividad 39** as an Avenue task.

## Differentiated Learning
### Expand
Have students choose one city from the brochure in **Actividad 39** and research more about it. Have them create a brochure about the city, including visuals and tips for the best ways to travel there.

## Learning Styles
### Auditory Learners
Read through the brochure in **Actividad 39** as a class. Then check comprehension by naming a thing or an event associated with a particular city; students can hold up one, two, or three fingers to indicate the corresponding paragraph.

**Answers**

**Antes de leer**
*Las respuestas variarán.*

**40**

1. Porque se celebra el cuarto centenario de la publicación de la segunda parte de *Don Quijote*, que es una obra mundialmente famosa y el máximo referente para las letras españolas.
2. Es una novela que combina la comedia, la poesía, el drama y la caballería. Es también una parodia, una novela de aventuras, un tratado de la mente, un cuento picaresco y una historia de amor.
3. Es un héroe humanizado que se ha vuelto un ícono de libertad y justicia.

**41**  *Respuesta posible:*
Para que se convierta en un clásico, una obra no debe envejecer y no debe terminar de decir nunca lo que tiene que decir. Para que sea universal, deben poder disfrutarla lectores de distintas culturas.

**74**

---

# Lectura informativa

 **1.3, 2.2, 3.1** **Antes de leer**

Un personaje literario se convierte en un clásico universal cuando se sabe de él aunque no se haya leído la obra en la que aparece. ¿Qué sabe Ud. sobre don Quijote de La Mancha?

 **1.2, 2.2, 3.1, 3.2**

**40 Comprensión**

1. ¿Por qué el año 2015 es importante para el castellano y la literatura universal?
2. ¿Qué tipo de obra es *Don Quijote*?
3. ¿Qué clase de héroe es don Quijote?

 **1.3, 3.1**

**41 Analice**

¿Qué características cree Ud. que debe tener una obra literaria para convertirse en un clásico universal?

---

○○○   2015, Año del Quijote

## 2015, Año del Quijote  **1.2, 2.2, 3.1, 3.2**

**ALVARO OCTAVIO LARA HUERTA** 14 de enero 2015 20:11:52

Este 2015 será un año importante para el castellano y la literatura universal, ya que se cumple el cuarto centenario[1] de la publicación de *El ingenioso hidalgo don Quijote de la Mancha* (la segunda parte de la novela). [...]

A finales de 1615 salía a luz uno de los textos más importantes para el mundo de las letras y el máximo referente[2] para la lengua española. La primera novela moderna que ha sido traducida prácticamente a todos los idiomas y solo superada en ediciones por la Biblia.

Una obra que conjuga[3] la comedia, la poesía, el drama y la caballería[4] de una forma extraordinaria que ha cristalizado al personaje principal Alonso Quijano, don Quijote, en un símbolo de la cultura hispanoamericana que lo mismo ha tocado el cine, las artes visuales, la música y, por supuesto, la literatura, convirtiéndose en ese eterno espíritu libre, sabio e inquebrantable[5].

Seguramente el idealismo de don Quijote invadirá los eventos culturales del presente año, pues siempre es una delicia volver a los clásicos para redescubrir su actualidad y frescura, aun después de 400 años. La inventiva y "sabiduría popular" impregna cada frase, situación y diálogo a lo largo de los 74 capítulos que integran la obra con un sinfín[6] de recursos literarios.

El *Quijote* se ha vuelto un ícono de libertad y justicia, el héroe humanizado, la utopía alcanzable, la locura más realista, la razón de la sinrazón.

Cervantes con el *Quijote* se convirtió en el mayor y más longevo inspirador de la creación artística. La lucidez y grandeza reflejada en su obra cumbre[7] ha influenciado lo mismo a poetas, críticos, filósofos, literatos, intelectuales y dramaturgos, entre otros. [...]

El *Quijote* lo es todo: una parodia, una novela de aventuras, un tratado de la mente, un cuento picaresco, una historia de amor que no termina de sorprendernos en las rendijas del discurso[8].

---

[1] four hundred year anniversary   [2] example   [3] combines   [4] chivalry   [5] unyielding
[6] endless number   [7] masterpiece   [8] interwoven throughout the story

---

## Essential Instruction

1. Have pairs discuss the **Antes de leer** question. Make a list of students' responses on the board.
2. Go over the **Estrategia**. Ask students to give an example of how background knowledge can help them understand new information.
3. Give students 30 seconds to skim each reading and share what they discovered. Write notes on the board and verify them as you go through the readings as a class.
4. For Common Core practice, have students answer the **Analice** question. Go over the answer as a class.

CIUDADANOS | EMPRENDEDORES | GOBIERNO | PRESIDENTA

## Cospedal celebra que "nuestro personaje más universal" acercará Castilla-La Mancha al mundo para crear riqueza

 **1.2, 2.2, 3.1**

08/01/2015, Presidenta, Castilla-La Mancha

*Subraya que el año 2015 hará que Castilla-La Mancha sea un referente conocido en cualquier parte del mundo en ámbito de la producción artística*

*Asegura que el logotipo ganador, 'Gigantes', "constituye una representación del Quijote y de nuestra tierra, clara, sencilla y reconocible pero, a su vez, vanguardista e innovadora"*

La presidenta del Gobierno de Castilla-La Mancha, María Dolores de Cospedal, ha destacado que nuestra región va a utilizar este año "a nuestro personaje literario más conocido y a nuestro escritor más universal" para dar a conocer al resto del mundo las bellezas de nuestra cultura, patrimonio e historia, y a partir de ahí "que sean acicates[1], todos ellos, para nuestro crecimiento económico".

Así lo ha manifestado Cospedal durante la presentación del logo del IV Centenario de la publicación de la Segunda Parte del Quijote, donde se ha referido a la magnífica posibilidad que supondrá para el turismo cultural en nuestra tierra, "para que visitantes de otras partes de España y del mundo vengan atraídos por todo lo que representamos y que esa representación lo sea de lo que es esta tierra nuestra, el corazón de España".

Cospedal ha subrayado que este año 2015, "hará que en el ámbito de la producción artística, Castilla-La Mancha sea un referente conocido en cualquier parte del mundo". [...]

### Un reto[2] importante

María Dolores de Cospedal ha hecho hincapié en[3] el "importante reto" que supone la celebración del IV Centenario de la publicación de la Segunda Parte del Quijote, "porque esta conmemoración es muy nuestra, porque no hay un personaje de ficción más conocido que don Quijote y tenemos la obligación de mirar al frente y cumplir ese reto con creces[4], como estoy convencida que vamos a hacer".

Por ello, la presidenta regional ha hecho referencia a toda una serie de actividades que se llevarán a cabo[5] a lo largo del año, "que van a plasmar[6], a través de las artes escénicas, de la música y exposiciones, la conmemoración de la obra más universal en lengua castellana y también dar a conocer el talento que hay en nuestra región".

Estos acontecimientos, ha señalado la presidenta, tendrán su continuación en el año 2016 con la conmemoración del IV Centenario del fallecimiento de Miguel de Cervantes. [...]

[1] stimuli   [2] challenge   [3] has emphasized   [4] exceeding expectations   [5] will take place   [6] express

**Búsqueda:** don quijote, miguel de cervantes, cuarto centenario del quijote, castilla-la mancha

 **1.2, 2.1, 2.2, 3.2**

## 42 Comprensión

1. ¿Qué beneficios le traerá a Castilla-La Mancha la celebración del IV Centenario de la publicación de la Segunda Parte del Quijote?

2. ¿Por qué este aniversario es una oportunidad magnífica para el turismo cultural en la región?

3. ¿Qué tipo de actividades planea el gobierno de Castilla-La Mancha para celebrar el aniversario?

 **1.3, 3.1, 4.2**

## 43 Analice

¿Qué lugares de su país atraen visitantes por su relación con obras literarias famosas?

**Answers**

**44** *Las respuestas variarán.*

**45** *Las respuestas variarán.*

**1.** Before beginning **Actividad 44**, review the windmills episode from **Don Quijote**. Brainstorm vocabulary such as **molinos de viento**, **aspas**, **lanza**, etc.

**2.** You might have students submit their social media posts from **Actividad 45**, along with a summary of people's reactions, in an Avenue task.

**3.** As an alternative to **Actividad 45**, you may want to have students share their ideas on Flipgrid, where their classmates can respond.

### Critical Thinking

**Analyzing**

Ask students to think about how social media has changed the way people interact. Are these changes positive or negative overall? Why?

### Pre-AP

Have students complete the activities on pp. 76–77 to help them prepare for the writing sections of the AP® exam.

---

# Escritura

## Publicar en las redes sociales  1.3

Las redes sociales de la internet son comunidades virtuales donde los usuarios interactúan con contactos de todo el mundo con quienes tienen gustos o intereses en común. Funcionan como una plataforma donde se pueden publicar textos (en general, breves), fotos y videos.

### ¡Comunicación! 1.2, 1.3, 2.2, 3.1, 3.2

**44** **"Gigantes", logotipo ganador Quijote 2015** Interpretive Communication

Vuelva a leer lo que dice la presidenta de Castilla-La Mancha sobre el "Gigantes" ganador del concurso del logotipo del Quijote en la página anterior y lo que dice aquí su propia creadora, Ana María Escribano. A medida que lea, resuma los puntos principales en una tabla, como la que se da a continuación.

Para la realización de la marca e imagen de dicha conmemoración excluí los referentes básicos y realicé una interpretación actualizada y moderna de las aspas de los molinos, estas dentro de un marco cuadrado reflejando así, de manera muy conceptual y abstracta, el movimiento causado por sus aspas, elemento tan importante en el *Quijote*. Se juega con la abstracción para hacer referencia a la pérdida del juicio del personaje, la visión sin sentido de sus aventuras y al mismo tiempo conseguir una marca moderna y actual, un ícono limpio y visible con opción de escalar a diferentes formatos y no perder su legibilidad, apoyado por una tipografía moderna, diseñada para la ocasión con pequeños referentes tipográficos de la época.

| Interpretaciones del logo "Gigantes" | |
|---|---|
| **Según la presidenta de Castilla-La Mancha** | **Según Ana María Escribano** |
| | |
| | |
| | |
| | |

**45** **Mi propia interpretación** Presentational Communication  1.3, 2.2, 3.1, 5.1

¿Qué piensa Ud. de este ícono? ¿Qué cree que pensarán sus amigos o conocidos? Compare la información que acaba de reunir, haga su propio análisis del ícono y saque sus propias conclusiones. Luego, publique su interpetación en su red social favorita para ver cómo reaccionan los demás.

**Essential Instruction**

**1.** Introduce this section by asking students about their use of social networks.

**2.** Draw attention to the logo in **Actividad 44**. Ask students what they think is represented by the lines in the square. Then have them read the statement by Ana María Escribano. Complete the table as a class.

**3.** For **Actividad 45**, remind students that social media posts are generally succinct.

**4.** For **Actividad 46**, play the audio once and have students just listen. Play the audio a second time and have them take notes.

**5.** For **Actividad 47**, review good practices for peer-editing.

# Un folleto turístico  1.3

Un folleto turístico es un texto que se escribe para atraer visitantes a un lugar. Su objetivo principal es promocionar lo mejor de ese lugar y, por eso, su estilo es muy parecido al de los textos publicitarios. Las instituciones como las secretarías de turismo u otros organismos del gobierno son quienes se encargan de publicar este tipo de folletos.

Los folletos turísticos suelen tener forma de cuadernillo o desplegable y, en general, se distribuyen de manera gratuita. Combinan partes descriptivas con secciones de consejos prácticos y elementos gráficos, como fotografías o mapas, que ilustran el lugar.

En los textos, se describen las características más atractivas o interesantes de la geografía del lugar, su historia y cultura, su gastronomía, las actividades que se pueden realizar allí o los distintos tipos de alojamiento. Usan un lenguaje que combina adjetivos y sustantivos para que las descripciones sean más vívidas y atrayentes: "imponente castillo", "cálidas aguas", "espléndidas vistas", etc.

> ### Para escribir más
>
> Puede usar los siguientes adjetivos para agregar detalles a su folleto turístico.
>
> encantador
> espectacular
> fabuloso
> ideal
> increíble
> mágico
> sin comparación
> único

## ¡Comunicación!

**46 Turismo en Castilla y León**  Interpretive Communication 🌸 **1.2, 1.3, 2.2, 3.2**

Escuche el siguiente segmento sobre el turismo en la región de Castilla y León en España y tome notas de lo que dice Javier Ramírez, Presidente de la Junta de Castilla y León, al respecto. ¿Qué tiene para ofrecer esta región del país en términos de turismo, según Ramírez? Escriba sus respuestas en una hoja aparte.

**47 ¿Por qué España?** Presentational Communication 🌸 **1.3, 2.1, 2.2, 3.1**

Imagine que Ud. trabaja para la Secretaría de Turismo de España y está encargado/a de crear un folleto publicitario para promocionar el turismo en varias regiones del país. Primero, repase la información que se ha presentado en la unidad* hasta ahora y resuma los puntos principales en un organizador gráfico como el que se ve a continuación.

Ahora, escriba el primer borrador de su folleto con base en la información que reunió y pídale a un(a) compañero/a que lo revise. Haga las correcciones necesarias y cree la versión final. Agregue fotos llamativas para que su folleto sea más interesante y, para terminar, preséntelo enfrente de la clase.

*Ver páginas 45 (video), 59–62, 65, 66, 73

---

## Differentiated Learning
### Heritage Learners
Ask heritage speakers to compare and contrast the tourism opportunities in **Castilla y León** with those in the city or region of their family's origin.

## Special Needs Students
### Auditory Impairment
Allow these students to listen several times to the recording in **Actividad 46**. You may also want to provide them with a script so that they can follow along and highlight the main points as they listen.

RESOURCES

 Activity 46

**Answers**

**46 Script**

Bueno. Efectivamente estamos haciendo un esfuerzo muy especial, muy especial, para tratar de que la imagen que se tiene del turismo español en el exterior, el turismo español en todo el mundo, se limite al modelo turístico de sol y playa. Nosotros estamos convencidos que la oferta turística española tiene otros muchos más recursos que ofrecer, y que Castilla y León en ese sentido es un exponente fundamental. Nosotros estamos hablando de una comunidad que tiene ocho bienes declarados patrimonio de la humanidad, que tiene multitud de castillos, que tiene nueve denominaciones de origen que tiene una oferta de turismo de naturaleza muy potente, más de cuarenta espacios naturales con algún tipo de declaración, y eso sin duda es una oferta turística que debemos dar a conocer fuera. Es verdad que no es fácil, pero también hay que reconocer que estamos haciendo un trabajo muy intenso en colaboración con Turespaña, en colaboración con el Ministerio, para que esa oferta de turismo interior, esos recursos vinculados a la cultura, vinculados a la naturaleza, vinculados a la gastronomía, vinculados al vino, al enoturismo, sean también conocidos fuera y enriquezcan la oferta turística nacional y supongan también un factor de diversificación de esa oferta para no limitarla únicamente al sol y playa, *Continued on p. 89.*

*Las respuestas variarán.*

**47** *Los folletos variarán.*

### Reference Desk

**Actividad 46** contains authentic audio, which is an important component of the AP® Spanish exam.

### RESOURCES

 Mejore su comprensión

**Answers**

**48** *Las explicaciones variarán.*
*Respuestas posibles:*

1. *Camino* no se relaciona con beber.
2. *Melancólico* describe un sentimiento.
3. *Tristeza* describe un sentimiento.
4. *Sombra* no es una actitud.
5. *Vereda* no se relaciona con el mar.
6. *Soñar* no es un verbo de movimiento.
7. *Callar* es algo que hacen las personas.
8. *Molesto* describe una actitud o sentimiento.

### Reference Desk

1. Point out that students will use this vocabulary to complete the audio activity on p. 79, as well as to aid in comprehension of the **Lectura literaria** on pp. 87–88.
2. Remind students of dictionary abbreviations; ask a volunteer to explain them.
3. Allow for a variety of answers as well as explanations in **Actividad 48** provided that students can justify their choice.

### TPR

Have students work in pairs. They should take turns acting out the vocabulary for their partner to guess. Encourage students to exaggerate their gestures. Invite a few pairs to act out some terms for the class.

## Mejore su comprensión 🎧 ✿ 1.2

Familiarizarse con este vocabulario le ayudará a leer "He andado muchos caminos" más adelante, y a mejorar su comprensión auditiva.

**a lomos de mula vieja** *exp. figurada:* Sin prisa, como si fueran (*as if they were*) montados en una mula vieja que anda despacio por su edad.

**andar** *v.* Ir de un lugar a otro a pie.

**apestar** *v.* Dar muy mal olor.

**atracar** *v.* Llegar una embarcación a tierra.

**borracho** *s.m.* Persona que está bajo los efectos del alcohol.

**cabalgar** *v.* Ir a caballo.

**callar** *v.* No hablar, en silencio.

**camino** *s.m.* Por donde se va de un sitio a otro.

**caravana** *s.f.* Grupo de personas que viajan juntas.

**danzar** *v.* Bailar al ritmo de una música.

**¡Eso sí que es!** Exclamación de afirmación cuyas iniciales deletrean la palabra *socks*.

**fresco/a** *adj.* Temperatura agradablemente fría.

**laborar** *v.* Trabajar la tierra.

**mar** *s.m.* Masa de agua salada que cubre la mayor parte de la superficie de la tierra.

**melancólico/a** *adj.* Triste.

**navegar** *v.* Viajar en una nave.

**palmo** *s.m.* Medida de longitud.

**pedantones al paño** *exp.* Personas sabelotodo.

**ribera** *s.f.* Borde del mar o de un río.

**soberbio/a** *adj.* Orgulloso.

**sombra** *s.f.* Imagen oscura reflejada por la luz en una superficie.

**soñar** *v.* Representar algo en la mente mientras se duerme.

**taberna** *s.f.* Lugar sencillo donde se sirven comidas y bebidas.

**tierra** *s.f.* Mundo; suelo donde crecen las plantas.

**tristeza** *s.f.* Sentimiento que tiende al silencio y al llanto.

**un poco molesto/a** *adj.* Algo disgustado(a).

*Caminos y veredas del norte de España*

**vereda** *s.f.* Camino estrecho formado por el paso de personas y ganado.

**vino** *s.m.* Bebida alcohólica que se obtiene de las uvas.

### 48 Identifique al intruso ✿ 1.3

Diga qué palabra no pertenece al grupo y explique por qué.

MODELO    atracar / navegar / cabalgar

**Cabalgar no tiene que ver con embarcaciones.**

1. vino / camino / taberna
2. palmo / melancólico / tierra
3. tristeza / caminos / caravanas
4. pedantón / sombra / soberbio
5. mar / vereda / ribera
6. soñar / danzar / andar
7. atracar / callar / tierra
8. cabalgar / molesto / mula

### Essential Instruction

1. Model pronunciation of the new vocabulary words and have students repeat. Clarify any unfamiliar words in the definitions.
2. Have students complete **Actividades 48** and **49** in pairs.
3. Before beginning **Actividad 50**, remind students that they will hear some vocabulary from p. 78 in the story.
4. For **Actividad 50**, have students listen to the story with their eyes closed. Play it a second time, pausing to ask questions. Then play the rest of the audio and have students select their answers.

## 49 ¿Cuál corresponde?  1.2

Complete las oraciones que siguen con la palabra del recuadro que corresponda según el contexto.

| vino | laboran | melancólicas | navegan |
|------|---------|--------------|---------|
| andar | palmos | soberbia | camino |
| | atracan | borracho | |

1. Ese hombre es un ____ que se la pasa bebiendo ____ de taberna en taberna.

2. Esos barcos inmensos ____ por el mar y ____ en sus riberas.

3. Esos campesinos ____ de sol a sol y viven de trabajar su par de ____ de tierra.

4. La tristeza es el gran mal que afecta a las personas ____ .

5. Ella es una persona ____ y orgullosa que se cree mejor que todos los demás.

6. Mañana tenemos que llegar a nuestro destino y todavía nos falta ____ gran parte del ____ .

## 50 El problema de una turista  1.2

Escuche el relato "El problema de una turista". Luego, Ud. oirá la primera parte de una pregunta y tres terminaciones posibles. Seleccione la letra de la respuesta con la terminación más lógica. La oración y las terminaciones se leerán dos veces.

*Una señora quiere comprarle unos calcetines a su esposo.*

1. **A.** ... no puede comprar ropa en un almacén.
   **B.** ... puede comprar ropa sin saber hablar inglés.
   **C.** ... puede comprar ropa porque habla inglés.

2. **A.** ... no comprar nada más.
   **B.** ... salir del almacén.
   **C.** ... comprar unos calcetines.

3. **A.** ... trata de explicarle lo que quiere.
   **B.** ... le explica lo que quiere.
   **C.** ... le habla en inglés.

4. **A.** ... la sección para caballeros.
   **B.** ... donde debe pagar.
   **C.** ... varios artículos de vestir.

5. **A.** ¡Eso sí que es!
   **B.** ¿Qué es eso?
   **C.** ¡Eso no es!

---

## Answers

**49**
1. borracho, vino
2. navegan, atracan
3. laboran, palmos
4. melancólicas
5. soberbia
6. andar, camino

**50 Script**

Una turista hispana que visita por primera vez los Estados Unidos está sorprendida de la facilidad con que se puede comprar ropa en un almacén de los Estados Unidos sin tener que hablar inglés, idioma que ella comprende un poco, pero no lo habla.

Después de recorrer las diferentes secciones y tomar de las mesas lo que más le gusta, decide comprar unos calcetines para su esposo. Busca una mesa con calcetines pero no la ve por ninguna parte. Esta vez la señora se ve en un gran problema porque no encuentra los calcetines y no sabe la palabra en inglés.

La señora se acerca a un dependiente y trata de explicarle lo que quiere. El dependiente, muy amablemente, le va mostrando varios artículos de vestir: blusas, faldas, vestidos, abrigos. Cada vez la señora mueve la cabeza diciendo: "No, no es eso", "no eso".

*Continued on p. 91.*

1. Una turista que visita por primera vez los Estados Unidos está sorprendida porque...
2. Después de tomar la ropa que le gusta de las diferentes mesas, la señora decide...
3. La señora se acerca a un dependiente y...
4. El dependiente le muestra a la señora...
5. Cuando el dependiente le muestra unos calcetines, la turista exclama:

1. B; 2. C; 3. A; 4. C; 5. A

---

## Differentiated Learning

**Heritage Learners**
Encourage heritage learners to list synonyms for the new vocabulary terms.

## Learning Styles

**Visual Learners**
Ask students to create a deck of flash cards, with the new vocabulary words on one side and on the other, have them draw or paste a picture to illustrate the term.

**Special Needs Students**
**Auditory Impairment**
Provide students with the story and the sentence starters in **Actividad 50**.

**79**

# Gramática

## Las comparaciones  1.2, 4.1

Para hacer comparaciones de superioridad e inferioridad se usa **más** o **menos** como se ve a continuación.

- La palabra comparativa *than* se expresa con **que**, pero cuando ocurre antes de un número o una cantidad se expresa con **de**.

| Las comparaciones de superioridad e inferioridad | | |
|---|---|---|
| **más/menos** + | adjetivo + **que** | Los trenes de larga distancia son **más cómodos que** los trenes regionales. |
| | adverbio + **que** | Los vuelos directos llegan **más rápido que** los vuelos que hacen escalas. |
| | sustantivo + **que** | En primera clase hay **menos pasajeros que** en clase turista. |
| verbo + **más/menos que** | | Tú **viajas más que** yo pero **te diviertes menos que** yo. |
| **más/menos de** + | número | La empresa invertirá **más de** 2 millones en el nuevo proyecto. |
| | cantidad | Pienso que lo vendieron por **menos de** la mitad del precio. |

- Al contrario del inglés, después de **más que** y **menos que** se usan los negativos **nunca**, **nadie**, **nada** y **ninguno**.

Estoy trabajando **más que nunca**.
*I'm working more than ever.*

Yo me preocupo **más que nadie**.
*I worry more than anyone.*

| Comparativos irregulares | | |
|---|---|---|
| **Adjetivo** | **Adverbio** | **Forma comparativa** |
| bueno (buen) | bien | mejor |
| malo (mal) | mal | peor |
| poco | poco | menos |
| mucho | mucho | más |
| pequeño | | menor |
| grande (gran) | | mayor |

*Es más cómodo viajar en primera clase que en clase turista.*

- Cuando **bueno** y **malo** se refieren al carácter de una persona y no a la calidad de una cosa, se usan las formas regulares.

  **carácter:**   Antonio es **mucho más bueno** que tú: no se enfada nunca.
  Ese hombre es aún **más malo** que los otros.

  **calidad:**   El segundo concierto fue **mejor** que el primero.
  El clima está **peor** que ayer.

- Cuando los adjetivos **grande** y **pequeño** se refieren a tamaño y no a edad, se usan las formas regulares.

  **tamaño:**   Mi mochila es **más grande** que la tuya.
  Este aeropuerto es aún **más pequeño** que el aeropuerto de Granada.

  **edad:**   Soy **mayor** que mi hermano Antonio, pero **menor** que mi hermana Rebeca.

## ¡Comunicación!

**51  Alternativas y preferencias**   Interpersonal Communication  1.1

Piense en todas las alternativas que tiene cuando va de viaje: cómo viajar, dónde quedarse, qué hacer. ¿Cuáles serían sus preferidas? Con un(a) compañero/a, túrnense para expresar sus preferencias y sus razones, como se ve en el modelo.

MODELO   viajar en tren / viajar en coche
(¿flexible? ¿rápido? ¿interesante?)

**A:**  **A mí me gusta más viajar en tren porque es más interesante que viajar en coche.**

**B:**  **A mí me gusta más viajar en coche que viajar en tren porque es más rápido.**

1. comer en un restaurante / comer en una cafetería
   (¿caro? ¿interesante? ¿conveniente?)

2. quedarse en un hotel / quedarse en una pensión
   (¿económico? ¿cómodo? ¿grande?)

3. hacer un viaje en grupo / hacer un viaje independiente
   (¿limitado? ¿eficiente? ¿flexible?)

4. hacer turismo (*sightsee*) en autobús / hacer turismo a pie
   (¿divertido? ¿económico? ¿aburrido?)

*Siempre nos quedamos en un hotel cuando viajamos. Es mucho mejor.*

**Reference Desk**

Give additional examples to contrast the varied meanings of **bueno/malo** and **grande/ pequeño**, such as: **Sonia es más buena que el pan.** vs. **No hay nada mejor que un pan fresco.**

**Communication**

Presentational/Interpersonal: Paired Practice
In pairs, have students talk about one great travel experience, and one that was bad. Remind them to use comparisons of inequality in their stories. Tell students to ask follow-up questions about their partner's story.

## Differentiated Learning
**Decelerate**
Write the basic structures for comparisons of inequality on the board. With each one, generate a list of possible adjectives, people, things, and verbs. Work as a class to make comparative statements.

## Multiple Intelligences
**Visual-Spatial**
Create a portfolio of celebrities, politicians, animals, and objects. Cut out photographs or illustrations from magazines and glue them to sticks. Use the characters to create observations and comparisons.

## ¡Comunicación!

**52  Decisiones y más decisiones** 👥  Presentational Communication ❁ **1.1, 1.3**

Imagine que Ud. y un(a) compañero/a están en Palma de Mallorca y tienen la opción de quedarse en el Hotel Isla Mallorca & Spa o el Hotel Costa Azul. Lean la información sobre los dos hoteles y compárenlos según el precio, la ubicación (*location*), las comodidades y los servicios incluidos. Luego, infórmenle a la clase qué hotel eligieron y expliquen por qué. Escriban seis oraciones usando los comparativos y los verbos del recuadro, como se ve en el modelo.

| estar | ofrecer | contar con | costar | hay | tener | ser | encontrarse |

**MODELO**  El Hotel Isla Mallorca & Spa está más lejos del mar, pero ofrece…

**Hotel Isla Mallorca & Spa**
- Habitaciones con terraza
- Situado en una zona tranquila de Palma
- Restaurante (a la carta y buffet), Bar
- Piscina al aire libre, Jardín, Terraza
- Gimnasio, Spa, Wi-Fi gratis
- 180 euros al día

**Hotel Costa Azul**
- Habitaciones con vista al mar
- Ubicado frente al puerto deportivo de Palma
- Restaurante de tipo buffet y cafetería con terraza
- Sauna y piscina, cubierta en invierno
- Gimnasio, Wi-Fi gratuito, TV LED vía satélite
- 250 euros al día

**53  ¡Qué interesante!** 👥  ❁  **1.1**

**Interpersonal Communication**

Imagine una conversación entre dos pasajeros de un largo viaje en avión. Los dos son muy extrovertidos y comunicativos y terminan contándose, uno al otro, la historia de su vida. Con un(a) compañero/a representen la situación. Túrnense para hacerse las preguntas del caso y responderlas, como se ve en el modelo.

*¿Viajas con mucha frecuencia?*

**MODELO**  
Ud.:  ¿Tienes una familia grande?  
pasajero/a:  No. Solo tengo dos hermanos. ¿Y tú?  
Ud.:  Yo tengo cinco hermanos. Tengo muchos más que tú.

### Essential Instruction

1. Have students scan the lists in **Actividad 52** for cognates.
2. For **Actividad 53**, generate a list of conversation topics that the travelers might discuss.
3. Personalize the **Gramática** presentation by making comparisons of equality that are true for you.
4. Have students check their answers to **Actividad 54** in pairs.

# Gramática

## Las comparaciones de igualdad  1.2

Para expresar una comparación de igualdad usamos **tan** o **tanto(a, os, as)** como se ve a continuación.

| Comparaciones de igualdad | | |
|---|---|---|
| *as... as* | **tan** + adjetivo + **como** | —¿Serán menos seguros los aviones del futuro que los aviones actuales?<br>—No. Serán **tan** seguros **como** los actuales. |
| | **tan** + adverbio + **como** | —¿Volarán más rápido que los actuales?<br>—No. Volarán **tan** rápido **como** los actuales. |
| *as much as* | **tanto(a)** + sustantivo + **como** | —¿Consumirán más energía que los actuales?<br>—No. Probablemente consumirán **tanta** energía **como** los actuales. |
| | verbo + **tanto como** | —¿Costarán más que los actuales?<br>—No. Costarán **tanto como** los actuales o menos. |
| *as many as* | **tantos(as)** + sustantivo + **como** | —En los aviones del futuro, ¿viajarán menos pasajeros que en los actuales?<br>—No. Viajarán **tantos pasajeros** como en los actuales. |
| | verbo + **tantos(as) como** | —¿Y tendrán tantos problemas como los actuales?<br>—Claro que tendrán **tantos como** los actuales, pero serán diferentes. |

### 54 Estoy de acuerdo  1.3

Dos turistas hablan sobre su experiencia en un hotel en Palma de Mallorca. Exprese lo que dicen usando comparaciones de igualdad según el modelo.

MODELO  Los huéspedes son amables. (*el personal*)
**Estoy de acuerdo. Los huéspedes son tan amables como el personal.**

1. Puede ir de excursión en barco. (*autobús*)
2. Llegan bastantes norteamericanos al hotel. (*españoles*)
3. Los precios del restaurante son económicos. (*la cafetería*)
4. Los jardines son bonitos. (*los patios*)
5. Los cuartos sencillos son muy agradables. (*los cuartos dobles*)
6. Se consiguen revistas internacionales en la tienda. (*periódicos*)

## RESOURCES

| WB | Activity 14 |
|---|---|
| LA | Activity 7 |

### Answers

**54**
1. Puede ir de excursión tanto en barco como en autobús.
2. Llegan tantos norteamericanos como españoles al hotel.
3. Los precios del restaurante son tan económicos como los precios de la cafetería.
4. Los jardines son tan bonitos como los patios.
5. Los cuartos sencillos son tan agradables como los cuartos dobles.
6. Se consiguen tantas revistas internacionales como periódicos en la tienda.

### Reference Desk

Remind students that **tanto/a** must agree in gender and number when used to modify nouns.

### TPR

Prepare a series of sentences, some with comparisons of equality and others that contain comparisons of inequality. Tell students to write an equal sign on one piece of paper and an equal sign with a slash through it on another piece of paper. After you read each statement, students hold up the appropriate paper.

## Special Needs Students
### Dyslexia
Provide students with extra practice focusing on the need for agreement when using **tanto**, **tantos**, **tanta**, and **tantas** to express equal amounts. Instruct students to circle the object with which it must agree.

## Multiple Intelligences
### Visual-Spatial
Instruct students to draw pictures to show equality. Ask students to choose two objects (e.g., **zanahorias y tomates**) and draw an equal number of each. Then have students exchange pictures and write comparisons of equality. (**Juan tiene tantas zanahorias como tomates.**)

83

**Answers**

 **55**

1. Avianca tiene tantos pilotos como Aeroméxico, pero Avianca y Aeroméxico no tienen tantos pilotos como Iberia.
2. Los aviones de Avianca son tan modernos como los de Aeroméxico, pero los aviones de Avianca y de Aeroméxico no son tan modernos como los de Iberia.
3. Avianca tiene tantos aviones como Aeroméxico, pero Avianca y Aeroméxico no tienen tantos aviones como Iberia.
4. Los auxiliares de vuelo de Aeroméxico trabajan tantas horas al día como los de Iberia, pero los auxiliares de vuelo de Avianca no trabajan tantas horas al día como los de Aeroméxico y los de Iberia.

### Reference Desk

Ask students if they know which countries are associated with each airline (**Iberia**—Spain; **Avianca**—Colombia; **Aeroméxico**—Mexico). Founded in 1919, **Avianca** is the oldest continuously operating airline in the Americas.

---

# Gramática

## 55  Avianca, Iberia y Aeroméxico   1.3

Lea con atención los servicios que ofrecen las compañías de aviación Iberia, Avianca, y Aeroméxico y exprese una comparación de igualdad.

> **MODELO**  Aeroméxico e Iberia tienen cuarenta y dos vuelos diarios. Avianca tiene treinta y cuatro.
>
> **Aeroméxico tiene tantos vuelos como Iberia, pero Avianca no tiene tantos vuelos como Aeroméxico o Iberia.**

1. Avianca y Aeroméxico tienen veinte pilotos. Iberia tiene veintiséis.
2. Los aviones de Iberia son modernos. Los de Avianca y Aeroméxico son menos modernos.
3. Iberia tiene cincuenta aviones. Avianca y Aeroméxico tienen cuarenta.
4. Los auxiliares de vuelo de Avianca trabajan solo ocho horas al día. Los auxiliares de vuelo de Aeroméxico e Iberia trabajan diez horas al día.

## El superlativo  1.2, 4.1

- Para formar el superlativo con adjetivos se añade el artículo definido (**el**, **la**, **los**, **las**) a la forma comparativa.

| Adjetivo | Comparativo | Superlativo | |
|---|---|---|---|
| pesado (*heavy*) | más pesado | el más pesado | Mi equipaje es **el más pesado**. |
| bueno | mejor | el mejor | Estas son **las mejores** vacaciones que he tenido. (calidad) |
| malo | peor | el peor | Este es **el peor** asiento del avión. (calidad) |

- Para formar el superlativo con adverbios, se usa la construcción **lo más** + **adverbio**.

| Adjetivo | Comparativo | Superlativo | |
|---|---|---|---|
| claramente | más claramente | lo más claramente | Lea el informe **lo más claramente** posible. |
| bien | mejor | lo mejor | Haz **lo mejor** que puedas. |

- Para expresar el superlativo en relación con otros elementos, se usa la forma superlativa seguida de la preposición **de** (inglés: *in* o *of*).

artículo + **más** + adjetivo + **de**
o
**menos**

Este viaje es **el más costoso de** todos.
Clara es **la menos alta de** las chicas.
Uds. son **los más estudiosos de** la clase.

---

### Essential Instruction

1. Have students check their answers to **Actividad 55** in pairs.
2. As you go through **El superlativo**, give concrete examples by making statements about objects in your school, students, and community.
3. Draw a simple representation of the solar system on the board. Label the planets and model the pronunciation. Then have students complete **Actividad 56**.

- Para un superlativo independiente, se puede usar la siguiente construcción.

| muy | | | Este viaje es **muy** costoso. |
|---|---|---|---|
| sumamente | + | adjetivo o adverbio | Clara es **sumamente** alta. |
| extraordinariamente | | | Diana es **extraordinariamente** inteligente. |
| extremadamente | | | Viaja **extremadamente** lejos. |
| adjetivo + -**ísimo(a, os, as)**[1] | | | Tiene una vista **hermosísima**. |
| | | | Le dio un regalo **carísimo**. |
| adverbio + -**ísimo** | | | La excursión de hoy fue **muchísimo** mejor que la de ayer. |
| | | | Se levantó **tempranísimo**. |

[1] Se suprime la vocal final del adjetivo y se añade -**ísimo(a, os, as)**. Algunas formas sufren cambios.

**z → c:**  feliz → felicísimo  **c → qu:**  rico → riquísimo

**g → gu:**  largo → larguísimo  **ble → bil:**  amable → amabilísimo

---

### 56 Un viaje interplanetario   Conéctese: la astronomía  1.2, 3.1

Es muy posible que en el futuro cercano, Ud. pueda planear un viaje interplanetario. Por eso es importante informarse sobre los planetas. Complete las oraciones con una expresión de inferioridad, superioridad, igualdad o con el superlativo. Cada espacio en blanco requiere una palabra.

1. Júpiter es ____ ____ grande de todos los planetas.

2. Mercurio es ____ pequeño ____ Saturno.

3. Júpiter tiene ____ lunas ____ la Tierra; tiene más ____ once lunas.

4. El "día" de un planeta es el tiempo que dura una rotación sobre su eje (*axis*). Un día en Júpiter dura un poco menos ____ diez horas; mientras que un día en Venus dura más ____ 243 días terrestres. Un día en la Tierra es ____ largo que uno en Júpiter, pero ____ largo que uno en Venus.

5. El "año" de un planeta es el tiempo que dura una revolución alrededor del sol. Un año en Mercurio dura casi ochenta y ocho días; una revolución de Plutón dura 249 de nuestros años terrenales. Un año en Mercurio es muchísimo ____ corto ____ un año en Plutón. Un hecho interesante: una rotación de Venus sobre su eje dura 243 días, mientras una revolución alrededor del sol dura sólo 225 días. Es decir, su "día" dura ____ tiempo ____ su "año."

6. La temperatura de la Tierra es 59 °F; la de Marte, 55 °F. Es decir, Marte es casi ____ caliente como la Tierra. En 1970 los científicos rusos midieron una temperatura de 885 °F en Venus, comprobando que este planeta es ____ ____ caliente ____ todos.

---

Answers

56

1. el más
2. más, que
3. más, que, de
4. de, de, más, menos
5. más, que, más, que
6. tan, el, más, de

### Reference Desk

Point out that the absolute superlative stresses the adjective to the maximum degree. It does not compare the person or thing to others.

### Connections

**Science/Astronomy**
Have students research a Spanish-speaking scientist in the field of astronomy or planetary science. Have them write a brief profile of the person and his/her work.

### Expansion

After reviewing **Gramática**, provide students with a note card. Have students write five sentences using the superlative. They must hand this card to you when they leave class at the end of the hour as their exit card. Correct the sentences and hand them back the next day at the beginning of class.

---

### Learning Styles
**Visual Learners**

Encourage students to use symbols (such as equal and plus signs) to process the information in the sentences in **Actividad 55**. Have them represent the information visually before they attempt to write the comparative sentences.

### Multiple Intelligences
**Visual-Spatial**

Make an illustration of each planet on separate pieces of poster board. Display each planet and review the name of each one. Ask students to put the planets in the correct order. After the planets are aligned, have students orally give other comparisons of the planets.

57 *Las conversaciones variarán.*

58 *Las presentaciones variarán.*

## Reference Desk

As a homework assignment, ask students to bring in a picture of a place that they remember very well. Have students complete **Actividad 58** with the picture on their desk. While presenting their special place to the class, have students pass their picture around the room to share the image with classmates.

## Communication

**Presentational: Cooperative Groups**
Have students create an advertisement for an airline, hotel, or travel assistance service. They should use comparatives and superlatives. Have groups present their ads to the class.

## ¡Comunicación!

**57  El mejor y el peor**   Interpersonal Communication   **1.1**

Con su compañero(a), intercambien ideas sobre los siguientes temas. Digan cuál es el mejor y el peor en cada una de las categorías. Sigan el modelo como guía.

> **MODELO**  Un programa de la televisión
>
> **A:** ¿Cuál crees que es el mejor programa de la televisión?
>
> **B:** *The Ellen DeGeneres Show.*
>
> **A:** ¿Por qué?
>
> **B:** Porque es muy chistoso (*funny*) cuando entrevista a personas famosas.

1. Un libro que ha leído
2. La canción del momento
3. Una película que ha visto
4. Un viaje que ha hecho
5. El/La cantante del año
6. Un grupo musical

**58  ¿Cuál es su favorito?**  Presentational Communication  **1.3, 5.2**

¿Cuál de los lugares que ha conocido le ha llamado más la atención? Describa un país, una ciudad o un pueblo que Ud. conozca y que le haya fascinado. Acuérdese de usar los comparativos y los superlativos para expresar su opinión. Luego, comparta lo que escribió con la clase.

> **MODELO**  Bolivia es un país **sumamente** interesante. Su capital es La Paz. La ciudad está a 12.000 pies de altura. Es la capital **más** alta del mundo. Las montañas que rodean la ciudad son **altísimas**. La Paz es una ciudad colonial de calles **muy** estrechas que tienen un encanto **muy** especial.

*Copacabana, Bolivia*

## Essential Instruction

1. Have pairs share their opinions for **Actividad 57**. Are there common ideas in the class?
2. Before they write their descriptions, have students make a list of adjectives that they can use in **Actividad 58**.
3. As you go through **Sobre el autor**, pause to ask comprehension questions.
4. Read the **Estrategia** and ask students to give the theme of universally famous works, such as **Don Quijote**, **Cien años de soledad**, or **Romeo y Julieta**.
5. Have students complete **Antes de leer** and **Actividad 59** in pairs.

# Lectura literaria

## He andado muchos caminos
### de *Antonio Machado*  1.2, 2.2, 3.1, 3.2

### Sobre el autor

Antonio Machado (Sevilla 1875–Colliure 1939) es uno de los poetas más importantes de la Generación del 98 en España. Esta generación la formaron intelectuales españoles que reflexionaban sobre la situación de España tras la pérdida de sus últimas colonias en América y el Pacífico. Antonio Machado, conocido como "el poeta del pueblo," describió los pueblos de España y sus gentes en su poesía íntima y melancólica. Entre sus obras más importantes destacan *Soledades, Galerías y otros poemas* (1899–1907) y *Campos de Castilla* (1912).

*Antonio Machado*

### Antes de leer   1.3

Machado dice en sus poemas que la mejor forma de conocer un país y su gente es caminando por sus caminos.

1. ¿Ha viajado de esta forma alguna vez?
2. ¿Ha conocido a alguien especial durante un viaje? Comparta su experiencia con sus compañeros/as de clase.

### Estrategia 3.1

**El tema**

El tema de un poema es el punto de enfoque o concepto que el poeta desarrolla a través de sus ideas. En la poesía el tema no siempre es evidente. Por eso, para identificarlo, se requiere analizar el lenguaje y reflexionar sobre las ideas que el poeta trata de comunicar.

### 59 Practique la estrategia  1.2, 1.3, 3.1, 3.2

En "He andado muchos caminos" Machado hace alusión a la gente sencilla y humilde que ha conocido por los caminos y veredas de España (la buena gente), al tiempo que censura a la gente soberbia y arrogante que se siente superior a todos los demás (la mala gente). Es en el fondo una crítica de las clases sociales en España. Busque en el poema dos ejemplos que ilustren a estas personas y dé su interpretación.

| Versos del poema | Buena gente | Mala gente | Interpretación |
|---|---|---|---|
| "...y pedantones al paño que miran, callan y piensan que saben porque no beben el vino de las tabernas." | | ✓ | No beben en las tabernas porque son lugares frecuentados por gente humilde, y si lo hacen, solo miran a la gente y piensan que son mejores que ellos y, por eso, no se toman ni la molestia de hablarles. |
| | | | |
| | | | |

## RESOURCES

Avenue

He andado muchos caminos
Antes de leer

**Answers**

**Antes de leer**
*Las respuestas variarán.*

59 *Las respuestas variarán.*

## Reference Desk

1. Find out what students know about the Spanish-American War (**la Guerra del 98**). During this conflict, the United States attacked Spain's colonies in the Pacific and also intervened in the Cuban fight for independence. (Remind students of what they learned about José Martí in **Unidad 1**.) After just ten weeks, the territories were ceded to the United States, effectively ending the Spanish Empire. This devastating blow to the Spanish psyche gave birth to the literary movement known as **la Generación del 98**. Other members of this movement were Miguel de Unamuno and Ramón del Valle-Inclán.

2. "**He andado muchos caminos**" is from *Soledades*. This earlier work belongs to Modernism, which is often melancholy in tone, uses symbolism and lush descriptions of the senses, and can have a musical rhythm.

## Differentiated Learning
### Decelerate
For **Actividad 59**, guide students in identifying the different groups of people in the poem; tell students to highlight them. Then work together to find the descriptions that correspond to each group of people; have students highlight the key descriptive words in another color.

## Special Needs Students
### Social Anxiety
Allow these students to carry out their presentations from **Actividad 58** in another format, such as a one-on-one meeting with you outside of class, or in an Avenue task.

## Pre-AP

**Course Theme: La belleza y la estética**

He andado muchos caminos

---

**Answers**

1. Quiere decir que ha visto a cantidades de gente triste ("caravanas de tristeza") en todas partes y se refiere a la gente que tiene todo y sin embargo no puede ser feliz.
2. Se refiere a los labradores del campo que viven de trabajar su pedazo de tierra.
3. La capacidad de vivir conforme y feliz con lo que se tiene.

**61** **E**

*Respuesta posible:*
A través del poema, Machado resalta la actitud de prepotencia de los ricos que se sienten tan superiores a los demás que no se dignan compartir con ellos una palabra o una bebida. Sin embargo, al final, todos mueren y quedan enterrados bajo la misma tierra: "en un día como tantos, descansan bajo la tierra".

### Reference Desk

1. Point out **He andado** in the title and remind students that this is the present perfect tense. Ask a volunteer to translate the phrase. Then have students find other examples of this tense in the poem.
2. In **Para concluir**, students will read "**Caminante, son tus huellas**," another Machado poem that uses "path" symbolism.

### Critical Thinking

**Analyzing**
Ask students to analyze the techniques that Machado uses to convey the theme, and what he achieves by using a musical rhythm in this poem (it evokes movement and walking).

---

 **1.2, 3.2**

### 60 Comprensión

1. ¿Qué quiere decir Machado cuando habla de "caravanas de tristeza" en la segunda estrofa, y a quiénes se refiere con esta metáfora?
2. ¿A quiénes se refiere Machado en los versos 16 a 18?
3. ¿Qué actitud de la gente se refleja en los versos 25 y 26?

 **1.3, 3.2**

### 61 Analice

Explique la ironía que se expresa en los versos 29 y 30.

---

# He andado muchos caminos   1.2, 2.2, 3.1, 3.2
## de *Antonio Machado*

He andado muchos caminos,
he abierto muchas veredas[1];
he navegado en cien mares,
y atracado[2] en cien riberas[3].

5 En todas partes he visto
caravanas de tristeza,
soberbios[4] y melancólicos
borrachos de sombra negra,

y pedantones al paño[5]
10 que miran, callan y piensan
que saben, porque no beben
el vino de las tabernas.

Mala gente que camina
y va apestando[6] la tierra...

15 Y en todas partes he visto
gentes que danzan o juegan,
cuando pueden, y laboran
sus cuatro palmos de tierra[7].

Nunca, si llegan a un sitio,
20 preguntan adónde llegan.
Cuando caminan, cabalgan
a lomos de mula vieja[8],

*He andado muchos caminos.*

y no conocen la prisa
ni aun en los días de fiesta.
25 Donde hay vino, beben vino;
donde no hay vino, agua fresca.

Son buenas gentes que viven,
laboran, pasan y sueñan,
y en un día como tantos,
30 descansan bajo la tierra.

[1] paths, trails  [2] anchored  [3] shores  [4] haughty  [5] pretentious  [6] polluting
[7] handspans of land  [8] on the backs of old mules

### Después de leer

Cada paso que andamos ayuda a hacer nuestro camino en la vida. ¿Qué paso ha sido especialmente significativo en su vida? Compare su experiencia con la de un(a) compañero/a y, luego, compartan sus experiencias con el resto de la clase.

---

## Essential Instruction

1. Have students read the title and look at the painting. Ask them to guess what the poem is about.
2. Before they read, have students scan the poem for cognates and words they learned in **Vocabulario 3** on p. 78.
3. Play the recording, pausing for students to answer the during-reading questions.
4. Read through the **Proyectos** on pp. 89–90. Allow students to choose project(s) that most appeal to them. Provide detailed rubrics so that students are aware of the expectations for these tasks.

# *Para concluir*

## Proyectos

Pregunta clave

¿Qué se aprende cuando se viaja al extranjero?

### A ¡Manos a la obra!  1.1, 1.3, 2.2, 3.1

Imagine que su clase de español celebra el IV Centenario de la publicación de *Don Quijote* en una jornada especial para conmemorar la obra.

A su grupo, le han asignado hacer una representación con alguno de estos personajes:

- Don Quijote
- Sancho Panza
- Dulcinea del Toboso

Primero, deben buscar información en la internet sobre el personaje elegido. Tomen nota sobre sus características: su aspecto físico, su personalidad, la relación con otros personajes. Luego, elijan un diálogo breve del libro en el que participe el personaje elegido. Busquen las expresiones que no entiendan en el diccionario o pidan ayuda a su profesor. Por último, representen el diálogo frente al resto de sus compañeros.

*Don Quijote y Sancho Panza*

### B En resumen  1.3, 2.1, 2.2, 3.1

Imagine que Ud. ha hecho un largo viaje por España y, a su regreso, le piden que escriba un artículo sobre su experiencia para la sección de viajes de una revista.

Primero, imagine el itinerario de su viaje a partir de la información que se presenta en las tres lecturas de Cultura. Luego, complete la tabla para organizar lo que ha aprendido en su viaje por España en cada lugar que ha visitado.

| | |
|---|---|
| Atractivo natural | |
| Atractivo cultural | |
| Atractivo artístico | |
| Atractivo histórico | |

Por último, escriba su artículo haciendo énfasis en todo lo que ha aprendido sobre la cultura española gracias a su viaje.

---

## Learning Styles
### Visual Learners
Ask these students to draw an image to represent each stanza of **"He andado muchos caminos."** Display their drawings for the class to reference as they re-read the poem.

## Special Needs Students
### At-Risk Students
Help these students to connect with the poem by asking them how its imagery and references might differ if Machado were to write it today. What sorts of people might he criticize or praise?

---

**Answers**

**Script** *Continued from p. 77.*
y al mismo tiempo también sirva para desestacionalizar la demanda con productos que tienen vida y que tienen capacidad de atracción turística a lo largo de todo el año, no en otros productos más vinculados al clima, más vinculados a la playa, que tienen una estacionalidad mucho más marcada y un periodo de tiempo mucho más corto. Esa colaboración nos va a permitir mejorar esa internacionalización que pretendemos.

**A** *Los diálogos variarán.*

**B** *Los artículos variarán.*

### Reference Desk

1. Point out the **Pregunta clave**. Ask students to think again about the question, this time in relation to their own experiences if they have traveled abroad.
2. You may want to have students act out their dialogues from **Actividad A** for other Spanish classes at your school. Encourage the use of props and, if possible, simple costumes.

### Culture

**Products/Practices: Activity**
Ask students to repeat **Actividad B** in a different context. Tell them to imagine that they just walked the **Camino de Santiago**, from the French town **San Juan Pie de Puerto** to **Santiago de Compostela** in Galicia. They can use the Internet to explore the route and the sights and attractions along the way. Have them submit their articles via Avenue.

**89**

**Answers**

**C** *Los párrafos variarán.*

**D** *Las respuestas variarán.*

**E** *Las respuestas variarán.*

## Reference Desk

1. Make sure that students have the resources available to work on their **proyecto(s)**, such as dictionaries, computers, reference books, travel guides, etc. If possible, you may also want to have examples of student work from other years or classes.
2. You could create an Avenue task for students to present their findings from **Actividad D**.

## Culture

**Products: Activity**
Ask students to create a chart about Spain in their Culture Journals. Give them appropriate column headings, such as **Lugares de interés**, **Medios de transporte**, **Arte**, **Literatura**, and **Otros datos**.

## Connections

**Technology**
Have students video record a marketing piece promoting tourism in Spain based on what they learned in this unit. If possible, post the videos on your class website and share the link with parents.

**90**

---

**C   ¡A escribir!**   Conéctese: la geografía      **1.3, 2.2, 3.1, 5.1**

Investigue información en la internet sobre la Ruta de Don Quijote. Imagine que Ud. hizo una parte del recorrido de esa ruta cuando estuvo en España. Ud. acaba de llegar y todo el mundo quiere saber cómo le fue. Escriba un párrafo sobre su experiencia y publíquelo en su red social favorita para así compartir todo lo que aprendió sobre España y su cultura al hacer este recorrido.

**Para escribir más**

Primero...
Después...
Luego...
Al final...
Un día...
Al otro día..

---

**D   Paseo del Arte**   Conéctese: el arte      **1.3, 2.2, 3.1**

Elija uno de los museos del "Paseo del Arte" de Madrid. Busque su sitio web y averigüe qué colecciones de artistas españoles posee. Tome notas acerca de las obras más relevantes. Incluya datos como el título de la obra, el nombre del artista, el año en que fue terminada y el movimiento artístico al que pertenece. Busque imágenes de algunas de las obras y comparta la información que reunió con el resto de la clase.

---

**E   Se hace camino al andar**   Conéctese: la literatura      **1.3, 2.2, 3.1**

Lea y escuche el poema "Caminante, son tus huellas" de Antonio Machado y, luego, compárelo con "He andado muchos caminos", el poema que leyó en esta unidad. ¿En qué se parecen? ¿En qué se diferencian? Escriba sus respuestas en un diagrama de Venn y justifíquelas con citas textuales de los poemas.

**"Caminante, son tus huellas"**
de *Antonio Machado*

Caminante, son tus huellas
el camino, y nada más;
caminante, no hay camino,
se hace camino al andar.
Al andar se hace el camino,
y al volver la vista atrás
se ve la senda que nunca
se ha de volver a pisar.
Caminante, no hay camino,
sino estelas en la mar.

"Caminante, son tus huellas"   "He andando muchos caminos"

Los dos se refieren al camino de la vida.

## Essential Instruction

1. Begin **Actividad C** by reading through the list in **Para escribir más**. Model their use by relating a simple episode from a day trip.
2. You may want to assign **Actividad D** as a group activity; divide the class into three groups and assign each one a museum. Each group member should research two important works of art.
3. Tell students to close their eyes as you play the recording of the poem in **Actividad E**. Then have them read the poem individually and complete their Venn diagrams.
4. For the **Vocabulario de la Unidad 2**, ask students to determine a few categories that could be used to sort the words. Then have students list the words in those categories.

# Vowbulario de la Unidad 2  1.2

**a lomos de mula vieja** on the backs of old mules
**¿A qué hora...?** At what time...?
**abordar** to board
**abrocharse el cinturón** to fasten one's seatbelt
**acordarse/recordar** to remember
el **aeropuerto** airport
**andar** to walk
el **andén del tren** train platform
**apagar** to turn off
**aparecer** to appear, to be listed
**apestar** to pollute, to stink
el **asiento de pasillo** aisle seat
el **asiento de ventanilla** window seat
el **aterrizaje forzoso** forced landing
**aterrizar** to land
**atracar** to anchor
el/la **auxiliar de vuelo** flight attendant
el **avión** airplane
**ayudar** to help
**bajar** to go down, to bring down
el **barco** boat
el **borracho** drunkard
el **botones** bellman
**cabalgar** to ride
**callar** to keep quiet
el **camino** path, road
**cancelar** to cancel
la **caravana** caravan
la **clase turista** economy class
**consultar** to check
el **coche** car
el **coche cama** sleeping car
el **coche comedor** dining car
el **control de seguridad** security
**con tres horas de anticipación** three hours in advance
**confirmar las reservaciones** to confirm reservations
**¿Cuánto cuesta...?** How much does...cost?
**danzar** to dance
**dar** to give
**desear + inf.** to want, to wish
**despegar** to take off
el **despegue** takeoff
el **detector de metales** metal detector
**dirigirse a** to walk to

**¡Eso sí que es!** That's it!
**Estamos próximos a...** We are about to...
**estrellarse** to crash
**facturar el equipaje** to check luggage
el **ferrocarril** train
**fresco/a** fresh
el/la **gerente** manager
la **habitación** room
**hacer** to do, to make
**hacer camino** to forge a path
**hacer escala** to have a layover
**hacer una parada** to make a stop
**hacer reservaciones** to make reservations
el **hotel** hotel
**indicar** to indicate
la **inmigración** immigration
**inscribirse** to register
la **inspección de aduana** customs inspection
el/la **inspector(a)** inspector
**ir a + inf.** to be going + inf.
**laborar** to work
**¿Les interesa...?** Are you interested in...?
la **lista de huéspedes** guest list
la **llave** key
**llevar contrabando** to carry illegal goods
el **maletín de mano** carry-on luggage
**mantener la calma** to keep calm
**mantenerse** to stay, to remain
el **mar** sea
**melancólico/a** melancholy
el **monitor** monitor
el **mostrador de la línea aérea** airline counter
**navegar** to navigate
la **oficina de cambio (de moneda)** currency exchange office
**pagar por exceso de equipaje** to pay for excess baggage
el **palmo de tierra** handspan of land
el **pasaje de ida y vuelta** round trip ticket
el/la **pasajero/a** passenger
**¡Pasajeros al tren!** All aboard!
el **pasaporte** passport
**pasar por...** to go through...

los **pedantones al paño** people who are pedantic to the core
**perder el vuelo** to miss the flight
el/la **piloto** pilot
la **planta baja** ground floor
**posponer** to postpone
**presentar** to show
la **primera clase** first class
la **primera vez** the first time
la **propina** tip
**querer + inf.** to want + inf.
**quitarse** to remove, to take off
la **recepción del hotel** hotel lobby
la **recomendación** recommendation
**recoger** to pick up
**revisar** to inspect
la **ribera** shore
la **sala de espera** waiting room
la **salida y llegada de vuelo** flight departure and arrival
**salir** to leave
**seguir las indicaciones** to follow directions
el **servicio** service
**soberbio/a** pompous
la **sombra** shadow
**soñar** to dream
**subir** to go up, bring up
la **taberna** tavern
la **tierra** land, earth, soil
**tomar precauciones** to take precautions
la **tripulación** crew
la **tristeza** sadness
la **turbulencia** turbulence
la **última llamada** last call
**molesto/a** annoyed
la **vereda** path, trail
**viajar al extranjero** to travel abroad
el **viaje** trip
el/la **viajero/a** traveler
el **vino** wine
la **visa** visa
el **vuelo de conexión** connecting flight
el **vuelo directo** direct flight
el **vuelo internacional** international flight
el **vuelo nacional** domestic flight

## Answers

**Script** *Continued from p. 79.*
Finalmente, el dependiente, un poco molesto, le muestra unos calcetines y la turista exclama con alegría: "¡Eso sí que es!" El dependiente, sorprendido, le dice: *"If you can spell S-O-C-K-S, why can't you say the word?"*

## Reference Desk

Explain that since students are studying at an advanced level, they will not see the dramatic improvements in their language skills they experienced in their first years of study. Reassure them that this is normal, and that their progress may not be as noticeable because they are refining and building on previously acquired skills.

## Differentiated Learning
### Accelerate
Ask students to write a short story using as much vocabulary as possible from this page. Alternatively, you may want to have students create a story collectively via Flipgrid. One person starts the story, then others add to it via separate posts.

## Learning Styles
### Auditory Learners
These students will benefit from saying and spelling the vocabulary words aloud. Group similar students so that they can work together to review the vocabulary orally.

1. This unit's country of focus is Peru. Students will learn more about this South American country throughout the unit, especially in the **Cultura** and **Lectura informativa** sections.

2. Point out the Anglicism **laptops** in **¿Sabía que…?** Explain that many foreign nouns that end in a consonant form the plural by adding **-s**. See if students can remember synonyms for **laptop** (**la computadora portátil**, **el portátil**). Ask students if they can think of other technology-related loanwords from English.

3. You may want to point out that there are regional variations for *computer* in Spanish: **el ordenador** (*Spain*), **la computadora** (*L. Am.*), **el computador** (*Col.*), **el/la PC** (*many regions*).

4. Tell students that they may see other variations of **la internet**; it can appear masculine or feminine, with or without the article, and capitalized or lowercase.

5. Remind students with eBook access they can click on the red country on p. 93 to link directly to Wikipedia.

## Connections

**Technology**
Have students research how many school districts in the United States issue mobile devices (laptops, tablets, etc.) to their students and how many operate on a "bring your own device" system. Have them project out five years. How much will that number increase?

**¿Sabía que…?** ⚜ 1.2, 2.2

Hoy en día, la tecnología forma parte esencial de un sistema educativo de calidad. Por eso, el Ministerio de Educación de Perú se propone entregar 80 mil laptops para que los estudiantes tengan acceso a la internet durante sus clases.

### Essential Instruction

1. Begin with a discussion of the **Pregunta clave**. Ask students for examples of how sociocultural factors might affect the future of a country.

2. Point out Peru on the map. Ask students to share what they know about the country.

3. Mention the culture photo and question. Remind students to watch for the photo and the answer as they read **Cultura**.

4. Point out the QR code, the video question, and the screen shot from "**El bailarín**." Encourage students to watch the video as many times as they like.

5. Have students read through **Mis metas** and ask questions about the goals.

# Unidad

# 3

# Paso a paso hacia el futuro

Escanee el código QR para mirar el video "El bailarín".

Lucía tiene que hacer una entrevista para su clase de arte. ¿Qué dice Eneko, su entrevistado, sobre lo que tiene que hacer para ser un bailarín profesional? Explique en detalle su respuesta.

*Pregunta clave*

**?**

¿Qué aspectos socioculturales de un país afectan el futuro de su gente?

Perú

Estudio de Danza

*Alicia Broseta*
*Pilar Garcia*

¿Cómo se llama este colegio de Perú y por qué es importante?

## Mis metas

**En esta unidad:**

► Hablaré sobre profesiones y ocupaciones y lo que puedo hacer para contribuir a mi futuro.

► Distinguiré la forma reflexiva y no reflexiva de algunos verbos y su significado.

► Leeré sobre la educación en Perú y lo que se está haciendo para mejorarla.

► Distinguiré el significado de palabras y frases según el contexto.

► Distinguiré el uso de los verbos **ser**, **estar**, **haber**, **hacer**, **tener**, **nevar** y **llover**.

► Me familiarizaré con un programa de verano de la Universidad del Pacífico.

► Escribiré una carta para solicitar ingreso al programa de verano en Cusco.

► Escribiré una recomendación del programa de la Universidad del Pacífico y la publicaré en la internet.

► Desarrollaré nuevas destrezas de vocabulario.

► Usaré expresiones de obligación y de probabilidad y las preposiciones **en** y **de** en español.

► Leeré el cuento "El alacrán de fray Gómez", del peruano Ricardo Palma.

noventa y tres  **93**

Answers

**Video question** *Los párrafos variarán.*
Tiene que cursar tres años de carrera profesional, lo cual está haciendo gracias a una beca para estudiar en un conservatorio de Londres. Su día es pesado y tiene que compaginar su carrera de bailarín con sus otros estudios, los cuales realiza a distancia, por las tardes. Requiere muchos sacrificios, un buen estado físico y un cuerpo flexible.

**Culture question**
Se llama Colegio de Alto Rendimiento (COAR). Es importante porque es un colegio meritocrático: permite que jóvenes de todos los niveles socioeconómicos y de todas las regiones de Perú tengan acceso a una educación de calidad.

**Reference Desk**

1. Ask students to read the **Pregunta clave** and speculate about the theme of the unit and the vocabulary and culture they might encounter. Explain that **aspectos socioculturales** refers to customs, lifestyles, and values that characterize a society.
2. Draw attention to the screen shot from "**El bailarín**." Ask students what type of dance studio this is, and have them predict what Eneko might say.
3. Point out the culture photo and have students read the question. Remind them that **colegio** is a false cognate, and ask students to deduce its meaning based on the photo.

## Multiple Intelligences

**Mathematical-Logical**
After reading the information in **¿Sabía que...?**, have these students survey their classmates about their use of laptops and other technology during the school day. They can present their findings to the class in the form of a graphic.

**Verbal-Linguistic**
Review and preview the unit by asking these questions: **¿Cuáles son los requisitos para tener éxito en tu colegio? ¿Piensas ir a la universidad? ¿Cuáles son los pasos que debes seguir? Después de graduarte del colegio, ¿en qué parte del mundo quisieras estudiar? ¿Qué ocupaciones te interesan?**

## Reference Desk

1. Model the pronunciation of **catedráticos** and explain its meaning. Tell students that this term is used in Spain and indicates a high-ranking professor; **profesor(a)** is the preferred term in Latin America.
2. Point out the word **carreras**; clarify that in this context it means *majors*, but it can also mean *careers*.
3. Explain that a commonly used synonym for **el bachillerato** is **la escuela secundaria**.
4. Provide additional vocabulary, such as names of specific majors, as needed.

## Critical Thinking

**Analyzing and Comparing**
Have students compare and contrast high school and university campuses, schedules, administrations, etc.

### Así nos preparamos

1.2

la feria del trabajo

El rector y los decanos de la Universidad del Pacífico hacen entrega de diplomas a cientos de estudiantes.

### Consejos prácticos para ingresar a la universidad

**¿Qué puede hacer Ud. para prepararse?**

**¿Qué requisitos debe cumplir?**

- Aprobar todas las asignaturas requeridas para graduarse del bachillerato.
- Llenar los formularios requeridos.
- Presentarse al examen de admisión y aprobarlo con buenas calificaciones.
- Matricularse dentro del plazo indicado.

- Investigue diferentes universidades. ¿Cuáles son las ventajas y desventajas de cada una?
- Visite la universidad y asista a las conferencias de orientación dictadas por los catedráticos de cada facultad.
- Haga preguntas sobre las carreras y especializaciones que ofrecen. Acuérdese de que no es lo mismo estudiar para ser abogado que sacar una licenciatura en humanidades.
- Hable con un consejero sobre los planes de estudios —cursos optativos y obligatorios—, y los horarios de clases.

## Essential Instruction

1. Before playing the audio, have students scan pp. 94–95 for cognates. They can work in pairs and practice pronouncing these words. Then model pronunciation for the other new terms and have students repeat them.
2. Play the audio for **Así nos preparamos** and pause occasionally to ask comprehension questions.
3. After listening to **Para conversar**, ask students if they agree with each item and why.

# Familiarícese con las instalaciones de la universidad

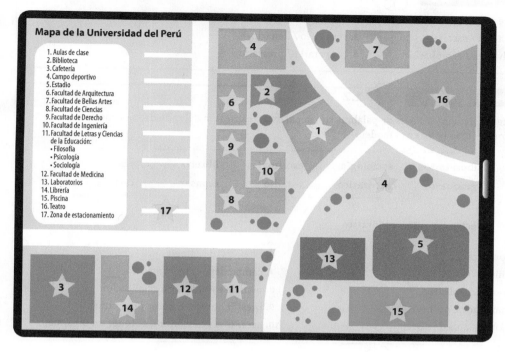

**Mapa de la Universidad del Perú**

1. Aulas de clase
2. Biblioteca
3. Cafetería
4. Campo deportivo
5. Estadio
6. Facultad de Arquitectura
7. Facultad de Bellas Artes
8. Facultad de Ciencias
9. Facultad de Derecho
10. Facultad de Ingeniería
11. Facultad de Letras y Ciencias
    de la Educación:
    • Filosofía
    • Psicología
    • Sociología
12. Facultad de Medicina
13. Laboratorios
14. Librería
15. Piscina
16. Teatro
17. Zona de estacionamiento

## Para conversar

**P**ara hablar de profesiones y campos de trabajo:

La informática es la carrera del futuro.
    No faltan trabajos para programadores.
La física, la química o la biología son buenas
    opciones si te gusta la investigación. Podrías
    volverte un científico famoso.
Para ser economista se necesita tener cabeza
    para los números y la estadística.
Puedes ser profesor de matemáticas si eres
    bueno para enseñar y resolver problemas.
Si eres sociólogo/a o psicólogo/a, puedes
    dar cursos en la universidad o tener una
    práctica privada.
La filosofía es un campo interesante, pero es
    difícil conseguir trabajo de filósofo.
Lo mismo pasa con las letras y las bellas artes
    (escritores, artistas, etc.). Es un campo muy
    competitivo y es difícil tener éxito si no se
    tiene mucho talento.

**P**ara hablar de lo que puedes hacer ahora para
contribuir a tu éxito futuro:

Primero que todo, desarrollar buenos hábitos
    de estudio.
Asistir a clase, aunque los profesores no
    pasen lista.
Prestar atención en clase, hacer preguntas
    y tomar apuntes.
Hacer todas las tareas y, si es necesario, quedarte
    después del colegio para estudiar y repasar
    para los exámenes.
Esforzarte por sacar buenas notas y no reprobar
    ninguna materia.

---

## Reference Desk

1. Draw attention to the map and to items 6–12 in the key. Tell students that **Facultad** is a false cognate and ask them to deduce its meaning (*School [of a university]*). Also ask them to guess the meaning of **Letras** (*Arts/Humanities*).
2. In **Para conversar**, point out **las bellas artes**, and clarify that **arte** is masculine in the singular and plural in the feminine. Also ask students to deduce the meaning of **pasar lista**.
3. Have students create a Flipgrid post in which they talk about their plans after high school graduation.

## Critical Thinking

**Analyzing**

Have students look at the right-hand column under **Para conversar**. Have them rank the recommendations in order of importance. They can explain their opinions in small groups.

## TPR

Have students write the numbers 1–17 on slips of paper or note cards, to correspond to the 17 items on the campus map on p. 95. Say a sentence about one of the locations on the map, and students hold up the corresponding number.

---

## Differentiated Learning

**Accelerate/Expand**

After listening to **Para conversar**, have students work in pairs and add items to each list. Have pairs share their ideas with the class. Create a master list on the board.

## Multiple Intelligences

**Visual-Spatial**

If your community has a university or college, obtain a campus map. Have students label the places using the new vocabulary.

95

Activity 1

## Answers

**1 Script**

1. Si Ud. quiere recibir ayuda financiera, debe…
2. Para no preocuparse más de sus problemas, debe…
3. Si quiere saber bien el material, debe…
4. Si quiere tener un buen horario de clases, debe…
5. Si quiere conseguir un buen trabajo, debe…

1. solicitarla
2. resolverlos
3. repasarlo
4. prepararlo
5. graduarse

**2**

1. catedrático
2. laboratorios
3. beca
4. escritor
5. librería
6. sociología
7. estadio
8. carrera
9. repasar
10. graduarse

**3**

1. D; 2. C; 3. A; 4. H; 5. I; 6. F; 7. J; 8. B; 9. G; 10. E

## Communication

**Interpersonal: Cooperative Groups**

In small groups, have students take turns describing the new vocabulary using circumlocution; their partners guess the word or phrase. Ex: **Es lo que pagas para estudiar en la universidad. (la matrícula)**

---

**1 Ud. escoge**   1.2

Escuche e indique la terminación correcta.

1. solicitarla / sacarla
2. resolverlos / reprobarlos
3. repasarlo / llenarlo
4. prepararlo / prestarlo
5. quedarse / graduarse

---

**2 Series de palabras**  1.2

Complete las siguientes series de palabras con la palabra o expresión del recuadro que mejor corresponda, como se ve en el modelo.

| laboratorios | sociología | escritor | librería | beca |
|---|---|---|---|---|
| graduarse | catedrático | estadio | repasar | carrera |

MODELO    rector, decano, <u>catedrático</u>

1. rector, decano, ____
2. química, física, ____
3. formulario, solicitud, ____
4. humanidades, profesor, ____
5. biblioteca, aula de clase, ____
6. filosofía, psicología, ____
7. campo deportivo, gimnasio, ____
8. plan de estudios, especialización, ____
9. prestar atención, hacer preguntas, ____
10. sacar una licenciatura, obtener un diploma, ____

---

**3 Definiciones**  1.2

Empareje cada definición con la profesión u ocupación que mejor le corresponda.

1. estudio de los seres vivos
2. persona que ejerce la carrera de leyes
3. estudio de las enfermedades y sus curas
4. persona que diseña construcciones y edificios
5. persona que trabaja en el mundo de las finanzas
6. estudio del proceso mental de las personas
7. estudio de la información por medio de las computadoras
8. la persona a cargo de la administración de una universidad
9. facultad donde estudian los futuros maestros o escritores
10. profesión en que se requiere de creatividad, talento y suerte para tener éxito

A. medicina
B. rector
C. abogado
D. biología
E. arte
F. psicología
G. letras
H. arquitecto
I. economista
J. informática

*Me gustaría ser profesor de matemáticas, pero no sé si tengo suficiente paciencia para enseñar.*

---

## Essential Instruction

1. Before playing the audio in **Actividad 1**, read through the answer choices as a class. Explain to students that they will hear a statement for which they must choose the logical ending.
2. Have students check answers to **Actividades 2** and **3** in pairs.
3. Follow up **Actividad 4** by asking students which things they have done or plan to do.
4. Check answers to **Actividad 5** chorally.
5. Ask students to report to the class about their partner's information from **Actividad 6**.

## 4 ¿Requisito o recomendación?  1.2

Diga si cada una de las siguientes declaraciones es una recomendación o un requisito que se debe cumplir para ingresar a la universidad.

| | Requisito | Recomendación |
|---|---|---|
| 1. Desarrollar buenos hábitos de estudio | | ✓ |
| 2. Llenar una solicitud si va a solicitar una beca | | |
| 3. Pedir ayuda financiera con anticipación | | |
| 4. Hablar con los consejeros sobre los programas de estudio | | |
| 5. Presentar y aprobar el examen de admisión | | |
| 6. Prestar atención en clase, hacer preguntas y tomar apuntes | | |
| 7. Llenar los formularios y matricularse dentro del plazo indicado | | |

## 5 Una buena decisión  1.2

Este estudiante universitario decide cambiar su especialización. Llene los espacios con la forma correcta de las palabras del recuadro, según el contexto.

| | | | | |
|---|---|---|---|---|
| aprobar | horario | catedrático | facultad | asistir |
| dictar | carrera | laboratorio | informática | nota |

Comencé mis estudios en la Universidad de Lima en septiembre de este año e ingresé en la **(1)** de arquitectura. Los **(2)** son extraordinarios y el programa es fascinante, pero es muy difícil para mí. Saco malas **(3)** en mis clases de física y estoy seguro de que no puedo **(4)** el curso básico de diseño (*design*). ¡Qué lata! En esta situación es mejor cambiar de **(5)**, ¿verdad? Voy a estudiar **(6)** porque me encantan las computadoras. Esta noche, uno de los profesores va a **(7)** una conferencia sobre metodologías para el desarrollo de *software* y pienso ir a escucharla después de trabajar. Creo que el semestre entrante va a ser mejor porque tengo un **(8)** de clases que coordina perfecto con mis horas de trabajo. Voy a **(9)** a clases cuatro veces por semana y voy a trabajar como asistente en el **(10)** de lenguas los miércoles.

## ¡Comunicación!

## 6 ¿Qué nos falta hacer? 👥 Interpersonal Communication  1.1

Imagine que Ud. y su mejor amigo/a se van a graduar este año y están preparándose para ingresar a la universidad. Mencionen: lo que han hecho ya, los problemas que han encontrado y cómo los han resuelto. Túrnense para hacerse preguntas y responderlas, como se ve en el modelo.

MODELO    A:  ¿Qué carrera vas a seguir: ciencias o humanidades?

B:  No he decidido. Estoy considerando las ventajas y desventajas de cada una. ¿Y tú?

---

## Differentiated Learning

### Accelerate/Adapt

To provide an extra challenge, adapt **Actividad 3**. You can eliminate the lettered items, or provide only the words, and students must write the definitions.

### Heritage Learners

Ask heritage learners to research a college or university in their family's country of origin. Ask them to find out where it is located, how many undergraduates it has, the majors and schools, how much tuition costs, and what the application process involves.

---

**4**
1. Recomendación
2. Requisito
3. Recomendación
4. Recomendación
5. Requisito
6. Recomendación
7. Requisito

**5**
1. facultad
2. catedráticos
3. notas
4. aprobar
5. carrera
6. informática
7. dictar
8. horario
9. asistir
10. laboratorio

**6** *Las conversaciones variarán.*

## Communication

**Interpersonal/Presentational: Cooperative Group**

Bring in campus maps from several different universities. Divide the class into groups and give each one a map. They should write a skit in which one person gives a tour of the university to some prospective students, who should ask questions about the various places on the tour. Encourage students to look up information about their university as needed, so that the "guides" can answer the questions accurately. Have groups role-play their tours for the class.

## TPR

Have students complete **Actividad 4** as a TPR activity. Read aloud each item and have them raise one hand for **Requisito** or two hands for **Recomendación**.

97

## Communication

**Interpersonal/Presentational: Paired Practice**

Have students tell a partner ten things they do every morning before 9:00. Then have students report to the class about their partner's routine.

## Communication

**Interpersonal/Presentational: Cooperative Groups**

Divide the class into groups. Tell them to work together to write a skit using at least eight different reflexive verbs. Allow groups time to rehearse, and then have them video record their skits or role-play them for the class.

## TPR

As a preview to the **Gramática**, have students act out reflexive verbs they learned in *¡Qué chévere! 1–3*. Create a list on the board for review.

# Gramática

## Los verbos reflexivos  1.2, 4.1

Los verbos reflexivos se usan para indicar que la persona que realiza la acción del verbo también la recibe. En otras palabras, la misma persona hace las veces de sujeto y objeto directo de la oración. Los verbos reflexivos se conocen porque terminan en **se** en la forma del infinitivo. En la forma conjugada, esa terminación se reemplaza por los pronombres reflexivos correspondientes de acuerdo a la conjugación.

| Levantar**se:** | **me** levant**o** | **te** levant**as** | **se** levant**a** | **nos** levant**amos** | **os** levant**áis** | **se** levant**an** |

Yo **me** levanto a las siete, pero mi hermana **se** levanta a las seis.

- La posición de los pronombres reflexivos varía según las formas del verbo.

| | |
|---|---|
| **con verbos conjugados:** | Todos los días **me** levanto temprano, **me** ducho y **me** visto mientras mi hermana Adela **se** prepara para salir. |
| **con el infinitivo:** | **Nos** tenemos que ir al colegio al mismo tiempo —yo la llevo en mi carro—, pero es un gran problema porque ella tarda eternidades en arreglar**se**. |
| **con el gerundio:** | Es un lío. Hace un momento estaba pintándo**se** las uñas y ahora **se** está maquillando. |
| **con el participio:** | Y todavía no **se** ha secado el pelo. ¡Qué horror! |
| **con los mandatos afirmativos y negativos:** | —Adela, da**te** prisa que ya son casi las ocho. Vamos a llegar tarde. <br> —Cálma**te**. Ya casi estoy lista. |

- Los pronombres reflexivos **nos**, **os** y **se** pueden usarse para expresar una acción recíproca equivalente a *each other* o *one another* en inglés.

  Mi amiga y yo **nos** hablamos por teléfono todos los días y **nos** vemos los lunes y los jueves.

- Algunas veces es necesario aclarar a quiénes se refiere el pronombre **se**. En ese caso, se puede añadir **uno a otro** (**una a otra**, **unos a otros**, **unas a otras**).

  **Se** miraban **los unos a los otros** con asombro, sin poder explicarse lo que estaba pasando.

*Mi hermana tarda mucho en arreglarse.*

## Essential Instruction

1. As a preview to **Gramática**, ask students if they can recall any reflexive verbs from **Vocabulario 1** (e.g., **matricularse**). If they can't, have them scan pp. 94–95.
2. Read through the introduction, and then ask personalized questions using **levantarse**: **¿Hoy te levantaste tarde o temprano?**
3. Review the various positions for placement of reflexive pronouns.
4. After going over the lists of verbs on p. 99, ask volunteers to create pairs of sentences that illustrate the changes in meaning.

- Muchos verbos transitivos (aquellos que admiten complemento directo) cambian de significado según se usen en forma reflexiva o no reflexiva.

  Yo **me despierto** a las seis de la mañana todos los días.

  A las siete **despierto a mis niños** para que **se levanten** y **se alisten** para ir al colegio.

  **Me visto** y luego **visto a mi niño** menor pues es muy pequeño. Mi hijo mayor **se viste** solo.

| Forma no reflexiva | |
|---|---|
| aburrir | *to bore* |
| acostar (ue) | *to put to bed* |
| calmar | *to calm* |
| casar | *to marry* |
| despertar (ie) | *to wake someone* |
| mover (ue) | *to move something* |
| mudar | *to change* |
| preparar | *to prepare* |
| reunir | *to gather* |
| sentar (ie) | *to seat (someone)* |
| sentir (ie) (+ sust.) | *to feel* |

| Forma reflexiva | |
|---|---|
| aburrirse | *to get bored* |
| acostarse | *to go to bed* |
| calmarse | *to calm down* |
| casarse | *to get married* |
| despertarse | *to wake up* |
| moverse | *to make a movement* |
| mudarse | *to move (change address)* |
| prepararse | *to get ready* |
| reunirse | *to get together* |
| sentarse | *to sit down* |
| sentirse (+ adj.) | *to feel* |

- Algunos verbos toman un significado algo diferente al hacerse reflexivos.

  —¿Cómo **se llama** ese chico al que **llamas** a toda hora?
  —¿No **te acuerdas**? Ya te lo he dicho muchas veces.
  —No, no me acuerdo, pero ya es tarde. **Despídete** y ve a acostarte.
  —Mamá…
  —Lo siento, pero es lo que **acordamos**.

| Forma no reflexiva | |
|---|---|
| acordar (ue) | *to agree* |
| beber | *to drink* |
| comer | *to eat* |
| despedir (i) | *to dismiss, fire* |
| dormir (ue) | *to sleep* |
| ir | *to go* |
| llamar | *to call* |
| parecer | *to seem* |
| perder (ie) | *to lose* |
| poner | *to put, place* |

| Forma reflexiva | |
|---|---|
| acordarse de | *to remember* |
| beberse | *to drink something all up* |
| comerse | *to eat something all up* |
| despedirse | *to say good-bye* |
| dormirse | *to fall asleep* |
| irse | *to leave; to go away* |
| llamarse | *to be named* |
| parecerse | *to resemble* |
| perderse | *to get lost; to miss out on something* |
| ponerse | *to put on* |

## Reference Desk

1. Remind students that **reunirse** has an accent on all forms except **nosotros** and **vosotros**.
2. You may want to present additional verbs that change meaning in the reflexive: **acercar** = *to bring near* / **acercarse** = *to approach*; **negar** = *to deny* / **negarse (a)** = *to refuse*; **probar** = *to taste* / **probarse** = *to try on*.
3. Ask students to create a Flipgrid post in which they ask a question using a reflexive verb. It can be about everyday life, e.g., **¿Qué haces cuando te aburres?** or silly/hypothetical in nature, such as **¿Qué haces si un oso se come toda tu comida?** Their classmates can respond with another posting. Encourage them to give details in their responses.

## TPR

Contrast the use of reflexive and nonreflexive verbs by giving examples, such as **A las siete acuesto a mi hijo. Luego me acuesto a las diez.** Vary the order in which you give the statements. Have students raise their hands whenever they hear the reflexive form.

## Special Needs Students
### Dyslexia/AD(H)D
Help these students review the four possible positions of pronoun placement by using color coding. For example, give them a copy of the table on p. 98, and highlight in yellow the pronouns placed before the conjugated verb, in pink the pronouns attached to the infinitive, in blue the pronouns attached to the present participle, and in green the ones attached to the command.

## Multiple Intelligences
### Bodily-Kinesthetic
To practice reflexive verbs used in a reciprocal manner, create sets of note cards with a different verb on each. Have pairs of students take turns choosing a card and acting out the reciprocal action.

**7**

1. te reúnes
2. te empeñas
3. te mudas
4. te pones
5. te duermes
6. te quejas
7. casarse
8. te vas

- Otros verbos se usan siempre en forma reflexiva. Frecuentemente van seguidos de las preposiciones **a**, **de** o **en**.[1]

    —¿**Te enteraste** de que aumentaron la cantidad de becas del gobierno para algunas profesiones?
    —Sí, **me di cuenta**. Parece que puedes obtener gran ayuda si **te decides** por enseñar.

| | | | |
|---|---|---|---|
| **acercarse a** | *to approach* | **darse cuenta de** | *to realize* |
| **alegrarse de** | *to be glad* | **decidirse a** | *to make up one's mind to* |
| **apresurarse a** | *to hasten to* | **empeñarse en** | *to insist on; to persist* |
| **atreverse a** | *to dare to* | **enterarse de** | *to find out* |
| **burlarse de** | *to make fun of* | **fijarse en** | *to notice* |
| **convertirse en (ie)** | *to become* | **quejarse de** | *to complain about* |

- Hay algunos verbos que al usarse en forma reflexiva toman en inglés el significado de *to become*.

    **Hacerse:** Expresa un cambio basado en el esfuerzo personal.
    He hecho muchos esfuerzos para **hacerme** abogado.
    **Nos haremos** dueños de este negocio.

    **Ponerse:** Expresa un cambio físico o emocional.
    —**Me pongo** muy nerviosa cuando lo veo.
    —Y cuando no lo ves, **te pones** triste. ¿Quién te entiende?

    **Volverse:** Expresa un cambio de un estado a otro. No hay esfuerzo personal.
    **Se está volviendo** loco.

[1] Para una lista más completa de los verbos reflexivos que llevan preposición, consulte el Apéndice 5: **¿Lleva el verbo una preposición?**

---

**7  No más preguntas, por favor**  **1.2**

Consulte la lista de verbos y complete las preguntas de la columna I con base en las respuestas correspondientes de la columna II.

| | | | |
|---|---|---|---|
| reunirse | quejarse | irse | casarse |
| dormirse | mudarse | ponerse | empeñarse |

| **I** | **II** |
|---|---|
| 1. ¿Por qué ____ siempre con esos chicos? | Estudiamos en grupo para el examen. |
| 2. ¿Por qué ____ en llamar a Sara? | Me cae bien y quiero conocerla mejor. |
| 3. ¿Por qué ____ fuera de la universidad? | Soy muy independiente y prefiero vivir solo. |
| 4. ¿Por qué ____ esa camiseta? | Voy al gimnasio después de clases. |
| 5. ¿Por qué ____ en la clase? | Me acuesto muy tarde y no duermo bien. |
| 6. ¿Por qué ____ tanto de esa clase? | No me gusta y la estoy reprobando. |
| 7. ¿Por qué no van a ____ como planearon? | Decidieron hacerlo después de graduarse. |
| 8. ¿Por qué ____ ahora? | ¡Ya estoy cansado de tantas preguntas! |

## 8 Una buena motivación  1.2, 1.3

Escriba la forma del verbo entre paréntesis que complete cada oración correctamente. Luego, conteste las siguientes preguntas.

Por lo general yo no (*1. sentir / sentirse*) muy motivada para (*2. despertar / despertarse*) temprano por la mañana. Me gusta mucho (*3. dormir / dormirse*) y prefiero (*4. quedar / quedarse*) tranquila y cómoda en la cama hasta que mi compañera de cuarto me saca con gritos y reclamos. Pero este semestre es diferente. Tengo una motivación muy fuerte para (*5. levantar / levantarse*). (*6. llamar / llamarse*) Andrés Camacho y es un nuevo compañero de clase. Normalmente las clases de historia me (*7. aburrir / aburrirse*), pero *Historia contemporánea 101* se ha convertido en mi asignatura favorita. Tres veces por semana, a las nueve de la mañana, nosotros (*8. reunir / reunirse*) en una pequeña aula, y durante una hora intento prestarle atención al profesor. ¡No es nada fácil! (*9. parecer / parecerse*) que le gusto a Andrés porque, aunque todavía no se ha atrevido a invitarme a salir, él (*10. sentar / sentarse*) junto a mí y siempre (*11. acordar / acordarse*) de traerme algún detalle... un café, una fruta, un bagel. ¿Faltar a esta clase? ¡Ni hablar! Tengo que aprobar este curso para poder tomar *Historia contemporánea 102*.

1. ¿Por qué se siente más motivada la joven para asistir a su clase de historia contemporánea?

2. ¿Cree Ud. que Andrés se da cuenta de sus sentimientos?

3. En su opinión, ¿por qué Andrés no se atreve a invitarla a salir?

4. ¿Cree que el profesor y los otros estudiantes se fijan en lo que está pasando entre ellos dos?

5. ¿Por qué se empeña ella en tomar otra clase de historia?

## 9 Ya no aguanto más  1.2

Amalia no se lleva bien con Cristina, su compañera de dormitorio, en la universidad. Complete el párrafo con la forma presente de los verbos **hacerse**, **ponerse** y **volverse**, según corresponda de acuerdo al contexto.

La situación con mi compañera de dormitorio, Cristina, __(1)__ insoportable (*unbearable*). Es que somos muy diferentes. Normalmente, soy una persona responsable y razonable. Mi compañera de dormitorio, en cambio, se enoja y __(2)__ nerviosa fácil y frecuentemente. Tengo metas (*goals*). Mi vida está bien planeada y me estoy esforzando mucho para __(3)__ bióloga. Cristina vive de día en día. Se levanta cuando quiere, falta mucho a las clases y nunca limpia el apartamento. Cuando regreso a casa después de un día largo y difícil y veo que todavía está en la cama, ¡ __(4)__ histérica! Si este problema no se resuelve pronto, creo que voy a __(5)__ loca.

---

**8**
1. me siento
2. despertarme
3. dormir
4. quedarme
5. levantarme
6. Se llama
7. aburren
8. nos reunimos
9. Parece
10. se sienta
11. se acuerda

*Respuestas posibles:*
1. A ella le gusta uno de sus compañeros.
2. Sí, porque él se sienta junto a ella y siempre le trae algún detalle.
3. Puede ser que Andrés sea muy tímido.
4. Sí, porque ella dice que es muy difícil prestarle atención al profesor.
5. Se empeña en tomar otra clase de historia para poder seguir viendo a Andrés.

**9**
1. se hace/se pone
2. se pone
3. hacerme
4. me pongo
5. volverme

### Expansion

In pairs, have students rewrite **Actividad 9** as a phone conversation. Have them role-play the call.

---

## Differentiated Learning
### Decelerate
If students struggle with **Actividad 7**, use a scaffolded approach. First read through each question/answer pair and help them identify the subject in the question. Then guide them to select the correct verb for each one. Finally, have students conjugate the verbs.

## Multiple Intelligences
### Mathematical-Logical
Ask these students to create a survey to find out at what times their classmates do various activities throughout the day (**levantarse**, **salir de la casa**, etc.). Tell them to use a mix of reflexive and nonreflexive verbs. Have students graph the results for the class, who can comment on them.

**101**

## ¡Comunicación!

### 10 Programa de orientación · Interpersonal Communication · 1.1

Imagine que está en el programa de orientación de una universidad que está considerando, y que tiene que pasar los siguientes dos días con uno de los estudiantes que le servirá de guía. Ud. tiene muchas preguntas con relación a la rutina diaria, los horarios, las clases y las diferentes actividades que van a realizar. Represente la situación con un(a) compañero/a y túrnense para hacer las preguntas del caso y responderlas. Usen los verbos del recuadro y otros que recuerden en su conversación, como se ve en el modelo.

*Todos los días me despierto a las siete de la mañana.*

| | | | |
|---|---|---|---|
| levantarse | arreglarse | almorzar | estacionar |
| ducharse | divertirse | ver la tele | hacer deporte |
| reunirse | enterarse | prepararse | acordarse |

**MODELO** A: ¿A qué hora te acuestas todas las noches?

B: Casi siempre me acuesto a eso de las once o doce de la noche.

A: ¿Por qué tan tarde?

B: ...

### 11 Bienvenidos · Presentational Communication · 1.3

Imagine que Ud. es uno de los guías en el programa de orientación que ofrece su universidad y le han encargado hacer una presentación de tres minutos para motivar a los estudiantes a decidirse por su universidad. Primero que todo, haga un borrador con los puntos principales que debe tratar, con base en las preguntas que se dan a continuación. Desarrolle sus ideas y ensaye su presentación frente al espejo para asegurarse de no pasarse de los tres minutos. Para terminar, haga la presentación enfrente de su clase.

- ¿Por qué se decidió Ud. por esta universidad?
- ¿Qué carrera eligió y por qué lo hizo?
- ¿Cómo se enteró de los diferentes planes de estudio?
- ¿Qué requisitos tuvo que cumplir para ingresar?
- ¿Qué clase de ayuda financiera pudo conseguir?

- ¿Cómo se sintió cuando recibió la notificación de admisión?
- ¿Cuántos años dura su carrera?
- ¿Qué podrá hacer después de graduarse?
- ¿Qué pueden hacer los estudiantes hoy mismo para prepararse?
- ¿Cuál es el mejor consejo que les puede dar?

### Essential Instruction

1. Before students begin their role-plays in **Actividad 10**, go over the verbs in the list and have students identify the reflexive ones. Invite them to brainstorm additional verbs, and write them on the board.
2. You may want to allow students to use note cards or an outline for their presentations in **Actividad 11**.
3. Point out the **Pregunta clave**, and tell students to keep it in mind as they complete the cultural readings.
4. Play the recording as students follow along in their books. Pause periodically to ask **sí/no** comprehension questions.
5. For Common Core practice, have students answer the **Analice** questions.

emcpassport.com
LA 2

 **¿Pregunta clave**
¿Qué aspectos socioculturales de un país afectan el futuro de su gente?

# Con la mira puesta en el futuro  1.2, 2.1, 2.2

Ciertas características socioculturales de Perú son alarmantes y afectan el futuro de su gente. En términos educativos, la sociedad peruana presenta condiciones que causan preocupación. Los peruanos pobres crecen con problemas nutricionales que les impiden desarrollar todo su potencial. Estudian en colegios estatales de bajos recursos y en general no pueden acceder a la universidad ni conseguir trabajos competitivos. Por su parte, quienes pertenecen a los sectores más privilegiados sí logran desarrollar todo su potencial y estudian en buenos colegios, acceden a la universidad y consiguen trabajos bien remunerados. En consecuencia, se perpetúa la brecha[1] entre pobres y ricos.

Todos los estudiantes peruanos quieren una buena educación.

Los resultados del Programa para la Evaluación Internacional de Alumnos (PISA) indican que el rendimiento académico[2] de Perú se encuentra en los últimos lugares a nivel mundial. Estos resultados no pueden atribuirse exclusivamente a las diferencias individuales, sino que están condicionados por las desigualdades económicas y sociales. Los especialistas en el campo de la educación afirman que el sistema educativo de Perú necesita cambios dramáticos y urgentes.

La buena noticia es que algunos de esos cambios ya se han puesto en marcha. El Ministerio de Educación peruano tiene varios proyectos alentadores[3]. Se anticipa que el proyecto de jornada escolar completa para secundaria se termine de implementar en todos los colegios del país en 2021. Los estudiantes tendrán diez horas más de clases semanales para reforzar la enseñanza de asignaturas clave. Otra iniciativa muy importante es el programa de apoyo escolar. Los estudiantes con dificultades podrán tomar clases adicionales fuera del horario escolar. Así, podrán recibir la ayuda necesaria para no repetir el grado y seguir adelante con sus estudios.

[1] gap    [2] academic performance    [3] encouraging

 **Búsqueda:** sistema educativo en perú, programa pisa

## Productos  1.2, 2.2

*Para que la educación (pública) eduque*, de J.F. Vega Ganoza (exjefe de planificación del Ministerio de Educación), es un libro publicado en 2005 que permite conocer cuáles son las causas profundas de la baja calidad de la educación peruana. Este breve ensayo habla con suma franqueza acerca del carácter sistémico y de las inercias sociales contra las que lucha y entre las que se debate la escuela pública. El autor quita la máscara al gobierno y a los maestros, alumnos, padres y expertos educativos.

Los estudiantes peruanos tienen ganas de aprender.

### 1.2, 2.1, 2.2
## 12 Comprensión

1. ¿Qué consecuencias trae a las personas la desigualdad en el sistema educativo?

2. ¿Por qué necesita cambios urgentes el sistema educativo de Perú?

3. ¿Qué cambios se están implementando para mejorar la educación?

### 1.3, 2.2, 3.1, 4.2
## 13 Analice

1. ¿Por qué cree Ud. que la educación ocupa un lugar tan importante en el desarrollo de las personas?

2. Compare las iniciativas para mejorar el sistema educativo en Perú con las que se llevan adelante en su región o país.

## RESOURCES

| | |
|---|---|
| fg | Flipgrid |
| ave | Avenue |
| 🎧 | Con la mira puesta en el futuro Productos |
| LA | Activity 2 |

**Answers**

**12** *Respuestas posibles:*
1. Si el sistema educativo no ofrece las mismas oportunidades para todos, los que nacen pobres no tienen la posibilidad de progresar y los más ricos conservan sus privilegios.
2. Porque se encuentra en los últimos lugares de los estudios que evalúan el rendimiento educativo.
3. Se están implementando el proyecto de jornada completa en secundaria y el programa de apoyo escolar.

**13** *Respuesta posible:*
1. Porque les permite acceder a los conocimientos y destrezas que necesitarán para cumplir sus objetivos.
2. *Las respuestas variarán.*

### Reference Desk

Students can do a Flipgrid post reacting to any of these cultural readings.

### Pre-AP

Have students respond to the **Pregunta clave**, in spoken or written form, using information from the readings on pp. 103–105. Students should also include a comparison between their own community/culture and Peru.

### Differentiated Learning
**Heritage Learners/Accelerate**
Ask heritage learners or accelerated students to make cultural comparisons using reflexive and reciprocal verbs. For example: **En [país hispano], la gente se saluda con dos besos en la mejilla. En este país generalmente se dan la mano.**

### Special Needs Students
**Social Anxiety**
Allow students with social anxiety the opportunity to complete their presentations for **Actividad 11** in alternate ways, such as privately outside of class, or as an Avenue task.

Del elitismo a la meritocracia
Prácticas

### Answers

**14**

1. Influyen factores del ambiente familiar, como el nivel económico, la educación de los padres y la lengua materna, y otros factores como el tipo de colegio, la región donde se encuentra y su ubicación.

2. Es un modelo que da la oportunidad a los estudiantes más talentosos y esforzados de acceder a una educación de calidad.

3. A los Colegios de Alto Rendimiento, pueden acceder los estudiantes más destacados de todo el país que aprueban evaluaciones muy exigentes. A la Educación Básica Alternativa, acceden jóvenes y adultos que no pudieron completar su educación antes y necesitan compatibilizar el estudio con el trabajo.

**15**  *Respuesta posible:*

1. No, porque solo pueden acceder a ellos los mejores estudiantes y no mejora la situación de los estudiantes pobres que tienen un rendimiento medio o bajo.

2. *Las respuestas variarán.*

### Critical Thinking

**Comparing**

Have students research alternative education programs in your community or state. In pairs, they can compare their findings to the **EBA** system in Peru.

---

 **1.2, 2.1, 2.2**

### 14 Comprensión

1. ¿Qué factores influyen en el rendimiento educativo de los estudiantes peruanos?

2. ¿Qué es un modelo educativo meritocrático?

3. ¿Quiénes pueden acceder a los Colegios de Alto Rendimiento? ¿Quiénes acceden a la Educación Básica Alternativa?

 **1.3, 2.2, 4.2**

### 15 Analice

1. ¿Cree Ud. que los COAR solucionan el problema del acceso a una educación de calidad? ¿Por qué?

2. ¿Qué semejanzas y qué diferencias encuentra entre la situación de la educación en Perú y la de su país?

---

# Del elitismo a la meritocracia   1.2, 2.1, 2.2

*Estudiantes peruanos en un COAR*

Según diversas investigaciones, el pobre desempeño[1] de los estudiantes peruanos estaría asociado en primer lugar a factores del ambiente familiar, como el nivel económico de la familia, el nivel educativo de los padres y la lengua materna. Otras variables importantes son el tipo de colegio (público o privado), la región natural del colegio (costa, sierra o selva) y su ubicación (Lima u otros lugares), situación que evidencia la desigualdad de la calidad educativa en Perú. Así, un niño peruano que vive en un hogar no pobre, con padres educados, tiene el castellano como lengua materna, estudia en un colegio privado, de la costa y en Lima, obtendría mejores resultados que aquella vasta mayoría que no cumple estas condiciones.

Una manera de mejorar esta situación es pasar de un modelo educativo elitista a un modelo meritocrático[2] que dé la oportunidad a los jóvenes más talentosos y esforzados, de todos los niveles socioeconómicos y de todas las regiones, de acceder a una educación de calidad. Esa idea es la razón de ser de los Colegios de Alto Rendimiento (COAR) de Perú. Los estudiantes más destacados[3] de todo el país, tras aprobar evaluaciones muy exigentes, acceden a una beca integral[4] otorgada por el Estado que cubre todas sus necesidades, desde los materiales educativos hasta el alojamiento y la alimentación. Los COAR brindan[5] una formación académica de excelencia que permite a los estudiantes continuar con éxito su educación en el nivel superior.

[1] performance   [2] based on individual merit   [3] outstanding   [4] full scholarship   [5] provide

**Búsqueda:** modelo educativo elitista perú, modelo educativo meritocrático perú, colegios de alto rendimiento perú

---

**Prácticas**  **1.2, 2.1**

La Educación Básica Alternativa (EBA) es una modalidad del sistema educativo peruano dirigida a jóvenes y adultos, así como a adolescentes en extra-edad escolar a partir de los 14 años de edad, que necesitan compatibilizar el estudio con el trabajo. Los estudiantes de la EBA son aquellos que no se insertaron oportunamente en el sistema educativo, no pudieron culminar su educación básica, requieren compatibilizar el trabajo con el estudio, desean continuar sus estudios después de un proceso de alfabetización o se encuentran en extra-edad para la Educación Básica Regular.

*Escuela de Educación Básica Alternativa Carlos W. Sutton en La Joya, Perú*

---

### Essential Instruction

1. Have students glance at the photos and titles on these pages. Ask them to predict what else they will learn about Peru.

2. Remind students of the culture photo and question from the unit opener. Ask them to skim the second paragraph of the reading on p. 104 to find the answer.

3. After reading **Prácticas**, ask the class to think of comparable programs in the United States.

# Diversidad y educación en Perú  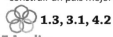 1.2, 2.1, 2.2

Perú presenta una diversidad cultural y lingüística muy amplia. Algo más de cuatro millones de personas hablan como lengua materna una lengua originaria[1] (quechua, aymara y otras). Durante mucho tiempo, las comunidades indígenas que hablan lenguas distintas del español fueron excluidas de un sistema educativo centrado en el idioma español, ajeno[2] a su realidad cultural. En la actualidad[3], Perú se ha sumado a la tendencia universal de respetar la diversidad y reconoce el derecho de las culturas indígenas a una educación intercultural y bilingüe. Los niños asisten a escuelas donde aprenden en su lengua natal y en español, con docentes[4] bilingües. Los contenidos y la forma de enseñarlos se corresponden con su realidad cultural y su contexto social. Gracias a este enfoque educativo, los estudiantes pueden conservar su lengua y sus raíces culturales. Así se evita que la cultura dominante las vuelva invisibles y se reconoce la riqueza que aporta la diversidad; en el pasado, esa diversidad era considerada un obstáculo para la educación.

*Estudiantes indígenas disfrutan de una educación bilingüe.*

En el marco de la educación intercultural bilingüe, el Ministerio de Educación implementó el programa "Tinkuy" ("encuentro" en quechua) para promover el diálogo entre alumnos de distintos contextos sociales, culturales y lingüísticos. En 2014, más de cien niños indígenas de entre diez y trece años que hablan 47 lenguas originarias y pertenecen a comunidades de distintas regiones visitaron Lima para compartir su cultura y sus experiencias con estudiantes limeños[5]. Además, tuvieron la oportunidad de visitar museos, un zoológico, el Palacio de Gobierno y conocer el mar. Al evento asistieron también profesores y autoridades de educación a escuchar a los estudiantes, para informarse sobre cómo ven su educación, qué problemas tienen y cuáles son sus perspectivas para el futuro. Este tipo de iniciativas favorece la integración de estudiantes que provienen de distintos contextos.

[1] indigenous language  [2] unconnected  [3] currently  [4] teachers
[5] from Lima

**Búsqueda:** comunidades indígenas perú, lenguas originarias perú, educación intercultural bilingüe, programa tinkuy

##  1.2, 2.1, 2.2, 3.2

### 16 Comprensión

1. ¿En qué consiste la educación intercultural bilingüe?

2. ¿En qué consiste el programa Tinkuy? ¿Qué se hizo en 2014?

3. Según el ministro de Educación, ¿de qué manera se puede construir un país mejor?

### 1.3, 3.1, 4.2

### 17 Analice

1. ¿Qué dificultades cree Ud. que puede tener un niño que debe aprender en una lengua distinta a su lengua materna?

2. ¿Qué comunidades de su país se benefician o podrían beneficiarse con la educación intercultural bilingüe?

###  1.2, 3.2

### *Perspectivas*

Durante la cita, el ministro de Educación, Jaime Saavedra Chanduví, manifestó su emoción. "Es una linda experiencia estar en este Tinkuy 2014 porque refleja la inmensa diversidad del país", declaró. "A pesar de las diferencias todos estamos juntos y queremos que los niños peruanos tengan igualdad de acceso a la educación, sin perder sus costumbres y valores. Hay que explotar esa diversidad cultural que tenemos para construir un país mejor", agregó. ¿De qué manera afectará esta experiencia el futuro de los niños peruanos que la vivieron?

RESOURCES

 Diversidad y educación en Perú

Answers

**Perspectivas**
*Las respuestas variarán.*

**16**

1. Los niños van a escuelas donde aprenden en su lengua originaria y en español, con docentes bilingües. La enseñanza se adecua a su realidad cultural y su contexto social.

2. Es un programa del Ministerio de Educación para promover el diálogo entre alumnos de distintos contexto sociales, culturales y lingüísticos. En 2014, un grupo de estudiantes de distintas comunidades indígenas viajaron a Lima a compartir sus experiencias con estudiantes de la ciudad.

3. Explotando la diversidad cultural y dándole la oportunidad a todos los niños peruanos de educarse sin perder sus costumbres y valores.

**17** *Respuestas posibles:*

1. Puede costarle más aprender si piensa en una lengua y le hablan en otra. También puede tener dificultades para expresarse en la segunda lengua.

2. En Estados Unidos, hay escuelas bilingües para la comunidad que habla español.

### Reference Desk

Jaime Saavedra Chanduví became Minister of Education in 2013; prior to that he held a variety of positions in Peruvian government, academia, and the World Bank.

## Multiple Intelligences

### Bodily-Kinesthetic
Prepare statements about these cultural readings, and write related acronyms or names on the board. Divide the class into two groups and have a member from each group stand. After you read the statement, students walk to the correct name. Continue with the rest of the statements.

### Verbal-Linguistic
Ask students to research the variety of indigenous groups in modern-day Peru, and their respective languages. Encourage them to find out about any influences that the indigenous languages and Spanish have had on each other.

# Vocabulario 2

## Comparación y contraste: ¡Ojo con estas palabras! 🍀 1.2, 4.1

En español, al igual que en inglés, hay varias formas de expresar estas palabras. Preste atención, pues su uso depende del contexto.

*Estas jóvenes están tomando un examen para ingresar a la universidad.*

**fracasar**   *to fail, to be unsuccessful*

Muchos estudiantes **fracasaron** en las pruebas estandarizadas.

Puedes hacer algo hoy para no **fracasar** mañana.

**reprobar (a alguien)**   *to fail (someone)*

En muchos colegios hispanos, si **repruebas** tres materias **repruebas** el curso y tienes que repetirlo.

**dejar de**   *to fail (to do something); to stop*

¿No te dije que no debías **dejar de** asistir al colegio? ¿Por qué no me haces caso?

Ya **deja de** aconsejarme que yo tengo mis razones.

**faltar (a)**   *to fail (to fulfill); to be lacking; to miss (an appointment)*

Si **faltas** a clase una vez más, te van a suspender.

Te recojo cuando **falten** quince minutos para las siete.

**tomar**   *to take; to get hold of; to drink; to take (a bus, cab, etc.)*

¿Cuántas materias vas a **tomar** este semestre?

¿Por qué no vamos y nos **tomamos** un café?

¿Quieres **tomar** el autobús o vamos caminando?

**llevar**[1]   *to take a person somewhere; to take or carry something*

¿Quién te va a **llevar** a la entrevista?

¿Qué papeles debo **llevar** a la entrevista?

**llevarse**   *to take away; to carry off*

**Llévese** solo lo que necesite.

**Se llevó** a su hija a vivir a otro país.

[1] **Llevar** se usa también con el significado de *to wear*:
La novia **llevaba** un vestido muy elegante.

### Essential Instruction
1. Model the pronunciation of the vocabulary and have students repeat the words.
2. Encourage volunteers to create additional example sentences about their own life.
3. Work with the class to create a poster with the expressions from **Vocabulario 2**.
4. Check the answers to **Actividad 18** by having students call out the answers.

Expresiones con acabar
- acabar
- acabarse
- acabar de + infinitivo

**acabar**  *to finish*

Voy a **acabar** mis estudios de bachillerato y, luego, me voy a conseguir un trabajo.

**acabarse**  *to run out; to terminate*

Va a conseguir una beca porque ya **se** le **acabó** el dinero que tenía para la matrícula de este semestre.

Mis sentimientos cambiaron… ya todo **se acabó**.

**acabar de + infinitivo**  *to have just… ; (past tense) had just…*

**Acabo de llenar** los formularios para solicitar ayuda financiera.

**Acabábamos de salir** cuando empezó a nevar.

**Otras expresiones idiomáticas**

**seguir una carrera**  *to pursue a career*

¿Qué carrera piensas **seguir**?

Me gustaría **seguir** una carrera en Humanidades.

**examinarse (de)**  *to take an exam*

Ese día van a **examinarse** más de trescientos estudiantes.

**quitarse**  *to take off (clothing)*

Tuve que **quitarme** el abrigo antes de entrar al aula donde iba a examinarme.

**sacar**  *to take out*

Solo nos permitieron **sacar** un lápiz y una hoja en blanco para el examen.

**tener lugar/suceder**  *to take place*

El concierto **tuvo lugar** anoche a las siete.

---

**18  ¿Cuál corresponde?**  **1.2**

Complete las oraciones con la palabra que corresponda según el contexto.

1. (*faltan / toman*) cinco minutos para que comience la ceremonia.
2. Los muchachos (*se llevarán / tomarán*) un vuelo directo a Lima.
3. En diez minutos te (*llevo / tomo*) a la estación. Debes (*llevar / tomar*) el primer tren de la tarde.
4. No (*faltes a / dejes de*) llamarnos por teléfono los fines de semana.

5. Si estudias todo el año no vas a (*fracasar / faltar*).
6. ¿Sabes si Alfredo piensa (*llevar / llevarse*) a Beatriz a la fiesta?
7. El profesor me (*fracasó / reprobó*) en matemáticas.
8. Cuando entra a la sala (*suspende / se quita*) el sombrero y (*deja de/falta a*) hablar.

**Answers**

**18**
1. Faltan
2. tomarán
3. llevo, tomar
4. dejes de
5. fracasar
6. llevar
7. reprobó
8. se quita, deja de

**Reference Desk**

1. Review the conjugations of **seguir** and **tener**.
2. You may want to explain that in some countries, such as Peru and Argentina, the "opposite" words are used for taking/giving an exam: **Los alumnos van a dar un examen.** = *The students are going to take an exam.* **El profesor tomó un examen.** = *The professor gave an exam.*

**Critical Thinking**

**Analyzing**
Create a worksheet using the expressions from **Vocabulario 2** incorrectly. Instruct students to make corrections to the expressions, and then explain their answers to a partner.

---

**Special Needs Students**
**Speech Impairment**
Model patience and an encouraging attitude to foster a positive learning environment. It is important to let students finish their own sentences. If you do not understand something that is said, indicate what you did understand. Finally, allow students to give short answers or answers in written form.

**Multiple Intelligences**
**Verbal-Linguistic**
Ask pairs of students to create a phone conversation between two friends who are discussing their schoolwork. They should use at least six expressions from **Vocabulario 2**. Have students rehearse their conversations, and then role-play them for the class, using props.

### Reference Desk

1. James Rodríguez is a Colombian-born midfielder who plays for Real Madrid. His performance in the 2014 World Cup won him the Golden Boot for being top scorer.
2. In **Actividad 19**, a synonym for **acabarse** is **agotarse**.

### Culture

**Productos/Prácticas: Activity**
Ask students to research Peru's participation in the history of the **Copa Mundial de Fútbol**. Ask them to find out as much as they can about Peru's national soccer team and its fans: the colors they wear, songs/chants sung during games, star players, etc. Have them summarize their findings in an Avenue task.

---

**19  Copa Mundial de Fútbol**  **1.2**

Complete el siguiente diálogo con los verbos del recuadro en presente o futuro, según corresponda. Los verbos pueden usarse más de una vez.

| acabar de | acabarse | faltar | llevar | tener lugar |
|---|---|---|---|---|

— ¿Sabes que solo **(1)** una semana para la Copa Mundial de Fútbol?

— ¡No me digas! Por la tele el reportero **(2)** decir que James Rodríguez no jugará para la selección nacional de Colombia.

— ¿Dónde **(3)** los partidos?

— En los estadios que **(4)** construir en varias ciudades por Europa. Iremos todos en grupo y **(5)** a varios amigos para que hagan barra (*to cheer*) con nosotros.

— En ese caso, avísame si vas a **(6)** a tu primo. Tenemos que comprar los boletos cuanto antes. Ya sabes que si **(7)** los boletos tendremos que comprarlos de los revendedores (*scalpers*), y eso, hermano, nos va a costar muy caro.

## ¡Comunicación!

**20  Cita con el consejero**  **Interpersonal Communication**  **1.1**

Imagine que Ud. acaba de graduarse y está en la oficina de su consejero/a solicitando la siguiente información sobre la universidad a la que quiere asistir. Con un(a) compañero/a, túrnense para hacerse las preguntas y responderlas, como se ve en el modelo.

**MODELO**

**Consejero:** ¿Piensa solicitar ayuda financiera?

**Estudiante:** Sí. Me gustaría dejar de trabajar y dedicarme por completo al estudio.

- Los requisitos para ingresar a la universidad
- Las carreras y los planes de estudio
- Las posibilidades de ayuda financiera
- Los formularios que se deben llenar
- Los plazos de matrícula
- Los cursos de orientación

**21  Mi nueva rutina**  **Presentational Communication**  **1.3**

Imagine que es su primera semana en la universidad y su familia está ansiosa por saber cómo le está yendo. Escríbales un correo electrónico contándoles todo sobre su nueva rutina diaria. Use verbos reflexivos y los adverbios del recuadro para hablar de sus actividades, como se ve en el modelo.

| casi siempre | enseguida | a veces | luego |
|---|---|---|---|
| de vez en cuando | a menudo | después | nunca |

**MODELO**

**Generalmente me levanto tarde los domingos. Casi siempre desayuno algo ligero y luego salgo a correr.**

○ ○ ○  Nuevo mensaje
De:
Para:
Asunto:

---

## Essential Instruction

1. Check answers to **Actividad 19** by having two students role-play the dialogue.
2. Arrange the desks in the classroom to create "offices" for students to role-play their conversations in **Actividad 20**. Brainstorm possible questions for each bullet point.
3. Before beginning **Actividad 21**, have students generate common phrases used in informal e-mails.
4. As a follow-up to **Actividad 22**, hold a class debate about topic three.
5. You may want to divide the class into two groups and assign each a topic from **Actividad 23**.

 **¡Comunicación!**

## 22 ¿Cuál es su opinión?  Interpersonal Communication 🏵 **1.1, 3.1**

Intercambie información con su compañero/a sobre los siguientes temas. Túrnense para hacer las preguntas y den respuestas según su propia opinión y experiencia.

- ¿Es importante saber hablar muchos idiomas si se vive en EE. UU.? Explica. ¿Qué quiere decir "tener buenos conocimientos de un idioma" y "dominio y fluidez de una lengua"? ¿Cuáles son dos idiomas muy útiles (aparte del inglés)? Explique.

- En Estados Unidos, ¿es importante tener un título para obtener trabajo? ¿Qué tipo de trabajo se puede obtener con un título universitario en artes (B.A.) o en ciencias (B.S.)? ¿Con un máster? ¿Con un doctorado?

- ¿Qué opinas del movimiento político en Estados Unidos que quiere exigir que el inglés sea la lengua oficial? ¿Qué opinas de la educación bilingüe?

- ¿Crees que con una fuerte preparación en idiomas se puede conseguir un buen trabajo? Explica.

## 23 Intercambio de ideas 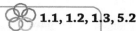 Interpersonal/Presentational Communication 🏵 **1.1, 1.2, 1.3, 5.2**

Reúnase con tres o cuatro compañeros para comentar de los siguientes temas. Intercambien ideas y opiniones, lleguen a acuerdos, saquen conclusiones y presenten un informe al resto de la clase.

- **Sistema de enseñanza actual**

  Se dice que la filosofía de la enseñanza está cambiando día a día. ¿Está Ud. de acuerdo con esta afirmación? ¿Podría Ud. explicar qué le gusta del sistema de enseñanza de hoy? ¿Qué no le gusta? ¿Qué tipo de enseñanza le gustaría tener para sus hijos? ¿Más estricto? ¿Más liberal? ¿Cuáles son algunas ventajas o desventajas de un sistema de educación más liberal o de uno más estricto? Se dice también que los estudiantes de ciencias ya no estudian humanidades. ¿Opina Ud. que deben hacerlo o no?

- **¿Trabajar, viajar o ingresar a la universidad?**

  Hoy en día, muchos estudiantes deciden empezar a trabajar tan pronto se gradúan del bachillerato, en lugar de asistir a la universidad. Otros deciden viajar para conocer el mundo, ya sea con programas de intercambio o por su propia cuenta. ¿Cuáles son las ventajas y las desventajas de esas decisiones?

## 24 ¿Qué diría Ud.?  Interpersonal/Presentational Communication 🏵 **1.1, 1.2, 1.3**

Reúnanse en grupos de tres estudiantes y comenten la siguiente situación. ¿Qué dirían y harían Uds. en el lugar del director y los padres de familia? Escriban el diálogo que tiene lugar entre ellos y, luego, represéntenlo enfrente de la clase.

Tres padres de alumnos de la escuela primaria hablan con el/la director(a) y reclaman para sus hijos una educación bilingüe. El/La director(a) les explica que no hay fondos, que no es conveniente para los niños y que no hay suficientes maestros bilingües. Además los estudiantes, en su papel de padres y madres de familia, deben dar razones poderosas para establecer los programas que desean para sus hijos.

**RESOURCES**

 Avenue

**Answers**

22 *Las respuestas variarán.*

23 *Las presentaciones variarán.*

24 *Los diálogos variarán.*

### Reference Desk

1. Tell students to choose a topic from **Actividad 22** that interests them. Create an Avenue task in which students summarize possible arguments for and against the issue. Tell them to conclude the report by giving their own opinion.
2. Remind students to use the formal register for their conversations in **Actividad 24**.

### TPR

Write a list of expressions from **Vocabulario 2** on the board. Have students stand and form a circle. Give them an object (a ball, hat, stuffed animal, etc.). One student begins by naming an expression and passing the object to another student. If this student can use the expression correctly in a sentence, s/he picks the next expression and passes the object again. If the sentence is incorrect, s/he must turn and face outside the circle.

---

## Differentiated Learning
### Expand
As a homework assignment, ask students to peruse Peruvian news sites for articles about primary and secondary education. Tell them to bring in one or two articles. In small groups, have students discuss the salient points of each article.

## Multiple Intelligences
### Verbal-Linguistic
Ask students to use the second bullet in **Actividad 23** to interview family or community members. Tell them to find out what they did after high school, and whether they would do anything differently. Have students summarize their findings in a brief report.

# Gramática

## Los usos de *ser* y *estar* 🌼 1.2, 4.1

Los verbos **ser** y **estar** expresan *to be*. Se debe prestar mucha atención al uso de estos verbos.

**ser + adjetivo**
Expresa las características esenciales del sustantivo.

> El amigo de Juan **es** guapo.
> La profesora de música **es** joven.

**estar + adjetivo**
Expresa una condición o estado especial en un determinado momento.

> El amigo de Juan **está** guapo (*looks handsome*) hoy.
> ¡Qué joven **está** la profesora de música!

**ser de**
Expresa propiedad, origen o material.

> Ese apartamento **es de** Lucas.
> Esos jóvenes **son de** Lima.
> Aquel trofeo **es de** plata.

**estar de**
Es equivalente a "trabajar como..." (*to be working as...*).

> Ernesto **estaba de** arquero en el equipo de fútbol. Ahora **está de** delantero y ha marcado muchos goles.

**ser para**
Expresa destino, propósito o plazo.

> Estos formularios **son para** Ricardo.
> La investigación **es para** entregar el lunes.

**estar para + infinitivo**
Es equivalente a "listo para..." (*to be about to...*).

> Después de recibir mis notas **estaba para** llorar.

**sustantivo o pronombre + ser + sustantivo**
Iguala el sujeto al sustantivo.

> Ellos **son** amigos.
> Este laboratorio **es** de física.

**estar + sustantivo o pronombre**
Se refiere a: listo, aquí, allí, en casa.

> ¿**Está** Mariana? (*Is Juanita there/here/at home?*)
> Llegué a tiempo a la clase, pero el profesor no **estaba** (allí).
> ¿Ya **están** los ejercicios (listos)?

**ser y el tiempo cronológico**
Expresa el día, la fecha y la hora.

> Hoy **es** viernes.
> **Es** el diez de marzo.
> **Son** las dos menos cuarto.

**estar y el tiempo atmosférico**
Expresa el estado del tiempo.

> Hoy **está** muy húmedo.
> El día **está** caluroso.

**ser = tener lugar**
(*to take place [an event]*)

> El concierto **será** en el auditorio.
> El ensayo **es** a las siete.

**estar en**
Expresa el lugar de las personas o cosas.

> Los estudiantes **están** en la cafetería.
> Los libros **están** en el escritorio.

### Essential Instruction

1. Open the **Gramática** presentation by having students recall as many **ser** vs. **estar** uses as they can.
2. As you go through the presentation, ask questions that elicit the use of **ser** and **estar**.
3. Check answers to **Actividad 25** by asking students to report whether they and their partner are in agreement or not.

**sujeto + *ser* + adjetivo de nacionalidad (región) o religión**

Expresa origen o religión.

> Todos **somos** cristianos.
> ¿Uds. **son** peruanos?

***ser* en expresiones impersonales**

Expresa una idea general.

> **Es** la clase más importante de la carrera.
> ¿**Es** necesario ir a la biblioteca?

***estar* + gerundio (-*ando*, -*iendo*)**

Expresa una acción en progreso.[1]

> **Estás estudiando** poco.
> Ellas no **están escuchando** al conferencista.

***estar* + participio[2] pasado**

Expresa el resultado de una acción anterior.

> El partido ya **está** terminado.
> ¿**Está cerrada** la cafetería?

| Expresiones con el verbo *estar* | |
|---|---|
| estar atrasado/a | to be late, be behind |
| estar de acuerdo con | to be in agreement with |
| estar de buen/mal humor | to be in a good/bad mood |
| estar de regreso | to be back |
| estar de vacaciones | to be on vacation |
| estar de viaje | to be on a trip |
| estar equivocado/a | to be wrong |
| estar harto/a de | to be fed up with |
| estar listo/a para | to be ready to (for) |

*Ellos están de vacaciones.*

[1] Vea el Capítulo 10 para estudiar más sobre el gerundio. Recuerde que los verbos que terminan en **-ar** forman el gerundio en **-ando** (**caminar → caminando**) y los verbos en **-er** y en **-ir** en **-iendo** (**comprender → comprendiendo**, **escribir → escribiendo**).

[2] Después de **estar**, el participio pasado funciona como adjetivo y concuerda en género y en número con el sustantivo.

---

**25 ¿Están de acuerdo?**  **1.1**

Conteste las siguientes preguntas. Luego, compare sus respuestas con las de un(a) compañero/a de clase. ¿Están de acuerdo o en desacuerdo?

sí   no

1. ____ ____ ¿Está Ud. satisfecho/a con la enseñanza que recibe en este colegio?

2. ¿Está Ud. de acuerdo con el establecimiento de los siguientes cursos con carácter obligatorio?

   ____ ____ **A.** idiomas extranjeros

   ____ ____ **B.** estudios étnicos

3. ____ ____ ¿Piensa Ud. que debemos usar uniformes en el colegio?

sí   no

4. ____ ____ Para Ud., ¿es mejor el sistema de trimestres?

   ____ ____ ¿De semestres?

5. ¿Le gustaría que el semestre terminara...

   ____ ____ **A.** antes de las fiestas de fin de año?

   ____ ____ **B.** después de las fiestas de fin de año?

## Reference Desk

You may want to briefly review the formation of past participles, especially irregulars. Emphasize that when a past participle is used as an adjective, it must agree in number and in gender with the noun it modifies.

## Communication

**Interpersonal: Cooperative Groups**

Create cards with **ser** and **estar** phrases. Divide the class into groups and provide each group with a set of cards. Have students review these verbs by pulling a card from the pile, discussing the definition, and giving an example.

## Expansion

Divide the class into five teams. Each team is responsible for debating one of the items in **Actividad 25**. Half of the team must take the "**sí**" side of the argument, and the other half must take the "**no**" side. Bring the class back together and allow students to present their arguments to the entire group.

## Learning Styles

### Kinesthetic Learners

Divide the board into two columns and label them **ser** and **estar**. Call out a use of one of the verbs (e.g., **características esenciales**) and call on a student, who must go to the board and write an example sentence (**Mi profesora es súper inteligente.**).

### Visual Learners

Ask students to create a simple drawing for each use on these pages. Encourage creativity. For example, for **ser de**, students can draw a close-up of a T-shirt label that says **Es de algodón**.

**27**

1. estás; 2. de; 3. Estoy; 4. para;
5. estoy; 6. de; 7. está; 8. de; 9. es;
10. de; 11. Estoy; 12. de; 13. está;
14. en; 15. estar; 16. de; 17. es;
18. para; 19. Es; 20. de

---

### Reference Desk

1. Display a map of Peru and show the locations of Lima, Cusco, and Machu Picchu.
2. Machu Picchu is one of the most important archaeological centers in South America. It is Peru's biggest tourist draw, with over 400,000 annual visitors.
3. Cusco is sometimes spelled Cuzco. Students will learn more about this city in the **Lectura informativa**.

---

### Culture

**Products: Activity**
Divide the class into small groups and ask each one to research a topic about Machu Picchu, such as its history, geography/location in Peru, the site's layout and structures, the Inca Trail, and possible itineraries for tourists to visit the site. As each group presents their information to the class, have students take notes in their Culture Journals.

---

### Expansion

If time allows, show excerpts from the 2004 film *The Motorcycle Diaries*, that show Machu Picchu.

---

## ¡Comunicación!

**26  ¿Dónde está y cómo es?**  Interpersonal Communication   **1.1**

Imagine que es su primera semana en la universidad y todavía no se ha familiarizado con los diferentes lugares adónde tiene que ir. Represente la conversación que tendría con su compañero/a de cuarto, quien quiere ayudarlo. Túrnense para hacerse preguntas sobre las instalaciones de la universidad, su ubicación, descripción y horas de servicio. Usen el mapa de la universidad del Perú en la página 95 y el vocabulario que se da a continuación, como guía.

**Ubicación:**   a la izquierda, a la derecha, cerca de, lejos de, al frente de, detrás de, lejos de, al norte / sur /este / oeste

**Descripción:**  limpio/a, sucio/a, viejo/a, nuevo/a, moderno/a, cómodo/a, incómodo

MODELO   la biblioteca

> A:  ¿Dónde está la biblioteca?
>
> B:  Está a la derecha de la cafetería.
>
> A:  ¿Y cómo es?
>
> B:  Es muy grande y completa. Está abierta de 7:00 AM a 10:00 PM.

**27  *Ser, estar* y las preposiciones**   **1.2**

El año académico en la Universidad de Lima va a terminar muy pronto. Jackie, una estudiante norteamericana, quiere conocer Machu Picchu antes de volver a Estados Unidos. Consulte las listas de las páginas 110 y 111 y complete el siguiente diálogo con el presente del verbo **ser** o **estar** y las preposiciones que correspondan según el contexto.

**Alberto:**  Jackie, __(1)__ __(2)__ muy mal humor. ¿Qué te pasa?

**Jackie:**  __(3)__ lista __(4)__ regresar a los Estados Unidos y aún no he visto Machu Picchu. No puedo volver a casa sin ver ese asombroso santuario inca.

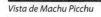
*Vista de Machu Picchu*

**Alberto:**  No te puedo acompañar porque no __(5)__ __(6)__ vacaciones. ¿Por qué no vas con Miguel y Sandra? Ahora Miguel __(7)__ __(8)__ guía turístico y sabrá muy bien orientarte en Machu Picchu, Sandra __(9)__ __(10)__ la ciudad del Cusco, que no está muy lejos de las ruinas. De Cusco salen muchos trenes diarios para Machu Picchu. ¿No te parece una excelente idea?

**Jackie:**  __(11)__ __(12)__ acuerdo contigo, Alberto. Sandra __(13)__ __(14)__ clase ahora, pero va a __(15)__ __(16)__ regreso en una hora más o menos. Entonces hablaré con ella sobre el viaje. Hoy es tu cumpleaños, ¿no es cierto, Alberto? Este regalo __(17)__ __(18)__ ti, querido amigo. ¡Feliz cumpleaños!

**Alberto:**  Gracias, ¡qué suéter más interesante! __(19)__ __(20)__ lana peruana, ¿verdad? Me gusta mucho.

---

### Essential Instruction

1. Circulate around the room as pairs work on **Actividad 26** to make sure that they are using the verbs correctly.
2. Open **Actividad 27** by having students share what they know about Machu Picchu.
3. Before students begin **Actividad 27**, emphasize that each pair of blanks will take a form of **ser** or **estar** and a preposition. After checking answers as a class, have students role-play the dialogue.
4. Encourage students to add at least three more lines to each dialogue in **Actividad 28**.

# ¡Comunicación!

**28** **Use su imaginación** 👥 Interpersonal/Presentational Communication  **1.1, 1.3**

Prepare los siguientes diálogos. Llene los espacios con la forma correcta de **ser** o **estar** y use su imaginación para terminar las oraciones. Compare sus diálogos con los de un(a) compañero/a, hagan los cambios necesarios y elijan uno para presentar a la clase.

**A. La ducha no funciona.**

—Oiga, la ducha no funciona desde hace tres días, no puedo **(1)** sin ducharme por tanto tiempo.

—Lo siento muchísimo. Voy a ver qué es lo que **(2)** roto y vuelvo...

—Esta es la segunda vez que... ¿Cree Ud. que para la noche... ?

—...

**B. En busca de alojamiento.**

—¡Estoy harta de **(3)** aquí!

—¿ **(4)** pensando en buscar otra residencia?

—Sí, **(5)** mejor para...

—¿Crees que **(6)** difícil... ?

—Francamente no lo sé, pero si quieres...

—...

**C. Una llamada telefónica.**

—¡Aló!, ¿... ? ¿Qué **(7)** haciendo?

—Estoy esperando a un amigo para...

—¿ **(8)** seguro de que irá por ti?

—...

—Bueno, en ese caso...

—...

**D. ¿Por qué tan serio/a?**

—¿Qué te pasa, chico/a? ¡ **(9)** muy serio/a!

—Creo que mi novio/a **(10)** saliendo con otro/a.

—¡No puede ser! ¿Por qué?

—...

**RESOURCES**

 Avenue

**Answers**

**28**

1. estar; 2. está; 3. estar; 4. Estás;
5. es; 6. será; 7. estás; 8. Estás;
9. Estás; 10. está

*Los diálogos variarán.*

**Culture**

**Products: Activity**
Ask students to research additional tourist sites in Peru, such as the Nazca Lines, Chan Chan, Lake Titicaca, etc. Have them prepare a travel brochure that contains a feature of each site. Encourage the use of visuals. They can submit their brochures via Avenue.

**Critical Thinking**

**Analyzing**
After students have completed **Actividades 27** and **28**, have them get together with another pair and explain why they chose which verb in each answer.

**Expansion**

Ask students to create their own mini-dialogues. Have them use blanks instead of the forms of **ser** and **estar**. Then have them exchange papers with a classmate and fill in the blanks.

## Multiple Intelligences

**Visual–Spatial**
Ask students to describe their neighborhood to a classmate, who will draw a simple map based on what they hear. Then have them take turns giving directions to different locations on the map. Finally, have students describe the places using **ser**.

**Naturalist**
Ask students to research Peru's varied geography. Have them find out the impact of tourists in heavily visited areas, such as Machu Picchu and Saksaywaman.

**113**

### Reference Desk

You may want to have students recall other **tener** expressions they know, such as **tener celos**, **tener éxito**, **tener dolor de cabeza**, **tener vergüenza**, and so on.

### Culture

**Products/Practices: Activity**
Divide the class into groups and assign each one a different Peruvian city. Ask the group to prepare a report on the city, including its history, sites of interest, cuisine, festivals, etc. Have each group prepare a presentation for the class. Tell them to include visuals. Students should take notes in their Culture Journal while listening to their classmates' presentations.

### Expansion

Ask students weather- and season-related questions, such as: **Cuando es invierno en los Estados Unidos, ¿en qué estación está Lima, Perú? ¿Cuándo nieva mucho? ¿Cuándo hace calor? ¿Cuándo hay muchas flores?**

# Gramática

## Los verbos *haber, hacer, tener, nevar y llover*  1.2

- **Haber**, en la tercera personal del singular, expresa existencia.

  **hay** (*there is/are*)
  En Colombia **hay** muchas universidades.

  **hubo** (*there was/were; took place*)
  Anoche **hubo** un accidente fatal.

  **había** (*there was/were*)
  **Había** unos tipos desconocidos en la residencia.

- **Hacer** y **tener** se usan en expresiones de tiempo en los siguientes casos.

  **hacer**
  En la tercera persona singular, expresa el tiempo meteorológico: **hace frío**, **hace calor**, **hace buen/mal tiempo**, **hace viento**, **hace sol**.
  —¿Qué tiempo **hace** en Barcelona?
  —**Hace buen tiempo**. **Hace** mucho **sol**.

  **tener**
  Expresa el efecto de la temperatura en las personas y animales: **tener frío**, **tener calor**.
  Si **tienes calor**, quítate la bufanda.

- Otros verbos que describen el tiempo son **nevar** y **llover**. Estos verbos siempre se usan en la tercera persona singular. Observe que tienen cambios en el radical.

  **nevar**
  **Nieva** mucho en los Andes.

  **llover**
  Cuando **llueve** prefiero quedarme en casa.

| Otras expresiones con el verbo *tener* | |
|---|---|
| **tener cuidado** | *to be careful* |
| **tener prisa** | *to be in a hurry* |
| **tener ganas de** | *to be in the mood for, to feel like* |
| **tener razón** | *to be right* |
| **tener sed** | *to be thirsty* |
| **tener hambre** | *to be hungry* |
| **tener sueño** | *to be sleepy* |
| **tener miedo de** | *to be afraid of* |
| **tener suerte** | *to be lucky* |

—¿**Tienes ganas de** salir con este frío?
—Ni hablar, hay demasiada nieve.

## Essential Instruction

1. As you work through the **Gramática** presentation, invite students to make example sentences about current events, yesterday's and today's weather, and how they feel.

2. Before beginning **Actividad 29**, go over the weather symbols as a class. Model pronunciation of the cities on the map.

3. Have students report on their partner's answers to **Actividad 30**.

emcpassport.com

 WB 10-11
LA 6

# ¡Comunicación!

## 29 ¿Cómo está el tiempo en Perú?  Interpersonal Communication ✿ 1.1, 1.2

Diga qué tiempo hace en este momento en las siguientes ciudades peruanas según el mapa. Luego, pregúntele a su compañero/a de clase sobre el tiempo en otras ciudades del mundo, consultando un mapa metereológico en el periódico o la internet.

> **MODELO**   Lima
>
> A: ¿Cómo está el tiempo en Lima?
>
> B: Hace sol. (Está despejado.)

**1.** Arequipa     **3.** Trujillo     **5.** Iquitos

**2.** Cusco     **4.** Machu Picchu     **6.** Huancayo

| | | | |
|---|---|---|---|
| Hace sol./Está despejado. | ☀ | Heladas. | **H** |
| Está nublado. | ☁ | Hay niebla. | ◯ |
| Llueve. | ☂ | Hace viento. | → |
| Hay tormenta. | ⚡ | | |

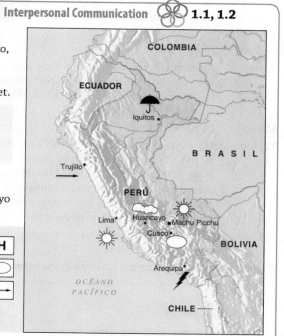

## 30 Situaciones  Interpersonal Communication ✿ 1.1

Con un(a) compañero/a, hablen de lo que hacen en las siguientes situaciones. Túrnense para hacer preguntas y responderlas como se ve en el modelo.

> **MODELO**   estar de buen humor
>
> A: ¿Qué haces cuando estás de buen humor?
>
> B: Salgo con mis amigos. ¿Y tú?
>
> A: ...

**1.** hacer calor     **4.** estar atrasado/a     **7.** hacer buen tiempo

**2.** tener miedo     **5.** tener hambre     **8.** estar de buen humor

**3.** llover     **6.** estar furioso/a

---

## Answers

**29**
1. En Arequipa hay tormenta.
2. En Cusco hay niebla.
3. En Trujillo hace viento.
4. En Machu Picchu hace sol/ está despejado.
5. En Iquitos llueve.
6. En Huancayo está nublado.
*Las respuestas variarán.*

**30** *Las respuestas variarán.*

### Reference Desk

Go through the weather expressions in **Actividad 29**. You may want to clarify that **tormenta** can be a general word for *storm*, not just a thunder/lightning storm. When students look up information for other cities, you may want to brainstorm additional weather vocabulary, such as **hace brisa**, **hace fresco**, **la temperatura está a... grados**, etc.

### Connections

**Science/Meteorology**
Have students work in groups to study Peru's climate and weather patterns. You may want to have them do online research and follow Peru's weather during a set time period.

---

## Differentiated Learning

### Accelerate/Adapt
Challenge students by having them repeat **Actividad 30** with information from when they were small children.

### Decelerate/Adapt
If students struggle with **Actividad 30**, change this to a matching activity. Provide sentence starters (e.g., **Cuando hace calor...**) and two possible answers for each one; students can choose the one that is most true for them. After students successfully match the items, encourage them to use these sentences to carry out the dialogue.

Answers

**31**

1. tengo ganas de
2. Tengo prisa
3. tienes hambre
4. Tienes sueño
5. tener cuidado
6. tienes frío
7. tienen miedo
8. tienes suerte
9. tienes razón

**32** *Las presentaciones variarán.*

### Reference Desk

1. The Amigos School in Cambridge began as a program in 1986, and follows a dual-language immersion model, in which the students are expected to emerge biliterate and bilingual.
2. You may want to have students submit their reports from **Actividad 32** via Avenue.

### Expansion

Follow up **Actividad 31** by asking students if they have someone in their life like Tía Emilia. Have students write a similar dialogue that they might have with their family member.

---

**31 ¡Deja de quejarte!**  **1.2**

Darío y Manuel viven juntos en un apartamento cerca de la universidad. Hoy la tía de Darío viene de visita. Consulte la página 114 y llene los espacios con la forma apropiada de las expresiones con el verbo **tener**.

**Manuel:** ¿Y esa cara?

**Darío:** Ay, es que hoy viene mi tía Emilia, y tú sabes cómo es ella. Yo no **(1)** escuchar sus comentarios y críticas sobre el apartamento, mi forma de comer, de limpiar, etc. Me trata como si fuera un niño de cinco años... Alguien llama a la puerta. ¡Es ella! ¿Adónde vas, Manuel? Quédate un rato más.

**Manuel:** Solo unos minutos. **(2)** por llegar al campus. No quiero perder mi clase de historia.

**Tía Emilia:** Hola, muchachos. Déjame verte, Darío. ¡Estás hecho un esqueleto (*skeleton*)! Seguramente tú **(3)** . Te voy a preparar unos espaguettis sabrosos. ¿Y esas ojeras (*dark eye circles*)? ¿ **(4)** ? Debes **(5)** con tu salud (*health*) aquí en la universidad. Ponte este suéter porque parece que tú **(6)** . ¿No tienes calefacción (*heating*) en este apartamento? Siempre leo en los diarios que por aquí hay mucho crimen. ¿Tú y Manuel no **(7)** de vivir aquí, solos, en este barrio? Ya sabes que siempre son bienvenidos en mi casa.

**Manuel:** No entiendo por qué te quejas tanto de tu tía. Creo que tú **(8)** de tener alguien que se preocupa tanto por ti.

**Darío:** Sí, tú **(9)** , amigo. No voy a quejarme más de mi tía Emilia.

---

**¡Comunicación!** **1.1, 1.3**

**32 El inglés como segundo idioma**  **Interpersonal/Presentational Communication**

Para poder tener éxito en los EE. UU. es esencial saber leer, entender, escribir y hablar bien el inglés. Las familias hispanas recién llegadas a nuestro país, ¿qué pueden hacer para asegurarse de que sus niños reciban una buena educación en la escuela si no saben hablar inglés? Muchas ciudades con grandes poblaciones de hispanos ofrecen varias soluciones. Por ejemplo, en Cambridge, Massachusetts, el programa "Amigos" les ofrece a los estudiantes hispanohablantes y los estudiantes angloparlantes la oportunidad de compartir su cultura y su idioma.

Busque información en la internet sobre este programa y, con un(a) compañero/a, túrnense para contestar las siguientes preguntas.

- ¿Qué son los "Programas intensivos de inglés"?

- ¿Cuál es el enfoque del programa?

- ¿Cuáles son algunas de las universidades que ofrecen este programa?

- ¿Son grandes las clases? Explique.

- ¿Cómo se consigue una visa para poder estudiar en los EE. UU.?

Ahora, investiguen programas similares en el área donde viven. ¿Qué opciones tienen las personas que no saben hablar inglés pero quieren aprender? Hagan un resumen de la información y preséntenla al resto de la clase.

---

### Essential Instruction

1. Open **Actividad 31** by reading the first two lines of dialogue. Ask students to imagine what Darío's face looked like.
2. Encourage students to use visuals in their presentations for **Actividad 32**.
3. Have pairs discuss the **Antes de leer** question. Have them jot down a few ideas to share with the class.
4. Go over the **Estrategia**. Have students read the title and subheadings of the reading to determine its topic.
5. For Common Core practice, have students answer the **Analice** questions.

# Lectura informativa

## Antes de leer

¿Cómo se imagina que puede ser la experiencia de estudiar en otro país donde la lengua y la cultura son distintas de las propias?

 **1.3, 4.2, 5.2**

### Estrategia  1.2, 3.1

**Leer para buscar información**

Antes de leer, mire los títulos, los subtítulos y las ilustraciones para identificar el tema. Haga una primera lectura para tener una idea general del contenido. Luego, vuelva a leer el texto y concéntrese en las ideas principales. Preste atención al contexto cuando no comprenda algo.

○ ○ ○  Verano en Cusco

**UNIVERSIDAD DEL PACÍFICO**

INFORMACIÓN PARA: SELECCIONAR  Buscar...

ADMISIÓN  CARRERAS  ESCUELA DE POSTGRADO  CENTRO DE IDIOMAS  FONDO EDITORIAL  INVESTIGACIÓN  VIDA EN EL CAMPUS

## Verano en Cusco  1.2, 2.2

### Bienvenido a la Universidad del Pacífico

En las tres últimas décadas, la Universidad del Pacífico (UP) ha sido clasificada como la más prestigiosa institución de educación superior en sus campos de especialización en Perú. Fortaleciendo nuestros esfuerzos de internacionalización, la UP ha abierto un Programa Internacional en Cusco para ofrecer a los estudiantes la oportunidad de aprender más sobre el entorno[1] de negocios en el Perú y América Latina, que cuenta con uno de los mercados emergentes más importantes del mundo. Los participantes podrán estudiar en un entorno arqueológico e histórico único, vivir una experiencia intercultural y obtener créditos académicos.

### Curso de verano: "Del conocimiento local a los negocios globales"

Este curso de dos semanas de duración ofrece una combinación de temas especializados relacionados con el comercio, el espíritu empresarial y la cooperación internacional desde la perspectiva de un país en desarrollo[2]. Los estudiantes examinarán cuestiones conceptuales aplicadas a casos prácticos en una dimensión de la vida real, con el objetivo de producir estrategias adecuadas para el entorno empresarial internacional, y tendrán la oportunidad de participar en excursiones de aprendizaje, talleres[3] culturales, y conocer a gente de todo el mundo en uno de los mejores destinos turísticos de Perú: Cusco.

### Acerca del curso

**Requisitos:** Los estudiantes de pregrado y postgrado[4] de ciencias sociales, negocios, economía y campos relacionados. Conocimiento de comercio internacional, los entornos socioculturales, economía, gestión[5], y temas relacionados.

### Alojamiento en casas de familia

La Universidad del Pacífico apoya a los estudiantes en la búsqueda de alojamiento en Cusco. Contamos con una red de alojamiento familiar especializada en la recepción de estudiantes internacionales. Los estudiantes interesados en vivir con familias locales para una experiencia intercultural real deben enviar un correo electrónico a: cuscoprograms@up.edu.pe y nosotros nos encargaremos de coordinar su alojamiento en Cusco.

[1] environment   [2] developing country   [3] workshops
[4] undergraduate and graduate students   [5] management

**1.2, 2.2**

## 33 Comprensión

1. ¿En qué consiste el Programa Internacional de Cusco?

2. ¿Qué temas incluye el curso de verano?

3. Además de los contenidos del curso, ¿qué otras cosas se ofrecen a los participantes?

**1.3, 5.2**

## 34 Analice

¿Por qué cree Ud. que alojarse en una casa de familia en el extranjero puede ser una experiencia enriquecedora?

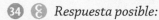 
**117**

**Answers**

 35

1. Es Patrimonio Cultural de la Humanidad y Machu Picchu es una de las Nuevas Siete Maravillas del Mundo.
2. La forma más conveniente es llegar por avión. Es importante reservar el vuelo lo antes posible y es preferible organizar el viaje desde la ciudad donde uno viva.
3. El clima es subtropical, seco y templado, con dos estaciones definidas: una estación seca y una temporada de lluvias.

36 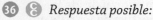 *Respuesta posible:*
Los estudiantes internacionales suelen estar interesados en viajar y conocer nuevos lugares además de estudiar. Si los cursos se dan en un lugar turístico, pueden atraer a más participantes.

## Culture

### Products: Information
Cusco was the capital of the Inca Empire from the thirteenth century until the Spanish arrived in the sixteenth century. As the center of a vast empire, the city was—and still is—an important agricultural region. Until the late 1700s, Cusco was the most populous city in South America. Today, the population is about 430,000.

 **1.2, 2.2**

### 35 Comprensión

1. ¿Con qué dos importantes reconocimientos internacionales cuenta la ciudad de Cusco?

2. ¿Cuál es la forma más conveniente de llegar a Cusco? ¿Qué precauciones hay que tomar?

3. ¿Cómo es el clima en Cusco?

 **1.3, 2.1, 3.2**

### 36 Analice

¿Por qué cree Ud. que la universidad eligió un destino turístico famoso en todo el mundo para su Centro Internacional?

○ ○ ○  Vida en Cusco

**UNIVERSIDAD DEL PACÍFICO**

INFORMACIÓN PARA: SELECCIONAR | Buscar...

ADMISIÓN | CARRERAS | ESCUELA DE POSTGRADO | CENTRO DE IDIOMAS | FONDO EDITORIAL | INVESTIGACIÓN | VIDA EN EL CAMPUS

## Vida en Cusco

### Acerca de Cusco
Cusco es una ciudad en el sureste de Perú, cerca del Valle de Urubamba en la cordillera de los Andes. Cusco no es solo una ciudad, Cusco fue el escenario de la histórica capital del Imperio inca y declarada Patrimonio de la Humanidad en 1983 por la UNESCO.

A pesar de que tendrá muchos lugares para visitar en la ciudad, Machu Picchu es el más popular, especialmente desde 2007, cuando la Fundación New7Wonders designó a Machu Picchu como una de las Nuevas Siete Maravillas del Mundo. Si no conoces Cusco, te estás perdiendo de mucho. No hay otro lugar como este. Y esa es la razón por la que la Universidad del Pacífico decidió colocar su Nuevo Centro Internacional en "La Capital Arqueológica de América".

### Cómo llegar a Cusco
#### Por avión
La forma más conveniente de llegar a Cusco es por avión. Si llegas por primera vez a Lima, podrás tomar un avión directo a Cusco. Hay vuelos diarios a Cusco en horarios diferentes, pero es importante reservar su vuelo lo antes posible. Por favor, tenga en cuenta que si no está planeando quedarse en Lima unos días es preferible organizar su viaje a Cusco desde su ciudad local, ya que podría no encontrar vuelos disponibles y los precios pueden ser considerablemente más altos. El vuelo dura unos 60 minutos. Algunas líneas aéreas: LAN PERÚ, STAR PERÚ, PERUVIAN AIRLINES. El costo aproximado del vuelo es (Lima-Cusco-Lima) US$ 120 o más.

#### Por tierra
Aunque es posible acceder a Cusco por tierra, esto no es lo más conveniente, dado que la ruta es larga y el viaje puede ser agotador[6], ya que toma aproximadamente 24 horas. Las empresas de transporte: Cruz del Sur, Excluciva, Civa, Oltursa. El costo aproximado (Lima-Cusco): US$ 40 a 60.

### Clima
Cusco tiene un clima subtropical. Su clima es generalmente seco y templado, con dos estaciones definidas. La estación seca se extiende de abril a octubre, con abundante sol, y ocasionales heladas[7] nocturnas: julio es el mes más frío con una media de 9,6 °C (49,3 °F). La temporada de lluvias dura de noviembre a marzo, con heladas nocturnas menos comunes: el promedio de noviembre es de 13,4 °C (56,1 °F). A pesar de que las heladas y el granizo[8] son comunes, la nieve es prácticamente desconocida.

[6] exhausting    [7] frost    [8] hail

🔍 **Búsqueda:** universidad del pacífico, cusco, estudiantes internacionales en perú, machu picchu

## Essential Instruction
1. Bring in photos of Cusco and the surrounding areas so that students can reference them as they read **Vida en Cusco**.
2. Go over the introductory information about formal letter writing. As you review the parts, show proper formatting on the board, or bring in a sample letter.
3. Have students peer-edit their letters from **Actividad 37**.

## Una carta formal 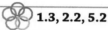 1.3

Una carta formal es un mensaje que se envía a una persona (que muchas veces no se conoce) para tratar temas relacionados con el trabajo, el comercio, las instituciones educativas, etc. Las cartas formales ofrecen información concreta y completa y están organizadas con claridad y precisión. El lenguaje debe ser formal y el tratamiento al destinatario será de "usted". En esta actividad, escribirá una carta formal para solicitar que lo acepten en el curso de la Universidad del Pacífico.

Una carta formal debe incluir:

- El **lugar** donde se encuentra la persona que escribe y el **día** en que se escribió la carta
- El **nombre completo del destinatario**, su tratamiento (Dr., Sra., etc.) y el puesto que ocupa
- Una forma de **saludo formal**, por ejemplo: *Estimado señor...*
- El **cuerpo**, donde se presenta quien escribe y explica el motivo de la carta
- La **despedida**, que es un pequeño párrafo donde se cierra la comunicación

### Para escribir más

Use las siguientes frases para el saludo y la despedida en las cartas formales.

*Estimado señor...*

*De mi consideración*

*Quedo a la espera de su pronta respuesta*

*Lo saluda atentamente*

*Me despido cordialmente*

### ¡Comunicación!

**37** | **Por medio de la presente...** Presentational Communication  1.3, 2.2, 5.2

Vuelva a leer la información sobre el curso de verano en Cusco que ofrece la Universidad del Pacífico. Preste atención a los contenidos del curso y a los requisitos que se deben cumplir para inscribirse. Luego, escriba una carta formal al rector de la universidad solicitando que lo acepten para el curso de este verano. Dé información detallada sobre sus estudios previos para explicar por qué Ud. es un buen candidato para el programa. Antes de escribir su carta, complete el organizador gráfico para hacer un borrador con sus ideas.

| | |
|---|---|
| ¿A quién va dirigida la carta? | |
| ¿Cuál es el propósito de la carta? | |
| ¿Por qué le interesa asistir a este programa? | |
| ¿Por qué es Ud. un buen candidato? | |
| ¿Cuáles son sus estudios previos y cómo se relacionan con el contenido de este curso? | |
| ¿Cuáles son sus planes de estudio en el futuro y cómo se beneficiarían si Ud. asiste a este curso de verano? | |

# Una recomendación  1.3, 3.1

Una recomendación es un relato en primera persona en el que se describe una experiencia positiva. El propósito es que otras personas conozcan las virtudes de una película, un libro, un destino turístico, etc. y aconsejarlas para que ellas también vivan esa experiencia.

##  ¡Comunicación!

**38 Un verano en Cusco**  Interpretive Communication 1.2, 1.3, 3.2

Escuche los siguientes comentarios de estudiantes que asistieron al curso de la Universidad del Pacífico que ofrece a los estudiantes extranjeros la oportunidad de familiarizarse con el entorno de los negocios en Perú y América Latina. Tome apuntes en una hoja aparte.

**39 Una experiencia maravillosa** Presentational Communication  1.2, 1.3, 2.2

Vuelva a leer la información sobre el programa de verano de la Universidad del Pacífico y tome apuntes de los puntos principales. Imagine que Ud. participó de este programa intercultural y escriba una recomendación en la que comente su experiencia, con base en la lectura, los comentarios que acaba de escuchar y los temas que se dan enseguida, como guía. Asegúrese de mencionar todo lo que le haya parecido agradable y positivo, con un tono entusiasta que invite a otras personas a inscribirse en el curso. Para finalizar, publique su recomendación en línea y agregue fotos para hacerla más llamativa.

*Con la Universidad del Pacífico se pueden visitar sitios inolvidables como Machu Picchu.*

- La geografía del lugar
- Las instalaciones de la universidad
- El contenido del curso
- El horario de clases y actividades diarias
- Su relación con los demás estudiantes

## Essential Instruction

1. Read about recommendations as a class.
2. For **Actividad 38**, play the audio once and have students just listen. Play the audio a second time and have them take notes.
3. Remind students that they should be persuasive in their recommendations. Brainstorm phrases or expressions that students can use in their writing.
4. Model pronunciation of the new vocabulary words and have students repeat. Clarify any unfamiliar words in the definitions.
5. You may want to have students complete **Actividad 40** in pairs.

# Vocabulario 3

## Mejore su comprensión   1.2

Familiarizarse con este vocabulario le ayudará a leer "El alacrán de fray Gómez" más adelante, y a mejorar su comprensión auditiva.

**alacrán** *s.m.* Animal venenoso, escorpión.

**alhaja** *s.f.* Joya de metal o piedras preciosas.

**apuro** *s.m.* Problema, necesidad de dinero.

**buhonero** *s.m.* Vendedor ambulante.

**celda** *s.f.* Cuarto individual de un convento.

**codicia** *s.f.* Deseo excesivo de riqueza.

**convento** *s.m.* Casa de religiosos/as.

**desbocado/a** *adj.* Se dice del caballo que corre sin control.

**descalabrarse** *v.* Herirse en la cabeza.

**desempeñar** *v.* Realizar las funciones propias de un trabajo; recuperar algo empeñado.

**deuda** *s.f.* Dinero que se le debe a alguien.

**devoto/a** *adj.* Dedicado a una causa.

**empeñar** *v.* Dejar una cosa en garantía de dinero prestado.

**empeñarse en** *v.* Insistir.

**esconder** *v.* Poner algo donde no se lo pueda encontrar.

**estar de vuelta a** *exp.* Volver a un lugar.

**holgazanería** *s.f.* Pereza, falta de ganas de trabajar.

**jaqueca** *s.f.* Dolor fuerte de cabeza.

**lucirse** *v.* Impresionar.

**milagro** *s.m.* Hecho que se explica por intervención divina.

**patitieso/a** *adj.* Que se queda sin sentido y no puede mover los pies o las piernas.

**perseverar** *v.* Insistir sin perder el ánimo.

**pícaro/a** *adj.* Que es listo y tiene habilidad para conseguir lo que quiere.

**prendedor** *s.m.* Joya que se lleva en la ropa.

*Un prendedor en forma de alacrán*

**préstamo** *s.m.* Entrega de algo con la condición de que sea devuelto.

**principiar** *v.* Empezar o dar comienzo.

**quejumbroso/a** *adj.* Con voz de dolor o pena.

**sabandija** *s.f.* Insecto.

**usurero** *s.m.* Persona que presta dinero a cambio de interés o ganancia excesiva.

---

**40 Identifique al intruso**  1.3

Diga qué expresión no pertenece al grupo y explique por qué.

1. préstamo   deuda   celda
2. pícaro   devoto   convento
3. alhaja   prendedor   milagro
4. codicia   usurero   sabandija
5. empeñarse   lucirse   perseverar
6. empeñar   desempeñar   principiar

---

## RESOURCES

 Mejore su comprensión

### Answers

**40** *Las explicaciones variarán; respuestas posibles:*

1. *Celda* no se relaciona con dinero.
2. *Pícaro* no se relaciona con la religión.
3. *Milagro* no se relaciona con joyas.
4. *Sabandija* no se relaciona con dinero.
5. *Lucirse* no se relaciona con hacer esfuerzos.
6. *Principiar* no se relaciona con cosas que se cambian por dinero.

### Reference Desk

1. The words in **Vocabulario 3** are extracted from the audio in **Actividad 42** and the **Lectura literaria** that appears later in the unit. These words are intended for comprehension and expansion only; they will not appear on assessments.
2. Allow for a variety of answers in the **Identifique al intruso** activity provided that students can justify their choice.

### Expansion

Create a matching worksheet with vocabulary words and their definitions to help students review their meanings.

---

## Special Needs Students
### Auditory Impairment

Ask these students to listen several times to the recording in **Actividad 38**. You may also want to provide them with a script so that they can follow along and highlight the main points as they listen.

## Multiple Intelligences
### Verbal-Linguistic

Ask students to create crossword puzzles with the new vocabulary. Have them exchange papers with a classmate and complete the puzzles.

**121**

**41**
1. desbocado
2. se descalabró
3. buhonero
4. patitieso
5. convento
6. jaqueca
7. de vuelta
8. devotos

**42 Script**
De vuelta a su pueblo un joven estudiante quiere lucirse mientras almuerza con sus padres.
De dos huevos que hay en un plato esconde uno de ellos rápidamente. Después pregunta a su padre:
—¿Cuántos huevos hay en el plato?
El padre contesta:
—Hay un huevo.
El estudiante pone en el plato el otro huevo y pregunta al padre:
—Y ahora, ¿cuántos huevos hay?
El padre contesta muy tranquilo:
—Ahora hay dos.
—Pues entonces—dice el estudiante—dos que hay ahora y uno de antes suman tres. Entonces son tres los huevos que hay en el plato. El padre se sorprende de los estudios de su hijo. La vista le dice que en el plato hay solo dos huevos; pero la dialéctica profunda le obliga a afirmar que hay tres huevos.
Al fin, la madre decide la cuestión prácticamente. Pone un huevo en el plato de su esposo, toma otro huevo para ella y le dice al hijo:
—Tú, que sabes tanto, cómete el tercer huevo.

1. ¿Cómo empieza la historia?
2. ¿Qué hace el joven estudiante para lucirse con sus padres?
3. Según el hijo, ¿cuántos huevos hay en total en el plato?
4. ¿Cómo reaccionan los padres?
5. ¿Cómo decide la cuestión la madre?

1. C; 2. A; 3. C; 4. A; 5. C

## 41 De puro milagro  1.2

Complete los párrafos con la palabra del recuadro que corresponda según el contexto.

| desbocado | convento | buhonero | jaqueca |
|---|---|---|---|
| se descalabró | devotos | patitieso | de vuelta |

El hombre cabalgaba por el campo cuando su caballo se paró de repente y echó a correr __(1)__ . El hombre salió a volar por el aire y al caer al suelo __(2)__ . Un __(3)__ que andaba de pueblo en pueblo vendiendo mercancía lo encontró __(4)__ y quejumbroso en medio del camino y lo llevó a un __(5)__ cercano donde lo ayudaron. Pasó un par de días con una gran __(6)__ , pero pronto estuvo bien y __(7)__ con su familia. Estaba agradecido porque, como dijeron los __(8)__ padres: "No se mató de puro milagro".

## 42 El milagro de la dialéctica  1.2

Escuche el relato "El milagro de la dialéctica". Luego, Ud. oirá unas preguntas y tres respuestas posibles. Seleccione la letra de la respuesta con la terminación más lógica. La pregunta y las terminaciones se leerán dos veces.

1. **A.** Un joven estudiante no quiere volver a su pueblo.
   **B.** Un joven estudiante, de vuelta a su pueblo, no quiere almorzar con sus padres.
   **C.** Un joven estudiante, de vuelta a su pueblo, quiere lucirse con sus padres.
2. **A.** Esconde uno de los huevos que hay en el plato.
   **B.** Se come uno de los huevos que hay en el plato.
   **C.** Rompe uno de los huevos que hay en el plato.
3. **A.** Uno.
   **B.** Dos.
   **C.** Tres.

*El joven almuerza con su padre.*

4. **A.** El padre se sorprende de los estudios de su hijo.
   **B.** La madre se sorprende de los conocimientos de su hijo.
   **C.** Los padres se miran sorprendidos.

5. **A.** Pone un huevo en el plato de su hijo.
   **B.** Pone dos huevos en el plato de su hijo.
   **C.** No pone huevos en el plato de su hijo.

**Essential Instruction**
1. Have students check their answers to **Actividad 41** in pairs.
2. Before playing the audio in **Actividad 42**, remind students that they will hear some of the words from p. 121.
3. For **Actividad 42**, have students listen to the story with their eyes closed. Play it a second time, pausing to ask questions. Then play the rest of the audio and have students select their answers.
4. Personalize the **Gramática** by giving examples from your own life.
5. Emphasize that there are many possible answers in **Actividad 43**. Have students write some examples on the board.

# Gramática

## Expresiones de obligación y probabilidad  1.2

- **Tener que + infinitivo** (*to have to, must*) expresa una fuerte obligación personal.

  Ellos **tienen que estudiar** mucho para el examen final.
  Mi mejor amigo **tendrá que presentarse** pronto.

- **Haber (hay) que + infinitivo** expresa una necesidad u obligación impersonal (*one must, it is necessary to…*).

  **Hay que disfrutar** las vacaciones al máximo.
  **Había que cancelar** el concierto por mal tiempo.
  **Habrá que resolver** la situación.

- **Deber (de) + infinitivo** y **haber de + infinitivo** expresan…

  obligación moral (*to be supposed to, should*)

  **Debo estudiar** para aprobar todas las materias.
  Ahora que estamos jóvenes, **hemos de aprovechar** mejor el tiempo libre.

  probabilidad (*must, probably*)

  **Debe (de) ser** muy buen profesor.
  **Ha de tener** mucha experiencia.

### ¡Comunicación!

**43** ¿Qué sabes? 👥 Interpersonal Communication  1.1

En parejas, creen diálogos como los del modelo.

MODELO  la rectora

A:  ¿Qué sabes de la rectora?
B:  Sé que tiene que dar una conferencia.

| | | |
|---|---|---|
| la rectora | | dar una conferencia |
| los profesores | | prisa por salir |
| la consejera | | muy equivocado/a |
| el ingeniero | tener | de vacaciones |
| los hombres | tener que | repasar la materia |
| el filósofo | deber de | mucha hambre |
| la abogada | estar | ser muy talentoso |
| los estudiantes | | ayudar a sus clientes |
| esa estudiante | | miedo de los exámenes |
| nosotros | | solicitar una beca |
| | | pensar en el futuro |

## RESOURCES

**WB** Activities 12–13

### Answers
**43** *Los diálogos variarán.*

### Reference Desk

Point out that **haber de** to express obligation and probability is more formal/literary; **deber de** is more common in everyday speech.

### Communication

**Interpersonal/Presentational: Paired Practice**
Have students work in pairs to draft a list of rules and recommendations for studying a second language. Have pairs share their ideas with the class, and summarize their ideas on the board. Finally, work as a class to make a poster with the most useful tips. You may want to have students make copies of the poster for other Spanish classes at your school.

## Differentiated Learning
### Accelerate/Expand
Tell students to imagine that a friend wants to apply to college, but needs some advice on how to prepare him/herself and go through with the application process. Tell them to write the friend an e-mail with at least eight recommendations.

## Learning Styles
### Visual Learners
Bring in photos that show people in a variety of situations, such as a traffic accident, winning the lottery, etc. Invite students to state what probably happened, how the people probably feel, and what they should do or have to do next.

**Answers**

44 *Las respuestas variarán.*

## Critical Thinking

**Analyzing**
Create sentences that do not follow the rules discussed on pp. 124–125. After reviewing this information, correct the sentences as a class and discuss how **en** and **de** were used incorrectly.

## Expansion

Have pairs of students repeat **Actividad 44** in the context of another class at school, or an extracurricular activity.

# Gramática

**44 La clase de ciencias**  **1.1**

Ud. estuvo enfermo/a y no ha podido asistir a los primeros días de clase. Pregúntele a su compañero/a lo siguiente.

MODELO     los requisitos para estar en la clase

A: ¿Cuáles son los requisitos para estar en la clase?

B: Tenemos que asistir a cuatro clases semanales y hay que ir una vez al laboratorio.

1. Los requisitos para estar en la clase
2. Los libros
3. El número de pruebas
4. El día del examen final
5. El número de estudiantes matriculados en la clase
6. Las horas de consulta del/de la profesor(a)
7. La hora a la que comienza y termina la clase
8. El horario del laboratorio

## Las preposiciones *en* y *de*  1.2

### *En* se usa...

- para designar el lugar donde algo ocurre o se localiza (*in, at*).
- con el significado de **encima de** (*on*) o **dentro de** (*in*).
- en expresiones de tiempo para designar lo que ocurre en un momento dado (*in*).

### Ejemplos

Mi familia vive **en** Cusco.
La fuente está **en** la plaza principal.

Los exámenes están **en** la mesa.
Colgué tu abrigo **en** el armario.

**En** esos días todo era más fácil.
Viviremos en Marte **en** el siglo XXII.

### *De* se usa...

- para indicar posesión (*of*).

- para indicar origen o nacionalidad (*from*).

- con un sustantivo para indicar el material de que esta hecho algo (*of*).
- para designar una hora específica (*in*).

### Ejemplos

Este suéter es **del** profesor.
El carro no es **de** Lucía; es mío.

Es una flor **de** esta región.
Ellos son **de** Chile.

Se ganó una medalla **de** oro.
Su cama es **de** madera.

Ya van a ser las ocho **de** la noche.
Viajarán a las dos **de** la tarde.

**Essential Instruction**

1. Model question formation for the first four items in **Actividad 44** to show the variety of interrogatives needed.
2. As you review the **Gramática** content, invite volunteers to create examples about your classroom and students.
3. As you review the answers for **Actividad 45**, ask students to justify their answers by citing the corresponding use listed in **Gramática**.
4. Have pairs role-play the dialogue in **Actividad 45**.

Answers_____

**45**
1. de; 2. en; 3. en; 4. de; 5. de;
6. del; 7. de; 8. de; 9. en; 10. de;
11. de; 12. de; 13. en; 14. de;
15. En

*De* **también se usa…**

- para designar el lugar al que pertenecen personas o cosas (*in, on*).
- seguido de un sustantivo, para indicar la condición, la función o el estado de algo, y expresa la idea de **como** (*as a*).
- después de un adjetivo para expresar la causa de un estado o una acción (*of, with*).
- para describir el uso práctico o el contenido de un objeto (*of*).

Lo encontré en la tienda **de** la esquina.
Él es mi amigo **de** la calle Sol.

El niño se viste siempre **de** vaquero.
Vino para ser nuestro profesor **de** idiomas.
**De** niño, era mi mejor amigo.

Regresaron cansados **de** tanto jugar.
Estoy contento **del** trabajo que hizo.

Encontraron el libro **de** recetas.

🌸 **1.1, 1.2**

## 45 Lo vamos a echar de menos 👥

Luis Bonilla estudia economía en la universidad. Al salir de clase, su compañera lo invita a tomar un café. Con un(a) compañero/a de clase, completen la conversación entre los dos amigos, utilizando **en**, **de** o **del**.

—¿Dónde es la fiesta __(1)__ los estudiantes para el profesor Azpillaga?

—Es __(2)__ casa de Juan Carlos.

—Es una pena que el profesor se jubile __(3)__ junio. ¿No crees?

—Sí, la verdad es que es un profesor excelente. Yo, __(4)__ viejo, quisiera ser como el profesor Azpillaga.

—¿Sí? ¿Por qué dices eso?

—Porque es un hombre __(5)__ gran corazón y gran cabeza. Uno de los reporteros __(6)__ periódico *El Mundo* ha escrito hoy un artículo sobre su vida.

—¿En serio? ¿Qué periodista?

—Ese que siempre lleva pantalones __(7)__ cuero negro.

—Pero, volviendo al tema __(8)__ la fiesta para el profesor Azpillaga, ¿vamos a comprarle algo entre todos los estudiantes del máster?

—Creo que es una buena idea. El otro día vi, __(9)__ la mesa __(10)__ su despacho, un librito __(11)__ poesía __(12)__ Mario Benedetti. Podemos ir a la librería que está __(13)__ la esquina para preguntar qué otros libros __(14)__ Benedetti tienen.

—Perfecto. __(15)__ este momento no tengo nada que hacer. ¡Vamos!

*Los jugadores son de Perú.*

### Reference Desk

The Uruguayan novelist and poet Mario Benedetti (1920–2009) is one of Latin America's most important writers of the last century.

### Critical Thinking

**Analyzing**
Have students review their answers for **Actividad 45** and explain their reasoning for each one.

### Communication

**Presentational: Paired Practice**
For additional practice, have students prepare their own sentences that require **de** or **en**, but have them leave out the preposition. In pairs, students fill in each other's sentences.

### Differentiated Learning
**Accelerate**
Bring in several poems by Mario Benedetti that use **en**, **de**, or **del**, such as "**El aguafiestas falta sin aviso**," "**Como si nada**," or "**La crisis**." Have students get together in small groups and analyze the uses of these words in the poems.

### Special Needs Students
**Linguistically Challenged/AD(H)D**
For these students, you may want to summarize the uses of **en** and **de** in English. To help solidify the information, give simpler example sentences for each use and have them circle **en** or **de** in each one.

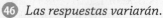
## Reference Desk

1. Point out the title of this selection. Explain the meaning of **fray** (*brother, monk*).

2. Ricardo Palma is best known for his masterpiece ***Tradiciones peruanas***, which was originally published in volumes between 1872 and 1910. The **tradiciones** are short stories that combine fiction and Peruvian history. They are written for amusement as well as education, although they are not necessarily historically accurate. Although Palma called his works **tradiciones**, his contemporaries in Peru and elsewhere in Latin America called this genre **costumbrismo**. However, Palma is considered a Romantic writer due to the time period and themes of his works.

## Pre-AP

**Course Theme: La belleza y la estética**

---

# Lectura literaria

## El alacrán de fray Gómez  1.2, 3.1
### de *Ricardo Palma*

### Sobre el autor

Ricardo Palma nació en Lima, Perú, en 1833. Periodista y literato, empezó publicando poesía y obras de teatro, aunque su obra más importante la componen sus relatos breves. En estos cuentos, Palma describe la sociedad colonial, con sus usos y lenguaje propios. Palma trabajó para fijar y tratar de que se reconociera el léxico propio del español de Perú, un lenguaje popular que caracteriza su literatura. Murió en Miraflores, Perú, en 1919.

*Busto de Ricardo Palma*

### Antes de leer   1.3

¿Sabe algún dicho popular o frase hecha del inglés que no tenga sentido al traducirse literalmente al español?

### Estrategia  3.1

**Los dichos populares o frases hechas**

Los dichos populares o frases hechas son expresiones de la cultura popular que, por lo general, no pueden traducirse literalmente. Analizar el uso y el significado de estas frases sirve como ayuda para entender mejor el texto.

### 46 Practique la estrategia  1.3, 3.1

Identifique el contexto de los siguientes dichos populares a medida que lea "El alacrán de fray Gómez". Explique su significado y piense en un dicho del inglés que pueda tener un significado similar.

| Frases hechas o dichos populares | Contexto | Interpretación | Frases o dichos similares en inglés |
|---|---|---|---|
| hacerse el sordo | **Pero es el caso, padre, que hasta ahora Dios se me hace el sordo**, y en acorrerme (ayudarme) tarda... | finge no escucharme | *to turn a deaf ear* |
| a mantas | | | |
| no gastar tinta | | | |
| estar en vena | | | |
| como por ensalmo | | | |
| ser paja picada | | | |
| ser a carta cabal | | | |
| con cerrojo y cerrojillo | | | |

## Essential Instruction

1. Go through **Sobre el autor**, pausing to ask comprehension questions.
2. Call on several students to share their answers to **Antes de leer** with the class.
3. For the **Estrategia**, give examples of expressions and show how they can't be translated literally into English.
4. For **Actividad 46**, guide students in finding each expression in the reading.
5. Go over the introduction on p. 127; then have students scan the reading for cognates and words from **Vocabulario 3**.

# El alacrán de fray Gómez
## de *Ricardo Palma*  1.2, 3.1

*"El alacrán de fray Gómez" es una tradición. Las
tradiciones son una forma literaria en la que se describen
costumbres de otras épocas. En las tradiciones se mezclan
elementos históricos y ficticios, y se utiliza un lenguaje
arcaico con frases y dichos de la cultura popular. Muchas
veces contienen elementos fantásticos y maravillosos,
como es frecuente en los cuentos hispanoamericanos.
En esta tradición, Ricardo Palma describe costumbres
limeñas de la época de la colonia.*

*El personaje de fray Gómez es un monje conocido porque
hace milagros. En este caso, el monje toma un alacrán,
un ser de la naturaleza que provoca rechazo y miedo
por ser venenoso, y lo usa mágicamente para ayudar
a un trabajador pobre.*

*Fray Gómez era conocido por
todos porque hacía milagros.*

A *Casimiro Prieto Valdés*
Principio, principiando;
principiar quiero
por ver si principiando
5   principiar puedo.

*In diebus illis*[1], digo, cuando yo era muchacho, oía con frecuencia a las viejas
exclamar, ponderando[2] el mérito y precio de una alhaja:

—¡Esto vale tanto como el alacrán de fray Gómez!

Tengo una chica, remate de lo bueno, flor de la gracia y espumita de la sal,
10   con unos ojos más pícaros y trapisondistas[3] que un par de escribanos:

chica que se parece
al lucero del alba[4]
cuando amanece,

al cual pimpollo[5] he bautizado, en mi paternal chochera[6], con el mote[7] de
15   *alacrancito de fray Gómez*. Y explicar el dicho de las viejas y el sentido del
piropo con que agasajo[8] a mi Angélica es lo que me propongo, amigo y
camarada Prieto, con esta tradición.

El sastre paga deudas con puntadas[9], y yo no tengo otra manera de
satisfacer la literaria que con usted he contraído que dedicándole estos
20   cuatro palotes[10].

[1] (Latin) In those days   [2] considering   [3] intriguing   [4] morning star
[5] beautiful young person   [6] affection   [7] nickname   [8] I praise, I honor
[9] stitches   [10] scribbles

## 47 Comprensión 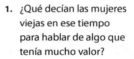 1.2

1. ¿Qué decían las mujeres
viejas en ese tiempo
para hablar de algo que
tenía mucho valor?

2. ¿Cómo es la chica a
quien el autor quiere
dedicar esta tradición y
cómo se llama?

3. ¿Qué piropo usa el
autor para agasajarla?

## 48 Analice 1.3, 3.2

¿Qué quiere decir el autor
cuando compara la chica
con el "lucero del alba"?

### Answers

**47**
1. Decían ¡*Esto vale tanto como el
alacrán de fray Gómez!*
2. Es joven, graciosa y pícara. Se
llama Angélica.
3. Le dio el mote *alacrancito de
fray Gómez*.

**48** *Respuesta posible:*
Quiere decir que es tan hermosa
como Venus cuando es visible en el
cielo.

## Reference Desk

1. This story is divided into
three parts. The first part
tells us that the purpose
of this story is to explain
the popular expression
**¡Eso vale tanto como un
alacrán de fray Gómez!**
Parts two and three (desig-
nated by Roman numerals I
and II) contain descriptions
of miracles carried out by
**fray Gómez**.
2. The story talks about miracles during the time of San
Francisco Solano, a Fran-
ciscan friar and missionary
who lived and worked in
Lima from 1595 to 1610.

## Critical Thinking

**Analyzing**
After reading this page, ask
students to explain why the
author would choose to write in
the first person.

## Differentiated Learning
### Heritage Learners/Accelerate
Ask students to discuss the following questions: **¿Existe alguna leyenda asociada a su
región o país? ¿Conoce algún dicho popular
que esté basado en un hecho verdadero o
en una leyenda?** For heritage learners, modify
the questions so that they refer to their cultural
communities.

## Special Needs Students
### Reading Difficulties/AD(H)D
Tell students to make a chart and label the headings **Lugar**, **Personajes**, **Milagros**. As students
read, have them fill in information about the
setting, characters, and miracles that occur.

**49**

1. Se encargaba de la comida en la enfermería del convento.
2. Se descalabró y quedó patitieso en el suelo.
3. Fray Gómez le puso el cordón de su hábito sobre la boca y le echó tres bendiciones y el hombre se levantó como si no le hubiera pasado nada.
4. Trataron de levantar al fraile en triunfo porque había hecho un milagro.
5. Cuando dice que fray Gómez, para escapar de la gente, se elevó en los aires y voló desde el puente hasta la torre de su convento.

**50**

La gente gritaba así porque el santo óleo se trae cuando alguien está a punto de morirse.

## Critical Thinking

### Analyzing
Have students re-read the last paragraph on p. 128. Ask them to consider why the author emphasizes a neutral stance regarding this fantastical element of the story.

---

 **1.2**

### 49 Comprensión

1. ¿Qué trabajo desempeñaba fray Gómez en el convento?

2. ¿Qué le pasó al jinete cuando el caballo lo arrojó al suelo?

3. ¿Qué hizo fray Gómez y cuál fue el resultado?

4. ¿Cómo reaccionó la gente ante los hechos?

5. ¿Qué versión de la crónica se basa claramente en la fantasía?

**1.3**

### 50 Analice

¿Por qué gritaba la gente que fueran por el santo óleo cuando el jinete se descalabró? Explique.

---

Este era un lego[11] contemporáneo de don Juan de la Pipirindica, el de la valiente pica, y de San Francisco Solano; el cual lego desempeñaba en Lima, en el convento de los padres seráficos[12], las funciones de refitolero[13]
25 en la enfermería u hospital de los devotos frailes. El pueblo lo llamaba fray Gómez, y fray Gómez lo llaman las crónicas conventuales, y la tradición lo conoce por fray Gómez. Creo que hasta en el expediente que para su beatificación y canonización existe en Roma no se le da otro nombre.

Fray Gómez hizo en mi tierra milagros a mantas, sin darse cuenta de ellos
30 y como quien no quiere la cosa. Era de suyo milagroso, como aquel que hablaba en prosa sin sospecharlo.

Sucedió que un día iba el lego por el puente, cuando un caballo desbocado arrojó sobre las losas[14] al jinete. El infeliz quedó patitieso, con la cabeza hecha una criba[15] y arrojando sangre por boca y narices.

35 —¡Se descalabró, se descalabró! —gritaba la gente—. ¡Que vayan a San Lázaro por el santo óleo[16]!

Y todo era bullicio y alharaca[17].

Fray Gómez acercóse pausadamente al que yacía en la tierra, púsole sobre la boca el cordón de su hábito, echóle tres bendiciones, y sin más médico
40 ni más botica el descalabrado se levantó tan fresco, como si golpe no hubiera recibido.

—¡Milagro, milagro! ¡Viva fray Gómez! —exclamaron los infinitos espectadores.

Y en su entusiasmo intentaron llevar en triunfo al lego. Este, para
45 substraerse[18] a la popular ovación, echó a correr camino de su convento y se encerró en su celda.

La crónica franciscana cuenta esto último de manera distinta. Dice que fray Gómez, para escapar de sus aplaudidores, se elevó en los aires y voló desde el puente hasta la torre de su convento. Yo ni lo niego ni lo afirmo.
50 Puede que sí y puede que no. Tratándose de maravillas, no gasto tinta en defenderlas ni en refutarlas.

[11] layman    [12] belonging to the order of Saint Francis of Assisi
[13] man in charge of the dining hall in a monastery    [14] flagstones    [15] sieve (full of holes)
[16] holy oil    [17] noise and fuss    [18] to get away from

---

### Essential Instruction
1. Play the recording, pausing for students to answer the during-reading questions.
2. For Common Core practice, have students answer the **Analice** questions.

Aquel día estaba fray Gómez en vena de hacer milagros, pues cuando salió de su celda se encaminó a la enfermería, donde encontró a San Francisco Solano acostado sobre una tarima, víctima de una furiosa jaqueca.

55 Pulsólo[19] el lego y le dijo:

—Su paternidad está muy débil, y haría bien en tomar algún alimento.

—Hermano —contestó el santo—, no tengo apetito.

—Haga un esfuerzo, reverendo padre, y pase siquiera un bocado.

Y tanto insistió el refitolero, que el enfermo, por librarse de exigencias que 60 picaban ya en majadería[20], ideó pedirle lo que hasta para el virrey habría sido imposible conseguir, por no ser la estación propicia para satisfacer el antojo[21].

—Pues mire, hermanito, solo comería con gusto un par de pejerreyes[22].

Fray Gómez metió la mano derecha dentro de la manga[23] izquierda, y sacó 65 un par de pejerreyes tan fresquitos que parecían acabados de salir del mar.

—Aquí los tiene su paternidad, y que en salud se le conviertan. Voy a guisarlos.

Y ello es que con los benditos pejerreyes quedó San Francisco curado como por ensalmo.

70 Me parece que estos dos milagritos de que incidentalmente me he ocupado no son paja picada. Dejo en mi tintero otros muchos de nuestro lego, porque no me he propuesto relatar su vida y milagros.

Sin embargo, apuntaré, para satisfacer curiosidades exigentes, que sobre la puerta de la primera celda del pequeño claustro, que hasta hoy sirve de 75 enfermería, hay un lienzo pintado al óleo representando estos dos milagros, con la siguiente inscripción:

"El Venerable Fray Gómez. —Nació en Extremadura en 1560. Vistió el hábito en Chuquisaca[24] en 1580. Vino a Lima en 1587. —Enfermero fue cuarenta años, Ejercitando todas las virtudes, dotado de favores y 80 dones celestiales. Fue su vida un continuado milagro. Falleció en 2 de mayo de 1631, con fama de santidad. En el año siguiente se colocó el cadáver en la capilla de Aranzazú, y en 13 de octubre de 1810 se pasó debajo del altar mayor, a la bóveda donde son sepultados los padres del convento. Presenció la traslación de los restos el Señor doctor don 85 Bartolomé María de las Heras. Se restauró este venerable retrato en 30 noviembre de 1882, por M. Zamudio".

[19] took his pulse    [20] foolishness    [21] whim    [22] a type of fish    [23] sleeve

[24] today, the city of Sucre

## 51 Comprensión  1.2

1. ¿Qué le recomendó fray Gómez al hermano San Francisco Solano después de tomarle el pulso?

2. ¿Qué antojo tenía el hermano?

3. ¿Por qué habría sido imposible hasta para el virrey conseguir los pejerreyes que quería el hermano y qué hizo fray Gómez para conseguirlos?

4. Explique por qué se considera que este suceso fue un milagro.

5. ¿Qué quiere decir la expresión "dejo en mi tintero"?

 1.3, 3.1, 3.2

## 52 Analice

1. ¿Conoce Ud. otros relatos de personas como fray Gómez a quienes se les atribuye el poder de hacer milagros? Explique.

2. ¿Por qué cree Ud. que el autor consideró importante incluir la información sobre la muerte y el lugar donde descansan los restos (remains) de fray Gómez?

*Unidad 3* | ciento veintinueve  **129**

Answers

 51

1. Le recomendó que tomara algún alimento.

2. Quería comerse un par de pejerreyes.

3. No era la estación del año para conseguir esa clase de pescado. Fray Gómez metió la mano dentro de la manga izquierda y los sacó de ahí, tan frescos como si hubieran acabado de salir del mar.

4. No es posible hacer aparecer dos pescados de la nada.

5. El autor quiere decir que hay muchos otros milagros, pero que no va a escribir sobre ellos.

52

1. *Las respuestas variarán.*

2. *Respuesta posible:* Para darle más credibilidad a la existencia de fray Gómez, quien fue un personaje de la vida real.

### Reference Desk

The painting Palma refers to on p. 129 in the second-to-the-last paragraph is kept at the **Museo San Francisco y Catacumbas** in Lima. The painting can be viewed online; if possible, display it in class so that students can see the inscription.

### Connections

**History**
At the end of part one, ask students to contextualize the events of the story by researching other events in Peru during the same time period.

## Differentiated Learning
### Accelerate
Students with high-level reading skills will probably be able to read the excerpt and complete **Actividades 49–52** independently. After these students complete the activities, pair them with students who have reading difficulties; students at both levels can benefit from this pairing.

## Learning Styles
### Visual Learners
Ask these students to create a vignette of three or four panels to illustrate the scenes described on pp. 128–129. Have them do a second vignette for the section on pp. 130–131.

**53**

1. un hombre pobre
2. Era muy pobre, pero con cara de honrado.
3. Era simple y un poco sucio. Tenía pocos muebles: cuatro sillones, una mesa, una cama sin colchón ni sábanas ni mantas y una piedra por almohada.
4. Era una buhonero cuyo negocio no estaba prosperando por falta de medios.
5. Le pide que le preste un poco de dinero para poder sacar adelante su negocio.

**54** *Respuesta posible:*

El hombre está esperando que fray Gómez le haga un milagro.

---

 **1.2**

### 53 Comprensión

1. ¿Quién golpeó a la puerta de fray Gómez?

2. ¿Cómo era el hombre que vino a visitarlo?

3. ¿Cómo era la celda de fray Gómez?

4. ¿Qué ocupación tenía el hombre y cuál era su problema?

5. ¿Qué le pidió el hombre a fray Gómez?

**1.3, 3.2**

### 54 Analice

¿Por qué cree el hombre que fray Gómez, pobre y mendicante como es, puede sacarlo del apuro? Explique.

---

**II**

Estaba una mañana fray Gómez en su celda entregado a la meditación, cuando dieron a la puerta unos discretos golpecitos, y una voz de quejumbroso timbre dijo:

90 —*Deo gratias*[25]... ¡alabado sea el Señor!

—Por siempre jamás, amén. Entre, hermanito —contestó fray Gómez.

Y penetró en la humildísima celda un individuo algo desarrapado, *vera efigies*[26] del hombre a quien acongojan pobrezas, pero en cuyo rostro se dejaba adivinar la proverbial honradez del castellano viejo.

95 Todo el mobiliario de la celda se componía de cuatro sillones de vaqueta[27], una mesa mugrienta[28], y una tarima sin colchón, sábanas ni abrigo, y con una piedra por cabezal o almohada.

—Tome asiento, hermano, y dígame sin rodeos lo que por acá le trae —dijo fray Gómez.

100 —Es el caso, padre, que yo soy hombre de bien a carta cabal...

—Se le conoce y que persevere deseo, que así merecerá en esta vida terrena la paz de la conciencia, y en la otra la bienaventuranza.

—Y es el caso que soy buhonero, que vivo cargado de familia y que mi comercio no cunde[29] por falta de medios, que no por holgazanería[30] y
105 escasez de industria en mí.

—Me alegro, hermano, que a quien honradamente trabaja Dios le acude.

—Pero es el caso, padre, que hasta ahora Dios se me hace el sordo, y en acorrerme tarda...

—No desespere, hermano, no desespere.

110 —Pues es el caso que a muchas puertas he llegado en demanda de habilitación[31] por quinientos duros, y todas las he encontrado con cerrojo y cerrojillo. Y es el caso que anoche, en mis cavilaciones[32], yo mismo me dije a mí mismo:

—¡Ea!, Jeromo, buen ánimo y vete a pedirle el dinero a fray Gómez, que si
115 él lo quiere, mendicante y pobre como es, medio[33] encontrará para sacarte del apuro. Y es el caso que aquí estoy porque he venido, y a su paternidad le pido y ruego que me preste esa puchuela[34] por seis meses, seguro que no será por mí quien se diga:

En el mundo hay devotos
120 de ciertos santos;
la gratitud les dura
lo que el milagro;
que un beneficio
da siempre vida a ingratos
125 desconocidos.

25 (Latin) Thank God    26 (Latin) the real image of    27 calfskin    28 filthy    29 isn't doing well
30 laziness    31 loan    32 thoughts    33 means, way    34 small amount of money

---

### Essential Instruction

1. Read aloud the narration as students read along in their books. Have volunteers read the dialogue portions.
2. Pause periodically to ask simple comprehension questions, and for students to answer the during-reading questions.
3. After reading through the bottom of p. 130, ask students to predict how the story will end.

—¿Cómo ha podido imaginarse, hijo, que en esta triste celda encontraría ese caudal?

—Es el caso, padre, que no acertaría a responderle; pero tengo fe en que no me dejará ir desconsolado.

130 —La fe lo salvará, hermano. Espere un momento.

Y paseando los ojos por las desnudas y blanqueadas paredes de la celda, vio un alacrán que caminaba tranquilamente sobre el marco de la ventana. Fray Gómez arrancó una página de un libro viejo, dirigióse a la ventana, cogió con delicadeza a la sabandija, la envolvió en el papel, y tornándose
135 hacia el castellano viejo le dijo:

—Tome, buen hombre, y empeñe esta alhajita³⁵; no olvide, sí, devolvérmela dentro de seis meses.

El buhonero se deshizo en frases de agradecimiento, se despidió de fray Gómez y más que de prisa se encaminó a la tienda de un usurero.

140 La joya era espléndida, verdadera <u>alhaja de reina morisca</u>³⁶, por decir lo menos. Era un prendedor figurando un alacrán. El cuerpo lo formaba una magnífica esmeralda engarzada sobre oro, y la cabeza un grueso brillante con dos rubíes por ojos.

El usurero, que era hombre conocedor, vio la
145 alhaja con codicia, y ofreció al necesitado adelantarle dos mil duros por ella; pero nuestro español se empeñó en no aceptar otro préstamo que el de quinientos duros por seis meses, y con un interés judaico, se entiende.

150 Extendiéronse y firmáronse los documentos o papeletas de estilo, acariciando el agiotista³⁷ la esperanza de que a la postre³⁸ el dueño de la prenda acudiría por más dinero, que con el recargo de intereses lo convertiría en
155 propietario de joya tan valiosa por su mérito intrínseco y artístico.

*El alacrán negro.*

Y con este capitalito fuele tan prósperamente en su comercio, que a la terminación del plazo pudo desempeñar³⁹ la prenda, y, envuelta en el mismo papel en que la recibiera, se la devolvió a
160 fray Gómez.

Este tomó el alacrán, lo puso sobre el alféizar de la ventana, le echó una bendición y dijo:

—Animalito de Dios, sigue tu camino.

Y el alacrán echó a andar libremente por las paredes de la celda.

165     Y vieja, pelleja,
        aquí dio fin la conseja⁴⁰.

³⁵ small jewel    ³⁶ exotic, precious jewel    ³⁷ moneylender    ³⁸ in the end
³⁹ redeem, get out of pawn    ⁴⁰ advice

## 55 Comprensión  1.2

1. ¿Qué tomó fray Gómez del marco de la ventana?

2. ¿Qué le dijo al buhonero cuando se lo dio?

3. ¿Adónde se dirigió el buhonero y por qué?

4. ¿Cómo era la joya?

5. ¿Qué esperanza tenía el usurero?

6. ¿Qué pasó cuando el buhonero le devolvió la joya a fray Gómez?

## 56 Analice  1.3, 3.2

¿Por que cree Ud. que el autor le dio a Angélica el apodo de "el alacrancito de fray Gómez"? Explique su respuesta.

## Después de leer  1.2

Conteste las siguientes preguntas sobre la lectura.

1. El alacrán es...
   A. una joya de reina mora de oro, esmeraldas y rubíes.
   B. un libro de texto religioso que usa fray Gómez todos los días.
   C. un insecto venenoso y peligroso.
   D. una olla donde fray Gómez prepara la comida todos los días.

2. ¿Qué le sucede al jinete caído?
   A. Se hirió y se recuperó.
   B. Se fue corriendo a encerrarse al convento.
   C. Se hirió y murió.
   D. Se elevó y voló hasta el convento.

3. ¿Cómo curó fray Gómez a San Francisco Solano?
   A. Le cocinó un par de pescados.
   B. Le pidió al virrey un par de pescados.
   C. Lo llevó a la enfermería.
   D. Le preparó un bocadillo.

4. ¿Cuál es la situación del hombre que visita a fray Gómez?
   A. Es holgazán y no le rinde el comercio.
   B. Es un vendedor pobre que necesita un préstamo.
   C. Tiene fe y necesita que recen por él.
   D. Es vendedor y no tiene suficientes hijos que lo ayuden.

5. ¿Qué le da fray Gómez para ayudarle?
   A. Un libro viejo.
   B. Un escorpión.
   C. Unos buenos consejos.
   D. El dinero que necesita.

6. ¿Qué decide hacer el vendedor?
   A. Dejar libre al alacrán.
   B. Empeñar la joya por más dinero del que necesita.
   C. Vender la joya en su comercio.
   D. Empeñar la joya por el dinero que necesita.

## Extensión  1.3, 3.1

A. ¿Qué consejo o moraleja cree Ud. que se da en esta leyenda? Explique su respuesta.

B. El autor nos cuenta que la leyenda sobre fray Gómez dio origen a un dicho popular: "¡Esto vale más que el alacrán de fray Gómez!" Ricardo Palma busca en el folclore literario de Perú esta leyenda como fuente para su relato. ¿Existe alguna leyenda asociada con la región donde Ud. vive? ¿Conoce algún dicho popular que esté basado en un hecho verdadero o en una leyenda?

### Essential Instruction

1. Check answers to **Después de leer** orally as a class.
2. Place students in small groups to answer the **Extensión** questions.
3. Read through the **Proyectos** and brainstorm ideas for the tasks. If time is limited, you may want to let students pick a project that appeals most to them.

# Para concluir

## Proyectos

? Pregunta clave

¿Qué aspectos socioculturales de un país afectan el futuro de su gente?

Answers_____

Ⓐ *Las entrevistas variarán.*

Ⓑ *Las respuestas variarán.*

### A ¡Manos a la obra! 1.1, 1.3, 2.2

Trabaje con un(a) compañero/a. Imagine que Ud. es el director de uno de los Colegios de Alto Rendimiento de Perú y que su compañero/a es un estudiante peruano que recién va a comenzar en este nuevo programa educativo.

Busquen más información sobre estos colegios en la internet y usen esos datos para inventar un cronograma con la rutina diaria de los estudiantes del COAR.

Luego, preparen una entrevista entre el director y el estudiante, que hará preguntas sobre las materias de estudio, los horarios, el alojamiento, la alimentación, etc. El director responderá a las preguntas del estudiante siguiendo el cronograma que sigue. Usen verbos reflexivos en la entrevista.

|  | LUNES | MARTES | MIÉRCOLES | JUEVES | VIERNES | SÁBADO | DOMINGO |
|---|---|---|---|---|---|---|---|
| mañana |  |  |  |  |  |  |  |
| tarde |  |  |  |  |  |  |  |
| noche |  |  |  |  |  |  |  |

### B En resumen 1.3, 2.1, 2.2, 4.2

Relea la información de las páginas de Cultura sobre la educación en Perú. Piense en los datos que le parezcan más llamativos o interesantes y compárelos con la situación del sistema educativo de su estado o país. Por ejemplo, ¿cómo son los resultados PISA en cada caso?, ¿qué tipo de proyectos de mejora educativa hay?, ¿cómo se maneja la diversidad lingüística?, ¿qué diferencias hay entre escuelas estatales y privadas?

Si es necesario, busque información adicional en la internet. Luego, complete el organizador gráfico para presentar su comparación a la clase. Explique qué aspectos socioculturales pueden explicar las diferencias entre ambos sistemas educativos.

|  | Sistema educativo de Perú | Sistema educativo de Estados Unidos |
|---|---|---|
| Resultados PISA |  |  |
| Mejoras educativas |  |  |
| Diversidad lingüística |  |  |
| Estatales versus privadas |  |  |
| Otros |  |  |

---

### Reference Desk

Point out the **Pregunta clave**. Ask students to think again about the question, this time in relation to their own culture.

### Culture

**Products/Practices: Activity**
Have students go online to watch the award-winning 2011 documentary **Marca Perú**, in which a group of Peruvians travel to Peru, Nebraska. Tell students to make a five-column chart in their Culture Journals with the headings **Comidas/Bebidas**, **Música/Baile**, **Ropa**, **Deporte/Juego**, and **Costumbres**. As they watch, have students fill in the chart with the elements of Peruvian culture that they see. Afterward, have a class discussion to find out what parts of the documentary were surprising to them, or looked most interesting.

---

## Differentiated Learning
### Expand
Ask students to read another **tradición** by Ricardo Palma. Have them briefly summarize the story in their own words, and then compare and contrast the themes with those found in "**El alacrán de fray Gómez.**"

## Multiple Intelligences
### Bodily-Kinesthetic/Verbal-Linguistic
Divide students into three groups and assign each one a miracle from the story. Allow groups time to prepare and rehearse their scene. Finally have each group perform their skit for the class.

**Answers**

**C** *Los discursos variarán.*

**D** *Las gráficas variarán.*

**E** *Los carteles variarán.*

### Reference Desk

You could create an Avenue task for students to compare and contrast the information from **Actividad D**.

### Expansion

Display students' posters from **Actividad E** in the classroom. Have students browse the posters, and then create a Flipgrid post stating where they would like to study and why.

---

 **1.3, 2.1, 2.2, 3.1, 5.1**

**C** **¡A escribir!** **Conéctese: las ciencias sociales**

Repase los problemas y complejidades que presenta el sistema educativo peruano. Imagine que Ud. quiere ser presidente de Perú y escriba un discurso en el que presente nuevas ideas y proyectos para enfrentar esos problemas. Puede incluir en su discurso algunos de los programas que ya están en funcionamiento en Perú, pero también puede pensar propuestas innovadoras. Luego, lea su discurso a la clase.

### Estrategia

**Problema/Solución**

Muchas veces es bueno organizar las ideas antes de empezar a escribir. Primero, haga una lista de los problemas. Luego, piense en una o más soluciones para cada uno.

**D** **El sistema educativo peruano**  **1.1, 1.3, 3.1, 4.2**

En la gráfica de abajo, se muestra cómo está organizado el sistema educativo peruano. Trabaje con un(a) compañero/a y preparen una gráfica similar con la organización del sistema educativo en su país. ¿Cuáles son las diferencias más llamativas? ¿A qué cree que se deben estas diferencias?

**Educación básica o inicial**
Edad: niños de hasta 5 años
Obligatoria para los niños de 5 años

**Educación primaria**
Edad: niños de entre 6 y 12 años
Duración: seis años
Obligatoria
Un solo maestro dicta todas las materias, excepto música, educación física, idiomas y religión.

**Educación secundaria**
Edad: entre 12 y 17 años
Duración: cinco años
Obligatoria
Todas las materias de estudio son impartidas por profesores especializados.

**Educación superior**
Edad: a partir de los 17 años
Se brinda en institutos superiores y universidades
Los institutos superiores otorgan títulos de profesional, técnico y experto, y también los de segunda y ulterior especialización profesional. Las universidades otorgan títulos de bachiller, maestro y doctor, así como certificados y títulos profesionales, incluso los de segunda y ulterior especialización.

**E** **Una experiencia intercultural** **1.1, 1.3, 2.2**

Los viajes de estudio son una experiencia única. Vuelva a leer el texto sobre el curso que ofrece la Universidad del Pacífico. Trabaje en grupo para inventar un curso nuevo que se dictará en otra ciudad de Perú. Investiguen en la internet sobre ciudades peruanas que presenten características particularmente interesantes. Piensen en los temas que se enseñarán en el curso, los

*Descubra las bellezas de Perú en un viaje de estudio.*

requisitos que deben cumplir los aspirantes, los detalles del alojamiento, etc. Luego, creen un cartel para promocionar el curso. Pueden incluir fotos y una tipografía que resulte atractiva.

### Essential Instruction

1. Begin **Actividad C** by reading through the **Estrategia**. You may want to have students use a graphic organizer to map out their ideas.

2. For **Actividad D**, have pairs get together with another pair and compare their responses.

3. For the **Vocabulario de la Unidad 3**, ask students to place the words into categories such as nouns, verbs, greetings, etc.

el/la **abogado/a** lawyer
**acabar(se)** to finish; to run out
**acabar de + inf.** to have just
el **alacrán** scorpion
la **alhaja** jewel
**aprobar (ue)** to pass
el **apuro** financial bind
el/la **arquitecto/a** architect
la **arquitectura** architecture
el/la **artista** artist
la **asignatura** subject
**asistir a clase** to attend classes
el **aula de clase** classroom
el **bachillerato** high school
la **beca** scholarship
las **bellas artes** arts
la **biblioteca** library
la **biología** biology
el **buhonero** peddler
las **calificaciones** grades
el **campo deportivo** athletic field
el **campo de trabajo** field of work
la **carrera** profession
el/la **catedrático/a** full professor
la **celda** cell
las **ciencias** sciences
el/la **científico/a** scientist
la **codicia** greed
**competitivo/a** competitive
**conseguir un trabajo** to get
a job
el/la **consejero/a** counselor
**contribuir** to contribute
el **convento** monastery
**cumplir con los requisitos**
to fulfill the requirements
el **curso obligatorio/optativo**
mandatory/elective course
**dar un curso de...** to teach a
course on...
el/la **decano/a** dean
**dejar de** to fail to do something
el **derecho (leyes)** law
**desarrollar buenos hábitos**
**de estudio** to develop good
study habits
**desbocado/a** runaway
**descalabrarse** to be hurt
**desempeñar** to hold a position;
to redeem
la **deuda** debt
**devoto/a** devout, pious
**dictar una conferencia** to give
a lecture
el **diploma** diploma

el/la **economista** economist
**empeñar** to pawn
**empeñarse** to be determined
**enseñar** to teach
**esconder** to hide
el/la **escritor(a)** writer
**esforzarse** to make an effort
la **especialización** major
el **estadio** stadium
la **estadística** statistics
**estar de vuelta** to be back
el **examen de admisión**
admission test
**examinarse** to take an exam
la **facultad** school (of a university)
**faltar a** to fail to fulfill
**familiarizarse** to become
familiar
la **filosofía** philosophy
el/la **filósofo/a** philosopher
la **física** physics
**fracasar** to fail
el **futuro** future
**graduarse** to graduate
**hacer entrega** to award
**hacer las tareas** to do
homework
la **holgazanería** laziness
el **horario** schedule
la **informática** computer science
la **ingeniería** engineering
el/la **ingeniero/a** engineer
**ingresar** to enroll
la **investigación** research
la **jaqueca** migraine headache
los **laboratorios** laboratories
las **letras** humanities
la **librería** bookstore
la **licenciatura** university degree
**llenar formularios** to fill out
forms
**llenar una solicitud** to fill out
an application
**llevar(se)** to take; to take away
**lucirse** to show off
la **matrícula** registration (fee)
**matricularse** to register
la **medicina** medicine
el/la **médico/a** doctor
el **milagro** miracle
**ofrecer** to offer
**pasar lista** to call the roll
**patitieso/a** paralyzed
**perseverar** to persevere
**pícaro/a** mischevious

la **piscina** pool
el **plan de estudios** curriculum
el **plazo (de matrícula)**
(registration) period, deadline
la **práctica privada**
private practice
el **prendedor** brooch
**presentarse** to show up
el **préstamo** loan
**prestar atención** to pay
attention
**primero que todo** first of all
**principiar** to begin
la **profesión** profession
el/la **profesor(a)** professor
el/la **programador(a)** programmer
la **psicología** psychology
el/la **psicólogo/a** psychologist
**quedarse** to stay
**¡Qué padre!** How cool!
**quejumbroso/a** in a painful
tone
la **química** chemistry
**quitarse** to take off (clothing)
el/la **rector(a)** president
(of a university)
**repasar** to review
**reprobar (una materia)**
to flunk, fail (a subject)
**requerido/a** required
**resolver problemas** to solve
problems
la **sabandija** creepy-crawly
**sacar (buenas notas)** to take
out; to get good grades
la **sociología** sociology
el/la **sociólogo/a** sociologist
**solicitar ayuda financiera**
to apply for financial aid
el **teatro** theater
**tener cabeza para los números**
to be good with numbers
**tener éxito** to be successful
**tener lugar** to take place
**tener talento** to have talent
**título (diploma)** title
**tomar (apuntes)** to take (notes)
el/la **usurero/a** money lender, usurer
las **ventajas (desventajas) de...**
advantages (disadvantages)
of...
la **zona de estacionamiento**
parking zone

## Reference Desk

1. Have students prepare a Flipgrid post in which they lay out their post-graduation plans. They should include as much unit vocabulary as possible and use the future tense. Play the posts in class and take a tally on how many students plan to work, how many plan to attend a community or technical college, and how many plan to attend a four-year college or university.

2. Create an Avenue task in which students create a detailed plan for the next nine months.

## Differentiated Learning
### Expand
Ask students to write a blog post about how their view of Peruvian culture has changed or expanded after studying **Unidad 3**.

## Multiple Intelligences
### Verbal-Linguistic
Ask pairs of students to write four conversations using as much of the vocabulary as they can. You may want to set a time limit.

**135**

1. This unit features Bolivia, a landlocked country in South America that shares borders with Brazil, Paraguay, Argentina, Chile, and Peru.
2. Bolivia is named after the military leader Simón Bolívar (also known as **El Libertador**), who was instrumental in helping several Latin American countries gain independence from Spain and establish sovereign nations.
3. After students read through **¿Sabía que...?**, see if they can guess the meaning of **aguayos** based on the photo. Explain that an **aguayo** is a rectangular woven cloth made by indigenous women. These cloths have many uses; they can be used to carry young children, as a blanket on which to make offerings to **Pachamama**, etc. Students will read more about **aguayos** in the cultural reading on p. 152.
4. Draw students' attention to the **bombín**, the traditional hat worn by indigenous Bolivian women. Students will read more about this item in the e-mail on p. 146.

### Culture

**Practices: Information**
**El conteo de regalos** is a Bolivian custom that takes place the day after a wedding. All the wedding presents received by the couple are laid out on **aguayos** and counted. If there is an uneven number of presents, the godparents will contribute an additional gift so that the total number is even.

**¿Sabía que...?** 1.2, 2.1, 2.2

El aguayo boliviano forma parte de la vida familiar desde su inicio: antes de casarse la mujer teje un par de aguayos con el nombre de los novios. Al día siguiente de la boda, sobre esos aguayos se exponen los regalos que recibieron los recién casados en un ritual tradicional de "conteo de regalos".

### Essential Instruction

1. Begin with a discussion of the **Pregunta clave**. Ask students for examples of family traditions that reflect one's cultural heritage. Have them draw on personal experience, if possible.
2. Point out Bolivia on the map. Ask students to share what they know about the country.
3. Draw attention to the culture photo and question. Encourage students to watch for the photo and the answer later in the unit.
4. Point out the QR code, the video question, and the screen shot from "**Las tareas del hogar**." Encourage students to watch the video as many times as they like.
5. Have students read and ask questions about **Mis metas**.

# Unidad 4

# La vida del hogar

 Escanee el código QR para mirar el video "Las tareas del hogar".

Alex y su amigo Joaquín hablan de cómo se hace la limpieza en sus respectivas casas. ¿Qué hace Alex para ayudar con los quehaceres y cómo se compara con lo que hace Joaquín? Explique su respuesta.

### Pregunta clave

?

¿Cómo se refleja la herencia cultural de un país en las prácticas familiares?

¿En qué fecha se celebra el Día Internacional de la Familia en Bolivia?

Bolivia

## Mis metas

### En esta unidad:

▶ Usaré expresiones relacionadas con la casa, la familia y los quehaceres.

▶ Repasaré las formas del pretérito y el imperfecto.

▶ Leeré sobre la familia y las prácticas familiares en Bolivia.

▶ Distinguiré el significado de palabras y frases según el contexto.

▶ Distinguiré el uso del pretérito y el imperfecto.

▶ Leeré un artículo sobre las trabajadoras del hogar en Bolivia.

▶ Trataré el tema de la vida del hogar en Bolivia y Estados Unidos en una carta.

▶ Escribiré un relato comparando la vida de una trabajadora del hogar antes y ahora.

▶ Desarrollaré nuevas destrezas de vocabulario.

▶ Usaré expresiones con **hace que...** y **hacía que...**

▶ Leeré el cuento "Las medias rojas" de la española Emilia Pardo Bazán.

ciento treinta y siete **137**

## Answers

**Video question** *Respuesta posible:* Alex no hace mucho para ayudar con la limpieza de la casa, excepto estorbar el trabajo de su madre y de su hermana, quienes son las que realmente hacen la limpieza. Por otro lado, su amigo Joaquín sí ayuda de verdad. Él hace su cama, recoge la ropa, sacude, barre y para terminar, lava el suelo. Es muy organizado.

**Culture question**
Se celebra el 15 de mayo.

## Reference Desk

1. Ask students to read the **Pregunta clave** and speculate about the theme of the unit and the vocabulary and culture they might encounter.

2. Draw attention to the screen shot from "**Las tareas del hogar.**" Ask students to guess how the people might be related, and what the boy is doing.

3. Remind students with eBook access they can click on the red country on p. 137 to link directly to Wikipedia.

4. Point out the culture photo and have students read the question. Ask them to speculate when this holiday might be celebrated in Bolivia and whether it is celebrated in other parts of the world.

## Learning Styles
### Visual Learners

As a class, create a concept web about Bolivia. Ask students to share what they already know about the country. As you progress through the unit, have students fill in more information. At the end of the unit, have them copy the concept webs into their Culture Journals.

## Multiple Intelligences
### Verbal-Linguistic

Review and preview the unit vocabulary and grammar by asking questions such as: **¿Cómo es tu casa? ¿Quiénes viven allí? ¿Cómo se reparten los quehaceres domésticos en tu casa? ¿Qué hiciste para ayudar en casa la semana pasada? ¿Cómo ayudabas a tus padres cuando eras niño/a?**

### Reference Desk

1. Read the title of this section, and ask a volunteer to deduce the meaning of **nos repartimos** (*we divide up among ourselves*). Inform students that this is not a reflexive verb in the traditional sense but rather it is being used to show a reciprocal action. See *¡Qué chévere! 3* p. 86.
2. Point out the photo of the house at the top of p. 138. Explain that this architecture is typical of Spanish houses, and that many colonial-era buildings in Latin America were also built in this style.
3. Mention that **chimenea** can refer to both the fireplace (as on p. 138) and the chimney.

### Expansion

Have students make their own flash cards for the new terms from **Vocabulario 1**. Tell them to use note cards, and to write the Spanish term on one side and draw or paste a picture on the other side.

### TPR

In pairs, have students take turns acting out chores from **Vocabulario 1** for their partner to guess. Then have them get together with another pair and repeat the activity.

**138**

---

## *Vocabulario 1*

### En casa nos repartimos los quehaceres  1.2

Acabamos de comprar una nueva casa y estamos muy contentos.

Es una casa de techo rojo con puertas y ventanas de madera. La casa tiene nueve habitaciones: cuatro dormitorios, sala, comedor, cocina y dos baños. Es bastante grande.

En la sala hay una gran chimenea que podemos encender en el invierno y un sofá muy cómodo para ver la tele. El comedor es amplio, perfecto para las cenas familiares. Tan pronto como nos mudamos dimos una gran fiesta de bienvenida.

Todos los electrodomésticos de la cocina (la estufa, la nevera, el lavaplatos, el horno y el microondas) son de acero inoxidable, súper modernos, al igual que el fregadero.

Mamá se encarga de cocinar. A mi hermanita le encanta ayudarla a hornear. Es feliz batiendo huevos para hacer nuestras tortas favoritas.

En casa nos repartimos los quehaceres. Mi hermanastra Ana recoge la mesa y siempre lava y seca los platos después del desayuno y el almuerzo.

**138** ciento treinta y ocho | *Unidad 4*

---

### Essential Instruction

1. Before playing the audio, have students look at the vocabulary on pp. 138–140 and pick out cognates. They can work in pairs and practice pronouncing these words.
2. Play the audio for **En casa nos repartimos los quehaceres**. Pause to ask comprehension questions.
3. Personalize the vocabulary presentation by having students say what items they have in their homes, and what chores they like and don't like.

Mi hermano y yo ayudamos a papá. Pasamos la aspiradora por las alfombras, y sacudimos los sillones, las lámparas y los cuadros de las paredes.

Nuestra abuelita vive con nosotros desde que quedó viuda. A ella le encanta regar las plantas y trabajar en el jardín.

En mi dormitorio hay una cama y una cómoda para guardar la ropa. También tengo un escritorio, un equipo de sonido y una computadora, donde puedo escuchar mis CDs o mirar mis DVDs.

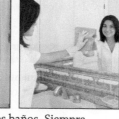

Mi hermana mayor arregla los baños. Siempre limpia los espejos del botiquín, los inodoros, los lavabos y las tinas y se asegura de que no falte jabón, papel higiénico o pasta de dientes.

## Para conversar

**P**ara hablar de otros artículos de la casa:

En el cuarto de la lavandería hay una lavadora y una secadora eléctricas que usamos todo el tiempo.

También hay una mesa para planchar y una plancha (aunque casi nadie las usa), y un clóset para guardar la escoba y otras cosas para limpiar.

En la cocina hay muchos gabinetes para guardar las ollas, las sartenes y otros electrodomésticos, como la licuadora, el exprimidor de frutas y la batidora.

La cafetera y la tostadora para tostar el pan están sobre el mostrador de la cocina pues las usamos a toda hora.

Siempre nos reunimos en la cocina a la hora de desayunar, almorzar y cenar.

En todas las habitaciones hay armarios para colgar abrigos y guardar las colchas, mantas, sábanas y almohadas que no estén en uso.

También hay ventiladores y conexiones de teléfono, aunque todos tenemos celular.

La abuela tiene un teléfono con contestador automático en su habitación y un despertador para despertarse todas las mañanas.

También tiene un radio para escuchar las noticias y hasta tiene un televisor con videocasetera. Ella es muy chapada a la antigua.

*Unidad 4* | ciento treinta y nueve **139**

**1**

1. jabón
2. dormitorio
3. plancha
4. nevera
5. almohadas
6. batidora
7. cenar
8. radio

**2**

1. B; 2. A; 3. D; 4. E; 5. F; 6. C

## Reference Desk

1. Review additional family vocabulary, such as **ahijado/a**, **bisabuelo/a**, **nuera**, **yerno**, **suegro/a**, etc.
2. Remind students that **parientes** is a false cognate.

## Communication

**Interpersonal/Presentational: Cooperative Groups**

Divide students into large groups. Tell each group that they are a family, and they must work together to determine their relationships, names, ages, professions, etc. Encourage creativity. Finally, have each family introduce themselves to the class.

## Expansion

Have students create a description of their family, following the structure of **Para contar la historia de la famila** at the top of p. 140.

---

**P**ara contar la historia de la familia:

En mi familia no somos muchos. Apenas once, entre padres, hijos, hermanos y cuñados y sin contar a mi madre Cristina Soto, quien murió hace mucho tiempo.

Mi padre, Alberto Echeverría Agudelo, quedó viudo muy joven, cuando yo tenía dos años. Después de unos años se enamoró de Elena Salazar y se casó con ella. Ellos tuvieron dos hijas, Julia y Adriana, mis medio-hermanas.

Yo quiero mucho a mi madrastra, pues me ha criado como si fuera su propio hijo.

También quiero mucho a mis medio-hermanas aunque de niños peleábamos y estábamos celosos los unos de los otros.

Julia y Adriana ya están las dos casadas. Julia y su esposo Fernando Sánchez tienen una niña pequeña. Se llama Carolina y es mi sobrina favorita.

Adriana y su esposo Alberto Correa, mi cuñado, acaban de tener gemelos, Tony y Dany. Sus suegros están encantados pues los niños son sus únicos nietos.

Elena es hija única y mi padre solo tiene una hermana, mi tía Carmen, divorciada y sin hijos. Por eso es que no tengo primos ni primas.

¿Y yo? Pues yo soy César, el soltero de la familia. Tengo una novia a la que amo mucho y vivo muy feliz.

---

**1 Series de palabras**  **1.2**

Complete las siguientes series de palabras con la palabra o expresión del recuadro que mejor corresponda, como se ve en el modelo.

| jabón | dormitorio | radio | almohadas |
|-------|-----------|-------|-----------|
| nevera | plancha | cenar | batidora |

MODELO  lavabo, tina, ____

lavabo, tina, **jabón**

1. lavabo, tina, ____
2. sala, comedor, ____
3. lavadora, secadora, ____
4. estufa, microondas, ____
5. colchas, sábanas, ____
6. tostadora, licuadora, ____
7. desayunar, almorzar, ____
8. equipo de sonido, televisor, ____

---

**2 ¿Para qué sirven?**  **1.2**

Complete cada oración de la columna I con la frase que le corresponda de la columna II.

**I**

1. El armario sirve para ____
2. La escoba sirve para ____
3. El fregadero sirve para ____
4. Los gabinetes sirven para ____
5. Los sillones y el sofá sirven para ____
6. La aspiradora sirve para ____

**II**

A. barrer el piso.
B. colgar la ropa.
C. limpiar las alfombras.
D. lavar los platos.
E. guardar las ollas y las sartenes.
F. sentarse a ver la tele.

## Essential Instruction

1. Review family vocabulary by describing relationships, e.g., **Es el padre de mi primo**; have students give the term (**tío**).
2. Have students check their answers to **Actividades 1** and **2** in pairs.
3. Go over **Un poco más**, and guide students in filling in the first oval in **Actividad 3**. Explain that the ovals are color-coded to help them determine gender.
4. Before playing the audio in **Actividad 4**, have students read the answer choices. Explain that they will hear sentence starters and they must choose the correct ending.

## 3 Un árbol genealógico   1.2

Vuelva a leer la información sobre la familia de César en la página 140 y complete el árbol genealógico con los nombres y apellidos de los diferentes miembros de su familia.

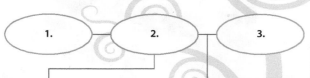

César Echeverría Soto

1. 2. 3.
4. 5. 6. 7.
8. 9. 10.

### Un poco más  2.1

Por lo general, los hispanos tienen dos apellidos. Julia Torres Parra lleva el apellido de su padre, Torres, seguido por el apellido de su madre, Parra. Al casarse, muchas mujeres mantienen el apellido de su padre seguido del apellido de su esposo. Así, si Julia se casa con Osvaldo Medina, su nombre completo será: Julia Torres de Medina.

## 4 La vida de todos los días   1.2

La familia Camacho sigue la misma rutina todas las mañanas. Escuche e indique la terminación correcta.

1. enciende el televisor / apaga el televisor
2. pone la mesa / recoge la mesa
3. los cuelga / los seca
4. la cuelgan / la riegan
5. la deja para congelar / la deja para descongelar
6. hacen la cama / hacen una llamada
7. regarlas / arreglarlas

*La señora Camacho se encarga de cuidar el jardín.*

---

**RESOURCES**

fg   Flipgrid

🎧   Activity 4

**Answers**_____

**3**
1. Carmen Echeverría Agudelo;
2. Alberto Echeverría Agudelo;
3. Elena Salazar de Echeverría;
4. Julia Echeverría de Sánchez;
5. Fernando Sánchez; 6. Adriana Echeverría de Correa; 7. Alberto Correa; 8. Carolina Sánchez Echeverría; 9. Tony Correa Echeverría; 10. Dany Correa Echeverría

**4**  **Script**
1. Para enterarse de las noticias, la señora Ruiz de Camacho...
2. Después de desayunar ella...
3. El señor Camacho lava los platos y la señora...
4. Los dos sacan la ropa de la lavadora y...
5. Antes de irse a trabajar, la señora saca la carne congelada de la nevera y...
6. Les gusta dejar el dormitorio arreglado y por eso siempre...
7. Para mantener sus plantas bonitas y verdes nunca salen de la casa sin...

1. enciende el televisor
2. recoge la mesa
3. los seca
4. la cuelgan
5. la deja para descongelar
6. hacen la cama
7. regarlas

**Reference Desk**

Ask students to create a Flipgrid post in which they introduce themselves using the Hispanic naming convention. Then they should say their parents' full names and state any other family members who live with them.

---

## Differentiated Learning
### Accelerate/Adapt
Activities can be adapted for accelerated students. For example, the word bank can be eliminated in **Actividad 1**, as well as the lettered items in **Actividad 2**. You can also ask students who finish early to create additional activity items for a classmate to complete.

## Learning Styles
### Visual Learners
Search online for an illustration showing the cross-section of a home. Provide students with a copy of the drawing and ask them to label the rooms, furniture, and other objects. Ask them to list a few chores that could be done in each room.

**5** *Respuestas posibles:*

Muebles: comedor
Adornos: lámparas; cuadros
Electrodomésticos: televisor; equipo de sonido; nevera; licuadora; tostadora; batidora; aspiradora
Otros: ventiladores; gabinetes; fregadero; alfombra

**6** *Las conversaciones variarán.*

### Reference Desk

Some students may not feel comfortable talking about their own families or homes in class. Reassure them that they can talk about a fictitious family/home or another family/home that they know.

### Communication

**Presentational: Paired Practice**
Ask students to create their own family trees. Encourage students to use pictures of their family members. Use the family trees to initiate conversations as a class.

### Expansion

Ask students to design their dream home, including a floor plan with labels. They should also create a storyboard where they write descriptions and provide pictures for each room. Encourage students to present their dream home to the class, who will ask follow-up questions.

## ¡Comunicación!

### 5 ¡Ya estoy harta de cosas viejas!   Presentational Communication   1.2

Imagine que sus padres acaban de comprar una casa nueva y su madre, que está harta de tener muebles, arreglos y electrodomésticos de hace veinte años, se va a ir de compras para reemplazarlos todos.

Mire el dibujo de la cocina de sus padres cuando estaban recién casados y haga una lista de todo lo que su mamá va a tener que comprar. Organice su lista según las categorías que se dan.

| Lista de cosas que vamos a comprar | | | |
| --- | --- | --- | --- |
| Muebles | Adornos | Electrodomésticos | Otros |
| | | | |
| | | | |
| | | | |

### 6 ¿Se llevaban muy bien?   Interpersonal Communication   1.1

Imagine que Tania le está mostrando fotos de su familia a su novio, Javier. Él quiere saber cómo era la vida de Tania cuando era niña y le hace muchas preguntas. Con un(a) compañero/a, hagan el papel de Tania y Javier y túrnense para hacerse preguntas y responderlas. Usen el pretérito y el imperfecto para hablar de Tania, su casa y sus costumbres familiares en ese tiempo, como se ve en el modelo.

MODELO   Javier: ¿Cuántos años tenías en esta foto?
Tania: Tenía solo siete años.
Javier: Y tus padres... ¡Qué jóvenes eran! ¿Se llevaban muy bien?
Tania: Sí, y siempre compartían el trabajo de la casa.
Javier: ...

*Mis padres siempre hacían fiestas para toda la familia.*

## Essential Instruction

1. For **Actividad 5**, you may want to allot students a certain amount of money for each category.
2. Before beginning **Actividad 6**, briefly review uses of the preterite and imperfect. Tell students that they will practice these tenses more in depth throughout the unit.
3. For **Actividad 6**, you may want to have students bring in several family photos from home (or print out images from the Internet of a fictitious family) for use in the activity.
4. Point out that the **El tiempo pretérito** presentation focuses on conjugation.

# Gramática

## El tiempo pretérito  1.2

El pretérito se usa para narrar acciones que ocurrieron en momentos específicos del pasado.

| Conjugación de los verbos regulares en pretérito | | | | | | |
|---|---|---|---|---|---|---|
| lavar | lavé | lavaste | lavó | lavamos | lavasteis | lavaron |
| barrer | barrí | barriste | barrió | barrimos | barristeis | barrieron |
| sacudir | sacudí | sacudiste | sacudió | sacudimos | sacudisteis | sacudieron |

### Verbos de cambio ortográfico

Los siguientes verbos tienen cambios de ortografía en la conjugación del pretérito, en la primera persona del singular.

- Los verbos que terminan en **-car** cambian la **-c** a **-qu** antes de **-e**.

| secar | sequé | secaste | secó | secamos | secasteis | secaron |
|---|---|---|---|---|---|---|

  Verbos como **secar**: buscar, colocar, dedicar, explicar, sacar, tocar

- Los verbos que terminan en **-gar** cambian la **-g** a **-gu** antes de **-e**.

| apagar | apagué | apagaste | apagó | apagamos | apagasteis | apagaron |
|---|---|---|---|---|---|---|

  Verbos como **apagar**: colgar, entregar, jugar, llegar, pagar, regar

- Los verbos que terminan en **-zar** cambian la **-z** a **-c** antes de **-e**.

| almorzar | almorcé | almorzaste | almorzó | almorzamos | almorzasteis | almorzaron |
|---|---|---|---|---|---|---|

  Verbos como **almorzar**: abrazar, comenzar, empezar, gozar

- Los verbos que terminan en **-aer** y **-eer**, al igual que **oír**, cambian la **-i** a **-y** en la tercera persona del singular y del plural, y todas las otras personas llevan tilde sobre la **-í**.

| caer | caí | caíste | cayó | caímos | caísteis | cayeron |
|---|---|---|---|---|---|---|
| leer | leí | leíste | leyó | leímos | leísteis | leyeron |
| oír | oí | oíste | oyó | oímos | oísteis | oyeron |

  Verbos que siguen la misma regla: creer, poseer

---

## RESOURCES

| WB | Activity 3 |
|---|---|
| LA | Activities 1–2 |

## Reference Desk

1. Remind students that the spelling changes occur in **-car** and **-gar** verbs in order to maintain the hard consonant sounds.
2. Point out the need for written accents to avoid diphthongs. Contrast the pronunciation of these verb forms with and without the accent.

## Expansion

Ask students to recount what happened at the beginning of class today. For example, say: **La clase empezó a las dos y cuarto. Y luego, ¿qué pasó?**

---

## Differentiated Learning

### Heritage Learners

Ask heritage learners to share information regarding families in their cultural communities. For example, is it common for different generations to live under the same roof? What role do **padrinos/madrinas** play?

## Multiple Intelligences

### Bodily-Kinesthetic/Verbal-Linguistic

Divide the class into groups and ask them to prepare a skit involving several family members who are working out how to divide up the household chores. Allow students time to rehearse, and then have them role-play their skits for the class.

## Reference Desk

Remind students that **ir** and **ser** have identical conjugations in the preterite. Tell students that they must use context to determine which verb is being used.

## Communication

**Interpersonal/Presentational: Cooperative Groups**
Have students write five sentences telling what they did last week. Three of the sentences should be true, and two should be false. Then have students get together in groups of three and take turns reading their sentences aloud. Their partners should say whether they think the statement is **la verdad** or **una mentira**.

## Game

**Charada**
Students can practice the preterite tense by playing charades. In pairs, students take turns acting out a variety of activities for their partner to guess (e.g., **¿Jugaste al tenis?**). Once their partner guesses correctly, they should confirm using the **yo** form: **Sí, jugué al tenis.**

## Verbos de cambio radical

Los verbos regulares de la tercera conjugación (**-ir**), que cambian el radical en el presente, sufren en el pretérito un cambio en la vocal de la tercera persona del singular y del plural.

### Cambio e → i

| sentir | sentí | sentiste | sintió | sentimos | sentisteis | sintieron |
|---|---|---|---|---|---|---|

Verbos como **sentir**: advertir, conseguir, divertirse, mentir, pedir, preferir, repetir, vestirse

### Cambio o → ue

| dormir | dormí | dormiste | durmió | dormimos | dormisteis | durmieron |
|---|---|---|---|---|---|---|
| morir | morí | moriste | murió | morimos | moristeis | murieron |

## Verbos irregulares

- Los siguientes verbos son irregulares. Tienen cambios de radical, pero comparten las mismas terminaciones.

| Infinitivo | Radical | Terminaciones en común | | | | | |
|---|---|---|---|---|---|---|---|
| andar | anduv- | anduve | anduviste | anduvo | anduvimos | anduvisteis | anduvieron |
| caber | cup- | cupe | cupiste | cupo | cupimos | cupisteis | cupieron |
| estar | estuv- | estuve | estuviste | estuvo | estuvimos | estuvisteis | estuvieron |
| haber | hub- | hube | hubiste | hubo | hubimos | hubisteis | hubieron |
| hacer | hic- | hice | hiciste | hizo | hicimos | hicisteis | hicieron |
| poder | pud- | pude | pudiste | pudo | pudimos | pudisteis | pudieron |
| poner | pus- | puse | pusiste | puso | pusimos | pusisteis | pusieron |
| saber | sup- | supe | supiste | supo | supimos | supisteis | supieron |
| tener | tuv- | tuve | tuviste | tuvo | tuvimos | tuvisteis | tuvieron |
| querer | quis- | quise | quisiste | quiso | quisimos | quisisteis | quisieron |
| venir | vin- | vine | viniste | vino | vinimos | vinisteis | vinieron |
| decir | dij- | dije | dijiste | dijo | dijimos | dijisteis | dijeron |
| producir | produj- | produje | produjiste | produjo | produjimos | produjisteis | produjeron |
| traer | traj- | traje | trajiste | trajo | trajimos | trajisteis | trajeron |

- Los verbos **ir**, **ser**, **dar** y **ver** son completamente irregulares.

| ir/ser | fui | fuiste | fue | fuimos | fuisteis | fueron |
|---|---|---|---|---|---|---|
| dar | di | diste | dio | dimos | disteis | dieron |
| ver | vi | viste | vio | vimos | visteis | vieron |

## Essential Instruction

1. Review the meaning of any unfamiliar infinitives in **Gramática**.
2. Working as a class, create a graphic organizer of irregular verbs in the preterite tense. Categories can include: stem-changing verbs, verbs with spelling changes, etc.
3. After checking answers to **Actividad 7**, have students role-play the dialogue in pairs.

## 7 ¿Hiciste tus quehaceres?  1.2

Complete la conversación entre estas dos hermanas con la forma correcta del verbo entre paréntesis.

**Ana:** ¿Qué (**1.** *hacer*) tú ayer?

**Andrea:** (**2.** *estar*) todo el día en casa ayudando a mamá con todos los quehaceres.

**Ana:** ¿Por dónde (**3.** *comenzar*) tú?

**Andrea:** ¡Por la cocina, por supuesto! (**4.** *lavar*) los platos y (**5.** *ordenar*) los estantes. Mamá y yo (**6.** *poner*) todo en orden.

**Ana:** ¿No me digas que tú (**7.** *barrer*) el piso? Sé que odias hacerlo.

**Andrea:** Por supuesto. No solo (**8.** *barrer*) el piso, sino que lo (**9.** *limpiar*) con un nuevo producto que es una maravilla.

**Ana:** Me imagino que tú también (**10.** *poner*) en orden mi habitación. ¿Verdad?

**Andrea:** ¡Qué va! Si tú no la (**11.** *arreglar*), ¿por qué tenía que hacerlo yo? Yo (**12.** *hacer*) mi cama, (**13.** *cambiar*) las sábanas y (**14.** *andar*) de un lugar a otro sacudiendo los muebles.

**Ana:** ¿Y por qué no (**15.** *salir*) de casa después de que acabaste de ayudar con los quehaceres?

**Andrea:** No (**16.** *poder*). Mamá (**17.** *tener*) que salir y yo (**18.** *tener*) que quedarme a cuidar a Luisito. Pero no importa, ella me (**19.** *pagar*) muy bien por cuidarlo.

## ¡Comunicación!

## 8 ¿Qué hiciste? 👥 Interpersonal Communication  1.1

Con un(a) compañero/a, hablen sobre lo que han hecho últimamente. Usen el pretérito y los temas que se dan como guía y túrnense para hacerse preguntas y responderlas, como se ve en el modelo.

MODELO   por la mañana / por la tarde

A: ¿Qué hiciste ayer por la mañana?

B: Fui a la biblioteca y preparé un informe.

A: Y por la tarde, ¿qué hiciste?

B: Me fui al cine con Sara. Vimos una buena película.

**1.** ayer / anoche

**2.** por la mañana / por la tarde

**3.** en la clase de español / en la clase de inglés

**4.** después de llegar a casa / antes de acostarse

**5.** después de clase / antes del examen

**6.** la semana pasada / el mes pasado

**7.** después de la escuela / después de hacer la tarea

**8.** después del almuerzo / después de la cena

*Estuve en la biblioteca unas tres horas.*

### Answers

**7**
1. hiciste
2. Estuve
3. comenzaste
4. Lavé
5. ordené
6. pusimos
7. barriste
8. barrí
9. limpié
10. pusiste
11. arreglaste
12. hice
13. cambié
14. anduve
15. saliste
16. pude
17. tuvo
18. tuve
19. pagó

**8** *Las respuestas variarán.*

### Game

**¡A conjugar!**
Play a dice game to give students practice conjugating verbs in the preterite. List the subject pronouns on the board and number them from 1 to 6. Point out the correspondence between the six sides of a die and the six subject pronouns. Divide the class into pairs and give each pair a die and a list of infinitives. They should take turns rolling the die and conjugating a verb from the list. You may want to have students write the conjugated forms so that their partner can verify the spelling and any accents.

## Differentiated Learning
### Heritage Learners
Ask heritage learners to retell a recent event or news story from their family's country of origin.

### Special Needs Students
#### Dyslexia/AD(H)D
Give these students extra support for open-ended activities such as **Actividad 8**. Have students brainstorm one or two verbs for each time period. Tell them to check pp. 143–144 for any irregularities, and then conjugate the verbs in the **yo** form (or **nosotros**, if the activity is shared). Finally, have them use their notes as they complete the activity in pairs.

**9**

1. A los novios les dieron muchos regalos.
2. Mamá no pudo hablar de la emoción.
3. Papá recibió a los invitados en la sala.
4. Los invitados se divirtieron mucho.
5. Como siempre, Carlos llegó tardísimo.
6. Tú trajiste un regalo magnífico.
7. El abuelo invitó a bailar a la abuela.
8. Todos bailaron y cantaron sin parar.
9. La fiesta fue estupenda.
10. Yo saqué muchas fotos de los novios.

**10** *Las respuestas variarán.*

**11** *Respuestas posibles:*

1. Porque estaba muy ocupada.
2. Llegó a Santa Bárbara hace cinco días.
3. Primero vio el campus, las playas y la laguna.
4. Empezaron el lunes.
5. Ella se enojó con él.
6. No pudo matricularse en sus clases favoritas y casi tuvo un accidente de bicicleta.

**12** *Los mensajes variarán.*

### Reference Desk

Point out the word **cruda** in the text message; students may know this word as *raw*. Explain that in colloquial Spanish it means *difficult*.

---

**9  Comentarios**  **1.3**

Cambie los siguientes comentarios que oyó sobre la boda de su hermana al tiempo pretérito.

1. A los novios les dan muchos regalos.
2. Mamá no puede hablar de la emoción.
3. Papá recibe a los invitados en la sala.
4. Los invitados se divierten muchísimo.
5. Como siempre, Carlos llega tardísimo.
6. Tú traes un regalo magnífico.
7. El abuelo invita a bailar a la abuela.
8. Todos bailan y cantan sin parar.
9. La fiesta es estupenda.
10. Yo saco muchas fotos de los novios.

 **¡Comunicación!**

**10  ¡Hablemos!**  👥  **Interpersonal Communication**  **1.1**

Cuéntele a su compañero todos los detalles de la boda de su hermana: quiénes asistieron, qué regalos le dieron, dónde hicieron la recepción, qué comieron y otras cosas que se le ocurran.

**1.2, 1.3**

**11  ¿Qué tal está Marta?  Interpretive Communication**

Marta acaba de mudarse a Santa Bárbara para estudiar en la universidad y le envía un mensaje de texto a su amiga Julia para contarle cómo le ha ido. Conteste las siguientes preguntas sobre el mensaje que Marta le envió a su amiga.

1. ¿Por qué no llamó Marta a su amiga cuando llegó a la universidad?
2. ¿Cuándo llegó a Santa Bárbara?
3. ¿Qué lugares vio primero?
4. ¿Cuándo empezaron las clases?
5. ¿Qué pasó con su novio?
6. ¿Qué otros problemas tuvo?

> Iba a llamarte cuando llegué a Santa Bárbara, hace cinco días, pero no pude. No te imaginas lo ocupada que he estado. Al principio me encantó el campus. Cuando vi las playas y la laguna creí estar en el cielo.
>
> Pero el lunes, cuando comenzaron las clases, volví a la cruda realidad. No pude matricularme en mis clases favoritas, me enojé con mi novio y casi tuve un accidente de bicicleta. ¡Qué día tan horrible!

**12  Desde la universidad   Presentational Communication   1.3**

Imagínese que Ud. acaba de ingresar a la universidad. Escríbale mensaje de texto a un(a) amigo/a, contándole cuándo llegó y a qué se dedicó los primeros días. Después, léale el mensaje a la clase.

---

### Essential Instruction

1. Begin **Actividad 9** by having students circle the verbs in the present tense and underline the subjects. Then have them give the preterite verb forms orally. Finally, have them write the full sentences.
2. Encourage creativity in **Actividad 10**.
3. Open **Actividad 11** by asking students how often they use text messages to communicate with friends.
4. Read aloud the e-mail in **Actividad 13**. Point out to students the words in bold in the preterite tense. They will be using them to answer questions in **Actividad 14**.

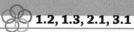 **1.2, 1.3, 2.1, 3.1**

## 13 ¡Qué maravilla! · Interpretive Communication

Alicia y su amiga Eugenia acaban de licenciarse en una universidad española y ahora están de viaje en Sudamérica. Desde Bolivia, Alicia le envía un correo electrónico a su prima Lucía. Lea el mensaje, y luego, complete las oraciones que le siguen con la información que corresponda de acuerdo al mensaje.

---

| ○○○ | ¿Sabes qué? | ⤢ |
|---|---|---|
| De: | Alicia | |
| Para: | Lucía | |
| Asunto: | ¿Sabes qué? | |

Querida Lucía:

¿Sabes qué, primita? Este país es una maravilla. Al llegar a Bolivia **quedé** tan impresionada con una de sus tradiciones que **decidí** dedicar unas líneas para describírtela. ¡Es el sombrero! No me vas a creer pero la gente indígena, tanto los niños como los adultos, usa más de 300 estilos de sombreros, gorros[1] y tocados[2]. Ojalá estuvieras aquí para verlos.

Hace casi quinientos años que Francisco Pizarro y sus hombres **desembarcaron**[3] en este continente y **conquistaron** el Imperio inca, primero en Perú y luego en Bolivia. Hoy se ven indígenas que llevan cascos[4] similares a los usados por los conquistadores, aunque ya no son de acero[5] sino de cuero con adornos de lana. El otro día en el mercado de una pequeña población **pude** ver los sombreros y gorros más extraordinarios. La variedad de colores y de formas era infinita y tan impresionante como cualquier desfile de modas[6] de París. Cuando **fui** a La Paz, en seguida me di cuenta de que el compañero inseparable de las mujeres era el bombín londinense[7]. Mientras **estuve** allí no **vi** a ninguna mujer indígena que no llevara bombín. Nuestro guía turístico nos **dijo** que en el pasado los hombres se los daban a las mujeres indígenas a cambio de favores. **Explicó** que ninguna mujer saldría a la calle sin él y que ningún hombre se atrevería[8] a llevarlo. Hay más bombines en La Paz que los que ha habido en Londres en cualquier época.

Con cariño,
Alicia

---

[1] caps   [2] headdresses   [3] arrived   [4] helmets
[5] steel   [6] fashion show   [7] British bowler hat
[8] would dare

1. Alicia es de ____ pero está de ____ en Sudamérica. Le escribe una carta a Lucía, su ____.
2. Algo que le impresionó mucho a Alicia es la costumbre boliviana de llevar ____.
3. Hay más de 300 ____.
4. Para las mujeres bolivianas, el estilo más popular es el ____.

*El volcán Licancabur, cerca del lago Blanca, en Bolivia*

---

**RESOURCES**

 Avenue

**Answers**

 13

1. España, viaje, prima
2. sombreros
3. estilos de sombreros, gorros y tocados
4. bombín londinense

### Reference Desk

1. As students read the e-mail, have them refer to p. 148 for a photo of a woman wearing a **bombín**. If possible, bring in images of other Bolivian headwear.
2. The Incan Empire was the largest in pre-Columbian America; by the time of Pizarro's conquest in 1532, it included parts of present-day Colombia, Ecuador, Peru, Bolivia, Chile, and Argentina.
3. Bolivia is the only Latin American country with two capitals: Sucre (official capital, seat of justice) and La Paz (administrative capital, seat of government).
4. The Licancabur Volcano is on the border of Bolivia and Chile.

### Connections

**History**
Divide the class into groups. Have each group research Bolivian history (starting with the founding of Tiahuanaco and finishing with the present) and construct a timeline of events. Emphasize that they should focus on major events, and include no more than ten. Ask them to narrate the events using the preterite tense. Have students present the information via an Avenue task.

---

## Differentiated Learning
### Accelerate/Expand
Have students choose a place in Bolivia and imagine they visited it recently. They should research more about the place. Tell them to write an e-mail to a friend in which they talk about what they did and saw.

## Multiple Intelligences
### Naturalist
Ask students to research more about Bolivia's geography and ecology. Ask them to make a list of geographic features such as Lake Titicaca, the Altiplano, volcanoes, salt flats, etc., and explain why they make Bolivia unique.

**147**

### Answers

**14** *Respuestas posibles:*
1. A Alicia le impresionó la tradición de llevar sombrero. Decidió escribirle a su prima.
2. Desembarcó hace casi 500 años.
3. Pizarro y sus hombres conquistaron el Imperio inca.
4. Vio los sombreros y gorros más extraordinarios.
5. El guía turístico le dijo que, en el pasado, los hombres les daban sombreros a las mujeres indígenas a cambio de favores.

### Reference Desk

Remind students that there are no stem changes in the imperfect tense. Emphasize that there are only three irregular verbs.

### Expansion

As a wrap up to the preterite tense, before moving into the imperfect, ask students to think about the most important news stories of the past year (or another time period). Tell them to choose the three events that they consider the most important and create a Flipgrid post in which they name the events and say what happened, using the preterite tense.

# Gramática

## ¡Comunicación!

**14  ¿Qué cuenta Alicia de Bolivia?**   Interpretive Communication  **1.3**

Conteste las preguntas sobre el correo electrónico en la página 147 que Alicia le escribió a su prima.

1. ¿Qué le impresionó a Alicia al llegar a Bolivia? Como resultado, ¿qué decidió hacer?
2. Según Alicia, ¿cuándo desembarcó Francisco Pizarro en Bolivia?
3. ¿Qué hicieron Pizarro y sus hombres?
4. ¿Qué vio Alicia cuando estuvo en el mercado?
5. ¿Qué le dijo su guía turístico?

*Una mujer boliviana con bombín*

*Unas mantas típicas de lana*

## El tiempo imperfecto  **1.2**

El imperfecto se usa para hacer descripciones de las personas, las cosas y los hechos en el pasado y para indicar su ubicación.

| Conjugación de los verbos regulares en imperfecto | | | | | | |
|---|---|---|---|---|---|---|
| guard**ar** | guard**aba** | guard**abas** | guard**aba** | guard**ábamos** | guard**abais** | guard**aban** |
| recog**er** | recog**ía** | recog**ías** | recog**ía** | recog**íamos** | recog**íais** | recog**ían** |
| compart**ir** | compart**ía** | compart**ías** | compart**ía** | compart**íamos** | compart**íais** | compart**ían** |

### Verbos irregulares

Los únicos verbos irregulares en imperfecto son los verbos **ir**, **ser** y **ver**.

| Verbos irregulares en imperfecto | | | | | | |
|---|---|---|---|---|---|---|
| **ir** | iba | ibas | iba | íbamos | ibais | iban |
| **ser** | era | eras | era | éramos | erais | eran |
| **ver** | veía | veías | veía | veíamos | veíais | veían |

### Essential Instruction

1. Before students answer the questions in **Actividad 14**, point out the words in bold in the e-mail on p. 147.
2. Personalize the grammar presentation by describing your family life when you were young: where you lived, what you played, the name of your school, etc.
3. After completing **Actividad 15**, ask students to summarize what life was like in those times.
4. Remind students to use only the imperfect in **Actividad 16**. Encourage partners to ask follow-up questions.

**15 ¡Qué suerte!**  **1.2**

Complete la conversación entre una madre y su hija con el imperfecto de los verbos entre paréntesis.

**Madre:** Te digo, hija, que los tiempos han cambiado. Tu abuela, por ejemplo, (**1.** *ser*) la perfecta ama de casa (*housewife*), aunque no le gustaba para nada.

**Hija:** ¿Por qué dices eso?

**Madre:** Bueno, pues porque ella (**2.** *tener*) que quedarse en casa todo el tiempo. Casi nunca (**3.** *poder*) salir porque (**4.** *pasar*) todo el tiempo haciendo quehaceres domésticos. Primero (**5.** *arreglar*) la casa: (**6.** *hacer*) las camas, (**7.** *sacudir*) los muebles y (**8.** *pasar*) la aspiradora. Luego, (**9.** *lavar*) la ropa a mano, porque no había lavadoras, y la (**10.** *colgar*) a secar en el patio. Cuando (**11.** *estar*) seca, la (**12.** *traer*) adentro, la (**13.** *planchar*), la (**14.** *doblar*) y la (**15.** *guardar*) en los armarios.

**Hija:** Y..., ¿quién (**16.** *preparar*) las comidas?

**Madre:** Ella, ella lo (**17.** *hacer*) todo, pues era lo que se (**18.** *esperar*) de las mujeres en esa época. ¡Es una suerte que no te tocó vivir en los tiempos de la abuela!

**Hija:** Sí, ¡gracias a Dios!

## ¡Comunicación!

**16 Uno de los mejores recuerdos** 👥 Interpersonal Communication  **1.1**

¿Qué recuerda Ud. con más cariño de su niñez? Con un(a) compañero/a, hablen de las actividades que más recuerdan de su infancia. Usen los temas que se dan como guía y túrnense para hacerse preguntas y responderlas, como se ve en el modelo.

**MODELO**

**A:** ¿Qué hacían durante las vacaciones de verano?

**B:** Durante las vacaciones nos gustaba viajar a las montañas. Mi papá conducía el coche y todos cantábamos en coro hasta que nos quedábamos dormidos de cansancio. Es uno de los mejores recuerdos de mi infancia.

- Vacaciones de verano
- Navidad y Año Nuevo
- Compañeros de juego
- En la escuela primaria
- Familiares preferidos
- En mi cumpleaños

*Cuando era niño me divertía mucho jugando con mi hermana.*

## Differentiated Learning
### Expand

Ask students to analyze their family life when they were five years old and compare it to now. Brainstorm a list of aspects to consider, such as lifestyles, family size, their home, pets, their parents' jobs, getting along with siblings, etc. Have students submit their comparisons via Avenue.

## Multiple Intelligences
### Verbal-Linguistic

Ask students to interview a favorite relative about his or her life as a child. Instruct students to write a composition describing the relative and telling about the person's life in the past.

## RESOURCES

 Flipgrid

 Mujeres: El eje central de la familia boliviana Prácticas

 **LA** Activity 4

### Answers

 **17**

1. Tiene un papel fundamental ya que muchas veces es quien se ocupa de mantener y criar a los hijos.
2. Está relacionado con el 27 de mayo de 1812, cuando las madres de Cochabamba fueron masacradas por las tropas españolas.
3. Las trabajadoras de hogar, porque se encargan de los quehaceres y el cuidado de los niños.

 **18** *Las respuestas variarán.*

---

### Reference Desk

Students can do a Flipgrid post reacting to any of these cultural readings.

---

### Critical Thinking

**Analyzing and Comparing**
Reread the last paragraph on p. 150, and ask students what factors allow domestic help to be very common in Bolivia. Is it as common in the United States? Why not?

---

### Pre-AP

Have students respond to the **Pregunta clave**, in spoken or written form, using information from the readings on pp. 150–152. Students should also include a comparison between their own community/culture and Bolivia.

---

**1.2, 2.1**
**17 Comprensión**

1. ¿Qué importancia tiene la madre en la familia boliviana?

2. ¿Con qué hecho histórico está relacionado el Día de la Madre en Bolivia?

3. Además de las madres, ¿qué otras mujeres desempeñan un rol importante en la vida familiar boliviana? ¿Por qué?

**1.3, 2.1, 4.2**
**18 Analice**

1. ¿Cómo se celebra el Día de la Madre en su país?

2. Compare el rol de la madre en Bolivia con el que tiene en su cultura. ¿Qué semejanzas y diferencias encuentra?

---

# Mujeres: El eje central de la familia boliviana

**1.2, 2.1**

*Las madres se encargan de cuidar a los hijos.*

En Bolivia, la madre es el pilar fundamental del hogar, ya que la mayoría de las familias se caracterizan por la ausencia del padre, que suele migrar[1] a otras regiones del país o a países vecinos en busca de trabajo. En muchísimos casos, son las mujeres quienes quedan a cargo de mantener y criar a los hijos.

El papel central de las madres en Bolivia está relacionado con las celebraciones tradicionales. En el mes de mayo se las homenajea[2] por razones históricas peculiares. El 27 de mayo de 1812, un grupo de mujeres de Cochabamba sacrificó su vida combatiendo contra las tropas realistas[3] españolas. Con el fin de proteger a sus hijos, se organizaron con la consigna[4] "nuestro hogar es sagrado". Todas fueron masacradas. En 1927, en reconocimiento a la valentía de estas heroínas, se consagró[5] oficialmente el 27 de mayo como Día de la Madre en Bolivia. Desde entonces, es un día muy especial para el que se preparan actividades, homenajes y regalos con anticipación.

Las trabajadoras del hogar son otro ejemplo de mujeres que desempeñan un rol destacado en la vida familiar. En Bolivia, es muy común pagarle a una persona para que se ocupe de los quehaceres y del cuidado de los niños. Las trabajadoras del hogar suelen vivir en las casas donde trabajan.

[1] move  [2] are honored  [3] royalist  [4] slogan  [5] established

**Búsqueda:** día de la madre en bolivia, heroínas de la coronilla

---

**Prácticas**  **2.1**

El Día Internacional de la Familia, que se celebra cada 15 de mayo y fue establecido por la ONU, es una ocasión para celebrar los vínculos que existen entre los miembros de una familia. En 2013, la Cámara de Senadores boliviana sancionó (*passed*) una ley para convertir a esa fecha en fiesta nacional, reconociendo la importancia de la familia como núcleo fundamental de la sociedad boliviana.

*Una familia boliviana*

---

### Essential Instruction

1. Point out the **Pregunta clave**, and tell students to keep it in mind as they complete the cultural readings.
2. Have students preview pp. 150–152. Ask them to predict what they will learn about Bolivia.
3. Remind students of the photo and question from the unit opener. Ask where they can find the answer (in the **Prácticas** section).

# El matrimonio en la cultura aymara  1.2, 2.1

El matrimonio entre los aymaras, que es el grupo de pobladores originarios más numeroso de Bolivia y representa el 30 % de la población, no es un asunto personal, sino un acontecimiento[1] social que concierne a la comunidad. El noviazgo no se practica y es común que las uniones sean concertadas[2] por los padres. Los jóvenes pueden casarse si cumplen algunos requisitos de carácter social y cultural.

*Una pareja aymara contrae matrimonio.*

Uno de los requisitos para el varón es haber ejercido cargos de autoridad en la comunidad, como haber supervisado los bailes que se realizan antes de los carnavales. Se considera que un joven puede ser responsable con su familia solo si ha demostrado ser responsable con la comunidad. Otros requisitos incluyen tener ahijados[3], tener cantidad suficiente de vestimentas y saber arar[4], techar una casa y tejer[5]. Para la mujer, los requisitos son similares. Después de casarse, pasan a ser considerados "personas completas".

Los padrinos[6] son los responsables directos de los novios. No es solo una responsabilidad espiritual sino total, porque deben apoyar y ayudar en los trabajos comunales a la nueva pareja. Se los considera segundos padres y su responsabilidad es tal que se dice que de ellos depende el éxito de la nueva pareja.

[1] event   [2] arranged   [3] godchildren   [4] plow   [5] weave   [6] godparents

 **Búsqueda:** matrimonio aymara, padrinazgo en la comunidad aymara

## Productos  1.2, 2.2

La "enramada" es la primera residencia de los recién casados en la cultura aymara. Se trata de una construcción provisional hecha con varas de eucalipto y un toldo. La entrada se decora por completo con hojas frescas y flores de kantuta, típicas del altiplano. En ese lugar se recibe y agasaja (*are honored*) a los novios, los padrinos y las autoridades comunitarias.

*Flores de kantuta*

### 1.2, 2.1, 2.2
## 19 Comprensión

1. ¿Qué importancia tiene la comunidad en los matrimonios aymara?

2. ¿Qué papel desempeñan los padrinos de un matrimonio aymara?

3. ¿Qué es la "enramada"?

### 1.3, 2.1
## 20 Analice

1. ¿Qué ventajas y desventajas opina Ud. que puede tener el hecho de que la comunidad tenga tanta influencia en los matrimonios?

2. ¿Por qué cree Ud. que tener ahijados es un requisito para casarse?

## Answers

**19**

1. Es muy importante porque el matrimonio es considerado un asunto social más que personal. La comunidad exige que los novios cumplan una serie de requisitos para poder casarse.

2. Son responsables directos de los novios. Deben apoyarlos y ayudarlos en los trabajos comunales y se los considera sus segundos padres.

3. Es la primera residencia de los recién casados, una construcción provisional donde se recibe a los novios, los padrinos y las autoridades de la comunidad.

**20**

1. *Las respuestas variarán.*

2. *Respuesta posible:* Porque que a una persona la elijan como padrino o madrina de un niño demuestra que es respetada por otros miembros de la comunidad.

## Reference Desk

1. The man in the photo is wearing a small **wiphala**, or Aymara flag, on his clothing.

2. The **kantuta** is one of Bolivia's national flowers.

## Critical Thinking

**Comparing**
Have students compare and contrast the Aymara wedding traditions with other marriage customs with which they are familiar.

## Differentiated Learning
**Expand**
Have students research online to learn more about the Aymara in Bolivia. Ask students to write a report about the indigenous group's history in the area, their customs, language, cuisine, etc. Tell students to summarize this information in their Culture Journals.

## Multiple Intelligences
**Musical-Rhythmic**
Have students research musical instruments that are traditional in Andean music, such as the **charango**, **zampoña**, **quena**, etc. Then have students search online and listen to songs by Bolivian groups that use these instruments, such as Los K'jarkas or Grupo Aymara.

# El aguayo 🎧 🌼 **1.2, 2.1, 2.2, 3.2**

El aguayo es un tejido colorido hecho a mano que usan las mujeres del altiplano[1] para cargar bebés, sentarse y exponer[2] productos. Su uso se consolidó en el siglo XIX debido a la presencia masiva de mujeres aymaras, que habían migrado del campo a la ciudad. Actualmente, está íntimamente relacionado con las cholas (mujeres de raíces aymaras y de corte urbano[3]) y es un accesorio imprescindible de su atuendo[4], como la falda y el sombrero.

🌼 **1.2, 2.1, 2.2, 3.2**

### 21 Comprensión

1. ¿Qué es el aguayo y para qué se usa?
2. ¿Quiénes son las cholas?
3. ¿Qué concepción del tiempo tienen los aymaras?

*El aguayo es bonito además de útil.*

🌼 **1.3, 2.1, 2.2**

### 22 Analice

1. ¿Qué ventajas o desventajas cree Ud. que tiene el uso del aguayo para las madres?
2. Algunas teorías sobre la crianza de los niños sostienen que el uso de aguayos o elementos similares para cargar a los bebés son beneficiosos para los niños. ¿Qué opina Ud. al respecto?

Tradicionalmente, se envuelve al bebé en un aguayo pequeño, con los brazos pegados al cuerpo para que no pase frío ni se arañe[5] la cara. Luego se coloca al bebé en el aguayo más grande y la mujer lo pone sobre su espalda y lo amarra[6] a su cuerpo.

Detrás de esta costumbre cotidiana, se encierra una concepción del tiempo. En el mundo aymara, el tiempo no es lineal, sino que es un círculo en el cual las personas caminan mirando al pasado, que es lo conocido, y de espaldas al futuro, que es lo desconocido. Por eso, al bebé, que representa el futuro, se lo lleva en la espalda.

🌼 **1.2, 3.2**

### Perspectivas

La psicóloga Ivonne Ramírez Martínez, que realizó una investigación sobre el uso del aguayo para cargar niños, señaló: "Es un elemento totalmente correlacionado con un aspecto antropológico que implica que el ser humano hasta la edad de dos años no puede valerse por sí mismo". Según esta cita, ¿cuál cree que es la relación entre el uso del aguayo y los valores familiares de la cultura aymara?

[1] Andean plateau   [2] display   [3] urban style   [4] outfit   [5] scratch   [6] ties

🔍 **Búsqueda: aguayo boliviano, chola boliviana, tejidos bolivianos**

# Vocabulario 2

## Comparación y contraste: ¡Ojo con estas palabras!  1.2, 4.1

En español, a diferencia del inglés, *to know* tiene dos significados diferentes.
Preste atención, pues el uso del uno o el otro depende del contexto.

to know ⟨ saber / conocer ⟩

### Saber

*to have knowledge of facts, concepts, or information*
**¿Sabes** cuándo se celebra en Bolivia el Día de la Madre?

*to know by heart*
**Sé** de memoria los nombres de todos los países del mundo hispano.

*to know how to do something*
¿Cuántos de Uds. **saben** hablar dos idiomas?

### Conocer

*to be acquainted with a person or place; to be familiar with*
No **conozco** bien esta área del país y tampoco **conozco** bien las señales de tránsito en español.

*to meet (someone) for the first time*
Ayer **conocí** a los hermanos de mi esposo por primera vez.
Hoy voy a **conocer** a mis suegros y estoy muy nerviosa.

*To meet* tiene otras variaciones de significado, además de **conocer**, como se ve a continuación.

to meet ⟨ reunirse / encontrarse / toparse con ⟩

**reunirse**   *to meet with a group or club*
Siempre **nos reunimos** para hacer las tareas después de clases.

**encontrarse**   *to meet by appointment or chance*
Ayer **me encontré** con tu madre en el supermercado.

**toparse (tropezarse) con**   *to meet by accident; to run into*
A que no adivinas **con** quién **me topé/me tropecé** a la salida del cine.

*Nos divertimos mucho cuando nos reunimos en grupo a trabajar.*

## RESOURCES

**Avenue**

**WB** Activities 5–6

## Reference Desk

1. Remind students that **saber** and **conocer** have irregular **yo** forms in the present indicative; **saber** also has an irregular conjugation in the future and preterite tenses.
2. Emphasize the use of the personal **a** after **conocer** when referring to people. Contrast this use by giving statements such as: **¿Conoces al presidente de los Estados Unidos? ¿No? Pero sabes quién es, ¿verdad? ¡Claro que sí!**
3. Remind students that **reunirse** carries a written accent in its present indicative conjugations, with the exception of **nosotros**.

## Expansion

Write sentences on the board that use the verbs from p. 153 incorrectly. Ask volunteers to correct the sentences.

---

## Differentiated Learning
### Heritage Learners
Ask heritage learners to compare and contrast the customs and cultural information described on pp. 150–152 with their own cultural communities.

## Multiple Intelligences
### Verbal-Linguistic
Have students create questions using the verbs on p. 153, e.g., **¿Conoces a una persona famosa?** Encourage creativity. Have students survey their classmates and summarize the results in an Avenue task.

**153**

**23**
1. conocía, sabía
2. conocía, sabía
3. supo
4. conocimos
5. sabía
6. conocimos
7. conoció, sabe
8. sabía
9. supieron
10. sabía
11. sabe
12. sabía
13. se conocieron
14. sabían
15. sabemos
16. Sabía

**24** *Las conversaciones variarán.*

### Expansion

For additional practice, ask pairs of students to write two cloze sentences for each verb. They can exchange papers with another pair and complete the sentences.

---

## 23 ¿Saber o conocer?  1.2

Complete las oraciones con la forma de **saber** o **conocer** según corresponda de acuerdo al contexto.

1. Hacía mucho tiempo que yo (*conocía / sabía*) a Marcela y (*conocía / sabía*) que era boliviana.

2. No (*conocía / sabía*) su casa pero (*conocía / sabía*) que era agradable y moderna.

3. Cuando Marcela (*conoció / supo*) que mi prima y yo estábamos de vacaciones en La Paz, nos invitó a su casa.

4. Allí (*conocimos / supimos*) a toda su familia.

5. Yo (*conocía / sabía*) que a Marcela le gustaba cocinar y, como era de esperar, la cena que preparó estaba riquísima.

6. Nos divertimos mucho en La Paz y en compañía de Marcela (*conocimos / supimos*) muchos lugares interesantes.

7. Hoy recibí una carta de Marcela. Dice que hace seis meses (*conoció / supo*) a un muchacho boliviano pero no (*conoce / sabe*) si se casarán pronto o no.

8. Yo (*conocía / sabía*) que tarde o temprano encontraría en su país al hombre de sus sueños.

9. Ellas (*conocieron / supieron*) del accidente durante la cena.

10. Yo (*conocía / sabía*) las capitales de los países del mundo cuando era niña. Ahora no recuerdo ninguna.

11. Mi mejor amigo (*conoce / sabe*) mucho sobre autos de carrera.

12. Mi padre (*conocía / sabía*) que yo estaba triste, pero él me hizo reír de todos modos.

13. Mi hermano y su novio (*se conocieron / se supieron*) hace un año.

14. Mis padres (*sabían / conocían*) conducir bien en La Paz.

15. Nosotros (*conocemos / sabemos*) llegar al aeropuerto.

16. ¿(*conocía / sabía*) la respuesta a su pregunta? ¡Yo no!

### Un poco más

El verbo **saber** toma el significado de **enterarse** (*to find out*) cuando se usa en pretérito.

¿Cuándo supiste la noticia de la boda?

*When did you find out the news about the wedding?*

---

## ¡Comunicación!

## 24 ¿Qué sabes de su vida? 👥 Interpersonal Communication 1.1

Imagine que lleva varios años en la universidad y un día se encuentra en la calle con un(a) compañero/a de colegio a quien no ha visto desde hace mucho tiempo. Los dos se ponen a conversar sobre todos los amigos que tenían en la secundaria y lo que ha sido de sus vidas. Con un(a) compañero/a, representen la conversación entre los dos amigos. Usen los verbos del recuadro y túrnense para hacerse preguntas y responderlas, como se ve en el modelo.

| saber | conocer | reunirse | encontrarse | toparse |
|-------|---------|----------|-------------|---------|

MODELO
A: ¿Qué sabes de la vida de Hannah?

B: No mucho. Me la encontré un día saliendo de un concierto, pero no tuvimos tiempo de hablar. Unos días después supe que se había casado.

---

## Essential Instruction

1. When checking answers to **Actividad 23**, ask students to explain why they chose each verb.

2. For **Actividad 24**, have a few pairs role-play their conversations for the class.

3. Circulate around the room as students complete **Actividad 25**. Provide additional vocabulary as needed.

# ¡Comunicación!

## 25 Una boda fuera de lo normal    Interpersonal Communication    1.1

Imagine que Ud. iba de regreso a casa después de su trabajo cuando se encontró en medio del terrible embotellamiento de tráfico que se muestra en la ilustración. Al principio no sabía qué estaba pasando, pero luego supo que en ese mismo momento estaba teniendo lugar una boda completamente fuera de lo normal.

Ud. decide avisarle a su esposa la razón de su retraso y, al enterarse, ella empieza a hacerle muchas preguntas. Tiene gran curiosidad de saber todos los detalles de una boda tan extravagante. Con un(a) compañero/a representen la conversación entre el esposo y su esposa, con base en los temas que se dan como guía y otros de su propia imaginación. Túrnense para intercambiar información, como se ve en el modelo.

© Quino

MODELO

> **Leo:** Ana, perdona pero voy a llegar tarde a cenar.
>
> **Ana:** ¿Por qué? ¿Qué pasa? ¿Estás bien?
>
> **Leo:** ¿No sabes lo que está pasando en el puro centro de la ciudad?
>
> **Ana:** Supe algo en las noticias sobre una boda que ha paralizado todo el tráfico, pero no sé detalles. Cuéntame más.
>
> **Leo:** ...

- El lugar de la boda
- La iglesia
- Los alrededores
- La ropa del novio
- La ropa de la novia
- El sombrero de la madrina (*godmother*)

- El traje del padrino
- El clima esa mañana
- Los conductores
- El tráfico
- Los transeúntes (*passersby*)
- La actitud de los transeúntes

**Answers**

㉕ *Las conversaciones variarán.*

## Reference Desk

Joaquín Salvador Lavado, better known as Quino, is an Argentine cartoonist. His comic strip *Mafalda*, which ran from 1964 to 1973, is immensely popular in Latin America and parts of Europe.

## Culture

**Practices: Activity**
Invite a Spanish speaker (if possible, from Bolivia) to the class to discuss wedding traditions in their country of origin. Encourage students to ask follow-up questions. For homework, ask them to compare and contrast the wedding customs with ones from their community.

## Differentiated Learning
### Expand
Ask students to look up some *Mafalda* comics online, and bring to class two or three that they think are funny or thought-provoking. Have students get together in small groups to discuss the comic strips.

## Multiple Intelligences
### Verbal-Linguistic
Ask students to create their own story of what is happening in the cartoon on p. 155. Tell students to use the preterite and the imperfect to narrate the story.

### Reference Desk

In **Actividad 27**, point out the term **juego de comedor** and explain that in this context, **juego** means *set*. This word can be used with many home items: **juego de sillas**, **juego de sábanas**, **juego de baño**, etc.

### Connections

**Architecture**

In recent years, a new architectural phenomenon has emerged in El Alto, Bolivia: the "New Andean" style. Ask students to research Freddy Mamani's buildings and describe them. What elements are typically Andean? What features give the designs a futuristic feel? Who is commissioning these homes? Finally, have students give their opinion of this design trend.

## ¡Comunicación!

### 26 ¿En qué se parecen? · Interpersonal Communication · 1.1

Trabajen con un(a) compañero/a e imaginen que la casa que se muestra es la casa donde cada uno pasó su niñez. Observen la fachada y el plano de la casa y digan en qué se parece o se diferencia de la casa donde viven hoy en día. Hagan las comparaciones con base en los puntos que se dan a continuación y túrnense para hacerse preguntas y responderlas como se ve en el modelo.

> **MODELO**
>
> A: ¿Qué tienen en común tu casa de hoy en día y la casa de tu niñez?
>
> B: No se parecen mucho. La casa de mi niñez era mucho más pequeña que la casa donde vivimos ahora.

- Tamaño de la casa y número de plantas
- Cantidad y tamaño de las habitaciones
- Distribución de las habitaciones
- Estilo y arquitectura

### 27 ¿Estás loco? · Interpersonal Communication · 1.1

Imagine que Ud. y su esposo/a viven con sus padres hace tiempo, pero ellos se van a jubilar (*retire*) y se van a ir a vivir lejos. Ud. y su esposo van a mudarse a un nuevo apartamento que es mucho más pequeño y por eso van a tener que vender muchas cosas. El problema es que no pueden ponerse de acuerdo en lo que van a vender. Siempre que su esposo sugiere vender una cosa u otra, Ud. encuentra una razón para no querer venderla. Con un(a) compañero/a, hagan los papeles del esposo y la esposa y representen la situación. Intercambien información sobre las cosas que deben vender y las razones por las cuales quieren o no quieren deshacerse de ellas, como se ve en el modelo.

> **MODELO**
>
> Esposo: **Tenemos que vender el juego de comedor. Es demasiado grande, pero es fino. Lo podremos vender bien.**
>
> Esposa: **¿El comedor? ¿Estás bromeando? En esos muebles está la historia de mi niñez, de todas las veces que nos reuníamos a comer o a celebrar en familia.**
>
> Esposo: **...**

### 28 Querida mamá · Presentational Communication · 1.3

Ahora, escríbale un correo electrónico a su madre y cuéntele en detalle cómo Ud. y su esposo resolvieron el problema de la actividad anterior. ¿Cómo hicieron para ponerse de acuerdo, qué cosas vendieron y a qué precio y qué compraron para el nuevo apartamento con el dinero que reunieron?

### Essential Instruction

1. In **Actividad 26**, encourage students to draw the floor plan of their current home and make a simple drawing of the exterior. Tell students to use the drawings for reference during their conversations.

2. Open **Actividad 27** by talking about a time when you moved from one home to another.

3. Have students peer-edit their e-mails from **Actividad 28**.

4. Survey the class to find out if there is a general consensus on the topics in **Actividades 29** and **30**.

# ¡Comunicación!

## 29 Soltero por gusto propio
**Interpersonal Communication**  1.1

¿Qué piensa Ud. de las personas que llevan una vida de soltero/a por gusto propio, no por falta de pareja? Primero, complete las oraciones según su opinión. Luego, compare sus respuestas y sus razones con las de un(a) compañero/a de clase. ¿Están de acuerdo o en desacuerdo?

1. Ser soltero/a es muy conveniente y significa...
   A. no tener que darle explicaciones a nadie si...
   B. poder dejar... amontonados (*piled up*) sin que esto le moleste a nadie.
   C. poder quedarse todo el día... o toda la noche...
   D. poder comer...
   E. nunca tener que...

2. Pero ser soltero/a tiene sus desventajas y puede significar...
   A. que los fines de semana...
   B. tener que quedarse...
   C. que en la casa...
   D. no tener excusas para...
   E. no tener con quién...

3. ¿Cuáles son tres razones convincentes para quedarse soltero/a?

4. ¿Cuáles son tres razones convincentes para casarse?

## 30 Intercambio de ideas
**Interpersonal/Presentational Communication**  1.1, 3.1

Reúnanse en grupos de tres o cuatro estudiantes para hablar de los siguientes temas. Intercambien información y tomen nota de los puntos en que estén de acuerdo y en desacuerdo. Luego, nombren a un representante para que presente las conclusiones de su grupo al resto de la clase.

1. La edad perfecta para casarse

   Los muchachos de hoy en día no desean casarse muy jóvenes. ¿Cuál es la mejor edad para casarse? ¿Cuáles son algunas ventajas de casarse joven? ¿Es mejor vivir un tiempo con su pareja antes de casarse? ¿Qué ventajas hay en esta convivencia? ¿Qué desventajas?

2. Cambios en la familia

   ¿Creen Uds. que en una familia donde existe unión, afecto y diálogo los problemas se resuelven más rápido? ¿Saben Uds. cómo ha cambiado la familia en los últimos diez o veinte años? ¿Qué razones ha habido para esos cambios? Expliquen su respuesta.

3. El matrimonio como institución

   ¿Piensan Uds. que el matrimonio está pasado de moda? ¿Por qué tantas parejas se divorcian hoy en día? ¿Cómo han cambiado nuestras ideas sobre las obligaciones de los esposos? ¿Cómo ven Uds. el papel de la mujer y del hombre en la familia?

*¿El matrimonio está pasado de moda?*

## RESOURCES

 Flipgrid

**Answers**
29 *Las respuestas variarán.*
30 *Las respuestas variarán.*

### Reference Desk

1. For **Actividad 29**, you may want to introduce some popular sayings related to the topic, e.g., **Mejor solo que mal acompañado.**
2. Have students choose one topic from **Actividad 30** and briefly state their opinions on the topic via a Flipgrid post. Tell students to respond to each other's ideas.

### Culture

**Practices: Information**
Bolivia legalized divorce in 1932; it was the second-to-last Latin American country to do so. There are about 6,000 divorces administered each year. The process can now be carried out entirely online. In 2014, Bolivia updated their **Código de Familia** to include no-fault divorce.

### Expansion

After students complete **Actividad 29**, hold a class debate about staying single vs. getting married.

## Learning Styles
### Auditory/Visual Learners
Read the description of a floor plan of a house or apartment. Tell students to listen to the descriptions and draw what they hear. To check answers, display a floor plan of what the house should look like.

## Multiple Intelligences
### Mathematical-Logical
Encourage students to research marriage, divorce, and family (e.g., average family size) statistics for Bolivia. Have them compare and contrast the numbers with data for the United States. They can chart their findings in a graph or chart to show the class.

**Reference Desk**

1. For the second bullet point on p. 158, emphasize that the speaker's perspective is key.
2. Create a list of key words and phrases that signal use of the preterite and the imperfect. Preterite: **ayer**, **aquel día**, **anoche**, **el lunes pasado**, **anteayer**, **de repente**, **una vez**, **por unos días**, **el otro día**, **hace cinco días**, **la semana pasada**, etc. Imperfect: **siempre**, **todos los días**, **cada mañana**, **muchas veces**, **diariamente**, etc.

**Expansion**

Write a simplified version of a well-known fairy tale. Read the story aloud and have students just listen. Then distribute copies of the fairy tale that have the verbs removed. Working as a class, read through the sentences and have students first determine whether the preterite or imperfect should be used, and write a "P" or an "I" next to each blank. Then have them identify the subject for each verb and conjugate the verbs.

# *Gramática*

## El pretérito vs. el imperfecto 🌸 1.2, 4.1

En general, el pretérito se usa para narrar acciones que se completaron en el pasado, que empezaron y terminaron en un momento específico.

- Narra acciones que ocurrieron en un momento específico.
  Mi primo Eduardo **vino** a cenar anoche.
  Eduardo **llegó** a las seis en punto.

- Narra acciones sucesivas que se consideran terminadas en el pasado.
  Después de cenar, yo **barrí** el suelo, **lavé** y **sequé** los platos, y **pasé** la aspiradora.

El imperfecto se usa para describir acciones que transcurrían (*were taking place*) en el pasado y que pueden haber o no haber terminado.

- Se usa para describir acciones que se repiten de forma habitual en el pasado (*would, used*)
  Eduardo **venía** a visitarnos todas las vacaciones. Siempre **llegaba** el viernes por la noche y **se marchaba** el domingo.

- Describe acciones que ocurren al mismo tiempo en el pasado, sin precisar su duración.
  Cuando él nos **visitaba** siempre **hacíamos** una cena especial.

- Describe escenas y condiciones que ocurren en el pasado sin prestar atención a su duración o resultado.
  Eduardo nos **contaba** de su vida, su trabajo y sus amigos.
  Siempre **salía** con chicas muy bonitas.

- Describe acciones que ocurren en el pasado como parte del escenario (*background*) de otras acciones que ocurren durante ese tiempo. Ese uso es equivalente del inglés *was/ were + -ing form of the verb*.
  Cuando **viajaba** por Sudamérica, **conoció** a Nancy, una chica muy especial.
  Cuando **estaba viajando** por Sudamérica, **conoció** a Nancy, una chica muy especial.

*Ya se imaginaba vestida con su traje de novia.*

- Se usa para describir los estados y características de las personas y las características de las cosas, los hechos o acontecimientos.
  De niña **me ponía** muy feliz cuando mi primo Eduardo nos visitaba. Él **era** muy simpático y **tenía** buen sentido del humor.

- Se usa para decir la hora y la edad en el pasado.
  **Tenía** cinco años cuando nos mudamos a esta ciudad y conocí a mi primo por primera vez.
  **Eran** las ocho cuando Eduardo llegó a cenar anoche y **era** muy tarde cuando se marchó.

**Essential Instruction**

1. Begin this grammar presentation by asking volunteers to recall as many uses of the preterite as they can. Repeat the process for the imperfect.
2. Personalize the **Gramática** by telling a memorable story from your past. Be sure to include all the uses presented on pp. 158–159.
3. Model pronunciation of the phrases in **Para decir más**. Give example sentences.

Answers_____

**31**
1. conociste
2. conocí
3. sabías
4. era
5. supe
6. visité
7. pasó
8. fuiste
9. Pudiste
10. quería
11. quería
12. decía
13. podía
14. supiste

En la misma oración, el imperfecto puede describir el escenario o ambiente en el que otra acción (en el pretérito) parece ser una interrupción.

Después de la cena, **hablábamos** en el salón cuando Eduardo **anunció** que **estaba** comprometido.

Como resultado de la diferencia entre el pretérito y el imperfecto, algunos verbos se traducen al inglés usando palabras diferentes.

| conocer | to know, be acquainted with | **Conocía** a Eduardo desde que era pequeña. |
| | to meet for the first time | Anoche **conocimos** a su novia durante la cena. |
| saber | to know | Yo **sabía** que eran novios desde hacía tiempo. |
| | to find out | Apenas hoy **supimos** que iban a casarse este verano. |
| poder | to be able | Él no **podía** venir a vernos con frecuencia. |
| | to manage to, succeed in | Por fin **pudo** venir con ella por unos días. |
| querer | to want, to try to | **Quería** que la conociéramos personalmente. |
| no querer | not to want, to refuse | Mi tía **estaba** muy disgustada y no **quiso** venir a la cena a conocerla. |

 **1.2, 1.3**

## 31 Antes de que te cases, mira lo que haces

Complete la conversación entre dos amigos, Jorge y Lucas, con la forma del pretérito o del imperfecto que corresponda de acuerdo al contexto.

**Jorge:** Y tú, Lucas, ¿dónde (**1.** *conocer*) a Mariela?

**Lucas:** La (**2.** *conocer*) una noche en una fiesta, el verano pasado.

**Jorge:** Esa noche, ¿tú (**3.** *saber*) que su familia (**4.** *ser*) tan, tan… fuera de lo común?

**Lucas:** ¡Para nada, Jorge! Lo (**5.** *saber*) mucho más tarde, una noche cuando (**6.** *visitar*) su casa.

**Jorge:** Cuéntame. ¿Qué (**7.** *pasar*) esa noche? Recuerdo que tú (**8.** *ir*) a su casa para pedir su mano. ¿(**9.** *poder*) hacerlo?

**Lucas:** ¡Claro que no! Yo (**10.** *querer*) hablar con el padre de Mariela, como había intentado muchas veces antes, pero…

**Jorge:** No entiendo.

**Lucas:** Pues, cada vez que (**11.** *querer*) hablar con su padre, Mariela me (**12.** *decir*) que no (**13.** *poder*) porque….

Ahora, use la imaginación y diga por qué no podía Lucas hablar con su padre.

**Jorge:** ¡No lo puedo creer, Lucas! Menos mal que tú (**14.** *saber*) eso antes, para no casarte con Mariela. Ya sabes el viejo refrán, "Antes de que te cases, mira lo que haces."

### Para decir más

| | |
| --- | --- |
| Fíjense que… | Notice that… |
| ¿Se pueden imaginar que…? | Can you imagine that…? |
| Fue algo espantoso… | It was something frightening… |
| Escuchen lo que les voy a contar… | Listen to what I'm going to tell you… |
| Fue algo muy divertido… | It was something very funny… |
| Cuando tenía… años… | When I was… years old… |
| Les cuento que… | I'm telling you that… |
| No me van a creer, pero… | You are not going to believe me, but… |
| A mí me gustaba… | I liked… |

## Reference Desk

1. Point out that **tener que** also changes meaning: in the preterite, it conveys *had to and did*, whereas in the imperfect it means *had to* or *was supposed to* (unknown outcome).
2. Remind students that **poder** in the imperfect describes a person's capability, regardless of whether he or she tried to do it. The preterite of **poder** describes what someone did (not) manage or succeed to do.

## Culture

**Products: Information**
Other proverbs about marriage:
**Los martes ni te cases, ni te embarques, ni de tu casa te apartes.**

## Learning Styles
### Visual Learners
Bring in several series of photographs. As you display the images, have students use the preterite and the imperfect to narrate what happened in the scenes.

## Special Needs Students
### Dyslexia/AD(H)D
Summarize the grammar presentation by creating a two-column chart on the board. Use one color for the preterite and a contrasting color for the imperfect.

## Answers

**32**
1. era
2. me levantaba
3. corría
4. estaba
5. leían
6. escuchaban
7. hacían
8. ponía
9. preparaba
10. me levanté
11. me sentía
12. Tenía
13. vio
14. preguntó
15. empecé
16. quería
17. entró
18. dijo
19. llovía
20. era

**33** *Las respuestas variarán.*

### Communication

**Presentational: Paired Practice**
Ask pairs of students to write a short story in the present indicative. Then tell them to rewrite the story using past narration. Students can present their narration to the class. Their classmates can check to be sure that the preterite and imperfect are used correctly.

### Expansion

Create two sets of index cards. The first set should have **pretérito** or **imperfecto** written on them. The other set of cards should have the verbs **conocer**, **saber**, **poder**, **querer**, and **no querer**. Put students in groups and have them draw a card from each pile. They must say a sentence with the correct form of the verb to get a point. Encourage students to use a variety of subjects when doing this activity.

---

**32 Una vieja costumbre**  **1.2**

Complete las oraciones con el imperfecto o el pretérito del verbo que está entre paréntesis según corresponda al contexto.

*Siempre disfrutábamos una excursión al campo.*

En mi familia, el sábado (**1.** *ser*) día de excursiones al campo. Todos los fines de semana yo (**2.** *levantarse*) temprano y (**3.** *correr*) a la cocina para desayunar. Allí (**4.** *estar*) mi papá, sentado a la mesa con mis dos hermanos. Ellos (**5.** *leer*) el periódico y (**6.** *escuchar*) las noticias en la radio. Mi mamá y la abuelita (**7.** *hacer*) los preparativos para nuestro día de campo. Mientras mi mamá (**8.** *poner*) frutas en bolsas de plástico, la abuelita (**9.** *preparar*) los tamales y el pollo picante. ¡Qué rico!

Un día yo (**10.** *levantarse*) temprano para ir al campo, como siempre, pero no (**11.** *sentirse*) bien. (**12.** *tener*) náuseas y dolor de cabeza. Cuando mi mamá me (**13.** *ver*) me (**14.** *preguntar*) qué pasaba. Yo (**15.** *empezar*) a llorar porque (**16.** *querer*) ir al campo a pesar de (*in spite of*) estar enfermo. En ese momento mi papá (**17.** *entrar*) al cuarto y (**18.** *decir*) que (**19.** *llover*) muy fuerte y que no (**20.** *ser*) posible ir de excursión.

---

**33 ¿Qué, cuándo y por qué?**  **1.3**

Forme oraciones completas con un elemento de cada columna. Use el pretérito con los verbos de la columna B y el imperfecto con los verbos de la columna C.

MODELO    **Ayer me levanté tarde porque era día de fiesta.**

| A | B | | C |
|---|---|---|---|
| El domingo... | ...ponerme el impermeable... | ...porque... | ...llover. |
| La semana pasada... | ...llamar a mi amigo(a)... | | ...ser mi (su) cumpleaños. |
| | ...levantarme tarde... | | ...no tener ganas de salir. |
| Anoche... | ...recoger la mesa... | | ...ser día de fiesta. |
| El otro día... | ...limpiar la casa... | | ...acabar de almorzar. |
| Ayer... | ...quedarme en casa... | | ...tener una cita a las siete y media. |
| Esta tarde... | ...ir al mercado... | | ...querer ver las noticias. |
| Esta mañana... | ...encender el televisor... | | ...venir mis padres a visitar. |
| El año pasado... | ...lavar la cafetera... | | ...necesitar ir de compras. |
| | ...salir de casa a las siete... | | ...estar sucia. |

**160**   ciento sesenta   |   *Unidad 4*

### Essential Instruction

1. Check answers to **Actividad 32** by having a different volunteer read aloud each sentence.
2. For **Actividad 33**, tell students that the columns can be combined in many different ways, but that they must use the preterite for column B and the imperfect for column C.
3. Have students explain their answers for **Actividad 34**.
4. Brainstorm a list of additional vocabulary for students to use in **Actividad 35**.

## 34 Problemas sin solución  1.2

Complete el párrafo con el pretérito o imperfecto de los verbos entre paréntesis según corresponda de acuerdo al contexto.

Mientras (**1.** *estoy, estaba*) en el aeropuerto, me (**2.** *di, daba*) cuenta de que no (**3.** *tuve, tenía*) el pasaporte. No (**4.** *estuvo, estaba*) en la maleta. Pensé que tal vez (**5.** *estuvo, estaba*) en casa. Pero yo me acuerdo que anoche lo (**6.** *puse, ponía*) en la maleta. Estoy seguro: (**7.** *fue, era*) un robo. Tenía que serlo. También me (**8.** *faltó, faltaba*) el cambio que me (**9.** *dio, daba*) el taxista. (**10.** *pensé, pensaba*) que todavía (**11.** *pude, podía*) arreglar el asunto, pero eso no (**12.** *fui, iba*) a suceder. Me (**13.** *fastidió, fastidiaba*) pensar que no (**14.** *hubo, había*) solución. Pero lo cierto es que debo llamar a la policía y volver a casa. No puedo resolver mi problema. ¡Qué bobada!

## ¡Comunicación!

## 35 Una pequeña equivocación 👥 Interpersonal Communication 🌸 1.1, 1.2

En parejas, miren la ilustración a la derecha y piensen en posibles escenarios que expliquen lo que pasó en el hospital cuando nacieron estos niños. Usen el pretérito y el imperfecto para describir la situación: qué pasó con los bebés, qué hacían las madres cuando eso sucedió, qué estarán pensando ahora que se están enterando de la realidad. Túrnense para dar su opinión, como se ve en el modelo.

MODELO    A: ¿Crees que apenas ahora se enteraron de que se había cometido una gran equivocación?

       B: No sé. Seguramente sospechaban algo, pero solo ahora lo saben con certeza.

—Esta es la señora que ocupaba la cama contigua a la mía en la maternidad.

Answers

**34**
1. estaba
2. di
3. tenía
4. estaba
5. estaba
6. puse
7. fue
8. faltaba
9. dio
10. Pensé
11. podía
12. iba
13. fastidió
14. había

**35** *Las conversaciones variarán.*

### Expansion

Provide students with a large piece of paper to write out their story from **Actividad 35**. Encourage students to share their stories with the class.

### Differentiated Learning
**Accelerate**
Ask students to take one of their sentences from **Actividad 33** and develop it into a short story or dialogue.

### Special Needs Students
**Dyslexia/AD(H)D**
Create a slide show presentation of **Actividad 34**. Work as a class to complete the activity. Circle the correct preterite responses in red and the imperfect responses in blue.

## ¡Comunicación!

### 36 El teléfono roto  Interpersonal Communication  1.1

Divídanse en dos grupos para hacer el siguiente juego y formen dos círculos.

- Para empezar, un(a) estudiante comienza el juego en cada círculo, diciendo que ayer/la noche anterior/la semana pasada vio a uno de sus cantantes favoritos (o a uno de sus amigos) salir de un lugar.

- El/la siguiente estudiante repite lo que recuerda y agrega algo más. Uno a uno, los estudiantes van agrandando la increíble historia hasta completarla.

**MODELO**

**Estudiante 1:** Escuchen lo que les voy a contar. Anoche vi a Ricky Martin salir de un lugar muy extraño.

**Estudiante 2:** Anoche vi a Ricky Martin salir de un lugar muy extraño. Iba de jeans y chaqueta negra.

**Estudiante 3:** Anoche vi a Ricky Martin salir de un lugar muy extraño. Iba de jeans y chaqueta negra y estaba con un hombre que yo no reconocí.

### 37 Anécdotas del pasado  Presentational Communication 1.1

En un grupo de tres o cuatro compañeros(as) de clase, cuenten una historia interesante o divertida de su pasado. Túrnense para contar sus anécdotas y usen las expresiones que se dan como guía.

- Una caída en público
- Un viaje al extranjero
- Una fiesta inolvidable
- Un regalo importante
- Una equivocación graciosa
- Un paseo increíble

*Me encantaba abrir los regalos que me daba mi novio.*

### Essential Instruction

1. Model **Actividad 36** by having volunteers read the sample dialogue aloud. Tell students that they should use well-known celebrities so that everyone in the group can visualize the story. Encourage creativity.

2. Have students make notes for **Actividad 37** before getting together in groups. Encourage students to ask their classmates follow-up questions. Call on a few groups to share their favorite story with the class.

3. Read aloud the e-mail in **Actividad 38** as students follow along. Then have students answer the questions in pairs.

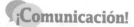

## ¡Comunicación!

### 38 ¡A que no sabes qué pasó!

Interpretive Communication 1.2, 1.3

Lea el correo electrónico que Alicia le escribió a su amiga Cristina, en el que explica por qué tuvo que acortar su viaje por Sudamérica y, luego, conteste las preguntas que siguen.

Nuevo mensaje

De: Alicia
Para: Cristina
Asunto: ¡A que no sabes qué pasó!

Querida Cristina:

Seguramente estás preocupada por mi silencio. Pensé enviarte unas líneas cuando estuve en Perú pero sucedieron muchas cosas.

Después de licenciarme en la Universidad de Salamanca pude realizar uno de mis sueños: hacer un viaje largo por Sudamérica. Esta vez fui con mi amiga Eugenia. Decidimos ir a Brasil, Argentina, Chile, Perú y Bolivia. Todo iba muy bien hasta el día que llegamos a Lima. En lugar de enviarle a mis padres el típico correo electrónico se me ocurrió llamar por teléfono a casa para saber cómo estaba la familia.

Mi sorpresa fue grande al oír que mi hermana Lucía, la menor de todos los hermanos, se había comprometido y se casaba muy pronto. Eugenia tuvo que continuar el viaje sola y a mí no me quedó más remedio[1] que volver a España.

Cuando llegué a casa, todos estaban muy nerviosos y ocupados. Mi madre llevaba un mes haciendo el vestido de novia y los trajes de gala de mis sobrinos. Mi padre intentaba, sin mucho éxito, mantener la calma y vigilar los preparativos de la boda. Mis primos, mis hermanos y yo nos pasamos los días que precedieron a la boda junto a mis tías y a la abuela, que ayudaban a mi madre.

Felizmente, todo salió bien. La boda fue muy bonita y los novios se veían muy contentos. Ya te enviaré algunas fotos.

Escríbeme pronto,
Tu amiga de siempre,
Alicia

[1] I had no choice

1. ¿Por qué seguramente estaba preocupada Cristina, la amiga de Alicia?
2. ¿Qué hizo Alicia después de terminar sus estudios?
3. ¿Por qué no les envió un correo electrónico a sus padres?
4. ¿Por qué tuvo que interrumpir su viaje?
5. ¿Cómo estaba la familia días antes de la boda?
6. ¿Cómo fue la boda de Lucía? ¿Cómo se veían los novios?



### Answers

38

1. Seguramente estaba preocupada por el silencio de Alicia.
2. Hizo un viaje largo por Sudamérica.
3. Se le ocurrió llamar por teléfono a casa para saber cómo estaba la familia.
4. Tuvo que interrumpir su viaje porque su hermana Lucía se casaba muy pronto.
5. La familia estaba muy nerviosa y ocupada.
6. La boda fue muy bonita. Los novios se veían muy contentos.

### Communication

**Interpersonal/Presentational: Cooperative Groups**

Create a list of family- and home-related survey topics, such as **tener hermano/a menor**, **saber cocinar algo**, etc. Tell students to circulate and ask questions (e.g., **¿Tienes un hermano menor?**) until they get someone who answers affirmatively. They should write down the person's name and ask one follow-up question using the preterite and/or imperfect (**¿Cuántos años tenías cuando nació tu hermanito?**). When they are finished, have students share what they learned about their classmates.

### Differentiated Learning

**Accelerate/Expand**

After completing **Actividad 38**, ask students to write two more e-mails: a response from Cristina in which she asks about the wedding, and a detailed reply from Alicia.

### Learning Styles

**Visual Learners**

Encourage these students to create icons for each use of the preterite and imperfect. For example, three check marks can represent a series of completed actions. Have them make a poster of the symbols; tell them to use one color for the preterite and another for the imperfect. Display the poster in the classroom for all students to reference during this unit.

**Answers**

### Antes de leer

*Las respuestas variarán.*

 **39**

1. La necesidad de mejorar la calidad de su trabajo y mejorar los resultados.
2. Ofrece lavado y planchado de ropa, limpieza de casas y departamentos, y cuidado de niños. Cuenta también con un restaurante y un servicio de catering.
3. Como las trabajadoras cobran por hora trabajada, pueden disponer de su tiempo y no necesitan pedirle permiso a nadie para realizar sus actividades.

**40** **CC** *Respuesta posible:*

Porque las trabajadoras de la cooperativa no tienen un empleo fijo. Si se tiene un empleo estable, aunque las condiciones no sean buenas, puede dar miedo tomar la decisión de trabajar por cuenta propia sin saber cómo puede resultar.

---

# *Lectura informativa*

 **1.3, 2.1** Antes de leer

En Bolivia, es usual que las trabajadoras del hogar vivan en la casa en la que trabajan. ¿Qué ventajas y desventajas cree Ud. que pueda tener este sistema?

### Estrategia  **3.1**

**Claves del contexto**

Puede usar las claves del contexto para deducir el significado de palabras desconocidas en un texto. Preste atención a las palabras que rodean la palabra desconocida y a las oraciones que están antes y después de la oración que la contiene.

 **1.2, 2.1, 2.2**

### 39 Comprensión

1. ¿Qué motivó la creación de la cooperativa *Sin patrón ni patrona*?
2. ¿Qué servicios ofrece la cooperativa?
3. ¿Qué ventajas tiene este sistema de trabajo?

 **1.3, 3.2**

### 40 Analice

¿Por qué cree Ud. que a muchas trabajadoras podría resultarles difícil tomar la decisión de sumarse a esta iniciativa?

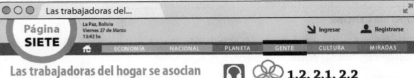

○ ○ ○   Las trabajadoras del...

**Página SIETE** · La Paz, Bolivia · Viernes 27 de Marzo · 13:42 hs · ↘ Ingresar · ▲ Registrarse

ECONOMÍA · NACIONAL · PLANETA · GENTE · CULTURA · MIRADAS

## Las trabajadoras del hogar se asocian y ofrecen servicios domésticos por hora   **1.2, 2.1, 2.2**

La ropa bien planchada luego de un lavado exigente, la casa reluciente y unos niños bien cuidados son los principios de la autodenominada "cooperativa" de trabajadoras del hogar *Sin patrón ni patrona*. Este emprendimiento[1] lo lidera un grupo de trabajadoras que optaron por la oferta de servicios para mejorar la calidad de su trabajo y optimizar los resultados.

Un piso de machimbre[2], limpio y brillante, se deja ver luego de abrir la puerta de una casa antigua típica del paceñísimo[3] barrio de Sopocachi. Se trata de la sede de *Sin patrón ni patrona*. La iniciativa surgió hace un año cuando siete mujeres decidieron dejar de ser trabajadoras del hogar para ofrecer servicios como lavado y planchado de ropa, limpieza de casas y departamentos, además de cuidado de niños y niñas. La principal característica de esta oferta es que se cobra por hora trabajada.

Recientemente inauguraron un restaurante con capacidad para 16 personas, donde ofrecen almuerzos diarios con ensalada bufet. También brindan servicio de *catering* y bocaditos[4] para reuniones sociales. [...]

Desde que emergió esta iniciativa, quienes la lideran buscan que se diferencie de las agencias de empleos, donde se "coloca"[5] a la gente. En *Sin patrón ni patrona*, en cambio, se ofrecen servicios; las trabajadoras disponen de su tiempo y ya no tienen que pedir permiso a nadie para realizar sus actividades, dado que el trabajo que realizan es por horas, a causa de la flexibilidad de los horarios que tienen.

Al subir las cuidadas y limpias gradas[6] de la sede no se encuentra ni rastro de polvo en las barandas[7] de madera. Allá, arriba, están los cuartos principales, donde habitan las socias de la "cooperativa". En la planta baja está el cuarto de Victoria que fue trabajadora del hogar durante 30 años. [...]

Los recursos que ganan con los servicios que ofertan los comparten entre ellas. Victoria explica que todas las socias de este emprendimiento trabajan y que del total del monto que ganan, el 10 % se destina para el mantenimiento y sustento de *Sin patrón ni patrona*. [...]

[1] undertaking   [2] tongue-and-groove boards   [3] very typical of La Paz   [4] snacks   [5] place
[6] steps   [7] handrail

### Essential Instruction

1. Have pairs discuss the **Antes de leer** question. Make a list of students' responses on the board.
2. Go over the **Estrategia**. Give an example of how to use context clues to understand an unknown word.
3. Give students 30 seconds to skim the reading and share what they discovered. Write notes on the board and verify them as you go through the readings as a class.
4. For Common Core practice, have students answer the **Analice** questions. Go over the answers as a class.

**Página SIETE**

Las trabajadoras del...

La Paz, Bolivia
Viernes 27 de Marzo
13:42 hs

↘ Ingresar    👤 Registrarse

🏠 ECONOMÍA    NACIONAL    PLANETA    GENTE    CULTURA    MIRADAS

Son las 10:30. Se oyen pasos apresurados en el primer piso. Alguien baja trotando las gradas. "Ella es Cristina Ibáñez", dice Victoria. [...] "Está yendo a la radio", justifica ante las miradas de este periodista y el fotógrafo, que preguntan "¿A dónde se dirige?". "Tenemos nuestro programa, pues... Hasta para eso nos turnamos, para atender eso por días y horarios", añade.

El espacio radial se denomina *Soy trabajadora del hogar con orgullo y dignidad*, desde donde publicitan su emprendimiento cooperativo. A través de este medio, que transmite de lunes a viernes con una duración de una hora, también difunden[8] historias e investigaciones de su ámbito de trabajo.

[...] También cuentan con una página en Facebook, llamada *Sin patrón ni patrona*, donde los posibles clientes pueden realizar las reservas para el restaurante y consultar sobre las tarifas[9] de sus servicios. [...]

Ellas consideran que es mejor trabajar de esta forma, a estar expuestas a una situación de explotación laboral, cuando desempeñan su labor "cama adentro". "A cualquier hora, los empleadores llegan y te dicen 'sírveme un té o un café', porque vives en la misma casa", comenta Yolanda, luego de explicar que esa fue una de las razones por las cuales se creó la "cooperativa".

*Trabajadoras del hogar*

Esta iniciativa —según ella— es una alternativa para que las trabajadoras del hogar se den cuenta del valor de su trabajo y aprovechen de mejor manera su tiempo. Es para que tengan suficiente margen para realizar otras actividades como dedicarse al estudio. [...]

**Entre micrófonos, plumeros y detergente**

*En Facebook* El 12 de junio *Sin patrón ni patrona* creó su página de Facebook, en la que los potenciales clientes pueden solicitar información sobre tarifas además de reservar almuerzos.

*Programa Soy trabajadora del hogar, con orgullo y dignidad* se llama el programa de radio en el cual se habla sobre la temática[10] relacionada con este sector laboral. Se emite de lunes a viernes por radio Deseo 103.3 FM de 14:00 a 15:00.

*Capacitación in situ* Las capacitaciones[11] en limpieza para nuevas integrantes las realiza la encargada del área, Yolanda Mamani, en los mismos ambientes donde contratan los servicios de *Sin patrón ni patrona*. En las primeras sesiones llevan sus propios implementos de limpieza.

*Niñeras 24 horas* Dentro de la oferta está establecido el servicio de cuidado de niños y niñas las 24 horas del día con previa reserva. [...]

[8] spread    [9] rates    [10] topics    [11] training sessions

🔍 **Búsqueda:** trabajadoras del hogar en bolivia, sin patrón ni patrona, soy trabajadora del hogar con orgullo y dignidad

---

❀ **1.2, 2.1, 2.2**

## 41 Comprensión

1. ¿Qué medios usa la cooperativa para darse a conocer?

2. ¿Qué significa "trabajar cama adentro"?

3. ¿Qué servicio les ofrece *Sin patrón ni patrona* a las nuevas integrantes de la cooperativa?

❀ **1.3, 2.1, 4.2**

## 42 Analice

Emplear a mujeres para que realicen las tareas del hogar es una práctica muy común en Bolivia. ¿Es esta una práctica común en su país o región? ¿Cómo se organizan las familias con las tareas domésticas en el lugar donde vive?

---

Answers _____

**41**

1. Tienen un programa de radio y una página en Facebook.
2. Quiere decir que la persona vive en la misma casa en la que trabaja.
3. Les ofrece capacitación en los mismos ambientes donde se contratan sus servicios.

**42** 🧑‍🤝‍🧑

*Las respuestas variarán.*

### Critical Thinking

**Analyzing**
Ask students to consider how working **cama adentro** can lead to exploitation of domestic workers.

---

## Differentiated Learning
**Heritage Learners**
Ask heritage learners to share what they know about domestic workers in their family's country of origin.

## Multiple Intelligences
**Verbal-Linguistic**
Ask students to imagine that they are a new member of **Sin patrón ni patrona**. Tell them to write a journal entry about their first day at work. They can compare and contrast the first day's events with what their job was like in the past.

**Answers**

43 *Las cartas variarán.*

# Escritura

## Una carta informal  1.3

Al igual que la carta formal, la carta informal es un mensaje que se envía a otra persona. La diferencia principal es que la carta informal está dirigida a un destinatario conocido, con el que se tiene un vínculo de cierta confianza. Por lo tanto, no aparecerán aquí fórmulas de tratamiento ni elementos formales sino un tono más personal y hasta cariñoso y tratamiento de "tú" para el destinatario.

Recuerde que, de todos modos, la carta informal debe incluir:

- El **saludo**, por ejemplo: *Hola, José.*
- El **cuerpo**, donde aparece el motivo por el que escribe.
- La **despedida**, donde se cierra la comunicación, por ejemplo: *Escríbeme pronto.*

### Para escribir más

Otras expresiones de saludo y despedida en una carta informal.

**Querido/a**
**Recordado/a**
**Con cariño**
**Un fuerte abrazo**
**Recuerdos**

### ¡Comunicación!

**43 Querido Ernesto** | Presentational Communication 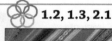 **1.2, 1.3, 2.1**

Escriba una carta informal a un amigo boliviano en el que comente las características típicas relacionadas con la vida en el hogar en Estados Unidos. Compare y contraste esas características con las que son tradicionales en Bolivia. Vuelva a leer los textos de Cultura de la unidad si es necesario y considere las siguientes preguntas como punto de partida:

- ¿Qué papel ocupan las madres y los padres, o las mujeres y los hombres en general, en el hogar de cada país?
- ¿Hay celebraciones típicas en las que se refleje ese papel?
- ¿Qué costumbres cotidianas se practican en el hogar, como el uso del aguayo en Bolivia?
- ¿Qué prácticas y requisitos son tradicionales para los jóvenes que quieren formar un nuevo hogar?

*Una novia boliviana*

# Un relato  1.3

Un relato es un texto narrativo, cuya extensión puede variar, en el que se cuentan o narran una sucesión de hechos. Además de las acciones, que suelen estar encadenadas en una sucesión causal o lógica, en un relato hay uno o más personajes y un conflicto o un desencadenante de la acción. El propósito de un relato puede ser desde entretener al lector hasta enseñarle una lección o moraleja.

Puede tratarse de hechos reales o ficticios, puede estar escrito en prosa o en verso y el punto de vista puede ser de primera persona (el narrador usa el pronombre "yo") o de tercera persona (el narrador no se menciona a sí mismo en el relato).

En resumen, las características del relato son:

• Los hechos pueden ser reales o ficticios, o una mezcla de ambos.

• Suele estar escrito en prosa.

• El punto de vista puede ser de primera persona (el narrador se identifica con un "yo") o de tercera persona.

## ¡Comunicación!

### 44  Soy trabajadora del hogar   Interpretive Communication  1.2, 2.1, 2.2, 3.1, 3.2

Escuche la canción del programa de radio *Soy trabajadora del hogar con orgullo y dignidad* y diga si las siguientes afirmaciones son verdaderas o falsas.

1. Las trabajadoras del hogar se avergüenzan de su oficio y por eso luchan.

2. Una de las formas de maltrato que destacan en la canción son los nombres o apodos con que las patronas se dirigen a las trabajadoras del hogar.

3. Es común que las patronas piensen que las trabajadoras del hogar roban por necesidad.

4. Las trabajadoras del hogar creen que su situación laboral nunca va a cambiar.

5. En Bolivia no hay ninguna ley que ampare y proteja el oficio de trabajadora del hogar.

1.3

### 45  Ya no soy una empleada   Presentational Communication

Vuelva a leer la lectura informativa teniendo en cuenta lo que se dice en la canción. Imagine que Ud. es una trabajadora del hogar boliviana que se ha independizado y escriba un relato en primera persona en el que cuente cómo era su vida antes y cómo es ahora. ¿Cómo han cambiado las cosas? Incluya detalles en el relato, no solo sobre la vida laboral de esta trabajadora del hogar sino también sobre su historia personal. Luego, comparta su relato con el resto de la clase.

*Ya trabajo con dignidad y orgullo.*

**Para escribir más**

Puede incluir algunas de estas expresiones en su relato.

Mi vida dio un vuelco cuando...

Las limitaciones que tenía antes...

Ahora gozo de más libertad para...

---

## Special Needs Students

**Linguistically Challenged**
Review the concepts of narration and the omniscient narrator. Bring in examples of prose written in the first person and the third person, and have students identify the point of view.

**Auditory Impairment**
Allow these students to listen several times to the recording in **Actividad 44**. You may also want to provide them with a script so that they can follow along as they listen.

---

**RESOURCES**

 Activity 44

**Answers**

**44  Script**
Soy trabajadora del hogar
con orgullo y dignidad.
De que me llames "empleada"
estoy cansada ya.
Ahora todo esto va a cambiar.
[bis]
Soy trabajadora del hogar
con orgullo y dignidad.
De tener este oficio nunca me he
sentido avergonzada.
Pero sí estoy cansada de que me
llames "empleada",
de que mi vida, mis pensamientos,
sentimientos, sueños e ilusiones
a usted, señora, no le importe
nada.
Porque, según usted, nada vale más
que su orden y su palabra.
Porque al verme emigrar del
campo a la ciudad usted me quiso
humillar.
"India, campesina" me denomina;
sin embargo, soy yo la que ordena
su vida.
Gracias a mi habilidad de cocinar,
lavar, planchar, su día tranquilo
está.
Muchas veces maltrato, explotación, acusaciones falsas
tuvimos que aguantar creyendo que
nuestra necesidad
a robar nos iba a llevar.
Pero usted equivocada está.
Somos mujeres que luchamos día a
día para llevar un plato de comida
a su hogar, y así el hambre de sus
hijos poder calmar, culminar esas
metas que tenemos trazadas ya.
Y aunque usted las quiera truncar
creyéndome incapaz de estudiar,
de poder ser algo más.
*Continued on p. 177.*

1. F; 2. V;  3. V; 4. F; 5. F
**45**  *Los relatos variarán.*

### Reference Desk

1. Point out that students will use this vocabulary to complete the audio activity on p. 169, as well as to aid in comprehension of the **Lectura literaria** on pp. 174–176.
2. Although its origins are ambiguous, variations of the legend of "**La llorona**" exist throughout Latin America. Some parents tell their children this story to discourage them from going outdoors after dark.

### TPR

Have students work in pairs. They should take turns acting out the vocabulary for their partner to guess. Encourage students to exaggerate their gestures. Invite a few pairs to act out some terms for the class.

# *Vocabulario 3*

## Mejore su comprensión  1.2

Familiarizarse con este vocabulario le ayudará a leer "Las medias rojas" más adelante, y a mejorar su comprensión auditiva.

**a la moda** *exp.* De actualidad.

**acosar** *v.* Perseguir a alguien sin darle descanso.

**agarrar** *v.* Coger o sujetar con la mano.

**amenazador(a)** *adj.* Que supone un peligro.

**amilanarse** *v.* Intimidarse.

**aporrear** *v.* Golpear algo de forma repetida y violenta.

**apretando los dientes** *exp.* Cerrar con fuerza los dientes.

**arrojar** *v.* Lanzar de manera violenta.

**aturdido/a** *adj.* Confuso.

**aturdir** *v.* Confundir.

**bosque** *s.m.* Terreno grande poblado de árboles.

**chillar** *v.* Dar gritos.

**cosecha** *s.f.* El producto de la siembra.

**defenderse** *v.* Protegerse de algún peligro.

**en arriendo** *exp.* Dado en alquiler.

**escudarse** *v.* Defenderse de un peligro o amenaza.

**espanto** *s.m.* Terror, susto.

**esperanza** *s.f.* Confianza de que ocurra lo que se desea.

**fantasma** *s.m.* Ser irreal que vive en la imaginación.

**fiambre** *s.m.* Alimento que se come frío.

**gritar** *v.* Levantar la voz más de lo acostumbrado.

**herir** *v.* Hacer daño físico a una persona.

**insólito/a** *adj.* Poco frecuente, no común.

**ira** *s.f.* Enfado muy fuerte o violento.

**lastimado/a** *adj.* Herido o con daño físico.

**leña** *s.f.* Madera de los árboles que se corta en trozos y se usa para hacer fuego.

**lujo** *s.m.* Riqueza y comodidades que no son necesarias.

**moza** *s.f.* Mujer que presta servicios domésticos.

**pegar** *v.* Dar golpes.

**por falta de pago** *exp.* Por no haber pagado.

**puño** *s.m.* Mano cerrada.

**sano/a** *adj.* Con buena salud.

**sin previo aviso** *exp.* Sin decir anteriormente.

**temor** *s.m.* Sentimiento de miedo y desprotección.

**trémulo/a** *adj.* Temblorosa o que tiembla.

**tuerto/a** *adj.* Que no tiene visión en un ojo.

**zarandear** *v.* Mover de un lado a otro con violencia.

*Los cuentos de fantasmas me dan espanto.*

---

**46 Sinónimos**  1.2

Elija la respuesta correcta.

1. *Espanto* es sinónimo de ____ .
   A. ira      B. trémulo      C. temor

2. *Gritar* es sinónimo de ____ .
   A. amilanarse    B. chillar    C. acosar

3. *Herir* es sinónimo de ____ .
   A. zarandear    B. lastimar    C. amenazar

4. *Aporrear* es sinónimo de ____ .
   A. aturdir    B. chillar    C. pegar

---

### Essential Instruction

1. Model pronunciation of the new vocabulary and have students repeat the words. Clarify any unfamiliar words in the definitions.
2. Have students complete **Actividades 46** and **47** in pairs.
3. Before beginning **Actividad 48**, remind students that they will hear some vocabulary from p. 168 in the story.
4. For **Actividad 48**, have students listen to the story with their eyes closed. Play it a second time, pausing to ask questions. Then play the rest of the audio and have students select their answers.

## 47 Otra versión  1.2

Complete esta versión de "La llorona" con la palabra del recuadro que corresponda según el contexto.

| | | | | | |
|---|---|---|---|---|---|
| espanto | bosque | leña | esperanza | confundida | fantasma |
| gritando | fiambre | insólito | en arriendo | amilanarse | indefensos |

Dice la leyenda que hace mucho, mucho tiempo, en un pueblo del norte de México, siempre al toque de las doce, ocurría este __(1)__ suceso. Se veía la figura de una mujer, toda vestida de blanco, que corría desesperada y __(2)__ por las calles, chillando de dolor y __(3)__ el nombre de sus hijos y, así, tan de repente como aparecía, se desaparecía camino del __(4)__ . Dicen que es el __(5)__ de La llorona, una pobre mujer cuyo esposo murió, dejándola viuda y con tres hijos y sin forma de valerse por sí misma. Cuentan que ni siquiera tenía __(6)__ con que hacer fuego para calentar a sus hijos, ni un trozo de __(7)__ con que alimentarlos y que para completar, por falta de pago, perdió la casa que tenía __(8)__ . Dicen que al verse en la calle sin __(9)__ alguna de salir adelante, agarró a sus hijos y los ahogó en el río. Luego de que realizó con __(10)__ el horror de sus acciones, ella misma, sin temor y sin __(11)__ se arrojó al mismo río donde había acabado con la vida de sus pobres inocentes e __(12)__ hijos.

## 48 Un original día de campo  1.2, 3.1

Escuche el relato "Un original día de campo". Luego, Ud. oirá la primera parte de una oración y tres terminaciones posibles. Seleccione la letra de la respuesta con la terminación más lógica. La oración y las terminaciones se leerán dos veces.

1. **A.** … pasaron el fin de semana en el bosque.
   **B.** … le hicieron una cortesía a la compañía de luz y gas.
   **C.** … tuvieron un original día de campo en su casa.

2. **A.** … les cortó los servicios domésticos sin previo aviso.
   **B.** … les cortó los servicios domésticos por tres meses.
   **C.** … consumió muchísima luz y gas.

3. **A.** … vio con sorpresa que eran las nueve de la noche.
   **B.** … se lavó la cara con agua caliente.
   **C.** … bajó a la cocina a preparar el desayuno, pero no había electricidad.

4. **A.** … le reinstalaron los servicios.
   **B.** … nadie contestó porque era sábado.
   **C.** … alarmó a sus niños.

*Los pequeños se divirtieron enormemente.*

5. **A.** … para ir al bosque a pasar el fin de semana.
   **B.** … para enseñar a los niños a sobrevivir en el bosque.
   **C.** … para jugar a que todos estaban perdidos en el bosque.

6. **A.** … porque los hijos tenían miedo de los fantasmas.
   **B.** … porque no tenía ni electricidad ni agua caliente.
   **C.** … porque la Sra. Morales había pagado sus deudas.

---

**Answers**

**47**
1. insólito
2. confundida
3. gritando
4. bosque
5. fantasma
6. leña
7. fiambre
8. en arriendo
9. esperanza
10. espanto
11. amilanarse
12. indefensos

**48 Script**
El último fin de semana la Sra. Elvira Morales y sus hijos tuvieron un original día de campo en el interior de su casa y según ella fue una cortesía de la compañía de gas y electricidad.
Como la Sra. Morales debía varios meses de consumo de gas y electricidad, la compañía decidió cortarle estos servicios domésticos sin previo aviso.
El día sábado, al despertarse, la Sra. Morales se dio cuenta que hacía mucho tiempo que el sol brillaba. Consultó la hora y vio, con sorpresa, que eran las nueve de la mañana. Bajó a la cocina a preparar el desayuno para sus hijos, pero no había electricidad ni agua caliente. Solo entonces comprendió la terrible realidad. La compañía de gas y electricidad le había cortado los servicios domésticos por falta de pago.
*Continued on p. 179.*

1. La Sra. Elvira Morales y sus hijos…
2. La compañía de luz y gas…
3. Al despertarse la Sra. Morales…
4. Cuando la Sra. Morales trató de comunicarse con la compañía…
5. La Sra. Morales sacó el equipo de campamento del armario…
6. La familia comió fiambres y no se bañó…

1. C; 2. A; 3. C; 4. B; 5. C; 6. B

**169**

---

## Differentiated Learning
### Accelerate/Expand
Have students go online and listen to a song or watch a short film inspired by "**La llorona**." Have them compare and contrast the representation of the legend with what they learned in **Actividad 47**.

## Special Needs Students
### Auditory Impairment
Provide students with the script of the story and the sentence starters in **Actividad 48**.

# Gramática

## Expresiones con *Hace que...* y *Hacía que...*  1.2

**Hace que...** y **Hacía que...** se usan para expresar el tiempo transcurrido (*that has passed*) de una acción, con relación a un momento del presente y del pasado, respectivamente.

- Use **hace** + tiempo + **que** + **presente o presente progresivo** para hablar del tiempo transcurrido de una acción que comenzó en el pasado y todavía continúa en momento presente.

| | |
|---|---|
| ¿Cuánto tiempo **hace que vives** en Estados Unidos? | *How long have you been living in the United States?* |
| **Hace** diez años **que vivo** en Estados Unidos. | *I have been living in the United States for ten years.* |
| **Hace** diez años **que estoy viviendo** en Estados Unidos. | |

- Use **hace** + tiempo + **que** + **pretérito** para hablar del tiempo transcurrido de una acción que comenzó y terminó en el pasado.

| | |
|---|---|
| ¿Cuánto **hace que te mudaste** a esta ciudad? | *How long ago did you move to this city?* |
| **Hace** dos años **que me mudé** a esta ciudad. | *I moved to this city two years ago.* |

- Use **hacía** + tiempo + **que** + **imperfecto** para hablar de la duración de una acción en el pasado.

| | |
|---|---|
| ¿Cuánto **hacía que no ibas** de regreso a tu país? | *How long had it been since you went back to your country?* |
| **Hacía** casi seis años **que no iba** de regreso a mi país. | *I had not been back to my country in almost six years.* |

## ¡Comunicación!

**49** **¿Cuánto hace que...?** 👥 **Interpersonal Communication**  1.1

Con un(a) compañero/a, túrnense para hacerse las siguientes preguntas y responderlas. Usen **hace que** + **presente** como se ve en el modelo.

> **MODELO** no ir a cine
>
> A: **¿Cuánto tiempo hace que no vas al cine?**
> B: **Hace un mes que no voy al cine.**

1. no ir al cine
2. no visitar a tu familia
3. estudiar español
4. conocer a tu mejor amigo/a
5. terminar con tu novio
6. vivir en la casa de tus padres

## ¡Comunicación!

### 50 Con imaginación 👥 Interpersonal Communication ✿ 1.1

Con un(a) compañero/a, túrnense para formular preguntas usando **hace que** + **pretérito** y los temas que se dan a continuación. Usen su imaginación para ampliar sus respuestas como se ve en el modelo.

MODELO  casarse (*tus padres*)

A: ¿Cuánto tiempo hace que se casaron tus padres?

B: Hace veinticinco años que se casaron.

A: Increíble cómo pasa el tiempo, ¿verdad?

B: Sí. Este año van a celebrar sus bodas de plata.

1. casarse (*tus padres*)
2. ir de vacaciones a Bolivia (*Uds.*)
3. aprender a conducir (*tú*)

4. comer en tu restaurante favorito (*tú*)
5. conocer a tu novio/a (*tú*)
6. graduarse de la universidad (*tu hermano/a*)

### 51 Amigas de por vida 👥 Interpersonal Communication ✿ 1.1, 5.2

Imagine que Ud. y su mejor amiga se gradúan de la secundaria este año y se van a ir a estudiar a universidades distintas. El día antes de la partida, se sientan a recordar todo lo que han compartido desde que se conocieron, el primer día de cuarto año de primaria. Represente la situación con un(a) compañero/a y usen el **pretérito**, el **imperfecto** y **hace que** en su conversación, como se ve en el modelo.

MODELO  A: ¿Cuánto tiempo hace que somos amigas?

B: Hace casi ocho años que nos conocimos. ¿Te acuerdas?

A: Como si fuera ayer. Estabas sentada en un rincón del patio del colegio.

B: Sí, hacía un mes que...

*Hacía un mes que llevaba puesto un yeso en el brazo.*

### 52 Ahora le toca a Ud. Presentational Communication ✿ 1.3

A todos nos encanta que nos cuenten historias de suspenso. Ahora le toca a Ud. contar un cuento de suspenso, ya sea inventado o basado en la realidad. Empiece su relato con la fórmula: "**hacía + tiempo + que + verbo en el imperfecto...**" y preste atención al uso del pretérito y el imperfecto. Cuando termine de escribir, lea su relato en voz alta, enfrente de la clase.

MODELO  Hacía una hora que miraba tele en mi cuarto, mientras afuera caía una lluvia torrencial: rayos y relámpagos y, de repente, silencio y oscuridad total. Solo se oía el sonido del viento golpeando las ventanas...

## Differentiated Learning
### Decelerate
Write the basic structures for **hace que** + **presente** and **hace que** + **pretérito** on the board. Under each one, generate simple sentences that use the same verb phrases (e.g., **estudiar español**). Have students circle the sentence that is true for them.

## Multiple Intelligences
### Mathmatical-Logical
Instruct students to make a list of ten important events in their life. They should write the list in a random order. Have students work with a partner to determine the order in which the events occurred.

## Culture

**Products/Practices: Activity**
La Paz sits about 12,000 feet above sea level. Have students research **el soroche**, or altitude sickness. Have them find out what some Bolivians do to combat this ailment.

## ¡Comunicación!

**53  Amor y despedida**  👥  Interpersonal/Presentational Communication  **1.1, 1.3**

¡Anoche fue la noche más triste de su vida! Salió a cenar solo/a a un restaurante y terminó enamorándose y despidiéndose, todo al mismo tiempo. Use el pretérito y el imperfecto para completar las oraciones y, luego, cuéntele la historia a un(a) compañero/a de clase. Al final, intercambien información, turnándose para hacerse preguntas y saber más sobre la historia.

**1.** Anoche yo... y conocí a un(a) muchacho/a muy... en... y...

**2.** Él/Ella era..., tenía... y le gustaba...

**3.** Fuimos a... y allí... Todo...

**4.** Durante toda la noche...

**5.** Al final de la cena él/ella me dijo que... y que...

**6.** La despedida fue muy... Yo... y él/ella...

**54  ¿Hace cuánto que celebraron las bodas de oro?**  👥  Conéctese: las matemáticas

Interpretive/Interpersonal Communication  **1.1, 1.2**

Martín habla de los momentos más importantes de su vida. En grupos de tres estudiantes, lean los datos, calculen las fechas y contesten las preguntas que siguen. ¡A ver cuál es el grupo más rápido de la clase! Al final, comparen sus respuestas con las de otros grupos para ver si acertaron en las fechas.

• Hace cincuenta y cinco años que Antonia y yo somos marido y mujer.

• Hace cuarenta y cinco años que estamos viviendo en la misma casita en Bolivia.

• Hace cincuenta y siete años que Antonia y yo nos conocimos en la clase de ciencias cuando los dos éramos estudiantes de la universidad en La Paz.

• Cuando nos conocimos, hacía tres años que yo estaba estudiando en La Paz y hacía solo un año que Antonia estudiaba allí.

• Hace cincuenta y siete años que terminé mi licenciatura y hace cincuenta y cinco que Antonia terminó la suya. El mismo año en que Antonia terminó, nos casamos.

• Hoy es nuestro aniversario de bodas. Hace cincuenta y cinco años que nos casamos y hace cinco años que celebramos nuestras bodas de oro.

• Durante nuestros dos primeros años de casados, trabajábamos juntos en la biblioteca de la universidad.

• Dos años más tarde cambiamos de trabajo porque estábamos cansados de vivir entre libros.

• Por muchos años ahorramos para poder hacer un viaje largo. Hace un año hicimos nuestro sueño realidad cuando le dimos la vuelta al mundo.

**1.** ¿En qué año comenzó Martín sus estudios universitarios? ¿Y Antonia?

**2.** ¿Cuándo se mudaron a su casita? ¿En qué año?

**3.** ¿En qué año se conocieron Martín y Antonia?

**4.** ¿Cuándo pudieron hacer el viaje de sus sueños? ¿En qué año fue?

**5.** ¿En qué año comenzaron a trabajar en la biblioteca? ¿En qué año terminaron?

**6.** ¿En qué año se casaron?

**7.** ¿En qué año celebraron sus bodas de oro?

## Essential Instruction

**1.** Call on a few volunteers to share their stories from **Actividad 53** with the class. Have the class vote for the saddest one.

**2.** For **Actividad 54**, read through the list of descriptions as a class. Then have students work in groups to figure out the answers. Remind them to use only Spanish when speaking in their groups.

**3.** Give groups plenty of time to write their scripts in **Actividad 55**. Have groups rehearse and act out the situations for the class.

## 55 Minidrama en dos actos  1.1

En grupos de tres personas, representen el siguiente minidrama.

**Lugar:** Una vivienda modesta

**Personajes:**

Paco Juárez, esposo de Josefina;

Josefina Méndez de Juárez, esposa de Paco;

Doña Matilde, madre de Josefina

**Antecedentes:** Paco y Josefina Juárez se casaron hace cinco años. Los primeros años de matrimonio fueron muy felices. Por supuesto que discutían de vez en cuando, como todas las parejas jóvenes, pero muy pronto hacían las paces.

Cuando Josefina dio a luz a su primer bebé, doña Matilde fue para ayudar con la niñita y con los quehaceres de la casa.

Al principio, Paco estaba muy contento con su suegra porque ella se encargaba de todo y ni él ni Josefina tenían que preocuparse de nada. Pero después de seis meses de hacer las cosas como quería la mamá de Josefina, Paco comenzó a sentirse como un extraño en su propia casa, y desde hace dos semanas busca la oportunidad de hablar con su esposa sobre esta situación.

*¿Cómo crees que me siento? Hace más de seis meses que no hago más que escuchar los consejos y reproches de mi madre día tras día.*

### Guía para la escenificación

**Primer acto:**

¿Qué dirá Paco? ¿Cómo reaccionará la esposa? ¿Estará enojada con Paco? ¿O estará de acuerdo con él y tendrá ganas de independizarse de su madre y cuidar personalmente a su niña?

**Segundo acto:**

Paco y Josefina han discutido el asunto y ahora están en presencia de doña Matilde. ¿Qué le dirán? ¿Le agradecerán por todo y la devolverán a su propio hogar donde su esposo la necesita más? ¿Cuál será la reacción de la suegra?

---

## RESOURCES

**WB** Activities 15–17

**LA** Activities 7–8

**Answers**

55 *Los minidramas variarán.*

### Expansion

Ask students: **Si fueras Paco, ¿qué harías en esta situación y cómo te sentirías?**

---

## Special Needs Students

**Social Anxiety**

Some students may find it difficult to speak in front of the class. Give these students the option of a non-speaking or minimal-speaking role in **Actividad 55**, or have the group record their role-play outside of class.

## Multiple Intelligences

**Mathematical-Logical**

Encourage students to make a timeline of the events in **Actividad 54**.

**Answers**

### Antes de leer
*Las respuestas variarán.*

 **56**

1. Una luz de ira cruzó por los ojos pequeños del labrador.
2. Y con el cerrado puño hirió primero la cabeza, luego, el rostro...
3. El cachete más violento cayó sobre un ojo...
4. El padre estaba viejo y cansado de una vida de trabajar en el campo.
5. Aquellos que viajaban debían estar sanos, con capacidad en todos sus sentidos para valerse por sí mismos y con su dentadura completa.

---

### Reference Desk

Emilia Pardo Bazán's works, including "**Las medias rojas**," were heavily influenced by the Naturalist literary movement. Naturalist works describe harsh, authentic life experiences in a detailed and realistic manner, and the characters are often subject to determinism (i.e., they do not have free will).

---

### Critical Thinking

**Comparing**

After completing **Antes de leer**, ask students to consider whether the typical arguments between parents and children are universal, or if there are cultural differences. Then ask them if they think these arguments would have been the same during Emilia Pardo Bazán's era.

---

### Pre-AP

**Course Theme: Las identidades personales y públicas**

---

# *Lectura literaria*

## Las medias rojas  1.2, 2.2, 3.1
### de *Emilia Pardo Bazán*

*Emilia Pardo Bazán*

### Sobre la autora

Emilia Pardo Bazán nació en 1851 en Galicia, España, en el seno de una familia culta que la motivó a leer los clásicos y a escribir. Viajó por Europa y entró en contacto con el movimiento naturalista y las obras de Zolá. La publicación de sus artículos explicando este movimiento literario en *La cuestión palpitante* (1882) causó un escándalo que la llevó a separarse de su marido. A pesar de la fuerte oposición machista de la época, Pardo Bazán fue la primera mujer que tuvo una cátedra de literatura en la Universidad Central de Madrid. Allí murió en 1921.

### Antes de leer  1.3

Este relato describe una escena rural entre un padre y su hija. Las medias rojas son algo más que un objeto de lujo para la hija de un labrador. Representan otro tipo de vida que ella tiene la esperanza de alcanzar y, por eso, se convierten en la causa de la fatal discusión entre ella y su padre. ¿Qué motivos de discusión cree Ud. que son frecuentes entre padres e hijos?

### Estrategia  3.1

**Causa y efecto**

Las relaciones de causa y efecto en una lectura explican qué pasa y por qué. La causa es la razón de lo que pasa y el efecto es el resultado de esa acción. Si la causa y el efecto no están explícitas en la lectura, el lector tiene que inferirlas basándose en su conocimiento previo y su propia experiencia.

### 56 Practique la estrategia 1.2, 1.3, 3.1

A medida que lea, identifique las causas que dieron lugar a los siguientes efectos y escríbalas en sus propias palabras como se muestra a continuación.

| Causa | Efecto |
|---|---|
| Había llovido mucho la semana anterior. | La leña estaba húmeda y ardía mal. |
| 1. | Saltó del banco donde estaba, agarró a su hija por los hombros y la zarandeó brutalmente. |
| 2. | Un diente bonito, juvenil, le quedó en la mano. |
| 3. | El médico dijo que sufrió un desprendimiento de la retina (*detachment of the retina*). |
| 4. | El padre no quería emigrar. |
| 5. | Nunca pudo irse en el barco que la hubiera llevado a nuevos horizontes de holganza (*pleasure*). |

## Essential Instruction

1. As you go through **Sobre la autora**, pause to ask comprehension questions.
2. Read the **Estrategia**. Bring in an example of writing where the cause and effect are explicit, and one example in which they are inferred.
3. Have students complete **Antes de leer** and **Actividad 56** in pairs.
4. Have students look at the image on p. 175. Ask them to guess what the story is about.
5. Before they read, have students scan the story for cognates and words they learned in **Vocabulario 3**.
6. Play the recording, pausing for students to answer the during-reading questions.

# Las medias rojas   1.2, 2.2, 3.1
## de *Emilia Pardo Bazán*

Cuando la rapaza[1] entró, cargada con el <u>haz de leña</u>[2] que acababa de merodear[3] en el monte del señor amo, el tío Clodio no levantó la cabeza[...].

Ildara soltó el peso en tierra y se atusó[4] el cabello, peinado a la moda «de las señoritas» y revuelto por los enganchones de las ramillas que se agarraban a él. Después, con la lentitud de las faenas[5] aldeanas, preparó el fuego, lo prendió, desgarró las berzas[6], las echó en el pote[7] negro, en compañía de unas patatas mal troceadas y de unas judías asaz secas, de la cosecha[8] anterior, sin remojar[9]. Al cabo de estas operaciones, tenía el tío Clodio liado su cigarrillo, y lo chupaba desgarbadamente, haciendo en los carrillos dos hoyos como sumideros, grises, entre el azuloso de la descuidada barba.

Sin duda la leña estaba húmeda de tanto llover la semana entera, y ardía mal, soltando una humareda acre; pero el labriego[10] no reparaba: al humo ¡bah!, estaba él bien hecho desde niño. Como Ildara se inclinase para soplar y activar la llama, observó el viejo cosa más insólita: algo de color vivo, que emergía de las <u>remendadas y encharcadas sayas</u>[11] de la moza... Una pierna robusta, aprisionada en una media roja, de algodón...

—¡Ey! ¡Ildara!

—¡Señor padre!

—¿Qué novidá[12] es esa?

—¿Cuál novidá?

—¿Ahora me gastas medias, como la hirmán[13] del abade[14]?

Incorporóse la muchacha, y la llama, que empezaba a alzarse, dorada, lamedora[15] de la negra panza del pote, alumbró su cara redonda, bonita, de facciones pequeñas, de boca apetecible, de pupilas claras, golosas de vivir.

—Gasto medias, gasto medias —repitió sin amilanarse—. Y si las gasto, <u>no se las debo a ninguén</u>[16].

—Luego nacen los cuartos[17] en el monte —insistió el tío Clodio con amenazadora sorna[18].

—¡No nacen!... Vendí al abade unos huevos, que no dirá menos él... Y con eso merqué[19] las medias.

Una luz de ira cruzó por los ojos pequeños, engarzados en duros párpados, bajo cejas hirsutas, del labrador...

Saltó del banco donde estaba escarrancado, y agarrando a su hija por los hombros, la zarandeó brutalmente, arrojándola contra la pared, mientras barbotaba[20]:

[1] young girl  [2] bundle of firewood  [3] to collect  [4] fixed  [5] chores  [6] cabbages
[7] pot  [8] harvest  [9] without soaking  [10] farmworker  [11] patched and soaked skirts
[12] novelty  [13] sister  [14] priest  [15] licking  [16] I don't owe them to anyone (*nadie*)
[17] the money  [18] malice  [19] to trade, to buy  [20] said through his teeth

## 57 Comprensión  1.2

1. ¿Qué faenas hizo Ildara después de regresar del bosque?

2. ¿Qué notó el viejo cuando Ildara se inclinó a soplar la llama del fuego?

3. ¿Cómo dijo Ildara que consiguió el dinero para comprar las medias rojas y cómo reaccionó su padre cuando se lo dijo?

*Agarró a su hija por los hombros y la arrojó contra la pared.*

## 58 Analice  1.3, 3.1

¿Qué recurso literario usa el autor cuando el tío Clodio dice con sorna: "Luego nacen los cuartos en el monte"? Explique.

**59**

1. Se defendió la cara con las manos.
2. Era importante porque su porvenir dependía de su belleza, ahora que iba a marcharse a otras tierras.
3. El gancho le había dado a Ildara cinco pesos de señal para el viaje. Con ese dinero ella compró las medias.
4. Adivinó que ella tenía planes de marcharse. Le dio furia porque él quedaría solo.
5. No logra marcharse porque su padre la golpea y la deja tuerta.

**60** *Respuestas posibles:*

1. La autora usa la hipérbole que consiste en exagerar algo con la intención de crear en el lector una imagen difícil de olvidar.
2. Si ser joven, sano y capaz eran los requisitos para poder emigrar, se puede asumir que les esperaba una vida de trabajo duro y mal pago. Esa es la vida de los inmigrantes en muchos países.

### Reference Desk

In the second paragraph, point out **Peinóse** and explain that attaching the pronoun to the conjugated verb is an archaic form.

### Critical Thinking

**Analyzing**
Ask students to answer the following questions after reading the story: **¿Quién es el narrador del cuento? ¿Cuál es el tema del cuento? ¿Qué colores se usan en el cuento y qué representan?**

---

## 1.2
### 59 Comprensión

1. ¿Qué hizo Ildara para defenderse?

2. ¿Por qué era importante que Ildara protegiera su belleza?

3. ¿Qué trato había hecho Ildara con el gancho y cómo se relaciona con el incidente de las medias?

4. ¿Qué adivinó el padre que iba a suceder y por qué le dio eso tanta furia?

5. ¿Por qué no logra Ildara realizar el sueño de tener un porvenir distinto del que le espera con su padre?

## 1.3, 3.1
### 60 Analice

1. ¿Qué figura literaria usa la autora cuando dice: "...donde el oro rueda por las calles y no hay sino bajarse para cogerlo...."? Explique.

2. ¿Qué clase de vida se puede deducir que en realidad les esperaba a aquellos que viajaban en el barco si tenían que ser jóvenes, capaces y sanos?

---

—¡Engañosa! ¡Engañosa! ¡Cluecas[21] andan las gallinas que no ponen!

Ildara, apretando los dientes por no gritar de dolor, se defendía la cara con las manos. Era siempre su temor de mociña[22] guapa y requebrada[23], que el padre la mancase[24], como le había sucedido a la Mariola, su prima, señalada por su propia madre en la frente con el aro de la criba[25], que le desgarró los tejidos. Y tanto más defendía su belleza, hoy que se acercaba el momento de fundar en ella un sueño de porvenir[26]. Cumplida la mayor edad, libre de la autoridad paterna, la esperaba el barco, en cuyas entrañas tanto de su parroquia[27] y de las parroquias circunvecinas se habían ido hacia la suerte, hacia lo desconocido de los lejanos países donde el oro rueda por las calles y no hay sino bajarse para cogerlo. El padre no quería emigrar, cansado de una vida de labor, indiferente de la esperanza tardía: pues que se quedase él... Ella iría sin falta; ya estaba de acuerdo con el gancho[28], que le adelantaba los pesos para el viaje, y hasta le había dado cinco de señal[29], de los cuales habían salido las famosas medias... Y el tío Clodio, ladino[30], sagaz, adivinador o sabedor, sin dejar de tener acorralada y acosada[31] a la moza, repetía:

—Ya te cansaste de andar descalza de pie y pierna[32], como las mujeres de bien, ¿eh, condenada? ¿Llevó medias alguna vez tu madre? ¿Peinóse como tú, que siempre estás dale que tienes con el cacho[33] de espejo? Toma, para que te acuerdes...

Y con el cerrado puño hirió primero la cabeza, luego, el rostro, apartando las medrosas[34] manecitas, de forma no alterada aún por el trabajo, con que se escudaba Ildara, trémula. El cachete[35] más violento cayó sobre un ojo, y la rapaza vio como un cielo estrellado[36], miles de puntos brillantes envueltos en una radiación de intensos coloridos sobre un negro terciopeloso[37]. Luego, el labrador aporreó la nariz, los carrillos. Fue un instante de furor, en que sin escrúpulo[38] la hubiese matado, antes que verla marchar, dejándole a él solo, viudo, casi imposibilitado de cultivar la tierra que llevaba en arriendo, que fecundó[39] con sudores tantos años, a la cual profesaba un cariño maquinal, absurdo. Cesó al fin de pegar; Ildara, aturdida de espanto, ya no chillaba siquiera.

Salió fuera, silenciosa, y en el regato[40] próximo se lavó la sangre. Un diente bonito, juvenil, le quedó en la mano. Del ojo lastimado, no veía.

Como que el médico, consultado tarde y de mala gana, según es uso de labriegos, habló de un desprendimiento de la retina, cosa que no entendió la muchacha, pero que consistía... en quedarse tuerta.

Y nunca más el barco la recibió en sus concavidades para llevarla hacia nuevos horizontes de holganza y lujo. Los que allá vayan, han de ir sanos, válidos, y las mujeres, con sus ojos alumbrando y su dentadura completa...

[21] broody     [22] young girl     [23] short     [24] hurt, leaving a permanent mark
[25] the ring of a sieve     [26] future     [27] church parish     [28] middleman
[29] as a downpayment     [30] astute, cunning     [31] cornered and harassed
[32] barefoot and barelegged     [33] a piece     [34] fearful     [35] slap     [36] saw stars
[37] velvety black     [38] without scruples     [39] sowed     [40] puddle

---

### Essential Instruction

1. For Common Core practice, have students answer the **Analice** questions.
2. Point out the **Pregunta clave** on p. 177.
3. Read through the **Proyectos** on pp. 177–178. Allow students to choose project(s) that most appeal to them. Provide detailed rubrics so that students are aware of the expectations for these tasks.

4. Have students peer-edit their essays from **Actividad C**.

# Para concluir

## Proyectos

**Pregunta clave**

¿Cómo se refleja la herencia cultural de un país en las prácticas familiares?

**A** | ¡Manos a la obra!  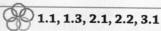 1.1, 1.3, 2.1, 2.2, 3.1

Trabaje con un compañero. Vuelvan a escuchar la canción del programa de radio *Soy trabajadora del hogar con orgullo y dignidad*. Conversen sobre otros aspectos del oficio que no aparecen mencionados en la canción, por ejemplo, la cantidad de horas que trabajan, el sueldo que cobran, los beneficios que reciben o las distintas maneras en que pueden luchar por sus derechos.

Pueden buscar más información en la internet, por ejemplo, leer la Ley 2450 para enterarse de los derechos que tienen las trabajadoras del hogar en Bolivia. Luego, usen esas ideas para escribir una nueva estrofa de cuatro versos para la canción. Canten juntos la nueva estrofa frente al resto de la clase.

**B** | En resumen  1.3, 2.1, 2.2, 3.1

Ud. está de visita en Bolivia y decide enviar un correo electrónico a un amigo para contarle los aspectos que más le han llamado la atención de la vida familiar boliviana. En particular, quiere describir el papel central que desempeñan las mujeres en esa cultura.

Complete el siguiente organizador gráfico y use esos apuntes para escribir su correo electrónico.

| Papel de las mujeres en la cultura boliviana | ¿Por qué es importante? |
|---|---|
| Papel de la madre en el hogar | |
| Papel de la trabajadora del hogar | |
| Papel histórico de las mujeres en las luchas por la independencia | |

**C** | ¡A escribir!  1.3, 2.1, 2.2

Lea el siguiente resumen sobre uno de los ritos de paso que atraviesan los jóvenes aymara a la hora de conformar su propia vida familiar: el matrimonio de prueba. Escriba un breve ensayo de opinión en el que exprese dos ventajas y dos desventajas del matrimonio de prueba.

*En todo el mundo andino, se practica el matrimonio de prueba o noviciado del matrimonio. Se trata de una etapa de pasaje o ritual de paso en el que, antes de casarse formalmente en una ceremonia civil y religiosa, los futuros esposos conviven durante un tiempo (alrededor de uno o dos años). Este período de prueba se toma muy en serio en la cultura aymara. Se espera que los jóvenes se ajusten mutuamente y evalúen si el matrimonio tendrá éxito. En ocasiones, después de algunos meses de ensayo, los jóvenes deciden separarse y quedan en libertad de formar una nueva pareja.*

---

## Answers

**Script** *Continued from p. 167.*
Soy trabajadora del hogar
con orgullo y dignidad.
De que me llames "empleada"
estoy cansada ya.
Ahora todo esto va a cambiar.
Luchando por el respeto y la igualdad desde hace 25 años ya.
Juntas de una sola mano
conformando sindicatos para que
nuestros derechos sean escuchados.
Y así de una vez cambiar todo este
cuento de que tú vales más por el
sueldo que me das.
Pero no quiero olvidar de aquella
gente que no me ha tratado mal y
mi trabajo ha sabido valorar.

**A** *Las estrofas variarán.*

**B** *Los correos electrónicos variarán.*

**C** *Los ensayos variarán.*

### Reference Desk

Point out the **Pregunta clave**. Ask students to think again about the question, this time in relation to their own culture.

---

## Differentiated Learning
### Accelerate/Expand
Ask students to write an alternate ending to the story. Have them share the new endings in groups and discuss how the change affects the message of the story.

## Multiple Intelligences
### Bodily-Kinesthetic/Musical-Rhythmic
Ask students to create dance steps and/or gestures to accompany the song (and additional verse) in **Actividad A**.

### Reference Desk

You could create an Avenue task for students to present their reports from **Actividad D**.

### Culture

**Practices/Products: Activity**
Ask students to research textile weaving in Bolivia. Ask them to find out whether men and/or women are weavers, what materials and dyes they use, and how the art of weaving is passed on through generations. Finally, tell students to find out what projects or organizations have been established to financially assist women weavers. Have students summarize their findings in an Avenue task.

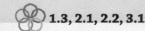 1.3, 2.1, 2.2, 3.1

### D El aguayo, tradición y familia — Conéctese: la publicidad

A lo largo de esta unidad, Ud. ha leído sobre los distintos usos del aguayo, un objeto tradicional de la cultura boliviana, que tiene mucho peso en la vida cotidiana y familiar. Imagine que Ud. es publicista y está preparando un anuncio para el periódico que promocione la compra de aguayos para fomentar la economía de su producción artesanal.

Use las siguientes preguntas como guía de los aspectos que puede mencionar en su anuncio. Busque más información en la internet si la necesita.

*¿Qué características del diseño del aguayo son llamativas? ¿Qué tipos de diseños hay? ¿Qué usos se le da al aguayo? ¿Usos cotidianos? ¿Usos comerciales? ¿Usos rituales? ¿Qué tradiciones aymaras se reflejan en esos usos?*

Prepare su anuncio e incluya fotografías que lo ilustren.

*¡Qué diseños más llamativos!*

### E El matrimonio  Conéctese: las ciencias sociales — 1.1, 1.3, 2.1, 2.2

Con un(a) compañero/a, conversen sobre las características del matrimonio en la comunidad aymara. Luego, comparen y contrasten esos datos con las características del matrimonio en su país. ¿Hay puntos en común? ¿Qué diferencias son las más notables? Completen la tabla.

| El matrimonio | Comunidad aymara | Su comunidad |
|---|---|---|
| ¿Se trata de un evento íntimo, personal, familiar, comunitario? | | |
| ¿Hay un noviazgo previo? ¿Cómo se suelen formar las parejas? | | |
| ¿Se puede saber si el matrimonio tendrá éxito? | | |
| ¿Qué requisitos deben cumplir los futuros esposos? | | |
| ¿Qué papel cumplen los padrinos de boda? | | |
| ¿Cómo son los ritos que rodean a la boda? ¿Hay ceremonias, agasajos, fiestas, regalos? | | |

### Essential Instruction

1. You may want to assign **Actividad D** as a pair or small group activity.
2. After students discuss marriage in **Actividad E**, you could have them compare and contrast marriage using Venn diagrams.
3. For the **Vocabulario de la Unidad 4**, ask students to determine a few categories that could be used to sort the words. Then have students list the words in those categories.

# Vocabulario de la Unidad 4  1.2

a la moda  in style
el/la **abuelo/a**  grandfather/grandmother
el **acero inoxidable**  stainless steel
**agarrar**  to grab
la **alfombra**  rug, carpet
las **almohadas**  pillows
el **almuerzo**  lunch
**amar**  to love
**amenazador(a)**  threatening
**amilanarse**  to be frightened
**aporrear**  to hit
**apretando los dientes**  clenching teeth
el **armario**  closet
**arrojar**  to fling, to hurl
**aturdido/a**  stunned
**aturdir**  to stun
el **baño**  bathroom
la **batidora**  beater
**batir**  to beat
el **bosque**  forest
el **botiquín**  medicine cabinet
la **cafetera**  coffeepot
la **cama**  bed
la **casa**  house
**casado/a**  married
el **celular**  cell (phone)
**chapado/a a la antigua**  old-fashioned
**chillar**  to scream
la **chimenea**  fireplace
la **cocina**  kitchen
**cocinar**  to cook
la **colcha**  bedspread
el **comedor**  dining room
**como si fuera**  as if (he/she) were
la **cómoda**  dresser
**cómodo/a**  comfortable
la **conexión de teléfono**  telephone connection
**conocer**  to know, to meet, to be familiar with
el **contestador automático**  answering machine
la **cosecha**  harvest
**criar**  to raise
el **cuadro**  framed picture
el/la **cuñado/a**  brother-/sister-in-law
**de poco uso**  not used much
**defenderse**  to defend oneself
el **despertador**  alarm clock
**divorciado/a**  divorced

el **dormitorio**  bedroom
los **electrodomésticos**  household appliances
**en arriendo**  in lease
**encargarse de**  to be in charge of
**encender**  to light
**encontrarse**  to meet
el **equipo de sonido**  sound system
la **escoba**  broom
**escudarse**  to shield oneself
el **espanto**  terror, panic, fright
el **espejo**  mirror
la **esperanza**  hope
el/la **esposo/a**  husband/wife
**estar celoso/a**  to be jealous
la **estufa**  stove
el **exprimidor**  juicer
el **fantasma**  ghost
el **fiambre**  cold cuts
el **gabinete**  cabinet
los **gemelos/as**  twins
**gritar**  to cry out
**guardar**  to put away
la **habitación**  room
**herir**  to injure
el/la **hermanastro/a**  stepbrother/stepsister
el/la **hermano/a**  brother/sister
el/la **hijo/a único/a**  only child
**hornear**  to bake
el **horno**  oven
**incorporarse**  to stand up
el **inodoro**  toilet
**insólito/a**  unusual
la **ira**  fury
el **jabón**  soap
la **lámpara**  lamp
**lastimado/a**  injured
el **lavabo**  sink
la **lavadora**  washer
la **lavandería**  laundry
el **lavaplatos**  dishwasher
**lavar**  to wash
la **leña**  firewood
la **licuadora**  blender
**limpiar**  to clean
el **lujo**  luxury
la **madera**  wood
la **madrastra**  stepmother
la **madre**  mother
la **manta**  blanket
el **microondas**  microwave

el **mostrador**  counter
la **nevera**  refrigerator
el/la **nieto/a**  grandson/granddaughter
las **ollas**  pots
el **padre**  father
el **papel higiénico**  toilet paper
**pasar la aspiradora**  to vacuum
la **pasta de dientes**  toothpaste
**pegar**  to hit
**pelear**  to fight
la **plancha**  iron
**planchar**  to iron
los **platos**  dishes
**por falta de pago**  for lack of payment
el/la **primo/a**  cousin
**propio/a**  own
la **puerta**  door
el **puño**  fist
los **quehaceres**  chores
**recoger la mesa**  to clear the table
**regar las plantas**  to water the plants
**repartirse**  to divide up
**reunirse**  to get together
las **sábanas**  sheets
**saber**  to know (information)
la **sala**  living room
**sano/a**  healthy
la **sartén**  frying pan
la **secadora**  dryer
**secar**  to dry
el **sillón**  armchair
**sin previo aviso**  without previous warning
el/la **sobrino/a**  nephew/niece
**soltero/a**  single
los **suegros**  parents-in-law
el **techo**  roof
el **temor**  fear
la **tina**  bathtub
el/la **tío/a**  uncle/aunt
**toparse con**  to meet by accident, to run into
la **torta**  cake
la **tostadora**  toaster
**tostar el pan**  to toast bread
**trémulo/a**  trembling
**tuerto/a**  blind in one eye
los **ventiladores**  house fans
**viudo/a**  widower/widow
**zarandear**  to shake

## RESOURCES

**T**  Unidad 4

Answers

**Script** *Continued from p. 169.*
En vano trató de comunicarse con la compañía para que le reinstalaran los servicios. Era sábado y nadie contestaba el teléfono. Como la Sra. Morales no quería alarmar a sus hijos, convirtió la falta de gas y electricidad en una gran aventura. Sacó el equipo de campamento y la familia pasó el fin de semana en la casa jugando a que todos estaban perdidos en el bosque y que tenían que sobrevivir. Comieron fiambres y fruta, no se bañaron y a la luz de las candelas la madre les contó historias de fantasmas.
Los pequeños se divirtieron enormemente, pero la pobre Sra. Morales sufría pensando en sus deudas.

## Differentiated Learning
### Heritage Learners
Remind heritage learners that regional differences in Spanish language occur not only in lexical terms, but in pronunciation as well. Reassure them that it is normal if their pronunciation differs from yours due to regional differences.

## Multiple Intelligences
### Verbal-Linguistic
Ask students to create crossword puzzles or word searches using the vocabulary from this unit.

1. Mexico is part of North America, but shares a greater cultural relation with its neighbors in Central America.

2. *Mesoamerica* refers to the cultural region composed of present-day Mexico, Guatemala, El Salvador, Belize, western Honduras, Nicaragua, and Costa Rica. The area is populated by an array of indigenous groups, including Maya, Nahua, Olmec, and Chibcha.

3. Explain that **tameme** comes from Nahuatl (*tlamama*, "to carry"), the language of the Aztecs. (You may want to point out that in present-day Mexican Spanish, the term has a negative connotation.) **Tamemes** were widely used in Mesoamerica before the arrival of the Spanish, given that there weren't any beasts of burden in the region to help transport goods, offerings, etc. If possible, display images of **tamemes** (depicted in the **Códice Mendoza**, available online) so that students can see the **mecapal**, or apparatus that they used to carry heavy loads.

### ¿Sabía que...?

Las culturas mesoamericanas en México ya practicaban el comercio en red. La diferencia es que en la actualidad usamos enlaces electrónicos y en aquel entonces se usaban enlaces con "tamemes" (cargadores humanos) y canoas que transportaban mercancías entre los diferentes poblados.

1.2, 2

### Essential Instruction

1. Begin with a discussion of the **Pregunta clave**. Ask students to cite examples of factors that affect a country's economic situation and its people.

2. Point out Mexico on the map. Ask students to share what they know about the country.

3. Draw attention to the culture photo and question. Encourage students to watch for the photo and the answer later in the unit.

4. Point out the QR code, the video question, and the screen shot from "**Entrevista de trabajo**." Encourage students to watch the video as many times as they like.

5. Have students read and ask questions about **Mis metas**.

# Unidad

# 5

# Empleos y finanzas

Escanee el código QR para mirar el video "Entrevista de trabajo".

**Pedro Valentín asiste a una entrevista para un puesto que ofrecen en un centro comercial de la ciudad. El entrevistador le pide que se describa a sí mismo y le cuente por qué quiere ese trabajo. ¿Qué contesta Pedro? Explique en detalle su respuesta.**

*Pregunta clave*

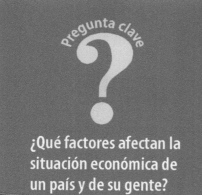

?

**¿Qué factores afectan la situación económica de un país y de su gente?**

¿Cómo se denominó la crisis económica que ocurrió en México en 1994 y cuáles fueron sus repercusiones?

México

## Mis metas

**En esta unidad:**

▶ Usaré expresiones relacionadas con la búsqueda de empleo y las finanzas personales.

▶ Repasaré las formas y usos del pretérito perfecto y el pluscuamperfecto.

▶ Leeré sobre la economía de México a nivel nacional y personal.

▶ Distinguiré el significado de palabras y frases según el contexto.

▶ Usaré correctamente los pronombres de complemento directo, indirecto y de preposición.

▶ Leeré sobre la situación actual del empleo en México.

▶ Crearé una hoja de vida para solicitar empleo.

▶ Escucharé un segmento donde dan consejos para una entrevista laboral y haré un resumen de este.

▶ Desarrollaré nuevas destrezas de vocabulario.

▶ Usaré el verbo **gustar** y verbos similares.

▶ Distinguiré los usos especiales del pronombre **se**.

▶ Repasaré el uso de las preposiciones **a** y **con**.

▶ Leeré el poema "Autorretrato" de la mexicana Rosario Castellanos.

ciento ochenta y uno **181**

**Answers**

**Video question** *Respuesta posible:* Pedro dice que es alegre, simpático y responsable y que siempre se implica en todo lo que hace. Explica que quiere conseguir ese trabajo porque quiere trabajar para no depender de sus padres y ganarse la vida por sí mismo. Además, le gustaría poder colaborar con la economía familiar.

**Culture question**
Se le denominó el "efecto Tequila". Las repercusiones sociales de esta crisis fueron incalculables: muchas familias mexicanas lo perdieron todo y el 50 % de la población cayó en pobreza. Llegó a plantearse que era el fin de la clase media en México.

### Reference Desk

1. Ask students to read the **Pregunta clave** and speculate about the theme of the unit and the vocabulary and culture they might encounter.
2. Draw attention to the screen shot from "**Entrevista de trabajo**." Ask students to guess how Pedro is feeling and to predict whether the interview will go well.
3. Remind students with eBook access they can click on the red country on p. 181 to link directly to Wikipedia.

## Differentiated Learning
### Heritage Learners
Ask students whose families originate from Mexico to share what they know about the country's culture. Have the class contribute what they know and ask follow-up questions. Be sure to create a classroom atmosphere that discourages stereotypes and misinformation when discussing cultural heritage.

## Multiple Intelligences
### Verbal-Linguistic
Review and preview the unit vocabulary and grammar by asking questions such as: **¿Tienes cuenta de ahorros? ¿cuenta corriente? ¿Trabajas? ¿Cuántos trabajos has tenido? ¿Has tenido entrevistas de trabajo? ¿Cómo te preparas para ellas? ¿Qué información incluyes en tu CV?**

# Vocabulario 1

## Aduéñate de tus finanzas  1.2

https://ubicaempleos.com

EMPLEOS | CURRÍCULUM VITAE | EMPRESAS | ENTREVISTAS | INICIA SESIÓN

¿Está cansado de andar sin chamba, de solicitar empleo y de tratar en vano de que le den una entrevista? Si es así, no se preocupe más. ¡Deje su búsqueda en nuestras manos! Somos la solución a sus necesidades de empleo: UbicaEmpleos.com.

NUEVO

¿Quiere ser su propio jefe, trabajar horas flexibles, ganar un buen sueldo y jubilarse joven? Si eso es lo que busca, únase a nuestro grupo de agentes de bienes raíces.
¡Lo invitamos a hacerse socio de nuestra empresa!

Se ofrece puesto de jornada completa como gerente de ventas de prestigiosa empresa internacional. Se requiere estar capacitado en cuestiones de finanzas (cambios de moneda, tasas de interés y préstamos). También se requiere tener experiencia tratando con ejecutivos, compradores y otros hombres y mujeres de negocios en el extranjero.

NUEVO

Se busca persona capacitada para desempeñar el puesto de jefe de personal en gran empresa nacional. Se necesita alguien que sepa de recursos humanos y pueda supervisar a los empleados sin contratiempos. Se ofrecen beneficios y posibilidades de ascenso.

### Essential Instruction

1. Begin by having students look at the photos and describe what they see.
2. Before playing the audio, have students look at the vocabulary on pp. 182–183 and pick out cognates. They can work in pairs and practice pronouncing these words.
3. Play the audio for **Aduéñate de tus finanzas**. Pause to ask comprehension questions.
4. Personalize the vocabulary presentation by asking students if they work part-time, and what knowledge or experience they have with personal finances.

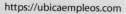

https://ubicaempleos.com

**EMPLEOS** | **CURRÍCULUM VITAE** | **EMPRESAS** | **ENTREVISTAS** | **INICIA SESIÓN**

NUEVO

Estamos contratando a cajeros que tengan experiencia atendiendo a los clientes y se lleven bien con los otros trabajadores. Postulantes, favor de llenar la solicitud de empleo y enviarla a la sucursal principal del Banco de la República: Avenida Juárez #124, Ciudad de México. Se entrevistará a los candidatos del 15 al 20 este mes.

**En una entrevista**

¿Alguna vez la han despedido de un puesto o le han pedido que renuncie voluntariamente?

¿Solo ofrecen puestos de media jornada en esta fábrica? Yo necesito un puesto de jornada completa.

## Para conversar

**P**ara hablar de las finanzas personales y cómo manejarlas:

Debes abrir una cuenta corriente y una cuenta de ahorros tan pronto tengas un empleo.

Debes revisar el saldo de tu cuenta antes de girar un cheque o usar tu tarjeta de débito. Así evitas sobregirarte.

Acuérdate de endosar cualquier cheque que vayas a cobrar o a ingresar, ya sea en el banco o en el cajero automático.

Es importante ahorrar un poco cada mes y nunca gastar más de lo que se gana.

También es buena idea invertir algo de dinero, por ejemplo en acciones de una compañía. Pero primero se debe averiguar cuáles tienden a producir ganancias en lugar de pérdidas.

Es mejor pagar al contado (en efectivo) que usar tarjetas de crédito o pedir préstamos.

Es importante regatear con los vendedores, especialmente cuando se compra algo costoso. Si no te rebajan el precio en ese almacén, en otro te lo darán con descuento.

Si compras mercancía a plazos, debes averiguar el total que vas a deber al banco, el porcentaje de interés (tanto por ciento) que debes pagar y el número de cuotas mensuales y su fecha de vencimiento.

No te olvides de abrir toda tu correspondencia a diario. Es mejor resolver cualquier problema a tiempo que tener que irritarse más tarde.

Acuérdate, tú eres la persona encargada de tus propias finanzas, ¡nadie más!

*Unidad 5* | ciento ochenta y tres **183**

**Answers**

**1 Script**
1. Una joven recién graduada viene a las oficinas para solicitar empleo.
2. Este señor también es miembro del club.
3. La semana pasada el señor Camacho se jubiló después de cuarenta años de trabajo.
4. Roberto Vega decidió no rebajar el precio de la mercancía.
5. Susana Martínez tiene la responsabilidad de contratar a los empleados.
6. Esa señora puede regatear el precio con cualquier vendedor.
7. Marcos quiere cambiar su horario de media jornada a jornada completa.

1. la postulante
2. el socio
3. el empleado
4. el vendedor
5. la encargada
6. la compradora
7. el trabajador

**2**
1. puesto
2. regatear
3. empresa
4. invertir
5. interés
6. precio
7. saldo
8. cheques

**3**
1. D; 2. A; 3. E; 4. C; 5. B

## Expansion

Ask students to explain how each group of words is related in **Actividad 2**.

---

**1 ¿Quién?**  1.2

Escuche e indique la persona que corresponde a cada descripción.

1. la postulante / la encargada
2. el comprador / el socio
3. el postulante / el empleado
4. el vendedor / el comprador
5. la encargada / la cajera
6. la socia / la compradora
7. el ejecutivo / el trabajador

**2 Series de palabras**  1.2

Complete las siguientes series de palabras con la palabra del recuadro que mejor corresponda, como se ve en el modelo.

| empresa | precio | invertir | regatear | saldo |
|---------|--------|----------|----------|-------|
| puesto | cheques | | interés | gerente |

MODELO  jefe, ejecutivo, ____
**jefe, ejecutivo, gerente**

1. chamba, empleo, ____
2. vendedor, comprador, ____
3. acciones, socio, ____
4. pérdidas, ganancias, ____
5. a plazos, préstamos, ____
6. rebajar, mercancía, ____
7. sobregirarse, cuenta corriente, ____
8. tarjeta de crédito, tarjeta de débito, ____

**3 Consejos**  1.2

Complete cada oración de la primera columna con la información que le corresponda de la segunda, según el contexto.

**I**
1. No puedes cobrar este cheque porque...
2. Es mejor cerrar tu cuenta de ahorros porque...
3. Debes ingresar tu cheque cuanto antes porque...
4. No es necesario llevar mucho dinero en efectivo porque...
5. Piensa bien antes de pedir un préstamo porque...

**II**
A. solo pagan un interés del dos por ciento.
B. la tasa de interés es muy alta.
C. puedes usar el cajero automático.
D. no lo has endosado.
E. estás sobregirado.

## Essential Instruction

1. Have students read through the items in **Actividad 1**; explain that they have to choose the person that corresponds to the description they hear.
2. Have students check their answers to **Actividades 2** and **3** in pairs.
3. If students finish **Actividad 4** early, encourage them to write the first few lines of the recommendation letter.
4. Before students begin **Actividad 5**, review the reading strategy of scanning for key information. Tell them that they do not need to read nor understand every word on the deposit slip in order to answer the questions.

## 4 Una recomendación  1.2

La jefa de personal de un banco en Ciudad de México piensa renunciar a su puesto y le pide a uno de los gerentes que le dé una carta de recomendación. Complete esta parte de la recomendación con la forma correcta de los verbos y expresiones del recuadro, de acuerdo al contexto.

| irritarse | atender | preocuparse por | resolver | llevarse bien | ponerse furiosa |
|---|---|---|---|---|---|

...y la señora de la Cruz __(1)__ a todos los clientes con la mayor cortesía. Es eficiente y está muy capacitada para __(2)__ cualquier problema que pueda surgir. En cuanto al personal, la señora de la Cruz __(3)__ con todos en el departamento; __(4)__ nuestro bienestar, nunca __(5)__ por los contratiempos inevitables que ocurren con frecuencia en un banco y solo una vez la he visto __(6)__ con un empleado, y este bien se lo merecía (*deserved it*). Para mí, ha sido un placer trabajar con la señora Patricia de la Cruz y, por tanto, la recomiendo sin reservaciones.

## ¡Comunicación!

## 5 Comprobante de depósito   Interpretive Communication  1.2

Observe este comprobante de depósito y conteste las preguntas que siguen.

1. ¿En qué banco se hizo este depósito?
2. ¿Quién hizo el depósito?
3. ¿Cuál es el número de la cuenta?
4. ¿Qué clase de cuenta es?
5. ¿Cuántos cheques se incluyen en el depósito y por qué cantidades?
6. ¿Cuánto dinero se depositó en efectivo?
7. ¿Cuánto dinero se depositó en total?

**6**

1. empresas
2. sucursales
3. sueldos
4. venden
5. emplean
6. capacitados
7. ganancias
8. contratar
9. fábricas
10. ganan
11. ascenso
12. encargados
13. despedir

**7**

1. depósito
2. ahorro
3. compra/comprador
4. empleado/empleo
5. encargado
6. fábrica
7. ingreso
8. pérdida
9. solicitud
10. venta/vendedor
*Las oraciones variarán.*

## Reference Desk

The factories mentioned in **Actividad 6** are **maquiladoras**, which were first opened in 1965 as a way to address unemployment near the border. Following NAFTA in 1994, the number of **maquilas** increased greatly. It is unknown exactly how many **maquilas** operate in Mexico today—some think around 7,000—but they constitute the second-largest industry in Mexico, after petroleum.

---

**6** **Situaciones difíciles**  1.2

Complete esta descripción sobre el mundo de los negocios en México con las palabras del recuadro que correspondan según el contexto. Asegúrese de cambiar las formas de los verbos, sustantivos y adjetivos según sea necesario.

| contratar | ascenso | encargado | sucursal | despedir |
|---|---|---|---|---|
| emplear | fábrica | sueldo | ganar | empresa |
| | ganancias | capacitado | vender | |

Las principales ciudades mexicanas cuentan con grandes __(1)__ que tienen __(2)__ en muchas partes del país. Los empresarios ganan __(3)__ impresionantes y muchos se han hecho riquísimos. Sin embargo, la mayoría de las compañías mexicanas están en manos de pequeños y medianos empresarios, cuya situación resulta difícil. Ellos __(4)__ suficientes productos para sobrevivir y trabajan solos o __(5)__ a familiares. Hay expertos en mercadeo que están __(6)__ para sacar adelante estas pequeñas compañías, pero las __(7)__ reducidas de los dueños no les permiten __(8)__ a estos especialistas.

Una situación aún más deprimente existe a lo largo de la frontera entre México y Estados Unidos. Allí han surgido una larga cadena de compañías extranjeras en cuyas __(9)__ trabajan miles de mexicanos que han venido para el norte en busca de empleo. La vida para estos mexicanos pobres suele ser muy difícil. __(10)__ un sueldo miserable, no existen posibilidades de __(11)__ para ellos y los __(12)__ están obligados a __(13)__ a las mujeres embarazadas. ¡Es un callejón de miseria sin salida!

**7** **Formación de palabras**  1.3

Forme sustantivos a partir de los verbos que se dan a continuación y luego úselos en oraciones como se ve en el modelo.

MODELO   ganar > **ganancias**
   **Las acciones de la empresa subieron y los empleados obtuvieron grandes ganancias.**

1. depositar ____
2. ahorrar ____
3. comprar ____
4. emplear ____
5. encargarse ____

6. fabricar ____
7. ingresar ____
8. perder ____
9. solicitar ____
10. vender ____

## Essential Instruction

1. For **Actividad 6**, emphasize that students will need to make the necessary changes to the words in the word bank.
2. Have pairs compare the sentences they wrote for **Actividad 7**.
3. Choose a few questions from **Actividad 8** for class discussion.
4. For **Actividad 9**, have students jot down phrases and ideas for their roles. Then have them role-play the situation. Encourage spontaneity.

# ¡Comunicación!

## 8 UbicaEmpleos.com  Interpretive/Interpersonal Communication ✿ 1.2, 1.3

Vuelva a leer los anuncios de empleo en UbicaEmpleos.com en *Vocabulario 1* y luego túrnese con un(a) compañero/a para contestar las preguntas que siguen. Usen su conocimiento y su imaginación para ampliar las respuestas, según sea el caso.

*Lo mejor de UbicaEmpleos.com es que puedo buscar empleo sin tener que ir de empresa en empresa.*

1. ¿Por qué cree Ud. que es conveniente usar una agencia de empleo en línea?

2. ¿Qué anuncio ofrece la posibilidad de ganar un buen sueldo y un horario flexible?

3. ¿Qué requisitos se necesitan para solicitar el puesto de gerente de ventas?

4. ¿Por qué cree que la persona que solicite el puesto de jefe de personal debe estar familiarizada con recursos humanos?

5. ¿Por qué es importante conseguir un puesto donde ofrezcan posibilidades de ascenso?

6. ¿Qué clase de beneficios cree Ud. que quiera alguien que busca trabajo?

7. ¿Qué clase de experiencia deben tener las personas interesadas en solicitar el puesto de cajero en un banco?

8. ¿Qué diferencia cree Ud. que hay entre renunciar voluntariamente a un puesto y ser despedido de un puesto? Explique su respuesta.

## 9 Aduéñate de tus finanzas  Interpersonal Communication ✿ 1.1

Imagine que Ud. acaba de mudarse a vivir por su cuenta. Ahora tiene un trabajo, independencia y, por supuesto, responsabilidades. Sin embargo, su madre se preocupa mucho y todas las noches lo/la llama para saber cómo está manejando sus finanzas. Represente la situación con un(a) compañero/a y túrnense para hacerse preguntas y responderlas con base en los temas que se dan como guía y en su propia experiencia e imaginación.

**MODELO**

| | |
|---|---|
| **Madre:** | ¿Ya abriste la cuenta corriente, como te dije? |
| **Hijo/a:** | No, mamá, todavía no. |
| **Madre:** | ¿Por qué? No entiendo. ¿No sabes que es algo importante? |
| **Hijo/a:** | La voy a abrir pronto, mamá. Tan pronto me paguen. ¡No te preocupes! |

• Estado de su cuenta

• Tarjeta de crédito

• Cuenta de ahorros

• Cajeros automáticos

• Problemas con sobregiros

• Compras en efectivo y a plazos

## RESOURCES

 Avenue

**Answers**

**8** *Respuestas posibles:*

1. La agencia de empleo hace la búsqueda de trabajos, en lugar del cliente.

2. El empleo de agente de bienes raíces.

3. Se requiere estar capacitado en cuestiones de finanzas y tener experiencia en tratar con ejecutivos, compradores y otros hombres y mujeres de negocios en el extranjero.

4. Porque es la persona a cargo de supervisar a los empleados y debe tener conocimiento de las reglas para tratar a los empleados, sus derechos y obligaciones.

5. Porque un ascenso representa progreso profesional y, generalmente, un aumento de sueldo.

6. Generalmente se espera recibir seguro médico y alguna contribución hacia la jubilación.

7. Deben tener experiencia profesional en atender a los clientes.

8. *Las respuestas variarán.*

**9** *Las conversaciones variarán.*

## Critical Thinking

**Analyzing and Evaluating**
In pairs, have students research a job search site in Mexico and in the United States. They should compare the user experience for each and evaluate which they think is easier to navigate.

## Differentiated Learning

### Expand
After completing **Actividad 8**, ask students to debate whether technology is a great help or enormous hindrance to today's office workers.

### Accelerate/Expand
Ask students to go online to watch *Maquilapolis: City of Factories* (2006) or *Maquila: A Tale of Two Mexicos* (1999). Tell them to take notes on the devastating effects of these factories, in terms of labor exploitation (especially of women) and environmental damage. Finally, ask students to write a review of the film and submit it via Avenue.

**187**

# *Gramática*

## El pretérito perfecto  1.2

El pretérito perfecto se forma con el presente del verbo **haber** y el participio pasado del verbo principal. El participio pasado de los verbos regulares se forma reemplazando la terminación **-ar** del infinitivo por **-ado** y las terminaciones **-er**, **-ir** por **-ido**.

| Formación del pretérito perfecto | | |
|---|---|---|
| **Infinitivo** | **Presente del verbo *haber*** | **Participio pasado** |
| ahorr**ar** vend**er** consegu**ir** | he has ha hemos habéis han | ahorr**ado** vend**ido** consegu**ido**[1] |

**Un poco más**

En ciertas regiones de España y en algunos países hispanoamericanos, se usa el pretérito perfecto en lugar del pretérito para expresar una acción terminada en un pasado no muy reciente.

Jaime **ha pedido** (pidió) un préstamo.

*Jaime **has requested** (requested) a loan.*

- El pretérito perfecto se usa para referirse a una acción que ha o no ha terminado en el pasado inmediato o a una acción pasada que continúa o puede repetirse en el presente.

  —¿Ya conseguiste empleo?

  —No, todavía no **he conseguido**. **He enviado** cantidades de solicitudes en los últimos meses y nadie me **ha respondido**.

- Algunos participios pasados son irregulares.[2]

| Participios pasados irregulares | | |
|---|---|---|
| **Infinitivo** | **Terminación irregular** | **Participio pasado** |
| **abrir** **cubrir** **describir** **escribir** **morir** **poner** **resolver** **romper** **ver** **volver** | -to | abierto cubierto descrito escrito muerto puesto resuelto roto visto vuelto |
| **decir** **hacer** **satisfacer** | -cho | dicho hecho satisfecho |
| **imprimir** | -so | impreso |

[1] Los verbos con cambios en el radical no tienen cambios en la forma del participio pasado: **encontrar → encontrado, conseguir → conseguido**.

[2] Las formas compuestas de estos verbos llevan la misma irregularidad en el participio pasado: **suponer → supuesto, devolver → devuelto, descubrir → descubierto**.

## 10 Todo en un día  1.2

Hoy ha sido un día difícil en el Departamento de Recursos Humanos de una empresa. Use el pretérito perfecto de los verbos entre paréntesis y, luego, forme oraciones lógicas con la información de las dos columnas.

**I**

1. El jefe del departamento (*ponerse furioso*)
2. Silvia, muy ofendida, (*renunciar*)
3. Otra secretaria, Ana, (*jubilarse*)
4. Dos candidatos capacitados (*solicitar*)
5. El jefe (*entrevistar*)
6. Pero no (*contratar*)

**II**

A. a su trabajo.
B. los puestos de Silvia y Ana.
C. a ninguno de ellos.
D. después de 30 años de servicio.
E. con su secretaria, Silvia.
F. a los dos candidatos para el puesto.

## 11 ¿Qué ha sido de su vida?  1.2

Imagine que Ud. se encuentra con Alex, un compañero de la universidad que no ve hace tiempo, y se ponen a charlar sobre la vida de sus otros compañeros. Complete sus conversaciones con el pretérito perfecto de los verbos entre paréntesis.

**Ud.:** ¿Tú (*1. ver*) a Felipe últimamente?

**Alex:** Sí, ¡cómo (*2. cambiar*)! Parece más viejo. ¿Qué le (*3. pasar*)?

**Ud.:** Alguien me (*4. decir*) que le va mal con su negocio.

**Alex:** ¡Qué lástima! Pero hablando de algo más alegre, ¿te enteraste de que Lucía y Jaime (*5. casarse*)?

**Ud.:** ¡No me digas! Y ¿qué tal les va?

**Alex:** ¡Estupendamente! Ellos (*6. poner*) un negocio de comida italiana y les está yendo muy bien.

**Ud.:** ¡Cuánto me alegro!

**Alex:** Bueno, ¿y tú? ¿Cómo (*7. estar*)? ¿Cómo va tu empresa?

**Ud.:** Bastante bien. La empresa (*8. crecer*) enormemente y nosotros (*9. tener*) que emplear a mucho personal nuevo.

*Hemos entrevistado a muchos jóvenes de talento.*

**Learning Styles**
**Auditory Learners**
Play the role of newscaster, and read aloud a series of descriptions about events that just happened (**El candidato ha dado un discurso en que…**). Have students identify the event (**elecciones presidenciales**). You may want to list the events on the board for reference.

**Multiple Intelligences**
**Musical-Rhythmic**
Play a portion of the song "**Muerte en Hawaii**" by **Calle 13**. Have students identify the uses of the present perfect. Ask them to create their own hyperbolic raps/rhymes about things they have done.

189

**Answers**

1. había aceptado
2. había solicitado
3. había endosado
4. habían sobregirado
5. había dado
6. habían perdido
7. habían ahorrado

# Gramática

## El pluscuamperfecto  1.2

El pluscuamperfecto se forma con el imperfecto del verbo **haber** y el participio pasado del verbo principal.

### Formación del pluscuamperfecto

| Infinitivo | Imperfecto del verbo *haber* | Participio pasado |
|------------|------------------------------|-------------------|
| pag**ar** ofrec**er** invert**ir** | había | pag**ado** ofrec**ido** invert**ido** |
| | habías | |
| | había | |
| | habíamos | |
| | habíais | |
| | habían | |

- El pluscuamperfecto se usa para referirse a una acción que ocurrió antes de otra acción en el pasado.

  Cuando mi jefa **llegó** a la oficina ayer, yo ya **había atendido** a dos clientes, **había escrito** tres cartas y **había resuelto** muchos problemas.
  *When my boss **arrived** at the office yesterday, I **had** already **waited** on two clients, I **had written** three letters, and I **had resolved** many problems.*

  Tuvimos que cerrar la empresa y **perdimos** todo el dinero que **habíamos invertido**.
  *We had to go out of business and **lost** all the money we **had invested**.*

---

### 12 ¿Qué había pasado antes?  1.2

Complete las oraciones con el pluscuamperfecto del verbo entre paréntesis para explicar qué había pasado antes en las siguientes situaciones.

1. Lo llamaron para ofrecerle una entrevista, pero él ya (*aceptar*) otro empleo.

2. Le ofrecieron un puesto de jornada completa, pero ella (*solicitar*) uno de media jornada.

3. No pudo depositar el cheque de su esposo porque él no lo (*endosar*).

4. El banco les cobró un recargo (*fee*) porque ellos se (*sobregirar*) en su cuenta corriente.

5. No me rebajaron más el precio del carro porque el vendedor ya me (*dar*) un descuento.

*Cancelé todas mis tarjetas de crédito porque pensé que me las habían robado.*

6. El mercado se recuperó, pero muchas personas ya (*perder*) todo su dinero.

7. No tuvieron que preocuparse al jubilarse pues (*ahorrar*) dinero por muchos años.

## 13 Antes y después  1.3

Diga qué había hecho antes de encontrarse en las siguientes situaciones. Use el pluscuamperfecto, incluya la palabra **ya** y no repita los verbos de las frases.

MODELO   visitar la Ciudad de México

**Antes de visitar la Ciudad de México, ya había estado en Guadalajara y Monterrey.**

1. tomar esta clase de español
2. cumplir dieciocho años
3. desayunar esta mañana
4. estudiar para el examen con un grupo de compañeros
5. ser estudiante en este colegio
6. salir con mi novio/a actual

## 14 ¿Pretérito perfecto o pluscuamperfecto?  1.2

Complete el siguiente párrafo con el pretérito perfecto o el pluscuamperfecto, según corresponda al contexto.

Ese día, antes de salir de la oficina, yo (**1.** *cobrar*) mi sueldo y quería hacerle un regalo a mi madre. Ella me (**2.** *decir*) que le gustaría tener una blusa de seda. Sus amigas la (**3.** *invitar*) a una fiesta y deseaba estar muy elegante.

Entré a un almacén pensando en una blusa que (**4.** *ver, yo*) la semana anterior. Aún no la (**5.** *encontrar, yo*) cuando oí a la vendedora que me decía:

—La compañía (**6.** *rebajar*) el precio de estas blusas y son muy bonitas. (**7.** *vender, nosotros*) muchísimas. ¿Las (**8.** *ver, Ud.*)?

## 15 ¿Qué hay en los clasificados? 1.2, 1.3

Lea los clasificados de la siguiente página y conteste estas preguntas.

1. ¿Cuántos años de experiencia requiere el puesto de sous chef?
2. ¿Qué tipo de gastronomía hay que dominar para el puesto de chef?
3. ¿Qué nivel de inglés requiere el puesto de ingeniero mecánico o eléctrico?
4. ¿Qué salario se ofrece para el puesto de asistente ejecutiva?
5. ¿Qué estudios requiere el puesto de asistente dental?
6. ¿Qué debe tener quien se postule como técnico plomero?

---

### RESOURCES

 Avenue

**Answers**

**13** *Las respuestas variarán.*

**14**
1. había cobrado
2. había dicho
3. habían invitado
4. había visto
5. había encontrado
6. ha rebajado
7. Hemos vendido
8. ha visto

**15**
1. cinco años
2. gastronomía mexicana y vasca
3. nivel avanzado
4. $13.000 a $15.000
5. estudios sobre asistencia dental o auxiliar de enfermería
6. medio de transporte y herramientas propias

### Connections

**History**
Ask students to study the history of Tenochtitlán and Mexico City. Have them find out the legend involved in Tenochtitlán's founding, and ask them to summarize the watershed moments from pre-Columbian times to the present. Have students present the information as an Avenue task.

---

**Learning Styles**
**Auditory Learners**
Prepare sentences with the past perfect, e.g.:
**Ya habíamos sacado todo nuestro dinero cuando ese banco se quebró. Habíamos salido del centro comerical cuando la bomba explotó. Como ya habíamos hecho los depósitos, hubo suficiente dinero en la cuenta.** Read the sentences aloud, and have students give a thumbs-up sign if it describes a positive outcome, or thumbs-down for a negative outcome.

**Multiple Intelligences**
**Musical-Rhythmic**
Note that the past participles make the past perfect ideal for rhyming. Ask students to create songs, chants, or raps using the past perfect.

**191**

## Reference Desk

1. You may want to remind students that **el D.F.** and **Ciudad de México** are used interchangeably for *Mexico City*.
2. Under **Plomería**, point out **Estado de México**. Explain that Mexico has thirty-one states, each one with its own constitution and congress. Governors (**gobernadores**), who serve six-year terms, and representatives (**diputados locales**), who serve three-year terms, are elected by popular vote.
3. Remind students to use formal register in **Actividad 16**.

## Expansion

Have students switch roles and repeat **Actividad 16**, but for a different job listing.

○○○ PORTADA CLASIFICADOS

**ANUNCIOSCLASIFICADOS.COM**  http://anunciosclasificados.com

PORTADA CLASIFICADOS >> EMPLEOS

**RESTAURANTE/COMIDA**

| | |
|---|---|
| • Cocinero • con experiencia, medio tiempo. Dirigirse a Zaragoza No. 17, Tepoztlán, Morelos. | Publicado: 28 de abril Fuente: Diario de Morelos |
| • Cocinero • con experiencia. Turno diurno y nocturno. Tiempo completo. San Luis Potosí. ►(444) 813-1113 | Publicado: 28 de abril Fuente: El Sol de San Luis |
| • Sous chef • Gastronomía local gourmet. Cinco años de experiencia, dominio del inglés. Postularse en Tonalá 111, Colonia Roma, D.F. | Publicado: 26 de abril Fuente: Excélsior, México |
| • Chef • con experiencia en gastronomía mexicana y vasca. Presentarse de 11 AM – 5 PM en 500 Polanco, Miguel Hidalgo, Ciudad de México. ►(55) 5282-2222 | Publicado: 25 de abril Fuente: El Universal, México |

**INGENIERÍA**

| | |
|---|---|
| • Ingeniero mecánico o eléctrico • Recién graduado con disponibilidad para recibir entrenamiento. Nivel de inglés avanzado. Sueldo mensual $18.000 a $21.000, más las prestaciones de ley. Enviar currículum y concertar entrevista por Adecco reclutador@adecco.com | Publicado: 28 de abril Fuente: El Heraldo |

**ADMINISTRATIVOS/OFICINA**

| | |
|---|---|
| • Asistente ejecutiva • Lic. en Administración o carrera afín. Inglés intermedio. $13.000 a $15.000 netos + beneficios. Llene la solicitud de másRH Consultores | Publicado: 28 de abril Fuente: La Prensa |
| • Asistente legal • Bufete de abogados. Mínimo dos años de experiencia en auditorías legales. Paseo de la Reforma, Cuauhtémoc, Ciudad de México ►(55) 5207-3997 | Publicado: 27 de abril Fuente: Reforma |

**SALUD**

| | |
|---|---|
| • Asistente dental • en consultorio dental Carrera en área de salud (asistencia dental, auxiliar de enfermería). Nezahualcóyotl. Contactar a la Dra. Villa al ►(668) 462-5734 | Publicado: 25 de abril Fuente: Diario de Nezahualcóyotl |

**ELECTRICIDAD**

| | |
|---|---|
| • Electricista liniero • Técnico electricista. Experiencia en instalación de líneas aéreas y subterráneas. Guanajuato ►(477) 470-3566 | Publicado: 28 de abril Fuente: El Sol de León |

**PLOMERÍA**

| | |
|---|---|
| • Técnico plomero • con medio de transporte y herramientas propias. Sueldo según experiencia. Toluca, Estado de México ►(723) 564-6066 | Publicado: 28 de abril Fuente: Impulso, Estado de México |

◄ Guardar anuncio ★ 🔄 💾

## ¡Comunicación!

**16 Una entrevista** 👥 **Interpretive/Interpersonal Communication** ✿ **1.1**

Imagine que Ud. ha enviado su hoja de vida en respuesta a algunos de los clasificados arriba mencionados y que acaban de llamarlo para invitarlo a una entrevista. Con un(a) compañero/a, hagan el papel del entrevistador y el entrevistado y representen la conversación. Usen el pretérito perfecto, el pluscuamperfecto, y los temas que se dan como guía, como se ve en el modelo.

| MODELO | Entrevistador: | Veo que Ud. está solicitando el puesto de asistente legal. Cuénteme, ¿qué experiencia ha tenido en ese campo? |
|---|---|---|
| | Entrevistado: | Bueno, en realidad no he tenido mucha experiencia, pero he tomado varios cursos sobre auditorías. Solicité un puesto similar a este cuando salí de la universidad, pero, desafortunadamente, ya habían empleado a alguien. |

- Experiencia
- Estudios
- Intereses
- Sueldo
- Beneficios
- Recomendaciones
- Disponibilidad de tiempo
- Posibilidades de ascenso

## Essential Instruction

1. Before students begin **Actividad 16**, have them carefully read through the classified ads one more time. Encourage them to use props and sit facing each other to simulate a real interview.
2. Point out the **Pregunta clave**, and tell students to keep it in mind as they complete the cultural readings.
3. Have students preview pp. 193–195. Ask them to predict what they will learn about Mexico.
4. Remind students of the culture photo and question from the unit opener. Have them scan the first reading on p. 193 for the answer.

# Cultura

1.2, 2.2, 3.1

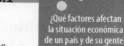**Pregunta clave**

¿Qué factores afectan la situación económica de un país y de su gente?

emcpassport.com

 LA 3

## La importancia de la economía

La economía de un país es el sistema que administra los recursos para satisfacer las necesidades de su gente. Esos recursos son los bienes y servicios que se producen e intercambian en el mercado. El problema es que los recursos son escasos[1], por lo que es necesario utilizarlos de manera eficaz y razonable para evitar que se produzca una crisis.

*Las crisis económicas pueden cambiar la vida de la gente.*

En México, en 1994, se produjo una crisis económica de magnitud[2], cuyas causas fueron, entre otras, una moneda nacional sobrevalorada[3], el fuerte endeudamiento en dólares y un gran déficit del sector público. Fue la primera crisis financiera de alcance global y en el mundo se la conoció como "efecto Tequila". Las repercusiones sociales de esta crisis fueron incalculables: muchas familias mexicanas lo perdieron todo y el 50 % de la población cayó en pobreza. Llegó a plantearse que era el fin de la clase media en México.

Con el tiempo, y mediante algunas medidas macroeconómicas que reestructuraron las finanzas del país, México pudo mejorar su situación y empezar a salir de la crisis. El NAFTA y otros acuerdos comerciales hicieron crecer exponencialmente las exportaciones, lo que tuvo resultados significativos en la reducción de la tasa[4] de pobreza.

[1] scarce   [2] major   [3] overrated   [4] rate

 **Búsqueda:** efecto tequila, nafta, crisis económica en méxico

### Productos  2.2

Las remesas son envíos de dinero que los mexicanos que trabajan en el extranjero, en especial en Estados Unidos, mandan a sus familias de México. Ese dinero es una fuente de ingresos considerable para la economía de esas familias en particular, pero también para la economía mexicana en general. Para incentivar este flujo de divisas al país, se ha implementado el programa ***Dos por Uno***: por cada peso de las remesas que contribuyan voluntariamente las familias de los emigrantes, el Estado aporta dos pesos para la construcción de infraestructura en sus comunidades.

*Por cada peso que se envía, el estado aporta dos.*

---

1.2, 2.2

### 17 Comprensión

1. ¿Por qué es importante administrar bien los recursos de un país?

2. ¿Qué ocurrió en México en 1994? ¿Cuáles fueron sus consecuencias?

3. ¿Cómo se logró salir de la crisis?

1.3, 2.2, 4.2

### 18 Analice

1. Piense en alguna crisis económica que haya atravesado su país y en las medidas que lo ayudaron a salir de ella. ¿Hay similitudes o diferencias con la crisis mexicana de 1994?

2. ¿Qué efecto cree Ud. que tienen las remesas que envían los trabajadores mexicanos sobre la economía de su país?

---

**Answers**

⑰
1. Los recursos son escasos, no son infinitos, y si no se distribuyen bien puede generarse una crisis.
2. Se produjo una gran crisis económica y financiera que afectó mucho al pueblo mexicano e incrementó la tasa de pobreza al 50 %.
3. Se implementaron medidas de reestructuración y acuerdos comerciales.

⑱ Las respuestas variarán.

## Reference Desk

Students can do a Flipgrid post reacting to any of these cultural readings.

## Critical Thinking

**Comparing**
Ask students to compare and contrast the U.S. 2007–2008 housing bubble and ensuing recession with Mexico's 1994 financial crisis.

## Pre-AP

Have students respond to the **Pregunta clave**, in spoken or written form, using information from the readings on pp. 193–195. Students should also include a comparison between their own community/culture and Mexico.

---

## Differentiated Learning

### Expand

Hold a job fair during class, using expanded versions of the ads from p. 192 and others. Also bring in sample job applications in Spanish. Divide the class into two groups: employers and job seekers. The job seekers should visit the various "booths" at the fair, choose a job they are interested in, and fill out an application. The employers should conduct interviews and make job offers. Finally, have the groups switch roles and repeat the activity.

### Heritage Learners

Ask heritage learners to share any insight they might have into the custom of remittances in their family's country of origin.

**1.2, 2.1, 2.2**

### 19 Comprensión

1. ¿Qué aspectos de la vida diaria están relacionados con la economía?

2. ¿En qué sentido es la educación un factor económico importante?

3. ¿Qué papel puede jugar el gobierno en la economía de una familia?

*A veces es difícil tomar decisiones económicas.*

**1.3, 4.2**
### 20 Analice

1. Además de la vivienda, ¿qué otros gastos importantes cree Ud. que incluye un presupuesto familiar?

2. ¿Hay alguna frase que refleje la visión cultural de su país sobre el ahorro? ¿Hay similitudes o diferencias con la frase "Ya Dios proveerá"?

## La economía real  **1.2, 2.1, 2.2**

Muchas veces los temas económicos, con todas sus estadísticas e indicadores, nos parecen un asunto abstracto que no tiene ningún punto de contacto con nuestra vida real. Pero lo cierto es que tanto nuestra forma de vida en general como nuestras decisiones diarias se ven afectadas por la economía: ¿Tenemos un trabajo que nos dé ingresos[1]?¿Cuáles son nuestros gastos?¿Podemos solventarlos[2] con esos ingresos? ¿Tenemos capacidad de ahorro?

Por ejemplo, tomar la decisión de continuar o abandonar nuestros estudios puede afectar económicamente nuestros futuros ingresos. En México, tener un buen nivel educativo es un requisito importante para encontrar empleo: si bien alrededor del 61 % de las personas en edad de trabajar tienen un empleo remunerado, ese porcentaje varía mucho si las personas no han obtenido un título secundario[3].

Elegir una casa donde vivir es otra decisión que puede afectar mucho nuestra economía. Una gran proporción del presupuesto familiar mexicano está destinada a los costos de vivienda. El pago de un alquiler[4] suele representar el gasto individual más grande de muchas familias, a lo que debe sumarse el pago de los servicios. En México, las familias gastan en promedio el 21 % de su ingreso solo en mantener su vivienda.

En este contexto, el apoyo que puede brindar el gobierno en prestaciones y servicios públicos gratuitos o de muy bajo costo, como la salud, la educación o el transporte, es clave para reducir los riesgos de pobreza, fomentar[5] el desarrollo infantil y mejorar la calidad de vida de su gente.

[1] income  [2] cover them  [3] high school diploma  [4] rent  [5] promote

**Búsqueda:** empleo remunerado en méxico, servicios públicos en méxico

**1.2, 3.2**
### Perspectivas

La frase "Ya Dios proveerá" dice mucho sobre la visión que tienen los mexicanos de la planificación financiera y el ahorro. Es una expresión arraigada en la cultura, que delega en Dios la responsabilidad de proveer bienes materiales en el futuro. Originalmente, la frase fue acuñada en el ámbito rural, donde las circunstancias cambiantes de la naturaleza determinaban la suerte de las cosechas.

*Una frase que refleja la visión mexicana sobre el ahorro*

## Essential Instruction

1. As you play the audio for each cultural reading, pause occasionally to check comprehension by asking **sí/no** questions.
2. Have students complete the **Analice** activities for Common Core practice.

3. As you discuss **Perspectivas** and **Prácticas**, mention that these sayings, beliefs, and practices are described in general terms; as with most cultural descriptions there are exceptions (i.e., people who act or feel a different way).

# Beneficios del teletrabajo

El teletrabajo[1] es el esquema que permite a los empleados de una empresa desarrollar sus actividades a distancia, sin necesidad de asistir a la oficina. Esta modalidad es una tendencia global que llegó de la mano del desarrollo tecnológico y que presenta múltiples ventajas económicas: reduce los costos fijos de la empresa en materia de infraestructura y servicios; aumenta la productividad, ya que motiva a los empleados; y ahorra el tiempo invertido en traslados[2] del hogar al trabajo.

*No hace falta salir de casa para estar "en el trabajo".*

Sin embargo, en México esta metodología no ha logrado afianzarse[3]. Mientras que uno de cada cinco puestos utiliza esta modalidad en Estados Unidos, la mayoría de las empresas mexicanas se resisten a implementarla. Algunas argumentan[4] motivos de seguridad, ya que no cuentan con plataformas que garanticen la protección de información corporativa importante y confidencial. Otros dicen que es necesario actualizar las regulaciones laborales antes de ponerla en práctica.

Pero ocurre que el cambio va más allá de las cuestiones prácticas: se trata de una concepción nueva del trabajo a la que las personas no están acostumbradas. Los jefes quieren seguir teniendo a sus empleados enfrente, y los empleados, a su vez, lo ven como una oportunidad para trabajar menos.

Todavía hay mucho por hacer para que el teletrabajo se generalice en México. La tecnología existe y está disponible, pero todavía no hay una cultura de "ser productivo" sin estar en la oficina.

[1] telecommuting    [2] commuting    [3] establish itself    [4] contend

 **Búsqueda:** teletrabajo en méxico, portales de empleo de méxico

## Prácticas  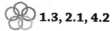 1.2, 2.1, 3.2

Hay un dicho en México: "Los estadounidenses viven para trabajar, pero los mexicanos trabajamos para vivir". En realidad, no se trata solo de un dicho; es algo que ponen en práctica a diario. El trabajo no es más que el medio de conseguir los bienes esenciales para subsistir. Una vez que se obtiene lo necesario, ya no se trabaja tiempo extra, sino que se prefiere pasar el tiempo en familia o con amigos. La dedicación al trabajo no es considerada una virtud moral y no hay una actitud competitiva, ya que en general no se ve compensada por una motivación al logro.

*Los mexicanos disfrutan su tiempo libre en familia.*

---

## 21 Comprensión  1.2, 2.1

1. ¿Cuáles son las ventajas del teletrabajo?

2. ¿Por qué dicen las empresas mexicanas que no quieren implementar el teletrabajo?

3. ¿Qué aspecto cultural de México impide que se implemente el teletrabajo?

 1.3, 2.1, 4.2

## 22 Analice

1. ¿Por qué cree Ud. que el teletrabajo logró implementarse en su país pero no en México?

2. ¿Qué diferencia importante cree Ud. que hay entre la filosofía del trabajo entre México y Estados Unidos?

---

**RESOURCES**

Beneficios del teletrabajo Prácticas

**Answers**

**21**

1. Reduce los costos en infraestructura, aumenta la productividad y ahorra tiempo perdido en trasladarse de casa al trabajo.
2. Por motivos de seguridad, para resguardar información confidencial, y por motivos legales, debido a la falta de regulación.
3. Hace falta un cambio en la concepción del trabajo tanto en la mentalidad de los jefes como en la de los empleados.

**22** *Las respuestas variarán.*

## Critical Thinking

**Analyzing**
After reading about **teletrabajo** and **Prácticas**, ask students to consider why bosses in any culture are reluctant to have their employees out of sight while working. What can employees do to counteract that hesitation?

---

## Differentiated Learning
**Expand**
Ask students to research the economy of the Aztecs. Ask them to find out the function of trade and currency, farming, marketplaces, and merchandise. Tell students to summarize this information in their Culture Journal.

## Multiple Intelligences
**Mathematical-Logical**
Have students go online to find out the current exchange rate of the Mexican peso and the U.S. dollar. Tell them that they are going to spend the weekend in Mexico City, and they need to determine how much money to bring. They should look up cost of hotel, food, sightseeing/ entertainment, and calculate totals.

**WB** Activity 10

**Answers**

 **23**

1. de
2. que
3. ir
4. en
5. llegar
6. piensa
7. pienso
8. venir
9. voy

## Critical Thinking

**Analyzing**
When checking answers to **Actividad 23**, ask students to explain why they chose each answer.

## Connections

**Literature**
Ask students to read a short story set in Mexico, such as one from Juan Rulfo's collection **El llano en llamas** or "**La noche boca arriba**" by Julio Cortázar. Ask students to analyze the elements of Mexican culture depicted in the story.

---

## *Vocabulario 2*

### Comparación y contraste: ¡Ojo con estas palabras! 1.2, 4.1

En español, al igual que en inglés, el verbo **pensar** tiene variaciones de significado cuando se usa con diferentes preposiciones o sin ellas. Preste atención a estas variaciones de significado.

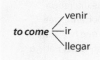

to think
- pensar de
- pensar (que)
- pensar en + infinitivo
- pensar en

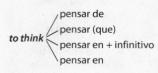

¿Qué **piensa** del horario de trabajo? ¿No va a interferir con sus estudios?

No, **pienso** terminar mis estudios de noche para poder trabajar la jornada completa.

**pensar de**   *to think of, have an opinion of*
—¿Qué **piensas de** la frase "Ya Dios proveerá", tan popular en México?

**pensar (que)**   *to think, to think that*
—**Pienso que** refleja la mentalidad de muchos hispanos.

**pensar + infinitivo**   *to intend/to plan + infinitive*
—¿Qué **piensas hacer** después de graduarte?

**pensar en**   *to think of, consider doing something*
—Estoy **pensando en** hacer un viaje a México.

El concepto de **ir** y **venir** también se expresa de manera diferente en inglés y en español y, por eso, es importante prestar atención a su uso.

to come
- venir
- ir
- llegar

**venir**   *to come*

**ir**   *to go*

**llegar (a)**   *to come to, arrive*

**ir**   *to come (when you move toward the person being spoken to)*

—¿**Vienes** en avión o en carro?

—**Voy** en avión.

—¡Qué bueno! ¿A qué hora **llega** tu vuelo?

—Marisa, ven a hablar con tu hermana. Apúrate.

—Ya **voy**, mamá, ya **voy**.

### 23 Piense en una solución  1.2

Complete esta conversación con la palabra del recuadro que corresponda según el contexto.

| ir | pienso | llegar | de | que | venir | en | voy | piensa |
|----|--------|--------|-----|-----|-------|-----|-----|--------|

**Sr. Salazar:** Srta. Gómez, como le digo, estamos muy interesados. Cuénteme, ¿qué piensa **(1)** la oferta de empleo?

**Srta. Gómez:** Pienso **(2)** es una gran oportunidad, pero **(3)** y venir desde tan lejos va a ser un poco difícil. Tengo que pensar **(4)** alguna solución.

**Sr. Salazar:** Le cuento que Cristina, una de nuestras empleadas, vive cerca de su barrio. Podrían **(5)** a un acuerdo y viajar juntas. ¿Qué **(6)** ?

**Srta. Gómez:** Perfecto. ¿Cuándo me la puede presentar?

**Sr. Salazar:** Pues, **(7)** hacerlo ahora mismo. Permítame un momento.

**Sr. Salazar:** ¿Aló? ¿Cristina? ¿Puede **(8)** un momento a mi oficina?

**Cristina:** Por supuesto Sr. Salazar. Ya mismo **(9)** .

---

## Essential Instruction

1. Personalize the **Vocabulario 2** presentation by talking about your own opinions and plans.
2. Write the **Para decir más** expressions on the board so that students are not looking in their books during their role-plays.
3. For **Actividad 25**, have a few pairs role-play their conversations for the class.
4. Encourage groups to develop dialogues that they can role-play for **Actividad 26**. Choose groups to act out each situation for the class, or have students video record them outside of class and plan a viewing day to watch them in class.

## 24 ¿Qué prefieres?  1.2

Complete estos mensajes de texto con el presente de los verbos **ir**, **venir** o **llegar** según corresponda.

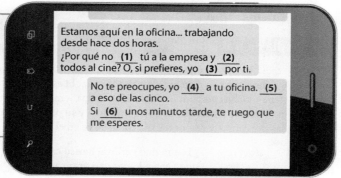

Estamos aquí en la oficina... trabajando desde hace dos horas.

¿Por qué no **(1)** tú a la empresa y **(2)** todos al cine? O, si prefieres, yo **(3)** por ti.

No te preocupes, yo **(4)** a tu oficina. **(5)** a eso de las cinco.

Si **(6)** unos minutos tarde, te ruego que me esperes.

## ¡Comunicación!  1.1

### 25 A que no te imaginas 👥 Interpersonal Communication

Imagine que Ud. acaba de conseguir un puesto en el centro de la ciudad y llama a su madre para contarle la noticia. Represente la situación con un(a) compañero/a con base en los temas que se dan y su imaginación, como se ve en el modelo.

MODELO

Luis: Mamá, a que no te imaginas... ¡acabo de conseguir un puesto fabuloso!

Madre: ¿Cómo? No puedo creerlo. ¿Dónde?

Luis: Aquí en el centro de la ciudad.

Madre: ...

- El nombre de la empresa
- La clase de negocio
- El tipo de trabajo
- El sueldo que va a ganar
- La jornada de trabajo
- Los beneficios que le ofrecen
- Las posibilidades de ascenso
- ¿...?

### Para decir más

Use estas expresiones como ayuda para hacer las Actividades 25 y 26.

Estupendo.
Fantástico.
No me digas.
Qué alegría.
Qué sorpresa.
Qué suerte.
Es muy importante que...
Es una lástima que...
No puedo entender por qué...
Siento decirle que...
Tienen que esforzarse, porque...

### 26 Cosas del oficio 👥 Interpersonal Communication  1.1

Imagine que Ud. es el/la jefe/a de personal de una empresa y tiene que resolver los siguientes problemas que han surgido con sus empleados. En parejas y en grupos pequeños, representen una de las siguientes situaciones.

- Clara, una de sus mejores empleadas, ha empezado a llegar unos quince minutos tarde todas las mañanas. ¿Qué va a hacer para resolver este problema?

- Ud. ha decidido despedir a Berta, una secretaria que nunca ha sido muy eficiente. Además, últimamente sus cartas han estado llenas de errores. ¿Qué debe hacer?

- Dos de sus mejores empleados se han peleado. Se cruzan sin mirarse y no se dirigen la palabra. Además, están dividiendo la oficina en dos campos enemigos. ¿Qué hará Ud. para mantener la armonía en la oficina?

### RESOURCES

 Avenue

Answers

**24**
1. vienes
2. vamos
3. voy
4. voy
5. Llego
6. llego

**25** *Las conversaciones variarán.*

**26** *Las conversaciones variarán.*

### Culture

**Products/Practices: Activity**
Ask students to research cell phone use in Mexico: which phones are most popular, the major service providers, popular smartphone apps, etc. Ask students to compare and contrast what they learned with their own cell phone usage. You may want to have them summarize the information in an Avenue task.

### Expansion

After students complete **Actividad 24**, ask them to write one more text message that might appear in the thread.

## Differentiated Learning
### Heritage Learners
Ask heritage learners to write on the board any abbreviations they know that people often use in text or chat messages (e.g., **x** = **por**; **k** = **qué**; **xq** = **porque**; **salu2** = **saludos**; **tb** = **también**). Have the class try to decipher the words.

## Learning Styles
### Auditory Learners
While completing the second question in **Actividad 26**, ask students to select a replacement for Berta. Read aloud (or make recordings) of people listing their qualifications and why they want the job. Instruct students to listen and decide which person would make the best new secretary.

### Reference Desk

Encourage students to use vocabulary from pp. 182–183 for **Actividad 27**.

### Culture

**Products: Activity**
Ask students to research the business empire of Carlos Slim, who is the richest man in the world and known as the "Warren Buffet of Mexico." Ask them to write a profile of Slim detailing his beginnings in business and how he proceeded to amass his fortune, as well as his role in Mexico's economy.

# ¡Comunicación!

## 27 Un día de trabajo en el banco  Interpersonal Communication  1.1

Imagine que Ud. trabaja en un banco y tiene que atender a un joven que acaba de conseguir su primer trabajo y quiere abrir su primera cuenta bancaria. Él está muy interesado en manejar bien sus finanzas, así que tiene muchas preguntas. Con un(a) compañero/a, representen la conversación entre el empleado y el joven. Usen los temas que se dan como guía y su propia experiencia e imaginación y túrnense para hacerse las preguntas y responderlas, como se ve en el modelo.

| MODELO | | |
|---|---|---|
| **Joven:** | ¿Tengo que venir al banco cada vez que vaya a hacer una transacción? | |
| **Empleado:** | No, no. Contamos con el servicio de Banca Móvil. Ud. puede realizar muchas de sus transacciones en su celular, 24 horas al día. | |
| **Joven:** | ¿De veras? ¿Y cuánto cuesta ese servicio? | |
| **Empleado:** | … | |

*Uso mi celular para hacer mis transacciones bancarias.*

- Productos y servicios que ofrece su banco
- Cuentas corrientes y de ahorros
- Depósitos de cheques y efectivo
- Cheques y sobregiros
- El cajero automático
- Las tarjetas de débito
- Las tarjetas de crédito
- Préstamos, intereses y pagos mensuales

## 28 ¿Por qué lo despidieron?  Interpersonal/Presentational Communication  1.1

Imagine que Ud. trabaja en una empresa y su supervisora acaba de despedirlo/a. Ud. piensa que ella ha sido injusta (*unfair*) y decide ir a hablar con el jefe de personal. Con un(a) compañero/a, representen la situación. Túrnense para hacer preguntas sobre el incidente y dar las explicaciones del caso, como se ve en el modelo.

| MODELO | |
|---|---|
| **Empleado:** | Gracias por atenderme sin previo aviso, Sr. Sánchez. |
| **Jefe de personal:** | Por supuesto. Explíqueme con calma lo que pasó. |
| **Empleado:** | Verá Ud. Yo he trabajado bajo la supervisión de la Sra. de Alarcón por más de un año, desde que ella llegó. Y la verdad es que me ha tratado mal desde el primer instante en que me vio. |
| **Jefe de personal:** | Ya veo… Ud. piensa que ella lo despidió por razones personales, ¿verdad? |
| **Empleado:** | … |

## Essential Instruction

1. For **Actividad 27**, you may want to have students base their role-play on a local bank.
2. Before students begin **Actividad 28**, have them generate questions and explanations for their respective roles. Tell them to try to reach a resolution about the matter.
3. Have groups summarize their ideas for each topic in **Actividad 29** and present them to the class.
4. Allow groups time to rehearse their dialogues from **Actividad 30**. Provide students with a rubric so that they know how the task will be graded.

 **¡Comunicación!**

**29 Intercambio de ideas**  Interpersonal Communication ✿ **1.1, 5.2**

Reúnase con tres o cuatro compañeros/as e intercambien ideas sobre uno de los siguientes temas.

- La adicción al trabajo

  El ritmo de la vida actual hace que los que trabajan en grandes empresas comerciales, bancarias, etc., sientan la necesidad de estar ocupados todo el día. ¿Creen Uds. que esta adicción al trabajo es una clase de enfermedad? ¿Conocen Uds. a personas que se sienten culpables si no están trabajando? ¿Tienen Uds. esa sensación? ¿Trabajan en su tiempo libre? ¿Necesitan informarles a los demás del motivo por el cual no están trabajando en un determinado momento? ¿A qué se debe este problema?

- Sugerencias para una entrevista de empleo

  ¿Han tenido alguna vez una entrevista de trabajo? Intercambien algunas ideas para salir bien en una entrevista de trabajo. ¡De una buena entrevista puede depender su futuro! Aquí van algunas preguntas importantes: ¿Qué ropa se debe llevar el día de la entrevista? ¿Qué debe decir uno? ¿Qué debe preguntar? Si uno ha sido despedido, ¿se debe mencionar el empleo anterior? ¿Es importante averiguar el sueldo? Si a uno le ofrecen el puesto, ¿hay que aceptarlo de inmediato?

**30 Situaciones**  Interpersonal Communication ✿ **1.1**

Reúnanse en grupos pequeños para representar una de las siguientes situaciones. ¡Usen la imaginación!

- Convenza a sus padres de que ellos deben dejarlo/a estudiar para ser maestro/a de yoga. Insisten en que estudie derecho.

- Es dentista pero no le gusta su profesión por varias razones. Explíquele estas razones a un(a) consejero/a, quien tratará de ayudarlo/a a cambiar de profesión.

- Quiere pedirle su jefe/a un aumento de sueldo, pero al llegar a la oficina todo le sale mal.

*Necesito un aumento de sueldo.*

 **RESOURCES**

🔵 Avenue

**Answers**

🔵 *Las respuestas variarán.*

🔵 *Las conversaciones variarán.*

**Reference Desk**

1. In **Actividad 29**, you may want to teach the terms **trabajólico** (a neologism) and **workaholic** (a loan-word from English).
2. Create an Avenue task in which students answer the questions for the topic that their group did not discuss in **Actividad 29**.

**Expansion**

Find out what job assistance organizations in your area offer help with resumes, interview skills and practice, and even proper attire. Ask students to make a brochure for the Spanish speakers of your community that would visit the center. Tell them to include a section of "dos and don'ts" that Spanish speakers may not be aware of in U.S. business culture.

**Differentiated Learning**
**Accelerate/Expand**
After completing **Actividad 29**, ask students to imagine that a friend or family member is a workaholic. Have them write an e-mail to the person, giving them advice to achieve a greater work-life balance.

**Multiple Intelligences**
**Verbal-Linguistic**
Ask students to search the TED Talks website for videos that deal with Mexico. Have them watch the talk and write a summary of it, giving their opinion of the speaker and the issue being discussed. Have students submit their summaries via Avenue.

# Gramática

## Los pronombres de complemento  1.2

### Los pronombres de complemento directo

Los pronombres de complemento directo se usan para referirse al complemento directo de la oración, el cual se conoce, y evitar repetición.

—Conseguí un empleo.
    Complemento directo

—¿Dónde **lo** conseguiste?
    p.c.d.

| Formas de los pronombres de complemento directo | | | |
|---|---|---|---|
| yo | **me** | nosotros(as) | **nos** |
| tú | **te** | vosotros(as) | **os** |
| él, ella, Ud. | **lo, la** | ellos(as), Ud. | **los, las** |

- El pronombre de complemento directo hace las veces del complemento directo, la persona o cosa sobre la que recae la acción del verbo. Cuando se trata de una persona se debe usar la **a** personal.

—¿Sabes si aprobaron el aumento de sueldo?
—Sí, **lo** aprobaron.

—¿Y emplearon a los nuevos vendedores?
—No, todavía no **los** han empleado.

- Cuando el pronombre que hace el papel del complemento directo es ambiguo, se puede aclarar mencionando a la persona o personas a quien(es) se refiere.

—**Los** van a despedir hoy.
—¿A quiénes? ¿A ellos?
—No, a Uds.

### *Lo* como complemento directo invariable

- Se usa **lo** como pronombre del complemento directo invariable para referirse a una idea o conceptos ya expresados.

—¿Decidiste aceptar la oferta de trabajo?
—No, todavía **lo** estoy pensando.

- También se usa en oraciones que constan únicamente del verbo **ser** o **estar**, generalmente en respuesta a una pregunta.

—¿Crees que es una buena inversión?
—Sí, **lo** es.

—¿Están interesados en el negocio?
—Sí, **lo** están.

- Tiene el mismo uso con los verbos **hacer**, **decir**, **pedir**, **preguntar** y **saber** cuando no se expresa el complemento.

—¡Tú eres el encargado de tus finanzas!
—Sí, **lo** sé.

—Llama al banco y pide una explicación.
—Sí, **lo** haré.

> **Un poco más**
>
> En algunas regiones de España e Hispanoamérica se usa **le** y **les** en lugar de los complementos directos **lo** y **los** cuando se refieren a personas:
>
> —¿Atendiste al cliente?
> —Sí, **le** atendí.
>
> —¿Y viste a los compradores?
> —Sí, **les** vi.

## Los pronombres de complemento indirecto

Los pronombres de complemento directo hacen las veces del complemento indirecto de la oración.

Amalia fue a la entrevista ayer, pero no **le** dieron el puesto.

p.c.i.

| Formas de los pronombres de complemento indirecto | | | |
|---|---|---|---|
| yo | **me** | nosotros(as) | **nos** |
| tú | **te** | vosotros(as) | **os** |
| él, ella, Ud. | **le** | ellos(as), Ud. | **les** |

- El pronombre de complemento indirecto indica la persona o las personas que se benefician indirectamente de la acción del verbo.

  —¿**Te** dieron una buena recomendación?     —Sí, **me** dieron una gran recomendación.

- Cuando el pronombre que hace el papel del complemento indirecto es ambiguo, se puede aclarar mencionando a la persona o personas a quien(es) se refiere.

                         →    ¿a Ud.?
  **Le** prestó mucho dinero.    →    ¿a él?
                         →    ¿a ella?

- El pronombre de complemento indirecto se usa con verbos de comunicación como **decir**, **pedir**, **preguntar** y **rogar**, y con verbos como **agradecer**, **ayudar**, **impedir**, **pagar** y **prohibir** para indicar a quién se dirige la acción.

  —¿Qué **les** dijo el gerente sobre el aumento de sueldo?
  —**Nos** dijo que lo empezarían a pagar a partir del próximo mes.

## Posición de los pronombres de complemento directo e indirecto

- Los pronombres de complemento directo e indirecto se colocan antes de un verbo conjugado.

  **La** llamaremos más tarde y **le** comunicaremos nuestra decisión.

- Se colocan antes del verbo en construcciones con el participio pasado (-*ado*, -*ido*).

  No **la** han llamado y no **le** han dicho nada.

- Los pronombres se pueden colocar antes o después del verbo en infinitivo o en gerundio[1].

  Compré el carro y **lo** estoy pagando a plazos.    Compré el carro y estoy pagándo**lo** a plazos.
  **Me** están dando muy buen interés.    Están dándo**me** muy buen interés.

  **Lo** voy a pagar en seis cuotas mensuales.    **Le** voy a girar un cheque ahora mismo.
  Voy a pagar**lo** en seis cuotas mensuales.    Voy a girar**le** un cheque ahora mismo.

- Se colocan después del verbo en los mandatos afirmativos y antes en los mandatos negativos.

  Aquí tiene su tarjeta de crédito. Guárde**la** en un lugar seguro y no **la** use en exceso.
  Somos clientes aquí desde hace años. Hága**nos** un descuento o no **nos** cobre tanto interés.

[1] Recuerde que el gerundio exige un acento escrito cuando se añaden los pronombres. Asimismo, el infinitivo y el mandato afirmativo exigen acento escrito si se añaden dos pronombres.

## Reference Desk

1. Emphasize that with double object pronouns, the indirect object pronoun always comes first.
2. Point out that **ti** does not have an accent, but that **mí** does in order to distinguish it from the possessive **mi**. Also point out the accent on **sí**.
3. You may want to explain that **consigo** is not often used in everyday speech.
4. Emphasize that the phrase **a** + *prepositional pronoun* does not take the place of the indirect object pronoun, but rather reinforces it.

## Expansion

Ask students to create a Flipgrid post in which they show and describe their favorite possession. Play the posts in class and have other students ask follow-up questions using object pronouns, e.g., **¿Quién te lo regaló?**

## TPR

Practice double object pronouns by using common objects in the classroom. For example, give a pen to a student, and ask the class **¿Debe pasarle el bolígrafo a Erin?** The class should tell the student what to do: **¡Sí, pásaselo!** or **No, no se lo pases. Pásaselo a Derek.** The student with the pen should perform the action corresponding to the command.

### Posición de los dos pronombres en la misma oración

- Cuando se usan los dos pronombres en la misma oración, el pronombre de complemento indirecto precede al complemento directo.

    Vendí las acciones pero no **me las** han pagado.

- Se usa el pronombre **se** en lugar de **le** y **les** delante de los pronombres **lo**, **la**, **los** y **las**.

    **Le** enviaremos <u>la mercancía</u> esta misma tarde. **Se la** enviaremos por correo aéreo.

### Los pronombres de complemento de preposición

| Pronombres de preposición ||
| Singular | Plural |
| --- | --- |
| mí | nosotros(as) |
| ti | vosotros(as) |
| él, ella, Ud. | ellos, ellas, Uds. |
| sí (reflexivo) | sí (reflexivo) |

- Los pronombres preposicionales, con excepción de **mí** y **ti**, tienen las mismas formas que los pronombres personales. Se usan después de una preposición.

    Compré una calculadora **para ti** y otra **para él**.

- Si el sujeto del verbo está en la tercera persona del singular o del plural o en la forma Ud., y la acción es reflexiva, se usa el pronombre **sí** después de la preposición.

    El candidato tímido vino para una entrevista, pero prefirió no hablar **de sí**.
    Ellos ahorraron mucho dinero y lo guardaron **para sí**.

- La preposición **con** seguida de **mí**, **ti** o **sí** tiene formas especiales:

    con + mí = **conmigo**      con + ti = **contigo**      con + sí = **consigo**

    —¿Quieres ir **conmigo** al salón de exhibiciones?
    —Sí, me gustaría ir **contigo**. Juan irá también, y llevará los documentos **consigo**.

- Cuando el sujeto del verbo y el pronombre se refieren a la misma persona, es frecuente el uso de **mismo** (**-a**, **-os**, **-as**) después de los pronombres.

    Marta, investígalo **por ti misma**.
    Pienso **en mí mismo** y no en los demás.
    Él tiene confianza **en sí mismo** y por eso tiene éxito.

- Las preposiciones **entre**, **según**, **salvo**, **excepto** y **menos** se usan con pronombres personales en vez de preposicionales.

    Te diré algo, pero tiene que quedar **entre tú** y **yo**, porque es un secreto: todos están enterados de la fiesta sorpresa para Carlos, **excepto él**, claro.

### Essential Instruction

1. Introduce prepositional pronouns by inviting students to do activities.
2. Go over the example sentences. Ask volunteers to create sentences for the words that do not have examples.
3. Check answers to **Actividad 31** by having two volunteers role-play the dialogue.
4. Point out that students will answer all questions affirmatively in **Actividad 32**; you may want to have them switch roles after item 3.

## 31 Qué casualidad  1.2

Complete la siguiente conversación entre Janet y Óscar con el pronombre de complemento directo que corresponda según el contexto.

**Janet:** ¿Has conocido a María Elena Reyes ya?

**Óscar:** Sí, claro que __(1)__ conocí.

**Janet:** ¿Dónde __(2)__ conociste?

**Óscar:** __(3)__ conocí en la reunión el martes. Pero, ¡qué casualidad! Ella __(4)__ había visto (a mí) hace un mes cuando vino a la oficina para su entrevista. Resulta que ella quería conocer __(5)__ a mí, y le preguntó a Pablo si él sabía mi número de teléfono. ¡Claro que él __(6)__ sabía! Es mi compañero de cuarto.

**Janet:** Y, ¿ __(7)__ llamó (a ti)?

**Óscar:** Sí. Ella __(8)__ llamó. Hablamos por una hora, y después yo __(9)__ invité a cenar.

**Janet:** ¿Vas a volver a ver __(10)__ ?

**Óscar:** ¡Sí, __(11)__ voy a ver esta noche. Vamos a ver la nueva película de Salma Hayek. ¿ __(12)__ has visto tú?

**Janet:** No, no __(13)__ he visto todavía. Espero ver __(14)__ el domingo.

## 32 Todo está en orden  1.3

Imagine que Ud. trabaja para la empresa mexicana SIDEC S.A. Su jefe acaba de volver de un viaje de negocios y quiere saber si todo está en orden y si se cumplieron sus instrucciones durante su ausencia. Conteste las preguntas sustituyendo el complemento directo por el pronombre de complemento directo correspondiente, como se ve en el modelo.

MODELO   ¿Contestó la correspondencia que le indiqué?
**Sí, la contesté.**

*¿Se cumplieron mis instrucciones durante mi ausencia?*

1. ¿Entrevistó a los postulantes para el puesto de secretario?
2. ¿Mandó el documento al banco en el D.F.?
3. ¿Resolvieron los abogados el problema con la sucursal en Acapulco?
4. ¿Consiguió Ud. las salas para la reunión?
5. ¿Aprobó la fecha de la reunión el licenciado del Castillo?
6. ¿Hizo Ud. todo lo que le pedí?

## Differentiated Learning
### Accelerate
For **Actividad 32**, tell the employees to answer all the questions in the negative (**No, no la contesté.**). The boss should ask follow-up questions, which the employee will have to answer creatively (**¿Por qué no la contestaste? No la contesté porque…**).

## Learning Styles
### Visual/Auditory Learners
Bring in several photographs. As you display the images, make false statements about them and have students correct what you say, using object pronouns. Follow up by having pairs of students create a story to go with each image.

**33**

1. nos
2. lo
3. le
4. le
5. le
6. le
7. le
8. la
9. lo
10. les
11. los
12. las
13. le

**34** *Las respuestas variarán.*

## Expansion

Bring in articles from newspapers or magazines. Ask students to identify where direct and indirect object pronouns were used. Discuss what the pronouns mean or to what they are referring.

---

**33 Consejos útiles**  **1.2**

Complete el párrafo con el pronombre de complemento directo o indirecto que corresponda según el contexto.

El costo de vida aumenta y sentimos la necesidad de ganar más y más dinero. Nuestros clientes siempre **(1)** preguntan: "¿Cómo podemos obtener **(2)** ? ¿Cómo **(3)** decimos a nuestro jefe que necesitamos un aumento de sueldo?" Pues bien, a continuación **(4)** sugerimos a Ud. algunos consejos útiles para estos casos.

- Primero, es importante que Ud. **(5)** pida a uno de sus superiores que hable con el jefe sobre Ud. y que **(6)** dé información positiva acerca de su trabajo.

- Demuéstre **(7)** a su jefe que le gusta su profesión y que **(8)** toma muy en serio.

- Tenga una actitud positiva. Ser optimista **(9)** ayudará mucho con su jefe. El optimismo es contagioso.

- Si tiene problemas con algunos compañeros en la oficina, muéstre **(10)** a todos que Ud. es capaz de resolver **(11)** .

- Si tiene ideas creativas, compárta **(12)** con su jefe. Quizás él **(13)** agradecerá con un aumento de salario.

---

**34 ¿Qué hicieron?**  **1.3**

Forme oraciones con información de cada columna para hablar de lo que hicieron las siguientes personas. Luego, vuelva a escribir cada oración con los pronombres de complemento directo e indirecto, como se ve en el modelo.

MODELO    La compañía le pagó **al postulante pasajes de ida y vuelta** para la entrevista.
               La compañía **se los** pagó.

| A | B | C |
|---|---|---|
| Mi hermano/a... | ...describir los trabajos... | ...a los clientes. |
| El/La jefe/a... | ...dictar una carta... | ...al botones. |
| La compañía... | ...querer vender sus productos... | ...al/a la gerente/a. |
| El/La empleado/a... | ...enviar la mercadería... | ...a las niñas. |
| Mi amigo/a... | ...desear escribir cartas... | ...a los viajeros. |
| La abuela... | ...pedir un descuento... | ...a su novio/a. |
| La azafata... | ...dar un consejo... | ...a los turistas. |
| El turista... | ...dar una propina... | ...a mí. |
| Los estudiantes... | ...hablar por teléfono... | ...al/a la secretario/a. |
| | ...mandar una tarjeta... | ...a mi padre. |
| | | ...a nosotros. |
| | | ...al/a la profesor(a). |

---

## Essential Instruction

1. Have students check their answers to **Actividad 33** in small groups.
2. You could do **Actividad 34** orally; have all students stand. In order to sit down, they have to form a logical and grammatically correct sentence, and a classmate must give the correct follow-up sentence with the pronouns.
3. Allow students time to practice their dialogues for **Actividad 35**. Remind them to use proper intonation.
4. **Actividad 36** can be repeated for other types of stores or businesses.

# ¡Comunicación!

## 35 Intercambios  Presentational Communication 1.2, 1.3

Con un(a) compañero/a, túrnense para completar las conversaciones con el pronombre preposicional que corresponda según el contexto y, luego, representen sus diálogos delante de la clase.

**A.** Entre tú y yo

—Ya me has dicho muchas veces que no te gusta deber dinero y que para __(1)__ es muy importante pagar en efectivo.

—¡Ya lo creo! Los intereses de las tarjetas de crédito son muy altos.

—Estoy de acuerdo con __(2)__ . Más vale no tener deudas.

**B.** Entre Ud. y yo

—¿Podría hablar con Ud.?

—Si Ud. quiere hablar con __(3)__ , le ruego que pase por mi despacho. Ud. sabe que las relaciones entre __(4)__ y __(5)__ han sido últimamente muy difíciles.

—Ya lo sé. A __(6)__ me parece que a Ud. le molestan mis ofertas. ¿No le interesa hacer negocios con __(7)__ ?

—Me interesan los negocios, pero no los malos negocios.

## 36 En un almacén de ropa Interpersonal Communication 1.1

Imagine que Ud. está en un almacén de ropa y habla con el vendedor o a la vendedora sobre lo que desea: el color, la talla, el estilo, etc. Represente la conversación con un(a) compañero/a con base en los temas que se dan y su propia imaginación, como se ve en el modelo.

MODELO
A: **Quisiera comprar una blusa.**
B: **¿De qué color la desea?**
A: **La deseo amarilla.**
B: **Aquí la tiene.**

1. Deseo unos pantalones.
2. Busco un abrigo.
3. Necesito unas medias.
4. Quiero un buen paraguas.
5. Desearía ver camisas.
6. ...

*Quisiera comprar una blusa.*

---

**RESOURCES**

 Avenue

**Answers**

**35**
1. ti
2. tigo
3. migo
4. Ud.
5. yo
6. mí
7. migo

**36** *Las conversaciones variarán.*

## Communication

**Interpersonal/Presentational: Cooperative Groups**
Ask students to make a list of places they like to visit during their free time. Divide the class into small groups and have students talk about the places. Encourage them to use: **¿Conoces....? Sí, lo/la conozco. ¿Me lo/la recomiendas? Sí, te lo/la recomiendo.**

## Expansion

Ask students to research the cost of living in Mexico and in the United States. Tell them to compare and contrast their findings and make note of any statistics that were surprising to them. Finally, have them present the information via Avenue.

---

## Differentiated Learning
**Accelerate/Expand**
After completing **Actividad 33**, ask students to develop one or two examples of how each piece of advice can be implemented.

## Multiple Intelligences
**Musical-Rhythmic**
Create a worksheet from a song by a Mexican singer or band, such as Julieta Venegas, Café Tacuba, or Los Tigres del Norte. Type up the lyrics, leaving a blank space for every pronoun. Instruct students to listen to the song a few times and fill in the blanks.

Answers

**Antes de leer**
*Las respuestas variarán.*

**37**

1. Más de la mitad se encuentra sin trabajo, un cuarto de los encuestados tiene trabajo pero quisiera cambiarlo y un pequeño porcentaje combina el estudio y el trabajo.
2. La mayoría de los encuestados, el 88 %, no están satisfechos con su situación actual.
3. Las posibilidades que mencionan son: tener un trabajo que les permita desarrollarse profesionalmente, conseguir un trabajo con un buen salario y grandes beneficios, seguir estudiando y trabajar o estudiar en el extranjero.

**38** *Las respuestas variarán.*

**206**

---

# Lectura informativa

**1.3, 5.2** **Antes de leer**
¿Cree Ud. que tener un título universitario facilita la búsqueda de empleo?

**Estrategia**  **3.1**

**Usar los conocimientos previos**
Antes de empezar a leer, piense en el tema y en lo que sabe sobre él. Mientras lee, relacione la información nueva con sus conocimientos previos.

**1.2, 2.2, 3.2**

## 37 Comprensión

1. ¿Qué condiciones laborales presentan los mexicanos encuestados?

2. ¿Qué opina la mayoría de los mexicanos encuestados sobre su situación laboral actual?

3. Según los mexicanos encuestados, ¿qué posibilidades consideran para cambiar su realidad quienes no están contentos con ella?

**1.3, 4.2**

## 38 Analice

¿Cómo es la situación laboral de los universitarios en su país? ¿Varía según la carrera que han seguido?

---

El 59 % de los universita...

INICIO    EL ABC    DE INTERÉS    BIBLIOTECA    NOTAS    VACANTES    TOP JOB NEWS

**ul Universo Laboral**    **1.2, 2.2, 3.2**    Buscar...    Follow @

### El 59 % de los universitarios mexicanos no cuenta actualmente con un empleo

**Trabajando.com y Universia consultaron a los usuarios en el marco de las Encuestas de Empleo que realizan en conjunto.**

**Entre los datos recogidos, el 88 % no está contento con su situación actual y pretende cambiar: el 38 % se imagina como jefe de área[1] en los próximos 5 años.**

En el estudio participaron 25.788 personas de Argentina, Brasil, Chile, Colombia, España, México, Perú, Puerto Rico y Uruguay. Entre los encuestados, aparece una mayor presencia masculina (51 %) por sobre la femenina (49 %). En cuanto a edad, el 71 % reveló tener más de 27 años, seguido por un 24 % de entre 21 y 26. Por su parte, el 5 % tiene entre 18 y 20 años. **La muestra[2] de México fue de 1394 usuarios que contestaron.**

Los resultados marcan un panorama[3] difícil en materia de empleo para Iberoamérica: el 63 % reveló estar sin trabajo, mientras que el 21 % tiene uno pero desea cambiarlo. Entre los restantes, el 11 % tiene trabajo y el 5 % trabaja y estudia a la vez. **En México el panorama tampoco resulta muy alentador[4] ya que el 59 % de los usuarios que contestaron esta encuesta se encuentra sin trabajo; el 24 % cuenta con empleo pero quiere cambiarse y apenas el 2 % combina el estudio y el trabajo.**

De la mano del resultado antes señalado y conscientes de la situación que atraviesan, el 88 % manifestó no estar contento con la situación en la que se encuentra; solo el 12 % está satisfecho.

**Para el 88 % de los mexicanos encuestados, la situación actual en la que se encuentran tampoco resulta satisfactoria.**

¿Cómo cambiar la realidad con la que la mayoría dice no estar contento? Para el 59 % una posibilidad es tener un trabajo donde pueda desarrollarse profesionalmente. Se aprecia aquí el valor que los encuestados le otorgan a la formación obtenida en sus carreras[5]. Mientras que el 31 % persigue un propósito que le otorgue rendimientos[6] a corto plazo: conseguir un trabajo donde tenga un buen salario y grandes beneficios. Otras opciones que los encuestados consideran son seguir estudiando (5 %) y viajar al extranjero a estudiar o trabajar (5 %).

[1] department head    [2] sample    [3] scenario    [4] encouraging    [5] majors (in college)
[6] yields results

---

**206**

INICIO     EL ABC     DE INTERÉS     BIBLIOTECA     NOTAS     VACANTES     TOP JOB NEWS

**ul** Universo Laboral     Buscar...     Follow @

**En México, el 61 % se visualiza mejorando su situación actual teniendo un trabajo donde se puedan desarrollar profesionalmente; el 34 % de los encuestados consideran que estarían mejor con un trabajo donde tengan un buen salario y grandes beneficios, y tan solo el 4 % cree que irse al extranjero a estudiar y/o trabajar favorecería su futuro.**

A la hora de elegir el tipo de empresa en la que les gustaría trabajar a los encuestados, los resultados ponen de manifiesto una clara preferencia de la empresa privada (57 %) frente a la pública (29 %). Por su parte, un 10 % de los encuestados muestran interés por el emprendimiento[7] como modo de desarrollo profesional, mientras que al 4 % le interesaría trabajar en una Organización No Gubernamental (ONG).

**En México, el 54 % de los encuestados manifestaron que les gustaría trabajar en una empresa privada, el 32 % quisiera desempeñarse en una entidad de gobierno, mientras que el 12 % buscaría oportunidades de emprender y tan solo el 2 % quisiera trabajar en una ONG.**

Entre el 12 % de los encuestados que estaban satisfechos con su situación laboral, el 42 % lo justificó indicando que su actual empleo le permitirá tener mejores oportunidades de futuro. Similar es el pensamiento del 17 %, que argumentó tener grandes proyecciones de crecimiento. En ambos casos, se desprende una visión a medio-largo plazo, como resultado de la formación y la experiencia profesional adquirida. En tanto, el 30 % lo justificó por estar haciendo lo que le gusta y el 11 % porque tiene una buena renta[8] y beneficios.

Finalmente, las proyecciones sobre el puesto de trabajo a 5 años vista son ambiciosas. El 41 % se imagina como jefe de área, el 17 % dueño de su propia empresa y el 16 % como encargado[9]. Es decir, se esperan pronósticos favorables en el futuro laboral de los encuestados. El 15 %, en tanto, se proyecta como empleado y el 11 % entiende que tiene posibilidades de ser nombrado gerente general[10].

A comparación de los resultados a nivel Iberoamérica, los encuestados en **México** indican que en 5 años el **38 % de los usuarios se visualizan como jefes de área; el 32 % se ve como gerente general de alguna empresa; el 20 % de los encuestados quisiera ser dueño de su propia empresa y tan solo el 3 % se ve como empleado.**

¿En qué tipo de empresa te gustaría trabajar?
- Privada: 57 %
- Pública: 29 %
- ONG: 4 %
- Emprendimiento personal: 10 %

¿En qué puesto te imaginas trabajando en los próximos 5 años?
- Jefe de área: 41 %
- Encargado: 16 %
- Empleado: 15 %
- Dueño de un emprendimiento: 17 %
- Gerente general: 11 %

[7] entrepreneurship     [8] income     [9] manager     [10] general manager

🔍 **Búsqueda:** inserción laboral de los universitarios latinoamericanos, desempleo entre los universitarios mexicanos

---

🎴 **1.2, 2.2, 3.2**

**39 Comprensión**

1. ¿Qué preferencias muestran los encuestados mexicanos en cuanto al lugar de trabajo?

2. ¿Por qué puede concluirse que el pronóstico es favorable con respecto a la proyección a cinco años que tienen los encuestados?

3. ¿Qué diferencia hay entre los resultados de Iberoamérica y México entre quienes se proyectan como empleados dentro de cinco años?

 **1.3, 3.1**

**40 Analice**

¿Qué ventajas y desventajas cree Ud. que tiene una persona que se dedica a su propia empresa?

---

**39**

1. La mayoría prefiere las empresas privadas, el 32 % prefiere una entidad gubernamental, el 12 % prefiere trabajar en emprendimientos propios y solo el 2 %, en una ONG.

2. Porque un alto porcentaje imagina que logrará progresar en su trabajo, ya sea consiguiendo un ascenso o convirtiéndose en dueño de su propia empresa.

3. Entre los encuestados de Iberoamérica, el 15 % se proyecta como empleado, mientras que solamente el 3 % de los encuestados mexicanos se ve como empleado dentro de 5 años.

**40**   *Respuesta posible:*

Si uno tiene un emprendimiento propio, puede trabajar de lo que a uno le gusta y ser su propio jefe, pero se corren más riesgos y el trabajo es más inestable.

**Critical Thinking**

**Analyzing**
Ask students to think about the effects of having so many unemployed young people, such as living at home longer, having less disposable income to spend on products aimed at their demographic, a highly competitive job market, some people may extend their studies, they may get married later, etc.

---

**Differentiated Learning**
**Heritage Learners**
Ask heritage learners to share what they know about employment statistics in their family's country of origin.

**Multiple Intelligences**
**Verbal-Linguistic**
Ask students to imagine that they are an unemployed college student in Mexico. Tell them to write an e-mail to a friend detailing their outlook for the coming year.

# Escritura

## Una hoja de vida  1.3

Una hoja de vida, o currículum vitae, es un texto que presenta los datos personales, los antecedentes académicos y la experiencia laboral de una persona que desea obtener un empleo. Debe ser breve para que, a simple vista, el lector se dé una idea del perfil del postulante. La información debe estar bien organizada e incluir solo datos veraces y relevantes.

Algunas consideraciones para redactar una hoja de vida:

- Datos personales: Debe incluir el nombre, la dirección de residencia, los teléfonos y el correo electrónico.

- Perfil profesional: Debe resumir las características distintivas puntuales (conocimientos, intereses, habilidades, experiencia previa) por las que se considera idóneo para ese puesto en particular.

- Formación académica: Debe enumerar los estudios cursados, con el nombre del título obtenido, la fecha y la institución.

- Experiencia laboral: Debe enumerar los puestos de trabajo anteriores, con fecha, nombre de la empresa y una descripción del cargo.

### ¡Comunicación!

**41** **¿Cómo es su hoja de vida?** Presentational Communication  1.2, 1.3

Escriba una hoja de vida para solicitar el empleo que se ofrece en el siguiente anuncio. Tenga en cuenta las consideraciones dadas para redactar una hoja de vida y use su imaginación para dar la información que se requiere.

**OFERTAS DE EMPLEO**

**VENDEDORES**
**Tienda por departamentos**
hace 1 día

**Requisitos**
Edad: 18 a 50 años
Educación: Bachillerato/Secundaria
Experiencia laboral: 1 año mínimo
Otros:   Puntualidad
          Gusto por las ventas

**Beneficios**
Sueldo: Acorde con experiencia
Comisiones
Cálido ambiente laboral
Oportunidades de crecimiento

**Contacto**
empleos@tienda.com

### Essential Instruction

1. Introduce this section by going over the information about **hojas de vida**. If possible, bring in sample resumes.
2. Before students begin drafting their resumes for **Actividad 41**, read through the job ad as a class. Ask comprehension questions.

3. Go over the information on summaries. Bring in a short text and use it to model, finding main ideas and paraphrasing.
4. Begin **Actividad 43** by reading through the questions; emphasize that students need to answer these questions in their e-mails. Have students review their summaries from **Actividad 42** to pick out the main advice.

# Un resumen  1.3

Un resumen es una versión abreviada de otro texto que contiene solo las ideas principales. Para hacer un resumen, se debe sintetizar, en términos breves y precisos, el contenido fundamental de lo dicho por el autor original. Resumir es una técnica muy útil para comprender textos y diferenciar ideas principales y secundarias.

A la hora de hacer un resumen, puede seguir las siguientes pautas:

- Haga una lectura general.
- Asegúrese de haber comprendido el texto.
- Avance párrafo por párrafo subrayando lo más importante.
- Parafrasee con sus propias palabras las ideas principales.

## ¡Comunicación!

### 42 Siga estos consejos 🎧  1.2, 1.3
**Interpretive Communication**

Escuche esta entrevista con la psicóloga Antonella Greco quien nos habla de cómo prepararnos para una entrevista laboral. Luego, prepare un resumen teniendo en cuenta lo que ella dice con relación a los siguientes temas.

- Preparación previa
- Puntualidad
- Presentación personal
- Veracidad
- Forma de expresarse

*Entrevista laboral*

### 43 Favor de responder   Presentational Communication  1.3

Imagine que recibe un correo electrónico del gerente de la tienda por departamentos, en el que le informan que están interesados en su perfil como vendedor. Le piden que responda una serie de preguntas específicas, antes de decidir si lo convocarán para una entrevista personal. Escriba un correo electrónico de respuesta, teniendo en cuenta los consejos que escuchó en el audio.

- ¿Qué características de su personalidad lo hacen un buen vendedor?
- ¿Qué aspectos del trabajo de vendedor son los que más le gustan?
- ¿Hay algún sector de la tienda que le interese por sobre los demás?
- ¿Tiene flexibilidad en cuanto a los horarios?
- ¿Está interesado en trabajar medio día?
- ¿Cuál es la remuneración mensual que pretende?

## Differentiated Learning
### Expand
After students complete the activities on these pages, ask them to work in pairs to conduct an interview between the job applicant and the store manager. They should use their resumes and e-mails from **Actividades 41** and **43**.

## Special Needs Students
### Auditory Impairment
Allow these students to listen several times to the recording in **Actividad 42**. You may also want to provide them with a script so that they can follow along as they listen.

RESOURCES

 Activity 42

Answers

**42 Script**

—Buenos días. Bienvenida a una semana más. Pues hoy, vamos a hablar, como decimos, de las entrevistas de trabajo: cómo afrontarlas, cómo dirigirse al que puede ser tu futuro jefe. Y vamos a comenzar la charla. Antonella, las entrevistas de trabajo, ¿por dónde empezamos?

— Las entrevistas se deben preparar con anterioridad, es decir, tenemos que un poco prepararnos, el saber qué vamos a decir y el cómo lo vamos a decir. Cuanto más preparada, menos sorpresa y menos nervios. Luego, también se recomienda que lleguemos un poquito antes de la hora. ¿Por qué? Para lo mismo, para controlar el tema de los nervios, ¿no?

—Tengo muchas preguntas al respecto ¿no? Punto importante también es el aspecto.

—Exacto, el tema del aspecto importantísimo, es ir aseados y si puede ser bien descansados y con buena presencia. La elección del vestuario, lo deberíamos de hacer, ya sería un punto bastante a favor, pues, en función del puesto de trabajo, si por ejemplo nos estamos presentando para un puesto de una sucursal bancaria iríamos trajeados. Si nos presentamos en un puesto más del sector primario, a alguna de obras, entonces iríamos aseados pero más sencillos vestidos. Luego aparte de no mentir porque eso es un punto muy importante, porque luego al final si mentimos, estas cosas al final se acaban sabiendo y lo que decía antes, la sinceridad es muy importante porque además nos sirve mucho también a nosotros mismos ¿no? Vamos a vendernos también nuestras cualidades personales.
*Continued on p. 223.*

*Los resúmenes variarán.*

**43** *Los correos electrónicos variarán.*

**209**

### Reference Desk

Point out that students will use this vocabulary to complete the audio activity on p. 211, as well as to aid in comprehension of the **Lectura literaria** on pp. 220–222.

### Game

**¡A dibujar!**
Divide the class into groups of four. Students should work in teams of two to play a Pictionary-type game to practice the vocabulary from **Mejore su comprensión**.

# Vocabulario 3

## Mejore su comprensión  1.2

Familiarizarse con este vocabulario le ayudará a leer "Autorretrato" más adelante, y a mejorar su comprensión auditiva.

**acariciar** *v.* Rozar con la mano de forma muy suave.

**amistad** *s.f.* Relación de cariño y simpatía entre dos personas.

**campesino** *s.m.* Persona que vive y trabaja en el campo.

**charlar** *v.* Conversar por pasatiempo.

**colaborar** *v.* Trabajar con otras personas en algo.

**con frecuencia** *exp.* Acto o suceso que se repite.

**corteza** *s.f.* Capa exterior de los árboles.

**descompuesto/a** *adj.* Que está estropeado o que ha dejado de funcionar.

**docena** *s.f.* Conjunto de doce cosas.

**encanecer** *v.* Ponerse el pelo blanco.

**espejo** *s.m.* Objeto de vidrio que refleja o da la imagen de algo.

**estreno teatral** *exp.* Espectáculo de teatro que se representa por primero vez.

**felicitación** *s.f.* Palabras con las que nos alegramos por algo bueno que le ha ocurrido a alguien.

**gafas** *s.f.* Anteojos que se apoyan en la nariz y en las orejas y que sirven para ver mejor.

**inapelable** *adj.* Referido esp. a una sentencia que no se puede modificar o anular.

**ir** *v.* Moverse de un lugar a otro.

**juez** *s.m.* Persona con la autoridad de juzgar a alguien y darle una sentencia.

**llanto** *s.m.* Salida de lágrimas generalmente acompañada de lamentos.

**mediocre** *adj.* Que no tiene la capacidad para la actividad que realiza.

**mostrador** *s.m.* Especie de mesa alargada sobre la que se muestran las mercancías o las bebidas en un bar.

**obligatorio** *adj.* Que se debe cumplir u obedecer.

**óptico** *s.m.* Persona que se dedica a la venta de objetos relacionados con la visión.

**pasear** *v.* Andar para pasar el rato.

**rehuir** *v.* Evitar algo o a alguien.

**rugoso/a** *adj.* Que tiene arrugas o pequeños desniveles.

**sufrir** *v.* Soportar o aceptar algo que resulta doloroso.

**verdugo** *s.m.* Persona encargada de ejecutar las penas de muerte u otros castigos corporales.

**whisky sobre las rocas** *exp.* Whisky solo servido sobre cubos de hielo.

*La sentencia del juez es inapelable.*

---

### 44 Antónimos  1.2

Elija el antónimo correspondiente a cada una de las siguientes palabras.

**1.** mediocre
  **A.** descompuesto
  **B.** competente
  **C.** inapelable

**2.** obligatorio
  **A.** rugoso
  **B.** óptico
  **C.** opcional

**3.** rehuir
  **A.** charlar
  **B.** colaborar
  **C.** pasear

**4.** verdugo
  **A.** amigo
  **B.** campesino
  **C.** juez

## Essential Instruction

1. Model pronunciation of the new vocabulary and have students repeat the words. Clarify any unfamiliar words in the definitions.
2. Have students complete **Actividades 45** and **46** in pairs. Be open to other answers in **Actividad 45** if students can justify their choice.
3. Before beginning **Actividad 47**, remind students that they will hear some vocabulary from p. 210 in the story.
4. For **Actividad 47**, have students listen to the story with their eyes closed. Play it a second time, pausing to ask questions. Then play the rest of the audio and have students select their answers.

## 45 Identifique al intruso  1.3

Diga qué palabra no pertenece al grupo y explique por qué.

**MODELO**   charlar / encanecer / pasear
**Encanecer no es algo que se hace por diversión.**

1. sufrir / llanto / rehuir
2. corteza / óptico / gafas
3. amistad / amigos / verdugo
4. juez / inapelable / campesino
5. estreno teatral / felicitación / corteza
6. whisky sobre las rocas / mostrador / espejo

## 46 Solo ha sido un sueño  1.2

Complete el párrafo con la palabra del recuadro que corresponda según el contexto.

| mediocre | docenas | llanto | charlaba |
|---|---|---|---|
| felicitación | rehuían | espejo | verdugos |

Un día, mientras __(1)__ con una amiga mía, una actriz famosa, me contó este sueño que tenía con frecuencia.

Había fracasado (*failed*). Solo unas cuantas __(2)__ de personas se habían presentado a su estreno teatral. Estaba sola en su cuarto. Sufría y no podía resistir su propio __(3)__. Se miraba al __(4)__ y se preguntaba si en realidad era tan __(5)__ que no merecía ni una simple __(6)__. Pero no, todos se habían vuelto jueces y __(7)__ y hasta sus propias amistades la __(8)__ al pasar. Luego se despertaba con alivio (*relief*) al darse cuenta de que solo había sido un sueño.

## 47 Las gafas  1.2, 3.1

Escuche el relato "Las gafas". Luego, Ud. oirá la primera parte de una oración y tres respuestas posibles. Seleccione la letra de la respuesta con la terminación más lógica. La oración y las terminaciones se leerán dos veces.

1. **A.** ... para la fiesta de San Isidro.
   **B.** ... para la fiesta de Santa Isidora.
   **C.** ... para comprarse gafas.
2. **A.** ... para ver todo, contemplarlo y admirarlo.
   **B.** ... porque nunca habían visitado Madrid.
   **C.** ... porque eran campesinos.
3. **A.** ... vio a una señora con gafas.
   **B.** ... vio a un señor que quería comprar gafas.
   **C.** ... vio a una señora que quería comprar gafas.
4. **A.** ... empezó a leer el periódico.
   **B.** ... empezó a ponerse gafas.
   **C.** ... se compró unas gafas.
5. **A.** ... si sabía leer.
   **B.** ... si podía ver.
   **C.** ... si quería leer.
6. **A.** ... si pudiera ver, no compraría las gafas.
   **B.** ... si tuviera dinero, compraría las gafas.
   **C.** ... si supiera leer, no necesitaría gafas.

---

## Special Needs Students
**Auditory Impairment**
Provide students with the script of the story and the sentence starters in **Actividad 47**.

## Multiple Intelligences
**Bodily-Kinesthetic/Verbal-Linguistic**
Have students work in groups of four to role-play "**Las gafas**." Three students can act out the dialogue and actions, and the fourth student can serve as narrator. To challenge students, do not provide them with the script, but rather have them improvise the narration and dialogue in their own words.

---

## RESOURCES

   Activity 47

**Answers**

**45** *Las explicaciones variarán.*
1. *Rehuir* no tiene que ver con sentimientos de tristeza.
2. *Corteza* no tiene que ver con la vista.
3. *Verdugo* no tiene que ver con la amistad.
4. *Campesino* no tiene que ver con la justicia.
5. *Corteza* no se relaciona con ocasiones de celebración y felicitación.
6. *Espejo* no tiene que ver con bebidas y dónde se sirven.

**46**
1. charlaba
2. docenas
3. llanto
4. espejo
5. mediocre
6. felicitación
7. verdugos
8. rehuían

**47 Script**
Como se acercaba el día de San Isidro, muchos campesinos habían venido a Madrid desde los pequeños pueblos de Castilla.
Llenos de curiosidad circulaban los forasteros por calles y plazas y entraban en las tiendas para ver todo, contemplarlo y admirarlo.
Uno de estos campesinos entró en la tienda de un óptico en el momento que estaba allí una señora que quería comprar unas gafas.
*Continued on p. 225.*

1. Muchos campesinos habían venido a Madrid...
2. Los forasteros entraban en las tiendas y los almacenes...
3. Un campesino entró en la tienda de un óptico y...
4. El campesino quiso imitar a la señora y...
5. El vendedor le preguntó al campesino...
6. El campesino le dijo que...

1. A; 2. A; 3. C; 4. B; 5. A; 6. C

**211**

## 48 No solo son negocios  1.2

Complete las oraciones sobre cómo hacer negocios en México con el pronombre de complemento indirecto que corresponda según el contexto.

A la persona que quiere hacer negocios en México __(1)__ conviene seguir algunos consejos. Por ejemplo, por lo general, a los mexicanos __(2)__ importan mucho los lazos personales y por eso __(3)__ gusta conocer bien a la gente primero, y hacer negocios después. A nosotros, los estadounidenses, no __(4)__ interesan tanto esas consideraciones. Pasar tiempo conociendo a la gente nos parece una pérdida de tiempo. A nosotros __(5)__ gusta ser breves y eficientes.

A los mexicanos __(6)__ gusta saber qué nos parece su país. Si contestamos: "A mí __(7)__ encanta el clima, la cocina, y la gente", se sienten satisfechos y abren el paso para hacer negocios con toda confianza.

## ¡Comunicación!

## 49 ¿Ha cambiado de forma de pensar?  Interpersonal Communication  1.1, 5.2

Cuando era niño/a quizás Ud. tenía una idea de lo que quería ser. ¿Han cambiado sus ideas? Con un(a) compañero/a, túrnense para hacerse las siguientes preguntas y responderlas, como se ve en el modelo.

MODELO   A: ¿Qué querías ser cuando tenías 13 años y qué quieres ser ahora?
B: Yo quería ser artista. Ahora quiero tener mi propia empresa.
A: ¿Por qué?
B: Porque me interesa ganar dinero. Y tú, ¿qué querías ser?
A: …

**A los trece años…**

• ¿Qué quería ser y por qué?

• ¿Qué cosas o actividades le interesaban?

• Después de las clases y los fines de semana, ¿qué le gustaba hacer y con quién(es)?

• ¿Qué le importaba más a esa edad? ¿Y qué les importaba mucho a sus padres?

**Ahora…**

• ¿Qué quiere ser y por qué?

• ¿Qué cosas o actividades le interesan?

• Después de las clases y los fines de semana, ¿qué le gusta hacer y con quién(es)?

• ¿Qué le importa más en la vida? ¿Y qué les importa a sus padres? ¿Le importa mucho a Ud. la opinión de sus padres y la de sus amigos? Explique.

• ¿Qué es lo que más le molesta a Ud.?

• ¿Hay algo que le encanta hacer después de las clases o del trabajo? ¿Qué es?

---

## RESOURCES

 Flipgrid

**Answers**

**48**
1. le
2. les
3. les
4. nos
5. nos
6. les
7. me

**49** *Las conversaciones variarán.*

## Expansion

After students complete **Actividad 49**, have them predict the type of person they will be twenty years from now. Have them answer questions such as: **¿Qué cosas o actividades te interesarán? ¿Qué te encantará hacer los fines de semana? ¿Qué te molestará? ¿Qué te importará más en la vida?** You may want to have them answer the questions via Flipgrid.

---

## Differentiated Learning
**Decelerate/Adapt**
Before putting students in pairs for **Actividad 49**, tell them to make a Venn diagram with the labels **A los 13 años** and **Ahora**, and write their answers to the questions in short form. They should note any similarities in the space where the circles overlap.

## Learning Styles
**Visual Learners**
Bring in photographs of people engaged in a variety of activities. Hold up the photos and have students make statements about the people's likes and dislikes. Encourage creativity.

## Communication

**Interpersonal/Presentational: Cooperative Groups**

Divide the class into small groups. Ask them to create a description of a famous person from the present day or in history. They should focus on using verbs like **gustar** to describe the person's preferences. Then have groups read their descriptions for the class, who should guess the person's identity.

## Expansion

Tell students to take notes during their conversations in **Actividad 51**. Follow up by having students report back to the class about their partner's responses.

**50 Dígame...**  1.3

Forme diez oraciones con una frase o palabra de cada columna, como se ve en el modelo.

MODELO    **A mí me duele el estómago.**

| I | II | III |
|---|---|---|
| A mí... | ...(no) convenir... | ...los ojos. |
| A vosotras... | ...(no) gustar... | ...los exámenes finales. |
| Al jefe... | ...(no) doler... | ...la lluvia. |
| A las personas de negocios... | ...(no) encantar... | ...la vendedora. |
| A ti... | ...(no) faltar... | ...las vacaciones largas. |
| A la profesora... | ...(no) importar... | ...dos horas para salir. |
| A Ud. ... | ...(no) molestar... | ...este trabajo. |
| A los estudiantes... | ...(no) quedar... | ...tiempo para divertirse. |
| A mi hermana... | ...(no) caer bien... | ...el estómago. |
| A mi jefe... | | ...sobregirarse. |
| Al banquero... | | ...renunciar al empleo. |
| | | ...atender a los clientes. |
| | | ...invertir mucho dinero. |
| | | ...los socios. |
| | | ...pagar al contado. |

**¡Comunicación!**  1.1, 5.2

**51 Gustos e intereses** 👥 **Interpersonal Communication**

Intercambie información con un(a) compañero/a sobre los siguientes temas. Usen verbos como **gustar** para hablar de lo que les gusta, les interesa o les disgusta. Túrnense para hacerse preguntas y responderlas, como se ve en el modelo.

*A mí me encanta el campo de la tecnología.*

MODELO    A: **¿Cuánto tiempo te falta para terminar tus estudios?**
          B: **Me falta un año solamente.**
          A: **¡Qué bueno! ¿Qué te interesa hacer después de graduarte?**
          B: **...**

• Su vida de colegio: clases, horarios, compañeros y profesores.

• Su vida en casa: padres, amigos, vecinos y familiares.

• Sus actividades fuera del colegio: trabajo, deporte, arte, comunidad.

• Sus planes de trabajo futuro: profesiones, ocupaciones, campos de trabajo.

• Sus finanzas personales ahora o en el futuro: sueldo, cuentas bancarias, ahorros, inversiones.

## Essential Instruction

1. For **Actividad 50**, emphasize that there are a myriad of possible combinations for these columns.

2. For **Actividad 51**, have students report to the class about their partner's answers.

3. Read through the four uses of **se** and give additional examples. Then, to practice the impersonal **se**, ask: **¿Dónde se come bien en esta ciudad?** Finally, drop your keys on the floor and say, **Se me cayeron las llaves.** and hold up your cell phone and say, **Se me acaba la batería.**

# Gramática

## Usos del pronombre *se*  1.2

El pronombre **se** tiene diferentes significados según el contexto de las oraciones en que se usa, ya sea que funcione como pronombre de complemento indirecto o como pronombre de carácter reflexivo, recíproco o impersonal.

| | |
|---|---|
| **Como pronombre de complemento:** | **Se** lo dije pero no quiso oír. |
| **Como pronombre reflexivo:** | **Se** esfuerzan por salir adelante. |
| **Como pronombre recíproco:** | **Se** apoyan mutuamente. |
| **Como pronombre impersonal:** | **Se** habla español. |

### El *se* impersonal

El *se* impersonal se usa en expresiones que hacen énfasis en la acción, no en el sujeto, el cual es indefinido. Es el equivalente del inglés *one*, *people* o *they* y siempre se usa con el verbo en tercera persona singular.

**Se puede** ganar mucho dinero si **se invierte** bien.
**Se cree** que ese campo de trabajo es muy lucrativo.

### *Se* en acciones inesperadas o involuntarias

También se usa **se** para hablar de acciones inesperadas o involuntarias que son el resultado de un acto no deliberado y fuera del control del sujeto que las realiza. En estas construcciones, **se** va acompañado del pronombre de complemento indirecto (que indica el sujeto) y el verbo en tercera persona singular o plural. En estos casos, el verbo concuerda en número con el sustantivo al que modifica.

| | |
|---|---|
| **Se me perdió** la tarjeta de crédito. | *My credit card was lost.* |
| **Se nos acabaron** los ahorros. | *Our savings ran out.* |

- Compare las dos oraciones:

| | |
|---|---|
| **Yo perdí** las llaves. | (Yo acepto la responsabilidad.) |
| *I lost my keys.* | |
| **Se me perdieron** las llaves. | (Yo no acepto la responsabilidad.) |
| *My keys got lost.* | |

- Estos son algunos de los verbos que se usan con esta construcción.

| | |
|---|---|
| acabarse | pararse |
| agotarse (terminarse) | perderse (ie) |
| caerse | quedarse |
| olvidarse | romperse |

*Qué pena. Se me olvidó avisarte que voy a llegar tarde.*

---

---

**215**

**52   Otros consejos para hacer negocios en México**   **1.2**

Cambie la estructura de las frases entre paréntesis (Ud. + verbo o la gente + verbo) a la estructura con **se** impersonal (se + tercera persona singular del verbo).

Para poder quedar bien con los colegas mexicanos (**1.** *Ud. debe saber*) algunas "reglas sociales". Por ejemplo, en México y muchas partes de América Latina, en reuniones formales e informales (**2.** *la gente tiende*) a estrecharse la mano (*shake hands*) con más frecuencia que en Estados Unidos. (**3.** *la gente hace*) esto al saludarse y al despedirse. (**4.** *la gente también suele*) acercarse más a la persona con quien se habla. (**5.** *la gente mantiene*) contacto visual al conversar. También (**6.** *la gente habla*) más con las manos (aunque no tanto como algunos europeos). Pero, (**7.** *Ud. debe*) evitar hacer los gestos si (**8.** *Ud. no sabe*) bien qué significan. Por ejemplo, cuando (**9.** *Ud. hace*) un gesto con la mano que para un mexicano significa "Muchas gracias," el mismo gesto para un argentino significa "¿Qué diablos quieres?" Por eso, (**10.** *Ud. tiene que*) tener cuidado.

## ¡Comunicación!

**53   Situaciones inesperadas**   **Interpersonal Communication**  **1.1**

Hable con su compañero/a sobre las siguientes situaciones inesperadas. Usen la estructura con **se** y túrnense para hacerse preguntas y responderlas, como se ve en el modelo.

MODELO   Olvidarse de pagar la cuenta de una tarjeta de crédito

**A:  ¿Qué pasa si se te olvida pagar la cuenta de una tarjeta de crédito?**

**B:  Si se me olvida pagar una cuenta, me cobran intereses altos y me enfado.**

• Acabarse el dinero antes del fin de mes

• Pararse el coche en la carretera

• Perderse las llaves de la casa

• Romperse un espejo

• Caerse los libros al subir a un autobús

• Olvidarse de hacer la tarea y estudiar para el examen

*¿Quién sabe?*

**Essential Instruction**

1. Check answers to **Actividad 52** by reading the paragraph aloud and having students call out the answers chorally.
2. Call on students to share their answers from **Actividad 53** with the class.
3. Go over the expressions in **Para decir más** and the drawings in **Actividad 54**, and model the pronunciation. Make sure that everyone is familiar with the game "Bingo."

## ¡Comunicación!

**54 ¿Cómo se juega?** Interpersonal Communication   **1.1, 1.3, 2.2, 4.2**

La lotería es un juego sumamente conocido y popular en México. Es similar al "Bingo" que se juega en EE. UU., pero emplea ilustraciones como las siguientes en vez de números y letras. En parejas, usen el **se** indefinido y el vocabulario de *Para decir más* para explicar cómo se juega.

### Para decir más

| | |
|---|---|
| la baraja | *deck of cards* |
| cantar o pregonar las figuras | *to call out or announce the figures* |
| el montón de frijoles o piedras | *pile of beans or stones* |
| llenar una hilera o tablero entero | *to complete a line or the whole board* |
| recibir un premio | *to receive a prize* |
| ganar el derecho de cantar | *to win the right to call out* |
| la siguiente tanda | *the next round* |

## RESOURCES

(fg) Flipgrid

Answers

**54** *Las respuestas variarán.*

### Expansion

Have students use Flipgrid to tell a chain story about a day in which everything goes wrong (**Un día terrible**). One person begins the story, and then other students continue the story via postings.

### Game

**Lotería**
Obtain an authentic **Lotería** game and play it with the class. (Spanish-language **Lotería** board games designed for young children are widely available.) Alternatively, have students design and create their own game boards and deck of images.

## Differentiated Learning
**Expand**
Ask students to research other popular games and pastimes in Mexico. Ask them to compare and contrast the activities with ones that they and their friends do.

## Multiple Intelligences
**Verbal-Linguistic**
Ask students to write creative sentences using the words from **Para decir más**.

# Gramática

## Las preposiciones *a* y *con*  1.2, 4.1

### Usos de la preposición *a*

- La preposición **a**, también llamada **a personal**, se usa cuando el complemento directo de la oración es una persona, una mascota (*pet*) o una cosa o idea personificada.

    El empleado no oyó **a** su jefe cuando le dijo que no llevara **a** su perro a la oficina.
    Los abuelos no temen **a** la muerte.

- También se usa con los pronombres indefinidos **alguien**, **nadie**, **alguno** y con **ninguno** y **cualquiera** cuando se refieren a un ser animado, pero se omite después del verbo tener y cuando las personas a quienes se refiere son indefinidas.

    —¿Conoces **a alguien** que haya tenido ese trabajo? —No, no conozco **a nadie**.
    —¿Tienes muchos parientes? —No, solo tengo un hermano.
    Busco un hombre viejo que recuerde cómo era la fábrica hace cincuenta años.

- La preposición **a** se usa para introducir el complemento indirecto (*to, for*).

    José nos debe dinero **a** nosotros, pero le dijimos **a** su madre que no tiene que devolvérnoslo.

- Se usa después de un verbo de movimiento (**ir**, **venir**, **bajar**, **subir**, **dirigirse**, **acercarse**) para indicar dirección hacia una persona, cosa o lugar (*to*).

    Se va **a** Chile para hacer las investigaciones.
    Nos acercamos con gran respeto **al** presidente.

- Se usa para designar la hora a la que ocurre una acción (*at*).

    Terminamos **a** las siete esta noche, y **a** las ocho iré a tu casa.

- Se usa para señalar lo que ocurrió después de un período de tiempo (*at, on, within*).

    **A** los dos meses de conocerse, se casaron y **al** día siguiente se mudaron a Taxco.

- Se usa seguida de un sustantivo para indicar manera o método (*by*).

    Antes la gente prefería pagar **al** contado.

- Se usa para indicar dos acciones que ocurren al mismo tiempo: **al** + infinitivo (*upon*).

    Se me ocurrió esa idea **al** entrar al banco. **Al** salir, me olvidé de despedirme.

### Usos de la preposición *con*

- Para expresar acompañamiento (*with*).

    Voy **contigo** al banco si vas **conmigo** al cine.

- Seguido de un sustantivo como sustituto del adverbio (*with*).

    Llenó la solicitud **con** cuidado (cuidadosamente).
    Llamó por teléfono **con** frecuencia (frecuentemente) para saber si había conseguido el puesto.

- Para caracterizar a una persona por algo que la acompaña (*with*).

    El hombre **con** barba es el jefe de la empresa.

## 55 En la oficina  1.2

Complete las conversaciones con **a**, **al** o **con** según se necesite de acuerdo al contexto.

**A.** —¿Qué busca Ud.?

— Busco __(1)__ los documentos que me dieron __(2)__ entrar __(3)__ la empresa esta mañana.

—¿No los encuentra?

—No. Se me perdieron __(4)__ los dos minutos de entrar en mi despacho.

—Y la jefa, ¿qué dice?

—¡Qué va a decir! Me los está pidiendo __(5)__ impaciencia.

**B.** — Esta noche viajo __(6)__ el gerente de ventas __(7)__ Nueva York. Esperamos encontrar __(8)__ un jefe de empresa que desee invertir dinero en México.

—¿Conocen __(9)__ alguien?

—¡Qué va! No conocemos __(10)__ nadie.

—¿Tienen algunas referencias?

—Le pregunté __(11)__ gerente y dijo que no tiene ninguna.

—Hermano, __(12)__ todo mi respeto te digo que así no se hacen los negocios.

¿Conoce a alguien que haya estudiado para ser artista?

No, no conozco a nadie. Conozco a alguien que es científico.

## Connections

**Art/History**
Display artwork by Mexican artists such as Diego Rivera, Frida Kahlo, José Clemente Orozco, and David Alfaro Siqueiros. Discuss the Mexican Revolution and the impact these artists' works had on society.

## Differentiated Learning
**Expand**
Have pairs of students write two more dialogues similar to the ones in **Actividad 55** and act them out for the class. Encourage them to use humor.

## Multiple Intelligences
**Verbal-Linguistic**
Have these students research the Nahuatl language and its influences on Spanish. How many Spanish words do they know that are derived from Nahuatl? How many English words?

**219**

# *Lectura literaria*

## Autorretrato   1.2, 2.2, 3.1
### de *Rosario Castellanos*

*Rosario Castellanos*

### Sobre la autora

Rosario Castellanos nació en México en 1925. Pasó su infancia en Chiapas, zona rural mayoritariamente indígena, lo que marcaría para siempre su obra literaria. Siempre tuvo presente una conciencia de las injusticias sociales. Se dedicó a la enseñanza de la literatura. Cultivó todos los géneros, pero es más que todo conocida por su obra poética, recogida en 1972 en el volumen *Poesía no eres tú*. Murió en 1971 en Tel Aviv, Israel, adonde se había trasladado como embajadora de México.

### Antes de leer  1.3, 5.2

En "Autorretrato" (*Self-portrait*), la autora hace una descripción poética de sí misma. ¿Cómo se describiría Ud. a sí mismo? ¿Cómo es físicamente? ¿A qué se dedica? ¿Qué le gusta hacer y qué no? ¿Qué lo hace feliz y qué lo hace llorar?

### Estrategia  3.1

**La inferencia**

La inferencia es una deducción que el lector hace de información que no está explícita en un texto. Hacer inferencias requiere de ánalisis y conexiones entre lo que está explícito en el texto y el conocimiento previo del lector. Es un proceso mental que contribuye a una mayor compresión de lo que se está leyendo.

### 56 Practique la estrategia 1.2, 1.3, 3.1

En "Autorretrato", Rosario Castellanos describe aspectos de su forma de pensar y de su vida cotidiana. Pero, a través de sus vivencias personales, se pueden percibir los prejuicios de la gente de su época. Analice las siguientes estrofas del poema, interprete su significado y diga qué información sobre la gente de la época podría inferirse del texto, como se muestra en la primera estrofa.

| Texto explícito | → | Análisis e inferencias |
|---|---|---|
| 1. "Yo soy una señora: tratamiento arduo de conseguir, en mi caso, y más útil para alternar (socializar) con los demás que un título extendido a mi nombre en cualquier academia". | → | **Estar casado es un símbolo de "status de sociedad" más importante y más útil que haber adquirido una eduación. Se puede deducir que las mujeres en esa época no valían por sus propios méritos sino por los méritos de sus maridos.** |
| 2. "Soy madre de Gabriel: ya usted sabe, ese niño que un día se erigirá (*will rise*) en juez inapelable y que acaso, además, ejerza de verdugo. Mientras tanto lo amo". | → | |
| 3. "Sé que es obligatorio escuchar música pero la eludo (*avoid*) con frecuencia. Sé que es bueno ver pintura pero no voy jamás a las exposiciones ni al estreno teatral ni al cine-club". | → | |
| 4. "Sería feliz si yo supiera cómo. Es decir, si me hubieran enseñado los gestos, los parlamentos (*speeches*), las decoraciones". | → | |

### Essential Instruction

1. As you go through **Sobre la autora**, pause to ask comprehension questions.
2. Read the **Estrategia**. Bring in example texts that convey information both explicitly and implicitly.
3. Have students complete **Antes de leer** and **Actividad 56** in pairs.
4. Have students look at the image on p. 221 and guess how the woman feels about herself.
5. Have students scan the poem for cognates and words they learned in **Vocabulario 3**.
6. Play the recording, pausing for students to answer the during-reading questions.

# Autorretrato   1.2, 2.2, 3.1
## de *Rosario Castellanos*

Yo soy una señora: tratamiento
arduo de conseguir, en mi caso, y más útil
para alternar con los demás que un título
extendido a mi nombre en cualquier academia.

5   Así, pues, luzco mi trofeo[1] y repito:
yo soy una señora. Gorda o flaca
según las posiciones de los astros[2],
los ciclos glandulares
y otros fenómenos que no comprendo.

10  Rubia, si elijo una peluca[3] rubia.
O morena, según la alternativa.
(En realidad, mi pelo encanece[4], encanece.)

Soy más o menos fea. Eso depende mucho
de la mano que aplica el maquillaje.

15  Mi apariencia ha cambiado a lo largo del tiempo
—aunque no tanto como dice Weininger[5]
que cambia la apariencia del genio—. Soy mediocre.
Lo cual, por una parte, me exime[6] de enemigos
y, por la otra, me da la devoción
20  de algún admirador y la amistad
de esos hombres que hablan por teléfono
y envían largas cartas de felicitación.
Que beben lentamente whisky sobre las rocas
y charlan de política y de literatura.

25  Amigas... hmmm... a veces, raras veces
y en muy pequeñas dosis.
En general, rehúyo[7] los espejos.
Me dirían lo de siempre: que me visto muy mal
y que hago el ridículo
30  cuando pretendo coquetear[8] con alguien.

[1] I display my trophy   [2] stars   [3] wig   [4] turns white   [5] Austrian philosopher (XIX c.)
[6] exempts   [7] avoid   [8] to flirt

*Rubia, si elijo una peluca rubia.*
*O morena, según la alternativa.*

 **1.2**
## 57 Comprensión

1. ¿A qué se refiere la autora cuando habla del "trofeo" y por qué lo luce?

2. ¿Qué tipo de admiradores le garantiza el ser mediocre?

3. ¿Qué tienen en común sus amigas y los espejos?

 **1.3**
## 58 Analice

¿Por qué cree Ud. que ser mediocre libra a alguien de tener enemigos? Explique.

## RESOURCES

 Autorretrato

Answers

**57**
1. Se refiere al título de señora y lo luce porque es un símbolo de status social más importante que cualquier título de estudios.
2. Le garantiza la amistad de hombres de medios que se pueden dar el lujo de hablar por teléfono, escribir largas cartas de felicitación, beber whisky en las rocas y charlar de política y de literatura.
3. Los dos le dicen que se viste mal y que hace el ridículo cuando pretende coquetear con los demás.

**58**
*Respuesta posible:*
La razón de muchas enemistades es la competencia, el deseo de ser mejor y más reconocido que los demás. Si la persona en cuestión es mediocre, se acaba la razón de la enemistad.

### Reference Desk

1. Before reading, ask students to write a list of adjectives to describe a woman in the 1960s and 70s.
2. Otto Weininger (1880–1903) was an Austrian philosopher. His book *Sex and Character* deals with the roles of men and women and the nature of genius. Today this book is widely considered misogynistic and anti-Semitic.

## Differentiated Learning
### Accelerate/Heritage Learners
Ask these students to compare and contrast the themes in "**Autorretrato**" with "**A Julia de Burgos**" by Julia de Burgos.

## Multiple Intelligences
### Visual-Spatial
Instruct students to draw a self-portrait and to answer the **Antes de leer** questions on their drawing. Display the portraits throughout the classroom. Ask students to circulate around the room to look at the portraits and responses.

**59**

1. En los versos 5 a 8. La autora es escritora de poemas y artículos que publica en un periódico. También es profesora de la universidad.

2. Le gusta leer y pensar y meditar en la oscuridad. No le gusta escuchar música, ni ver pintura. Tampoco le gusta ir al estreno del teatro o al cine-club.

3. Porque no llora ni al momento adecuado ni por las razones que se espera. Por ejemplo, no llora en la cámara mortuoria (a la muerte de alguien), pero en cambio llora cuando se le quema el arroz.

**60** *Respuesta posible:*

Se puede decir que la autora es una mujer culta e independiente que aprendió a pensar por sí misma y, por tanto, no está de acuerdo con el molde de comportamiento establecido para las mujeres de su época. Sin embargo, por más de que trata de ser diferente de ellas no logra hacerlo completamente y eso le causa sufrimiento.

---

### Reference Desk

Explain that **Bosque** in line 39 refers to Mexico City's **Bosque de Chapultepec**, one of the largest parks in the world (1,700 acres). It contains many attractions, such as a zoo, the Museum of Anthropology, art museums, and performance halls.

---

### Critical Thinking

**Analyzing**

Ask students to answer the following questions after reading the story: **¿Por qué creen que dice la autora "soy madre de Gabriel" en vez de "tengo un hijo"? ¿Cuál es su oficio? ¿Creen que está feliz con su trabajo?**

---

 **1.2**

### 59 Comprensión

1. ¿En qué versos hace la autora referencia a su oficio? ¿A qué se dedica?

2. ¿Qué le gusta hacer y qué prefiere no hacer?

3. ¿Por qué dice la autora que el llanto en ella es un mecanismo descompuesto? Dé ejemplos del texto.

**1.3, 3.2**

### 60 Analice

¿Por qué cree Ud. que no poder diferenciarse más de sus congéneres es causa de sufrimiento para la autora? ¿Qué dice eso de su persona y de su vida? Explique.

---

Soy madre de Gabriel: ya usted sabe, ese niño
que un día se erigirá en juez inapelable
y que acaso, además, ejerza de verdugo.
Mientras tanto lo amo.

35 Escribo. Este poema. Y otros. Y otros.
Hablo desde una cátedra[9].
Colaboro[10] en revistas de mi especialidad
y un día a la semana publico en un periódico.

Vivo enfrente del Bosque. Pero casi
40 nunca <u>vuelvo los ojos</u>[11] para mirarlo. Y nunca
atravieso[12] la calle que me separa de él
y paseo y respiro y acaricio
la corteza rugosa de los árboles.

Sé que es obligatorio escuchar música
45 pero la eludo con frecuencia. Sé
que es bueno ver pintura
pero no voy jamás a las exposiciones
ni al estreno teatral ni al cine-club.

Prefiero estar aquí, como ahora, leyendo
50 y, si apago la luz, <u>pensando un rato</u>
<u>en musarañas</u>[13] y otros menesteres[14].

Sufro más bien por hábito, por herencia, por no
diferenciarme más de mis congéneres[15]
que por causas concretas.

55 Sería feliz si yo supiera cómo.
Es decir, si me hubieran enseñado los gestos,
los parlamentos, las decoraciones.

En cambio me enseñaron a llorar. Pero el llanto
es en mí un mecanismo descompuesto
60 y no lloro en la cámara mortuoria[16]
ni en la ocasión sublime ni frente a la catástrofe.

Lloro cuando se quema el arroz o cuando pierdo
el último recibo del impuesto predial[17].

[9] professor's position    [10] contribute    [11] turn my gaze    [12] cross    [13] daydreaming
[14] (thinking about) business, errands, duties    [15] peers    [16] mortuary    [17] property tax

---

### Essential Instruction

1. For Common Core practice, have students answer the **Analice** questions.

2. Point out the **Pregunta clave** on p. 223 and have students reflect on the information they have gathered in this unit that will help them respond to the question.

3. Read through the **Proyectos** on pp. 223–224. Allow students to choose project(s) that most appeal to them. Provide detailed rubrics so that students are aware of the expectations for these tasks.

4. Have students peer-edit their articles from **Actividad B**.

# *Para concluir*

## Proyectos

**?** **Pregunta clave**

¿Qué factores afectan la situación económica de un país y de su gente?

### A ¡Manos a la obra! 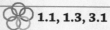 1.1, 1.3, 3.1

Trabaje con un(a) compañero/a. Preparen juntos un cuestionario de cinco preguntas para hacer una encuesta entre sus compañeros sobre sus expectativas en el mundo laboral. Hagan preguntas que ofrezcan opciones múltiples de respuesta para que los encuestados elijan una y Uds. puedan analizar los porcentajes.

Pueden tener en cuenta los siguientes temas o pensar otros por su cuenta:

- Cualidades importantes para conseguir trabajo
- Importancia de la formación y los estudios
- Campo del mercado laboral que les parece más fácil/difícil para conseguir trabajo
- Tiempo que puede demorar una persona en conseguir trabajo
- Si es más fácil para los jóvenes que para las personas de más edad

Luego, resuman los resultados de la encuesta y preparen gráficas de barras o de torta para ilustrarlos. Presenten la información a la clase.

*Los jóvenes opinan sobre su futuro laboral.*

### B En resumen  1.3, 2.1, 2.2, 3.1, 4.2

Ud. acaba de regresar de México y debe escribir un breve artículo para el periódico escolar sobre algunos de los problemas económicos de ese país. Puede escribir sobre la crisis económico-financiera de 1994, sobre la falta de una cultura del ahorro, sobre lo que opinan los empresarios mexicanos del teletrabajo, etc. En su artículo, comente las semejanzas y diferencias que encuentra con lo que ocurre en su país. Puede buscar más información en la internet si lo necesita.

*Un artículo sobre la economía en México*

---

**C** **¡A escribir!**  **1.3**

Imagine que Ud. es empresario y necesita contratar a un nuevo empleado para su empresa. Muchos aspirantes se presentarán a la entrevista. Piense en el perfil de empleado que le gustaría contratar: edad, estudios, experiencia, rasgos de personalidad. Luego, prepare un cuestionario de diez preguntas para los candidatos. Piense en opciones originales que los sorprendan y que los inviten a hablar con sinceridad.

*Una aspirante al empleo contestando las preguntas del cuestionario*

**D** **El mundo del trabajo**  **Conéctese: las estadísticas**  **1.3, 2.2, 3.1**

Vuelva a leer el texto de la *Lectura informativa*. Busque información estadística en la internet sobre el nivel de empleo entre los universitarios estadounidenses. Complete el cuadro comparativo con esa información, aunque también puede agregar otros datos. Analice las diferencias que le parezcan más llamativas. Luego, presente sus conclusiones a la clase.

| Los universitarios | en México | en Estados Unidos |
|---|---|---|
| No tiene empleo. | 59 % | |
| No está contento con su situación actual. | 88 % | |
| Estudian y trabajan. | 2 % | |
| Prefieren un empleo en el sector privado. | 54 % | |
| Quiere tener su propia empresa en el futuro. | 20 % | |

**E** **Sistemas de intercambio**  **Conéctese: la historia** **1.1, 2.1, 2.2, 3.1**

En la cultura maya, las rutas de intercambio comercial favorecieron la integración de diversos grupos que entraron en contacto para proveerse de productos que no estaban disponibles en su entorno inmediato. El comercio abarcaba artículos de consumo básico que se negociaban en mercados regionales, pero también objetos de lujo que se transportaban largas distancias por tierra o por mar y estaban reservados a un grupo social restringido. El acceso a estos bienes escasos o foráneos fue un factor importante en la constitución de las clases sociales superiores.

Converse con un(a) compañero/a y reflexionen sobre los puntos de contacto que hay entre el sistema de intercambio comercial en la cultura maya y la sociedad actual:

- ¿Creen que los bienes básicos de consumo siguen proviniendo en su mayoría de economías regionales o locales?

- ¿Creen que las rutas comerciales terrestres y marítimas siguen siendo las más importantes?

- ¿Qué factores económicos creen que mantienen hoy en día a las clases sociales más altas?

### Essential Instruction

1. For **Actividad C**, tell students to take into account the type of company they keep, in order to strike the correct tone in their questionnaires.

2. In **Actividad E**, tell students to give a few examples for each answer.

3. For the **Vocabulario de la Unidad 5**, ask students to determine several categories that could be used to sort the words. Then have students list the words in those categories.

# Vocabulario de la Unidad 5  1.2

**a diario** daily
**el/la agente de bienes raíces** real estate agent
**abrir una cuenta corriente/de ahorros** to open a checking/savings account
**acariciar** to caress
**las acciones** shares, stock
**ahorrar** to save
**el almacén** warehouse
**la amistad** friendship
**el ascenso** promotion
**atender a los clientes** to take care of (wait on) the customers
**averiguar** to find out
**los beneficios** benefits
**buscar** to look for
**la búsqueda** search
**el cajero automático** ATM
**el/la cajero/a** teller, cashier
**el cambio de moneda** currency exchange
**el/la campesino/a** peasant
**capacitado/a** trained
**la chamba** job (slang)
**charlar** to chat
**el/la cliente/a** client
**cobrar un cheque** to cash a check
**colaborar** to contribute
**el/la comprador(a)** buyer
**comprar a plazos** to buy in installments
**con frecuencia** frequently
**contratar** to hire
**contratiempos** setbacks
**la correspondencia** mail
**la corteza** bark
**costoso/a** expensive
**la cuota mensual** monthly payment
**dárselo** to let you have it for
**deber al banco** to owe the bank
**dejar** to leave
**descompuesto/a** broken
**el descuento** discount
**desempeñar** to work as
**despedir de un trabajo** to fire from a job
**la docena** dozen
**el/la ejecutivo/a** executive
**el/la empleado/a** employee, clerk
**la empresa** company
**encanecer** to turn white (hair)

**el/la encargado/a** person in charge
**endosar** to endorse
**la entrevista** interview
**entrevistar** to interview
**enviar** to send
**el espejo** mirror
**estar cansado/a** to be tired
**el estreno teatral** theatrical debut
**la experiencia** experience
**la fábrica** factory
**la fecha de vencimiento** due date
**la felicitación** congratulations
**las finanzas** finances
**las gafas** glasses
**las ganancias** profits
**ganar un sueldo** to earn a salary
**gastar** to spend (money, time)
**el/la gerente** manager
**girar/firmar un cheque** to draw/sign a check
**el/la hombre/mujer de negocios** businessman/woman
**las horas flexibles** flexible hours
**inapelable** unappealable
**ingresar/depositar un cheque** to deposit a check
**invertir dinero** to invest money
**invitar** to invite
**ir** to go
**irritarse** to get irritated
**el/la jefe/a** boss
**joven** young
**jubilarse** to retire
**el/la juez** judge
**el llanto** crying
**llenar una solicitud de empleo** to fill out a job application
**llevarse bien (con)** to get along (with)
**mediocre** mediocre
**la mercancía** merchandise
**el mostrador** counter
**las necesidades de empleo** employment needs
**obligatorio/a** compulsory
**olvidar** to forget
**el/la óptico/a** optician
**pagar al contado (en efectivo)** to pay cash
**pasear** to go for a walk
**pedir un préstamo** to apply (ask) for a loan
**las pérdidas** losses

**el personal** personnel, staff
**el porcentaje/por ciento** percentage, per cent
**el/la postulante/candidato/a** job seeker, candidate
**preocuparse** to worry about
**prestigioso/a** prestigious
**el puesto de jornada completa/tiempo completo** full-time position
**el puesto de media jornada/tiempo parcial** part-time position
**rebajar el precio** to lower the price
**los recursos humanos** human resources
**regatear** to bargain
**rehuir** to avoid
**renunciar a un trabajo** to resign from the job
**resolver problemas** to solve problems
**revisar el saldo** to check the balance
**rugoso/a** rough
**se busca** wanted
**se requiere** required
**sobregirarse** to overdraw
**el/la socio/a** partner, member
**solicitar un empleo** to apply for a position
**la solución** solution
**la sucursal** branch
**sufrir** to suffer
**supervisar** to supervise
**la tarjeta de crédito/de débito** credit/debit card
**la tasa de interés** interest rate
**tienden a producir** tend to yield
**el trabajador** worker
**tratar con** to deal with
**tratar en vano** to try in vain
**unirse** to join
**usar** to use
**el/la vendedor/a** salesperson
**el verdugo** executioner
**voluntariamente** voluntarily
**whisky sobre las rocas** whiskey on the rocks

---

Answers

**Script** *Continued from p. 211.*

La señora tenía muchas docenas de gafas extendidas sobre el mostrador. Se las ponía, miraba después en un periódico y decía:
—Con estas gafas no leo.
Siete u ocho veces repitió la operación, hasta que al final, después de ponerse otras gafas, miró en el periódico y dijo muy contenta:
—Con estas gafas leo perfectamente.
Al ver lo que había hecho la señora, el campesino quiso imitarla, y empezó a ponerse gafas y a mirar en el mismo periódico. Pero siempre decía:
—Con estas gafas no leo.
Así se pasó más de media hora; el campesino se puso tres o cuatro docenas de gafas, y como no podía leer con ninguna, las devolvía todas, repitiendo siempre:
—No leo con estas gafas.
El vendedor entonces le dijo:
—Pero, ¿Ud. sabe leer?
—Pues si yo supiera leer, respondió el campesino, ¿para qué necesitaría las gafas?

---

## Differentiated Learning
### Accelerate/Heritage Learners
Ask these students to write a short story using as much of the unit vocabulary and grammar as they can.

## Learning Styles
### Auditory Learners
Have students sit in a circle and play the game of telephone. Tell them that their sentences must use at least one word from **Vocabulario de la Unidad**.

1. This unit's country of focus is Chile, which occupies a long and narrow coastal strip of land wedged between the Andes mountains and the Pacific Ocean. The country borders Peru, Bolivia, and Argentina, and also includes Easter Island, Desventuradas, Salas y Gómez, and the Juan Fernández Islands.

2. Chile has the longest seacoast in the world, stretching from Peru all the way to Punta Arenas, one of the southernmost cities in the world. However, its widest point measures just 217 miles.

## Culture

**Products/Practices: Information**
The Mapuche are the original inhabitants of central and southern Chile, and the most numerous indigenous population in South America (about 1.4 million). **Machis** are central to Mapuche medicine; they possess knowledge of herbal remedies and are also believed to have spiritual powers. **Machis** are usually women.

## Culture

**Products/Practices: Activity**
Ask students to create a list of questions they have about Chile. As students progress through the unit, encourage them to document the answers they find in their Culture Journals. If any questions remain unanswered, provide suggestions for resources where students might find this information.

**¿Sabía que...?** 1.2, 2.1, 2.2

La medicina ancestral mapuche todavía se practica y convive con la medicina moderna. Para hacer un diagnóstico, el machi o chamán canta acompañado por el *kultrún* (tambor ritual) en una ceremonia llamada *machitún*. Todos los productos curativos de la medicina mapuche provienen de la tierra.

## Essential Instruction

1. Begin with a discussion of the **Pregunta clave**. Ask students to consider how health care changes over time.
2. Point out Chile on the map. Ask students to share what they know about the country.
3. Draw attention to the culture photo and question. Encourage students to watch for the photo and the answer later in the unit.
4. Point out the QR code, the video question, and the screen shot from "**Visitas inesperadas**." Encourage students to watch the video as many times as they like.
5. Have students read and ask questions about **Mis metas**.

# 6

# Salud y bienestar

## RESOURCES

 Visitas inesperadas

 Avenue

Escanee el código QR para mirar el video "Visitas inesperadas".

En esta historia de visitas y situaciones inesperadas, la madre de Alex se da cuenta de que él está enfermo y llama al médico para que vaya a hacerle una consulta en casa. ¿Qué síntomas tiene Alex, qué dice el médico y qué le recomienda?

*Pregunta clave*

# ?

¿Cómo cambia el cuidado de la salud según la época?

¿Qué papel desempeña el *machi* o *chamán* en la cultura mapuche?

Chile

## Mis metas

### En esta unidad:

▶ Usaré expresiones relacionadas con la salud y el bienestar, enfermedades, diagnósticos y tratamientos.

▶ Repasaré las formas y usos del presente del subjuntivo.

▶ Leeré sobre la medicina mapuche en Chile, la medicina rural y la salud en el mundo virtual.

▶ Distinguiré el significado de palabras y frases según el contexto.

▶ Usaré correctamente los mandatos de **Ud.** y **Uds.**

▶ Leeré un artículo sobre los momentos que marcaron la evolución de la medicina y la salud en Chile.

▶ Crearé una historia clínica con base en una entrevista entre un médico y un paciente.

▶ Escribiré un ensayo argumentativo con base en un segmento sobre la medicina complementaria y la medicina convencional.

▶ Desarrollaré nuevas destrezas de vocabulario.

▶ Usaré correctamente los mandatos de **tú**, **vosotros/as** y **nosotros/as.**

▶ Leeré el poema *"Walking Around"* del chileno Pablo Neruda.

doscientos veintisiete 227

## Multiple Intelligences

### Naturalist
Ask these students to research the varied landscapes and habitats of Chile, and prepare a geographical profile of the country. They can submit their profiles via Avenue.

### Verbal-Linguistic
Review and preview the unit vocabulary and grammar by asking questions such as: **¿Qué podemos hacer para mantener la salud? ¿Alguna vez has sufrido una fractura o golpe fuerte? ¿Dónde? ¿Qué le recomiendas a una persona que se siente muy estresada?**

# Vocabulario 1

## ¡Más vale prevenir que curar!  1.2

### Cuándo ir al consultorio del médico

*Respire profundo.*

Es importante que te hagas un examen médico cada año aunque te sientas bien. La enfermera revisará tu peso y tu presión arterial, te tomará la temperatura y te hará un análisis de sangre y de orina. Luego, el médico te examinará.

Ve al médico si tienes fiebre y dificultad para respirar y si te duele la garganta y no dejas de toser. Puede ser solo gripe, pero también es posible que tengas otra enfermedad o una infección que requiera antibióticos o algún otro tratamiento.

### Cuándo ir a la sala de emergencias

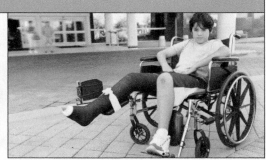

Ve a la sala de emergencias si te enfermas de gravedad o si tienes un dolor agudo constante en cualquier parte del cuerpo. Puede ser algo grave que necesite atención inmediata. Si ese es el caso, es posible que te lleven ahí mismo al quirófano para hacerte una operación.

También debes ir a la sala de emergencias si te caes y te rompes algún hueso. Allá te tomarán rayos equis para hacer un diagnóstico. Si te fracturas la pierna o el pie, es posible que tengas que estar enyesado por un tiempo y que tengas que caminar con muletas o usar una silla de ruedas.

### Cuándo pedir auxilio

Pide auxilio y llama una ambulancia si presencias un accidente, si alguien se estrella o es atropellado y debe ser llevado al hospital. Y recuerda: conduce siempre con cuidado. ¡No quieres ser el muerto o el herido de gravedad en esa camilla!

**228** doscientos veintiocho | *Unidad 6*

### Essential Instruction

1. Before playing the audio, have students scan the vocabulary on pp. 228–229 and pick out cognates. They can work in pairs and practice pronouncing these words.
2. Ask students to brainstorm a list of reasons why someone would visit a doctor.
3. Play the audio for **¡Más vale prevenir que curar!** Pause occasionally to ask comprehension questions.
4. Personalize the vocabulary presentation by asking students how long it has been since their last physical. Depending on your class's comfort level, you could ask about any emergency room trips or hospital stays.

## El cuerpo humano: partes externas

la cabeza
la espalda
la rodilla
la pantorrilla
el pie
la mano
la muñeca
las uñas

la boca
el pelo
el pecho
el cuello
el brazo
el codo
el hombro
la cintura
los dedos
la pierna
el tobillo

### La cara

el ojo
la nariz
los labios
la ceja
las pestañas
la mejilla
la oreja

### El cuerpo humano: órganos internos

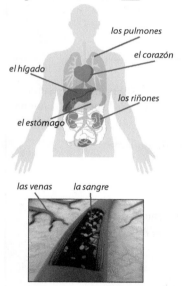

los pulmones
el corazón
el hígado
los riñones
el estómago
las venas
la sangre

### Para conversar

**P**ara intercambiar información en el consultorio del médico:

—Tengo los ojos superirritados y no dejo de estornudar. Creo que tengo una infección, pero soy alérgico a los antibióticos y no sé qué hacer.

—No se preocupe. Lo que tiene es alergia. Le recetaré otros medicamentos para aliviar los síntomas. Mientras tanto, póngase boca abajo que ya mismo le voy a aplicar una inyección. Verá que pronto se sentirá mucho mejor.

—Generalmente duermo bien, pero ya llevo varios días sin poder hacerlo y, luego, paso el día entero bostezando. Estoy preocupado.

—No se preocupe. Ud. sufre de insomnio. Le voy a recetar unas pastillas para dormir, pero sería buena idea ver a un psicólogo si el problema continúa.

*Unidad 6* | doscientos veintinueve **229**

RESOURCES

El cuerpo humano: partes externas
El cuerpo humano: órganos internos
Para conversar

### Reference Desk

1. You may want to present additional words for the body, such as **la barbilla**, **la cadera**, **el cerebro**, **el dedo del pie**, **la frente**, **la lengua**, **el muslo**, and **la piel**. The terms **los intestinos** and **el ombligo** are presented later in the unit.

2. Explain that **la oreja** refers to the outer ear, and **el oído** indicates the inner ear.

### Communication

**Interpersonal: Paired Practice**
In pairs, have students take turns describing a part of the body, for example, **Los uso para nadar y para abrazar a mi madre.** Their partner must guess the word (**los brazos**).

### Expansion

Give sentences that use expressions related to parts of the body, e.g., **Luis se encogió de hombros; Marta tiene cara de enojada; ¿Tengo monos en la cara o qué?** Have the class try to guess their meaning.

### TPR

Say aloud the names of different parts of the body. Have students point to where they are located on the body.

### Differentiated Learning
**Heritage Learners**
Health and medical vocabulary may vary by region; for example, most Spanish speakers use **la gripe** for *flu*, but in Colombia and Mexico **la gripa** is more common. Ask heritage learners what terms they know that are synonyms of the ones presented on pp. 228–230.

### Learning Styles
**Visual Learners**
Have students make their own flash cards for the new terms from **Vocabulario 1**. Tell them to use note cards, and to write the Spanish term on one side and draw or paste a picture on the other side.

### Reference Desk

1. Review additional medical vocabulary, such as **la homeopatía**, **sano/a**, **el seguro médico**, etc.
2. Students may also encounter **estar constipado/a** (*to have a cold*). Point out that this is a false cognate. Students will study a variety of false cognates in **Vocabulario 2**.

### Communication

**Interpersonal: Cooperative Groups**
In small groups, have students ask each other questions using a variety of verb tenses, e.g., **¿Alguna vez te has desmayado? Cuando eras niño/a, ¿tenías gripe a menudo?**

---

## Para conversar

**P**ara dar recomendaciones y consejos:

- Si te sientes débil y mareado/a a toda hora, como si te fueras a desmayar, es mejor que vayas al médico. Puede que sea una simple dolencia, pero es mejor prevenir que curar.

- Si estás embarazada y tienes náuseas y ganas de vomitar, es mejor que tomes remedios caseros para aliviar el malestar. Haz ejercicio para estar en forma y aliméntate bien para que tu bebé esté fuerte y goce de buena salud. Cuando sea la hora de dar a luz, ve de inmediato al hospital y dirígete a la sala de maternidad.

- Si tienes un resfriado o un simple catarro, no es necesario que vayas al médico. Toma jarabe para la tos. El farmacéutico te puede ayudar si no sabes cuál comprar.

- Cuando tengas una cita médica, chequea con la persona que está en el mostrador de información y, luego, espera en la sala de espera junto con los otros pacientes. Después de la cita, no te olvides de pagar la consulta o pedir que te pasen la cuenta.

**1 Una consulta médica**   **1.2**

Ud. tuvo una consulta médica porque se sentía enfermo/a y ahora le cuenta a su compañero/a cómo le fue en el consultorio. Escuche e indique la terminación correcta.

1. me tomó la temperatura / me recetó píldoras
2. tos / fiebre
3. el estómago / la lengua
4. la garganta / la nariz
5. me puse una inyección / me tomó la presión arterial
6. dar a luz / hacer el análisis de sangre
7. recetarme píldoras / recomendarme una buena dieta
8. pedí auxilio / pagué la consulta

*El médico me recetó unas pastillas.*

**2 Una emergencia en la sala de urgencias**  **1.2**

Imagine que Ud. es enfermero/a y tiene que preparar un informe para el médico sobre una señora que acaban de traer a la sala de urgencias después de un accidente. Combine las frases de la primera columna con las que correspondan de la segunda para hacer su informe.

MODELO    **Dr. Lara, la Sra. Ruiz tuvo un accidente. Tiene ocho meses de embarazo.**

1. Ella goza...
2. Aunque está...
3. Se queja de un fuerte dolor...
4. Su hermana dice que es alérgica...
5. Afortunadamente, no sufre...
6. Ya hemos pedido el análisis...
7. Parece estar a punto...

A. de cabeza.
B. de dar a luz.
C. de un buen estado de salud.
D. en forma, el embarazo es de riesgo por su edad.
E. de sangre.
F. a la penicilina.
G. de presión arterial alta.

### Essential Instruction

1. Ask students what they do when feeling dizzy or nauseous, have a cold or fever, etc.
2. Before playing the audio in **Actividad 1**, read aloud the answer choices. Tell students that they will hear sentence starters and must choose the correct ending.
3. Check their answers to **Actividades 1** and **2** orally as a class.
4. For **Actividad 3**, tell students that they can write information that is true for them or someone they know, or they could use impersonal expressions such as **Es bueno...** or **Hay que...**.

# ¡Comunicación!

## 3 ¿Qué haces para mantenerte saludable?   Presentational Communication  1.3

Complete las siguientes oraciones de manera lógica, como se ve en el modelo. Luego, comparta sus ideas con el resto de la clase.

**MODELO**   ....porque es bueno para la salud.

**Me alimento con comida sana porque es bueno para la salud.**

1. ...porque es bueno para la salud.
2. ...es mejor que tomar jarabe para la tos.
3. ...para evitar los dolores de estómago.
4. ...para dormir bien y evitar el insomnio.
5. ...y por eso creo que las mujeres embarazadas deben evitarlo.
6. ...es un síntoma de la gripe.
7. ...para estar en forma y tener una mejor calidad de vida.
8. ...para aliviar calambres o dolores por el deporte.

## 4 ¡Qué larga espera!   Interpersonal Communication  1.1

Imagine que Ud. tiene una cita con su médico, pero ha tenido que esperar por mucho rato pues hay muchos pacientes esperando turno. Con un(a) compañero/a, hagan el papel de los siguientes pacientes, imaginen su situación y representen su conversación. Túrnense para hacerse preguntas y responderlas, como se ve en el modelo.

**MODELO**   Una madre que trata de calmar a su hijo pequeño que no deja de llorar.

Madre:   **Cálmate, por favor, cálmate. Tan pronto te vea el doctor te sentirás mejor.**

Hijo:   **No quiero ver al doctor. ¡No quiero! Sé que me va a poner una inyección.**

- Una madre que trata de calmar a su hijo pequeño que no deja de llorar.
- Una señora que entra empujando a un muchacho en una silla de ruedas.
- Una señora que discute con su esposo quien no deja de bostezar.
- Una joven embarazada que le hace confidencias a una señora de edad.
- Dos ancianos que se conocen desde hace tiempo y se encuentran por casualidad (*by chance*) en la sala de espera.
- Un niño que habla con la recepcionista mientras su mamá llena el historial médico.
- Una joven que no deja de toser y estornudar y el muchacho que la acompaña.
- Un(a) paciente que se queja con la enfermera por que tiene una cita y está cansado/a de esperar.

*¿Sabes si me van a poner una inyección?*

---

## RESOURCES

  Flipgrid

Answers
3   *Las respuestas variarán.*
4   *Las conversaciones variarán.*

### Reference Desk

Before assigning **Actividad 4**, ask students to name ways to pass the time while waiting at the doctor's office.

### Communication

**Interpersonal/Presentational: Cooperative Groups**
Ask students to research and make a list of as many idiomatic expressions as they can that involve parts of the body (e.g., **tomarle el pelo a alguien**, **no tener pelos en la lengua**, **no tener dos dedos de frente**, **buscarle tres pies al gato**). In small groups, have students take turns reading their expressions to see if their classmates can guess the meanings. Finally, tell groups to write a skit that incorporates several of the expressions. Have groups perform their skits for the class.

### Expansion

After completing **Actividad 4**, ask students to create a Flipgrid post in which they describe a time when they experienced a long wait at a doctor's office or hospital.

---

## Learning Styles
### Visual Learners
Search online for anatomical illustrations and scenes from medical offices or hospitals. Provide students with a copy of the drawing and ask them to label the people, actions, and things.

## Multiple Intelligences
### Bodily-Kinesthetic/Verbal-Linguistic
Ask pairs of students to develop a skit between a doctor or nurse and a patient. Encourage them to use humor in their conversations. Allow the pairs time to rehearse and then role-play their scenes for the class.

**231**

# Gramática

## El modo subjuntivo  1.2

El **modo indicativo** se usa para referirse a hechos objetivos que tuvieron, tienen o tendrán lugar, como se ha visto en las unidades anteriores.

**Pasado:** **Tuvo** que ir a la sala de emergencia esta mañana por que **se sentía** muy mal.

**Presente:** **Está** en la sala de espera esperando los resultados de los rayos equis.

**Futuro:** El médico **analizará** los resultados y le **dará** un diagnóstico.

El **modo subjuntivo**, en cambio, se usa para referirse a estados o hechos hipotéticos, o a dudas, emociones o deseos.

En el modo subjuntivo, la acción del verbo generalmente depende de una acción en la cláusula principal que está en el modo indicativo. Las dos cláusulas van unidas por medio de la conjunción **que**.

cláusula principal      cláusula subordinada
El doctor me **recomienda**      **que descanse**.
Ind.      Subj.

### Conjugación de verbos regulares en el presente del subjuntivo

| tom**ar** | tom**e** | tom**es** | tom**e** | tom**emos** | tom**éis** | tom**en** |
|---|---|---|---|---|---|---|
| tos**er** | tos**a** | tos**as** | tos**a** | tos**amos** | tos**áis** | tos**an** |
| sufr**ir** | sufr**a** | sufr**as** | sufr**a** | sufr**amos** | sufr**áis** | sufr**an** |

- Los siguientes verbos tienen cambios en la terminación antes de -**o** (en la primera persona del presente del indicativo) y antes de -**a** (en todas las personas del presente del subjuntivo).

| g → j | c → zc | i → y | gu → g |
|---|---|---|---|
| **recoger** | **conocer** | **construir** | **distinguir** |
| reco**j**a | cono**zc**a | constru**y**a | distin**g**a |
| reco**j**as | cono**zc**as | constru**y**as | distin**g**as |
| reco**j**a | cono**zc**a | constru**y**a | distin**g**a |
| reco**j**amos | cono**zc**amos | constru**y**amos | distin**g**amos |
| reco**j**áis | cono**zc**áis | constru**y**áis | distin**g**áis |
| reco**j**an | cono**zc**an | constru**y**an | distin**g**an |

### Un poco más

La conjugación del presente del subjuntivo se obtiene fácilmente si se cambia la vocal -**o** de la primera persona singular del presente de indicativo por la vocal -**e** en los verbos terminados en -**ar** y por la vocal -**a** en los verbos terminados en -**er** e -**ir**.

recet**ar** → recet**o** → recet**e**

tos**er** → tos**o** → tos**a**

sufr**ir** → sufr**o** → sufr**a**

Esta regla también se aplica a los verbos de cambio radical y ortográfico, y a los irregulares que terminan en -**go** en la primera persona del presente del indicativo.

s**e**ntir → s**ie**nto → s**ie**nta

ele**g**ir → eli**j**o → eli**j**a

ten**er** → ten**g**o → ten**g**a

## Essential Instruction

1. Review the concept of grammatical mood; just like English, Spanish has three moods: indicative, subjunctive, and imperative. In this grammar presentation, students will learn the subjunctive; later in the unit they will study the imperative.

2. Go over **Un poco más**; ask students to give the full conjugations for the verbs in the box.

3. Emphasize that there are only six irregular verbs in the subjunctive.

- Los verbos terminados en **-car**, **-gar** y **-zar** cambian de ortografía en todas las personas del subjuntivo.

| g → gu | c → qu | z → c |
|--------|--------|-------|
| **pagar** | **sacar** | **gozar** |
| pa**gu**e | sa**qu**e | go**c**e |
| pa**gu**es | sa**qu**es | go**c**es |
| pa**gu**e | sa**qu**e | go**c**e |
| pa**gu**emos | sa**qu**emos | go**c**emos |
| pa**gu**éis | sa**qu**éis | go**c**éis |
| pa**gu**en | sa**qu**en | go**c**en |

*Es una lástima que la abuelita no goce de buena salud.*

- Los verbos que tienen cambios de raíz en el presente del indicativo también los tienen en el presente del subjuntivo. Los verbos terminados en **-ir** tienen un cambio adicional en la primera y segunda persona del plural.[1]

| e → ie | o → ue | o → ue, u | e → ie, i | e → i, i |
|--------|--------|-----------|-----------|----------|
| **pensar** | **volver** | **dormir** | **sentir** | **pedir** |
| p**ie**nse | v**ue**lva | d**ue**rma | s**ie**nta | p**i**da |
| p**ie**nses | v**ue**lvas | d**ue**rmas | s**ie**ntas | p**i**das |
| p**ie**nse | v**ue**lva | d**ue**rma | s**ie**nta | p**i**da |
| pensemos | volvamos | d**u**rmamos | s**i**ntamos | p**i**damos |
| penséis | volváis | d**u**rmáis | s**i**ntáis | p**i**dáis |
| p**ie**nsen | v**ue**lvan | d**ue**rman | s**ie**ntan | p**i**dan |

- Los verbos irregulares que terminan en **-go** en la primera persona cambian de la misma forma en el presente del subjuntivo.

| hacer | poner | decir | salir | venir |
|-------|-------|-------|-------|-------|
| **hago → haga** | **pongo → ponga** | **digo → diga** | **salgo → salga** | **vengo → venga** |
| hagas | pongas | digas | salgas | vengas |
| haga | ponga | diga | salga | venga |
| hagamos | pongamos | digamos | salgamos | vengamos |
| hagáis | pongáis | digáis | salgáis | vengáis |
| hagan | pongan | digan | salgan | vengan |

- En el presente del subjuntivo, hay seis verbos que son completamente irregulares.

| haber | ir | saber | ser | dar | estar |
|-------|-----|-------|-----|-----|-------|
| haya | vaya | sepa | sea | dé | esté |
| hayas | vayas | sepas | seas | des | estés |
| haya | vaya | sepa | sea | dé | esté |
| hayamos | vayamos | sepamos | seamos | demos | estemos |
| hayáis | vayáis | sepáis | seáis | deis | estéis |
| hayan | vayan | sepan | sean | den | estén |

[1] En el Apéndice C, consulte una lista de verbos en los que el radical cambia en el presente del indicativo.

## Reference Desk

1. You may want to review the conjugations of **jugar**, which has **u → ue** stem change and a spelling change (**juegue**, **juegues**...), and **oler**, which is a unique **o → ue** verb (**huela**, **huelas**...).
2. You may want to teach students the mnemonic device *DISHES* to help them remember irregular present subjunctive verbs (**dar**, **ir**, **ser**, **haber**, **estar**, **saber**).
3. Point out the accent on **dé** and explain that it is needed to distinguish the verb from the preposition **de**.
4. Explain that **haber** is an auxiliary verb; students will only use the third-person singular without a past participle.

## Game

### Concurso de ortografía

Hold a spelling bee to practice present subjunctive forms. Arrange students' desks in rows, and tell students to have paper and pencils ready on their desks. Explain that students within the row cannot communicate with each other during the activity. Call out a present subjunctive form that the row must spell (for example, **construyas**). Have the first person in the row say the first letter in Spanish, the second person the next letter, and so on until the row has spelled the verb correctly. If the row does not spell the word correctly, go to the next row and start the word over. Encourage students to write the letters that they have heard. Remind students they must include appropriate accents in order for the word to be correct.

## Learning Styles
### Auditory Learners

Read aloud sentences that use the present subjunctive, for example, **Es importante que durmamos ocho horas.** Have students listen for the subjunctive form, determine the infinitive, and call out the verb (**dormir**).

## Special Needs Students
### Dyslexia/AD(H)D

Create three-column worksheets with the headings **Infinitivo**, *yo - indicativo*, and **Presente del subjuntivo**. Provide infinitives in the first column, and model how to complete the second and third columns. Create separate worksheets for regular verbs, spelling-change verbs, and stem-changing verbs.

# El subjuntivo vs. el indicativo en cláusulas nominales

El verbo de la cláusula principal de la oración determina si se usa el indicativo o el subjuntivo en la cláusula subordinada.

> Verbo principal + que + $\begin{cases} \text{indicativo} \\ \text{o} \\ \text{subjuntivo} \end{cases}$

*La enfermera le pide a la paciente que conteste algunas preguntas.*

- Cuando el verbo de la cláusula principal se refiere a hechos objetivos que han tenido, tienen o tendrán lugar, se usa el indicativo en la cláusula subordinada.

    Él **sabe** que la anestesióloga **va** a ponerle anestesia local en la operación de mañana.

- Cuando el verbo de la cláusula principal se refiere a estados o hechos hipotéticos, o a dudas, emociones o deseos, se usa el subjuntivo en la cláusula subordinada.

    Ella **duda** que la anestesióloga **vaya** a ponerle anestesia local en la operación de mañana.

### El indicativo

El indicativo se usa cuando el verbo de la cláusula principal denota...

- percepción física o mental (**escuchar**, **notar**, **observar**, **oír**, **ver**, **saber**)

    **Supe** que **hay** especialidades nuevas en esta clínica.

    ¿**Notaron** que el paciente **tiene** una infección?

- comunicación verbal (**comentar**, **decir**, **explicar**, **opinar**)

    Los noticieros **dicen** que las enfermeras **irán** a la huelga.

    El paciente **opina** que no **existe** nada para aliviar el dolor tan fuerte que siente.

- procesos mentales (**creer**, **imaginar**, **pensar**, **recordar**, **suponer**)

    Mis abuelos **creen** que la tía Teresa **está** embarazada.

    Los tíos **suponen** que **dará** a luz en diciembre.

### El subjuntivo

El subjuntivo se usa cuando el verbo de la cláusula principal expresa...

- petición o mandato (**decir**, **exigir**, **mandar**, **pedir**, **ordenar**, **insistir en**, **requerir**, **hacer**)

    Los doctores **exigen** (**mandan**) que los enfermeros **se desinfecten** bien antes de ir al quirófano.

    El paciente **pide** que lo **atiendan** cuanto antes.

- deseo (**desear**, **esperar**, **preferir**, **proponer**, **querer**)

    **Espero** que te **haya ido** bien en el parto.

    ¿**Prefieres** que te **traiga** las medicinas al cuarto?

- consejo o ruego (**aconsejar**, **recomendar**, **rogar**, **sugerir**, **suplicar**)

  Los nutricionistas **recomiendan** que **consumamos** mucha fibra.
  ¡Camila **ruega** que **pidan** una ambulancia!

- permiso o prohibición (**aprobar**, **impedir**, **oponerse a**, **permitir**, **dejar**, **prohibir**)

  El traumatólogo no **permite** que **camine** sin muletas.
  La clínica **prohíbe** que **suban** visitas después de las nueve de la noche.

- emociones (**alegrarse de**, **tener miedo de**, **temer**, **gustar[le]**, **esperar**, **importar[le]**, **lamentar**, **molestar[le]**, **sentir**, **sorprenderse de**)

  Me **molesta** que no **atiendan** rápido a mi abuela.
  **Nos alegramos de** que **haya** buena atención médica en ese hospital.

| Otros usos del indicativo y del subjuntivo | |
|---|---|
| **Indicativo** | **Subjuntivo** |
| El indicativo se usa cuando la cláusula principal expresa seguridad (**saber**, **estar seguro de**, **no ignorar**, **no dudar**, **no negar**)<br><br>La doctora **está segura** de que el bebé **tiene** fiebre.<br><br>Los especialistas **no dudan** que **hay** una solución. | El subjuntivo se usa cuando la cláusula principal expresa duda o negación (**no estar seguro de**, **ignorar**, **dudar**, **negar**)<br><br>La mamá **no está segura** de que el bebé **tenga** fiebre.<br><br>Los pacientes **dudan** que **haya** una solución. |
| Se usa con los verbos **creer** y **pensar** cuando la cláusula principal es afirmativa y en oraciones interrogativas cuando el que habla expresa seguridad.<br><br>Él **cree** que **está** curado.<br><br>¿No **piensas** que **debes** ir al médico?<br><br>¿**Crees** que el doctor **está** mañana? | Se usa con los verbos **creer** y **pensar** cuando la cláusula principal es negativa y en oraciones interrogativas cuando el que habla expresa duda o falta de seguridad.<br><br>Juan **no cree** que **se cure** pronto.<br><br>¿Acaso **no piensas** que **debas** ir al médico?<br><br>¿**Crees** que el doctor **esté** mañana? |
| El indicativo también se usa en oraciones impersonales que expresan certidumbre o niegan la duda (**es evidente**, **verdad**, **obvio**, **indudable**, **cierto**, **seguro**; **está claro**, **no es dudoso**)<br><br>**Es seguro** que hoy **estará** el resultado.<br><br>**No dudo** que esta terapia **funciona**. | El subjuntivo se usa en oraciones impersonales que expresan duda o niegan la certidumbre (**dudo**, **es dudoso**, **no es verdad**, **no es cierto**, **no es evidente**, **no es obvio**, etc.)<br><br>**Dudo** que hoy **esté** el resultado.<br><br>**No es verdad** que yo **sea** alérgico.<br><br>También se usa en expresiones impersonales que expresan una opinión subjetiva o personal (**es bueno**, **mejor**, **malo**, **necesario**, **conveniente**, **preciso**, **importante**, **urgente**, **lástima**, **probable**, **posible**; **está bien**, **mal**)<br><br>**Es probable** que la niña **tenga** miedo. |

**RESOURCES**

 Flipgrid

**Communication**

**Interpersonal/Presentational: Cooperative Groups**
Write a list of ailments on the board (such as **el mal aliento**, **la artritis**, **la caspa**, **la indigestión**, **el resfriado**, etc.) and tell students that you suffer from all of these and need help. Divide the class into small groups where they should make a list of at least two home remedies for each ailment. Have groups share their remedies with the class using verbs such as **aconsejar**, **recomendar**, and **sugerir**; for example: **Recomendamos que usted tome té de jengibre para combatir la indigestión.** The other groups should voice their agreement or disagreement: **Sí, es cierto que el té de jengibre sirve para combatir la indigestión. / Dudamos que el té de jengibre pueda combatir la indigestión.**

**Expansion**

Ask students to create a Flipgrid post in which they express their wishes for their next birthday, e.g., **Espero que mis padres me den un carro. Es importante que celebre con mis amigos.** Invite students to post follow-up comments about each other's wishes, for example: **Recomiendo que tus padres te compren un carro híbrido. Es importante que cuidemos el planeta.**

**Differentiated Learning**
**Heritage Learners**
Ask students to write five sentences comparing U.S. social customs and customs in their family's country of origin. For example: **En EE. UU., es importante que seamos puntuales. En [país], es normal que lleguemos un poco tarde.**

**Multiple Intelligences**
**Visual-Spatial**
Ask students to create comic strips that use the present subjunctive. You may want to give a context, such as a doctor's office, or health class at your school. Display the comics in the classroom.

**235**

**5**

1. Es vital que apruebes este curso con buena nota.
2. Es mejor que empieces con un repaso de anatomía funcional.
3. También es conveniente que repases los conocimientos de fisiología.
4. Más vale que practiques con los modelos anatómicos, maniquíes y simuladores.
5. Es preciso que te aprendas de memoria los síntomas de los traumas para poder hacer un diagnóstico diferencial.
6. Conviene que seas cuidadoso a la hora de recetar medicamentos.

**6** *Respuestas posibles:*

1. J; Señora Lopera, es evidente que puede estar embarazada.
2. D; Lamento que tenga náuseas y mareos.
3. F; Es indudable que se siente mal y tiene cambios de humor.
4. I; Opino que necesite un análisis de orina y sangre.
5. G; Le prohíbo que fume y tome bebidas alcohólicas.
6. B; Le recomiendo que siga una dieta saludable.
7. K; Es mejor que camine mucho y tome mucha agua.
8. H; Supongo que se acuesta temprano o duerme ocho horas.
9. A; Es conveniente que haga ejercicio moderado.
10. C; Le sugiero que tome vitaminas y suplementos.

### Reference Desk

Remind students that they will have to add **que** to each sentence in **Actividad 5**.

### Expansion

After completing **Actividad 5**, ask students to write a list of advice for students interested in studying upper-level Spanish.

---

**5**  **La facultad de concentrarse**  👥  **1.1, 1.2**

Imagine que Ud. estudia en la Facultad de Medicina y necesita ayuda en su curso de traumatología porque es muy difícil. Con un(a) compañero/a, túrnense para convertir los siguientes comentarios en consejos, como se ve en el modelo.

MODELO  Es necesario estudiar mucho.

**Es necesario que estudies mucho.**

1. Es vital aprobar este curso con buena nota.
2. Es mejor empezar con un repaso de anatomía funcional.
3. También es conveniente repasar los conocimientos de fisiología.
4. Más vale practicar con los modelos anatómicos, maniquíes y simuladores.

*Es importante que entienda los resultados de su radiografía.*

5. Es preciso aprenderse de memoria los síntomas de los traumas para poder hacer un diagnóstico diferencial.
6. Conviene ser cuidadoso a la hora de recetar medicamentos.

---

**6**  **¡Jennifer Lopera está embarazada!**  **1.2**

El doctor Burgos sospecha que Jennifer Lopera está embarazada por los síntomas que presenta: náuseas, fatiga y edema. Mientras esperan el resultado de los análisis, el doctor habla con la Sra. Lopera. Forme oraciones con frases de ambas columnas, usando el indicativo o el subjuntivo, según la situación.

**I**

1. Señora Lopera, es evidente que....
2. Lamento que....
3. Es indudable que...
4. Opino que...
5. Le prohíbo que...
6. Le recomiendo que...
7. Es mejor que...
8. Supongo que...
9. Es conveniente que...
10. Le sugiero que...

**II**

A. hacer ejercicio moderado.
B. seguir una dieta saludable.
C. tomar vitaminas y suplementos.
D. tener náuseas y mareos.
E. no tener fiebre ni la presión alta.
F. sentirse mal y tener cambios de humor.
G. fumar y tomar bebidas alcohólicas.
H. acostarse temprano o dormir ocho horas.
I. necesitar un análisis de orina y sangre.
J. poder estar embarazada.
K. caminar mucho y tomar mucha agua.

### Essential Instruction

1. For **Actividad 5**, practice other subjunctive forms when checking answers by having students call out the sentences with **nosotros/as**, e.g., **Es vital que aprobemos este curso con buena nota.**
2. For **Actividad 6**, tell students first to match the columns, then conjugate the verbs, and finally write the complete sentences.

Remind them that all the verbs in the subordinate clause will be in the **Ud.** form.

3. Before assigning **Actividades 7** and **8**, go through the items and have students identify which ones will take the subjunctive.
4. Survey the class to see if they gave similar advice in **Actividad 9**.

 **¡Comunicación!**

 **1.1, 1.3**

## 7 La tensión y el estrés, enemigos de la salud  Interpersonal Communication

Un(a) colega y Ud. son expertos en el tema del estrés y su efecto negativo sobre la salud. Juntos darán una conferencia sobre el tema. En parejas, terminen las siguientes oraciones. Luego, comparen sus comentarios con el resto de la clase.

1. Es evidente que la tensión emocional y el exceso de preocupaciones...

2. Sabemos que las personas nerviosas o las que viven bajo un estado continuo de tensión...

3. Está comprobado que muchas enfermedades, desde un resfriado hasta el cáncer...

4. Los resultados de las investigaciones no evidencian que...

5. Para evitar que el estrés tenga efectos negativos en la salud, recomendamos...

6. Es una lástima que un ritmo de vida acelerado cause que...

7. Los pacientes dudan que su salud se vea afectada, pero el estrés excesivo...

## 8 ¡Auxilio, no puedo dormir! Interpersonal Communication **1.1**

Imagine que un(a) amigo/a le cuenta que sufre de insomnio y no sabe qué hacer. Túrnense con un(a) compañero/a para hablar sobre el tema y darle consejos. Use las siguientes expresiones y el indicativo y el subjuntivo según corresponda, como se ve en el modelo.

MODELO
A: He notado que pasas todo el día bostezando. ¿Qué pasa?
B: No sé qué hacer. Me lo paso bostezando todo el día porque llevo varias noches sin poder dormir.
A: Es probable que sufras de insomnio. Creo que debes ir al médico.

1. Te sugiero que...
2. No es conveniente que...
3. Supongo que...
4. Noto que...
5. Es mejor que...
6. Los médicos recomiendan que...
7. Creo que...
8. Es obvio que...
9. No dudo que...
10. Es probable que...

## 9 ¿Qué debo hacer?  Interpersonal Communication **1.1**

Imagine que Ud. es estudiante de medicina y todo el mundo le pide consejos sobre cómo prevenir ciertas condiciones y enfermedades. Represente la situación con un(a) compañero/a. Intercambien información con base en los siguientes temas y usen el indicativo o el subjuntivo según corresponda.

MODELO
A: ¿Qué me recomiendas para aliviarme de esta gripe?
B: Sugiero que descanses y tomes jarabe para la tos.

1. Los dolores de cabeza
2. Los catarros y la gripe
3. La diabetes
4. Las enfermedades cardíacas
5. Las caries (cavities) y los dolores de muela
6. Los dolores de estómago

### RESOURCES

 Avenue

Answers

7 *Las respuestas variarán.*

8 *Las conversaciones variarán.*

9 *Las conversaciones variarán.*

### Communication

**Presentational: Cooperative Groups**
As a class, brainstorm a list of areas that could use improvement in your school. Then divide the class into groups and have them choose the three improvements that they feel are most important. Tell them to write a formal letter to school officials politely pointing out the issues and using the subjunctive to request improvements.

### Communication

**Interpersonal: Paired Practice**
Have pairs of students talk about their favorite and least favorite movies. Tell them to make positive or negative recommendations using the subjunctive.

### Connections

**Health**
Ask students to create posters with their top ten recommendations for being healthy. Encourage them to use visuals and to give the poster a catchy title. Display the posters in the classroom; you may want to have the class choose one poster to be displayed at a local community center or gym.

## Differentiated Learning
**Adapt/Expand**
Expand **Actividad 7** by having students develop the sentences into the script of a TV news report on the negative effects of stress. Have students submit their reports via Avenue.

## Multiple Intelligences
**Musical-Rhythmic**
Choose a song that uses the present subjunctive, such as "**A Dios le pido**" by Juanes or "**Tortura**" by Shakira. Create a cloze worksheet using song lyrics; make a blank space for each subjunctive verb. Play the song one or two times and tell students to fill in the missing verbs.

**Answers**

**10**

1. Debido a la migración masiva a las ciudades.
2. Los machis y los médicos convencionales se derivan pacientes unos a otros según la dolencia que padezca.
3. Para los mapuches, es una manera de mantener vivas sus tradiciones, aun en la gran ciudad. Para el resto de la población, es una manera de acceder a tratamientos alternativos.

**11** *Las respuestas variarán.*

### Reference Desk

Students can do a Flipgrid post reacting to any of these cultural readings.

### Critical Thinking

**Analyzing and Comparing**
Ask students to consider what impediments there are to alternative medicine in the United States.

### Pre-AP

Have students respond to the **Pregunta clave**, in spoken or written form, using information from the readings on pp. 238–240. Students should also include a comparison between their own community/culture and Chile.

---

 *Cultura*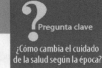

**Pregunta clave**
¿Cómo cambia el cuidado de la salud según la época?

**1.2, 2.1, 2.2**
### 10 Comprensión

1. ¿Por qué se pueden encontrar chamanes mapuches en la gran ciudad?

2. ¿Cómo se combinan la medicina mapuche y la convencional?

3. ¿Qué ventajas tiene la colaboración entre medicina mapuche y medicina convencional?

**1.3, 2.1, 2.2, 4.2**
### 11 Analice

1. ¿Qué opina Ud. de los tratamientos alternativos, naturales o tradicionales?

2. ¿Cree Ud. que en su país las personas recurren a la medicina alternativa tanto como en Chile?

## Medicina mapuche en el siglo XXI

Puede parecer de ciencia ficción, pero no lo es: en Chile es posible encontrar un chamán o médico mapuche en una gran ciudad moderna como Santiago. Históricamente, la medicina tradicional de los mapuches (los indígenas del sur chileno) se limitaba al ámbito rural. Sin embargo, con la migración masiva a las grandes ciudades, muchos sanadores[1] mapuches han abierto en ellas consultorios privados donde ofrecen una alternativa terapéutica.

*Los chamanes mapuches siguen teniendo vigencia en la actualidad.*

La medicina mapuche se basa en la herbolaria, que es el uso de plantas y hierbas con fines curativos, y es ejercida por el machi o chamán. Pero lo más interesante de esta alternativa es que no excluye las prácticas médicas convencionales. Por el contrario, ambas se combinan y complementan. Los machis ofrecen a los pacientes tratamientos muy distintos a los de la medicina occidental, pero los pacientes aseguran que no hay conflicto: a veces son los mismos médicos quienes los derivan[2] a un machi (por ejemplo, cuando se trata de problemas asociados con el estrés) o viceversa: el machi manda los pacientes al médico (por ejemplo, cuando sus dolencias[3] requieren una cirugía).

Esta colaboración intercultural recibe el apoyo del Ministerio de Salud de Chile, que desde hace años reconoce la medicina mapuche y permite el ejercicio libre[4] de los machis. De hecho, hay más de 150 plantas medicinales estudiadas y reconocidas por ese organismo. Para la comunidad mapuche, es una oportunidad imperdible[5] de mantener su cultura viva dentro de una gran ciudad. Para el resto de los chilenos, es una posibilidad de complementar y mejorar el cuidado de su salud.

[1] healers  [2] refer  [3] ailments  [4] free practice  [5] unique

**Búsqueda:** medicina mapuche, machi mapuche, chamán mapuche, programa salud y pueblos indígenas chile

---

### Prácticas   **2.1**

En Chile, según una encuesta del Ministerio de Salud, más de la mitad de las personas han recurrido en algún momento a la medicina alternativa para tratar problemas de salud. Esta práctica se ha difundido tanto entre los chilenos porque los mismos profesionales de la medicina convencional tienen una mirada positiva al respecto y muchos de ellos se especializan también en disciplinas de la medicina complementaria, como la homeopatía y la acupuntura.

*Muchos médicos chilenos recurren también a la medicina alternativa.*

---

### Essential Instruction

1. Point out the **Pregunta clave**, and tell students to keep it in mind as they complete these cultural readings.
2. Have students preview the titles and photos on pp. 238–240. Ask them to predict what they will learn about Chile.
3. Remind students of the photo and question from the unit opener. Ask where they can find the answer (in the second paragraph on p. 238).

# Un médico rural, un médico integral   1.2, 2.1, 2.2

Es posible que, al pensar en la medicina rural en América Latina, imaginemos un médico que, en solitario y maletín en mano, visita muy esporádicamente[1] a sus pacientes en lugares remotos. Pero las cosas cambian. Si bien es cierto que en el ámbito rural hay factores que dificultan el acceso a la salud, como las largas distancias o la falta de equipamiento especializado en las pequeñas clínicas, también hay muchos programas en los que los médicos trabajan en equipo para mejorar el sistema rural de salud.

En la Universidad de Chile, los estudiantes de medicina del último año de la carrera deben cursar un Internado Rural. Se trata de una experiencia integradora, en la que los internos se incorporan durante cuatro semanas a la vida rural: viven allí, se relacionan estrechamente con la comunidad y aprenden a apreciar sus condiciones de vida.

Los médicos rurales tienen una relación muy cercana con sus pacientes.

Durante esta experiencia, ponen en práctica sus conocimientos mediante actividades de promoción, prevención y atención primaria. Uno de los aspectos más enriquecedores es que los internos visitan a pacientes que no pueden asistir a la clínica. Así, entran en su hogar, conocen a su familia y forma de vida, conversan con ellos, les entregan medicamentos y resuelven situaciones clínicas agudas[2]. Este tipo de atención personalizada no es habitual ni posible en un consultorio moderno del sistema urbano de salud. En el internado rural, los futuros médicos adquieren una visión abarcadora[3] y alternativa de los problemas del paciente, sin dejar de lado ningún detalle. Así se preparan para ser médicos integrales.

[1] seldom  [2] acute  [3] wide-ranging

 **Búsqueda:** medicina rural en chile, internado rural universidad de chile

## Productos  1.2, 2.2

El Museo Nacional de Medicina de Chile contiene equipos e instrumental médico, libros, documentos y fotografías de la historia de la salud chilena. Los visitantes pueden acceder allí al patrimonio histórico no solo de la medicina convencional sino también de la medicina mapuche. En el museo hay un rehue (tronco de árbol que simboliza el poder), dos cultrum, o tambores, y una pipa usada por los machis. Hay también una pequeña muestra de las plantas medicinales de varias culturas precolombinas, que luego se incorporaron a la farmacopea española durante la conquista y, junto con los baños termales, sirvieron para aliviar las enfermedades de los conquistadores.

Los cultrum usados por los machis en la medicina mapuche

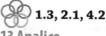 **12 Comprensión** 1.2, 2.1, 2.2

1. ¿Qué dificultades presenta el ámbito rural para el acceso a la salud?

2. ¿Qué se hace en Chile para mejorar el sistema de salud rural?

3. ¿Qué tiene de particular el ejercicio de la medicina rural?

**13 Analice** 1.3, 2.1, 4.2

1. ¿Qué opina Ud. de la mirada más abarcadora de la medicina rural u otras medicinas alternativas?

2. ¿Hay alguna práctica de la medicina de los pueblos originarios de su país que esté reconocida por la medicina convencional? ¿Cuáles?

---

---

**Answers**

**Perspectivas**
*Las respuestas variarán. Respuesta posible:*
La posibilidad de conectarse por la internet con los médicos y centros de salud es solo una herramienta de ayuda útil para obtener información, no para obtener tratamiento.

**14**

1. Permiten brindar servicios de medicina a distancia llamados "salud conectada".
2. El paciente se relaciona con su médico y obtiene información; los médicos se comunican entre ellos para capacitarse o hacer interconsultas.
3. Concentran todos los datos médicos de un paciente de modo que cualquier médico que lo atienda pueda tener una visión global de su estado.

**15** Las respuestas variarán.

---

 **1.2, 2.1, 2.2**
**14 Comprensión**

1. ¿Qué aplicación tienen las nuevas tecnologías de la información en la medicina?

2. ¿Cuáles son los usos de la salud conectada?

3. ¿Cuáles son las ventajas de la salud conectada?

**1.3, 2.1, 2.2, 4.2**
**15 Analice**

1. ¿Qué aplicaciones tiene la tecnología de la información en la medicina en su país?

2. ¿Cuáles cree Ud. que serían las desventajas de un sistema como la salud conectada?

---

# La salud en el mundo virtual   1.2, 2.1, 2.2

*Cada vez más personas tratan su salud a distancia.*

Desde hace mucho tiempo, la medicina usa la tecnología para mejorar su calidad de atención. Ya en el siglo XIX se transmitían datos clínicos por telégrafo; con la aparición del teléfono, se empezaron a intercambiar interpretaciones de exámenes y la televisión aumentó enormemente el volumen y el alcance de la información sobre la salud.

Hoy en día, gracias a las nuevas tecnologías de la información y las comunicaciones, se brindan servicios de medicina a distancia[1] llamados "salud conectada". Esto permite que los pacientes puedan supervisar su estado sin necesidad de acudir[2] a consultas u hospitales.

En Chile, hay varias empresas que brindan este servicio de vinculación[3] directa entre médico y paciente para el monitoreo a distancia de enfermedades crónicas como la diabetes o la hipertensión arterial. Pero hay otros usos para la salud conectada, por ejemplo, es una fuente de información para educar al paciente y también es un foro de capacitación[4] e interconsulta entre profesionales de la salud. Una ventaja importante es que en un único lugar se concentran todos los datos médicos del paciente, por lo que cada especialista que consulte su historia puede tener una visión global de su estado e indicar el tratamiento que resulte más apropiado.

Por supuesto que la salud conectada no reemplazará a las tradicionales consultas cara a cara. La idea es aprovechar[5] las posibilidades tecnológicas para integrar e intercambiar la información y avanzar hacia una medicina de mejor calidad.

[1] remote   [2] show up   [3] relationship   [4] training   [5] take advantage of

**Búsqueda:** salud conectada, portales de salud chile

**Perspectivas**  1.2, 3.2

Con el acceso a la internet, muchas personas pueden participar de la salud conectada, pero el servicio debe tener un sustento científico y profesional responsable. Xavier Urtubey, médico y presidente para América Latina y El Caribe de la Asociación Americana de Telemedicina (ATALACC), sostiene: "Se trata de la vida humana y no es cuestión de pasarle un *smartphone* con aplicaciones a un paciente y pretender que con eso vaya a tener una buena salud o se mejore. El hecho de que el teléfono tenga acceso a la internet no se traduce en la solución al problema del paciente".

¿Por qué las nuevas tecnologías en sí mismas no son suficientes para resolver los problemas de salud?

*Los servicios de salud siempre deben brindarse de manera responsable.*

---

# Vocabulario 2

## Comparación y contraste: ¡Ojo con estas palabras!  1.2, 4.1

Hay muchas palabras que tienen la misma raíz etimológica en español y en inglés. Estas palabras se llaman **cognados** y, a veces, tienen el mismo significado; por ejemplo: computadora = *computer*; universidad = *university*; composición = *composition*. Otras veces no tienen el mismo significado y, en esos casos, se conocen como falsos amigos o falsos cognados. Preste atención al uso de estas palabras pues su significado depende del contexto.

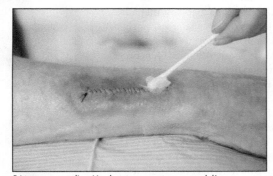

*Póngase una aplicación de esta crema tres veces al día.*

**asistir (a)**   *to attend*
¿Piensas **asistir** a la reunión del viernes?

*to assist*   **ayudar**
La instrumentista **ayudó** durante la cirugía.

**aplicación**   *application (of a cream, ointment)*
Tengo que ponerme una **aplicación** de esta crema tres veces al día.

*application*   **solicitud**
Él presentó una **solicitud** para trabajar como enfermero en la clínica.

**mover**   *to change the position of an object*
**Mueve** esa silla, por favor.

*to move*   **mudarse (cambiar de residencia)**
¿Cuándo **se mudaron** a este edificio?

**realizar**   *to fulfill, to achieve*
Carolina se propuso **realizar** sus sueños.

*to realize*   **darse cuenta de**
¿No **te diste cuenta de** que tenías fiebre?

**registrar**   *to examine, to inspect*
Le **registraron** todas las maletas en la aduana.

*to register*   **matricularse, inscribirse**
Mi prima **se matriculó** en la Facultad de Medicina.

**retirar(se)**   *to take away; to withdraw, to retreat*
Voy a **retirar** el dinero de mi cuenta de ahorros.
Estaba muy cansada y **se retiró** a su habitación.

*to retire*   **jubilarse**
La Sra. Pérez **se jubiló** de su puesto de enfermera hace un año.

**soportar**   *to put up with, to bear*
No **soporto** esta picazón en los ojos.

*to support*   **mantener, sostener**
Gano suficiente para **mantener** a mis hijos.

**embarazada**   *pregnant*
Ana está **embarazada**, pero no le ha dicho nada a su familia.

*embarrassed*   **apenado(a), avergonzado(a)**
Está **avergonzada** de decirles la verdad.

---

**16**
1. se jubiló
2. nos mudamos
3. ayudar
4. me doy cuenta de
5. embarazada
6. soportar
7. se mueva
8. ayudé
9. avergonzada
10. matricularme
11. solicitud

**17** *Las respuestas variarán.*

## Reference Desk

Santiago, located in Chile's central valley, is the country's capital and largest city. Although Santiago is the capital, Chile's legislative bodies meet in the city of Valparaíso, which is located approximately 75 miles northwest of Santiago on the Pacific coast. Viña del Mar is one of five cities that make up the greater Valparaíso metropolitan area.

## Expansion

For additional practice, ask pairs of students to write two cloze sentences for each verb from **Vocabulario 2**. They can exchange papers with another pair and complete the sentences.

### 16 ¡Me encanta mi profesión!  1.2

Complete el siguiente párrafo con la palabra entre paréntesis que corresponda según el contexto.

Mi nombre es Eugenia. Soy enfermera en un Hospital en Santiago, Chile. Trabajé por dos años aproximadamente en un hospital en Viña del Mar, cuando el año pasado, después de más de treinta años con una compañía de seguros médicos, mi padre (**1.** *retiró, se jubiló*). Nosotros (**2.** *nos mudamos, movimos*) a la capital. Me gusta lo que hago porque puedo (**3.** *asistir, ayudar*) a mucha gente. Además, (**4.** *me doy cuenta de, realizo*) que tengo muchas responsabilidades y de que es un trabajo maravilloso. Esta mañana, por ejemplo, una mujer (**5.** *apenada, embarazada*) llegó en ambulancia. Estaba sufriendo mucho, casi no podía (**6.** *sostener, soportar*) el dolor. Le dije: "Señora, no (**7.** *se mueva, se mude*). Tengo que tomarle la presión arterial". También le tomé la temperatura y la llevé a la sala de maternidad. Una hora más tarde, dio a luz a gemelos y me dio las gracias delante de todos. Dijo que yo la (**8.** *ayudé, asistí*) mucho y que soy la mejor enfermera del mundo. Yo estaba un poco (**9.** *embarazada, avergonzada*), pero me sentí feliz.

*Soy enfermera y me encanta mi profesión.*

Es obvio que me fascina la medicina. De hecho, me gusta tanto que he decidido (**10.** *matricularme, registrarme*) en la Facultad de Medicina de la universidad. Hace dos meses que presenté los exámenes de entrada y llené la (**11.** *aplicación, solicitud*). ¡Ya fui aceptada! Seré doctora dentro de siete años.

## ¡Comunicación!

### 17 Consejos y recomendaciones  Interpersonal Communication 1.1

Día a día se presentan situaciones en que los médicos, dentistas, familiares y maestros se ven en la obligación de dar consejos y recomendaciones. Con un(a) compañero/a, túrnense para dar las recomendaciones del caso en cada una de las situaciones que se dan a continuación, como se ve en el modelo.

MODELO  de un siquiatra a una paciente que sufre de depresión
**Le recomiendo que tome sus pastillas diariamente y se mantenga ocupada.**

**1.** De un maestro de español a sus estudiantes

**2.** De un doctor a una niña que se fracturó el brazo

**3.** De un profesor de música a sus alumnos de piano

**4.** De una madre a su hijo que ve mucha televisión y no le gusta hacer sus tareas

**5.** De la instructora de un gimnasio a un grupo de personas que quiere perder peso

### Essential Instruction

1. When checking answers to **Actividad 16**, ask students to explain why they chose each word.
2. For **Actividad 17**, ask students to brainstorm some verbs that they can use in their recommendations.
3. As pairs share their lists of characteristics in **Actividad 18**, write the ideas on the board. Work as a class to create a coherent profile of a hypochondriac.

# ¡Comunicación!

## 18 ¿Es Ud. hipocondríaco/a? Interpersonal/Presentational Communication 1.1, 1.3

Con un(a) compañero/a, túrnense para hacerse las siguientes preguntas y contestarlas. Luego, piensen en otras cinco características de los hipocondríacos y preséntenlas al resto de la clase.

1. ¿Cree que sufre de alguna enfermedad grave cuando le duele la cabeza o el estómago o tiene alguna irritación en la piel?

2. Cuando su amigo/a se enferma y le cuenta sus síntomas, ¿empieza a sentir los mismos dolores?

3. ¿Guarda un termómetro en su mesilla de noche?

4. ¿Está hipervitaminado/a? O sea, ¿consume la cantidad doble o más de vitaminas de la que debiera?

5. Cada vez que le duele algo o se siente mal, ¿consulta los síntomas en la internet para hacerse su propio diagnóstico?

6. ¿Va al consultorio de su médico/a o a la sala de urgencias cada vez que tiene cualquier dolencia o malestar?

## 19 ¡Defiendan su punto de vista! Interpersonal/Presentational Communication 1.1, 1.3, 3.1, 5.2

Reúnanse en grupos de tres o cuatro estudiantes para discutir los siguientes temas. Túrnense para hacer preguntas y responderlas y justifiquen sus razones, ya sea que estén de acuerdo o en desacuerdo. Al final, presenten sus conclusiones al resto de la clase.

### El derecho a la vida

En los últimos años, ha habido varios casos en que los familiares de un(a) enfermo/a terminal han dejado de prolongarle la vida para evitarle sufrimiento.

- ¿Piensan que es justo que los familiares de un(a) enfermo/a terminal decidan si debe o no debe vivir?

- ¿Creen que es justo que la medicina prolongue la vida artificialmente?

*Siento mucho que estés sufriendo.*

### El derecho a la salud

La Organización Mundial de la Salud decreta que la salud es un derecho del ser humano sin distinción de razas, religiones, partidos políticos ni condiciones sociales o económicas.

- ¿Consideran Uds. que los gobiernos deben cuidar de la salud pública o esta debe ser una obligación individual? ¿Qué ventajas y desventajas tiene que el gobierno sea responsable del mantenimiento de la salud pública?

- La desnutrición es una de las enfermedades características de la pobreza. ¿Creen Uds. que al socializar la medicina se daría fin a esta enfermedad cada vez mayor en el mundo?

**Answers**

18 *Las respuestas variarán.*

19 *Las respuestas variarán.*

### Reference Desk

You may want to choose one of the topics from **Actividad 19** for a class debate. Remind each team that as they formulate their arguments, they should take into account the evidence and opinions both for and against their position.

### Expansion

Have students watch the 2004 film *Mar adentro*. Then have them revisit their answers to **El derecho a la vida** in **Actividad 19**.

## Differentiated Learning

### Accelerate/Adapt

For accelerated students, modify **Actividad 16** so that there aren't answer choices for each blank. For **Actividad 17**, ask them to provide at least two pieces of advice for each context.

### Expand

Ask pairs to choose one situation from **Actividad 17** and turn it into a dialogue. Have pairs role-play the situation for the class.

### Adapt

Have students turn **Actividad 18** into a quiz that asks the frequency (**siempre**, **a veces**, **nunca**) with which people act in these ways. Tell them to assign a point value for each answer.

**Answers**

**20**
1. Estírense, se olviden
2. Hágale, enyésele
3. Tengan, la crucen
4. Tome, tome
5. Prevengan, Lávense
6. Llame, vaya

## Reference Desk

1. Point out that the use of **Ud.** or **Uds.** after the command form is optional, but that doing so is more polite.
2. Emphasize that since these command forms are identical to the third-person present subjunctive forms, students already know how to conjugate them.
3. Draw attention to **comida chuchería** in **Actividad 21**. Another term for this is **comida chatarra**. Ask students if they enjoy reading **lectura chuchería**, and to give some examples.
4. Point out **hacerle un control** in **Actividad 22**. Ask students to guess its meaning (*medical checkup*).

---

# Gramática

## El modo imperativo  1.2

El imperativo de Ud. y Uds (los mandatos formales) se forma de la misma manera que la tercera persona singular y plural del presente de subjuntivo.

| Formas de los mandatos formales | | | | |
|---|---|---|---|---|
| | **Afirmativo** | | **Negativo** | |
| | **Singular** | **Plural** | **Singular** | **Plural** |
| **preguntar** | pregunte Ud. | pregunten Uds. | no pregunte Ud. | no pregunten Uds. |
| **vender** | venda Ud. | vendan Uds. | no venda Ud. | no vendan Uds. |
| **dormir** | duerma Ud. | duerman Uds. | no duerma Ud. | no duerman Uds. |

### El uso del imperativo

- El imperativo se usa para dar órdenes directas. Los pronombres **Ud.** y **Uds.**, si se necesitan para dar énfasis, se colocan después del verbo.

  **Espere** Ud. un momento, por favor.

  Si quiere mantenerse saludable, **haga** ejercicio y **siga** una dieta saludable.

  **Practique** ejercicios aeróbicos, **camine**, **corra** o **ande** en bicicleta.

  Antes de trotar, **haga** estiramiento lento por cinco minutos.

  **Duerma** por lo menos ocho horas diarias.

*Estírese antes de hacer cualquier clase de ejercicio.*

- Los pronombres reflexivos y de complemento directo e indirecto se colocan después del verbo en la forma afirmativa y antes del verbo en la forma negativa.

  **Explíquele** al doctor o a la doctora todos sus síntomas y **no se olvide** de darle su historial médico si no lo ha hecho antes.

  **Tómese Ud.** todos los antibióticos y **llámenos** si no se siente mejor después de terminarlos.

  **Relájense** y **no se preocupen** por cosas sin importancia.

  **Aliméntense** bien y **beban** suficientes líquidos.

---

### 20 Consejos prácticos  1.2

Complete las siguientes oraciones con el mandato formal del verbo entre paréntesis, prestando atención al uso de los pronombres reflexivos, de complemento directo e indirecto, según sea el caso.

1. (*estirarse-Uds.*) antes de hacer ejercicio y no (*olvidarse*) de beber mucho líquido.
2. (*hacerle-Ud.*) una radiografía al paciente y (*enyesarle*) el brazo si es necesario.
3. (*tener-Uds.*) cuidado al cruzar la calle. No (*cruzarla*) sin antes mirar a lado y lado.
4. (*tomar-Ud.*) estas pastillas para el dolor, pero no (*tomar*) más de dos al día.
5. (*prevenir-Uds.*) el contagio de infecciones. (*lavarse*) las manos antes y después de atender a cada paciente.
6. (*llamar-Ud.*) a su médico si se siente enfermo/a. No (*ir*) a la sala de urgencias si no es algo grave.

---

## Essential Instruction

1. Begin this grammar presentation by asking a volunteer to describe the imperative mood in his or her own words.
2. Give simple **Uds.** commands (e.g., **levántense**; **salten sobre un pie**, etc.) and have students act them out. Then switch the activity by inviting students to say **Ud.** commands that you must act out.
3. Have students complete **Actividades 20–22** for homework. In class, have them check their answers in pairs.
4. Model completing a sentence in a logical way for **Actividad 23**.

## 21 ¡Sí, se puede!  1.2, 1.3

Para mucha gente que trabaja o estudia y hace dieta, el peor momento es el tiempo entre la llegada a la casa y la hora de comer. Pero hay algunos trucos (*tricks*) que le ayudarán para no caer en la tentación de comer. Complete las siguientes oraciones con el mandato de **Ud.** del verbo entre paréntesis y una recomendación adicional de acuerdo a su experiencia.

1. (*lavarse*) los dientes. Sentir la frescura en la boca, le ayudará a mantenerla así. También...

2. (*empezar*) a hacer la comida y (*ponerse*) de inmediato a hacer algún ejercicio. (*correr*), (*estirarse*), (*saltar la cuerda*) o (*pedalear*) una bicicleta estacionaria. El ejercicio, contrariamente a lo que se cree, hace perder el apetito. También...

3. (*cambiar*) su rutina de "al fin en casa." (*hacer*) algo que le ayude a mantener ocupada la mente durante aquel tiempo que antes pasaba en un sillón comiendo papitas y viendo televisión. Por ejemplo, (*revisar*) su correo electrónico, (*hacer*) sus tareas, (*darse*) un baño o (*llamar*) por teléfono a sus amigos/as También...

4. (*sustituir*) su "comida chuchería" (*junk food*) por "lectura chuchería," esas novelas tan fáciles de leer que uno no puede abandonar. También...

## 22 Examen físico 1.2, 1.3

El doctor Camacho examinó a su paciente, el Sr. Torres, y descubrió que tenía la presión arterial muy baja. Cambie las instrucciones del doctor por mandatos formales, como se ve en el modelo.

MODELO   Debe respirar profundo.
**Respire profundo.**

1. Ud. puede desvestirse y ponerse la bata en esa sala.

2. No debe acostarse boca abajo, debe acostarse boca arriba.

3. Debe respirar profundamente.

4. Ahora puede vestirse y sentarse en mi oficina.

5. Al llegar a casa, debe tomar la medicina cada tres horas.

6. Debe descansar mucho y no salir por las noches.

7. No debe consumir bebidas alcohólicas.

8. Es conveniente que sustituya la carne por el pescado.

9. Debe venir a la clínica dos veces por mes para hacerle un control.

10. Es importante traer los resultados de los análisis de sangre y de orina.

## 23 Segunda opinión  1.3

El paciente de la actividad anterior no quedó satisfecho con las recomendaciones del doctor Camacho y optó por buscar una segunda opinión. Aquí tiene las instrucciones del segundo doctor. Forme el imperativo formal de los verbos y complete las instrucciones de manera lógica.

1. Mantener...
2. Aprender a...
3. Decirles a otras personas...
4. Dejar de...
5. Informarse sobre...
6. Cambiar...
7. Pensar en...
8. No preocuparse...
9. Asegurarse de...

### Answers

**21**
1. Lávese
2. Empiece, póngase, Corra, estírese, salte la cuerda, pedalee
3. Cambie, Haga, revise, haga, dese, llame
4. Sustituya
*Las recomendaciones variarán.*

**22**
1. Desvístase y póngase la bata en esa sala.
2. No se acueste boca abajo; acuéstese boca arriba.
3. Respire profundamente.
4. Ahora vístase y siéntese en mi oficina.
5. Al llegar a casa, tome la medicina cada tres horas.
6. Descanse mucho y no salga por las noches.
7. No consuma bebidas alcohólicas.
8. Sustituya la carne por el pescado.
9. Venga a la clínica dos veces por mes para hacerle un control.
10. Traiga los resultados de los análisis de sangre y de orina.

**23** *Las respuestas variarán. Respuestas posibles:*
1. Mantenga la calma ante los problemas que se presenten.
2. Aprenda a relajarse.
3. Dígale a otras personas "no" cuando no quiere participar en ciertas actividades.
4. Deje de comer cosas con tanta sal.
5. Infórmese sobre síntomas problemáticos.
6. Cambie de actitud ante la tarea y la escuela.
7. Piense en hacer ejercicios.
8. No se preocupe demasiado por los problemas de la vida diaria.
9. Asegúrese de reducir el tiempo que pasa enfrente del televisor.

## Differentiated Learning
### Heritage Learners
Explain that in some regions of Latin America, it is common for parents to speak to their children in the formal register. Ask heritage learners what commands might be given to children in their cultural communities.

## Multiple Intelligences
### Verbal-Linguistic
Ask students to write a list of at least 12 **reglas de oro** for academic success. For example: **Duerman ocho horas todas las noches. Estudien cada día; no esperen hasta la noche antes del examen.**

## ¡Comunicación!

**24 ¡Ya puede pasar!** Interpersonal/Presentational Communication **1.1, 1.3**

Imagine que Ud. va por primera vez al consultorio de su nuevo/a doctor(a) porque últimamente no se siente muy bien. En grupos de cuatro, escriban el diálogo que tiene lugar entre las diferentes personas: el/la paciente, la recepcionista, el/la enfermero/a y el/la médico/a y representen la situación enfrente de la clase. Usen los mandatos formales y las pautas y temas que se dan a continuación en su conversación.

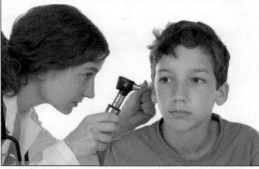
*¿Te duele el oído?*

### Escena 1
**Conversación recepcionista-paciente:**

- Historial médico
- Seguro médico
- Costo de la consulta
- Formas de pago

### Escena 2
**Conversación enfermero/a-paciente:**

- Preguntas generales sobre su salud y su historia médica
- Razones para su visita y chequeo general de su peso, temperatura y presión arterial

### Escena 3
**Conversación médico/a-paciente:**

- Explicación de los síntomas y dolencias del paciente
- Comentarios y preguntas del doctor o la doctora
- Comentarios y aclaraciones del paciente o la paciente
- Recetas, recomendaciones y tratamientos por parte del doctor o la doctora

### Essential Instruction

1. Encourage students to dress up for their roles and to use props (such as a child's doctor kit, a clipboard and pen for paperwork, etc.) in their skits for **Actividad 24**.

2. Before beginning **Actividad 25**, read through the nutritional information as a class. Clarify any unfamiliar words. Ask students to think of additional foods/drinks for each category.

# ¡Comunicación!

## 25 Una dieta sana y saludable 👥 Interpersonal Communication  1.1, 1.2

Lea el anuncio. Luego, con un(a) compañero/a, representen la conversación entre un paciente y un especialista en nutrición en cada uno de los casos que se dan. Túrnense para hacerse preguntas y responderlas con base en la lectura y su propia experiencia. Usen los mandatos formales en su conversación, como se ve en el modelo.

- Una joven que sufre de sobrepeso y aun así solo se alimenta de comida chuchería.

- Una señora que lleva una vida muy ocupada y no le queda tiempo de cocinar o de comer.

- Un señor de edad que come mucho y con gran gusto, pero tuvo un ataque al corazón y tiene que modificar su dieta.

- Una pareja que acaba de tener un bebé y quiere consejos sobre cómo alimentarlo bien desde el principio.

MODELO
**A:** Doctora, la verdad es que a mí me encanta comer de todo, salado, dulce, y en cantidades, y no quiero dejar de hacerlo.

**B:** Bueno, nadie dice que tiene que dejar de comer lo que le gusta. Es solo cuestión de balancear lo que come y las porciones que come.

# EL PLATO PARA COMER SALUDABLE

Use aceites saludables (como aceite de oliva o canola) para cocinar, en ensaladas, y en la mesa. Limite la margarina (mantequilla). Evite las grasas trans.

**ACEITES SALUDABLES**

**AGUA** Tome agua, té, o café (con poco o nada de azúcar). Limite la leche y lácteos (1-2 porciones al día) y el jugo (1 vaso pequeño al día). Evite las bebidas azucaradas.

Mientras más vegetales y mayor variedad, mejor. Las patatas (papas) y las patatas fritas (papas fritas/papitas) no cuentan.

**VEGETALES**

**GRANOS INTEGRALES** Coma una variedad de granos (cereales) integrales (como pan de trigo integral, pasta de granos integrales, y arroz integral). Limite los granos refinados (como arroz blanco y pan blanco).

Coma muchas frutas, de todos los colores.

**FRUTAS**

**PROTEINA SALUDABLE** Escoja pescados, aves, legumbres (habichuelas/leguminosas/frijoles), y nueces; limite las carnes rojas y el queso; evite la tocineta ("bacon"), carnes frías (fiambres), y otras carnes procesadas.

**¡MANTÉNGASE ACTIVO!**

© Harvard University

Harvard T.H. Chan School of Public Health
The Nutrition Source
www.hsph.harvard.edu/nutritionsource

Harvard Medical School
Harvard Health Publications
www.health.harvard.edu

---

Answers
25 *Las conversaciones variarán.*

## Communication

**Interpersonal/Presentational: Cooperative Groups**
Ask students to work in small groups. Tell them to think of a new diet- or health-related product and give it a name. Ask them to create a television ad to promote the product. Finally, have groups act out (or record and play) their ads for the class.

## Expansion

Tell students to think of something that they know how to do well (**preparar un cappuccino**; **sacar una foto**). Ask them to create a "how to" presentation. They should use **Ud.** commands to give very detailed and specific step-by-step instructions.

## TPR

Ask students to write a variety of **Uds.** commands on index cards. Have students take turns reading the commands to the class, who will perform the actions.

---

## Learning Styles
### Auditory Learners
Read aloud a series of situations, e.g., **Olvidé mi tarea en casa**; **Mis amigos y yo perdimos el autobús**. For each one, have students call out commands that provide a solution for the situation (**Vuelva a la casa para buscarla**; **Vayan a pie**).

## Multiple Intelligences
### Bodily-Kinesthetic/Musical-Rhythmic
Have students research the **cueca**, Chile's national dance, and learn the steps. Tell them to create a presentation in which they teach the class how to dance the **cueca**. They should give the instructions using **Uds.** commands.

# Lectura informativa

 **1.3, 2.1, 2.2  Antes de leer**

¿Por qué cree Ud. que la medicina está en permanente desarrollo? ¿Qué avances de la medicina le parecen los más impactantes?

## Estrategia  **3.1**

**Secuencia**

Mientras lee, preste atención a la secuencia para entender mejor en qué orden temporal ocurrieron los sucesos.

 **1.2, 2.1, 2.2**

### 26 Comprensión

1. ¿Cuál era la base de la medicina en el siglo xv en Chile?

2. ¿Cómo aumentó Chile sus posiblidades de ganar la Guerra del Pacífico?

3. ¿Cuál era la explicación religiosa para las enfermedades mentales?

 **1.3, 4.2**

### 27 Analice

En Chile, los primeros pasos de la medicina están vinculados con lo religioso. ¿Qué papel desempeña la religión en la salud de su país?

---

○○○  Los momentos que...

LA TERCERA  Política | Nacional | Mundo | Negocios | Opinión | Santiago | Tendencias | Educación | Cultura | Entretención | Deportes | LaTercera TV

## LA TERCERA  MARTES 14 DE SEPTIEMBRE DE 2010

# Los momentos que marcaron la evolución de la medicina y la salud en Chile

 **1.2, 2.1, 2.2, 3.1**

Las pestes, la guerra y la economía industrial hicieron que la medicina y la ciencia fueran una necesidad de desarrollo.

por Teresita Quezada

### La Botica[1] de los Jesuitas

Aceite de alacranes para el dolor de oídos, agüita de llantén[2] para la fiebre y tirar las orejas en dirección opuesta para la amigdalitis[3]. La Botica de Los Jesuitas ya existía en el siglo xv en Chile y perduró[4] hasta inicios del siglo xIX. Sus ungüentos[5] y remedios eran la base de la medicina por esos días. Tenía más de 916 productos, unos que no curaban y otros que sí, como el hollín[6], utilizado como desinfectante. "Era similar a la pastilla de carbón. Fue el producto principal de Roche, la productora de fármacos suiza", cuenta César Leyton, historiador del Museo Nacional de Medicina.

### De París a la guerra

Uno de los mayores problemas en tiempos de guerra fue que no había técnicas de desinfección del material y de las salas donde se curaba a los heridos. De hecho, casi todos morían de gangrena. Buscando una solución, la Universidad de Chile envió un grupo de médicos a París, en 1878, a aprender las técnicas de antisepsia de Joseph Lister. Los procedimientos consistían en un rociador[7] que limpiaba y desinfectaba el ambiente, además de hervir[8] el instrumental quirúrgico con ácido fénico. Los becados llegaron a la Guerra del Pacífico y lo incorporan, logrando que el Ejército chileno desarrollara una sanidad militar que no tenían ni Perú ni Bolivia. "Eso hizo que hubiera más jóvenes dispuestos a ser soldados, porque aumentaron enormemente las posibilidades de ganar", agrega el también profesor de la U. de Chile.

### La Endemoniada de Santiago

"En Chile, si te volvías loco y eras pobre te ibas al Hospital San Juan de Dios; si eras rico, al San Andrés, en Lima, o también podías terminar en un monasterio por endemoniamiento", cuenta Leyton. En 1857 se produjo la primera gran discusión pública al respecto. Carmen Marín yacía amarrada[9] en una cama hablando en latín, insultando en francés y alemán. Se calmaba sólo con el Evangelio de San Juan. Entonces, se concluyó que estaba poseída por el demonio.

[1] pharmacy  [2] fleawort infusion  [3] tonsilitis  [4] endured  [5] ointments  [6] soot
[7] spray  [8] boil  [9] tied down

 **248**  doscientos cuarenta y ocho  |  *Unidad 6*

---

## RESOURCES

 Antes de leer
Los momentos que marcaron la evolución de la medicina y la salud en Chile

### Answers

**Antes de leer**
*Las respuestas variarán.*

**26**
1. Los remedios y ungüentos de la Botica de los Jesuitas.
2. Envió un grupo de médicos a París para aprender técnicas de desinfección que mejoraron la salud de los soldados.
3. Se creía que estaban poseídos por el demonio.

**27** *Las respuestas variarán.*

## Reference Desk

Jesuits are priests and brothers who are members of a Catholic religious order called the Society of Jesus, which was formed in 1540 and now has about 17,000 members worldwide. Jesuits have a long tradition of working in education and research, promoting peace and social justice, and ministering in hospitals, prisons, and parishes.

## Pre-AP

**Course Theme: La ciencia y la tecnología**

---

### Essential Instruction

1. Discuss the **Antes de leer** questions as a class. Write common ideas on the board.
2. Go over the **Estrategia**. Ask volunteers to give examples of sequencing words and other cues that indicate the order of events.
3. Give students 30 seconds to skim the reading and share what they discovered. Write notes on the board and verify them as you go through the readings as a class.
4. For Common Core practice, have students answer the **Analice** questions. Go over the answers as a class.

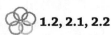

## LA TERCERA
LA TERCERA | Política | Nacional | Mundo | Negocios | Opinión | Santiago | Tendencias | Educación | Cultura | Entretención | Deportes | LaTercera TV

MARTES 14 DE SEPTIEMBRE DE 2010

La mujer se había convertido en un fenómeno: la gente iba a verla como a un show de rarezas[10], a rezar[11] por ella, los sacerdotes[12] pedían hacerle un exorcismo y los médicos estaban divididos entre simulación e histeria. Andrés de Carmona, médico chileno de la época, planteó que Carmen Marín era histérica, que aprendió latín porque vivió con las monjas[13] en orfanatos, que huyó[14] a Valparaíso con marinos franceses y alemanes, y que tuvo una desilusión amorosa con un hombre llamado Juan, dándole una explicación sicosocial de la enfermedad. "Fue el triunfo de la medicina y la siquiatría sobre la Iglesia y también en la opinión pública", dice Leyton.

### Orden saludable
Con la industrialización se formaron cordones marginales[15] en la periferia. Ahí nacieron los conventillos[16], donde vivían muchas familias en condiciones de higiene mínimas y altísimas posibilidades de contagiarse de enfermedades. Como la industrialización necesitaba gente sana, la salud se convirtió en una cuestión económica. En el gobierno de José Manuel Balmaceda se ordena el incipiente sistema de salud público con hospitales y educación. El Estado comienza a encargarse totalmente de la salud y la ciencia.

#### El pulverizador
La desinfección de las salas de operación a través de rociar químicos en el aire permitió, a finales del siglo XIX, disminuir las infecciones de gangrena, una de las principales razones de muerte entre los heridos de la Guerra del Pacífico.

#### El opio y la herbolaria
A principios del siglo XIX, las enfermedades se curaban con plantas medicinales indígenas, como el curare (anestesia) y el llantén (bajar la fiebre). El jarabe de opio era para la tos y los resfríos de adultos y niños, con buenos resultados.

#### La anestesia eléctrica y el cloroformo
Aunque a principios del siglo XX se trajo a Chile un método de anestesia eléctrica, no funcionó. El cloroformo, en cambio, se siguió usando y sigue vigente[17] desde que se descubrió como anestesia, en 1848.

[10] freak show [11] pray [12] priests [13] nuns [14] ran away [15] slums [16] tenements [17] in use

🔍 **Búsqueda:** la botica de los jesuitas, técnicas de antisepsia, carmen marín

 **1.2, 2.1, 2.2**

## 28 Comprensión

1. ¿Qué posición tuvo el médico chileno Andrés de Carmona con relación a la enfermedad de Carmen Marín?

2. ¿Qué efecto tuvo la industrialización sobre el cuidado de la salud?

3. ¿Qué remedios o técnicas se han usado a lo largo de los años para anestesiar pacientes?

## 29 Analice  **1.3, 2.1, 2.2**

¿Qué ventajas y desventajas cree Ud. que tiene el hecho de que la salud sea una política de Estado?

---

**Answers**

**28**

1. Dio razones lógicas para la enfermedad basadas en la psicología social (el estudio del ser humano dentro del contexto social). Explicó que Carmen era histérica, que aprendió latín con las monjas de los orfanatos donde vivió y que aprendió francés y alemán con los marinos con quienes huyó.

2. Se necesitaba mucha mano de obra sana y fue necesario hacer de la salud una cuestión de Estado.

3. Plantas como el curare, anestesia eléctrica, cloroformo.

**29** *Las respuestas variarán.*

### Reference Desk
José Manuel Balmaceda was president of Chile from 1886 to 1891. His political disagreements eventually plunged Chile into civil war in 1891, during which 10,000 lives were lost.

### Culture

**Products: Information**
Industrial engineer María Constanza Correa studied hospital-acquired infections and found that hospital bed safety rails were a major source of contagion. Constanza Correa then founded CopperBioHealth and began replacing standard bed rails with ones made of copper, which has anti-microbial properties and can kill viruses, fungi, and bacteria on contact. So far the copper bed rails are now used in four hospitals in Chile, and CopperBioHealth is developing other copper-based products.

---

## Differentiated Learning
### Expand
Ask students to research Chile's health statistics, including life expectancy, infant mortality rate, leading causes of death, and also figures for how much Chile spends on health costs. Have students compare what they learned with data for the United States.

## Multiple Intelligences
### Naturalist
Ask students to research the medicinal plants mentioned in this reading. Tell them to find out each plant's classification and chemical structure, where it grows, its pharmacological properties, and history of use.

Answers_____

**30** *Las conversaciones variarán.*

# Escritura

## Una historia clínica 1.3

La historia clínica es un documento confidencial en el que el médico anota los datos necesarios para atender a un paciente. Durante la entrevista clínica, el médico hace preguntas que le permiten reunir la información que necesita para poder ayudar al paciente con el motivo de su consulta.

### ¡Comunicación!

**30 En el consultorio** — Interpersonal/Presentational Communication — 1.1, 1.3

Imagine que Ud. es medico/a y está atendiendo a un(a) paciente que viene a su consultorio por primera vez. Represente la situación con un(a) compañero/a asegurándose de hacer las preguntas necesarias para completar la siguiente historia clínica.

**HISTORIA CLÍNICA**     N.º _____

Nombre y apellido: _____     Edad: _____
Teléfono: _____     Sexo: _____
Dirección: _____     Estado civil: _____
_____
_____

Nivel de estudios: _____     Ocupación: _____

Motivo de la consulta: _____
_____

Diagnóstico: _____
_____

Evolución: _____
_____

Tratamiento: _____
_____

Antecedentes personales (enfermedades previas, alergias, cirugías, etc.): _____
_____

Antecedentes familiares (enfermedades del padre o la madre): _____
_____
_____

Informe sobre el examen físico: _____
_____
_____

**250**

# Un texto argumentativo  1.3, 3.1

En un texto argumentativo, el autor presenta claramente su punto de vista sobre un tema. Para ello, plantea su posición y luego enumera las razones que la justifican. Al final, presenta una conclusión que puede extraerse de todo lo que ha dicho antes.

A la hora de escribir un texto argumentativo, se pueden usar los siguientes recursos:

• Citas: Se incluyen palabras de otra persona, que puede ser una autoridad en el tema o alguien que da un testimonio personal.

• Ejemplos: Se dan casos concretos y específicos que ilustran el punto de vista del autor.

• Estadísticas: Se dan datos objetivos con números, porcentajes, etc.

• Preguntas retóricas: Se invitan al lector a reflexionar.

## ¡Comunicación!

### 31 Ventajas y desventajas · Interpretive Communication 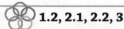 1.2, 2.1, 2.2, 3.2

Escuche el siguiente segmento de *A tu salud*, un programa de Radio de la Universidad de Chile dirigido por la periodista Cecilia Espinosa, quien, en esta oportunidad, aborda el tema de la medicina complementaria y la medicina convencional con el doctor Juan Carlos Salinas. Luego, complete el organizador de ideas con las ventajas y desventajas de la medicina complementaria con base en lo que escuchó y su propio conocimiento del tema.

| | Ventajas | Desventajas |
|---|---|---|
| Medicina complementaria | | |
| Medicina convencional | | |

### 32 ¿Está Ud. a favor o en contra? 1.3

**Presentational Communication**

Use la información del organizador de ideas para escribir un texto argumentativo en el que presente su opinión sobre la medicina complementaria. Incluya razones de apoyo y una conclusión.

**Para escribir más**

Desde mi punto de vista,…

En mi opinión,…

Creo firmemente que…

Prueba de ello es…

Los especialistas afirman que…

Según las estadísticas,…

En resumen, es obvio que…

Por todo lo dicho, repito que…

## RESOURCES

 Activity 31

**Answers**

**31 Script**

—Yo creo que tenemos en este momento una gran ventaja como país, que es que el Ministerio de Salud haya acogido el tomar las riendas en el sentido de hacer regulación respecto a las prácticas de las medicinas complementarias, y digo medicinas complementarias porque y no alternativas porque la verdad es que cuando uno practica esta medicina no elige entre una y otra, sino que las utiliza racionalmente y de una manera personalizada dependiendo del caso. Va a haber casos que definitivamente la solución más biológica sea la utilización de un antibiótico, para resolver el caso, pero en otros, vamos a requerir otro tipo de prácticas y de elementos terapéuticos, que van a ser precisamente más biológicos que muchos otros medicamentos que son drogas, más, que podrían tener reacciones adversas, y finalmente el costo/beneficio es menor.

—De algún modo, doctor, no se trata de desconocer todo el mundo y los aportes de la medicina alópata sino que…

—En ningún caso, en ningún caso, al contrario, yo creo que una de las grandes virtudes que tiene la medicina convencional es la rigurosidad científica, y precisamente la medicina complementaria en la medida que va mostrando *Continued on p. 261.*

*Las respuestas variarán.*

**32** *Los textos variarán.*

## Differentiated Learning
### Accelerate/Expand
After completing **Actividad 30**, tell students to imagine that the patient's condition has worsened, and he/she needs to visit a specialist. Have students pair up with a different classmate and role-play a conversation in the specialist's office. The specialist should be given the patient's **historia clínica** for reference.

## Special Needs Students
### Auditory Impairment
Allow these students to listen several times to the recording in **Actividad 31**. You may also want to provide them with a script so that they can follow along as they listen.

## Reference Desk

**Actividad 31** contains authentic audio, which is an important component of the AP® Spanish exam.

# Vocabulario 3

## Mejore su comprensión  1.2

Familiarizarse con este vocabulario le ayudará a leer "*Walking Around*" más adelante, y a mejorar su comprensión auditiva.

**aterido/a** *adj.* Paralizado por el frío.

**bodega** *s.f.* Local donde se deposita mercancía.

**cárcel** *s.f.* Lugar en el que se encierra a una persona para castigarla por un delito.

*Los lirios están marchitos.*

**desgracia** *s.f.* Mala suerte.

**espantoso/a** *adj.* Terrible, que da miedo.

**establecimiento** *s.m.* Lugar donde se ejerce una industria o profesión.

**fiel** *adj.* Honrado/a, que cumple sus compromisos.

**furia** *s.f.* Enfado muy grande.

**golpe** *s.m.* Encuentro violento de un cuerpo contra otro.

**hacerse viejo/a** *v.* Envejecer.

**intestino** *s.m.* Órgano del cuerpo en el que se completa la digestión.

**lágrimas** *s.f.* Gotas de agua que salen de los ojos cuando lloramos.

**lento/a** *adj.* Que se mueve muy despacio.

**lirio** *s.m.* Planta de tallos largos y flores grandes de colores fuertes.

**llorar a gritos** *exp.* Derramar lágrimas dando voces.

**marchito/a** *adj.* Seco, envejecido.

**mercaderías** *s.f.* Lo que se compra o se vende.

**microbio** *s.m.* Nombre genérico de microorganismos unicelulares.

**morir de frío** *exp.* Sentir un frío muy intenso.

**notario** *s.m.* Persona cuyo trabajo consiste en asegurar que algo es verdad.

**ombligo** *s.m.* Pequeño agujero que tenemos en el centro del vientre.

**paraguas** *s.m.* Instrumento que sirve para protegerse de la lluvia.

**peluquería** *s.f.* Lugar en el que se corta el pelo.

**raíz** *s.f.* Parte de una planta que crece bajo tierra.

**recompensar** *v.* Remunerar un servicio o un trabajo.

**sastrería** *s.f.* Lugar en el que se hacen o se arreglan trajes.

**suceder** *v.* Producirse un hecho.

**tiniebla** *s.f.* Oscuridad.

**veneno** *s.m.* Sustancia que al ingerirse produce la muerte o daños graves.

**vergüenza** *s.f.* Sensación producida por algo humillante o ridículo.

---

**33 ¿Cómo se relacionan?**  1.3

Escriba una oración con cada uno de los siguientes pares de palabras.

**1.** raíz / lirio

**2.** furia / golpe

**3.** recompensar / fiel

**4.** desgracia / espantoso

**5.** microbios / intestino

**6.** aterido / morir de frío

**7.** llorar a gritos / lágrimas

**8.** peluquería / establecimiento

## 34 Solo el recuerdo  1.2

Complete las oraciones con la palabra del recuadro que corresponda según el contexto.

| mercadería | bodegas | sastrería | vieja | furia | marchitos | a gritos |
|---|---|---|---|---|---|---|
| establecimiento | lágrimas | paraguas | aterida | cárcel | peluquería | desgracia |

Aunque se estaba haciendo __(1)__, quería verse bien para el funeral de su esposo. Por eso, se mandó a hacer un traje negro, elegante y a la medida en una __(2)__ muy reconocida. Empezó a caminar por la avenida principal en busca de una __(3)__. Quería hacerse cortar y arreglar el pelo, pero no halló ninguna. Solo había lugares donde compraban y vendían __(4)__. Pensó que sería mejor regresar. Llovía a cántaros y ella sin un abrigo o un __(5)__ para protegerse de la lluvia. Estaba cansada y __(6)__ de frío, así es que decidió refugiarse bajo la entrada de un __(7)__ que halló abierto.

*Sus lágrimas expresaban profunda tristeza y desconsuelo.*

Se sentía triste y desconsolada. Quería llorar __(8)__ pero no podía. Tampoco podía contener las __(9)__ que le rodaban por el rostro cada vez que recordaba con incredulidad la espantosa __(10)__. El barco se había hundido por el peso mal distribuido de la carga en sus __(11)__. Se había hundido y más de doscientos pasajeros, su esposo entre ellos, habían muerto. Ella sentía una inmensa __(12)__ al pensar que no se había culpado a nadie de la tragedia. Nadie había ido a la __(13)__ a pagar por el descuido del cual solo habían quedado de recuerdo lirios __(14)__ flotando en el mar.

## 35 El triste futuro de Jacinta  1.2, 3.1

Escuche el relato "El triste futuro de Jacinta". Luego, Ud. oirá una pregunta sobre el relato y tres respuestas posibles. Seleccione la letra de la respuesta con la terminación más lógica. La oración y las terminaciones se leerán dos veces.

1. **A.** Era un mal médico.
   **B.** Era muy buen médico.
   **C.** Cobraba poco dinero.

2. **A.** Porque no tenía tiempo.
   **B.** Porque le gustaba ser soltero.
   **C.** Porque no le gustaba gastar dinero.

3. **A.** Porque iba a darle mucho dinero.
   **B.** Porque quería recompensarla por sus servicios.
   **C.** Porque iba a casarse con ella.

4. **A.** Recibir mucho dinero.
   **B.** Casarse con el médico.
   **C.** Librarse del viejo.

5. **A.** Dar su dinero a los pobres.
   **B.** Dar el nombre de Jacinta a un microbio.
   **C.** Dar su dinero a Jacinta.

## Multiple Intelligences

**Mathematical-Logical**
Ask students to organize the words from **Mejore su comprensión** into four categories: **lugares**, **el mundo natural**, **acciones y emociones**, **otras palabras**.

**Visual-Spatial**
After checking answers to **Actividad 34**, add a visual component to the exercise: as you read the completed paragraph aloud, have students compose a drawing of the widow, the weather, and her thoughts. Have students compare their drawings in small groups.

# Gramática

## Mandatos de *tú* y de *vosotros* ✿ 1.2

El mandato positivo de **tú** tiene las mismas formas que la tercera persona singular del presente del indicativo. Sin embargo, para el mandato negativo se usa la forma de la segunda persona singular del presente del subjuntivo.

| Mandatos de *tú* | | |
|---|---|---|
| | **Afirmativo** | **Negativo** |
| mirar | **mira** (tú) | **no mires** |
| volver | **vuelve** (tú) | **no vuelvas** |
| pedir | **pide** (tú) | **no pidas** |

- Algunos verbos son irregulares en la forma afirmativa del imperativo, pero siguen la regla anterior en la forma negativa.

| Mandatos irregulares en la forma de *tú* | | |
|---|---|---|
| | **Afirmativo** | **Negativo** |
| decir | di | no digas |
| hacer | haz | no hagas |
| ir | ve | no vayas |
| poner | pon | no pongas |
| salir | sal | no salgas |
| ser | sé | no seas |
| tener | ten | no tengas |
| venir | ven | no vengas |

- El mandato positivo de **vosotros** se forma cambiando la **-r** del infinitivo por **-d**. Para el mandato negativo se usa la forma de la segunda persona plural del presente del subjuntivo.

| Mandatos de *vosotros* | | |
|---|---|---|
| | **Afirmativo** | **Negativo** |
| descansar | descansad | **no descanséis** |
| comer | comed | **no comáis** |
| vivir | vivid | **no viváis** |

Si se usa la forma afirmativa del imperativo de **vosotros** con el pronombre reflexivo **os**, se suprime la **-d** final. (*Excepción:* **irse: id** + **os** = **idos**)

| Mandatos de *vosotros* con pronombres reflexivos | | |
|---|---|---|
| | **Afirmativo** | **Negativo** |
| sentarse | (sentad + os) = **sentaos** | **no os sentéis** |
| ponerse | (poned + os) = **poneos** | **no os pongáis** |
| vestirse | (vestid + os) = **vestíos** | **no os vistáis** |

### Essential Instruction

1. As you present **Gramática**, give **tú** commands (e.g., **Cierra el libro**) while pointing to individual students and have them react accordingly. Then indicate two or more students and give **vosotros/as** commands (e.g., **Levantad la mano**).
2. When checking answers to **Actividad 36**, ask students which pieces of advice they follow, or which they feel are most important.
3. Expand **Actividad 37** by having students write a follow-up sentence for each item using a negative command. For example: 1. **No dejes de informarte sobre los avances.**

Answers

## 36 Para mantener una buena condición física  1.2

El siguiente artículo fue publicado en una revista sobre la salud. Complete el siguiente párrafo sobre la salud con el mandato de **tú** del verbo entre paréntesis.

(*1. masticar*) despacio. (*2. eludir*) las tentaciones. (*3. eliminar*) los alimentos de alto contenido calórico de tu lista de mercado. (*4. comprar*) solo lo que te propones comer en tu dieta. (*5. endulzar*) con azúcar natural de arroz y con frutas. No (*6. consumir*) muchos productos lácteos ni aderezos (*dressing*) para ensaladas. (*7. asar*) las carnes al horno o a la parrilla, no (*8. freírlas*). (*9. hacer*) ejercicio diariamente. (*10. realizar*) actividades divertidas y al aire libre. (*11. recurrir*) a la terapia si no puedes de ninguna manera mantener tu peso. No (*12. lucharlo*) solo.

## 37 Medicina alternativa  1.2

Complete las oraciones sobre medicina alternativa con el mandato de **tú** de los verbos del recuadro que mejor corresponda según el contexto.

*Relájate y te sentirás mejor.*

| | | | |
|---|---|---|---|
| aprender | mantenerse | ponerse | comprar |
| incluir | mejorar | acordarse | combatir |

1. ____ al día con estas nuevas opciones para la salud.
2. ____ el estrés con esta hierba mágica.
3. ____ nuestra guía de plantas medicinales.
4. ____ el aumento de peso con el ejercicio.
5. ____ estas hierbas en tu dieta.
6. ____ de leer este artículo sobre las vitaminas.
7. ____ cinco técnicas para acabar con el insomnio.
8. ____ saludable con una dieta de frutas y verduras.

**36**
1. Mastica
2. Elude
3. Elimina
4. Compra
5. Endulza
6. consumas
7. Asa
8. las frías
9. Haz
10. Realiza
11. Recurre
12. lo luches

**37**
1. Ponte
2. Mejora
3. Compra
4. Combate
5. Incluye
6. Acuérdate
7. Aprende
8. Mantente

### Communication

**Presentational: Paired Practice**
Instruct students to make a list of things they were told not to do as a child. Have students compare their lists in pairs.

### Expansion

Repeat **Actividades 36** and **37** with **vosotros** commands.

### Special Needs Students
**Linguistically Challenged/Speech Impairment**
Read aloud sentences that express obligation or need, using **deber** + *infinitive* or **tener que** + *infinitive*, e.g., **Tienes que salir de aquí.** Hold up two pieces of paper that have command forms (**Sal de aquí**; **Ven aquí**). Have students point to the correct answer. Model pronunciation of the imperative form and have students repeat.

### Multiple Intelligences
**Visual-Spatial**
Instruct students to write a list of ten rules for a happy and healthy life, using **tú** commands. Ask students to create a collage with drawings or photos of things that make them happy and healthy. Ask students to present their rules and collage to the class.

## 38 ¡Mantente saludable… por la internet!  1.2

Lea las siguientes recomendaciones para llevar una dieta saludable y complételas con el mandato de **tú** del verbo entre paréntesis.

1. (*incrementar*) el consumo de vegetales de colores vivos (*bright*) como brócoli, espinaca y tomate.

2. (*disminuir*) drásticamente los alimentos con un alto contenido en azúcar, grasas y calorías.

3. (*ingerir*) de 1.000 a 1.500 miligramos de calcio por día, pero (*reemplazar*) la leche entera por leche descremada.

4. (*elegir*) otros alimentos ricos en calcio como col, nabo, pescado enlatado, jugo de naranja, granos y frijoles.

5. No (*consumir*) quesos que sean altos en grasa, no (*beber*) alcohol y no (*fumar*).

6. (*hacer*) ejercicios diariamente, (*fortalecer*) los huesos caminando y trabajando en el jardín, y (*acordarse*) de tomar vitaminas.

## ¡Comunicación!

## 39 ¡Por favor, doctor! 1.1, 1.2

**Interpersonal Communication**

En parejas, lean esta caricatura y, luego, representen el papel del médico y el paciente en esta situación. El médico le recomienda una dieta saludable al paciente, pero él no quiere seguir su consejo. Usen las expresiones que se dan como guía en su conversación, prestando atención al uso del imperativo y el subjuntivo, como se ve en el modelo.

### Para decir más

| El médico dice: | El paciente resiste: |
|---|---|
| Le recomiendo que… | Le ruego que… |
| Le prohíbo que… | Insisto en que… |
| No apruebo que… | Le pido que… |
| No permito que… | Le suplico que… |
| No coma… | Déjeme… |

MODELO

**Médico:** Deje de comer alimentos altos en grasa y consuma más vegetales.

**Paciente:** No me diga qué debo comer y no comer. Yo estoy bien y no necesito estar a dieta.

**Médico:** Le suplico que sea más razonable.

### Essential Instruction

1. Ask students to check their answers to **Actividad 38** in pairs, and have them tell their partner whether a doctor has ever given them any of this advice.

2. For **Actividad 39**, remind students that they will use the formal register. Have students arrange their desks to simulate a doctor's office. Encourage the use of props.

3. As you go over **Gramática**, hold mini-conversations with students in which you suggest doing various activities. Encourage them to either accept or decline your invitations.

4. Have students complete **Actividad 40** in pairs.

256

# Gramática

## Mandatos de *nosotros*  1.2, 4.1

Los mandatos de **nosotros** (inglés: *let's* + verbo[1]), afirmativos y negativos, siguen la conjugación de la primera persona plural del presente del subjuntivo.

### Mandatos de *nosotros*

|  | Afirmativo | Negativo |
|---|---|---|
| entregar | entreguemos | no entreguemos |
| correr | corramos | no corramos |
| salir | salgamos | no salgamos |

• Los verbos reflexivos pierden la **-s** final en el mandato afirmativo antes de que se agregue el pronombre reflexivo. En el negativo siguen la forma del subjuntivo.

### Mandatos de *nosotros* con verbos reflexivos

|  | Afirmativo | Negativo |
|---|---|---|
| quedarse | (quedemos + nos) = **quedémonos**[2] | no nos quedemos |
| levantarse | (levantemos + nos) = **levantémonos** | no nos levantemos |
| ponerse | (pongamos + nos) = **pongámonos** | no nos pongamos |

• El verbo **ir** es irregular en el mandato afirmativo. En el negativo sigue la forma del subjuntivo.

### Mandatos de *ir*

|  | Afirmativo | Negativo |
|---|---|---|
| ir | vamos | no vayamos |
| irse | vámonos | no nos vayamos |
| salir | salgamos | no salgamos |

[1] *Let's* se puede expresar también usando el modo indicativo **vamos a** + infinitivo en el afirmativo: **Vamos a estudiar ahora.** En el negativo solo se usa la forma del subjuntivo.

[2] **Atención:** Cuando se agrega el pronombre hay que escribir un acento sobre la antepenúltima sílaba.

### 40 Vivamos una vida sana  1.2, 1.3

Constantemente vemos en revistas y periódicos anuncios que nos recuerdan la necesidad de evitar las tensiones y vivir una vida sana. Cambie cada oración para formar el imperativo de nosotros, según el modelo.

*¡Divirtámonos!*

**MODELO** Hay que vivir una vida sana.
**¡Vivamos una vida sana!**

1. Hay que transformar la tensión en actividad.
2. Hay que correr y montar en bicicleta porque ambos ejercicios nos ponen en contacto con la naturaleza.
3. Hay que practicar ejercicios respiratorios.
4. Hay que relajar los músculos de los brazos, la cara, los hombros, el abdomen y las piernas.
5. Hay que levantarse y acostarse temprano para gozar de las mejores horas del día.
6. Hay que tratar de mantener siempre un cuerpo sano.

---

**Answers**

**40**
1. ¡Transformemos la tensión en actividad!
2. ¡Corramos y montemos en bicicleta! ¡Pongámonos en contacto con la naturaleza!
3. ¡Practiquemos ejercicios respiratorios!
4. ¡Relajemos los músculos de los brazos, la cara, los hombros, el abdomen y las piernas!
5. ¡Levantémonos y acostémonos temprano! ¡Gocemos de las mejores horas del día!
6. ¡Tratemos de mantener siempre un cuerpo sano!

**Reference Desk**

1. Emphasize that **nosotros/as** commands are identical to the **nosotros/as** form of the present subjunctive.
2. Point out that **-ir** stem-changing verbs have a stem change in the **nosotros/as** command. For example: **dormir - durmamos**, **mentir - mintamos**, **pedir - pidamos**.

**Expansion**

Provide groups with a set of cards. Each card should have an infinitive written on it and a + or – sign. Have students conjugate **nosotros** commands using the cards with their group. To challenge students, add reflexive, direct, and indirect object pronouns to some cards.

---

## Differentiated Learning

### Adapt/Expand

Have students turn the statements from **Actividad 38** into a health brochure. Tell them to add a title and illustrations for each section.

### Multiple Intelligences

**Visual-Spatial/Verbal-Linguistic**

Hold a caption contest. Bring in a few single-panel cartoons that deal with medical situations, and white out any captions or speech bubbles. Display the cartoons for a week, and allow students to submit one entry per cartoon. At the end of the week, have the class vote, and award first, second, and third place for each cartoon.

# Lectura literaria

## Walking Around  1.2, 2.2, 3.1
### de *Pablo Neruda*

### Sobre el autor

Neftalí Ricardo Reyes Basoalto, conocido mundialmente como Pablo Neruda, nació en Chile en 1904. Poeta consagrado, su vida estuvo siempre marcada por la literatura y por su activismo político. En 1927 empezó su larga carrera diplomática, gracias a la que realizó múltiples viajes. Comprometido con el movimiento republicano primero, tras ser testigo de la guerra civil española, y con el comunismo después, Neruda se exilió en 1949. Recibió prestigiosos premios que culminaron con el Premio Nobel de Literatura en 1971. Neruda murió en septiembre de 1973 en Chile, días después del golpe de estado del general Pinochet contra el gobierno de Salvador Allende, durante el cual la casa de Neruda fue saqueada y sus libros, quemados.

*Pablo Neruda*

### Antes de leer  1.3

En *"Walking Around"* el poeta camina solo por la ciudad. Se siente desamparado en un mundo impersonal que da la espalda a los valores naturales en favor de la hipocresía, el materialismo y la rutina. ¿Qué sensaciones le causa a Ud. la ciudad?

### Estrategia 3.1

El símbolo es un recurso literario mediante el cual se relacionan dos elementos, uno concreto y otro abstracto que va más allá de la interpretación literal, y que puede no estar explícito en el texto. Entender la naturaleza de los símbolos y su significado lo ayudará a comprender el poema con mayor profundidad.

### 41 Practique la estrategia 1.2, 3.1

En *"Walking Around"* Neruda usa el simbolismo para describir la desesperación y el rechazo que le produce vivir rodeado de una civilización inhóspita y antinatural. A medida que lea el poema, empareje los versos de la primera columna con el significado simbólico que mejor corresponda de la segunda.

**Versos del poema**

1. ...entro en las sastrerías y en los cines marchito,...

2. ...como un cisne de fieltro (*swan (made) of felt*)...

3. Sólo quiero un descanso de piedras o de lana (*wool*)

4. sólo quiero no ver establecimientos ni jardines, ni mercaderías, ni anteojos, ni ascensores

5. asustar (*frighten*) a un notario con un lirio cortado o dar muerte a una monja (*nun*) con un golpe de oreja

6. No quiero seguir siendo raíz (*root*) en las tinieblas,

7. extendido, tiritando de sueño, hacia abajo, en las tripas (*guts*) mojadas de la tierra, absorbiendo y pensando, comiendo cada día.

**Simbolismo**

A. la muerte del espíritu natural del hombre, que vive en una sociedad que lo anula

B. la poesía como arma para rebelarse contra las convenciones sociales y las instituciones

C. el deseo de una existencia más natural, la búsqueda de refugio en la naturaleza

D. el rechazo hacia lo artificial, lo moderno y la tecnología

E. el deseo de iluminación y repugnancia por lo oscuro y escondido

F. la ciudad desnaturalizada, donde es más importante vestir a la moda y embotar la mente con entretenimiento artificial

G. la pureza de lo natural transformada en algo artificial

### Essential Instruction

1. As you go through **Sobre el autor**, pause to ask comprehension questions.
2. Read the **Estrategia**. Bring in examples of symbolic writing, or cite memorable symbols from famous pieces of literature.
3. Have students complete **Antes de leer** and **Actividad 41** in pairs.
4. Have students look at the image on p. 259. Ask them to guess what the tone of the poem will be.
5. Before they read, have students scan the story for cognates and words they learned in **Vocabulario 3**.
6. Play the recording, pausing for students to answer the during-reading questions.

# Walking Around   1.2, 2.2, 3.1
### de *Pablo Neruda*

Sucede[1] que me canso de ser hombre.
Sucede que entro en las sastrerías y en los cines
marchito, impenetrable[2], como un cisne de fieltro[3]
navegando en un agua de origen y ceniza[4].

5   El olor de las peluquerías me hace llorar a gritos
Sólo quiero un descanso de piedras[5] o de lana[6]
sólo quiero no ver establecimientos ni jardines,
ni mercaderías, ni anteojos, ni ascensores.

Sucede que me canso de mis pies y mis uñas
10   y mi pelo y mi sombra.
Sucede que me canso de ser hombre.

Sin embargo sería delicioso
asustar a un notario con un lirio cortado
o dar muerte a una monja[7] con un golpe de oreja.
15   Sería bello
ir por las calles con un cuchillo verde
y dando gritos[8] hasta morir de frío.

No quiero seguir siendo raíz en las tinieblas,
vacilante[9], extendido, tiritando[10] de sueño,
20   hacia abajo, en las tripas mojadas de la tierra,
absorbiendo y pensando, comiendo cada día.

No quiero para mí tantas desgracias.
No quiero continuar de raíz y de tumba,
de subterráneo solo, de bodega con muertos,
25   aterido[11], muriéndome de pena.

[1] it so happens  [2] impervious  [3] swan (made) of felt  [4] ash  [5] stones  [6] wool
[7] nun  [8] yelling  [9] wavering  [10] shivering  [11] frozen stiff

*...sólo quiero no ver establecimientos ni jardines, ni mercaderías, ni anteojos, ni ascensores.*

 **1.2**

## 42 Comprensión

1. ¿De qué se cansa el poeta?

2. ¿Qué le gustaría hacer?

3. ¿Qué no quiere para él, el poeta?

 **1.3, 3.1**

## 43 Analice

¿Qué cree Ud. que simboliza la imagen "asustar a un notario con un lirio cortado"?

RESOURCES

 Walking Around

**Answers**

**42**

1. Se cansa de su existencia, de su ser (de ser hombre, de sus pies, sus uñas, su pelo, su sombra).
2. Le gustaría rebelarse contra las instituciones (asustar a un notario con un lirio cortado o dar muerte a una monja con un golpe de oreja).
3. No quiere seguir siendo raíz en las tinieblas, en la oscuridad, solo sobreviviendo (absorbiendo y pensando, comiendo día a día). No quiere tantas desgracias, la pena de vivir como si fuera un muerto.

**43** *Respuesta posible:*

El poeta quiere rebelarse contra el gobierno, las instituciones, pero de forma pacífica. El notario simboliza el gobierno, las leyes, las instituciones. El lirio blanco es un símbolo de paz.

### Reference Desk

As they read, tell students to make a list of the things the author doesn't want (**No quiere...**).

### Critical Thinking

**Analyzing**
Ask students to consider why Neruda might have chosen a title in English for this poem.

## Differentiated Learning
### Accelerate/Heritage Learners
Encourage these students to read the selection independently. You may want to have them research more about the author.

## Multiple Intelligences
### Visual-Spatial
Encourage students to represent the poem visually. Ask students to paint, draw, or use newspaper or magazine clippings.

# Answers

**44** *Respuestas posibles:*

1. Describe rincones, casas, hospitales, zapaterías, calles, oficinas, tiendas de ortopedia, patios.

2. Describe casas húmedas de cuyas puertas cuelgan horribles intestinos. Habla de hospitales de donde salen huesos por la ventana, de zapaterías que huelen a vinagre y de calles espantosas como grietas.

**45** **⚙** *Respuesta posible:*

Los espejos deberían haberse avergonzado y espantado de reflejar una realidad tan horrible, una realidad vulgar, uniforme y deshumanizada.

**Después de leer**
*Las respuestas variarán.*

---

## Connections

### Literature
Ask students to compare and contrast "Walking Around" with another poem that presents the city as a hostile environment, such as "**Vuelta de paseo**" from Federico García Lorca's collection **Poeta en Nueva York** (1930).

---

 **1.2**

## 44 Comprensión

1. ¿Qué lugares de la ciudad describe el poeta?

2. ¿Cómo describe el poeta la fealdad de esos lugares?

 **1.3, 3.1**

## 45 Analice

¿Qué cree que quiso decir el poeta en este verso: "...hay espejos que debieran haber llorado de vergüenza y espanto"? ¿Qué debería haber avergonzado y espantado a los espejos?

---

Por eso el día lunes arde[12] como el petróleo
cuando me ve llegar con mi cara de cárcel,
y aúlla[13] en su transcurso[14] como una rueda herida,
y da pasos de sangre caliente hacia la noche.

30 Y me empuja[15] a ciertos rincones[16], a ciertas casas húmedas,
a hospitales donde los huesos salen por la ventana,
a ciertas zapaterías con olor a vinagre,
a calles espantosas como grietas[17].

Hay pájaros de color de azufre[18] y horribles intestinos
35 colgando de las puertas de las casas que odio,
hay dentaduras olvidadas en una cafetera[19], hay espejos
que debieran haber llorado de vergüenza y espanto[20],
hay paraguas en todas partes, y venenos[21], y ombligos[22].

Yo paseo con calma, con ojos, con zapatos, con furia, con olvido
40 paso, cruzo oficinas y tiendas de ortopedia,
y patios donde hay ropas colgadas de un alambre[23]:
calzoncillos[24], toallas y camisas que lloran
lentas lágrimas sucias.

[12] burns    [13] howls    [14] path    [15] leads    [16] corners    [17] cracks    [18] sulfur
[19] coffee pot    [20] shock    [21] poison    [22] navels    [23] wire    [24] underpants

---

## Después de leer  **1.1, 1.3**

En "*Walking Around*", Neruda describe una ciudad árida, que vive de espaldas a la naturaleza y a los sentimientos. Con un(a) compañero/a, contesten las siguientes preguntas y, luego, comparen sus respuestas con las del resto de la clase.

• ¿Qué piensa Ud. de la vida en la ciudad?

• ¿Cómo se compara su opinión con la de Neruda?

• ¿Le gusta vivir en la ciudad o prefiere el campo? ¿Por qué?

• ¿Cómo compararía ambos estilos de vida en la actualidad?

**260** doscientos sesenta | *Unidad 6*

---

## Essential Instruction

1. For Common Core practice, have students answer the **Analice** questions.
2. Point out the **Pregunta clave** on p. 261.

3. Read through the **Proyectos** on pp. 261–262. Allow students to choose project(s) that most appeal to them. Provide detailed rubrics so that students are aware of the expectations for these tasks.

**260**

# Para concluir

## Proyectos

### A  ¡Manos a la obra! 👥   1.1, 1.3, 2.1, 2.2

Trabaje con un(a) compañero/a. Imaginen que son estudiantes del último año de la carrera de medicina en la Universidad de Chile. Acaban de regresar de su experiencia en el Internado Rural y deben escribir un informe sobre lo que vivieron allí.

Pueden incluir en su informe:

- Detalles específicos del internado: dónde estuvieron, cuánto tiempo, con quién, etc.

- Un programa de prevención del que hayan participado

- Una anécdota emotiva o graciosa con alguno de sus pacientes

- El relato de una visita en la vivienda de algún paciente

- Qué cosas deberían mejorar en el cuidado de la salud en el ámbito rural

- Las cosas que aprendieron de esta experiencia

Luego, presenten el informe al resto de sus compañeros.

*Los estudiantes escriben un informe sobre su experiencia.*

### B  En resumen  🌸 1.3, 2.1, 2.2

Repase lo que aprendió sobre la salud en Chile. ¿Qué cosas pasaban antes? ¿Qué cosas pasan ahora? Complete el cuadro comparativo y luego converse con un(a) compañero/a sobre los cambios que les hayan parecido más interesantes.

|  | Antes | Ahora |
|---|---|---|
| Usos de la medicina complementaria |  |  |
| La medicina rural |  |  |
| Usos de la tecnología aplicada a la salud |  |  |
| Prevención de infecciones |  |  |

### Extensión

Busque información acerca de la historia de la salud en otro país de habla hispana y compárela con la información de Chile. ¿En qué se parecen? ¿En qué se diferencian? ¿Son más o menos importantes las influencias de los pueblos indígenas y de la iglesia?

---

## Answers

**Script** *Continued from p. 251.*
 y existen artículos en donde ya se está viendo la efectividad de las terapias complementarias, por ejemplo en acupuntura, o en algunos preparados homeopáticos o de homeotoxicología, se está viendo como hay respuestas que pueden ser objetivables y por lo tanto válidas. Ahora, yo quiero también definir siguiendo tu pregunta y continuar comentando que el sistema de salud en este momento ha tomado un poco las riendas de garantizar a la población de que aquellos que practican estas terapias tengan las competencias adecuadas.
—Asegurar también la calidad.
—Exactamente. Y de esa manera entonces hacerla más válida hacia la población, darle más seguridad a la población.

**A** *Los informes variarán.*

**B** *Las respuestas variarán.*

### Reference Desk

Point out the **Pregunta clave**. Ask students to think again about the question, this time in relation to their own culture.

---

## Differentiated Learning

### Accelerate/Expand

Ask students to read other poems by Neruda, such as "**Poema 20**" from ***Veinte poemas de amor y una canción desesperada***, or one of his **odas elementales**. Tell students to identify the tone, theme(s), and symbolism in each poem.

### Heritage Learners

Ask heritage learners to read Antonio Skármeta's short novel ***No pasó nada*** (alternatively, provide students with excerpts). Ask them to analyze the protagonist's feelings of alienation, homesickness, and hostility. In what ways are the protagonist's feelings universal to the immigrant experience? In what ways are his feelings unique?

Answers

**C** *Los artículos variarán.*

**D** *Los carteles variarán.*

**E** *Los poemas variarán.*

## Reference Desk

1. Elicura Chihuailaf Nahuelpán is a Mapuche Chilean poet. He writes in both Mapudungun and Spanish. His work ***Recado confidencial a los chilenos*** expresses a defense of Mother Nature, which he believes is threatened by modern society.

2. You could have students create Flipgrid posts of their poems from **Actividad E**.

## Culture

**Products: Activity**
Ask students to watch a few videos by Chilean comedian and video blogger Germán Garmendia. Tell them to choose one video and write an e-mail to a friend to tell him/her about it. Students should recommend the video positively or negatively, using the subjunctive, and explain why.

---

**C** **¡A escribir!**  1.3, 2.1, 2.2

Imagine que Ud. es médico/a en Chile y quiere escribir un artículo para una revista especializada. Su artículo será una crítica al sistema de salud conectada. Ud. defenderá la atención tradicional cara a cara con el paciente.

Primero, complete el organizador de ideas. Piense en todas las desventajas que se le ocurran sobre la salud conectada: ¿Qué problemas representa para los médicos? ¿Qué problemas representa para el paciente? Enumere también las ventajas de atender a un paciente en una consulta personal.

| DESVENTAJAS de la salud conectada | VENTAJAS de la atención personal |
| --- | --- |
| | |

Por último, escriba su artículo respaldando su opinión con todas las razones que incluyó en el organizador de ideas.

**D** **El arte de curar con plantas** Conéctese: la botánica  1.3, 2.1, 2.2, 3.1

Busque información en la internet sobre la herbolaria mapuche. Elija cinco plantas o hierbas utilizadas por los chamanes con fines curativos. Tome notas acerca de los beneficios de cada una. Incluya información sobre cómo debe prepararse, qué efectos produce, etc. Busque imágenes de algunas de las plantas o hierbas y prepare un cartel para presentarlo al resto de la clase.

**E** **El árbol del canelo**  Conéctese: la literatura 1.1, 1.2, 1.3, 2.2, 3.1

Lea el siguiente fragmento de un poema del chileno Elicura Chihuailaf. Habla del canelo, un árbol considerado sagrado entre los mapuches, no solo por sus poderes curativos sino por razones simbólicas.

**Para sanarte vine, me habló el canelo**
de *Elicura Chihuailaf*

Para sanarte vine, me habló el Árbol Sagrado
Ve y recoge mis hojas, mis semillas
me está diciendo
De todas partes vinieron tus buenas Machi
mis buenos Machi
desde las cuatro Tierras, desde las cuatro Aguas
mediaremos, me están diciendo sus poderes
en tus nervios, en tus huesos, en tus venas
[…]

Comente el fragmento con un(a) compañero/a. Observen el lugar que ocupa la naturaleza en general y el canelo en particular como interlocutor en el poema. Juntos elijan alguna de las hierbas tradicionales de la medicina mapuche que investigaron en la actividad anterior y escriban un poema sobre la misma.

## Essential Instruction

1. Have students peer-edit their articles from **Actividad C**.
2. You may want to assign **Actividad D** as a pair or small group activity.
3. Read the poem in **Actividad E** and discuss it as a class. Then have pairs write their poems.
4. For the **Vocabulario de la Unidad 6**, ask students to determine a few categories that could be used to sort the words. Then have students list the words in those categories.

# Vocabulario de la Unidad 6 🌸 1.2

el **accidente** accident
**aguantar** to put up with, to stand
las **alergias** allergies
**alimentar(se)** to feed (oneself)
**aliviar** to relieve
la **ambulancia** ambulance
el **análisis de sangre/de orina** blood test/urine test
los **antibióticos** antibiotics
la **aplicación** application (of an ointment)
**asistir** to attend
**ateridos/as** terrified
**atropellar** to run over
**avergonzado/a** embarrassed
la **bodega** warehouse
**bostezar** to yawn
**caerse** to fall
la **camilla** stretcher
**caminar** to walk
la **cárcel** jail
el **catarro/resfriado** cold
**con cuidado** carefully
**conducir** to drive
**constante** continous
**continuar** to continue
el **corazón** heart
el **cuerpo** body*
**curar(se)** to cure; to be cured
**dar a luz** to give birth
la **desgracia** misfortune
**desmayarse** to faint
el **diagnóstico** diagnosis
la **dificultad en respirar** difficulty breathing
la **dolencia** complaint, ailment
**doler** to hurt
el **dolor agudo** sharp pain
el **dolor de garganta** sore throat
**dormir** to sleep
**enfermarse** to become ill
la **enfermedad** sickness
el/la **enfermero/a** nurse
**espantoso/a** frightening
el **establecimiento** establishment
**estar embarazada** to be pregnant
**estar en forma** to be in good shape
**estar enfermo/a** to be sick
**estar enyesado/a** to be in a cast
**estar mareado/a** to feel dizzy
**estornudar** to sneeze

*Ver partes del cuerpo en la página 229.

el **examen médico** medical exam
**examinar** to examine
el/la **farmacéutico/a** pharmacist
**fiel** faithful
**fracturarse/romperse una pierna** to fracture/break a leg
**fuerte** strong
la **furia** fury
los **gastos** bills, debts
el **golpe** blow
**gozar de buena salud** to be healthy
**grave** serious
la **gripe** flu
**hacer ejercicio** to exercise
**hacerse viejo/a** to become old
**herido/a de gravedad** seriously injured
el **hígado** liver
el **hueso** bone
la **infección** infection
los **intestinos** intestines
**irritado/a** irritated
el **jarabe para la tos** cough syrup
las **lágrimas** tears
**lento/a** slow
el **lirio** lily
**llevar días sin…** to go days without…
**llorar a gritos** to cry your heart out
el **malestar** discomfort
**marchito/a** wilted
los **medicamentos** medicines, medications
las **mercaderías** wares
el **microbio** virus, microbe
**morir de frío** to freeze to death
el **mostrador de información** information desk
**mover** to move
el/la **muerto/a** dead person
las **muletas** crutches
el/la **notario/a** notary
el **ombligo** navel
la **operación** surgery
el/la **paciente** patient
**pagar la consulta** to pay for the visit
el **paraguas** umbrella
**pasar la cuenta** to submit the bill
las **pastillas** pills
**pedir auxilio** to ask for help

la **peluquería** hair salon
**poner una inyección** to give a shot
**ponerse boca abajo (arriba)** to lie face down (up)
**presenciar** to witness
la **presión arterial** blood pressure
**prevenir** to prevent
los **pulmones** lungs
el **quirófano** operating room
la **raíz** root
los **rayos equis** X-rays
**realizar** to fulfill, to achieve
**recetar** to prescribe
**recompensar** to compensate
**registrar** to examine, to inspect
los **remedios caseros** home remedies
**respirar profundamente** to breathe deeply
**retirarse** to retreat
los **riñones** kidneys
la **sala de emergencias/urgencias** emergency room
la **sala de maternidad** maternity room
la **salud** health
la **sangre** blood
la **sastrería** tailor shop
**sentirse bien/mejor** to feel well/better
**sentirse débil** to feel weak
**ser alérgico/a** to be allergic
la **silla de ruedas** wheelchair
**soportar** to put up with, to bear
**suceder** to happen
**sufrir de insomnio** to suffer from insomnia
**tener fiebre** to run a fever
**tener ganas de vomitar** to feel like throwing up
**tener náuseas** to feel nauseated
**tener una cita** to have an appointment
las **tinieblas** darkness
**tomarte la temperatura** to take your temperature
**toser** to cough
el **tratamiento** treatment
las **venas** veins
el **veneno** poison
la **vergüenza** shame
**ya mismo** right away

Unidad 6 | doscientos sesenta y tres **263**

## RESOURCES

 Avenue

 Unidad 6

## Connections

**Art**
Ask students to research the paintings of Chilean artist Roberto Matta. Ask them to look at his works that have political or social themes, and choose one to analyze in depth. What figures are visible in the painting, and how are they portrayed? How does the painting relate to contemporary events? What feelings does the work capture? Have students submit their analyses via Avenue.

## Connections

**Science**
Have students share interesting facts they know about the human body, e.g., **¿Sabían que la piel es el órgano más grande del cuerpo humano?**

## Differentiated Learning
### Accelerate
Ask students to write a diary entry of a busy emergency room doctor or nurse. Tell them to use as much vocabulary as possible from this unit.

## Multiple Intelligences
### Musical-Rhythmic
Ask students to research the **nueva canción** in Chile, and listen to some songs by Víctor Jara, Violeta Parra, or Inti-Illimani. Have students analyze the instrumentation and themes in the songs, and explain this musical genre's association with politics.

## Reference Desk

1. Argentina is the second largest South American country in area, and the eighth largest in the world. Argentina has about 41 million inhabitants, 13 million of whom reside in the Buenos Aires metropolitan area.
2. Buenos Aires is an autonomous district in Argentina, meaning it does not belong to Buenos Aires Province nor any other region; its formal name is **Ciudad Autónoma de Buenos Aires**.
3. Buenos Aires is a port city located on the shores of the Río de la Plata estuary, which flows into the Atlantic Ocean just beyond Buenos Aires. Puerto Madero, built in the nineteenth century in an ambitious and costly project overseen by Eduardo Madero, was created by filling in a large area of coastal water with earth and reinforced concrete.

## Culture

**Products/Practices: Activity**
Introduce cultural information about Argentina by giving groups of three sentences: two false and one true. Have students guess which pieces of information are not true. Example: **La capital es Córdoba. Argentina se conoce por la música y baile de la salsa. Argentina tiene fronteras con Paraguay and Bolivia.** (**La capital es Buenos Aires; Argentina se conoce por el tango.**) Continue this activity with other information about Argentina. Have students write the correct information in their Culture Journals.

### ¿Sabía que...? 1.2, 2.2

Puerto Madero, el barrio más moderno de Buenos Aires, fue durante décadas una de las zonas más abandonadas de la ciudad. Los grandes galpones de ladrillo a la vista del viejo puerto no albergaban más que basura y soledad. En la actualidad, son un paseo obligado del turista que quiera disfrutar de un bello paisaje urbano.

## Essential Instruction

1. Begin with a discussion of the **Pregunta clave**. Ask students to describe urban life and cite examples of its problems. Then ask them to consider some solutions.
2. Point out Argentina on the map. Ask students to share what they know about the country.
3. Draw attention to the culture photo and question. Encourage students to watch for the photo and the answer later in the unit.
4. Point out the QR code, the video question, and the screen shot from "**Direcciones**." Encourage students to watch the video as many times as they like.
5. Have students read and ask questions about **Mis metas**.

# 7

# La vida urbana

Escanee el código QR para mirar el video "Direcciones".

Álavaro habla por teléfono con su amiga Sarah para saber dónde está, pues habían quedado de encontrarse en la parada del tranvía y ella no ha llegado. Explique qué sucedió y qué deciden hacer al respecto.

*Pregunta clave*

?

¿Qué problemas conlleva la vida urbana y cómo se resuelven?

¿En qué consiste el programa de ferias itinerantes de Buenos Aires?

Argentina

## Mis metas

### En esta unidad:

▶ Usaré expresiones relacionadas con las ventajas y desventajas de la vida en la ciudad.

▶ Usaré el presente del subjuntivo en cláusulas adjetivales y adverbiales.

▶ Leeré sobre el transporte en Buenos Aires, el mercado de Abasto y la tragedia ocurrida en la ciudad de La Plata.

▶ Distinguiré el significado de palabras y frases según el contexto.

▶ Usaré correctamente el imperfecto del subjuntivo.

▶ Leeré un artículo sobre los daños causados por una inundación en Buenos Aires.

▶ Escribiré un ensayo comparativo sobre la vida en el campo y la ciudad.

▶ Escucharé un segmento sobre la construcción de bicisendas en Buenos Aires y escribiré una carta de lectores al respecto.

▶ Desarrollaré nuevas destrezas de vocabulario.

▶ Usaré el subjuntivo en oraciones independientes y repasaré el uso de los adverbios.

▶ Leeré el cuento "Los dos reyes y los dos laberintos" del argentino Jorge Luis Borges.

doscientos sesenta y cinco **265**

## RESOURCES

 Direcciones

**Answers**

**Video question** *Respuesta posible:* Álvaro estaba esperando a Sarah en la parada de Puerto de Mar pero ella estaba en la parada de Luceros, donde pensaba que habían quedado de encontrarse. Ellos aclaran el malentendido y Álvaro le da direcciones por teléfono para que puedan encontrarse en el puerto.

**Culture question**
Son puestos móviles que cada día de la semana se ubican en distintos puntos de la ciudad para vender productos frescos: frutas, verduras, carnes, pescados, mariscos, etc.

## Reference Desk

1. Ask students to read the **Pregunta clave** and speculate about the theme of the unit and the vocabulary and culture they might encounter. Be sure students understand the meaning of **conllevar** (*to entail*).
2. Draw attention to the screen shot from "**Direcciones.**" Ask students to guess where Álvaro is and to whom he is speaking on the phone.
3. Remind students with eBook access they can click on the red country on p. 265 to link directly to Wikipedia.

## Differentiated Learning
### Expand
Ask students to research the five largest cities in Argentina based on population. Have them create an urban profile for each place. Finally, have them tell a partner where they would most like to visit and why.

## Multiple Intelligences
### Verbal-Linguistic
Review and preview the unit vocabulary and grammar by asking questions such as: **¿Cómo es la vida en la ciudad? ¿Qué es lo bueno de vivir en la ciudad? ¿Y lo malo? Cuando termines los estudios, ¿dónde te gustaría vivir? ¿Qué idioma hablarías si fueras argentino/a? ¿Cómo sería tu vida si vivieras en Buenos Aires?**

## RESOURCES

 Avenue

 Así se vive en
la ciudad
Para conversar

**WB** Activities 1–2

**FC** Unidad 7

### Reference Desk

1. Explain that **ciudadela** means *citadel*, but it is often used to refer to a residential area or community within a city.
2. You may want to mention that **contar con** in this context is a synonym of **tener**.

### Culture

**Practices: Activity**
Ask students about what they know about **huelgas**, and if they or anyone they know has ever participated in one, or another type of public protest. Then ask students to research the **cacerolazo**, a popular form of street protest in Latin America and Spain. Ask them to find out what people do during a **cacerolazo**, and what the most recent ones in Argentina were about. Ask them to write a summary of their findings and submit it via Avenue.

### Game

**El ahorcado**
Have students practice the new vocabulary by playing Hangman. First have a volunteer demonstrate the game on the board with a short word, such as **seda**.

**266**

---

# *Vocabulario 1*

## Así se vive en la ciudad   1.2

### Diario TIERRA VERDE

| NOTICIAS | NEGOCIOS | CULTURA | DEPORTES | ENTRETENIMIENTO |

TRANSPORTE
SEGURIDAD

**CIUDADELA TIERRA VERDE**

La alcaldesa de la ciudad anunció la inauguración de Ciudadela Tierra Verde, un inmenso conjunto residencial que proporcionará vivienda a miles de personas.

Ciudadela Tierra Verde se compone de más de veinte edificios de apartamentos, además de establecimientos comerciales diseñados para suplir las necesidades de toda la comunidad.

Cuenta con amplios medios de transporte público, líneas del metro y redes de autobuses que movilizarán a cientos de pasajeros desde las afueras, a cualquier lugar de la ciudad y a cualquier hora.

Contribuya a la seguridad en Tierra Verde. Preste atención a los semáforos y a las señales de tránsito antes de cruzar las calles o doblar las esquinas. Hay muchos casos de peatones que son atropellados por falta de cuidado de ellos mismos o de los conductores.

## Para conversar

**P**ara hablar de problemas relacionados con la vida en la ciudad:

Se necesitan soluciones a los problemas de transporte. ¡Colabore! Camine o monte en bicicleta en cuanto sea posible. Con menos coches y motocicletas en las vías habrá menos embotellamientos de tránsito.

Se aumentarán las tarifas del transporte urbano para satisfacer las demandas de sus empleados que reclaman aumentos de sueldo y amenazan con hacer huelga, según comunicado de la alcaldía municipal.

Se aumentará el patrullaje de la policía para combatir la injusticia social, el crimen y la delincuencia. Si Ud. sufre un atraco o presencia algo sospechoso repórtelo a la estación de policía.

Tenga cuidado con los mendigos en las paradas de autobuses y en los kioskos. Aunque muchos son desamparados, otros son solo delincuentes que se quieren aprovechar del buen corazón de los ciudadanos.

---

## Essential Instruction

1. Begin by having students look at the photos on pp. 266–268 and describe what they see.
2. Before playing the audio, have students look at the vocabulary and pick out cognates.
3. Play the audio for **Así se vive en la ciudad**. Pause occasionally to ask comprehension questions.
4. Remind students that the expressions in the **¡Acuérdese!** boxes (pp. 267 and 268) are considered active vocabulary.
5. Personalize the vocabulary presentation by asking students to describe residential and shopping areas in your community.

Diario TIERRA VERDE

| MODA | NOTICIAS | CULTURA | DEPORTES | ENTRETENIMIENTO |

**TIENDAS**

**CIUDADELA TIERRA VERDE >> EL BOSQUE >> CENTRO COMERCIAL DE VENTAS DE FÁBRICAS**

En Tierra Verde se halla el mayor centro comercial de ventas de fábrica y liquidación donde encontrará las mejores gangas en ropa y accesorios de vestir.

Hallará lo mejor en ropa para damas: vestidos, suéteres, blusas, faldas, vaqueros y pantalones en todos los colores y estilos.

Encontrará todo lo que necesite en ropa para caballeros: trajes, camisas, impermeables, etc., y todo de la mejor calidad.

Cuenta con tiendas de calzado y artículos de cuero para todas las ocasiones: botas, zapatos, sandalias, cinturones y carteras.

## Para conversar

**P**ara hablar de artículos de vestir:

—¿Cuáles zapatos le gustan más, los planos o los de tacón?
—Los de tacón. Están de moda y hacen juego perfecto con el vestido que llevo puesto.
—Aquí tiene una falda de lana a cuadros y una a rayas. ¿Se las quiere medir?
—No. Las dos se ven pasadas de moda. Prefiero llevarme la falda lisa, de un solo color, y la de algodón.
—Bueno. Y también se va a llevar el abrigo de piel, la blusa de seda de manga corta y la camisa de manga larga, ¿verdad?
—Por supuesto, pero solo si todo está en rebaja.

### ¡Acuérdese!

**Otras prendas y accesorios de vestir** ♻

- los calcetines
- los calzoncillos
- las corbatas
- los guantes
- los pañuelos
- los sombreros

RESOURCES

fg   Flipgrid

🎧   Para conversar

### Communication

**Interpersonal/Presentational: Paired Practice**
Ask students to write a detailed description of their favorite outfit. Divide the class into pairs and provide them with blank paper and colored pencils or markers. Have students read their description to their partner, who must draw the outfit. You may want to follow up this activity in the next class period with a fashion show; tell students that they must wear the outfit in their description. Have students "model" their clothing while volunteers take turns playing the role of emcee and reading the descriptions of the models' clothing aloud.

### Expansion

Tell students to imagine that they are spending winter break in Buenos Aires. (Tell them to keep in mind that Argentina is in the southern hemisphere.) Have them write a list of what they would pack in their suitcase. Then repeat the activity for a July vacation.

### Expansion

Introduce the phrase **bueno, bonito y barato**. Ask students to create a Flipgrid post in which they say which of **las tres bes** is most important to them and why, and where they like to shop for clothes.

## Differentiated Learning
### Heritage Speakers
Remind heritage speakers often to be aware of spelling: the use of capital and lowercase letters, accentuation, and ambiguous letters such as **b/v**, **c/s/z**, **x/h**, **ll/y**, and **j/g**. For example, in **Vocabulario 1**, point out the spelling of **movilización**; draw attention to **halla** and contrast it with **haya**; remind students to accent all interrogative words, etc.

## Learning Styles
### Visual Learners
Bring in department store circulars and have pairs discuss the clothing and accessories advertised in each one.

**267**

Diario TIERRA VERDE

| MERCADOS | NOTICIAS | CULTURA | DEPORTES | ENTRETENIMIENTO |

PUESTOS

**CIUDADELA TIERRA VERDE  >>  MERCADO DEL PROGRESO**

Otro beneficio de Tierra Verde es su cercanía al Mercado del Progreso, famoso por sus carnicerías y ventas de verduras y vegetales.

Hallará puestos de toda clase de frutas: uvas, fresas, peras, naranjas, sandías y manzanas, y ventas de los mejores jugos de fruta fresca.

## Para conversar

**P**ara hacer compras en el mercado:

—Véndame una libra de carne de res, dos libras de costilla de cordero y dos libras de mariscos, por favor.
—Con mucho gusto. ¿No quiere llevarse unos chorizos? Dice el carnicero que acaban de prepararlos.

—¿Llevamos estos plátanos para los frijoles?
—No sé. Se ven muy maduros. Busquemos unos que estén más verdes.

> **¡Acuérdese!**
>
> **Otras carnes, frutas y verduras**
>
> | | |
> |---|---|
> | la cebolla | el pavo |
> | los champiñones | el pepino |
> | las habichuelas | el pescado |
> | los hongos | el pollo |
> | el jamón | el repollo |
> | la lechuga | la ternera |

### 1  Problemas urbanos y soluciones  1.2

Elija la solución de la segunda columna que mejor corresponda a cada problema de la primera.

| Problemas | Soluciones |
|---|---|
| **1.** Embotellamientos causados por exceso de automóviles. | **A.** Comprar en almacenes de descuento |
| **2.** Exceso de crimen y delincuencia | **B.** Crear más rutas de autobuses y líneas del metro |
| **3.** Casos de peatones atropellados | **C.** Consumir más frutas, verduras y vegetales |
| **4.** Consumo excesivo de comida basura | **D.** Caminar o ir en bicicleta |
| **5.** Poco presupuesto familiar para gastos | **E.** Prestar atención a las señales de tránsito |
| **6.** Pocos medios de transporte público | **F.** Reportar situaciones sospechosas a la policía |

## 2 Una zona agrícola  1.2

Además de sus centros de esquí, Mendoza, Argentina se conoce por su producción agrícola. Escuche la descripción de algunos aspectos de la agricultura de esta zona y escoja la opción correcta para cada oración.

1. A nivel nacional, Mendoza es la primera productora de (*frutas / verduras*).

2. Dos frutas principales son las manzanas y (*los plátanos / las peras*).

3. Una parte de la producción de (*la lechuga / la cebolla*) está destinada al consumo fresco.

4. Casi toda la producción de (*la pera / la uva*) se usa para fabricar vino.

5. (*la carne / la verdura*) ecológica es una industria reciente en la provincia de Mendoza.

## ¡Comunicación!

## 3 De excursión por Mendoza Interpersonal Communication  1.1

La ciudad de Mendoza, Argentina, ubicada junto a los Andes, es un lugar ideal para practicar *rafting*, *trekking*, montañismo y esquí. Imagine que Ud. va a Mendoza por unos días con unos amigos y que está haciendo su maleta. Sus amigos insisten en que no necesita llevar algunos artículos de ropa y accesorios, pero Ud. no está de acuerdo con ellos. Justifique por qué considera que no puede eliminar ninguno de los siguientes artículos.

1. pantalones térmicos
2. chaqueta alpina
3. vaqueros
4. abrigo de piel
5. guantes "polar"
6. sandalias
7. vestido / corbata de seda
8. calcetines de lana

## 4 El *look* de Cristina Presentational Communication 1.3

La ex presidenta de Argentina, Cristina Fernández de Kirchner, es conocida por su *look* y su pasión por la ropa, la cual es siempre centro de discusión en todas sus presentaciones dentro y fuera del país. Busque fotos de varias de estas presentaciones y describa en forma breve la ropa que la ex presidenta llevaba puesta para la ocasión, como se ve en el modelo. Luego, describa el *look* de Cristina en un párrafo, en sus propias palabras y preséntelo enfrente de la clase.

MODELO: **Para su presentación en la Asamblea General de Las Naciones Unidas, la ex presidenta Cristina Fernández de Kirchner llevaba puesta una chaqueta de seda de color lila y una falda blanca plisada de organza (*organdi*).**

| Ocasión | Descripción de su vestuario |
|---|---|
| | |
| | |
| | |
| | |

*Cristina Fernández de Kirchner en la Asamblea General*

### RESOURCES

 Activity 2

Answers

**2 Script**

Por su clima árido, la provincia de Mendoza se ha convertido en la primera productora de fruta fresca en el país. Las frutas principales son las manzanas y las peras. Hay un importante mercado nacional e internacional para ellas. Las verduras, en especial la cebolla y las papas, no se quedan atrás. Estas dos verduras están destinadas al consumo fresco y conservado. Por las excelentes condiciones climáticas, la producción de las uvas es una industria próspera. El 99 % de la producción de uvas está destinada a la fabricación de vinos que tienen fama internacional. Últimamente en la provincia de Mendoza han empezado a producir carnes ecológicas.

1. frutas
2. las peras
3. la cebolla
4. la uva
5. La carne

**3** *Las respuestas variarán.*

**4** *Las respuestas variarán.*

### Reference Desk

Cristina Fernández de Kirchner began her first term as President of Argentina in 2007; her second term began in 2011. She is the second female to serve as president of Argentina (first was Isabel Martínez de Perón, from 1974–1976), but the first woman to be elected to the post. Argentine presidents may serve an unlimited number of terms, but not more than two consecutively.

## Reference Desk

Draw attention to the name ***Davivienda***, and have a volunteer explain its meaning.

## Culture

**Products: Activity**
Ask students to research Argentine cuisine. Have them pick a dish and find a recipe online. Ask them to write a shopping list of the ingredients needed to prepare the dish. Have students read their shopping lists to the class, who will try to guess the food (e.g., **¿Es un tipo de galletas?**).

## Critical Thinking

**Comparing**
Have students compare and contrast ***Davivienda*** with a similar program in this country.

# ¡Comunicación!

**5** **Proyecto *Davivienda*** **👥** Interpretive/Interpersonal Communication  **1.1, 1.2**

Imagine que Ud. quiere participar en el proyecto de vivienda que acaba de anunciar la Alcaldía Municipal. Con un(a) compañero/a, represente la conversación que Ud. tiene con el/la representante de la alcaldía cuando llama para pedir más información. Turnénse para hacer preguntas y responderlas. Usen la información del anuncio y los siguientes puntos, como se ve en el modelo.

- Objetivo principal de *Davivienda*
- Condiciones para participar en el proyecto y obtener un préstamo de vivienda
- Información sobre los tipos y precios de las viviendas
- Fases de construcción y fechas de finalización

MODELO

| | |
|---|---|
| Ciudadano: | **Dígame, ¿qué condiciones debo cumplir para poder conseguir el préstamo de *Davivienda*?** |
| Representante: | **Bueno, para empezar, debe ser cabeza de familia.** |
| Ciudadano: | **¿Y tengo que cumplir algún requisito de salario?** |
| Representante: | **...** |

## *Davivienda:*
### Una solución a los problemas de vivienda

**La Alcaldía Municipal** de la ciudad acaba de anunciar la creación de *Davivienda*, un programa de vivienda para que las familias de bajos ingresos tengan la oportunidad de comprar casa. Gracias a este programa, todas las personas que trabajen y puedan documentar sus ingresos podrán obtener un préstamo para conseguir una casa cómoda, con tal de que sean cabeza de familia y que piensen ocupar permanentemente la vivienda.

A fin de que los beneficios lleguen a las masas, *Davivienda* cuenta con varios tipos de casas económicas. Los precios exactos de estas viviendas aún no se han dado a conocer, pero en cuanto la Alcaldía Municipal tenga esta información, se notificará a los interesados.

La construcción de estas viviendas se hará en diferentes fases, que se iniciarán en el año en curso y se completarán en el transcurso de los siguientes dos años.

Las personas que deseen más información sobre *Davivienda* pueden dirigirse a las oficinas de la Alcaldía Municipal para que les envíen más detalles.

*El programa de vivienda es un proyecto de la Alcaldía Municipal.*

## Essential Instruction

1. Read through the article about ***Davivienda*** as a class. Then have pairs read the bulleted items and prepare for their roles in **Actividad 5**.

2. Brainstorm a list of place names and verbs that students might use in **Actividad 6**. You may want to have students describe places in your community.

3. For **Actividad 7**, you may want to have groups exchange the finished articles and peer-edit them.

## ¡Comunicación!

### 6 ¡Ventajas de vivir en la ciudad!  Interpersonal Communication  1.1

Una ventaja de vivir en la ciudad es estar cerca de las tiendas, los negocios y los centros municipales y comerciales. Imagine que Ud. se siente enfermo hoy y le pide a su mejor amigo/a que le ayude con algunas diligencias (*errands*). Él/Ella lo hace y luego le da un informe de cómo le fue. Con un(a) compañero/a, represente la conversación relacionada con cada diligencia, turnándose para hacer el papel de quien pide el favor y quien lo hace. Usen términos del vocabulario y un mínimo de dos mandatos, como se ve en el modelo.

*Edificios en el centro de Buenos Aires*

**MODELO** Solicitar una copia de su acta de nacimiento

**Estudiante 1:** Necesito con urgencia una copia de mi acta de nacimiento, por favor. Si tomas el autobús número 23 o el metro, llegas directamente al centro. En el ayuntamiento vas al registro (*hall of records*). Entrégales mi carnet de identidad y diles que nací en el Hospital del Carmen.

**Estudiante 2:** Fui al ayuntamiento pero me dijeron que tú tenías que ir personalmente para solicitar el documento. Lo siento, amigo.

- Hacer una denuncia del delincuente que le quitó a la fuerza su computadora
- Averiguar las ofertas y los productos que están en rebaja en los almacenes
- Hacer una lista de los ingredientes necesarios para una comida frugal y nutritiva
- Conseguir los horarios y la disponibilidad del transporte urbano

### 7 Artículo periodístico  Presentational Communication 1.3

Formen grupos pequeños y usen palabras y expresiones del vocabulario para escribir la primera parte de un artículo del periódico sobre alguna situación complicada que haya ocurrido en la ciudad. Luego, entréguenla a otro grupo para que termine el artículo. Sigan el modelo.

**MODELO**

**Primer grupo: Un pasajero golpeó (*struck*) a una señora en un autobús cuando esta le exigió que le devolviera la billetera que acababa de robarle. El conductor sorprendido le ordenó al ladrón que devolviera lo robado y que se bajara del autobús inmediatamente. Cuando este se negó a obedecer, el conductor apagó el motor del autobús, llamó a la policía y dijo que no iba a seguir su marcha hasta que lo entregara a la policía.**

**Segundo grupo: Cuando los otros pasajeros se enteraron del problema...**

## RESOURCES

**ave** Avenue

**Answers**

**6** *Las conversaciones variarán.*

**7** *Los artículos variarán.*

### Reference Desk

**Actividad 7** previews the imperfect subjunctive, which is presented later in the unit. Before starting the activity, point out an example of imperfect subjunctive and see if students can identify the tense and find examples in the **Modelo**. Ask students if they recall the rules for usage or if they can deduce them from the example.

### Communication

**Interpersonal: Paired Practice**
Ask students to use the Internet to find city center maps for various cities in Argentina. Make copies of the maps and distribute them to pairs of students. Have them take turns naming two locations on a map; their partner must give the directions from point A to point B.

### Expansion

Discuss the emerging trend of **microcasas**. Ask students to consider the advantages and disadvantages of these dwellings.

### Differentiated Learning
#### Accelerate/Expand
Ask students to identify an area of your community that needs housing. Ask them to draft a proposal for a new home, group of homes, apartment complex, or other solution. Tell them to consider how the new housing will be integrated into the community, and explain the benefits of their housing development. Have students submit their proposals as an Avenue task.

#### Learning Styles
#### Auditory Learners
Research current headlines of new stories from your city or area. Ask students to listen to each headline and speculate the details of the event.

# Gramática

## El subjuntivo en cláusulas adjetivales  1.2

Una cláusula adjetival es una cláusula que funciona como un adjetivo y modifica al sustantivo en la cláusula principal.

| Vivo en | una ciudad | pequeña. |
| | *sustantivo* | *adjetivo* |

| Quiero vivir en | una ciudad | que sea grande. |
| | *sustantivo antecedente* | *cláusula adjetival* |

*La Boca es un barrio de Buenos Aires que es muy famoso.*

### Subjuntivo vs. indicativo en cláusulas adjetivales

$$\text{sustantivo} + \text{que} + \begin{cases} \text{indicativo (existe o se conoce)} \\ \text{subjuntivo (no existe o no se conoce)} \end{cases}$$

- Se usa el indicativo en la cláusula adjetival cuando el antecedente (el sustantivo en la cláusula principal) es algo o alguien definido, que existe y se conoce.

- Se usa el subjuntivo en la cláusula adjetival cuando el antecedente es algo o alguien indefinido, desconocido o que no existe.

| Indicativo | Subjuntivo |
|---|---|
| Conozco un mercado donde **tienen** productos orgánicos. | ¿Conoce Ud. un mercado donde **tengan** productos orgánicos? |
| Vamos a ir al almacén donde **venden** zapatos a precios de fábrica. | Buscamos un almacén donde **vendan** zapatos a precios de fábrica. |
| En las afueras hay un centro comercial que **ofrece** productos de calidad. | Cerca de aquí, no hay ningún lugar que **ofrezca** productos de calidad. |
| Conozco a varios empleados que **quieren** hacer huelga. | No conozco a nadie que **quiera** hacer huelga. |

### Un poco más

Las palabras **algo**, **alguien**, **alguno/a** y **nada**, **nadie**, **ninguno/a** se usan con frecuencia en oraciones con cláusulas adjetivales.

Yo conozco a **alguien** que trabaja en la alcaldía, ¿y tú?

No, yo no conozco a **nadie** que trabaje en la alcaldía.

Answers

8
1. pertenezca
2. vivimos
3. se preocupa
4. luche
5. sepa
6. tenga
7. quieren
8. comprenda
9 *Las respuestas variarán.*
10 *Los anuncios variarán.*

## 8  Participe en las elecciones  1.2

Complete las siguientes oraciones sobre la elección de un(a) nuevo/a alcalde o alcaldesa. Use el presente del indicativo o del subjuntivo del verbo entre paréntesis según el contexto.

1. Debemos elegir a alguien que (*pertenecer*) a nuestra comunidad.

2. La ciudad en que nosotros (*vivir*) es algo peligrosa.

3. Ahora tenemos un alcalde que no (*preocuparse*) por los grupos étnicos.

4. La ciudad necesita a alguien que (*luchar*) contra las injusticias sociales.

5. Necesitamos un político que (*saber*) decir "no" a la delincuencia.

6. Buscamos un alcalde que (*tener*) experiencia en los asuntos de la ciudad.

7. Hay muchos candidatos que (*querer*) el puesto, pero no tienen suficiente experiencia.

8. Debe ser alguien que (*comprender*) el grave problema de la delincuencia juvenil.

## 9  Tener y querer  1.3

Todos tenemos cosas que nos gustan, y sin embargo quisiéramos tener cosas mejores. Consulte la lista de vocabulario, elija cinco prendas de vestir y describa las que Ud. ya tiene y las que quiere comprar.

MODELO **Tengo un abrigo de lana pero quiero comprarme uno de piel que esté más de moda y abrigue más en el invierno.**

## ¡Comunicación!

## 10  En busca de... 👥 Presentational Communication  1.1, 1.3

El periódico *La Nación*, de Buenos Aires, saca los domingos una sección titulada "Búsqueda de la semana". Allí se encuentran los anuncios más diversos, escritos por personas que están deseosas por encontrar lo que necesitan. Para cada una de las siguientes categorías, escriba un anuncio de periódico con la ayuda de un(a) compañero/a.

MODELO **Necesito un(a) vendedor(a) con experiencia laboral mínima de un año, que hable inglés y que esté dispuesto/a a desplazarse por el interior del país. Llame al 33-42-21. Pregunte por Mónica.**

1. Un(a) director(a) de proyectos
2. Un(a) compañero/a de apartamento
3. Un taxi usado
4. Un(a) profesor(a) de inglés
5. Un(a) compañero/a para bailar tango

### Communication

**Presentational/Interpersonal: Cooperative Groups**
Ask each student to write one quality that they look for in a teacher. Then, working as a class, create a job description for hiring a new teacher at your school. Work through drafting the description on the board.

### Expansion

Find newspaper or magazine articles that use adjective clauses. Distribute copies of the articles and have students identify and highlight the adjective clauses that were used. Have them explain why the subjunctive or indicative was used in each highlighted sentence.

### Differentiated Learning
**Adapt/Expand**
Have students share their sentences from **Actividad 9** with a partner. They should follow up each sentence by asking where they can buy or find the clothing that they want, e.g., **¿Hay alguna tienda por aquí que venda gorros de lana baratos?** Tell them to use a variety of questions.

### Special Needs Students
**AD(H)D/Dyslexia**
For **Actividad 8**, guide students in identifying and underlining the words that determine if the subjunctive or indicative should be used. Tell them to write "S" or "I" next to the sentence. Then have them circle the subject and conjugate the verb.

273

### Reference Desk

1. La Boca is located just south of Puerto Madero and near Buenos Aires's old port. Many of La Boca's early inhabitants were immigrants from Genoa, Italy.
2. Explain that **colectivos** are a form of public transportation in Buenos Aires. Students will learn more about **colectivos** in the **Cultura** readings.
3. Benito Quinquela Martín (1890–1977) was born in La Boca. He is one of Argentina's most famous and beloved artists.
4. If possible, play the tango "**Caminito**" in class.

### Connections

**Art**

Bring in or display examples of paintings by Benito Quinquela Martín that show La Boca. Have students analyze his use of color and brushstrokes. How does the artist capture the essence of La Boca in his works?

## ¡Comunicación!

**11  El Caminito**  Interpersonal Communication ✿ **1.1, 1.2**

Lea el folleto sobre la calle Caminito en La Boca, una de las zonas más pintorescas y antiguas de la ciudad de Buenos Aires. Luego, con un(a) compañero/a, representen la conversación entre una turista que quiere conocer todos los sitios de atracción y un(a) guía de turismo que le hace recomendaciones. Usen los verbos del recuadro con el subjuntivo o el indicativo según corresponda, como se ve en el modelo.

| buscar | querer | esperar | necesitar | conocer | haber (hay) |
|---|---|---|---|---|---|
| recomendar | sugerir | aconsejar | es importante | es recomendable | es buena idea |

**MODELO**   **Turista:**  Quiero conocer un lugar que tenga algo de historia.

**Guía:**  Le sugiero que vaya a conocer el barrio de La Boca. Es uno de los lugares más históricos de Buenos Aires.

○○○   Calle Caminito, La Boca

**BuenosAires123**   Paseos y turismo   La guía más completa de la ciudad

### Calle Caminito, La Boca

**Caminito** es la calle más famosa y colorida de la ciudad de **Buenos Aires**. También es la más visitada por los turistas extranjeros. La **calle Caminito** está ubicada en el corazón del **barrio de La Boca**, en la zona conocida como Vuelta de Rocha, frente a la orilla del Riachuelo. **Caminito** se encuentra a 400 metros de "**La Bombonera**", el estadio del **Club Atlético Boca Juniors**.

### Cómo llegar a Caminito en La Boca

**Colectivos:** 29, 33, 64, 53, 152

**Nota:** La **calle Caminito** recibe miles de turistas cada día, la zona es segura. Sin embargo, el barrio de **La Boca** puede ser peligroso a causa de los robos. Por tal motivo, no se recomienda llevar objetos de valor ni caminar por las calles solitarias del interior del barrio.

### Historia de la calle Caminito

Por la zona donde en la actualidad se encuentra **Caminito**, en 1898 pasaba el tren. En 1928, esa vía del ferrocarril cerró y el terreno quedó abandonado. En 1950 un grupo de vecinos, entre ellos el reconocido pintor Quinquela Martín, decidieron limpiar y recuperar el espacio para hacer un paseo público. Así comienza la apertura de la calle, a la cual bautizaron **Caminito**, en homenaje al tango de Gabino Coria Peñaloza y Juan de Dios Filiberto.

El paseo fue decorado con esculturas y murales de diferentes artistas. En 1959 **Caminito** fue transformado en un museo a cielo abierto, donde muchos pintores del barrio exponían sus obras.

*Calle Caminito, La Boca, Buenos Aires*

### Los conventillos (casas típicas)

En la zona de **Caminito** se encuentran unas viviendas muy singulares, conocidas como "**conventillos**". Estas casas fueron las viviendas típicas de los inmigrantes italianos que se instalaron en el barrio. Las casas son viviendas colectivas, donde viven muchas familias que comparten patios, cocinas, etc. Las condiciones de vida no son muy buenas en el interior de los **conventillos**. El material utilizado para la construcción de las viviendas fueron las chapas de zinc, que se pintaban con las sobras de las pinturas de los talleres cercanos.

Hoy la tradición de pintar las casas con diferentes colores permanece. Muchos **conventillos** hoy se utilizan como tiendas de ventas de suvenires.

### Essential Instruction

1. Begin **Actividad 11** by having volunteers take turns reading aloud the article about **Caminito**. Ask **sí/no** comprehension questions.
2. Display a map of Buenos Aires and show the location of La Boca.
3. Go over **Gramática**. Give example sentences for each of the words in **Un poco más**.

# Gramática

## El subjuntivo en cláusulas adverbiales  1.2

- Una cláusula adverbial es una cláusula que funciona como un adverbio y modifica el verbo de la cláusula principal.

Te llamo    después.
*verbo*      *adverbio*

Te llamo    después de que llegues a casa.
*verbo*                *cláusula adverbial*

### Un poco más

**Estos adverbios introducen cláusulas adverbiales de tiempo**

| | |
|---|---|
| **cuando** | *when* |
| **después (de) que** | *after* |
| **en cuanto** | *as soon as* |
| **hasta que** | *until* |
| **mientras¹ (que)** | *while* |
| **tan pronto (como)** | *as soon as* |

### Subjuntivo vs. indicativo en cláusulas adverbiales de tiempo

> **Cláusula principal + expresión de tiempo +** { **indicativo (acción pasada o habitual)**
> **subjuntivo (acción futura)** }

- Se usa el indicativo en la cláusula adverbial cuando se trata de una acción que ya ocurrió o que ocurre habitualmente. En estos casos generalmente el verbo de la cláusula principal está en el pasado o en el presente.

    Nombraron a otro alcalde después de que su periodo de gobierno **terminó**.

- Se usa el subjuntivo en la cláusula adverbial de tiempo cuando se trata de una acción pendiente (que no ha pasado todavía). En este caso, generalmente el verbo de la cláusula principal está en el tiempo futuro o en el modo imperativo.

    Nombrarán a otro alcade después de que su periodo de gobierno **termine**.

¹ Mientras + indicativo = *while*. Mientras (que) + subjuntivo = *We don't know how long.*

*Se inaugurarán las nuevas líneas del metro tan pronto como termine la construcción.*

---

### RESOURCES

| | |
|---|---|
| **WB** | Activities 9–11 |
| **LA** | Activity 2 |

### Reference Desk

Give a few examples of **mientras** + indicative and **mientras que** + subjunctive.

### Expansion

Have students write about something they are planning to do that has not yet occurred. Ask students to share their work with a partner. In groups of two, students should write sentences using adverbial clauses about the event that is yet to occur.

---

## Learning Styles

### Auditory Learners

Read aloud a series of sentences that use the indicative and subjunctive in adverbial clauses. Have students raise their hands whenever they hear the subjunctive.

### Special Needs Students

### Reading Difficulties

Bring in a few news articles that use the subjunctive and indicative in adverbial clauses. Pair accelerated students with weaker ones and tell them to underline the verbs in the main clause and identify the tenses used. They should then highlight the verbs in the adverbial clauses, using one color for the indicative and another for the subjunctive.

### Reference Desk

Point out that in English, we often use dependent clauses when there isn't any change in subject, e.g., *I work so that I have money*. Explain that in Spanish, the infinitive is used: **Trabajo para tener dinero.**

### Communication

**Interpersonal/Presentational: Cooperative Groups**
Divide the class into groups. Distribute copies of a tourist map of Buenos Aires and label as many sites of interest as possible, such as **La Recoleta**, **La Casa Rosada**, **la Plaza San Telmo**, **el Obelisco**, etc. Tell groups that they have to decide which places to visit and use adverbial clauses to write sentences about their plans, e.g., **Visitaremos el Obelisco salvo que haya mucho tráfico.**

### Culture

**Products/Practices: Activity**
Have students research the Argentinean custom of drinking **mate**. Have them learn how to prepare this infusion, how it is served and consumed socially, and what health benefits it has.

### Expansion

As an example, write on the board a sentence using an adverbial clause that requires the subjunctive. Ask each student to create a sentence that would require the subjunctive, using the expressions from pp. 275 and 276. Have each student write his/her sentence on the board. Read the sentences to the class, and underline each adverbial clause.

## Las cláusulas adverbiales de propósito, condición y anticipación

- Se usa el subjuntivo en cláusulas adverbiales de propósito, condición y anticipación cuando se refieren a acciones que aún no se han realizado.

$$\text{Cláusula principal + expresión de} \left\{ \begin{array}{l} \text{propósito} \\ \text{condición o} \\ \text{anticipación} \end{array} \right. \text{+ subjuntivo}$$

Vamos al mercado antes de que **llueva**.

| Conjunciones que introducen cláusulas adverbiales en subjuntivo | | |
|---|---|---|
| **Propósito** | **Condición** | **Anticipación** |
| a fin de que  *in order that, so that* | a menos que  *unless* | antes (de) que  *before* |
| para que  *in order that, so that* | a no ser que  *unless* | |
| en caso (de) que  *in case* | con tal (de) que  *provided that* | |
| | salvo que  *except* | |
| | sin que  *without* | |

- **A pesar (de) que** (*although*), **aun cuando** (*even though*) y **aunque** (*even if*) introducen cláusulas en indicativo si se implica seguridad. Introducen cláusulas en subjuntivo si se implica inseguridad.

  Fuimos al mercado aunque **llovía**.

  Iremos al mercado aunque **llueva**.

- **Mientras (que)** introduce cláusulas en subjuntivo cuando tiene el significado de *as long as* (condición). Introduce cláusulas en indicativo o subjuntivo cuando tiene el significado de *while* (tiempo), según sea el caso.

  Te esperé mientras **tuve** tiempo.

  Te esperaré mientras **tenga** tiempo.

*Voy a tomarme un mate, aunque no sé si me guste.*

### Essential Instruction

1. Ask volunteers to create example sentences for each conjunction given in **Gramática**.
2. For the last two bullets, ask students to explain in their own words the difference in meaning between the two example sentences.
3. Have students check their answers to **Actividad 12** in pairs.
4. Point out that there are a variety of possible answers for **Actividad 13**; students should make sure that their combinations are logical.
5. Model completing item 1 in **Actividad 14**. You may want to have students work in pairs to complete the conversation.

## 12 Preparativos para la fiesta  1.3

Complete los siguientes preparativos para una fiesta con el subjuntivo del verbo entre paréntesis, y explique por qué es necesario usarlo.

1. Los muchachos se alegrarán cuando tú les (*decir*) ____ que haremos una fiesta.

2. Ellos van a alegrarse mucho cuando (*saber*) ____ que la fiesta es este fin de semana.

3. Yo iré al supermercado, con tal de que mis hermanos (*ir*) ____ a la pescadería.

4. Carlos preparará el flan sin que nosotras lo (*ayudar*) ____ .

5. Compraré las carnes hoy, para que mañana nosotras no (*tener*) ____ que salir.

6. Tendremos que preparar ensaladas y verduras en caso de que algunos de los invitados (*ser*) ____ vegetarianos.

7. Andrés puede traer los refrescos, a menos que Enrique (*querer*) ____ hacerlo.

8. Disfrutaremos hasta que (*salir*) ____ el sol.

## 13 De compras  1.3

Combine la información de las dos columnas con las conjunciones del recuadro para formar oraciones lógicas, como se ve en el modelo.

| tan pronto como | a menos que | en caso de que | con tal de que | para que | cuando | hasta que |

**MODELO** **Voy a llevar dinero en caso de que tú quieras comprar algo de ropa.**

1. Voy a llevar dinero...

2. Te regalaré esos guantes...

3. Esperaré en casa...

4. Me probaré estas sandalias...

5. Cenaremos juntos...

6. No compraré esos vaqueros...

7. Compraré las botas...

...no (*costar*) demasiado.

...tú (*venir*) a recogerme.

...tú (*querer*) comprar algo de ropa.

...(*estar*) en rebaja.

...(*llegar*) a la tienda.

...nosotros (*poder*) ir a esquiar.

...nosotros (*acabar*) de comprar.

## 14 Use su imaginación  1.3

Imagínese que un(a) amigo/a que visita su ciudad por primera vez le hace varias preguntas. Use su imaginación para completar la conversación.

1. **A:** ¿Cómo voy al centro histórico?
   **B:** Primero, caminas tres cuadras y después doblas a la izquierda **cuando** (tú)...

2. **A:** ¿Hay mucho tráfico?
   **B:** Sí. No cruces la calle **hasta que** el semáforo...

3. **A:** ¿Crees que habrá boletos para el cine?
   **B:** Seguro, pero **tan pronto como** el cine...

4. **A:** ¿Puedo regresar del centro en autobús **después de que**... ?
   **B:** Sí, **a menos que**...

5. **A:** En caso de que me pierda, ¿qué hago?
   **B:** Me llamas por teléfono **para que**...

### Answers

12 *Las explicaciones variarán.*
1. digas
2. sepan
3. vayan
4. ayudemos
5. tengamos
6. sean
7. quiera
8. salga

13 *Las respuestas variarán.*
*Respuestas posibles:*
1. Voy a llevar dinero en caso de que tú quieras comprar algo de ropa.
2. Te regalaré esos guantes cuando nosotros podamos ir a esquiar.
3. Esperaré en casa hasta que tú vengas a recogerme.
4. Me probaré estas sandalias con tal que no cuesten demasiado.
5. Cenaremos juntos cuando nosotros acabemos de comprar.
6. No compraré esos vaqueros a menos que estén en rebaja.
7. Compraré las botas tan pronto como llegue a la tienda.

14 *Las respuestas variarán.*

### Connections

**Environmental Science**
Ask students to think of pollution and its consequences for the environment. Have students give oral responses that use **a menos que**.

## Differentiated Learning
**Accelerate**
Create situations and ask students to create advice for each situation using the subjunctive. **Mi hermano nunca limpia su parte de nuestra habitación. Creo que mi novio salió con otra.**

## Special Needs Students
**Linguistically Challenged**
Modify **Actividades 12** and **13**. For **Actividad 12**, work with students to underline words that trigger the use of the subjunctive and model verb conjugations. Convert **Actividad 13** into a dehydrated sentences activity, matching up fragments for them.

277

### 15 Condiciones y precauciones  1.1

Siempre queremos hacer cosas, pero hay condiciones para todo. En parejas, terminen las oraciones de una forma lógica.

1. Un padre le dice a su hijo/a:
   A. No corras en la calle en caso de que…
   B. No salgas del coche sin que…
   C. No hables con nadie a menos que…
   D. No toques las cosas en el almacén a no ser que…
   E. No te muevas de aquí hasta que…

2. El policía le dice al conductor o a la conductora:
   A. Podrá aparcar su coche allí mientras que…
   B. No debe manejar a menos que…
   C. Quédese aquí hasta que el semáforo…
   D. Muéstreme su licencia de conducir para que…
   E. Tome un taxi en caso de que…

3. El alcalde le dice a los ciudadanos:
   A. Yo trabajaré para todos Uds. después de que…
   B. Bajaré los impuestos (*taxes*) tan pronto como…
   C. Encontraré viviendas para los desamparados cuando…
   D. Todos tendrán trabajo con tal de que…
   E. No habrá delincuencia mientras que…

## ¡Comunicación!

### 16 Ventas por comisión   Interpersonal Communication   1.1

Imagine que Ud. trabaja como vendedor(a) en un almacén de ropa donde le pagan comisión por las ventas. Con un(a) compañero/a, representen una conversación entre el vendedor o la vendedora y un(a) cliente que está buscando un regalo para su novio/a, pero no sabe qué comprarle. Ofrézcale cuanto pueda para poder ganarse su comisión. Use las expresiones del recuadro y el subjuntivo o indicativo en cláusulas adverbiales, como se ve en el modelo.

| | | | | |
|---|---|---|---|---|
| aunque | mientras que | sin que | a no ser que | después de que |
| para que | con tal de que | salvo que | antes de que | a pesar de que |

**MODELO**

| | |
|---|---|
| Vendedor: | Cómprele una de estas corbatas antes de que se vendan. Aproveche la oferta. |
| Cliente: | No, quisiera comprarle algo mejor, aunque sea más costoso. |

# Buenos Aires y el tránsito  1.2, 2.2, 3.1

*El caos de tránsito en Buenos Aires*

La capital de la República Argentina es una metrópolis enorme, cosmopolita y maravillosa, pero no por eso exenta[1] de problemas. Y uno de los principales dolores de cabeza para sus habitantes es trasladarse de un lugar a otro: la ciudad es un enjambre[2] enloquecido de tránsito.

El parque automotor[3] de Buenos Aires, con casi dos millones de automóviles, ha crecido exponencialmente en los últimos años, a lo que debe sumarse la gran cantidad de taxis, colectivos[4], motos y bicicletas que recorren a diario la ciudad. Así, Buenos Aires presenta altas tasas de accidentes de tránsito, escasez de estacionamientos, y se puede tardar horas en hacer trayectos cortos.

Con los años, distintas estrategias se pusieron en marcha[5] para mejorar esta situación. Por ejemplo, en el marco de un plan de restricción vehicular, más de 40 cuadras del microcentro se transformaron en calles peatonales, lo que favorece la circulación de las personas y valoriza los comercios de la zona, y a la vez disminuye el ruido y el esmog. Asimismo, desde 2009 se está construyendo una red de ciclovías de unos 150 km que une distintos puntos estratégicos de interconexión con otros medios de transporte. Además, el gobierno local otorga préstamos[6] muy económicos para impulsar la compra de bicicletas y se instaló el sistema público Ecobici de préstamo de bicicletas.

Todas estas alternativas forman parte del plan de movilidad sustentable de Buenos Aires, cuyo eje es que el ciudadano se movilice en transporte público o en bicicleta, en lugar de usar el automóvil.

[1] free    [2] swarm    [3] total number of vehicles    [4] buses    [5] were set in motion    [6] loans

**Búsqueda:** problemas de tránsito en buenos aires, restricción vehicular en buenos aires, sistema ecobici buenos aires

## Productos  2.2

El colectivo es un medio de transporte tradicional con mucha historia en la ciudad de Buenos Aires. Sus coloridas decoraciones pintadas a mano nunca dejan de sorprender a los visitantes. Sin embargo, recién en 2011, la ciudad decidió dedicarles un sistema de carriles exclusivos: el Metrobús. Gracias a este sistema, se redujo el tiempo del recorrido, y los choferes se sienten más cómodos y seguros.

*Carriles exclusivos para los colectivos*

*Pregunta clave*
¿Qué problemas conlleva la vida urbana y cómo se resuelven?

emcpassport.com
LA 3

 1.2, 2.2, 3.1

## 17 Comprensión

1. ¿Cuáles son las consecuencias del gran tránsito vehicular en Buenos Aires?

2. ¿Mediante qué estrategias se intenta resolver el problema del tránsito?

3. ¿En qué sentido contribuyen estas estrategias al medio ambiente?

## 18 Analice  1.3, 2.2, 4.2

1. ¿Cree Ud. que los problemas de tránsito son similares en todas las grandes ciudades del mundo?

2. Compare las soluciones que propone Buenos Aires para el tránsito con los sistemas implementados en alguna gran ciudad de su país.

---

## RESOURCES

| | |
|---|---|
| fg | Flipgrid |
| 🎧 | Buenos Aires y el tránsito Productos |
| LA | Activity 3 |

### Answers

**17**

1. Altas tasas de accidentes de tránsito, escasez de estacionamientos y demoras para llegar de un lugar a otro.
2. Calles peatonales en el microcentro y fomento del uso de bicicletas.
3. Disminuyen el ruido y el esmog producido por los automóviles.

**18**  *Las respuestas variarán.*

### Reference Desk

Students can do a Flipgrid post reacting to any of these cultural readings.

### Expansion

Have students take a virtual tour of one of Buenos Aires's most famous streets, **Avenida 9 de Julio**. Also ask them to find out how wide it is and what challenges the street presents in terms of congestion and safety.

### Pre-AP

Have students respond to the **Pregunta clave**, in spoken or written form, using information from the readings on pp. 279–281. Students should also include a comparison between their own community/culture and Argentina.

---

## Differentiated Learning
### Accelerate/Expand
Create an additional category for **Actividad 15**: **El profesor de español les dice a los estudiantes...**. Have pairs write five complete sentences using the subjunctive.

## Multiple Intelligences
### Visual-Spatial
Have students explore the Buenos Aires government website to learn more about Ecobici. Have students create a brochure promoting **Ecobici** to tourists. The brochure should include examples of the street signs and symbols used by **Ecobici**, safety tips, and a map of the **ciclovías**.

## Answers

**19**

1. Era un mercado proveedor de frutas, verduras y carnes muy importante que llenaba de vida el barrio.
2. En 1984 el gobierno decidió trasladar todas sus actividades a otro mercado en las afueras de la ciudad.
3. Se instalaron allí nuevos comercios, hoteles, edificios, teatros y otros espacios destinados a actividades culturales.

**20** *Las respuestas variarán.*

### Reference Desk

1. The word **abasto** means *provisions* or *supplies*.
2. Carlos Gardel (1890–1935) was Argentina's most famous tango singer and composer. Gardel died in a plane crash in Colombia while at the height of his fame.
3. The word **porteño/a** means *of the port*, and is a popular way to refer to the residents of Buenos Aires. Students may also encounter the more formal adjective **bonaerense**.

### Culture

**Products: Activity**
Ask students to research the history of **lunfardo** and its usage in tango lyrics and everyday speech. You may want to have them focus on **vesre**, and have them find out the equivalents of words they already know, e.g., **ñoba** (**baño**), **colo** (**loco**); **gotán** (**tango**).

---

 **1.2, 2.2**

## 19 Comprensión

1. ¿Qué era, en sus orígenes, el Mercado de Abasto? ¿Cuál era su importancia?
2. ¿Cuándo y por qué cerró sus puertas el Mercado de Abasto?
3. ¿En qué sentido la apertura del centro comercial reactivó toda la zona?

**1.3, 4.2**

## 20 Analice

1. ¿Qué barrios o zonas de su ciudad han atravesado mutaciones como las del barrio del Abasto?
2. ¿Qué lugares de compras alternativos (que no sean supermercados) para productos frescos hay en su ciudad?

---

## Cuando lo abandonado vuelve a cobrar vida

*El hermoso edificio del Mercado de Abasto*

En toda gran ciudad, los espacios van mutando. Según la época, y en función de los cambios poblacionales o incluso a causa de modas pasajeras[1], algunos barrios prosperan y otros "caen en desgracia". Así ocurrió con la zona del Mercado de Abasto de Buenos Aires.

El mercado se creó a fines del siglo XIX y era uno de los centros de comercialización de frutas, verduras y carnes más importantes de la ciudad. Funcionaba en un edificio imponente, con techos abovedados[2], y estaba ubicado en el corazón de la ciudad, en un barrio de tradición tanguera, hogar de Carlos Gardel. Durante años, el mercado llenó de vida la zona con su bullicio de camiones, vendedores y clientes.

Sin embargo, en 1984 tuvo que cerrar sus puertas porque el gobierno decidió trasladar todas las actividades a un nuevo mercado central en las afueras de Buenos Aires. El edificio quedó abandonado, todo ese movimiento de proveedores y compradores desapareció, y el barrio todo perdió su encanto. Los periódicos de la época decían que era el "Bronx porteño", una zona de "marginalidad y delincuencia"[3].

Finalmente, a mediados de la década de 1990, este espacio público pasó a manos privadas: el magnate George Soros compró el edificio y lo transformó en un gran centro comercial. La apertura del Abasto Shopping dio un nuevo impulso a la zona. A su alrededor se abrieron muchísimos comercios, se construyeron nuevos hoteles y edificios, y surgieron numerosos teatros independientes y otros espacios destinados a actividades culturales.

[1] temporary    [2] vaulted    [3] deprivation and crime

🔍 **Búsqueda:** mercado de abasto de buenos aires, barrio del abasto, abasto shopping

---

### Prácticas  **1.2, 2.1**

A pesar de que ya no quedan en la ciudad grandes mercados de abastecimiento, los porteños todavía pueden seguir con la costumbre de ir a comprar los productos frescos al "mercado barrial". El programa de Ferias Itinerantes consiste en puestos móviles que cada día de la semana se ubican en distintos puntos de la ciudad para ofrecer sus productos a los vecinos. Allí pueden comprar, entre otras cosas, frutas, verduras, carnes, productos de granja, pescados y mariscos.

*Puestos de productos frescos en las ferias itinerantes*

---

### Essential Instruction

1. Remind students of the culture photo and question from the unit opener. Have them scan p. 280 for the answer.
2. As you play the audio for each cultural reading, pause occasionally to check comprehension by asking **sí/no** questions.
3. Have students complete the **Analice** activities for Common Core practice.

# De ciudad ideal a ciudad sumergida   1.2, 2.2

La ciudad de La Plata, fundada en 1882, fue planificada y construida específicamente para funcionar como capital de la provincia de Buenos Aires. Es reconocida por su trazado[1] —un cuadrado perfecto—, por las diagonales que la cruzan formando rombos dentro de su contorno, por sus bosques y por sus plazas, colocadas con exactitud cada seis cuadras. La Plata fue concebida como una ciudad ideal y representó para el mundo entero un modelo de planificación urbana.

*La ciudad de La Plata es reconocida como un modelo de planificación urbana.*

Lamentablemente, con el correr de los años, el espíritu que dio a luz a la ciudad se fue perdiendo. La urbanización irresponsable y la falta de previsión[2] de los distintos gobiernos de turno hicieron que la construcción creciera sin control y que nuevos pobladores se asentaran[3] en zonas inadecuadas.

Fue una tragedia sin precedentes la que puso sobre el tapete[4] esa falta de previsión. El 2 de abril de 2013, fuertes precipitaciones que marcaron un récord histórico tuvieron como consecuencia casi un centenar de muertos, miles de evacuados, decenas de miles de viviendas inundadas y pérdidas materiales incalculables. La ciudad quedó devastada y sus habitantes, que recibieron ayuda desde todos los rincones del país, terriblemente golpeados.

Después de la inundación, se puso en marcha un plan de obras para reconstruir la ciudad y prepararla para soportar fenómenos climáticos extremos. El plan incluye, por ejemplo, obras hidráulicas estructurales, obras viales[5], la adecuación y limpieza de arroyos[6], la relocalización de asentamientos[7] y la creación de reservorios. Los platenses se merecen vivir en la ciudad ideal que pensaron para ellos sus fundadores.

[1] layout   [2] foresight   [3] settle   [4] brought to light   [5] road works
[6] stream   [7] settlements

**Búsqueda:** inundación de la plata 2 de abril de 2013

## Perspectivas 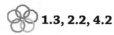  1.2, 3.2

Refiriéndose a la inundación de abril de 2013, el titular de la cátedra de Hidrología de la Universidad Nacional de La Plata, Pablo Romanazzi, declaró: "Hay diagnóstico, sabemos lo que pasa cuando llueve así y que las obras hidráulicas no tienen un nivel de servicio para atender este tipo de tormentas. Pero hay medidas que se pueden tomar, como no seguir asentando población en los márgenes de los arroyos. Es una locura y lo venimos denunciando hace tiempo". Señaló también: "Paremos la presión inmobiliaria (*real state*) de querer urbanizar todo. Hay que hacerlo responsablemente".

Según Romanazzi, ¿qué medidas son esenciales para disminuir los riesgos de las tormentas fuertes?

*Imagen de la inundación de la ciudad de La Plata en 2013*

  1.2, 2.2

## 21 Comprensión

1. ¿Qué tiene de especial la ciudad de La Plata?

2. ¿Qué ocurrió en la ciudad con el correr de los años?

3. ¿Qué ocurrió el 2 de abril de 2013?

1.3, 2.2, 4.2

## 22 Analice

1. ¿Por qué es importante que exista la planificación urbana a largo plazo?

2. ¿Cree que la ciudad en la que vive está preparada para afrontar fuertes precipitaciones? ¿Por qué?

## Reference Desk

1. Draw attention to **ponerse** and explain that it is used with adjectives only to indicate temporary changes in mood or health: **ponerse furioso**, **ponerse enfermo**.

2. Review other ways to express *to become*. Give examples with **hacerse** (can be used with noun or adjective: **hacerse médico**, **hacerse rico**); **llegar a ser** (change over time, does not imply effort: **llegar a ser director**); **volverse** (radical, irreversible change: **volverse loco**); **convertirse en** (radical professional or life change: **convertirse en actriz**, **convertirse en una sombra de sí mismo**).

## Critical Thinking

**Analyzing**
After students complete **Actividad 23** on p. 283, ask them to explain why each possible answer is used. Also have them explain why similar verbs are not possible; for example, in item 1, **ir** cannot be used because it isn't the reflexive form (**irse**).

# Vocabulario 2

## Comparación y contraste: ¡Ojo con estas palabras!  1.2, 4.1

En español, al igual que en inglés, estas palabras tienen distintas connotaciones y significados. Preste atención, pues su uso depende del contexto.

**salir** *to go out (with someone)*
Hace un año que Enrique **sale** con Ana.

**salir (de)** *to leave (a place), to go out (from a place), to depart*
Recuerda que **salgo** de clase a las diez.
El crucero **sale** de la ciudad de Cartagena.

**irse (de) / marcharse (de)** *to leave, to go away*
Se paró y **se fue** sin decir nada.
**Me marcho** de vacaciones por un mes.

**dejar** *to leave behind; to drop off*
**Dejemos** las chamarras en el carro; hace calor.
¿Me **dejan** en el estadio de fútbol, por favor?

**poner** *to put, to place, to set (the table)*
**Pon** los platos y los vasos en el fregadero.
Niños, **pongan** la mesa para desayunar.

**ponerse** *to put on (clothing); to become*
Sarita, **ponte** el abrigo que hace frío.
No **te pongas** nervioso.

**meter** *to put (in)*
Por favor, **mete** el postre en la nevera, para que no se dañe.

**colocar** *to put (in place); to place*
**Coloquen** los platos sucios en el lavaplatos.
**Colocaron** el anuncio en primera página para que todos lo vieran.

## Essential Instruction

1. Personalize the **Vocabulario 2** presentation by talking about your morning routine.
2. Before beginning **Actividad 23**, explain that several of the blanks can take more than one verb. Model this with item 1 (**salir**, **marcharse**). When checking answers, survey the class for all possible responses.
3. Have students check answers to **Actividad 24** and then role-play the dialogue.

## 23 Olvidé mi dinero en casa  1.2

Elija el verbo adecuado y complete el párrafo con el pretérito o el pluscuamperfecto del indicativo, según el caso.

| colocar | ir | meter | ponerse |
|---|---|---|---|
| dejar | marcharse | poner | salir |

Ayer yo **(1)** temprano de la casa y **(2)** de compras sin darme cuenta de que **(3)** mi billetera en la casa. Cuando quise pagar el regalo que había comprado, **(4)** la mano en la bolsa. De pronto recordé que antes de salir de la casa, **(5)** la billetera sobre la mesa de la cocina. Con mucha discreción **(6)** el regalo sobre el mostrador, **(7)** los guantes y **(8)** del almacén.

## 24 Un atraco en la ciudad  1.2

Complete el diálogo con la palabra entre paréntesis que corresponda según el contexto.

**María:** ¿De dónde (**1.** *vienes / vas*) tan alterada?

**Patricia:** (**2.** *me marcho / vengo*) del centro comercial. Acabo de ver (**3.** *una huelga / un atraco*) que me dejó muy asustada.

**María:** ¿Qué sucedió?

**Patricia:** Un hombre atracó a una joven cuando ella (**4.** *dejaba / salía*) del centro comercial.

**María:** ¿Cuándo pasó todo eso?

**Patricia:** Hace más o menos media hora. Ella (**5.** *puso / metió*) su bolso en el suelo un segundo mientras (**6.** *se ponía / ponía*) sus paquetes en el baúl del coche. El ladrón (**7.** *tomó / colocó*) el bolso con fuerza y, aunque ella trató de evitarlo, él se lo quitó y (**8.** *se marchó / se salió*) corriendo.

**María:** ¿Alguien dio aviso a la policía?

**Patricia:** ¡Desde luego! Yo llamé ahí mismo al 9-1-1.

**María:** ¿Y qué pasó con la joven?

**Patricia:** La pobre chica (**9.** *puso / se puso*) muy pálida y empezó a gritar pidiendo ayuda.

*Trataba de acordarme dónde había dejado mi coche.*

*El ladrón aprovechó para agarrar el bolso y salir corriendo.*

*Me puse muy nerviosa y empecé a gritar pidiendo ayuda.*

### Answers

**23**
1. salí/me marché
2. fui
3. había dejado
4. metí
5. había puesto/había dejado/había colocado
6. coloqué/puse/dejé
7. me puse
8. me marché/salí

**24**
1. vienes
2. Vengo
3. un atraco
4. salía
5. puso
6. ponía
7. tomó
8. se marchó
9. se puso

### Reference Desk

In **Actividad 24**, remind students that the structure **al** + *infinitive* indicates simultaneity of action.

### Culture

**Practices: Information**
There are several emergency numbers in Argentina. To reach the police, people dial 9-1-1 (this was adopted in 2006; it used to be 1-0-1). Each day, 9-1-1 in Argentina receives about 12,500 calls. In a medical emergency, one can call 1-0-7 for free ambulance service and EMTs. When there's a fire or similar emergency, people call 1-0-0 and firefighters will respond. Finally, for cases such as floods or a toxic chemical spill, people dial 1-0-3 to reach **Defensa Civil**.

## Differentiated Learning
### Accelerate/Expand
As a follow-up to **Actividad 24**, ask students to write the dialogue of an interview between the police officer and the woman.

## Learning Styles
### Visual Learners
Bring in photos of people engaged in activities that use the verbs from **Comparación y contraste**. As you hold up each image, have students describe what they see.

## Culture

**Practices: Activity**
Tell students about the concept of **lucir bien** in Spanish-speaking countries, the importance of dressing well in social situations, and how it generally isn't considered fashionable to "dress down" or dress too casually, or in clothing that is ripped or too baggy. Give examples of how young people in the Spanish-speaking world would dress to go to a party or to go to a college class. Have students compare and contrast this with how they would dress for such occasions.

## Culture

**Practices: Activity**
Explain that in Spanish-speaking countries, many people usually buy just a few select, high-quality pieces per season. It can also be socially acceptable to repeat articles of clothing during the week. Ask students to compare and contrast this with their own clothing use: Do they ever repeat an outfit during the week? Which do they prefer: to have many inexpensive clothes, or fewer expensive but well-made clothing items?

# ¡Comunicación!

**25  ¿Qué reloj quieres comprar?**   Interpersonal Communication  **1.1**

En parejas, completen el siguiente diálogo.

**Vendedor:** ¿En qué puedo... ?

**Ud.:** Me gustaría comprar un reloj que...

**Vendedor:** Aquí tiene Ud. este reloj de oro blanco que...

**Ud.:** Es demasiado caro...

**Vendedor:** ¿Qué le parece uno que... ?

**Ud.:** Me gusta y no es tan caro. ¿Podría Ud. ponerlo en una caja de regalos que... ?

**Vendedor:** Claro que sí. Escoja el papel de regalo que...

**Ud.:** Este papel me gusta porque...

**Vendedor:** Aquí lo tiene.

**Ud.:** Gracias.

**1.1, 5.2**

**26  En gustos no hay disgustos**

**Interpersonal Communication**

Formen parejas y túrnense para responder las siguientes preguntas e intercambiar opiniones sobre el tema.

1. ¿Dónde prefieres comprar ropa, en una pequeña tienda exclusiva o en un almacén de cadena? ¿Por qué te parece ventajoso comprar en los almacenes de cadena? ¿Y en las pequeñas tiendas exclusivas?

2. ¿Qué prefieres: vestir a la última moda o tener tu propio estilo? ¿Piensas que para ser elegante hay que estar a la moda? Si te gusta estar a la moda, ¿qué haces con la ropa que ya pasó de moda? ¿La regalas? ¿La vendes? ¿La dejas en tu armario pensando que más adelante la usarás de nuevo?

3. ¿Cómo te gusta vestirte para ir al colegio? ¿A una fiesta? ¿Al cine? ¿Qué significa para ti la elegancia?

*¿Qué prefieres: vestir a la moda o tener tu propio estilo?*

4. Describe a alguien que, a tu modo de ver, se vista bien. ¿Qué quiere decir "vestirse bien"? ¿Es primordial? ¿Se puede identificar el nivel socioeconómico de una persona por su manera de vestir? Explica.

5. ¿Eres un(a) comprador(a) compulsivo/a que va a las tiendas a comprar, pero no sabe precisamente qué quiere y termina comprando lo que menos necesita? ¿Has revisado cuánta ropa hay en tu armario que te has puesto solo una o dos veces?

## Essential Instruction

1. Before students begin **Actividad 25**, read through the dialogue as a class and have them identify sentences where the subjunctive would be used.

2. Have pairs share some of their responses to **Actividad 26** with the class. Are there any general tendencies among your students?

3. Follow up **Actividad 27** by holding a class debate about question 1 or 2.

4. If most of your students have smartphones, you may want to have them take photos of about 12–15 of their outfits. They can use the photos as they complete **Actividad 29**. Alternatively, have students draw or write a list of their clothing items.

 **¡Comunicación!**

**27** **Problemas de vivir en la ciudad** 👥 Interpersonal Communication 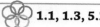 **1.1, 1.3, 5.2**

Conteste las siguientes preguntas. Luego, compare sus respuestas con las de un(a) compañero/a y comenten sus diferencias de opinión, si las tienen.

1. ¿Cuál consideras que es el origen de la delincuencia juvenil? ¿Piensas que se deba a las injusticias sociales? ¿Al exceso de libertad que tienen los niños? ¿A una influencia negativa de la televisión? ¿A la falta de atención y presencia de los padres?

2. ¿Estás de acuerdo en que el gobierno debe aumentar los impuestos para construir más cárceles y entrenar un mayor número de policías? ¿Por qué?

3. ¿Piensas que algunas zonas de la ciudad donde vives son peligrosas y por eso las evitas? ¿Cuáles? Si has estado de día o de noche en alguna de esas zonas, ¿podrías describirla?

4. ¿Qué es para ti una ciudad ideal? ¿Una que tenga un millón de habitantes? ¿O una que esté a orillas del mar? Descríbela, por favor.

**28** **No sé qué comprar** 👥 Interpersonal Communication  **1.1**

Imagine que Ud. va a un almacén a comprar los regalos de Navidad para sus suegros y necesita ayuda. Con un(a) compañero/a, hagan el papel del cliente o la clienta que no sabe qué comprar y el/la dependiente que le da sugerencias y consejos. Use cláusulas adjetivales y adverbiales en su conversación y las expresiones de *Para decir más* y el vocabulario de la unidad, como se ve en el modelo.

> **Para decir más**
>
> ¿En qué puedo ayudarlo/a?
> ¿Qué le parece…?
> ¿Qué talla usa?
> ¿Desea probarse…?
> Me queda… /No me queda…
> ¿Qué precio tiene…?

MODELO   Cliente:   Tengo que comprar un regalo para mi suegro, algo que no sea muy personal. ¿Qué me recomienda?

Dependiente:   ¿Qué le parece este pañuelo para que lo ponga en el bolsillo de su traje? Es de pura seda. Muy fino.

Cliente:   …

**29** **Para dejar y para regalar** 👥 Interpersonal Communication  **1.1**

Imagine que su mejor amiga se va a ir a vivir a otra ciudad y no quiere llevarse toda la ropa que tiene. Ella le pide a Ud. que le ayude a decidir qué dejar y qué regalar o donar a gente más necesitada. Represente la situación con un(a) compañero/a. Usen el vocabulario de la unidad en su conversación, como se ve en el modelo.

MODELO   A: ¿Qué piensas de esta falda a cuadros? ¿Cómo me queda?

B: No sé. Te queda bien y es fina, pero se ve bien pasada de moda.

A: Tienes razón. Colócala en el montón de ropa para regalar.

**RESOURCES**

 Flipgrid

Avenue

**Answers**

27 *Las respuestas variarán.*

28 *Las conversaciones variarán.*

29 *Las conversaciones variarán.*

**Reference Desk**

Ask students to create a Flipgrid post with their response from question 4 in **Actividad 27**.

**Critical Thinking**

**Analyzing**
Ask students to analyze clothing trends from the last 100 years. Ask them to consider in what ways the trend of each era is a reaction to the styles of the preceding time period.

**Connections**

**Art**
Have students research recent collections of Argentinean fashion designers, such as Jazmín Chebar, Gustavo Cadile, or Elsa Serrano. Ask them to choose the designer whose clothing they like most and write a review of their latest collection. Have students describe in detail their most and least favorite pieces. You may want to have students submit their reviews in an Avenue task.

**Differentiated Learning**
**Expand**
After completing **Actividad 27**, ask students to use travel websites and blogs to investigate more about neighborhoods in Buenos Aires. Are there ones that are not recommended for tourists? Why?

**Multiple Intelligences**
**Verbal-Linguistic**
Ask students to describe the clothing trends of a certain era (e.g., **la época victoriana**, **los 70**, etc.) to a classmate. Their partner will try to guess the era to which the clothing styles belong.

**285**

Answers

**30**

1. Buscan reafirmar su propia identidad y reflejar lo especial y original que es su personalidad.
2. La ropa de marca es un símbolo de estatus social, de juventud, originalidad y estilo.
3. En la realidad, todos los adolescentes se visten de forma parecida y muestran lo que caracteriza a su generación.
4. *Las respuestas variarán.*
5. *Las respuestas variarán.*

### Critical Thinking

**Analyzing**

Ask students to consider the concept of conformity. You may want to share famous quotes about the topic, such as "**Cada generación se ríe de las viejas modas, pero sigue rigurosamente las nuevas**" (Henry David Thoreau) or "**La recompensa por la conformidad es que todo el mundo te quiere, excepto tú mismo**" (Rita Mae Brown). Ask students if they consider themselves conformists in terms of personal dress and style. Why or why not? Is it possible for one not to conform?

### Expansion

Ask students to create a Flipgrid post in which they describe their **estilo personal**. Their classmates can reply with posts in which they recommend where the person should shop, either in your community or online.

286

---

## ¡Comunicación!

 **1.1, 1.2, 1.3, 5.2**

**30  La moda no incomoda**   Interpersonal/Presentational Communication

Lea el artículo sobre la moda y conteste las preguntas que siguen. Luego, intercambie opiniones con dos compañeros de clase para ver qué opinan y presenten sus conclusiones al resto de la clase.

Moda: influencia en...

*Laurita y Alejandrita*

### Moda: influencia en adolescentes

Uno de los temas más polémicos con los adolescentes es la ropa.

**La ropa comunica**

La ropa es un medio de comunicación: con ella se dicen muchas cosas y los adolescentes se han dado cuenta de que una imagen vale 3 mil palabras y quieren utilizarla para expresarse.

Con la ropa, los peinados y los adornos buscan reafirmar su propia identidad, reflejar una personalidad única y original, aunque en realidad todos los adolescentes se visten de forma parecida y lo que logran es mostrar y comunicar lo que caracteriza a su generación.

Están orgullosos de su vestimenta [...] y [...] se sienten apreciados por parecerse a su grupo; [...] cada elemento del vestuario es un signo de pertenencia.

**Los afanes adolescentes por la ropa de marca**

Lujos y razones suelen ser un punto de contradicción que rebasa a muchos adolescentes. [...] Para muchos de ellos se vuelve un problema vital el hecho de comprar los artículos que la publicidad les sugiere.

[...] Cuando los tenis sirven para algo más que caminar, son una señal de identidad y una forma simbólica de juventud, estatus, originalidad y estilo personal.

[...] Un(a) adolescente puede ser discriminado/a por no llevar ropa de marca [...] y a veces ese pensamiento hace que muchos jóvenes [...] no tengan su propio estilo por [...] miedo a ser desplazados del grupo o criticados.

1. ¿Qué quieren expresar los adolescentes a través de la ropa que se ponen?
2. ¿Qué simboliza la ropa de marca?
3. ¿Qué muestra en realidad el estilo de vestir de los adolescentes?
4. ¿Cuál es la contradicción que hay entre vestir a la moda y ser auténtico? Explique su respuesta.
5. ¿Cómo se viste Ud. y cuáles son las influencias que tiene?

**Essential Instruction**

1. Open **Actividad 30** by asking students where they shop, and if brands matter to them.
2. Begin the **Gramática** presentation by telling students that the imperfect subjunctive is triggered by the same uses as the present subjunctive, but it refers to the past.
3. Check answers to **Actividad 31** by having volunteers role-play the dialogue for the class.

# Gramática

## El imperfecto del subjuntivo  1.2

Para formar el imperfecto del subjuntivo se toma la tercera persona del plural del pretérito del indicativo y se cambia la terminación **-on** por **-a**.[1]

| Pretérito | Radical | Terminación | Imperfecto del subjuntivo |
|---|---|---|---|
| dijeron | dijer- | -a | dijera |
| durmieron | durmier- | -as | durmieras |
| escribieron | escribier- | -a | escribiera |
| hablaron | hablar- | -amos | habláramos[2] |
| oyeron[3] | oyer- | -ais | oyerais |
| supieron | supier- | -an | supieran |

[1] Esta es la forma del imperfecto del subjuntivo que se usa en la mayoría de los países de Hispanoamérica. En muchos lugares de España las terminaciones del imperfecto del subjuntivo son **-se, -ses, -se, -semos, -seis, -sen**. Por ejemplo: **decir: dijese, dijeses, dijese, dijésemos, dijeseis, dijesen**.

[2] La primera persona del plural se convierte en una palabra esdrújula, por lo tanto lleva acento ortográfico en la tercera sílaba contando de la derecha: ha-**blá**-ra-mos. Recuerde que todas las palabras esdrújulas llevan acento ortográfico.

[3] Si el radical del verbo tuvo el cambio ortográfico **i → y** (**oír → oyeron**) en la tercera persona del plural del pretérito, tendrá el mismo cambio ortográfico en todas las personas del imperfecto del subjuntivo.

### 31 ¿Cómo te fue de compras?  1.2

Juanita quiere saber cómo le fue a Susana cuando fue de compras con su amiga Marcela. Complete su conversación con el imperfecto del subjuntivo del verbo entre paréntesis.

**Juanita:** Finalmente... ¿pudieron ir de compras?

**Susana:** Sí. Salimos tarde de casa y temíamos que algunos almacenes ya no (**1.** *estar*) abiertos.

**Juanita:** ¿Tuvieron que darse mucha prisa?

**Susana:** ¡Seguro! Era indispensable que (**2.** *llegar*) lo antes posible.

**Juanita:** ¿Y adónde fueron?

**Susana:** Yo fui a la tienda de accesorios. Le sugerí a Marcela que (**3.** *subir*) a la sección de ropa femenina para que (**4.** *comprar*) el regalo de su madre.

**Juanita:** ¿Qué le compró?

**Susana:** Su madre le había pedido que le (**5.** *dar*) una blusa elegante.

**Juanita:** ¿La encontró?

**Susana:** Sí, y la compró, aunque no estaba segura de que la blusa le (**6.** *quedar*) bien a su madre.

**Juanita:** ¿Regresaron a casa para la comida?

**Susana:** ¡Sí! Carlos nos había dicho que (**7.** *regresar*) temprano para poder ir al concierto de Navidad en la plaza.

**Answers**

**31**
1. estuvieran
2. llegáramos
3. subiera
4. comprara
5. diera
6. quedara
7. regresáramos

## Reference Desk

1. Mention that the **yo** and **usted/él/ella** forms are identical.
2. Point out that there are irregular verbs in the present subjunctive, but that they follow a regular pattern: any irregular verbs in the third-person plural of the preterite tense (such as stem changes or spelling changes) will have the same irregularity in the imperfect subjunctive.
3. Write the imperfect subjunctive forms of **ir** and **ser** on the board and explain that they are identical, and students will have to use context to determine which verb is used.
4. Remind students that it is a good idea to familiarize themselves with the **-se** endings, as they are sometimes used in literary and formal contexts.

## Expansion

Ask students to make a list of verbs that are irregular in the preterite. Write the list on the board and show imperfect subjunctive conjugations.

## Differentiated Learning
### Expand
Follow up **Actividad 30** with a class debate about school uniforms. Divide the class into two groups, those for and against. Remind each group to keep in mind both sides of the issue as they develop their arguments.

## Multiple Intelligences
### Musical-Rhythmic
Teach students a cheer to help them remember imperfect subjunctive conjugations: **¡Ra, ras, ra-ra-ra, ramos, rais, ran-ran-ran!**

## 32 Unicenter 🏵 1.2

Lea el anuncio de Unicenter, uno de los centros comerciales más populares de Buenos Aires. Luego, complete los comentarios que un turista puso al respecto en su red social con el imperfecto del subjuntivo del verbo entre paréntesis.

> ○○○   Panamericana & Paraná...
>
> **f facester**
>
> ### Unicenter
>
> Ubicado en la localidad de Martínez, a solo 15 minutos del centro de la ciudad, Unicenter cuenta con 300 locales de las mejores marcas nacionales e internacionales, patio de comidas para 1.800 personas, 14 salas de cine, parque de diversiones y estacionamiento para 6.500 autos. Es el único shopping que ofrece a los turistas un tour de compras con traslados[1] gratuitos desde puntos estratégicos de la capital, Welcome Drink, y descuentos en más de 40 locales. Además, muchos de sus locales cuentan con el sistema TAX FREE que permite —presentando las facturas[2] de estos locales en los aeropuertos internacionales y en las terminales de Buquebús del Puerto de Buenos Aires— recuperar el valor del IVA (hasta el 16 %) incluido en sus compras. Para realizar el tour contáctese con el conserje de su hotel, con la agencia de viajes o llamando a Unicenter al 4733-1166. Traslados gratuitos.

Unicenter

[1] rides    [2] receipts

El portero del hotel donde nos hospedamos nos recomendó que (**1.** *ir*) a Unicenter porque quedaba a solo 15 cuadras del centro de la ciudad. Dijo que era bueno que (**2.** *hacer*) nuestras compras allá porque era el único centro comercial que ofrecía un tour de compras con transporte gratis desde cualquier lugar de la ciudad. También dijo que era el único centro que contaba con el sistema de TAX FREE, el cual permitía que los turistas (**3.** *recuperar*) hasta el 16 % del valor del IVA (impuesto a turistas extranjeros) a la salida del país. Obviamente, era muy importante que (**4.** *guardar*) todas las facturas de las compras y que las (**5.** *presentar*) en el aeropuerto para poder obtener el descuento. Sabía que vendían ropa de calidad, pero yo no estaba seguro que (**6.** *tener*) ropa de las mejores marcas en mi talla (mido 6 pies de estatura). Aún así, decidí que valdría la pena ir. Como dijo el portero, a lo mejor no encontraba ropa para mí, pero con más de 300 locales, era imposible que no (**7.** *encontrar*) regalos para mi familia y mis amigos. Quería ir al cine, pero no creía que (**8.** *dar*) películas con subtítulos en inglés. Más tarde supe que, al contrario de lo que pensaba, en todas las 14 salas de cine daban películas en inglés con subtítulos en español. En fin, el portero mencionó que si me interesaba ir, era importante que me (**9.** *poner*) en contacto con la agencia de viajes para hacer una reservación y que era necesario que (**10.** *llamar*) enseguida porque los tours se llenaban rápidamente. Así lo hice y me alegro de haberlo hecho, pues fue una de las mejores experiencias de mi viaje.

# Gramática

## Los usos del imperfecto del subjuntivo  1.2

En la **Unidad 6** vimos los verbos que exigen el uso del subjuntivo y, en esta unidad, los usos del subjuntivo en cláusulas adjetivales y adverbiales en tiempo presente. En general, se aplica el mismo criterio para usar el imperfecto del subjuntivo en el tiempo pasado.

- El indicativo se usa para expresar hechos o certeza, mientras que el subjuntivo se usa para expresar subjetividad (deseos, emociones, recomendaciones, expresiones impersonales, dudas o negación y *Ojalá*).

*Querían una casa que quedara en La Boca.*

| Presente del subjuntivo | Imperfecto del subjuntivo |
|---|---|
| **Quiero** que **vayas** de compras al mercado de agricultores. | **Quería** que **fueras** de compras al mercado de agricultores. |
| **Es** importante que **sepamos** sobre nuestra herencia cultural. | **Era** importante que **supiéramos** sobre nuestra herencia cultural. |
| **Me encanta** probar restaurantes que **tengan** chefs famosos. | **Me encantaría** probar restaurantes que **tuvieran** chefs famosos. |
| **Vamos** temprano para que **tengamos** suficiente tiempo. | **Fuimos** temprano para que **tuviéramos** suficiente tiempo. |

- Se usa el imperfecto del subjuntivo cuando el verbo de la oración principal está en pasado o condicional simple y la acción de la cláusula subordinada ocurre de forma simultánea o posterior a la acción de la oración principal.

  **Necesitábamos/Necesitaríamos** un voluntario que nos **ayudara/ayudase** en el centro comunitario.

  **Buscaba** una persona que **conociera** la ciudad.

- También se usa después de la locución **como si…** (*as if…* ) cuando la cláusula principal está en presente o en pasado del indicativo.

  Se **ven** incómodos, como si no **cupieran** en el carro.

  Se **veían** incómodos, como si no **cupieran** en el carro.

- Se usa cuando la acción de la oración principal está en presente y la acción de la cláusula subordinada ocurrió en el pasado y no está vinculada al presente.

  El dueño **se alegra** (hoy) de que tú **colaboraras** (ayer).

  **Dudamos** que Federico **supiera** hablar francés.

### Un poco más

El imperfecto del subjuntivo también se usa para hacer una solicitud formal o una sugerencia cortés (solamente con los verbos *deber, poder y querer*).

Quisiera pedirte un favor.
*I would like to ask you a favor.*

¿Pudiera Ud. prestarme ese libro?
*Could you lend me that book?*

---

## Differentiated Learning
### Expand
Have students research other Buenos Aires shopping malls (such as **Galerías Pacífico**, **Alto Palermo**, **Patio Bullrich**, etc.) and compare and contrast them with **Unicenter**. They can also map the locations of the shopping centers within Buenos Aires and explain how to get from one to the other.

## Multiple Intelligences
### Naturalist
Ask students to research environmental issues affecting Argentina, such as erosion of the grasslands, receding glaciers in Patagonia, etc. Have them state what measures conservationists have proposed, using the imperfect subjunctive, e.g., **Pidieron que se implementara una ganadería sustentable en las pampas.**

### RESOURCES

**WB** Activities 15–17

**LA** Activity 5

### Reference Desk

You may want to explain that the imperfect subjunctive is often used in **si** clauses, for example, **Si tuviera un millón de dólares, viajaría por el mundo.**

### Game

**Caramba**
Create sets of note cards; each card should contain an infinitive and a subject. Also, on five cards, write the word **caramba**. Shuffle the card sets and place each set in a bag. Divide the class into groups and give each one a set of cards. Students take turns drawing a card and conjugating the verb. If they do so correctly, they keep the card and earn one point. If they don't conjugate it correctly, they put the card back in the bag. If students draw a **caramba** card, they lose all their points.

### Game

**¿Quién es?**
Divide the class into small groups and tell students to share strange or funny beliefs and wishes that they had as children, using phrases such as **Quería que…**; **Esperaba que…**; **Deseaba que….** Then have each group choose one or two stories to present to the class, who will try to identify whose story it is (allow the class to ask follow-up questions). Award one point to groups that can correctly identify a person, and two points to groups that can stump the class.

**33**
1. estuviera
2. tuviéramos
3. diéramos
4. pudiera
5. nos quedáramos, encontrara
6. acompañara
7. enviara, llevara

**34**
1. llamara
2. invitara
3. se animara
4. fuera
5. ayudara
6. comprarse
7. se probaba
8. había
9. debía
10. escogiera
11. viera
12. marcharse
13. tenía
14. pagar
15. eligiera
16. esperara
17. viniera
18. eligiera
19. estuviera

## Expansion

Ask groups of students to create a skit based on the story in **Actividad 33**. Allow groups time to rehearse; then have them perform the skit for the class.

---

### 33 ¡Qué fastidio que nos asaltaran!  1.2

Estando de viaje, Ud. acaba de regresar de una caminata por un parque y le cuenta a su compañero/a de habitación en el hotel que su amiga Cristina y Ud. fueron asaltados/as en la calle por dos delincuentes. Use el imperfecto del subjuntivo de los verbos entre paréntesis.

1. Cuando subíamos al metro, le aconsejé a Cristina que (*estar*) ____ pendiente de la mochila.

2. Era inevitable que nosotros/as (*tener*) ____ que caminar entre la multitud al bajarnos del metro.

3. Después de cruzar la calle, un par de jóvenes nos pidieron que les (*dar*) ____ indicaciones para llegar a una farmacia que supuestamente estaba en esa parte de la ciudad.

4. Antes de que Cristina (*poder*) ____ abrir la mochila para sacar papel y bolígrafo, uno de los jóvenes se la arrebató (*snatched it from her*) y los dos se fueron corriendo.

5. Menos mal que en ese momento llegó un policía y nos recomendó que (*quedarse*) ____ en el hotel hasta que él (*encontrar*) ____ a los delincuentes.

6. Yo prefería que el policía nos (*acompañar*) ____ al hotel porque estaba muy asustado/a.

7. El policía pidió a la Jefatura de Policía más cercana que (*enviar*) ____ un taxi para que nos (*llevar*) ____ al hotel.

### 34 ¡Quiero ir de compras!  1.2

Martha y Cecilia son dos adolescentes que se interesan más por divertirse que por estudiar. Martha estaba hoy con la "depre" (*depression*) porque no tenía planes. Complete los párrafos con el imperfecto del subjuntivo o indicativo del verbo entre paréntesis. Use el infinitivo cuando no haya cambio de sujeto.

Martha estuvo esperando a que Eduardo la (**1.** *llamar*) y la (**2.** *invitar*) a salir, pero el teléfono jamás sonó. A fin de que Martha (**3.** *animarse*) un poco, Cecilia le pidió que (**4.** *ir*) con ella al centro comercial para que la (**5.** *ayudar*) a (**6.** *comprarse*) unas botas que había visto hacía unos días.

Mientras Cecilia (**7.** *probarse*) las botas, Martha vio que (**8.** *haber*) unas ofertas súper y pensó que (**9.** *deber*) aprovecharlas.

*Las compras son una buena terapia para mí.*

**Martha:** Sería estupendo que yo (**10.** *escoger*) estos dos pares de zapatos, esta blusa de seda y una chaqueta de cuero para combinar con este pantalón. ¡No tengo nada que ponerme para salir de fiesta! No me gustaría que Eduardo me (**11.** *ver*) con estos jeans viejos que me quedan mal.

Cecilia quería (**12.** *marcharse*) enseguida de la tienda porque sabía que su amiga no (**13.** *tener*) suficiente dinero en la billetera para (**14.** *pagar*) tantas cosas. Le sugirió a Martha que (**15.** *elegir*) uno o dos prendas y que (**16.** *esperar*) unas semanas para buscar las demás.

**Martha:** ¡Qué bobada! No sé para qué me pediste que (**17.** *venir*) contigo si no querías que (**18.** *elegir*) nada. ¡Y... por favor! Deja de mirarme como si (**19.** *estar*) loca. Tengo la depre y las compras son una buena terapia para mí.

## Essential Instruction

1. Have students check their answers to **Actividad 33** in small groups.
2. After checking answers to **Actividad 34**, ask students if they know anyone with shopping habits similar to Martha's.
3. Have students share their sentences from **Actividad 35** with the class, who can vote for their favorite ones.
4. In **Actividad 37** reinforce for students that the expressions in **Para decir más** trigger the present subjunctive and will be used with the first part of the activity.

## 35 Como si...  1.3

Complete las oraciones.

1. Cuando invito a mi pareja a un restaurante exclusivo, me comporto como si...
2. Cuando veo que el menú está en italiano, hago como si...
3. Cuando veo lo que vale cada plato, me siento como si...
4. Cuando el camarero me trae la cuenta, la pago como si...
5. Cuando llegamos a su casa, me despido como si...

## ¡Comunicación!

### 36 Nuestro primer encuentro   Presentational Communication  1.3

Aunque llevan diez años de casados y tienen hijos, Liliana y Edgar mantienen vivo su amor, como en el día que se conocieron. Complete el mensaje que Liliana le escribió a Edgar con motivo de su aniversario, con el imperfecto del subjuntivo de los verbos entre paréntesis para saber cómo fue ese primer encuentro.

Cuando nos encontramos por primera vez en ese café, deseé que (**1.** *habernos*) conocido antes. No podía creer que (**2.** *ser*) tan querido y espontáneo. Me hablabas como si (**3.** *conocernos*) de toda la vida y eso me encantaba. Teníamos tantos intereses en común que parecía que (**4.** *estar*) hechos el uno para el otro. Me enamoré de ti de golpe y rogaba en el fondo de mi alma que tú también (**5.** *enamorarse*) de mí. "Pura ilusión de juventud", pensaba. Seguramente preferirías a una persona que (**6.** *ser*) más sofisticada, que (**7.** *pertencer*) a tu misma esfera social. Aun así seguía soñando. Quería de todo corazón que (**8.** *verme*) por lo que soy y lo que valgo y no por lo que tengo. Fue entonces cuando dijiste que querías conocerme mejor e insististe que (**9.** *volver*) a vernos. El destino quiso que nosotros (**10.** *cruzar*) caminos ese día. Cuando se llegó el momento de despedirnos ansiaba que (**11.** *besarme*) y no me desilusionaste. Me diste un beso inolvidable y así empezó la historia de un gram amor, que lleva diez años y sigue creciendo con el tiempo.

### 37 Problemas y soluciones   Interpersonal/Presentational Communication  1.1, 1.3

En grupos pequeños, comenten los siguientes problemas y propongan soluciones a los mismos. Luego, elijan a una persona del grupo para que dé un informe al resto de la clase. Usen el presente del subjuntivo y las expresiones de *Para decir más* para comentar los problemas y hacer las propuestas, y el imperfecto del subjuntivo para hacer el informe, como se ve en el modelo.

- La contaminación
- Los desamparados
- La vivienda
- El tráfico de drogas
- La delincuencia juvenil
- El transporte urbano

**Para decir más**

Es importante que…
Es preferible que…
Hay que pedir a las autoridades que…
Es una lástima que…
Sugiero que…
Es necesario que…
Propongo que…
Recomiendo que…

| MODELO | Roberto: | Es una lástima que haya tantas personas sin un lugar donde vivir. Propongo que creemos un programa de apoyo a los desamparados. |
|---|---|---|
| | Informe: | Roberto propuso que se creara un programa de apoyo a los desamparados. |

**Answers**

**Antes de leer**
*Las respuestas variarán.*

**38** *Respuestas posibles:*

1. Porque no solo produjo muertes, grandes pérdidas materiales y angustia entre los ciudadanos, sino también porque fue consecuencia de la falta de previsión de la dirigencia política.

2. Porque no hubo la planificación necesaria para recibir tanta cantidad de gente en la ciudad, que se asentó en lugares poco adecuados.

3. Crecieron de forma desmedida y sin prestar atención al comportamiento de la naturaleza, lo que produjo superpoblación y colapso de los servicios.

**39** **C** *Las respuestas variarán.*

**Pre-AP**

**Course Theme: Los desafíos mundiales**

---

# Lectura informativa

## Antes de leer   1.3

1. ¿Qué clase de problemas cree Ud. que puede provocar la falta de previsión y planificación en las ciudades?

2. ¿Qué clase de medidas cree Ud. que se pueden tomar para minimizar las consecuencias de los fenómenos naturales?

**Estrategia**  3.1

**Identificar las opiniones**

Los textos argumentativos suelen incluir datos objetivos además de opiniones subjetivas. Identificar los datos y las opiniones mientras lee un texto argumentativo lo ayudará a comprender la postura del autor.

 1.2, 2.2, 3.2

## 38 Comprensión

1. ¿Por qué fue la inundación una "catástrofe en varios sentidos"?

2. ¿Por qué es problemático el enorme crecimiento de la ciudad de Buenos Aires?

3. ¿Qué ocurrió en los barrios de clase media y alta?

 1.3

## 39 Analice

¿Qué medidas cree Ud. que se deberían tomar para ordenar el crecimiento de las ciudades?

---

○ ○ ○　Una tragedia que no…

**lanacion·com**　Archivo Edición impresa　1.2, 2.2, 3.2

Últimas noticias　|　Secciones　|　Edición impresa　|　Blogs　|　LN Data　|　Servicios　|　Guía LA NACION

**Una tragedia que no admite más disputas ni dilaciones[1]**

*publicado en La Nación, Argentina, 4 de abril de 2013, Editoriales*

La falta de previsión y de políticas de Estado debe ser rápidamente superada en busca de soluciones que prioricen la seguridad y el bienestar de la población

Decenas de muertos, cuantiosas[2] pérdidas materiales en centenares de hogares y una enorme angustia por un presente perdido y un futuro impredecible representan apenas una pequeña enumeración de los daños que causó la última inundación registrada en la ciudad y en numerosos partidos bonaerenses[3]. Fue una catástrofe en varios sentidos, no solo climáticos.

No pocas tragedias humanas, individuales o colectivas en nuestro país vienen casi siempre precedidas por una tragedia social y política, una suma de oportunismos, de desaprensiones[4] y actitudes egoístas de quienes solo parecen pensar y actuar para el corto plazo.

La ciudad de Buenos Aires ha crecido enormemente a lo largo de los años. La gran masa de gente que se ha ido asentando en ella y en sus alrededores no ha contado con la necesaria planificación de las autoridades de turno para que, con el tiempo, su llegada no resultara un problema habitacional y sanitario. Los loteos[5] y las usurpaciones[6] en zonas bajas, inundables, son una práctica habitual y no solo en la Capital. Las posibilidades de trabajo que ofrecían y ofrecen las grandes urbes han derivado en que mucha gente se asentara en lugares donde se sabe que la vida es muy riesgosa, cuando no imposible. Las márgenes de ríos como la contaminada cuenca[7] del Riachuelo son un ejemplo de ello. La política habitacional corrió siempre detrás de los hechos consumados.

Pero no se trata solamente de zonas que hoy podrían considerarse marginales. El desapego[8] por el comportamiento de la naturaleza y el desconocimiento o el uso impropio de la tierra determinaron que barrios enteros de clases media y alta se erigieran hacia el cielo clausurando drenajes naturales y provocando una superpoblación que colapsa los más elementales servicios. El exceso de pavimento ha hecho menos permeables los suelos.

[1] delays　　[2] substantial　　[3] from the province of Buenos Aires　　[4] unscrupulousness
[5] division of land into lots　　[6] misappropriation of property　　[7] basin　　[8] indifference

---

**Essential Instruction**

1. Discuss the **Antes de leer** question as a class. Ask students to give examples.
2. Go over the **Estrategia**. Go through each paragraph of the reading as a class and have students identify the objective and subjective statements.
3. Play the recording, pausing to ask comprehension questions.
4. For Common Core practice, have students answer the **Analice** questions. Go over the answers as a class.

Cuando los problemas comenzaron a hacerse evidentes, las soluciones siempre fueron parciales. A las contadas oportunidades en que se intentó planificar a largo plazo, se opuso una serie interminable de mezquindades[9] políticas. El bloqueo de eventuales réditos[10] del adversario dejó en el camino obras que hubieran significado un alivio de fondo, duradero. [...]

¿No hubo dinero en todos estos años? Probablemente sí, pero no fue priorizado para esas obras. Se mire por donde se mire, la solución no ha llegado y las responsabilidades no son privativas de un solo sector. Lamentablemente, es una situación que se reproduce en casi todos los distritos del país.

A eso hay que sumar los nefastos[11] efectos del cambio climático. Habrá más inundaciones, más copiosas y más seguidas. Los expertos ya dieron sus alertas. Los gobiernos, en cambio, no atinan a[12] ponerse de acuerdo para afrontarlos, menos aún, para intentar prevenirlos. [...]

De esta última tormenta se sabía un par de días antes, aunque su dimensión resultó mayor de la esperada, con disímiles precipitaciones aun en lugares muy próximos. No solo las autoridades demostraron falta de reacción para paliar sus efectos mediante una profunda limpieza de calles y desagües[13]. Tampoco estuvieron a la altura de los hechos los vecinos que siguieron depositando bolsones de residuos en las calles, incluso cuando la lluvia ya había comenzado.

Un nuevo entubado[14] no resuelve por sí solo el problema. Como se dijo, la catástrofe climática no es ajena[15] a la situación social que la precede. Hay muchas cosas que cambiar, no solo los drenajes subterráneos. Las zancadillas[16] políticas de las últimas horas, tendientes a eludir responsabilidades, traen a la memoria otros tristes recuerdos de hechos trágicos en los que nuestra dirigencia ha sucumbido ante su propia ineficiencia.

En contradicción con este tipo de actitudes, numerosas instituciones y particulares, entre los que también se incluyen dirigentes partidarios y gremiales[17], han salido prestamente en auxilio de los damnificados[18]. [...]

Como se dijo, es tiempo de ayudar en la contingencia, pero también de pensar todos juntos en salidas viables a las crisis que se nos puedan presentar y de ponerlas en práctica asumiendo la necesidad de considerar el tema como una verdadera política de Estado entre la Nación, las provincias y los municipios. Por mucho tiempo más tendremos que convivir con las inundaciones. De todos nosotros depende que esa convivencia no se traduzca en nuevas muertes.

[9] stinginess    [10] possible returns    [11] disastrous    [12] succeed in    [13] drains    [14] tubing
[15] disconnected    [16] impediments    [17] party and union leaders    [18] victims

🔍 **Búsqueda: inundaciones buenos aires abril 2013**

 **1.2, 2.2, 3.1, 3.2**

## 40 Comprensión

1. ¿Qué ocurrió cuando los problemas comenzaron a hacerse evidentes?

2. Si se sabía desde antes que habría una fuerte tormenta, ¿por qué fueron tan desastrosas las consecuencias?

3. ¿Por qué es importante considerar al cambio climático seriamente y poner en práctica políticas de Estado?

 **1.3, 4.2**

## 41 Analice

¿Qué fenómenos naturales extremos han tenido lugar en su país con consecuencias graves para la población?

**Answers**

**40**
1. Las soluciones siempre fueron parciales y a corto plazo.
2. *Respuesta posible:* Porque las autoridades mostraron falta de reacción y no limpiaron las calles y los desagües; los vecinos, por su parte, siguieron depositando residuos en las calles.
3. *Respuesta posible:* Porque es muy probable que se repitan fenómenos climáticos extremos y el Estado debe estar preparado para minimizar las consecuencias.

**41**  *Las respuestas variarán.*

## Critical Thinking

**Analyzing**
Create an Avenue task in which students answer this unit's **Pregunta clave** in relation to this **Lectura**.

## Differentiated Learning

**Heritage Learners**
Ask heritage learners to share what they know about the problems that cities in their family's country of origin are facing. Have the class compare and contrast the issues with what they learned in the **Lectura informativa**.

**Expand**
Have students research the Buenos Aires **villas miserias**. Tell them to find out how many **villas** there are, how many people live there, and what **FONAVI** is and what the organization is doing to help those who live in **villas**. Finally, ask students to imagine how the scenarios outlined in the reading might affect the **villas**.

# Escritura

## Un ensayo comparativo  1.3

En un ensayo comparativo, el autor señala las similitudes (lo que tienen en común) y diferencias (lo que los distingue) entre dos objetos, ideas, lugares, personas, etc. Previamente, el autor realiza un trabajo de investigación y análisis de esos dos objetos de comparación para poder presentar razones y ejemplos que fundamenten sus afirmaciones.

> **Consejos para un ensayo comparativo**
>
> • Estructure el texto con claridad, dividiendo en párrafos los distintos puntos de contraste y comparación.
>
> • Utilice palabras de enlace que organicen su discurso.
>
> • Si utiliza citas, no olvide incluir las fuentes.

### ¡Comunicación!

**42 El campo y la ciudad** Presentational Communication  1.3

Piense en los textos que ha leído en esta unidad sobre los problemas de vivir en una gran ciudad. Luego, escriba un ensayo comparativo en el que indique cuáles son las diferencias que Ud. considera más significativas entre la vida urbana y la vida rural.

Considere los siguientes puntos:

• El trabajo

• El transporte

• El estrés

• El tiempo libre

• La seguridad

Complete el diagrama de Venn con sus ideas. Busque más información en la internet para poder incluir en su ensayo ejemplos y evidencias que fundamenten su comparación.

El campo    La ciudad

*La vida en la ciudad puede ser muy activa e interesante, pero a la vez puede causar estrés.*

### Essential Instruction

1. Go over the information about comparative essays. Remind students of the difference between subjective and objective statements (**Estrategia**, p. 292), and tell them that their essay may include both.
2. For **Actividad 42**, tell students that they can also write about other points of comparison.
3. Begin **Actividad 43** by having students read the statements. Play the audio and pause to ask comprehension questions. Play it again for students to select their answers.
4. Generate a list of phrases (such as **sin embargo**, **a pesar de eso**, **por lo tanto**, **por otro lado**, etc.) for students to use in **Actividades 44** and **45**.

# ¡Comunicación!

### 43 ¡Al trabajo en bicicleta!  Interpretive Communication  1.2

Escuche el audio en el que el Jefe de Gobierno de la Ciudad de Buenos Aires anunciaba el inicio de las obras de construcción de bicisendas o ciclovías para fomentar el uso de la bicicleta en la ciudad. Según lo que se dice en el audio, indique si las siguientes afirmaciones son verdaderas o falsas.

1. La bicisenda fue uno de los temas más importantes de la Cumbre sobre cambio climático en Copenhague.

2. La bicisenda es importante por motivos de medio ambiente, pero también por motivos económicos.

3. La idea es que en Buenos Aires haya 200 km de bicisendas.

4. El uso de la bicicleta empeora los índices de accidentes de tránsito y de inseguridad.

5. La bicicleta es un medio de transporte que no contamina y mejora la salud de la gente.

6. El viaje promedio en Buenos Aires es de 5 km, una distancia ideal para hacer ejercicio.

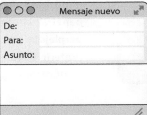

### 44 No te imaginas cómo ha mejorado mi vida

**Presentational Communication**

Imagine que Ud. vive en Buenos Aires. Escriba un correo electrónico informal a un(a) amigo/a en el que le cuente cómo mejoró su vida desde que empezó a usar la bicicleta para ir al trabajo. Incluya al menos dos datos o detalles de lo que escuchó en el audio.

*Ir al trabajo en bicicleta es una manera de hacer ejercicio físico, ahorrar dinero y cuidar el medio ambiente.*

### 45 Carta de lectores · Presentational Communication · 1.3

En una carta de lectores, el autor se dirige al director de un periódico para comentar, criticar o hacer elogios con relación a algún tema cotidiano o de interés de la comunidad.

Escriba una carta de lectores sobre las ventajas de fomentar el uso de la bicicleta en Buenos Aires, basada en el correo electrónico que escribió en la actividad anterior. Su carta de lectores expresará las mismas ideas que el correo electrónico, pero con un registro formal. Tenga en cuenta que la carta aparecerá en el periódico y será leída por muchas personas.

*Unidad 7* | doscientos noventa y cinco **295**

---

## RESOURCES

 Activity 43

Answers_____

**43 Script**

—Vi la bicisenda; me pareció una maravilla de… eso que uno ve normalmente en Europa que, distraídos como somos, hay que decirle a la gente, ahora hay que crear el conocimiento de esto, porque la gente, si no camina sin advertirlo, eso a mí me pasa cuando estoy de viaje, ando por la bicisenda y me tie…

—Hay que decirles que estén atentos pero también que se animen porque… la última… se acuerda que yo estuve… que hablamos, creo que yo estaba allá en la Cumbre de cambio climático en Copenhague y el capítulo más importante, Víctor Hugo, aunque parece increíble, fue el de la bicisenda.

—Es que hay razones de medio ambiente, hay razones económicas y hay razones muy poderosas para presentar la bicisenda de esa manera, claro ellos tienen bicisenda prácticamente por cada una de las ciudades, toda la ciudad.

—No, bueno, por supuesto, pero… y además nosotros vamos veinticinco kilómetros ahora y vamos a rumbo a cien antes de fin de año que se va a conectar gran parte de la ciudad.

—Usted sabe que es muy buena idea…

—Es fantástico y lo más notable de todo es que como ya son muchos años de experiencia que tienen todas las ciudades, han ido midiendo y le bajaron los índices de accidentes de tránsito pues la gente maneja con más cuidado cuando está la bicicleta al lado.

*Continued on p. 303.*

1. V; 2. V; 3. F; 4. F; 5. V; 6. V

**44** *Los correos electrónicos variarán.*

**45** *Las cartas variarán.*

---

## Differentiated Learning

### Expand

Ask students to research another measure designed to reduce pollution and ease vehicle traffic: Mexico City's **Hoy No Circula** program. Have students write a summary of how the program works, and state whether they think the program would be useful or successful in your town or city.

## Special Needs Students

### At-Risk Students

Give these students additional support as they complete **Actividades 44** and **45**. Bring in examples of an informal e-mail and a letter to the editor. Encourage them to use the samples as a model for their writing.

1. *Huésped* no se refiere a la forma en que se siente una persona.
2. *Congregar* no se relaciona con actividades impuestas a una persona.
3. *Cabalgar* no se relaciona con la acción de destruir.
4. *Fatigoso* no se relaciona con el azar, arriesgarse y tener suerte.
5. *Mago* no se relaciona con lo que una persona en peligro podría hacer.
6. *Perplejo* no se relaciona con acciones que se pueden infligir a una persona.

### Reference Desk

1. Point out that students will use this vocabulary to complete the audio activity on p. 297, as well as to aid in comprehension of the **Lectura literaria** on pp. 301–302.
2. Draw attention to the word **huésped** and explain that **s.com.** stands for **sustantivo común**. See if students can deduce the meaning of **sustantivo común** based on the definition of **huésped** (it can be used to refer to both males or females).

### Expansion

Ask students to create sentences using the new vocabulary terms; they should try to use at least two of the terms in each sentence.

# Vocabulario 3

## Mejore su comprensión 🎧 ✿ 1.2

Familiarizarse con este vocabulario le ayudará a leer "Dos reyes y dos laberintos" más adelante, y a mejorar su comprensión auditiva.

**asesinado/a** *adj.* Matado con premeditación.

**afrentado/a** *adj.* Ofendido, insultado.

**amarrar** *v.* Atar con cuerdas.

**aventurar** *v.* Arriesgar, poner en peligro.

**bronce** *s.m.* Material muy resistente y de un color parecido al rojo.

**cabalgar** *v.* Ir a caballo.

**cautivo/a** *adj. y sus.* Prisionero o retenido en un lugar a la fuerza.

**confundido/a** *adj.* Perturbado, desconcertado.

**congregar** *v.* Reunir a un gran número de personas.

**derribar** *v.* Destruir una construcción echándola abajo.

La explosión derribó muchos muros de la ciudad.

**desatar** *v.* Soltar o quitar las ataduras.

**digno/a** *adj.* Merecedor de algo.

**estragar** *v.* Estropear o deteriorar.

**estrangulado/a** *adj.* Muerto por asfixia causada por presión en el cuello.

**fatigoso/a** *adj.* Que causa cansancio.

**galería** *s.f.* Camino largo y estrecho que está bajo tierra.

**hacer burla** *v.* Decir o hacer algo con intención de ridiculizar a alguien.

**huésped** *s.com.* Persona que se aloja en una casa que no es propia.

**implorar** *v.* Pedir con ruegos o con lágrimas.

**laberinto** *s.m.* Lugar formado por muchos caminos que se cruzan de modo que es difícil encontrar la salida.

**ligadura** *s.f.* Cuerda, correa u otro material que sirve para atar.

**mago** *s.m.* Persona que usa poderes mágicos para conseguir algo.

**muro** *s.m.* Pared o tapia.

**penetrar** *v.* Introducirse en el interior.

**perplejo/a** *adj.* Confuso.

**proferir** *v.* Pronunciar palabras con voz muy alta.

**venturoso/a** *adj.* Que tiene buena suerte.

---

**46 Identifique al intruso**  1.3

Diga qué palabra no pertenece al grupo y explique por qué.

MODELO  asesinado / estrangulado / afrentado
**Afrentado no se refiere a formas en que se ha matado a alguien.**

1. huésped / confundido / perplejo
2. amarrar / congregar / desatar
3. derribar / estragar / cabalgar
4. venturoso / aventurar / fatigoso
5. cautivo / implorar / mago
6. hacer burla / afrentado / perplejo

## Essential Instruction

1. Model pronunciation of the new vocabulary and have students repeat the words. Clarify any unfamiliar words in the definitions.
2. Have students complete **Actividades 46** and **47** in pairs.
3. Before beginning **Actividad 48**, remind students that they will hear some vocabulary from p. 296 in the story.
4. For **Actividad 48**, have students listen to the story with their eyes closed. Play it a second time, pausing to ask **sí/no** questions. Then play the rest of the audio and have students select their answers.

## 47 Sin compasión  1.2

Complete el párrafo con las palabras del recuadro que mejor correspondan según el contexto.

| amarrado | asesinado | digno | cautivo |
|----------|-----------|-------|---------|
| perplejos | implorado | bronce | ligaduras |

Sabían que lo habían **(1)**, pero no sabían quién lo había hecho ni el motivo que habían tenido para hacerlo. Estaban confundidos y **(2)** en la escena del crimen. Se veía que el hombre había estado **(3)** por muchos días, **(4)** a dos columnas de **(5)** que sostenían el techo de una de las galerías. Tenía **(6)** en sus manos y pies y marcas profundas en el cuello, como si hubieran tratado de estrangularlo varias veces, pero esa no había sido la causa de su muerte. Su rostro reflejaba terror. Seguramente había **(7)** a gritos por su vida, pues era obvio que lo habían torturado sin compasión y que había sufrido una muerte que, para ningún ser humano, era **(8)** de sufrir.

*Los detectives de la policía están investigando el crimen.*

## 48 La mano  1.2, 3.1

Escuche el relato de "La mano". Luego, Ud. oirá la primera parte de una oración y tres terminaciones posibles. Seleccione la letra de la respuesta con la terminación más lógica. La oración y las terminaciones se leerán dos veces.

1. A. … el doctor no murió.
   B. … nadie había entrado en su apartamento.
   C. … dormía con el balcón cerrado.

2. A. … una mano solitaria y viva las había mirado.
   B. … la policía quería abandonar el caso.
   C. … una araña había saltado del armario.

3. A. … porque habían abandonado el caso.
   B. … para ver la mano de un hombre fuerte.
   C. … para cazar la mano y sentenciarla.

4. A. … la mano escribió con la pluma que le dio el juez.
   B. … la mano se paró después de una larga pausa.
   C. … el juez vio que era su propia mano.

5. A. … que era la mano del doctor Alejo.
   B. … que había destrozado la sala de disección.
   C. … que era la mano de Ramiro Ruiz, asesinado por el doctor.

---

## Learning Styles
### Visual Learners

Ask these students to create simple drawings to illustrate the new vocabulary terms. Tell them to use the drawings to create a deck of flash cards. Make copies of the cards and distribute them to the class.

## Multiple Intelligences
### Visual-Spatial

Ask students to illustrate the story of "**La mano**" in the style of a graphic novel.

---

## RESOURCES

 Activity 48

**Answers**

**47**
1. asesinado
2. perplejos
3. cautivo
4. amarrado
5. bronce
6. ligaduras
7. implorado
8. digno

**48 Script**

El doctor Alejo murió asesinado. Indudablemente murió estrangulado. Nadie había entrado en la casa. El doctor Alejo dormía con el balcón abierto, pero era tan alto su piso que no era posible que por allí hubiera entrado el asesino.

La policía no encontraba al criminal y ya iba a abandonar el caso, cuando la esposa y la criada del muerto llegaron llenas de miedo a la policía. Ellas dijeron que una mano solitaria y viva como una araña, saltando de un armario, las había mirado y después había huido por la habitación. Allí la esposa y la criada la habían dejado encerrada con llave en el cuarto.

Allí llegaron la policía y el juez. Fue un trabajo difícil cazar la mano, pero la cazaron y todos le agarraron un dedo, porque era vigorosa como si ella tuviera toda la fuerza de un hombre fuerte.

*Continued on p. 305.*

1. Era difícil resolver el misterio del asesinato del doctor Alejo porque…
2. La criada y la esposa del doctor Alejo llegaron a la policía porque…
3. La policía y el juez llegaron al apartamento del muerto…
4. El misterio se resolvió cuando…
5. La mano escribió…

1. B; 2. A; 3. C; 4. A; 5. C

**297**

# Gramática

## El subjuntivo en oraciones independientes  1.2

Se usa el subjuntivo en oraciones independientes cuando se expresa duda o probabilidad y deseo o exhortación, como se ve a continuación.

| Para expresar duda o probabilidad | |
|---|---|
| **Acaso, quizá(s), tal vez** (*maybe, perhaps*), **posiblemente, probablemente** | |
| Se usan con el indicativo o el subjuntivo. El indicativo expresa más certidumbre; el subjuntivo hace énfasis en la duda. | Tal vez **sabrá** preparar la receta. (Creo que lo sabe.)<br>Probablemente **sepa** preparar la receta. (Es posible que lo sepa, pero lo dudo.) |
| Nota: recuerde que después de "a lo mejor" se usa el indicativo. | A lo mejor **salimos** hoy por la noche.<br>A lo mejor ya **está** listo para salir. |
| Ojo: cuando el adverbio va después del verbo, el verbo va en indicativo. | **Vienen**, tal vez, mañana.<br>**Pensó**, quizá, que le hacía un favor a su papá. |

| Para expresar deseo o exhortación | |
|---|---|
| **Que*** | |
| Se usa en oraciones en las que se ha eliminado la cláusula principal. | (Deseo…) ¡Que **se diviertan**!<br>¡Que les **vaya** bien! |
| **Quién** | |
| Se usa para expresar un deseo en forma exclamativa. Se refiere al hablante y es imposible de realizar o no se ha realizado. Va en imperfecto o pluscuamperfecto del subjuntivo. | ¡Quién **fuera** millonario!<br>¡Quién **supiera** hablar cinco idiomas!<br>¡Quién **hubiera sabido** lo que iba a pasar! |
| **Querer, poder** y **deber** | |
| Se usan en el imperfecto del subjuntivo para expresar cortesía. Equivalen al condicional (*would, could, should*). | **Quisiera** (Querría) hablar con Ud.<br>**Debieras** salir ahora para evitar el embotellamiento. |
| **¡Ojalá (que)… !** | |
| Siempre se usa con el subjuntivo. | |
| • Cuando se usa el presente del subjuntivo expresa el deseo de que algo ocurra en el presente o futuro. | ¡Ojalá **deje** de llover pronto! (*I hope it stops raining soon!*)<br>¡Ojalá te **sirva** esta información! |
| • Cuando se usa el imperfecto del subjuntivo expresa un deseo hipotético, improbable o irrealizable. | ¡Ojalá **dejara** de llover! (*I wish it would stop raining!*) |
| **Imperativo** | |
| Siempre van en subjuntivo la tercera persona singular/plural y la forma negativa de todas las personas. | ¡**Jueguen** afuera!<br>¡No **llegues** tarde! |

* No hay que confundir la exclamación **qué** —como en ¡**Qué** extraordinario!— y la conjunción **que** usada para unir una cláusula principal con una cláusula subordinada —como en (Espero) **Que** seas feliz—.

# Gramática

emcpassport.com
WB 18–23
LA 6–9

## 49 Rumbo a la Argentina  1.2

La familia y amigos de Enrique han ido a despedirlo al puerto de La Guaira en Venezuela. Saldrá de viaje con su novia, Amanda, en un crucero rumbo a la Argentina. Todo el mundo les expresa buenos deseos.

*¡Que les vaya bien!*

Complete cada oración con el presente o el imperfecto del subjuntivo según el contexto.

1. ¡Que (*tener*) ____ buen tiempo en la travesía!
2. ¡Ojalá que su viaje (*ser*) ____ maravilloso!
3. Lástima que el barco no (*hacer*) ____ escala en Río de Janeiro. ¡Ojalá lo (*hacer*) ____!
4. ¡Quién (*poder*) ____ viajar con Uds.!
5. ¡Que (*volver*) ____ bronceados!
6. ¡Que todo (*salir*) ____ muy bien!
7. ¡Les pido que nos (*traer*) ____ cositas de allá!

## ¡Comunicación!

### 50 A cada guía le toca su visitante 👥 Interpersonal Communication  1.1

Un primo visita su ciudad para decidir si vendrá a la universidad aquí. Como buen guía, Ud. contesta sus preguntas. Túrnese con un(a) compañero/a para hacer el papel de visitante y guía. Usen fórmulas de cortesía con los verbos **poder**, **querer** y **deber** para preguntar y el imperativo para responder, como se ve en el modelo.

MODELO
A: ¿Pudieras decirme cómo llegar a la universidad?
B: Ve hacia el norte y toma el metro. Luego, bájate en la estación…

## Los adverbios  1.2

- Un adverbio es una palabra que modifica a un verbo, a un adjetivo o a otro adverbio.

  Ve **rápidamente**, por favor.
  Estos libros son **bastante** económicos.
  Para que te dure más el celular, trátalo **muy** cuidadosamente.

- Muchos adverbios terminan en **-mente**. Para formarlos se usa la forma femenina del adjetivo + **-mente**:

| Forma masculina | Forma femenina | Adverbio |
|---|---|---|
| tranquilo | tranquila | tranquilamente |
| principal | principal | principalmente |
| elegante | elegante | elegantemente |

> **Un poco más**
>
> Cuando hay dos o más adverbios que terminan en **-mente** en la misma oración, la terminación se añade solo al último.
>
> Ella bailaba **graciosa** y **elegantemente**.

A menudo, la forma terminada en **-mente** se puede sustituir por una **preposición** + **un sustantivo**.

generalmente = por lo general, en general
frecuentemente = con frecuencia, a menudo
repentinamente = de repente, de golpe

A menudo, un adjetivo puede funcionar como adverbio. En este caso toma la forma masculina, excepto cuando también modifica al sujeto.

Los diseñadores trabajan **lento**.
Pero: Las niñas iban muy **contentas**.

---

## RESOURCES

WB   Activities 19–23

### Answers

**49**
1. tengan
2. sea
3. haga, hiciera
4. pudiera
5. vuelvan
6. salga
7. traigan

**50** *Las conversaciones variarán.*

### Reference Desk

1. Remind students that adverbs retain the accent mark when adding **-mente**: **hábil - hábilmente**.
2. Point out that irregular adverbs must be memorized, such as **despacio**, **bastante**, **demasiado**, **bien**, **mal**, **peor**, **así**, **apenas**, etc. Remind students that some adverbs, like **bastante** and **poco**, have identical adjective forms.
3. Other adverbs that can be replaced by adverbial phrases are **cuidadosamente - con cuidado; cariñosamente - con cariño**.

---

## Differentiated Learning
### Accelerate/Heritage Learners

Ask pairs of accelerated students or heritage learners to play the role of teacher and present these grammar topics. Allow them time to prepare, and encourage them to use visuals and their own examples in the presentations.

## Learning Styles
### Visual Learners

Bring in photographs of people engaged in a variety of activities. As you display the images, have students make statements about the people using adverbs.

299

**51** *Las respuestas variarán.*

**52**

1. amorosamente
2. pesadamente
3. sarcásticamente
4. tranquilamente, verdaderamente
5. desesperadamente
6. repentinamente
7. puntualmente

## Expansion

Ask students to go online to learn more about **el subte** in Buenos Aires. Tell them to investigate its history, how many lines it has, how much fares cost, and a current map.

## TPR

Have pairs of students take turns acting out adverbs for their partner to identify.

---

### 51 Así me gusta vivir  1.1

Descríbale a su compañero/a de qué manera hace Ud. tres actividades. Para hacerlo, forme adverbios que terminen en **-mente** con los adjetivos en las dos columnas de la derecha u otros.

> **MODELO** Usualmente, me despierto a las seis de la mañana.
>
> Desayuno ligeramente con jugo de naranja y cereal.
>
> Voy a clases puntualmente a las ocho.

| | | |
|---|---|---|
| 1. levantarse, despertarse | amable | frecuente |
| 2. desayunar, almorzar, cenar | claro | general |
| 3. vestirse | cómodo | inteligente |
| 4. salir, volver | normal | lento |
| 5. conducir el coche | cuidadoso | nervioso |
| 6. ir a clases | diligente | profundo |
| 7. estudiar | rápido | inmediato |
| 8. ir al centro | elegante | tranquilo |
| 9. hacer las compras | excesivo | triste |
| 10. divertirse | fácil | verdadero |
| 11. hacer deportes | usual | juicioso |
| 12. dormir(se) | disciplinado | alegre |

---

### 52 Lo que Enrique vio en el subte  1.2

Los porteños le dicen "subte" —que viene de la palabra subterráneo— al metro. Para saber lo que observó Enrique en el "subte" cuando visitó Buenos Aires, reemplace la preposición y el sustantivo por un adverbio que termine en **-mente**.

> **MODELO** En general, mucha gente toma el metro.
>
> Generalmente, mucha gente toma el metro.

*Una pareja en el subte se miraba cariñosamente.*

1. Una pareja se miraba **con amor**.
2. Un joven pasó caminando **con pesadez** y lo pisó (*stepped on*) con una botas claveteadas (*hobnailed*).
3. **Con sarcasmo**, el joven dijo, "¡Tenga cuidado, por favor!"
4. Enrique miró a la señora **con tranquilidad**, pero **de verdad**, estaba molesto.
5. Una niña se había perdido y llamaba **con desesperación** a su madre.
6. **De repente**, el conductor anunció que había encontrado a una niña.
7. A pesar de todo, Enrique llegó a su destino con **puntualidad** y se bajó.

---

## Essential Instruction

1. Tell students to keep track of their partner's answers in **Actividad 51**, so that they can report to the class.
2. For **Actividad 52**, point out that students will need to first determine the adjective form of the words in bold.
3. After students read through **Sobre el autor**, ask a few comprehension questions.
4. Read the **Estrategia**. Ask volunteers to give everyday examples of causality.
5. Have students complete **Antes de leer** and **Actividad 53** in pairs.

# Lectura literaria

## Los dos reyes y los dos laberintos
### de *Jorge Luis Borges*  1.2, 2.2, 3.1

### Sobre el autor

Jorge Luis Borges (Buenos Aires, Argentina, 1899–Ginebra, Suiza, 1986) tuvo una temprana vocación literaria, promovida por su padre y la amplia biblioteca familiar. Vivió con su familia en varios países de Europa (Suiza, Italia, España) y fue a su regreso a Buenos Aires (1921) cuando redescubrió los suburbios porteños que aparecen en sus primeras obras. Escribió en revistas y periódicos antes de publicar sus primeros poemas y ensayos. Trabajó en una biblioteca municipal, donde empezó a escribir los cuentos de sus libros *Ficciones* (1944) y *El Aleph* (1949). A partir del año 1955, Borges se convirtió en una figura literaria internacional y recibió múltiples premios y reconocimientos. Su amor por la lectura se refleja en este célebre par de versos: «Que otros se jacten de las páginas que han escrito; a mí me enorgullecen las que he leído.»

*Jorge Luis Borges, uno de los grandes exponentes de la literatura argentina*

### Antes de leer   1.3, 5.2

Borges soñaba con frecuencia que estaba atrapado en un cuarto y que, al tratar de salir, se encontraba en otro cuarto. ¿Era el mismo cuarto o era un cuarto exterior? Ese sueño le dio el tema del laberinto. ¿Alguna vez ha estado en un laberinto? ¿Ha tenido algún sueño parecido al de Borges? ¿Qué sensación le produce no encontrar la salida o perderse en un lugar?

### *Estrategia*  3.1

**La causalidad**

Filosóficamente, la causalidad es la ley según la cual un determinado efecto o consecuencia tiene una causa. Según Borges, cada causa y efecto están condicionados por infinitas series de causas y consecuencias anteriores, que no siempre están explícitas en el texto. Identificar las causas de las consecuencias que se insinúan en la narración mejorará su comprensión de la lectura.

### 53  Practique la estrategia  1.2, 1.3, 3.1

A medida que lea "Los dos reyes y los dos laberintos", identifique las palabras o expresiones que indican una causa y escríbalas en la primera columna del cuadro. En la segunda columna, escriba las consecuencias correspondientes.

| Causa | Consecuencia |
|---|---|
| 1. "...un laberinto perplejo y sutil..." | "...los que entraban se perdían." |
| 2. | |
| 3. | |
| 4. | |
| 5. | |

## RESOURCES

 Los dos reyes y los dos laberintos
Antes de leer

### Answers

**Antes de leer**
*Las respuestas variarán.*

53  *Las respuestas variarán.*

## Reference Desk

Borges's stories often combine literature and philosophy; his goal was to convey abstract philosophical principles in literature in order to explore the enigmas of time and space. His works generated the Borgesian conundrum, a philosophical concept that questions "whether the writer writes the story, or it writes him."

## Critical Thinking

**Analyzing**
Ask students if they have encountered labyrinth metaphors in literature, and if so, how they were used. If not, ask them to think how a labyrinth might be used symbolically.

## Pre-AP

**Course Theme: La belleza y la estética**

---

**Differentiated Learning**
**Accelerate**
Ask students to write recommendations for tourists in Buenos Aires; each piece of advice should use a different adverb.

**Special Needs Students**
**Linguistically Challenged**
Provide extra practice for these students. Create a worksheet of multiple-choice items for students to answer; each item can have a situation (e.g., **Veo un atraco en la calle**) and two or three answer choices (**a. Bailo alegremente**; **b. Llamo inmediatamente a la policía**; **c. Camino tranquilamente a casa**).

Answers

**54**

1. Lo hace entrar en el laberinto para burlarse de él.
2. *Respuesta posible:* Simboliza el valor de la simplicidad la cual no se debe menospreciar. El laberinto del rey de Arabia no iguala al del rey de Babilonia en perplejidad y sutileza, pero es igual de mortal si alguien se pierde allí.
3. El babilonio lo hacen personas, arquitectos y magos. El árabe lo hace Dios.

**55**

1. Su pecado es el orgullo.
2. *Las respuestas pueden variar, pero deben contrastar lo que es hecho por Dios y lo que es hecho por el hombre.*

### Reference Desk

Make sure that students understand the setting of the story; **Babilonia** was an important city in ancient Mesopotamia, located on the Euphrates River about 50 miles south of what is now Baghdad, Iraq. **Arabia** refers to the Arabian Peninsula.

### Critical Thinking

**Analyzing and Comparing**
Have students use Venn diagrams to compare and contrast the two kings and the two labyrinths.

---

 **1.2, 3.1**

### 54 Comprensión

1. ¿Por qué hace entrar el rey babilonio al rey árabe en el laberinto?

2. ¿Qué simboliza un laberinto sin "escaleras que subir, [...] ni muros que veden el paso"?

3. ¿Quién hace el laberinto babilonio y quién el árabe?

**1.3, 3.1**

### 55 Analice

1. ¿Cuál es el pecado del rey babilonio?

2. Analice las dualidades y contrastes del cuento, así como el equilibrio o la falta de él entre los extremos.

---

# Los dos reyes y los dos laberintos   1.2, 2.2, 3.1
## de *Jorge Luis Borges*

Cuentan los hombres <u>dignos de fe</u>[1] (pero Alá sabe más) que en los primeros días hubo un rey de las islas de Babilonia que congregó a sus arquitectos y magos y les mandó a construir un laberinto tan perplejo y sutil que los varones más prudentes no se aventuraban a entrar, y los que entraban se perdían. Esa obra era un escándalo, porque la confusión y la maravilla son operaciones propias de Dios y no de los hombres. <u>Con el andar del tiempo</u>[2] vino a su corte un rey de los árabes, y el rey de Babilonia (para hacer burla de la simplicidad de su huésped) lo hizo penetrar en el laberinto, donde <u>vagó afrentado</u>[3] y confundido hasta la <u>declinación de la tarde</u>[4]. Entonces imploró socorro divino y dio con la puerta.

*"Mandó a construir un laberinto tan perplejo y sutil que los que entraban se perdían".*

Sus labios no profirieron queja ninguna, pero le dijo al rey de Babilonia que él en Arabia tenía otro laberinto y que, <u>si Dios era servido</u>[5], se lo daría a conocer algún día. Luego regresó a Arabia, juntó sus capitanes y sus <u>alcaides</u>[6] y <u>estragó</u>[7] los reinos de Babilonia con tan venturosa fortuna que derribó sus castillos, <u>rompió sus gentes</u>[8] e hizo cautivo al mismo rey. Lo amarró encima de un camello veloz y lo llevó al desierto. <u>Cabalgaron</u>[9] tres días, y le dijo: "¡Oh, rey del tiempo y substancia y <u>cifra del siglo</u>![10], en Babilonia me quisiste perder en un laberinto de bronce con muchas escaleras, puertas y muros; ahora el Poderoso ha tenido a bien que te muestre el mío, donde no hay escaleras que subir, ni puertas que forzar, ni fatigosas galerías que recorrer, ni muros que veden[11] el paso." Luego le desató las <u>ligaduras</u>[12] y lo abandonó en la mitad del desierto, donde murió de hambre y de sed. <u>La gloria sea con aquel que no muere</u>[13].

[1] trustworthy, credible, believable    [2] with the passage of time
[3] wandered feeling offended    [4] sunset    [5] God willing; (literally) if God be served
[6] governor of a fortress or castle    [7] wreak havoc    [8] scatter; cause an army to break ranks
[9] rode    [10] crown of the century (king of the age)    [11] stop, impede    [12] bonds
[13] Glory be to the living who dieth not.

---

## Essential Instruction

1. Have students look at the image on p. 302 and describe what they see.
2. Have students scan the story for cognates and words they learned in **Vocabulario 3**.
3. Play the recording, pausing for students to answer the during-reading questions.
4. For Common Core practice, have students answer the **Analice** questions.

5. Point out the **Pregunta clave** on p. 303.
6. Read through the **Proyectos** on pp. 303–304. Allow students to choose project(s) that most appeal to them. Provide detailed rubrics so that students are aware of the expectations for these tasks.

# *Para concluir*

## Proyectos

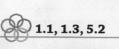

### A ¡Manos a la obra!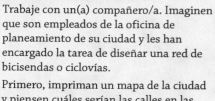

**1.1, 1.3, 5.2**

Trabaje con un(a) compañero/a. Imaginen
que son empleados de la oficina de
planeamiento de su ciudad y les han
encargado la tarea de diseñar una red de
bicisendas o ciclovías.

Primero, impriman un mapa de la ciudad
y piensen cuáles serían las calles en las
que debería haber ciclovías. Piensen en la
importancia de conectar lugares donde se
concentra mucha gente, como terminales
de transporte público, zonas de oficinas,
áreas comerciales, centros de salud,
universidades, etc.

*Las bicisendas conectan puntos clave de una ciudad.*

Luego, piensen en distintas estrategias para promover el uso de esas ciclovías: carteles para colgar en la
vía pública, anuncios en la radio o la televisión, publicidad en los periódicos. ¿Qué imágenes usarían?
¿Qué frases serían atractivas para que las personas viajaran más en bicicleta? Preparen juntos un primer
borrador para esa estrategia publicitaria.

Por último, muestren a la clase el mapa con el recorrido de la ciclovía y el modelo para publicitarlo.

### B En resumen

**1.3, 2.2, 3.1**

Repase lo que aprendió sobre las ciudades de Argentina. Piense en los distintos problemas que
presentan esas ciudades y en las soluciones que se ofrecen. Complete el cuadro de problema-solución
de abajo, proponiendo una solución distinta que se le ocurra.

| Problema | Solución implementada | Nueva propuesta |
|---|---|---|
| Tránsito intenso | | |
| Espacios abandonados | | |
| Inundaciones | | |
| Gran crecimiento de la población | | |

**?** Pregunta clave

¿Qué problemas conlleva
la vida urbana y cómo
se resuelven?

Answers

**Script** *Continued from p. 295.*

Mejoran los índices de seguridad…
y ni hablar del tema del medio
ambiente, ¿no? Porque el medio
ambiente, la bicicleta es cero
contaminante y encima mejora los
indicadores de la salud de la gente
porque hace más gimnasia, así que
es todo para ganar. La verdad que
a mí me entusiasma mucho pero
mucho la idea (sí es un avance)
el viaje promedio, Víctor Hugo,
el viaje promedio en la ciudad
de Buenos Aires por los estudios
estadísticos que hicimos no es
más de cinco kilómetros. Es una
distancia perfecta para hacer un
poco de ejercicio, es perfecta de
hacer.

—Comparto plenamente, por
eso queríamos resaltarlo, cuando
tenemos algo así bueno y positivo
lo dejamos quietito, sin tocarlo
con otros temas, porque me parece
que es fantástico, verdaderamente.
Insisto que la ciudad de Buenos
Aires pueda empezar ese recorrido.

**A** *Las presentaciones variarán.*

**B** *Las respuestas variarán.*

### Reference Desk

Point out the **Pregunta
clave**. Ask students to think
again about the question, this
time in relation to their own
community/culture.

## Differentiated Learning
### Accelerate/Expand
Ask students to read another short story by
Borges that uses the labyrinth motif, such as "**El
inmortal**" or "**El jardín de senderos que se
bifurcan**." Tell them to compare how the meta-
phor is used in the stories.

## Multiple Intelligences
### Bodily-Kinesthetic/Visual-Spatial
Students form two teams: **Babilonia** and
**Arabia**. **Babilonia** must make a labyrinth using
the furniture in your classroom, and **Arabia**,
an open space at school. Blindfold one student from each group, and have him/her try to
escape the labyrinth; the "kings" can ask their
team for help. Follow up with a class discussion.

**Answers**

**C** *Los informes variarán.*

**D** *Las respuestas variarán.*

**E** *Las estrofas variarán.*

### Reference Desk

You could create an Avenue task for students to present their reports from **Actividad C**.

### Connections

**History/Art**
Have students research and make a timeline of Argentina's **guerra sucia** and military dictatorship. Then ask them to watch a movie that deals with the topic, such as **No habrá más penas ni olvido** (1983), **La historia oficial** (1985), **La noche de los lápices** (1986), **Cautiva** (2003), or **Hermanas** (2005). Ask students to write a review of the film and its representation of the dirty war and its consequences. They can submit their timelines and reviews via Avenue.

**C** **¡A escribir!**  **1.2, 1.3**

Lea el siguiente resumen de la historia de Puerto Madero. Luego, escriba un informe en el que compare en qué se parece la evolución de este barrio de Buenos Aires a lo que ocurrió en el barrio del Abasto. Puede buscar más información en la internet si lo desea.

A fines del siglo XIX, se construyeron en Buenos Aires las instalaciones portuarias de Puerto Madero, que consistían en una serie de diques cerrados, interconectados por puentes. Sin embargo, apenas una década después quedó claro que esas instalaciones eran insuficientes para el volumen creciente del intercambio comercial y el espacio quedó obsoleto y abandonado. En 1989, se decidió comenzar a urbanizar la zona, que se transformó finalmente en el barrio más moderno de la ciudad, lleno de restaurantes, edificios corporativos, oficinas comerciales, hoteles cinco estrellas y departamentos de lujo.

*Puerto Madero, el barrio más moderno de Buenos Aires*

**D** **Ciudades planificadas** **Conéctese: los estudios sociales**  **1.3, 2.2, 3.1**

A diferencia de las ciudades que se desarrollan a partir del movimiento espontáneo de la población, una ciudad planificada, como la ciudad de La Plata, es una ciudad creada con un propósito determinado y de acuerdo con un plan urbanístico global. Busque en la internet algún otro ejemplo de ciudad planificada del mundo y haga una lista de sus características más llamativas. Luego, compare esas características con las que ya conoce de la ciudad de La Plata.

**E** **Antes y después** **Conéctese: la música**  **1.1, 1.2, 1.3, 2.2, 3.1**

Lea el siguiente fragmento de una canción de Luca Prodan, músico de origen italiano radicado en Argentina y fundador del famoso grupo de rock Sumo. La canción habla del barrio del Abasto.

**Mañana en el Abasto**
por *Luca Prodan*

[...]

Tomates podridos por las calles del Abasto,
podridos por el sol que quiebra las calles del Abasto.
Hombre sentado ahí, con su botella de Resero*,
los bares tristes y vacíos ya, por la clausura del Abasto.

[...]

*marca popular de vino argentino

Con un(a) compañero/a, comenten a qué época del barrio creen que hace referencia la canción. Luego, escriban otra estrofa en la que hagan referencia a una época distinta del barrio, que puede ser anterior o posterior a la que ilustra la canción.

### Essential Instruction

1. For **Actividad C**, encourage students to look up images of Abasto and Puerto Madero throughout different eras.
2. In **Actividad E**, you may want to play the song as students read the verse on p. 304.
3. For the **Vocabulario de la Unidad 7**, ask students to determine several categories that could be used to sort the words. Then have students list the words in those categories.

# Vocabulario de la Unidad 7  1.2

a cuadros plaid
a rayas striped
el abrigo de piel fur coat*
los accesorios de vestir accessories
afrentado/a offended
las afueras suburbs
el/la alcalde/alcaldesa mayor
la alcaldía municipal city hall
el algodón cotton
amarrar to tie up
amenazar to threaten
anunciar to announce
aprovecharse (de) to take advantage (of)
los artículos de cuero leather items
asesinado/a murdered
aumentar to increase
aventurar to venture
las botas boots
el bronce bronze
la calidad quality
la camisa shirt
la carne de res beef
la carnicería butcher shop
el/la carnicero/a butcher
la cartera woman's purse
el/la cautivo/a captive
la cebolla onion
la cercanía proximity
la chaqueta jacket
el chorizo sausage
el cinturón belt
el/la ciudadano/a citizen
colocar to put (in place)
combatir to fight, to battle
comercial commercial
la comunidad community
el/la conductor(a) driver
confundido/a confused
congregar to bring together
el conjunto residencial residential complex
contar con to rely on
el cordero lamb
cruzar la calle to cross the street
de manga corta/larga short/long-sleeved
la delincuencia delinquency
el/la delincuente delinquent
derribar to tear down
desamparado/a homeless
desatar to untie
digno/a worthy

diseñado/a designed
doblar la esquina to turn the corner
el edificio de apartamentos apartment building
el embotellamiento de tránsito traffic jam
encerrado/a locked up
la estación de policía police station
estar de moda/pasado de moda to be in style/out of style
estar en rebaja to be on sale
estragar to ravage
estrangulado/a strangled
la falda skirt
la falta de cuidado lack of attention
famoso/a famous
fatigoso/a exhausting
la fresa strawberry
los frijoles beans (black, kidney)
la galería gallery
las gangas bargains
hacer burla to make fun
hacer juego con to match
la huelga strike
el impermeable raincoat
implorar to implore
la inauguración opening
la injusticia social social injustice
irse (de)/marcharse (de) to leave, to go away
el kiosko newspaper stand
el laberinto maze
la lana wool
la ligadura tie, cord
las líneas del metro metro lines
la liquidación final sale
liso/de un solo color plain
llevar puesto to be wearing
el/la mago/a magician
la manzana apple
los mariscos seafood, shellfish
el mayor centro comercial largest shopping center
los medios de transporte means of transportation
el/la mendigo/a beggar
montar en bicicleta to ride a bike
la moto(cicleta) motorcycle
el muro wall

la naranja orange
los pantalones pants
el pañuelo handkerchief
las papas/patatas potatoes
la parada de autobuses bus stop
el patrullaje patrol
el pavo turkey
el/la peatón/peatona pedestrian
penetrar to penetrate
el pepino cucumber
la pera pear
perplejo/a bewildered
el pescado fish
el plátano maduro/verde ripe/green plantain
el pollo chicken
poner(se) to put (on)
proferir to utter
proporcionar to provide
el repollo cabbage
reportar to report
la ropa para mujeres/caballeros clothes for women/men
las rutas de autobuses bus routes
las sandalias sandals
la sandía watermelon
satisfacer las demandas/necesidades to meet the demands/needs
la seda silk
el semáforo traffic light
las señales de tránsito traffic signs
sospechoso/a suspicious
el suéter sweater
sufrir un atraco to be mugged
la tarifa transportation fare
tener cuidado to be careful
la ternera veal
la tienda de calzado footwear store
el traje suit
transportar to transport
el transporte público/urbano public/urban transportation
las uvas grapes
los vaqueros jeans
los vegetales vegetables
las ventas de fábrica factory sales
venturoso/a fortunate
las verduras greens
el vestido dress
la vivienda housing
los zapatos planos/de tacón flat shoes/heels

*Ver otras prendas y accesorios de vestir en la página 267 y otras carnes, frutas y verduras en la página 268

## RESOURCES

 Flipgrid

 Unidad 7

## Answers

**Script** *Continued from p. 297.*

¿Qué hacer con la mano? ¿Cómo sentenciarla? ¿De quién era aquella mano?
Después de una larga pausa, al juez se le ocurrió darle una pluma para que escribiera. La mano entonces escribió: "Soy la mano de Ramiro Ruiz, asesinado vilmente por el doctor Alejo en el hospital y destrozado cruelmente en la sala de disección. He hecho justicia."

## Differentiated Learning
### Accelerate/Expand

Ask students to search online for videos about Argentinean recipes. Have them watch a video and write an e-mail to a friend or do a Flipgrid post describing how to make the dish in their own words. Have them use the unit vocabulary and grammar when possible, e.g., **Separa las yemas de las claras cuidadosamente**; **Debes sofreír la cebolla a fuego lento para que no se queme**.

## Multiple Intelligences
### Verbal-Linguistic

Have students work in small groups to play **20 preguntas**. First, have them make a list of only the nouns in **Vocabulario de la Unidad 7**. Students take turns thinking of a noun; their partners can ask up to 20 **sí/no** questions and guess the word.

305

1. This unit's country of focus is Puerto Rico (officially known as the Commonwealth of Puerto Rico or **Estado Libre Asociado de Puerto Rico**), an unincorporated U.S. territory in the Caribbean. Puerto Rico is an archipelago made up of the main island and a few smaller islands; of these, only the main island, Vieques, and Culebra are inhabited.

2. New York's first Puerto Rican Day Parade was held on April 12, 1958, and was attended by Puerto Rico's first elected Governor, Luis Muñoz Marín.

## Culture

**Products/Practices: Information** New York City has long been a hub for Puerto Rican immigrants to the United States. Large waves of immigration occurred after 1917 (when Puerto Ricans were given limited U.S. citizenship and no longer needed a passport), in the 1950s (with the advent of commercial air travel), and after 2006 (due to economic crisis on the island). Puerto Rican immigrants quickly formed **barrios** in the Bronx, East Harlem (thereafter known as Spanish Harlem), and the Lower East Side; in these neighborhoods **bodegas** are ubiquitous and one can find street vendors selling **piraguas** (shaved ice treats). It is now estimated that Puerto Ricans represent 9% of New York City's population. Puerto Ricans form an integral part of the city's cultural landscape in artistic, musical, political, and commercial areas.

**¿Sabía que…?**  1.2, 2.1, 2.2

El segundo domingo de junio es una fiesta para los puertorriqueños que viven en Nueva York. Al Desfile del Día Nacional de Puerto Rico asisten casi dos millones de espectadores y muchas personalidades puertorriqueñas relacionadas con la cultura, la política y el espectáculo.

## Essential Instruction

1. Begin with a discussion of the **Pregunta clave**. Give an example of a political decision (such as immigration legislation), and ask students how it might affect a country's cultural identity.

2. Display a map of Puerto Rico and label the main cities, towns, and El Yunque. Ask if any students have visited the country, and find out where they went.

3. Draw attention to the culture photo and question. Encourage students to watch for the photo and the answer later in the unit.

4. Point out the QR code, the video question, and the screen shot from "**El clima**." Encourage students to watch the video as many times as they like.

5. Have students read and ask questions about **Mis metas**.

# 8

# A nuestro alrededor

**Escanee el código QR para mirar el video "El clima".**

**Si piensa viajar, es recomendable estar informado sobre el tiempo que hará en su lugar de destino. ¿Cuál es el pronóstico del tiempo para este fin de semana, según María Laura Pérez, y qué recomendaciones tiene ella para los viajeros?**

*Pregunta clave*

**?**

**¿Cómo afectan las decisiones políticas la identidad cultural de un país?**

## Mis metas

### En esta unidad:

▶ Usaré expresiones relacionadas con nuestro entorno natural y sociocultural.

▶ Usaré el condicional y las cláusulas condicionales con **si**.

▶ Leeré sobre la identidad de los puertorriqueños, su historia, su idioma y su cultura.

▶ Distinguiré el significado de palabras y frases según el contexto.

▶ Usaré el presente perfecto del subjuntivo.

▶ Repasaré el uso de expresiones afirmativas y negativas.

▶ Leeré un artículo sobre los universitarios puertorriqueños que emigran a Estados Unidos.

▶ Escribiré una biografía sobre la vida de un emigrante.

▶ Escucharé un segmento informativo sobre una puertorriqueña que ha realizado una gran labor comunitaria en Nueva York y le dirigiré una carta en nombre de alguien que agradece su ayuda.

▶ Desarrollaré nuevas destrezas de vocabulario.

▶ Distinguiré los usos de la voz activa y la voz pasiva.

▶ Leeré un fragmento del libro *Cuando era puertorriqueña*, de Esmeralda Santiago.

¿Por qué emigran tantos puertorriqueños a los Estados Unidos?

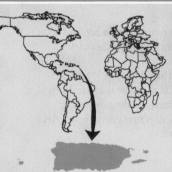

Puerto Rico

trescientos siete **307**

# *Vocabulario 1*

## Nuestro entorno natural y sociocultural   1.2

https://PuertoRico.org

| PUERTO RICO | CULTURA | NOTICIAS | POLÍTICA | RECURSOS NATURALES |

 **PUERTO RICO**

Puerto Rico es una isla de clima tropical entre el mar Caribe y el océano Atlántico. Es un lugar de grandes contrastes geográficos, de cordilleras de montañas, valles, llanos, costas y playas de arenas blancas.

Al este de la isla está el Bosque Nacional del Caribe conocido como el Yunque, una selva tropical donde viven numerosas especies de plantas y de árboles y donde nacen muchos de los ríos de la isla.

En el sur, donde el clima es como de desierto, hay épocas de sequía prolongada que perjudican la vida de muchos campesinos que viven de la agricultura y la ganadería, dos industrias importantes de la isla.

En la isla, debido a su ubicación, se tienen que afrontar con frecuencia desastres naturales como tormentas y huracanes que, en épocas de lluvia, dejan a su paso inundaciones, destrucción y escombros.

### Para conversar

**P**ara hablar de nuestro entorno natural y social:

En Puerto Rico nunca cae nieve y nunca se han registrado temperaturas por debajo de cero.

Las olas producidas por el huracán Isabel tenían hasta 4,3 metros de altura.

Los rayos, relámpagos y truenos son fenómenos eléctricos que acompañan a las tormentas.

En Puerto Rico no hay lagos naturales, solo lagos artificiales.

Puerto Rico no cuenta con volcanes activos pero sí se encuentra en riesgo de sufrir terremotos.

En Puerto Rico hay un alto nivel de contaminación de la atmósfera causado en parte por el alto consumo de gasolina.

A pesar de los esfuerzos, el nivel de pobreza del país no ha disminuido.

https://PuertoRico.org

**PUERTO RICO** | **CULTURA** | **NOTICIAS** | **POLÍTICA** | **RECURSOS NATURALES**

Puerto Rico fue una colonia española durante cuatro siglos. Su población, que es hispana, es una mezcla de blancos (descendientes de los españoles), mestizos (de sangre europea e indígena) y mulatos (descendientes de europeos y negros africanos).

Puerto Rico pasó a ser parte de Estados Unidos durante la guerra hispano-estadounidense en 1898 y se constituyó como Estado Libre Asociado de Puerto Rico, con su propio gobierno, el 25 de julio de 1952.

En 1947, el Congreso de Estados Unidos aprobó una ley que permitía que los puertorriqueños eligieran a su propio gobernante. Luis Muñoz Marín fue el primer gobernador elegido por voto popular en la historia de Puerto Rico.

Los puertorriqueños, aunque son ciudadanos de EE. UU., solo pueden votar en las elecciones presidenciales si son residentes permanentes de alguno de los cincuenta estados del país.

## Para conversar

**P**ara hablar de política y asuntos de gobierno:

El gobierno fue derrocado por un régimen militar mediante un golpe de estado.

En muchas dictaduras se imponen doctrinas y censuras, y se cometen violaciones de los derechos humanos, encarcelamientos y muertes a manos del ejército.

El comunismo y el socialismo son regímenes de izquierda en favor de la igualdad de las clases sociales y en contra de los prejuicios raciales.

En una democracia, la libertad de expresión, el proceso electoral y la existencia de partidos políticos son parte de la constitución.

El representante del partido liberal obtuvo la victoria en las elecciones para presidente.

Los miembros del partido conservador ganaron las elecciones del Senado y la Cámara de diputados.

Solo los obreros apoyaron al candidato del partido socialista. Su derrota fue total.

La huelga declarada por los gremios de agricultores, ganaderos e industriales causó una crisis económica que no se ha podido resolver.

Se hicieron acuerdos con los líderes sindicales y se aprobaron leyes en favor de esos sindicatos.

Se pidieron reformas salariales para los políticos y miembros del gabinete presidencial.

---

## Differentiated Learning
### Accelerate/Expand
Have students research basic information about Puerto Rican citizens and politics. Ask them to find the answers to questions such as: **¿Los puertorriqueños tienen representación en el gobierno estadounidense? ¿Podría un(a) puertorriqueño/a llegar a ser presidente/a de los EE. UU.? ¿Cómo es el gobierno de**

**Puerto Rico y cómo funciona? ¿Quién es el jefe del estado?**

### Learning Styles
**Auditory/Visual Learners**
Find clips of TV reports about Puerto Rican weather or politics. Play the clips and have students listen for words from **Vocabulario 1**. Then have students describe what they saw.

**Answers**

**1**

1. C; 2. A; 3. C; 4. B; 5. A; 6. B; 7. C;
8. D; 9. B; 10. D

**2**

1. H; 2. J; 3. A; 4. G; 5. E; 6. I; 7. B;
8. D; 9. C; 10. F

**3** **Script**

1. Ciudadanos, con su ayuda
   prometo...
2. Iniciaré programas culturales
   para los niños en las escuelas
   para poner fin a...
3. Trabajaré noche y día para
   proteger... para todos.
4. En mi programa no habrá nada
   más importante que resolver...
5. ¡Ecologistas, confíen en mí!
   El asunto número uno de mi
   programa es acabar con...
6. ¡Trabajadores, escúchenme!
   Ya no habrá más necesidad de
   declarar...

1. disminuir la pobreza
2. los prejuicios raciales
3. los derechos humanos
4. la crisis económica
5. la contaminación ambiental
6. la huelga

## Critical Thinking

**Analyzing**

After students listen to the audio in **Actividad 3**, ask them if they would support this candidate. Why or why not?

## Connections

**Social Studies**

Ask students to scan the list of vocabulary in **Actividad 2**. Have them give examples of the types of governments that other countries have. Make a list on the board to show the different types.

---

**1 Categorías**  **1.2**

Clasifique las siguientes expresiones de acuerdo con las siguientes categorías.

**A.** entorno natural   **B.** entorno social   **C.** entorno político   **D.** entorno económico

1. Dar un golpe de estado
2. Sufrir huracanes y terremotos
3. Imponer doctrinas y censuras
4. Aumentar el nivel de pobreza
5. Disminuir el nivel de contaminación
6. Ser blanco, mestizo o mulato
7. Tener libertad de expresión
8. Pertenecer a un sindicato
9. Ser descendiente de españoles
10. Declararse una huelga de obreros

**2 Definiciones**  **1.2**

Empareje las palabras de la columna I con las definiciones que correspondan de la columna II.

| I | II |
|---|---|
| 1. el golpe de estado | **A.** Un grupo que se organiza para defender sus intereses económicos |
| 2. la democracia | **B.** El totalitarismo; el despotismo |
| 3. el sindicato | **C.** El conjunto de soldados bajo el mando de un general |
| 4. el gabinete | **D.** La opinión sobre algo antes de tener conocimiento de ello |
| 5. el ciudadano | **E.** El individuo que puede participar en el gobierno de un país |
| 6. el comunismo | **F.** Una de las asambleas legislativas de un país |
| 7. la dictadura | **G.** El conjunto de colaboradores de un gobierno |
| 8. el prejuicio | **H.** La apropiación ilegal del poder político de un país |
| 9. el ejército | **I.** La colectivización de los medios de producción y la supresión de las clases sociales |
| 10. el Senado | **J.** El ejercicio de la autoridad por los ciudadanos de un país |

**3 Promesas del candidato**  **1.2**

Para ganar el apoyo popular, este candidato hace muchas promesas. ¡Ojalá las cumpla! Escuche e indique la terminación correcta.

1. aumentar la pobreza / disminuir la pobreza
2. los paros generales / los prejuicios raciales
3. los derechos humanos / la dictadura
4. el proceso electoral / la crisis económica
5. la contaminación ambiental / la cámara de diputados
6. la victoria / la huelga

*En una democracia hay libertad de expresión.*

**Essential Instruction**

1. Before assigning **Actividad 1**, tell students that more than one response may be possible, but that they should justify their answers.
2. Complete **Actividad 1** as a class: Write the categories on the board and have students list the expressions for each.
3. Check answers to **Actividad 2** by having volunteers read the items as complete sentences.
4. For **Actividad 4**, encourage students to use their own words to converse about the storm.

## ¡Comunicación!

**4** | **Noticias de última hora** 👥 Interpretive/Interpersonal Communication ✿ **1.1, 1.2**

Complete el artículo sobre una catástrofe ocurrida en Puerto Rico y el comentario de un turista de vacaciones en la isla con la palabra del recuadro que corresponda según el contexto. Luego, con un(a) compañero/a, hagan el papel del reportero de televisión y el turista y túrnense para hacer preguntas y dar más detalles de la catástrofe, según su imaginación, como se ve en el modelo.

| costa | desierto | huracanes | inundaciones | isla | lluvias |
|-------|----------|-----------|--------------|------|---------|
| playa | rayo | ríos | tormenta | trueno | |

**MODELO**

**Reportero:** ¿Dónde estaban sus compañeros de viaje cuando empezó la tormenta?

**Turista:** Estaban visitando a unos familiares y quedaron atrapados por la inundación.

**Reportero:** ¡Increíble! Cuéntenos…

---

○ ○ ○  ¡Puerto Rico devastado!

Hace 1 hora    Hace 3 horas    Hace 5 horas    Hace 20 minutos    Ahora

### ¡Puerto Rico devastado!

Martes, 2 de junio, 2015 — 12 m

SAN JUAN, Puerto Rico—"En las zonas de la __(1)__ y del centro de la __(2)__ caribeña, más de 300 personas tuvieron que evacuar su casa debido a fuertes __(3)__ repentinas que provocaron __(4)__ y desbordaron (*overflowed*) __(5)__," dijo el director de la Agencia de Control de Emergencias.

1 comentario   >> Enviar nuevo comentario

Usuario: **Euroturista**   Hace 10 minutos

"Estoy de vacaciones aquí en San Juan, mi lugar favorito del Caribe latinoamericano. Descansaba en la __(6)__ contemplando cómo crecían las olas, cuando de repente aparecieron enormes nubes negras en el cielo. Entonces vi zigzaguear en el cielo un __(7)__ y el tremendo ruido del __(8)__ me asustó. Como es agosto, la época de __(9)__, empecé a preocuparme. No sabía qué pensar porque soy de Andalucía, y en el __(10)__ casi nunca llueve. El hotelero me dijo que me tranquilizara y me aseguró que solo era una __(11)__ tropical y que pronto pasaría…"

### Reference Desk

Tornadoes, hurricanes, earth-quakes, floods, and electrical storms are all natural occurrences in Puerto Rico. However, the island does not have any volcanoes. Additionally, Puerto Rico does not have any natural lakes, only artificial ones.

### Connections

**History/Civics**
Follow up **Actividad 6** by brainstorming historical examples of **golpes de estado**, **comunismo**, and **democracia**. Ask students to research one example of each that occurred (or presently exists) in Spanish-speaking countries. You could have students summarize what they learned in an Avenue task.

## ¡Comunicación!

**5  Fenómenos naturales**     Interpersonal/Presentational Communication   1.1, 1.3

En grupos de tres o cuatro, intercambien información sobre los siguientes fenómenos naturales, los peligros que presentan, las precauciones que deben tomarse y los efectos que tienen en la economía de un lugar. Tomen apuntes y luego compartan sus conclusiones con el resto de la clase.

- Tornados
- Huracanes
- Terremotos
- Inundaciones
- Volcanes activos
- Tormentas eléctricas

*Uno de los 12 volcanes activos entra en erupción cada tres o cuatro años en las islas Galápagos.*

**6  ¿Qué es?**  Presentational Communication   1.3

Describa los términos que se dan a continuación en un breve párrafo y, luego, comparta sus descripciones con el resto de la clase. Use el vocabulario que se da como guía, como se ve en el modelo.

> **MODELO**  la censura: la dictadura, el gobierno, la libertad de expresión, aprobar
>
> **Cuando un gobierno nacional impone la censura, no existe la libertad de expresión.**
>
> **Por ejemplo, en una dictadura el gobierno tiene que aprobar toda la información contenida en los periódicos, los libros, las películas y las obras de teatro.**

**el golpe de estado:**   la injusticia, los derechos humanos, derrocar al gobierno, el ejército

**el comunismo:**   la censura, el partido político, la igualdad de las clases sociales, la libertad de expresión

**la democracia:**   votar por, el presidente, aprobar una ley, el senado

### Essential Instruction

1. For **Actividad 5**, you may want to assign one topic to each group, or give each group a geographical area on which to focus.
2. Before assigning **Actividad 6**, ask volunteers to complete the **modelo** in their own words.
3. As you introduce **Gramática**, emphasize the similarities in form between the conditional and the future.
4. Give an additional example sentence for each use of the conditional.

# Gramática

## El condicional  1.2

- El condicional simple tiene la misma raíz que el futuro simple. En los verbos regulares, se forma tomando el infinitivo y añadiendo las siguientes terminaciones:

| Formación del condicional | | |
|---|---|---|
| **Infinitivo + Terminación = Condicional** | | |
| votar | -ía | votaría |
| llover | -ía | llovería |
| elegir | -ían | elegirían |

- Los verbos con futuro irregular también son irregulares en el condicional, pero mantienen las mismas terminaciones que los verbos regulares.

| Infinitivo | Raíz | Condicional |
|---|---|---|
| caber (to fit) | **cabr-** | cabría |
| decir | **dir-** | diría |
| hacer | **har-** | haría |
| haber | **habr-** | habría |
| poder | **podr-** | podría |
| poner | **pondr-** | pondría |
| querer | **querr-** | querría |
| saber | **sabr-** | sabría |
| salir | **saldr-** | saldría |
| tener | **tendr-** | tendría |
| valer | **valdr-** | valdría |
| venir | **vendr-** | vendría |

### Un poco más

Cuando *would* significa *used to*, se traduce al español con el imperfecto.

Antes **salíamos** los viernes.

Cuando *would* expresa voluntad o deseo, se traduce al español con **querer**.

Le pedí que fuera, pero no **quería**.

## Usos del condicional

El condicional expresa probabilidad, posibilidad, conjetura o especulación, así como invitación, petición, deseo o sugerencia corteses. Se usa principalmente para hablar sobre situaciones hipotéticas que pueden ocurrir o no; también se le dice el "futuro hipotético". Básicamente, corresponde a *would, could, must have* y *probably* en inglés. Se usa...

- para hacer una conjetura o especular sobre el futuro desde el pasado.

- para hacer una conjetura o especular sobre el pasado.

- para expresar una solicitud, deseo, invitación o sugerencia con suavidad o cortesía.

- para expresar una acción hipotética o una acción que depende de una condición implícita que no se enuncia.

- para expresar una acción posible o deseable que depende de una condición hipotética que empieza con **si**.

Pensé que **habría** (*there would be*) alerta de huracán hoy.

Creímos que **sería** una tormenta terrible.

Nos **gustaría** que vinieran temprano.

Les **encantaría** que fuéramos con ellos.

Yo **votaría** por ella (si tuviera la edad para votar).

Yo **votaría** por ella, si supiera que tiene experiencia.

*Repase el uso del futuro para expresar probabilidad en el presente en la Unidad 2, página 71.

## RESOURCES

 Flipgrid

**WB** Activities 3–4

**LA** Activity 1

### Reference Desk

1. Remind students that conditional endings are the same for **-ar**, **-er**, and **-ir** verbs. Also point out that the **yo** and **usted/él/ella** forms are identical for all verb types.
2. Remind students that all conditional endings are accented; demonstrate the need for the written accent by contrasting the pronunciation of a word with a diphthong (such as **comedia**) with an accented word (such as **zapatería**).
3. Point out that there is no Spanish equivalent for the English auxiliary *would* (*I would vote* — **yo votaría**).

### Expansion

Ask students to create a Flipgrid post in which they state what they would put in a time capsule that would be opened 100 years from now.

## Learning Styles
### Visual Learners

Create drawings (or bring in photos) that portray dangerous, difficult, or unfortunate situations. Display the images and have students react by saying what they would or wouldn't do. For example, a photo of a shark near an ocean beach could elicit **Saldría del agua**; **No nadaría**; **Se lo diría al salvavidas**; etc.

## Special Needs Students
### Linguistically Challenged

Provide these students with all conjugated forms, together with the subject pronouns, of the verbs presented in **Gramática**. Work with students to make flash cards for the irregular forms.

**313**

**7** **¿Qué haría un candidato independiente?**  **1.2**

En los países latinoamericanos, se suele hablar mucho de política y en Puerto Rico es igual. Una familia puertorriqueña habla sobre un candidato independiente que hace campaña para gobernador de la isla. Complete el diálogo, usando el condicional.

**Padre:** Yo no (**1.** *apoyar*) a un candidato independiente, ¿y Uds.?

**Madre:** Me (**2.** *gustar*) saber más sobre su programa.

**Padre:** Pero, ¿crees que la gente (**3.** *votar*) por él?

**Madre:** No lo sé. Creo que un candidato independiente (**4.** *tener*) que conseguir apoyo para ganar las elecciones.

**Hijo:** Un gobernador independiente (**5.** *poder*) introducir muchos cambios. El candidato prometió que a los pobres no les (**6.** *faltar*) ni comida, ni vivienda, ni atención médica.

**Padre:** ¿Tú crees en lo que dicen los políticos? ¿Piensas que un gobernador independiente (**7.** *disminuir*) la pobreza en Puerto Rico?

**Hijo:** Creo que es posible, papá, pero me imagino que (**8.** *llevar*) algún tiempo.

## ¡Comunicación!

**8** **Promesas de campaña**  Interpersonal Communication **1.1, 1.2, 1.3**

Muchos ciudadanos desconfían de las promesas que hacen los candidatos en sus campañas políticas. Lea el siguiente segmento de un discurso político y haga las actividades con un(a) compañero/a.

Conciudadanos (*fellow citizens*):

Jamás permitiremos ni el hambre ni la pobreza en nuestra isla. <u>Reinará</u> la justicia en todas partes. Ahora <u>habrá</u> elecciones y el pueblo <u>podrá</u> votar por el cambio. <u>Mejoraré</u> las condiciones sociales. ¡Prometo que <u>habrá</u> trabajo para todos y que los pobres no <u>sufrirán</u> más!

*Los discursos de campaña presentan las propuestas de los candidatos.*

- Ud. escuchó las promesas hechas por un candidato en su discurso político y le parecieron tan interesantes que ahora quiere reportárselas a un(a) compañero/a de clase. Empiece con la frase, "El candidato dijo que..." y el condicional de los verbos subrayados. Recuerde que el condicional representa el futuro en relación con el pasado.

- Aunque Ud. sí confía en las promesas de este candidato, su compañero/a no tiene mucha confianza en él. Sostengan un diálogo acalorado (*heated*) donde presentan y justifican sus ideas y opiniones. Intercambien ideas sobre las promesas de los políticos. ¿Qué tienen todos ellos en común? ¿Cumplen los políticos todas sus promesas? Explique.

- Ud. decide lanzar su propia campaña política ¡y su compañero/a será su asistente! Preparen juntos un discurso político para presentárselo a la clase. Usen el condicional para formular sus promesas de campaña.

### Essential Instruction

1. After students complete **Actividad 7**, have pairs role-play the dialogue.
2. For the second bullet in **Actividad 8**, students can talk about a current candidate at the local, state, or national level. For the third bullet, so that both students have speaking time, you may want to have the assistant give an introductory speech for the candidate.
3. Open **Actividad 10** by talking about the problems (for the United States and other countries) associated with drug trafficking.
4. Invite pairs to share their answers to **Actividad 11** with the class, who can vote for their favorite solution.

## 9 Quizá, quizá, quizá...  1.1

Ud. había planificado un asado con sus amigos del colegio, pero hubo un grupo de tres muchachos que nunca llegaron. Practique el siguiente diálogo con un(a) compañero/a, haciendo conjeturas en el tiempo pasado para expresar probabilidad. Sigan el modelo.

MODELO ¿Por qué no vendrían al asado los muchachos?
(Quizá se les olvidó la fecha.)
**Se les olvidaría la fecha.**

1. ¿A dónde habrán ido? (Quizá fueron a ver el partido de béisbol de los Cangrejeros de Santurce.)
2. Pues, que yo sepa, no tenían entradas. (Posiblemente consiguieron entradas en la taquilla.)
3. ¿En qué irían, si queda lejos? (Tal vez tomaron la guagua[1].)
4. ¿A qué hora hablaste con ellos? (Aproximadamente eran las once y media.)
5. ¿Por qué no nos avisaron? (A lo mejor no tenían señal.)

[1] *Guagua* significa autobús en Puerto Rico.

## ¡Comunicación!

## 10 ¿Qué medidas deberían tomar?  Interpersonal Communication  1.1

Hoy en día, el narcotráfico es uno de las calamidades más graves de todos los tiempos. ¿Qué medidas y precauciones se deberían tomar en Estados Unidos y en los países latinoamericanos? Intercambie opiniones con un(a) compañero/a y usen el condicional para hablar de las medidas que debería tomar cada una de las siguientes personas e instituciones.

- El (la) presidente/a
- El (la) gobernador(a) del estado
- La policía de la ciudad
- Los ciudadanos

## 11 Según las circunstancias Interpersonal Communication 1.1

A veces, se nos presentan situaciones difíciles en la vida. ¿Qué haríamos en esas circunstancias? Con un(a) compañero/a, túrnense para hablar sobre lo que harían o dirían en cada una de las siguientes situaciones, usando el condicional.

MODELO Sus amigos quieren nadar, pero se oyen truenos a lo lejos.
**Les diría que es peligroso nadar con una tormenta eléctrica.**

*¡Podría haber una tormenta eléctrica!*

- A un amigo/a suyo/a le gusta la investigación médica, pero está deprimido/a porque le parece muy difícil hacer carrera en esa área.
- Sus abuelos se acaban de jubilar y están decidiendo qué harán de ahora en adelante.
- Sus primos habían planificado una excursión este fin de semana, pero hay lluvias torrenciales y alerta de tornado en esa zona.

---

## Differentiated Learning
### Expand
Provide students with the links to a few well-known Puerto Rican political blogs. Tell students to read a few entries and print the ones that they find most interesting. Divide the class into groups and have students discuss what they read.

## Learning Styles
### Visual Learners
Ask students to watch a film that deals with **narcotráfico**, such as **María, llena eres de gracia** (2004). Ask students to write a brief synopsis of the film and then say what they would and would not do if they were the protagonist.

### Reference Desk

1. **Los Cangrejeros de Santurce** are a basketball team from the Santurce neighborhood of San Juan. The **Cangrejeros**, whose mascot is a crab, are one of 10 teams that make up **BSN (Baloncesto Superior Nacional)**, a professional men's league on the island.
2. **Guagua**, a word of unknown etymology, is also used to refer to buses in Cuba and the Canary Islands. In the Andes region, the word (from the Quechua *wawa*) means *baby*.

### Communication

**Presentational/Interpersonal: Paired Practice**
Ask students to write a list of three or four problems (big or small) that they are facing. (If students do not wish to share personal information, they can invent problems.) Have them form pairs and share their problems; their partner can commiserate and offer solutions by saying what he/she would do. For this purpose (and as a preview of the **si** clause concept on the next page), you may wish to introduce the expressions **yo que tú** or **yo en tu lugar**: **Yo que tú, hablaría con un consejero académico.**

# *Gramática*

## Las cláusulas condicionales con *si*  1.2

Las oraciones condicionales son aquellas donde hay una condición que se debe cumplir para que otra sea verdadera. Las cláusulas condicionales con **si** expresan situaciones posibles, probables o hipotéticas, en el presente y el futuro.

- **Cláusula con *si* en presente del indicativo**

  Cuando la condición es real o posible, se usa el presente del indicativo —nunca el presente del subjuntivo—, en la cláusula condicional y otro verbo en indicativo —presente o futuro— o en imperativo en la oración principal.

| Cláusula con *si* | Oración principal |
|---|---|
| *Si* + presente del indicativo + **(condición posible)** | presente del indicativo<br>futuro del indicativo<br>imperativo |

Si **tienes** un momento libre, **pasa** a visitarnos.

Si ella **tiene** un momento libre mañana, **vendrá** a visitarnos.

**Llámame** si **tienes** un momento libre.

- **Cláusulas con *si* en imperfecto del subjuntivo**

  Se usa el imperfecto del subjuntivo y el condicional si la situación es improbable, hipotética o contraria a la realidad.

| Cláusula con *si* | Oración principal |
|---|---|
| *Si* + imperfecto del subjuntivo + **(condición hipótetica o improbable)** | condicional |

Si **tuvieran** una democracia (pero no la tienen), **tendrían** libertad de expresión.

Si **usáramos** menos gasolina, **habría** menos contaminación.

*Si tú no me hablas, yo tampoco te hablaré.*

*Si estuvieras acá, podrías salir con nosotros.*

emcpassport.com

WB 5
LA 2

 **¡Comunicación!**

**12** **La participación social**  **Interpretive Communication** 🍀 **1.1, 1.2, 5.2**

Ud. puede contribuir con su comunidad apoyando distintos programas para mejorar la sociedad en la que vive. Por ejemplo, puede hacer voluntariado, puede contribuir con dinero o hacer donaciones para distintas causas. Lea la información sobre la Fundación de Niños San Jorge y, luego, túrnese con un(a) compañero/a para contestar las preguntas con base en la información y dar su opinión al respecto.

---

 San Jorge Children's...

**San Jorge Children's Foundation** es una organización sin fines de lucro dedicada a la salud y el bienestar de los niños de Puerto Rico. Ayudamos a las familias de escasos recursos económicos a sufragar los costos para que los pacientitos puedan recibir los tratamientos médicos necesarios.

**Cómo puede ayudarnos**

Nuestra Fundación depende en gran medida de las aportaciones realizadas por personas y entidades comprometidas con el bienestar de nuestros niños. Entre otras modalidades, puede contribuir con dinero, donando su tiempo o con donativos de juguetes y material escolar. A continuación, verá el contenido de nuestros programas:

| Subvenciones | Programa escolar |
|---|---|
| Ofrecemos ayudas económicas para sufragar costos de: | Coordinación de servicios educativos y sociales |
| • evaluaciones | • Educación hospitalaria |
| • laboratorios | • Educación domiciliaria |
| • estudios médicos | • Talleres de arte |
| • medicamentos | • Orientación de programas y servicios que ofrece el Departamento de Educación |
| • tratamientos médicos | • Seguimiento académico (durante y después de la hospitalización) |
| • anestesias | • Repasos para las Pruebas Puertorriqueñas / College Board |
| • sala de operaciones | • Refuerzo académico durante el verano |
| • honorarios de cirugías | • Acceso a materiales y equipo |
| • hospitalizaciones | • Orientación / Consejería |
| • seguimiento médico | |
| • apoyo sicológico y siquiátrico | |

**¡Cualquier aporte es valioso! ¡Contamos con usted!**

---

**1.** ¿Cómo podría ayudar Ud. a niños sin recursos económicos que necesitan tratamiento?

**2.** Si Ud. decidiera contribuir con la Fundación San Jorge, ¿de qué forma lo haría?

**3.** ¿Cómo cree que podría cambiar la vida de un niño beneficiado?

**4.** ¿Cómo cree que se sentiría el niño y cómo se sentiría Ud.? ¿Qué haría para ayudar?

**5.** ¿Qué tipo de relación le gustaría tener con el/la niño/a? ¿Le gustaría seguir en contacto con él o ella?

**6.** ¿Cómo podría ayudar a otras personas en su propia comunidad o ciudad? ¿Hay algún centro comunitario cerca de su casa?

**7.** ¿Cómo podría colaborar en un orfanato, un hogar para ancianos, un hospital u otros sitios donde se necesite ayuda?

---

**Differentiated Learning**
**Expand**
Ask students to research other well-known nonprofit organizations that benefit children in Spanish-speaking countries, such as **Pies Descalzos** in Colombia or **AMAPerú** in Peru. Have them find out the foundation's history and mission, as well as volunteer and donation opportunities.

**Multiple Intelligences**
**Musical-Rhythmic**
Select songs that use **si** clauses with the indicative and subjunctive, such as "**Si tú te vas**" by Enrique Iglesias and "**Si tuviera un ukulele**" by Eduardo Zambrano. Create a cloze worksheet using song lyrics; make a blank space for each verb. Play the song once or twice and tell students to fill in the blanks.

## Communication

**Interpersonal/Presentational: Cooperative Groups**

Hold a class debate about one of the topics in **Actividad 15**, or another controversial topic that the class chooses. Divide the class into teams that are **a favor** and **en contra**. Remind teams to consider their opponent's point of view when formulating their arguments.

 **¡Comunicación!**

**13** **Me gustaría saber más** **Presentational Communication**  **1.3**

Antes de hacer un donativo —ya sea en tiempo, dinero o en especie (*in kind*)—, quizá le gustaría obtener información más específica sobre la agencia con la cual desea colaborar. Investigue alguna organización que brinde ayuda a los niños, ya sea una internacional como UNICEF u otro programa semejante como *Save the Children*. Después, comparta la información con la clase.

Si hiciera un donativo...

1. ¿qué necesidades básicas de los niños cubriría la contribución?

2. ¿qué tipo de alimentación recibirían los niños?

3. ¿sería posible enviarles regalos y otras cosas además del dinero?

4. ¿conocería personalmente a niños beneficiados?

5. ¿podría hacer algo especial en épocas festivas, como Navidad, Año Nuevo u otro día de fiesta?

**14** **Si yo ganara la lotería...** **Interpersonal Communication**  **1.1**

Todo el mundo sueña con ganarse la lotería. Con un(a) compañero/a, túrnense para hablar de lo que harían en esa situación. Sigan el modelo como guía.

> MODELO
> A: **Si yo ganara la lotería, viajaría alrededor del mundo. ¿Y tú?**
> B: **Yo compraría un carro deportivo de último modelo y una casa en la playa.**

**15** **¡Si se lograran esos cambios!** **Interpersonal Communication** **1.1**

¿Qué pasaría si se modificaran ciertas medidas adoptadas por la ciudad, el ayuntamiento, el gobierno federal u otras instituciones? Con un(a) compañero/a, pónganse en las siguientes situaciones y túrnense para dar su opinión al respecto.

> MODELO
> Las autoridades de tránsito declaran un día a la semana libre de dióxido de carbono y se prohíbe el tránsito de vehículos ese día.
>
> A: **Si las autoridades declararan un día semanal libre de dióxido de carbono, las emisiones de gases tóxicos disminuirían significativamente.**
> B: **Sí, y más personas caminarían y usarían bicicletas.**

- Las autoridades reducen a quince años la edad legal para conducir un automóvil.
- Se decreta el servicio militar obligatorio para las mujeres.
- Los gobiernos del mundo deciden limitar el derecho a la privacidad por razones de seguridad internacional.
- El concepto de matrimonio se amplía legalmente para incluir todo tipo de parejas.
- Se abren las fronteras de toda América para transitar sin visa de un país a otro.

**Essential Instruction**

1. You may want to have students perform their presentations from **Actividad 13** in small groups. Encourage the group members to ask follow-up questions.

2. Encourage students to elaborate and explain the reasons for their choices in **Actividad 14**.

3. Have pairs share any responses that they agree on from **Actividad 16**; have them answer using the **nosotros/as** form.

4. Open **Actividad 17** by asking students if they remember the story of "**Aladino y la lámpara maravillosa**."

##  ¡Comunicación!

**16** **¿Qué podríamos hacer?**  **Interpersonal Communication** **1.1**

Un desastre o una calamidad puede ocurrir repentinamente en cualquier lugar del mundo. Con un(a) compañero/a, piensen en las siguientes situaciones y túrnense para decir qué harían en cada una.

- Si hubiera una inundación súbita...
- Si ocurriera un terremoto en su ciudad...
- Si su banco tuviera una grave crisis de liquidez (*liquidity*)...
- Si se restringiera la libertad de expresión...

**17** **¡Si mis deseos se cumplieran!** **Interpersonal/Presentational Communication** **1.1, 1.3**

La literatura infantil tiene muchos cuentos y relatos en los que se le otorgan tres deseos a alguien. Formen grupos de cuatro o cinco estudiantes. Primero, piensen en lo que harían si en este momento alguien les ofreciera concederles tres grandes deseos. Luego, compartan sus respuestas con sus compañeros de grupo y compárenlas con las de los otros grupos.

**18** **El caso del contrabandista** **Interpersonal/Presentational Communication** **1.1, 1.3**

Trabajen en grupos de tres o cuatro estudiantes para resolver el siguiente caso de contrabando. Representen la situación, turnándose para resolver los interrogantes del caso. Luego, hagan un informe y preséntenlo al resto de la clase.

Los agentes de aduana vigilan el tránsito de los pasajeros en los aeropuertos y toman medidas para evitar el contrabando. Todos los meses, hay una señora que viaja con una maleta. Un mes, lleva la maleta llena de libros, al mes siguiente lleva ropa usada, al otro la lleva repleta de juguetes (*toys*), y así sucesivamente. Los agentes de la aduana sospechan que la señora contrabandea algo, pero no saben qué podrá ser.

*Si fuera el agente de aduana, revisaría el equipaje.*

- Si fueran los agentes, ¿qué harían cuando pasara la señora todos los meses?
- ¿Qué estrategia usarían para averiguar si es una contrabandista o no?
- ¿Qué preguntas le harían? Si la señora resultara ser contrabandista, ¿qué podría estar contrabandeando? (¿Ropa, juguetes, libros u otra cosa?)

---

**Answers**

**16** *Las respuestas variarán.*

**17** *Las respuestas variarán.*

**18** *Los informes variarán.*

### Reference Desk

For **Actividad 17**, as is often done in stories of this type, you may wish to set some restrictions, such as not being able to wish for more wishes, not wishing for someone to die, etc.

### Communication

**Interpersonal: Paired Practice**
After completing **Actividad 18**, divide the class into pairs. Tell students to take turns convincing their partner why they should or should not report **un(a) contrabandista**.

### Expansion

Tell students to choose a Spanish-speaking country that they would like to visit. They should use the Internet to find out customs regulations for traveling to this country. Ask students to share useful travel information with the class.

---

## Differentiated Learning

**Expand**
Ask students to research other types of charitable organizations in Spanish-speaking countries. Have them choose one organization and answer the questions in **Actividad 14** (modify the questions as needed given the type of organization).

**Heritage Learners**
Ask heritage learners to write a paragraph about what their life would be like if they lived in their family's country of origin.

La construcción de la puertorriqueñidad Prácticas

 LA Activity 3

**Answers**

**19**

1. Hubo una política de americanización. Las tradiciones puertorriqueñas se consideraban anticuadas. Surgieron sentimientos de resistencia frente a Estados Unidos.

2. Porque comparte con Estados Unidos la ciudadanía y las fronteras políticas, pero a su vez quiere diferenciarse.

3. Porque todos los puertorriqueños construyen su identidad en el contexto de una relación compleja con Estados Unidos.

**20** *Las respuestas variarán.*

### Reference Desk

The photo in **Prácticas** shows a mural on the exterior of the Nuyorican Poets Cafe, painted by local artist Antonio "Chico" García. Chico's art can be found on many buildings in the Lower East Side, Bronx, and Spanish Harlem. His bright, contemporary murals depict socially conscious themes.

### Pre-AP

Have students respond to the **Pregunta clave**, in spoken or written form, using information from the readings on pp. 320–322. Students should also include a comparison between their own community/culture and Puerto Rico.

---

# Cultura

1.2, 2.1, 2.2, 3.2

 **Pregunta clave**
¿Cómo afectan las decisiones políticas la identidad cultural de un país?

 **1.2, 2.1, 2.2, 3.2**

## 19 Comprensión

*Los puertorriqueños comparten la ciudadanía con los estadounidenses.*

1. ¿Qué cambios hubo en la identidad puertorriqueña durante la primera mitad del siglo XX?

2. ¿Por qué puede decirse que la identidad puertorriqueña es "ambigua"?

3. ¿Por qué tanto los emigrantes como los que se quedan en la isla sufren transformaciones en su identidad cultural?

 **1.3, 2.1, 2.2, 3.2, 4.2**

## 20 Analice

1. Además de los factores políticos, ¿qué otros factores cree Ud. que pueden afectar la identidad de los puertorriqueños?

2. Compare su propia identidad cultural con la que se describe para los puertorriqueños. ¿Hay diferencias? ¿Hay similitudes?

### Prácticas   2.1

A partir de la década de los setenta y hasta el día de hoy, muchos poetas puertorriqueños de Nueva York se reúnen en el Nuyorican Poets Cafe a leer sus poemas. En esas sesiones poéticas, surgió el término "nuyorriqueño" para referirse a los emigrantes de la isla que vivían en la ciudad. Algunos de los más conocidos escritores que han relatado su experiencia como "nuyorriqueños" son Miguel Piñero, Giannina Braschi y Nancy Mercado.

## La construcción de la puertorriqueñidad

Para los puertorriqueños, la identidad nacional y cultural es una cuestión compleja que está históricamente relacionada con su estatus político: la isla fue colonizada por dos culturas muy distintas y luego, sus habitantes se convirtieron en un pueblo emigrante.

Puerto Rico fue colonia española hasta 1898. En los primeros cincuenta años de dominio estadounidense, se llevó a cabo una política[1] de americanización que impuso, por ejemplo, un nuevo estilo alimenticio: se recomendaba una tabla diaria de alimentos en la que no aparecían frutas ni verduras que se cultivaran en la isla. Hacia mediados de siglo, muchas costumbres tradicionales habían quedado estigmatizadas como retrógradas y anticuadas[2]. Ante esta amenaza de asimilación, surgió un sentimiento de resistencia que defendía la autodeterminación política y la soberanía[3] cultural.

En 1952, la isla pasó a ser un Estado Libre Asociado (ELA) de Estados Unidos. Este proyecto político se planteaba como una oportunidad de modernización y progreso para Puerto Rico. Pero la situación de identidad cultural seguía siendo ambigua: ahora los puertorriqueños compartían la ciudadanía y las fronteras[4] políticas con un Estado del que llevaban años intentado diferenciarse.

La adquisición de la ciudadanía estadounidense, junto con las políticas económicas del ELA, incentivaron la emigración masiva a Estados Unidos. Allí surgió una gran comunidad que, a pesar de vivir fuera de la isla, se identifica culturalmente con Puerto Rico. Para ellos, "ser puertorriqueño" adquiere otra dimensión, ya que desarrollan una personalidad bicultural y bilingüe.

Los que se quedan en la isla mantienen una ilusión de identidad pura, pero la transformación cultural no es un fenómeno exclusivo del emigrante. Hace más de cien años que los puertorriqueños construyen su identidad en el contexto de una relación estrecha[5], pero tensionada por el deseo de diferenciación, con Estados Unidos.

[1] policy  [2] old-fashioned and obsolete  [3] sovereignty  [4] borders  [5] close

 **Búsqueda:** estatus político de puerto rico, asimilación cultural en puerto rico, estado libre asociado de estados unidos

*Nuyorican Poets Cafe*

---

**Essential Instruction**

1. Point out the **Pregunta clave**, and tell students to keep it in mind as they complete these cultural readings.

2. Have students preview the titles and photos on pp. 320–322. Ask them to predict what they will learn about Puerto Rico.

3. Remind students of the photo and question from the unit opener. Have them scan the readings to find the answer (on p. 322).

4. As you work through these cultural readings, create a timeline of the events on the board. Contextualize the information further by adding other relevant dates, such as Columbus's arrival on the island.

# El idioma y la cultura   1.2, 2.1, 2.1

Es un hecho: en Puerto Rico se habla español. Esta realidad lingüística surge de un proceso histórico de idas y vueltas[1] frente a los intentos de Estados Unidos de introducir el inglés en esta isla caribeña desde 1898.

Cuando la antigua colonia española pasó a manos estadounidenses, entró en vigencia[2] una ley de uso indistinto de los dos idiomas en las esferas[3] importantes del país. Como eran esferas dirigidas por funcionarios norteamericanos que no hablaban español, había un predominio implícito del inglés. Sin embargo, en los ámbitos más masivos siempre predominó[4] el español. Por ejemplo, aunque se intentó que el inglés fuera el único idioma de enseñanza en las escuelas, esta imposición fracasó porque ni los maestros ni los niños sabían hablarlo.

*El español es el idioma que predomina en la isla.*

En 1991, en un gesto de reafirmación de sus raíces culturales, Puerto Rico declaró el español como única lengua oficial. Pero ese logro no duró mucho tiempo: dos años más tarde, esa ley fue derogada[5] y se aprobó otra que establece el español y el inglés como idiomas oficiales.

En 2009, se inició un programa de escuelas bilingües, en las que se enseña inglés como segunda lengua y aunque muchos entienden que su enseñanza no necesariamente erosiona la cultura puertorriqueña, los defensores del idioma español redactaron un manifiesto en contra. Por otra parte, muchos isleños opinan que no es una buena idea solicitar que el español sea el único idioma oficial del país porque, desde el punto de vista político, esa actitud podría verse como un intento de alejarse de Estados Unidos.

Está claro que el debate por el idioma en Puerto Rico no es solo una cuestión lingüística, sino también política. Para muchos puertorriqueños, el español ha sido el escudo de resistencia y reafirmación de la identidad nacional.

[1] back and forth   [2] was enacted   [3] areas   [4] prevailed   [5] repealed

 1.2, 2.1, 2.2

## 21 Comprensión

1. ¿Cómo intentó Estados Unidos imponer el uso del inglés en la isla?
2. ¿Qué postura defienden los que se oponen a las escuelas bilingües?
3. ¿En qué sentido es político el debate por el idioma?

 1.3, 2.1, 4.2

## 22 Analice

1. ¿Qué lugar cree Ud. que ocupa el idioma en la conformación de la identidad de un pueblo?
2. Compare la realidad del uso del inglés y el español en Puerto Rico con lo que sucede actualmente con esas dos lenguas en Estados Unidos.

### Perspectivas 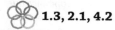 1.2, 3.2

El director de la Academia Puertorriqueña de la Lengua Española, José Luis Vega, explica que el español en Puerto Rico es "una lengua del pueblo. Quien verdaderamente lo ha mantenido vivo y vibrante son los hablantes", lo que le da al idioma una "fortaleza muy difícil de minar por una ley, un reglamento o una imposición".

Según Vega, ¿qué papel tienen las decisiones políticas en el uso del español en Puerto Rico?

## RESOURCES

 Flipgrid

 El idioma y la cultura

### Answers

**Perspectivas**
Según José Luis Vega, el uso del español en Puerto Rico está principalmente determinado por la gente, no las decisiones políticas.

**21**
1. A través de leyes que imponían su uso en las esferas importantes y en las escuelas.
2. Creen que la enseñanza del inglés erosiona la cultura puertorriqueña.
3. Según la postura política que tengan sobre la relación de Puerto Rico con Estados Unidos, hay opiniones opuestas sobre cuál debe ser el idioma oficial del país.

**22** *Las respuestas variarán.*

### Reference Desk

1. Students can do a Flipgrid post reacting to any of these cultural readings.
2. Each Spanish-speaking country has its own Academy of the Spanish Language, or association of academics and experts that regulate the use of the language in their respective country. Puerto Rico's was established in 1953.
3. Remind students that the Spanish-American War took place in 1898.

### Connections

**History**
Have students research more about the Spanish-American War and how its outcome helped shape the Puerto Rico of today.

## Differentiated Learning
**Expand**
Ask students to research the **Castillo San Felipe del Morro**. Have them create a tourist brochure about the fort, including important historical information and points of interest, as well as hours of operation, ticket cost, and visitor tips. Encourage students to include at least three visuals.

## Multiple Intelligences
**Verbal-Linguistic**
Invite students to explore the website of the **Academia Puertorriqueña de la Lengua Española**. Have them write important information about the organization. Ask students to share two facts that were surprising or interesting to them.

Answers

**23**

1. La población envejece y disminuye notablemente en Puerto Rico.
2. Porque tienen la ciudadanía estadounidense y no necesitan permisos especiales.
3. La eliminación del programa de exenciones contributivas, que había impulsado a la industria y lo había convertido en el primer destino de las inversiones estadounidenses.

**24** *Las respuestas variarán.*

 **1.2, 2.1, 2.2**

### 23 Comprensión

1. ¿Qué consecuencias tiene para Puerto Rico la emigración masiva hacia Estados Unidos?

2. ¿Por qué los puertorriqueños que deciden emigrar eligen Estados Unidos?

3. ¿Cuál fue la causa de la crisis económica que comenzó en el año 2006 en Puerto Rico?

### 24 Analice  **1.3, 2.1, 2.2**

1. ¿Qué crisis ocurridas en otros países impulsaron oleadas migratorias hacia Estados Unidos?

2. ¿Qué ventajas y desventajas cree Ud. que implica ser un Estado Libre Asociado?

3. ¿En qué ámbitos de la cultura se refleja la mezcla de culturas estadounidense y puertorriqueña?

 **1.2, 2.1, 2.2**

# Nueva ola migratoria de la isla al continente

*Emigración masiva de puertorriqueños rumbo a Estados Unidos*

Desde hace varios años, hay más puertorriqueños viviendo en Estados Unidos que en Puerto Rico. En la isla, la población envejece y disminuye notablemente en medio de una crisis económica que comenzó en el año 2006 y que ha impulsado la más reciente ola migratoria hacia el continente.

La inmensa mayoría de los emigrantes puertorriqueños elige trasladarse a Estados Unidos porque al ser Puerto Rico un Estado Libre Asociado, sus habitantes tienen la ciudadanía estadounidense y no requieren permisos especiales. Entre 1940 y 1970, una gran ola migratoria generó una comunidad importantísima de puertorriqueños que se concentraban en la ciudad de Nueva York y alrededores, por lo que recibieron el nombre de *nuyoricans*. En los últimos años, la tendencia ha cambiado: en lugar de emigrar al norte del país, un gran porcentaje de puertorriqueños se afianzó[1] en el sur, principalmente en el estado de la Florida, y se los conoce como *disneyricans*.

En 2006 se eliminó el programa federal de exenciones contributivas[2] que había impulsado a la industria manufacturera en Puerto Rico y lo había convertido en el primer destino de las inversiones estadounidenses. La eliminación de este programa provocó un colapso económico que ha sido una de las causas principales de la huida[3] hacia el continente desde entonces.

La población que se va de la isla no tiene reemplazo en el futuro, ya que las actuales tasas de fecundidad[4] del país están entre las más bajas de su historia. A menos que se revierta esta tendencia, Puerto Rico se irá convirtiendo, poco a poco, en una isla vacía.

[1] established itself    [2] tax exemptions    [3] flight    [4] fertility rates

**Búsqueda:** nueva ola migratoria de puertorriqueños a estados unidos, nuyorriqueño, disneyricans

### Productos  **1.2, 2.2**

La experiencia de los puertorriqueños residentes en Nueva York derivó en el surgimiento de una nueva lengua, el *Nuyorican* o nuyorriqueño. Se trata de una mezcla de inglés y español que busca recrear literariamente la realidad de los puertorriqueños que viven en Estados Unidos. Los poetas nuyorriqueños, atentos a los cambios que observaban en la lengua de la calle, se abocaron a representar esa fusión entre dos lenguas y la realidad que la motivaba. Así como el encuentro de las culturas dio origen a nuevos estilos musicales como la salsa y el jazz latino, la mezcla cultural también es el motor que impulsa cambios lingüísticos y movimientos literarios.

*Tato Laviera es un reconocido poeta nuyorriqueño.*

## Essential Instruction

1. As you play the audio for each cultural reading, pause occasionally to check comprehension by asking **sí/no** questions.
2. Have students complete the **Analice** activities for Common Core practice.
3. Open the vocabulary presentation by asking volunteers to provide as many definitions for **quedar** as possible. Then have students open their books and review the definitions on p. 323.
4. As you work through expressions in **Vocabulario 2**, make statements about your own life and community.

# Comparación y contraste: ¡Ojo con estas palabras!  1.2, 4.1

En español, el verbo **quedar** tiene distintos significados y connotaciones. Preste atención, pues su uso depende del contexto.

¿Será que me **queda bien** esta chaqueta para ir al restaurante con Frank?

Hola, ¿podrías decirnos dónde **queda** el Museo de Arte Contemporáneo?

Déjame ver bien. No quiero **quedar mal** con Uds.

Gracias. Es que **quedamos** con unos amigos a las 2.

Bueno. Todavía les **queda** una media hora para llegar, pero es lejos. ¿Pueden agarrar un taxi?

A ver. Me **quedan** unos cincuenta dólares en efectivo…

**quedar**
- to be located
- to arrange to meet
- to agree on
- to make a good/bad impression
- to have left, remain
- to suit/become/flatter
- to stay (behind), to leave
- to keep (sth)

**quedar**    *to be (located)*
¿Dónde **queda** la Universidad de Puerto Rico?
La sede de Río Piedras **queda** cerca de aquí.

**quedar**    *to arrange to meet*
¿**Quedamos** a las 10?
Habíamos **quedado**, pero no voy a poder.

**quedar (en)**    *to agree on*
Ellos **quedaron en** llamarnos por celular.
¿**Quedaron en** que harían eso?

**quedar bien (mal) con**    *to make a good/bad impression, to do the right thing*
Voy a hacer voluntariado; quiero **quedar bien** con la fundación.
Ella no fue y **quedó muy mal**.

**quedarle a uno**    *to have left, to remain*
**Nos quedan** unos diez mil pesos de la quincena.
**Les queda** mucho por hacer.

**quedarle bien (mal)/grande (pequeño)**    *to suit, become, flatter; to fit; (clothes) to be too big (small)*
Te **queda mal** esa chaqueta; ese color no te favorece.
A Juanita le **quedaron pequeños** los zapatos.

**quedarse**    *to stay (behind), to remain, to leave, to be left*
¿Por qué **te quedaste** en la casa?
Ese estudiante **se quedó** atrás en matemáticas.

**quedarse (con/sin)**    *to keep, to be left without*
Puedes **quedarte con** el libro.
**Me quedé sin** almuerzo.

**RESOURCES**

 Flipgrid

Avenue

WB   Activity 6

**Reference Desk**

Guide students in identifying the expressions in **Vocabulario 2** that are reflexive or use an indirect object pronoun.

**Culture**

**Practices/Products: Activity**
Ask students to research more about Losaida, the Manhattan neighborhood with a large Puerto Rican population and the location of the Nuyorican Poets Cafe. They can visit The Losaida Center's website to learn more about the organization's mission and goals. Tell students to investigate the Center's two main projects, the annual **Festival Losaida** and the Plenatorium. Ask them to create a Flipgrid post in which they state which project they would like to participate in and why.

**Expansion**

Ask students to research online to learn more about the Nuyorican Movement, including its literary, musical, and visual arts components. Have students choose one writer or artist and research his/her life and works. Ask them to write a profile of the person and a description of their favorite work by the artist. Students can submit their writing via Avenue.

**Multiple Intelligences**
**Mathematical-Logical**
Ask students to research and analyze Puerto Rico's population statistics throughout history, as well as the most recent years for which data exists. If the population continues to fall at the current rate, have them project how long will it take until Puerto Rico is, as the reading states, **una isla vacía**.

**Musical-Rhythmic**
Divide the class into groups. Assign each one a Puerto Rican musical style: **bomba**, **plena**, **salsa**, **jazz latino**, **reggaetón**. Groups should prepare a presentation about the history of the musical style, describe its rhythms and influences, and identify a few of its most famous performers. Have groups choose a song or two to play during their presentation.

**25**

1. quedamos
2. quedaron en
3. queda
4. le quedan
5. se quedaron
6. quedamos mal
7. quedarse
8. nos quedemos
9. le quedó
10. se quedan

**26** *Las respuestas variarán.*

**27** *Los diálogos variarán.*

---

## Communication

### Presentational/Interpersonal: Cooperative Groups

Tell students to work individually to write a list of situations similar to **Actividad 26**. Then have them use the items to survey their classmates. Tell students to interview a few classmates for each question. When finished, have volunteers share any answers that are similar, or humorous/creative responses.

---

## Expansion

Record a podcast about Puerto Rico and create a worksheet with questions about the podcast. Each question should have multiple-choice answers. After listening to the podcast, give students two minutes to complete the worksheet.

---

**25  ¿Qué queda?**   **1.2**

Complete las oraciones con el uso de **quedar** que corresponda según el contexto.

1. ¿A qué hora ____ tú y yo para ir al cine?
2. Mariana y Miguel ____ ayudar a preparar la comida.
3. Me gusta el cibercafé que ____ por Santa Rita.
4. A Juan no ____ esos colores tan llamativos.
5. Los niños ____ esta mañana en el ensayo del coro.
6. Si no llevamos nada a la fiesta ____ con los anfitriones.
7. Dile a tu hermano que puede ____ con la camisa.
8. El plan es que nosotros ____ una semana en Puerto Rico.
9. A mi mamá ____ perfecta la blusa que le regalé.
10. ¡Levántense rápido!, porque si no, ____ sin desayuno.

---

**26  Situaciones**   **1.1, 1.3, 5.2**

¿Qué hace Ud. si se encuentra en las siguientes situaciones? Preste atención a los usos de **quedar** y complete las respuestas de manera lógica.

1. Si me regalan un vestido que me queda grande...
2. Si mi vecino/a se queda con la calculadora que le presté hace un mes...
3. Si tengo que ir a un laboratorio para hacerme unos exámenes pero no sé dónde queda...
4. Si quedé de encontrarme con mi amigo/a a las diez, pero voy a llegar tarde...
5. Si tengo que pagar la cuenta de mi celular pero ya no me queda ni un peso del sueldo de esta semana...

---

**¡Comunicación!**

**27  Espere lo mejor, pero prepárese para lo peor**   **1.1, 5.2**  Interpersonal Communication

Imagine que Ud. va a hacer un largo viaje por carretera y su madre, que está muy preocupada, quiere saber qué haría Ud. si se encontrara en las siguientes situaciones. Con un(a) compañero/a, túrnense para hacerse las preguntas y responderlas según sea el caso. Usen cláusulas con si y el imperfecto del subjuntivo en su conversación, como se ve en el modelo.

> **MODELO**  Te quedas varado en medio de la carretera.
>
> A: ¿Qué harías si te quedaras varado en medio de la carretera?
> B: Si me quedara varado en medio de la carretera, llamaría a la policía de transporte para pedir ayuda.

- Tienes que quedarte en un hotel, pero no sabes dónde hay uno bueno.
- Al registrarte en el hotel te das cuenta de que se te quedó la tarjeta de crédito en casa.
- El mecánico, que había quedado de arreglarte el carro en un día, dice que se tardará dos días más.

---

## Essential Instruction

1. When checking answers to **Actividades 25** and **26**, ask students to explain which use of **quedar** is represented in each sentence.
2. Have students share their answers from **Actividad 26** in small groups.
3. Have students complete **Actividad 28** in pairs or small groups.
4. Have a class discussion about students' ideas from **Actividad 29**.
5. Give students a rubric for **Actividad 30** so that they are aware of the expectations.

## 28 Eco conciencia  1.3, 3.1

Según las siguientes categorías, indique cómo Ud. solo/a puede ayudar a resolver el grave problema de la contaminación del medio ambiente.

| | mejorar la huella ecológica | reducir, reusar, reciclar mejor | promover el uso de energía limpia |
|---|---|---|---|
| en el hogar | | | |
| en la escuela | | | |
| en el vecindario | | | |
| en la ciudad | | | |

## ¡Comunicación!

## 29 El aporte individual 👥 Presentational Communication  1.1

Formen grupos pequeños para hacer una lluvia de ideas sobre cómo cada individuo puede hacer aportes importantes para ayudar a solucionar los siguientes problemas.

- La pobreza y la falta de educación
- Los altos índices de depresión entre los jóvenes
- El maltrato físico y sexual
- El tráfico humano
- La discriminación por motivos de raza, creencias o preferencias sexuales

## 30 ¡Bienvenidos a Puerto Rico! 👥 Interpersonal/Presentational Communication 1.1, 1.3, 2.2

Trabajen en grupos para seleccionar un sitio interesante de Puerto Rico y preparar un folleto de turismo sobre ese lugar. Pueden buscar la información en la internet o en una biblioteca. En el folleto, deben resaltar los atractivos con palabras e imágenes y presentarlos breve y concisamente. De los siguientes datos, incluyan aquellos que sean más relevantes.

*El puente para viandantes en la selva tropical de El Yunque*

- Destino turístico
  - atractivos naturales: las montañas, los volcanes, los valles, la selva
  - atractivos culturales: edificaciones antiguas, museos, bibliotecas, teatros, festivales
- Transporte
  - maneras de llegar: en avión, en barco
- Excursiones
  - lugares importantes que se deben visitar
  - compras que se pueden hacer
- Hoteles
  - categoría
  - ubicación
  - ambiente
  - servicios e instalaciones
- Restaurantes
  - comida internacional
  - comida típica
- Recomendaciones prácticas para los turistas
  - vestimenta adecuada
  - precauciones de seguridad

## Multiple Intelligences

### Naturalist
Ask students to prepare a report about the flora and fauna found in El Yunque, as well as the challenges the park faces due to climate change.

### Verbal-Linguistic
Divide the class into small groups. Have students use their brochures from **Actividad 30** in a role-play between a travel agent and friends who are planning a trip to Puerto Rico.

## RESOURCES

 fg  Flipgrid

**Answers**

28 *Las respuestas variarán.*

29 *Las respuestas variarán.*

30 *Los folletos variarán.*

### Reference Desk

1. Display a map of Puerto Rico and show the location of El Yunque. Bring in a few photos that show different areas of the park.
2. El Yunque National Forest is located in the northeastern part of the island. It is the U.S. national park system's only tropical rain forest. The name may derive from the Spanish word for *anvil* (**yunque**) or the Taino *yuke* (*white earth*, perhaps referring to the clouds that cover the mountains in the area). The highest peaks in the park are El Toro and El Yunque.

### Communication

**Presentational: Cooperative Groups**
After students complete **Actividad 29**, tell groups to choose one topic and create a public service announcement to be played on a Puerto Rican TV or radio station. Students can post their PSAs via Flipgrid.

### Expansion

Ask students to create a recycling campaign for their community.

# *Gramática*

## El presente perfecto del subjuntivo  1.2

El presente perfecto del subjuntivo se forma con el presente del subjuntivo del verbo **haber** y el **participio pasado** del verbo conjugado[1].

| Formación del presente perfecto del subjuntivo | | | | | | |
|---|---|---|---|---|---|---|
| **Presente del subjuntivo de *haber*** | **Participio pasado del verbo conjugado** | | | | | |
| | dar | estar | hacer | ver | abrir | ir |
| haya | | | | | | |
| hayas | | | | | | |
| haya | dado | estado | hecho | visto | abierto | ido |
| hayamos | | | | | | |
| hayáis | | | | | | |
| hayan | | | | | | |

### Usos del presente perfecto del subjuntivo

El presente perfecto del subjuntivo, al igual que el presente perfecto del indicativo, se usa en cláusulas nominales, adjetivales y adverbiales[1].

- **En cláusulas nominales**

  El presente perfecto del subjuntivo se usa para expresar una reacción, opinión o juicio en relación a una acción pasada que es relevante en el presente. El juicio u opinión en la cláusula principal requiere el uso del subjuntivo en la cláusula subordinada[2].

  **Indicativo:**     El avión no ha llegado todavía. No sé que ha pasado.

  **Subjuntivo:**     Es posible que el vuelo se haya retrasado debido a la tormenta.

- **En cláusulas adjetivales**

  Se usa el presente perfecto del subjuntivo en oraciones con cláusulas adjetivales cuando el antecedente es desconocido o no existe. Se usa el presente perfecto del indicativo cuando el antecedente es conocido.

  **Indicativo:**     **Emplearon** a alguien que **ha tenido** experiencia previa en ese campo.

  **Subjuntivo:**     **Emplearán** a alguien que **haya tenido** experiencia previa en ese campo.

- **En cláusulas adverbiales**

  En oraciones con cláusulas adverbiales se usa el presente perfecto del subjuntivo para referirse a acciones que no han sucedido. Se usan los tiempos perfectos del indicativo para referirse a acciones que han o habían sucedido en el momento del habla.

  **Indicativo:**     El vuelo no **había aterrizado** cuando **llegamos** al aeropuerto.

  **Subjuntivo:**     **Te llamaremos** en cuanto el vuelo **haya aterrizado**.

[1] Repase la explicación del presente perfecto del indicativo en la Unidad 5, página 188.

[2] Repase el uso del subjuntivo en cláusulas nominales (Unidad 6, página 234), y en cláusulas adjetivales y adverbiales (Unidad 7, páginas 287 y 289).

## 31 Un viaje solos  1.2

Sus padres le han enviado a Ud. con su hermano menor a Puerto Rico para visitar a sus parientes. Su hermano aprende mucho y se divierte más de lo que había imaginado. Complete las oraciones con el presente perfecto del subjuntivo del verbo entre paréntesis.

1. Nuestros padres están preocupados por el viaje. Les llamaremos tan pronto como (*llegar*).
2. Nuestras primas se alegran de que mi hermanito (*darse cuenta*) de que es mejor hablar español en Puerto Rico.
3. En Puerto Rico hay muchos paisajes bonitos. Es una lástima que mi hermanito (*perder*) la cámara, pero podemos usar mi celular para sacar fotos.
4. Me sorprende mucho que mi hermanito (*ponerse*) triste cuando fue la hora de regresar.

## 32 Requisitos y limitaciones  1.2, 1.3

Complete las oraciones con el presente perfecto del subjuntivo de las expresiones del recuadro que correspondan según el contexto.

| | | |
|---|---|---|
| aprobar los planos | pasar la tormenta | tener experiencia |
| aumentar el sueldo | terminar la votación | tomar posesión |

1. Esperamos que elijan a un gobernante que...
2. Se sabrá quien ha ganado las elecciones cuando...
3. El nuevo alcalde firmará las reformas después de que...
4. Los obreros terminarán la huelga tan pronto como...
5. Empezarán la construcción del complejo residencial en cuanto...
6. No podrán estimar los daños causados por la inundación hasta que...

## 33 Testigo de primera mano  1.3

Un huracán ha pasado por Puerto Rico y no dejó más que destrucción y escombros a su paso. Después de dos días, Alejandra logra comunicarse con su amigo Samuel para contarle esa experiencia traumática. Complete el diálogo con el presente perfecto del indicativo o del subjuntivo, según el caso.

**Samuel:** Alejandra, ¿cómo estás? Espero que ya (*1. reponerse, tú*) del susto.

**Alejandra:** Sí, lo (*2. lograr*) poco a poco. Confío en que (*3. recibir, tú*) el mensaje que te envié por celular.

**Samuel:** Sí, sí, (*4. llegar*) hace poco. Me alegra que tu casa no (*5. sufrir*) muchos desperfectos.

**Alejandra:** Afortunadamente, mi casa no (*6. quedar*) tan mal. Aunque es terrible que la de mi abuela (*7. destruirse*) con los vientos.

**Samuel:** ¿Qué ayuda (*8. ofrecer*) las autoridades?

**Alejandra:** (*9. decir*) que van a estudiar cada caso.

**Samuel:** ¡Es una lástima que tanta gente (*10. perder*) su casa!

**Alejandra:** Sí, desastroso. Cuando (*11. pasar*) lo peor, vamos a ayudar en lo que se pueda.

*¡Es espantoso que el huracán haya arruinado tantas casas!*

---

**Answers**

**31**
1. hayamos llegado
2. se haya dado cuenta
3. haya perdido
4. se haya puesto

**32**
1. Esperamos que elijan a un gobernante que haya tenido experiencia.
2. Se sabrá quien ha ganado las elecciones cuando haya terminado la votación.
3. El nuevo alcalde firmará las reformas después de que haya tomado posesión.
4. Los obreros terminarán la huelga tan pronto como les hayan aumentado el sueldo.
5. Empezarán la construcción del complejo residencial en cuanto hayan aprobado los planos.
6. No podrán estimar los daños causados por la inundación hasta que haya pasado la tormenta.

**33**
1. te hayas repuesto
2. he logrado
3. hayas recibido
4. ha llegado
5. haya sufrido
6. ha quedado
7. se haya destruido
8. han ofrecido
9. Han dicho
10. haya perdido
11. haya pasado

### Critical Thinking

**Analyzing**
Have students justify their answers for **Actividad 33**.

---

### Differentiated Learning

**Adapt**
Modify these activities according to your students' level. For accelerated students, use word banks instead of parentheses for the verbs in **Actividades 31** and **33**; to decelerate, make these activities multiple choice. **Actividad 32** can be adapted to a matching activity, or made more challenging as an activity in which students must combine elements from three columns of prompts.

### Special Needs Students

**Linguistically Challenged**
Review the formation of regular and irregular past participles. Remind students that with the past perfect subjunctive, the participle does not change in gender or number. Then review verbs that trigger the use of the subjunctive.

### Reference Desk

1. Remind students that **ninguno/a** is always used in the singular, even when elicited by a plural noun. For example: **¿Hay políticos totalmente honestos en Washington? No, no hay ninguno.**

2. You may want to remind students of phrases such as **de ninguna manera**, **de ningún modo**, and **ni siquiera**.

# Gramática

## Expresiones afirmativas y negativas 🌸 1.2

| Expresiones afirmativas | Expresiones negativas |
|---|---|
| algo (*something, anything*) | nada (*nothing*) |
| alguien (*someone, anyone*) | nadie (*no one, nobody*) |
| todo el mundo (*everyone*) | |
| algún, alguno(a, os, as) (*some, someone*) | ningún, ninguno(a) (*none, no one, not any*) |
| unos(as) (*a few*) | |
| siempre (*always*) | |
| alguna vez (*ever*) | nunca, jamás (*never*) |
| algunas veces (*sometimes*) | |
| algún día (*someday*) | |
| o… o (*either…or*) | ni… ni (*neither…nor*) |
| también (*also, too*) | tampoco (*neither*) |

### Usos de las expresiones

- **algo ≠ nada** (pronombres)
  Son invariables y se refieren a cosas.

- **alguien ≠ nadie** (pronombres)
  Son invariables y se refieren a personas.

- **alguno/a/os/as ≠ ninguno/a** (pronombres y adjetivos)

  **Alguno** concuerda en género y número (o/a, os/as), pero **ninguno** concuerda solo en género. Generalmente se usa solo en singular.

  Como adjetivos, pierden la **o** final cuando van antes de un sustantivo masculino singular (**algún**, **ningún**).

- **siempre ≠ nunca, jamás** (adverbios)
  Son invariables. **Jamás** es más enfático.

- **también ≠ tampoco** (adverbios)
  Son invariables.

### Ejemplos

Sé que tienes **algo** que decirme.

No tengo **nada** que decirte.

¿Hay **alguien** que sepa preparar sushi?

No, no hay **nadie** que sepa prepararlo.

**Algunos** libros son difíciles de entender. (adjetivo)

No hay **ninguno** imposible de entender. (pronombre)

¿Tienes **alguna** receta para preparar tarta de manzana?

No, no tengo **ninguna** receta de esas.

¿Viste **algún** libro sobre ese tema?

No vi **ningún** libro sobre ese tema.

**Siempre** vamos al cine los viernes.

**Nunca** me has invitado a ir.
¡**Jamás** he ido con Uds.!

Les encantan las montañas y la nieve **también**.

No les gusta el calor; **tampoco** les gusta el mar.

### Essential Instruction

1. Introduce the **Gramática** by making complaints in a melodramatic, gloomy tone, e.g., **Ningún amigo me llama por teléfono**; **Nadie quiere visitarme**, etc. Switch to a cheerful tone and give affirmative statements: **Todo el mundo me quiere**, etc.

2. Brainstorm additional words that begin with **in-, im-**, and **des-**. Encourage students to make lists for their own reference.

3. Have volunteers create additional examples for **Un poco más**.

4. Have students exchange papers with a classmate and check answers to **Actividad 34**.

- o... o ≠ ni... ni (conjunciones)

    O... o se usa para ofrecer dos alternativas.

    Ni... ni niega dos alternativas. El verbo con dos sujetos unidos por ni... ni se usa en plural.

- in-, im- y des- (prefijos)

    Son prefijos de negación que se usan con varios adjetivos, sustantivos y verbos.

O se toman medidas ecológicas o el clima cambiará irremediablemente.

Ni la extrema derecha ni la extrema izquierda ofrecen algo nuevo.

Los terremotos son **im**predecibles.
No hay que **des**estimar todas las propuestas.
Sería un final **in**deseable.

## 34 ¿Hacer siempre o nunca hacer?  1.3

Debido a los conflictos bélicos, sean guerras civiles o guerras internacionales, los países del mundo deben abordar los temas de cómo mantener la paz. Conteste las preguntas, usando las siguientes palabras:

| | | | |
|---|---|---|---|
| algún, alguno(s) | alguna(s) | algo | ni... ni |
| ningún, ninguno(s) | alguien | nada | tampoco |
| ninguna(s) | nadie | o... o | nunca |

MODELO ¿Hay algo de bueno en la guerra?
**No, no hay nada de bueno en la guerra.**
**(La guerra no tiene nada de bueno).**

1. ¿Debe alguien discriminar por razones de raza, nacionalidad, clase social, edad, religión o sexo?
2. Si sucediera alguna tragedia en un país de las Naciones Unidas, ¿irían algunos países en su auxilio?
3. ¿Debe algún país atacar a otro sin razón alguna?
4. ¿Algún día deberían permitirse las invasiones extranjeras?
5. ¿Deben los países capitalistas y los países comunistas tratar de imponer sus doctrinas políticas?
6. Quienes tienen creencias religiosas muy firmes ¿deben también tratar de imponer sus creencias?
7. ¿Cuándo es importante luchar por la paz?
8. O cruzarse de brazos o ignorar el problema, ¿qué es lo mejor? (Ni... ni)

*¡La guerra no tiene nada de bueno!*

### Un poco más

- Si la negación va delante del verbo, se omite la doble negación.

    **No** bailan **nunca** solos. **Nunca** bailan solos.

    **No** se lo pidió **nadie**. **Nadie** se lo pidió.

- Para contestar una pregunta de forma negativa cuya respuesta es sí o no, se debe repetir la palabra **no**.

    ¿Hay tornados en tu área?
    **No**, **no** hay tornados en mi área.

- Cuando los indefinidos y negativos se refieren a personas y funcionan como complementos directos del verbo, se requiere la "a" personal.

    ¿Conoces **a algún** chef?
    No, no conozco **a ningún** chef.

- Para cambiar la expresión "algún día" al negativo se dice nunca o jamás.

    **¿Algún día** piensas retirarte de tu profesión?
    No, **nunca** pienso retirarme de mi profesión.

*Unidad 8* | trescientos veintinueve  **329**

### Critical Thinking

**Analyzing**
Have a class discussion about ways that people can reduce their carbon footprint. Then have students name things that their families buy regularly. Finally, ask them to think of ways that these products could be made more environmentally friendly.

### Expansion

Tell students to write their sentences from **Actividad 35**. Have them associate each one with a politician who is currently in office or campaigning.

## ¡Comunicación!

**35 O lo uno o lo otro...** 👥 **Interpersonal Communication** ✿ **1.1**

Enriqueta y Aníbal son candidatos para el Senado en Puerto Rico. Como buenos políticos que son, les gusta hacer promesas, pero tienen ideas muy diferentes. Trabajen en parejas para terminar las promesas de cada candidato sobre algún tema, como la educación, la pobreza, la salud, el trabajo, el crimen, el ambiente, etc.

| **Enriqueta** | **Aníbal** |
|---|---|
| Yo siempre… | Yo nunca… |
| Algún día… | Jamás… |
| Alguien… | Nadie… |
| Algunos/as… | Ningún, Ninguno/a… |
| También voy a… | Tampoco voy a… |

**36 Prometo que siempre...** 👥 **Interpersonal/Presentational Communication** ✿ **1.1, 1.3**

Trabajen en parejas para escribir un discurso sobre algún tema polémico, como…

• La minimización del efecto invernadero

• El mejoramiento de los mecanismos regionales e internacionales para lograr y mantener la paz

• La desigualdad de género

• La libertad de expresión

• Otro tema

Elijan sus palabras con cuidado y usen las expresiones de la unidad. Después lean el discurso ante la clase.

Expresiones para comunicarse:

*¡Los políticos siempre prometen mucho!*

| | |
|---|---|
| Nunca / Jamás permitiremos que… | Nada es más importante que… |
| Que nadie se atreva a… | Siempre trataremos de… |
| Si a alguien se le ocurriera… | Si algo le sucediera a… |
| Nadie debería… | O hacemos eso o… |

### Essential Instruction

1. For **Actividad 35**, tell students to complete the statements for Enriqueta. Then have them write Aníbal's statements.

2. You may want to have pairs divide their speeches from **Actividad 36** into two parts, so that each student has a turn to speak in front of the class. If possible, provide a lectern.

3. Discuss the **Antes de leer** question as a class.

4. Go over the **Estrategia**; work as a class to scan the reading and make a list of each type of cognate.

5. Play the audio for the reading as students follow along in their books.

# Lectura informativa

## Antes de leer   1.3

¿Qué clase de problemas influyen en las personas que deciden emigrar a otro país?

### Estrategia  3.1

**Identificar cognados y falsos cognados**

Los cognados son palabras que tienen una forma similar en dos lenguas distintas. Muchas de ellas significan lo mismo en ambos idiomas, como *familia* y *family*. Sin embargo, también existen los falsos cognados: palabras semejantes en su forma con significados muy distintos, como *policía* y *policy*. Identificar ambos al leer puede ayudar a comprender mejor un texto.

⚪⚪⚪ La crisis lleva a...

### VÍVELO HOY 🔍

## La crisis lleva a universitarios puertorriqueños a emigrar en masa a EE. UU.  1.2, 2.1, 2.2, 3.2

**Por Jorge J. Muñiz Ortiz — Agencia EFE en EEUU 07/22/14 10:24 a. m.**

**SAN JUAN** — La crisis económica y la falta de empleos de su ámbito en Puerto Rico lleva a miles de universitarios puertorriqueños con experiencia profesional a emigrar a EE. UU., como es el caso de tres jóvenes ingenieros que en el último mes han emprendido una nueva vida en ese país.

Pedro Eloy Guzmán, Jesús Manuel de León y Jaime Rodríguez, de entre 27 y 33 años, comentan cómo se vieron forzados a emigrar ante la dificultad de conseguir trabajo en su isla natal relacionado con su especialidad, pese a que los tres tienen experiencia y méritos profesionales.

Según datos del Instituto de Estadísticas de Puerto Rico, durante 2012 emigraron a EE. UU. unas 75.000 personas, que tenían una edad media de 33 años. De todas ellas, el 52 % tenía algún tipo de formación universitaria [...] y el 35 % estaban casadas.

Guzmán encarna[1] por tanto a la perfección el perfil del emigrante puertorriqueño: tiene 33 años, está casado, es padre de un hijo y tiene una licenciatura[2] en Ingeniería Eléctrica con licencia de Ingeniero Profesional.

En su opinión, el ámbito de la ingeniería en Puerto Rico está "supersaturado" debido a la gran cantidad de jóvenes que se gradúan de Ingeniería en la isla, frente a las pocas oportunidades que hay porque las empresas no generan suficiente dinero para contratarlos.

"Eso, junto a que el mercado laboral es un ecosistema relativamente cerrado, hace que el ingeniero se vea como uno más del montón", relata Guzmán, quien quedó desempleado en noviembre, después de haber trabajado en Alternate Concepts, Microsoft, Boston Scientific y Doral Bank.

Tras esas experiencias, cinco empresas lo contactaron para ofrecerle trabajo, pero todas le decían lo mismo: "Te queremos hacer una oferta pero la economía no aguanta[3]. Te avisaremos".

Ante la incertidumbre[4] y tras cinco meses buscando una oportunidad de empleo, su esposa le sugirió que buscara trabajo en las oficinas de Microsoft en Seattle, donde está la sede del gigante estadounidense.

Finalmente, Amazon, con oficinas también en Seattle, contrató a Guzmán, quien lleva menos de un mes en esa ciudad y habla ya de "un cambio bastante grande, a nivel profesional y personal". [...]

[1] embodies  [2] degree  [3] restrain  [4] uncertainty

---

 1.2, 2.1, 2.2

## 37 Comprensión

1. ¿Cuáles son las causas de la emigración masiva de universitarios puertorriqueños a Estados Unidos?

2. ¿Qué dos características presenta gran parte de los puertorriqueños que emigran a Estados Unidos?

3. ¿Qué problema enfrentan los ingenieros en Puerto Rico?

4. ¿Qué problema enfrentan las empresas que quieren contratar ingenieros?

 1.3, 2.2

## 38 Analice

¿Qué política cree Ud. que se podría implementar para mejorar la situación de los ingenieros en el futuro?

---

**Answers**

**Antes de leer**
*Las respuestas variarán.*

**37**
1. Son la crisis económica y la falta de empleo en Puerto Rico.
2. Tienen algún tipo de formación universitaria y están casados.
3. Hay muchos ingenieros y pocos puestos de trabajo para ellos en las empresas de su país.
4. La economía no se lo permite.

**38** *Respuesta posible:*
Como el mercado está saturado de ingenieros, el Estado podría incentivar el estudio de otras carreras para que los universitarios puedan conseguir empleo más fácilmente.

---

## Differentiated Learning
### Accelerate/Expand
Ask students to develop their sentences from **Actividad 35** into a role-play of a contentious political debate between two candidates with opposing views. Have a few pairs perform their debates for the class.

## Multiple Intelligences
### Mathematical-Logical
Ask students to research employment statistics for Puerto Rico in the last few decades. Ask them to analyze the trends and share their findings with the class.

**39**

1. Florida, Pennsylvania y Nueva York.
2. Se sienten que no tenían otra opción. Por un lado, están contentos de haber conseguido trabajo. Por otro lado, hubieran preferido quedarse en su país.
3. Lo logran por amiguismo, es decir, gracias a sus contactos personales.
4. Porque como ingeniero ganaba menos dinero y solo consiguió contratos sin cobertura social.

**40** *Las respuestas variarán.*

 **1.2, 2.1, 2.2, 3.2**

### 39 Comprensión

1. ¿Cuáles son los tres estados de Estados Unidos más elegidos por los emigrantes puertorriqueños?

2. ¿Cómo se sienten los puertorriqueños con respecto a la decisión de emigrar a Estados Unidos?

3. Según Rodríguez, ¿cómo logran conseguir trabajo los pocos que lo consiguen?

4. ¿Por qué para Rodríguez era mejor trabajar como camarero que como ingeniero?

 **1.3, 4.2**

### 40 Analice

Si Ud. estuviera en una situación similar a la de los ingenieros puertorriqueños, ¿qué cree que haría? ¿Intentaría trabajar en otro ámbito o pensaría en emigrar para ejercer su profesión? ¿Por qué?

---

○○○    La crisis lleva a...

VÍVELO **HOY**

Similar historia describe De León, de 33 años, también, casado y con estudios en Ingeniería Eléctrica y una maestría[5] en Administración de Empresas.

Luego de trabajar desde 2006 como ingeniero en varias compañías de telecomunicaciones, la última de ellas no renovó su contrato y quedó desempleado en una isla que acumula ya casi ocho años en recesión.

"El campo está saturado: Hay mucha más oferta que demanda", indica De León, quien desde hace tan solo unas semanas vive y trabaja en Nueva York, un estado donde reside una amplísima comunidad puertorriqueña y que en la actualidad es el tercer destino más frecuente entre los emigrantes de la isla, antecedido por Florida y Pennsylvania.

Hasta ahora, De León nunca había pensado en emigrar, porque siempre había querido quedarse en su isla natal, pero cuando se vio sin empleo se dio cuenta de que "me iba a ser difícil encontrar trabajo en Puerto Rico".

Según las estadísticas oficiales más recientes, durante 2012 Puerto Rico perdió 1,5 % de su población a causa de la emigración [...]. Por su parte, Rodríguez, el más joven de este trío de ingenieros (27 años), coincide con sus colegas en que la ingeniería en Puerto Rico está "sumamente saturada" de profesionales.

"Hay muchísimos estudiantes que terminan la universidad con notas perfectas, revalidan estudios y obtienen certificaciones, pero aún así no consiguen trabajo y muchos de los que sí lo logran es por amiguismo[6]", asegura.

Rodríguez cuenta con estudios graduados en Ingeniería Civil y una maestría en Administración de Proyectos de Construcción, pero en su isla natal únicamente ha podido encontrar trabajo como camarero.

Admite que como mozo lograba más dinero que cuando alguna empresa lo contrataba por horas trabajando bajo contratos de servicios profesionales, una modalidad que no le garantiza ningún tipo de protección o cobertura social[7].

Ahora, el joven ingeniero se encuentra en la ciudad de Saint Joseph, Missouri, desde donde dice sentirse "asustado, solo, nervioso" porque no conoce a nadie, pero a la vez "contento de haber iniciado una aventura o un capítulo nuevo" en el libro de su vida.

Al igual que sus colegas de estudios, Rodríguez hubiera preferido seguir viviendo en Puerto Rico, pero, ante la falta de perspectivas profesionales que se ajusten a sus estudios, "no me quedaba otra opción".

[5] master's degree    [6] thanks to personal contacts    [7] social security

🔍 **Búsqueda:** migración de universitarios puertorriqueños a estados unidos

### Essential Instruction

1. For Common Core practice, have students answer the **Analice** questions. Go over the answers as a class.
2. Introduce **Escritura** by asking students about interesting biographies they have read. Then go over the introduction about biographies.
3. Before students begin **Actividad 41**, allow them time to prepare their immigrant backstories.

# Escritura

## Una biografía  1.3

Una biografía es un relato escrito que narra la vida de una persona desde su nacimiento hasta su muerte. Suele estar escrita en tercera persona y describe los sucesos más sobresalientes de la vida de esa persona, incluidos aspectos de su infancia, sus logros y fracasos personales o profesionales, y cualquier otro aspecto que resulte de interés.

### ¡Comunicación!

**41 La vida del emigrante** 👥 Interpersonal/Presentational Communication  1.1, 1.3

Trabaje con un(a) compañero/a. Imagine que uno es periodista y el otro es un emigrante puertorriqueño que vive en Estados Unidos. Túrnense para hacer las preguntas del siguiente cuestionario. Tomen nota de las respuestas y usen esa información para escribir una biografía en la que relate la historia del emigrante.

#### Cuestionario para la biografía

- ¿En qué lugar de Puerto Rico nació?
- ¿Cómo era su vida y su familia allí?
- ¿A qué se dedicaban sus padres?
- ¿A qué edad emigró a Estados Unidos?
- ¿Emigró solo o con alguien más?
- ¿Cuáles fueron los motivos para emigrar?
- ¿A qué lugar de Estados Unidos emigró?
- ¿Conocía a alguien allí?
- ¿Cómo fue su vida en Estados Unidos en los primeros tiempos?
- ¿Cómo es su vida ahora?
- ¿Regresa a menudo a Puerto Rico? ¿Por qué?
- ¿Qué aspectos de la vida puertorriqueña le provocan cierta nostalgia?
- ¿Cómo cree que sería su vida si se hubiera quedado en la isla?

Tenga en cuenta que el entrevistado dará sus respuestas en primera persona, pero Ud. deberá cambiar el punto de vista y redactar la biografía en tercera persona.

*Puerto Rico, Estado Libre Asociado de Estados Unidos*

### RESOURCES

 Avenue

Answers _____
**41** *Las biografías variarán.*

### Reference Desk

Before students begin writing their biographies in **Actividad 41**, remind them that their biographies should include an introduction and a closing paragraph. You may want to tell students to give the profile a catchy title as well.

### Pre-AP

Have students complete the activities on pp. 333–334 to help them prepare for the writing sections of the AP® exam.

## Differentiated Learning

### Heritage Learners
Have heritage learners use the questions from **Actividad 41** to interview a family member or friend about their experiences. They can submit their biographical reports via Avenue.

### Accelerate/Expand
Tell students to imagine that they are a Puerto Rican engineer who has recently emigrated to the United States. Ask them to write an e-mail to a friend or family member back home in which they talk about their experiences during the first month.

## Extensión    Conéctese: los estudios sociales

*La Voz del Centro* es un programa radial en el que se tratan temas interesantes sobre la historia, la cultura y la sociedad de Puerto Rico y el Caribe. El eje central del programa son las entrevistas que realiza el conductor del programa, Ángel Collado Schwarz.

A continuación, escuchará dos segmentos de la emisión N.° 50, una entrevista con el profesor Amilcar Tirado sobre el tema de la emigración puertorriqueña a los Estados Unidos.

### ¡Comunicación!

**42  Antonia Pantoja, una puertorriqueña visionaria**   **1.2, 1.3**

**Interpretive/Presentational Communication**

Escuche el segmento inicial de la entrevista sobre Antonia Pantoja, una puertorriqueña que emigró a Estados Unidos, y responda las siguientes preguntas.

1. ¿Dónde realizó su labor comunitaria Antonia Pantoja?
2. ¿En qué década realizó ese trabajo?
3. ¿A qué nivel de estudios quería Pantoja que accedieran los puertorriqueños?
4. ¿Qué medalla recibió por su labor?

Busque más información en la internet sobre la vida y la obra de Antonia Pantoja. Luego, imagine que Ud. es un emigrante puertorriqueño que pudo prosperar en Nueva York en la década de 1950 gracias al trabajo comunitario realizado por Antonia Pantoja. Escriba una nota de agradecimiento para ella con los detalles de la ayuda que recibió.

**43  Puertorriqueños en Orlando**   **Interpretive/Presentational Communication**  **1.2, 1.3**

Escuche el segmento final de la entrevista sobre la gran emigración de puertorriqueños a la Florida, principalmente a Orlando. Diga si las siguientes afirmaciones son verdaderas o falsas.

1. Como parte de la ola migratoria, se han instalado en Orlando bancos, medios de comunicación y centros de educación puertorriqueños.
2. Este movimiento migratorio tiene exactamente las mismas características que la emigración puertorriqueña de mediados del siglo pasado.
3. Los puertorriqueños que emigran a Orlando son en su mayoría profesionales.
4. Estos inmigrantes rompen todos los lazos que los unían a Puerto Rico.
5. Hay un cuento de Magali García Ramis que habla de esos emigrantes.

Piense en lo que leyó en la Lectura informativa sobre la emigración actual de puertorriqueños a Estados Unidos. Sume a esa información lo que se aporta en el archivo de audio. Escriba un párrafo donde detalle las principales características de esta emigración. Puede buscar más datos en la internet si lo necesita.

# Vocabulario 3

## Mejore su comprensión   1.2

Familiarizarse con este vocabulario le ayudará a leer el fragmento de *Cuando era puertorriqueña* más adelante, y a mejorar su comprensión auditiva.

**aptitud** *s.f.* Capacidad para realizar una actividad, profesión o empleo.

**artes domésticas** *exp.* Conocimientos o reglas relacionadas con las tareas de la casa o el hogar.

**artes dramáticas** *exp.* La rama de las artes escénicas relacionadas con la actuación.

**calificar** *v.* Ilustrar, servir como ejemplo.

**cartógrafa** *s.f.* Persona que traza mapas geográficos.

**consejero** *s.m.* Persona que da consejos.

**decepcionar** *v.* No responder a las expectativas.

**desempeñar** *v.* Realizar las funciones propias de un trabajo.

**entrenamiento** *s.m.* Preparación que se lleva a cabo para realizar una actividad.

**entrenar** *v.* Preparar a una persona para practicar una actividad.

**escena** *s.f.* Parte de una obra de teatro.

**modelo** *s.m.f.* Persona que trabaja poniéndose prendas de vestir para mostrarlas.

**papel dramático** *s.m.* Personaje que representa un actor.

*Se dice que Javier Bardem hará el papel de villano en Piratas del Caribe.*

**rebuscar** *v.* Buscar con cuidado en un montón de cosas.

**recitar** *v.* Decir un poema en voz alta.

**topógrafa** *s.f.* Persona que se dedica profesionalmente al estudio de la superficie de un terreno.

**vocacional** *adj.* Relacionado con una vocación o profesión.

### 44 Según su experiencia  1.3

Piense en los siguientes temas e ilústrelos con ejemplos de acuerdo con su propia experiencia.

1. Su modelo favorito/a
2. Su actor o actriz favorita y su papel más famoso
3. Película, libro o actuación que lo ha decepcionado
4. Sus propias aptitudes vocacionales
5. Entrenamiento necesario para ser topógrafo/a
6. Papel que desempeña el consejero en un colegio
7. Materias sobre artes domésticas que se enseñan en el colegio
8. Requisitos o aptitudes necesarias para estudiar artes dramáticas

---

## RESOURCES

 Mejore su comprensión

### Answers

44 *Las respuestas variarán.*

### Reference Desk

1. **Actividades 42** and **43** on p. 334 contain authentic audio, which is an important component of the AP® Spanish exam.
2. In the script for **Actividad 43**, you may want to point out the question: **¿Qué tú comentarías?** Explain that in Puerto Rico, Cuba, and the Dominican Republic, it is common to use the subject pronoun before the verb in short questions with **qué** (**¿Qué tú haces?**).
3. Javier Bardem is a Spanish actor from the Canary Islands. His first major role was in the 1992 Spanish film *Jamón jamón*. Since then, he has starred in numerous productions in both Spain and Hollywood, and has won dozens of awards.
4. Explain that the abbreviation **exp.** in the vocabulary presentation stands for **expresión**.

---

## Differentiated Learning
### Expand
Ask students to research other Puerto Rican civil or political activists. Tell them to chose one person and create a poster featuring a biographical profile and his/her accomplishments. Display the posters in the classroom.

## Special Needs Students
### Auditory Impairment
Allow these students to listen several times to the recordings in **Actividades 42** and **43**. You may also want to provide them with the scripts so that they can follow along as they listen.

**335**

**Answers**

**45 Script**

Isapí era una muchacha india muy hermosa. Su padre era el jefe de la tribu. A la joven india venían a verla los mejores guerreros pero Isapí no quería a nadie porque no podía amar. Era muy fría de corazón. Como nadie la había visto llorar en el pueblo, la llamaban "la que nunca lloró."
La tribu sufrió muchas desgracias. Los hombres morían en las guerras. Viejos y jóvenes lloraban, pero Isapí no lloraba. Ella era indiferente al dolor de todos. El brujo del pueblo consultó con las estrellas y al fin habló: "Para que no tengamos más desgracias, Isapí tiene que llorar". Pero, ¿cómo hacerla llorar si ella no sentía la menor compasión ante el dolor de los otros?
Un día que Isapí iba por un camino del bosque, se le acercó llorando una mujer joven con un niño en los brazos y le mostró a su niño casi muerto. La joven madre le pidió a Isapí que buscara unas hierbas buenas para curar a su hijo pero la muchacha india continuó su camino indiferente.
*Continued on p. 344.*

*Continued on p. 344.*

1. La muchacha india Isapí no quería a nadie porque...
2. La tribu sufrió muchas desgracias y el brujo que consultó a las estrellas dijo...
3. Una mujer en el bosque le pidió a Isapí...
4. El brujo, ante la indiferencia de Isapí, llamó al diablo en esta forma:
5. Desde la primera palabra del brujo...

1. B; 2. A; 3. C; 4. C; 5. A

---

**45  Isapí: La leyenda del sauce llorón**   **1.2, 3.1**

Escuche el relato de "Isapí: La leyenda del sauce llorón". Luego, Ud. oirá la primera parte de una oración y tres terminaciones posibles. Seleccione la letra de la respuesta con la terminación más lógica. La oración y las terminaciones se leerán dos veces.

1. A. ... su padre era el jefe de la tribu.
   B. ... era muy fría de corazón.
   C. ... no venían a verla los mejores guerreros.
2. A. ... que Isapí tenía que llorar.
   B. ... que los hombres morían en las guerras.
   C. ... que Isapí mostraba compasión por todos.
3. A. ... que cuidara un momento a su niño.
   B. ... que viera si su niño estaba muerto.
   C. ... que buscara hierbas buenas para curar a su niño.
4. A. Señor de las sombras, haz que esta mujer no tenga corazón.
   B. Señor de las sombras, haz que esta mujer sea madre.
   C. Señor de las tinieblas, haz que esta mujer viva eternamente llorando.
5. A. ... Isapí fue convirtiéndose en un árbol fresco.
   B. ... Isapí se puso a llorar.
   C. ... Isapí vio crecer un árbol lleno de hojas.

*Un sauce llorón*

**Essential Instruction**

1. For **Actividad 45**, have students listen to the story with their eyes closed. Replay the story and then have students listen to the sentence starters and select the correct endings.
2. After presenting **Gramática**, give additional sentences in the active voice and have students convert them to the passive voice.

# Gramática

## La voz pasiva  1.2, 4.1

### La voz pasiva con *ser*

El uso de la voz pasiva en español es mucho menos frecuente que en inglés. El orden natural de la oración en la voz activa se invierte en la voz pasiva y el sujeto recibe la acción del verbo. Se usa la preposición **por**, seguida de un agente.

La oración se escribe con el participio pasado[1] del verbo conjugado en la voz activa, el cual concuerda en género y en número con el sujeto pasivo.

**Voz activa:** La tormenta **causó** las inundaciones.

**Voz pasiva:** Las inundaciones **fueron causadas por** la tormenta.

- En la construcción pasiva, el verbo **ser** siempre está en el mismo tiempo que el verbo correspondiente de la oración activa.

*Se espera mucha lluvia.*

### Formación de la voz pasiva con *ser*

| Sujeto pasivo | + *ser* + | participio pasado como adjetivo | + *por* + | agente |
|---|---|---|---|---|
| Las lluvias torrenciales | son | pronosticadas | por | los medios. |
| Algunos árboles y casas | fueron | arrasados | por | el tornado. |
| La ayuda humanitaria | será | dada | por | los cooperantes. |

### La voz pasiva con *se*

La voz pasiva con **se** es mucho más común que la pasiva con **ser** y se usa cuando no se menciona al agente de la acción. La construcción es la siguiente:

### Formación de la voz pasiva con *se*

| *Se* + | tercera persona singular o plural del verbo | + | sujeto pasivo |
|---|---|---|---|
| Se | pronostican | | lluvias torrenciales. |
| Se | arrasaron | | algunos árboles y casas. |
| Se | dará | | ayuda humanitaria. |

Cuando el **a** personal precede al sujeto de la voz pasiva con **se**, el verbo siempre está en singular: **Se auxilió** a los damnificados.

[1] El participio pasado funciona como adjetivo en la voz pasiva; por lo tanto, concuerda en género y número con el sujeto pasivo.

## Reference Desk

1. Remind students that while **por** and **para** can both be translated as *for* in certain circumstances, **por** is the only preposition used with the passive voice in Spanish. Tell students to think of **por** in this context as meaning *by*.
2. Point out that with the passive voice using **ser**, the past participle functions as an adjective, and therefore must agree in number and gender with the passive subject (not the agent).

## Culture

**Products/Practices: Activity**
Have students research a Puerto Rican festival or event, such as **Fiestas de la Calle San Sebastián** in San Juan. Ask them to describe the customs surrounding the event using the passive voice.

## Connections

**Literature**
Bring in copies of Taino myths and legends. Have students work in small groups to analyze the stories and then retell them in their own words using the passive voice.

## Differentiated Learning
### Accelerate/Expand
Ask students to research the symbolism of the Weeping Willow in other cultures. Have them compare and contrast what they learned with the story of Isapí.

### Heritage Learners
Ask heritage learners to retell a legend or myth from their family's country of origin.

## Learning Styles
### Kinesthetic Learners
Replay the audio for **Actividad 45** and have students act out the story as they listen.

**337**

---

### Reference Desk

1. See if students can name all the Spanish-speaking countries that have part of the Amazon Rainforest (Colombia, Peru, Venezuela, Ecuador, and Bolivia).
2. As students listen to their classmates' presentations from **Actividad 47**, have them take notes in their Culture Journals.

---

### Critical Thinking

**Analyzing**

Ask the class to brainstorm a list of environmental issues in their community. Have them write sentences, using the passive voice, about what caused these issues.

---

### Connections

**Science**

Ask students to read studies of Puerto Ricans' genetic makeup. Ask students to find out the following: What percentage of Puerto Ricans' ancestry is Taino? African? European? Why have studies found different results in terms of Taino ancestry?

---

**46  Amazonía, pulmón del mundo**  **1.2, 1.3**

Brasil tiene muchos problemas ambientales, al igual que Puerto Rico. Por ejemplo, la tala (*felling*) de árboles en la selva amazónica para despejar pastizales para el ganado causa deforestación. Esta práctica tiene un impacto grave sobre el ambiente, por ejemplo, pérdida de biodiversidad, degradación del hábitat, pérdida del ciclo del agua y modificación del clima global. Cambie las siguientes oraciones a la forma pasiva.

MODELO  La deforestación destruye la selva amazónica.
**La selva amazónica es destruida por la deforestación.**

1. Los ganaderos talan los árboles para hacer pastizales.
2. La desaparición del hábitat de las especies daña la biodiversidad.
3. Los bosques pierden la capacidad de absorber $CO_2$.
4. Los ecologistas estudian el ciclo del agua.
5. La falta de recursos naturales aumenta la pobreza.

*En la selva del Amazonas se talan árboles para despejar campos destinados a pastizales del ganado.*

**¡Comunicación!**  **1.1, 1.3, 2.1, 2.2, 3.1**

**47  Puerto Rico, Isla del Encanto**  **Interpersonal/Presentational Communication**

Puerto Rico es la Isla del Encanto. Para aprender más sobre ella, formen equipos de tres o cuatro personas y preparen una presentación sobre uno de los siguientes temas u otro similar que Uds. elijan.

El mestizaje de personas y culturas en Puerto Rico:

- Los diversos orígenes étnicos: taínos, africanos y españoles
- Las migraciones más recientes de Europa y de Asia

La historia de Puerto Rico:

- Desde la prehistoria hasta la llegada de Cristóbal Colón
- El período colonial español entre 1492 y 1898
- Los piratas del mar Caribe; Puerto Rico en el siglo XX
- La doctrina Monroe y las relaciones con EE. UU.

La geografía de Puerto Rico:

- La isla principal y las islas pequeñas

- Las ciudades más grandes: San Juan y Ponce
- El contraste entre las playas de la costa y las montañas
- La naturaleza: flora y fauna

*A Puerto Rico se lo conoce como la Isla del Encanto.*

La economía de Puerto Rico:

- La importancia del turismo
- El estancamiento de las industrias tradicionales, como la producción de caña de azúcar
- El desarrollo de nuevas industrias: ganadería, industria y construcción
- La alta tasa de desempleo y su relación con los movimientos migratorios

### Essential Instruction

1. Check answers to **Actividad 46** orally as a class.
2. For **Actividad 47**, have each student in the group choose an area of focus to research and present. Group members should share equal presentation time.
3. Have students check their answers to **Actividades 48** and **49** in pairs.
4. Brainstorm definitions for the terms in **Actividad 50** as a class. Then have groups discuss possible solutions and present their ideas to the class. You may want to have them research statistics to support their proposals.

### 48 Puerto Rico a lo largo de la historia  1.2, 1.3, 3.1

Aprenda más sobre la historia de Puerto Rico, poniendo las siguientes oraciones en la forma pasiva.

**MODELO** Los españoles conquistaron a los indígenas taínos en poco tiempo.
**En poco tiempo, los indígenas taínos fueron conquistados por los españoles.**

1. En 1493, Colón descubrió Puerto Rico.
2. En 1509, nombraron gobernador de Puerto Rico a Juan Ponce de León.
3. Los indígenas taínos cultivaban la tierra.
4. En 1522, los españoles llevaron esclavos africanos a la isla.
5. En 1898, expulsaron a España de Puerto Rico.
6. En 1952, los puertorriqueños eligieron por primera vez a un gobernador.

### 49 ¡Quedan cosas por resolver!  1.2, 1.3

Forme oraciones pasivas con **se**, eliminando el agente en negrita.

**MODELO** El acuerdo de paz será logrado por **las partes**.
**Se logrará el acuerdo de paz.**

1. En poco tiempo, la zona de desastre fue atendida por **agencias humanitarias**.
2. Fue aprobada una nueva constitución por **los asambleístas**.
3. Los ciudadanos son representados por **los diputados** de cada circuito.
4. Los actos racistas serán castigados por **la ley**.
5. La ayuda humanitaria para los afectados es solicitada por la **Cruz Roja**.
6. Lo que queda por resolver será abordado por **las nuevas generaciones**.

*Se solicitó ayuda humanitaria para los afectados.*

## ¡Comunicación!

### 50 La protección ambiental  Interpersonal/Presentational Communication  1.1, 1.3, 3.1

En grupos de tres o cuatro comenten el impacto ambiental que tiene la actividad humana.

**Definición de términos**: Primero, hagan una lluvia de ideas sobre las nociones básicas. Definan los siguientes conceptos en sus propias palabras:

| | | | |
|---|---|---|---|
| La erosión | La contaminación | La deforestación | El efecto invernadero |
| El ciclo del agua | La huella ecológica | La biodiversidad | El reciclaje |

**Discusión**: Ahora comenten las medidas que consideren son las mejores para proteger el planeta.
**Presentación**: Presenten sus conclusiones ante la clase.

---

## Differentiated Learning

### Accelerate/Adapt
Have students write additional sentences for **Actividad 48**, using what they learned in the **Cultura** readings.

### Expand
Ask students to research online to find out as much as they can about the Taino people. Have them investigate Taino culture in Puerto Rico at the time of Columbus's arrival: their societal structure, language, homes, agriculture and diet, and religion. Also have them find out why the Taino vanished from the region so rapidly. Have students summarize what they learned in their Culture Journals.

---

### RESOURCES

**WB** Activity 12

**LA** Activity 8

### Answers

**48**
1. Puerto Rico fue descubierto por Colón en 1493.
2. Juan Ponce de León fue nombrado gobernador de Puerto Rico en 1509.
3. La tierra era cultivada por los indígenas taínos.
4. Los esclavos africanos fueron llevados por los españoles a la isla en 1522.
5. España fue expulsada de Puerto Rico en 1898.
6. Un gobernador fue elegido por los puertorriqueños por primera vez en 1952.

**49**
1. En poco tiempo, se atendió la zona de desastre.
2. Se aprobó una nueva constitución.
3. Se representa a los ciudadanos de cada circuito.
4. Se castigarán los actos racistas.
5. Se solicita ayuda humanitaria para los afectados.
6. Se abordará lo que queda por resolver.

**50** *Las respuestas variarán.*

### Reference Desk

Juan Ponce de León (1474–1521) was a Spanish explorer. In 1513 he led an expedition to Florida, which he named.

### Connections

**Technology**
Brainstorm a list of the most important inventions in history. Have students choose 10, find out when they were invented or discovered and by whom, and write sentences using the passive voice. Ex: **El teléfono fue inventado por Alexander Graham Bell en 1876.**

**339**

### Reference Desk

1. As students read through **Sobre la autora**, invite them to guess the meaning of **está a caballo entre dos culturas** (*to be divided between cultures*).
2. The term *Spanglish* was coined by the Puerto Rican author Salvador Tió in the 1940s.

### Connections

**Linguistics**
Explain that Spanglish can involve hybrid words (e.g., **rentar**, **lonchar**); semantic extensions (**carpeta** to mean *carpet*); calques (literal translations such as **te llamo para atrás**); loan words (**sándwich**); or code switching (alternating between languages, e.g., **tengo que firmar un nuevo** lease **mañana**). Ask students to look up or invent examples of each type.

### Pre-AP

**Course Theme: La belleza y la estética**

---

# *Lectura literaria*

## Cuando era puertorriqueña   1.2, 2.2, 3.1
### de *Esmeralda Santiago*

*Esmeralda "Negi" Santiago*

### Sobre la autora

Esmeralda "Negi" Santiago nació en San Juan de Puerto Rico en 1948 y se crió en Macún y Santurce. En 1961, a los trece años, su mamá decidió mudar a la familia a Nueva York. Santiago aprendió inglés mientras se adaptaba a su nuevo entorno y, luego, fue aceptada en la escuela secundaria Performing Arts de Nueva York donde estudió teatro y danza. Se graduó magna cum laude de la Universidad de Harvard y tiene una maestría en escritura creativa del Sarah Lawrence College. Su esposo, el director Frank Cantor, y ella tienen una compañía de producción cinematográfica llamada Cantomedia. Empezó su carrera literaria como productora y escritora de documentales y películas educativas.

Su primer libro, *Cuando era puertorriqueña*, son sus memorias sobre su niñez en Puerto Rico y Estados Unidos, publicado originalmente en inglés como *When I was Puerto Rican* en 1993. Como tantos otros emigrantes, ya no se siente puertorriqueña, pero tampoco es completamente estadounidense: está a caballo entre dos culturas.

### Antes de leer  1.3

Piense en una palabra o expresión que le resulte difícil decir en español o en inglés. ¿Cómo se siente cuando le cuesta expresar algo en otro idioma? ¿Cómo se ayuda con las manos, la expresión de la cara y el tono de voz para comunicar algo nuevo o difícil a otra persona?

### Estrategia 3.1

**El *espanglés* como forma de bilingüismo**

Hablar ***espanglés***, o Spanglish, es combinar fluidamente palabras del español y del inglés, cuando no se hablan bien ambos idiomas o cuando se vive inmerso en una cultura donde se entienden ambos idiomas. ¿Qué palabras diría Ud. en *espanglés* por prisa o porque el significado le parece más preciso? Las palabras en *espanglés* indican una cultura mezclada. No serán difíciles de entender si Ud. las pronuncia en voz alta.

### 51 Practique la estrategia  1.2, 3.1

¿Qué significan las expresiones en cursiva en esta conversación entre Esmeralda y su amiga Yolanda? En una hoja aparte, escriba las expresiones correctamente en inglés y su traducción al español, como se ve en la tabla a continuación.

—¿Te preguntó el Míster Barone, *llu no*, lo que querías hacer *juen llu gro up*?

— Sí, pero *ay dint no*. ¿Y tú?

—Yo tampoco sé. *Ji sed* que *ay laik tu jelp pipel*. Pero, *llu no*, a mí no me gusta mucho la gente.

| Diálogo en *Espanglés* | Diálogo en inglés | Traducción al español |
|---|---|---|
| ¿Tienes *jobis*? | *Do you have a hobby?* | ¿Tienes un pasatiempo? |

---

### Essential Instruction

1. As you go through **Sobre la autora**, pause to ask comprehension questions.
2. Read the **Estrategia**. Write examples of Spanglish on the board; have students pronounce them aloud and determine their meaning.
3. Have students complete **Antes de leer** and **Actividad 51** in small groups.
4. Before they read, have students scan the story for cognates and words they learned in **Vocabulario 3**.
5. Play the recording, pausing for students to answer the during-reading questions.

## Cuando era puertorriqueña
### de *Esmeralda Santiago*

*"Quería ser una jíbara, quería ser cartógrafa y, después, topógrafa".*

 **1.2, 2.2, 3.1**

[...] Nos habíamos mudado a la Ellery Street. [...] Tuve que cambiar de escuelas, así que Mami me llevó a la P.S., donde haría mi noveno grado. [...] Me dieron una serie de exámenes, los cuales indicaron que, aunque no podía hablar el inglés muy bien, lo podía escribir y leer al nivel del décimo grado. [...]

Un día, Míster Barone, el consejero vocacional de la escuela, me llamó a su oficina.

[...]—Bueno —[...] hablándome despacio para que yo entendiera— ¿qué quieres ser cuando seas grande?

—Yo no sé.

Rebuscó[1] entre sus papeles.

[...] —¿Y no has pensado en lo que vas a ser cuando seas grande?

Cuando yo era nena, quería ser una jíbara[2]. Cuando me hice mayor, quería ser cartógrafa, después topógrafa. Pero desde que llegamos a Brooklyn, no había pensado mucho en el futuro.

—No, señor.

Bajó los lentes a sus ojos y rebuscó entre los papeles otra vez.

—¿Tienes *jobis*? —no entendí lo que me decía—. *Jobis. Jobis* [...] cosas que te gustan hacer en tu tiempo libre.

—¡Ah, sí! —traté de imaginar qué yo hacía en casa que pudiera calificar[3] como un *jobi.* —Me gusta leer.

[...] —Sí, eso ya lo sabemos —sacó un papel de su escritorio y lo estudió—. [...] También puede ser que te guste la comunicación. Como maestra, por ejemplo.

Recordé a Miss Brown parada al frente de un salón lleno de *tineyers* desordenados[4][...].

—No creo que me gustaría.

[...] —¿Por qué no lo piensas, y hablamos otro día? [...] —Eres una chica inteligente, Esmeralda. [...]

Camino a casa, me acompañaba otra niña del noveno grado, Yolanda. Llevaba tres años en Nueva York, pero hablaba tan poco inglés como yo. Hablábamos en *espanglés*, una combinación de inglés y español [...].

[...] Unos días más tarde, el Míster Barone me llamó a su oficina.

[...] —Quisiera ser una modelo —le dije al Míster Barone. [...] —Yo quiero aparecer en la televisión.

[1] search through    [2] peasant    [3] qualify    [4] unruly

**RESOURCES**

 Cuando era puertorriqueña

**Answers**

1. Para orientarla sobre su vocación profesional.
2. Es una mezcla de español e inglés; la ortografía fonética muestra lo difícil que resulta pronunciar una lengua germánica para alguien que habla una lengua romance.
3. Realmente no lo sabe. Quería ser jíbara, quería ser cartógrafa y quería ser topógrafa.

**53** *Las respuestas variarán, pero deben relacionarse con el hecho de que Esmeralda tiene que empezar una nueva vida, tiene que aprender un nuevo idioma y, básicamente, tiene que volver a planear su futuro.*

**1.2**

### 52 Comprensión

1. ¿Para qué llama Míster Barone a Esmeralda?

2. ¿Qué es el *espanglés* y cómo se nota la dificultad para pronunciar un idioma muy distinto?

3. ¿Sabe Esmeralda realmente qué quiere ser? Cite ideas del texto que lo reflejen.

**1.3**

### 53 Analice

¿Cómo afecta el choque de culturas a Esmeralda? Analice los diálogos y explique cómo se refleja el efecto en Esmeralda.

---

**Differentiated Learning**
**Heritage Learners**
Ask heritage learners whether they or members of their community feel **a caballo entre dos culturas**. Also ask them to describe any use of Spanglish in their cultural communities.

**Learning Styles**
**Visual Learners**
Encourage students to use a graphic organizer, such as a story map, as they read pp. 341–342.

**54**

1. Tenía que aprender una escena dramática.
2. Solo sabía pronunciar las palabras, pero no sabía lo que significaban todas.
3. Porque Esmeralda se preparó muy bien para la prueba.

**55** *Respuesta posible:*

Cuando Mister Barone menciona que podría ingresar a la Escuela Superior de Artes Dramáticas, Esmeralda decide que eso es lo que debe hacer para poder irse de Brooklyn. Ella se prepara con esfuerzo y disciplina para poder pasar los exámenes de admisión y así lo logra.

### Expansion

Have students read newspaper interviews with the sociolinguist and professor Ilán Stavans, a world authority on Spanglish. Alternatively, bring in excerpts of his book *Spanglish: The Making of a New American Language.* Use Stavan's assertions about Spanglish as a starting point for class discussion.

 **1.2**

## 54 Comprensión

1. ¿Qué debía hacer Esmeralda para que la aceptaran en la escuela de actuación?

2. ¿Qué sabía Esmeralda del soliloquio que se aprendió?

3. ¿Por qué dice Míster Barone que "nos va a salir la cosa"?

 **1.3**

## 55 Analice

Esmeralda quería irse de Brooklyn. ¿Por qué y qué hace para lograrlo? Analice los eventos del pasaje.

—Ah, pues entonces quieres ser actriz. [...] Yo solo sé de una escuela que entrena actores. [...] Dice aquí que tienes que ir a una prueba. [...] ¿Has desempeñado alguna vez un papel dramático en frente del público?

—Un año fui la maestra de ceremonias en el programa musical de mi escuela. En Puerto Rico. [...]

[...] —Déjame llamarles y averiguar lo que necesitas hacer. [...]

Salí de su oficina feliz, confiando[5] en que algo bueno había pasado. [...]

"No tengo miedo...No tengo miedo...No tengo miedo...". Todos los días andaba de la escuela a casa repitiéndome esas palabras. [...] Fue en estas caminatas angustiadas[6] que decidí que me tenía que salir de Brooklyn. [...] Cuando el Mister Barone me habló de Performing Arts High School, supe lo que tenía que hacer.

—¡Las pruebas son en menos de un mes! Tienes que aprender una escena dramática [...] en frente de un jurado[7]. [...]

El Míster Barone se encargó de prepararme para la prueba. Seleccionó un soliloquio[8] de una obra de Sydney Howard titulada *The Silver Cord* [...].

—Míster Garri, el maestro de gramática, te dirigirá... Y *Missis* Johnson te hablará acerca de lo que debes de poner y esas cosas.

Mi parte era la de Cristina, una joven casada confrontando[9] a su suegra. Aprendí el soliloquio fonéticamente, bajo la dirección de Míster Gatti. [...]

—No tenemos tiempo de aprender lo que quiere decir cada palabra –dijo Míster Gatti—. Solo asegúrate de que las pronuncies todas.

*Missis* Jonson, quien era la maestra de artes domésticas[10], me llamó a su oficina.

[...]Me senté tiesa[11] mientras *Missis* Jonson y Míster Barone me hacían preguntas que se imaginaban el jurado en Performing Arts me iba a preguntar.

—¿De dónde eres?

—De Puerto Rico.

—¡No! —dijo *Missis* Johnson—, *Porto Rico.* Pronuncia la r suave. Otra vez.

—¿Tienes algún *jobi*? –me preguntó Míster Barone, y esta vez supe cómo contestar.

—Me gusta bailar y me gusta el cine.

—¿Por qué quieres estudiar en esta escuela?

*Missis* Johnson y Míster Barone me habían hecho memorizar lo que debía decir si me preguntaban eso.

—Quiero estudiar en la Performing Arts High School por su reputación académica y para recibir entrenamiento en las artes dramáticas.

—¡Muy bien! ¡Muy bien! —Míster Barone se frotó las manos[12] y le guiñó a *Missis* Johnson—. Creo que nos va a salir la cosa.

[5] trust   [6] anguished   [7] panel of judges   [8] soliloquy   [9] confront   [10] home economics
[11] stiff   [12] rub one's hands (together)

## Essential Instruction

1. For Common Core practice, have students answer the **Analice** questions. Discuss the answers as a class.
2. Point out the **Pregunta clave** on p. 343.
3. Read through the **Proyectos** on pp. 343–344. Allow students to choose project(s) that most appeal to them. Provide detailed rubrics so that students are aware of the expectations for these tasks.
4. In **Actividad A**, allow your heritage learners to start with a poem in Spanish rather than in English.
5. After students complete their presentations in **Actividad A**, display the groups of poems in the classroom.

# Para concluir

## Proyectos

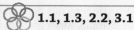
¿Pregunta clave

¿Cómo afectan las decisiones políticas la identidad cultural de un país?

### A  ¡Manos a la obra!    1.1, 1.3, 2.2, 3.1

Trabaje con un(a) compañero/a. Busquen en la internet algún poema de los poetas del Nuyorican Poets Cafe, por ejemplo, de sus fundadores Miguel Algarín, Miguel Piñero o Lucky Cienfuegos. Elijan un poema que esté escrito en inglés.

- Primero, analicen y comenten el poema en detalle. Tengan en cuenta su contenido, es decir, el tema del que habla el poema, pero también su forma (la métrica, la rima, el uso del lenguaje).

- Luego, hagan una traducción del poema al español. Puede ser una versión libre, o una traducción más literal, palabra por palabra.

- Por último, hagan una tercera versión en la que incluyan una mezcla de ambos idiomas, dejando algunas palabras en inglés e insertando algunos términos que fusionen ambos idiomas.

Presenten las tres versiones a la clase.

Nuyorican Poets Cafe

### B  En resumen  1.3, 2.1, 2.2

Repase lo que aprendió sobre los aspectos políticos de Puerto Rico que han ido marcando la identidad de su pueblo a lo largo de la historia. Complete el cuadro de abajo, con los efectos que tuvo cada suceso político y luego debata con un(a) compañero/a su opinión: ¿los efectos son positivos o negativos para los puertorriqueños?

| Suceso político | Efectos sobre los puertorriqueños | ¿Es positivo o negativo? |
|---|---|---|
| Colonización española | | |
| Colonización estadounidense | | |
| Incorporación como Estado Libre Asociado | | |
| Establecimiento de dos idiomas oficiales | | |
| Eliminación de exenciones contributivas | | |

Answers

**Script** *Continued from p. 334.*
Antonia Pantoja, pues, dejó sus memorias. Ella murió en el año pasado, lamentablemente; dejó poco antes de morir unas memorias sobre su participación, sobre su vida. Y me parece que en algún momento ya sea muy pronto, lo más pronto posible debe haber una un reconocimiento a toda la labor que realizó Antonia Pantoja. Inclusive Antonia Pantoja, pues, recibió la Medalla Presidencial de los Estados Unidos que muy pocos puertorriqueños en ese sentido pues la han recibido por su labor meritoria en el trabajo de comunidad.

A  *Las presentaciones variarán.*

B  *Las respuestas variarán.*

### Reference Desk

Point out the **Pregunta clave**. Ask students to think again about the question, this time in relation to their own culture.

## Differentiated Learning

### Accelerate/Expand

Bring in other literary examples in which Hispanic-Americans explore their feelings about being caught between two cultures, such as **"América"** by Richard Blanco, "Half-Mexican" by Juan Felipe Herrera, or "Bilingual Blues" by Gustavo Pérez Firmat.

### Heritage Learners

Have heritage learners ask their family members about any stories, songs, or movies they like that capture their own feelings as immigrants. Have these students read, listen to, or watch the piece and write a reaction piece to it.

**Script** *Continued from p. 336.*
De pronto, una misteriosa fuerza la obligó a detenerse en el camino y oyó la voz del brujo que llamaba al diablo: —Señor de las sombras, haz que esta fría mujer que no tiene compasión de una madre, no sea nunca madre. Señor de las tinieblas, haz que esta mujer sin corazón, que no ha llorado nunca, viva eternamente llorando... Isapí no oyó más. Desde la primera palabra del brujo, había ido poco a poco transformándose, metiendo los pies en la tierra como duras raíces, sintiendo su cuerpo endurecerse como un tronco y crecer su pelo como grandes ramas llenas de hojas. Al acabar de hablar el brujo, la hermosa Isapí estaba convertida en un árbol fresco y verde que hoy se conoce con el nombre de sauce llorón.

**C** *Los resúmenes variarán.*

**D** *Las respuestas variarán.*

**E** *Los comentarios variarán.*
1898; 1940, 1970; Puerto Rico declara el español como única lengua oficial; Puerto Rico declara el español y el inglés como lenguas oficiales; 2006

---

**C    ¡A escribir!**  **1.3, 2.2**

Investigue en la internet la vida de algún puertorriqueño que haya emigrado a Estados Unidos y se haya hecho famoso, por ejemplo, Ricky Martin, Chayanne, Rita Moreno o Luis Guzmán. Escriba un resumen de su historia. ¿Cree Ud. que estos personajes enfrentaron dificultades adicionales en su camino a la fama por tratarse de emigrantes? Justifique su opinión con datos concretos sobre el personaje elegido.

*Chayanne*

**D    Una fusión de dos idiomas    Conéctese: el lenguaje** 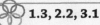 **1.3, 2.2, 3.1**

En la tabla de abajo se muestran algunos ejemplos de términos del *espanglés*, esa mezcla de español e inglés que es la herramienta cultural de integración e identidad para millones de hispanos que viven en Estados Unidos. Los poetas y dramaturgos nuyorriqueños fueron unos de los primeros en llevar el *espanglés* a la literatura. Investigue en la internet otros términos del *espanglés* para agregar a la tabla.

| espanglés | español |
|---|---|
| remembrear | recordar |
| printear | imprimir |
| webear | navegar en la internet |
| hasta sun | hasta pronto |
| monchar | comer con apetito |
| janguear | salir con amigos |
| | |
| | |
| | |
| | |

**E    Puerto Rico y su historia    Conéctese: la historia    1.1, 1.3, 2.2, 3.1**

Investigue los principales sucesos de la vida política de Puerto Rico y complete la línea de tiempo con los datos que faltan. Luego, compare y comente los sucesos con un(a) compañero/a.

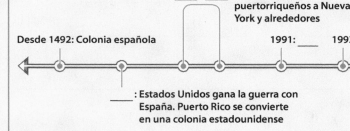

**Essential Instruction**

1. Before assigning **Actividad C**, have students review the information on biographies on p. 333.
2. Have students share their answers to **Actividad D** with the class; create a class dictionary of Spanglish terms.
3. Check **Actividad E** by drawing a timeline on the board with only the years filled in. See if students can fill in the information without consulting their papers from **Actividad E**.
4. For the **Vocabulario de la Unidad 8**, ask students to determine a few categories that could be used to sort the words. Then have students list the words in those categories.

# Vocabulario de la Unidad 8  1.2

| | | | | | | |
|---|---|---|---|---|---|---|
| | **al este/al sur** to the east/south | | la | **derrota** defeat | el/la | **mulato/a** person of mixed |
| | **acompañar** to accompany | | | **desempeñar** to perform | | blood (African and European) |
| el | **acuerdo** treaty | | el | **desierto** desert | | **nacer** to be born |
| | **afrontar** to face | | la | **dictadura** dictatorship | los | **negros africanos** black people |
| el/la | **agricultor/a** farmer | | | **disminuir la pobreza** to | | from Africa |
| la | **agricultura** agriculture | | | decrease the poverty level | la | **nieve** snow |
| el | **alto nivel** high level | | el | **ejército** army | el/la | **obrero/a** blue-collar worker |
| | **apoyar** to support | | | **elegir (i)** to elect | la | **ola** wave |
| | **aprobar (ue) una ley** to pass | | | **en favor/en contra** in | el | **papel dramático** theater role |
| | a law | | | favor/against | el | **partido político** political party |
| el | **árbol** tree | | el | **encarcelamiento** imprisonment | | **perjudicar** to harm |
| la | **arena** sand | | | **encontrarse en riesgo** to be | la | **playa** beach |
| las | **artes domésticas** | | | at risk | la | **población** population |
| | Home Economics | | el | **entorno** surroundings | el | **poder militar** military power |
| las | **artes dramáticas** | | el | **entrenamiento** training | el/la | **político/a** politician |
| | Performing Arts | | | **entrenar** to train | | **por debajo de cero** below zero |
| la | **atmósfera** atmosphere | | la | **época de lluvias** rainy season | los | **prejuicios raciales** |
| | **blanco/a** white person | | la | **escena** scene | | racial prejudices |
| | **caer** to fall | | los | **escombros** rubble | el/la | **presidente/a** president |
| | **calificar** to qualify | | los | **esfuerzos** efforts | el | **proceso electoral** |
| la | **Cámara de Diputados** House | | el | **gabinete presidencial** | | electoral process |
| | of Representatives | | | president's cabinet | | **prolongado/a** extended |
| el/la | **campesino/a** peasant | | la | **ganadería** cattle raising | | **quedar*** to be located |
| el/la | **candidato/a** candidate | | el/la | **ganadero/a** cattle rancher | el | **rayo** lightning bolt |
| el/la | **cartógrafo/a** cartographer | | | **ganar las elecciones** | | **rebuscar** to search carefully |
| la | **censura** censorship | | | to win elections | | **recitar** to recite |
| el | **clima tropical** tropical weather | | el | **gobernador** governor | las | **reformas** reforms |
| | **cometer violaciones** | | el | **gobernante** ruler | el | **régimen militar** military regime |
| | to commit violations | | el | **golpe de estado** coup d'état | | **registrarse** to register |
| el | **comunismo** communism | | | (government takeover) | el | **relámpago** lightning |
| el/la | **consejero/a vocacional** | | los | **gremios** unions | el/la | **representante** representative |
| | vocational adviser | | la | **guerra** war | | **resolver** to solve |
| | **conservador/a** (adj.) | | el/la | **hispano/a** Hispanic person | el | **río** river |
| | conservative | | el | **huracán** hurricane | la | **selva** jungle |
| | **constituirse** to become | | la | **igualdad de clases sociales** | el | **Senado** Senate |
| el | **consumo de gasolina** | | | equality of social classes | la | **sequía** drought |
| | gas consumption | | | **imponer una doctrina** | el | **siglo** century |
| la | **contaminación ambiental** | | | to impose a doctrine | el | **sindicato** worker's union |
| | environmental pollution | | la | **industria** industry | el | **socialismo** socialism |
| la | **costa** coast | | el | **industrial** industrialist | el/la | **socialista** socialist |
| la | **crisis económica** economic crisis | | la | **inundación** flood | el | **terremoto** earthquake |
| | **de sangre indígena** | | la | **isla** island | el/la | **topógrafo/a** topographer |
| | of indigenous blood | | | **liberal** (adj.) liberal | la | **tormenta** storm |
| | **decepcionar** to disappoint | | la | **libertad de expresión** freedom | el | **trueno** thunder |
| | **declarar huelga/paro** to | | | of speech | la | **ubicación** location |
| | declare a strike | | el | **líder sindical** union leader | el | **valle** valley |
| | **dejar a su paso** to leave in | | el | **llano** prairie | la | **victoria** victory |
| | its wake | | el/la | **mestizo/a** person of | la | **vida** life |
| la | **democracia** democracy | | | mixed blood (indigenous | | **vivir** to live |
| los | **derechos humanos** | | | and European) | el | **volcán activo** active volcano |
| | human rights | | la | **mezcla** mix | | **votar por** to vote for |
| | **derrocar el gobierno** to | | las | **montañas** mountains | el | **voto popular** popular vote |
| | overthrow the government | | las | **muertes** deaths | | |

*Ver otros significados de **quedar** en la página 323.

---

## Differentiated Learning
### Accelerate
Ask students to brainstorm the biggest environmental or political problems that their generation will face. Have them choose one problem and write a blog post about it; they should propose a few solutions. Students can submit their posts via Avenue.

## Learning Styles
### Visual Learners
Have students create word webs for the unit vocabulary. For example, they can create one web with **la política** at the center, another with **la naturaleza** at the center, etc.

## Answers

*Script from p. 334, Act. 43.*
—Hablando de Florida, como sabemos, en los últimos años ha habido una gran emigración de puertorriqueños a Florida, particularmente Orlando. Y más aún, en estos últimos años vemos como la banca se está moviendo allí, Banco Popular, la Hora RG, vemos los medios de comunicación, el *Nuevo Día* que abre su versión en Orlando, vemos los centros de educación, como Ana G. Méndez que está abriendo allí. ¿Qué tú comentarías sobre todo este tipo de emigración distinta a la que ocurrió en los cincuenta?
—Definitivamente esto es un cambio, o un momento, o un nuevo elemento, dentro de la emigración puertorriqueña, porque no es una emigración de trabajadores no diestros, sino, mayormente son personas preparadas profesionales que emigran a Estados Unidos. Y en ese sentido muchas de ellas no tienen problemas de empleo, conseguir empleo o vincularse con más seguridad dentro de la sociedad norteamericana, pero manteniendo sus lazos culturales con Puerto Rico. De hecho hay un cuento de la profesora Magali García Ramis sobre, que toca este tema, ¿no? Los puertorriqueños que emigran a estos lugares que siempre van, pero vienen y compran cuando vienen en las Navidades. Siempre están en la en la búsqueda de comprar artesanía, maraca, lo que sea puertorriqueño para llevárselo a Estados Unidos a sus lugares de vivienda. Y mantienen unos lazos de algunas tradiciones, costumbres puertorriqueñas en los lugares que ellos están viviendo.

**345**

## ¿Sabía que...?

El Carnaval del Diablo se viene realizando en Colombia desde 1847 para celebrar la paz entre dos pueblos del municipio de Riosucio que, según cuentan, se unieron para evitar el castigo que el diablo les tenía reservado si no acababan con su enemistad.

### Essential Instruction

1. Begin with a discussion of the **Pregunta clave**. Ask students to think about cultural elements that form part of celebrations and festivals.
2. Point out Colombia on the map. Ask students to share what they know about the country.
3. Draw attention to the culture photo and question. Encourage students to watch for the photo and the answer later in the unit.
4. Point out the QR code, the video question, and the screen shot from "**El Día de los Muertos**." Encourage students to watch the video as often as they like.
5. Have students read and ask questions about **Mis metas**.

# Unidad

# 9

# Festejos con tradición

Escanee el código QR para mirar el video "El Día de los Muertos".

El Día de los Muertos es una celebración que se hace en honor de los difuntos. ¿En qué fechas y en qué lugares tiene lugar esta celebración y qué actividades se realizan para celebrarla? Explique en detalle su respuesta.

Colombia

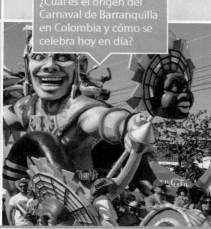

¿Cuál es el origen del Carnaval de Barranquilla en Colombia y cómo se celebra hoy en día?

## Pregunta clave

?

¿Qué aspectos de la cultura de un país se reflejan en sus fiestas y tradiciones?

## Mis metas

### En esta unidad:

- ▶ Usaré expresiones relacionadas con las celebraciones del mundo hispano.
- ▶ Distinguiré los usos del infinitivo y las preposiciones **por** y **para**.
- ▶ Aprenderé sobre varias festividades tradicionales de Colombia y cómo se celebran.
- ▶ Distinguiré el significado de palabras y frases según el contexto.
- ▶ Repasaré los usos de las preposiciones y las frases preposicionales.
- ▶ Leeré un artículo sobre la fiesta de las 'brujitas' y la celebración tradicional de los 'angelitos'.
- ▶ Escucharé una entrevista con un colombiano sobre las celebraciones de su país.
- ▶ Escribiré una publicación en una red social sobre las fiestas colombianas desde el punto de vista de un extranjero cuya estadía coincide con una celebración.
- ▶ Desarrollaré nuevas destrezas de vocabulario.
- ▶ Repasaré el uso de los diminutivos y los aumentativos en español.
- ▶ Leeré el cuento "Un señor muy viejo con unas alas enormes" del colombiano Gabriel García Márquez.

trescientos cuarenta y siete | 347

Answers

**Video question** *Respuesta posible:* El Día de los Muertos se celebra el primero y el dos de noviembre en México, América Central y en muchas comunidades de Estados Unidos. Las personas hacen altares en honor de los muertos y los adornan con fotos de los difuntos, flores amarillas y papel picado. También ponen agua (porque el viaje es largo y los difuntos vienen sedientos) y platos con sal (porque la sal purifica). Las familias cocinan las comidas que les gustaban a los difuntos y pasan el día recordando anécdotas de los momentos que pasaron con ellos antes de morir.

**Culture question**
Tiene raíces en la mezcla de tres culturas: la española, la africana y la indígena. Hoy en día, se celebra con música, bailes, disfraces y carrozas, máscaras y ferias de artesanías.

## Reference Desk

1. Ask students to read the **Pregunta clave** and speculate about the theme of the unit and the vocabulary and culture they might encounter.
2. Draw attention to the screen shot from "**El Día de los Muertos.**" See if students can identify any of the items (**papel picado, velas, flores, una calavera pintada**).
3. Remind students with eBook access they can click on the red country on p. 347 to link directly to Wikipedia.

## Differentiated Learning
### Heritage Learners
Ask heritage learners if the Day of the Dead is celebrated in their family's country of origin. If so, ask them to describe the celebration, and have the class compare and contrast it with what they saw in the video "**El Día de los Muertos.**"

## Multiple Intelligences
### Verbal-Linguistic
Review and preview the unit vocabulary and grammar by asking questions such as: **¿Cuáles son los días festivos que celebra tu familia? ¿Qué haces para celebrarlos? Al terminar las fiestas, ¿cómo te sientes?**

## Reference Desk

1. Draw attention to the words **víspera** and **Belén**; have students deduce the meanings.
2. You may want to model pronunciation of the Three Kings' names for students: **Baltasar**, **Melchor**, **Gaspar**.
3. Search online for a recording of "**Las mañanitas**" to play for the class, or sing the lyrics.
4. **La misa de gallo** is the Roman Catholic name for the Mass that is celebrated at midnight on Christmas Eve.

## Culture

**Products/Practices: Information**
In many Spanish-speaking countries, children receive gifts from the Three Kings on January 6th. For example, in Mexico on the night of January 5th, children will leave their shoes outside filled with grass or hay for the Three Wise Men's camels. Another widespread Three Kings' Day tradition is eating **rosca de reyes**, a ring-shaped cake in which a small figurine is hidden. Whoever finds the figurine in their piece is named **rey** or **reina** of the party.

# *Vocabulario 1*

## ¡De celebración en celebración! 🎧 ✿ 1.2, 2.1, 2.2

"Hoy es domingo y mañana es fiesta, qué buena vida es esta."

Este proverbio o refrán sirve para ilustrar la cantidad de festividades que celebramos en el mundo hispano, la mayoría heredadas de nuestros antepasados.

Cada día, millones de personas celebran su cumpleaños. Es una tradición inmemorial, al igual que la costumbre de soplar las velas del pastel de cumpleaños y pedir un deseo antes de apagarlas.

### Festividades de diciembre y enero

La Navidad es una de las celebraciones más queridas de todos. Los hogares se decoran con árboles de Navidad, y luces y adornos navideños. Las familias se reúnen para celebrar el 24 de diciembre por la noche y el 25 por la mañana los niños abren los regalos de Navidad que les trae el Niño Dios o Papá Noel.

El Año Nuevo se celebra el primero de enero. En la víspera, a la medianoche, en medio de la bulla y el ruido de los fuegos artificiales, la gente se besa y se abraza y hace un brindis por que el Año Nuevo traiga salud, dinero y amor, y mucha felicidad. Es una de las celebraciones más alegres del mundo entero.

El 6 de enero se celebra el Día de los Reyes Magos. Cuentan que ellos llegaron a Belén guiados por una estrella, para honrar al niño nacido en un pesebre.

### Para conversar

**P**ara hablar de celebraciones y tradiciones:
"Las mañanitas" es una canción que se canta cuando alguien cumple años. Es típica de México, al igual que los mariachis cuyas serenatas son populares en las bodas, aniversarios, graduaciones y cualquier otra ocasión de celebración.

En la víspera de Navidad, al repicar de las campanas a la medianoche, es costumbre asistir a la Misa de Gallo y cantar villancicos para conmemorar el nacimiento de Jesús.

## Essential Instruction

1. Begin by having students look at the photos and describe what they see.
2. Before playing the audio, have students look at the vocabulary on pp. 348–350 and pick cognates. They can work in pairs and practice pronouncing these words.
3. Play the audio for **¡De celebración en celebración!** Pause to ask **sí/no** comprehension questions.
4. Personalize the vocabulary presentation by asking students to compare and contrast their family's celebrations with the information on these pages.

## Festividades de febrero a noviembre

El Carnaval es una fiesta folclórica que se realiza en muchos países hispanos entre febrero y marzo, según el año. El carnaval se da en una atmósfera de fiesta sin igual, con desfiles de carrozas y reinas que lucen disfraces y tocados de plumas y cintas de gran sofisticación.

La Semana Santa se celebra a finales de marzo o a principios de abril. Comienza con el Domingo de Ramos. El Viernes Santo se conmemora la muerte de Cristo y el Domingo de Pascua, su resurrección. Es costumbre dar a los niños huevos teñidos de colores que les trae el conejo de Pascua.

El Día de la Independencia es una fiesta nacional. En Colombia se celebra el 20 de julio. Ese día se hacen desfiles cívicos, se realizan ceremonias en que se saluda la bandera y se toca el himno nacional para honrar a los héroes de la independencia.

El Día de los Muertos y el Día de Todos los Santos son celebraciones para honrar el alma de los difuntos. La gente visita los cementerios y hace altares con flores y decoraciones de esqueletos y calaveras en honor del espíritu de sus seres queridos.

### Para conversar

**P**ara hablar de fiestas familiares:

En las fiestas de independencia también hay fuegos artificiales, festivales, bailes con trajes regionales, bandas y barbacoas familiares.

El Día de Acción de Gracias es una fiesta tradicional de Estados Unidos que se celebra a finales de noviembre. Ese día, las familias se reúnen y comparten una gran cena que típicamente incluye pavo relleno, papas, ensaladas, verduras y una variedad de tortas.

> ### ¡Acuérdese!
>
> **Frases de felicitación y buenos deseos**
>
> Muchas felicidades
> Muchas felicitaciones
> Feliz cumpleaños
> Que los cumplas felices
> Que lo pases bien
> Que lo pases muy feliz

---

## RESOURCES

🎧 Para conversar

### Reference Desk

1. **El Día de los Muertos** is a Mexican holiday celebrated on November 1st and 2nd.
2. **El Día de Todos los Santos** is a Catholic holiday that is celebrated on November 1st.

### Culture

**Products/Practices: Information**
**Carnaval** is a frenetic, playful celebration that takes place over several days leading up to the solemn period of **Cuaresma** (*Lent*), which always begins on **Miércoles de Ceniza** (*Ash Wednesday*).

### Culture

**Products/Practices: Activity**
Ask students to research and analyze the fusion of indigenous and Catholic influences in **el Día de los Muertos**. Then have them compare and contrast this holiday with **el Día de Todos los Santos**.

### Expansion

Ask students to make **cierto/falso** statements about the information presented in **Vocabulario 1**. Have them exchange papers with a classmate and correct the false sentences.

---

## Differentiated Learning
### Heritage Learners
Ask heritage learners to share birthday traditions from their cultural communities. Have the class compare and contrast what they hear with their own experiences.

## Special Needs Students
### AD(H)D/Dyslexia
Work as a class to create a calendar of the celebrations mentioned in **Vocabulario 1**. Add to the calendar as you work through the unit.

## Para conversar

**P**ara hablar de las ferias artesanales:

Las ferias artesanales son muy populares pues allí se venden artesanías para todas las ocasiones y se ofrecen actividades para toda la familia.

Para Navidad se consiguen lindos pesebres o nacimientos con figuras de cerámica o de madera tallada y adornos de vidrio soplado para el árbol de Navidad. También se consiguen decoraciones de Papá Noel de acero, hierro u hojalata para adornar el jardín.

En las ferias se encuentran toda clase de regalos, incluyendo dulces y chocolates típicos envueltos en lindo papel de regalo con motivos navideños.

Asistir a la feria de artesanías es un buen programa para pasar un domingo en familia. Para los niños, hay puestos de juegos y globos para reventar, y puestos de cuentacuentos donde les cuentan chistes, mitos, leyendas y las fábulas con las mejores moralejas.

---

**1 Una fiesta sorpresa**  1.2

Los amigos y familiares de Susana le hacen una fiesta sorpresa para su cumpleaños. Escuche la serie de oraciones incompletas e indique la terminación correcta.

1. bulla / banda
2. ¡Salud, dinero y amor! / ¡Felicitaciones!
3. cumplía / contaba
4. bailó / besó

5. pavo / pastel
6. los globos / los huevos
7. brindis / chiste

---

**2 Sin cambiar el significado**  1.2

Elija la palabra del recuadro que pueda reemplazar la palabra en negrilla en cada oración, sin cambiar su significado.

| torta | refranes | nacimiento | bulla | adornos | villancicos | se conmemora |

1. El Domingo de Pascua **se celebra** la resurrección Jesús.
2. Durante la Misa de Gallo se acostumbra cantar **canciones de Navidad**.
3. No pude oír tu brindis de Año Nuevo por la cantidad de **ruido** que había.
4. En nuestra casa ponemos un lindo **pesebre** de madera junto al árbol de Navidad.

5. Los **proverbios**, al igual que las fábulas, generalmente tienen una moraleja.
6. La ciudad se llena de luces y **decoraciones** en Navidad.
7. Pedí un deseo antes de apagar las velitas de mi **pastel** de cumpleaños. Espero que se cumpla.

**Essential Instruction**

1. Have students read through the items in **Actividad 1**, and then play the audio.
2. Check answers to **Actividad 2** orally as a class. Brainstorm examples where appropriate, e.g., in item 2, names of **villancicos**.
3. Have students check their answers to **Actividades 3** and **4** in pairs.
4. Ask comprehension questions about the information in **Actividad 4**.

## 3 Dos por una  1.2, 2.1

En la columna I se dan dos oraciones por cada una de las celebraciones de la columna II. Empareje las celebraciones con sus actividades según corresponda.

**I**
**Actividades**

1. Se toca el himno nacional.
2. Se dan dulces en forma de conejo.
3. Se hacen desfiles de carrozas.
4. Se tocan "Las mañanitas".
5. Se hacen ceremonias y se saluda la bandera.
6. Se abren los regalos que trae el Niño Dios.
7. Se hacen decoraciones en forma de calaveras.
8. Se soplan velas mientras se piensa en un deseo.
9. Se abraza y se besa a los demás y se les desea felicidad.
10. Se tiñen huevos de colores.
11. Se hace un altar en honor de los seres queridos.
12. Se asiste a la Misa de Gallo y se cantan villancicos.
13. Se hace un brindis al repicar de las doce de la noche y se prenden fuegos artificiales.
14. Se presentan comparsas y personas en disfraces sofisticados.

**II**
**Celebraciones**

A. el Año Nuevo
B. el Carnaval
C. el cumpleaños
D. el Día de la Independencia
E. el Día de los Muertos
F. la Navidad
G. la Semana Santa

*Hermosas mujeres desfilan en carrozas en el Carnaval de Barranquilla.*

## 4 Locura de Carnaval  1.2, 2.1, 2.2

Aunque no es tan grande como Mardi Gras en Nueva Orleans ni tan lujoso como el Carnaval de Río de Janeiro, los colombianos creen que su Carnaval de Barranquilla es el mejor carnaval del mundo. Complete la lectura con la palabra del recuadro que corresponda según el contexto.

| celebrar | fiesta | honrar | disfraces | regionales |
|----------|--------|--------|-----------|------------|
| carrozas | bandas | plumas | sin igual | festividades |

Las **(1)** son un elemento fundamental de la cultura colombiana. No hay semana sin una **(2)** religiosa, ni mes sin un día cívico para **(3)** a algún héroe de la independencia. Los colombianos viven para **(4)**, y el mejor momento para hacerlo es la temporada de Carnaval, la máxima celebración del calendario colombiano. Esta fiesta folclórica **(5)** atrae todos los años a más de un millón de personas, entre locales y visitantes, que se entregan de lleno a celebrar y a disfrutar de toda una serie de eventos y actividades: **(6)** musicales, bailes **(7)** y, sobretodo, desfiles de gente con absurdos **(8)** y reinas luciendo tocados de **(9)** y de luces en llamativas **(10)**. El carnaval de Barranquilla es algo planeado y espontáneo a la vez. Es una celebración de las raíces y la identidad de un pueblo. Es el mejor carnaval del mundo.

## Culture

**Products/Practices: Activity**
Ask students to research Colombian New Year's Eve traditions, such as popular songs (e.g., "**Año Nuevo, vida nueva**" by Billo's Caracas Boys or "**Faltan cinco pa' las doce**" by Aníbal Velásquez), colors, foods, or other traditions (such as **el portazo**, **las 12 uvas**, or **el muñeco de Año Viejo**). Have students work as a group to plan a Colombian-style New Year's Eve celebration to hold in class, complete with the music, foods, and traditions that they researched.

## Culture

**Practices: Information**
In the nine days leading up to Christmas Eve, some Spanish-speaking countries celebrate **las posadas**, a reenactment of Mary and Joseph searching for lodging. In Colombia, Venezuela, and Ecuador, however, it is customary for families to gather each day during this period, eat **buñuelos** and **natillas**, and say a special set of prayers and sing **villancicos**. This tradition is called **las Novenas (de Aguinaldos)**.

## ¡Comunicación!

### 5  ¿Uvas o maletas?  👥  Interpersonal /Presentational Communication   1.1

El Año Nuevo es una fecha de festejo casi universal, tanto así que su celebración se pasa por televisión en países del mundo entero. Sin embargo, aunque el motivo de la celebración es el mismo, las actividades que se hacen para celebrar varían de acuerdo a la región, las tradiciones y las supersticiones de la gente. ¿Cuáles son las actividades más emocionantes, las más divertidas, y hasta las más ridículas, inesperadas o inexplicables que la gente realiza con la esperanza de tener buena suerte en el nuevo año? Con un(a) compañero/a intercambien la información u opiniones que tengan al respecto, como se ve en el modelo. Luego, hagan una lista de las actividades más sobresalientes y, para finalizar, compartan su lista con sus compañeros/as de clase.

MODELO
> **A:** Yo tengo una amiga de España que se come doce uvas al repicar de las doce de la noche. Me contó que era una costumbre que había heredado de sus abuelos y que, supuestamente, traía buena suerte en el año venidero. Y tú, ¿qué costumbres conoces?
>
> **B:** Bueno… No sé del mundo hispano, pero mi abuela siempre espera el toque de las doce con una maleta en la mano. Según dice, eso asegura que el nuevo año le traiga posibilidades de viajar y conocer otros lugares y a otra gente.

### 6  Diferencias y similitudes  👥  Interpersonal/Presentational Communication  🌸 1.1, 1.3, 2.1, 2.2, 4.2

Trabajen en grupos de tres o cuatro estudiantes para hacer una presentación sobre las fiestas tradicionales del mundo hispano en comparación con las de su país o región. Primero, elijan una festividad del mundo hispano que también se celebre donde Uds. viven e intercambien ideas al respecto, teniendo en cuenta los temas que se dan y otros de su creación. Si es necesario, busquen información adicional en la internet. Indiquen diferencias y similitudes entre las dos celebraciones, como se ve en el modelo, y túrnense para hacer sus presentaciones enfrente del resto de la clase.

MODELO
> **La Navidad es una celebración que tiene siglos de tradición popular y religiosa. Se celebra el 25 de diciembre, pero en los países hispanos la mayor parte de la celebración ocurre la noche del 24, llamada la Nochebuena.**

- Nombre y razón de la celebración
- Fecha y lugar donde se celebra
- Historia y tradición
- Actividades típicas
- Entretenimiento
- Diferencias
- Similitudes
- …

*Mi ciudad se llena de luces y decoraciones en Navidad.*

**Essential Instruction**

1. For **Actividad 5**, have students jot down a few ideas before getting together with a partner.
2. Encourage students to incorporate visual and/or audio components into their presentations for **Actividad 6**.
3. Open the **Gramática** presentation by asking a volunteer to define **infinitivo** and give examples. Then review the information on pp. 353–354.

# *Gramática*

## Los usos del infinitivo  1.2, 4.1

Las construcciones con el infinitivo se usan con algunas palabras, preposiciones y expresiones y pueden desempeñar diferentes funciones en la oración.

- El infinitivo puede funcionar como el sujeto de la oración, en cuyo caso, el uso del artículo definido es optativo.

    (El) **llevar** un regalo a los anfitriones se considera de buen gusto.

    En una fiesta, **poner** música alegre hace que el ambiente sea divertido.

- También puede funcionar como complemento de la oración o como predicado de la oración después del verbo **ser**.

    Nos piden **colaborar** con un plato cada uno para la fiesta.

    Lo que más queremos los seres humanos **es lograr** la felicidad.

- Cuando no hay cambio de sujeto, funciona como complemento de un verbo.

    Me **encantaría viajar** por todo el mundo y me **gustaría aprender** varios idiomas.

- En oraciones que no tienen cambio de sujeto, se puede usar el infinitivo después de una preposición o frase preposicional. Tenga en cuenta que en inglés se suele usar el gerundio en esos casos: *after eating, before shopping*.

    **Antes de irse** de parranda, durmieron una buena siesta.

    No descansarán **hasta**[1] **terminar** de **preparar** todos los canapés.

    **Sin atender** ni a ruegos ni a súplicas, decidió abandonar sus estudios.

- También se usa el infinitivo después de verbos de percepción (**escuchar**, **mirar**, **oír**, **sentir**, **ver**, etc.). En estos casos, suele haber otro agente para la acción indicada por el infinitivo y se requiere el pronombre del complemento directo.

    Una y otra vez, su público **los ha oído tocar** su famosa salsa brava.

    Fue después del tercer cuento que **la vimos sonreír** tímidamente.

[1] Cuando la cláusula adverbial se refiere a una acción pendiente —generalmente en futuro o en imperativo—, se usa la conjunción **hasta que** y el **subjuntivo**: No se detendrán **hasta que** lleguen a la cima de la montaña. (Vea la página 275 de la Unidad 7).

*Antes de soplar las velas, abuelita pidió un deseo.*

---

### RESOURCES

**WB** Activity 4

**LA** Activities 1–4

### Reference Desk

1. Remind students that the infinitive is the unconjugated form of the verb, and that all Spanish infinitives end in either **-ar**, **-er**, or **-ir**.
2. Remind students that **gerundio** is a false cognate. Ask for a volunteer to explain the difference between the **gerundio**, a gerund, and a present participle.

### Expansion

Ask students to create additional example sentences for each bullet point in **Gramática**, using what they have learned about Hispanic celebrations in this unit.

---

### Differentiated Learning
#### Accelerate/Heritage Learners
Ask accelerated students or heritage learners to become a professor for the day and present this grammar point. Allow them time to prepare, and encourage them to come up with their own examples.

### Multiple Intelligences
#### Bodily-Kinesthetic
Have students work in groups to research the Christmas ritual of **las posadas**. Tell groups to create a skit in which they act out asking for lodging; they should also include the traditions of breaking a **piñata** and singing **villancicos**.

**353**

El infinitivo también se usa:

- Después de las expresiones impersonales (**es difícil**, **es necesario** y otras) y después de ciertos verbos de voluntad o influencia (**aconsejar**, **dejar**, **hacer**, **invitar**, **mandar**, **(im)pedir**, **obligar a**, **ordenar**, **permitir**, **prohibir**). Generalmente, esta construcción requiere el pronombre del complemento indirecto.

  **Nos urge conseguir** donaciones para hacer la fiesta de Navidad en el ancianato.

  Mi madre **no me permitía estar** fuera de casa después de las 12 de la noche.

- Para expresar obligación personal se usa **tener que** + **infinitivo** (*to have to*) o **haber de** + **infinitivo** (*should, to be supposed to*).

  **Tenéis que recoger** a los abuelos y **habéis de comprar** el postre también.

  Uds. **han de** hacer la ensalada y yo **tengo que** meter el pavo al horno.

- Para expresar obligación impersonal se usa **haber que** + **infinitivo** (*one must... /it is necessary*).

  Explicaron que para meditar **había que relajarse** y despejar la mente.

  Siempre **hay que tener cuidado** al manejar cuando hay nieve.

- En expresiones temporales como equivalente de **en el momento de** (*upon + -ing*) se usa **al** + **infinitivo**.

  **Al terminar de envolver** los regalos, los pusimos debajo del arbolito de Navidad.

  Cuando dieron las doce, se pusieron emotivos **al recordar** a los que no estaban.

- Como equivalente de las oraciones **si** + **indicativo** o **si** + **subjuntivo** se usa **de** + **infinitivo**.

  Viajaremos a Colombia en Pascua, **de conseguir** pasajes. (...si conseguimos pasajes).

  **De poder hacerlo**, llevaría regalos para todos en Navidad. (Si pudiera hacerlo...).

- Como equivalente del imperativo en anuncios impersonales.

  Prohibido **pisar** el césped. (No pise...)

  No **fumar** en el avión. (No fume...)

*Al repicar de las campanas a la medianoche, mis amigos y yo celebramos el Año Nuevo.*

### Essential Instruction

1. Ask volunteers to create additional examples for each bullet point in **Gramática**.
2. Check answers to **Actividad 7** chorally.
3. Encourage students to compare their answers to **Actividad 8** in pairs.

## 7  La mañana de Navidad   1.2

Era la mañana de Navidad y los niños se levantaron a ver qué les había traído Papá Noel. Ellos pegaban brincos de emoción, ansiosos por abrir los regalos que había debajo del arbolito. Modifique las oraciones para incorporar infinitivos y cambie cualquier otra cosa que haga falta, según el modelo.

MODELO   Era la mañana de Navidad y yo oía que los niños se reían de alegría.
**Era la mañana de Navidad y yo los oía reír de alegría.**

*Veíamos a los niños reír de alegría.*

1. En la víspera, fue indispensable que yo tranquilizara a los niños para que se fueran a dormir.
2. La mañana de Navidad, nosotros oímos que los niños se habían levantado.
3. De pronto, escuchamos que bajaban corriendo.
4. En el momento que entraron, vimos que los chicos saltaban de la emoción.
5. Papá les ordenó que desayunaran antes de abrir los regalos.
6. Cuando vimos sus caritas tristes, dejamos que abrieran uno antes del desayuno.
7. La comprensión con los chiquillos es necesaria.
8. Si nos sentimos como niños, recordaremos el gran gozo de la Navidad.

## 8  Los funerales de la mamá grande  1.2

Hace unos días, se murió la abuelita de Gabriel. Cambie el subjuntivo por el infinitivo para saber qué pasó en el funeral.

MODELO   Fue indispensable que consiguieran pasajes enseguida.
**(Les) fue indispensable conseguir pasajes enseguida.**

1. La tía Juana permitió que el primo Roberto escribiera el homenaje para la abuelita.
2. Los tíos no permitieron que los niños vieran a la abuelita difunta.
3. La etiqueta demanda que se vistieran de colores oscuros.
4. Fue necesario que se pidieran muchas flores para el funeral.
5. Los tíos aconsejaron que todos comieran algo antes de que fueran al cementerio.
6. Era difícil que los familiares no lloraran de dolor ante el féretro.
7. La mamá de Gabriel le pidió al coro que cantara el himno favorito de la abuelita.
8. Cuando escucharon el homenaje, fue inevitable que manifestaran su tristeza.

---

---

**Answers**

**9** *Las respuestas variarán.*

**10** *Las respuestas variarán.*

### Reference Desk

1. **La Fiesta Nacional del Café** takes place in Calarcá, a town in the department of Quindío. Besides the **yipaos**, the main attraction of the festival is **el Reinado Nacional del Café**, the winner of which goes on to represent Colombia in **el Reinado Internacional de Café** in Manizales.
2. Colombian coffee is considered to be some of the best in the world, and the country's coffee production is placed third worldwide, after Brazil and Vietnam. Most Colombian coffee is grown in a central-western region of the country known as **el Eje Cafetero**, or **el Triángulo del Café**. The area represents a vital part of the Colombian economy, because of the coffee it produces and also agritourism; for example, each year about 45,000 tourists visit **el Parque Nacional del Café** in the department of Quindío.
3. Medellín, in the department of Antioquia, is the second-largest city in Colombia. Due to its average annual temperature of 72 degrees, the city is known as **la Ciudad de la Eterna Primavera**.
4. Encourage students to share their celebration memories from **Actividad 10** in a Flipgrid post.

**356**

---

**9** *Yipaos* **en la Fiesta del Café en Colombia**  **1.2, 2.1, 2.2**

La Fiesta Nacional del Café en Colombia tiene como simpático protagonista al *yipao*. Lea sobre la historia del *yipao* y conteste las preguntas. Al leer, fíjese en el uso del infinitivo.

Desde 1960, **celebrar** la Fiesta del Café es un evento anual lleno de colorido y alegría. Entre sus protagonistas, hay que **destacar** al *yipao*. La palabra *yipao* surge de **adaptar** al español la pronunciación de la palabra *jeep*. Los *jeep* Willys llegaron en 1946 para **sustituir** a los animales de carga. Por eso, llegaron a **convertirse** en emblemas del eje cafetero al **ser** usados para **transportar** de todo, desde personas y enseres hasta el muy importante café. De allí, pasaron a **figurar** en la Fiesta del Café como un gran espectáculo, a partir de 1988. **Picar** y **girar** los *yipaos* con las ruedas en el aire es una de las proezas de sus orgullosos dueños. **Montarse** sobre la carrocería y **hacer** piruetas es otra de sus hazañas. ¡Realmente es algo digno de **verse**!

*Hacer gala de una gran versatilidad es típico de los* yipaos.

1. ¿Alguna vez ha visto a un *jeep* hacer piruetas? Si no lo ha visto, ¿le gustaría verlo? ¿Por qué?
2. ¿Qué opina sobre usar vehículos en lugar de mulas? Como medida para favorecer el ambiente, ¿cuál le parece mejor? Como medida para proteger a los animales, ¿qué otra alternativa puede sugerir?

 **¡Comunicación!**

**10** **¡La pasamos muy bien!** 👥 **Interpersonal Communication**  **1.1, 5.2**

Piense en la última fiesta familiar que celebraron Ud. y su familia y, luego, intercambie anécdotas con un(a) compañero/a. Túrnense para hacer preguntas y responderlas teniendo en cuenta la siguiente información.

- La ocasión que estaban celebrando
- La fecha y el lugar de la celebración
- El número de invitados y quiénes eran
- Los platos que se sirvieron
- Actividades que realizaron para celebrar

*Al terminar la fiesta, mis tías regresaron a Medellín.*

### Essential Instruction

1. Have volunteers take turns reading aloud the paragraph in **Actividad 9**. Then have students discuss the questions in small groups.
2. Encourage students to bring in photos or other memorabilia from the celebrations that they discuss in **Actividad 10**.
3. Begin the grammar presentation by asking students to name as many uses of **por** and **para** as they can. Write the uses on the board; then add in any uses that they missed. Then continue with the **modismos** on pp. 357–358.

# Gramática

## Usos de *por* y *para*  1.2, 4.1

### Usos de *por*

La preposición **por** se usa...

- para expresar motivo o razón (*out of, because of*)

  Me gusta leer **por** amor al arte, no **por** obligación.
  En Colombia hay muchos días festivos **por** motivos religiosos.

- para expresar lugar o tiempo impreciso (*around*)

  **Por** estos tiempos, hay muchas festividades.
  ¿Dónde queda un restaurante **por** aquí cerca?

- para expresar **a través** o **a lo largo de** (*through, along, by*)

  Viajábamos **por** las carreteras menos conocidas.
  Llegamos a la casa de Manolo **por** la ruta de la selva.

- con el significado de **durante** para indicar períodos de tiempo (*in, during, for*)

  Me han gustado los idiomas **por** muchos años.
  **Por** toda la Navidad, hay alumbrados especiales en Medellín.

- para introducir el agente de la voz pasiva (*by*[1])

  El fútbol es celebrado como una fiesta **por** los fanáticos.
  Las leyendas fueron transmitidas **por** los antepasados.

- para indicar el medio o el modo de una acción (*by*)

  Mis tíos viajaron **por** barco en un crucero por el Caribe.
  Los chicos hablaron tres horas **por** video **por** la internet.

- con el significado de **a cambio de** (*for*)

  Arturo cambió sus videojuegos **por** una guitarra eléctrica.
  La fiesta de quinceañera salió **por** quinientos mil pesos.

- con el significado de **en busca de** con los verbos **ir, venir, volver, regresar, enviar, mandar** (*for*)

  Los primos fueron **por** los canapés para la fiesta.
  Cuando se acabó, enviaron a los chicos **por** hielo.
  Mandaron **por** flores para adornar el salón de fiesta.

- con el significado de **por amor a**, **en consideración de** (*on behalf of, for the sake of*)

  No fuimos a la fiesta **por** acompañar a nuestro padre enfermo.
  ¡**Por** amor de Dios! Te pido que me comprendas.

- con expresiones de cantidad (*per, by*)

  Los trenes de alta velocidad alcanzan más de 200 km **por** hora.
  La receta lleva cuatro huevos **por** libra de harina.

- con el infinitivo, para expresar una acción pendiente, no terminada

  Todavía hay mucho **por** hacer.
  Son las siete y aún quedan **por** preparar los tentempiés.

[1] Para el estudio de la voz pasiva, vea la Unidad 8, página 337.

### Modismos con *por*

| | |
|---|---|
| **por fin** (*finally*) | ¡**Por fin** llegaron los invitados!, una hora tarde. |
| **por lo general/común** (*in general*) | **Por lo general**, ponemos música suave con la cena. |
| **por esto/eso**; **por lo tanto** (*therefore*) | Está lloviendo, **por lo tanto**, no iremos al festival. |

## Reference Desk

See if students can recall additional expressions with **por**, such as **por casualidad**, **por cierto**, **por ejemplo**, **por favor**, **por primera vez**, **por si acaso**, **por última vez**.

## Expansion

Ask students to write a composition about their last family gathering based on the information they discussed in **Actividad 10**. Tell them to include at least five infinitives and **por** and **para**. Have students peer-edit each other's work.

## TPR

Read cloze sentences to the class; they must decide if **por** or **para** would be used and raise their right hands for **por** or their left hands for **para**.

## Differentiated Learning
### Accelerate/Expand

Ask students to research another Colombian festival and write a paragraph about it using infinitives. They should refer to **Actividad 9** as a model.

## Multiple Intelligences
### Musical-Rhythmic

Demonstrate how infinitives can easily lend themselves to rhyme due to their endings. Ask students to create songs, chants, or raps using infinitives.

357

1. Contrast the difference between verbs that take both **por** and **para**. For example: **trabajar por** – *to work in someone's place* (i.e., fill in when someone is sick) or *to work in exchange for something* (i.e., money) versus **trabajar para** – to work for a company/person; **ir por** – *to go get something* versus **ir para** – *to go to/toward*.
2. You may want to introduce additional expressions with **para**, such as **estar para** (*to be about to*), **para colmo** (*to top it off*), **para entonces**, **ser tal para cual** (*to be two of a kind*).
3. Remind students that the following verbs do not take **por** and **para**: **buscar**, **esperar**, **pagar**, **pedir**.
4. Review the differences between the two words for *to ask* in Spanish. Ask students in what contexts you would use **pedir** and **preguntar**.

**Critical Thinking**

**Analyzing**
Bring in magazine or newspaper articles. Have students work in pairs to find and circle the words **por** and **para**. Ask students to explain why each word was used.

| | |
|---|---|
| **por supuesto** (*of course*) | **Por supuesto** que en el festival habrá música. |
| **por más/mucho que** (*however much*) | **Por mucho que** quiera, no podré ir al baile esta noche. |
| **por poco** (*almost*) | ¡**Por poco** pasamos de largo! No vimos bien la dirección. |
| **por otra parte** (*on the other hand*) | ¡Se nos hizo tarde! **Por otra parte**, no queda muy lejos. |
| **tomar por** (*to take for*) | Como es muy alta, la **toman por** alguien mayor de lo que es. |
| **por lo menos** (*at least*) | Aunque no vimos todo, **por lo menos** vimos lo mejor. |

## Usos de *para*

La preposición **para** se usa...

| | |
|---|---|
| • con el infinitivo para expresar propósito (*in order to*) | Hicieron un agasajo **para** celebrar su nombramiento. Él le cantó una serenata **para** expresarle su amor. |
| • para indicar el destino de cosas o acciones (*for*) | Van **para** Cartagena **para** pasar las vacaciones. Prepararé una torta **para** la verbena. |
| • para indicar el uso o la conveniencia de algo (*for*) | Compramos una cafetera **para** preparar cappuccino. Harán una piñata **para** los niños. |
| • para marcar un límite de tiempo (*by, for*) | **Para** fines de mes, estará todo listo para el festival. Habrá que tener listos los canapés **para** las cinco de la tarde. |
| • para expresar una comparación o falta de correspondencia con algo o alguien (*for, considering*) | Mi abuelita es muy lúcida **para** alguien de su edad. **Para** los tiempos que corren, hay que ser muy sereno. |
| • en sustitución de **según**, **en la opinión de** (*for*) | La paz es un tema muy importante **para** todo el mundo. **Para** la ONU, las metas del milenio son prioritarias. |

## Modismos con *para*

| | |
|---|---|
| **para siempre** (*forever*) | García Márquez se consagró como autor **para siempre**. |
| **no ser para tanto** (*not to be so important*) | ¡Quédate tranquilo! El problema **no es para tanto**. |
| **no estar para bromas** (*not to be in the mood for joking*) | Mejor dejen a papá en paz; se ve que **no está para bromas**. |

**Essential Instruction**
1. Open **Actividad 11** by asking students if they used to have **piñatas** at their birthday parties.
2. Have students check their answers to **Actividad 11** in pairs.
3. Before beginning **Actividad 12**, point out that there are many possible combinations.
4. After completing the activities on p. 359, have students explain why they chose **por** or **para** for each item.

## 11 La piñata de Panchito  1.2

Panchito va a cumplir cinco años el próximo sábado y la familia Rodríguez Pérez está preparando alegremente una gran fiesta con piñata. Complete las siguientes oraciones con **por** o **para**.

**1.** Los primos Pérez llegarán el sábado ____ la tarde ____ celebrar el cumpleaños de Panchito.

**2.** Panchito es muy alto ____ su edad y, a veces, lo toman ____ un niño de ocho años, pero apenas es un chiquillo.

**3.** Los tíos Alejandro e Isabel viajarán ____ avión ____ asistir a la fiesta.

**4.** ____ lo tanto, Papá conversó con la tía Isabel ____ teléfono.

**5.** Le avisó que iríamos ____ ellos al aeropuerto, el sábado ____ la mañana.

**6.** ____ la fiesta de cumpleaños, mamá compró una divertida piñata del Chapulín Colorado.

**7.** Hemos rellenado la piñata con juguetes y golosinas ____ que los chicos se diviertan.

**8.** Queda pendiente ir ____ la torta del Chapulín que se encargó a la pastelería. Es un poco cara, a unos veinte mil pesos ____ kilo.

**9.** ____ mañana en la mañana, debemos tener todos los preparativos listos.

**10.** Queremos que la fiesta sea inolvidable y que Panchito la recuerde ____ siempre.

**11.** ____ amor a Panchito, vienen muchos familiares y sus amigos de la escuela ____ compartir con él.

**12.** ____ nosotros, las celebraciones familiares son muy importantes.

*Hay una gran piñata para el cumpleaños de Panchito.*

## 12 Navidad, Navidad, dulce Navidad...  1.3

Use un elemento de cada columna para formar oraciones lógicas con **por** o **para**.

**MODELO**   Todos viajamos a casa de la abuelita Teresa en Navidad **para** reunirnos en familia.

**1.** Algunos primos volaron desde Nueva York...

**2.** Se compró un bello pino...

**3.** Colgamos muérdago (*mistletoe*)...

**4.** Vinieron por tierra, mar y aire...

**5.** La comida fue preparada...

**6.** Pusimos los regalos debajo del pino...

**7.** Preparamos un ponche crema...

**8.** Los niños estaban emocionados...

**9.** Algunos se quedaron...

**10.** Nos encantan las reuniones familiares...

**A.** seguir la tradición familiar.

**B.** poder compartir con todos.

**C.** pasar más días juntos.

**D.** celebrar las fiestas juntos.

**E.** hacer otra cosa divertida.

**F.** llegar a tiempo para las fiestas.

**G.** petición de lo que les gusta.

**H.** todos los que quisieron ayudar.

**I.** esperar la llegada del Niño Dios.

**J.** divertirse colgando adornos.

*Unidad 9* | trescientos cincuenta y nueve  **359**

## RESOURCES

 Avenue

**Answers**

**11**
1. por, para
2. para, por
3. por, para
4. Por, por
5. por, por
6. Para
7. para
8. por, por
9. Para
10. para
11. Por, para
12. Para

**12** *Las respuestas variarán.*

## Reference Desk

**1.** **Chapulín Colorado** (Red Grasshopper) was the main character of a Mexican TV show of the same name. The program, which aired from 1972 to 1981, parodied superhero shows. The show has enjoyed renewed popularity in Colombia and Peru in recent years, and an animated version of the series is being produced.

**2.** Remind students that **pedir**, **preguntar**, **preguntar por**, **hacer una pregunta**, and **preguntarse** have separate meanings and are not interchangeable. **Pedir** has the additional meaning of *to order* in a restaurant context.

## Special Needs Students
### Linguistically Challenged
Encourage these students not to rely on English when working with **por** and **para**. Provide additional cloze activities for practice, and display a list of the uses with simplified language in the classroom for easy reference.

## Multiple Intelligences
### Verbal-Linguistic
Ask students to write a thank-you letter to someone who recently gave them a gift or did something nice for them. Tell students to exchange letters and peer-edit them. Instruct them to focus on unit grammar, punctuation, and spelling. Have students submit their final drafts via Avenue.

**13**
1. por
2. Para
3. por
4. Por
5. Para
6. por
7. para
8. por
9. por
10. Por
11. para

**14** *Las respuestas variarán.*

**15** *Los párrafos variarán.*

---

## Reference Desk

1. The **gitano** population in Spain is currently estimated at one million. Their population in Colombia is unknown; estimates vary between 5,000 and 80,000.
2. As in English, the word **gitano/a** derives from the word for *Egyptian* (**egipcio/a**), due to an erroneous belief in medieval times that these people came from Egypt.
3. Encourage the class to ask follow-up questions during the presentations in **Actividad 15**.

---

## Connections

**Music/Literature**
Have groups of students research Gypsy-inspired musical or literary forms in Spain, such as **flamenco** and **sevillanas** or Lorca's ***Romancero gitano***. Tell groups to create a short presentation, including audio and/or visual elements.

---

### 13 Cómo llegaron los gitanos a Colombia  1.2, 2.2

Lea el siguiente párrafo sobre la historia de los gitanos. Sustituya las palabras entre paréntesis por las preposiciones **por** o **para**, según el contexto.

Se cree que los gitanos salieron de la India y se dispersaron (**1.** *a lo largo de*) toda Europa. (**2.** *hacia*) fines del siglo XVI, muchos de ellos recorrían los pueblos europeos, especialmente de España y el sur de Francia. La gente les tenía miedo (**3.** *a causa de*) su manera exótica de vivir. (**4.** *durante*) las noches adivinaban la suerte (*would tell fortunes*), tocaban música y bailaban. (**5.** *en la opinión de*) mucha gente, su historia se resume en la vida nómada, la adivinación y el rebusque, aunque nadie puede negar que (**6.** *debido a*) sus aires enigmáticos se han tejido misteriosas leyendas.

*Los gitanos conservan su lengua, su manera de vestir y sus celebraciones para preservar su cultura.*

Los gitanos llevan menos de cien años viviendo en Colombia. Provienen de Rusia y Egipto, y parece que llegaron (**7.** *con el propósito de*) quedarse. Han echado raíces en tierra colombiana y (**8.** *a causa de*) eso han cambiado sus viviendas temporales (**9.** *a cambio de*) casas de madera y ladrillo. Conservan su lengua, su antigua manera de vestir y sus celebraciones. (**10.** *en consideración de*) sus tradiciones patriarcales, la mujer soltera debe estar en casa (**11.** *antes de*) las cinco de la tarde.

---

### 14 Una fiesta inolvidable  1.3

Jacobo dio tremenda fiesta. Complete las oraciones con expresiones que usen **por** o **para** de manera original para crear su propia versión de qué ocurrió en la fiesta.

1. Jacobo planeó la fiesta...
2. Varios llegaron...
3. Todos estaban muy alegres...
4. Había varios regalos...
5. Los canapés fueron preparados...
6. Como había piscina, los invitados cambiaron la ropa...
7. Hubo distintos juegos y actividades...
8. Al amanecer, todos se fueron...

---

## ¡Comunicación!

### 15 Recuerdos de una celebración   Presentational Communication   1.3

Recuerde una fiesta o celebración a la que Ud. haya asistido o que haya dado. Describa lo que sucedió en un breve párrafo, incluyendo las expresiones del recuadro y, luego, comparta su párrafo con el resto de la clase.

| | | |
|---|---|---|
| por fin | por eso | por lo general |
| por lo menos | por poco | por más/mucho que |

---

## Essential Instruction

1. Read aloud the paragraph in **Actividad 13**. Then have students read it a second time and select their answers.
2. Check answers to **Actividad 14** orally as a class; for each sentence starter, have a few volunteers provide their endings.
3. Have students preview pp. 361–363. Ask them to predict what they will learn about Colombia.
4. Point out the **Pregunta clave**, and tell students to keep it in mind as they complete the cultural readings.
5. Remind students of the culture photo and question from the unit opener. Have them scan p. 361 for the answer.

# El carnaval y la cumbia  1.2, 2.1, 2.2

En la ciudad portuaria de Barranquilla, ubicada al norte de Colombia, se celebra todos los años (a fines de febrero o principios de marzo) una de las fiestas folclóricas y culturales más importantes del país: el Carnaval de Barranquilla. Música, bailes, disfraces y carrozas[1] llenan de color y alegría las calles.

Su historia se remonta[2] al siglo XIX, pero su origen tiene raíces más profundas en la mezcla de tres culturas: la tradición española y portuguesa de celebrar los carnavales, los ritmos africanos traídos por los negros esclavizados y la herencia indígena.

*Desfile de carrozas en el Carnaval de Barranquilla*

Fruto de este sincretismo[3] cultural que se dio en la época de la conquista y la colonia, surgió en Colombia una de las danzas típicas del país en general y del Carnaval de Barranquilla en particular: la cumbia. En esta danza, se mezclan elementos de las tres tradiciones. Entre sus instrumentos están los tambores de origen africano, el guache (una especie de maraca) y los pitos (flautas y gaitas) de origen indígena. Los cantos y coplas[4] provienen de la poética española, aunque con el tiempo se han transformado bastante. El baile en sí mismo contiene movimientos sensuales, galantes y seductores característicos de las danzas africanas. Los trajes típicos tienen claros rasgos españoles: faldas largas, encajes[5], lentejuelas[6], candongas[7] y tocados[8] de flores y maquillaje intenso en las mujeres; camisa y pantalón blancos, pañolón rojo anudado al cuello y sombrero en los hombres.

Más de un millón de personas, entre visitantes y locales, participan de este popular carnaval en Barranquilla que, por su importancia y legado cultural, ha sido declarado Obra Maestra del Patrimonio Oral e Intangible de la Humanidad por la UNESCO en 2003. Desde entonces, ha crecido exponencialmente la cantidad de "hacedores" del carnaval (músicos, grupos de baile, confeccionistas de trajes) y la actividad comercial que lo rodea (venta de comidas, bebidas, artesanías, servicios de hotelería).

[1] floats  [2] dates back  [3] fusion  [4] popular songs  [5] lace  [6] sequin
[7] Colombian word for earrings  [8] headdress

 **Búsqueda:** carnaval de barranquilla, danzas colombianas, cumbia

## Productos  2.2

El Carnaval de Barranquilla se destaca por las artesanías que le dan colorido y elegancia a la fiesta. Para la ocasión, se crean vestidos, máscaras, disfraces, instrumentos musicales, adornos, sombreros, etc. Los artesanos provenientes de diferentes municipios se reúnen en ferias o puestos ambulantes y la venta de sus productos contribuye en gran medida a la dinámica comercial de la fiesta.

*Las máscaras son una tradición del carnaval.*

 **Pregunta clave**

¿Qué aspectos de la cultura de un país se reflejan en sus fiestas y tradiciones?

## 16 Comprensión 1.2, 2.2

1. ¿Cuáles son las raíces del Carnaval de Barranquilla?

2. ¿Qué elementos de la cumbia muestran el sincretismo de tres culturas?

3. Además de su importancia cultural, ¿cuál es la importancia comercial de un evento tan popular como el Carnaval de Barranquilla?

## 17 Analice 1.3, 2.2, 4.2

1. ¿Cómo cree Ud. que influye en el Carnaval de Barranquilla haber sido declarado Patrimonio de la Humanidad por la UNESCO?

2. ¿Qué evento de su cultura se celebra con música, bailes o desfiles que reflejen una mezcla de tradiciones?

**RESOURCES**

 Avenue

El carnaval y la cumbia Productos

**Answers**

**16**

1. La mezcla de tres culturas: la tradición española y portuguesa de celebrar los carnavales, los ritmos africanos traídos por los negros esclavizados y la herencia indígena.

2. Instrumentos de origen africano e indígena; canciones y trajes de origen español; movimientos típicos de danzas africanas.

3. El evento genera puestos de trabajo para muchas personas: artesanos, músicos, bailarines, vendedores de comidas y bebidas, etc.

**17** *Las respuestas variarán.*

## Culture

**Practices/Products: Activity**
Have students learn more about the events that take place before and during Barranquilla's **Carnaval**, including the **Lectura del Bando**, **la Guacherna**, **Batalla de Flores**, **Gran Parada**, **Festival de Orquestas**, and the burial of **Joselito Carnaval**.

## Pre-AP

Have students respond to the **Pregunta clave**, in spoken or written form, using information from the readings on pp. 361–363. Students should also include a comparison between their own community/culture and Colombia.

## Differentiated Learning

**Accelerate/Heritage Learners**
Create an Avenue task in which students watch an episode of the controversial program *Mi gran boda gitana* and write a critique answering: Are the portrayals of Gypsies and Gypsy life accurate? Does the show reinforce or break down stereotypes? For someone who does not know much about Gypsies, does the show give a positive or negative image?

## Multiple Intelligences

**Musical-Rhythmic**
Create a cloze activity using the lyrics from a song about Barranquilla's **Carnaval**, such as "**La Guacherna**" by Esther Forero or "**Frutos del Carnaval**" by Cuco Valoy.

**Answers**

**Perspectivas** Porque es la bandera de la cultura colombiana y los representa ante el mundo.

**18**

1. Se promociona el vallenato, un género musical colombiano, y sus ritmos: el paseo, el merengue, el son y la puya.
2. Son bailarines que desfilan y bailan una danza con pilones o morteros para pisar el maíz o el arroz.
3. Porque relata una historia en la que hay grupos indígenas que se enfrentan a los colonizadores españoles, tal como ocurrió en la época de la colonia.

**19** *Las respuestas variarán.*

## Culture

**Products: Information**
The man in the **Perspectivas** photo is wearing a **sombrero vueltiao** ("turned" hat), a traditional hat from Colombia that has grown to be one of its great cultural symbols. The name **vueltiao** refers to the turns or laps (**vueltas**) in the hat. Originally worn by peasants, it is often worn by **cumbia** or **vallenato** artists, and by the general public during national festivals. Most **sombreros vueltiaos** are made by the Zenú indigenous group using a local plant called **caña flecha**.

 **1.2, 2.1, 2.2**

### 18 Comprensión

1. ¿Qué se promociona en el Festival de la Leyenda Vallenata?
2. ¿Qué son los "piloneros"?
3. ¿Por qué se puede decir que la Leyenda del Milagro se relaciona con la historia de Colombia?

**1.3, 4.2**

### 19 Analice

1. ¿Qué importancia cree Ud. que tiene la televisación de eventos culturales como el Festival de la Leyenda Vallenata?
2. ¿Cree Ud. que este tipo de celebraciones y festivales son realmente útiles a la hora de expresar y preservar las tradiciones culturales de un país?

## La Leyenda Vallenata   **1.2, 2.1, 2.2**

El Festival de la Leyenda Vallenata es un evento muy popular en el que el protagonista indiscutido es el "vallenato", género musical originario de Colombia. El festival se realiza en abril desde 1968 en Valledupar en el noreste del país y allí se difunden[1] y promocionan los ritmos o "aires" del vallenato: el paseo, el merengue, el son y la puya.

*En el Festival de la Leyenda Vallenata, se difunden y promocionan los ritmos del vallenato.*

Además de los conciertos y concursos musicales, donde se elige el Rey Vallenato, uno de los momentos más tradicionales del festival son los desfiles de los "piloneros". Se trata de bailarines que participan de una danza en la cual usan como parte de su coreografía un pilón o mortero[2] para pisar el maíz o el arroz. Esta danza está inspirada en las labores tradicionales del hogar.

Otra de las propuestas interesantes del festival son las obras de teatro callejero[3] en las que se representa la famosa Leyenda del Milagro. Esta leyenda data de 1576 y cuenta la conversión de los grupos indígenas chimilas, tupes y cariachiles a la religión católica en la época de la colonia. En el relato se describen los crueles enfrentamientos[4] entre los ejércitos españoles y los indígenas, que finalmente deciden convertirse después de ver el poder de Dios manifestado a través de la resurrección de los combatientes de ambos bandos.

El Festival de la Leyenda Vallenata de 1999 marcó sin lugar a duda un hito[5] en su historia ya que por primera vez fue transmitido por televisión a nivel nacional e internacional.

[1] become known   [2] kitchen mortar   [3] street theater   [4] confrontations   [5] milestone

 **Búsqueda:** festival de la leyenda vallenata, rey vallenato, baile del pilón

*Perspectivas* **1.2, 3.2**

"[…] el folclor vallenato hoy en día es la bandera colombiana de la cultura en el exterior, así que para mí ganar este certamen es de gran satisfacción, que me compromete a trabajar de la mejor forma posible y haré todo lo que esté a mi alcance para seguir aportando un granito de arena en cuanto al fortalecimiento y la salvaguarda del vallenato tradicional", sostiene Mauricio de Santis, el Rey Vallenato de la edición 2015 del Festival de la Leyenda Vallenata. Según de Santis, ¿por qué hay que salvaguardar el vallenato?

*Todos los años se elige un Rey Vallenato en el festival.*

**Essential Instruction**

1. If time allows, play video clips of people performing **cumbia** or **vallenato**.
2. Display a map of Colombia and highlight the cities and places mentioned in these cultural readings.
3. As you play the audio for each cultural reading, pause occasionally to check comprehension by asking **sí/no** questions.
4. Have students complete the **Analice** activities for Common Core practice.

# Noviembre es pura fiesta en Cartagena  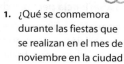 1.2, 2.1, 2.2

Cartagena de Indias, uno de los puertos más importantes de América durante la época colonial, se declaró independiente de España el 11 de noviembre de 1811. El aniversario de este importante acontecimiento histórico se festeja con gran pompa a lo largo de varias jornadas cada noviembre. Desde 1934, para esas fechas se realiza también el Concurso Nacional de Belleza de Colombia, que congrega[1] a locales y visitantes en torno a la belleza de la mujer colombiana.

Cartagena se llena de gente, colores y alegría durante las Fiestas de Independencia.

Durante las fiestas novembrinas, la ciudad amurallada se colma[2] de colombianos y extranjeros atraídos por eventos para todos los gustos. Se realizan conciertos en todas las plazas, donde se puede disfrutar de los distintos ritmos colombianos. Hay también desfiles cívico-militares en homenaje a los héroes de la independencia. En el Desfile Folclórico participan decenas de grupos con carrozas[3] y disfraces junto a las candidatas al reinado y múltiples artistas. Uno de los eventos más esperados es el Cabildo de Getsemaní, una gran fiesta con desfiles y comparsas[4] en las calles del tradicional barrio de Getsemaní. Los vecinos se preparan durante meses para este espectáculo.

El broche de oro[5] del mes entero es la coronación de la reina. El concurso no solo premia la belleza y el carisma, ya que en la Señorita Colombia se reconocen los valores de toda la nación representados en su personalidad integral. Por tanto, las reinas deben reflejar un sentido de responsabilidad social que les permita involucrarse en causas y actividades sociales para colaborar con su país.

[1] brings together    [2] is inundated    [3] floats    [4] group of people that participates in a parade
[5] crowning glory

 **Búsqueda:** fiestas de independencia de cartagena, cabildo de getsemaní, concurso nacional de belleza de colombia, desfile de balleneras

## 20 Comprensión  1.2, 2.1, 2.2

1. ¿Qué se conmemora durante las fiestas que se realizan en el mes de noviembre en la ciudad de Cartagena?

2. ¿Qué actividades se realizan en la ciudad durante las fiestas?

3. ¿En qué consiste el Desfile de Balleneras?

## 21 Analice 1.3, 2.1

1. ¿Cómo cree Ud. que las festividades que convocan a tanto público pueden beneficiar a una ciudad?

2. ¿Qué opinión tiene Ud. de los concursos de belleza como Señorita Colombia?

Una de las actividades más concurridas del Concurso Nacional de Belleza es el Desfile de Balleneras, durante el cual las aspirantes al título de Señorita Colombia se pasean en bote por la Bahía de Cartagena. Los pobladores pueden ver de cerca a las candidatas sin tener que pagar por una entrada. Ellas se presentan en traje de baño y tienen la oportunidad de saludar al pueblo y enamorarlo con su belleza y su carisma. Por su parte, los cartageneros admiran a las mujeres más hermosas del país y demuestran sus preferencias. Juntos hacen de la tarde una verdadera fiesta costera.

---

## RESOURCES

**fg**  Flipgrid

🎧  Noviembre es pura fiesta en Cartagena Prácticas

**Answers**

**20**
1. Se conmemora la independencia de España, que se declaró el 11 de noviembre de 1810.
2. Hay espectáculos musicales, un desfile en homenaje a los héroes de la independencia, un desfile folclórico y un concurso nacional de belleza.
3. Las aspirantes al título de Señorita Colombia desfilan en bote por la Bahía de Cartagena en traje de baño.

**21** *Las respuestas variarán.*

### Reference Desk

1. Students can do a Flipgrid post reacting to any of these cultural readings.
2. In **Prácticas**, the word **Balleneras** refers to the whaling boats that are used as floats during the parade.

### Critical Thinking

**Analyzing**
Provide students with a brief excerpt from ***Los funerales de la Mamá Grande*** by Gabriel García Márquez, in which he enumerates a list of pageant winners. As a class, analyze and discuss how the author satirizes Colombian culture in the passage.

---

## Differentiated Learning
**Expand**
After completing the readings on p. 363, have the class debate the issue of whether beauty pageants have a place in modern society. If they do, should they include both men and women? Should the participants be required to wear bathing suits?

## Multiple Intelligences
**Musical-Rhythmic**
Have students choose one of the types of music mentioned in **Cultura**, or other typical Colombian genre, such as **porro**, **gaita**, **puya**, or **salsa**. Ask students to research the genre's influences and instruments, and listen to some songs.

# Vocabulario 2

## Comparación y contraste: ¡Ojo con estas palabras! 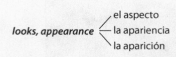 1.2, 4.1

En español, estas palabras tienen distintos significados y connotaciones. Preste atención, pues su uso
depende del contexto.

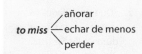

*looks, appearance* —
- el aspecto
- la apariencia
- la aparición

> ¡Qué buena **apariencia** tenemos juntos! ¿No te parece, mi amor?

> Sí, mi vida. Además, todo tiene un **aspecto** hermoso hoy.

**el aspecto** *features, looks*
Ese plato tiene un **aspecto** delicioso.

**la apariencia** *outward appearance, looks*
La **apariencia** personal da una primera impresión.

**la aparición** *appearance, presence, apparition*
La **aparición** de los trapecistas en el escenario
ocurrió como por arte de magia.

*to miss* —
- añorar
- echar de menos
- perder

> Esta **cita** fue una gran idea para nuestro aniversario.

> Sí, ¿verdad? Mmm, y estos **dátiles** están deliciosos.

**añorar** *to long for*
A veces, uno **añora** momentos del pasado.

**echar de menos (extrañar)** *to miss (a person or
thing), to feel a lack of*
Es normal **echar de menos** a las personas ausentes.

**perder** *to miss (a bus or an event), to lose*
No me **pierdo** ni un solo libro de ese autor.

*date* —
- la cita
- la fecha
- el dátil

**la cita** *date, appointment*
Los abogados tienen una **cita** a las 11 con el cliente.

**la fecha** *date (day, month, year)*
Hay **fechas** que marcan acontecimientos
especiales.

**el dátil** *date (fruit)*
En Oriente Medio se consiguen **dátiles** frescos.

---

**22 A ver ¿cómo dijiste?** 1.2

Complete las oraciones con la palabra entre
paréntesis que corresponda según el contexto.

1. Martha tenía una (*cita / fecha*) con el
   fisioterapeuta, pero (*perdió / extrañó*) la
   agenda y se le olvidó.

2. Hijo mío, te (*perdemos / echamos de menos*).
   Esperamos que regreses pronto.

3. Con (*la aparición / el aspecto*) de los elefantes
   en la arena del circo, los niños se animaron
   mucho.

4. Debido a la mezcla genética, los colombianos
   tienen (*una aparición / un aspecto*) físico que
   varía mucho.

5. (*los dátiles / las fechas*) del jardín de mi tía
   son deliciosos.

**Essential Instruction**

1. After going through **Vocabulario 2**, ask
   volunteers to create additional example
   sentences.
2. Have pairs read aloud the dialogues in the
   speech bubbles.
3. After completing **Actividad 23**, ask students which sayings they believe are most
   true.

4. In **Actividad 24**, encourage students to
   take notes for any items that they marked
   **Depende**. They can incorporate those ideas
   in their partner and large-group discussions.

**¡Comunicación!** **1.1, 1.2**

## 23 Proverbios  Interpersonal Communication

Los proverbios son una expresión de la sabiduría popular. Detrás de cada refrán suele haber una filosofía más o menos profunda. En la literatura Sancho Panza, el compañero de don Quijote de la Mancha, es famoso por sus proverbios, un reflejo de su actitud práctica hacia la vida. Los refranes son una parte esencial de nuestro idioma. Con un(a) compañero/a, túrnense para explicar el significado de los siguientes refranes e identificar su equivalente en inglés.

*A caballo regalado no se le mira el diente.*

- A caballo regalado no se le mira el diente.
- Cada loco con su tema.
- Más vale tarde que nunca.
- Camarón que se duerme se lo lleva la corriente.
- Cuando el río suena, piedras lleva.

- De tal palo, tal astilla.
- Dime con quién andas y te diré quién eres.
- No hay mal que por bien no venga.
- Más vale pájaro en mano que cien volando.
- Más sabe el diablo por viejo que por diablo.

## 24 El arte de hacer regalos  Interpersonal /Presentational Communication  **1.1, 1.3**

Regalar puede ser divertido y bonito. Sin embargo, para muchas personas es un invento comercial que aligera (*lighten*) el bolsillo y quita tiempo. También puede significar un gasto de horas para buscar algo elusivo que no se logra encontrar. Complete el cuestionario. Luego, compare sus respuestas con las de un(a) compañero/a de clase y comenten sus conclusiones con el resto de la clase.

| Cuestionario | Sí | No | Depende |
|---|---|---|---|
| 1. Mediante los regalos se usa un lenguaje mudo (*silent*) para expresar sentimientos de... | | | |
| A. amor. | | | |
| B. amistad. | | | |
| C. aprecio. | | | |
| D. gratitud. | | | |
| E. respeto. | | | |
| 2. Los comerciantes se inventaron los regalos para que gastemos dinero. | | | |
| 3. Obsequiar un bono de regalo de una tienda es más práctico. | | | |
| 4. Dar lo que a uno le gustaría recibir es el mejor regalo. | | | |
| 5. Si la persona es rica, hay que darle un regalo caro. | | | |
| 6. No es acertado regalar ropa. | | | |
| 7. Los ejecutivos mandan a su secretario/a a comprar los regalos. | | | |
| 8. Si uno hace el regalo en lugar de comprarlo, tiene más significado. | | | |
| 9. Hay que hacerle un regalo al jefe o a la jefa. | | | |
| 10. Es aceptable regalar a otra persona algo que le hayan dado a Ud. | | | |

## Differentiated Learning
### Heritage Learners
Ask heritage learners to share popular sayings that they hear in their cultural communities. Have the class try to guess the meaning of the phrases and the English equivalents.

## Learning Styles
### Visual Learners
Ask students to create drawings for the **proverbios** in **Actividad 23**. Display the illustrations and have the class identify the **proverbio**.

Communication

Interpersonal/Presentational: Paired Practice
Ask pairs of students to write a dialogue between two friends or family members who have very different opinions about gift-giving. Tell students that they can use ideas from **Actividad 24** if needed. Allow pairs time to rehearse and then perform their conversations for the class.

**25** *Las conversaciones variarán.*

**26**

1. F
2. V
3. F
4. F
5. V

*Las conversaciones variarán.*

## Reference Desk

Make sure that students understand the name **Domingo de Ramos** (*Palm Sunday*).

## Culture

### Practices: Information

In recent years, many parishes throughout Colombia have taken measures to celebrate Palm Sunday in a more "ecological" way, by encouraging people to carry live plants (rather than cut branches) or artificial fronds made from recycled materials.

## Expansion

Share with students this popular saying about Palm Sunday: **Domingo de Ramos, quien no estrena algo no tiene manos.** See if students can decipher the meaning.

# ¡Comunicación!

## 25 La Semana Santa en Estados Unidos — Interpersonal Communication — 1.1

Imagine que un estudiante extranjero desea saber cómo se celebra la Semana Santa en Estados Unidos. Represente la conversación con un(a) compañero/a, teniendo en cuenta la siguiente información.

- Tradiciones religiosas
- Tradiciones familiares
- Actividades para niños
- El conejo de Pascua
- El comercio de chocolates y caramelos
- ¿...?

*¡Oh! ¡Los huevitos que dejó el conejito de Pascua!*

## 26 El Domingo de Ramos — Interpretive/Interpersonal Communication — 1.1, 1.2, 2.1, 2.2, 4.2

Lea esta información sobre la Semana Santa y diga si las oraciones que siguen son verdaderas o falsas. Luego, hable con un(a) compañero/a sobre las tradiciones del Domingo de Ramos en su ciudad o país y en sus respectivas familias. ¿Son muy diferentes las tradiciones en distintas regiones de Estados Unidos?

*Celebración tradicional del Domingo de Ramos*

El Domingo de Ramos da inicio a la Semana Santa en la tradición iberoamericana. Es una fiesta religiosa que conmemora la entrada triunfal de Jesús de Nazaret a Jerusalén, en medio de una multitud que lo aclamaba como el Hijo de Dios. Por eso, se celebra con una alegre procesión en la que los fieles (*believer, faithful*) llevan ramos en la mano como recuerdo de ese glorioso día.

Algunos montan borriquillas o mulas. En España, las tradicionales cofradías llevan algunas de las escenas pascuales en hombros. Las cofradías son hermandades piadosas de orígenes medievales que visten una capucha, capirote o capuz (*hood*), una túnica y una capa del color de su orden.

Antes de la procesión, se bendicen ramas de olivo, palmera o laurel. En Latinoamérica, hay un sincretismo con las tradiciones indígenas en las que se recolectan ramas de diversa índole, según el país. Por ejemplo, en Perú llevan "chamizo", una retama seca, y en otros países llevan palmas, u hojas de palmera, verde.

¡Las distintas procesiones del Domingo de Ramos dan un bello comienzo a la llamada Semana Mayor!

1. El Domingo de Ramos finaliza la Semana Mayor en la tradición iberoamericana.
2. La procesión celebra la entrada triunfal de Jesús a Jerusalén.
3. Todos los fieles llevan ramos y visten los colores de su cofradía.
4. Las cofradías son los hermanos de los fieles.
5. Entre los ramos que se llevan, hay hojas de palmera verde, olivo, laurel y chamizo.

## Essential Instruction

1. After checking answers to **Actividad 25**, you may want to have a few students share favorite Easter memories.
2. Before students begin **Actividad 26**, have them skim the text. Clarify any unfamiliar vocabulary. Then have students complete the activity.
3. As you go through **Gramática**, make simple line drawings on the board to illustrate the prepositions.

# Gramática

## Usos de algunas preposiciones comunes  1.2, 4.1

| Usos | Ejemplos |
|---|---|
| ***Bajo se usa…*** | |
| • para indicar una posición inferior con respecto a algo (*under, below*) | Hay muchos huevos de Pascua **bajo** los árboles.<br>La temperatura de la nevera es de cinco grados **bajo** cero. |
| • en sentido figurado, para indicar dependencia o subordinación (*under*) | Habrá un cese al fuego **bajo** las siguientes condiciones.<br>**Bajo** nuevas reglas del juego, se busca firmar la paz. |
| ***Desde se usa…*** | |
| • para indicar un punto de partida en el espacio (*from*) | Los gitanos salieron **desde** la India sin rumbo fijo.<br>El crucero sale **desde** Cartagena y va por el Caribe. |
| • para indicar un punto de partida en el tiempo (*since*) | Trabajamos **desde** las 7:30 AM **hasta** las 5:30 PM (**hasta** indica el final o término). |
| ***Entre se usa…*** | |
| • para indicar una posición intermedia espacial, temporal o figurada (*between, among*) | La romería empieza **entre** las 6:00 PM y las 6:30 PM.<br>Hay algo eléctrico **entre** tú y yo. |
| ***Hasta se usa…*** | |
| • para marcar el término de lugar y tiempo (*until, up to, as far as*) | Los niños creen en los cuentos **hasta** la pubertad.<br>Caminaron **hasta** el centro de la ciudad. |
| • para expresar inclusión con el sentido de **aun**, **incluso** (*even*) | **Hasta** los abuelitos han aprendido a usar la internet.<br>En esta era, **hasta** los más chicos usan la tecnología. |
| ***Sin se usa…*** | |
| • para indicar algo que falta (*without*) | Se dieron cuenta de que se habían quedado **sin** hielo. |
| • con el infinitivo para indicar algo que no sucedió (inglés: *without + -ing*) | Ellos se miraron **sin** mediar palabra.<br>Entraron a la fiesta **sin** saludar. |
| • con el infinitivo para expresar acciones no terminadas (inglés: *un- + past participle*) | El vino se quedó **sin destapar**.<br>**Sin avergonzarse**, empezó a cantar otra vez suavemente. |
| ***Sobre se usa…*** | |
| • para indicar que algo está **encima de** una superficie o en una posición más alta (*on, upon*) | Mariposas amarillas volaban **sobre** Mauricio Babilonia.<br>Por favor, pon el libro **sobre** la mesa. |
| • con el significado de **acerca de**, para indicar el tema de algo (*on, about*) | Estaba leyendo un artículo **sobre** García Márquez.<br>Hay una conferencia **sobre** las fiestas iberoamericanas. |

### Reference Desk

1. Point out that **bajo** is not used as an adjective here, and therefore does not change in number or gender.
2. Explain that **entre** is used to express *between* as well as *among*.
3. You may want to introduce common phrases with these prepositions, such as **desde luego**, **hasta la fecha**, **sin duda**, **sin embargo**, etc.

### Expansion

Ask students to write one additional sentence using the prepositions **bajo**, **desde**, **hasta**, **entre**, **sobre**, and **sin**.

## Learning Styles
### Auditory Learners
Read aloud sentences that use the prepositions from pp. 367–368. Have students raise a hand each time they hear a preposition from the **Gramática** presentation.

## Multiple Intelligences
### Verbal-Linguistic
Have students use Flipgrid to create a chain story about Easter or another holiday of their choosing. Each student should add one or two sentences to the story. Encourage creativity and humor.

### Critical Thinking

**Analyzing**
Ask students questions about the location of places in your school and community: **¿Dónde está la cafetería? ¿Dónde está la calle Oak?**

### TPR

Have pairs of students take turns giving each other commands using these prepositions, e.g., **Pon la mano sobre el escritorio.** Their partner should carry out the action.

## Los pronombres usados como objeto de la preposición

| Pronombres como objeto de preposición | | | |
|---|---|---|---|
| yo | mí | nosotros/as | **nosotros/as** |
| tú | ti | vosotros/as | **vosotros/as** |
| él, ella, Ud. | **él, ella, Ud.** | ellos/as, Uds. | **ellos/as, Uds.** |

- Después de las preposiciones **entre**, **excepto**, **hasta**, **incluso**, **menos**, **salvo** y **según**, use los pronombres personales.

  Me gustaría que este secreto quedara **entre tú** y **yo**.

  Todos vinieron, **hasta ella** que tenía que estudiar.

- Con las demás preposiciones, use **mí** y **ti** para **yo** y **tú**, la primera y segunda persona del singular.

  La organización de la fiesta cayó **sobre ti**.

  Diles que no lo hagan **sin mí**.

- **Con** se combina con los pronombres **mí**, **ti** y **si** para formar **conmigo**, **contigo** y **consigo**.

  —¿Te gustaría ir **conmigo** al carnaval?

  —Me encantaría ir **contigo**. No querría perderme una fiesta que trae **consigo** tanta celebración.

### Un poco más

Estas son otras preposiciones y frases preposicionales comunes.

| | |
|---|---|
| acerca de | *about* |
| al lado de | *beside* |
| arriba de | *above* |
| cerca de | *near* |
| debajo de | *beneath* |
| delante de | *in front of* |
| dentro de | *within, inside of* |
| detrás de | *in back of, behind* |
| encima de | *on top of, above* |
| en lugar de | *in place of* |
| en vez de | *instead of* |
| excepto (menos, salvo) | *except* |
| frente a | *in front of, opposite, across from* |
| fuera de | *outside of* |
| hacia | *toward* |
| incluso | *including* |
| junto | *next to* |
| lejos de | *far from* |
| según | *according to* |

*El conejo de chocolate está colocado entre todos los dulces.*

### Essential Instruction
1. Model the use of the prepositions on this page by holding an item in various positions to elicit the preposition, e.g., **El libro está dentro de la mochila.**
2. Encourage students to write as many sentences as possible for each child in **Actividad 27**. Have them compare their answers with a partner.

Answers

**27** *Las respuestas variarán.*
*Respuestas posibles:*
Fátima y Sofía están detrás de la ventana.
Claudia está al lado de la planta.
Andrés está encima de la chimenea.
Ismael está entre el librero y la puerta.
Jacobo está dentro del armario.
Patricia está detrás del sofá.
Isabel está en el dormitorio.
Francisco está montado encima de la lámpara.
Noemí está bajo la lámpara.

**27** **¡Listos o no, allá voy!**  **1.3**

Hoy es la fiesta de cumpleaños de Claudia. Sus amigos vinieron y ahora están jugando a las escondidas, o al escondite (*hide-and-seek*). Diga dónde está ubicado cada niño usando las preposiciones correspondientes, como se ve en el modelo.

MODELO    Claudia está parada **hacia** un lado de la planta.

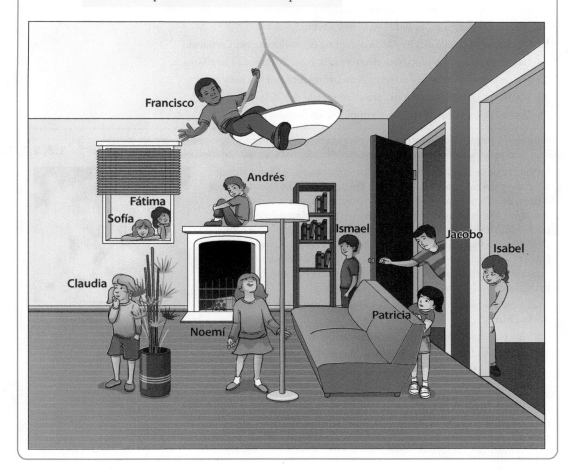

**Differentiated Learning**
**Decelerate/Adapt**
Before assigning **Actividad 27**, review furniture and house vocabulary. This activity can also be adapted according to your students' needs; you could provide a word bank, or create **cierto/falso** sentences about the children.

**Multiple Intelligences**
**Visual-Spatial**
Draw a square on the board. Call on two volunteers to come to the board. Have the class give the volunteers commands about where to draw objects relative to the square. Change volunteers after about six to eight drawings.

**28**

1. antes de
2. desde arriba
3. Encima de
4. Detrás de
5. Al lado del
6. detrás del
7. Delante de
8. después de
9. Hacia

**29**

1. desde
2. en, de
3. En
4. de, con
5. con, para
6. a, entre
7. a, para, de
8. Para, con, de
9. de, para
10. de, hasta
11. Por, encima de, entre
12. Con, para

## Reference Desk

1. **Rey Momo**, usually a tall, heavyset man, is the male counterpart of the carnival queen. In Barranquilla, King Momo has been part of the festivities since 1888.

2. Draw attention to the title of **Actividad 29**; explain that this is a line of a song that is sung while people are taking turns trying to break the **piñata**. Share the first verse with students.

---

**28 El desfile de Carnaval**  **1.2, 2.1, 2.2**

Es Carnaval y la familia Sánchez está viendo el desfile de carrozas. Elija la preposición que corresponda según el contexto.

1. Las comparsas se organizan (*detrás de / antes de*) arrancar el desfile.

2. La familia ve pasar el desfile de carrozas (*desde arriba / desde encima*), en su balcón.

3. (*encima de / debajo de*) una carroza llena de flores va la Reina del Carnaval.

4. (*detrás de / debajo de*) la Reina va el Rey Momo.

5. (*encima del / al lado del*) Rey Momo camina el Presidente del Carnaval.

6. Las carrozas de las comparsas desfilan (*abajo del / detrás del*) Rey Momo.

7. (*delante de / frente a*) las carrozas, una banda toca música muy alegre.

8. Los fuegos artificiales darán comienzo (*detrás de / después de*) las ocho.

9. (*hasta / hacia*) la medianoche terminarán los festejos del día.

---

**29 ¡No quiero oro, ni quiero plata, yo lo que quiero es romper la piñata!** 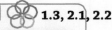 **1.3, 2.1, 2.2**

La piñata tiene una larga tradición, que empieza en la China, donde se usaba para celebrar el Año Nuevo. Entonces, tenían forma de vaca o buey, se rellenaban con cinco tipos de semillas, y se adornaban con símbolos y colores para una buena cosecha. Marco Polo llevó la tradición a Italia, donde se adaptó a las festividades de la cuaresma, y de allí pasó a España. Los españoles la llevaron al Nuevo Mundo; los frailes las hacían con siete picos, que simbolizaban los siete pecados capitales. Eventualmente, perdieron el sentido religioso. Elija la preposición que corresponda según el contexto.

*Una piñata estrella*

1. La piñata tiene una larga tradición que viene (*desde / hasta*) la China.

2. Hoy (*en / por*) día, son un elemento central (*con / de*) la Navidad y los cumpleaños.

3. (*en / sobre*) los mercados lucen sus alegres formas y colores.

4. Antes se rellenaban (*de / en*) semillas y ahora se rellenan (*con / sin*) dulces, cacahuates, frutas y juguetes.

5. Jugar (*con / por*) la piñata es un divertido juego (*por / para*) toda la familia.

6. Primero, se elige (*a / por*) una persona (*entre / sobre*) los invitados a la fiesta.

7. Los primeros turnos se dan (*a / ante*) los más pequeños (*para / por*) que tengan la oportunidad (*en / de*) romper la piñata.

8. (*para / por*) que no puedan ver la piñata, les tapan los ojos (*con / sin*) un pañuelo (*de / desde*) tela opaca.

9. Entonces, se los toma (*de / en*) la mano y se les da vueltas (*por / para*) desorientarlos.

10. El participante trata (*a / de*) golpear la piñata (*hasta / desde*) que acaba su turno.

11. (*por / para*) fin, cuando alguien logra romper la piñata, el relleno cae (*debajo de / encima de*) todos, (*por / entre*) risas y gritos de alegría.

12. (*sin / con*) prisa, todos corren (*para / sobre*) agarrar los dulces y los juguetes.

## Essential Instruction

1. Check answers to **Actividad 28** by having volunteers read aloud the complete sentences.

2. Complete **Actividad 29** as a class.

3. Before assigning **Actividad 30**, brainstorm necessary vocabulary and write it on the board. Then divide the class into pairs and have them complete the activity.

# ¡Comunicación!

## 30 El ayer y el ahora... 👥 Interpersonal Communication ✿ 1.1, 1.3, 3.1

Con un(a) compañero/a, observen y describan los detalles de esta escena usando las preposiciones del recuadro. Luego, túrnense para responder las preguntas que se dan a continuación.

| bajo | de | sin | para | con | hasta |
|------|-----|-----|------|-----|-------|

- ¿Se ve esta escena en las típicas fiestas infantiles de hoy en día? ¿En qué se parece y en qué se diferencia?

- ¿Cuál puede ser el evento o acontecimiento que están celebrando?

- ¿Con qué se rellena una piñata de cumpleaños en la actualidad?

---

### Connections

**Art**
Ask students to look up three paintings by Fernando Botero and print them. Tell students to write a description of the locations of the people and objects in each painting. Then, in class, have pairs of students take turns reading their descriptions; their partner should point to the corresponding painting.

---

## Differentiated Learning
### Accelerate/Expand
In pairs, have one student's desk face the front of the room and the other face the back. The student facing the back of the room will have a blank piece of paper. Display an image that contains several people and objects. The student facing the front must explain the scene to his/her partner, who must draw it. Finally, students can compare the drawing with the original scene. Have pairs switch roles and repeat the activity with another image.

### Learning Styles
**Visual Learners**
After choosing answers for **Actividad 28**, tell students to draw the carnival scene as described in the sentences.

Antes de leer
¿Triqui triqui enfrentado a los angelitos?

## Answers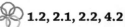

### Antes de leer

*Las respuestas variarán.*

**31**

1. Se celebran prácticamente en la misma fecha. En ambos casos, los niños salen a pedir dulces de casa en casa mientras cantan. Ambas se celebran en la ciudad de Barranquilla. Ambas celebraciones provienen de la fiesta de Todos los Santos.
2. En *Halloween* participan tanto los niños como los adultos, mientras que en el Día de los Angelitos participan solo los niños. *Halloween* tiene origen celta, mientras que el Día de los Angelitos proviene de la cultura española. El Día de los Angelitos tiene un sentido religioso del que carece *Halloween*.
3. Es una fiesta cristiana heredada de los españoles. En Extremadura se celebraba la Chaquetía el Día de Todos los Santos el 1 de noviembre, que consistía en que los niños salían a pedir aguinaldos como premio adelantado por tocar las campanas en memoria de los fallecidos el 2 de noviembre, que es el Día de Todos los Difuntos.
4. Constaba de niños saliendo por la mañana a pedir dulces, caña de azúcar y panela entre familiares y vecinos. Algunas veces recogían ingredientes para hacer una merienda, un almuerzo o un sancocho al aire libre ese mismo día.

**32**  *Las respuestas variarán.*

### Pre-AP

**Course Theme: La vida contemporánea**

**372**

---

# Lectura informativa

## Antes de leer  1.3, 5.2

1. ¿Cuáles son sus festividades favoritas?
2. ¿Qué tradiciones conoce que se hayan perdido con el tiempo?

### Estrategia  3.1

**Comparar y contrastar**

Identificar las semejanzas y diferencias que presentan las prácticas, los sucesos o las personas que se describen en un texto lo ayudará a comprenderlo mejor.

 1.2, 2.1, 2.2, 4.2

### 31 Comprensión

1. ¿En qué se parecen *Halloween* y el Día de los Angelitos?
2. ¿En qué se diferencian las dos celebraciones?
3. ¿Cuál es el origen del Día de los Angelitos?
4. ¿En qué consistía la tradición del Día de los Angelitos en el Caribe?

### 32 Analice 1.3

¿Cómo cree Ud. que influye la globalización y el avance de los medios de comunicación en la llegada de celebraciones extranjeras a otras culturas?

**VIERNES 26 DE JUNIO**  CONTÁCTENOS | OBITUARIOS | OFERTAS H | CLASIFICADOS | SUSCRIPCIONES

**ELHERALDO.CO**  BUSCAR

HOME   LOCAL   REGIÓN   DEPORTES   TENDENCIAS   ENTRETENIMIENTO   JUDICIAL   NOTICIAS   MULTIMEDIA   OPINIÓN   REVISTAS   USUARIOS

## ¿Triqui triqui enfrentado a los angelitos? 1.2, 2.1, 2.2, 3.2
**Por Melissa Zuleta Bandera**

**La fiesta de las 'brujitas', a pesar de no ser propia, tiene gran acogida en la ciudad. La celebración tradicional de 'angelitos' aún vive y lucha por imponerse.**

El final de octubre y el principio de noviembre traen consigo dos celebraciones distintas en origen pero similares en ejecución: tanto en Halloween (o Día de las Brujitas) como en el Día de los Angelitos, los niños salen a pedir dulces de casa en casa mientras entonan cánticos[1].

Mientras el *Halloween* viene de la fiesta celta *All Hallows' Eve* (víspera de todos los santos), la otra surge de la fiesta española de Todos los Santos. La diferencia es que en la primera tanto niños como adultos se disfrazan[2]. En la segunda, arraigada en Barranquilla, el sentido es más religioso. Y en esta ciudad ambas dan su pelea por demostrar su prevalencia.

**Desde Europa.** El Día de los Angelitos, celebrado en algunas ciudades del Caribe colombiano, es una fiesta cristiana heredada de los españoles.

Nanet Mercado, miembro de la comisión de la Pastoral Infantil de la Arquidiócesis de Barranquilla, explica que en la comunidad española de Extremadura se celebraba una fiesta llamada Chaquetía el Día de Todos los Santos (primero de noviembre) como preámbulo al Día de Todos los Difuntos, que consistía en que los niños salían a pedir aguinaldos[3] como premio adelantado por tocar las campanas en memoria de los fallecidos el 2 de noviembre. "Es una fiesta netamente[4] católica", cuenta Mercado.

La tradición en la región Caribe constaba de niños saliendo en la mañana a pedir dulces, caña de azúcar y panela[5] entre familiares y vecinos. Algunas veces recogían ingredientes para hacer una merienda, un almuerzo o un sancocho[6] al aire libre ese mismo día. [...]

**Lo propio versus lo ajeno.** Desde hace doce años, la Pastoral Infantil viene trabajando para recuperar la tradición del Día de los Angelitos. [...]

[1] chant  [2] wear costumes  [3] gifts  [4] purely  [5] brown sugar loaf  [6] stew

---

## Essential Instruction

1. Discuss the **Antes de leer** question as a class. Ask students to give examples.
2. Go over the **Estrategia**. Encourage students to use a Venn diagram to compare and contrast the two holidays discussed in the reading.
3. Play the recording, pausing to ask comprehension questions.
4. For Common Core practice, have students answer the **Analice** questions. Go over the answers as a class.

**¿Triqui triqui enfrentado...**

VIERNES 26 DE JUNIO

CONTÁCTENOS | OBITUARIOS | OFERTAS H | CLASIFICADOS | SUSCRIPCIONES

**H** | **ELHERALDO**.CO

BUSCAR

HOME | LOCAL | REGIÓN | DEPORTES | TENDENCIAS | ENTRETENIMIENTO | JUDICIAL | NOTICIAS | MULTIMEDIA | OPINIÓN | REVISTAS | USUARIOS

Desde el punto de vista de la Iglesia Católica, la tradición se ha ido perdiendo ante el auge del Día de las Brujitas. "Es fácil que la gente se deje deslumbrar, sobre todo en los sectores populares, que era donde más se celebraba. *Halloween* llega por las clases sociales altas que tenían la posibilidad de viajar y traer costumbres de otros países. En los clubes para estas fechas se daban fiestas llenas de colorido, disfraces, máscaras y vestidos pomposos, y poco a poco se fue metiendo en los sectores populares", sopesa Mercado. Considera que disfrazarse y pedir dulces "no está del todo mal", pero que "es mejor" celebrar lo tradicional.

Jair Vega, sociólogo y docente[7] de la Universidad del Norte, considera que la proliferación de esta fiesta extranjera "hace parte de la comunicación global que va a la par de la expansión de los mercados, hace parte de ese proceso mediante el cual todas las celebraciones se van asociando al consumo".

"Recibimos mucha influencia de la forma como se vive en Estados Unidos, a través del cine, la televisión y muchos elementos, lo cual hace que ese tipo de referentes se vayan convirtiendo también en referentes locales".

Es ahí donde, para él, está el problema: "Esto debe verse más allá de un asunto meramente moral, de que *Halloween* sea 'diabólico' o que Día de los Angelitos sea 'religioso'. Es un asunto que tiene más que ver con la identidad de lo propio y lo foráneo[8], porque siempre habrá influencias, pero también hay que ver hasta qué punto las influencias las resumimos, las procesamos y las readecuamos a nuestro contexto o en qué medida esos referentes externos reemplazan nuestros propios referentes. Entre más referentes propios perdemos nosotros, más estamos al vaivén[9] de lo externo y perdemos autonomía", sostiene el docente.

**Comercio y educación.** Otras posturas no son tan radicales. Según un experto, los gastos de los colombianos relativos al día de las "brujitas" mueven la economía. [...]

Otros aprovechan la coyuntura[10]. Aurora de Guete, rectora[11] del Colegio Real – Royal School, explica que a cada festividad le sacan algo positivo para que los niños aprendan.

"Es un aprendizaje. Es volverte alguien más, caracterizar su voz, explicar a los otros por qué lo escogiste. Facilitar que los niños hagan caracterizaciones en este día es aprendizaje y diversión", detalla Guete, quien sostiene que desde la institución no están ni de acuerdo ni en desacuerdo con la celebración, sino que apoyan "todo lo que sea un aprendizaje a través de la diversión". Por eso mismo, abren un espacio similar para el Día de los Angelitos. [...]

[7] professor    [8] foreign    [9] we are exposed    [10] circumstances    [11] principal

**Búsqueda:** *halloween* en colombia, día de las brujitas, día de los angelitos

 **1.2, 2.1, 2.2, 3.2**

## 33 Comprensión

1. ¿Cómo llegó *Halloween* a Colombia?

2. ¿Qué explicación le encuentra Jair Vega a la difusión de *Halloween*?

3. ¿Por qué para Jair Vega el reemplazo de una tradición local por una extranjera es un problema?

4. Según Aurora de Guete, ¿qué aspecto positivo tienen las festividades?

## 34 Analice **1.3, 3.2**

¿Por qué cree Ud. que *Halloween* se convirtió en una celebración popular en otras culturas? ¿Qué aspectos de la celebración cree Ud. que resultan más atractivos para los extranjeros?

---

**Answers**

**33**

1. Llegó de la mano de las personas de clase alta que tenían la posibilidad de viajar y llevar al país costumbres de otros lugares. Con el tiempo se difundió también entre los sectores populares.

2. Cree que tiene que ver con la comunicación global y la expansión de los mercados, que hace que todas las celebraciones se asocien al consumo. También influye mucho la cultura estadounidense, ya que a través del cine, la televisión y otros medios sus referentes se terminan convirtiendo en referentes locales en otras culturas.

3. Porque al perder los referentes propios se pierde autonomía.

4. Las festividades se pueden aprovechar para el aprendizaje mediante la diversión.

**34** *Las respuestas variarán.*

### Reference Desk

The words **Triqui triqui** in the title refer to the rhyme that children in Colombia say when asking for Halloween treats: **Triqui triqui *Halloween*, Quiero dulces para mí, Si no hay dulces para mí, Se le crece la nariz.**

### Critical Thinking

**Analyzing**
Ask students if they think it's true that "**todas las celebraciones se van asociando con el consumo.**"

---

**Differentiated Learning**
**Accelerate/Expand**
Ask students to read and analyze the themes in **Don Juan Tenorio**, the play that is traditionally performed in Spain and Mexico on All Saints' Day.

**Multiple Intelligences**
**Verbal-Linguistic**
Ask students to reread the first and last paragraphs on this page. Tell them to write a short paragraph stating whether they agree more with Nanet Mercado's assertions or Aurora del Guete's, and why.

# Escritura

## Una carta persuasiva  1.3

El propósito de una carta persuasiva es presentar a una persona, a una organización o al público en general (cuando se envía a un periódico o una revista) el propio punto de vista sobre algún tema controvertido.

Las cartas persuasivas, además de presentar las características de las cartas formales (que puede consultar en la Unidad 3), cuentan con características similares a las del ensayo persuasivo.

- El punto de vista o la postura de quien la escribe debe presentarse claramente al principio.
- Debe incluir argumentos para fundamentar el punto de vista, en forma de evidencia, explicaciones o ejemplos.
- Al final de la carta, se debe incluir una conclusión en la que se resuma el punto de vista.

### ¡Comunicación!

**35  Decisiones antipáticas**   Presentational Communication  1.3, 2.1, 2.2

Imagínese que Ud. vive en Barranquilla, Valledupar o Cartagena y que el alcalde de la ciudad que elija ha decidido suspender las celebraciones populares por un año por razones económicas. Escriba una carta persuasiva al alcalde en la que explique la importancia de realizar la celebración de todas maneras. Antes de comenzar a escribir, organice sus ideas en el siguiente gráfico, colocando el punto de vista en el círculo superior y las razones que lo apoyen en los círculos inferiores.

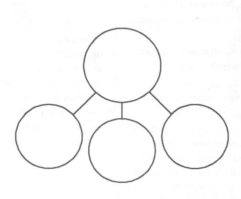

*Los trajes tradicionales dan un toque de elegancia a las celebraciones colombianas.*

## Essential Instruction

1. Introduce this section by going over the information about **cartas persuasivas**. If needed, briefly review formal letter-writing.
2. Before students begin filling in their outlines for **Actividad 35**, remind them of the celebrations associated with the three cities.

   Have students peer-edit their letters.
3. Play the audio in **Actividad 36** once for students just to listen. Then replay it and have them check the appropriate box.
4. Encourage students to use Venn diagrams to organize their ideas in **Actividad 38**.

 ¡Comunicación!

**36 De fiesta en Colombia**  Interpretive Communication  **1.2, 2.1, 2.2**

Escuche la entrevista a un joven colombiano que habla sobre las celebraciones de su país. Luego, diga a qué celebración corresponde cada una de las siguientes actividades.

| Actividades | Carnavales de negros y blancos | Navidad |
|---|---|---|
| 1. Todos cenan en casa de los padres o los abuelos. | | |
| 2. Se realiza en honor a los españoles. | | |
| 3. Se realiza en honor a los esclavos. | | |
| 4. Se celebra con mucho calor humano. | | |
| 5. Se utilizan cosméticos para pintarse la cara. | | |
| 6. Se celebra en familia. | | |
| 7. Se cantan villancicos. | | |
| 8. Hay un desfile de artesanos. | | |

**37 ¡Ud. también participa!** Presentational Communication  **1.3, 2.1, 2.2**

Imagine que un amigo colombiano lo ha invitado a pasar las vacaciones en su casa y que su estadía en Colombia coincide con una de las dos fiestas que se mencionan en el audio de la actividad anterior. Escriba una publicación en una red social en la que relate su experiencia.

**38 Fiestas de aquí y de allá** Presentational Communication **1.3, 2.1, 2.2, 4.2**

Piense en un festival, un desfile o una celebración que se realice en la región donde vive o de donde proviene y compárelo/a con una o más de las celebraciones colombianas sobre las que ha leído. ¿Tienen alguna característica en común? ¿Cuáles son las diferencias más notables? Escriba un párrafo en el que compare y contraste las celebraciones.

**Differentiated Learning**

**Expand**

Work as a class to prepare a **día de celebraciones**. Divide the class into groups and have them choose a Colombian holiday or festival. Each group member should be responsible for researching, preparing, and bringing to class a different aspect of their holiday, such as music, food, dances, clothing/masks/accessories, or another traditional aspect. Allow each group a separate space in the classroom to set up their holiday. The class can visit each festival in turn to sample the food, listen to music, and learn dance steps, etc. At the end of the day, have students share their impressions of the day via Flipgrid.

**RESOURCES**

 Flipgrid

 Activity 36

**Answers**

**36 Script**

—Bueno, pues, me contaste que las fiestas son una cosa importante en Colombia. ¿Cómo son las fiestas?
—Bueno, sí, mira, nosotros los colombianos tenemos de trascendencia celebrar muchísimas fiestas en cada una de las regiones y en cada uno de los departamentos. Para darte una leve idea de cómo se viven las fiestas en Colombia, se comienza en enero. A principios del dos, tres, cuatro, cinco y seis de enero se celebran los tradicionales carnavales de negros y blancos en la ciudad de Pasto, que es al sur de Colombia. Es una experiencia maravillosa, en donde el día cuatro se realiza la llegada de la familia Castañeda, que es una remembranza de los primeros familias que quisieron unificarse y celebrar un carnaval en aquella región del sur. El día cinco la población, en honor a los esclavos, se pinta la cara de cosmético negro, y el día seis, que es el día más importante, es todo lo contrario, y se celebra el día de los blancos, que es una remembranza a los españoles, en donde uno se coloca cosmético en la cara de color blanco, y hay un desfile muy importante que lo realizan los artesanos de Nariño.

*Continued on p. 385.*

1. Navidad
2. Carnavales de negros y blancos
3. Carnavales de negros y blancos
4. Navidad
5. Carnavales de negros y blancos
6. Navidad
7. Navidad
8. Carnavales de negros y blancos

**37** *Las respuestas variarán.*

**38** *Los párrafos variarán.*

### Reference Desk

Point out that students will use this vocabulary to complete the audio activity on p. 377, as well as to aid in comprehension of the **Lectura literaria** on pp. 380–384.

### Expansion

Ask students to define the terms in **Actividad 39** in their own words.

### Game

**Dibujos**
Divide the class into teams. Give one member of each group a word from **Mejore su comprensión**. The team member with the word or phrase then draws clues for his or her team members. Each team has one minute to guess the word or phrase from the drawn clues. Award points to the fastest team and continue with different vocabulary and artists until a team reaches a point total determined in advance.

# Vocabulario 3

## Mejore su comprensión  1.2

Familiarizarse con este vocabulario le ayudará a leer "Un señor muy viejo con unas alas enormes" más adelante, y a mejorar su comprensión auditiva.

**alboroto** *s.m.* Ruido, conmoción.

**anegado/a** *adj.* Inundado de agua u otro líquido.

**caritativo/a** *adj.* Generoso, compasivo.

**codiciar** *v.* Desear con fuerza algo.

**criterio** *s.m.* Capacidad para comprender algo y formar una opinión.

**decrépito/a** *adj.* Persona de edad avanzada cuyas facultades físicas y mentales han disminuido.

**desbaratar** *v.* Deshacer o arruinar algo.

**despectivo/a** *adj.* Que expresa desprecio y arrogancia.

**despotricar** *v.* Criticar algo sin consideración.

**displicente** *adj.* Que expresa indiferencia y falta de interés.

**encallar** *v.* Quedar inmovilizada una embarcación en piedras o en la arena.

**escarmiento** *s.m.* Enseñanza que se saca de una experiencia negativa para evitar repetirla.

**exasperado/a** *adj.* Irritado al punto de perder la paciencia.

**fuera de quicio** *exp.* Sin control de sí mismo.

**incauto/a** *adj.* Crédulo, inocente.

**ingenuidad** *s.f.* Sinceridad, inocencia o ausencia de malicia.

**intemperie** *s.f.* Al aire libre, sin ningún techo o protección.

**juicio** *s.m.* Facultad que permite discernir y valorar.

**magnánimo/a** *adj.* Noble, generoso.

**náufrago** *s.m.* Persona que viajaba en un barco que se ha hundido.

**peregrino** *s.m.* Que viaja a un lugar sagrado o va por tierras remotas.

**podrido/a** *adj.* Algo descompuesto o alterado.

**prudencia** *s.f.* Capacidad de reflexión y uso de precaución para evitar problemas.

**quebrantar** *v.* Dañar o destrozar algo.

**senil** *adj.* Característica de los ancianos y la vejez.

**tumulto** *s.m.* Bulla o desorden producido por una multitud.

**veredicto** *s.m.* Decisión de un jurado en un tribunal.

*Muchos peregrinos hacen el recorrido del Camino de Santiago en España.*

### 39 Sinónimos  1.2

Empareje cada palabra con su sinónimo.

| Palabras | Sinónimos |
|---|---|
| 1. decrépito | A. juicio |
| 2. exasperado | B. ingenuo |
| 3. alboroto | C. senil |
| 4. veredicto | D. desbaratar |
| 5. incauto | E. displicente |
| 6. despectivo | F. tumulto |
| 7. magnánimo | G. caritativo |
| 8. quebrantar | H. fuera de quicio |

### Essential Instruction

1. Model pronunciation of the new vocabulary and have students repeat the words. Clarify any unfamiliar words in the definitions.
2. Have students complete **Actividades 39** and **40** in pairs.
3. Before beginning **Actividad 41**, remind students that they will hear some vocabulary from p. 376 in the story.
4. For **Actividad 41**, have students listen to the story with their eyes closed. Play it a second time, pausing to ask questions. Then play the rest of the audio and have students select their answers.

## 40 Según el contexto  1.2

Complete las siguientes oraciones con la palabra entre paréntesis que corresponda según el contexto.

1. Las tierras quedaron (*anegadas / podridas*) después de la tormenta tropical.
2. Confío en la sentencia del juez. Sé que será (*decrépito / magnánimo*) en su decisión.
3. El anciano se pasaba el día (*desbaratando / despotricando*) sobre los inventos modernos.
4. Esperaban que el castigo del prisionero les sirviera de (*alboroto / escarmiento*) a los demás.
5. Tal era su (*ingenuidad / prudencia*) que no se daba cuenta que no le convenía lograr lo que codiciaba.
6. Los (*náufragos / peregrinos*) estuvieron muchos días a la intemperie después de que encalló su embarcación.

## 41 El secreto de la viña  1.2, 3.1

Escuche el relato "El secreto de la viña". Luego, Ud. oirá la primera parte de una oración y tres terminaciones posibles. Seleccione la letra de la respuesta con la terminación más lógica. La oración y las terminaciones se leerán dos veces.

1. **A.** ... llamó a sus hijos.
   **B.** ... fue llamado por sus hijos.
   **C.** ... no quería hablar con sus hijos.
2. **A.** ... que él tenía muchas deudas.
   **B.** ... que él iba a morir muy pronto.
   **C.** ... que en la viña había un tesoro de gran valor.
3. **A.** ... que era necesario cavar mucho para encontrar el tesoro.
   **B.** ... que él no había podido encontrar el tesoro.
   **C.** ... que los hijos tenían que enterrar un tesoro.

4. **A.** ... encontraron mucho dinero enterrado.
   **B.** ... cavaron durante mucho tiempo sin encontrar el tesoro.
   **C.** ... comieron mucha fruta de la viña.
5. **A.** ... que el tesoro de la viña era el trabajo.
   **B.** ... que la viña ese año no daría frutos.
   **C.** ... que no había un tesoro en la viña.

 Activity 41

**Answers**

**40**
1. anegadas
2. magnánimo
3. despotricando
4. escarmiento
5. ingenuidad
6. náufragos

**41 Script**
Un campesino que estaba para morir llamó a sus hijos y les dijo:
—Hijos míos, como mi vida llega a su fin, quiero decirles mi secreto. En la viña tengo enterrado un tesoro de gran valor. Será necesario mucho trabajo si quieren encontrarlo.
Y sin decir más, murió el campesino.
Los hijos, después de enterrar al padre, fueron a la viña y durante mucho tiempo cavaron la tierra, a veces en una parte y a veces en otra. Pero no encontraron el tesoro que buscaban.
Como aquel año los hijos cavaron tanto la tierra, la viña dio mucha más fruta que los años anteriores. El hermano mayor, al ver cuánto se había aprovechado, les dijo a sus hermanos menores:
—Con esta experiencia, ahora comprendo que el tesoro de la viña de nuestro padre es nuestro trabajo.

1. Un campesino que estaba para morir...
2. El secreto que el campesino quería decirles a sus hijos era...
3. El campesino les dijo a sus hijos...
4. Después de enterrar al padre, los hijos...
5. El hermano mayor comprendió...

1. A; 2. C; 3. A; 4. B; 5. A

## Special Needs Students
**Auditory Impairment**
Provide students with the script of the story and the sentence starters in **Actividad 41**. Allow them to listen as many times as needed.

## Multiple Intelligences
**Bodily-Kinesthetic/Verbal-Linguistic**
Have students work in small groups to role-play "**El secreto de la viña**." Tell groups to create dialogue for the various scenes that do not have it, and that they can give their characters names if they wish. Have groups role-play their skits for the class, who can vote for the most original dialogue, best acting, etc.

# Gramática

## Los diminutivos y los aumentativos ✿ 1.2

En español, se usan frecuentemente los diminutivos y los aumentativos, especialmente en el habla cotidiana. Para formarlos, se usan sufijos, terminaciones para dar a las palabras un significado específico.

| Los diminutivos | | |
|---|---|---|
| **Sufijos** | **Expresan...** | **Ejemplos** |
| **-ito, -ita**[1] | • pequeñez, menor intensidad, aprecio, cariño (son los más usados) | Mi sobrin**ito** tiene dos añ**itos**. |
| **-cito, -cita**[2] | | A la Virgen**cita** de Chiquinquirá también le dicen la Chin**ita** por cariño. |
| **-uelo, -uela** | • juventud, pequeñez o pureza; también menosprecio | Las moz**uelas** usaban pañoleta y chal. |
| | | La tachaban de mujerz**uela**. |
| **-illo, -illa** | • juventud, pequeñez o afecto; también menosprecio o conmiseración | Son unos chiqu**illos** muy simpáticos. |
| **-cillo, -cilla** | | Era un jefe**cillo** de una tribu menor. |
| | | Pobre**cilla** ella, ¡cómo sufría! |

| Los aumentativos | | |
|---|---|---|
| **Sufijos** | **Expresan...** | **Ejemplos** |
| **-ón, -ona** | • tamaño grande o apariencia llamativa; también menosprecio o disgusto | Es un bebé precioso y cachet**ón**. |
| | | Es muy guapa, ¡todo un mujer**ón**! |
| | | ¡Qué hombret**ón** tan desagradable! |
| **-ote, -ota** | • gran tamaño, intensidad o poder; también menosprecio o desestimación | Abría esa boc**ota** desmedidamente. |
| **-azo, -aza** | | Me encanta trabajar con él. ¡Es todo un jef**azo**! |
| **-aco, -aca** | | El pobre patito era un bicharr**aco** feo y torpe. |
| **-uco, -uca** | • menosprecio o desestimación (muy despectivo); aprecio o conmiseración | Se asomaba desde un ventan**uco** oscuro. |
| **-ucho, -ucha** | | Era una muchachita larguir**ucha** y apocada. |

[1] En Latinoamérica, muchos adjetivos o adverbios toman la forma diminutiva: **grande** → **grandecito**, **ahora** → **ahorita**.

[2] No hay reglas fijas para usar **-ito** o **-cito**. Sin embargo, se tiende a usar **-ito** con palabras terminadas en **a** y **o**: tostad**ita**, pajar**ito**; y se tiende a usar **-cito** con palabras terminadas en las vocales **e, i**, o las consonantes **n** o **r**: cafe**cito**, aji**cito**, vagon**cito**, calor**cito**.

### Essential Instruction

1. Open **Gramática** by asking what suffixes are added to English names to express endearment (*-y* or *-ie*, as in *Johnny, Jennie*).

2. As you work through the grammar presentation, model the pronunciation of the suffixes and have students repeat after you. Also model how tone of voice coupled with diminutives and augmentatives can show either affection or disgust.

3. Check answers to **Actividad 42** chorally.

4. Have students complete **Actividad 43** in pairs. Then have pairs join together to discuss their responses.

5. Play or sing the full songs in **Actividad 44** for the class.

## 42 Halloween, fiesta de espíritus  1.2

*Halloween* es una fiesta muy antigua. Se creía que los espíritus deambulaban (*wandered*) libremente al finalizar el otoño, en la víspera del invierno. Por eso, se hacían lámparas para alejar espíritus malignos, y se ofrendaba comida y bebida. También había juegos y adivinanzas. Las personas se disfrazaban para engañar a los espíritus, imitándolos; iban de casa en casa pidiendo comida y haciendo travesuras si no les daban nada. Use sufijos diminutivos para cambiar las palabras en negrita. *¡Trick or treat!*

1. Cuando era un **chico**, disfrutaba *Halloween* con mis **primos**.
2. Poníamos **calabazas** a la entrada de casa.
3. Nos poníamos disfraces y **máscaras**.
4. Algunos iban de piratas, algunas **niñas** de hadas.
5. Íbamos de puerta en puerta con nuestras **bolsas**.
6. Cantábamos una **canción** al abrirse cada puerta.
7. Queríamos que nos dieran **juguetes** o **golosinas**.
8. Si no nos daban nada, hacíamos un **truco**.
9. Corríamos entre **risas** y algarabía.
10. A medianoche, caíamos rendidos como **ángeles**.

## 43 Pajarraco o pajarito  1.2

Javier y Juan son gemelos, pero tienen temperamentos muy diferentes. Javier es pesimista y a veces sarcástico. Use el aumentativo que corresponda a las palabras en negrita.

Mis **vecinos** son **antipáticos**. No soporto las **palabras** que sueltan a cada rato esos **señores** de al lado. La **gran casa** donde habitan no se ve acogedora y nunca saludan. Encima, tienen un **perro grande** y una gata **fea** que es **flaca**.

En cambio, Juan es un optimista. Use el diminutivo que corresponda.

Estuvimos en un **pueblo** muy **cerca** de un lindo **lago**. Por las mañanas, los **pájaros** cantaban sus melodiosas **canciones**, mientras las dulces **viejas** ordeñaban las vacas y las **chicas** recogían **flores**.

## 44 Cancionero musical  1.2, 3.1

Muchas canciones latinoamericanas están llenas de diminutivos. ¿Conoce Ud. alguna de las siguientes canciones? Escriba los diminutivos y diga de qué palabra proviene cada una. Recuerde que, en Latinoamérica, muchos adjetivos y adverbios toman la forma diminutiva, como **chico/a → chiquito/a**, **ahora → ahorita**.

**Cielito lindo**

¡Ay, ay, ay, ay!
Canta y no llores,
porque cantando
se alegran, cielito lindo,
los corazones.

**Muñequita linda**

Muñequita linda
de cabellos de oro,
de dientes de perla,
labios de rubí.
Dime si me quieres
como yo te quiero,
si de mí te acuerdas
como yo de ti.

**La casita**

¿Que de dónde, amigo, vengo?
De una casita que tengo
más abajo del trigal.
De una casita chiquita
para la mujer bonita
que me quiera acompañar.

---

emcpassport.com
WB 10–13
LA 6–8

## RESOURCES

 Flipgrid

**Answers**

**42** *Respuestas posibles:*
1. chiquillo, primitos
2. calabacitas
3. mascaritas
4. niñitas
5. bolsitas
6. cancioncita
7. juguetitos, golosinitas
8. truquito
9. risitas
10. angelitos

**43** *Respuestas posibles:*
*Javier:* vecinotes, antipaticones, palabrotas, señorones, casona, perrote/perrazo, feúcha/feona, flacuchenta
*Juan:* pueblito/pueblecillo, cerquita, laguito, pajaritos/pajarillos, cancioncitas/cancioncillas, viejecillas/viejecitas, chicuelas/chiquillas, florecitas/florecillas

**44**
cielito — cielo
muñequita — muñeca
casita — casa
chiquita — chica

## Connections

**Language Arts**
Bring in copies of a fairy tale in Spanish, such as "**Caperucita roja**." Have students work in pairs to read the story and analyze its use of diminutives and augmentatives. Then ask students to create a Flipgrid post in which they give the synopsis of another favorite fairy tale from childhood.

---

## Differentiated Learning
### Heritage Learners
Ask heritage learners to share which diminutive and augmentative suffixes are most common in their family's country of origin. Have the class create diminutive and augmentative forms using these suffixes.

## Learning Styles
### Visual Learners
Bring in caricatures of people and things, or cartoons in which sizes are exaggeratedly large or small. Display the images and have students describe what they see using diminutives and augmentatives.

**Answers**

**Antes de leer**
*Las respuestas variarán.*

**45** *Las respuestas variarán.*

## Reference Desk

1. This story was first published as part of the collection ***La increíble y triste historia de la cándida Eréndira y su abuela desalmada*** (1968).
2. In the 1960s and 70s, Latin America experienced a literary "boom," of which Gabriel García Márquez was a main figure, along with Julio Cortázar, Carlos Fuentes, Mario Vargas Llosa, and others.
3. Make sure that students understand the concepts of literal and symbolic interpretations before reading the story.

## Critical Thinking

**Analyzing**
Tell students that this story's subtitle is **Un cuento para niños**, but that it is not a story for children. Ask them why they think the author may have chosen this subtitle.

## Expansion

Make a timeline of the life and works of Gabriel García Márquez and discuss them as a class.

## Pre-AP

**Course Theme: La belleza y la estética**

---

# *Lectura literaria*

## Un señor muy viejo con unas alas enormes
### de *Gabriel García Márquez*  1.2, 2.2, 3.1

### Sobre el autor

Gabriel García Márquez nació en Aracataca, Colombia, en 1927. Estudió en Bogotá y trabajó como periodista en varias publicaciones de su país, aunque vivió también en Europa, Venezuela, Nueva York y México. Publicó su novela más aclamada, *Cien años de soledad*, en 1967 y se convirtió en referente del realismo mágico, un estilo característico que seguirían otros autores hispanoamericanos y en el cual se tratan hechos o personajes sobrenaturales o fantásticos con naturalidad, como si fueran parte de la realidad. En 1982 se le concedió el Premio Nobel de Literatura. Una de las eminencias más internacionales de la literatura hispanoamericana, García Márquez publicó su autobiografía *Vivir para contarla* en 2002. Falleció el 17 de abril de 2014 en la Ciudad de México.

*Gabriel García Márquez*

### Antes de leer  1.3, 3.1

El título de este cuento, "Un señor muy viejo con unas alas enormes", ya nos sitúa en el ambiente del realismo mágico, no por la referencia al "señor viejo", algo común, sino por la mención de las "alas enormes", un elemento de fantasía típico de los cuentos infantiles. ¿Qué tipo de personaje le sugiere este título y qué elementos mágicos o fantásticos cree que Ud. que lo caracterizan?

### Estrategia 3.1

**La hipérbole**

La hipérbole es una figura literaria que consiste en presentar la realidad de forma exagerada para producir un efecto más conmovedor. La hipérbole describe situaciones que no se dan en la práctica pero que ayudan a enfatizar los sucesos o acontecimientos que el escritor quiere grabar en la mente del lector. Saber interpretar este recurso literario le ayudará a distinguir lo real de lo irreal y a comprender el mensaje del autor, que no siempre está explícito en el texto.

### 45 Practique la estrategia 1.2, 1.3, 3.1

A medida que lea, identifique tres ejemplos de hipérbole y escríbalos en una hoja aparte. Subraye lo irreal de la situación y dé su interpretación. Diga lo que quería comunicar o resaltar el autor con la exageración, como se ve a continuación.

| Ejemplos de hipérboles | Interpretación |
|---|---|
| "…siendo casi una niña se había escapado de la casa de sus padres para ir a un baile, y cuando regresaba por el bosque después de haber bailado toda la noche sin permiso, un trueno pavoroso abrió el cielo en dos mitades, y por aquella grieta salió el relámpago de azufre <u>que la convirtió en araña</u>." | Que un rayo (elemento que acompaña al relámpago) le caiga a una persona es poco común, pero es posible. Que le caiga a una persona y la convierta en araña es imposible, pero la idea de que eso le pueda suceder a alguien como castigo por desobeder a sus padres es tan terrible que definitivamente serviría de escarmiento a los demás. Quizá este sea el mensaje que quería comunicar el autor: "No hay que desobedecer a los padres". |

---

### Essential Instruction

1. As you go through **Sobre el autor**, pause to ask **sí/no** comprehension questions.
2. Read the **Estrategia**. Give an example by making hyperbolic statements about your day so far. Then give purely factual statements about the same events. Have students compare and contrast the two accounts.
3. Have students discuss their answers to **Antes de leer** and **Actividad 45** in small groups.

# Un señor muy viejo con unas alas enormes
## de *Gabriel García Márquez*   1.2, 2.2, 3.1

Al tercer día de lluvia habían matado tantos cangrejos dentro de la casa, que Pelayo tuvo que atravesar su patio anegado para tirarlos al mar, pues el niño recién nacido había pasado la noche con calenturas[1] y se pensaba que era causa de la pestilencia. El mundo estaba triste desde el martes. El cielo y el mar eran una misma cosa de ceniza, y las arenas de la playa, que en marzo fulguraban[2] como polvo de lumbre, se habían convertido en un caldo de lodo[3] y mariscos podridos. La luz era tan mansa[4] al mediodía, que cuando Pelayo regresaba a la casa después de haber tirado los cangrejos, le costó trabajo ver qué era lo que se movía y se quejaba en el fondo del patio. Tuvo que acercarse mucho para descubrir que era un hombre viejo, que estaba tumbado boca abajo en el lodazal[5], y a pesar de sus grandes esfuerzos no podía levantarse, porque se lo impedían sus enormes alas.

Asustado por aquella pesadilla[6], Pelayo corrió en busca de Elisenda, su mujer, [...] Ambos observaron el cuerpo caído con un callado estupor[7]. Estaba vestido como un trapero[8]. Le quedaban apenas unas hilachas descoloridas en el cráneo pelado y muy pocos dientes en la boca, y su lastimosa condición de bisabuelo ensopado[9] lo había desprovisto de toda grandeza. Sus alas de gallinazo grande, sucias y medio desplumadas, estaban encalladas para siempre en el lodazal. Tanto lo observaron, y con tanta atención, que Pelayo y Elisenda se sobrepusieron[10] muy pronto del asombro y acabaron por encontrarlo familiar. Entonces se atrevieron a hablarle, y él les contestó en un dialecto incomprensible pero con una buena voz de navegante. Fue así como pasaron por alto el inconveniente de las alas, y concluyeron con muy buen juicio que era un náufrago solitario de alguna nave extranjera abatida[11] por el temporal. Sin embargo, llamaron para que lo viera a una vecina que sabía todas las cosas de la vida y la muerte, y a ella le bastó con una mirada para sacarlos del error. —Es un ángel —les dijo—. Seguro que venía por el niño, pero el pobre está tan viejo que lo ha tumbado[12] la lluvia.

[...] Contra el criterio de la vecina sabia, para quien los ángeles de estos tiempos eran sobrevivientes[13] fugitivos de una conspiración celestial, no habían tenido corazón para matarlo a palos. Pelayo estuvo vigilándolo toda la tarde desde la cocina, armado con un garrote de alguacil[14], y antes de acostarse lo sacó a rastras[15] del lodazal y lo encerró con las gallinas en el gallinero alumbrado. [...] Poco después el niño despertó sin fiebre y con deseos de comer. Entonces se sintieron magnánimos y decidieron poner al ángel en una balsa con agua dulce y provisiones para tres días, y abandonarlo a su suerte en alta mar. Pero cuando salieron al patio con las primeras luces, encontraron a todo el vecindario[16] frente al gallinero, retozando con el ángel sin la menor devoción y echándole cosas de comer por los huecos de las alambradas, como si no fuera una criatura sobrenatural sino un animal de circo.

[1]feverish  [2]glowed  [3]mud  [4]mild  [5]marsh  [6]nightmare  [7]silent astonishment
[8]ragman  [9]drenched  [10]recovered  [11]run aground  [12]knocked him down
[13]survivors  [14]truncheon  [15]dragged him out  [16]neighborhood

## 46 Comprensión  1.2

1. ¿Qué significa que "el mundo estaba triste"?

2. ¿Por qué el ángel parecía una pesadilla?

3. ¿Por qué había recomendado la vecina sabia que mataran al ángel a palos?

## 47 Analice  1.3

¿Qué demuestran las distintas reacciones frente al ángel? Analice los efectos de los prejuicios sobre las actitudes de las personas frente a personas o experiencias nuevas.

---

## RESOURCES

 Un señor muy viejo con unas alas enormes

**Answers**

**46**
1. Significa que estaba lloviendo mucho y todo se veía gris.
2. Porque era un viejito empapado, con poco pelo y pocos dientes, y las alas sucias y desplumadas.
3. Porque creía que era un fugitivo de una conspiración celestial.

**47**
*Respuesta posible:* temor a lo desconocido y dificultades de comunicación

### Reference Desk

1. Ask students to make a list of words in the reading they don't recognize. Have students try to understand their meaning from context. If this is not successful, tell them to look up the words in a dictionary.
2. Remind students that the word **criterio** in the last paragraph on this page is a false cognate. Ask a volunteer to recall the definition given in **Vocabulario 3**.

### Critical Thinking

**Analyzing**
After reading the first two paragraphs, ask students:
**¿En qué mes estamos cuando el cuento empieza? ¿Cuál es la relación entre Pelayo y Elisenda? ¿Dónde encontraron al hombre?**

---

## Differentiated Learning
**Accelerate/Heritage Learners**
Divide the story into sections. At the end of each section, ask these students to summarize the events of that portion of the story in their own words.

## Special Needs Students
**AD(H)D/Reading Difficulties**
Aid these students with their reading comprehension. Guide them in completing a chart as they read; the chart categories can be **Lugar**, **Personajes**, etc.

**48**

1. Porque no hablaba latín, olía mal y no tenía la dignidad que él espera de los ángeles.
2. Decidió cobrar cinco centavos de entrada a quienes quisieran ver al ángel.
3. Porque gastaron tiempo discutiendo si el ángel tenía ombligo, si hablaba un dialecto relacionado con el arameo, si podía caber muchas veces en la punta de un alfiler o si sería un noruego con alas.

**49** 🌐 *Respuesta posible:*
Los ángeles generalmente son idealizados y son descritos como bebés inocentes, puros, blancos y limpios, mientras que este supuesto ángel es descrito como un hombre viejo, sucio y apestoso.

### Critical Thinking

**Analyzing**
Ask students: **¿Por qué había gente en la casa? ¿Por qué no se podían comunicar con el hombre? ¿Dónde vivió el hombre cuando llegó? ¿Por qué vino el padre Gonzaga? ¿Cuánto costaba la entrada?**

### Connections

**Art**
Display a picture of Diego Rivera's mural titled *Man at the Crossroads*. Ask students to compare and contrast the figure in the mural to the man with wings in the story.

 **1.2**

## 48 Comprensión

1. ¿Por qué desconfía el padre Gonzaga del carácter angelical del señor con alas?

2. ¿Cómo aprovechó Elisenda la situación?

3. ¿Por qué se demoraban las cartas de Roma?

## 49 Analice  **1.3**

Describa el estereotipo de ángel que todo el mundo esperaba y en qué se diferencia el señor con alas.

El padre Gonzaga llegó antes de las siete alarmado por la desproporción de la noticia. [...] [P]idió que le abrieran la puerta para examinar de cerca a aquel varón de lástima que más parecía una enorme gallina decrépita entre las gallinas absortas. Ajeno[17] a las impertinencias[18] del mundo, apenas si levantó sus ojos de anticuario y murmuró algo en su dialecto cuando el padre Gonzaga entró en el gallinero y le dio los buenos días en latín. El párroco tuvo la primera sospecha de impostura[19] al comprobar que no entendía la lengua de Dios ni sabía saludar a sus ministros. Luego observó que visto de cerca resultaba demasiado humano: tenía un insoportable olor de intemperie, el revés de las alas sembrado de algas parasitarias y las plumas mayores maltratadas por vientos terrestres [...] Entonces abandonó el gallinero, y con un breve sermón previno[20] a los curiosos contra los riesgos de la ingenuidad. Les recordó que el demonio tenía la mala costumbre de recurrir a artificios de carnaval para confundir a los incautos. Argumentó que si las alas no eran el elemento esencial para determinar las diferencias entre un gavilán[21] y un aeroplano, mucho menos podían serlo para reconocer a los ángeles. Sin embargo, prometió escribir una carta a su obispo, para que éste escribiera otra al Sumo Pontífice, de modo que el veredicto final viniera de los tribunales más altos.

Su prudencia cayó en corazones estériles. La noticia del ángel cautivo se divulgó[22] con tanta rapidez, que al cabo de pocas horas había en el patio un alboroto[23] de mercado, y tuvieron que llevar la tropa con bayonetas para espantar el tumulto que ya estaba a punto de tumbar la casa. Elisenda, con el espinazo[24] torcido de tanto barrer basura de feria, tuvo entonces la buena idea de tapiar el patio y cobrar cinco centavos por la entrada para ver al ángel.

Vinieron curiosos hasta de la Martinica. [...] Vinieron en busca de salud los enfermos más desdichados del Caribe: [...] En medio de aquel desorden de naufragio que hacía temblar la tierra, Pelayo y Elisenda estaban felices de cansancio, porque en menos de una semana atiborraron de plata los dormitorios, y todavía la fila de peregrinos que esperaban su turno para entrar llegaba hasta el otro lado del horizonte.

El ángel era el único que no participaba de su propio acontecimiento. [...] Su única virtud sobrenatural parecía ser la paciencia. [...] La única vez que consiguieron alterarlo fue cuando le abrasaron el costado con un hierro de marcar novillos, porque llevaba tantas horas de estar inmóvil que lo creyeron muerto. Despertó sobresaltado, despotricando en lengua hermética y con los ojos en lágrimas, y dio un par de aletazos que provocaron un remolino de estiércol de gallinero [...]

El padre Gonzaga se enfrentó a la frivolidad de la muchedumbre con fórmulas de inspiración doméstica, mientras le llegaba un juicio terminante[25] sobre la naturaleza del cautivo. Pero el correo de Roma había perdido la noción de la urgencia. El tiempo se les iba[26] en averiguar si el convicto tenía ombligo, si su dialecto tenía algo que ver con el arameo, si podía caber muchas veces en la punta de un alfiler, o si no sería simplemente un noruego con alas. Aquellas

---

[17] disregarding  [18] insolence, impudence  [19] deception  [20] warned  [21] hawk, falcon
[22] spread  [23] commotion  [24] spine  [25] definitive  [26] they wasted time

**Essential Instruction**
1. Have students scan the story for cognates and words they learned in **Vocabulario 3**.
2. Play the recording, pausing for students to answer the during-reading questions.
3. For Common Core practice, have students answer the **Analice** questions.

cartas de parsimonia habrían ido y venido hasta el fin de los siglos, si un acontecimiento providencial no hubiera puesto término a las tribulaciones del párroco.

Sucedió que por esos días, entre muchas otras atracciones de las ferias errantes del Caribe, llevaron al pueblo el espectáculo triste de la mujer que se había convertido en araña por desobedecer a sus padres. La entrada para verla no solo costaba menos que la entrada para ver al ángel, sino que permitían hacerle toda clase de preguntas sobre su absurda condición, y examinarla al derecho y al revés, de modo que nadie pusiera en duda la verdad del horror.

Era una tarántula espantosa del tamaño de un carnero y con la cabeza de una doncella triste. Pero lo más desgarrador[27] no era su figura de disparate[28], sino la sincera aflicción con que contaba los pormenores[29] de su desgracia: siendo casi una niña se había escapado de la casa de sus padres para ir a un baile, y cuando regresaba por el bosque después de haber bailado toda la noche sin permiso, un trueno pavoroso abrió el cielo en dos mitades, y por aquella grieta salió el relámpago de azufre que la convirtió en araña. Su único alimento eran las bolitas de carne molida que las almas caritativas quisieran echarle en la boca. Semejante espectáculo, cargado de tanta verdad humana y de tan temible escarmiento, tenía que derrotar sin proponérselo al de un ángel despectivo[30] que apenas si se dignaba mirar a los mortales. Además los escasos milagros que se le atribuían al ángel revelaban un cierto desorden mental, [...] Aquellos milagros de consolación que más bien parecían entretenimientos de burla, habían quebrantado ya la reputación del ángel cuando la mujer convertida en araña terminó de aniquilarla. Fue así como el padre Gonzaga se curó para siempre del insomnio, y el patio de Pelayo volvió a quedar tan solitario como en los tiempos en que llovió tres días y los cangrejos caminaban por los dormitorios.

Los dueños de la casa no tuvieron nada que lamentar. Con el dinero recaudado construyeron una mansión de dos plantas, con balcones y jardines, y con sardineles muy altos para que no se metieran los cangrejos del invierno, y con barras de hierro en las ventanas para que no se metieran los ángeles. Pelayo estableció además un criadero de conejos muy cerca del pueblo y renunció para siempre a su mal empleo de alguacil, y Elisenda se compró unas zapatillas satinadas de tacones altos y muchos vestidos de seda tornasol, de los que usaban las señoras más codiciadas en los domingos de aquellos tiempos. El gallinero fue lo único que no mereció atención. Si alguna vez lo lavaron con creolina y quemaron las lágrimas de mirra en su interior, no fue por hacerle honor al ángel, sino por conjurar la pestilencia de muladar[31] que ya andaba como un fantasma por todas partes y estaba volviendo vieja la casa nueva. Al principio, cuando el niño aprendió a caminar, se cuidaron de que no estuviera cerca del gallinero. Pero luego se fueron olvidando del temor y acostumbrándose a la peste, y antes de que el niño mudara[32] los dientes se había metido a jugar dentro del gallinero, cuyas alambradas podridas se caían

[27]heartbreaking    [28]nonsensical    [29]particulars    [30]scornful    [31]dung heap    [32]lost

## 50 Comprensión  1.2

1. ¿Cómo se convirtió en araña la mujer tarántula? ¿Por qué fue castigada?

2. ¿Cómo cambió la vida de Elisenda y su familia?

## 51 Analice  1.3

Analice la diferencia entre la vida que lograron Elisenda y Pelayo, y cómo trataban al ángel. ¿Le parece justo? ¿Por qué?

**50**

1. Le cayó un relámpago de azufre. Por desobedecer a sus padres.
2. Construyeron una gran mansión, Pelayo estableció un negocio y dejó el oficio de alguacil, Elisenda se compró ropa y zapatos lujosos.

**51**

*Las respuestas variarán, pero deben mencionar la riqueza en que terminó viviendo la familia de Elisenda en comparación con la miseria en que tenían viviendo al ángel y el maltrato que le daban.*

### Expansion

Encourage students to discuss their feelings as they read the story. Ask questions such as: **¿Cómo se sienten? ¿Les da miedo? ¿disgusto?**

## Differentiated Learning

### Expand

When students have finished reading the story, ask them to watch the 1988 film version by Argentine director Fernando Birri. Ask students to compare and contrast the two works, and state whether they think the film is a successful interpretation of the story.

## Multiple Intelligences

### Visual-Spatial

Ask students to retell the story in the form of a graphic novel.

### Bodily-Kinesthetic

Encourage small groups of students to choose a scene from the story to perform for the class.

**52**

1. Se arrastraba de acá para allá, apareciendo por todas partes en la casa. Parecía que hubiera muchos ángeles.

2. Durante el invierno, casi no comía, tenía los ojos turbios, andaba a tropezones y casi no le quedaban plumas. Parecía que se iba a morir.

3. Después del invierno, mejoró con el calor, se quedaba inmóvil en un rincón y empezaron a nacerle plumas grandes y duras.

**53** **E** *Las respuestas variarán.*
*Respuesta posible:* A pesar de ser un ángel, el hombre viejo con alas enormes fue rechazado por ser diferente de lo que la gente esperaba.

---

### Communication

**Presentational: Paired Practice**
Tell students to work with a partner to create a timeline of events in the story.

---

### Critical Thinking

**Analyzing**
Ask students: **¿Qué representa el hombre con las alas enormes? ¿Y la mujer araña? ¿Por cuánto tiempo estuvo el hombre con Pelayo y Elisenda? ¿Cómo se representa el tema de la prosperidad en el cuento?**

---

 **1.2**

### 52 Comprensión

1. ¿Qué hacía el ángel que sacaba de quicio a Elisenda?

2. ¿Qué le pasó al ángel durante el invierno?

3. ¿Qué le pasó al ángel después del invierno?

### 53 Analice  **1.3**

Analice el desenlace del cuento. ¿Por qué el ángel nunca fue aceptado, a pesar de su naturaleza mística? ¿Qué conclusiones puede sacar sobre la naturaleza humana? ¿Cree que puede haber ángeles que pasan desapercibidos?

*"Pelayo le echó encima una manta y le hizo la caridad de dejarlo dormir en el cobertizo..."*

a pedazos. El ángel no fue menos displicente con él que con el resto de los mortales, pero soportaba las infamias[33] más ingeniosas con una mansedumbre[34] de perro sin ilusiones. Ambos contrajeron la varicela al mismo tiempo. El médico que atendió al niño no resistió la tentación de auscultar[35] al ángel, y encontró tantos soplos en el corazón y tantos ruidos en los riñones, que no le pareció posible que estuviera vivo. [...]

Cuando el niño fue a la escuela, hacía mucho tiempo que el sol y la lluvia habían desbaratado el gallinero. El ángel andaba arrastrándose por acá y por allá como un moribundo sin dueño. [...] Parecía estar en tantos lugares al mismo tiempo, que llegaron a pensar que se desdoblaba, que se repetía a sí mismo por toda la casa, y la exasperada Elisenda gritaba fuera de quicio[36] que era una desgracia vivir en aquel infierno lleno de ángeles. Apenas si podía comer, sus ojos de anticuario se le habían vuelto tan turbios que andaba tropezando con los horcones, y ya no le quedaban sino las cánulas peladas de las últimas plumas. Pelayo le echó encima una manta y le hizo la caridad de dejarlo dormir en el cobertizo, y solo entonces advirtieron que pasaba la noche con calenturas delirantes en trabalenguas de noruego viejo. Fue esa una de las pocas veces en que se alarmaron, porque pensaban que se iba a morir, y ni siquiera la vecina sabia había podido decirles qué se hacía con los ángeles muertos.

Sin embargo, no solo sobrevivió a su peor invierno, sino que pareció mejor con los primeros soles. Se quedó inmóvil muchos días en el rincón más apartado del patio, donde nadie lo viera, y a principios de diciembre empezaron a nacerle en las alas unas plumas grandes y duras, plumas de pajarraco viejo, que más bien parecían un nuevo percance de la decrepitud. [...] Una mañana, Elisenda estaba cortando rebanadas de cebolla para el almuerzo, cuando un viento que parecía de alta mar se metió en la cocina. Entonces se asomó por la ventana, y sorprendió al ángel en las primeras tentativas[37] del vuelo. Eran tan torpes, que abrió con las uñas un surco de arado en las hortalizas y estuvo a punto de desbaratar el cobertizo con aquellos aletazos indignos que resbalaban en la luz y no encontraban asidero en el aire. Pero logró ganar altura. Elisenda exhaló un suspiro de descanso, por ella y por él, cuando lo vio pasar por encima de las últimas casas, sustentándose de cualquier modo con un azaroso aleteo de buitre senil. Siguió viéndolo hasta cuando acabó de cortar la cebolla, y siguió viéndolo hasta cuando ya no era posible que lo pudiera ver, porque entonces ya no era un estorbo[38] en su vida, sino un punto imaginario en el horizonte del mar.

[33] wicked acts    [34] docility    [35] auscultate, examine    [36] exasperated    [37] attempts
[38] nuisance

---

### Essential Instruction

1. Ask students to complete the following after reading the story: **El narrador es...** and **El tema del cuento es...**

2. Point out the **Pregunta clave** on p. 385.

3. Read through the **Proyectos** on pp. 385–386. Allow students to choose project(s) that most appeal to them. Provide detailed rubrics so that students are aware of the expectations for these tasks.

4. For **Actividad A**, you may want to assign a celebration to each group to ensure that there are not duplicates.

# Para concluir

## Proyectos

¿Pregunta clave

¿Qué aspectos de la cultura de un país se reflejan en sus fiestas y tradiciones?

### A ¡Manos a la obra!  1.1, 1.3, 2.1, 2.2

Trabaje con un grupo de cuatro compañeros/as.
Elijan alguna de las celebraciones colombianas que se
mencionan en esta unidad e imaginen que los contrataron
para diseñar el cartel publicitario de esa fiesta.

Recopilen la siguiente información sobre el evento para
incluirla en el cartel:

- Nombre de la celebración
- Lugar donde se celebra
- Fecha en la que se celebra
- Actividades atractivas
- Razones para participar

Pueden buscar en la internet otros datos y fotografías
relacionadas con esa fiesta.

Por último, presenten el cartel a la clase.

*Colombia asombra al mundo entero con sus celebraciones alegres y coloridas.*

### B En resumen 1.3, 2.1, 2.2

En esta unidad, se mencionan distintas fiestas y celebraciones de Colombia. Repase las características
de cada una, en especial teniendo en cuenta las tradiciones culturales que se reflejan en ellas, las
actividades y su origen. Complete el cuadro que sigue con información de los textos que leyó en la
unidad o información adicional que encuentre en la internet, si es necesario.

| Celebración | Fecha | Actividades | Origen |
|---|---|---|---|
| Carnaval de Barranquilla | | | |
| Festival de la Leyenda Vallenata | | | |
| Fiestas de Independencia | | | |
| Día de los Angelitos | | | |
| Carnavales de Negros y Blancos | | | |

---

---

**C** **¡A escribir!**  1.3, 2.1, 2.2

Imagínese que Ud. trabaja como corresponsal extranjero en Colombia y lo envían a cubrir una fiesta popular. Busque información en la internet acerca de otras celebraciones que se realicen en Colombia y que no se hayan visto en esta unidad. Elija la que le resulte más atractiva y escriba un artículo informativo en el que describa la celebración a los lectores extranjeros.

**D** **La otra Cartagena** **Conéctese: la historia**  1.3, 2.2, 3.1

La ciudad de Cartagena de Indias debe su nombre a la ciudad española de Cartagena de Levante. Fue la segunda ciudad sudamericana, después de Caracas, en declarar su independencia de España en 1811. Ese suceso histórico fue de tal magnitud que hoy es el eje conmemorativo de las populares fiestas novembrinas.

Busque información en la internet sobre el proceso de independencia de Cartagena y prepare una presentación a la clase: puede incluir una línea de tiempo, mapas, imágenes, grabados de los protagonistas, etc.

1.1, 1.3, 2.1, 2.2, 3.1

**E** **Máscaras de carnaval** 👥 **Conéctese: el arte**

Uno de los elementos más representativos del Carnaval de Barranquilla son las coloridas máscaras artesanales que representan animales o figuras divinas como el diablo o la muerte.

En un principio, las máscaras se usaban en los desfiles y representaban a animales salvajes y domésticos, en una tradición instaurada por los esclavos africanos: leones, tigres, toros, burros, micos, perros, diablos, guacamayas, cebras, caimanes.

Más recientemente, estas máscaras pasaron de ser objetos exclusivos del carnaval y se convirtieron en obras de exposición.

Trabaje con un(a) compañero/a. Busquen en la internet imágenes de las bellas máscaras del Carnaval de Barranquilla. Elijan un animal o una figura divina y diseñen su propia máscara de carnaval en una hoja grande. Incluyan al pie una breve explicación del animal o figura elegida que indique en qué danza o desfile se usará y por qué.

*Las máscaras del Carnaval de Barranquilla no solo se exponen en los desfiles sino también en galerías de arte.*

### Essential Instruction

1. For **Actividad C**, encourage students to briefly explain the history of the celebration and highlight aspects of the celebration that would be particularly striking for foreigners. Tell them to give their article a catchy title.

2. You could have students work in pairs or small groups for **Actividad D**.

3. Emphasize that students should create original masks of their own design for **Actividad E**.

4. For the **Vocabulario de la Unidad 9**, ask students to determine several categories that could be used to sort the words. Then have students list the words in those categories.

abrazar y besar  to hug and kiss
el **acero**  steel
**adornar**  to decorate
los **adornos**  decorations
el **alboroto**  commotion
el **alma**  soul
**anegado/a**  flooded
el **Año Nuevo**  New Year
los **antepasados**  ancestors
el **árbol de navidad**
Christmas tree
las **artesanías**  crafts
la **atmósfera de fiesta**
party atmosphere
el **baile**  dance
la **banda**  band
la **barbacoa**  barbecue
la **bulla**  commotion
la **calavera**  skull
**caritativo/a**  generous
el **Carnaval**  Carnival
la **carroza**  float
**celebrar**  to celebrate
el **cementerio**  cemetery
la **cena**  dinner
la **cerámica**  ceramic
el **chiste**  joke
la **cinta**  ribbon
**codiciar**  to covet
**compartir**  to share
el **conejo de Pascua**  Easter Bunny
**conmemorar**  to commemorate
**contar**  to tell
la **costumbre**  custom
el **criterio**  opinion, judgment
**cumplir... años**  to turn...
years old
**decrépito/a**  very old
**desbaratar**  to ruin, to wreck
los **desfiles cívicos**  civic parades
**despotricar**  to rant and rave
el **Día de Acción de Gracias**
Thanksgiving
el **Día de la Independencia**
Independence Day
el **Día de los Muertos/Difuntos**
the Day of the Dead
el **Día de los Reyes Magos**  Three
Kings' Day
el **Día de Todos los Santos**
All Saints Day
el **disfraz**  costume
**displicente**  rude

el **Domingo de Pascua**
Easter Sunday
los **dulces**  candy
**encallar**  to run aground
**envolver**  to wrap
el **escarmiento**  punishment
los **espíritus**  spirits
el **esqueleto**  skeleton
la **fábula**  fable
**¡Felicitaciones!**
Congratulations!
la **feria artesanal**  artisan fair
las **festividades**  festivities
la **fiesta nacional**  national holiday
la **fiesta familiar**
family celebration
las **flores**  flowers
los **fuegos artificiales**  fireworks
**fuera de quicio**  to be out of
your mind
los **gorros y tocados**  caps and
headdresses
**guiados por una estrella**
guided by a star
**hacer un brindis**  to make
a toast
**heredar**  to inherit
los **héroes**  heroes
el **hierro**  iron
el **hogar**  home
la **hojalata**  tin
**honrar**  to honor
**incauto/a**  gullible
**incluir**  to include
la **ingenuidad**  naivety
la **intemperie**  in the open
el **jardín**  garden
el **juicio**  judgment
**"Las mañanitas" (México)**
"Happy Birthday" song
la **leyenda**  legend
**llegar**  to arrive
las **luces**  lights
**lucir**  to wear
la **madera tallada**  carved wood
**magnánimo/a**  magnanimous
la **medianoche**  midnight
la **misa de gallo**  midnight Mass
el **mito**  myth
la **moraleja**  moral
el **mundo hispano**  Hispanic world
el **nacimiento**  birth
el **náufrago**  shipwreck survivor

la **Navidad**  Christmas
el **Papá Noel**  Santa Claus
el **papel de regalo**
wrapping paper
el **pavo relleno**  stuffed turkey
**pedir un deseo**  to make a wish
el/la **peregrino/a**  pilgrim
el **pesebre (nacimiento)**
nativity scene
las **plumas**  feathers
**podrido/a**  rotten
la **prudencia**  good sense
los **puestos**  stalls
**¡Que lo pases bien! ¡Que lo
pases muy feliz!**  Have a
great day!
**¡Que los cumplas feliz!**  Happy
birthday!
**quebrantar**  to break, shatter
**querido/a**  cherished
**realizarse**  to take place
el **refrán/proverbio**  proverb
**repicar las campanas**  to ring
the bells
**reventar (ie) los globos**  to pop
the balloons
el **ruido**  noise
**¡Salud, dinero y amor!**  To your
health! (literally: Health, money,
and love!)
**saludar la bandera**  to salute
the flag
la **Semana Santa**  Holy Week
**senil**  senile
la **serenata**  serenade
los **seres queridos**  loved ones
**servir para**  to be used for
**sin igual**  unsurpassed
**soplar/apagar las velas**  to blow
out the candles
**teñir (huevos)**  to dye (eggs)
**tocar el himno nacional**  to play
the national anthem
la **torta (el pastel)**  cake
**traer regalos**  to bring gifts
el **traje regional**  traditional dress
las **tumbas**  graves
el **tumulto**  turmoil, commotion
el **vidrio soplado**  blown glass
el **Viernes Santo**  Good Friday
los **villancicos**  Christmas carols
la **víspera de Navidad**
Christmas Eve

*Ver ¡Ojo con estas palabras! en la página 364.

1. This unit's country of focus, Honduras, borders Guatemala, El Salvador, and Nicaragua, as well as the Pacific Ocean and the Caribbean Sea. Its largest city is the capital, Tegucigalpa, which the inhabitants refer to as **Tegus**.
2. It is believed that Honduras was named by Christopher Columbus, in reference to the deep waters near the coast.
3. Hondurans are often referred to by the nickname of **catracho/a**, after General Florencio Xatruch, who in 1857 successfully led a coalition of Central American armies against the troops of American expeditioner William Walker.

## Culture

**Practices: Information**
About half of Honduran households possess at least one television.

## Connections

**Geography**
Ask students to list the countries of Central America. To challenge them, ask them also to name the capital of each country.

**¿Sabía que...?** 1.2, 2.2

La primera transmisión de televisión en Honduras se realizó el 15 de septiembre de 1959 —día en que se conmemoraba un nuevo aniversario de la independencia— para unos veinticinco televisores instalados en las vitrinas de los centros comerciales de Tegucigalpa.

## Essential Instruction

1. Begin with a discussion of the **Pregunta clave**. Ask students to consider how political or social situations within a country might affect its media.
2. Point out Honduras on the map. Then invite students to share what they know about the country.
3. Draw attention to the culture photo and question. Encourage students to watch for the photo and the answer later in the unit.
4. Point out the QR code, the video question, and the screen shot from "**El taller de radio**." Encourage students to watch the video as many times as they like.
5. Have students read and ask questions about **Mis metas**.

# Unidad

# 10 Fuentes de información

Escanee el código QR para mirar el video "El taller de radio".

Varios estudiantes participan en la creación de un taller de radio. ¿Qué hacen y qué aprenden de esta experiencia?

Pregunta clave

**?**

¿Cómo afecta la situación política y social de un país a los medios de comunicación?

¿Cuál es el objetivo de la RDS, Red de Desarrollo Sostenible de Honduras, y dónde funciona?

Honduras

ON AIR

## Mis metas

### En esta unidad:

▶ Usaré expresiones relacionadas con la información y la comunicación.

▶ Repasaré las formas y los usos del gerundio.

▶ Aprenderé sobre los medios de comunicación en Honduras.

▶ Distinguiré el significado de palabras y frases según el contexto.

▶ Repasaré las formas y los usos del futuro perfecto y el condicional perfecto.

▶ Distinguiré las formas y los usos del pluscuamperfecto del subjuntivo.

▶ Leeré una entrevista con un locutor hondureño que lleva 40 años al frente de un programa de radio.

▶ Escribiré un ensayo persuasivo sobre la libertad de expresión.

▶ Escucharé un segmento de un programa radial hondureño y escribiré una entrada de blog al respecto.

▶ Distinguiré los pronombres relativos en español.

▶ Leeré dos poemas, "Hombres necios" de Sor Juana Inés de la Cruz y "Peso ancestral" de Alfonsina Storni.

trescientos ochenta y nueve **389**

**389**

## Differentiated Learning
### Expand
Ask students to work in groups and create a radio station for your school. Have them give the station a name and devise a programming schedule. They should describe what steps would be necessary to set up the station.

## Multiple Intelligences
### Verbal-Linguistic
Review and preview the unit vocabulary and grammar by asking questions such as: **¿Cómo te enteras de las noticias? ¿Cuántas veces al día te contectas a la internet? Si se hubieran cancelado las clases hoy, ¿qué habrías hecho? Dentro de diez años, ¿qué habrás logrado?**

### Reference Desk

In addition to **La Prensa**, Honduras's main newspapers are **El Heraldo**, **Diario Tiempo**, and **La Tribuna**. The official government paper is **La Gaceta**.

### Communication

**Interpersonal: Paired Practice**
Have pairs of students take turns giving the first and last letter of a vocabulary word. Their partner must identify the term and spell it aloud.

### Expansion

Set up a news bulletin board in the classroom. Each day, update the board with news stories and advertisements from Spanish-language media.

# Vocabulario 1

## ¿Cómo nos comunicamos?    1.2, 2.2

### Ξ ENTÉRATE AL INSTANTE

| NOTICIAS Y ESPECTÁCULOS | PÁGINAS SOCIALES | ENTRETENIMIENTO | CLASIFICADOS | HISTORIETAS | HORÓSCOPO |

**Directora del diario *La Prensa* recibe el mayor premio otorgado a periodistas en Honduras**

Se hace entrega del premio Álvaro Contreras a la periodista Marlen Perdomo de Zelaya, directora del diario *La Prensa* (periódico de publicación semanal) de Honduras. En este acontecimiento que tuvo lugar en Expocentro, el presidente Juan Orlando Hernández ratificó su absoluto respeto a la libertad de expresión. VER MÁS...

**Festival Internacional de Cine**

Esta semana tiene lugar el Festival Internacional de Cine, el cual contará con la actuación de las grandes estrellas de la pantalla cinematográfica. No se pierda los reportajes sobre los mejores estrenos y la entrega de premios, la cual será transmitida en directo a millones de televidentes por varias cadenas de televisión. Ahórrese las horas de hacer cola y compre sus entradas ya mismo. Boletos a la venta en todas las taquillas de la ciudad. VER MÁS...

 Proteja su información
¡NO HAGA CLIC!

**NO** No haga clic en ningún enlace que reciba en salas para chatear, en mensajes de texto y de correo electrónico, especialmente correo basura, si no sabe de dónde vienen.

### Ξ CLIMA DE HOY · HONDURAS

Mayormente nublado
32 °C

⇨ Ver informe meteorológico para la semana

### Ξ TELERADIO EN LÍNEA

Escucha a tus locutores y comentaristas favoritos y mira todas tus telenovelas en vivo, sin propagandas y sin tener que navegar la red.

 RADIO

 TV

En este sitio web hallarás software que te permitirá acceder a radioemisoras y programas de televisión del mundo entero, completamente gratis. Descárgalo y conéctate ahora mismo. VER MÁS...

## Essential Instruction

1. Begin by having students look at the photos and describe what they see.
2. Play the audio for **¿Cómo nos comunicamos?** Pause to check comprehension making **cierto/falso** statements. Have students correct the false information.
3. Give examples of the different movie genres and have volunteers give a few titles for each genre.
4. Personalize the vocabulary presentation by asking students which news item from these pages they would click on first, and why.

≡ VBD · VIDEO BAJO DEMANDA                                    ENTRAR

**Servicios de emisión continua** | **Normas editoriales** | **Contáctenos**

Los corales de Honduras · Documental

| DOCUMENTALES | DEPORTES | NOTICIEROS | PELÍCULAS | VIDEOJUEGOS |
|---|---|---|---|---|
| ≡ NUEVO DOCUMENTAL · HONDURAS | | NOTICIAS LOCALES | CÓMICAS | |
| | | NOTICIAS INTERNACIONALES | DE CIENCIA FICCIÓN | |
| | | TITULARES DE PRIMERA PLANA | DE DIBUJOS ANIMADOS | |
| | | | DE GUERRA | |
| | | | DE MISTERIO | |
| | | | POLICÍACAS | |
| | | | DE VAQUEROS | |

DVD

Pruebe un plan de DVD por un mes sin costo alguno.

≡ TODOS CONTRA TODOS

Este martes, en el ciclo de cine "Todos contra todos", se pasa la película *Gente en sitios*, dirigida por Juan Cavestany. Rodada cámara en mano y sin presupuesto, *Gente en sitios*, que es comedia y drama a la vez, te atrapa desde la primera escena y te enreda con su hilera de argumentos y su ir y venir de personajes y papeles protagonizados, no por uno, sino por casi todos los actores y actrices españoles de renombre. Si quieres ver algo diferente de cuánto hayas visto, esta es una película que no te quieres perder. VER MÁS...

gente en sitios
una película de juan cavestany

## Para conversar

**P**ara hacer llamadas telefónicas en línea:

Para hacer llamadas telefónicas por la internet no necesita hardware especializado, solo su computadora y una cuenta con un proveedor de servicio telefónico en línea.

Siga las indicaciones en la pantalla, usando su teclado o su ratón, para descargar la aplicación del servidor del proveedor que haya elegido.

Esta aplicación le permitirá hacer llamadas locales y de larga distancia, dejar recados y consultar la guía telefónica de la misma forma que lo hace desde su celular o el teléfono de su casa, pero a menor costo.

Para hacer llamadas de cobro revertido, comuníquese con la operadora y dígale qué número debe marcar, con quién desea hablar y de parte de quién es la llamada. Si no aceptan los cargos, asegúrese de no tener el número equivocado. Si la línea está ocupada, vuelva a llamar más tarde.

---

## RESOURCES

 Flipgrid

Para conversar

## Reference Desk

1. The islands off the Caribbean coast of Honduras are famous for their scuba diving and snorkeling opportunities. **Las Islas de la Bahía** are part of the Mesoamerican Reef, which is the second-largest barrier reef in the world.
2. *Gente en sitios* is a 2013 Spanish film.

## Critical Thinking

**Analyzing**
Survey the class to find out the most popular ways for viewing television, finding news, making phone calls, etc. Then ask students to predict how they think this will change over their lifetime, and why.

## Expansion

Ask students to watch *Gente en sitios* or another modern Spanish-language film and post their opinion of the movie on Flipgrid.

---

**Differentiated Learning**
**Heritage Learners**
Ask heritage learners to describe what the media and technology are like in their family's country of origin.

**Multiple Intelligences**
**Verbal-Linguistic**
Tell pairs of students to create analogies using the words from **Vocabulario 1**. They can eliminate one word from each analogy, swap papers with another pair, and fill in the blanks.

**Answers**

**1** **Script**

1. El abuelo lee un artículo sobre el turismo en la costa norte del país en...
2. El hijo, Rafael, busca un coche usado en...
3. El señor Vargas busca noticias sobre el campeonato de fútbol en...
4. Ana Vargas, la hija mayor, lee una entrevista con el Rey de España en...
5. Para leer *Garfield*, el hermanito de Ana pide...
6. A la abuelita le gusta saber quién se casó y por eso lee...

1. las noticias nacionales
2. los anuncios clasificados
3. los deportes
4. las noticias internacionales
5. las tiras cómicas
6. las notas sociales

**2** *Las respuestas variarán.*
*Respuestas posibles:*

1. Es la persona que vende boletos en una taquilla.
2. Es el nombre de la persona a quien se le envía correspondencia.
3. Es el nombre de la persona que envía la correspondencia.
4. Es una persona que mira televisión.
5. Es una persona que representa un papel en el teatro, el cine o la televisión.
6. Es una persona que habla ante el micrófono en las estaciones de radio o ante la cámara en las estaciones de televisión.
7. Es una persona que elabora las noticias.
8. Es una persona que hace comentarios en los medios de comunicación.

≡ SERVICIOS PUERTA A PUERTA  ENTRAR

**VUELA SEGURO**

Mi cuenta
Nombre del usuario
Contraseña

**HERRAMIENTAS RÁPIDAS**

DIRECTORIO DE DISTRITOS POSTALES
VENTA DE SELLOS, SOBRES Y ETIQUETAS

**SERVICIOS**

ENVÍOS NACIONALES
ENVÍOS INTERNACIONALES
CORREO AÉREO CERTIFICADO
PAQUETES Y ENCOMIENDAS
APARTADOS DE CORREOS

## Para conversar

**P**ara enviar paquetes y correspondencia:

Verifique el nombre y dirección del destinatario y del remitente en sus cartas y tarjetas postales antes de echarlas al buzón. Cierre los sobres y pegue los sellos correspondientes al franqueo.

Para enviar paquetes, es necesario que vaya a la oficina de correos para que los pesen y los aseguren si Ud. lo desea, y para pedir un comprobante por si tiene que reclamar más tarde.

**1  El periódico**  1.2

Los miembros de la familia Vargas, que viven en la capital de Honduras, están leyendo el periódico hondureño *La Prensa*. Ud. oirá una serie de oraciones incompletas. Escuche e indique la terminación correcta.

1. las noticias locales / las noticias nacionales
2. primera plana / los anuncios clasificados
3. los deportes / los titulares
4. las noticias internacionales / las historietas
5. el horóscopo / las tiras cómicas
6. las notas sociales / los editoriales

**2  En sus propias palabras** 1.3

Defina los siguientes términos en español en sus propias palabras, como se ve en el modelo.

MODELO  taquillero
**Es la persona que vende boletos en una taquilla.**

1. taquillero
2. destinatario
3. remitente
4. televidente
5. actor
6. locutor
7. reportero
8. comentarista

**Essential Instruction**

1. Have students read through the answer choices in **Actividad 1**, and then play the audio.
2. Tell students to get together in small groups to compare their definitions from **Actividad 2**.
3. Have students check their answers to **Actividades 3** and **4** in pairs.
4. Encourage students to be nuanced in their explanations in **Actividad 5**. Are there certain conditions under which they *would* do these things?

## 3  ¿Qué significa?  1.2

Empareje cada palabra con la definición correspondiente.

1. franqueo
2. chatear
3. enlace
4. buzón
5. ratón
6. reportaje
7. descargar
8. contraseña

**A.** Charlar con alguien en línea
**B.** Lugar donde uno recibe su correo
**C.** Bajar información en línea
**D.** Texto informativo sobre un tema de actualidad
**E.** Código que usan los usuarios para acceder a sitios en la red
**F.** Dispositivo que permite interactuar con una computadora
**G.** Cantidad que se paga en sellos para enviar algo por correo
**H.** Expresión que conecta información en línea con otra que se le relaciona

## 4  Véala en VBD  1.2

Complete esta reseña sobre la película *Los 33* con las palabras del recuadro que correspondan según el contexto.

| | | | | |
|---|---|---|---|---|
| protagonizada | papeles | DVD | prensa | actuación |
| acontecimientos | dirigida | rodaje | en vivo | argumento |

Si no ha visto *Los 33*, una película chilena **(1)** por la mexicana Patricia Riggen y **(2)** por Antonio Banderas, es posible que ya la pueda ver en VBD o en **(3)** . No se la pierda. *Los 33* es un drama cuyo **(4)** se basa en los tristes **(5)** que ocurrieron en Chile en 2010 después del derrumbe (*collapse*) de la mina San José, en la cual quedaron atrapados 33 mineros chilenos. La película fue filmada en Chile y en Colombia y en su **(6)** se requirió la **(7)** de mil extras para representar los **(8)** de los familares de los mineros, los miembros de las operaciones de rescate y los reporteros de **(9)** y televisión quienes hicieron campamento en el lugar y transmitieron las noticias **(10)** por 70 días.

## ¡Comunicación!

## 5  ¿Con razón o sin razón? 👥 Interpersonal Communication 1.1

Todo el mundo tiene sus razones para hacer lo que hace. Con un(a) compañero/a, intercambien información sobre los siguientes temas. Digan si harían o no harían estas actividades y expliquen por qué.

1. Usar el celular en el carro
2. Hacer llamadas de cobro revertido
3. Hacer clic en cualquier enlace recibido en línea
4. Descargar información de la red indiscriminadamente
5. Usar un apartado de correos para recibir su correspondencia
6. Salir solo/a con alguien que se acaba de conocer en un sitio web

*Siempre uso el GPS de mi celular para buscar direcciones.*

**¡Comunicación!**

**6** **¡Nunca podré olvidarlo!**  **Interpersonal Communication** **1.1, 3.1**

Con un(a) compañero/a, intercambien impresiones sobre algún dato informativo importante que les haya causado gran impresión. Usen las siguientes ideas como guía.

- una emisión de radio
- un reportaje periodístico
- una noticia de primera plana
- una actuación en vivo
- un documental de televisión
- el argumento de un libro o una película

**7** **Lo mejor de lo mejor** **Interpersonal/Presentational Communication** **1.1, 1.3**

Divídanse en grupos de tres o cuatro estudiantes e intercambien opiniones sobre sus fuentes de información preferidas y lo mejor del mundo de las noticias y el entretenimiento. Usen los temas que se dan a continuación como guía. Luego, hagan una lista en orden de preferencia y sométanla a votación del resto de la clase. Para finalizar, publiquen los resultados de la votación en la página web de su colegio o en su red social favorita.

| Lo mejor de lo mejor | | |
|---|---|---|
| periódicos | películas | periodistas |
| radioemisoras | noticieros | estrellas de cine |
| cadenas de televisión | telenovelas | actores de televisión |
| proveedores de servicios en la red | documentales | locutores de radio |
| proveedores de servicios telefónicos | sitios web | comentaristas de televisón |

**8** **Tutoría básica**  **Interpersonal Communication** **1.1**

Imagine que su abuela, que hasta ahora se oponía al uso de la tecnología, decide actualizarse y le pide su ayuda. Con un(a) compañero/a, represente la situación, turnándose para hacer las preguntas del caso y responderlas. Usen los términos del recuadro y otros que necesiten, para darle a su abuelita nociones básicas de lo que necesita para actualizarse, como se ve en el modelo.

| | | | |
|---|---|---|---|
| descargar | pantalla | correo basura | ratón |
| contraseña | en línea | navegar en la red | enlace |
| computadora | hacer clic | correo electrónico | teclado |

MODELO   A: ¿Qué debo hacer para comprar algo en línea?
         B: Primero, debes registrarte y, para hacerlo, debes crear un nombre de usuario y una contraseña.

*Haz clic en este ícono de la pantalla para ver tu correo electrónico.*

# Gramática

## El gerundio  1.2, 4.1

### Formas del gerundio

El gerundio o participio presente es una forma verbal impersonal invariable pues no se conjuga.

- Los verbos regulares forman el gerundio con las siguientes terminaciones.

| Formación del gerundio regular | | | |
|---|---|---|---|
| **Verbo** | **Radical** | **+ Terminación** | **= Gerundio** |
| llamar | llam- | **ando** | llam**ando** |
| encender | encend- | **iendo** | encend**iendo** |
| transmitir | transmit- | **iendo** | transmit**iendo** |

- Los verbos de las conjugaciones **-er** e **-ir** cuyo radical termina en una vocal toman la terminación **-yendo** en lugar de **-iendo**.

| **Verbo** | **Radical** | **+ Terminación** | **= Gerundio** |
|---|---|---|---|
| caer | ca- | | ca**yendo** |
| creer | cre- | | cre**yendo** |
| leer | le- | **yendo** | le**yendo** |
| construir | constru- | | constru**yendo** |
| oír | o- | | o**yendo** |

- Los verbos de la conjugación **-ir** que cambian la vocal del radical (**o → u**, **e → i**) en la tercera persona del pretérito tienen el mismo cambio de vocal en gerundio.

| **Infinitivo** | **Pretérito** | **Gerundio** |
|---|---|---|
| decir | dijo | diciendo |
| dormir | durmió | durmiendo |
| pedir | pidió | pidiendo |
| repetir | repitió | repitiendo |
| sentir | sintió | sintiendo |
| venir | vino | viniendo |

- El único verbo con gerundio irregular es **ir → yendo**.

   Pasa la vida **yendo** de un lugar a otro, como si fuera un peregrino errante.

## Reference Desk

1. Remind students that **gerundio** is a false cognate. Ask for a volunteer to explain the difference between the **gerundio**, a *gerund*, and a *present participle*.
2. Remind students that when pronouns (indirect, direct, or reflexive) are attached to a present participle, a written accent on the **a** or the **e** of the participle is required: **hablándome**, **peinándose**, **leyéndolo**.
3. You may want to mention that **yendo** is not often used.

## Expansion

Create flash cards to review present participles. Write the infinitive on one side and show the class. Ask students to say and spell the present participle.

## TPR

Give sentences using the present progressive and have students act out what they hear. Then have students continue the activity in pairs.

## Special Needs Students
### Linguistically Challenged

Work with these students to develop their ideas and provide linguistic support before pairing them for activities such as **Actividades 6** and **8**. Allow them to give short answers or answers in written form. For **Gramática**, review the formation of present participles.

## Multiple Intelligences
### Bodily-Kinesthetic/Verbal-Linguistic

Have students use the information from **Actividad 7** to role-play an awards ceremony night in class. Assign students to play the roles of nominated people for each category, the awards show host, and reporters on the red carpet.

## Communication

**Interpersonal/Presentational: Cooperative Groups**

To review the present progressive, have the class sit in a circle and do a round-robin activity. Tell students to imagine it is 7:30 on a Saturday night. One student begins by saying what he/she is doing, e.g., **Estoy cenando con mi familia.** The next student must repeat the information and add his/her own sentence (**Alicia está cenando con su familia y yo estoy leyendo un libro.**), and so on around the circle. Encourage students to support and correct each other's mistakes. See how far around the circle students can go. Repeat the exercise with other days and times.

## Expansion

Ask students to create a Flipgrid post with their predictions for the future of the country. What will be the same in the next election cycle or political administration? What will be different? Tell them to use the structures on these pages when possible, e.g., **El nuevo presidente seguirá fortaleciendo lazos diplomáticos con Cuba. La economía irá mejorando. Los políticos andarán haciendo las mismas promesas de siempre, pero no las cumplirán.** Encourage students to post follow-up comments to at least three classmates' posts.

---

## Usos del gerundio

- El uso más corriente del gerundio es con el verbo **estar** para expresar una acción en progreso.

  En la internet **están comentando** una noticia de última hora.

  El comentarista de televisión **estaba hablando** sobre las tendencias del momento.

  Muchas personas **estarán siguiendo** las noticias con atención.

- Los verbos de movimiento como **ir**, **venir**, **andar**, **entrar**, **salir** y **llegar** + gerundio describen una acción que se desarrolla gradualmente.

  El número de usuarios de las redes sociales **viene aumentando** exponencialmente.

  Los expertos dicen que las economías **irán solucionando** los problemas paulatinamente.

- Hay dos verbos que tienen un matiz diferente cuando se traducen al inglés: **venir** + gerundio (*to keep doing something*) y **andar** + gerundio (*to go around doing something*).

  El clima **viene comportándose** erráticamente desde hace un tiempo a esta parte.

  Los científicos **andan diciendo** que vamos hacia la extinción de muchas especies.

- Los verbos **continuar** y **seguir** + gerundio refuerzan la acción continua.

  Gracias a las redes sociales, los ciudadanos **continúan reportando** noticias en tiempo real.

  De esa manera, **seguirán cambiando** el panorama político mundial.

- El gerundio se puede usar con los verbos de percepción en vez del infinitivo.

  Los **vimos yendo** (ir) hacia la concentración en la plaza.

  Lo **oíamos cantando** (cantar) en la ducha.

*La reportera está transmitiendo en vivo.*

## Essential Instruction

1. Ask a volunteer to remind the class of the uses of the present progressive.
2. Ask students to create additional examples for each bullet point in **Gramática**.
3. Give additional example sentences for students to act out.

- El gerundio se puede usar como adverbio para modificar un verbo.

  Todos **reaccionamos sonriendo** con los mohines del bebé.

  Era un gran jefe: solía **hablarnos animándonos**.

- Se puede usar para explicar cómo se puede hacer algo (inglés: *by* + gerundio).

  **Arriesgándose** valientemente, estas mujeres luchan por la paz.

  Tanto niños como adultos cultivan la conciencia ecológica **viendo** documentales ambientales.

- También se puede usar cuando está subordinado a otro verbo y las dos acciones coinciden en algún momento del tiempo.

  **Agradeciendo** a sus seguidores, anunció su retiro del periodismo.

  Explicamos quiénes son los refugiados **haciendo** una actividad lúdica con los niños.

- Cuando el gerundio va acompañado de los pronombres de complemento directo e indirecto, lleva tilde si los pronombres van pospuestos[1].

  El guarda está **pidiéndole** la credencial al reportero.
  Pero: El guarda **le** está **pidiendo** la credencial al reportero.

  El guarda está **pidiéndosela** al reportero.
  Pero: El guarda **se la** está **pidiendo** al reportero.

[1] Repase la Unidad 5, página 201.

[2] Repase la Unidad 9, página 353.

> ### Un poco más
>
> En español, a diferencia del inglés, no se usa el gerundio después de las preposiciones. Se usa el infinitivo[2].
>
> Después de **ver** la película podemos ir a cenar.
>
> Podremos seguir el reportaje del evento sin **salir** de casa.
>
> Antes de **venir**, por favor, compra pan y leche.

*Mi mamá y yo siempre vivíamos riéndonos.*

**Answers**

**9** *Las respuestas variarán.*

## Reference Desk

1. Remind students that another way to say **hacer cola** is **hacer fila**.
2. Guatemalan singer-song-writer Ricardo Arjona is one of Central America's most successful artists. Besides love songs, Arjona is known for addressing sociopolitical themes such as globaliza-tion, racism, and immigra-tion in his music.
3. Guillermo Anderson is one of Honduras's most famous musicians. Many of his songs are dedicated to the beauty of his country, as well as social issues.

## Culture

**Practices/Products: Activity**
Ask students to read five or six entries from Guillermo Anderson's blog. Have them take notes and create a Flipgrid post about three things they learned, what they thought was most interesting, and one thing that surprised them.

## Expansion

Ask students to identify the **gerundios** in **Actividad 9** and explain their use.

---

**9** **Boletos en reventa**  **1.2, 1.3**

Lea la conversación entre un señor que hacía cola para comprar boletos para un concierto y un revendedor de boletos y conteste las preguntas que siguen.

—Hombre, parece que se están agotando los boletos para el concierto de Arjona. ¿Tendría Ud., por casualidad, dos boletos?

—Un momentito, déjeme ver si todavía me queda alguno. A ver, sí, aquí tengo dos.

—Dígame, ¿a cuánto los está revendiendo?

—Los tengo a diez mil pesos cada uno.

—¿Cómo va a ser? ¡Pero si en la taquilla los estaban vendiendo a cinco mil pesos!

—Bueno, ¡siga haciendo cola! Ya le está dando la vuelta a la esquina y, como anunciaron, se están acabando los boletos de hoy. Vaya preparándose para comprar entradas para mañana o pasado.

—Tranquilo, no me estoy quejando. Solo estaba haciendo un comentario. Por favor, deme las dos entradas que le quedan.

—Aquí tiene.

Mientras el revendedor se va alejando, se le oye promocionando su mercancía:

—¡Corran, aprovechen! Solo me quedan dos entradas para Arjona y Guillermo Anderson... y me queda una sola para Café Guancasco.

1. ¿Qué le pasó al señor que estaba haciendo cola para comprar los boletos del concierto?
2. ¿Qué le dijo el revendedor de boletos? ¿Cuál cree que fue su intención al decir esto?
3. ¿Qué alternativa le quedó al señor?
4. ¿Alguna vez tuvo Ud. que hacer cola durante horas para ver una película? ¿Qué película? ¿Valió la pena esperar?
5. ¿Qué podría hacer Ud. si está haciendo cola para comprar boletos para algún espectáculo y anuncian que se están acabando?

*Haciendo cola para comprar boletos*

## Essential Instruction

1. Open these activities by asking students if they or anyone they know has ever bought tickets from scalpers.
2. Begin **Actividad 9** by having two volunteers read the dialogue aloud. Have students work individually to write the answers to the questions, and then share their answers in small groups.
3. Check answers to **Actividad 10** chorally.
4. After pairs answer the questions in **Actividad 11**, open up the topic for class discussion.

## 10 ¿Revender o no revender? Esa es la pregunta  1.2

Complete las oraciones con el gerundio del verbo del recuadro que corresponda según el contexto.

| premiar | comprar | fortalecer | aprender | generar |
|---------|---------|-----------|----------|---------|
| remunerar | analizar | dedicarse | descuidar | |

1. La Asamblea de Padres ha estado ____ el asunto de la reventa de boletos.

2. Los revendedores continúan ____ en preventa para obtener un buen margen de ganancia.

3. Atraídos por las ganancias, algunos chicos han estado ____ sus estudios por estar ____ al negocio de la reventa.

4. Al aprender a planear con anticipación, los chicos están ____ buenos hábitos de consumo.

5. Para disuadir a los estudiantes revendedores, se pueden crear otros medios para que vayan ____ ingresos propios.

6. Por ejemplo, ____ horas de tutoría, se crean otras fuentes de ingresos para estudiantes avanzados.

7. ____ el buen desempeño, se están ____ otras destrezas deseables.

## ¡Comunicación!

## 11 ¿Qué opina Ud.? 👥 Interpersonal Communication  1.1

Acudir a los revendedores cuando los boletos para grandes funciones están a punto de agotarse o ya se han agotado es una práctica común. Ellos siempre están listos para aprovechar la oportunidad de ganarse un buen margen a costa de los desprevenidos. Según ellos, su trabajo es honesto y por eso se consideran con derecho de trabajar en ese oficio. ¿Qué opina Ud.? Con un(a) compañero/a, túrnense para contestar las preguntas y dar su opinión sobre el tema.

*Boleto de reventa para un concierto*

1. ¿Por qué cree que los revendedores suelen tener boletos para estas funciones?

2. ¿Opina que revender boletos es un trabajo honesto? ¿Por qué?

3. ¿Cree que los revendedores tienen acuerdos especiales con la taquilla para revender los boletos? ¿Qué alternativa puede haber a la reventa de boletos?

4. ¿Se permite la reventa de boletos en Estados Unidos?

5. ¿Alguna vez le ha comprado boletos a un revendedor?

6. ¿Cuánto más alto fue el precio que pagó?

**12**

1. pasando
2. pensando
3. contando
4. corriendo
5. sintiendo
6. matando
7. enamorando
8. alimentando
9. sufriendo
10. siendo

*Las opiniones y consejos variarán.*

**13** *Las respuestas variarán.*

## Expansion

Invite groups to role-play their radio programs from **Actividad 12** for the class. Allow them time to rehearse.

## Game

**20 Preguntas**
Ask a student to come to the front of the classroom. Provide him or her with the name of a famous person. The class can ask up to 20 **sí/no** questions to reveal the identity of the famous person.

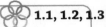

## ¡Comunicación!

**12 ¡Locamente enamorado!** 👥 Interpersonal/Presentational Communication ✿ **1.1, 1.2, 1.3**

Imagine que Ud. está escuchando un programa de radio donde dan consejos sentimentales. Primero, lea la nota de "Locamente enamorado" y complétela con el gerundio del verbo entre paréntesis. Luego, con dos o tres compañeros/as túrnense para hacer el papel de los oyentes que llaman a participar en el programa dando su opinión y consejo al respecto.

No sé lo que me está (**1.** *pasar*). Conocí a una chica hace poco y, por más que trato, no puedo sacarla de mi mente. Estoy a punto de reprobar varias materias en el colegio porque vivo (**2.** *pensar*) en ella. Igual me sucede en el trabajo. Paso el tiempo (**3.** *contar*) los minutos para salir (**4.** *correr*) a verla.

Pero no sé si ella siente lo mismo que yo estoy (**5.** *sentir*). A veces, cuando está conmigo, parece distraída, como ausente. ¿Me quiere o no me quiere? La duda me está (**6.** *matar*).

Mis amigos dicen que me estoy (**7.** *enamorar*) impulsivamente y sienten lástima de mí. Según ellos, estoy (**8.** *alimentar*) una relación que no existe y voy a seguir (**9.** *sufrir*) hasta que acepte que este amor es y seguirá (**10.** *ser*) solo una ilusión de mi loco e insconsciente corazón.

**13 Ha nacido una estrella** 👥 Interpersonal/Presentational Communication ✿ **1.1, 1.3**

Intercambie ideas con un(a) compañero/a sobre cómo se puede llegar a ser lo que uno quiera. Usen el gerundio de los verbos y las profesiones que se dan como guía, como se ve en el modelo. Luego, elijan la profesión que más les llama la atención y díganle a la clase qué harían para tener éxito en ese campo.

MODELO   un(a) gran cineasta
**Se puede llegar a ser un gran cineasta estudiando cine, viendo los clásicos y haciendo sus propios documentales.**

- un(a) gran comediante
- una estrella de cine
- un(a) locutor/a de radio
- un(a) periodista famoso/a
- un(a) buen(a) comentarista de televisión
- un(a) bloguero/a influyente
- un(a) tuitero/a con muchos seguidores

*Un gran cineasta se forma desarrollando su propio estilo.*

## Essential Instruction

1. Check answers to **Actividad 12** orally as a group. Then divide the class into small groups and have them conduct their role-plays. Allow each student time to prepare for his/her role.
2. Open **Actividad 13** by reading through the bulleted list and asking students to name famous people for each occupation.
3. Point out the **Pregunta clave**, and tell students to keep it in mind as they complete the cultural readings.
4. Have students preview pp. 401–403. Ask them to predict what they will learn about Honduras.
5. Open the first cultural reading by asking students what they know about journalism ethics.

emcpassport.com
LA 3

# Los medios de comunicación hondureños  1.2, 2.1, 2.2

**? Pregunta clave**

¿Cómo afecta la situación política y social de un país a los medios de comunicación?

La relación entre los medios de comunicación y el poder político suele ser compleja y estar mediada por intereses que, según el caso, los acercan o los enfrentan.

En Honduras, hay una gran cantidad de medios: cuatro periódicos nacionales, varias estaciones de televisión y numerosas radioemisoras; sin embargo, la propiedad de esos medios está concentrada en pocas manos, y sus dueños mantienen una relación estrecha e influyente con la cima[1] del poder político del país. En este contexto de concentración mediática, ejercer[2] el periodismo independiente representa un desafío.

*Los medios independientes de Honduras enfrentan tiempos difíciles.*

Desde que el presidente Manuel Zelaya fue derrocado[3] por un golpe militar el 28 de junio de 2009 —después de que el grupo opositor encabezado por Roberto Micheletti lo acusó de querer cambiar la constitución para permitir la reelección presidencial—, Honduras se ha hundido[4] en una crisis política grave.

Desde entonces, forma parte de los países más peligrosos de América Latina para el gremio[5] periodístico: diversos medios de comunicación independientes han denunciado casos de censura, amenazas y agresiones; muchos periodistas fueron despedidos[6]; y lo más grave: más de 50 periodistas han sido asesinados, y la mayoría de esos crímenes siguen impunes[7].

Esta situación pone en riesgo la libertad de expresión y el derecho a la información: dos derechos fundamentales de los ciudadanos hondureños.

[1] heights    [2] practice    [3] overthrown    [4] sunk    [5] trade    [6] fired    [7] unpunished

 **Búsqueda:** medios de comunicación en honduras, golpe militar en honduras

## Prácticas  2.1

Uno de los problemas graves de la práctica profesional del periodismo en Honduras es lo que se conoce como "prensa tarifada". Cualquier persona que tenga los recursos económicos necesarios puede "pagarse un periodista" para difundir información que sirva a sus intereses personales aunque se trate de datos falsos o manipulados.

*Prácticas como la censura, las amenazas o la prensa tarifada ponen en riesgo la libertad de expresión.*

## 14 Comprensión  1.2, 2.1, 2.2

1. ¿Qué tipo de relación pueden tener los medios de comunicación y el poder político?

2. ¿Por qué es un desafío ejercer el periodismo independiente en Honduras?

3. ¿Por qué Honduras es un país peligroso para los periodistas independientes?

## 15 Analice  1.3, 4.2

1. ¿Qué relación cree Ud. que hay entre una situación de crisis política y la inseguridad del periodismo independiente?

2. ¿Qué semejanzas o diferencias encuentra Ud. entre la situación de los medios de comunicación en Honduras y en Estados Unidos?

**Differentiated Learning**

**Accelerate/Heritage Learners**
Ask students to research the life and works of Rafael Murillo Selva, Honduras's most famous playwright. Ask them to find out why his play ***Loubavagu*** is so popular and long-running, and how it depicts the history and culture of the indigenous Garifuna people. If possible, have students read or watch parts of the play online.

**Expand**
Discuss different types of media bias: corporate, racial, liberal, conservative, etc. Hold a class debate on the topic, and whether bias can ever be completely eliminated. If so, how? If not, what measures can be taken to control it as much as possible?

### Answers

**Perspectivas** *Respuesta posible:* Para que haya pluralidad de voces y se escuchen distintas opiniones.

**16**
1. Reporteros sin Fronteras, la OEA, la ONU, etc.
2. Explican los peligros que implica ejercer el periodismo, el estado de inseguridad en el que trabajan y la autocensura.
3. El Parlamento aprobó una ley para protegerlos.

**17**  *Las respuestas variarán.*

### Reference Desk

1. The Organization of American States, headquartered in Washington, D.C., was founded in 1948.
2. **El premio Álvaro Contreras** was created in 1926, and is awarded annually to writers, politicians, and national and international journalists.
3. Students can do a Flipgrid post reacting to any of these cultural readings.

### Critical Thinking

**Comparing and Contrasting**
Ask students to compare and contrast Honduras's laws regarding free speech and press with those of the United States.

---

**1.2, 2.1, 2.2**

## 16 Comprensión

1. ¿Qué organizaciones han analizado la situación de los medios en Honduras?
2. ¿Qué dicen los informes de esas organizaciones?
3. ¿Cómo actuó Honduras a raíz de estos informes?

## 17 Analice  **1.3**

1. ¿Qué otras medidas cree Ud. que podría tomar el gobierno de Honduras para garantizar la protección de los periodistas?
2. ¿Por qué cree Ud. que los organismos internacionales se interesan por asuntos como lo que ocurre en Honduras?

---

# Una ley para el periodismo   1.2, 2.1, 2.2

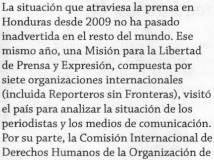

*El Parlamento hondureño aprobó una ley de defensa del periodismo.*

La situación que atraviesa la prensa en Honduras desde 2009 no ha pasado inadvertida en el resto del mundo. Ese mismo año, una Misión para la Libertad de Prensa y Expresión, compuesta por siete organizaciones internacionales (incluida Reporteros sin Fronteras), visitó el país para analizar la situación de los periodistas y los medios de comunicación. Por su parte, la Comisión Internacional de Derechos Humanos de la Organización de los Estados Americanos (OEA) también visitó Honduras en 2014 para evaluar los problemas de violencia e inseguridad en distintos ámbitos[1], incluido el periodismo.

Los informes dan cuenta[2] de los peligros que rodean al ejercicio del periodismo, del estado de inseguridad en el que realizan su labor[3] profesional y de la autocensura que surge en consecuencia. Honduras se encuentra en el lugar 132, entre 180 países, en la Clasificación Mundial de la Libertad de Prensa de Reporteros sin Fronteras publicada en febrero de 2015. Además, en su Examen Periódico Universal (EPU) de 2010 y 2014, la Organización de las Naciones Unidas (ONU) ha instado[4] a Honduras a proteger a los periodistas.

A raíz de este llamado de atención y para cumplir con las recomendaciones de la ONU, el Parlamento hondureño aprobó en 2015 la ley de protección a periodistas, comunicadores sociales y defensores de los derechos humanos. Se pretende así frenar los asesinatos de los profesionales de la comunicación y proporcionar un marco legal[5] para el resurgimiento de la libertad de expresión.

[1] spheres    [2] explain    [3] work    [4] urged    [5] legal framework

🔍 **Búsqueda:** misión para la libertad de prensa y expresión en honduras, clasificación mundial de la libertad de prensa, ley de protección a periodistas

---

*Perspectivas*  **1.2, 3.2**

"Quienes gobiernan, los empresarios y los políticos no deben temer a la prensa independiente ni a la pluralidad de medios, no deben sentirse cómodos con una prensa incondicional, al contrario, porque una sociedad democrática solo puede enfrentarse a sus desafíos cuando tiene a su alcance información contrastada y opinión crítica", afirmó la directora ejecutiva de diario *La Prensa*, María Antonia Martínez de Fuentes, en su discurso de agradecimiento por el premio Álvaro Contreras. Según Martínez de Fuentes, ¿por qué son necesarias las opiniones críticas en una democracia?

*María Antonia Martínez de Fuentes recibe el premio Álvaro Contreras.*

---

### Essential Instruction

1. Remind students of the culture photo and question from the unit opener. Have them scan p. 403 for the answer.
2. As you play the audio for each cultural reading, pause occasionally to check comprehension by asking **sí/no** questions.
3. Have students complete the **Analice** activities for Common Core practice.

## Asociación de Medios Comunitarios en Honduras

 **1.2, 2.1, 2.2**

Gracias a la iniciativa de más de treinta organizaciones de la sociedad civil y representantes de medios de comunicación alternativos, en el año 2013 se conformó la primera Asociación Nacional de Medios Comunitarios de Honduras (AMCH). Su objetivo es servir como interlocutora[1] con el Estado en los temas relacionados con la radio y la televisión, para que la ciudadanía y las instituciones puedan tener el derecho de operar sus propios medios de comunicación.

*Gracias a los medios comunitarios, se escuchan nuevas voces y se difunden otros temas y opiniones.*

La asociación surgió en el marco[2] del debate nacional por la democratización del espectro radioeléctrico. Este debate adquirió una relevancia particular a partir del golpe de estado de 2009, cuando los oligopolios fueron capaces de manipular la información y la población no tenía casi ninguna opción para defenderse de ese comportamiento. En ese contexto, el ánimo[3] que impulsó la asociación fue permitir que la población pudiera tener acceso a la información por parte de medios de comunicación alternativos.

En cuanto a los contenidos, los medios comunitarios se proponen divulgar[4] procesos sociales y reflejar la voz de distintas organizaciones —representantes de grupos de jóvenes, empresas de transformación social, indígenas, mujeres feministas, entre otros— para dar lugar a la expresión de la pluralidad. Los medios comunitarios se caracterizan por ser defendidos y promovidos por las comunidades y son estas las que se encargan de establecer la agenda informativa y editorial.

[1] spokesperson    [2] framework    [3] intention    [4] spread

 **Búsqueda:** asociación de medios comunitarios en honduras, amch, red de desarrollo sostenible de honduras, rds radio

### Productos   1.2, 2.2

RDS Radio es una radioemisora con fines educativos y de entretenimiento creada por la Red de Desarrollo Sostenible de Honduras, una organización que surgió a partir de un proyecto de la ONU. La radio funciona en el Distrito Central de Tegucigalpa y forma parte de la AMCH. Tiene como objetivo promover y construir ciudadanía fomentando la cultura, el arte y los valores para el crecimiento sano e integral de la comunidad. Se trata de un medio de comunicación comunitario e independiente, que hace radio por medio de una programación educativa y entretenida que incluye temas que abarcan la música, las letras, el cine, la ciencia, la economía, entre otros.

*Los medios comunitarios difunden contenidos que promueven valores democráticos y plurales.*

---

**1.2, 2.1, 2.2**

### 18 Comprensión

1. ¿Con qué objetivo se formó la Asociación de Medios Comunitarios en Honduras?

2. ¿Por qué el debate por la democratización de los medios se volvió más relevante a partir de 2009?

3. ¿Qué clase de contenidos promueven los medios comunitarios?

### 19 Analice   **1.3, 2.2**

1. Teniendo en cuenta lo que ha leído sobre los medios de comunicación en Honduras, ¿cree Ud. que esta es una iniciativa positiva? ¿Por qué?

2. ¿Qué ventajas cree Ud. que tiene para la población poder acceder a medios comunitarios además de los medios operados por grandes empresas?

---

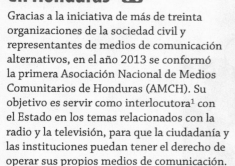
---

**Differentiated Learning**

**Expand**
Encourage students to research more about the OAS's founding, mission, and principles.

**Learning Styles**
**Auditory Learners**
Ask students to go online to listen to a few recent Honduran radio broadcasts or podcasts. Have them analyze the broadcasts for content, and indicate how they think they would be different before the 2015 **ley de protección a los periodistas**. Then ask them to listen to a few broadcasts from before 2015 to verify their predictions.

## Comparación y contraste: ¡Ojo con estas palabras! 1.2, 4.1

Preste atención a las siguientes palabras pues su uso, tanto en español como en inglés, varía de acuerdo al contexto.

*but* — pero / sino / sino que

**pero** + (sujeto) + verbo
   **Pero** equivale a *but*. Sirve para unir dos cláusulas independientes.

   Queríamos ir al estreno de la película, **pero** no tuvimos tiempo.

   Había muchos reporteros, **pero** la conferencia de prensa se canceló.

**sino** + sustantivo
   **No... sino** *but (rather)* tiene el sentido de **al contrario**. Sirve para introducir una oración negativa seguida de una idea opuesta.

   No tengo pereza **sino** sueño atrasado.

   No hubo un solo comunicado de prensa **sino** varios.

**sino** + **que** + verbo
   **No... sino que** se usa cuando los verbos de las dos cláusulas son distintos y se oponen.

   **No** cancelaron el estreno, **sino que** cambiaron el día.

   El Cascadas Mall en Tegucigalpa **no** solamente tiene tiendas y restaurantes, **sino que** también tiene la zona de Experiencias Creativas para los más chicos.

**No solo... sino (también)**   *Not only... but also*
   Sirve para hacer una afirmación, eliminando la restricción impuesta por **solo**.

   Mis primos planean visitar **no solo** Comayagua, **sino también** Santa Rosa de Copán.

   En Tegucigalpa **no solo** irán al Festival de la Mora, **sino también** al Festival Gastronómico del Choro y el Vino.

### Essential Instruction

1. After going over the information in **Vocabulario 2**, ask volunteers to create additional example sentences using information about themselves.
2. After completing **Actividad 20**, ask students to role-play the dialogue.
3. Begin **Actividad 21** by brainstorming examples of movie titles for each category listed.

## 20 ¿Qué hay en cartelera?  1.2

Complete el diálogo con **pero**, **sino**, **sino que** o **sino también**.

**Karina:** ¿Aló, Rodrigo? Te estoy esperando. No quedamos en que me llamaras a las siete __(1)__ pasaras por mí para ir al cine.

**Rodrigo:** Sí, sí, Karina. Ya lo sé, __(2)__ acabo de confirmar que hoy no pasan la película de Almodóvar que queríamos ver. Revisé la cartelera en línea y no la vi en Cinépolis de Cascadas Mall.

**Karina:** Yo creo que no la están pasando en Cascadas Mall __(3)__ en Cinemark del Citymall.

**Rodrigo:** ¡Qué lástima! No solo se nos está haciendo tarde __(4)__ debo poner gasolina y el Citymall queda muy lejos de aquí.

**Karina:** Bueno, tranquilo. Sí tenía muchas ganas de ver la película de Almodóvar, __(5)__ podemos verla otro día. Oye, como ya se hizo tarde, ¿qué te parece si vamos a la Librería Universitaria? Podemos ver no solo una peli con Andy García __(6)__ una con Salma Hayek.

**Rodrigo:** ¡Excelente idea! __(7)__ tienes que prometerme que verás ambas películas. La vez pasada nos fuimos a la mitad de la segunda película porque te pareció aburrida.

**Karina:** No solo era aburrida __(8)__ demasiado larga.

**Rodrigo:** Bueno, bueno. Paso a recogerte en cinco minutos.

## ¡Comunicación!

## 21 En gustos no hay disgustos... 👥 Interpersonal Communication  1.1

Imagine que Ud. y su compañero/a quieren ir al cine, pero no pueden ponerse de acuerdo sobre qué tipo de película quieren ver. ¡Tienen gustos cinematográficos muy diferentes! Representen la conversación que tienen con base en los géneros que se dan a continuación, como se ve en el modelo.

**MODELO**
**A:** ¿Qué película quieres ir a ver?

**B:** Me gustaría ver una película de suspenso, pero no creo que estén pasando ninguna que sea muy buena. ¿Qué tal si vemos una película de romance? Me encantan.

**A:** ¿De romance? Mejor vamos a ver una película de ciencia ficción. No es que no me gusten las películas románticas, sino que es que hoy no estoy de humor.

**B:** ...

- Ciencia ficción
- *Anime*
- Acción
- *Neo-noir*
- Suspenso
- Comedia
- Romance
- Drama

*Sabíamos que era una buena película de acción, pero también resultó siendo una película de suspenso fabulosa.*

**Answers**

**20**
1. sino que
2. pero
3. sino
4. sino que
5. pero
6. sino también
7. Pero
8. sino

**21** *Las conversaciones variarán.*

## Reference Desk

1. City Mall opened in 2006 in San Pedro Sula and in 2012 in Tegucigalpa. The location in the capital is Central America's largest mall.
2. Andy García and Salma Hayek have both enjoyed success in Hollywood; García is a Cuban-born actor and director, and Hayek is a Mexican-born actress of Lebanese descent. Ask students what films they have seen with these actors.
3. Survey the class to find out which Almodóvar films they have seen, and which they like best.

## Expansion

Ask students to create a Flipgrid post in which they talk about their favorite movie and summarize the plot. Their classmates can create follow-up posts in which they state their own opinions of the movie, and make recommendations for similar ones in the genre.

## Differentiated Learning
### Heritage Learners
Ask heritage learners to name titles of movies that are popular in their cultural communities. Also have them share whether their family's country of origin has a flourishing film industry, and/or any film festivals that are held there.

## Special Needs Students
### AD(H)D
Make a graphic organizer with three columns labeled **pero**, **sino**, and **sino que**. Work with students to write in each column additional examples of each use of **pero**, **sino**, and **sino que**.

# ¡Comunicación!

**1.1, 1.2, 1.3, 3.1**

**22  Clásicos del séptimo arte**  Interpersonal /Presentational Communication

Hay películas que se consideran clásicas porque se tienen como modelos dignos de ser emulados o tratan sobre temas que permanecen vigentes. En grupos de tres o cuatro, intercambien opiniones sobre las películas que se dan a continuación, turnándose para hacer las preguntas y responderlas. Decidan qué películas les gustan más (tanto las clásicas como las más recientes) y pónganlas en orden de preferencia eliminando o añadiendo las que crean que deben estar o no en cada lista. Para finalizar, elijan una película, hagan un resumen de su argumento en un breve párrafo y preséntenlo enfrente de la clase.

1. ¿Cuáles de estos títulos reconocen? ¿Saben cuál es el título original de estas películas? ¿Cuáles han visto Uds.? ¿Quiénes son los protagonistas? ¿Cuál es el argumento?

| | |
|---|---|
| *Nosferatu* | *Fantasía* |
| *El perro andaluz* | *101 dálmatas* |
| *El Mago de Oz* | *Vértigo* |
| *Lo que el viento se llevó* | *La dolce vita* |
| *Casablanca* | *Psicosis* |
| *Tiempos modernos* | *2001: Una odisea del espacio* |
| *Ciudadano Kane* | *El padrino I, II y III* |
| *El halcón maltés* | *Apocalipsis ahora* |
| *El ladrón de bicicletas* | *La lista de Schindler* |
| *Los siete samuráis* | *Mujeres al borde de un ataque de nervios* |

2. ¿Cuál es el título original de las siguientes películas? ¿Cuáles creen Uds. que se convertirán en clásicos y cuáles no? ¿Por qué?

*Tiempos violentos* (*Pulp Fiction*)

*La guerra de las galaxias* y su saga

La saga de *Harry Potter*

La saga de *El señor de los anillos* (*Las dos torres*, *El retorno del rey*...)

La saga de *El hobbit*

La saga del universo Marvel: *Los vengadores*, *Daredevil*, *Capitán América*, *El Hombre Araña*, *Thor*, *Iron Man*, *Hulk*, etc.

La saga de *Piratas del Caribe*

*Matrix* y su trilogía

*Toy Story*

*Buscando a Nemo*

*Amélie*

*Tron* y *Tron: El legado*

*El laberinto del fauno*

*El Mago de Oz es un clásico del cine. Ha inspirado a generaciones y sus imágenes son emblemáticas.*

## Essential Instruction

1. As groups work through **Actividad 22**, encourage them to fill in gaps in each other's knowledge.

2. For their presentations in **Actividad 22**, you may want to ask groups to research interesting facts about their movie.

3. Begin **Actividad 23** by asking students if they are familiar with *The Avengers* films. Have volunteers read the review aloud while students follow along in their books.

4. Open **Actividad 24** by asking students if they have ever binge-watched a TV show, and to share their experiences.

# ¡Comunicación!

## 23 Una crítica de cine | Presentational Communication  1.2, 1.3, 3.1

Imagine que Ud. trabaja en un periódico y está encargado/a de hacer una crítica (*critique*) de cine para la sección de ocio y entretenimiento. Elija una película que haya visto recientemente y escriba una reseña para publicar en la internet. Incluya una breve sinópsis del argumento y la crítica, como se ve a continuación.

---

○ ○ ○   RESEÑAS DE CINE

## OCIO Y ENTRETENIMIENTO

**RESEÑAS DE CINE**   *Los vengadores: La era de Ultrón*   **Duración: 141 minutos**   **Calificación: 8/10**
**Género: Aventuras**

**Sinopsis:** Tony Stark estaba desarrollando un programa para mantener la paz mundial e intentó completarlo con inteligencia artificial hallada en el cetro de Loki. Sin embargo, al hacerlo, el androide Ultrón se descontrola y cree que debe erradicar a la humanidad para salvar a la Tierra. Ultrón se escapa y desarrolla otro cuerpo, mejor que el rudimentario que tenía, y construye un ejército de drones. Los Vengadores —el Capitán América, Iron Man, Thor, Hulk, la Viuda Negra y Ojo de Halcón, junto con Nick Furia, María Hill y los agentes de Shield— deberán unirse y urdir un plan para detener a Ultrón.

**Crítica:** ¿Cómo lograr que un elenco (*cast*) de mega estrellas del cine logren trabajar juntas y generar un éxito de taquilla? En *Vengadores: La Era de Ultrón*, el director Joss Whedon tiene la receta perfecta. Él logra entrelazar el argumento de manera que todos los personajes sean protagonistas y nos mantengan pegados a los asientos por las casi dos horas y media que dura la película. Las escenas de acción de alto voltaje se suceden sin dar respiro al espectador salvo por las usuales dosis de humor y hasta alguna que otra situación romántica... Ultrón se ha convertido en una nueva amenaza para nuestro planeta, pero gracias a nuestros superhéroes y a sus superpoderes y destrezas extraordinarias sobreviviremos para ver las secuelas anunciadas para los próximos años.

---

## 24 Televisión a la carta  Interpersonal Communication 1.1

El VBD, o video bajo demanda, cambió la forma de ver televisión. Los espectadores ya no tienen que depender de horarios de programación fija; pueden adelantar, devolver, pausar y reanudar el programa. Antiguamente, se repartían películas en DVD por correo. Ahora, los servicios de emisión continua (*streaming*) de video se han convertido en videoclubes virtuales. Sus suscriptores pueden acceder a una gran oferta de series, películas y documentales. La manera de ver televisión cambió al liberarse todos los episodios de la temporada de una sola vez. De allí, han surgido las maratones (*binge watching*) para ver una serie de un tirón.

Comente con un(a) compañero/a los pros y los contra de esta nueva modalidad.

- Pros y contras de la televisión a la carta / de las maratones / de la publicidad en televisión
- Opinión sobre los programas de la televisión tradicional en horario de máxima audiencia
- Ventajas de la televisión tradicional y el cine versus los videos en emisión continua
- Géneros preferidos de películas o series

---

---

## Differentiated Learning
### Accelerate/Expand
Ask students to watch a film from a Spanish-speaking country that has a strong film industry, such as Mexico, Spain, or Argentina. Tell them to write a brief summary of the plot and assign it a star rating. Have students get together in small groups; they should take turns sharing information about the films and making recommendations.

## Learning Styles
### Visual Learners
Ask these students to create a slide presentation or other visual component to accompany their group's summary in **Actividad 22**.

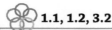

## ¡Comunicación!

 **1.1, 1.2, 3.2**

**25  Para quejarse mejor** 👥 **Interpersonal Communication**

Lea y comente con un(a) compañero/a de clase la siguiente reseña y, luego, conteste las preguntas.

«El otro día en una tienda de telefonía móvil escuché una conversación de dos personas sobre cómo realizaban sus reclamaciones a la marca de esta compañía de móviles: "Yo ya nunca llamo por teléfono, que te tienen en espera dos años para luego marearte de un departamento a otro. Prueba Twitter, les dejas un *tweet* y pones un *hashtag* tipo #engaño o #estafa y te responden al segundo".

Esto no es un hecho aislado, cada vez más el usuario se ha percatado de que escribir un *tweet* citando a la marca y expresando su problema es una vía directa para que la empresa te responda y entre en contacto contigo. Es curioso que funcione mejor una red social que un servicio de atención al cliente vía telefónica.»

—de "Twitter como canal de atención al cliente" por Isabel Romero en www.enredandoporlared.com

1. ¿Por qué cree que las redes sociales funcionan mejor para hacer quejas o reclamos?
2. ¿Qué tipo de experiencias ha tenido para presentar una queja?
3. ¿Alguna vez ha usado una red social para hacer reclamos?

**26  ¿Por avión o por carretera?** 👥 **Interpersonal Communication**  **1.1**

Imagine que Tina, una estudiante de intercambio, está en la oficina de una compañía de transporte averiguando la mejor forma de hacer enviar parte de su equipaje desde Honduras. Con un(a) compañero/a, hagan el papel de Tina, que tiene muchas preguntas, y el empleado que le da consejos y recomendaciones. Usen los servicios que se dan como guía en su conversación y su propia imaginación, como se ve en el modelo.

*Puede hacer seguimiento de su envío en línea.*

MODELO

**A:** Necesito enviar un par de cajas de libros y regalos, porque llevarlas como equipaje me costaría una fortuna. ¿Cree que debo enviarlas por avión?

**B:** Francamente, no creo que sea buena idea. No es que el transporte aéreo no sea bueno, sino que el costo, como es por peso, sería prohibitivo.

- Servicio de transporte aéreo
- Servicio de envío por mar o carretera
- Tarifas, impuestos y seguros
- Costos de aduana
- Tiempo de entrega y seguimiento en línea

## Essential Instruction

1. Open **Actividad 25** by surveying the class about their experiences with Twitter.
2. For **Actividad 26**, you may want to have students look up the actual costs of shipping via the various methods from Tegucigalpa to your city.
3. As you go through **Gramática**, point out the similarities in the formation of the future perfect and the conditional perfect.

# Gramática

## El futuro perfecto y el condicional perfecto  1.2, 4.1

### Formación del futuro y el condicional perfecto

El futuro perfecto se forma con el futuro del verbo auxiliar **haber** y el **participio** del verbo principal.
El condicional perfecto se forma con el verbo auxiliar **haber** en condicional y el **participio** del verbo principal.

| Futuro perfecto | |
| --- | --- |
| **Futuro de** *haber* | **Participio pasado** |
| habré | apagado |
| habrás | apagado |
| habrá | encendido |
| habremos | encendido |
| habréis | dicho |
| habrán | dicho |

| Condicional perfecto | |
| --- | --- |
| **Condicional de** *haber* | **Participio pasado** |
| habría | abierto |
| habrías | abierto |
| habría | escrito |
| habríamos | escrito |
| habríais | visto |
| habrían | visto |

### Usos del futuro perfecto

- El futuro perfecto corresponde a *will have* (+ participio) en inglés. Indica una acción anterior a otro punto de referencia en el futuro.

  Clara **habrá terminado** todas las reseñas para esta tarde.

  *Clara **will have finished** all the press reviews by this afternoon.*

- El futuro perfecto también puede expresar probabilidad.

  Ella ya nos **habrá enviado** un mensaje de texto.
  (Probablemente ella ya **ha enviado** un mensaje de texto.)

  *She **has** probably **sent** us a text message.*

### Usos del condicional perfecto

- El condicional perfecto corresponde a *would have* (+ participio) en inglés. Indica una acción anterior a otro punto de referencia en el pasado.

  Ayer, Clara me dijo que **habría terminado** todas las reseñas para esta tarde.

  *Yesterday, Clara told me that **she would have finished** all the press reviews by this afternoon.*

- El condicional perfecto también puede expresar probabilidad.

  Ella **habría enviado** un mensaje de texto en cuanto llegara.
  (Probablemente **había enviado** un mensaje de texto en cuanto llegó.)

  *She **had** probably **sent** a text message as soon as she arrived.*

- El condicional perfecto también se usa para expresar deseo o posibilidad respecto de una condición contraria a la realidad.

  **Habríamos desayunado**, pero no nos dio tiempo.
  *We **would have had breakfast**, but we had no time.*

  **Habríamos desayunado** si nos hubiera dado tiempo.
  *We **would have had breakfast** if we had had time.*

---

### Reference Desk

1. Point out that past participles do not change in gender or number, and remain the same for every perfect tense.
2. Remind students that object pronouns precede the conjugated form of **haber**: **Ella me ha dicho**. When an expression uses the infinitive **haber**, the object pronoun attaches directly to the infinitive: **Siento no haberte ayudado.**
3. Remind students that past participles with two vowels next to each other require an accent mark, for example, **caído**, **creído**, **leído**, **oído**, **reído**, **sonreído**, **traído**. The **ui** combination does not require an accent mark: **construido**.

### Communication

**Interpersonal/Presentational:
Cooperative Groups**
Ask students to write predictions about their classmates using the future perfect tense. Collect the papers, shuffle them, and read them aloud. Have the class agree or disagree with the predictions.

### Expansion

Ask students to make a chart of the four perfect tenses: present, past, future, and conditional.

---

### Differentiated Learning
**Heritage Learners**
Ask students to write a paragraph about how their life would have been different if they had grown up in their family's country of origin. Encourage them to read their paragraphs for the class.

### Learning Styles
**Auditory Learners**
Prepare sentences that use the future perfect and the conditional perfect. Write **condicional perfecto** on the left side of the board, and **futuro perfecto** on the right side. Read the sentences aloud. Have students point to the tense they hear in each sentence.

**27** *Las respuestas variarán.*

**28**

1. Yo me habría levantado temprano, pero me acosté tarde.
2. Yo habría desayunado bien, pero tuve que salir corriendo para el colegio.
3. Yo habría ido al entrenamiento de gymnasia, pero tuve que quedarme a la reunión del club de español.
4. Yo habría salido a comer con amigos, pero tuve que ir de compras al supermercado.
5. Yo habría escrito mi ensayo de literatura, pero se descompuso mi computadora.
6. Yo habría visto la entrega de premios en la tele, pero tuve que llevar a mi hermanita a su clase de baile.
7. Yo habría comprado los boletos del concierto, pero dejé mi billetera en casa.

---

### Reference Desk

The term *phubbing* was coined as the result of a 2012 ad campaign by Macquarie Dictionary in Australia.

---

### Critical Thinking

**Analyzing**
Ask students to write sentences about how their lives would have been different if certain conditions in their lives had been very different, such as growing up very wealthy/poor, in an urban/rural area, in a larger/smaller family, etc.

---

## ¡Comunicación!

### 27 ¿Hipercomunicados o incomunicados?    Interpersonal Communication    1.1, 5.2

¿Qué nos habrá pasado camino a conectarnos mejor para terminar más aislados? Imagine que está con alguien que de repente empieza a reírse sin razón aparente. "¿Qué habré dicho que sea tan gracioso?" se pregunta Ud. algo desconcertado (*taken aback*), pero resulta que la persona no se estaba riendo por algo que Ud. dijo, sino por algo que leyó en su celular. ¿Le ha ocurrido a Ud. algo similar? Seguramente sí, porque es una práctica muy común hoy en día. Tanto, que hasta tiene nombre propio. Se llama *phubbing*, y consiste en ignorar a aquellos con quienes estamos por estar pendientes del celular. Este uso excesivo de la la tecnología afecta negativamente nuestras relaciones personales y debemos evitarlo porque, al final, no habrá valido la pena sacrificar la interacción cara a cara en nombre de la interacción virtual.

Con un(a) compañero/a, comenten la situación que se ilustra en la fotografía y contesten las preguntas que siguen teniendo en cuenta la información que acabaron de leer.

- ¿Para qué se habrán reunido estos amigos?
- ¿Por qué habrán preferido mirar el celular?
- ¿Con quién se habrán comunicado?
- Al analizar su impacto futuro, ¿Uds. creen que las redes sociales habrán ayudado a comunicarse más o menos?
- Diga escenarios futuros en los cuales la tecnología habrá mejorado la comunicación.
- Si comparan sus interacciones personales con sus interacciones en redes sociales, ¿cuáles creen que habrán reportado más beneficios en su futuro profesional?
- Si alguna vez les han hecho *phubbing*, especulen por qué habrá sido.
- ¿Qué medidas pueden tomar hoy que habrán resultado en mejores relaciones interpersonales en el futuro?

*El 87 % de los adolescentes prefiere comunicarse por mensaje de texto.*

### 28 Por una razón u otra    1.3

Imagine que hoy no ha sido un buen día, pues, por una razón u otra, no pudo hacer muchas cosas que quería o tenía que hacer. Diga qué habría hecho y por qué no lo hizo usando el condicional perfecto y el pretérito, como se ve en el modelo.

> **MODELO**   echar los DVDs al buzón / no encontrarlos por ninguna parte
> **Yo habría echado los DVDs al buzón, pero no los encontré por ninguna parte.**

1. levantarse temprano / acostarse tarde
2. desayunar bien / tener que salir corriendo para el colegio
3. ir al entrenamiento de gimnasia / tener que quedarse a la reunión del club de español
4. salir a comer con amigos / tener que ir de compras al supermercado
5. escribir el ensayo de literatura / descomponerse mi computadora
6. ver la entrega de premios en la tele / tener que llevar a mi hermanita a su clase de baile
7. comprar los boletos del concierto / dejar mi billetera en casa

---

---

### Essential Instruction

1. After pairs answer the questions in **Actividad 27**, have them get together in groups of four for further discussion.
2. Have students compare their sentences from **Actividad 28** in pairs.
3. For **Actividad 29**, point out that students can either agree and say that they would have done the same, or they can say what they would have done instead.
4. Open **Gramática** by telling students that they are going to review another perfect tense using past participles.

# *Gramática*

## RESOURCES

| WB | Activity 8 |

| LA | Activity 5 |

## ¡Comunicación!  1.1

### 29 Yo de ti... 👥 Interpersonal Communication

Un(a) compañero/a le cuenta algo que le pasó y Ud. le dice lo que habría hecho si hubiera estado en su lugar.

MODELO   Mis papás me pidieron que me conectara todos los días por Skype, pero hacía tantas actividades que se me olvidaba.

**Yo de ti también lo habría olvidado.**

Yo de ti no me habría salido de la banda. ¡Hoy serías famoso!

1. Quería ir al concierto de One Direction, pero tuve que quedarme estudiando.

2. Debía estudiar para los demás exámenes finales, pero estaba cansado/a y fui al cine.

3. Mi mamá me pidió que comprara leche y pan, pero se me olvidó.

4. Me encantan las artes escénicas, pero mis padres no las consideran una carrera seria.

5. Cuando envié los formularios de la universidad, puse medicina y derecho de primeros.

## Answers

**29** *Las respuestas variarán.*
*Respuestas posibles:*
1. Yo de ti habría ido al concierto.
2. Yo de ti me habría quedado estudiando.
3. Yo de ti lo habría comprado enseguida.
4. Yo de ti les habría dicho que quieres ser actor/actriz.
5. Yo de ti me habría ido por artes escénicas; tienes un gran talento dramático.

## Reference Desk

Point out that **yo de ti** is a colloquial expression; it takes the place of a more formal phrase such as **yo, de ser tú** or **yo, si fuera tú**. Other popular colloquial expressions are **yo que tú** and **yo en tu lugar**.

## El pluscuamperfecto del subjuntivo  1.2

Formamos el pluscuamperfecto del subjuntivo con el imperfecto del subjuntivo del verbo **haber** y el participio pasado del verbo principal.

| Formación del pluscuamperfecto del subjuntivo | | |
|---|---|---|
| **Infinitivo** | **Imperfecto del subjuntivo de** *haber* | **Participio pasado** |
| **enviar** | hubiera | **enviado** |
| | hubieras | |
| **ver** | hubiera | **visto** |
| | hubiéramos | |
| **dirigir** | hubierais | **dirigido** |
| | hubieran | |

### Usos del pluscuamperfecto del subjuntivo

- El pluscuamperfecto del subjuntivo se usa en el tiempo pasado, en oraciones en que en la cláusula principal se expresa una reacción de duda, emoción, sorpresa o incredulidad, entre otras, ante una acción previamente ocurrida. En estos casos, el verbo de la cláusula principal está en el pasado del indicativo y el verbo de la cláusula subordinada está en subjuntivo.

No podíamos creer que **hubieran cancelado** el concierto a última hora.

*We couldn't believe that they **had cancelled** the concert at the last minute.*

Nos sorprendió que el presidente mismo le **hubiera entregado** el premio.

*We were surprised that the president himself **had handed** her the award.*

## Learning Styles
### Auditory Learners
Create a worksheet containing sentence endings. Read aloud the sentence starters and have students select the correct ending for each one.

## Multiple Intelligences
### Verbal-Linguistic
Tell students to imagine that they are interns at an ad company, and they have been tasked with writing an anti-phubbing radio or TV spot for broadcast in Latin America. In small groups, have students create their ads and then present them to the class. Encourage humor and creativity.

**30** *Las respuestas variarán.*

### Communication

**Interpersonal/Presentational: Paired Practice**

Ask students to make a list of tasks that they have not completed. In pairs, students take turns asking each other why they haven't completed these activities. They should give excuses using the past perfect subjunctive and the conditional perfect.

### Expansion

Ask students to write sentences about events in their community for which the outcome would have been different if something had (not) happened. For example: **Yo habría ido al desfile para celebrar con el equipo de fútbol americano si hubiera terminado mis quehaceres.**

---

- También se usa para expresar una situación hipotética o contraria a la realidad en el pasado. En ese caso, el verbo de la cláusula principal está en el condicional y el verbo de la cláusula subordinada está en subjuntivo.

| | |
|---|---|
| Les asombraría muchísimo que las cosas **hubieran cambiado** mucho en dos años. | *They would be very surprised if things **had changed** much in two years.* |
| Sería un desperdicio que no se **hubiera logrado** nada con las conversaciones de paz. | *It would be a waste if nothing **had been accomplished** with the peace talks.* |

- El pluscuamperfecto del subjuntivo se usa especialmente en cláusulas con **si**, para expresar acciones o situaciones contrarias a la realidad, cosas que habrían podido ocurrir (si se hubieran dado ciertas circunstancias), pero no ocurrieron. En esos casos, la cláusula principal va en el condicional perfecto y la cláusula subordinada con **si** va en pluscuamperfecto del subjuntivo. Note que se puede cambiar el orden de las cláusulas sin que cambie el significado de la oración.

| | |
|---|---|
| **Si hubiera sabido** de la reunión (pero no supe), habría preparado algo. | *If I had known about the meeting (but I didn't know), I would have prepared something.* |
| Yo habría preparado algo **si hubiera sabido** de la reunión. | *I would have prepared something if I had known about the meeting.* |

- En la cláusulas con **si** en que se expresan acciones contrarias a la realidad, la construcción **de** + **infinitivo** puede tomar el lugar del pluscuamperfecto del subjuntivo.

| | |
|---|---|
| **Si hubieras dicho** algo a tiempo, se habría evitado el problema. | *If you had said something on time, the problem would have been averted.* |
| **De decir** algo a tiempo, se habría evitado el problema. | *By saying something on time, the problem would have been averted.* |

---

 **¡Comunicación!**

**30** **¿Qué habríamos hecho?** 👥 **Interpersonal Communication** ✿ **1.1, 5.2**

Con un(a) compañero/a, comenten qué habrían hecho...

- si hubieran estado enfermos hoy.
- si hubieran tenido entrenamiento ayer y un examen hoy.
- si llegaran a un restaurante y se hubieran dado cuenta de que no tenían dinero.
- si no hubieran estudiado español y viajaran a un país hispanohablante.
- si hubieran ahorrado mucho dinero en el verano.

---

**Essential Instruction**

1. Give example sentences (**Si hubiera tenido tiempo, habría ido a tu casa**) and have volunteers offer alternate endings (**...habría hecho la tarea**).

2. Have pairs share their responses to **Actividad 30** with the class.

3. Read through the article in **Actividad 31** as a class, and have students complete the cloze paragraph. Then have them role-play the dialogue in pairs.

## ¡Comunicación!

**31 Reportaje ciudadano** | Interpretive Communication  **1.2**

Lea el siguiente reportaje. Luego, complete el diálogo que se da a continuación con el pluscuamperfecto del subjuntivo o con el condicional perfecto, según corresponda de acuerdo al contexto.

### ¡Reportaje ciudadano en acción!
Martes 7 de julio – 12 PM

*Cada cual da su propia versión de los hechos.*

¿Alguna vez ha visto un evento importante en la calle, lo ha filmado y fotografiado, y, luego, compartido en las redes sociales? Eso es lo que hacen muchos ciudadanos en sitios donde los medios de comunicación no están cubriendo la noticia o porque ellos se encontraban en el lugar justo, en el momento justo.

En este tipo de "reportaje", los ciudadanos juegan un papel primordial en la recolección, reportaje, análisis y diseminación de noticias. Por ejemplo, pueden publicar su propia versión de un acontecimiento en un blog, sea propio o ajeno. También pueden enviar su versión como reacción o respuesta a una noticia en un medio de comunicación, la versión contemporánea de una carta al editor. Otra modalidad consiste en colaborar estrechamente con periodistas profesionales.

Cualquiera que sea el método, el objetivo es comunicar noticias. Sin embargo, ¿cuán confiable es una noticia difundida por un ciudadano privado? Esa es una de las preguntas que debe responderse. Ya ha habido instancias de subjetividad, errores y exageraciones en la transmisión de noticias, así como manipulaciones de imágenes. Por qué se reporta —la motivación— y cómo —la ética— son el quid.

—¿Viste el reportaje sobre los paraguas amarillos en Hong Kong? ¡Me (**1.** *encantar*) estar allá para cubrir la noticia! Si (**2.** *ir*) con mi primo, (**3.** *poder*) hacerlo de primera mano.

—Sí, pero no todo es confiable. Si tú (**4.** *estar*) allá, (**5.** *darse*) cuenta de que no es fácil ser objetivo estando sobre el terreno.

—Pero... ¡yo (**6.** *simpatizar*) mucho con los estudiantes de Hong Kong!

—Claro, yo también. Sin embargo, si (**7.** *querer*) que te siguieran muchas personas, (**8.** *tener*) que ser más imparcial.

—Te entiendo, ¡pero es difícil! Si tú (**9.** *vivir*) allá, ¿cómo crees que (**10.** *sentirse*)?

—Yo creo que (**11.** *emocionarse*) mucho.

—Sí, definitivamente. Hace diez años, ¿quién (**12.** *imaginarse*) que las redes sociales iban a cambiar tanto el mundo?

—Quizá no tanto como lo han hecho, ¡pero nuestros abuelitos nunca lo (**13.** *soñar*)!

Answers

**31**
1. hubiera encantado
2. hubiera ido
3. habría podido
4. hubieras estado
5. te habrías dado
6. habría simpatizado
7. hubieras querido
8. habrías tenido
9. hubieras vivido
10. te habrías sentido
11. me habría emocionado
12. se hubiera imaginado
13. hubieran soñado

### Critical Thinking

**Analyzing**
After checking answers to **Actividad 31**, ask students to think of recent or memorable examples of individuals posting photos or videos of events online. Which postings had a positive outcome? Which ones led to negative fallout? Why?

## Differentiated Learning
### Decelerate
To review the many uses of the subjunctive mood, set up stations around the classroom with listening, speaking, reading, and writing activities. Provide students with a worksheet to record written answers. You may want to have students work in pairs or groups of three to complete each activity.

## Special Needs Students
### All Categories
Review verbs and expressions that trigger the use of the subjunctive, and create an extra practice worksheet to review with students.

## ¡Comunicación!  1.1, 1.2

**32** *Spam*, ese correo no deseado    Interpretive/Interpersonal Communication

Lea esta interesante información sobre el *spam* y conteste las preguntas que siguen. Luego, haga una lista de los mensajes de *spam* más absurdos que haya recibido y compárelos con los de sus compañeros/as. ¿Qué tienen en común? ¿En qué se diferencian?

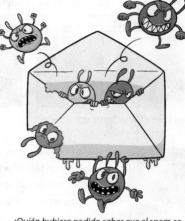

*¿Quién hubiera podido saber que el* spam *se volvería parte de nuestra vida cotidiana?*

En sus remotos orígenes —1937—, SPAM era, y sigue siendo, jamón enlatado. Muchos se preguntan de dónde salió el nombre y *Hormel*, la compañía que lo produce, perpetúa el misterio. Dicen en su sitio web que hubiera podido significar *SPiced hAM*, o jamón especiado, pero que solo lo sabe con certeza el inventor del nombre.

Los ingleses hubieran jurado que significaba *Specially Processed American Meat*, o carne americana procesada especialmente, como se le decía en el Reino Unido durante la II Guerra Mundial. Lo que sí es cierto es que, si no hubiera existido el SPAM, muchos soldados y civiles habrían pasado hambre. Una cifra que demuestra su popularidad es el hecho de que hubiera llegado a consumirse en 41 países y a comercializarse en 100 para el año 2003.

¿Qué ocurrió para que hubiera pasado de nombre de carne a denominar al correo no solicitado? Todo empezó en 1970, con una sátira de *Monty Python*: todos los platos de un menú tenían SPAM y, cada vez que la mesonera decía: "SPAM", un grupo de vikingos repetía: "¡SPAM, SPAM, SPAM, SPAM, SPAM, SPAM, SPAM, SPAM, delicioso SPAM, maravilloso SPAM!". Sofocaban la conversación hasta que los mandaban a callar.

Rápidamente, en las salas de *chat* y en los MUD (*multi-user dungeons*) se empezó a usar *spam* para referirse a mensajes excesivos o molestos que los grupos enviaban a sus rivales. La propagación accidental de mensajes masivos también se llamó *spam*, hasta que se convirtió en el término para denominar los correos electrónicos no deseados.

Ya habrían preferido los productores de SPAM que eso no hubiera sucedido nunca. Obviamente, jamás se le hubiera ocurrido a nadie de Hormel el desatino de asociar su marca con algo negativo.

La marca SPAM se debe escribir en mayúsculas —una batalla legal ganada— para distinguirla de los correos molestos. Desafortunadamente, ¿y quién lo hubiera adivinado?, *spam* está pasando a significar también cualquier tipo indeseado de publicidad, llamada o mensaje —sea digital o no—.

1. ¿Siempre lee todos sus mensajes electrónicos? ¿Por qué?
2. Diga la definición de *spam*.
3. Explique la conexión entre la carne SPAM y los correos *spam*.
4. ¿Por qué es paradójico que el SPAM haya pasado a significar correo indeseado?

# Lectura informativa

## Antes de leer  1.3

1. ¿Cómo cree Ud. que afecta la situación política y social de un país a los periodistas?

2. ¿Qué dificultades y peligros puede enfrentar un periodista que trabaja durante una dictadura?

### Estrategia  3.1

**Hacer un resumen**

Resumir es una buena estrategia para asegurarse de haber comprendido las partes más importantes de un texto. Cuando lea, identifique las ideas principales y las secundarias, pero incluya solamente las primeras en el resumen.

---

 Virgilio Andrade: en 50...

**ConexiHon** — comunicación para vencer el miedo

## Virgilio Andrade: en 50 años de radio sufrí amenazas, marginación y exilio  1.2, 2.1, 2.2, 3.2

*Inicio*

Por Israel Cruz

**San Pedro Sula, Honduras (Conexihon)**. En 40 años de estar al frente de su programa Sonriendo y Comentando, el locutor Virgilio Andrade dice haber experimentado desde problemas, amenazas[1], intimidación, marginamiento hasta el cruel exilio, pero que no puede negar que la jornada[2] le deja una enseñanza de amistad e interacción con la audiencia.

El polémico comunicador [...] expresa que el aprendizaje en radio es como una escuela o la universidad de la vida que le permite conocer a muchas personas de diferentes edades y culturas.

El controvertido comunicador que se hace llamar "el hombre de las verdades" asegura que haber alcanzado cuatro décadas con su programa el 15 de febrero anterior refleja la mitad de una larga vida.

**Conexihon.Info (CI): ¿Se puede vivir con dignidad del periodismo?**

**Virgilio Andrade (VA):** Sí, claro, hay que aferrarse a los principios de solidaridad y actitud positiva porque es una forma de entregarse al público.

**CI: ¿Qué opina que en algunas emisoras se irrespeta[3] al oyente?**

**VA:** Creo que los dueños de estas estaciones de radio sabrán de cómo se maneja una ferretería[4], pero no saben nada de radio, la cual no solo es el aparato que transmite sonidos sino, además, una cátedra[5] que sirve para entretener, enseñar e informar.

Al no saber del asunto y sus contenidos, "se convierten en simples mercaderes que contratan a un aprendiz de locutor para que diga lo que quiera a cambio de un comercial. Deberían de estar en la cárcel o un manicomio[6] por haber vulgarizado la radiodifusión", apostilló[7] con ademanes[8] de enojo.

El popular comunicador agregó que lo más grave de esto es que no se descarta[9] que exista una audiencia que les sigue porque está al mismo nivel de analfabetismo[10] y vulgaridad del locutor.

**CI: ¿Cómo ha incidido[11] la muerte de los comunicadores en su desempeño periodístico?**

**VA:** Son lamentables estos hechos, no estamos exentos de la violencia, es algo que está en todas partes, intimidan a la profesión, "el miedo está en el viento y nosotros lo percibimos".

[1] threats    [2] every work day    [3] be disrespectful to    [4] hardware store
[5] professor's podium    [6] madhouse    [7] added    [8] gestures    [9] dismiss    [10] illiteracy
[11] affect

---

 1.2, 2.1, 2.2, 3.2

## 33 Comprensión

1. ¿Qué aspectos positivos destaca Virgilio Andrade de su trabajo en la radio?

2. ¿Qué opina Andrade sobre los dueños de estaciones radiales en las que se falta el respeto a la audiencia?

3. ¿Qué opinión le merecen los oyentes que siguen programas vulgares?

## 34 Analice 1.3, 3.2

¿Por qué cree Ud. que un periodista que ha sufrido problemas graves a causa de su trabajo nunca dejó el ejercicio de su profesión?

---

**Answers**

### Antes de leer
*Las respuestas variarán.*

**33**
1. Destaca la amistad y la interacción con la audiencia y el conocimiento de muchas personas de distintas edades y culturas.
2. Cree que no saben nada de radio, que solo les interesa vender publicidad y que vulgarizan la radio.
3. Cree que son tan vulgares como los presentadores de esos programas.

**34** *Las respuestas variarán.*
*Respuesta posible:* Para él seguramente era más importante su vocación que el miedo.

### Pre-AP

**Course Theme: Los desafíos mundiales**

---

**Differentiated Learning**
**Accelerate/Expand**
Ask students to watch the RTVE report on violence in Honduras, "**En el reino del plomo**" (available online). Have students summarize what they saw and write their reactions to the piece. They can submit their reports via Avenue.

**Multiple Intelligences**
**Bodily-Kinesthetic/Verbal-Linguistic**
Ask groups of students to create a skit involving SPAM and/or spam. Encourage humor and creativity. Allow groups time to rehearse before performing their scenes for the class.

**415**

**35**

1. Cree que tiene que haber intereses que van más allá del trabajo periodístico, porque no tiene sentido que se mate a alguien por una noticia o una opinión.

2. Le clausuraron una radio; no le vendían espacios radiales; y sufrió intimidaciones, amenazas y marginamiento por parte de los dueños de los medios.

3. Porque hubo un golpe de estado y él era crítico de los militares.

**36** *Las respuestas variarán.*

## Expansion

Ask students to research more about Virgilio Andrade and write a biographical profile.

---

 **1.2, 2.1, 2.2, 3.2**

### 35 Comprensión

1. ¿Qué opina Andrade sobre la muerte de periodistas?

2. ¿Qué problemas enfrentó Andrade durante la dictadura militar?

3. ¿Por qué Andrade tuvo que escaparse de Honduras?

 **1.3, 3.2**

### 36 Analice

Andrade dice que no se puede decir todo lo que uno quiere decir porque a veces no es ético o no corresponde. ¿Está Ud. de acuerdo con su postura? ¿Por qué?

---

 Virgilio Andrade: en 50...

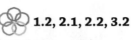 **comunicación para vencer el miedo**

Supongo... y solo supongo que las muertes de los periodistas tienen que ver con elementos más allá del trabajo periodístico... no tiene sentido que se sacrifique tan brutalmente a un comunicador porque diga una noticia, un comentario o una especulación, no le veo sentido.

Debe haber algo más, pero nunca se sabrá porque no tenemos policía de investigación [...].

**CI: ¿En alguna oportunidad fue objeto de amenazas a muerte?**

**VA:** Desde luego en la década de los ochentas. En esa época en la que los militares tenían la última palabra fui objeto de intimidación al extremo de clausurarme[12] una emisora[13] llamada Mi Favorita con el pretexto de que le cambié el nombre sin informar a Hondutel.

Esto tenía mensaje porque yo siempre fui crítico de los militares a pesar de haber pertenecido a esta rama. Después de ese incidente nadie me vendía espacios radiales; tuve que irme a Radio Progreso, en El Progreso, Yoro, donde la Compañía Jesuita me abrió las puertas.

En este periodo me la pasé con problemas, amenazas, marginamiento por parte de los dueños de los medios porque obedecían órdenes de los coroneles que eran los "dioses de Olimpo", de aquel entonces.

**CI: ¿La libertad se defiende con armas?**

**VA:** La autodefensa es importante, siempre anduve armado [...]. Últimamente no ha habido ese tipo de amenazas porque el ambiente es distinto; sin embargo, hay que guardar prudencia: no se puede decir todo lo que uno quiere decir porque a veces no es ético, no corresponde, lo que no evita seguir siendo crítico.

**CI: ¿Los anunciantes lo siguen a dónde va?**

**VA:** Decía mi amigo el analista financiero Carlos Urbizo Solís, el programa es como la comida que sirve el chef: la gente lo va a seguir al restaurante que él vaya: la audiencia me sintoniza[14] en la radio que yo esté.

**CI: ¿Estuvo fuera del país?**

**VA:** Me fui a El Salvador y trabajé en radio Ondas Orientales, me tocó dormir en una banca de madera que estaba en la casa donde funcionaba la radio.

Luego regresé a Honduras y laboré[15] para la emisora HRP1, pero en esos días el general Oswaldo López Arellano protagonizó el golpe de estado de 1963, y escapé a Nicaragua y, como el ambiente era caliente para los críticos de los militares, me quedé por nueve años por allá.

[12] close down      [13] radio station      [14] tunes in      [15] worked

**Búsqueda:** programa sonriendo y comentando honduras, periodista virgilio andrade honduras

---

## Essential Instruction

1. For Common Core practice, have students answer the **Analice** questions.

2. Introduce the **Escritura** section by reviewing persuasive essays.

3. Before students begin filling in their graphic organizers for **Actividad 37**, encourage them to reread the **Cultura** section.

4. Have students peer-edit their essays from **Actividad 37**. In addition to spelling and grammar, tell students to make sure that the essay is organized according to the guidelines at the top of p. 417.

# Escritura

## Un ensayo persuasivo  1.3

Recuerde que en un ensayo persuasivo Ud. tiene que convencer al lector de que adhiera a su punto de vista. Es importante que exprese ese punto de vista claramente en una oración y que luego lo fundamente con razones y evidencias. En la conclusión, debe reformular la idea central de su ensayo y resumir los argumentos de apoyo.

Partes de un ensayo persuasivo:

- Una introducción atractiva: incluya un dato interesante, una declaración controvertida o una pregunta retórica para despertar el interés del lector.

- En ese mismo párrafo introductorio, incluya una oración que exprese claramente la tesis u opinión sobre el tema del ensayo, para que el lector identifique la postura del autor.

- Oraciones que fundamenten con razones de peso la postura del autor. Para convencer al lector de que el punto de vista es atinado, es preciso incluir evidencia que lo demuestre.

- Una conclusión para reforzar la tesis. En el párrafo final, es recomendable resumir las razones presentadas en el cuerpo del ensayo y reformular la tesis para cerrar el ensayo.

### ¡Comunicación!   1.3, 2.1, 2.2, 3.1, 3.2

**37 La libertad de expresión**  Presentational Communication

Imagine que Ud. es periodista y vive en Honduras. Escriba un ensayo persuasivo donde explique por qué es necesario defender la libertad de expresión. Si es necesario, vuelva a leer la información de los textos de Cultura de esta unidad y tenga en cuenta estas ideas como guía:

- ¿Por qué es importante la libertad de expresión?
- ¿Qué relación hay entre la democracia y la libertad de expresión?
- ¿Qué papel tienen los periodistas en una democracia?
- ¿Qué medidas o acciones propone?
- ¿Qué efecto tendrán esas medidas?

Ingrese sus ideas en un organizador gráfico como el de abajo antes de empezar a escribir:

**Para escribir más**

Use las siguientes frases para introducir las razones que fundamenten su punto de vista.

porque...
ya que...
puesto que...
dado que...
debido a...
pues...

---

---

**Differentiated Learning**
**Accelerate/Expand**
Hold a journalism day in class. Divide the class into two groups, A and B. Group A will be journalists and bloggers who will interview members of Group B, who are people currently in the news. (You may want to assign a role/name to each person in Group B.) Allow both groups time to prepare questions and answers, and then have them circulate around the room, conduct their interviews, and take notes. Then have the groups switch roles and repeat the activity. At the end, have students write a mini-article or blog entry for each interview, and submit them via Avenue.

**417**

Activity 38

**38** **Script**

Lanzamos el gran Festival de la Alegría para poder decir que había una organización que empezaría a trabajar con esta gente, que empezaría a trabajar con toda la comunidad, la familia, la escuela, líderes comunitarios. Y partimos con una propuesta: era trabajar las oportunidades educativas desde los primeros años de vida. Entonces estábamos hablando una propuesta programática de Compartir que integraba componentes como estimulación temprana para niños desde tres a cinco años, de educación preescolar para niños de cinco años, el apoyo a la educación escolar para niños de seis a doce años, y toda una propuesta de apoyo para niños de seis a trece, de trece a dieciocho años que integraba toda la lúdica, el arte, el deporte.

*Continued on p. 431.*

1. V
2. F
3. V
4. F
5. V
6. V

**39** *Los blogs variarán.*

## Reference Desk

**Actividad 38** on p. 418 contains authentic audio, which is an important component of the AP® Spanish exam.

### Extensión

"Protagonistas del desarrollo" es un programa radial hondureño transmitido por la radioemisora comunitaria RDS Radio. El eje del programa son las noticias positivas sobre instituciones y organizaciones solidarias y comprometidas con el desarrollo de Honduras.

La Asociación Compartir es una organización no gubernamental de desarrollo que surge en 1990 para dar una solución a la problemática de los "niños en calle" en Honduras.

 **¡Comunicación!**

**38** **Proyectos de la asociación**  Interpretive Communication  **1.2, 2.2**

El 17 de noviembre de 2014 dos miembros de la Asociación Compartir participaron como invitadas del programa "Protagonistas del desarrollo" para difundir las actividades de la organización. Escuche el segmento sobre los proyectos de la Asociación Compartir y diga si las siguientes afirmaciones son verdaderas o falsas.

1. La Asociación Compartir partió de la propuesta de trabajar las oportunidades educativas de los primeros años de vida.
2. Según la entrevistada, es preferible trabajar con los problemas de forma aislada.
3. La propuesta educativa de la Asociación Compartir incluye estimulación temprana, educación preescolar, apoyo en la escuela primaria y un programa lúdico, artístico y deportivo.
4. La Asociación Compartir solo se dedica a programas educativos para la niñez y no trabaja con la comunidad ni la familia.
5. Los trabajadores sociales, psicólogos y pedagogos de la organización trabajan con alrededor de 1000 familias.
6. Uno de los objetivos del programa es ayudar a las personas a resolver sus problemas familiares.

**39** **El blog de la Asociación Compartir** Presentational Communication **1.2, 1.3, 2.2**

Imagine que Ud. es miembro de la Asociación Compartir y que se dedica a la difusión de sus actividades para promocionarlas. Escriba una entrada para el blog de la organización explicando los servicios que ofrece y su importancia para los niños y adolescentes de Honduras. Use referencias del segmento que escuchó y, si es necesario, busque en la internet más información al respecto. Por último, lea su entrada de blog al resto de la clase.

### Essential Instruction

1. Read aloud the sentences in **Actividad 38**. Play the audio once for students to just listen. Then replay it and have them indicate **verdadero** or **falso**.
2. Model pronunciation of the words in **Vocabulario 3** or play the audio, and have students repeat. Clarify any unfamiliar words in the definitions.
3. Have students study the vocabulary list, and then tell them to cover it with a piece of paper before completing **Actividad 40**.

# Vocabulario 3

## Mejore su comprensión  1.2

Familiarizarse con este vocabulario le ayudará a leer "Hombres necios" y "Peso ancestral" más adelante, y a mejorar su comprensión auditiva.

**amante** *s.m.* Persona que mantiene una relación de amor con otra sin estar casada con ella.

**ansia** *s.m.* Deseo fuerte de conseguir algo.

**blandir** *v.* Mover algo haciéndolo vibrar en el aire.

**brotar** *v.* Salir un líquido; nacer la planta de la tierra.

**burlarse** *v.* Reírse de algo y no tomarlo en serio.

**chillar** *v.* Gritar, levantar la voz.

*El cinematógrafo fue inventado en 1895.*

**cinematógrafo** *s.m.* Cine.

**consejo** *s.m.* Opinión que se da a alguien porque se considera que puede servirle de ayuda.

**culpa** *s.f.* Responsabilidad por haber cometido una falta.

**culpar** *v.* Echar la culpa de algo.

**de acero** *exp.* Que es muy duro y resiste mucho.

**débil** *adj.* Que tiene poca fuerza o resistencia.

**desdén** *s.m.* Indiferencia y falta de interés que denotan menosprecio.

**enfadar** *v.* Hacer que una persona pierda el buen humor.

**enfado** *s.m.* Disgusto que tiene una persona por algo.

**entender** *v.* Tener claro el significado de algo.

**incitar** *v.* Impulsar a alguien a actuar.

**ingrato/a** *adj.* Que no agradece los favores que se le han hecho.

**instancia** *s.f.* Petición solicitada por escrito según determinadas fórmulas.

**liviano/a** *adj.* Que pesa poco; se dice de una mujer que es ligera en su relación con los hombres.

**liviandad** *s.f.* Falta de dominio moral o que no observa control sexual.

**loco/a** *adj.* Que no piensa las cosas que hace o que se pone en peligro sin darse cuenta.

**necio/a** *adj.* Que no actúa con inteligencia.

**ofender** *v.* Hacer o decir algo que molesta o que demuestra desprecio o falta de respeto.

**pecar** *v.* No cumplir la ley de Dios.

**pena** *s.f.* Sensación que se tiene cuando pasa algo triste.

**quejarse** *v.* Expresar con la voz un dolor o una pena.

**rogar** *v.* Pedir con súplicas, con mucha educación o como favor.

**sentir** *v.* Lamentar, sentir contrariedad o disgusto.

**sombra** *s.f.* Imagen oscura que deja un cuerpo al lado contrario del sitio por donde le da la luz.

**soportar** *v.* Sufrir algo con paciencia.

**vacío/a** *adj.* Que no tiene nada en su interior.

**veneno** *s.m.* Sustancia que produce graves daños en los seres vivos y que puede llegar a matarlos.

---

### 40 Palabras relacionadas  1.2

Elija el verbo del vocabulario que se relaciona con las siguientes palabras.

1. culpa
2. burla
3. ruego
4. ofensa
5. chillido
6. enfado
7. pecado
8. queja

---

## RESOURCES

 Mejore su comprensión

### Answers

**40**
1. culpar
2. burlarse
3. rogar
4. ofender
5. chillar
6. enfadar
7. pecar
8. quejarse

### Reference Desk

Point out that students will use this vocabulary to complete the audio activity on p. 420, as well as to aid in comprehension of the **Lectura literaria** on pp. 427–430.

### Game

**Tabú**
Divide the class into groups to play **Tabú**. Prepare a set of cards; each card should list a target vocabulary word and several related words that are "taboo." Review the rules with students: team members take turns drawing a card and giving clues so that his/her teammates can guess the word. However, they cannot use the taboo words, gestures, drawings, or sounds. Teams receive one point for each correctly guessed word, and they lose a point for speaking any taboo words.

---

### Differentiated Learning
**Adapt/Accelerate/Decelerate**
**Actividades 38** and **39** can be adapted to fit your students' needs. Ask more advanced classes to correct the false information in **Actividad 38**. For weaker students, provide them with the script as they complete **Actividades 38** and **39**.

### Multiple Intelligences
**Verbal-Linguistic**
Encourage students to create word families for the words in **Vocabulario 3**, for example, **amante**, **amar**, **amor**, **amoroso**.

**419**

Answers

**41**

1. ofende, enfadado
2. brotar
3. culpa
4. ingratas
5. débil
6. siento
7. consejos
8. desdén, soportaba

**42** **Script**

Un hombre se presenta a la puerta de un cine. Va a la taquilla y le dice a la taquillera que su esposa está en la sala acompañada de su amante. —Quiero hablar con ella y sorprenderla —grita mostrando un paraguas.

Quiere hablarle, pero gratis, sin comprar ninguna entrada. La taquillera se asusta y mientras el marido chilla, ella telefonea al director. El director interrumpe la película, hace iluminar la sala y se dirige al público en estos términos: —A la entrada del cine hay un hombre cuya esposa se encuentra aquí en compañía de su amante. Ese hombre quiere hablar con ella. La espera en la puerta. Pero que nadie se asuste. El caballero y la señora podrán salir por la puerta de atrás.

*Continued on p. 433.*

1. Un hombre se presenta en el cinematógrafo y le dice a la taquillera que...
2. Como la taquillera se asusta...
3. El director interrumpe la película...
4. Se apaga la luz...
5. En la oscuridad...
6. Cuando se enciende la luz...

1. C; 2. C; 3. B; 4. A; 5. A; 6. B

**420**

---

**41** **¿Cuál corresponde?**  **1.2**

Complete las siguientes oraciones con la palabra del recuadro que corresponda según el contexto.

| ingratas | desdén | consejos | siento | culpa |
|----------|--------|----------|--------|-------|
| enfadado | soportaba | ofende | débil | brotar |

1. Me ____ que puedas pensar tan mal de mí y luego me culpes por sentirme ____ .
2. Todos los años ansiaba que llegara la primavera para ver ____ las primeras hojas de las plantas.
3. No me eches la ____ por tus resultados: te ayudé a estudiar, pero tú tomaste el examen.
4. Algunas personas son muy ____ . No importa lo que hagas por ellas, nunca te lo agradecen.
5. Tras su enfermedad se sentía muy ____ . Necesitó mucho reposo para recuperarse.
6. No sabes cuánto lo ____ . Realmente me entristece que no te saliera el proyecto.
7. Un necio es una persona que no entiende y no atiende los ____ de nadie.
8. Se quejaba de que su amante la trataba con indiferencia y ____ , a pesar de todas las penas y sufrimientos que ____ por él.

**42** **En las sombras del cinematógrafo**   **1.2, 3.1**

Escuche el relato "En las sombras del cinematógrafo". Luego, Ud. oirá la primera parte de una oración sobre el relato y tres terminaciones posibles. Seleccione la letra de la respuesta con la terminación más lógica. La oración y las terminaciones se leerán dos veces.

1. **A.** ... quiere matar a su esposa.
   **B.** ... quiere esperar a su esposa.
   **C.** ... quiere hablar con su esposa.
2. **A.** ... grita y sale corriendo.
   **B.** ... llama a la policía.
   **C.** ... telefonea al director.
3. **A.** ... para abrir la puerta de atrás.
   **B.** ... para dirigirse al público.
   **C.** ... para preguntar quién es la esposa del hombre.
4. **A.** ... para ocultar a la pareja que sale.
   **B.** ... para continuar con la película.
   **C.** ... porque el teatro está vacío.
5. **A.** ... se levantan muchas parejas.
   **B.** ... no se levanta nadie.
   **C.** ... se levanta solo una pareja.
6. **A.** ... el teatro está casi lleno.
   **B.** ... el teatro está casi vacío.
   **C.** ... el teatro está completamente vacío.

*Todos salieron y el teatro quedó vacío.*

**Essential Instruction**

1. Before beginning **Actividad 42**, remind students that they will hear some vocabulary from p. 419 in the story.
2. For **Actividad 42**, have students listen to the story with their eyes closed. Play it again, pausing to ask questions. Then play the rest of the audio and have students select their answers.
3. Open **Gramática** telling a brief story that includes many repeated nouns. Ask students what sounds odd about your story (repetition). Then repeat the story using relative pronouns.

# Gramática

## Los pronombres relativos *que* y *quien(es)*  1.2, 4.1

Los pronombres relativos sirven para unir dos oraciones simples o para formar una oración compuesta. El pronombre relativo reemplaza a un sustantivo ya mencionado.

> **El reportero** está cubriendo la noticia. (El reportero) es de Honduras.

> El reportero **que** está cubriendo la noticia es de Honduras.

El pronombre relativo puede ser sujeto o complemento del verbo.

| | |
|---|---|
| **Sujeto:** | **Los camarógrafos** llegaron. (Los camarógrafos) son de la prensa internacional. |
| | Los camarógrafos **que** llegaron son de la prensa internacional. |
| **Complemento:** | Compré **un regalo**. (El regalo) es para mi padre. |
| | El regalo **que** compré es para mi padre. |

Los pronombres relativos pueden introducir dos clases de cláusulas subordinadas. Se usan con…

- una cláusula restrictiva que completa el significado del antecedente y que no puede omitirse sin cambiar el sentido de la oración.

| | | |
|---|---|---|
| **Oración principal:** | El paquete | es para mi hermana. |
| **Pronombre relativo:** | que | |
| **Cláusula restrictiva:** | *envié hoy* | |

- una cláusula parentética que está separada de la oración principal por comas y sirve para ofrecer información adicional. Por lo tanto, esta información puede eliminarse sin alterar el sentido de la oración.

| | | |
|---|---|---|
| **Oración principal:** | La playa de Roatán, | es muy hermosa. |
| **Pronombre relativo:** | que | |
| **Cláusula restrictiva:** | *queda en el Caribe,* | |

| | | |
|---|---|---|
| **Oración principal:** | La presentadora, | es muy carismática. |
| **Pronombre relativo:** | quien | |
| **Cláusula restrictiva:** | *ha entrevistado a grandes personalidades,* | |

El pronombre relativo es indispensable en español y no puede omitirse como sucede frecuentemente en inglés.

> Esta es la playa **que** me encanta.
>
> *This is the beach (**that**) I love.*

La playa que me encanta es la de Roatán, en Honduras.

---

## RESOURCES

| | |
|---|---|
| **WB** | Activities 9–10 |
| **LA** | Activities 6–7 |

## Reference Desk

1. Point out that relative pronouns, unlike interrogative words, never carry accent marks.
2. Remind students that although in English *that* can be omitted, in Spanish **que** is not optional.

## Connections

**History**
Have students research more about the island of Roatán. Have them make a three-column chart with the headings **Época precolombina**, **Época colonial**, and **Hoy día**, and find out as much as they can about each time period.

---

**Learning Styles**
**Auditory Learners**
Read sentences to students that could require the use of relative pronouns, e.g., **Juana y Marta trabajan conmigo. Juana y Marta viven cerca de mi casa.** Ask them to rewrite the sentences using the relative pronouns **que** or **quien/es** (**Juana y Marta, quienes trabajan conmigo, viven cerca de mi casa.**).

**Special Needs Students**
**Auditory Impairment**
Provide students with the script of the story and the sentence starters in **Actividad 42**. Allow them to listen as many times as needed.

**43**

1. quien
2. quienes
3. que
4. quien
5. que
6. que

---

## Communication

**Interpersonal/Presentational: Cooperative Groups**

Have students work in small groups to write a simple plot summary of a movie or book. They should use relative pronouns, but no easily identifiable names of places or characters. Have groups take turns reading their descriptions for the class, who will try to guess the title of the work.

---

### Usos de *que*

- El pronombre relativo **que** reemplaza a personas o cosas, y es invariable. **Que** es el pronombre relativo más usado.

- **Que** va después del antecedente y, con frecuencia, introduce una cláusula restrictiva.

    La periodista **que** entrevistó al papa es muy famosa. (*who*)

    El amigo **que** les presenté estudió periodismo conmigo. (*whom*)

    Los medios de comunicación **que** buscan proyectarse también se publican en línea. (*that*)

### Usos de *quien(es)*

- El pronombre relativo **quien(es)** reemplaza solamente a personas y concuerda con el antecedente en número.

- **Quien(es)** introduce una cláusula parentética, separada de la cláusula principal por comas.

    Silvia, **quien** estudió Comunicación Social conmigo, cubre noticias políticas actualmente. (*who*)

- Cuando el pronombre relativo **quien** se usa como complemento directo, debe llevar la preposición **a** antepuesta a la persona.

    El sábado vi **al** actor Viggo Mortensen en una película. Él es de origen danés.

    El actor Viggo Mortensen, **a quien** vi el sábado en una película, es de origen danés. (*whom*)

- **Quien(es)** reemplaza a personas y siempre va pospuesto a las preposiciones.

    El director de medios, **con quien** mantengo correspondencia, dio los permisos de reproducción. (*with whom*)

    El candidato para editor, **de quien** hemos hablado, se llama Carlos. (*of whom*)

---

**43** **¿Que, quien o quienes?**  **1.2**

Elija el pronombre relativo adecuado para completar las oraciones correctamente.

1. El productor de cine para (*quien* / *que*) trabajo es muy exigente.

2. Las actrices, (*quien* / *quienes*) esperaban su turno en la audición, estaban ansiosas.

3. El reportero (*que* / *quien*) cubrió el estreno de la película hizo un trabajo estupendo.

4. El guionista de la serie, a (*que* / *quien*) admiro mucho, anunció que esta sería la última temporada.

5. La directora de la película (*que* / *quien*) vimos anoche está rodando una segunda parte con los mismos actores.

6. Los efectos especiales, (*quienes* / *que*) requirieron muchos meses de trabajo, merecen un premio.

---

### Essential Instruction

1. For **Actividad 43**, have students compare their answers with a partner's. When checking answers as a class, ask students to justify their answers.

2. As you work through the grammar presentation, work with the class to identify and highlight the antecedents in the example sentences.

3. Ask volunteers to create example sentences about people, places, or things in your school.

# Gramática

## Otros pronombres relativos  1.2, 4.1

### Usos de *el que, el cual*

- El pronombre relativo **el que** (**el cual**) se usa para reemplazar cosas. Concuerda en género y en número con el antecedente y va pospuesto a las preposiciones.

  La serie de fantasía **de la que** (**de la cual**) hemos conversado termina el viernes.

  Los libros **en los que** (**en los cuales**) aparecen dragones son muy populares entre los jóvenes.

- **El que** (**el cual**) se usa en lugar de **quien(es)** cuando va pospuesto a una preposición, para identificar con mayor claridad el antecedente.

  Los estudiantes **en los que** (**en los cuales**) me fijé para las pasantías ya consiguieron trabajo.

- **El que** también se usa para introducir una cláusula subordinada parentética (entre comas). **El** (**la, los, las**) **que** distingue uno (una, unos, unas) entre varios al referirse a personas, cosas o lugares.

  Aquel autor, **el que** escribió la trilogía sobre el señor de los anillos, se llama J. R. R. Tolkien. (*the one who*)

  Este reportaje no me parece tan certero como **el que** vimos anoche. (*the one that*)

- **El que** se usa después del verbo **ser** para referirse a personas o cosas.

  Autores como Galdós o Fernández y González eran **los que** publicaban sus novelas por entregas. (*the ones who*)

  Esta estación **es la que** sigo para mantenerme informado. (*the one that*)

- **El que** se usa para indicar un antecedente tácito que puede ser persona o cosa.

  **Los que** no se postularon a tiempo no pudieron participar en el concurso. (*Those who*)

  Me encantan los libros de suspenso, especialmente **los que** tienen un componente psicológico. (*the ones that*)

### Usos de *lo que*

- **Lo que** es el pronombre relativo neutro. Es invariable.

- Se usa **lo que** cuando el antecedente se refiere a una idea completa expresada en una cláusula.

  Los críticos de teatro no tuvieron comentarios positivos sobre la obra, **lo que** disgustó mucho al director. (*which*)

- También se usa **lo que** para referirse a una idea vaga o imprecisa.

  **Lo que** ellos le confiaron a su círculo más íntimo nunca se sabrá. (*that which, what*)

  En realidad, no sabemos **lo que** se va hacer con esas fotos. (*what*)

---

## RESOURCES

 Flipgrid

 Activities 11–13

 Activity 8

## Reference Desk

Point out that when these relative pronouns are used with the prepositions **a** or **de**, the contractions **al que/cual** and **del que/cual** are formed.

## Communication

**Interpersonal: Paired Practice**
Model circumlocution using relative pronouns. Then have students practice circumlocution in pairs. Tell pairs to sit back to back. Students should take turns describing a word that they do not know in Spanish to their partner, who will try to guess the word.

## Culture

**Products: Activity**
Divide the class into groups and assign each one a region of Honduras. Tell groups to research places of interest, tourist activities, lodging, and any other important information. Each group should create a radio or TV ad promoting tourism in their region. Tell groups to use at least five relative pronouns. Allow groups to perform or record their ads for the class to view.

---

## Differentiated Learning
### Accelerate
Ask students to write a personal ad in which they describe themselves and their ideal mate, or a description of their ideal home. Tell them to check their writing for correct use of relative pronouns. You may want to have students describe their ideal person/home via Flipgrid.

## Learning Styles
### Visual Learners
Bring in images of people and things. As you display each one, have students describe what they see using relative pronouns, e.g., **La mujer que está sentada lleva un vestido rojo.**

**423**

**44**

1. que
2. quien
3. que
4. que
5. que
6. quienes
7. que
8. que
9. quien
10. que
11. quien
12. que
13. quienes
14. que

## Reference Desk

1. **Univisión**, established in 1986 and headquartered in New York City, is the United States' largest commercial Spanish-language network, followed by **Telemundo** and **Azteca**.
2. Point out the Ricky Martin quote in the third paragraph. Explain that Martin is referring to his experiences in the Puerto Rican boy band Menudo, which was hugely popular throughout Latin America, especially in the 1980s. The members were all pre-teen and teenage boys, and as certain members grew too old for the group, new ones were recruited. Menudo formed in 1977 and was dissolved in 2009; Ricky Martin joined in 1984, at the height of their success.

---

**44 ¡Talento latino!**  **1.2**

Un nuevo programa de talentos busca formar una banda de muchachos latinos. Lea la reseña y complete las oraciones con el pronombre relativo **que** o **quien(es)**, según sea más apropiado.

Univisión y Syco Entertainment se han asociado para crear un concurso musical como aquellos con los __(1)__ Simon Cowell, __(2)__ es el dueño de Syco, ha tenido tanto éxito. Es el nuevo concurso llamado *La Banda*, __(3)__ busca la participación de muchachos talentosos de Estados Unidos y toda Latinoamérica. El programa, __(4)__ se estrenará en septiembre por Univisión, será transmitido en todas las plataformas __(5)__ tiene la emisora, tanto de televisión tradicional como digital.

Los participantes, __(6)__ representarán a toda la cultura latinoamericana, optarán también por un apetecido contrato con Sony Music Latin, así como con Syco Music, __(7)__ es el sello discográfico de Cowell. El objetivo es __(8)__ de allí salga la mejor banda latina de chicos, como logró Cowell con One Direction.

*Estos son los muchachos que ganaron el concurso.*

Ricky Martin, __(9)__ será productor ejecutivo y juez de la competencia, aseguró estar muy entusiasmado por participar en el proyecto. Dijo Martin: "Nuestra comunidad necesita proyectos musicales __(10)__ permitan el desarrollo de sus talentos". Cuando los miembros de la banda sean seleccionados, Martin será __(11)__ los guíe en calidad de mánager. Él recuerda sus propios inicios: "En mi caso, era un niño __(12)__ a los 12 años corría bicicleta en su barrio y de pronto se montó en un avión privado y empezó a dar literalmente la vuelta al mundo".

Por su parte, en su cuenta de redes sociales, Simon Cowell convocó a __(13)__ quisieran participar: "Me complace anunciar que las audiciones para formar parte del nuevo *boyband* latino están abiertas", invitándolos a creer en los sueños __(14)__ "sí se hacen realidad".

## Essential Instruction

1. Begin **Actividad 44** by asking students if they watch any talent shows on TV.
2. For **Actividad 45**, explain to students that they will need to furnish the information for the subordinate clauses.
3. For **Actividad 46**, check answers to the cloze sentences as a class. Then tell pairs to write the additional sentences and share them in groups of four.

## 45 Una fiesta inolvidable  1.3

Fernanda es una estudiante hondureña que vive en una universidad estadounidense. Esta semana, se celebrará la diversidad cultural que caracteriza a América con una feria internacional. Los estudiantes, quienes tienen ancestros diversos, van a preparar platos que sean típicos y a poner música que sea representativa de esos países.

Modifique cada una de las siguientes oraciones usando **que** o **quien(es)** y complétela con una cláusula subordinada, según el modelo.

MODELO  Habrá *cincuenta países* representados.
Los cincuenta países **que** van a participar representan a toda América.

1. Se está preparando *una feria internacional*.
2. Habrá distintos *platos regionales*.
3. Yo voy a preparar *caraotas negras*.
4. Conocí a unos *estudiantes puertorriqueños*.
5. Ayer te hablé de *las brasileras*.
6. Me pondré *un traje típico de mi país*.
7. Pondremos *música tradicional*.
8. Invitaremos por las redes sociales a *otros amigos*.

## 46 Trágica noticia  1.1, 1.3

Comente con un(a) compañero/a la noticia sobre la tragedia que ocurrió en Shanghai por una estampida. Primero, seleccionen el pronombre relativo apropiado; luego, terminen la oración de una manera original y lógica, como se ve en el modelo.

MODELO  Leí la noticia de una estampida (*el que / que / el cual*) ocurrió en Shanghai la noche de Año Nuevo.
Lo que leí fue que...
Leí la noticia de una estampida **que** ocurrió en Shanghai la noche de Año Nuevo.
**Lo que leí fue que la estampida se desató por la gran masa de personas subiendo y bajando de una plataforma.**

1. Hubo una estampida en (*la que / el que / las que*) murieron 36 personas y 47 resultaron heridas.
Lo que no sabía era que...
2. Las víctimas, (*quienes / las que / las cuales*) eran mujeres y estudiantes en su mayoría, quedaron aplastadas en el suelo.
¡Qué horror! Lo que me parece terrible es que...
3. Las personas (*que / el que / el cual*) se sentían arrinconadas empezaron a lanzarse por la escalera.
Lo que pasa cuando empieza el pánico es que...
4. La policía (*la que / que / las cuales*) acudió al sitio intentó controlar la muchedumbre, pero ya era demasiado tarde.
Lo que deberían haber hecho era que...

*Una celebración que terminó en tragedia*

**RESOURCES**

LA  Activities 9–10

**Answers**

45 *Las respuestas variarán, especialmente en la cláusula subordinada. Respuestas posibles:*
1. La feria internacional que se está preparando celebra la diversidad cultural.
2. Los platos regionales que habrá serán platos típicos de diferentes países.
3. Las caraotas negras que voy a preparar son un plato típico de Venezuela.
4. Los estudiantes puertorriqueños, a quienes conocí en la universidad, son muy alegres.
5. Las brasileras de quienes te hablé son muy lindas.
6. El traje típico de mi país, que me pondré para la fiesta, es muy colorido.
7. La música que pondremos es música bailable tradicional del Caribe.
8. Los amigos que invitaremos por las redes sociales asisten a otras universidades.

46
1. la que
2. quienes
3. que
4. que
*Las oraciones variarán.*

**Reference Desk**

The stampede mentioned in **Actividad 46** took place on December 31, 2014, during a New Year's celebration near Chen Yi square on the city's waterfront. The tragedy occurred on a stairway leading to a viewing platform that overlooked the water.

**Special Needs Students**
**At-Risk Students**
Provide extra practice by playing a game with two teams. One member from each team goes to the board. Read aloud a sentence that could use a relative pronoun. Students must change the sentence to include a relative pronoun and write it on the board. The first student to finish writing a correct sentence scores a point for his/her team.

**Multiple Intelligences**
**Bodily-Kinesthetic/Musical-Rhythmic**
Hold a musical talent show. The participants must sing a song in Spanish, perform a dance from any Spanish-speaking country, or play a musical piece by a Hispanic composer. Other students will play the role of judges, audience members (allow for input from the audience), and reporters on the red carpet.

**425**

**47**

1. Ellos son los camarógrafos a quienes te quería presentar.
2. Este es el estudio de grabación en el que se transmiten las noticias matutinas.
3. Esos son los videoclip de los que te he hablado varias veces.
4. Aquel es el *teleprompter*, o apuntador, en el que debes mirar tus intervenciones.
5. Aquí tienes la computadora portátil con la que escribirás tus artículos.
6. Tendrás un horario flexible, lo que estoy seguro será de tu agrado.

**48**

1. que
2. quien/que
3. la que/quien
4. la cual/la que
5. la cual
6. que/quien/la que
7. que
8. que/quien/la que
9. quien
10. la cual/la que
11. que
12. lo que

## Critical Thinking

### Analyzing

Ask students why they think urban legends are so popular and persistent, and how technology has affected their exposure.

## Expansion

Divide the class into groups. Give each one a large piece of paper and assign them a relative pronoun (**que**, **quien**, **el que**, **los que**, **la cual**, etc.). Each group must write 10 sentences that use that relative pronoun. Post each paper on the board and correct the examples as a class.

**426**

---

**47 El medio y el mensaje**  **1.2, 1.3**

Ud. comenzará a trabajar para un medio muy importante. El jefe de redacción, quien fue compañero de estudios de su padre, quiere mostrarle la oficina en la que va a trabajar. Una las dos oraciones con **el (la, los, las) que** o **lo que**, según se indica. Siga el modelo a continuación.

MODELO   Este es el edificio. La televisora queda en este edificio. (*in which*)
**Este es el edificio en el que queda la televisora.**

1. Ellos son los camarógrafos. Quería presentarte a los camarógrafos. (*whom*)
2. Este es el estudio de grabación. En el estudio se transmiten las noticias matutinas. (*in which*)
3. Esos son los videoclip. Te he hablado sobre los videoclip varias veces. (*of which*)
4. Aquel es el *teleprompter*, o apuntador. Debes mirar tus intervenciones en el apuntador. (*in which*)
5. Aquí tienes la computadora portátil. Escribirás tus artículos con la computadora. (*with which*)
6. Tendrás un horario flexible. Estoy seguro de que será de tu agrado. (*which*)

**48 Leyenda urbana**  **1.2**

¿Conoce alguna leyenda urbana? Complete las siguientes oraciones con el pronombre relativo **que**, **quien**, **el (la, los, las) que** o **el (la, los, las) cual**.

1. El encuentro ____ tuve hace un mes fue algo inexplicable.
2. Conocí a una muchacha, ____ me parecía familiar, pero no sabía por qué.
3. Era muy simpática esa chica con ____ bailé esa noche en la fiesta.
4. Me pidió que la dejara en una casa frente a ____ hay un parque muy emblemático.
5. Varios días después, volví a la casa delante de ____ había dejado a la hermosa muchacha.
6. Toqué a la puerta y pregunté por Claudia, la joven con ____ había bailado en la fiesta.
7. La madre reaccionó con una angustia ____ se reflejó en su pálido rostro.
8. —¿Está seguro de que la muchacha con ____ salió es Claudia?
9. Después fui yo ____ se quedó helado de espanto cuando me explicó.
10. Su hija Claudia era la muchacha sobre ____ habían hablado todos los periódicos hacía un año.
11. Era famoso el caso no resuelto de secuestro ____ tanto había entristecido a la comunidad.
12. ¡No podía creer ____ me había pasado!

*Era increíble lo que me decían sobre la hermosa muchacha con la que bailé esa noche.*

## Essential Instruction

1. After checking answers to **Actividad 47**, have pairs act out the situation.
2. Open **Actividad 48** by asking students if they know any urban legends.
3. As you go through **Sobre la autora**, pause to ask **sí/no** comprehension questions.
4. Read the **Estrategia**. Give examples by naming famous works and have students state the author's purpose in each.
5. Discuss answers to **Antes de leer** and **Actividad 49** as a class.

# Lectura literaria

## La voz femenina en Sor Juana Inés y Alfonsina Storni
## Hombres necios  1.2, 2.2, 3.1
### de *Sor Juana Inés de la Cruz*

### Sobre la autora

Juana Inés de Asbaje y Ramírez de Santillana nació en Nepantla, México, en 1651. Aprendió a leer y a escribir a los tres años de edad, pero su precoz afición a las letras y sus ansias de saber y estudiar chocaron con la actitud intolerante de la época. A los trece años ingresó a la corte del virrey Antonio Salazar de Toledo y, más tarde, se convirtió en dama de compañía de su esposa, la virreina Leonor Carreto, bajo cuya protección desarrolló su intelecto y capacidad literaria. Teniendo que elegir entre el matrimonio o ingresar al convento, eligió lo último y entró a una orden carmelita a los dieciséis años. De allí pasó a la Orden de San Jerónimo y fue allí donde se convirtió en Sor Juana Inés de la Cruz y donde vivió el resto de su vida.

*Sor Juana Inés de la Cruz*

En su obra se destaca la expresión de la voz femenina, que se manifiesta en la redondilla satírica "Hombres necios" donde señala la hipocresía de los hombres seductores. También escribió autos sacramentales por encargo; comedias de enredo como *Los empeños de una casa* y *La segunda Celestina*; la comedia mitológica *Amor es más laberinto*; loas, villancicos, poemas de situación, así como poesía jocosa y satírica.

### Antes de leer   1.3

Sor Juana Inés de la Cruz vivió en una época difícil para las mujeres, en una sociedad en que se las tenía menos y, por tanto, no se les permitía estudiar ni tener aspiraciones intelectuales. ¿Cómo cree que ha cambiado esta actitud a través del tiempo? Piense en ejemplos que evidencien ese cambio.

### Estrategia  3.1

**El propósito del autor**

El propósito del autor es la intención que tiene al escribir, ya sea la de entretener, informar o convencer al lector de algo. Esta intención a veces se presenta clara y explícitamente, pero otras veces se da a entender a través de lenguaje figurado o hay que deducirla. Entender el propósito del autor es importante para poder entender su obra y la perspectiva y la visión del mundo que quiso comunicarnos.

### 49 Practique la estrategia  1.2, 1.3, 3.1

En "Hombres necios", Sor Juana hace uso de la antítesis —oposición de palabras o de ideas— para denunciar la hipocresía de los hombres en su trato para con las mujeres de su época. A medida que lea, identifique tres ejemplos de antítesis y explique lo que significan en sus propias palabras como se ve a continuación.

| Verso del poema | Antítesis | Interpretación |
|---|---|---|
| "¿Por qué queréis que obren bien si las incitáis al mal?" | bien/mal | Ilustra la contradicción y sin razón en la actitud de los hombres que por un lado esperan que las mujeres sean buenas pero, por otro, quieren que sean malas. |
| 1. | | |
| 2. | | |
| 3. | | |

---

**Answers**

1. Ella quiere explicar por qué considera que los hombres son volubles pues acusan a las mujeres de actitudes que ellos mismos fomentan.
2. Se parecen en que cometen acciones que inducen actitudes en las mujeres y, luego, se asustan de lo que ocasionaron.

51 🅒 *Las respuestas variarán.*

---

**Reference Desk**

1. Have students read the first few lines of the poem and ask what type of narrative voice is used (second person/**vosotros**).
2. Ask students to make a list of words in the poem they don't recognize. Have students try to figure out their meaning from context. If this is not successful, tell them to look up the words in a dictionary.
3. To aid comprehension, remind students to take into account the time period in which it was written.

---

**Critical Thinking**

**Analyzing**
As students read, have them list the ways in which men view women. What sort of dichotomy is constructed in enumerating these perceptions?

---

 **1.2, 3.2**

## 50 Comprensión

1. ¿Qué quiere decir Sor Juana Inés en el versículo inicial, antes del poema?

2. ¿En qué se parecen los hombres a un niño?

## 51 Analice 🌸 1.3

Explique la referencia a Thais y a Lucrecia en el contexto de la época y diga cómo podría describirse en el contexto de la época actual.

---

# Hombres necios   1.2, 2.2, 3.1
## de *Sor Juana Inés de la Cruz*

*Arguye de inconsecuentes[1] el gusto y la censura de los hombres que en las mujeres acusan lo que causan.*

Hombres necios[2] que acusáis
a la mujer sin razón,
sin ver que sois la ocasión[3]
de lo mismo que culpáis:

5   si con ansia[4] sin igual
solicitáis[5] su desdén,
¿por qué queréis que obren bien[6]
si las incitáis[7] al mal?
Combatís[8] su resistencia

10   y luego, con gravedad,
decís que fue liviandad
lo que hizo la diligencia.
Parecer quiere el denuedo[9]
de vuestro parecer loco[10],

15   al niño que pone el coco[11]
y luego le tiene miedo.

Queréis con presunción necia,
hallar a la que buscáis,
para pretendida[12], Thais[13],

20   en la posesión, Lucrecia[14].
¿Qué humor[15] puede ser más raro
que el que, falto de consejo[16],
él mismo empaña[17] el espejo
y siente[18] que no esté claro?

25   Con el favor y el desdén
tenéis condición igual[19],
quejándoos, si os tratan mal,
burlándoos, si os quieren bien.
Opinión[20], ninguna gana;

30   pues la que más se recata[21],
si no os admite, es ingrata,
si os admite, es liviana.

---

[1] inconsequential, petty    [2] silly, foolish    [3] you are to blame    [4] urgent plea, zeal
[5] implore, beseech    [6] behave, be good    [7] spur, urge    [8] conquer, overcome
[9] Akin is the posturing    [10] of your foolish attitude    [11] who summons the bogeyman
[12] when courted    [13] Thais, famous Greek courtesan who accompanied Alexander the Great
[14] Lucretia, Roman lady who, to avoid shame, committed suicide after being raped; symbol of virtue
[15] whim, quirk    [16] lacking good judgment    [17] clouds, fogs    [18] laments, mourns
[19] your attitude does not change    [20] prestige    [21] acts modestly

---

**Essential Instruction**

1. Have students scan the poem for cognates and words they learned in **Vocabulario 3**.
2. Play the recording and pause as needed so that students can answer the during-reading questions.
3. After students read p. 428, ask them in what tone the poem is written.
4. For Common Core practice, have students answer the **Analice** questions.

*Queredlas cual las hacéis o hacedlas cual las buscáis.*

Siempre tan necios andáis
que, con <u>desigual nivel</u>[22],
35   a una culpáis por cruel
y a otra por fácil culpáis.
¿Pues <u>cómo ha de estar templada</u>[23]
la que vuestro amor pretende,
si la que es ingrata, ofende,
40   y la que es fácil, enfada?
Mas, entre el enfado y pena
que vuestro gusto <u>refiere</u>[24],
bien haya la que no os quiere
y <u>quejaos en hora buena</u>[25].
45   ¿Cuál mayor culpa ha tenido
en una pasión errada:
la que cae <u>de rogada</u>[26]
o el que ruega de caído?

¿O cuál es más de culpar,
50   aunque cualquiera mal haga:
la que <u>peca</u>[27] <u>por la paga</u>[28]
o el que paga <u>por pecar</u>[29]?
Pues ¿para qué os <u>espantáis</u>[30]
de la culpa que tenéis?
55   <u>Queredlas cual las hacéis</u>[31]
o hacedlas cual las buscáis.
Dejad de solicitar,
y después, con más razón,
acusaréis la afición
60   de la que <u>os fuere a rogar</u>[32].
Bien con muchas armas <u>fundo</u>[33]
que <u>lidia</u>[34] vuestra arrogancia,
pues en promesa e <u>instancia</u>[35]
juntáis diablo, carne y mundo.

[22] with inconsistent judgment    [23] how is she to be deemed temperate    [24] expresses, recounts
[25] you may complain at will    [26] while being courted    [27] the one who sins    [28] for a fee
[29] to sin    [30] why do you fear    [31] like them as you have made them    [32] might seek you out
[33] I assert    [34] wield    [35] request

 **1.2**

## 52 Comprensión

1. ¿Qué significa "cómo ha de estar templada"?

2. Explique el significado de "la que cae de rogada / o el que ruega de caído".

3. Explique el significado de "la que peca por la paga / o el que paga por pecar".

## 53 Analice   **1.3**

Analice el tema del poema y diga si los argumentos de Sor Juana en el siglo XVII tienen validez en la actualidad. Justifique su respuesta con ejemplos.

*Unidad 10*   |   cuatrocientos veintinueve   **429**

**Differentiated Learning**
**Heritage Learners**
Ask heritage learners to read another poem by Sor Juana, "**En perseguirme, Mundo, ¿qué interesas?**", and share their analysis of the poem with the class.

**Accelerate**
Ask students to imagine how a man from Sor Juana's era might react to reading "**Hombres necios.**" Ask them to write a short-response poem from the man's point of view.

**Answers**

**54**

1. Se refiere a la sociedad machista.
2. Es una hipérbole, o exageración para referirse al machismo; también hay una antítesis entre lágrima y acero.
3. Significa que la sociedad espera que las mujeres sean débiles y lloren, pero los hombres no. El veneno simboliza el profundo dolor de la mujer en una sociedad machista.

**55** *Las respuestas variarán.*

**Después de leer**
*Las respuestas variarán.*

### Critical Thinking

**Analyzing and Comparing**
Ask students to compare and contrast the tone, theme, and message in "**Hombres necios**" and "**Peso ancestral**."

---

# Peso ancestral   1.2, 2.2, 3.1
## de *Alfonsina Storni*

### Sobre la autora

Alfonsina Storni nació en Sala Carpiasca, Suiza, en 1892, pero a los cuatro años sus padres se mudaron a Argentina, el lugar donde ella se crió y vivió el resto de su vida. A los trece años, Alfonsina se independizó y trabajó como actriz. Luego, fue maestra en diversos colegios; escribió sus poemas y algunas obras de teatro durante esa época. Tuvo que afrontar la vida como madre soltera, al nacer su hijo en 1912, enfrentándose a la carga de los prejuicios morales de una sociedad hipócrita y estrecha.

*Alfonsina Storni*

Storni se considera una de las voces femeninas más potentes de principios del siglo xx. Con tono feminista, cambió las letras latinoamericanas mediante su originalidad.

En 1935 enfermó gravemente con cáncer y, cuando empeoró, se suicidó en Mar de Plata. Entre sus obras destacan "El dulce daño", "Irremediablemente", "Languidez", "¡Adiós!", "Alma desnuda", "La caricia perdida", "Razones y paisajes de amor", "Queja", "Tu dulzura", "Dolor" y "Frente al mar".

## 1.2
### 54 Comprensión

1. ¿A quién se refiere el yo poético en la primera estrofa?

2. ¿Qué quiere decir la primera estrofa con su conclusión "no han llorado los hombres de mi raza, eran de acero"?

3. ¿Qué significa que la lágrima también sea un veneno?

## 55 Analice  1.3

Analice a qué se refiere el "Peso ancestral". ¿Cree Ud. que ese "dolor de siglos" se refiere al dolor sufrido por la mujer, por el hombre o por ambos?

---

# Peso ancestral  1.2, 2.2, 3.1

Tú me dijiste: no lloró mi padre;
tú me dijiste: no lloró mi abuelo;
no han llorado los hombres de mi raza,
eran de acero[1].

5   Así diciendo te brotó[2] una lágrima
y me cayó en la boca; más veneno
yo no he bebido nunca en otro vaso
así pequeño.
Débil mujer, pobre mujer que entiende,

10  dolor de siglos conocí al beberlo.
Oh, el alma mía soportar[3] no puede
todo su peso.

[1] steel    [2] sprouted    [3] bear, carry

*No han llorado los hombres de mi raza, eran de acero.*

## Después de leer 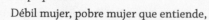 1.3, 4.2

Sor Juana y Alfonsina Storni se enmarcan en la tradición de escritoras latinoamericanas que "son mujeres" y escriben como tales. ¿Conoce a alguna escritora de su cultura que se pudiera enmarcar en la misma tradición? ¿Cuáles son los retos sobre los que escribe?

---

### Essential Instruction

1. As you go through **Sobre la autora**, pause to check comprehension by making **sí/no** statements.
2. Draw attention to the poem's title and ask students to predict its meaning.
3. Point out the **Pregunta clave** on p. 431.

4. Read through the **Proyectos** on pp. 431–432. Allow students to choose project(s) that most appeal to them. Provide detailed rubrics so that students are aware of the expectations for these tasks.

# *Para concluir*

## Proyectos

 **Pregunta clave**

¿Cómo afecta la situación política y social de un país a los medios de comunicación?

### A ¡Manos a la obra! 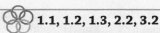 1.1, 1.2, 1.3, 2.2, 3.2

Trabaje con un grupo de tres compañeros/as. Prepararán un programa de radio en el que entrevistarán al periodista Virgilio Andrade. Primero, piensen de qué tipo de programa de radio se trata (noticias, entretenimiento, musical, etc.), cuál es su temática, qué duración tiene, qué tipo de música pasan, etc. Escriban una ficha de programa como la siguiente:

Nombre del programa:

Tipo de programa:

Radioemisora:

Días de emisión:

Horarios de emisión:

Temas que se tratan:

Música:

*Con nosotros hoy, Virigilio Andrade, que lleva 50 años como periodista en América Central...*

Luego, escriban las preguntas que le harán al entrevistado y las respuestas que dará. Relean la Lectura informativa para tomar ideas de allí. Pueden buscar en la internet más información sobre el periodista.

Por último, representen la entrevista frente a la clase. Dos de Uds. harán el papel de entrevistadores y uno hará el papel de Virgilio Andrade. Incluyan una breve introducción antes de empezar la entrevista con los datos de la ficha del programa.

### B En resumen  1.2, 1.3, 2.1, 2.2

La situación actual de los periodistas independientes en Honduras resulta compleja. Vuelva a leer los textos de Cultura de esta unidad y complete el cuadro de abajo con los problemas que enfrentan los periodistas hondureños. Incluya las soluciones que se han puesto en práctica para resolverlos y, si no se han ofrecido soluciones aún, proponga alguna que le parezca adecuada. Puede buscar más datos en la internet si lo desea.

| Problemas | Soluciones |
|-----------|------------|
|           |            |
|           |            |
|           |            |

---

**Differentiated Learning**

**Accelerate/Expand**

Ask students to write an original poem about societal constructs or pressures that they perceive in today's society. Have them recite their poems in front of the class or in a Flipgrid post.

**Multiple Intelligences**

**Visual-Spatial**

Ask these students to create a series of drawings or a collage to illustrate the imagery in "**Peso ancestral**."

---

**RESOURCES**

fg Flipgrid

**Answers**

**Script** *Continued from p. 418.*

Y a la par de todo este programa educativo, ¿verdad? que es el que el programa que yo coordino, toda una propuesta de un programa de participación comunitaria, participación y organización comunitaria. Porque no se puede, no se debe trabajar aislado en los problemas. El problema de niñez tiene que ver con una familia, y tiene que ver con un contexto, con un entorno, con una comunidad. Es así que entonces Compartir tiene todo un programa de organización y participación comunitaria que son trabajadores sociales, psicólogos, pedagogos, que trabajan directamente alrededor de mil familias que reciben un acompañamiento para su propio desarrollo, o sea tiene que ver con orientación familiar, visitas domiciliarias, capacitación, desarrollo vocacional de las madres, desarrollo de competencias para la vida, y todo un programa que sobre todo lo que busca es generar competencias en la gente para dar respuesta a su problemática familiar.

A *Las entrevistas variarán.*

B *Las respuestas variarán.*

**Reference Desk**

Point out the **Pregunta clave**. Ask students to think again about the question, this time in relation to their own culture.

**C** *Los ensayos variarán.*

**D** *Los resúmenes variarán.*

**E** *Las presentaciones variarán.*

## Culture

### Practices/Products: Activity

Ask students to research an aspect of Honduran culture, such as a festival (e.g., **Lluvia de Peces**), indigenous ruins (Copán), artist (José Antonio Velásquez), art form (**punta**), or indigenous group (Lenca, Misquito) and prepare a ten-minute presentation, including visuals. Have students take notes on the presentations in their Culture Journals.

## Connections

### History

The 2009 coup in Honduras was led by members of the military that were graduates of the United States School of the Americas (now WHINSEC). Ask students to find out more about the SOA's involvement in several of Honduras's dictatorships, as well as those of other Latin American countries. Ask them to prepare a report of their findings. They should state their reactions to the school's activities, as well as their opinions about the United States' moral obligations and standing in the Western Hemisphere.

## Expansion

Ask students to visit the blog **Atenas Hernández**. Tell them to read several entries in the section about Honduras: at least one each about a tourist attraction, food/drink, or restaurant. Ask them to write a detailed e-mail recommending the blog to a friend who wants to learn more about Honduras.

---

**C** **¡A escribir!**  **1.3, 3.1, 4.2**

Investigue cuál es la situación de los periodistas y los medios de comunicación en su estado o país. Luego, teniendo en cuenta lo que aprendió en esta unidad sobre el periodismo independiente en Honduras, piense en las diferencias y similitudes de las dos situaciones. Escriba un ensayo comparativo. Puede usar las siguientes preguntas como guía:

- ¿Hay medios concentrados en unas pocas manos?
- ¿La oferta de información es variada? ¿Hay pluralidad de voces?
- ¿Hay acusaciones de manipular la información?
- ¿Hay denuncias por amenazas o agresiones?
- ¿Hay medios alternativos comunitarios?

---

**D** **El golpe militar** **Conéctese: la historia**  **1.3, 2.2, 3.1**

Honduras sufrió un golpe de estado en junio de 2009 que derrocó al presidente Manuel Zelaya. Desde entonces, el país sufre una crisis política grave.

Investigue las causas que desencadenaron el golpe militar en Honduras y los sucesos políticos clave que se han sucedido hasta la fecha. Escriba un resumen de su investigación en forma de listado cronológico de sucesos.

---

**E** **Un programa comunitario** 👥 **Conéctese: los medios de comunicación** **1.1, 1.3, 3.1**

Imagine que le ofrecen un espacio en un canal de televisión comunitario de Honduras para hacer un programa. Trabaje con un(a) compañero/a para presentar un plan de trabajo al canal en el que den todos los detalles del programa que quieren hacer.

Estas preguntas le servirán de guía, pero puede incluir otra información que considere necesaria.

- ¿Qué tipo de programa sería? ¿Educativo? ¿Musical? ¿De noticias?
- ¿Qué tipo de servicios brindaría a la comunidad?
- ¿Cuánto tiempo duraría? ¿Qué días saldría al aire?
- ¿Cuántos conductores tendría? ¿Serían periodistas o especialistas de otras áreas?
- ¿Tendrían personajes invitados? ¿Quiénes?
- ¿Cuáles serían las fuentes de información?

*¿Se imagina trabajando en la televisión de Honduras?*

### Essential Instruction

1. Before assigning **Actividad C**, review comparative essays. Encourage students to organize their ideas and information using a Venn diagram.
2. You could have students work in pairs or small groups for **Actividad D**.
3. For the **Vocabulario de la Unidad 10**, ask students to determine several categories that could be used to sort the words. Then have students list the words in those categories.

# Vocabulario de la Unidad 10  1.2

**a la venta** on sale
**a la vez** at once
**a menor costo** at a lower cost
**acceder a** to access
**aceptar los cargos** to accept the charges
el **acontecimiento** event
el **actor (la actriz)** actor (actress)
la **actuación** performance
el **ansia** zeal
el **apartado de correos** P.O. Box
el **argumento** plot
**asegurar(se)** to ensure, to make sure
**atrapar** to capture
el/la **boleto, entrada** ticket
**brotar** to sprout
**burlarse** to ridicule
el **buzón** mailbox
la **cadena de televisión** television network
el **celular** cell phone
**cerrar (ie) el sobre** to seal the envelope
los **clasificados** classified ads
el/la **comentarista** commentator
el **comprobante** receipt
la **computadora** computer
**conectarse** to connect
el **consejo** advice
la **contraseña** password
el **correo basura** junk mail, spam
la **culpa** blame
**culpar** to blame, to condemn
**de la misma forma** in the same way
**¿De parte de quién?** Who is calling?
**de renombre** renown
**dejar un recado** to leave a message
**deportes** sports
**descargar** to download
el **desdén** disdain, scorn
el/la **destinatario(a)** addressee
**dirigir** to direct
el **distrito postal** ZIP Code
el **documental** documentary
el **DVD** DVD
**echar una carta al buzón** to drop a letter in the mail
**editorial** editorial
la **emisión** broadcast
**en directo, en vivo** live

**en línea** online
la **encomienda postal** parcel post
**enfadar** to make someone angry
el **enfado** annoyance
el **enlace (vínculo)** link
**enredar** to entangle
**entender** to understand
**enterarse** to find out
el **envío** delivery
el **espectáculo** show
el/la **estrella (del cine)** movie star
el **estreno** premiere
la **etiqueta** label, sticker
el **franqueo** postage
la **guía telefónica** telephone directory
**hacer clic** to click
**hacer cola** to stand in line
la **hard(soft)ware** hard(soft)ware
la **hilera** line
las **historietas** comic strips
el **horóscopo** horoscope
**incitar** to spur
el **informe meteorológico** weather report
**ingrato/a** ungrateful
la **instancia** request
la **internet** the Internet
la **línea ocupada** busy line
**liviana** loose woman
**liviandad** licentiousness
la **llamada local y de larga distancia** local and long distance call
la **llamada por cobrar (a cobro revertido)** collect call
el/la **locutor(a)** announcer
**marcar** to dial (a number)
**mayormente nublado** mostly cloudy
el **mensaje de correo electrónico** e-mail message
**navegar la red** to surf the web
**necio/a** foolish
las **noticias** news
el **noticiero** news broadcast
el **número equivocado** wrong number
la **oficina de correos** post office
**otorgar** to bestow
las **páginas sociales** society pages
la **pantalla** screen

la **pantalla (cinematográfica)** screen (film screen)
el **paquete** package
**pecar** to sin
**pegar los sellos** to put (stick) the stamps (on a letter)
las **películas** movies: **de ciencia ficción** science fiction; **cómicas** comedy; **de dibujos animados** cartoons; **de guerra** war; **policíacas** police (detective); **de vaqueros** cowboy
la **pena** pity, difficulty
el **periódico (diario)** newspaper
el/la **periodista** journalist
el **personaje** character
**pesar** to weigh
**por correo aéreo (certificado)** by air (registered) mail
la **prensa** press
la **primera plana** the front page
**probar** to try
**protagonizar** to play a main role
**proteger** to protect
el/la **proveedor(a)** provider
la **publicidad** advertising
**quejarse** to complain
la **radioemisora** radio station
**ratificar** to confirm
el **ratón** mouse
**recibir** to receive
**reclamar** to make a claim
el/la **remitente** sender
el **reportaje** news report
**rodar (filmar)** to make a movie
**rogar** to plead
el **servidor** server
**sin costo alguno** free of charge
**sin presupuesto** without budget
el **sitio web** website
la **taquilla** box office
la **tarjeta postal** postcard
el **teclado** keyboard
la **telenovela** soap opera
la **televisión** television (medium)
los **titulares** headlines
**transmitir** to broadcast
el/la **usuario/a** user
el **video bajo demanda** video on demand
el **videojuego** video game

---

## RESOURCES

**T**  Unidad 10

**Answers**

**Script** *Continued from p. 420.*
Después de estas palabras se abre la puerta de atrás y se apaga la luz para ocultar a la pareja. En la oscuridad se ven levantarse dos sombras. Detrás de estas se levantan otras dos y así hasta once parejas. Cuando se enciende la luz, el teatro se encuentra casi vacío. Mientras tanto, el marido continúa blandiendo su paraguas en la entrada.

## Game

### Culebra
Divide the class into two groups and tell them to form two lines at the board. Students will take turns writing a word on the board. The first student writes a word from the vocabulary list and moves to the end of the line. The next student must write a word from the list that begins with the last letter of the previous word. For example: **actor – rogar – ratón – navegar**. Students can use nouns, adjectives, and verbs. Keep a time limit in order to move students to the board and to the back of the line quickly. Students cannot repeat words or receive help from their teammates. If someone is unable to come up with a word, the other team gets a point.

## Learning Styles
### Kinesthetic Learners
Give a piece of construction paper to each student. Have each student write his/her name at the top. Tell students they should think of a category of vocabulary; they have one minute to write as many words from the unit that fit that category that they can recall. Then tell them to crumple their papers into "snowballs" and toss them to another spot in the room. Tell students to grab a snowball and open it. Give them one more minute to add new words to the list that belong to that same category. Finally, each student gets his/her own snowball back.

**433**

## Apéndice A

# Reglas de puntuación y ortografía

## La puntuación

Los signos de puntuación sirven para dar claridad a las ideas expresadas por escrito. Los más importantes son: el punto (.), la coma (,), los dos puntos (:), el punto y coma (;), los puntos suspensivos (...), los paréntesis ( ), las comillas (" "), la raya *(dash)* (—), el guión *(hyphen)* (-), los signos de interrogación (¿?) y los signos de admiración (¡!).

La puntuación en español y en inglés tiene mucho en común y generalmente sigue las mismas reglas. Algunas diferencias importantes son las siguientes:

1.  Se usa el punto y no la coma como en inglés para separar números.

    Después del inventario hay 2.420 libros en el almacén.

2.  Se usa la coma...

    A.  en la enumeración de una serie de elementos, excepto en las dos últimas palabras si van unidas por una conjunción.

        Compré manzanas, naranjas, peras y uvas.
        El proyecto es claro, preciso e interesante.

    B.  para indicar las fracciones decimales.

        3½ equivale a 3,5.

3.  La raya se usa para indicar el comienzo de un diálogo y se repite cada vez que cambia la persona que habla.

    —Buenos días, Raúl. ¿Hace cuánto tiempo que estás aquí?
    —Hace media hora.

    **Atención:** En español, como en inglés, las comillas se usan para indicar una cita.

    El mendigo me dijo: "Dios se lo pague."

4.  Los signos de interrogación se colocan al principio y al final de una pregunta.

    ¿Te gustaría ir al cine conmigo?

5.  Los signos de admiración se usan al principio y al final de una oración exclamativa.

    ¡Qué frío hace hoy!

# Las letras mayúsculas y minúsculas

## A. Las mayúsculas

1. Como en inglés, en español se escriben con mayúscula los nombres propios de personas, animales, cosas y lugares.

   **G**loria **I**turralde llegó de **C**osta **R**ica trayendo a su gata **M**ichica.
   El lago **T**iticaca está en los **A**ndes.

2. En títulos de obras literarias, artículos y películas, únicamente la primera palabra lleva la letra mayúscula.

   Gabriel García Márquez escribió *Los funerales de la mamá grande*.
   Cantinflas actuó en la película *La vuelta alrededor del mundo en ochenta días*.

## B. Las minúsculas

Al contrario del inglés, en español se escriben con minúscula los días de la semana, los meses del año, los adjetivos de nacionalidad y los nombres de los idiomas.

Enviamos su pedido el día **l**unes, 5 de **a**bril.
Para ser **e**spañola habla muy bien el **i**nglés.

# División de sílabas

## A. Las consonantes

1. Una consonante entre dos vocales se une a la vocal siguiente (las letras **ch**, **ll** y **rr** constituyen una sola consonante).

   e-**n**e-ro   za-**p**a-to   te-**ch**o   ca-**ll**a-**d**o   fe-**rr**o-**c**a-**rr**i-le-**r**o

2. Dos consonantes juntas generalmente se separan.

   a**l**-**t**o   co-men-**z**ar   tie**m**-**p**o   per-**s**o-na   a**c**-**c**ión

3. No se separan ni los grupos de consonantes con **b**, **c**, **f**, **g** o **p** seguidas de **l** o **r** ni los grupos **dr** o **tr**.

   a-**br**i-ré   a-**pr**en-de-mos   ha-**bl**ar   a-**gr**a-da-**bl**e   re-**tr**a-to

4. Si hay tres o más consonantes entre dos vocales, solo la última consonante se une a la vocal siguiente, a menos que la última consonante sea **l** o **r**.

   in**s**-**p**i-ra-ción   con**s**-**t**i-tuir   in**s**-**t**an-te

   **P ero:** os-**tr**a   ex-**pl**i-ca-ción

## B. Las vocales

1. Dos vocales abiertas (**a**, **e**, **o**) se separan.

   le-**e**-mos   ca-**e**-rán   lo-**a**-ble   em-ple-**a**-do

2. Los diptongos (combinación de dos vocales cerradas [**i**, **u**] o una abierta y una cerrada) no se separan.

    c**ue**-llo    t**ie**-nes    v**ie**-jo    a-ve-ri-g**ua**r    b**ai**-la-ri-na

3. Si la vocal abierta del diptongo lleva acento, las vocales no se separan.

    re-vi-s**ió**n    vi-v**ió**    tam-b**ié**n    pu-bli-ca-c**ió**n

4. Si la vocal cerrada lleva acento, se rompe el diptongo; por lo tanto, las vocales se separan.

    gra-d**ú**-an    r**í**-o    i-r**í**-a-mos    dor-m**í**-a-mos

## El acento en el lenguaje hablado y escrito

1. El acento de intensidad se refiere al lenguaje hablado. Es la mayor fuerza que se da a una sílaba en una palabra.

    per**so**na    re**cuer**do    univer**sal**

2. Si una palabra termina en vocal o en la consonante **n** o **s**, el acento de intensidad cae naturalmente en la penúltima sílaba.

    ma**ñ**ana    **co**men    **a**las

3. Si una palabra termina en consonante con la excepción de **n** o **s**, el acento de intensidad cae naturalmente en la última sílaba.

    pregun**tar**    pa**red**    carna**val**

4. Las palabras que no se pronuncian de acuerdo a estas reglas llevan acento ortográfico sobre la vocal de la sílaba acentuada.

    te**lé**fono    lad**rón**    **fá**cil    mate**má**ticas

5. Las palabras de una sola sílaba generalmente no llevan acento ortográfico. Sin embargo, se usa el acento ortográfico en algunos casos para indicar una diferencia de significado entre dos palabras que se pronuncian de la misma manera.

    | | | | |
    |---|---|---|---|
    | **de** | preposición | **dé** | presente de subjuntivo y mandato formal (**dar**) |
    | **el** | artículo definido | **él** | pronombre de la tercera persona singular |
    | **mas** | pero | **más** | *more* |
    | **mi** | adjetivo posesivo | **mí** | pronombre preposicional |
    | **se** | pronombre | **sé** | primera persona singular del presente del indicativo del verbo **saber** |
    | **si** | *if* | **sí** | *yes;* pronombre reflexivo |
    | **te** | pronombre complemento | **té** | *tea* |
    | **tu** | pronombre posesivo | **tú** | pronombre personal |

6. Las palabras interrogativas y exclamativas llevan acento ortográfico en la sílaba acentuada.

    ¿**Qué** hora es?        ¿**Cómo** estás?        ¡**Cuánto** lo quería!

## Apéndice B — Los posesivos

## Los adjetivos posesivos enfáticos

| Singular | | Plural | |
|---|---|---|---|
| mío(a) | nuestro(a) | míos(as) | nuestros(as) |
| tuyo(a) | vuestro(a) | tuyos(as) | vuestros(as) |
| suyo(a) | suyo(a) | suyos(as) | suyos(as) |

Los adjetivos posesivos enfáticos se colocan después del sustantivo. Su uso es menos común que el de los posesivos que preceden al sustantivo. Se usan principalmente en exclamaciones o con el verbo **ser** y concuerdan en género y número con la cosa poseída.

¡Dios **mío**! Esos papeles que acabas de romper no son **míos**. ¡Son de mi jefe!
Un amigo **nuestro** nos aconseja hacerlo.
Hija **mía**, ¡cuánto te quiero!

## Los pronombres posesivos

Los pronombres posesivos tienen las mismas formas que los adjetivos posesivos enfáticos, pero se usan con el artículo definido. Concuerdan en género y número con la cosa poseída. Se usan para reemplazar al sustantivo.

Este es mi vaso; **el tuyo** está en la cocina.
Tu libro no es igual que **el mío**; tiene más páginas.
Sus resultados son mejores que **los nuestros**.
**La suya** es una historia muy larga, pero muy interesante.

Si se necesita aclarar el significado del pronombre posesivo **el suyo**, **la suya**, **los suyos** o **las suyas**, se puede reemplazar el pronombre por una frase preposicional.

Las suyas [**Las de Ud.**] son las mejores estudiantes.
Los suyos [**Los libros de María**] le costaron mucho dinero.
Aquella tierra es la suya [**la de ellos**]; no es la nuestra.

## Lo + adjetivo posesivo

Se usa **lo** + adjetivo posesivo enfático para referirse a una idea general de cosas poseídas.

No te preocupes por **lo mío** (mis cosas, mis problemas).
**Lo nuestro** (nuestro amor, nuestra asociación) ha terminado.
Nos adorábamos tanto, que todo **lo mío** era suyo y **lo suyo** mío.

## Apéndice C — Los verbos

Verbo de la primera conjugación: **-ar**
Infinitivo: **hablar**
Gerundio: **hablando**
Participio pasado: **hablado**

### Tiempos simples

| Indicativo | | | | | Subjuntivo | | | Imperativo | |
|---|---|---|---|---|---|---|---|---|---|
| *Presente* | *Imperfecto* | *Pretérito* | *Futuro* | *Condicional* | *Presente* | *Imperfecto* | | *Afirmativo* | *Negativo* |
| hablo | hablaba | hablé | hablaré | hablaría | hable | hablara | hablase | | |
| hablas | hablabas | hablaste | hablarás | hablarías | hables | hablaras | hablases | habla (tú) | no hables |
| habla | hablaba | habló | hablará | hablaría | hable | hablara | hablase | hable (Ud.) | |
| hablamos | hablábamos | hablamos | hablaremos | hablaríamos | hablemos | habláramos | hablásemos | hablemos (nosotros) | |
| habláis | hablabais | hablasteis | hablaréis | hablaríais | habléis | hablarais | hablaseis | hablad (vosotros) | no habléis |
| hablan | hablaban | hablaron | hablarán | hablarían | hablen | hablaran | hablasen | hablen (Uds.) | |

### Tiempos compuestos

| Indicativo | | | | Subjuntivo | | |
|---|---|---|---|---|---|---|
| *Presente perfecto* | *Pluscuamperfecto* | *Futuro perfecto* | *Condicional perfecto* | *Presente perfecto* | *Pluscuamperfecto* | |
| he hablado | había hablado | habré hablado | habría hablado | haya hablado | hubiera hablado | hubiese hablado |
| has hablado | habías hablado | habrás hablado | habrías hablado | hayas hablado | hubieras hablado | hubieses hablado |
| ha hablado | había hablado | habrá hablado | habría hablado | haya hablado | hubiera hablado | hubiese hablado |
| hemos hablado | habíamos hablado | habremos hablado | habríamos hablado | hayamos hablado | hubiéramos hablado | hubiésemos hablado |
| habéis hablado | habíais hablado | habréis hablado | habríais hablado | hayáis hablado | hubierais hablado | hubieseis hablado |
| han hablado | habían hablado | habrán hablado | habrían hablado | hayan hablado | hubieran hablado | hubiesen hablado |

Verbo de la segunda conjugación: **-er**
Infinitivo: **aprender**
Gerundio: **aprendiendo**
Participio pasado: **aprendido**

## Tiempos simples

| Indicativo | | | | | Subjuntivo | | | Imperativo | |
|---|---|---|---|---|---|---|---|---|---|
| *Presente* | *Imperfecto* | *Pretérito* | *Futuro* | *Condicional* | *Presente* | *Imperfecto* | | *Afirmativo* | *Negativo* |
| aprendo | aprendía | aprendí | aprenderé | aprendería | aprenda | aprendiera | aprendiese | | |
| aprendes | aprendías | aprendiste | aprenderás | aprenderías | aprendas | aprendieras | aprendieses | aprende (tú) | no aprendas |
| aprende | aprendía | aprendió | aprenderá | aprendería | aprenda | aprendiera | aprendiese | aprenda (Ud.) | |
| aprendemos | aprendíamos | aprendimos | aprenderemos | aprenderíamos | aprendamos | aprendiéramos | aprendiésemos | aprendamos (nosotros) | |
| aprendéis | aprendíais | aprendisteis | aprenderéis | aprenderíais | aprendáis | aprendierais | aprendieseis | aprended (vosotros) | |
| aprenden | aprendían | aprendieron | aprenderán | aprenderían | aprendan | aprendieran | aprendiesen | aprendan (Uds.) | no aprendáis |

## Tiempos compuestos

| Indicativo | | | | Subjuntivo | | |
|---|---|---|---|---|---|---|
| *Presente perfecto* | *Pluscuamperfecto* | *Futuro perfecto* | *Condicional perfecto* | *Presente perfecto* | *Pluscuamperfecto* | |
| he aprendido | había aprendido | habré aprendido | habría aprendido | haya aprendido | hubiera aprendido | hubiese aprendido |
| has aprendido | habías aprendido | habrás aprendido | habrías aprendido | hayas aprendido | hubieras aprendido | hubieses aprendido |
| ha aprendido | había aprendido | habrá aprendido | habría aprendido | haya aprendido | hubiera aprendido | hubiese aprendido |
| hemos aprendido | habíamos aprendido | habremos aprendido | habríamos aprendido | hayamos aprendido | hubiéramos aprendido | hubiésemos aprendido |
| habéis aprendido | habíais aprendido | habréis aprendido | habríais aprendido | hayáis aprendido | hubierais aprendido | hubieseis aprendido |
| han aprendido | habían aprendido | habrán aprendido | habrían aprendido | hayan aprendido | hubieran aprendido | hubiesen aprendido |

Verbo de la tercera conjugación: **-ir**
Infinitivo: **vivir**
Gerundio: **viviendo**
Participio pasado: **vivido**

## Tiempos simples

| Indicativo | | | | | Subjuntivo | | | Imperativo | |
| --- | --- | --- | --- | --- | --- | --- | --- | --- | --- |
| Presente | Imperfecto | Pretérito | Futuro | Condicional | Presente | Imperfecto | | Afirmativo | Negativo |
| vivo | vivía | viví | viviré | viviría | viva | viviera | viviese | | |
| vives | vivías | viviste | vivirás | vivirías | vivas | vivieras | vivieses | vive (tú) | no vivas |
| vive | vivía | vivió | vivirá | viviría | viva | viviera | viviese | viva (Ud.) | |
| vivimos | vivíamos | vivimos | viviremos | viviríamos | vivamos | viviéramos | viviésemos | vivamos (nosotros) | |
| vivís | vivíais | vivisteis | viviréis | viviríais | viváis | vivierais | vivieseis | vivid (vosotros) | no viváis |
| viven | vivían | vivieron | vivirán | vivirían | vivan | vivieran | viviesen | vivan (Uds.) | |

## Tiempos compuestos

| Indicativo | | | | Subjuntivo | | |
| --- | --- | --- | --- | --- | --- | --- |
| Presente perfecto | Pluscuamperfecto | Futuro perfecto | Condicional perfecto | Presente perfecto | Pluscuamperfecto | |
| he vivido | había vivido | habré vivido | habría vivido | haya vivido | hubiera vivido | hubiese vivido |
| has vivido | habías vivido | habrás vivido | habrías vivido | hayas vivido | hubieras vivido | hubieses vivido |
| ha vivido | había vivido | habrá vivido | habría vivido | haya vivido | hubiera vivido | hubiese vivido |
| hemos vivido | habíamos vivido | habremos vivido | habríamos vivido | hayamos vivido | hubiéramos vivido | hubiésemos vivido |
| habéis vivido | habíais vivido | habréis vivido | habríais vivido | hayáis vivido | hubierais vivido | hubieseis vivido |
| han vivido | habían vivido | habrán vivido | habrían vivido | hayan vivido | hubieran vivido | hubiesen vivido |

# Verbos irregulares

| | Indicativo | | | | | Subjuntivo | | | Imperativo | |
|---|---|---|---|---|---|---|---|---|---|---|
| Verbo | Presente | Imperfecto | Pretérito | Futuro | Condicional | Presente | Imperfecto | | Afirmativo | Negativo |
| Infinitivo **Andar** | ando | andaba | anduve | andaré | andaría | ande | anduviera | anduviese | | |
| | andas | andabas | anduviste | andarás | andarías | andes | anduvieras | anduvieses | anda | no andes |
| Gerundio **andando** | anda | andaba | anduvo | andará | andaría | ande | anduviera | anduviese | ande | |
| | andamos | andábamos | anduvimos | andaremos | andaríamos | andemos | anduviéramos | anduviésemos | andemos | |
| Participio pasado **andado** | andáis | andabais | anduvisteis | andaréis | andaríais | andéis | anduvierais | anduvieseis | andad | no andéis |
| | andan | andaban | anduvieron | andarán | andarían | anden | anduvieran | anduviesen | anden | |
| Infinitivo **Caber** | quepo | cabía | cupe | cabré | cabría | quepa | cupiera | cupiese | | |
| | cabes | cabías | cupiste | cabrás | cabrías | quepas | cupieras | cupieses | | |
| Gerundio **cabiendo** | cabe | cabía | cupo | cabrá | cabría | quepa | cupiera | cupiese | | |
| | cabemos | cabíamos | cupimos | cabremos | cabríamos | quepamos | cupiéramos | cupiésemos | | |
| Participio pasado **cabido** | cabéis | cabíais | cupisteis | cabréis | cabríais | quepáis | cupierais | cupieseis | | |
| | caben | cabían | cupieron | cabrán | cabrían | quepan | cupieran | cupiesen | | |
| Infinitivo **Caer** | caigo | caía | caí | caeré | caería | caiga | cayera | cayese | | |
| | caes | caías | caíste | caerás | caerías | caigas | cayeras | cayeses | cae | no caigas |
| Gerundio **cayendo** | cae | caía | cayó | caerá | caería | caiga | cayera | cayese | caiga | |
| | caemos | caíamos | caímos | caeremos | caeríamos | caigamos | cayéramos | cayésemos | caigamos | |
| Participio pasado **caído** | caéis | caíais | caísteis | caeréis | caeríais | caigáis | cayerais | cayeseis | caed | no caigáis |
| | caen | caían | cayeron | caerán | caerían | caigan | cayeran | cayesen | caigan | |
| Infinitivo **Conducir** | conduzco | conducía | conduje | conduciré | conduciría | conduzca | condujera | condujese | | |
| | conduces | conducías | condujiste | conducirás | conducirías | conduzcas | condujeras | condujeses | conduce | no conduzcas |
| Gerundio **conduciendo** | conduce | conducía | condujo | conducirá | conduciría | conduzca | condujera | condujese | conduzca | |
| | conducimos | conducíamos | condujimos | conduciremos | conduciríamos | conduzcamos | condujéramos | condujésemos | conduzcamos | |
| Participio pasado **conducido** | conducís | conducíais | condujisteis | conduciréis | conduciríais | conduzcáis | condujerais | condujeseis | conducid | no conduzcáis |
| | conducen | conducían | condujeron | conducirán | conducirían | conduzcan | condujeran | condujesen | conduzcan | |
| Infinitivo **Dar** | doy | daba | di | daré | daría | dé | diera | diese | | |
| | das | dabas | diste | darás | darías | des | dieras | dieses | da | no des |
| Gerundio **dando** | da | daba | dio | dará | daría | dé | diera | diese | dé | |
| | damos | dábamos | dimos | daremos | daríamos | demos | diéramos | diésemos | demos | |
| Participio pasado **dado** | dais | dabais | disteis | daréis | daríais | deis | dierais | dieseis | dad | no deis |
| | dan | daban | dieron | darán | darían | den | dieran | diesen | den | |

| | **Indicativo** | | | | | **Subjuntivo** | | | **Imperativo** | |
|---|---|---|---|---|---|---|---|---|---|---|
| Verbo | Presente | Imperfecto | Pretérito | Futuro | Condicional | Presente | Imperfecto | | Afirmativo | Negativo |
| Infinitivo **Estar** Gerundio **estando** Participio pasado **estado** | estoy estás está estamos estáis están | estaba estabas estaba estábamos estabais estaban | estuve estuviste estuvo estuvimos estuvisteis estuvieron | estaré estarás estará estaremos estaréis estarán | estaría estarías estaría estaríamos estaríais estarían | esté estés esté estemos estéis estén | estuviera estuvieras estuviera estuviéramos estuvierais estuvieran | estuviese estuvieses estuviese estuviésemos estuvieseis estuviesen | está esté estemos estad estén | no estés no estéis |
| Infinitivo **Haber** Gerundio **habiendo** Participio pasado **habido** | he has ha hemos habéis han | había habías había habíamos habíais habían | hube hubiste hubo hubimos hubisteis hubieron | habré habrás habrá habremos habréis habrán | habría habrías habría habríamos habríais habrían | haya hayas haya hayamos hayáis hayan | hubiera hubieras hubiera hubiéramos hubierais hubieran | hubiese hubieses hubiese hubiésemos hubieseis hubiesen | | |
| Infinitivo **Hacer** Gerundio **haciendo** Participio pasado **hecho** | hago haces hace hacemos hacéis hacen | hacía hacías hacía hacíamos hacíais hacían | hice hiciste hizo hicimos hicisteis hicieron | haré harás hará haremos haréis harán | haría harías haría haríamos haríais harían | haga hagas haga hagamos hagáis hagan | hiciera hicieras hiciera hiciéramos hicierais hicieran | hiciese hicieses hiciese hiciésemos hicieseis hiciesen | haz haga hagamos haced hagan | no hagas no hagáis |
| Infinitivo **Ir** Gerundio **yendo** Participio pasado **ido** | voy vas va vamos vais van | iba ibas iba íbamos ibais iban | fui fuiste fue fuimos fuisteis fueron | iré irás irá iremos iréis irán | iría irías iría iríamos iríais irían | vaya vayas vaya vayamos vayáis vayan | fuera fueras fuera fuéramos fuerais fueran | fuese fueses fuese fuésemos fueseis fuesen | ve vaya vamos id vayan | no vayas no vayáis |
| Infinitivo **Oír** Gerundio **oyendo** Participio pasado **oído** | oigo oyes oye oímos oís oyen | oía oías oía oíamos oíais oían | oí oíste oyó oímos oísteis oyeron | oiré oirás oirá oiremos oiréis oirán | oiría oirías oiría oiríamos oiríais oirían | oiga oigas oiga oigamos oigáis oigan | oyera oyeras oyera oyéramos oyerais oyeran | oyese oyeses oyese oyésemos oyeseis oyesen | oye oiga oigamos oíd oigan | no oigas no oigáis |
| Infinitivo **Poder** Gerundio **pudiendo** Participio pasado **podido** | puedo puedes puede podemos podéis pueden | podía podías podía podíamos podíais podían | pude pudiste pudo pudimos pudisteis pudieron | podré podrás podrá podremos podréis podrán | podría podrías podría podríamos podríais podrían | pueda puedas pueda podamos podáis puedan | pudiera pudieras pudiera pudiéramos pudierais pudieran | pudiese pudieses pudiese pudiésemos pudieseis pudiesen | | |
| Infinitivo **Poner** Gerundio **poniendo** Participio pasado **puesto** | pongo pones pone ponemos ponéis ponen | ponía ponías ponía poníamos poníais ponían | puse pusiste puso pusimos pusisteis pusieron | pondré pondrás pondrá pondremos pondréis pondrán | pondría pondrías pondría pondríamos pondríais pondrían | ponga pongas ponga pongamos pongáis pongan | pusiera pusieras pusiera pusiéramos pusierais pusieran | pusiese pusieses pusiese pusiésemos pusieseis pusiesen | pon ponga pongamos poned pongan | no pongas no pongáis |
| Infinitivo **Querer** Gerundio **queriendo** Participio pasado **querido** | quiero quieres quiere queremos queréis quieren | quería querías quería queríamos queríais querían | quise quisiste quiso quisimos quisisteis quisieron | querré querrás querrá querremos querréis querrán | querría querrías querría querríamos querríais querrían | quiera quieras quiera queramos queráis quieran | quisiera quisieras quisiera quisiéramos quisierais quisieran | quisiese quisieses quisiese quisiésemos quisieseis quisiesen | | |

| | Indicativo | | | | | Subjuntivo | | | Imperativo | |
|---|---|---|---|---|---|---|---|---|---|---|
| Verbo | Presente | Imperfecto | Pretérito | Futuro | Condicional | Presente | Imperfecto | | Afirmativo | Negativo |
| Infinitivo **Saber** Gerundio **sabiendo** Participio pasado **sabido** | sé sabes sabe sabemos sabéis saben | sabía sabías sabía sabíamos sabíais sabían | supe supiste supo supimos supisteis supieron | sabré sabrás sabrá sabremos sabréis sabrán | sabría sabrías sabría sabríamos sabríais sabrían | sepa sepas sepa sepamos sepáis sepan | supiera supieras supiera supiéramos supierais supieran | supiese supieses supiese supiésemos supieseis supiesen | sabe sepa sepamos sabed sepan | no sepas no sepáis |
| Infinitivo **Salir** Gerundio **saliendo** Participio pasado **salido** | salgo sales sale salimos salís salen | salía salías salía salíamos salíais salían | salí saliste salió salimos salisteis salieron | saldré saldrás saldrá saldremos saldréis saldrán | saldría saldrías saldría saldríamos saldríais saldrían | salga salgas salga salgamos salgáis salgan | saliera salieras saliera saliéramos salierais salieran | saliese salieses saliese saliésemos salieseis saliesen | sal salga salgamos salid salgan | no salgas no salgáis |
| Infinitivo **Ser** Gerundio **siendo** Participio pasado **sido** | soy eres es somos sois son | era eras era éramos erais eran | fui fuiste fue fuimos fuisteis fueron | seré serás será seremos seréis serán | sería serías sería seríamos seríais serían | sea seas sea seamos seáis sean | fuera fueras fuera fuéramos fuerais fueran | fuese fueses fuese fuésemos fueseis fuesen | sé sea seamos sed sean | no seas no seáis |
| Infinitivo Tener Gerundio **teniendo** Participio pasado **tenido** | tengo tienes tiene tenemos tenéis tienen | tenía tenías tenía teníamos teníais tenían | tuve tuviste tuvo tuvimos tuvisteis tuvieron | tendré tendrás tendrá tendremos tendréis tendrán | tendría tendrías tendría tendríamos tendríais tendrían | tenga tengas tenga tengamos tengáis tengan | tuviera tuvieras tuviera tuviéramos tuvierais tuvieran | tuviese tuvieses tuviese tuviésemos tuvieseis tuviesen | ten tenga tengamos tened tengan | no tengas no tengáis |
| Infinitivo **Traer** Gerundio **trayendo** Participio pasado **traído** | traigo traes trae traemos traéis traen | traía traías traía traíamos traíais traían | traje trajiste trajo trajimos trajisteis trajeron | traeré traerás traerá traeremos traeréis traerán | traería traerías traería traeríamos traeríais traerían | traiga traigas traiga traigamos traigáis traigan | trajera trajeras trajera trajéramos trajerais trajeran | trajese trajeses trajese trajésemos trajeseis trajesen | trae traiga traigamos traed traigan | no traigas no traigáis |
| Infinitivo **Valer** Gerundio **valiendo** Participio pasado **valido** | valgo vales vale valemos valéis valen | valía valías valía valíamos valíais valían | valí valiste valió valimos valisteis valieron | valdré valdrás valdrá valdremos valdréis valdrán | valdría valdrías valdría valdríamos valdríais valdrían | valga valgas valga valgamos valgáis valgan | valiera valieras valiera valiéramos valierais valieran | valiese valieses valiese valiésemos valieseis valiesen | val valga valgamos valed valgan | no valgas no valgáis |
| Infinitivo **Venir** Gerundio **viniendo** Participio pasado **venido** | vengo vienes viene venimos venís vienen | venía venías venía veníamos veníais venían | vine viniste vino vinimos vinisteis vinieron | vendré vendrás vendrá vendremos vendréis vendrán | vendría vendrías vendría vendríamos vendríais vendrían | venga vengas venga vengamos vengáis vengan | viniera vinieras viniera viniéramos vinierais vinieran | viniese vinieses viniese viniésemos vinieseis viniesen | ven venga vengamos venid vengan | no vengas no vengáis |
| Infinitivo **Ver** viendo **Gerundio** Gerundio **visto** | veo ves ve vemos veis ven | veía veías veía veíamos veíais veían | vi viste vio vimos visteis vieron | veré verás verá veremos veréis verán | vería verías vería veríamos veríais verían | vea veas vea veamos veáis vean | viera vieras viera viéramos vierais vieran | viese vieses viese viésemos vieseis viesen | ve vea veamos ved vean | no veas no veáis |

# Verbos con cambios en la raíz

## Verbos de la primera y de la segunda conjugacion (-ar y -er): o→ue

| | Indicativo | | | | | Subjuntivo | | | Imperativo | |
| --- | --- | --- | --- | --- | --- | --- | --- | --- | --- | --- |
| Verbo | Presente | Imperfecto | Pretérito | Futuro | Condicional | Presente | Imperfecto | | Afirmativo | Negativo |
| Infinitivo Contar | cuento | contaba | conté | contaré | contaría | cuente | contara | contase | | |
| | cuentas | contabas | contaste | contarás | contarías | cuentes | contaras | contases | cuenta | no cuentes |
| Gerundio *contando* | cuenta | contaba | contó | contará | contaría | cuente | contara | contase | cuente | |
| | contamos | contábamos | contamos | contaremos | contaríamos | contemos | contáramos | contásemos | contemos | |
| Participio pasado *contado* | contáis | contabais | contasteis | contaréis | contaríais | contéis | contarais | contaseis | contad | no contéis |
| | cuentan | contaban | contaron | contarán | contarían | cuenten | contaran | contasen | cuenten | |
| Infinitivo *Volver* | vuelvo | volvía | volví | volveré | volvería | vuelva | volviera | volviese | | |
| | vuelves | volvías | volviste | volverás | volverías | vuelvas | volvieras | volvieses | vuelve | no vuelvas |
| Gerundio *volviendo* | vuelve | volvía | volvió | volverá | volvería | vuelva | volviera | volviese | vuelva | |
| | volvemos | volvíamos | volvimos | volveremos | volveríamos | volvamos | volviéramos | volviésemos | volvamos | |
| Participio pasado *vuelto* | volvéis | volvíais | volvisteis | volveréis | volveríais | volváis | volvierais | volvieseis | volved | no volváis |
| | vuelven | volvían | volvieron | volverán | volverían | vuelvan | volvieran | volviesen | vuelvan | |

Otros verbos: **acordarse, acostar(se), almorzar, colgar, costar, demostrar, doler, encontrar, llover, mostrar, mover, probar(se), recordar, rogar, soler, soñar, torcer**

## Verbos de la primera y de la segunda conjugacion (-ar y -er): e→ie

| | Indicativo | | | | | Subjuntivo | | | Imperativo | |
| --- | --- | --- | --- | --- | --- | --- | --- | --- | --- | --- |
| Verbo | Presente | Imperfecto | Pretérito | Futuro | Condicional | Presente | Imperfecto | | Afirmativo | Negativo |
| Infinitivo Pensar | pienso | pensaba | pensé | pensaré | pensaría | piense | pensara | pensase | | |
| | piensas | pensabas | pensaste | pensarás | pensarías | pienses | pensaras | pensases | piensa | no pienses |
| Gerundio pensando | piensa | pensaba | pensó | pensará | pensaría | piense | pensara | pensase | piense | |
| | pensamos | pensábamos | pensamos | pensaremos | pensaríamos | pensemos | pensáramos | pensásemos | pensemos | |
| Participio pasado pensado | pensáis | pensabais | pensasteis | pensaréis | pensaríais | penséis | pensarais | pensaseis | pensad | no penséis |
| | piensan | pensaban | pensaron | pensarán | pensarían | piensen | pensaran | pensasen | piensen | |
| Infinitivo Entender | entiendo | entendía | entendí | entenderé | entendería | entienda | entendiera | entendiese | | |
| | entiendes | entendías | entendiste | entenderás | entenderías | entiendas | entendieras | entendieses | entiende | no entiendas |
| Gerundio entendiendo | entiende | entendía | entendió | entenderá | entendería | entienda | entendiera | entendiese | entienda | |
| | entendemos | entendíamos | entendimos | entenderemos | entenderíamos | entendamos | entendiéramos | entendiésemos | entendamos | |
| Participio pasado entendido | entendéis | entendíais | entendisteis | entenderéis | entenderíais | entendáis | entendierais | entendieseis | entended | no entendáis |
| | entienden | entendían | entendieron | entenderán | entenderían | entiendan | entendieran | entendiesen | entiendan | |

Otros verbos: **atravesar, cerrar, comenzar, confesar, despertar(se), empezar, encender, entender, negar(se), nevar, perder, sentar(se), tender(se), tropezar**

## Verbos de la tercera conjugación (-ir): o→ue→u

| | Indicativo | | | | | Subjuntivo | | | Imperativo | |
| Verbo | Presente | Imperfecto | Pretérito | Futuro | Condicional | Presente | Imperfecto | | Afirmativo | Negativo |
|---|---|---|---|---|---|---|---|---|---|---|
| Infinitivo | duermo | dormía | dormí | dormiré | dormiría | duerma | durmiera | durmiese | | |
| Dormir | duermes | dormías | dormiste | dormirás | dormirías | duermas | durmieras | durmieses | duerme | no duermas |
| | duerme | dormía | durmió | dormirá | dormiría | duerma | durmiera | durmiese | duerma | |
| Gerundio | | | | | | | | | | |
| durmiendo | dormimos | dormíamos | dormimos | dormiremos | dormiríamos | durmamos | durmiéramos | durmiésemos | durmamos | |
| Participio pasado | dormís | dormíais | dormisteis | dormiréis | dormiríais | durmáis | durmierais | durmieseis | dormid | no durmáis |
| dormido | duermen | dormían | durmieron | dormirán | dormirían | duerman | durmieran | durmiesen | duerman | |

Otros verbos: **morir(se)**

## Verbos de la tercera conjugación (-ir): e→ie→i

| | Indicativo | | | | | Subjuntivo | | | Imperativo | |
| Verbo | Presente | Imperfecto | Pretérito | Futuro | Condicional | Presente | Imperfecto | | Afirmativo | Negativo |
|---|---|---|---|---|---|---|---|---|---|---|
| Infinitivo | miento | mentía | mentí | mentiré | mentiría | mienta | mintiera | mintiese | | |
| Mentir | mientes | mentías | mentiste | mentirás | mentirías | mientas | mintieras | mintieses | miente | no mientas |
| | miente | mentía | mintió | mentirá | mentiría | mienta | mintiera | mintiese | mienta | |
| Gerundio | | | | | | | | | | |
| mintiendo | mentimos | mentíamos | mentimos | mentiremos | mentiríamos | mintamos | mintiéramos | mintiésemos | mintamos | |
| Participio pasado | mentís | mentíais | mentisteis | mentiréis | mentiríais | mintáis | mintierais | mintieseis | mentid | no mintáis |
| mentido | mienten | mentían | mintieron | mentirán | mentirían | mientan | mintieran | mintiesen | mientan | |

Otros verbos: **advertir, arrepentirse, consentir, convertir(se), divertir(se), herir, preferir, referir(se), sugerir**

## Verbos de la tercera conjugación (-ir): e→i

| | Indicativo | | | | | Subjuntivo | | | Imperativo | |
| Verbo | Presente | Imperfecto | Pretérito | Futuro | Condicional | Presente | Imperfecto | | Afirmativo | Negativo |
|---|---|---|---|---|---|---|---|---|---|---|
| Infinitivo | pido | pedía | pedí | pediré | pediría | pida | pidiera | pidiese | | |
| Pedir | pides | pedías | pediste | pedirás | pedirías | pidas | pidieras | pidieses | pide | no pidas |
| | pide | pedía | pidió | pedirá | pediría | pida | pidiera | pidiese | pida | |
| Gerundio | | | | | | | | | | |
| pidiendo | pedimos | pedíamos | pedimos | pediremos | pediríamos | pidamos | pidiéramos | pidiésemos | pidamos | |
| Participio pasado | pedís | pedíais | pedisteis | pediréis | pediríais | pidáis | pidierais | pidieseis | pedid | no pidáis |
| pedido | piden | pedían | pidieron | pedirán | pedirían | pidan | pidieran | pidiesen | pidan | |

Otros verbos: **competir, concebir, despedir(se), elegir, impedir, persequir, reír(se), reñir, repetir, sequir, servir, vestir(se)**

# Verbos con cambio ortográfico

| **-gar g → gu delante de e** | | | **-ger, -gir g → j delante de a y o** | | | **-guar gu → gü delante de e** | | | **-guir gu → g delante de o y a** | | |
|---|---|---|---|---|---|---|---|---|---|---|---|
| *Verbo* | *Indicativo* | *Subjuntivo* | *Verbo* | *Indicativo* | *Subjuntivo* | *Verbo* | *Indicativo* | *Subjuntivo* | *Verbo* | *Indicativo* | *Subjuntivo* |
| | Pretérito | Presente | | Presente | Presente | | Pretérito | Presente | | Presente | Presente |
| *llegar* | llegué | llegue | *proteger* | protejo | proteja | *averiguar* | averigüé | averigüe | *seguir* | sigo | siga |
| | llegaste | llegues | | proteges | protejas | | averiguaste | averigües | | sigues | sigas |
| | llegó | llegue | | protege | proteja | | averiguó | averigüe | | sigue | siga |
| | llegamos | lleguemos | | protegemos | protejamos | | averiguamos | averigüemos | | seguimos | sigamos |
| | llegasteis | lleguéis | | protegéis | protejáis | | averiguasteis | averigüéis | | seguís | sigáis |
| | llegaron | lleguen | | protegen | protejan | | averiguaron | averigüen | | siguen | sigan |

Otros verbos: **colgar, jugar, navegar, pagar, rogar**

Otros verbos: **coger, corregir, dirigir, escoger, exigir, recoger**

Otros verbo: **apaciguar**

Otros verbos: **conseguir, distinguir, perseguir, proseguir**

| **-cer, -cir después de una vocal c → zu delante de o y a** | | | **-cer, -cir después de una consonante c → z delante de a y o** | | | **-car c → qu delante de e** | | | **-zar z → c delante de e** | | |
|---|---|---|---|---|---|---|---|---|---|---|---|
| *Verbo* | *Indicativo* | *Subjuntivo* | *Verbo* | *Indicativo* | *Subjuntivo* | *Verbo* | *Indicativo* | *Subjuntivo* | *Verbo* | *Indicativo* | *Subjuntivo* |
| | Presente | Presente | | Presente | Presente | | Pretérito | Presente | | Pretérito | Presente |
| *conocer* | conozco | conozca | *vencer* | venzo | venza | *buscar* | busqué | busque | *comenzar* | comencé | comience |
| | conoces | conozcas | | vences | venzas | | buscaste | busques | | comenzaste | comiences |
| | conoce | conozca | | vence | venza | | buscó | busque | | comenzó | comience |
| | conocemos | conozcamos | | vencemos | venzamos | | buscamos | busquemos | | comenzamos | comencemos |
| | conocéis | conozcáis | | vencéis | venzáis | | buscasteis | busquéis | | comenzasteis | comencéis |
| | conocen | conozcan | | vencen | venzan | | buscaron | busquen | | comenzaron | comiencen |

Otros verbos: **agradecer, aparecer, establecer, merecer, obedecer, ofrecer, producir**

Otros verbos: **convencer, esparcir, torcer**

Otros verbos: **comunicar(se), explicar, indicar, practicar, sacar, tocar**

Otros verbos: **abrazar, almorzar, cruzar, empezar, gozar**

## -uir i (no acentuada) → y entre vocales (menos -guir)

| Verbo | Indicativo | | Imperativo | Subjuntivo | |
|---|---|---|---|---|---|
| | Presente | Pretérito | | Presente | Imperfecto |
| **huir** | huyo | huí | | huya | huyera |
| | huyes | huiste | huye | huyas | huyeras |
| **huyendo** | huye | huyó | huya | huya | huyera |
| | huimos | huimos | huyamos | huyamos | huyéramos |
| **huido** | huís | huisteis | huid | huyáis | huyerais |
| | huyen | huyeron | huyan | huyan | huyeran |

Otros verbos: **construir, concluir, contribuir, destruir, instruir, sustituir**

## -aer, -eer, i (no acentuada) → y entre vocales / -eír pierde una e en la tercera persona / -iar i → í / -uar u → ú

| Verbo | Indicativo | Subjuntivo | Verbo | Indicativo | Subjuntivo | Verbo | Indicativo | Subjuntivo | Verbo | Indicativo | Subjuntivo |
|---|---|---|---|---|---|---|---|---|---|---|---|
| | Pretérito | Imperfecto | | Pretérito | Imperfecto | | Presente | Presente | | Presente | Presente |
| **creer** | creí | creyera | **reír** | reí | riera | | envío | envíe | | actúo | actúo |
| | creíste | creyeras | | reíste | rieras | | envías | envíes | | actúas | actúas |
| | creyó | creyera | | rió | riera | **enviar** | envía | envíe | **actuar** | actúa | actúe |
| **creyendo** | creímos | creyéramos | **riendo** | reímos | riéramos | | enviamos | enviemos | | actuamos | actuemos |
| | creísteis | creyerais | | reísteis | rierais | | enviáis | enviéis | | actuáis | actuéis |
| **creído** | creyeron | creyeran | **reído** | rieron | rieran | | envían | envíen | | actúan | actúen |

Otros verbos: **caer, leer, poseer**  Otros verbos: **sonreír, freír**  Otros verbos: **ampliar, criar, enfriar, guiar, variar**  Otros verbos: **acentuar, continuar, efectuar, graduar(se), situar**

# Apéndice D

## ¿Lleva el verbo una preposición?

### A

| | | |
|---|---|---|
| abandonarse a + *noun* | *to give oneself up to* | Me abandoné a la tristeza. |
| acabar con + *noun* | *to finish, to exhaust* | Acabé con mis tareas. |
| acabar de + *inf.* | *to have just + past participle* | Acabamos de llegar. |
| acabar por + *inf.* | *to end (up) by* | Acabaste por pedirle perdón. |
| acercarse a + *inf.* | *to approach* | Se acercó a ver el desfile. |
| + *noun* | | Se acercó a la casa. |
| aconsejar + *inf.* | *to advise* | Te aconsejo confesar tu falta. |
| acordarse (o → ue) de + *inf.* | *to remember* | ¿Te acordarás de escribirme? |
| + *noun* | | Me acordé de ti. |
| acostumbrarse a + *inf.* | *to get used to* | Se acostumbraron a salir temprano. |
| + *noun* | | Se acostumbró al país. |
| agradecer + *noun* | *to be thankful for* | Te agradezco tu compañía. |
| alegrarse de + *inf.* | *to be glad to (about)* | Me alegro de verlos sanos y contentos. |
| alejarse de + *noun* | *to go away from* | Nos alejamos del parque. |
| amenazar con + *inf.* | *to threaten to, with* | Me amenazó con no pagar. |
| + *noun* | *to threaten with* | Me amenazó con un palo. |
| animar a + *inf.* | *to encourage to* | Lo animé a salir. |
| animarse a + *inf.* | *to make up one's mind to* | Nos animamos a bailar. |
| apostar (o → ue) a + *subj.* | *to bet (that)* | Te apuesto a que tengo razón. |
| aprender a + *inf.* | *to learn to* | Aprendiste a cocinar. |
| apresurarse a + *inf.* | *to hasten to* | Se apresuraron a ir de compras. |
| aprovechar + *noun* | *to make good use of* | Aproveché la gran oportunidad. |
| aprovecharse de + *noun* | *to take advantage of* | Se aprovecharon del pobre viudo. |
| arrepentirse (e → ie, i) de + *inf.* | *to repent of, to be sorry for* | Se arrepintió de hacerlo. |
| + *noun* | | Me arrepiento de mis faltas. |
| arriesgarse a + *inf.* | *to risk* | Nos arriesgamos a perderlo todo. |
| asistir a + *noun* | *to attend* | Asistimos al concierto anoche. |
| asomarse a + *inf.* | *to appear (at), to look out of* | Me asomé a ver si venía. |
| + *noun* | | Me asomé a la ventana. |
| asombrarse de + *inf.* | *to be astonished at* | Se asombró de conducir tan rápido. |
| + *noun* | | Se asombró de los cuadros. |
| aspirar a + *inf.* | *to aspire to* | Aspira a ser astronauta. |
| asustarse de + *inf.* | *to be frightened at* | Se asustó de verme tan triste. |
| + *noun* | | Se asustó de su aspecto triste. |
| atreverse a + *inf.* | *to dare (to)* | Te atreviste a venir en la lluvia. |
| autorizar a (para) + *inf.* | *to authorize to* | ¿Me autorizas a comprar el coche? |
| aventurarse a + *inf.* | *to venture (to)* | Nos aventuramos a entrar en el castillo. |
| avergonzarse (o → üe) de + *inf.* | *to be ashamed of* | Me avergüenzo de no saber la lección. |
| ayudar a + *inf.* | *to help to* | Te ayudo a cocinar. |

## B

| | | |
|---|---|---|
| bastar con + *noun* | *to be enough* | Basta con eso para prepararlo. |
| burlarse de + *noun* | *to make fun of* | Se burlaron del enfermo. |
| buscar + *noun* | *to look for* | Busco mis libros. |
| + *inf.* | | Buscaban mejorar las condiciones higiénicas. |

## C

| | | |
|---|---|---|
| cambiar de + *noun* | *to change* | Cambiamos de avión. |
| cansarse de + *inf.* | *to grow tired of* | Se cansó de esperarla. |
| carecer de + *noun* | *to lack* | Carece de ideales. |
| casarse con + *noun* | *to get married to* | Se casó con José. |
| cesar de + *inf.* | *to cease, to stop* | Cesó de llover. |
| comenzar (e → ie) a + *inf.* | *to begin to* | Comenzaron a pintar la casa. |
| complacerse en + *inf.* | *to take pleasure in* | Se complacen en enviarme regalos. |
| comprometerse a + *inf.* | *to obligate oneself to* | Me comprometo a firmar el contrato. |
| comprometerse con + *noun* | *to get engaged to* | Se comprometió con Juan. |
| concluir de + *inf.* | *to finish* | Concluimos de trabajar a las ocho. |
| condenar a + *inf.* | *to condemn to* | Fue condenado a morir. |
| + *noun* | | Fue condenado a muerte. |
| confesar (e → ie) + *inf.* | *to confess* | Confesó tener miedo. |
| + *noun* | | Confiesa su miedo. |
| confiar en + *inf.* | *to trust* | Confío en saber pronto la verdad. |
| + *noun* | | Confío en la verdad. |
| conformarse con + *inf.* | *to resign oneself to* | Me conformo con vivir en la pobreza. |
| + *noun* | | Me conformo con la pobreza. |
| consagrarse a + *inf.* | *to devote oneself to* | Se consagró a trabajar día y noche. |
| + *noun* | | Se consagró al trabajo. |
| conseguir (e → i) + *inf.* | *to succeed in (doing)* | Consiguió llegar a la cumbre. |
| + *noun* | *to get, to obtain* | Consigo dinero para el viaje. |
| consentir (e → ie, i) + *inf.* | *to consent to* | No le consiento gritar. |
| contar (o → ue) con + *inf.* | *to count on, to rely upon* | Cuento con tener tu ayuda. |
| + *noun* | | Cuento con tu ayuda. |
| contentarse con + *inf.* | *to content oneself with* | Me contento con viajar. |
| + *noun* | | Me contento con un viaje. |
| contribuir a + *inf.* | *to contribute to* | Contribuyó a descubrir el crimen. |
| + *noun* | | Contribuyó al descubrimiento. |
| convenir (e → ie) + *inf.* | *to be convenient* | Conviene decírselo. |
| convenir (e → ie, i) en + *inf.* | *to agree to* | Convenimos en ir juntos. |
| convertirse (e → ie, i) en + *noun* | *to become* | La lluvia se convirtió en granizo. |
| creer + *inf.* | *to believe, to think* | Creo entender sus intenciones. |
| cuidar + *noun* | *to care for* | Cuidaba mucho sus plantas. |
| cuidar de + *inf.* | *to take care to* | Cuide de no perderlo. |
| cumplir con + *noun* | *to fulfill* | Cumplió con su obligación. |

## D

| deber + *inf.* | *ought, must* | Debe hablar en voz alta. |
| decidir + *inf.* | *to decide* | Decidieron enviar la carta. |
| decidirse a + *inf.* | *to make up one's mind to, to decide upon* | Nos decidimos a comenzar. |
| decidirse por + *noun* | *to decide on* | Me decidí por estos zapatos. |
| dedicarse a + *inf.* | *to devote oneself to* | Me dediqué a trabajar. |
| + *noun* | | Me dediqué al trabajo. |
| dejar + *inf.* | *to let, to allow, to permit* | Déjame probarlo. |
| dejar de + *inf.* | *to stop, to fail to do something* | Dejará de trabajar. |
| desafiar a + *inf.* | *to dare (someone) to,* | Te desafío a pelear. |
| + *noun* | *to challenge (someone) to* | Te desafío a un duelo. |
| desear + *inf.* | *to desire* | Deseo tener dos hijos. |
| despedirse (e → i, i) de + *noun* | *to take leave of* | Nos despedimos de ellos. |
| destinar a (para) + *noun* | *to destine to, to assign* | Fue destinado a (para) Perú. |
| determinarse a + *inf.* | *to make up one's mind to* | Me determiné a seguir mi carrera. |
| dirigirse a + *noun* | *to address, to make one's way toward* | Se dirigió a la policía. |
| disculparse por + *inf.* | *to excuse oneself for* | Se disculpó por llegar tarde. |
| + *noun* | | Se disculpó por su error. |
| disfrutar (de) + *noun* | *to enjoy (a thing)* | ¡Disfrute de la vida! |
| disponerse a + *inf.* | *to get ready to* | Se dispusieron a partir. |
| divertirse (i → ie, i) con + *persona* | *to amuse oneself with (a* | Me divierto con Juan. |
| en + *noun* | *person); by (an activity)* | Me divierto en las fiestas. |
| dudar + *inf.* | *to doubt* | Dudo saber la lección. |
| dudar de + *noun* | *to doubt* | Duda de todos. |
| dudar en + *inf.* | *to hesitate to* | ¿Por qué dudaste en llamarme? |

## E

| echarse a + *inf.* | *to start to, to begin* | Al ver el oso, se echó a correr. |
| empeñarse en + *inf.* | *to insist on, to persist in* | Se empeñó en golpearme. |
| enamorarse de + *noun* | *to fall in love with* | Se enamoraron de la niñita. |
| encargarse de + *inf.* | *to take it upon oneself to,* | Me encargo de organizar la fiesta. |
| + *noun* | *to take charge of* | Me encargo de las deudas. |
| enterarse de + *noun* | *to find out about* | Ayer me enteré del divorcio. |
| entrar en (a) + *noun* | *to enter* | Entramos en el (al) museo. |

## F

| faltar a + *noun* | *to be absent from, to fail to meet (an obligation)* | Faltaste a la reunión de anoche. |
| felicitar por + *noun* | *to congratulate for* | Te felicito por tu cumpleaños. |
| felicitarse de + *inf.* | *to congratulate oneself on* | Me felicito de conocerte tan bien. |
| fijarse en + *noun* | *to notice* | ¿Te fijaste en su sombrero? |
| fingir + *inf.* | *to pretend* | Fingió no vernos. |

## G

| | | |
|---|---|---|
| gozar de (con) + *noun* | *to enjoy* | Goza de (con) su familia. |
| gustar *(indirect object pronoun)* + *inf.* | *to like, to please* | Nos gusta bailar. |

## H

| | | |
|---|---|---|
| haber de + *inf.* | *to have to, to be going to* | Hoy he de verlo. |
| hacer + *inf.* | *to make, to cause* | No lo hagas llorar. |
| hay que + *inf.* | *to be necessary* | Hay que pagar los impuestos. |
| huir de + *noun* | *to flee from, to avoid* | Huimos del peligro. |

## I

| | | |
|---|---|---|
| imaginarse + *inf.* | *to imagine* | ¿Te imaginas tener tanto dinero? |
| impacientarse por + *inf.* | *to grow impatient for (to)* | Se impacienta por trabajar. |
| impedir (e → i, i) + *inf.* | *to prevent, to impede* | Me impidió llamar por teléfono. |
| importar(le) + *inf.* | *to matter* | No me importa ver tu desdén. |
| + *noun* | | No me importa tu desdén. |
| inclinarse a + *inf.* | *to be inclined to* | Me inclino a pensar así. |
| influir en + *noun* | *to influence* | Influyó en mis decisiones. |
| insistir en + *inf.* | *to insist on* | Insiste en vivir de ese modo. |
| inspirar a + *inf.* | *to inspire to* | Me inspiró a escribir. |
| intentar + *inf.* | *to attempt* | Intentará decírselo. |
| ir a + *inf.* | *to be going to* | Voy a rezar. |
| + *noun* | *to go to* | Voy a la iglesia. |
| irse de + *noun* | *to leave* | Me voy de esta casa. |

## J

| | | |
|---|---|---|
| jugar (u → ue) a + *noun* | *to play at, to practice (a sport)* | ¿Juegas al tenis? |
| jurar + *inf.* | *to swear* | Juró decir la verdad. |

## L

| | | |
|---|---|---|
| limitarse a + *inf.* | *to limit oneself to* | Me limité a viajar por México. |
| + *noun* | | Me limité a un viaje a México. |
| llegar a + *inf.* | *to manage to, to succeed in* | Llegamos a preparar la comida. |
| + *noun* | *to come to, to arrive at* | Llegamos a la posada. |
| lograr + *inf.* | *to succeed in, to manage to* | Lograste abrir la puerta. |
| luchar para + *inf.* | *to struggle in order to* | Lucho para darles de comer a los pobres. |
| luchar por + *noun* | *to struggle on behalf of* | Lucho por los pobres. |

## M

| | | |
|---|---|---|
| mandar + *inf.* | *to cause, to have, to order* | Nos mandó llamar. |
| maravillarse de + *inf.* | *to marvel at* | Me maravillo de escucharte cantar. |
| + *noun* | | Me maravillo de tu talento. |
| marcharse de + *noun* | *to leave* | Se marchó del pueblo. |
| merecer + *inf.* | *to deserve* | Merece recibir el premio. |
| meterse a + *inf.* | *to begin, to set oneself to* | Se metió a cantar. |

| | | |
|---|---|---|
| meterse en + *noun* | *to become involved in* | Se metió en malos negocios. |
| mirar + *inf.* | *to watch* | Miraba partir el tren. |
| + *noun* | *to look at* | Miró todos los cuadros. |
| morirse (o → ue, u) por + *inf.* | *to be dying to* | Me muero por conocerlos. |

## N

| | | |
|---|---|---|
| necesitar + *inf.* | *to need* | Necesito salir de compras. |
| negar (e → ie) + *inf.* | *to deny* | Negó conocerlo. |
| negarse (e → ie) a + *inf.* | *to refuse to* | Me niego a abrir la puerta. |

## O

| | | |
|---|---|---|
| obligar a + *inf.* | *to oblige to* | Nos obligan a firmar un contrato. |
| obstinarse en + *inf.* | *to persist in* | Se obstina en callar. |
| ocuparse de + *inf.* | *to take care of* | Se ocupa de hacer las compras. |
| + *noun* | | Se ocupa de las compras. |
| ocurrirse *(indirect object pronoun)* + *inf.* | *to occur (to someone)* | Se nos ocurrió ir al cine. |
| ofrecer + *inf.* | *to offer* | Te ofrezco dividir las ganancias. |
| + *noun* | | Te ofrezco las ganancias. |
| ofrecerse a + *inf.* | *to offer to, to promise* | Se ofreció a darnos una conferencia. |
| oír + *inf.* | *to hear* | Oímos rugir a las fieras. |
| oler (o → ue[hue]) a + *noun* | *to smell of, like* | La casa huele a pescado. |
| olvidar + *inf.* | *to forget* | Olvidaste traer un paraguas. |
| olvidarse de + *inf.* | *to forget* | Se olvidó de cerrar con llave la puerta. |
| oponerse a + *inf.* | *to be opposed to* | Nos oponemos a pagar tus deudas. |
| + *noun* | | Nos oponemos a tus proyectos. |
| optar por + *inf.* | *to choose* | Optaron por salir temprano. |
| ordenar + *inf.* | *to order* | Te ordeno cantar. |

## P

| | | |
|---|---|---|
| parar de + *inf.* | *to stop, to cease* | Pare de fumar. |
| pararse a + *inf.* | *to stop to* | Me paré a ver los vestidos de moda. |
| pararse en + *noun* | *to stop at* | Me paré en todas las tiendas. |
| parecer + *inf.* | *to seem* | Parece tener razón. |
| parecerse a + *noun* | *to resemble* | Se parece al abuelo. |
| pasar a + *inf.* | *to proceed to, to pass on to* | Pasó a pedir dinero para el proyecto. |
| + *noun* | | Pasó a la siguiente lección. |
| pedir (e → i) + *noun* | *to ask for* | Pides más ayuda. |
| pensar (e → ie) + *inf.* | *to intend* | Piensa escribir una novela. |
| pensar (e → ie) de + *noun* | *to have an opinion about* | ¿Qué piensas de mí? |
| pensar (e → ie) en + *noun* | *to think about (have in mind)* | Piensa en su madre. |
| permitir + *inf.* | *to permit* | No permiten hablar inglés en clase. |
| persistir en + *inf.* | *to persist in* | Persiste en mentir. |
| poder (o → ue) + *inf.* | *can, to be able to* | ¿Podemos entrar? |
| ponerse a + *inf.* | *to set oneself to, to begin to* | Nos pusimos a esquiar. |

|  |  |  |
|---|---|---|
| preferir (e → ie, i) + *inf.* | *to prefer* | Prefieren callar. |
| prepararse a (para) + *inf.* | *to prepare oneself to* | Se prepara a (para) salir. |
| prepararse para + *noun* | *to prepare oneself for* | Se prepara para los exámenes. |
| pretender + *inf.* | *to claim* | ¿Pretendes decir la verdad? |
| principiar a + *inf.* | *to begin to* | Principia a llover. |
| prohibir + *inf.* | *to forbid* | Te prohíbo salir. |
| prometer + *inf.* | *to promise* | Prometo decírtelo. |
| proponerse + *inf.* | *to propose* | Me propuse sacar buenas notas. |

## Q

|  |  |  |
|---|---|---|
| quedar en + *inf.* | *to agree to* | Quedamos en vernos más a menudo. |
| quedar por + *inf.* | *to remain to be* | Queda por ver lo que dirá. |
| quedarse a (para) + *inf.* | *to remain to* | Se quedó a (para) cuidar a los niños. |
| quedarse en + *noun* | *to remain in* | Se quedó en casa. |
| quejarse de + *inf.* | *to complain of (about)* | Se queja de no tener tiempo. |
| + *noun* | | Se queja de sus padres. |
| querer (e → ie) + *inf.* | *to want, to wish* | Quiero bailar. |

## R

|  |  |  |
|---|---|---|
| recordar (o → ue) + *inf.* | *to remember* | Recuerdo oírlo gritar. |
| reírse (e → i, i) de + *noun* (pronoun) | *to laugh at, to make fun of* | Todos se rieron de mí. |
| renunciar a + *inf.* | *to renounce, to give up* | Renunció a vivir en el campo. |
| + *noun* | *to resign* | Renunció a su puesto. |
| reparar en + *noun* | *to notice, to observe* | No reparé en sus defectos. |
| resignarse a + *inf.* | *to resign oneself to* | No me resigno a morir. |
| + *noun* | | No me resigno a la muerte. |
| resistirse a + *inf.* | *to resist, to refuse to* | Se resiste a salir. |
| resolverse (o → ue) a + *inf.* | *to decide to do something* | Me resolví a salir solo. |
| retirarse a + *inf.* | *to retire, withdraw to* | Se retiró a descansar. |
| rogar (o → ue) + *inf.* | *to beg, to ask, to request* | Te ruego hablar despacio. |
| romper a + *inf.* | *to begin (suddenly) to* | Al verlo rompimos a llorar. |
| romper con + *noun* | *to break off relations with* | Rompí con mi novio. |

## S

|  |  |  |
|---|---|---|
| saber + *inf.* | *to know (how)* | Sabe patinar muy bien. |
| salir de + *noun* | *to leave, come out of* | Salí de la casa temprano. |
| sentarse (e → ie) a (para) + *inf.* | *to sit down to* | Nos sentamos a (para) comer. |
| sentir (e → ie, i) + *inf.* | *to be sorry, regret* | Siento comunicarle esta noticia. |
| separarse de + *noun* | *to leave* | Me separé de mi esposa. |
| servir (e → i, i) de + *noun* | *to serve as, to function as* | Mi radio sirve también de reloj. |
| servir para + *noun* | *to be of use for* | Estas carpetas sirven para papeles. |
| servirse de + *noun* | *to use* | Me serví de estos documentos para el juicio. |
| soler (o → ue) + *inf.* | *to be in the habit of* | Suelo destarme temprano. |
| soñar (o → ue) con + *inf.* | *to dream of (about)* | Sueñas con via*jar.* |
| + *noun* | | *Sueñas con viajes.* |

| | | |
|---|---|---|
| sorprenderse de + *inf.* | *to be surprised to* | Se sorprendió de verte conmigo. |
| + *noun* | *to be surprised at* | Se sorprendió de mi casa. |
| sostener (e → ie) + *inf.* | *to maintain* | Sostiene saber la verdad. |
| subir a + *noun* | *to go up, to climb* | Subimos a las montañas. |
| suplicar + *inf.* | *to beg* | Te suplico contestar mis cartas. |

**T**

| | | |
|---|---|---|
| tardar en + *inf.* | *to take long to* | Tardaste en llegar. |
| temer + *inf.* | *to fear* | Temo recibir su carta. |
| terminar de + *inf.* | *to finish* | Terminaré de trabajar. |
| terminar por + *inf.* | *to end (up) by* | Terminamos por divorciarnos. |
| tirar de + *noun* | *to pull* | Tiré de la puerta. |
| tocar *(indirect object pronoun)* + *inf.* | *to be one's turn* | Te toca jugar a las cartas. |
| trabajar en + *noun* | *to work at* | Trabajamos en casa. |
| trabajar para + *inf.* | *to strive to, in order to, to work for* | Trabaja para mantener a su hijo. |
| trabajar por + *noun* | *to work on behalf of* | Trabaja por su hijo. |
| tratar de + *inf.* | *to try to* | ¿Trataste de verlo? |
| tratarse de + *noun* | *to be a question of, to be about* | Se trata de algo muy serio. |
| tropezar (e → ie) con + *noun* | *to come upon* | Tropecé con María en Lima. |

**V**

| | | |
|---|---|---|
| vacilar en + *inf.* | *to hesitate to* | Vacilé en decírselo. |
| valer más + *inf.* | *to be better* | Vale más hablar con él. |
| valerse de + *noun* | *to avail oneself of* | Me valí de él para conocer al jefe. |
| venir a + *inf.* | *to come to* | Vine a visitarte. |
| ver + *inf.* | *to see* | Vimos salir la luna. |
| volver (o → ue) a + *inf.* | *to do again* | Volvieron a llamarme. |
| + *noun* | *to return to* | Volvieron a Paraguay. |

# Vocabulario

## Español / Inglés

**Abbreviations:**

| | |
|---|---|
| *adj.* | **adjective** |
| *f.* | **feminine** |
| *colloq.* | **colloquial** |
| *m.* | **masculine** |
| *pl.* | **plural** |
| *s.* | **singular** |
| *n.* | **noun** |
| *adv.* | **adverb** |

## A

**a diario** daily
**a menor costo** at a lower cost
**abajo** (*adv.*) below, down
**abogado/a** (*n.*) lawyer
**abordar** to board
**aborto** abortion, miscarriage
**abrazar** to embrace, to hug
**abrigo** overcoat, shelter
**abrir** to open
**abrochar** to fasten
   **abrocharse el cinturón de seguridad** to fasten one's seatbelt
**abuelo/a** (*n.*) grandfather, grandmother
**abundar** to be abundant, to abound
**aburrir** to bore
**aburrirse** to get bored
**acabar** to end, to finish
**acabar de** + *inf.* to have just + past participle
**acabarse** to run out
**acceder a** to access
**accesorios de vestir** (*pl.*) accessories
**acciones** (*f., pl.*) stocks, shares
**acelerador** (*m.*) gas pedal
**aceptar los cargos** to accept the charges
**acercarse a** to approach
**acero** steel
  **acero inoxidable** stainless steel
**acompañar** to accompany
**aconsejar** to advise, to counsel
**acontecer** to happen
**acontecimiento** event, incident, happening
**acordar (ue)** to agree upon
**acordarse (ue) de** to remember
**acostar (ue)** to put to bed
**acostarse (ue)** to go to bed
**acostumbrarse a** to be customary; to get accustomed to
**actriz** (*f.*) actress
**actuación** (*f.*) performance

**actual** present-day
**actualidad** (*f.*) present time
**actuar** to act
**acuerdo** agreement
   **acuerdo de paz** peace treaty
   **¡de acuerdo!** O.K.!
   **de acuerdo con** according to
**adelante** ahead
**adelgazar** to lose weight
**además** in addition, besides
**adicción** (*f.*) addiction
**adicional** additional
**adiós** good-bye
**¿adónde?** to where?
**adornar** to decorate
**adornos** (*pl.*) decorations
**aduana** customs
**aéreo/a** (*adj.*) air
   **correo aéreo** air mail
   **línea aérea** airline
**aeropuerto** airport
**afán** (*m.*) eagerness, anxiety
**afecto** affection
**afeitar(se)** to shave (oneself)
**afirmación** (*f.*) statement
**afrontar** to face
**afuera** outside
**afueras** suburbs
**agencia** agency
   **de bienes raíces** real estate
**agente** (*m., f.*) agent
**agitar** to gesticulate; to excite; to stir
**agotar(se)** to exhaust; to run out
**agradable** pleasant
**agradecer** to thank
**agricultor/a** (*n.*) farmer
**agricultura** agriculture
**aguacate** (*m.*) avocado
**agudo/a** sharp
**ahorrar** to save
**ahorros** (*pl.*) savings
**aire** (*m.*) **acondicionado** air conditioning
**ajo** garlic
**alcalde(sa)** (*n.*) mayor
**alcaldía** municipal city hall
**alcanzar** to reach; to be sufficient

**aldea** village
**alegrarse de** to be glad of, about
**alegría** happiness
**alérgico/a** (*adj.*) allergic
**alfombra** rug, carpet
**alma** (*f.*) (uses **el**) soul
**almacén** (*m.*) department store
**algo** something; somewhat
**algodón** (*m.*) cotton
**alguien** someone
**algún** some; any
**alguno/a** (*pronoun*) someone; something
**aligerar** to lighten
**alimentación** (*f.*) nutrition; feeding
**aliviar** to relieve
**almohada** pillow
**almorzar (ue)** to eat lunch
**alojamiento** lodging
**alquiler** (*m., n.*) rent, rental
**alrededor de** around
**altas horas de la noche** very late at night
**alto/a** (*adj.*) tall; high
**alto nivel** high level
**alzar** to lift, to raise
**amanecer** (*m., n.*) dawn
**amar** to love
**ambiente** (*m.*) atmosphere
**ambulancia** ambulance
**ambulante** (*adj.*) traveling
**negociante** (*m., f.*) **ambulante** peddler
**amenazar** to threaten
**americana** jacket (Spain)
**amistad** (*f.*) friendship
**amor** (*m.*) love
**ampliar** to amplify; to expand
**amplio/a** (*adj.*) ample; broad
**analizar** to analyze
**ancho/a** (*adj.*) wide
**andén** (*m.*) platform
**ánimo** spirit
**antelación** (*f.*)**: con antelación** in advance
**antepasados** (*pl.*) ancestors
**anterior** previous, prior

**antes de** before
**anticipación** (*f.*) anticipation
    **con anticipación** in advance
**antiguo/a** (*adj.*) ancient
**antihéroe** (*m.*) antihero
**anunciar** to announce
**anuncio** advertisement
    **anuncio clasificado** classified ad
**Año Nuevo** New Year
**aparecer** to appear, to be listed
**apariencia** appearance
**apartado de correos** P.O. box
**apellido** last name
**aplicar** to apply
**apoyar** to support
**aprender** to learn
**aprestarse a** to get ready to
**apresurarse a** to hurry, to hasten to
**aprobar (ue)** to approve
  **aprobar el curso** to pass the course
**aprovechar** to make use of
**aprovecharse de** to take advantage of
**apuntar** to take notes
**apuntes** (*m., pl.*) notes
**apuro** problem
**árbol** (*m.*) tree
    **árbol de Navidad** Christmas tree
    **árbol genealógico** family tree
**archivo** file; archive
**arena** sand
**argumento** plot
**armario** closet, wardrobe
**armonía** harmony
**arquitecto/a** (*n.*) architect
**arquitectura** architecture
**arreglar** to arrange; to fix; to straighten
**arriba** above; upstairs
**artesanía** handicrafts
**ascenso** promotion
**asegurar** to assure; to insure
**asegurarse** to mke sure; to ensure
**asiento** seat
    **asiento delantero** front seat
    **asiento del pasillo** aisle seat
    **asiento de ventanilla** window seat
    **asiento trasero** back seat
**asignatura** course, subject
**asistencia** attendance
**asistir a** to attend
**asombroso/a** (*adj.*) astonishing
**aspiradora** vacuum cleaner
**atender (ie)** to attend to
**aterrizaje** (*m.*) landing
    **aterrizaje forzoso** forced landing

**aterrizar** to land
**atmósfera** atmosphere
**atraco** robbery; mugging
**atraer** to attract
**atrapar** to capture
**atrás** in the back
**atrasar(se)** to delay (to be late)
**atravesar (ie)** to cross
**atreverse a** to dare to
**atropellar** to run over
**aumentar** to increase
**aun** even
    **aun cuando** even though
**aún** still, yet
**aunque** although; even if
**ausencia** absence
**autobús** (*m.*) bus
**auxiliar** (*m., f.*) **de vuelo** flight attendant
**auxilio: pedir** (*i*) **auxilio** to cry for help
**avergonzado/a** (*adj.*) embarrassed
**averiguar** to verify; to find out
**avión** (*m.*) airplane
**aviso** warning; notice
**ayer** yesterday
**ayuda** help
**ayudar** to help
**ayuntamiento** city hall
**azteca** (*n., m., f., adj.*) Aztec person
**azúcar** (*n., m.*) sugar

## B

**bachillerato** high school
**bailar** to dance
**baile** (*m.*) dance
**bajar** to go down; to take down; to lose
    **bajar de peso** to lose weight
    **bajarse de** to get off
**bajo** (*prep.*) under
    **bajo demanda** on demand
**baloncesto** basketball
**bancario/a** (*adj.*) banking
**banco** bank
**bandera** flag
**bañera** bathtub
**baño** bathroom; bath
**barato/a** (*adj.*) cheap
**barbacoa** barbecue
**barbilla** chin
**barco** ship
    **por barco** by ship
**barra** bar

**barrer** to sweep
**barrio** neighborhood
**base** (*f.*) basis, base
**basta con** is enough to
**basura** garbage
**batidor** (*m.*) beater
**batir** to beat
**baúl** (*m.*) car trunk (**maletero** in some countries)
**bebida** drink
**beca** scholarship
**bélico/a** (*adj.*) warlike
**bellas artes** fine arts
**beneficio** benefit
**besar** to kiss
**biblioteca** library
**bicicleta** bicycle
**bienestar** (*m.*) welfare
**bienvenida** welcome
    **¡Bienvenido!** Welcome!
    **dar la bienvenida** to welcome
**billete** (*m.*) ticket
  **billete de ida y vuelta** round-trip ticket
**blusa** blouse
**boca** mouth
    **boca abajo** face down
    **boca arriba** face up
**bocadillo** sandwich
**boda** wedding
**bola** ball
**boletín** (*m.*) **de noticias** news bulletin
**boletín** (*m.*) **meteorológico** weather report
**boleto** ticket
  **boleto de ida y vuelta** round-trip ticket
**bolsa** purse, bag
**bolsillo** pocket
**bombín** (*m.*) bowler hat
**borla** tassel
**borrador** (*m.*) eraser; first draft
**borrar** to erase
**bostezar** to yawn
**botas** (*pl.*) boots
**bote** (*m.*) bottle, jar; boat
**botella** bottle
**botiquín** (*m.*) medicine cabinet
**botones** (*m., sing.*) bellboy
**bragas** (*pl.*) (women's) underwear
**brazo** arm
**brinco** jump
**brindar** to toast
**brindis** (*m.*) toast
**bulla** (*colloq.*) loud noise
**bulto** parcel
**burlarse de** to make fun of

**buscar** to look for

　**se busca** wanted

**búsqueda** search

**buzón** (*m.*) mailbox

# C

**cabeza** head

**cabina de mando** pilot's cabin

**cabina de teléfono** telephone booth

**cacique** (*m.*) political boss

**cada** each

**cadena** chain; network

**caer(se)** to fall

**cafetera** coffee pot

**caja** box; cashier's booth

**cajero/a** (*n.*) cashier

**cajuela** glove compartment

**calavera** skull

**calcetines** (*m., pl.*) (*sing.* **calcetín**) socks

**calidad** (*f.*) quality

**calificación** (*f.*) grade

**calificar** to qualify

**calle** (*f.*) street

**callejero/a** (*adj.*) street

**calma** (*f.*) calm

**calzoncillos** (*pl.*) (men's) underwear

**cama** bed

**cámara** chamber; camera

　**Cámara de Diputados** House of Representatives

**camarero/a** (*n.*) waiter, waitress

**cambio** change, exchange

　**casa de cambio de moneda** money exchange office

**caminar** to walk

**camilla** stretcher

**camisa** shirt

**campana** bell

**campesino/a** (*n.*) farmer; person who lives in the country

**campo** countryside

**canal** (*m.*) channel; canal

**canasta** basket

**cancha** court (tennis)

**canción** (*f.*) song

**cansado/a** tired

**cantar** to sing

**cantidad** (*f.*) quantity

**capacitado/a** (*adj.*) qualified; trained

**capital** (*m.*) capital (money)

**capital** (*f.*) capital (city)

**capó** car hood

**capricho** whim

**cara** face

**cárcel** (*f.*) jail

**cargador/a** (*n.*) loader

**cariño** affection, love

**cariñoso/a** (*adj.*) affectionate, loving

**carnaval** (*m.*) carnival; Mardi Gras

**carne** (*f.*) meat

　**carne de res** beef

　**carne de ternera** veal

**carné** (*m.*) card

　**carné de identidad** identification card

**carnicería** butcher shop

**carnicero/a** (*n.*) butcher

**caro/a** (*adj.*) expensive

**carrera** profession, career; race

**carretera** road, highway

**carroza** (parade) float

**carta** letter

**cartera** wallet

**cartero/a** (*n.*) mail carrier

**casa** house

**casado/a** (*n.*) married person; (*adj.*) married

**casar(se)** to marry (to get married)

**casco** helmet

**casero/a** (*adj.*) having to do with the home

**casi** almost

**castigar** to punish

**catálogo** catalogue

**catarro** cold

**catedrático/a** (*n.*) full professor

**causa** cause

　**a causa de** because of, due to

**cebolla** onion

**cejas** (*pl.*) eyebrows

**celoso/a** (*adj.*) jealous

**cementerio** cemetery

**cenar** to eat dinner

**censura** censorship

**centro** center

　**centro comercial** shopping center

**cepillo** brush

**cercanía** nearness, proximity

**cerdo** pig

**cerebro** brain

**cerradura** lock

**cesta** basket

**chamarra** (Mex.) jacket

**champiñón** (*m.*) mushroom

**chapado/a a la antigua** old-fashioned

**chaqueta** jacket

**charla** conversation

**cheque** (*m.*) check

**chimenea** fireplace

**chisme** (*m.*) gossip

**chiste** (*m.*) joke

**chofer** (*m., f.*) driver

**chorizo** sausage

**ciencia** science

　**ciencia ficción** science fiction

**científico/a** (*n.*) scientist; (*adj.*) scientific

**cierto/a** (*adj.*) certain, sure

**cilindro** cylinder

**cine** (*m.*) movies

**cintura** waist

**cinturón** (*m.*) belt

　**cinturón de seguridad** seat belt

**círculo** circle

**cita** appointment

**ciudad** (*f.*) city

**ciudadano/a** (*n.*) citizen

**claro/a** (*adj.*) clear

　**¡Claro que sí!** Of course!

**clima tropical** (*m.*) tropical climate

**cobrar** to cash (a check); to collect

**coche** (*m.*) car

　**coche-cama** sleeping car

　**coche-comedor** dining car

**cocina** kitchen

**cocinar** to cook

**codo** elbow

**coger** to pick; to take

**cojín** (*m.*) pillow, cushion

**col** (*f.*) cabbage

**cola** line; glue

　**hacer cola** to stand in line

**colcha** bedspread

**colegio** school

　**colegio mayor** dormitory (usage in Spain)

**colgar (ue)** to hang

**colocar** to put (in place)

**colorado/a** (*adj.*) red

**combatir** to fight, to battle

**comedor** (*m.*) dining room

**comentarista** (*m., f.*) commentator

**comenzar (ie)** to begin

**cometer** to commit, to do

**cómico/a** (*adj.*) funny

**comida** food

**como** as, like

　**¿cómo?** how? what?

　**¡cómo!** how!

　**¡cómo no!** of course!

　**como si fuera** as if (he/she) were

**cómoda** chest of drawers

**cómodo/a** (*adj.*) comfortable

**compañero/a** (*n.*) friend

　**compañero/a de cuarto** roommate

**compartir** to share

**compatriota** (*m., f.*) fellow citizen

**competencia** contest, competition
**competitivo/a** competitive
**comportarse** to behave
**comprador/a** (*n.*) shopper, buyer
**comprar** to buy, to purchase
**comprobante** (*m.*) receipt
**comprometerse** to get engaged; to commit oneself
**computadora** computer
**comunidad** (*f.*) community
**con** with
  **con tal (de) que** provided that
**concierto** concert
**concurso** contest
**conducir** to drive
**conductor/a** (*n.*) driver
**conejo de Pascua** Easter bunny
**conexión** (*f.*) connecting (flight)
**confirmar** to confirm
**congelar** to freeze
**conjetura** guess, conjecture
**conjugar** to conjugate
**conjunto residencial** residential complex
**conmemorar** to commemorate
**conocer** to know, to be acquainted with
**conseguir (i)** to obtain
**conservador/a** (*adj.*) conservative
**constante** continuous
**constituirse** to become
**construir** to build
**consulta** consultation, visit to a doctor's office
**consultar** to consult
**consumo** consumption
**contado: al contado** in cash
**contaminación** (*f.*) **ambiental** pollution
**contaminar** to pollute, to contaminate
**contar (ue)** to tell, to count
  **contar con** to rely on
**contestador** (*m.*) **automático** answering machine
**contestar** to answer
**continuar** to continue
**contrabandista** (*m., f.*) smuggler
**contrabando** illegal goods
**contratar** to contract; to hire
**contratiempo** mishap
**contribuir** to contribute
**control de seguridad** (*m.*) security
**convenir (ie)** to suit
**convertir (ie)** to convert
  **convertirse en** to become
**convivencia** living together

**convocatoria** notice of a meeting
**copa** wine glass
**corazón** (*m.*) heart
**corbata** necktie
**cordero** lamb
**cordillera** mountain range
  **correos: oficina de correos** post office
  **correo aéreo** air mail
  **correo certificado** registered mail
  **correo ordinario** surface mail
**corregir (i)** to correct
**correr** to run
  **correr las cortinas** to open or close the curtains
**correspondencia** correspondence
**corresponder** to correspond; to write
**corrida de toros** bullfight
**corriente** (*f.*) current
**cortés** (*adj.*) courteous
**cortesía** courtesy, politeness
**corto/a** (*adj.*) short
**costa** coast
**costar (ue)** to cost
**costillas** (*pl.*) ribs
**costoso/a** (*adj.*) expensive
**costumbre** (*f.*) custom
**cotidiano/a** (*adj.*) daily
**cotilleo** gossip
**crecimiento** growth
**crédito de vivienda** mortgage
**creencia** belief
**creer** to believe
**criar** to raise
**crimen** (*m.*) crime
**criminal** (*n., m., f.*) criminal, outlaw; delinquent, perpetrator
**crucero** cruise (ship)
**cruzar** to cross
**cuadra** block
  **a dos cuadras** two blocks away
**cuadro** painting; picture
**cuadros: a cuadros** plaid
**cual(es)** which
  **¿cuál(es)?** which (one[s])?
**cualquier/a** any, whatever
**cuando** when
  **¿cuándo?** when?
**¿cuánto/a?** how much?
**¿cuántos/as?** how many?
**cuarteto de cuerdas** string quartet
**cuarto** room; fourth; quarter
**cuello** neck
**cuenta** account; bill; calculation
  **cuenta corriente** checking account

**cuenta de ahorros** savings account
**cuento** story, tale
**cuero** leather
**cuerpo** body
**cuestión** (*f.*) issue, matter
**cuestionar** to question
**cuidado** care, attention
  **con cuidado** carefully
  **tener cuidado** to be careful
**culpable** (*adj.*) guilty
**cumpleaños** (*sing.*) birthday
**cumplir... años** to turn... years old
  **cumplir con los requisitos** to fulfill the requirements
**cursar** to take (a course)
**curso** course
**cuota** fee

# D

**daños** (*pl.*) damages
**dar** to give
  **dar a luz** to bear a child
  **dar fin a** to end
  **dar la bienvenida** to welcome
  **dar una clase** to teach a class
  **dar una película** to show a movie
  **dar una vuelta** to walk around; to go for a ride (a walk)
  **darse cita con** to meet
  **darse cuenta de** to realize
  **dárselo a** to sell for (give it to you for)
**de** from, of
  **¿de dónde?** from where?
  **de la misma forma** in the same way
  **de nada** you're welcome; not at all
  **de poco uso** not used much
  **de renombre** renown
  **¿De veras?** Really?
**debajo (de)** below, underneath
**deber** to owe; should, ought
**débil** weak
**decano/a** (*n.*) dean
**decidirse a** to make up one's mind to
**decir (i)** to say; to tell
  **es decir** that is to say
  **querer (ie) decir** to mean
**dedicarse a** to dedicate oneself to
**dedo** finger; toe; digit
**defectuoso/a** (*adj.*) defective
**defender (ie)** to defend
**dejar** to allow; to leave (behind)

**dejar a su paso** to leave in its wake.

**dejar de** to stop; to fail to (do something)

**dejar un recado** to leave a message

**delante de** in front of

**delincuencia** crime

**delincuente** (*m., f.*) criminal, delinquent

**demanda** claim; lawsuit

**demás: los demás** the others

**demonios: ¿dónde demonios... ?** where on earth... ?

**dentista** (*m., f.*) dentist

**dependiente/a** (*n.*) clerk

**deporte** (*m.*) sport

**deportivo/a** (*adj.*) related to sports

**derecho/a** (*adj.*) right; **derecho** (*n.*) law; privilege

**a la derecha** to the right

**derechos de aduana** import duties

**derrocar** to knock down, to overthrow

**derrota** defeat

**desafiar** to challenge; to defy

**desamparado/a** (*n.*) homeless

**desanimar** to discourage

**desarrollar(se)** to develop

**desayunar** to eat breakfast

**desayuno** breakfast

**descanso** rest

**descargar** to download

**descender (ie)** to go down

**descongelar** to defrost

**describir** to describe

**descuento** discount

**desde** since; from

**desde luego** of course

**desear** to want, to desire

**de desear** desirable

**desechable** disposable

**desempeñar** to work as

**desempleo** unemployment

**deseo** desire, wish

**desfile** (*m.*) parade

**desierto** desert

**desmayarse** to faint

**desmayo** fainting spell

**desnutrición** (*f.*) malnourishment

**despacho** office (lawyer's, doctor's)

**despedida** farewell

**despedir (i)** to fire, to dismiss

**despedirse (i) de** to say good-bye to

**despegar** to take off (plane)

**despegue** (*m.*) takeoff (plane)

**despertar (ie)** to awaken

**despertarse (ie)** to wake up

**después** after; afterward

**destapar** to open

**desteñido/a** (*adj.*) faded

**destinatario/a** (*n.*) recipient, addressee

**destrozar** to destroy, to rip apart

**destruir** to destroy

**desvelarse** to stay awake

**desventaja** disadvantage

**detalle** (*m.*) detail

**detener(se) (ie)** to stop

**detrás de** behind

**día** (*m.*) day

**Día de Acción de Gracias** Thanksgiving

**Día de los Muertos** All Souls' Day

**diablo** devil

**diagnóstico** diagnosis

**diario/a** (*adj.*) daily; **diario** (*n.*) newspaper

**dibujo** art drawing

**dibujos** (*pl.*) **animados** cartoons

**dictadura** dictatorship

**dictar** to dictate

**dictar una conferencia** to give a lecture

**diente** (*m.*) tooth

**difícil** difficult

**dilema** (*m.*) dilemma

**diminuto/a** (*adj.*) very small

**Dios** (*m.*) God

**diputado/a** (*n.*) deputy, representative

**directo: en directo** live (performance)

**dirigir** to manage; to direct

**dirigirse a** to approach, to address (a person)

**discoteca** dance club

**discriminado/a** (*adj.*) discriminated (against)

**disculpa** excuse

**discurso** speech

**diseñar** to design

**disfraz** (*m.*) costume

**disfrutar (de)** to enjoy

**disminuir** to decrease

**disponibilidad** (*f.*) availability

**dispuesto/a a** (*adj.*) willing to

**distrito postal** ZIP code

**diversión** (*f.*) entertainment

**divertido/a** (*adj.*) entertaining

**divertirse (ie)** to have a good time

**divorciado/a** (*adj.*) divorced

**divorcio** divorce

**doblar** to turn (at a corner), to fold

**doblarse** to bend over

**doble** double

**doctrina** doctrine

**documental** (*m.*) documentary

**doler (ue)** to hurt

**dolor** (*m.*) pain

**dolor agudo** sharp pain

**doloroso/a** (*adj.*) painful

**domicilio** place of residence

**donde** where

**¿dónde?** where?

**¿adónde?** to where?

**¿de dónde?** from where?

**dormir (ue)** to sleep

**dormirse (ue)** to fall asleep

**dormitorio** bedroom; dormitory

**ducha** shower

**dudable (dudoso/a)** doubtful

**dudar** to doubt

**dulce** sweet

**dulces** (*m., pl.*) candies; pastries

**durante** during

**durar** to last

## E

**echar** to throw

**echar al buzón** to mail

**edad** (*f.*) age

**edificios de apartamentos** (*pl.*) apartment buildings

**educador/a** (*n.*) educator

**efectivo** cash

**pagar en efectivo** to pay (in) cash

**efectuar** to bring about; to implement

**eficaz** (*adj.*) efficient; that works

**egresar** to leave; to graduate

**ejecutivo/a** (*n.*) executive

**ejercicio** exercise

**ejército** army

**elaborar** to prepare, to put together

**electrodoméstico** (home) appliance

**elegir (i)** to elect

**embarazada** (*adj.*) pregnant

**embotellamiento** traffic jam

**emoción** (*f.*) emotion

**empeñarse en** to insist on; to persist in

**empezar (ie)** to begin

**empleado/a** (*n.*) employee

**empleo** job; employment

**empresa** company; undertaking

**en favor/en contra** in favor/against

**en seguida** immediately

**enamorado/a** (*n.*) boyfriend, girlfriend

**enamorarse (de)** to fall in love (with)
**encajar en** to set in
**encantado/a** (*adj.*) delighted
**encantar** to enchant
**encarcelamiento** imprisonment
**encargado/a** (*n.*) person in charge, superintendent
**encargarse de** to be in charge of
**encariñarse con** to grow in affection for
**encender (ie)** to light; to turn on (lights, appliances)
**encima de** on top of
**encinta** pregnant
**encomienda postal** parcel post
**encontrar (ue)** to find
**encontrarse (ue) con** to meet
   **encontrarse en riesgo** to be at risk
**encuentro** meeting
**encuesta** survey, poll
**endosar** to endorse
**enfadado/a** (*adj.*) angry
**enfadarse** to get angry
**enfermarse** to get sick
**enfermedad** (*f.*) illness
**enfermero/a** (*n.*) nurse
**enfermo/a** (*adj.*) sick person, patient
**enfoque** (*m.*) focus
**enfrentarse** to confront
**enfriar** to cool down
**engordar** to get fat
**enhorabuena** congratulations
**enojarse** to get angry
**enredar** to entangle
**enseñanza** teaching
**enseñar** to show
  **enseñar a** to teach how to
**entender (ie)** to understand
**enterarse de** to find out, to hear about
**entibiar** to cool off
**entonces** then
**entorno** surroundings
**entrar** to enter
**entre** among, between
**entregar** to deliver, to hand over
**entrenarse** to train (for a sport, etc.)
**entretenido/a** entertaining
**entrevista** interview
**entusiasmado/a** (*adj.*) enthusiastic
**enviar** to send
**envío** delivery
**enyesado: estar enyesado** to be in a cast
**época** age, era
**equipaje** (*m.*) baggage, luggage
  **equipaje de mano** carry-on luggage

**equipo** team
  **equipo de sonido** sound system
  **equipo de video** video camera
**equivocado/a** mistaken
**equivocar(se)** to (make a) mistake
**escala** scale
  **hacer escala** to have a layover (airline flight)
**escapar** to escape
**escaso/a** (*adj.*) scant; a few
**escena** scene
**escenario** stage
**escenificación** (*f.*) staging
**escoba** broom
**escoger** to choose
**escombros** (*pl.*) rubble
**escribir** to write
**escritor(a)** (*n.*) writer
**esforzarse** to make an effort
**espalda** back
**espantoso/a** (*adj.*) horrible
**espárragos** (*pl.*) asparagus
**especialización** (*f.*) major (field of study)
**espectáculo** show
**espejo** mirror
**espera** wait
**espinacas** (*pl.*) spinach
**espíritu** (*m.*) spirit
**esposo/a** (*n.*) husband, wife
**esqueleto** skeleton
**esquina** corner
**estación** (*f.*) station; season
  **estación de ferrocarril** railroad station
**estadística** statistics
**estado** state
  **estado civil** marital status
**estampado/a** (*adj.*) printed, stamped
**estancia** room
**estar** to be
  **estar en forma** to be in good shape
  **estar en onda** (*colloq.*) to know what's going on
  **estar por** to be about to
**este** (*m.*) east
**estirar** to stretch
**estómago** stomach
**estornudar** to sneeze
**estrecho/a** (*adj.*) narrow
**estrella** star
  **estrella del cine** movie star
  **guiados por una estrella** guided by a star
**estrellarse** to crash
**estreno** première; new movie
**estricto/a** (*adj.*) strict
**estudiante** (*m., f.*) student

**estudiantil** (*adj.*) related to students
**estufa** stove
**estupendo/a** (*adj.*) wonderful
**etiqueta** label
**europeo/a** (*adj.*) European
**examen** (*m.*) exam
**examen de admisión** (*m.*) admission test
**examinar** to examine
**examinarse** to take an exam
**exigir** to demand
**éxito** success
**experiencia** experience
**explicar** to explain
**exponer** to exhibit
**exprimidor** (*m.*) juicer
**exprimir** to squeeze
**extender (ie)** to extend
**extranjero** abroad
**extraño/a** (*adj.*) strange; foreign; (*n.*) stranger

# F

**fábrica** factory
**fábula** fable
**fácil** (*adj.*) easy
**facilidad** (*f.*) ease
**factura** bill
**facturar el equipaje** to check the luggage
**facultad** (*f.*) school (in a university)
**falda** skirt
**faltar** to miss; to be lacking; to fail (to fulfill)
  **falta de cuidado** lack of attention
**familiar** (*adj.*) related to family; (*n.*) family member
**familiarizarse** to become familiar
**farmacéutico/a** (*n.*) pharmacist
**farmacia** pharmacy
**fastidiado/a** bothered
**fastidio** nuisance
**felicitar** to congratulate
  **¡Felicitaciones!** Congratulations!
**Feliz cumpleaños.** Happy birthday.
**feria** fair
**ferrocarril** (*m.*) railroad
  **estación** (*f.*) **de ferrocarril** railroad station
**festejar** to celebrate
**fiebre** (*f.*) fever
**fiesta** party
**fijarse en** to notice, to pay attention to
**filmar** to film

**filosofía** philosophy
**filósofo/a** (*n.*) philosopher
**fin** (*m.*) end
    **fin de año** New Year's Eve
    **fin de semana** weekend
    **por fin** finally
**financiero/a** financial
**finanzas** (*pl.*) finances
**firma** company
**flecha** arrow
**flor** (*f.*) flower
**folleto** pamphlet
**fondos** (*pl.*) funds
**formulario** printed form
**fortalecer** to strengthen
**foto(grafía)** (*f.*) photograph
**fracasar** to fail
**fracturarse** to fracture, to break
**franqueo** postage
**franqueza** frankness
    **con franqueza** frankly
**frasco** bottle
**frazada** blanket
**frecuencia** frequency
    **con frecuencia** frequently
**fregadero** kitchen sink
**freno** brake
**frente** (*f.*) forehead
**fresa** dentist's drill (mechanical); strawberry
**fresco/a** (*adj.*) fresh
**frescura** freshness
**frijoles** (*m., pl.*) beans
**frontera** border
**frutería** fruit store
**fuego** fire
    **fuegos artificiales** (*pl.*) fireworks
**fuera** outside
**fuerte** strong
**fumar** to smoke
**función** (*f.*) event, show; showing of a movie
**funcionar** to work
**funcionario/a** (*n.*) worker; officer
**funda** pillowcase
**furioso/a** (*adj.*) angry
**fútbol** (*m.*) soccer
    **fútbol americano** (*m.*) American football
**futuro** future

## G

**gabinete** (*m.*) office; cabinet
**gallo** rooster
    **misa del gallo** Christmas midnight Mass

**gamba** shrimp
**ganadería** cattle raising
**ganadero/a** (*n.*) cattle rancher; (*adj.*) related to livestock
**ganancias** (*pl.*) earnings; profit
**ganar** to earn; to win
**ganas** (*pl.*) desire
    **tener ganas de** to feel like
**ganga** bargain
**ganso** goose
**garaje** (*m.*) garage
**garganta** throat
**gaseosa** mineral water
**gastado/a** (*adj.*) worn out
**gastar** to spend
**gemelo/a** (*n.*) twin
**generalmente** generally, usually
**gerente** (*m., f.*) manager
**gimnasio** gymnasium
**ginecólogo/a** (*n.*) gynecologist
**girar: girar un cheque** to write a check
**giro** money order
    **giro bancario** bank draft
**globo** globe; balloon
**gobernador(a)** governor
**gobernante** (*m., f.*) ruler
**golpe: golpe de estado** coup d'état
**golpear** to beat up
**gorro** cap
**gozar** to enjoy
**grabar** to engrave; to record
**gracias** thanks
**graduación** (*f.*) commencement
**graduarse** to graduate
**grasa** grease
**gratis** free
**grato** pleasure
**gratuito/a** (*adj.*) free
**grave** serious
**gravedad** (*f.*) seriousness, gravity
**gremios** (*pl.*) unions
**grifo** water faucet
**gripe** (*f.*) flu
**grito** shout
    **a gritos** shouting
**grúa** crane
**guantes** (*m., pl.*) gloves
**guardarropa** wardrobe
**guerra** war
**guía** guide
    **guía telefónica** telephone directory
**guitarra** guitar
**gustar** to like, to be pleasing
**gusto** pleasure
    **mucho gusto en conocerlo(la)** a pleasure to meet you

## H

**haber** to possess, to have (auxiliary)
    **haber de** + inf. to be supposed to; to be going to
    **haber que** + inf. one must, it is necessary to
**había** there was, there were
**habichuelas** (*pl.*) (green) beans
**habilidad** (*f.*) ability
**habitación** (*f.*) room
    **habitación doble** double room
    **habitación sencilla** single room
**hablar** to speak
    **¡Ni hablar!** Don't even say it!, No way!
**hacer** to do, to make
    **hacer cola** to stand in line
    **hacer ejercicio** to exercise
    **hacer entrega** to award
    **hacer juego con** to match
    **hacer un brindis** to make a toast
    **hacerse** to become
**hambre** (*f.*, uses **el**) hunger
    **tener hambre** to be hungry
**harto/a** (*adj.*)**: estar harto/a** to be fed up
**hasta la vista** so long
**hasta luego** see you later
**hasta pronto** see you soon
**hasta que** until
**hay** there is, there are
    **hay que** one has to
    **no hay de qué** you are welcome
**heredar** to inherit
**herido/a** (*adj.*) wounded
**hermano/a** (*n.*) brother, sister
**herramienta** tool
**hierba** grass; herb
**hierro** iron
**hígado** liver
**hijo/a** (*n.*) son, daughter
    **hijo de vecino** any person
    **hijo/a único/a** only child
**hilera** row
**himno nacional** national anthem
**hipoteca** mortgage
**hispánico/a** (*adj.*) related to Hispanic culture
**hispano/a** (*n.*) Spanish-American (person)
**historietas** (*pl.*) comics
**hogar** (*m.*) home
**hoja** leaf; sheet (of paper)
    **hoja de maíz** corn husk
**hojalata** tin
**hombre** (*m.*) man

**hombro** shoulder
**hongos** (*pl.*) mushrooms
**honrar** to honor
**hora** hour (clock)
    **es hora de** it's time to
    **¿Qué hora es?** What time is it?
    **¡Ya es hora!** Time's up!
**horario** schedule
**hornear** to bake
**horno** oven
**hospitalizar(se)** to put (oneself) in
    the hospital
**hubo** there was, there were
**huelga** strike
**hueso** bone
**huésped** (*m., f.*) guest
**huevo** egg
**huir** to flee
**humillado/a** (*adj.*) humiliated
**huracán** (*m.*) hurricane

## I

**ida y vuelta** round trip
**idioma** (*m.*) language
**ídolo** idol
**iglesia** church
**igual** equal
**igualdad** (*f.*) equality
**igualmente** same here
**imagen** (*f.*) image
**imaginar** to imagine
**imperio** empire
**impermeable** (*m.*) raincoat
**imponer** to impose
**importar** to matter, to care
**importe** (*m.*) sum, amount charged
**impresionar** to impress
**impresos** (*pl.*) printed matter; forms
**impuesto** tax
**inauguración** (*f.*) opening
**inca** (*m., f.*) Inca; (*m.*) Peruvian money
**incendio** fire
**inclinarse** to bend over
**incluir** to include
**inconveniente** (*m.*) disadvantage,
    inconvenience
**indicar** to indicate
**indígena** (*m., f.*) native inhabitant
**indignarse** to get angry
**indudable** unquestionable
**infección** (*f.*) infection
**informática** computer science
**informe** (*m.*) report
**ingeniería** engineering
**ingeniero/a** (*n.*) engineer

**ingresar** to enter, to enroll
**ingresos** (*pl.*) income
**iniciar** to begin
**inmediato: de inmediato**
    immediately
**inmigración** (*f.*) immigration
**inodoro** toilet
**inquietud** (*f.*) concern, worry
**inscribirse** to register
**insomnio** insomnia, sleeplessness
**inspección** (*f.*) inspection
**intercambiar** to exchange
**interés** (*m.*) interest
  **tasa de interés** rate of interest
**internar** to place in (a hospital, jail)
**interrogar** to interrogate
**interrumpir** to interrupt
**intervenir (ie)** to intervene
**inundación** (*f.*) flood
**invertir (ie)** to invest
**investigación** research
**invitar** to invite
**inyección** (*f.*) injection
  **poner una inyección** to give an
    injection
**ir** to go
  **ir de compras** to go shopping
**irritado/a** irritated
**irritarse** to get angry
**irse** to go away, to leave
**isla** island
**itinerario** itinerary; schedule
**izquierdo/a** left
  **a la izquierda** to the left

## J

**jabón** (*m.*) soap
**jamás** never
**jamón** (*m.*) ham
**jarabe** (*m.*) syrup
**jardín** (*m.*) garden
**jardinero/a** (*n.*) gardener
**jefe/a** (*n.*) chief, boss
**jeringuilla** syringe
**jornada** day's work
  **jornada completa** full-time
  **media jornada** half-time
**joven** young
**jubilarse** to retire
**judío/a** (*adj.*) Jewish
**juego** game
**jugador/a** (*n.*) player
**jugar (ue)** to play
**jugo** juice
**juguete** (*m.*) toy

**justificar** to justify
**juventud** (*f.*) youth

## L

**labio** lip
**lago** lake
**lámpara** lamp
**lana** wool
**lápiz** (*m.*) pencil
**largo/a** (*adj.*) long
  **a lo largo** through; along; by
  **larga distancia** long distance
**lata** can
**latido** throb, beat
**lavabo** sink
**lavadora** washing machine
**lavaplatos** (*m., sing.*) dishwasher
**lecho** bed
**lechuga** lettuce
**lengua** language; tongue
  **sacar la lengua** to stick out one's
    tongue
**lenguaje** (*m.*) language
**letras** (*pl.*) letters; humanities
**letrero** sign
**levantar** to raise, to lift
**ley** (*f.*) law
**leyenda** legend
**libertad** (*f.*) **de expresión** freedom
  of speech
**libra** pound
**libre** (*adj.*) free
**librería** bookstore
**libreta de cheques** check book
**licenciatura** degree (equivalent to
  B.A.)
**licuadora** blender
**licuar** liquefy; to blend
**líder** (*m., f.*) leader
**ligar** to make close friends; to get a
  date
**ligue** (*m.*) close friend; date
**limosna** charitable donation
**limpiaparabrisas** (*m., sing.*)
  windshield wiper
**limpio/a** (*adj.*) clean
**línea** line
  **línea aérea** airline
**liso/a** (*adj.*) plain; straight
**lista** list
  **lista de espera** waiting list
  **pasar lista** to call the roll
**listo/a** (*adj.*) intelligent; ready
  **estar listo/a** to be ready
**llamada** call

**llamada de larga distancia** long distance call

**llamada equivocada** wrong number

**llamada local** local call

**llamada por cobrar** collect call

**llamar** to call

**llamarse** to call oneself, to be named

**llano** prairie

**llanta** car tire

**llave** (*f.*) key

**llegada** arrival

**llegar** to arrive

**llenar** to fill; to fill out

**llevar** to carry; to wear; to be... time in a place

**llevarse** to take away, to carry off

**llevarse bien** to get along well

**llover (ue)** to rain

**lluvia** rain

**loco/a** (*adj.*) crazy

**lograr** to achieve; to manage to

**luchar** to fight

**lucir trajes regionales** to wear the traditional dress

**luego** later

**lustrar** to shine

**luz** (*f.*), **luces** (*pl.*) light

## M

**madera** wood

**madre** (*f.*) mother

**madrina** godmother

**madrugada** dawn

**maduro/a** (*adj.*) mature; ripe

**maestría** Master of Arts (degree)

**mal** (*m.*) evil; sickness

**mal** badly

**mal aliento** bad breath

**malestar** (*m.*) discomfort

**malo/a** (*adj.*) bad

**maleta** suitcase

**maletín** (*m.*) small suitcase; briefcase

**maltratado/a** (*adj.*) mistreated

**mando** command

**mandón(-ona)** (*adj.*) bossy

**manejar** to drive

**manga** sleeve

**manguera** hose

**mano** (*f.*) hand

**manta** blanket

**mantener (ie)** to maintain

**mantenerse (ie) en forma** to stay in shape

**mantenimiento** maintenance

**manzana** apple

**mañana** tomorrow; morning

**mapa** (*m.*) map

**máquina** machine

**máquina de afeitar** shaver

**maravilla** marvel

**marca** brand

**marcar** to dial (a number)

**marcharse** to go away, to leave

**mareo** dizziness, seasickness

**mariachis** (*m., pl.*) Mexican musical group

**mariscos** (*pl.*) seafood; shellfish

**masa** dough

**materia** subject

**maternidad** (*f.*) maternity; motherhood

**matinal** (*adj.*) morning

**matrícula** registration (fee)

**matricularse** to register

**matrimonio** marriage, married couple

**maya** Mayan

**mayor** bigger; older

**el mayor** the biggest, oldest

**mayoría** majority

**mayormente nublado** mostly cloudy

**mayúscula** capital letter

**medicamento** medication

**médico/a** (*n.*) physician

**medianoche** midnight

**medio/a** (*adj.*) half

**medios** (*pl.*) means

**medios de comunicación** media

**medios de transporte** means of transportation

**mejilla** cheek

**mejor** better

**mejorar** to improve

**mendigo/a** (*n.*) beggar

**menor** smaller; younger

**menor de edad** minor

**mensaje** (*m.*) message

**mensual** monthly

**mentir (ie)** to lie

**menudo: a menudo** often

**mercadería** merchandise

**mercado** market

**mercancía** merchandise

**mestizo/a** (*adj.*) mixed-blood person

**meter** to insert

**mezcla** mix

**miedo** fear

**tener miedo** to be afraid

**miel** (*f.*) honey

**mientras (que)** while; as long as

**mientras tanto** meanwhile

**mimado/a** (*adj.*) spoiled

**minifalda** miniskirt

**mirar** to look at

**misa** (church) Mass

**misa del gallo** Christmas midnight Mass

**misionero/a** (*n.*) missionary

**mito** myth

**mochila** knapsack, backpack

**moda** fashion

**estar de moda** to be in style

**estar pasado de moda** to be out of style

**mojar(se)** to (get) wet

**molestar** to bother

**moneda** currency, coin

**mono/a** (*n.*) monkey

**montaña** mountain

**montar en bicicleta** to ride a bike

**moraleja** moral (of a story)

**moreno/a** (*adj.*) dark complexioned

**morir (ue)** to die

**mostrador** (*m.*) showcase; counter

**mostrar (ue)** to show

**moto(cicleta)** (*f.*) motorcycle

**moverse (ue)** to make a move

**mudar de** to change

**mudarse** to change clothes; to move (change address)

**mudo/a** (*adj.*) mute, silent

**mueble** (*m.*) piece of furniture

**muebles** (*pl.*) furniture

**muelle** (*m.*) (mechanical) spring; pier, wharf

**muertes** (*f.*) deaths

**muerto/a** (*adj.*) dead

**mujer** (*f.*) woman

**muleta** crutch

**mundo hispano** Hispanic world

**muñeca** wrist; doll

**muñeco** dummy, doll

**músculo** muscle

## N

**nacer** to be born

**Nacimiento** Nativity scene, crèche

**nacimiento** (*m.*) birth

**nada** nothing

**de nada** you're welcome; not at all

**nadar** to swim

**nadie** no one, nobody

**nalgas** (*pl.*) buttocks

**naranja** orange

**narcotraficante** (*m., f.*) drug dealer

**narcotráfico** drug traffic
**nariz** (*f.*) nose
**narrar** to narrate
**natación** (*f.*) swimming
**natal: ciudad natal** birthplace
**náuseas** nausea
**Navidad** (*f.*) Christmas
**necesidades de empleo** (*f.*)
    employment needs
**negar (ie)** to deny
**negocios** (*pl.*) business
    **hombre (mujer) de negocios**
      businessperson
**negro/a** (*n.*) black person
**neumático** tire
**nevar (ie)** to snow
**nevera** refrigerator
**ni... ni** neither... nor
**nieto/a** (*n.*) grandson,
    granddaughter
**nieve** (*f.*) snow
**ningún** not any
**ninguno/a** (*adj.*) not one, none
**no más** only (Mex.)
**noche** (*f.*) night
**nocturno/a** (*adj.*) evening, night
**nota** grade; note
**noticias** (*pl.*) news
**novio/a** (*n.*) boyfriend, girlfriend;
    bridegroom, bride
**nuevo/a** (*adj.*) new
**nunca** never
**número** number

## O

**obedecer** to obey
**obligatorio/a** (*adj.*) compulsory
**obrero/a** (*n.*) blue-collar worker
**obtener (ie)** to obtain
**océano** ocean
**ocupación** (*f.*) job, trade
**ocupado/a** (*adj.*) busy
**ofender** to offend
**oferta** offer
**oficina** office
**oficio** trade; job
**ofrecer** to offer
**oído** (*m.*) (inner) ear
**ojo** eye
**¡Ojo!** Careful!, Watch out!
**ola** wave
**olla** cooking pot
**olor** (*m.*) smell, odor
**olvidar** to forget
**operación** (*f.*) operation

**opinar** to express an opinion
**oprimir** to press
**optativo/a** elective
**orden** (*m.*) order, sequence
**orden** (*f.*) command; order of
    merchandise
**oreja** (outer) ear
**orejera** earflap
**orilla** shore
**orina** urine
**oscilar** to fluctuate
**otorgar** to bestow
**otro/a** another
**otros/as** others(s)

## P

**paciente** (*m., f.*) patient
**padecer (una enfermedad)** to suffer
    (an illness)
**padre** (*m.*) father
**padrino** godfather
**pagar** to pay
    **pagar con tarjeta de crédito** to
      pay with a credit card
    **pagar en cuotas mensuales**
      to make monthly payments
    **pagar en efectivo/al contado** to
      pay cash
**país** (*m.*) country
**pájaro** bird
**palabra** word
**paloma** dove
**palomita** pigeon
**palomitas de maiz** popcorn
**pan** (*m.*) (loaf) of bread
    **pan de molde** sandwich bread
**panadería** bakery
**panadero/a** (*n.*) baker
**pantalla** (movie or TV) screen
**pantalones** (*m., pl.*) pants, slacks
**pantorrilla** calf
**pañuelo** handkerchief
**papa** potato
**Papá Noel** Santa Claus
**papel** (*m.*) paper; role (in a play)
    **papel de envolver** wrapping
      paper
    **papel higiénico** toilet paper
**par** (*m.*) pair
**para** in order to, for
    **¿para qué?** for what purpose?;
      why?
**parada** stop
**paraguas** (*m., sing.*) umbrella
**parecer** to seem

**parecerse** to resemble, to look like
**pareja** pair, couple
**pariente** (*m., f.*) relative
**paro** strike, work stoppage
**partido** (political) party
**párrafo** paragraph
**pasaje** (*m.*) ticket, fare
**pasajero/a** (*n.*) traveler, passenger
**pasar** to pass; to come in
    **pasar lista** to call the roll
    **pasado de moda** out of fashion
**Pascua** Easter
**pasillo** aisle
**pasta de dientes** toothpaste
**pastel** (*m.*) cake
**pastilla** pill
    **pastilla para dormir** sleeping pill
**patata** potato
**patillas** (*pl.*) sideburns
**patinador(a)** (*n.*) skater
**patria** homeland
**patrocinador(a)** (*n.*) sponsor
**patrullaje** (*m.*) patrol
**pavo** turkey
**paz** (*f.*) peace
**peatón(ona)** (*n.*) pedestrian
**pecho** chest, breast
**pedir (i)** to ask for; to order
    **pedir la baja** to resign
    **pedir un préstamo** to ask for a
      loan
**pegar** to glue, to paste; to hit
**pelear** to fight
**película** film
**peligro** danger
**pelo** hair
**pendiente** hanging, pending;
    earring
**pensamiento** thought
**pensar (ie)** to think
    **pensar de** to think of
    **pensar en** to think about
    **pensar en un deseo** to make a
      wish
**peor** worse
**pepino** cucumber
**pera** pear
**percance** (*m.*) accident, mishap
**perder (ie)** to lose
    **perder el vuelo** to miss the flight
**perderse (ie)** to get lost
**pérdidas** (*pl.*) losses
**perdonar** to excuse
**periódico** newspaper
**periodismo** journalism
**periodista** (*m., f.*) journalist
**perjudicar** to harm
**permanencia** stay; green card

**permiso** permission; permit
**pero** but
**perseguir (i)** to pursue
**personaje** (*m.*) character (in a play)
**personajes** (*pl.*) **e intérpretes** (*pl.*) cast
**personal** (*adj.*) personal; (*m.*) personnel
**pertenencias** (*pl.*) belongings
**perturbar** to disturb
**pesar** to weigh
   **a pesar de (que)** in spite of; although
**pescadería** fish market
**pescado** fish
**peso** weight; currency of several Latin American countries
**pestaña** eyelash
**picar** to eat small bits
**pie** (*m.*) foot
   **pies de foto** (*m., pl.*) captions
**piel** (*f.*) skin
**pierna** leg
**píldora** pill
**piloto** (*m., f.*) pilot
**piratería aérea** hijacking
**piscina** pool
**piso** floor; apartment
**pista** roadway; clue; track
   **pista de aterrizaje** runway
**placa** license plate
**placer** (*m.*) pleasure
**plana: primera plana** front page
**plancha** iron
**planchar** to iron
**plano/a** (*adj.*) flat
**plano de la casa** floorplan
**planta baja** ground floor
**plantearse** to examine, to study
**plata** silver
**plátano** banana; plantain
**plato** plate; dish
**playa** beach
**plazos** (*pl.*)**: comprar a plazos** to buy on the installment plan
**pleno/a** (*adj.*) full
**plomo** lead
   **sin plomo** unleaded
**pluma** pen; feather
**población** (*f.*) town; population
**pobreza** poverty
**poder** (*m.*) power
**poder (ue)** to be able; can
**podría** could
**policía** (*f.*) police
**policía** (*m.*) policeman
  **mujer policía** (*f.*) policewoman
**político/a** (*n.*) politician

**pollo** chicken
**poner** to put, to place
   **poner una inyección** to give a shot
**ponerse** to put on, to wear; to become
**por** through; by
   **por debajo de cero** below zero
   **por favor** please
   **por fin** finally
   **por lo menos** at least
   **por poco** almost
   **¿Por qué?** why?
   **porque** because
   **por supuesto** of course
**porcentaje** (*m.*) percent
**posponer** to put off, to postpone
**postulante** (*m., f.*) applicant
**postular** to apply for
**práctica privada** private practice
**precio** price
**precisar** to need; to be specific
**preferir (ie)** to prefer
**pregonar** to announce publicly
**pregunta** question
   **hacer preguntas** to ask questions
**preguntar** to ask
**preguntarse** to wonder
**prejuicio** prejudice
**premiar** to give an award
**prenda** jewel
   **prenda de vestir** piece of clothing
**prensa** press, newspapers
**preocupar** to worry (another)
   **preocuparse por** to worry about
**preparar(se)** to prepare (oneself) (to get ready)
**preparativos** (*pl.*) preparations
**presenciar** to witness
**presentar** to present; to introduce; to show
   **me gustaría presentarle(te) a...** I would like you to meet...
   **presentarse al examen** to show up for the test
**presión** (*f.*) **arterial** blood pressure
   **presión alta** high blood pressure
**préstamo** loan
**prestar** to lend
   **prestar atención** to pay attention
**prestigioso/a** prestigious
**presupuesto** budget
**prevenir (ie)** to prevent; to warn
**primer, primero/a** (*adj.*) first
**primero que todo** first of all

**primo/a** (*n.*) cousin
**principio** beginning
**prisa** haste
   **tener prisa** to be in a hurry
**probar (ue)** to try; to taste
**procedencia** place of origin
**procedente de** coming from
**proceso** procedure; process; lawsuit
**programador/a** (*n.*) programmer
**prolongado/a** extended
**prometer** to promise
**pronto** soon
   **de pronto** soon
   **tan pronto como** as soon as
**propina** tip
**propio/a** own
**proponer** to propose
**proporcionar** to provide
**propósito** aim, purpose
**proteger** to protect
**proveedor/a** provider
**próximo/a** (*m.*) next
**proyecto** project
**prueba** test
**publicidad** (*f.*) advertising
**¿Puedo?** May I?
**puerta** door
**puesto** job, position; market stall
**pulmón** (*m.*) lung
**punto** point
   **punto de vista** point of view

## Q

**que** that, which
**¿Qué?** what?
   **¿Por qué?** why?
   **¡Qué lástima!** what a pity!
   **¿Qué tal?** how are you?
   **¡Qué va!** no way!
**quedar bien con** to make a good impression on
**quedar en** to agree on
**quedarle a uno** to have left
**quedarle bien a uno** to suit someone
**quedar(se)** to remain, to stay; to be located
   **quedarse con** to keep
**quedársele a uno** to be left (remaining) to one
**quehacer** (*m.*) task, chore
**queja** complaint
**quejarse (de)** to complain (about)
**quemar** to burn
**querer (ie)** to wish, to want; to love

**querer decir** to mean
**querido/a** (*adj.*) dear, beloved
**queso** cheese
**quien** who, whom
**¿quién?** who?, whom?
**quinceañera** fifteen-year-old girl
**quisiera** I would like
**quitar(se)** to remove; to take off
    (clothing)
**quizá, quizás** perhaps

# R

**racimo** bunch
**ración** (*f.*) portion, serving
**radio** (*m.*) radio set
**radio** (*f.*) radio
**radioemisora** radio station
**raspar** to scrape
**ratificar** to confirm
**rato** short while
**raya** stripe
    **a rayas** striped
**rayo** ray; thunderbolt, lightning
  **rayos equis** (*pl.*) X-rays
**raza** race
**razón** (*f.*) reason
    **tener razón** to be right
**realizar** to fulfill, to achieve
**realizarse** to take place
**rebaja** discount
    **en rebaja** reduced merchandise
**rebajar** to reduce
**rebozo** shawl (Mex.)
**recado** message
**recámara** bedroom (Mex.)
**recepción** (*f.*) hotel lobby
**receta** prescription
**recetar** to prescribe
**recibir** to receive
**reciclado** recycling
**reclamar** to claim
**recoger** to pick up
    **recoger la mesa** to clear the table
**recomendación** (*f.*)
    recommendation
**recordar (ue)** to remember
**recorrer** to travel through, to pass
    over
**recostarse (ue)** to lean back
**rector/a** (*n.*) president of a university;
    chancellor
**recuerdo** memory; souvenir
**recursos humanos** (*pl.*) human
    resources
**reemplazar** to replace

**referirse (ie) a** to refer to
**refrán** (*m.*) proverb, saying
**refresco** drink
**regalo** gift
**regar (ie)** to water
**regatear** to bargain
**régimen** (*m.*) **militar** military regime
**registrar** to examine, to look
    through, to inspect
**registrarse** to register
**relajar** to relax
**relámpago** lightning
**releer** to reread
**relleno** stuffing
**reloj** (*m.*) watch; clock
**remedio** remedy
    **no tener más remedio** to have
      no other choice
**remitente** (*m., f.*) sender
**renunciar** to quit, to resign
**reñir (i)** to fight; to scold
**repartirse** to share
**repasar** to review
**repetir (i)** to repeat
**repicar las campanas** to ring
    (church) bells
**reportaje** (*m.*) news report
**reportar** to report
**reprobar (ue)** to fail, to flunk
**requerido/a** required
    **se requiere** required
**requisito** requirement, requisite
**resfriado: coger un resfriado** to
    catch a cold
**resfrío** cold
**resistir** to resist
**resolver (ue)** to solve
**respirar** to breathe
**restar** to subtract
**retirar** to take away
**retirarse** to withdraw, to retreat
**retraso** delay
**reunir(se)** to gather; to meet
**reunión** (*f.*) meeting
**revendedor/a** (*m., f.*) reseller; scalper
**reventar (ie)** to pop, to burst, to
    explode
**revisar** to review; to check
    **revisar el saldo** to check the
      balance
**revista** magazine
**Reyes** (*m., pl.*) **Magos** the Three Wise
    Men
**rezongar** to mumble
**riesgo** risk
**riñón** (*m.*) kidney
**río** river
**ritmo** rhythm

**robo** robbery, theft
**rodar (ue)** to film (a movie)
**rodear** to surround
**rodilla** knee
**rogar (ue)** to beg, to plead
**romper** to break
**ropa** clothing
**ropero** closet; wardrobe
**ruborizado/a** (*adj.*) blushing
**rueda** wheel
**ruido** noise
**rumbo a** bound for
**rutas de autobuses** (*pl.*) bus routes

# S

**sábana** bed sheet
**saber** to know; to taste
    **¡sabe a demonios!** it tastes
      horrible!
**sacar** to take out
    **sacar buenas (malas) notas**
      to get good (bad) grades
**sacerdote** (*m.*) priest
**sala** room; living room
  **sala de espera** waiting room
**salida** exit
**salir** to leave; to depart
**salón** (*m.*) room
**saltar** to jump
**salud** (*f.*) health
    **¡Salud, dinero y amor!** To your
      health!
**saludable** (*adj.*) healthy
**saludar** to greet; to salute
**salvar** to save, to rescue
**sandalia** sandal
**sandía** watermelon
**sangre** (*f.*) blood
**santo** saint
**satisfacer las demandas/**
    **necesidades** to meet the
    demands/needs
**secadora** dryer
**secar los platos** to dry the dishes
**sed** (*f.*) thirst
  **tener sed** to be thirsty
**seda** silk
**seguir (i)** to follow
    **seguir las indicaciones** to follow
      directions
**segundo** second
**seguro/a** (*adj.*)**: estar seguro** to be
    safe; to be sure
**seguro** insurance
**seleccionar** to select

**sello** postage stamp
**selva** jungle
**Semana Santa** Holy Week
**semáforo** traffic light
**sencillo/a** (*adj.*) easy; simple
**sendero** path
**sentarse (ie)** to sit
**sentimiento** feeling
**sentir (ie)** to feel
**sentirse mal (bien)** to feel sick (well)
**señal** (*f.*) signal
    **señales** (*pl.*) **de tránsito** traffic
      signals
**sequía** drought
**serenata** serenade
**seres queridos** (*m.pl.*) loved ones
**servir (i)** to serve
    **servir para** to be used for
**sicólogo/a** (*m., f.*) psychologist
**sida** (*m.*) AIDS
**siempre** always
**siglo** century
**siguiente** following
**silbar** to whistle
**silla** chair
    **silla de ruedas** wheelchair
**sillón** (*m.*) armchair; rocking chair
**sin** without
    **sin cesar** ceaseless(ly)
    **sin costo alguno** free of charge
    **sin embargo** however
    **sin igual** unsurpassed
    **sin presupuesto** without budget
**sindicato** labor union
**sino** but; except
**síntoma** (*m.*) symptom
**sobre** (*m.*) envelope
**sobre** above; about
**sobregirarse** to overdraw
**sobreviviente** (*m., f.*) survivor
**socio/a** (*n.*) partner
**soldado** (*m., f.*) soldier
**soler (ue)** to be accustomed
**solicitante** (*m., f.*) applicant
**solicitar** to apply
    **solicitar un empleo** to apply for
      a job
**solicitud** (*f.*) application
**solo** only
**solo/a** (*adj.*) alone
**soltero/a** (*n.*) single (unmarried)
    person
**solución** (*m.*) solution
**sonreír (i)** to smile
**soñar (ue)** to dream
**soplado/a a mano** (*adj.*) hand-blown
**soplar** to blow out (candles)
**sorprender** to surprise

**sorpresa** surprise
**sortear** to draw lots
**sospechoso/a** (*adj.*) suspicious,
    suspect
**subasta** auction
**subir** to go up; to take up; to climb
    **subir(se) a** to get on
**subrayar** to underline
**suceder** to take place
**sucio/a** (*adj.*) dirty
**sucursal** (*f.*) branch (office, store)
**suegro/a** (*n.*) father-in-law, mother-
    in-law
**sueldo** salary
**suele ser** (it) usually is
**suelo** floor
**sueño** dream
    **tener sueño** to be sleepy
**suerte** (*f.*) luck
    **tener suerte** to be lucky
**sufrir** to suffer
**sugerir (ie)** to suggest
**sujetador** (*m.*) bra
**sumar** to total, to add
**supervisar** to supervise
**suponer** to suppose
**supuesto: por supuesto** of course
**sur** (*m.*) south
**suspender** to flunk (a student or a
    subject)
**sustituir** to substitute

# T

**tablón** (*m.*) **de anuncios**
    bulletin board
**tacaño/a** (*adj.*) cheap, stingy
**tacón** (*m.*) heel
**tal** such
    **¿Qué tal?** How are you?
**talla** size
**tallado/a** (*adj.*) carved
**tamaño** size
**tampoco** neither; (not) either
**tanque** (*m.*) **de gasolina** gas tank
**tapas** (*pl.*) snacks (Spain)
**taquilla** ticket office, ticket window
**tarea** task; work; homework
**tarifa** fare; fee
**tarjeta** card
    **tarjeta de crédito** credit card
    **tarjeta postal** postcard
**taza** cup
    **taza de café** cup of coffee
**teatro** theater
**techo** roof

**tejado** roof
**tejido/a** (*adj.*) knit
**telenovela** soap opera
**telepantalla** television screen
**televidente** (*m., f.*) television viewer
**telón** (*m.*) theater curtain
**temer** to be afraid of, to fear
**temporada** season
**tenderse (ie)** to lie down
**tener (ie)** to have, to possess
    **tener cabeza para los números**
      to be good with numbers
    **tener calor** to be hot
    **tener cuidado** to be careful
    **tener frío** to be cold
    **tener hambre** to be hungry
    **tener ganas de** to feel like
    **tener lugar** to take place
    **tener miedo** to be afraid
    **tener razón** to be right
    **tener sueño** to be sleepy
    **tener suerte** to be lucky
    **tener talento** to have talent
**tensión** (*f.*) stress
**teñir (i)** to dye
**terminar** to end, to finish
**ternera** veal
**terraza** terrace
**terremoto** earthquake
**tertulia** gathering, conversation
**testigo** (*m., f.*) witness
**tiempo** time
**tienda de calzado** shoe store
**tienden a producir** tend to yield
**tila, flor de** linden tree flower(s)
    (medicinal)
**tina** bathtub
**tinto: café tinto** black coffee
    (Colombia)
    **vino tinto** red wine
**tío/a** (*n.*) uncle, aunt
**titular** (*m.*) headline
**título** title; degree
**toalla** towel
**tobillo** ankle
**tocado** hairdo; headdress
**todo/a** (*adj.*) all, every
    **ante todo** above all
**tomar** to take; to drink
    **tomar apuntes** to take notes
    **tomar asiento** to sit down
    **tomar precauciones** to take
      precautions
**tontería** foolishness
    **¡Qué tontería!** What nonsense!
**toparse con** to meet (by chance)
**torear** to bullfight
**tormenta** storm

**torta** cake
**tortilla** corn or flour pancake
  **tortilla española** Spanish omelette
**tos** (*f.*) cough
**toser** to cough
**tostadora** toaster
**trabajador/a** (*n.*) worker
**traducir** to translate
**traer** to bring
**traje** (*m.*) suit
**trámite** (*m.*) procedure
**tranquilo/a** (*adj.*) calm, quiet
**tránsito** traffic; transit, passage
**transmitir** to broadcast
**transportar** to transport
**transporte** (*m.*) transportation
**trapo** rag, piece of cloth
**tratamiento** treatment
**tratar** to try
  **tratar con** to deal with
  **tratar en vano** to try in vain
**tratarse de** to be about
**tren** (*m.*) train
**tripulación** (*f.*) crew
**tropezarse con** to meet (by chance)
**trotar** to jog
**trueno** thunder
**tumba** grave
**turbulencia** turbulence
**turista** (*m., f.*) tourist

## U

**ubicación** (*f.*) location
**último/a** last
**único/a** (*adj.*) only
  **hijo/a único/a** only child
**unirse** to join
**universitario/a** (*n.*) university student

**unos (unas)** some; a few
**uña** (finger or toe) nail
**usuario/a** user
**uva** grape

## V

**¡Vale!** O.K.!
**valle** (*m.*) valley
**valor** (*m.*) value; courage
**vaquero** (*m.*) cowboy
**vaqueros** (*pl.*) jeans
**variedad** (*f.*) variety
**varón** (*m.*) male
**vecino/a** (*n.*) neighbor
**vehículo** vehicle
**vela** candle
**vena** vein
**vencimiento: fecha de vencimiento** expiration date
**vendedor/a** (*n.*) salesperson
**vender** to sell
**¡Venga!** Come on!
**venir (ie)** to come
**venta** sale
  **a la venta** on sale
  **ventas de fábrica** factory sales
**ventaja** advantage
**ventanilla** car window; ticket booth
**ventilador** (*m.*) vent; fan
**verano** summer
**verbena** conversational gathering; popular festival
**verde** (*adj.*) green; unripe
**verdura** vegetable; (edible) green
**verdulería** vegetable market
**verificar** to check
**vestido** dress
**vestimenta** clothes, garments
**vez** (*f.*) time, occasion
  **a la vez** at the same time

  **a veces** sometimes
  **otra vez** another time; once again
**viajar** to travel
**viaje** (*m.*) trip
**viajero/a** (*n.*) traveler
**vida** life
**vidrio** glass
**Viernes** (*m.*) **Santo** Good Friday
**villancico** Christmas carol
**vino** wine
**víspera de Navidad** Christmas Eve
**visto: por lo visto** apparently
**viudo/a** (*adj.*) widowed; (*n.*) widower, widow
**vivienda** housing
**vivir** to live
**volante** (*m.*) steering wheel
**voluntad** (*f.*) will; desire
**volver (ue)** to return
  **volver a** to (do something) again
  **volver en sí** to regain consciousness
**volverse (ue)** to become
**voto** vote
**voz** (*f.*) voice
**vuelo** flight
  **vuelo directo** direct flight
**vuelta** return; change (money)
  **estar de vuelta** to be back

## Y

**ya mismo** right away

## Z

**zapato** shoe
**zona** zone
**zumo** juice (Spain)

# Índice

a causa de (por), 16
a pesar (de) que, 276
acabar(se), 106
acentuación
    en palabras interrogativas, 7
adjetivos
    calificativos, 32–33
    cláusulas que funcionan como, 272
    como adverbios, 299
    comparaciones de superioridad
        e inferioridad, 80–81
    de igualdad, 83
    diminutivos y aumentativos, 378
    posesivos, 35–36
    superlativos, 84–85
adverbios
    cláusulas que funcionan como, 275
    como adjetivos, 299
    comparaciones de superioridad
        e inferioridad, 80–81
    de igualdad, 83
    formación, 299
    gerundios en función de, 397
    superlativos, 84–85
    usos de, 299
afirmativa/negativa
    expresiones, 329
al, 23
al + infinitivo, 354
andar + gerundio, 396
anticipación, expresiones de, 276
*appearance,* 23
artículos definidos
    formas, 23
    usos, 23–24
artículos indefinidos
    formas, 24
    omisión de, 24
*to ask,* 16
aumentativos, 378
aun cuando, 276
aunque, 276

*because,* 16
*to become,* 98–100
bueno(buen)/malo(mal)
    comparativos, 81
    formas adverbiales, 81
    superlativos, 84–85
*but,* 404
caer bien/mal, 212
cláusulas
    adjetivales, 272
    adverbiales, 275–276
    condicionales con si, 316
    independientes unidas por pero,
        404
    nominales, 234–235
    parentéticas, 421–423
    restrictivas, 421
cláusulas subordinadas
    imperfecto del subjuntivo en, 289
    indicativo vs. subjuntivo en, 234–
        235
    pluscuamperfecto del subjuntivo
        en, 411
    pronombres relativos en, 421–423
cognados falsos, 241
colocar, 282
*to come,* 196

¡cómo...! en frases exclamativas, 11
como si, 289
comparaciones
    de igualdad, 83
    de superioridad e inferioridad,
        80–81
    irregulares, 80–81
    superlativos, 84–85
con
    con pronombres de complemento,
        202
    usos, 218
condición, expresiones de, 276
condición expresado con si +
    imperfecto del subjuntivo
    usos, 316
condicional
    en cláusulas condicionales con si,
        316
    formacion, 313
    para expresar el futuro con relación
        al pasado, 313
    para expresar probabilidad en el
        pasado, 313
condicional perfecto
    formacion, 409
    usos, 409
conjunciones
    pero, sino, sino que, 404
conmigo (–sigo, –tigo), 202
conocer
    saber vs., 153
    significado en pretérito, imperfecto,
        159
convenir, 212
¿cuál?
    comparado con ¿qué?, 6
    para selección, 6
cuando, 275
¿cuánto... ?, 6
¡cuánto... ! en exclamaciones, 11
cuestión vs. pregunta, 16

*date,* 364
de
    + el, 23
    + infinitivo, 354, 412
    en comparaciones de número,
        cantidad, 80
    estar +, 110
de (continuado)
    omisión de artículo, 24
    usos, 124–125
deber (de)
    en expresiones de deseo, 298
    en expresiones de obligación, 123
    en expresiones de probabilidad,
        123
decir
    como mandato, 234
    uso de lo con, 200
dejar
    como verbo de permiso, 235
dejar de, 106
del, 23
desde, 367
deseo
    expresiones de, 298
    que como conjunción en
        expresiones de, 298

subjuntivo después de verbos de,
    298
    verbos de, 234
después (de) que, 275
diminutivos, 378

+ el, 23
el (la), 23
el (la) cual, 423
el (la) que, 423
en
    con significado de encima de, 110
    estar +, 110
    expresiones del tiempo, 110
    para designar lugar, 124
en cuanto, 275
encantar, 212
encima de, 124
encontrarse, 153
entrar + gerundio, 396
entre
    pronombres personales con, 50
    pronombres preposicionales con,
        202
    usos, 367
estar
    + de, 110
    + en, 110
    + para + infinitivo, 110
    + sustantivo o pronombre, 110
    con gerundio, 111, 396
    en expresiones del tiempo
        atmosférico, 110
    expresiones comunes con, 111
    participio pasado +, 111
    uso de lo con, 200
    y ser, 110–111
excepto
    pronombres personales con, 50
    pronombres preposicionales con,
        202
exclamaciones
    acentuación en, 11
expresiones impersonales
    haber, 114
    haber que + infinitivo, 123
    infinitivos después de, 353–354

*to fail,* 106
faltar, 106, 212
fracasar, 106
futuro
    cláusulas condicionales con, 316
    formación del, 68
    ir a + infinitivo, 71
    presente como, 71
    querer + infinitivo como, 71
    usos del, 71
futuro perfecto
    formación, 409
    usos, 409

gerundios
    con venir, andar, 396
    en lugar del infinitivo, 396
    estar +, 396
    formación, 395
    pronombres reflexivos con, 100
    verbos de continuidad +, 396
    verbos de movimiento +, 396

verbos de percepción +, 396
grande
  en comparaciones, 81
gustar
  con subjuntivo, 235
  construcción especial de, 212

haber
  con participio pasado tiempos,
    188, 190
    para expresar existencia (hay),
    114
haber de
  en expresiones de obligación
    personal, 123, 353–354
  en expresiones de probabilidad,
    122
haber (hay) que
  en expresiones de obligación
    impersonal, 122, 353–354
hacer
  en expresiones del tiempo
    atmosférico, 114
  en expresiones del tiempo
    transcurrido, 170
  hacerse, 100
  hasta, 367
  hasta que, 275

imperativo. véase también mandatos
  con pronombres de complemento
    directo e indirecto, 244
  con pronombres reflexivos, 244
  de nosotros, 257
  familiar (tú y vosotros), 254
  formal (Ud. y Uds.), 244
  usos del, 244
imperfecto del indicativo
  formación, 148
  usos, 158–159
  vs. pretérito, 158–159
imperfecto del subjuntivo
  cláusulas condicionales con, 316
  formación, 287
importar, 212
incluso, pronombres personales con,
  50
indicativo
  comunicación verbal, 234
  con el verbo creer, 235
  en cláusulas adjetivales, 272
  en cláusulas adverbiales, 275–276
  en oraciones impersonales +, 235
  en oraciones interrogativas, 235
  expresiones de seguridad +, 234
  percepción física o mental +, 234
  procesos mentales +, 234
indicativo vs. subjuntivo
  afirmativa/negativa, 234–235
  en cláusulas adjetivales, 272
  en cláusulas adverbiales, 275–276
  en cláusulas condicionales con si,
    316
  seguridad/inseguridad, 234–235
infinitivo
  como complementos de verbos,
    353
  como imperativo, 354
  con por, 357
  con sin, 368

de +, como equivalente de si +
  indicativo, 354
de +, como equivalente de si +
  subjuntivo, 354, 412
después de oraciones impersonales,
  354
después de preposiciones, 353
haber (hay) que +, 123
pronombres reflexivos con, 368
inseguridad/seguridad
  expresiones de, 276
  indicativo vs. subjuntivo después,
    234–235
interesar, 212
interrogativos
  acentuación de, 6–7
  expresiones, 6–7
  pronombres, 6–7
  usos, 6–7
ir
  + gerundio, 396
  vs. venir, llegar, 196
ir a + infinitivo, 71
irse (de)/marcharse (de), 282
–ísimo, 85

to leave, 282
llegar
  + gerundio, 296
  vs. ir, venir, 196
llevar(se)
  usos de, 106
  y artículo indefinido, 24
lo, 200
lo que, 423

malo(mal)/bueno(buen)
  comparativos, 81
  superlativos, 84
mandatos. véase también imperativo
  infinitivo como, 354
más/menos
  comparaciones de superioridad/
    inferioridad, 80–81
  superlativos, 84
to meet, 153
–mente, 299
meter, 282
mientras (que), 275
mismo(a)
  para énfasis, 50
  uso después de pronombres, 202
to miss, 364
molestar, 212

negativas, expresiones, 328–329
no querer
  significado en pretérito, imperfecto
    del indicativo, 159
no solo...sino (también), 404
obligación, expresiones de, 123, 354
oír, 52
oler, 51
ortografía
  acentuación, 7
  verbos con cambios en radical, 51
otro como artículo indefinido, 24

palabras interrogativas, 6
para

modismos con, 358
  pronombres de complemento con,
    352 028
  usos de, 358
participios pasados
  con estar, 111
  con haber en tiempos compuestos,
    188, 190, 326
  irregulares, 188
  pensar, 196
pero y sino, 404
pluscuamperfecto del indicativo
  formación, 190
  usos, 190
pluscuamperfecto del subjuntivo
  formación, 411
  usos, 411–412
poder
  en expresiones de deseo, 298
  significados diferentes, 159
poner(se)
  como verbo reflexivo, 99
  usos, 282
por
  en voz pasiva, 337
  usos de, 357
¿por qué?, 6, 16
porque, 6, 16
posesión
  adjetivos para expresar, 35
  de para expresar, 124
posibilidad, cláusulas condicionales
  con si, 316
pregunta vs. cuestión, 16
preguntar, 16
  uso de lo con, 200
preposiciones
  + infinitivo, 353
  antes de infinitivo, 353
preposiciones comunes, usos de,
  367–368
presente del indicativo
  cláusulas condicionales, 315
presente del subjuntivo
  formación, 232–233
  usos, 234–235
presente perfecto del indicativo
  formación, 188
  usos, 188
presente perfecto del subjuntivo
  formas, 326
  usos, 326
pretérito
  formación, 143–144
  usos, 158–159
  vs. imperfecto del indicativo, 158–
    159
probabilidad
  cláusulas condicionales para
    expresar, 316
  futuro perfecto para expresar, 409
pronombres de complemento de,
  200
pronombres de complemento directo
  e indirecto con gerundios, 397
  con imperativo, 244
  posición de, 200–202
  usos, 200–202
propósito, expresiones de, 276
to put, 282

que
  en cláusulas del subjuntivo, 234
  en comparaciones, 80–81
  para introducir cláusula restrictiva, 421–423
  para reemplazar a personas o cosas, 421–423
  pronombre relativo, 423
  uso de lo que, 423
¡qué...!
  en exclamaciones, 11
  y artículo indefinido, 24
¿qué?
  como adjetivo interrogativo, 6
  comparado con ¿cuál?, 6
  en expresiones interrogativas, 6
quedar, 212, 323
querer
  + infinitivo, 71
  significado en pretérito, imperfecto del indicativo, 159
quien (es)
  para reemplazar a personas, 422
  usos, 422

reflexivos
  pronombres, 98, 244
  verbos, 98–100
saber
  vs., 153
  significado en pretérito, imperfecto del indicativo, 159
  subjuntivo presente, 233
  uso de lo con, 200
salir (de), 282
salvo, 202
se
  como sujeto no responsable, 215
  con verbos reflexivos, 98
  con voz pasiva, 337
  indefinido, 215
según, 50
seguridad/inseguridad, expresiones de, 276
ser
  + de, 110
  + para, 110
  con voz pasiva, 337
  en expresiones impersonales, 111
  lo con, 200
  y estar, 110–111

y tiempo cronológico, 110
si + subjuntivo, 316
sin, 368
sino que, 404
sino y pero, 404
sobre, 367
subjuntivo. *véase también* tiempos específicos del subjuntivo
  con creer, pensar en negativo, 235
  con expresiones de consejo o ruego, 235
  con expresiones de deseo, 298
  con expresiones de duda/ inseguridad/negación, 234–235
  con expresiones de emociones, 235
  en cláusulas adjetivales, 272
  en cláusulas adverbiales, 275–276
  en cláusulas condicionales, 316
  en expresiones impersonales, 235
  en oraciones interrogativas, 235
  mandatos, 234
superlativos, 84–85
sustantivos
  artículos con, 21, 24
  comparaciones de igualdad, 83
  en comparaciones de superioridad e inferioridad, 80–81
  género de, 21

*to take*, 106
tan...como, 83
tanto(a)...como, 83
tantos(as)...como, 83
tener
tener que + infinitivo
  en expresiones de obligación, 123, 354
*to think*, 196
tiempo atmosférico
  estar con, 110
  hacer en expresiones del, 114
  palabras que describen, 114
tiempo cronológico
  al + infinitivo en expresiones de, 354
  de en expresiones de, 124–125
  en en expresiones de, 124–125
  expresiones de, 63
  hacer en expresiones de, 170

palabras para expresar aspectos de, 124–125
  ser para expresar, 110
tiempos compuestos, 188, 190
tiempos del verbos. *véase* tiempos específicos del verbos
*time*, 63
*to ask*, 16
*to become*, 100
*to come*, 196
*to fail*, 106
*to leave*, 282
*to meet*, 153
*to miss*, 364
*to put*, 282
*to take*, 106
*to think*, 196
tomar, 106
toparse con, 153
tropezar con, 153
tú vs. usted, 50

un(a)
  formas, 24
  omisión, 24
unos(as), 24
usted(es)
  de cortesia, 50
  tú vs., 50

venir
  + gerundio, 396
  vs. ir, llegar, 196
verbos. *véase también* modos específicos; tiempos específicos
  con cambios en vocal del radical, 51, 233
  construcción especial del gustar, 212
  irregulares, 52, 68, 233
  que terminan en –car, –gar, y –zar, 51–52, 233
  reflexivos, 98–99
vez (veces), 63
volverse, 100
voz pasiva, 337

*why*, 16

# Credits

## Acknowledgments

The authors wish to thank the many people of the Caribbean Islands, Central America, South America, Spain, and the United States who assisted in the photography used in the textbook. Also helpful in providing photos and materials were the National Tourist Offices of Argentina, Bolivia, Chile, Colombia, Honduras, Mexico, Perú, Puerto Rico, and Spain.

## Literary/Audio Credits

The Publisher would like to thank the following people and/or institutions for the right to reproduce their content:

10 "Una joven ofrece su testimonio sobre los efectos del bloqueo", en "Audiencia parlamentaria denunció violaciones del bloqueo contra Cuba". © *Juventud Rebelde — Edición Digital*, Cuba, 23 de octubre de 2014; 15 © Silvio Rodríguez, 1980. "Vamos a andar". *Rabo de nube*. La Habana, Cuba: http://zurrondelaprendiz.com; 26–27 Fragmentos del "Discurso de Barack Obama sobre la reanudación de relaciones entre EE. UU. y Cuba". *La Jornada*, México, 17 de diciembre de 2014. Used with permission of The Associated Press Copyright© 2015. All rights reserved. 29 www.rtve.es/alacarta/videos/programa/alegria-entre-cubanos-ante-levantamiento-restricciones-viajes-envios/476444/; 40 José Martí. 1913. "Dos patrias". En *Versos libres*. Dominio público; 58 Europ Assistance © Europ Assistance; 59 "El Madrid dorado", "Madrid de noche", "Tour de tapas" © SANDEMANs NEW Europe GmbH; 65–66 "Tipos de trenes en España", "Trenes internacionales de alta velocidad en España" © http://www.eurail.com/; 74 © Álvaro Octavio Lara Huerta. 2015. "2015, Año del Quijote". *Zacatecas en Imagen*, México, 14 de enero; 75 "Cospedal celebra que 'nuestro personaje más universal' acercará Castilla-La Mancha al mundo para crear riqueza". © *Presidente, Castilla-La Mancha*. 8 de enero de 2015. (http://www.castillalamancha.es/actualidad/notasdeprensa/cospedal-celebra-que-"nuestro-personaje-más-universal"-acercará-castilla-la-mancha-al-mundo-para); 76 © Ana María Escribano. 2015. "Logotipo ganador Qvixote 2015". 18 de enero de 2015. (https://www.behance.net/gallery/22857349/Logotipo-ganador-Qvixote-2015); 76 Logo Qvixote 2015 © Fundación Cultura y Deporte de Castilla-La Mancha; 77 mvod.lvlt.rtve.es/resources/TE_STURCOM/mp3/7/9/1379666091297.mp3; 87 Antonio Machado. 1907. "He andado muchos caminos". En *Soledades, galerías y otros poemas*. © Herederos de Antonio Machado; 117 Bienvenido a la Universidad del Pacífico © 2010 Universidad del Pacífico (http://www.up.edu.pe/internacional/programs.aspx?program=Summer in Cusco); 117 Curso de verano: "Del conocimiento local a los negocios globales" ©2010 Universidad del Pacífico (http://www.up.edu.pe/internacional/program-details.aspx?program=Summer in Cusco&detail=Acerca del curso); 117 Alojamiento en casas de familia ©2010 Universidad del Pacífico (http://www.up.edu.pe/internacional/program-details.aspx?program=Summer in Cusco&detail=Alojamiento); 118 Acerca de Cusco ©2010 Universidad del Pacífico (http://www.up.edu.pe/internacional/program-details.aspx?program=Summer in Cusco&detail=Vida en Cusco); 120 www.up.edu.pe/internacional/programs.aspx?program=Summer%20in%20Cusco; 127–131 Ricardo Palma. 1896. "El alacrán de Fray Gómez". En *Tradiciones peruanas*. Barcelona: Montaner y Simón; 164–165 Gabriel Díez Lacunza. 2014. "Las trabajadoras del hogar se asocian y ofrecen servicios domésticos por hora". *Página Siete*. 23 de junio; 167 Soy trabajadora del hogar © Radio Deseo, Mujeres Creando Bolivia www.radiodeseo.com, www.mujerescreando.org; 175–176 Emilia Pardo Bazán. 1922. "Las medias rojas". En *Cuentos de mi tierra*. Madrid: Atlántida; 206–207 "El 59% de los universitarios mexicanos no cuenta actualmente con un empleo". © *Universo Laboral: Redacción*, México. 12 de octubre de 2012; 209 https://archive.org/details/ANTONELLAGRECO_20131111; 221–222 "Autorretrato" por Rosario Castellanos. En *Poesía no eres tú: Obra poética 1948-1971 (1972)*. Copyright © 2004, Fondo de Cultura Económica. Todos los derechos reservados. México, D. F. Esta edición consta de 5.000 ejemplares impresos; 247 El plato para comer saludable: *Derechos de autor © 2011 Universidad de Harvard. Para más información sobre El Plato para Comer Saludable, por favor visite la Fuente de Nutrición, Departamento de Nutrición, Escuela de Salud Pública de Harvard, http://www.thenutritionsource.org y Publicaciones de Salud de Harvard, health.harvard.edu*; 248–249 Teresita Quezada. "Los momentos que marcaron la evolución de la medicina y la salud en Chile". @ *Diario La Tercera*, Chile. 14 de septiembre de 2010; 251 radio.uchile.cl/programas/a-tu-salud/la-periodista-cecilia-espinosa-junto-a-su-equipo-de-panelistas-abordo-el-tema-de-la-medicina-complementaria-con-sus-modalidades-teorias-y-creencias-que-la-acompanan-para-esto-tuvo-como-invitados-al; 259–260 Pablo Neruda. "Walking around", *RESIDENCIA EN LA TIERRA*, @ Fundación Pablo Neruda, 2015; 292–293 "Una tragedia que no admite más disputas ni dilaciones". @ *La Nación: Editoriales*, Argentina, 4 de abril de 2013; 295 www.continental.com.ar/noticias/sociedad/macri-construira-100-km-de-bicisendas-el-promedio-de-viaje-en-la-ciudad-no-es-de-mas-de-5-km-una-distancia-perfecta-para-hacer-ejercicio/20100311/nota/966241.aspx; 302 "Los dos reyes y los dos laberintos" de *El Aleph* por Jorge Luis Borges. Copyright © por María Kodama, usado con permiso de The Wylie Agency, LLC; 331–332 Jorge J. Muñiz Ortiz. "La crisis lleva a universitarios puertorriqueños a emigrar en masa a EE. UU." *Vívelo Hoy*. @ Agencia EFE en EEUU, 07/22/14 10:24 a. m.; 334 www.vozdelcentro.org/2003/11/30/la-emigracion-puertorriquena-a-los-estados-unidos/; 341–342 Extraído de *Cuando era puertorriqueña*. @ Esmeralda Santiago. 1994. Nueva York: Vintage Español; 372–373 Melissa Zuleta Bandera. "¿Triqui triqui enfrentado a los angelitos?". @ *El Heraldo*, Colombia, 1 de noviembre de 2013; 375 https://archive.org/details/LatinElective.blogspot.com_ColombiayFiestas; 381–384 Gabriel García Márquez. "Un señor muy viejo con unas alas enormes", *La increíble y triste historia de la cándida Eréndira y su abuela desalmada*. © Gabriel García Márquez, 1972, & Herederos de Gabriel García Márquez; 415–416 Israel Cruz. "Virgilio Andrade: en 50 años de radio sufrí amenazas, marginación y exilio". @ *ConexiHon*, Honduras, 27 de agosto de 2013; 418 https://soundcloud.com/rdsradiohn/protagonistas-del-desarrollo-17-noviembre-2014-asosiacion-compartir?in=rdsradiohn/sets/protagonistas-del-desarrollo; 428–429 Sor Juana Inés de la Cruz. 1689. "Hombres necios que acusáis". En *Inundación castálida*. Madrid: Juan García Infanzón; 430 Alfonsina Storni. 1919. "Peso ancestral". En *Irremediablemente*. Buenos Aires: Cooperativa Editorial Limitada

# Photo Credits

Cover photo Jess Kraft/Shutterstock 74421508; 0 Lya_Cattel/iStock; 1 (bottom) Zeroth/wikimedia; 2 (top left) monkeybusinessimages/iStock; (top right) Odua Images/Shutterstock; (center left) Yuri_Arcurs/iStock; (center right) Steve Debenport/iStock; (bottom) KatarzynaBialasiewicz/iStock; 3 (top left) Steve Debenport/iStock; (top right) Steve Debenport/iStock; 7 tomazl/iStock; 8 davidf/iStock; 9 XIIIfrom TOKYO/Wikimedia; 11 Chagin/iStock; 12 Jeremey Horner/Corbis; 13 (center) Susan Chiang/iStock; (bottom) andresr/iStock; 14 (top) Susan Chiang/iStock; (center) www.granma.cu; 15 (top) LaraBelova/iStock; (bottom) Zeroth/Wikimedia; 16 zoranm/iStock; 20 Chagin/iStock; 22 starfotograf/iStock; 28 rgbspace/iStock; 30 Lisa Klumpp/iStock; 35 (top left) Featureflash/Shutterstock; (top right) gdcgraphics/Wikimedia; 39 Public Domain/Wikimedia; 44 wallix/iStock; 45 (bottom) Diego Velázquez/Wikimedia; 46 (top left) Izabela Habur/iStock; (center left) andresr/iStock; (center center) Sorbis/Shutterstock.com; (center right) BraunS/iStock; (cb) Milkovasa/Shutterstock; (bottom right) andresrimaging/iStock; 47 (top left) Gannet77/iStock; (center left) gchutka/iStock; (center center) Prasit Rodphan/Shutterstock; (bottom left) Air Images/Shutterstock; (bottom center) dotshock/Shutterstock; (bottom right) OJO_Images/iStock; gchutka/iStock; 54 Sergio Pitamitz/Age Fotostock America, Inc.; 60 (top) Diego Velázquez/Wikimedia; (center) Puerta de Alcalá/Wikimedia; 61 (top) Lukasz Janyst/iStock; (bottom) Simon Pielow/Wikimedia; 62 (top) Claussmoon/wikipedia; (bottom) habari1/iStock; 63 Goodluz/Shutterstock; 64 vm/iStock; 65 Elenathewise/iStock; 67 (top) MarioGuti/iStock; (bottom) Holger Mette/iStock; 68 Arnau Design/iStock; 69 metoni/iStock; 73 (top) Gordito1869/Wikimedia; (left) Xauxa/Wikimedia; (bottom) Asier Sarasua Garmendia/Wikimedia; 74 rhoon/Istock; 76 Logo Qvixote 2015 © Fundación Cultura y Deporte de Castilla-La Mancha; 78 oscarcalero/iStock; 79 Cebas/iStock; 80 Avid Creative, Inc./iStock; 81 OJO_Images/iStock; 82 BraunS/iStock; 86 joelblit/iStock; 87 Archivo Iconografico/CORBIS; 88 Hansen, Clayton/iStockphoto; 89 rhoon/iStock; 92 Martin Mejia /ASSOCIATED PRESS; 93 (bottom) andina_Photografia@editoraperu.com.pe; 94 (top left) dboystudio/Shutterstock; (top right) MartaKimball; (top center) andresr/iStock; (center left) Syda Productions/Shutterstock; (bottom) Steve Debenport/iStock; 96 Lisa Klumpp/iStock; 98 ottokalman/iStock; 102 alvarez/iStock; 103 (top) www.bibliotecaobraje.blogspot.com; (bottom) www.deporteyarteparacrecer. .wordpress.com; 104 (top) 2014 Agencia Peruana de Noticias; (bottom) www.cebacarloswsutton.blogspot.com/; 105 Michael S. Lewis/National Geographic Creative/Corbis; 106 Soubrette/iStock; 111 Wavebreak Media Ltd/bigstock; 112 Tamboer, W./Masterfile/US; 113 hjalmeida/iStock; 120 tose/iStock; 121den3/Fotolia; 122 Aldo Murillo/iStock; 125 Aksonov/iStock; 126 Nicholson, Michael/CORBIS; 131 johnaudrey/iStock; 134 YinYang/iStock; 136 Bartosz Hadyniak/iStock; 137 (bottom) tirc83/iStock; 138 (top left) Aldo Murillo/iStock; (top right) Devasahayam Chandra Dhas/iStock; (center left) chandlerphoto/iStock; (center right) Iriana Shiyan/iStock; (bottom left) Rich Legg/iStock; (bottom right) Razumovskaya Marina Nikolaevna/Shutterstock; (top left) MJTH/Shutterstock; (top right) Carme Balcells/Shutterstock; (center left) MattSchia_/iStock; (center right) Iriana Shiyan/Shutterstoc; 141 Elenathewise/iStock; 142 (bottom) Erlanson Productions/Getty Images; 145 adamkaz/iStock; 147 Resiak, Tomasz/iStock; 148 (top center) Wolfgang Kaehler/Corbis; (top right) Murcova, Tatiana/iStock; 149 Mason, Bradley/iStock; 150 (top) tirc83/iStock; (bottom) Petrenko Andriy/Shutterstock; 151 (top) Juan Karita/AP; (bottom) Martin_Pescador/iStock; 152 James Brunker/Alamy; 153 (top) UmbertoPantalone/iStock; (bottom) starfotograf/iStock; 155 Quino; 157 Jean-philippe WALLET/iStock; 158 bobbieo/iStock; 160 rez-art; 162 'Doruk Sikman Photography/iStock; 165 Daniel Walker/Página Siete; 166 Scianna, Ferdinando/Magnum Photos Inc.; 167 clodio/iStock; 168 frenc/iStock; 169 SerrNovik/iStock; 171 Brown,Robert/iStock; 173 KatarzynaBialasiewicz/iStock; 174 Agencia EFE; 178 Gorivero; 180 Alina Solovyova-Vincent/iStock; 181 (bottom) Morrison1977/iStock; 182 (top left) wavebreakmedia/Shutterstock; (top right) IPGGutenbergUKLtd/iStock; (bottom left) Monkey Business Images/Shutterstock; (bottom right) Keepsmiling4u/Shutterstock; 183 (top) YinYang/iStock; (center left) Vgstockstudio/Shutterstock; (center right) stevecoleimages/iStock; 187 sidneybernstein/iStock; 189 deansanderson/iStock; 190 richcano/iStock; 193 (top) Morrison1977/iStock; (bottom) MaElena1/iStock; 194 (center) PeopleImages/iStock; (bottom) GeorgiosArt/iStock; 195 (top) monkeybusinessimages/iStock; (bottom) Vernon Wiley/iStock; 196 Brand X Pictures/Alamy; 198 orlando123/iStock; 199 YinYang/iStock; 203 arekmalang/iStock; 205 mediaphotos/iStock; 208 Pressmaster/Shutterstock; 209 Cathy Yeulet/iStock; 210 Newman, Michael/PhotoEdit; 212 blackwaterimages/iStock; 214 Odua Images/Fotolia; 215 ParkerDeen/iStock; 216 Onur Döngel/iStock; 219 (bottom left) Balcazar, Andres/iStock; (bottom right) Balcazar, Andres/iStock; 220 (top) Library of Congress; 223 (top) Danil Melekhin/iStock; (bottom) badahos/iStock; 224 PeopleImages/iStock; 226 Tituz/iStock; 227 (bottom) Tituz/iStock; 228 (top left) digitalskillet/Istock; (top right) Alexander Raths/Shutterstock; (center left) ChameleonsEye/Shutterstock; (center right) Juanmonino/iStock; (bottom) Larry St. Pierre/Shutterstock; 229 (top left) Rommel Canlas/Shutterstock; (top right) Lorraine Swanson/Shutterstock; (ct) kurhan/Shutterstock; (cb) BengLim/iStock; (bottom) Ugreen/istock; 230 dra_schwartz/iStock; 231 Rich Legg/iStock; 233 Mark Bowden/iStock; 234 JackF/iStock; 236 snapphoto/iStock; 238 (top) Tituz/iStock; (bottom) aabejon/iStock; 239 (top) Eugene Chernetsov/Shutterstock; (bottom) Internet Archive Book Images/Flickr Commons; 240 (top) fatihhoca/iStock; (bottom) racorn/Shutterstock; 241 Pamela Moore/iStock; 242 antsmarching/iStock; 243 Sean_Warren/iStock; 244 webphotographeer/iStock; 246 kickstand/iStock; 247 Harvard Medical School Harvard Health Productions www.health.harvard.edu Translation: http://gimenezm.blogspot.com; 252 Bodrov/iStock; 253 Rich Legg/iStock; 255 Yuri/iStock; 257 Deklofenak/iStock; 258 Bettmann/CORBIS; 261 goldenKB/iStock; 264 alex_black/iStock; 265 (bottom) Propiedad intelectual de la ciudad de Buenos Aires, bajo licencia de Creative Commons 2.5. de la Argentina; 266 (top left) wdstock/iStock; (top center) nancy10/Fotolia; (top right) De Visu/Shutterstock; (center) Anton_Ivanov/Shutterstock; 267 (top left) E. Schittenhelm/Fotolia; (top right) gpointstudio/iStock; (center left) Lana Smirnova/Shutterstock; (center right) Adisa/Shutterstock; 268 (top left) Boggy/Fotolia; (top right) JackF/Fotolia; 269 EdStock/iStock; 270 Christa Brunt/iStock; 271 alex_black/iStock; 272 Dennis Degna/